THE DAVIS RANCH SITE

AMERIND STUDIES IN ANTHROPOLOGY

Series Editor **Christine R. Szuter**

THE DAVIS RANCH SITE

A KAYENTA IMMIGRANT ENCLAVE IN SOUTHEASTERN ARIZONA

Rex E. Gerald

EDITED BY Patrick D. Lyons

THE UNIVERSITY OF ARIZONA PRESS
TUCSON

The University of Arizona Press
www.uapress.arizona.edu

ISBN-13: 978-0-8165-3854-6 (cloth)

Cover and interior design by Sara Thaxton
Cover photo courtesy of the Amerind Foundation, Inc., Dragoon, AZ

Publication of this book is made possible in part by funding from the Southwestern Foundation for Education and Historical Preservation and the Arizona Archaeological and Historical Society.

Library of Congress Cataloging-in-Publication Data are available at the Library of Congress.

Printed in the United States of America
♾ This paper meets the requirements of ANSI/NISO Z39.48-1992 (Permanence of Paper).

This volume is dedicated to the Smallhouse family of Redington, Arizona, stewards of the San Pedro Valley's ancient past for five generations.

Rex E. Gerald demonstrating the use of an atlatl at the University of Arizona Archaeological Field School at Point of Pines, 1949. Photograph by Paul H. Ezell, courtesy of the Arizona State Museum, University of Arizona (Negative No. 2446).

CONTENTS

Appendices

PREFACE AND ACKNOWLEDGMENTS

Patrick D. Lyons

Rex Gerald excavated the Davis Ranch Site in 1957, as a predoctoral research fellow at the Amerind Foundation, and it has taken more than 60 years for the results of his work to be fully published. I bear some blame for the delay, however, in that Gerald passed away in 1990, and I have been wrestling with his data, his writings, and my own analyses of his collections from the site for many years. Here, I provide a brief account of how this book finally came to be, a description of the materials used to produce it, and an overview of the end product.

HOW THIS BOOK CAME TO BE (AND WHY IT TOOK SO LONG)

In 1999, while a graduate student in the Department of Anthropology at the University of Arizona, I made two trips to the Amerind Museum to examine perforated ceramic plates from the Davis Ranch Site and nearby settlements in the San Pedro Valley. My goal was to include data from these sites in my doctoral dissertation: an examination of evidence of the migration of groups from the Hopi Mesas to the middle Little Colorado River Valley, the movement of groups from the Kayenta region of northern Arizona and southern Utah to the southern U.S. Southwest and northern Mexico, and the relationship between Kayenta immigrants and the Salado phenomenon (Lyons 1999a, 2001, 2003, 2004a; Lyons and Lindsay 2006). On the second of those two trips, Allan J. McIntyre, former Amerind Museum collections manager, showed me a copy of Rex Gerald's unfinished 1958 manuscript, the foundation of this volume, and suggested that I consider a reanalysis of all the pottery from the site. Given my desire to finish my dissertation and my need to look for a job after graduate school, I replied that someday I might be able to take on such a project, but not in the near future.

The following year, I found myself employed by the Center for Desert Archaeology (CDA, now Archaeology Southwest) as a preservation archaeologist doing fieldwork in, and analysis of ceramics from, the San Pedro Valley. As part of the San Pedro Preservation Project, CDA conducted test excavations at 29 sites in the lower stretch of the valley, between Benson and Winkelman, including the Davis Ranch Site (Clark and Lyons, eds. 2012). Information and insights produced as a result of these excavations and the survey that preceded them are discussed in chapters 7 and 8, as well as in editorial annotations to chapter 6.

In 2001, I researched Amerind Foundation collections from Reeve Ruin and the Davis Ranch Site in order to identify objects to be viewed by tribal representatives participating in CDA's San Pedro Ethnohistory Project (Ferguson and Colwell-Chanthaphonh 2006). By that time, I had come to appreciate the importance of the Davis Ranch

Site, and in December of that year, John A. Ware, then executive director of the Amerind Foundation, alerted me to a two-drawer filing cabinet at the Amerind Museum containing materials related to Rex Gerald's excavations. These had been found at the University of Texas at El Paso (UTEP), where Gerald was employed at the time of his death, and sent to Dragoon in 1998 by Deborah L. Martin, one of Gerald's former students.

In 2003, I assessed Gerald's manuscript, producing an initial outline of a proposed book that would incorporate the results of new analyses. Sally A. Thomas, then CDA's office manager, transcribed the manuscript, producing a series of word-processor files for my use in 2004. It was not until 2006, however, that I had sufficient time available to begin in earnest editing and annotating the manuscript and reanalyzing a large portion of the ceramic assemblage and other artifacts with the assistance of William J. Robinson and Gloria J. Fenner. Robinson, retired director of the University of Arizona Laboratory of Tree-Ring Research, had attended the Point of Pines archaeological field school with Gerald in the summer of 1956 and visited the Davis Ranch Site excavations in 1957. Fenner, former curator at the Western Archeological and Conservation Center (National Park Service), had worked at the Amerind Foundation from 1963 to 1979 as an assistant archaeologist, archaeologist, and laboratory chief.

In 2006, I submitted a successful grant proposal to the Southwestern Foundation for Education and Historical Preservation in support of the project, arguing that work with the Davis Ranch Site collections could provide stratigraphic verification of the new seriation-based Roosevelt Red Ware ("Salado polychrome pottery") typology and chronology I had recently developed (Lyons 2004b). Soon afterward, I left CDA, joining the faculty of the Arizona State Museum (ASM), at the University of Arizona, as associate curator and head of collections.

At ASM, I had new responsibilities, of course, and despite my change in employment, an ethical obligation to do my part in writing up the results of CDA's San Pedro Preservation Project (Clark and Lyons, eds. 2012) and its Precontact Population Decline and Coalescence Project (Clark et al. 2013; Hill et al. 2004, 2015; Lyons, Hill, and Clark 2011). I was also honor-bound to complete my contributions, as lead curator and co-principal investigator, to the CDA traveling exhibition entitled *Pieces of the Puzzle: New Perspectives on the Hohokam*. This exhibit, funded by a Communicating Research to Public Audiences grant from the National Science Foundation and based on the results of the Precontact Population Decline and Coalescence Project, opened at Pueblo Grande Museum in 2009 and since has been mounted at the Huhugam Ki Museum (Salt River Pima-Maricopa Indian Community), the Anasazi Heritage Center (Dolores, Colorado), the El Paso Museum of Archaeology (El Paso, Texas), Deer Valley Petroglyph Preserve (Phoenix, Arizona), and ASM.

I continued work on the Davis Ranch Site project, slowly, as I chipped away at my portions of the San Pedro Preservation Project volume, other publications, and the traveling exhibition. All the while, I was taking on additional administrative duties at ASM, becoming associate director in 2009 and director in 2013. I hope that readers find the resulting volume worth the wait.

SOURCE MATERIALS

The materials that made this publication possible are curated by the Amerind Museum. Aside from the artifacts, they include a copy of Gerald's 1958 manuscript, his original field notebook, 200 black-and-white photographs, catalog cards for 236 curated artifacts, and a catalog of 128 stone objects, many of which were not curated. A large (4′ × 12′) table (in pencil) of sherd counts and percentages by type and provenience and a large (3′ × 5′) site map executed with Le Roy pen and Zipatone on blue vellum are also present in the Amerind Museum's archives. The site map is the only illustration Gerald produced for publication yet located. Finally, there are the files that were in Gerald's possession, transferred to the

Amerind in 1998, limited correspondence germane to the project, and "Copy No. 2" of the 1958 manuscript. The latter was returned to the Amerind in 2004, two years after a chance encounter at the Velvet Elvis Pizza Company restaurant in Patagonia, Arizona, between William Robinson and Gerald's daughter, Netzin Gerald Steklis, now a lecturer in the University of Arizona's School of Family and Consumer Sciences and its School of Animal and Comparative Biomedical Sciences.

As mentioned above, many objects listed in the stone catalog were not retained, especially the larger items, such as metates. Gerald also mentions that many plain ware sherds were analyzed, recorded in the field, and discarded. He prepared no line drawings to illustrate his manuscript, except for the site map mentioned above. Consequently, Ronald J. Beckwith was hired to produce architectural plans, cross sections, and feature maps based on Gerald's field notebook sketches. Allen J. Denoyer, then at Desert Archaeology Inc., was engaged to draw the projectile points and a number of other flaked stone tools. The set of original black-and-white artifact photos curated by the Amerind Museum has been augmented, when necessary, with color images produced by Jannelle Weakly (ASM), Mathew A. Devitt (then at CDA), Samantha G. Fladd (then at ASM), and the volume's editor.

William H. Burt, then curator of mammals at the Museum of Zoology and professor in the Department of Zoology at the University of Michigan, analyzed the mammalian fauna from the Davis Ranch Site at Gerald's request. Burt also arranged for the avifauna to be identified by Harrison B. Tordoff, then curator of birds at the Museum of Zoology and assistant professor in the Department of Zoology at the University of Michigan. Burt sent his and Tordoff's species identifications to Gerald and presented a paper on the mammalian fauna at the 38th annual meeting of the American Society of Mammalogists, in Tucson, Arizona.

Gerald later had the mammal bone reexamined by Arthur H. Harris, then associate professor of biology and curator of vertebrate paleobiology at the Museum of Arid Land Biology at UTEP. R. Roy Johnson, then associate professor and head of biology at Prescott College, reanalyzed the avifauna with assistance from Lyndon L. Hargrave, who was also at Prescott College and then assistant research professor of ethnobiology. Gerald knew Johnson when the latter was an assistant and later associate professor of biology at UTEP.

The results of Burt's and Tordoff's analyses were not incorporated into Gerald's 1958 manuscript, although Gerald later made use of these data as well as species identifications by Harris and Johnson in his 1975 dissertation. The published version of Burt's (1961) paper, which includes a brief summary of Tordoff's data, is reprinted herein as appendix G. Contextual data associated with the mammalian and avian fauna, not included in Gerald's dissertation, are presented in appendices H and I, respectively.

At least one report of specialized analyses is known to be missing. Correspondence indicates that Hugh C. Cutler, then acting director of the Missouri Botanical Garden, received 10 or more macrobotanical items from Gerald for identification and that Cutler processed the material. However, a report has not been located, and apparently the items were never returned to the Amerind.

Four additional specialized studies were conducted specifically so that their results could be included in this volume (appendices A–C and J). In appendix A, Jeffrey S. Dean, emeritus professor of dendrochronology in the Laboratory of Tree-Ring Research at the University of Arizona, presents species identifications for the dendrochronological specimens Gerald submitted for analysis in 1957. These were examined in 1957 and again by Dean in 2004. Appendix B is a report by Ethne Barnes, an independent paleopathologist/physical anthropologist, researcher, and consultant, on her reanalysis of the human remains Gerald recovered from the site. Most of this study occurred in 2007, but one set of remains was not examined until 2011. Arthur W. Vokes, manager of ASM's Archaeological Repository, and Erika Heacock, formerly an ASM curatorial/museum specialist, contributed appendix C, a reanalysis of the Davis Ranch Site shell assemblage completed in 2013. The shell specimens previously had been identified as to species (in 1957) by George P. Kanakoff, then curator of paleontology at the Los Angeles County Museum, and Gerald had included this information in his manuscript. The study by Vokes and Heacock, however, juxtaposes the Davis Ranch Site sample with those recovered from other sites in the region, and the authors also consider the assemblage in the context of large-scale temporal patterns.

Appendix J, by James S. Schoenwetter (d. 2015), professor emeritus of anthropology at Arizona State University, is an update, written in 2008, of his 1965 report on the analysis of pollen samples from the Davis Ranch Site. Gerald had collected pollen samples in 1957 and submitted them to the Geochronology Laboratory at the University of Arizona, but they were subsequently misplaced. As a result, he obtained samples from different proveniences in 1965. Field notes associated with the 1965 excavations have not been located. Schoenwetter processed the 1965 samples when he was director of the Palynology Laboratory of the Laboratory of Anthropology at the Museum of New Mexico and submitted a report to Gerald for use in his dissertation. Ultimately, the 1957 samples resurfaced and were sent to Schoenwetter, but he was unable to process them due to other commitments and returned them to Gerald in El Paso, where they later disappeared.

ORGANIZATION OF THE VOLUME

Rex Gerald's 1958 manuscript forms the core of this volume (chapters 2–6) and is presented under his authorship. However, it has been edited (as all first drafts must be) and annotated extensively by the editor. Every effort has been made to check his text with the field notes and other materials; however, some inconsistencies remain. This is particularly true of Gerald's chapter on the ceramics he recovered.

In chapter 1, I place Gerald's excavations in the context of late pre-Hispanic southeastern Arizona culture history as well as the Amerind Foundation's long-term research focus and the conceptual scheme developed by then-director Charles Di Peso. Chapter 2 is Gerald's introduction to the report, written in 1958, in which he discusses the three research foci that guided fieldwork at the Davis Ranch Site (San Pedro Valley ceramic chronology, cultural and temporal relationships between the Sobaipuri and the inhabitants of Reeve Ruin, and temporal and spatial variability in Roosevelt Red Ware) and the methods he used, both in the field and in the laboratory. The architecture and miscellaneous features encountered at the site are described in chapter 3. Chapter 4 is a report on the inhumations and cremations recovered, and chapters 5 and 6 address non-ceramic and ceramic artifacts, respectively. In Gerald's chapters, in order to place the Davis Ranch Site within the recently developed regional chronology, phase designations developed as a result of the San Pedro Preservation Project (Clark and Lyons, eds. 2012) have been inserted. Where appropriate, the phase names Gerald used appear in parentheses, thus: Aravaipa (Sosa) phase.

Chapters 7 and 8, like chapter 1, were written for this volume. In chapter 7, I present the results of a reanalysis of the Roosevelt Red Ware, Maverick Mountain Series pottery, and perforated plates from the site. In chapter 8, Jeffery J. Clark and I consider Gerald's findings, the results of the ceramic reanalysis, and data presented in the appendices in relation to the key conclusions of Archaeology Southwest's studies of San Pedro Valley archaeology, conducted between 1990 and 2012. We argue that the record from the Davis Ranch Site is unlike that from any other settlement in terms of the opportunities it presents to shed light on Kayenta migrations, the relationship between northern immigrants and the genesis and spread of Roosevelt Red Ware, and the nature of the Salado phenomenon.

The final product comprising these chapters and appendices is a testament to the importance of long-term partnerships among researchers and institutions. Producing this book required cooperation and collaboration by personnel from the Arizona State

Museum, the Amerind Foundation, and Archaeology Southwest. In closing, I hope that readers come to accept one of the key tenets of preservation archaeology at the heart of this endeavor: that museum collections are invaluable sources of information, allowing contemporary researchers to ask old questions in new ways and to ask questions that previous generations of researchers never imagined could be addressed.

ACKNOWLEDGMENTS

William J. Robinson and Gloria J. Fenner contributed a great deal to this volume by reformatting large portions of Gerald's manuscript and cross-checking data with Amerind Museum catalog records. They were also instrumental in the initial reanalysis of Roosevelt Red Ware and Maverick Mountain Series pottery from the site. This work laid the foundation for the study reported on in chapter 7. In addition, Fenner made adjustments to Gerald's non-ceramic artifact categories to make them more internally consistent and updated avifaunal taxonomic nomenclature. Robinson secured the participation of Ethne Barnes, Jeffrey S. Dean, and the late James S. Schoenwetter in the project. Benjamin W. Smith provided editorial assistance to Robinson, and Katherine M. Cerino assisted with many different organizational tasks.

Mathew A. Devitt, then at CDA, took the photographs of whole and partial ceramic vessels used during the research process, one of which is reproduced herein. Jannelle Weakly, of ASM, is responsible for most of the images of whole and partial ceramic vessels, cataloged by Rex Gerald, that appear in this volume. Figures 1.1 and 1.2 are derived from a base map drawn by Ronald J. Beckwith. Catherine Gilman, of Desert Archaeology Inc., produced figures 1.5, 7.41, and 8.2–8.10.

Alan Ferg, of ASM, Marie-Blanche Roudaut, then of Tierra Right of Way Services Inc., and James M. Vint, of Desert Archaeology Inc., assisted in the identification of projectile points. Darrell G. Creel, emeritus professor of anthropology at the University of Texas at Austin, and Roger Anyon, of the Pima County Cultural Resources and Historic Preservation Office, classified the Mimbres Black-on-white pottery from the site according to style and provided age estimates.

Claire S. Barker and Samantha G. Fladd, then ASM graduate research assistants, and ASM volunteers Jaye S. Smith, Marilyn M. Marshall, and Don L. Burgess made crucial contributions to the final stages of the reanalysis of Roosevelt Red Ware and Maverick Mountain Series pottery from the site, including the search for conjoining and matching sherds and the documentation of partially reconstructible vessels. Donna Cook, also an ASM volunteer, made high-resolution scans of the black-and-white photos from Gerald's excavations and assisted in physically organizing the ceramic collection for analysis.

William H. Doelle, president and CEO of Archaeology Southwest, and John A. Ware, former executive director of the Amerind Foundation, provided advice and encouragement. Eric J. Kaldahl, deputy director and chief curator of the Amerind Museum, assisted me in countless ways. Generous financial support was contributed by the Southwestern Foundation for Education and Historical Preservation and the Arizona Archaeological and Historical Society. Carol Gifford Jelinek and Raymond H. Thompson read an earlier version of the manuscript and made many helpful suggestions. Finally, I wish to express my most sincere gratitude to the two anonymous reviewers whose recommendations substantially improved this book, the staff at the University of Arizona Press, copyeditor Maya Allen-Gallegos, and Christine R. Szuter, current executive director of the Amerind Foundation.

THE DAVIS RANCH SITE

1

Context

Patrick D. Lyons

More than 60 years have passed since Rex Gerald's excavations at the Davis Ranch Site (ARIZONA:BB:11:7[AF], AZ BB:11:10[ASM], AZ BB:11:36[ASM]), the results of which are published in this volume, in large part, for the first time. Gerald embarked on this project in 1957, as a graduate student in the University of Arizona's Department of Anthropology but working under the auspices of the Amerind Foundation. In 1958, he produced the manuscript that forms the foundation of this book.

Before presenting the results of Gerald's excavations (in chapters 2–6) and considering their relevance to recent and current research efforts (in chapter 8), in this chapter, I offer a brief overview of southeastern Arizona culture history intended to provide the reader with critical background information. I then discuss how the record from the Davis Ranch Site is unique in illuminating the nature of the relationship between immigrants from the Kayenta region and the Salado phenomenon. Next, I place Gerald's work in the context of the Amerind Foundation's long-term research program and the overarching conceptual framework established by Charles Di Peso, who was the institution's director at the time of Gerald's excavations. After considering likely points of contention between Gerald and Di Peso, I conclude with a brief summary and a look ahead to the chapters that follow.

A BRIEF CULTURE HISTORY OF LATE PRE-HISPANIC SOUTHEASTERN ARIZONA

Southeastern Arizona, within the Basin and Range physiographic province, is home to three major south-to-north flowing drainages, all tributaries of the Gila River. From west to east, these are the Santa Cruz River, the San Pedro River, and San Simon Creek (figures 1.1, 1.2). The north-to-south draining Sulphur Springs Valley lies between the San Pedro River and San Simon Creek, and east of the Sulphur Springs Valley is the San Bernardino Valley, which also drains from north to south. Other key hydrologically defined areas include Aravaipa Creek (a major tributary of the San Pedro River) and the Safford Basin (a portion of the Gila River Valley bounded by Sanchez Gorge on the southeast and the Mescal Mountains on the northwest, including the majority of the drainage of the San Carlos River and the lowermost portion of San Simon Creek; Gregory 1995a:38–39).

There is archaeological evidence indicating nearly continuous human occupation of southeastern Arizona beginning about 13,000 years ago (Bronitsky and Merritt 1986). The major ceramic period pre-Hispanic (ca. AD 50–1540) cultural traditions of the region were Hohokam (generally dominant in

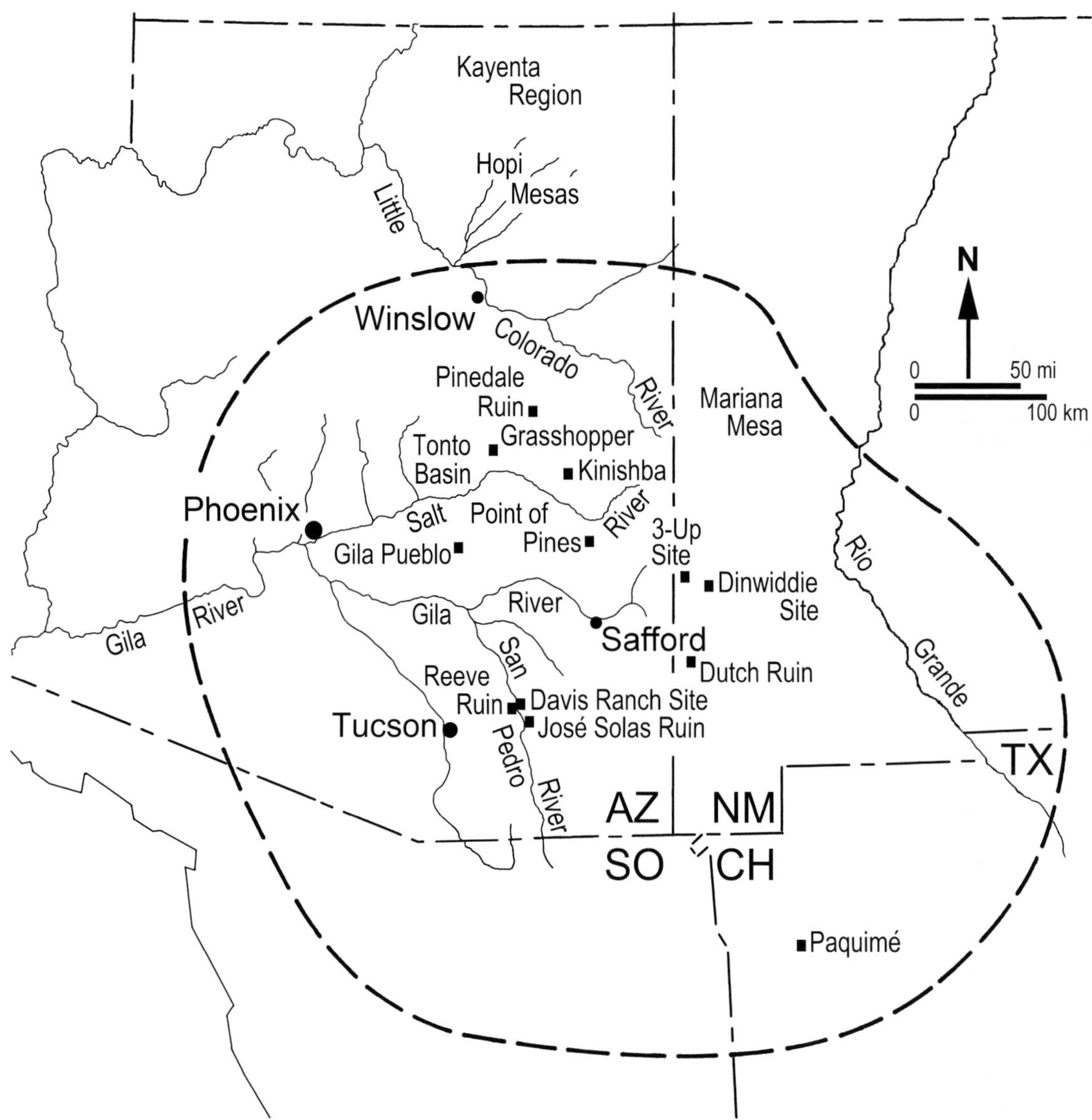

FIGURE 1.1 Map of Arizona, western New Mexico, northern Sonora, and northern Chihuahua, showing locations of sites and areas discussed in the text. Base map drawn by Ronald J. Beckwith. Dashed line (after Crown 1994:Figure 1.1) indicates the known distribution of Roosevelt Red Ware.

the west) and Mogollon (generally dominant in the east) (figure 1.3). However, many areas within southeastern Arizona (or portions thereof) were boundary zones or hinterlands. These places were inhabited by co-resident groups with disparate histories and practices (i.e., some maintaining Hohokam conventions living near others perpetuating Mogollon customs) and/or culturally homogenous local populations who negotiated identities distinct from various neighboring groups, while maintaining exchange relationship with them and sometimes emulating or adopting some of their behaviors and material culture (Altschul et al. 2014; Deaver and Van West 2001; Douglas 2007, 2014; Gilman 2011; Masse et al. 2014; Neuzil and Woodson 2008, 2014; Purcell and Clark 2008; Sayles 1945; Vanderpot

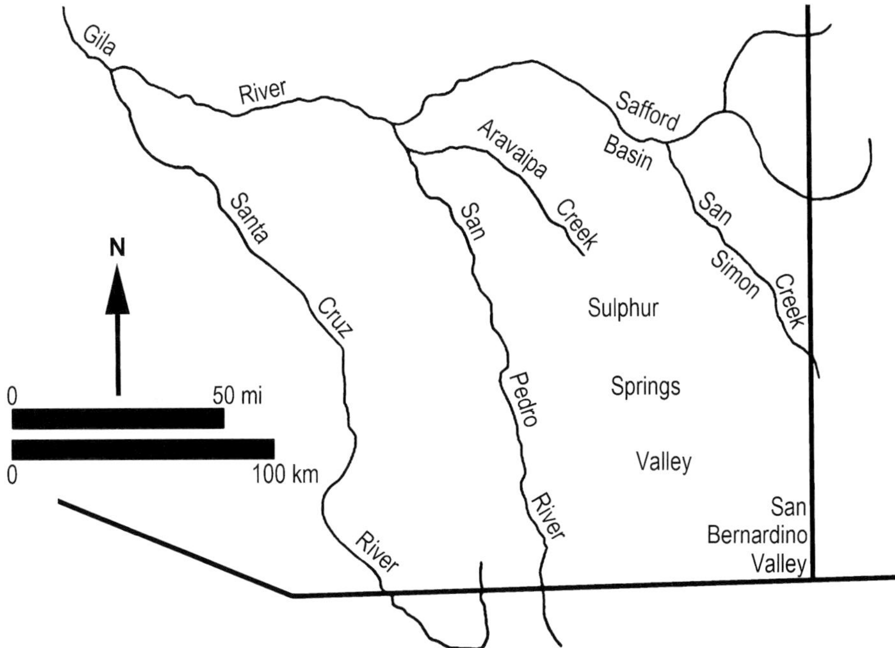

FIGURE 1.2 Map of southeastern Arizona. Base map drawn by Ronald J. Beckwith.

and Altschul 2007; Wallace 2014; Whittlesey et al. 1994; Whittlesey and Heckman 2000). These hinterlands include the upper Santa Cruz Valley, the upper San Pedro Valley, the Sulphur Springs Valley, the Safford Basin, the San Simon Valley, and the San Bernardino Valley. In addition, there has long been evidence suggesting an influx of immigrants from the Colorado Plateau to southeastern Arizona late in the pre-Hispanic sequence.

Many sites in southeastern Arizona built and/or occupied after circa AD 1300 have been classified as "Salado." Such sites are present in large numbers in all three of the study areas' major south-to-north flowing drainages, as well as the Safford Basin, the Aravaipa Valley, and the Sulphur Springs Valley (Lekson 1992; Nelson and LeBlanc 1986; Neuzil 2008). Some sites in the San Bernardino Valley have also been identified as Salado. The key problem with applying Salado as a cultural historical term, however, is that it does not hold together conceptually in the same way as Hohokam or Mogollon (Dean 2000:4; Elson et al. 2000:190; Rice 1990:25). In the sections that follow, I provide an overview of the patterns used to define the Hohokam and Mogollon archaeological cultures, I describe the local manifestations of these patterns in different parts of southeastern Arizona, I review evidence of ancient immigrants from the north in the study area, and I briefly examine the Salado concept.

Hohokam

Southeastern Arizona encompasses several areas that researchers consider peripheries of the Hohokam regional system's core, the Phoenix Basin (Wilcox 1979, 1980; Wilcox and Shenk 1977:173–199; Wilcox and Sternberg 1983:219–222; see also Crown 1991). These include the Santa Cruz Valley, the San Pedro Valley, and the Safford Basin. In these areas, Hohokam traditions of architecture, ceramics, flaked and ground stone, shell jewelry, and treatment of the dead predominated, and shifts in material culture over time generally tracked temporal changes in the Phoenix Basin.

Hohokam pre-Classic domestic architecture typically took the form of a house-in-a-pit (a structure built in a shallow depression), as opposed to a true

Date (AD)	Hohokam Period[a]	Hohokam Phase (Phoenix Basin)[a]	Mogollon Period[b]
1450			
1400		Civano	
1350			
1300	Classic		Pueblo
1250		Soho	
1200			
1150			
1100			
1050	Sedentary	Sacaton	
1000			
950			
900		Santa Cruz	
850	Colonial		Late Pit House
800		Gila Butte	
750		Snaketown	
700		Sweetwater	
650		Estrella	
600	Pioneer		
550		Vahki	
500			
450			Early Pit House (AD 100–550)
400	Early Ceramic Horizon (AD 50–450)		
350			
300			

[a]Henderson 2002; Wallace and others 1995; [b]Douglas 1987, 1995; Gilman 2011; Lekson 2014; Nelson and LeBlanc 1986

FIGURE 1.3 Southern Arizona archaeological chronology. Although local phase names are used in each valley, the Hohokam period sequence (Pioneer through Classic) and Phoenix Basin Hohokam phases (Gladwin and Gladwin 1929, 1934; Gladwin et al. 1937; Haury 1945, 1976) represent the basic framework for discussing change through time in most of southern Arizona. The Mogollon periods, as presented here (cf. Lekson 2014; Nelson and LeBlanc 1986), have been modified to better reflect the cultural dynamics of southeastern Arizona (see Douglas 1987, 1995; Gilman 2011).

pit house (a structure dug a substantial depth into the earth such that the walls of the pit formed part of the house's walls). Hohokam houses-in-pits were most often arranged in courtyard groups most likely representing extended households. Ballcourts, ceremonial structures designed to accommodate a version of the Mesoamerican ball game, were present in large pre-Classic villages. The overwhelmingly dominant pre-Classic Hohokam method of disposing of the dead was cremation.

During the Classic period, houses-in-pits were replaced by aboveground compounds, most often rectilinear domestic architectural spaces defined by courtyard walls connecting to and enclosing one or more square or rectangular rooms. Ballcourts fell out of use during the pre-Classic Sedentary period, and platform mounds were the ceremonial structures associated with the Classic period. Inhumation of the dead (typically supine and extended) began to be practiced widely during the Classic period. Cremation continued, but inhumations account for nearly half of all Classic period Hohokam human burials (Rice 2016:52).

Hohokam ceramics were produced using the paddle-and-anvil technique, and decorated pottery made in the Phoenix Basin, Middle Gila Buff Ware, bears red paint on a buff-colored (slipped) background (very early in the sequence, red-on-gray pottery was also produced) (Gladwin and Gladwin 1933; Haury 1937a, 1945, 1976). Stylistically analogous red-on-buff types were made locally using the same technology in the lower San Pedro Valley and in the Safford Basin (Doyel 2000:299; Johnson and Wasley 1966; Lyons 2004c, 2004d, 2012a, 2012b; Masse 1980a, 1982; Masse et al. 2014; Neuzil 2008:76–86; Wallace 1995, 1996). The Hohokam painted pottery tradition is manifest in the Santa Cruz Valley as red-on-brown types decorated in styles analogous to those of the red-on-buff types of the Phoenix Basin (Danson 1957; Deaver 1984, 1989; Heckman 2000a; Heckman and Whittlesey 1999; Heidke 1995, 2000; Kelly et al. 1978; Wallace 1986).

Late pre-Classic (Rincon Red-on-brown) and Classic period (Tanque Verde Red-on-brown) painted types made in the Santa Cruz Valley have intentionally smudged interiors. The interior surfaces of smudged bowls of these types most often bear painted decoration, creating designs that are, in effect, red-on-gray or red-on-black. Smudging, which increased in frequency over time, further distinguishes these types from those made contemporaneously in the Phoenix Basin. Recent research has documented local production of Rincon Red-on-brown and Tanque Verde Red-on-brown in the lower San Pedro Valley (Lyons 2012b).

San Carlos Red-on-brown is a Classic period type made in the Hohokam tradition but apparently was only produced outside the Phoenix Basin core. Local manufacture in the lower San Pedro Valley (Lyons 2012a, 2012b; Masse 1982), the Tonto Basin (Wallace 1995:76), and the Safford Basin (Lyons 2004c, 2004d; Neuzil 2008:76–86) has been demonstrated, and it may also have been made in the Globe-Miami area (Doyel 1978:36–37, 98). Distinguished from related types by its thin walls, lustrous polish on both interior and exterior surfaces, and dense black smudging on vessel interiors, San Carlos Red-on-brown is most common in the Safford Basin and the lower San Pedro Valley. It also occurs in the middle Santa Cruz Valley (the Tucson Basin), the Dripping Springs Valley, the Point of Pines area, and the Phoenix Basin.

The upper San Pedro Valley is home to Babocomari Polychrome, a Classic period pottery type used, in part, by Charles Di Peso (1951a:125, Figure 46) to define the Babocomari Culture. Today, most researchers view Babocomari Polychrome as related to the Hohokam ceramic tradition, in that it was produced using the paddle-and-anvil technique, and the painted designs it exhibits are quite similar to those characteristic of the Tucson Basin Brown Ware types Rincon Red-on-brown and Tanque Verde Red-on-brown, as well as the Middle Gila Buff Ware types Sacaton Red-on-buff and Casa Grande Red-on-buff (Bronitsky and Merritt 1986:199; Di Peso 1951a:232; Heckman 2000b:29). Robert Heckman (2000b; see also Jones 1996) has defined the Babocomari Tradition as a group of related pottery types that includes Babocomari Polychrome and Babocomari Bichrome. According to Heckman (2000b:23), the bichrome type, which can be decorated with either red or black paint, may date as early as AD 700 and likely was made until circa AD 1300.

Sites with ceramic assemblages dominated by Babocomari Polychrome are concentrated in the upper San Pedro Valley, south of the Babocomari River (Altschul et al. 2014; Heckman 2000b). The architecture of these sites is distinctive, in that rooms are appended to the outsides of compound walls, and many compounds are circular rather than rectilinear (Altschul and Shelley 1996; Altschul et al. 2014; Di Peso 1951a; Shelley and Altschul 1996). Although cremation appears to have been the dominant method of disposing of the dead, platform mounds are not present at Babocomari Culture sites, and only one possible ballcourt has been identified in the area (Altschul et al. 2014; Di Peso 1951a; Shelley and Altschul, eds. 1996).

Mogollon

Building on the work of Emil Haury (1936, 1940), Joe Ben Wheat (1955) defined six branches of the Mogollon archaeological culture. One of these, the San Simon Branch (ca. AD 450–1150/1200), previously described by E. B. Sayles (1945), is named for the San Simon Valley. Mogollon traditions characteristic of the San Simon Branch include true pit houses (although these are the shallowest associated with any Mogollon branch), pottery produced using the coil-and-scrape technique, and inhumation of the dead. The San Simon Branch is distinguished from other Mogollon branches by the absence of great kivas, although Hohokam-style ballcourts are present at some San Simon Branch villages. The San Simon Series (Sayles 1945; see also Franklin 1980:222; Heckman 2000c:63; Masse et al. 2014:194–195) of mostly red-on-brown pottery types bears decorations apparently derived from those of the Mogollon highlands to the north and east.

Many researchers consider the Dragoon Complex or Culture (ca. AD 700–1100) of the San Pedro Valley to represent a mixture of Mogollon and Hohokam traits, and some are explicit in considering the possibility that this pattern may indicate ethnic co-residence (Franklin 1980:219–229; Fulton and Tuthill 1940:55–56, 63; Masse et al. 2014:165, 177; Tuthill 1947:83–86, 1950; Wheat 1955:28; Whittlesey et al. 1994:65, 80). William Fulton and Carr Tuthill (1940; see also Tuthill 1947, 1950) describe the Dragoon Culture as basically Hohokam with "Mogollon influence." Others see the Dragoon Culture as a local Mogollon group who adopted some Hohokam practices (Franklin 1980:55–57, 222–223; Masse et al. 2014:194–195; Whittlesey et al. 1994:65–86).

Among those who classify the Dragoon Culture as a local expression of the larger Mogollon tradition are many who also consider Dragoon Series and San Simon Series pottery types to be spatial varieties of the same phenomenon (i.e., analogous types made by related or closely interacting groups; Franklin 1980:55–57, 109–114; Heckman 2000d:45; Masse et al. 2014). Fulton and Tuthill (1940:60), however, opine that Dragoon Series pottery "resembles both Hohokam and Mogollon and yet is neither." Some Dragoon Series pottery was made using the paddle-and-anvil technique associated with the Hohokam cultural tradition (Heckman 2000d:45), and some researchers point to a trend toward more Hohokam "influence" in Dragoon Series pottery in the San Pedro Valley (in contrast to San Simon Series pottery in the San Simon Valley) over time (Deaver 1984: 363–369; Franklin 1980:55–57; Heckman 2000d: 61–62; Jones 1996:17–21).

The final cultural tradition to discuss under the heading of Mogollon is referred to as the Animas phase (ca. AD 1150–1450). A group of sites in the San Bernardino, Sulphur Springs, and San Simon Valleys has long been considered to be similar to sites in far northern Sonora and Chihuahua as well as the San Luis, Animas, and Playas Valleys of southwestern New Mexico. The original concept of the Animas phase (Gladwin 1936; Gladwin and Gladwin 1934:Figure 9, endpapers; Kidder et al. 1949; Sayles 1936:86–88; see also Carpenter 2002; Douglas 1987) linked these settlements together, defining an archaeological culture that represents either a local expression of, or a group closely related to, the Mogollon tradition who were peripheral participants in the cultural dynamics of the Casas Grandes region of northern Chihuahua. Indeed, Alfred Kidder and his colleagues (1949:144) describe the group as "country cousins . . . of the Chihuahueños."

Animas phase sites share the following characteristics: surface architecture built of coursed adobe (many sites are large, plaza-focused pueblos), painted pottery assemblages with high frequencies of Chihuahuan Polychromes, utility ware assemblages with high frequencies of Cloverdale Corrugated (in the west) or Playas Red and Playas Red Incised (in the east), the presence of Chihuahuan-style ballcourts at some sites, and the occasional presence of distinctive architectural features associated with Casas Grandes and surrounding sites, such as hearths surrounded by raised adobe platforms and vertical roof posts encircled by adobe collars (Douglas 1987, 1990, 1995, 1996, 2007, 2014; Fish and Fish 1999, 2006; Johnson and Thompson 1963; McCluney 1962; Mills and Mills 1966, 1971; Skibo et al. 2002). Different methods of disposing of the dead are evident at Animas phase sites. Some have yielded only inhumations, others both inhumations and cremations, and sometimes cremations predominate. Reflecting strong ties to Paquimé, the inhabitants of some Animas phase sites appear to have locally produced Ramos Polychrome (Carpenter 2002; Woosley and Olinger 1993) and a feature at the Slaughter Ranch Site may have been a macaw pen like those documented at Paquimé (Fish and Fish 1999:39; Mills and Mills 1971:34). Because Roosevelt Red Ware has been recovered in considerable quantities from many late Animas phase sites (post-AD 1300/1325), particularly those in Arizona (Douglas 2014; Fish and Fish 1999; Lekson 1992), some researchers (e.g., Bronitsky and Merritt 1986; Hegmon et al. 1999; Nelson and LeBlanc 1986) include the late Animas phase under the rubric of Salado (see below).

Immigrants from the North

Artifacts and architecture in southeastern Arizona likely indicating the presence of immigrants from the northern Southwest were first noted by William Duffen (1937; see also Duffen and Hartmann 1997), who excavated a portion of Webb Ruin (76 Ranch Ruin; AZ BB:8:1[ASM]), a fourteenth-century AD site in the Sulphur Springs Valley. As more sites were investigated over the years, more such evidence accumulated. By the 1950s, in part based on discoveries made by the University of Arizona's archaeological field school at Point of Pines (Haury 1958, 1989), archaeologists working in the Tucson Basin and the San Pedro Valley were hypothesizing about population influxes during the late AD 1200s from the Kayenta area of the Four Corners region (Danson 1957:226–229; Hayden 1957:122) or a more vaguely defined "Western Pueblo" point of origin (sensu Reed 1948; see also Di Peso 1958a). During the 1970s and 1980s, traces of Kayenta immigrants in the Safford Basin came to light (Brown 1973, 1974), and previously reported data from the San Pedro Valley were placed in a larger comparative framework (Lindsay 1987).

Research focused on documenting and understanding the consequences of Kayenta migration into southeastern Arizona intensified during the 1990s and 2000s, as Eastern Arizona College, the University of Texas at Austin, and the Center for Desert Archaeology conducted survey and excavation projects in the Safford Basin, the San Pedro Valley, and the Aravaipa Valley (Clark and Lyons, eds. 2012; Jernigan 1993; Lyons 2001, 2003, 2004a; Neely 2005; Neuzil 2005, 2008; Rinker 1998; Woodson 1995, 1999; see also Clark 2004; Lyons and Lindsay 2006; Tyberg 2000; Welch 1995). Many of these projects were driven, in part, by previous studies (e.g., Brown 1973, 1974; Carlson 1961, 1970, 1982; Crown 1994) suggesting a relationship between Kayenta immigrants and the Salado phenomenon.

Salado

Archaeologists previously used the term "Salado" to refer to an archaeological culture, a consistent set of shared practices associated with particular groups of people with common origins and a shared history, similar to Hohokam or Mogollon (Gladwin and Gladwin 1930; Haury 1945). The Salado archaeological culture supposedly developed in the Salt River drainage, specifically the Lake Roosevelt area (the Tonto Basin), and during the late Hohokam Classic period (after ca. AD 1300), spread through migration over much of the southern Southwest. Subsequent work, however, has shown that so-called Salado archaeology is far from monolithic, varying in terms of domestic and ceremonial architecture, treatment of the dead, and other traditions, even within individual valleys (Crown 1994; Dean, ed. 2000; Doyel and Haury 1976; Lange and Germick 1992). Indeed, the only trait(s) shared by all the various sites labeled as Salado is one or more Roosevelt Red Ware pottery types referred to informally as "Salado polychromes" (Lindsay and Jennings 1968; Nelson and LeBlanc 1986:1–14).

Many researchers (e.g., Clark et al. 2013; Douglas 2007, 2014; Lekson 1992; Nelson and LeBlanc 1986) acknowledge that Salado, whatever it represents, is a thin veneer, underneath which lie Hohokam-affiliated populations and traditions in the western portions of central and southern Arizona and a Mogollon-affiliated demographic and cultural substrate in the eastern parts of central and southern Arizona, as well as southwestern New Mexico. Despite nearly 90 years of research on the problem, a universally accepted definition of Salado has not emerged. However, many archaeologists now use the term "Salado" (or "Salado phenomenon") to refer to a horizon between AD 1275 and 1450 characterized by migration, co-residence, and concomitant sociopolitical, religious, and economic changes in the southern Southwest (Clark 2001; Clark et al. 2013; Crown 1994; Dean 2000; Lekson 2000; Lyons 2003).

Salado as the Kayenta in Diaspora

Patricia Crown (1994) has done the most to establish the connection between immigrants from the Kayenta region and the origin of Roosevelt Red Ware, the ceramic component of the Salado phenomenon. She argues that Roosevelt Red Ware represents an innovation by part-time specialist, immigrant potters—an attempt by economically and socially marginal newcomers to gain a more secure foothold among their host populations in the context of established land tenure systems. Although Crown favors the idea that production of the ware quickly spread beyond the immigrants who developed it (in the context of a regional cult), she sketched out an alternative argument: that the manufacture of these pottery types remained tightly bound to immigrant groups and was spread as a result of waves of migration.

Crown (1994:204–206) suggested that, in evaluating the latter hypothesis, it would be fruitful to examine the co-occurrence of key markers of Kayenta immigrants and evidence of the local production of Roosevelt Red Ware throughout the temporal and geographical range of these types. Since then, Kayenta immigrant enclaves have increasingly been identified throughout central and southern Arizona, as well as southwestern New Mexico, based on the presence of perforated plates (Kayenta pottery-making tools), Maverick Mountain Series pottery (ceramics made in the southern Southwest, using forming techniques and exhibiting shapes and painted decoration characteristic of the Tsegi Orange Ware tradition of the Four Corners region), room-block architecture, entryboxes, and kivas, among other indicators (Di Peso 1958a; Haury 1958; Lindsay 1987; Lyons 2001, 2003, 2004a; Lyons and Lindsay 2006; Neuzil 2005, 2008; Woodson 1995, 1999). These markers are consistently associated with evidence of the local manufacture of Roosevelt Red Ware. Spatial and chronological patterns in these and other data indicate that Roosevelt Red Ware production remained closely tied to northern immigrants and their descendants rather than spreading quickly and easily to local host groups (Lyons 2001, 2003; Lyons and Clark 2012).

Building on these insights, my colleagues and I argue that the Salado phenomenon is best viewed as the material residue of Kayenta groups in diaspora (Lyons 2007, 2010, 2013a, 2014, 2015; Lyons and Clark 2012; Lyons, Hill, and Clark 2011; see also Clark and Lyons, eds. 2012; Clark et al. 2013). This model holds that groups of Kayenta immigrants mixing with disparate host groups, under different local economic and political circumstances, led, over generations, to varied, partially shared expressions of group identity (Lyons and Clark 2008; Lyons et al. 2008). In some places, such as the San Pedro Valley, immigrants were allowed to remake the homeland almost entirely, standing out from local groups in very visible ways. In others, such as the Tonto Basin (the putative Salado "heartland") and the Phoenix Basin (the Hohokam core), they had to deemphasize differences between themselves and their hosts. Regardless of local circumstances, however, a network linked these dispersed enclaves, and thus, a shared ceramic tradition, Roosevelt Red Ware, exhibited remarkable consistency across a large geographical area and persisted over many generations.

The Davis Ranch Site as a Salado Settlement

Gerald (1975; see also chapter 2; cf. Di Peso 1958a) considered the Davis Ranch Site a Salado settlement because Roosevelt Red Ware overwhelmingly dominates the painted ceramics he recovered. Other researchers have made the same identification on these grounds and also based on the site's architecture, noting that most Salado sites consist of pueblo-like room blocks (sets of contiguous rooms) often connected by walls to create compounds (Bronitsky and Merritt 1986:217–219; Franklin 1980:224–229, Table 9; Franklin and Masse 1976:50–51; Nelson and LeBlanc 1986:5, Table 1.2).

The Davis Ranch Site is critical to the model of Salado as the Kayenta in diaspora in that the evidence that the pueblo was built and occupied by Kayenta immigrants is both abundant and robust, Roosevelt Red Ware was produced by the people who lived there and intensively exchanged with local groups, and over time, its inhabitants began to abandon some Kayenta traditions and, presumably, adopted some local practices. Indeed, if Salado studies had begun in southeastern rather than central Arizona—in the context of the record from the San Pedro Valley, the Aravaipa Valley, the Sulphur Springs Valley, and the Safford Basin, rather than the Globe-Miami area and the Tonto and Phoenix Basins—the Salado phenomenon would not be nearly so puzzling to archaeologists as it has been. There would have been a notion of a Salado heartland south of the Gila rather than north of the Salt (Lyons and Lindsay 2006). Gerald, however, did not have the benefit of the recent discoveries that form the foundation of the diaspora model. Instead, his research, analyses, and inferences must be viewed within the context of what was known during the 1950s and against the institutional and intellectual backdrop of his employer, the Amerind Foundation.

THE AMERIND FOUNDATION

The Amerind Foundation, established in 1937 by William Shirley Fulton and based in Dragoon, Arizona, focused the majority of its research, through the mid-1950s, on the archaeology and history of southeastern Arizona. The San Pedro Valley was an especially important locus of activity, and during this period Amerind Foundation archaeologists excavated Tres Alamos (ARIZONA:BB:15:2[AF], AZ BB:15:1[ASM]; Tuthill 1947), the K.E.G. Site (ARIZONA:BB:15:3[AF]; Di Peso 1951b), Babocomari Village (ARIZONA:EE:7:1[AF], AZ EE:7:1[ASM]; Di Peso 1951a), the Presidio de Santa Cruz de Terrenate (ARIZONA:EE:8:1[AF], AZ EE:4:11[ASM]; Di Peso 1953), and Reeve Ruin (ARIZONA:BB:11:12[AF], AZ BB:11:26[ASM]; Di Peso 1958a), among other sites (see also Clark and Lyons, eds. 2012).

Amerind Foundation researchers interpreted the archaeology of the San Pedro Valley through the lens of the Dragoon Culture (or Complex), which had been defined earlier by Fulton and Tuthill (Fulton 1934a, 1934b, 1938; Fulton and Tuthill 1940; Tuthill 1950) based on materials recovered from sites in the Dragoon area and near Gleeson, Arizona. They also wrestled with the Salado phenomenon and focused much of their effort on the archaeology of the Sobaipuri, the Piman speakers who inhabited the San Pedro and Santa Cruz Valleys at Spanish contact, left the San Pedro Valley in the late 1700s, and were absorbed by other O'odham groups.

One of the stated goals of the Amerind Foundation and its former director, Charles C. Di Peso

(1952–1982), was to bridge "the gap" between the archaeological and historical records in southeastern Arizona. This objective became the driving force behind Di Peso's doctoral dissertation research, the results of which were published as *The Amerind Foundation* No. 6 (1953). The main focus of his fieldwork was a site on the west bank of the San Pedro River, just north of Fairbank, Arizona. Di Peso argued that under the remains of Santa Cruz de Terrenate, a Spanish presidio dating to the late eighteenth century, lay the protohistoric Sobaipuri village of Quiburi. Today, the consensus (Gerald 1968; Masse 1981; Seymour 1989; Williams 1986) is that the underlying architecture represents the founding stages of the presidio rather than a Sobaipuri village.

José Solas Ruin (AZ BB:11:5[AF], AZ BB: 11:91[ASM]) was another key site in Di Peso's reconstruction of continuity between the ancient and historic inhabitants of the San Pedro Valley. Di Peso (1953:26–28, 38, 49–50, 133) equated it with the protohistoric Sobaipuri settlement of San Salvador de Baicatcan, based on his interpretation of seventeenth-century Spanish documents describing spatial relationships among colonial installations, indigenous villages, and natural features. However, evidence available at the time of the site's excavation and additional information compiled in the intervening years indicate that, rather than a Sobaipuri village occupied during the seventeenth century, the component at José Solas Ruin investigated by the Amerind Foundation was a fourteenth-century AD village built and occupied, at least in part, by immigrants from the Kayenta region or their descendants (Lyons 2004a; see also Clark and Lyons, eds. 2012).

Di Peso's O'otam Model

Di Peso (1953, 1956, 1958a, 1979, 1980, 1981) argued for the existence of an O'otam, or "Desert Mogollon," culture that was indigenous to southern Arizona, portions of southwestern New Mexico, and parts of northern Mexico, manifest in the San Pedro Valley and surrounding areas in the form of the Dragoon Complex, the Babocomari Culture, the San Simon Branch, and the archaeology of other local groups who made red-on-brown painted pottery (as opposed to the red-on-buff painted ceramics of the Salt and Gila River valleys). He traced the origin of O'otam groups to the area's Archaic period inhabitants (or the "Cochise Culture," as they were formerly called; Sayles and Antevs 1941). Di Peso asserted that southern Arizona was colonized by the Hohokam (to whom he attributed a Mesoamerican origin) during the Colonial period (now dated ca. AD 750–950), and that puebloan immigrants (sometimes referred to as Salado) established themselves in the region during the Civano phase of the Classic period (now dated ca. AD 1300–1450). He also posited that the historic Sobaipuri people were the descendants of both the indigenous O'otam and puebloan immigrants.

In an effort to investigate the Salado presence in the San Pedro, as well as the impact of puebloan immigrants on the O'otam, Di Peso excavated the Reeve Ruin during the spring and summer of 1956 (Di Peso 1958a). He found the site to be lacking key traits characteristic of the Salado Culture (as defined by Haury [1945] in his report on Los Muertos; AZ U:9:56[ASM]), despite the fact that Roosevelt Red Ware was overwhelmingly dominant in the ceramic assemblage. Instead, he observed many traits associated with the Western Pueblo Complex (Reed 1948) and little evidence of the presence of O'otam groups. Therefore, he described the site as a Western Pueblo site-unit intrusion (Di Peso 1958a:6; see also Wauchope 1956). Because the results from the Reeve Ruin raised more questions than they answered, another site with similar features but more time depth, the Davis Ranch Site, was excavated.

REX GERALD AND THE DAVIS RANCH SITE

Rex Ervin Gerald (frontispiece) was born in Stanton, Texas, on March 18, 1928. He received his BA in anthropology from the University of Arizona in 1951

FIGURE 1.4 Rex E. Gerald (left) and Emil W. Haury (right) sorting potsherds at Point of Pines, 1946. Photograph by E. B. Sayles, courtesy of the Arizona State Museum, University of Arizona (Negative No. 1560).

and his AM in anthropology from the University of Pennsylvania in 1957. His master's thesis is entitled "An Historic House Site in Northwest Chihuahua, Mexico." Between his undergraduate and graduate school years, during the Korean War, he served in Japan and Korea as a physical anthropologist in the U.S. Army's Central Identification Unit.

Gerald attended the University of Arizona's archaeological field school at Point of Pines in 1946, 1948, 1949, and 1956 (figure 1.4). There, he met his first wife, Mary Virginia ("Ginny," or "Gini") Gould. They married in 1951 and had two children, Rosemary Elaine and Eric Campbell Gerald. In 1957, he joined the staff of the Amerind Foundation, filling its "first and only" predoctoral research position (Fenner 1977:325). The agreement that established the position called for Gerald to excavate the Davis Ranch Site, located across the San Pedro River from Reeve Ruin, and to publish the results of his work.

The Davis Ranch Site consists of a nine-room pueblo and an apparently isolated two-room unit in a plaza surrounded by three room blocks and a compound wall, a three-room and a four-room unit within a few meters of the exterior of the northwestern perimeter room block, a rectangular kiva a few meters outside (east of) the compound wall, a group of nine rooms about 75 m to the northeast of the kiva, several extramural features, and 10 pit houses that predate the pueblo (figure 1.5). In 1957, Gerald excavated 16 rooms, the kiva, and five of the pit houses in their entirety. He nearly completely excavated four of the pit houses (leaving overlying

FIGURE 1.5 The Davis Ranch Site (ARIZONA:BB:11:7[AF], AZ BB:11:10[ASM], AZ BB:11:36 [ASM]). Map produced by Catherine Gilman after original by Rex E. Gerald.

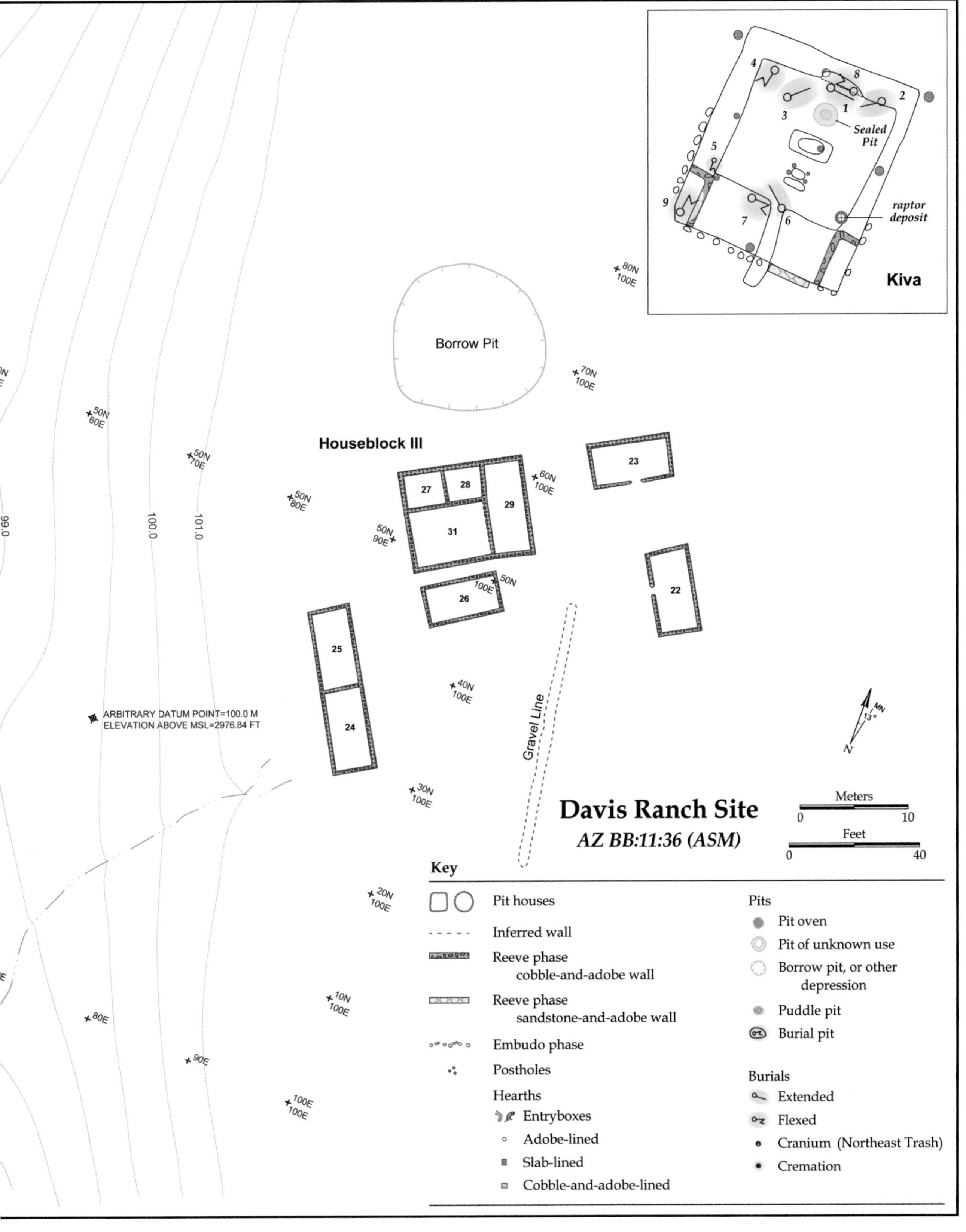

Kiva
Sealed Pit
raptor deposit
Borrow Pit
Houseblock III
ARBITRARY DATUM POINT=100.0 M
ELEVATION ABOVE MSL=2976.84 FT
Gravel Line
Davis Ranch Site
AZ BB:11:36 (ASM)
Meters
Feet
Key
Pit houses
Inferred wall
Reeve phase cobble-and-adobe wall
Reeve phase sandstone-and-adobe wall
Embudo phase
Postholes
Hearths
Entryboxes
Adobe-lined
Slab-lined
Cobble-and-adobe-lined
Pits
Pit oven
Pit of unknown use
Borrow pit, or other depression
Puddle pit
Burial pit
Burials
Extended
Flexed
Cranium (Northeast Trash)
Cremation

features in place), dug a small portion of one of the pit houses, substantially but incompletely excavated one room, and test-trenched 20 rooms as well as a number of extramural areas. This work yielded, by his reckoning, 50 whole or partial ceramic vessels, more than 41,000 sherds, more than 100 flaked stone tools and pieces of debitage, and more than 120 ground stone objects and resulted in the discovery of 15 interments and 3 cremations.

Gerald wrote a draft report of his excavations and analyses in 1958. However, this 238-page document was never completed or published. That same year, he left Arizona to work at Texas Western College of the University of Texas at El Paso (now the University of Texas at El Paso). He was hired as director of the Centennial Museum (a post he held for 22 years) and an assistant (later, associate) professor of anthropology (a position he held for 32 years) in the Department of Sociology and Anthropology. In 1961, Gerald married Maria Elgie Zaiz, with whom he had four children: Elgie Lisette, Rex Ervin II, Lorenzo Xocotzin, and Camille Nenetzin (Netzin) Gerald.

Despite the fact that Gerald never completed the Davis Ranch Site manuscript, parts of the dataset were disseminated. He delivered a paper on the kiva at the 23rd annual meeting of the Society for American Archaeology (SAA; Gerald 1958), and an analysis of the mammalian fauna was published by William Burt (1961; reprinted herein as appendix G) in *Journal of Mammalogy*. Gerald was awarded a PhD in anthropology by the University of Chicago in 1975. In his dissertation, he used palynological and faunal data, as well as the spatial distribution of ceramic design elements, to examine social responses to climate change at the Davis Ranch Site and Reeve Ruin.

Aside from completing his dissertation, Gerald very seldom turned his attention to archaeology in Arizona, focusing instead on the rich and varied cultural resources, both ancient and historic, of Texas and northern Chihuahua. He succumbed to liver cancer on May 13, 1990. He is remembered fondly by colleagues and former students as an excellent field archaeologist, a gifted teacher, a pioneer in the field of cultural resource management archaeology in Texas, the researcher largely responsible for the government's 1987 decision to restore federal recognition of the Tigua Tribe of Ysleta del Sur Pueblo, a key contributor to Spanish presidio studies, and a master of outreach to the general public (Martin 1990, 1997). In recognition of all this and more, he was posthumously honored by the El Paso Archaeological Society, which presented him its 1997 Award of Distinction.

Gerald's Dilemma

At the Davis Ranch Site, Gerald encountered many artifacts and architectural features known, by the 1950s, to be characteristic of groups in the northern Southwest and that, together, likely indicated the presence of immigrants. These included the kiva, Maverick Mountain Series pottery, a babe-in-cradle figurine (see chapter 6), a mealing bin, manos with pecked finger grips, flat metates, and perforated plates. In fact, in his manuscript, he calls attention to the northern origin of many, but not all, of these phenomena.

Prior to his work at the Davis Ranch Site, most of Gerald's field experience had been at Point of Pines. In all, Gerald spent four summers there, including the summer of 1956, when he served as dig foreman (figure 1.6). William J. Robinson (personal communication 2011) also attended the field school in 1956 and remembers discussions of the Maverick Mountain phase during the evening classroom sessions. Maverick Mountain phase was the name given to artifacts and architecture at Point of Pines that Haury (1958) inferred were associated with an influx of immigrants from the Kayenta region. Most, if not all, of the characteristics of the Maverick Mountain phase—including locally produced Kayenta-like painted pottery (the Maverick Mountain Series), the initial short-term use of pit houses and later construction of pueblo architecture, and a northern-style kiva (D-shaped, rather than rectangular, at Point of Pines)—were considered in those discussions.

FIGURE 1.6 Point of Pines field school crew at AZ W:9:39(ASM) in 1956. Left to right: Rex E. Gerald, Donald H. Morris, Katherine Major, William J. Robinson, Lloyd Rogers, and T. Patrick Culbert. Photographer unknown, courtesy of the Arizona State Museum, University of Arizona (Negative No. 3888).

The similarities between traces of northern immigrants at Point of Pines—to whom Haury had attributed a specific origin—and the material from the Davis Ranch Site could not possibly have gone unnoticed by Gerald. Indeed, in 1957, Gerald (R. Gerald to W. Burt, letter, July 6, 1957, Archives, Amerind Museum, Dragoon) wrote the following to William Burt, who analyzed the mammalian fauna from the site:

> We originally thought this site, i.e., the Davis Site, ARIZONA:BB:11:7, was the remains of the Sobaipuri village of Cusac visited by Kino, Manje and Bernal in the 1690s; but excavation revealed neither artifacts of Spanish origin nor architecture of Sobaipuri construction. . . . Incidentally, the Davis Site has produced the first indisputable kiva in southern Arizona—strong evidence, when combined with other architectural features and artifacts, of migration of a functioning social group (such as a village) into the area. After writing the above, I realized that you have identified the bone from Reeve Ruin (ARIZONA:BB:11:12), a site located immediately

> across the river from the Davis Site; therefore, to relate the two sites, I should say that Reeve Ruin is probably the first site in the area occupied by the Pueblo people migrating from northern Arizona. Shortly afterwards and probably before Reeve Ruin was abandoned, these migrants began occupying [the] Davis Site, a locality closer to the fields but less easily defended—possibly the need for defense had diminished by that time.

A few months later, Gerald corresponded with Harold Colton and Edward Danson of the Museum of Northern Arizona regarding pottery from the Davis Ranch Site that both Colton and Danson found to be like Kayenta Polychrome, Tusayan Polychrome, and also Maverick Mountain Polychrome from Point of Pines (see chapter 6). Danson (E. Danson to R. Gerald, letter, September 13, 1957, Archives, Amerind Museum, Dragoon) writes:

> Here is probably another situation, then, of people making northern pottery types in the south. This certainly does follow out my thinking on Point of Pines, which is that migrants from the Kayenta area to Point of Pines represent one of many groups who came south, mixing somewhat with the local people but retaining many of their old cultural patterns.

It is important to note here that, in 1954, Danson (1957) completed a study of Maverick Mountain Series pottery from University Indian Ruin (AZ BB:9:33[ASM]), in Tucson, some 40 km (25 miles) from the Davis Ranch Site. Thus, to him, the San Pedro Valley represented a third area where Kayenta immigrants had established themselves. Gerald (R. Gerald to E. Danson, letter, October 1, 1957, Archives, Amerind Museum, Dragoon), who later cited the University Indian Ruin report (Hayden 1957) in his manuscript, offers Danson a cryptic response, writing, "Your idea of a migration from the north into Southern Arizona is in line with our thoughts here. Unfortunately, however, we are forced to look to some as yet unknown region, probably below the Mogollon Rim, for the origin of our intrusive group."

Gerald never wrote a concluding chapter for his manuscript, but his correspondence and the paper he presented at the SAA annual meeting in 1958 (see also Gerald 1975) are likely good indicators of his thoughts at the time regarding the nature of the Davis Ranch Site. In the SAA paper, he writes:

> The Davis Ranch Site is slightly divergent [from the Western Pueblo Complex, sensu Reed (1948)] in so far as it has flexed burials and lambdoidal deformation. Both of these are Anasazi Pueblo traits though flexed burials are also characteristic of the Hopi-Zuni-Mimbres-Casas Grandes portion of the Western Pueblo area (Reed 1948:15). The pottery assemblage . . . suggest[s] an early Pueblo IV period of occupation by a Salado-like people (Gerald 1958:1).

Based on parallels between the kiva he excavated and those of the Hopi Mesas, he hypothesizes that Hopis may have been among those who built and occupied the village. He is puzzled, however, by the preponderance of Gila Polychrome at the site, considering its near absence on the Hopi Mesas.

Di Peso's published expectations regarding the Davis Ranch Site and Gerald's (1958; see also chapter 2) results and initial conclusions were very much in conflict. This friction may have contributed to Gerald's departure from the Amerind Foundation. Although Di Peso's ideas evolved over time, a key tenet of his San Pedro Valley model, and the intellectual device he used to "close the gap," was the notion that sites such as José Solas Ruin (Di Peso's San Salvador de Baicatcan) and the Davis Ranch Site (which he hypothesized was the Sobaipuri rancheria named Cusac) were occupied during the 1600s:

> Archaeological evidence was needed . . . to prove . . . [José Solas Ruin was occupied during the historic era] for the presence of Gila Polychrome alone suggested a prehistoric, and not an historic, occupation of the village. A room

> located centrally in the western cluster was chosen and excavated. . . . This room produced one complete plainware plate (very much like Sobaipuri Plainware), and parts of four other plates, as well as a crushed Gila Polychrome jar and a crushed Gila Polychrome bowl. . . . The association of Gila Polychrome with a Sobaipuri-like plainware supported the supposition that Gila Polychrome continued to be made into historic times (Di Peso 1953:133–134). . . . Surface collections taken from a late compound site near Redington, Arizona [the Davis Ranch Site] indicate that Gila Polychrome is a companion ware of Sobaipuri Plainware. Positive proof of this ceramic sequence will come only after the above-mentioned sites [José Solas Ruin and the Davis Ranch Site] are thoroughly examined (Di Peso 1953:273).

Indeed, as late as 1981, Di Peso continued to argue that the suite of material traces found at José Solas Ruin (the same associations between architectural features and artifacts evident at Reeve Ruin and the Davis Ranch Site) demonstrated continuity across the protohistoric period (Di Peso 1981:114–115; Lyons 2004a; see also Masse 1981).

Writing in 1956, the year before Gerald's excavations at the Davis Ranch Site, Joe Ben Wheat delivered a stinging critique of Di Peso's assertions in the pages of *American Antiquity*:

> The validity of much of Di Peso's reconstruction of events in southern Arizona depends on his contention that Gila Polychrome continued to be used into historic times. This in turn rests largely on the identification of the site of Baicatcan. The Sobaipuri moved from Baicatcan to Quiburi in 1692. His identification of this site is based on 2 assumptions: that the location is correct, and that the cultural complex forms a continuum with Quiburi. The pottery at "Baicatcan" consisted of plainware "similar to Sobaipuri Plainware" (p. 63) and "late" Gila Polychrome (46.97%, p. 274). At Quiburi only 2 sherds of Gila Polychrome were found; these were in the trash "in association with Spanish metal, ceramics, etc. . . ." (p. 262). To this reviewer it seems incredible that Sobaipuris living at Baicatcan in 1692 and using 47% Gila Polychrome should virtually stop using this type in moving to Quiburi. This is not to argue that prehistoric Sobaipuris may not have used Gila Polychrome, but that the evidence for the identification of Baicatcan, and hence for closing the "time gap," is not yet convincing (Wheat 1956:430–431).

Presumably, Wheat did not know that the pottery "very much like Sobaipuri Plainware" found at José Solas Ruin/Baicatcan and the Davis Ranch Site by Di Peso consisted almost entirely of perforated plates, a marker of thirteenth- or fourteenth-century AD immigrants from the Kayenta region, rather than an indicator of occupation by the seventeenth-century Sobaipuri (Lyons 2004a; see chapters 6 and 7). It is clear, however, that Gerald knew this, based on his work with Amerind Museum collections (see chapter 6). It is interesting to note that by 1963, Gerald (R. Gerald to C. Di Peso, letter, October 11, 1964, Archives, Amerind Museum, Dragoon; see also Gerald 1968:16–20), in a synthesis of historical documentation and archaeological data bearing on late eighteenth-century presidios in northern New Spain, had written his own critique of (1) Di Peso's (1953) identification of certain features and artifacts at the Presidio de Santa Cruz de Terrenate as the remains of the Sobaipuri rancheria called Quiburi, and (2) Di Peso's assertion that artifacts from the site help to establish continuity between the valley's pre-Hispanic and Spanish period inhabitants.

SUMMARY AND CONCLUSION

Above, I have presented a sketch of the long-lived ancient cultural traditions of southeastern Arizona, Hohokam and Mogollon, and provided an overview of the late pre-Hispanic Salado phenomenon. The Davis Ranch Site, unlike any other settlement yet investigated, allows archaeologists to see clearly the strong and enduring connection between immigrants from the Kayenta region and Roosevelt Red Ware, the ceramic component of the Salado phenomenon. Rex Gerald, based on his experience at Point of Pines, was well equipped to interpret the site as a Kayenta immigrant enclave inhabited during the AD 1300s and perhaps the early 1400s. The nature of the record at the Davis Ranch Site, as documented by Gerald, contradicts the regional cultural historical framework established by Charles Di Peso, then the director of the Amerind Foundation, where Gerald worked. Di Peso had hypothesized that the site's occupation bridged the gap between the pre-Hispanic era and the Spanish period, and I suggest that disagreement on this point may have been a factor in Gerald's departure from the Amerind Foundation and his manuscript remaining unfinished.

The chapter that immediately follows this one is the introduction to the excavation report that Gerald wrote in 1958. Chapters 3 through 6, also authored by Gerald, present the results of his analyses of the sites' architecture and the human remains, non-ceramic artifacts, and pottery he recovered. In chapter 7, I report the results of my reanalysis of Roosevelt Red Ware, Maverick Mountain Series pottery, and perforated plates from the site. The volume concludes with chapter 8, in which Jeffery J. Clark and I place Gerald's findings, and my conclusions based on the reanalysis, in the larger context of what is now known and hypothesized regarding late pre-Hispanic Kayenta migrations into the southern Southwest and the Salado phenomenon.

2

Background and Procedures

BACKGROUND

Problems

The Davis Ranch Site (ARIZONA:BB:11:7[AF]) was excavated in an attempt to find solutions to three problems of both a specific and a general nature.

Problem 1

The Davis Ranch Site exhibits surface features similar to those found at the Reeve Ruin, which is located immediately across the San Pedro River. The Reeve Ruin was excavated in the spring of 1956 by Charles C. Di Peso of the Amerind Foundation, but because of the absence of intrusive pottery types it could not be placed in a chronology relative to previously defined red-on-brown pottery–producing cultures of the area. Because of the presence of red-on-brown sherds on the surface at the Davis Ranch Site, as well as the polychrome sherds characteristic of the Reeve Ruin, it was hoped that stratigraphic relationships could be established for these pottery types and the cultures that produced them.

Problem 2

The Amerind Foundation published a report on the Sobaipuri Indians of the upper San Pedro River (Di Peso 1953) and has subsequently been interested in expanding that study to the Sobaipuri of the lower San Pedro Valley. The Davis Ranch Site is located in the vicinity of Cusac, the southernmost village of the lower Sobaipuri (Bolton 1936:364–365), and on the surface there were alignments of stone as well as fragments of pottery bearing the Sobaipuri rim coil (Di Peso 1953:149–150). All of these facts led us to hope that this might be the site of Cusac and that information might be recovered to show the cultural and temporal relationship between the cultural assemblage found at Reeve Ruin and the Sobaipuri.

Problem 3

Gila Polychrome (Haury 1945:63–80), a pottery type of wide geographical and temporal span, was found to be the most common decorated pottery at Reeve Ruin and was expected to be very popular at the Davis Ranch Site. With this large collection of Gila Polychrome from the briefly occupied Reeve Ruin and the expected stratified collection from the Davis Ranch Site, plus other site collections at the Amerind Foundation and the Arizona State Museum, it was expected that regional and temporal variants of Gila Polychrome would be recognized.

Site and Environment

The Davis Ranch Site is located on the first terrace above the riverbed on the east side of the San Pedro

River, approximately 4.8 km (3 mi) south of Redington and 64.4 km (40 mi) north of Benson, in southeastern Arizona. It is on land owned by Kingston J. Smallhouse. The site is 906.2 m (2,973 ft) above sea level and about 15.2 m (50 ft) above the present entrenched streambed.

The site is in the Lower Sonoran Life Zone characterized by saguaro (*Carnegiea gigantea*), prickly pear (*Opuntia engelmannii*), honey mesquite (*Prosopis juliflora*), greasewood (*Larrea tridentata*), and barrel cactus (*Ferocactus wislizeni*) in the flora, and by peccary (*Pecari tajacu*), white-tailed deer (*Odocoileus virginianus*), mule deer (*Odocoileus hemionus*), coyote (*Canis latrans*), and black-tailed jackrabbit (*Lepus californicus*) in the fauna. The Galiuro Mountains are about 24 km (15 mi) to the east, reaching an elevation of over 2,134 m (7,000 ft). The Santa Catalina Mountains, over 2,743 m (9,000 ft) in elevation, are some 19–24 km (12–15 mi) to the west. Within 32 km (20 mi) to the southwest are the Rincon Mountains, rising to more than 2,592 m (8,500 ft) in elevation. Foothills of these mountain ranges extend down to the San Pedro River to form a narrow, rugged, but not particularly deep canyon a mile south of the site.

The projection of the terrace on which the main part of the site is located is relatively flat and extends about 100 m north to south and some 80 m east to west. On the north, west, and south, the terrace drops abruptly to the valley floor, into which the river has recently cut a channel, while to the east there is a 2 m rise to a second terrace, on which a portion of the site (Houseblock III) is located. There is surface evidence of a Hohokam Colonial period occupation on this terrace, but no testing was done there.

The bedrock underlying the main portion of the site is apparently a down-faulted stratum of sandstone of the same type that underlies the Reeve Ruin. Gravel and caliche overlie this sandstone stratum in places. Above and often intermixed with this is red clay, which was apparently utilized by the occupants of the site as adobe for the construction of buildings; 15–20 cm of silty soil overlie the clay stratum.

PROCEDURES

Lease

A lease was negotiated with Mr. Smallhouse, owner of the property on which the Davis Ranch Site is located, for permission to excavate the site and to use private roads and gates, water from a well, and an abandoned farmhouse for living quarters and a field laboratory.

Mapping

A map of topographical and architectural features was made with the use of an alidade, a plane table, a Philadelphia rod calibrated in the metric system, a 50 m Wyteface steel tape, a 2 m steel tape, and a plumb bob. The topographical map was made using the alidade, plane table, and Philadelphia rod, while architectural and other man-made features were sighted in with the alidade and measured in with the 50 m tape for greater accuracy. A distance reading on the alidade was found to be accurate to within about 50 cm, while a distance measurement made with the 50 m tape is believed to be accurate to within about 5 cm (the inked lines denoting room walls on the final map are about 8 cm wide) on the field map, which was scaled so that 1 inch equals 3 m. Minor inaccuracies in mapping of architectural features undoubtedly occurred because of difficulty in locating room corners exactly and in determining wall thicknesses in the rooms with poorly preserved walls, as well as for other reasons at present unknown. Errors of a few centimeters in measurements of this sort are quite noticeable on the map but are difficult to correct at the scale employed.

A temporary benchmark located on the site was related to a USGS benchmark on the Pima County line by determining the bearing from true north, reading an angle from the horizontal from the USGS benchmark to the temporary benchmark with a transit, measuring the distance with the 50 m tape, and calculating the horizontal and vertical distances from the USGS benchmark.

To simplify taking field notes and to provide a systematic method of designating areas and trenches at the site, a grid system was used. At the site, a zero point was located near the center of the area of concentrated excavation, and a line was passed through this point parallel to the long axis of the pueblo enclosure. This line was oriented north-northwest to south-southeast on a bearing of 335° from true north. Another line was passed through the zero point at a right angle to the first. Stakes were driven at the zero point (0, 0) and at 10 m intervals along each of the lines and were marked 10N (i.e., 10 m north) in all four directions, the north-northwest line being taken as north. Using this system, any point in the site could be designated as so many meters north or south and so many meters east or west of the zero point. In practice, features were not located more accurately than to a square meter, each square meter of the surface of the site being arbitrarily designated by the name of the point at the northeast corner. Thus, the notation 20N 15E would indicate the square meter that lay to the southwest of a point 20 m north and 15 m east of the zero point. Any feature lying mostly within this square meter or between 19.01 m and 20.00 m north and 14.01 m and 15.00 m east of the zero point would also be given the locator designation 20N 15E.

Where practicable, an attempt was made to orient long trenches parallel to one of the lines through the zero point. In all but one instance it was possible to designate these trenches by indicating the distance to the trench from the line through the zero point that it paralleled, such as T10N to designate a trench parallel to the east-west line through the zero point and located immediately south of a line 10 m north of the east-west line. Since such a trench could extend to infinity in two directions, it was necessary to denote the meter squares at each end of the actual excavation by the method described above. However, instead of writing 10N before each east or west designation, it was recorded once, and the east or west designations were hyphenated. For example, T10N 12–18E indicates a trench parallel to the east-west line 10 m north of the zero point and delimited on the west and east by the meter squares 10N, 12E and 10N, 18E, respectively. Larger areas were indicated by hyphenating both the north-south and the east-west numbers, as 10–12N 12–18E.

Excavation

Three primary techniques were utilized: test trenching, stratigraphic testing, and architectural feature excavation. Test trenches were used to determine the depth to sterile soil in various areas and to search for cremations, burials, and architectural features. The earth removed from test trenches was not screened, except when searching for fragments of recently broken artifacts; sherds and other artifacts were recovered as they were noted during the excavation.

Stratigraphic tests, or stratitests, were made in attempts to find evidence of cultural change through time as manifested in changing styles in sherds and other artifact types from lower, earlier deposits to the higher, later deposits. Stratitests were made in areas of deep trash deposits and in the fill of most pueblo rooms and in pit houses. Stratitests in dwellings were made in order to get some indication of the types of artifacts in vogue at the site during the time the particular dwelling was being filled by man and nature. In practice, stratitests were made in vertical columns of fill that were excavated by carefully controlled levels and were passed through 1/4-inch or 1/8-inch screen, sherds and other artifacts being recovered on the screen. Controls of this type theoretically make it possible to recognize differences in the cultural material from the upper and lower layers, if such differences exist, and also give indications of the types and quantities of material being deposited in the structure during different stages of the filling.

Harold S. Colton (1946:297–299) has stated that most of the stratitests dug by the staff of the

Museum of Northern Arizona have proven to be of little value as indicators of culture change because of vertical movements of sherds and other artifacts in a deposit as a result of rodent burrowing, root action, and reworking of the trash by man. Of greater probable authenticity is the information to be gained from stratitests concerning the changing nature of the fill from level to level, particularly within dwellings.

Architectural feature excavation followed a pattern of outlining the walls of a dwelling with a trench extending to within about 10 cm of the floor, removing the fill from the center of the room, at least one square meter of which was removed as a stratitest, and then clearing the fill from 10 cm above the floor down to the level of the floor. Hearths, postholes, and floor pits were cleared during the latter stage of excavation, and artifacts found in contact with the floor were left in place until the room was photographed. All test trenches and stratitests were excavated down to sterile soil, and subfloor tests were dug down to sterile soil in all dwellings that were excavated completely.

One other excavation technique must be mentioned: strip tests, which are excavations in which the top 5–10 cm of soil is removed from an area with broom and trowel. This technique was utilized to search for and expose features lying close to the surface. Strip tests were made to clear the historic era (Embudo phase) enclosure, in defining relationships between historic era (Embudo phase) and Redfield and Romero (Reeve) phase features, and in excavating historic era (Embudo phase) structures. Strip tests were made inside the historic era (Embudo phase) enclosure in an attempt to locate jacal dwellings similar to those found at Santa Cruz de Gaybanipitea (Di Peso 1953:125, Plate 42) and at San Pablo de Quiburi (Di Peso 1953:111–122), but with negative results. Strip tests were not extended down to sterile soil.

Excavation equipment consisted of a one-yard International dump truck; three wheelbarrows; long-handled, round-pointed shovels; picks; four-inch pointing trowels; hand picks; whisk brooms; house brooms; push brooms; paint brushes; dental tools; and numerous other small tools for special purposes.

Four laborers were employed for 12 1/2 weeks, January 15–April 19, 1957, with an expenditure of 224 man-days of energy devoted to actual digging. [*Editor: Gerald's notes indicate that the following men were members of the excavation crew: Ramon Bernal, Mike Cañez, Pat Cañez, José Estrella, Dario Gordillo, Alfred Lujan, Andres Lujan, Adolfo Martinez, Marcello Padia, Chris Ramirez, Juliel Servin, and Robert Trujillo.*]

Photography

Photography was employed throughout the dig and in the laboratory to record data and to document the report. An aerial photograph was taken before the dig began and general views of the site were taken from a photographic ladder and from ground level during various stages of the excavation. Architectural features were recorded by photography as were artifacts or data that could not be removed to the laboratory for further study and photography. Removable artifacts were photographed in the laboratory.

Photographic equipment consisted of a 4 × 5-inch Graphic View camera with a 90 mm wide-angle lens and a 203 mm regular lens; a 35 mm Exakta VX for color slides with a 35 mm wide angle lens and a 50 mm regular lens; a Graflex Stroboflash unit with two lights; and a General Electric light meter. In addition to the actual photographic equipment, numerals and letters were used to designate features in the photographs, 25 cm and 50 cm arrows were used to indicate true north, and a 1 m stick was used for vertical scale.

Site Designation

The system utilized by the Amerind Foundation is identical to that of the Arizona State Museum and as described by Wasley (1957), except that the last number of a site designation is not usually the same for the same site in the two versions of the system. This inconsistency is the result of the freedom allowed in the assignment of numbers to sites within a limited geographical area rather than a result of a difference in the systems employed. The Davis Ranch Site is designated ARIZONA:BB:11:7 by the Amerind Foundation. [*Editor: The Arizona State Museum has designated the Davis Ranch Site AZ BB:11:10 and AZ BB:11:36.*]

Laboratory

All sherds, bones, and other specimens that were recovered in the field were examined in the laboratory. Where possible they were cleaned and subjected to a preliminary analysis in the field laboratory. All sherds were separated as to type and were counted, and all sherds except some of the most numerous plain ware types (Davis Plain) were stamped with their provenience and placed in boxes according to types. The unstamped Davis Plain sherds were returned to their respective marked bags and were saved until final analysis was completed, in the event they were needed for future reference. When the fieldwork was finished, the sherds, which were segregated according to types as recognized in the field, were again analyzed, a more careful identification was made, and a second count for each provenience was recorded. This second analysis of pottery types was of particular importance because the entire sample of a type could be examined and any sherds mistakenly identified in the preliminary analysis could be properly identified. Sherds of unrecognized types or sherds suspected of being from another area were sent to specialists in the archaeology of the areas of suspected origin for examination and identification.

Portable artifacts other than sherds were cataloged in either the regular Amerind Museum cataloging system or the Amerind Foundation stone cataloging system. The artifacts cataloged under the former system are those kept in the museum for exhibit, study, or exchange and are assigned numbers serially with an alphabetical prefix that denotes the site from which the artifacts came; Davis Ranch Site artifacts were assigned regular catalog numbers, such as D/123. Under the stone catalog system, artifacts that are not to be kept permanently in the museum are assigned numbers serially with the same site prefix plus the letter "s" to indicate that the number is a stone catalog number; Davis Ranch Site stone catalog numbers were written D/s123, and so on.

Burials were designated serially with the prefix letter "B" for inhumations. Cremations are similarly numbered with a "C" prefix. All nonhuman bones were saved and, after washing and packing in bags and boxes with their provenience, sent to specialists for identification.

3

Architecture and Miscellaneous Features

[Editor: Gerald arranged his discussion of architecture and features chronologically, from most recent to oldest, and did not always provide information under each of the headings he used to organize his descriptions. In this chapter, features are discussed in stratigraphic order, from oldest to most recent, and whenever possible, additional data have been added to flesh out individual descriptions, making the presentation more balanced. In addition, the following, brief introductory section has been added.

Architectural traits and the presence or absence of different classes of artifacts indicate the presence of five components at the Davis Ranch Site. These date to the Early Agricultural period, the Hohokam Colonial and Sedentary periods, the Aravaipa phase, the Redfield and Romero phases, and the historic era (table 3.1). Gerald applied phase names to four of these intervals but did not describe the criteria he used to assign deposits and features to them. Gerald's Davis phase apparently encompasses the Hohokam Colonial and Sedentary periods, his Sosa phase includes materials currently assigned to the Aravaipa phase, his Reeve phase is apparently coeval with the Redfield and Romero phases, and it is inferred that his Embudo phase represents evidence of historic use of the site. Gerald did not identify an Early Agricultural period (or as it would have been called at the time, San Pedro stage Cochise Culture) occupation. In order to place the results of Gerald's excavations at the Davis Ranch Site in the larger context of recent research in the lower San Pedro Valley, the phase sequence developed as a result of the San Pedro Preservation Project (Clark and Lyons, eds. 2012) is employed here, although Gerald's phase names are provided in parentheses.

The architectural units present at the Davis Ranch Site include two shallow, round houses-in-pits; a subrectangular house-in-a-pit; seven pit houses; a rectangular kiva; a 36-room pueblo composed of four room blocks, a plaza, a compound wall, rooms appended to the compound wall but unassociated with any identified room block, and a room whose relationship to the identified room blocks cannot be determined; two small room blocks outside the pueblo; and a separate group of nine room-spaces of unknown function (see figure 1.5).]

ROUND HOUSES

[Editor: As early as the 1940s, researchers had begun to recognize shallow, oval houses associated with the preceramic San Pedro phase (Sayles 1945:1–4), but architecture associated with what is now known as the Early Agricultural period (the San Pedro and Cienega phases, ca. 1200–800 BC and ca. 800 BC–AD 50, respectively; Vint 2017) remained poorly understood until the 1990s (Huckell 1995; Mabry 1998). Gerald's writings give no indication as to whether he considered the possibility that the round houses at the Davis Ranch Site (Houses 6 and 10) were preceramic in age.

TABLE 3.1 Correlation of Rex Gerald's (1958, 1975; see also Di Peso 1958a) phase sequence with Clark and Lyons's (eds. 2012) phase sequence and approximate dates (all AD)

Gerald phase	Approximate date(s)	Clark and Lyons phase or period	Approximate date(s)
Embudo	Post-1600	Historic	Post-1840
Reeve	1300–1500	Romero	1350/1375–1425/1450
		Redfield	1300/1325–1350/1375
Sosa	1250–1300	Aravaipa	1250/1275–1300/1325
Davis	Pre-1250	Sedentary	950–1150
		Colonial	750–950

Based on stratigraphic evidence, these houses must predate the Northeast Trash, the overlying refuse deposit generated initially by the occupants of the Colonial and Sedentary period pit houses at the site and later by those who inhabited the late Classic period pit houses and the late Classic period pueblo. The absence of artifacts clearly associated with Houses 6 and 10 hinders any attempt to assign a precise date to them. However, their size and shape, as well as the nature of their walls, suggest construction and use during the Early Agricultural period (see Huckell 1995:Figure 3.8; Mabry 1998). Furthermore, characteristic Early Agricultural period projectile points have been recovered from the site (see chapter 5). Gerald had not identified them as preceramic or Early Ceramic period in age, despite the fact that one is an excellent example of the well-known San Pedro point (Sayles 1941:Plate 16), and others, though not provided with names until the 1980s, were known by the 1950s to date later than the San Pedro phase and earlier than the Hohokam and Mogollon sequences (e.g., Haury 1957; Haury et al. 1950; Martin et al. 1952). Three specimens are identified in chapter 5 as Cienega points: one Cienega Short, one Cienega Long, and one Cienega Stemmed (Huckell 1988; Sliva 2005:95–98, Figure 3.16). Additional evidence includes a fragment of a knobbed stone tray (D/191) recovered from Pit 1 in House 6 and another fragment (D/170g) found near House 6, in the Northeast Trash. Such objects are known to occur in Early Agricultural period contexts in the Tucson Basin, the Cienega Valley, the Point of Pines region, and Sonora (Adams 2015; Ferg 1997, 1998; Haury 1957; see chapter 5).]

The two structures described below were called granaries for a time, but there is no direct evidence to support this designation; moreover, they are earlier than, and constructed differently from, the granaries of Tres Alamos (Tuthill 1947:27) and Chihuahua (Kidder 1939:229, Figure 7, Plate 17a; Lumholtz 1902:63–64; Sayles 1936:18, Plate 8a).

House 6

Located 12 m east of the north corner of the pueblo's compound wall, 22 m north of House 4, and near the southeast edge of the Northeast Trash mound, House 6 (figure 3.1) is a circular structure built, and apparently destroyed by fire, before the Northeast Trash had accumulated. The absence of charred organic material from the house's fill and from the area around it, the presence of clay casts encircling the floor but bereft of charred pole stubs, and the absence of plaster from most of the floor all suggest that the structure was cleaned out after it had burned and possibly some of its contents were salvaged. The discovery of a fragment of burned plaster bearing grass thatch impressions 6 m north of this structure, on sterile soil under the trash deposit, lends further support to the inference that House 6 predates the Northeast Trash.

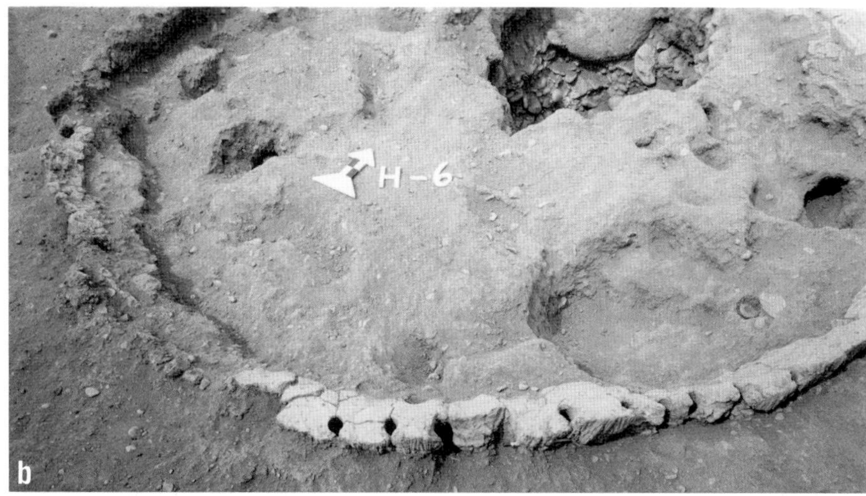

FIGURE 3.1 House 6: (a) overview, (b) close-up. Photographs D/117 (a) and D/120 (b) by Rex E. Gerald. Courtesy of the Amerind Foundation Inc., Dragoon, Arizona.

Orientation and Size

No doorway was found to indicate House 6's orientation; it is 2.80 m in diameter.

Floor

House 6 apparently once had a well-plastered floor with a ridge of plaster 10–20 cm high extending around the perimeter. Preserved in two places on the north side, the few fragments of plaster remaining are 1.2–2.5 cm thick and only as smooth as the viscous plaster would become after being patted into place by hand. In other areas, the plastered floor is missing. There remains only the underlying sterile red clay containing gravel, which is irregular and pitted as though disturbed by burrowing animals. The well-preserved and sharp edges of the remaining fragments of plaster suggest that the floor was removed intentionally after the structure burned.

Floor Features

None were found.

Walls

Evidence for the walls is manifest as nearly vertical holes, 2.5–3.5 cm in diameter, set around the perimeter of the floor. These holes are spaced 10–20 cm apart and are encased in a plaster rim extending up from the floor over the lower 10–20 cm of the inferred poles as they protruded above the floor. This plaster bears hand impressions in places. The poles were evidently driven into the ground and plastered around later because none of the plaster casts bear an impression of the end of a pole. These casts are smooth, showing neither relief nor texture. Poles placed in these casts form angles of from 85° to 116° (and average 105°) with a horizontal line passing through the center of the structure at floor level. This indicates that the diameter of the structure was greater above the base than at ground level; if the walls continued upward to a height of 2 m at this same angle, the diameter at that level would be about 3.8 m. It is also inferred that the poles were held in place by horizontal branches that ranged in diameter from 1.4 cm to 2.3 cm and were placed on the exterior of the circle of upright poles. These were held in place by two strips of fiber, which, used together, were wrapped around the horizontal branch and the vertical pole, one turn being made about each. A grass thatch was attached to the framework of vertical and horizontal poles. It was prevented from blowing inside the framework by strips of fiber crisscrossed between the upright poles.

Roofing

In the fill of House 6 and in the trash around it, a number of double-handful-size lumps of fired clay were found. These lumps of clay appear to have been placed close together around the top of the structure to form a rim of sorts. The 10 complete specimens range in size from 15.2 × 6.5 × 7.0 cm to 20.0 × 7.5 × 9.6 cm and average 18.0 × 7.4 × 8.8 cm. All surfaces are covered with a thin incrustation of lime, but broken surfaces are red, or in a few cases, light to dark brown. The surfaces of the whole specimens are, in general, smooth. The upper surfaces have a few protruding pebbles that resisted wind and rain erosion better than the adobe, which was not burned. The long sides of the adobe lumps usually bear one or two concave impressions on one side and one or two convex impressions on the opposite side where adjacent lumps of adobe were placed; a few have impressions on only one side and are rounded on the other. The ends are usually rounded, although occasionally the impressions of adjacent lumps of adobe are visible. The lower surfaces of almost all specimens bear impressions of the grass thatching, or of horizontal branches placed outside of and over the thatching, or both. The long axes of the lumps of clay are parallel to that of the branches and at right angles to that of the grass thatching. The upper and lower surfaces of these lumps are roughly parallel in the direction of the long axes but tend to converge on one side in the direction of the short axes, and in the specimens having impressions of the horizontal branches, the surfaces tend to converge in the direction of the center of the circle formed by the horizontal branches. This suggests that the lumps rested on a slanting, rather than a horizontal, surface. One clay lump was found that appears to form the inner edge of a circle. None was found that would have fit in the center of a domed roof, so apparently the entire roof was not covered, the center being exposed. No charred organic roofing material was found in the fill of the structure; only one burned fragment of charred cane was found in Pit 2, and this appears to have been deposited with the trash that covered the structure.

Intrusive Features

Pit 1 is near the northwest side of the structure, is circular in shape, 70–75 cm in diameter, and extends about 70 cm below the floor. It is unsealed, filled with cobbles and some trash (10 sherds), and appears to have been dug through the floor of the house after it had burned and was abandoned. Pit 2 is a shallow, poorly defined depression that is 30–35 cm in diameter and about 20 cm deep. It was filled with the same type of material that constituted the Northeast Trash and the fill above House 6.

Artifacts

None of these artifacts can be associated with House 6 without question because, as mentioned above, the structure was apparently cleaned out after it burned, and later, the Northeast Trash, probably including many of these artifacts, was deposited on top of it.

Fill. D/130a shell bead, D/130b shell bracelet.

Floor. D/131a bone awl, D/131b shell bracelet, D/131c shell bracelet, D/131d shell bead, D/s164 grinding slab.

Pit 1. D/132 shell tinkler, D/191 knobbed stone tray, D/s74 rubbing stone.

Pit 2. D/133 burned cane.

House 10

Located 5 m north of House 1, House 10 appears as a disturbed ring of burned adobe with pole impressions identical to those of House 6. In the small portion of this structure that was excavated, it was found that most of the adobe ring had been moved out of place. No floor plaster was found. Cremation 3 was found in a pit 10–15 cm above the northwest edge of House 10.

PIT HOUSES AND SUBRECTANGULAR HOUSE-IN-A-PIT

The term "pit house" as utilized here refers to isolated dwellings constructed in shallow or deep pits, whether or not the sides of the pit are used for walls, and having a superstructure of thatch, wattle and daub, or adobe. This is admittedly a broad definition, but each of the structures of this type found at the Davis Ranch Site are unique in one way or another, and rather than attempt a more specific classification on the basis of such sparse data, they are placed in a single class for the purposes of description. Wheat's (1955:196) distinction between Mogollon pit houses and Hohokam houses-in-pits may be applied to the Davis Ranch Site pit structures only with reservation because of the poor preservation of many of them. House 4 will undoubtedly fit into the house-in-a-pit class, but the remainder must be classed as pit houses in the absence of evidence, such as peripheral postholes or encircling grooves, that indicate walls inside the pit. There is indisputable evidence of superimposed pit houses and therefore of non-contemporaneity. [*Editor: Based on floor plan and depth, Gerald recognized four classes of these structures, three of which are placed in the interval defined by the Hohokam Colonial and Sedentary periods (Davis phase) (see chapter 7) and one in the Aravaipa (Sosa) phase. Structures are grouped and described here in order of age, stratigraphically, from oldest to youngest. Structures inhabited during the Colonial period or the Sedentary period (Houses 4, 5, 8, and 9) are addressed first, followed by the Aravaipa phase structures (Houses 1, 2, 3, and 7), which were built and occupied by the Kayenta immigrants who later constructed the kiva, the pueblo, and other features.*]

House 8

Located under House 5 and part of Room 2, House 8 is roughly rectangular in shape. The floor of House 8 is 47 cm below the floor of House 5 and 57 cm below the floor of Room 2. House 8 was mostly destroyed by the construction of House 5 (figure 3.2; see also figure 3.40).

Orientation and Size

The long axis of House 8 runs northwest-southeast, and it measures 1.90 × 3.00 m.

Floor

Built on sterile cobbles and reddish clay, with only a few spots of plaster remaining, the floor is about a meter below the present surface.

Floor Features

No hearth was found, although a circular depression 40 cm in diameter and 10 cm deep is located near the center of the structure; it contains no ash

FIGURE 3.2 Houses 4, 5, and 8 and Room 2: House 8 floor (A), Burial 10 (B), House 5 floor (C), House 4 floor (D), Room 2 floor (E), and stone-and-pole enclosure (F). Photograph D/136 by Rex E. Gerald. Courtesy of the Amerind Foundation Inc., Dragoon, Arizona.

or charcoal. [*Editor: This feature does not appear on the sketch of House 8 in the field notes.*]

A pit was located near the center of the northwest wall. It is oval in shape, 40–50 cm in diameter, and 40 cm deep. Only one posthole was found, near the south corner of the dwelling, and it is partially dug into the pit wall. It is 15 cm in diameter and extends 15 cm below the level of the floor.

Walls

Presumably, these were formed by the sides of the pit, although no plaster remains to support this belief. The sides of the pit stand to a height of 47 cm in places and may have been higher at one time. No entryway was found.

Roofing

No evidence was found.

Artifacts

Fill. D/137a perforated sherd disk, D/137b debitage.

Stratitest Level 3. D/138 clay coil.

[*Editor: House 8, the earliest pit structure in the stratigraphic sequence that also includes House 5 and House 4, yielded both Colonial period and Sedentary period decorated pottery. Curiously, there is a higher percentage of Sedentary period sherds on the floor than in the fill of this structure.*]

House 5

Located under the east corner of Room 2, House 5 (figure 3.3) is roughly oval in shape. House 5 overlies House 8. The excavations for House 4 and Burial 10 destroyed part of House 5 and are therefore later. The east corner of Room 2 is built over House 5, and the floor of Room 2 is 10 cm above a portion of the floor of House 5. The stone-and-pole enclosure overlies House 5 and is therefore later than House 5. A later pit for Burial 10 was dug through the floor of the house. [*Editor: This burial was accompanied by both Tucson Polychrome and Gila Polychrome vessels.*] This pit house is badly disturbed as a result of later excavations and is partially obscured by overlying walls that were not removed.

Orientation and Size

House 5 is roughly oval, 4.35 × 3.50 m, and its long axis runs northwest-southeast.

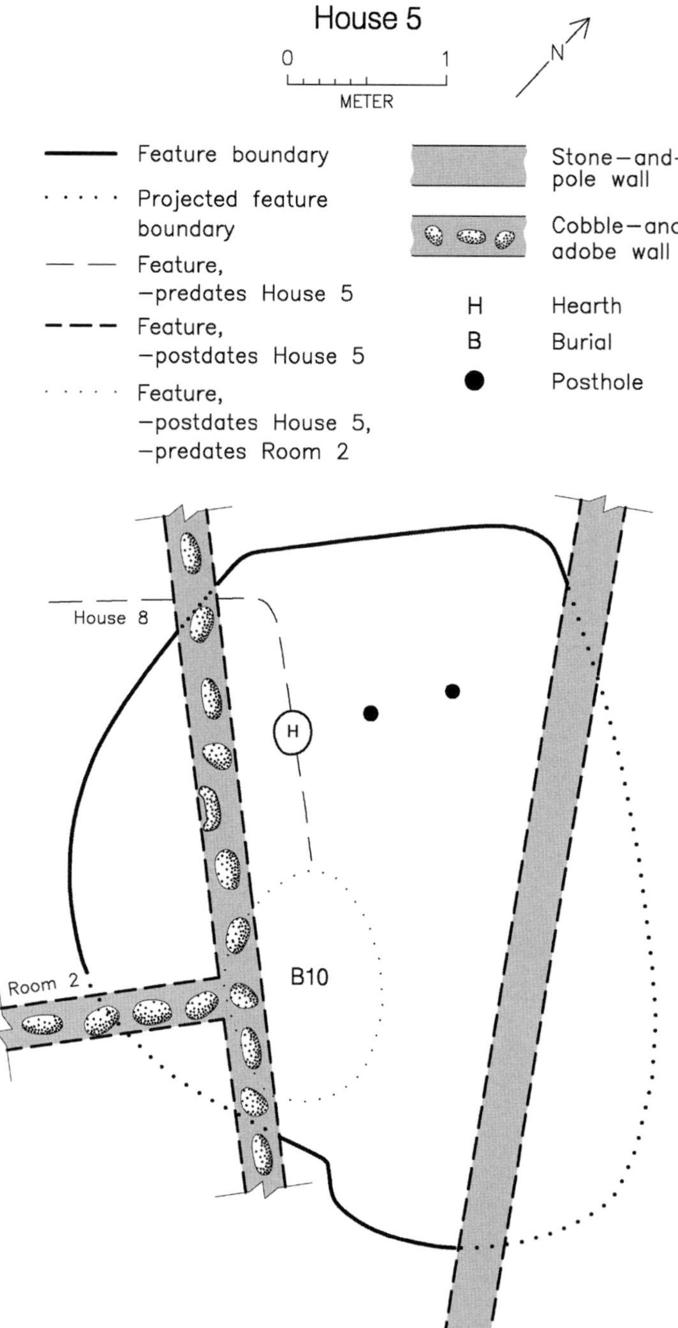

FIGURE 3.3 Plan of Houses 5 and 8, Burial 10, and Room 2. Drawing by Ronald J. Beckwith based on Rex E. Gerald's field map and notes.

Floor

Immediately around the hearth, the floor is plastered and well preserved. In the area under Room 2, it is not plastered but is easily distinguished. The floor is 50 cm below the present surface and is cut 30 cm into sterile red clay and gravel.

Floor Features

Two hearths were located, one directly above the other. The later hearth is circular in plan, basin shaped in cross section, 27–30 cm in diameter, and 13 cm deep. The adobe plaster with which it is lined is about 1.0 cm thick and extends above the floor about 1.5 cm to form a wide ridge on the south and west sides. The second hearth is immediately below the later one, slightly deeper and larger, and of similar construction. The adobe of both hearths is burned; the earlier hearth contains white ash.

Two small postholes are located 40 cm and 90 cm northeast of the hearth. They are 10 cm in diameter and about 10 cm deep.

Walls

The walls of the pit presumably formed the lower portions of the walls of this house; they are preserved on the northwest and southeast sides only, and there the original pit is discernable for only 30 cm above the floor. No wall plaster or impressions of grass, straw, wood, or indications of an entry were found.

Roofing

No evidence was found.

Artifacts

Fill. D/s104 mano, D/s105 mano or rubbing stone.

Floor. D/128 perforated sherd disk, D/129a pigment, D/129b projectile point, D/s115 mano.

[*Editor: More than half of the decorated sherds on the floor of House 5 and nearly 25% of those in its fill are specimens of Colonial period types.*]

House 4

A subrectangular house-in-a-pit, House 4 (figures 3.4, 3.5) is located 1.5 m east of Room 2 and the pueblo compound. House 4 is stratigraphically later than Pit 2. Part of the floor of House 5 was destroyed when House 4 was built, and therefore, House 5 is earlier than House 4. Pit 1 was apparently dug into the floor of House 4 after the house was abandoned and some fill had accumulated on the floor. Pit Oven 1 was also dug after the abandonment of House 4. The Embudo phase stone-and-pole enclosure was built over the southwest wall of House 4 after it was abandoned and after intrusive Pit 3 was dug.

Orientation and Size

House 4 measures 4.50 × 3.70 m, its long axis runs northwest-southeast, and its entrance is on the northeast side.

Floor

Although the floor is plastered and relatively well preserved, the underlying gravel and red clay show in places.

Floor Features

No hearth was found, but it may have been destroyed by intrusive Pit 1. Oval in shape, 1.20 × 1.30 m, and 60 cm deep, Pit 2 is located in the south corner of the house; part of the southeast wall channel passed over it. Pit 2 was filled with cobbles and trash and was sealed with red clay at the time House 4 was constructed.

Two main postholes divide the house into thirds along the long axis. The northwest posthole is 50 cm in diameter and extends 70 cm below floor level; the southeast posthole is 40–50 cm in diameter and 25 cm deep. The northwest wall channel terminates at the west corner in a posthole that is 14 cm in diameter and 20 cm deep, and that is partially dug into the edge of the pit. Two postholes, 20 cm and 26 cm in diameter, are located near the center of the southwest wall. Other postholes may have been located along this wall, but none were found because of the irregular nature of the pit at this edge of the floor.

Two shallow postholes, each 10 cm in diameter, are located on either side of the entryway near the middle of the northeast wall. To the north of these and near the center of the north half of the wall is half of a preserved posthole in the edge of Pit Oven 1. This posthole is 15 cm in diameter and about 15 cm deep. Other postholes in this area may have been destroyed by the excavation of Pit Oven 1. The south half of the northeast wall is marked by four postholes, the largest of which is 22 cm in diameter and about 20 cm deep. It is located at the junction of the south side of the entryway and the wall. The second and fourth postholes to the south are each about 10 cm in diameter and 10–20 cm deep; the latter

FIGURE 3.4 House 4: House 4 floor (A), House 5 floor (B), and stone-and-pole enclosure (D). Photograph D/119 by Rex E. Gerald. Courtesy of the Amerind Foundation Inc., Dragoon, Arizona.

posthole is located near, but not in, the east corner of the house. The third posthole south of the entryway is 16 cm in diameter and about 25 cm deep.

Walls

There is little direct evidence of wall construction materials, but from the arrangement of postholes and channels around the perimeter of this structure compared with similar houses in other sites, it can be suggested that the southwest and northeast walls were made of post-supported thatch or wattle and daub. The northwest and southeast walls did not have posts along them but made use of a channel 15 cm wide and 10 cm deep at the periphery of the floor, into which small vertical timbers may have been plastered. Unfortunately, no casts were found in the channel plaster. The walls of the original pit rose at the outer edges of the channels and at the outer edges of the postholes on all sides except the northeast. At the west corner, the side of the pit rose 55 cm above the floor.

The entryway is located in the center of the northeast wall, is 80 cm wide, and extends out 50 cm as a small nub on the wall. Two postholes, 10 cm and 12 cm in diameter, held posts that probably formed the doorframe. There is a low step up out of the house and a small compacted area outside the entryway.

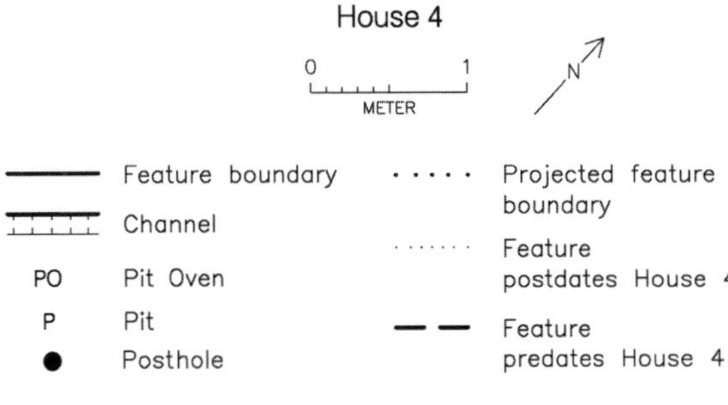

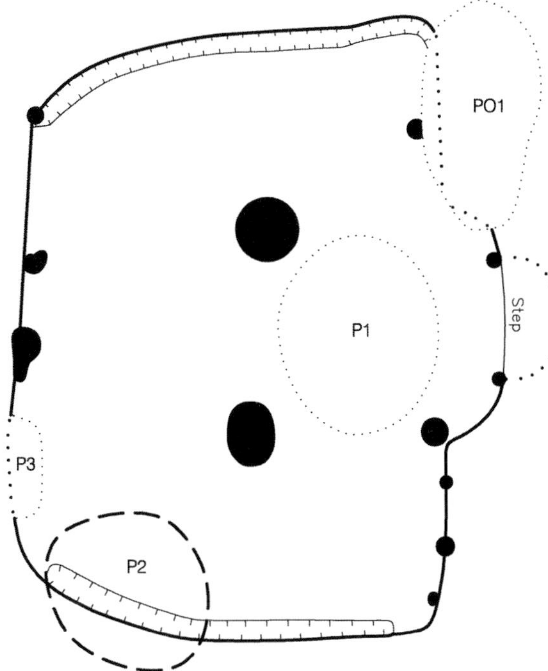

FIGURE 3.5 Plan of House 4. Drawing by Ronald J. Beckwith based on Rex E. Gerald's field map and notes.

Roofing

No evidence was found.

Intrusive Features

A large, shallow pit (Pit 1) is located between the center of the house and the entrance. It is oval in shape, 1.60 × 1.40 m, and 20 cm deep. The bottom is flat and the sides form sharp angles with the house floor. Neither the bottom nor the sides are plastered, being formed of the red clay and gravel that underlie much of the site. The configuration of this pit suggests that it was dug after the house was abandoned and partially filled, although evidence of the pit was not recognized in the fill above the floor. Pit 3 is located just west of Pit 2 and is cut through the south end of the southwest wall. It is oval in shape, 80 cm long, about 50 cm wide, and some 20 cm deep. It cuts through the floors of both House 4 and House 5 and is therefore later than both. Pit Oven 1 is located at the north corner of the house; part of the house floor was destroyed when this feature was created.

Artifacts

Fill. D/120 perforated sherd disk; D/122, D/124 shell bracelets; D/123 worked sherd; D/s70 metate; D/s71 mano.

Floor. D/121a flat abrader, D/121b clay coil, D/126 shell bracelet.

Pit 2. D/125a sherd disk, D/125b worked sherd, D/127 shell bracelet.

Pit Oven 1. D/3a drill, D/3b projectile point, D/11 worked sherd.

[*Editor: House 4 exhibits a number of features shared by many Colonial and Sedentary period Hohokam houses-in-pits in the Phoenix Basin, including main roof support beams on the long axis (about midway between the front and back walls), floor grooves, and circumferential postholes (Haury 1976:53–65). House 4, however, is more square than most Hohokam houses with a centrally placed two-post roof support arrangement, and its entry is wider and shorter than is typical. Ninety percent of the decorated sherds from the floor of the structure (*n *= 41) date to the Colonial period, the Sedentary period, or were in use during both periods. Pit 1, intrusive to House 4, yielded only six decorated sherds, four of Colonial period age and two of Sedentary period age. More than half of the decorated sherds from the fill (*n *= 94) date to the Colonial period or the Sedentary period.*]

House 9

Located under House 7, Room 6, and parts of Rooms 4 and 5, House 9 is subrectangular in shape, with rounded ends. The floor is 15–18 cm below Floor 2 of House 7 (figure 3.6).

FIGURE 3.6 House 9: House 9 floor (A), House 7 Pit 4 (B), House 7 Hearth 3 (C), House 7 Floor 2 (D), and Room 6 floor (E). Photograph D/151 by Rex E. Gerald. Courtesy of the Amerind Foundation Inc., Dragoon, Arizona.

Orientation and Size

Measuring 3.20 × 4.90 m, House 9's long axis runs northwest-southeast.

Floor

House 9's floor is gravelly and unplastered.

Floor Features

None were located, but portions of this house were not excavated due to the superimposed walls and hearths of House 7 and Room 6.

Walls

The walls of the pit are presumed to have been used as the lower portions of the house walls, although no plaster or other evidence of this was found. There is a short lateral entryway located near the center of the northeast side. It is 65 cm wide and 90 cm long, horizontal rather than inclined, and has a step about 10 cm high at the outer end.

Roofing

No evidence was found.

Artifacts

Fill. D/139 unworked stone.

Floor. D/s121 metate.

[*Editor: In terms of its shape, House 9 resembles Colonial and Sedentary period houses-in-pits at Snaketown (AZ U:13:1[ASM]; Haury 1976:53–65), as well as some structures at Tres Alamos (Tuthill 1947:Figure 3) and Type II houses at the Gleeson Site (ARIZONA:FF:5:1[AF], AZ FF:5:1[ASM]; Fulton and Tuthill 1940:16–17, Figure 1). Gerald reports only 5*

FIGURE 3.7 House 1. Photograph D/10 by Rex E. Gerald. Courtesy of the Amerind Foundation Inc., Dragoon, Arizona.

sherds from the fill and 11 from the floor. More than half of the floor sherds are specimens of Colonial period types, 9% are Sedentary period types, and nearly 20% were identified as specimens of types that straddle these two periods. The remaining sherds are intrusive, representing late Classic period types.]

House 1

Located 25 m east of the pueblo compound, House 1 is a rectangular pit house with rounded corners (figures 3.7, 3.8). No other roughly contemporaneous structure that might have faced on a common plaza could be found closer than 19 m to the north (an unexcavated house was located there) or 18 m to the west (House 2). The floor is 45 cm below the present surface; sterile red clay and gravel lie immediately below.

Orientation and Size

House 1 measures 2.62 × 2.73 m. Its orientation could not be determined with certainty. [*Editor: Based on the location of a feature that appears to be an entrybox, House 1 faced southwest. See below.*]

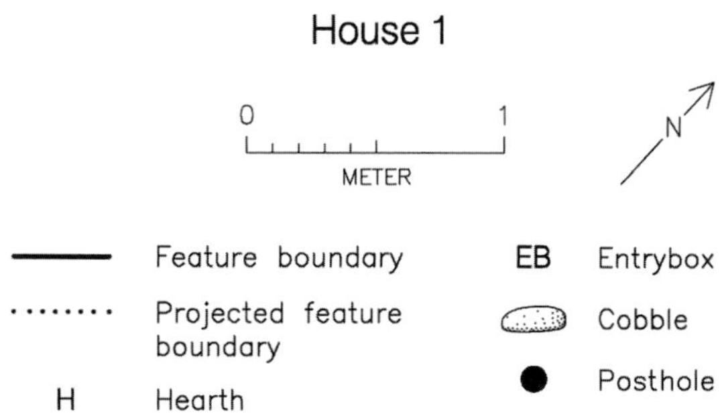

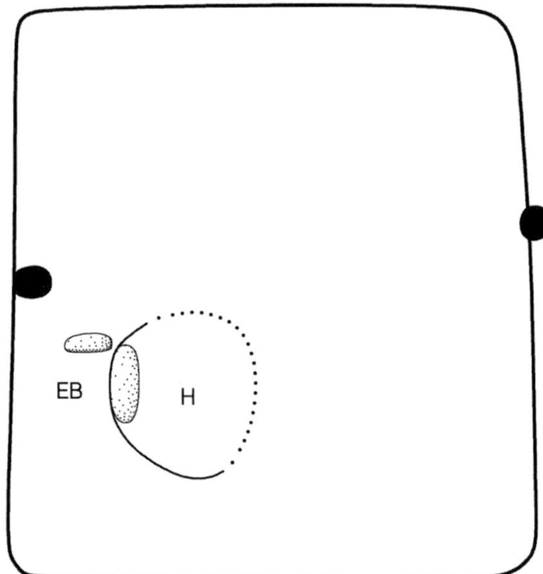

FIGURE 3.8 Plan of House 1. Drawing by Ronald J. Beckwith based on Rex E. Gerald's field map and notes.

Floor

House 1's floor is well preserved in the northwest quarter and easily located but unplastered in other areas. The soft, black fill of the house stops abruptly at the floor in most areas, and reddish-brown clay and gravel, darkened by use, mark the floor level and continue as the underlying sterile soil.

Floor Features

In the center of the south quarter of the pit house, a pit 80 cm in diameter and 25 cm deep is plastered over; the southwest edge is marked by an upright stone, 38 × 38 × 16 cm, set parallel to the southwest wall and extending about 25 cm above floor level. A second upright stone, 36 × 23 × 8 cm, is set at the northwest edge of the first upright stone and extends to the southwest at a right angle to it. It also stands some 25 cm above floor level. [*Editor: The L-shaped, upright-stone feature described by Gerald appears to have been a Kayenta entrybox, and the pit that abutted it was most likely a hearth. See the discussion of entryboxes that follows the description of Houseblock I, Room 3.*]

There are two postholes, one located against the southwest wall near its center and the other near the northeast wall just north of its center. The southwest posthole is 15 × 20 cm in diameter and extends 10 cm below the floor; the northeast posthole is 18 cm in diameter and extends 25 cm below the floor.

Walls

The sides of the pit probably formed the walls of the house, but no evidence of wall plaster is preserved. As stated above, the floor is about 45 cm below the present surface, but evidence of the original excavation could not be traced more than 30 cm above the floor. No entry was found.

Roofing

No evidence was found.

Artifacts

Floor. D/43 shell bracelet.

House 2

The existence of House 2 is confirmed by a floor area that is located 18 m west of House 1. The plastered floor gives way to a red clay and gravel surface, and that, in turn, gives way to an irregular gravel and clay mixed with trash as one proceeds away from the hearth. A regular outline of the defined floor area could not be discerned.

Orientation and Size

Neither could be determined.

Floor

The plastered floor is 30 cm below the surface and is well defined around the hearth but difficult to locate away from it. The floor level was followed out for 1–3 m from the hearth in all directions.

Floor Features

A circular, plastered pit, 20 cm in diameter, the hearth is 10 cm deep with a rim raised 2 cm above the floor.

Walls

No evidence remained.

Roofing

No evidence was found.

Artifacts

Fill. D/116 unclassified stone artifact, D/117 sherd disk, D/s103 mano.

House 3

Located under the north corner of Room 3 at a depth of 60–76 cm below the surface, or 30 cm below the floor of Room 3, House 3 is rectangular in shape. A large portion of the floor is disturbed where the later pueblo occupants dug through it to lay the foundation for the northwest and northeast walls of Room 3.

Orientation and Size

House 3 measures 2.75 × 2.65 m, and its long axis runs northeast-southwest.

Floor

The floor of this house is built over a pocket of water-deposited sand and trash and is not plastered or well defined; it is discernible only as a gravelly surface somewhat more firmly compacted than the trash above it.

Floor Features

None were found.

Walls

The edges of the pit that formed the walls of House 3 are soft, crumbly, and irregular, and no trace of plaster remains.

Roofing

No evidence was found.

Artifacts

Fill. D/118 palette, D/119a sherd disk, D/119b perforated sherd disk.

House 7

A rectangular pit house with adobe walls, House 7 (figures 3.9, 3.10) is located under the northwestern two-thirds of Room 6. The floor of House 9 is 15–18 cm below House 7 Floor 2. House 7 Subfloor 1 fill encompasses the space between Floors 1 and 2. Pits 1, 2, and 3 are all stratigraphically above or dug into House 7 Floor 1 and are therefore later. Room 6 is later than House 7 Floor 1 and its fill.

Orientation and Size

House 7 measures 3.38 × 2.67 m and is oriented with its long axis running northwest-southeast. Its doorway opens to the northeast.

Floor

Floor 1 is plastered and well preserved in all areas except along the southwest wall where Pits 1, 2, and 3 were dug through the floor after the house was abandoned. This floor rests on 20–27 cm of gravel, cobbles, and trash, apparently brought in to raise the floor to a higher level. Floor 1 is 27 cm above Floor 2.

Floor 2 is well preserved and has two coats of brown, sandy, adobe plaster, each coat of which is 8–10 cm thick. It is coved to join the wall plaster in the south corner and in the center of the northeast wall. This floor has 1–2 cm of sand and silt deposited on its north half.

FIGURE 3.9 House 7: House 9 floor (A), House 7 Floor 1 (B), and Room 6 floor (C). Photograph D/125 by Rex E. Gerald. Courtesy of the Amerind Foundation Inc., Dragoon, Arizona.

Floor Features

Contemporaneous with Floor 1, but not necessarily contemporaneous themselves, are Hearths 3, 4, and 5. Hearth 3 is a rectangular firebox, 37 × 40 cm and 12 cm deep, located 15 cm in from the northeast wall, near its center. Lined on three sides with sandstone slabs placed on edge, it is oriented with its long axis at right angles to that of the house. The portions of the sides lacking sandstone slabs are plastered with adobe.

Hearth 4 is superimposed on Hearth 5. Both are located 60–75 cm from the doorway toward the center of the room. Both are circular depressions lined with roughly finished adobe plaster. Both are filled with white ash, but Hearth 4 also contains sherds. Hearth 4 is 28–32 cm in diameter and 10 cm deep; it is located 2–3 cm above Hearth 5. Hearth 5 is 40 cm in diameter and 11 cm deep. The bottom of this hearth is 11 cm above Floor 2. No Floor 2 hearth was found, but one or more could have been located under features of the Floor 1 occupation.

Pit 4, the only pit associated with Floor 2, is located 40 cm from the northeast wall, near the center of the room. It is rectangular, with rounded corners, measures 1.00 m × 70 cm, is 14 cm deep, and is oriented with its long axis paralleling that of the house. It is plastered with brown adobe similar to that used on the floor and has a rim 3 cm high and 12 cm wide extending around it at floor level. This rim must have been added after the floor was plastered, because the rim can easily be separated from the floor.

One posthole, found near the center of the southeast half of the structure, does not extend above Floor 1. It is 23 cm in diameter and extends 14 cm below Floor 2. Tree-ring sample 6 (see appendix A) was found in this posthole. [*Editor: Neither this nor any other of the dendrochronological specimens yielded a date.*] The second posthole is associated with Floor 1 only and is located 25 cm from the northwest wall near its center. It is 13 cm in diameter and 5 cm deep. [*Editor: Two additional postholes are recorded in*

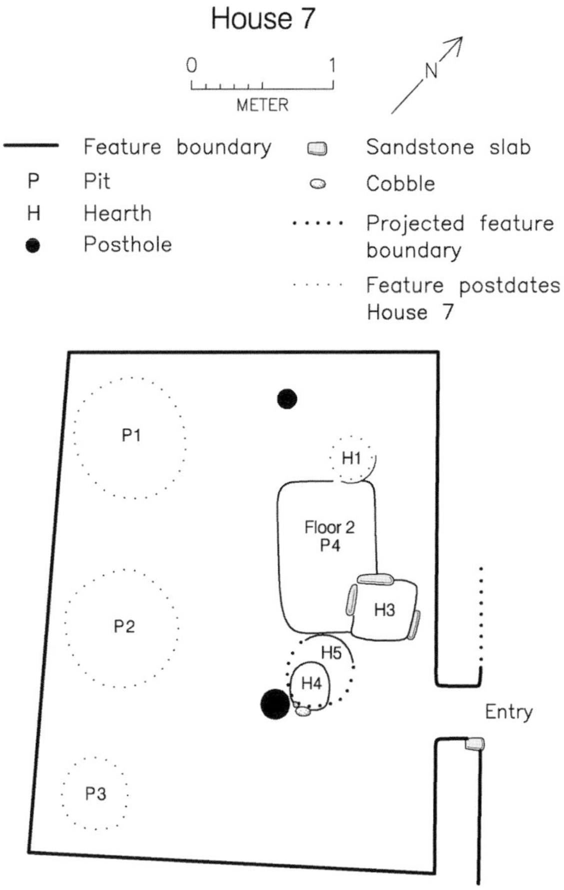

FIGURE 3.10 Plan of House 7. Drawing by Ronald J. Beckwith based on Rex E. Gerald's field map and notes.

the field notes and on a field map. Gerald associates them with Room 6.]

Walls

All are constructed of adobe containing some gravel and a few small cobbles and are well preserved below the floor of the superimposed Room 6. All the walls are straight or slightly bowed out, and they all meet with slightly coved corners. In almost all areas they stand to a height of 40–50 cm above Floor 2 and appear to have been cut off at this level prior to, or during the construction of, Room 6. The southwest wall is an exception; it extends 10–15 cm higher than the others in a few areas where it was preserved, because it served as a foundation for the northeast wall of Room 10. The northwest wall, which partially underlies the southeast wall of Room 4, and the southeast wall, which is just inside the corresponding wall of Room 6, do not appear to have been deliberately utilized as the foundations for the later walls. Reddish-brown wall plaster is well preserved on most walls but is absent from the majority of the southwest wall, except for one well-preserved portion of the southwest wall near the west corner above Floor 1.

No exterior surface could be recognized on any of the walls except on a short section of the northeast wall near the east corner, where the exterior surface appears to be 30 cm wide. In other areas, the exterior wall face is an irregular mass of adobe that appears to have been molded against the side of an irregular pit. The adobe of the southeast wall, which was exposed on the exterior for its entire length, ranged from 15 cm to 25 cm in thickness.

A doorway was located in the northeast wall, 90 cm from the east corner. It is 37 cm wide, and the adobe sill is 40 cm above Floor 2. A small, upright sandstone slab forms a portion of the south door frame.

Roofing

No evidence was found.

Intrusive Features

Five hearths are intrusive through Floor 1 of House 7. Hearths 1 and 2 are shallow, unplastered, circular, ash-filled depressions. Hearth 1, located in the north corner, is 25 cm in diameter and 12 cm deep. Hearth 2, located in the north-central portion of the house, is 32 cm in diameter and 13 cm deep; it was sealed over with a thin layer of silt. [*Editor: This hearth does not appear on Gerald's field map and thus is not shown on the plan (see figure 3.10).*]

The remaining hearths, labeled Pits 1, 2, and 3, are located along the southwest wall, Pit 1 being in the west corner, Pit 3 in the south corner, and Pit 2 in between. All three are circular and were dug through Floor 1 after trash and other debris had accumulated to a depth of about 15 cm. Pits 1, 2, and

3 have the following respective diameters at Floor 1 level: 80 cm, 78 cm, and 45 cm. They have the following respective depths measured from Floor 1 level: 30 cm, 34 cm, and 20 cm. All three pits contain white ash, but only Pit 2 has evidence of burning in the discoloration of the earth and cobbles into which it was dug. The white ash in Pit 2 extends 15 cm above Floor 1. Pit 3 was dug down to, and exposed a patch of, Floor 2.

Artifacts

Fill. D/134 pigment; D/s91 metate; D/s93 mano; D/s94, D/s95 hammerstones; D/s96 grinding slab.

Floor 1. D/s90 metate.

Subfloor 1 Fill. D/135 unworked stone.

Floor 2. D/136a sherd disk, D/136b quartz crystal, D/136c unworked shell, D/s112 mano.

[*Editor: Houses 1, 3, and 7, as a group, stand apart from the other pit houses based on their rectangular shape and their lack of projecting lateral entries. This form is dominant among Kayenta pit houses (Geib 1985; Harrill 1986; Schroedl 1989). Furthermore, these three structures, along with House 2 (of indeterminate shape), form an arc around the kiva, and the inferred entrances of Houses 1 and 7 face the kiva. As mentioned above, House 1 is outfitted with what appears to be a Kayenta entrybox.*

Fragments of perforated plates were recovered from the floor of House 2 and the lower floor (Floor 2) of House 7. Maverick Mountain Series sherds were found on the floors of Houses 1 and 2, on Floor 2 in House 7, and in the fill of House 3 (floor and fill proveniences were not differentiated when House 3 was excavated and artifacts were removed). Perforated plates and Maverick Mountain Series pottery are telltale markers of Kayenta immigrants (Lindsay 1987; Lyons and Lindsay 2006).]

Summary

On the basis of floor plan and depth, these houses may be divided into four classes.

Class I includes rectangular pit houses with rounded corners: Houses 1, 3, and 7. Class II includes pit houses of irregularly oval or roughly rectangular outline: Houses 5 and 8. Class III includes a subrectangular pit house with a lateral entryway: House 9. Class IV includes a subrectangular house-in-a-pit with a lateral entryway: House 4. [*Editor: Gerald's manuscript indicates that he believed House 2 might be included in Class I. As discussed above, Class I structures were built and occupied during the Aravaipa (Sosa) phase. The ceramics associated with House 2 place it in the Aravaipa phase. Class II, III, and IV structures were constructed and used during the Hohokam Colonial and Sedentary periods (Davis phase).*]

THE KIVA

[*Editor: This section combines portions Gerald's manuscript with excerpts from the paper he presented at the 1958 annual meeting of the Society for American Archaeology. Although Gerald inferred that the kiva was built during the Redfield (early Reeve) phase, based on its location and orientation relative to Houses 1, 2, 3, and 7, construction during the preceding Aravaipa (Sosa) phase is more likely.*]

One of the most interesting results of the Amerind Foundation's work at the Davis Ranch Site was the excavation of a rectangular, subsurface kiva of a type comparable to those reported from the Little Colorado River area (Fewkes 1904:Plate 58; Mindeleff 1891:111–137, Figures 22–23, 25). Pueblo kivas were not recognized in southeastern Arizona until the present structure was excavated. With the identification of this structure as a kiva, two previously excavated structures at nearby sites may now be identified as kivas with greater confidence, even though they lack the overwhelming number of kiva features found at the Davis Ranch Site. The pottery assemblages at these three sites suggest an early Pueblo IV period of occupation by Salado people.

[*Editor: It is almost certain that one of the structures to which Gerald refers is Room 15 at Reeve Ruin (Di Peso 1958a:60–61). The other is likely Room VIII at the 76 Ranch Ruin (AZ BB:8:1[ASM]; Duffen 1936a, 1937; Duffen and Hartmann 1997). Although Duffen*

(1936a; see also Duffen and Hartmann 1997) referred to the latter structure as a kiva in his unpublished field notes, and later concluded that the feature he initially identified as a filled doorway was more likely a ventilator shaft (notations by William Hartmann, 1995, in Duffen's [1936a] field notes), his published description employs a less precise term: "ceremonial room" (Duffen 1937:14).]

Watson Smith (1952a:162), in his discussion of "When Is a Kiva?" concludes that "a kiva was regarded as such [by the excavator] because it differed in some way from the other rooms of its unit, or stood apart from them positionally; and not primarily because it possessed or lacked any particular internal feature or complex of features." Smiley (1952a) gives a more detailed definition. He writes, "A kiva, archaeologically speaking, [is] . . . a room possessing a ventilator, a firepit, a hatchway over the firepit, and one or more of the following features: deflector, ashpit, sipapu, bench, platform, recess, wall niche, loom anchor, and subterranean or ground level placement" (Smiley 1952a:11).

The Davis Ranch Site kiva conforms to both definitions given above. It differs from the living and storage rooms, and it stands apart from them positionally. In addition, it possesses all of the traits listed by Smiley as characteristic of kivas, except the ashpit and wall niches. Furthermore, this kiva manifests two traits not listed by Smiley that are characteristic of some Hopi kivas. These are the foot drum/sipapu combination (Fewkes 1892:19–20; Mindeleff 1891:117, 121–122, 123, 125–126, 130–131, Figures 22, 27, 30; Parsons 1936:10–11, 17–23, 34, 48, 708, 720, 830–832, Figures 2, 6, 31.14, 140.9, 296f, 313h, 313i, 321d, 385, 448, 449.10; Smiley 1952a:33, 47; Smith 1952b:6) and constriction at the junction of the platform and the benches, on one or both sides of the platform (Dorsey and Voth 1902:170–171, Plate 81; Mindeleff 1891:122–133, Figures 22, 27; Parsons 1936:720, Figure 385; Smith 1952b:5).

[*Editor:* "Sipapu" *is the term archaeologists use to refer to the* sípàapuni *(Hill et al. 1998:504–505) of Hopi oral tradition. The sípàapuni is the hole of emergence, through which the Hopi entered this world (Mindeleff 1891:16–17; Nequatewa 1936:14–23; Simmons 1942:418–419; Voth 1905:10–11, 19, 26, 28, 36, 38). Many locate the hole of emergence north, west, or northwest of the inhabited Hopi villages (Fewkes 1899:535n3; Voth 1905:21–23, 36–38; see also Titiev 1944:177). Stephen (Parsons 1936:473, 849n1), Ferguson and Lomaomvaya (1999:76), and James (1990:7–8) all place the sípàapuni at or near the confluence of the Colorado and Little Colorado Rivers (see also Dongoske et al. 1993:27; Eiseman 1959; Geertz and Lomatuway'ma 1987:122, 187; Simmons 1942:237–241).*

Some Hopi kivas are outfitted with a feature meant to represent the hole of emergence, and archaeologists have applied the term sipapu to this as well. There are two kinds of sipapus in historic Hopi kivas. The first consists of a cylindrical hole drilled into one of the flagstones on the floor (Mindeleff 1891:125–126, 130–131, Figure 25; Parsons 1936:721–722, 724, Figure 387). The second is a combination foot drum/sipapu consisting of a floor pit (resonating chamber) covered by a wooden plank. The plank is perforated, creating a representation of the hole of emergence, which can be closed on occasion by means of a cottonwood plug. Participants in certain ceremonies dance, stamp their feet, or tap on the plank with its plug to communicate with the inhabitants of the underworld (Parsons 1936:10–11, 17–23, 34, 48, 514–518, 708, 720, 830–832, Figure 6). Hawley (1950a:294) reports a similar feature in the head kiva at Acoma.]

Location and Fill

The kiva is located outside the walled compound, 3 m east of the pueblo, near its south end (figure 3.11). The surface manifestation of the kiva was an area depressed some 30 cm below the general surface level. It was semirectangular in shape, with opposite sides neither parallel nor of equal length.

The fill of the kiva consists of adobe roofing material, trash containing sherds and artifacts, and windblown and water-deposited sand and silt. The lowest 15 cm of fill consists of windblown

FIGURE 3.11 The kiva. Gerald's notes indicate that the small wooden elements visible in the roof of the horizontal portion of the ventilator shaft are not original; these were added to indicate the former presence of supports laid perpendicular to the shaft and anchored in holes in the platform on both sides of the shaft (see figure 3.14). See figure 3.13 for key to feature labels. Feature K, not depicted in figure 3.13, is a pit of unknown function. Photograph D/78 by Rex E. Gerald. Courtesy of the Amerind Foundation Inc., Dragoon, Arizona.

and water-deposited sand, silt, and pebbles. Large amounts of adobe roofing material make up most of the fill above this level to about 60 cm above the floor. Some roofing adobe is found up to 1 m above the floor, but most of the fill, from 60 cm above the floor to the surface, consists of trash, sand, silt, and gravel.

From the debris in the fill of the kiva, it appears that the structure stood open and unused for a period of time during which sand, silt, and some trash accumulated on the floor.

[Editor: A concentration of raptor bones was recovered from the east corner of the kiva, near the point where the northeast bench and the platform meet, and assigned bone bag number 75. Precise provenience data are lacking, but an inventory sheet indicates this material was recovered "near the floor." The date on the bone bag places the find on the day the last of the kiva fill was cleared before photography. Examination of stratigraphy evident in field photographs leads to the inference that these bird elements were deposited somewhere between

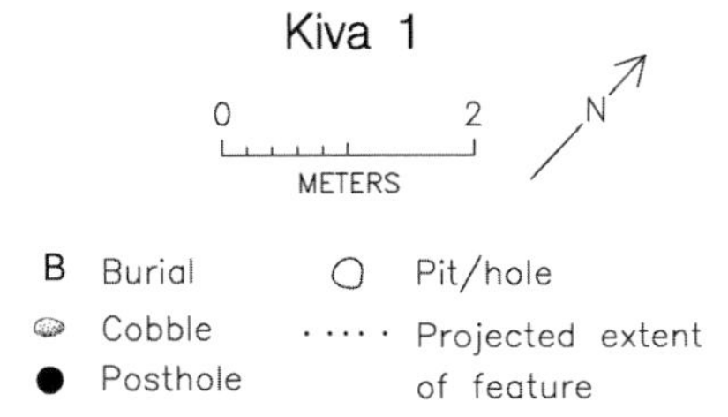

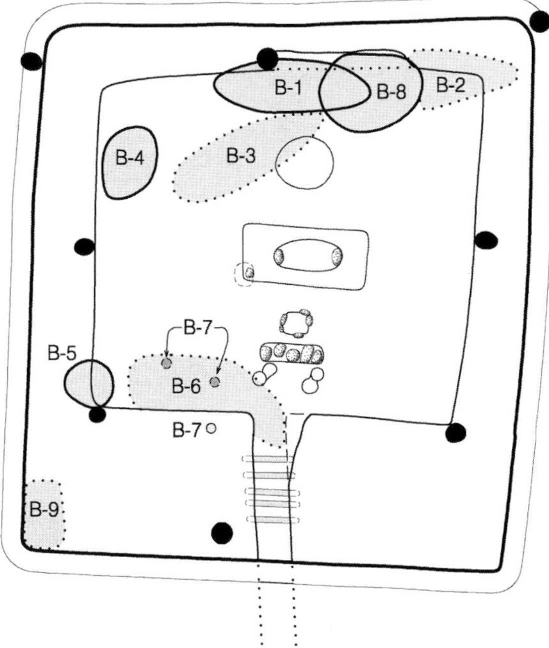

FIGURE 3.12 Plan of the kiva indicating the locations of the burials within and below it. Drawing by Ronald J. Beckwith based on Rex E. Gerald's field map and notes. In this composite, Gerald did not draw the outline of the pit for Burial 8 in such a way as to indicate that it disturbed Posthole 8 (see figure 3.13). The plan map of Burial 8 in the following chapter (see figure 4.3) shows that this posthole was disturbed by the burial pit.

the floor and the roof fall.] After the roof collapsed, the resulting depression was used extensively as a trash dump and as a place to inter both flexed inhumations and extended supine inhumations.

Eight burials were recovered during the removal of the fill (figure 3.12). Fifty cataloged artifacts, excluding those associated with the burials, eight stone catalog artifacts, and more than 17,000 sherds were recovered during the excavation. Several irregular pits were located in the north and east corners and along the southwest wall. These pits appear to have resulted from the action of burrowing animals.

Orientation and Size

The average dimensions above the bench and platform are 7.25 m in a northwest-southeast direction by 6.75 m northeast-southwest; the floor is 1.75 m below the present surface (figures 3.13, 3.14).

Floor

Hard plaster was present and well preserved in all areas except the following: between the mouth of the ventilator and the deflector; near the center of the northwest wall where the excavation for Burial 8 destroyed part of the floor; in the area of the sealed subfloor pit (Feature F), where the floor had sunk a few millimeters and cracked to reveal the perimeter of the pit; over Feature K (see figure 3.11), where the floor was soft; and over a few burrow-like pits probably made by rodents. In the south quarter of the kiva there is only a thin coat of plaster over the caliche bedrock, while in the north quarter there are two coats of plaster covering pockets of dark dirt as much as 10 cm deep. The upper coat of plaster is about 1 cm thick. The dark dirt was probably used to fill irregularities in the excavation during the preparation of the floor.

Hearth (Feature D)

On the opposite side of the deflector from the ventilator and 15 cm from the deflector is the hearth (Feature D), which was in use at the time the kiva was abandoned. This hearth is oval in shape, 28 × 32 cm, and is oriented with its long axis at right

A	Ventilator		Cobble–and–adobe wall
B	Ladder holes	G, H, M, N	Loom holes
C	Deflector	I, P, R	Paired holes
D	Hearth	O, Q, S, T	Unpaired holes
E	Foot drum/sipapu	——• B'	Profile line
F	Pit, subfloor	········	Projected extent of feature
L	Hearth, subfloor		
●	Posthole		

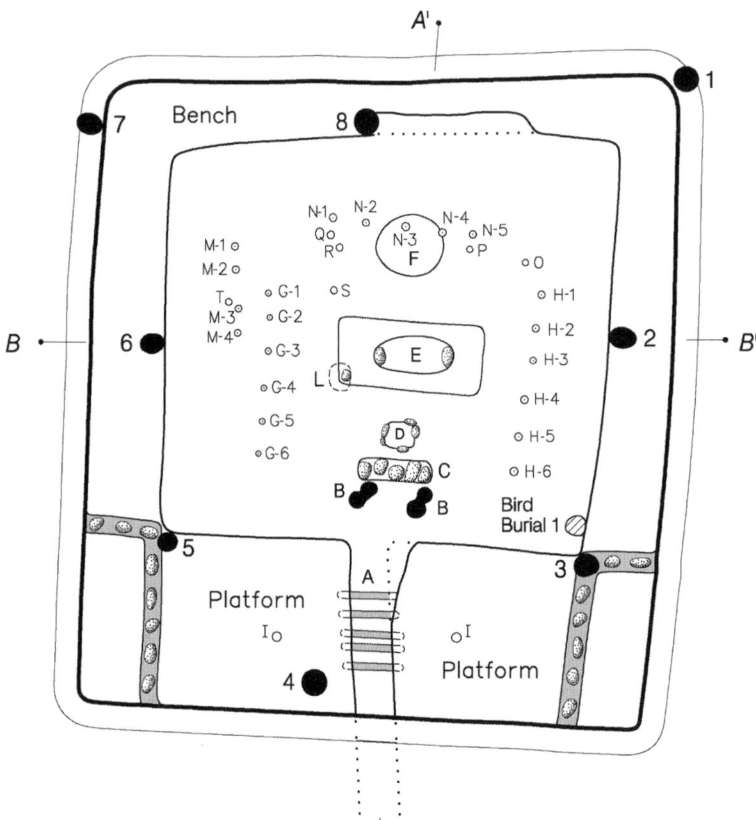

FIGURE 3.13 Plan of the kiva indicating the locations of floor features. Drawing by Ronald J. Beckwith based on Rex E. Gerald's field map and notes.

angles to the major axis of the kiva. It is constructed of five cobbles set in adobe, flush with the floor. The hearth is 22 cm deep and is filled with white ash. A second hearth (Feature L) is under 2–4 cm of floor plaster at the south corner of the foot drum. This hearth is also oval in shape, 40 × 32 cm in size, and is oriented such that its long axis is roughly perpendicular to that of the later hearth. It extends 19 cm below the level of the kiva floor and also is filled with white ash.

Foot Drum/Sipapu (Feature E)

In the center of the main floor of the kiva is a rectangular depression, near the center of which is a

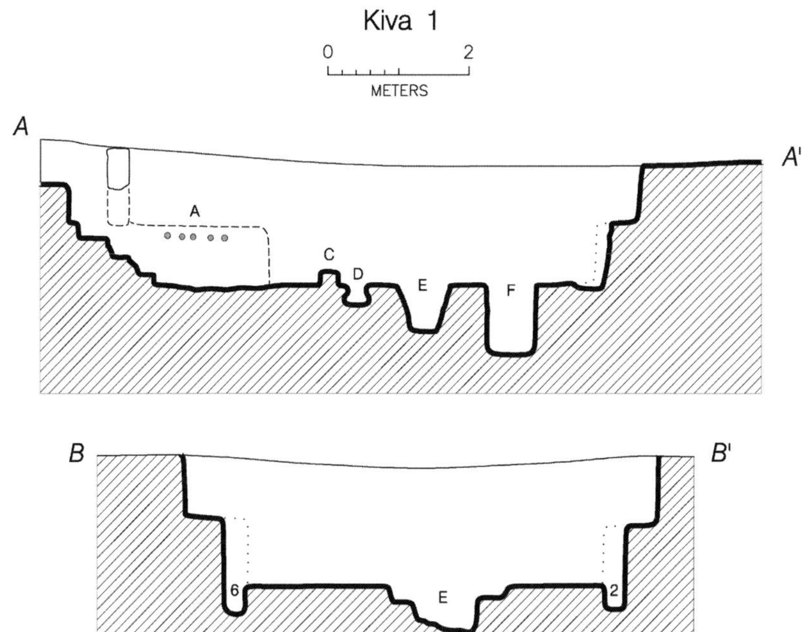

FIGURE 3.14 Kiva profiles. Drawings by Ronald J. Beckwith based on Rex E. Gerald's field map and notes.

deep, elongated, oval pit. The rectangular part of the depression is 1.62 m × 72 cm in size and 10 cm deep; the elongated oval pit measures 93 × 43 cm and extends 65 cm below the kiva floor. The long axis of these depressions is at right angles to the line between the ventilator and hearth. The oval pit is somewhat deeper near the east end. At each corner of the rectangular depression is a stone or a lump of caliche that may have supported the board over the foot drum pit.

Pits (Features F and K)

In line with the hearth and ventilator and centered in the space between the foot drum and the bench opposite the platform, there is a sealed cylindrical pit (Feature F) measuring 70 × 80 cm and extending 86 cm below the kiva floor. This pit was completely sealed over with hard floor plaster and was only revealed by a faint crack around the perimeter, where the plaster parted as a result of the compaction of the fill in the pit. This pit is flat bottomed and sufficiently large to hold an average-sized man with comfort.

Feature K is a 1 m long, straight-sided, round-ended pit located southwest of Feature F. It is 37 cm wide and 13 cm deep at the eastern end and 47 cm wide and 35 cm deep at the western end.

Deflector (Feature C)

Located directly in front of the ventilator opening and 80 cm from the face of the platform, the deflector is constructed of cobbles and adobe. It is 85 cm long and 25 cm thick and stands 20 cm above the floor, although originally it may have stood higher.

Postholes

Eight large postholes are located about the perimeter of the kiva. Most of them are oval in outline and range in diameter from 20.0 × 25.0 cm to 30.0 × 35.5 cm. They range in depth from 13.0 cm to 50.0 cm below the surface of the bench, the surface of the platform, or the floor (table 3.2). All postholes are dug down to or into caliche-cemented gravel and cobbles. Because of the unique placement of these postholes, each is described in detail; the posthole numbers in table 3.2 refer to the numbers on the plan (see figure 3.13).

Ladder Holes (Feature B)

Two figure-eight-shaped depressions are located near either end of the deflector in the area between the deflector and the platform. The easternmost of these depressions is 38 cm long and 18 cm wide at its widest part; it extends 27 cm below floor level at its deepest point, which is nearest the deflector. The westernmost depression is 35 cm long and 12 cm wide at its widest point; it extends 13 cm below floor level. In this location, these holes could have held the base of a ladder positioned to pass through a hatchway over the hearth.

Loom-Anchor Holes (Features G, H, M, and N)

Four rows of loom-anchor holes are located on the main floor of the kiva. These are cylindrical, vertical holes that have been filled with clean sand in most cases and plastered over except for a small circular hole left near the center of each row. Three of these rows of holes (G 1–6, H 1–6, M 1–4) are oriented northwest-southeast, parallel to the long axis of the kiva, and one row (N 1–5) is oriented at right angles to the long axis (table 3.3; see figure 3.13).

Paired Holes (Features I, P, and R)

Two pairs of circular holes dug vertically into the floor are arranged symmetrically along the long axis

TABLE 3.2 Characteristics of the kiva's postholes

Posthole no.	Diameter (cm)	Depth (cm)	Associated surface	Remarks
1	30.0	25.0	Bench	Plastered into wall near north corner; tree-ring sample 7 (see appendix A) recovered from this hole
2	25.0 × 34.0	35.0	Floor	Set into center edge of northeast bench; plastered around
3	25.0 × 30.0	13.0	Floor	Set in east corner between bench and platform; continues upward to form corner of rectangular area separating bench from platform
4	30.0 × 35.5	18.0	Platform	Placed on platform against southeast wall, on west side of ventilator shaft
5	20.0 × 25.0	20.0	Floor	Set in south corner, between bench and platform; continues upward beside wall of rectangular area at southwest end of platform
6	22.0 × 30.0	45.0	Floor	Set into edge of southwest bench near its center and plastered around
7	23.0 × 30.0	30.0	Bench	Wedged with cobbles and plastered into wall near west corner
8	28.0 × 30.0	50.0	Floor	Set into edge of northwest bench, near center, and probably plastered around; disturbed by Burial 8

TABLE 3.3 Characteristics of the kiva's four rows of loom-anchor holes

	Row			
Characteristic	G	H	M	N
Number of holes	6	6	4	5
Row length, center to center (m)	1.84	2.07	0.98	1.68
Distance between holes (cm)				
Range	27.0–43.0	37.0–47.0	27.0–43.0	37.0–45.0[a]
Average	37.0	41.0	33.0	41.0[a]
Diameter (cm)				
Range	7.5–9.5	9.0–10.0	8.5–10.5	8.5–10.0
Average	8.7	9.4	9.4	8.9
Depth (cm)				
Range	19.0–25.0	18.0–23.0	13.0–19.0	14.0–26.0
Average	22.0	20.6	17.0	20.0

[a]Approximate (center hole not measured before being destroyed)

of the kiva. One pair (Feature I) is located on the platform, midway between the edge and the southeast wall. Each of these holes is 12.0 cm in diameter; the eastern one is 18.0 cm deep, and the western one is 13.0 cm deep. Features P and R (the second pair of holes) are on opposite sides of the sealed subfloor pit (Feature F); they are also close to a row of loom-anchor holes (Feature N), of which one or both may be a part. The eastern hole (Feature P) is 8.5 cm in diameter and 17.0 cm deep; the western hole (Feature R) is 9.0 cm in diameter and 20.0 cm deep.

Unpaired Holes (Features O, Q, S, and T)

Four unpaired, circular holes dug vertically into the floor were located. Three of these are near rows of loom-anchor holes. Feature O is near the north end of Feature H; it is 10.5 cm in diameter and 17.0 cm deep. Feature Q is near the west end of Feature N; it is 8.5 cm in diameter and 23.0 cm deep. Feature T is near the center of Feature M; it is 8.0 cm in diameter and 15.0 cm deep. Feature S is near the west corner of the foot drum (Feature E); it is 8.5 in diameter and 20.0 cm deep.

Walls

The platform and bench rest on or near the surface of the caliche hardpan found under most of the site; therefore, the faces of these features, which extend all the way around the kiva, required no reinforcement, the caliche face being plastered only. Above the bench and platform the soft soil and trash presented more of a problem in the construction of walls. This problem was met in two different ways. In most areas, the walls were built simply by plastering a thick layer of adobe over the trash, but on the southwest, the upslope side, this adobe layer was thicker and cobbles were added. In the east-central portion of the southeast wall, where the vertical shaft of the ventilator was built before the wall was constructed, flat slabs of sandstone were utilized in rough courses separated by thick cushions of adobe mortar. The west-central portion of this wall contained more cobbles than sandstone slabs and was badly tumbled at the time of excavation.

These walls formed the perimeter of the rectangular structure above the level of the bench and platform. Merging imperceptibly into the silt and soil at the surface, the walls appear to stand to a height of 75 cm above the bench on the northwest side, 91 cm on the northeast, 102 cm above the platform on the southeast, and 84 cm above the bench on the northwest. The heights of these walls above the kiva floor are 1.60 m, 1.72 m, 1.80 m, and 1.77 m, respectively.

On the platform, in the south and east corners, the rectangular outline of the kiva was altered by the erection of walls of cobbles and adobe to partition small rectangular areas in each corner. These walled-off areas, which had no floors but contained trash with sherd counts similar to those from the kiva fill in general, were apparently left hollow and served to separate the platform from the bench.

Patches of brown plaster are preserved just above the bench on all walls except the northeast and on the portions of the walls that cut off the rectangular areas in the south and east corners and face onto the platform. All of this plaster is sandy and has a poor surface. There is no trace of paint on any of the walls.

Bench

The bench is continuous around three sides of the kiva, excluding the southeast, where the platform is located. It is 75 cm wide at the south end of the northeast bench and 62 cm wide at the north end; 85 cm wide at the east end of the northwest bench and 80 cm wide at the west end; 81 cm wide at the north end of the southwest bench and 82 cm wide at the south end. The bench is 81 cm above the floor on the northeast side, 87 cm above the floor on the northwest side, and 93 cm above the floor on the southwest side. The inside edge of the bench has crumbled away all around, but back from the edge it is plastered on the upper surface and is relatively smooth. The vertical face of the bench retains plaster in one area only, near the west corner. Where the bench turns at the north and west corners, the turns are coved rather than angular.

Platform

As stated above, the platform is at the southeast end of the kiva. It is centered against the wall, is 1.90 m wide at the east end, 2.10 m wide at the west end, and stands 82 cm above the floor. Passage between the platform and bench is cut off by cobble-and-adobe-walled, rectangular areas at each end of the platform. No plaster remains on the vertical face of the platform; on the surface of the platform, plaster remains only on portions of the western half and on areas adjacent to the walls on the eastern half.

Ventilator (Feature A)

The horizontal shaft of the ventilator transects the platform at a slight angle to its short axis. The floor of this shaft is at, or just below, the level of the kiva floor to within 35 cm of the point at which it passes under the southeast kiva wall. At this spot, the floor of the horizontal ventilator shaft begins to rise in a series of five irregular caliche steps. At the riser of what would be a sixth step, the horizontal shaft joins the vertical shaft of the ventilator and continues up to the old surface. Both the horizontal and the vertical shafts are 44 cm wide. The exact size of the aperture of the vertical shaft was not determined because the shaft was not stone lined and the soft earth has crumbled; however, it appears to have been about 44 × 60 cm in size.

The roofing method employed over the horizontal shaft is suggested by pairs of opposed holes in the vertical faces of the shaft located 60–65 cm above the floor and large enough to hold beams between 6 cm and 9 cm in diameter. Holes for five beams were found; they were spaced 7–18 cm apart. Placement of these paired holes suggests that there were originally eight or nine beams supporting the ventilator shaft roof; evidence for additional pairs of holes was not found.

Roofing

Roofing material found in the fill of the kiva was limited to lumps of adobe. There is no evidence that the kiva burned.

Artifacts

Fill

D/18, D/31, D48a, D/105 unworked shell; D/22, D/58 sherd disks; D/25, D/29, D/40, D/45, D/46, D/60, D/61, D/74a, D/74b, D/89, D/90 bone awls; D/27 bone handle; D/28 shell bracelet; D/37, D/51, D/144c, D/144d, D/144e, D/144f knives; D/39a, D/39b, D/59 sheet iron; D/41, D/53a, D/165 shell tinklers; D/47, D/48b shell rings; D/49 scraper; D/50 bone tube; D/52 pigment; D/53b shell bead; D/62, D/76 shaft smoothers/straighteners; D/63 worked sherd; D/75 projectile point; D/77 corncobs; D/97 miniature vessel; D/144a, D/s13 tabular tools; D/144b protopalette; D/144g, D/s129 debitage; D/144h tabular tool fragment; D/144i, D/144j, D/144k scrapers; D/145 ceramic figurine; D/146a core; D/s14 chopper; D/s38 stone slab; D/s43 mortar; D/s68 grinding stone; D/s127 mano fragment.

Floor

D/94 shell bracelet, D/99 sherd disk, D/151 lightning stone?

Ventilator (Feature A)

D/92 stone bead, D/98a bone awl, D/98b shell bead.

Level 3–5

D/146a core; D/146b, D/146c knives.

Level 6–8

D/147 debitage, concentration of raptor bones (no catalog number).

Stratitest Level 5

D/93a, D/93b projectile points; D/93c quartz crystal; D/148 perforated sherd disk.

Stratitest Level 6

D/149 debitage.

Stratitest Level 7

D/95 bone awl.

Platform

D/150 shell bracelet.

Foot Drum (Feature E)

D/152 pigment, D/s42 mano.

Summary and Discussion

The kiva at the Davis Ranch Site is similar in many respects to other rectangular kivas reported from prehistoric and modern Indian villages. The Davis Ranch Site kiva is a subsurface structure exhibiting nine of the characteristic features of kivas listed by Smiley (1952a). It is probable that this structure was built by a people intimately familiar with kivas of the Hopi area of the late thirteenth century AD or later. All modern Hopi kivas are rectangular, subsurface or partially subsurface, and have platforms (Fewkes 1892:19–24; Mindeleff 1891:111–137). Some have offsets in one or both side walls, benches on the sides as well as opposite the platform, loom anchors, and foot drum/sipapus (e.g., Mindeleff 1891:Figures 22, 24, 25, 27; Parsons 1936:Figure 385). Also like modern Hopi kivas, and unlike modern Zuni and Acoma kivas, the Davis Ranch Site kiva was built in the open and not incorporated into a houseblock (Lange 1958:38–39; Parsons 1939:9). Modern Hopi kivas differ from the Davis Ranch Site kiva in having flagstone floors and wall-supported instead of post-supported roofs, and in lacking ventilators and deflectors. The Davis Ranch Site kiva is also much larger than modern Hopi kivas, which average about 30 m^2 in area.

[*Editor: Smith's (1972) report on the ancient kivas of Antelope Mesa documents the use of ventilators by the Hopi as recently as the mid- to late AD 1600s. This same source indicates the use of perforations in flagstones as loom-anchor holes during the seventeenth century. By the nineteenth century, Hopi kivas lacked ventilators (Fewkes 1908:398) and a new type of loom-anchor apparatus had been introduced: perforated logs embedded horizontally in the floor, flush with surrounding flagstones and parallel to the side walls (e.g., Mindeleff 1891:128–129, 132–133, Figures 22, 25, 27, 31). Mindeleff (1891:124, Figures 23, 24, 26, 28; see also Fewkes 1892:21–22) reports that the roof design characteristic of modern Hopi kivas, which includes a raised hatchway chamber, "is said to . . . facilitate the egress of smoke." This innovation may have rendered ventilator shafts unnecessary.*]

Kivas most similar to the Davis Ranch Site structure are to be found at Awat'ovi (AZ J:7:1[ASM]; Smith 1952b). In his general description of the Awat'ovi kivas, Smith (1952b:5–9) says they are rectangular, partially subterranean, and often have offset walls. Each has a broad platform at one end and narrow benches along the side walls. Sometimes a bench along the wall opposite the platform is present. Each is outfitted with a ventilator shaft, a deflector, a hearth, and a hatchway entrance. Other floor features include loom-anchor holes and sometimes a foot drum/sipapu. All of these features are found in the Davis Ranch Site kiva.

The Awat'ovi kivas differ in that they are smaller (averaging about 20 m^2) and have flagstone floors and wall paintings. Also, in a typical Awat'ovi kiva, the hearth is rectangular rather than oval and the deflector is a sandstone slab rather than a cobble-and-adobe wall. [*Editor: Gerald based his comparisons on a brief description of kivas included in Smith's (1952b) report on murals at Awat'ovi and Kawàyka'a (AZ J:7:2[ASM]). Smith's (1972:118) later publication, devoted exclusively to kiva architecture, documents structures with rhomboidal and basin-shaped fire pits.*] The single early historic Zuni kiva reported (Hodge 1939) shares many of the traits of Awat'ovi kivas, exhibiting a rectangular shape, a flagstone floor, loom-anchor holes, a platform with a ventilator tunnel, a deflector, and a rectangular fire pit. [*Editor: The age of the rectangular, subterranean kiva at Hawikku (NM M:1:1[ASM]) remains an unresolved matter. Although Hodge (1939:202) and others (Douglass 1935:53, 1938:13; Smiley 1952b:19) reported tree-ring dates of AD 1381, 1391, 1405, and 1480, Bannister and others (1970:12) indicate that these could not be confirmed upon reanalysis. Ceramic data reported by Hodge (1939, 1966) and interpreted by Schachner (2006) suggest this kiva was abandoned during the early 1600s.*] The single modern Zuni kiva presented by Smiley (1952a:-Figure 3; see also Bunzel 1932:877) has a bench around its walls and a vestigial platform.

The floor, bench, and platform area of the Davis Ranch Site kiva is 44.9 m^2, much larger than any other rectangular kiva, ancient or historic, yet reported. *[Editor: This was likely true in 1958, but more recent work has documented rectangular kivas of similar size or larger at Chevelon Ruin (AZ P:2:11 [ASM]), Homol'ovi II (AZ J:14:15[ASM]), Homol'ovi III (AZ J:14:14[ASM]), and the Krider Kiva locus (AZ CC:1:43[ASM]) of the Spear Ranch Site (AZ CC:1:11[ASM]) (Adams 2002:Table 6.6; Jernigan 1993; Neuzil 2005, 2008).*] Another difference between this kiva and other rectangular kivas is the posthole pattern. Only one other kiva, a historic Hopi structure, is reported to have posts set on the bench and platform, and these are not matched by symmetrically placed posts on the opposite side of the structure (Parsons 1936:Figure 387). [*Editor: Although it is true that vertical support posts resting on the benches or platforms of rectangular kivas are rare, there are many rectangular kivas with vertical roof support beams set into or behind their walls (e.g., Fewkes 1904:137–138, Figure 87, Plate 58; Gann 1995; Jennings 1980:88–95, Figures 22, 23; Lyons 1997).*]

The sealed subfloor pit (Feature F) near the northwest bench of the Davis Ranch Site kiva is comparable to a pit used in the Jemez great kiva dedication ceremony (Ellis 1952:149). At Jemez, a man hiding in the hole during the ceremony speaks to the assembled kiva members in the voice of the Corn Mother (Ellis 1952:152–153). After the ceremony, the hole is secretly filled and all evidence of its existence is obliterated (Ellis 1952:152). The size of the pit in the Davis Ranch Site kiva, its location, and the fact that it was filled and sealed over fit the described practices at Jemez exactly. It seems plausible, therefore, to suggest that some sort of a dedication ceremony, possibly involving the hiding of a man in the pit, took place in this kiva. Numerous other uses of this pit can, of course, be suggested. [*Editor: Ceramics recovered from the pit indicate that it was sealed during the Romero phase, long after the kiva was constructed. This fact does not preclude earlier uses of the feature.*

A cluster of more than 80 associated hawk bones and bone fragments in the east corner of the kiva was identified in the field as a bird burial. Analysis by Harrison Tordoff in 1958 (appendices G and H) and R. Roy Johnson in 1969 (appendix I) revealed the presence of elements from at least four individual raptors. At least three individuals of Buteo jamaicensis *(red-tailed hawk) and/or* Buteo swainsoni *(Swainson's hawk) are represented by a complete cranium, 22 cranial fragments, 44 foot bones, 7 leg bones (including 3 or possibly 4 left tarsometatarsi), and at least 4 wing bones (a left ulna, a right radius, a right carpometacarpus, and a left carpometacarpus). A* Buteogallus anthracinus *(black hawk) tarsometatarsus was also identified.*

*A pit in the fill of a pit structure (a possible kiva) at the nearby José Solas Ruin yielded more than 100 raptor bones, including elements comprising 15 wings from a minimum of 9 different individuals. At least five species were represented, including red-tailed hawk (*Buteo jamaicensis*), Swainson's hawk (*Buteo swainsoni*), northern goshawk (*Accipiter gentilis*), northern harrier (*Circus cyaneus*), and American kestrel (*Falco sparverius*) (Clark and Lyons 2012; Lyons 2004a; Vint 2000).*

Such assemblages, which likely represent worn-out ritual objects, or "ceremonial trash," are often recovered in abandoned ceremonial structures within ancestral puebloan settlements (McKusick 2001; Walker 1995, 1999). Examples of this phenomenon have been documented at Awat'ovi (Olsen 1978:4–6, 33), Grasshopper Pueblo (AZ P:14:1[ASM]; McKusick 1982:91), Bailey Ruin (AZ P:11:1 [ASM]; Mills, Van Keuren et al. 1999:162–172), Point of Pines Pueblo (AZ W:10:50[ASM]; McKusick 2001:97; see also Light 1990), Homol'ovi I (AZ J:14:3[ASM]), Homol'ovi II, and Homol'ovi III (Lyons 1997; Strand 1998:284–295, 352–363, 382–386), among other sites.]

In view of the evidence presented here, the Davis Ranch Site kiva appears to be most similar to the kivas excavated at Awat'ovi and to the few modern Hopi kivas for which data are available. On the basis of kiva similarities alone, it may be suggested that the builders of the Davis Ranch Site kiva were Hopi. However, the predominant decorated pottery (Gila Polychrome) has never been reported in quantity from the Hopi area. [*Editor: In the years since Gerald's manuscript was prepared, more kivas have been identified in southern Arizona. These data and other evidence of the movement of Kayenta groups into the southern Southwest are addressed in detail in the concluding chapter.*]

THE PUEBLO

[*Editor: Gerald referred to the different parts of the pueblo using the following labels: Houseblock I (Rooms 3–11), Houseblock II (Rooms 16–21 and 33), and Miscellaneous Rooms (Rooms 2, 15, 36, and 37) (see figure 1.5). He also labeled on various maps Rooms 35, 45, 46, and 47 but did not discuss them in his draft report. He also identified "Rooms" 14 and 34 on some maps as possible ramadas ("Ramada?"). Each of these structures, with the exception of Room 35, is labeled in Gerald's (1975:Figure 3) dissertation; each yielded ceramics and most produced other artifacts as well. Gerald did not assign a number to the structure now designated Room 48. This identifier is used to facilitate discussion.*

Attention to overall spatial organization, bond/abut patterns, and other relationships makes it possible to reconceptualize and relabel the parts of the pueblo. Based on wall bonds, their proximity to Rooms 16–21 and 33, and the fact that they help to define a plaza-like area bounded by Houseblocks I and II, Rooms 15 and 14 are treated here as part of Houseblock II. As the space identified as Room 35 shares walls with Room 33, it is also considered part of Houseblock II.

The five conjoined rooms (including Room 47) west of, and separate from, Houseblock II have been given the label Houseblock VI, and the discrete set of 10 rooms (including Rooms 37 and 45) to the northwest of Houseblock VI has been designated Houseblock VII. The compound wall that abuts Houseblock VII and Houseblock II and the rooms directly attached to this wall (Rooms 2, 36, and 48) are treated as a separate unit of analysis (see Rooms Associated with the Compound Wall, below). Rooms 34 and 46 are also considered separately (see Other Rooms, below). Room 34 is an apparently unroofed space defined by the west wall of Room 36, the east wall of Room 5, and a wall that connects these two features. Room 46 and a possible room to the south appear isolated from all other architectural features, but this is likely a result of stone robbing. The west wall of Room 46 aligns with the west wall of Room 7, in Houseblock I, and intervening architectural features may have been destroyed.]

During preexcavation visits to the Davis Ranch Site, numerous short rows and a few long continuous rows of stones protruding above the surface were noted. After the brush had been removed, and with the commencement of excavation, it soon became apparent that these rows of stones were, as had been suspected, remnants of decomposed cobble-and-adobe walls. When digging and mapping had been completed, it was found that a cobble-and-adobe wall surrounded a rectangular area 66 m long in a northwest-southeast direction and 30 m wide. Three groups of contiguous, single-storied rooms and at least three isolated rooms are connected to this wall. There is one opening in the south corner and possibly others in the north corner and along the northeast side. In only one area, the center of the southeast side, was there evidence that additional rooms were attached to the perimeter row.

A cluster of nine contiguous-walled rooms was built in the center of the southern one-third of the plaza, and there is some evidence that a second, smaller cluster of rooms may have existed in the northern portion of the plaza. One other architectural feature, a rectangular subsurface kiva, is associated with this pueblo. It is located outside the compound and to the east.

The description of the architecture of this pueblo is based on the complete excavation of 9 rooms, the trenching of 10 others, and the mapping of 15 more. [*Editor: There are 41 total mapped spaces in the portion of the site referred to as the pueblo. Gerald assigned room numbers to 26 of these, including two apparently unroofed spaces (Rooms 14 and 34). Here, in describing his sample, Gerald refers to having excavated Rooms 2, 3, 4, 6, 7, 8, 9, 10, and 11 in their entirety; having trenched Rooms 5, 15, 16, 17, 18, 19, 20, 21, 33, and 37; and having mapped the five rooms that make up Houseblock VI, the nine rooms that along with Room 37 constitute Houseblock VII, and the space I have designated Room 48. However, he also conducted test excavations in Rooms 35, 36, 45, and 47. In addition, he dug test trenches and pits in Rooms 14 and 34. Finally, in addition to the spaces already discussed, he mapped Room 46, a possible room to the south of Room 46, and a three-walled space in Houseblock VI.*]

The walls of the pueblo buildings at the Davis Ranch Site were almost entirely constructed of puddled adobe and cobbles, with the ratio of cobbles to adobe ranging from a few cobbles in an entire wall of a room to walls composed of cobbles separated by only 5–10 cm of adobe. The cobbles range in size from 16 × 9 × 6 cm to 38 × 23 × 9 cm, and average about 27 × 18 × 8 cm. The vast majority of them are water-rounded basalt cobbles, while a few are cobbles of water-rounded tuff and andesite. Some angular basalt and sandstone slabs were used. Most of the stone probably was collected in the arroyos that join the San Pedro River on both sides of the site; there are relatively few cobbles in the riverbed itself.

The northwest and northeast walls of Room 4 were constructed of tabular sandstone laid in bands separated by 10–15 cm of adobe. Some sandstone-slab walls are present in Houseblock II as well. This sandstone was probably quarried on the slope of the terrace on which the pueblo is built. The lack of fallen sandstone slabs in the fill around these walls suggests that they were not used in the upper portions of the walls. The use of tabular sandstone in walls is characteristic of Reeve Ruin (Masonry Type 1). At that site, it is utilized in banded masonry, in which there is direct contact between slabs and spalls, creating a stone-supported wall (Di Peso 1958a:35). [*Editor: Di Peso (1958a:35) reports mortar thickness ranging from 3 cm to 12 cm in Type 1 walls.*] At the Davis Ranch Site, the sandstone slabs are in mortar-supported walls.

The greatest height to which walls were found standing at the Davis Ranch Site was 75 cm. Evidence from collapsed walls, however, suggests that some of them probably stood to heights of 1.95–2.20 m. Wall thicknesses range from 18 cm to 60 cm, with the majority falling between 25 cm and 30 cm.

Wall footings are unspecialized. In most cases, excavation for wall footings was less than 30 cm deep, and the earth removed from the excavation was mixed with water and a puddled adobe foundation made in place. Large cobbles and occasional boulders were usually placed in the puddled adobe footings. Footings are often 5–10 cm thicker than the walls above.

Traces of one or two coats of wall plaster are found in almost all rooms. This plaster ranges in thickness from 0.1 cm to 3.0 cm and averages about 0.8 cm; where two coats of plaster are discernible, the first coat is always thicker. When plaster reaches the floor level it is always coved to join the floor. Two colors of plaster are recognized, brown and reddish-brown. Since the reddish-brown plaster is always the latest coat and always occurs in burned rooms, it is thought to have resulted from the oxidization of the plaster when the room burned.

Doorways are located in five of the nine rooms excavated completely and in one of the trenched rooms. All are exterior doorways leading to the plaza and are located near the center of the room wall. Of these six doorways, four have deflector walls between the hearth and the doorway, and of these four, two also have deflector walls outside the doorway.

Doorway widths range from 30 cm to 47 cm and average 37 cm in the lower 20 cm of the opening. That the upper portions of some doorways may have been wider is indicated by the entrance to Room 16, which is 30 cm wide in the lower 20 cm and 45 cm wide above. The poor condition of the upper portions of doorways, however, prevented accurate measurements in most cases. Door sills range in height from 9 cm to 25 cm above floor level and were made of adobe. Elongated river cobbles were used to reinforce the central portions of the adobe sills in about half of the recorded cases.

Posthole patterns, to the extent they are discernible in the often poorly preserved floors, suggest that several different methods of roof support were used. Of the nine rooms excavated completely, three contained no postholes, one contained a single centrally located posthole, one contained two postholes equally spaced along the long axis, one contained a single posthole near a corner, and three contained a centrally located posthole with three or more additional postholes near the corners and along the walls.

The single (or double) central postholes are usually larger than other postholes in a room, ranging in diameter from 13.0 cm to 30.0 cm and averaging 19.0 cm. In depth they range from about 25 cm to 75 cm. The non-central postholes range from 8.0 cm to 20.0 cm in diameter and average 13.3 cm; in depth they range from 11.0 cm to 30.0 cm and average 18.0 cm. From this evidence it may be suggested that roofs were supported by the walls, supplemented by centrally located posts in most rooms, and that it was frequently necessary to place additional posts in the corners or along the walls.

Evidence of roofing material comes from burned wood, reeds, grass, and adobe in the fill and on the floors of the rooms. Rooms 3, 4, 6, 7, 9, 10, and 11 contained sufficient evidence of this nature to suggest that they were burned. The charred wood comes from fragments of logs ranging in diameter from 7.0 cm to 10.5 cm, although one specimen was probably somewhat larger originally. The largest specimen recovered (tree-ring sample 2 specimen group; see appendix A) is 78 cm long and more than

10.0 cm in diameter (the exterior has been burned and/or rotted away) and bears three burned notches that appear to have been made by burning crossbeams. These notches are separated by intervals of 28 cm and 32 cm.

Taken collectively, this evidence suggests that roofs were composed of main beams 10 cm or more in diameter that spanned the rooms with the aid of a central support post and that these were crossed at intervals of about 30 cm by rafters up to 10 cm in diameter. One or more layers of smaller sticks probably crossed the rafters, and these, in turn, were crossed by reeds and covered with grass. All of this was topped with adobe mud to a depth of 10 cm or more.

Floors in all but three rooms are broken up in places as a result of being built on trash, although each floor is well defined in some portion of the room. The basic adobe floor plaster is brown in color, but three rooms have reddish-brown plaster floors, possibly as a result of the rooms having burned. In the two rooms with replastered floors, the range in thickness of the plaster is 1.5–5.6 cm.

Seven excavated or tested rooms have hearths, and of these, two rooms have two hearths each. Five hearths are rectangular. Three of these are partially or completely slab lined, and two are lined with plaster and cobbles. They range in size from 30 × 32 cm to 47 × 50 cm and in depth from 15 cm to 25 cm. The rims of one or more sides of two rectangular hearths project at least 5 cm above the level of the floor. Four hearths are circular or oval in shape, and three of these are plastered with adobe. They range in size from 25 cm in diameter to 40 × 48 cm, and in depth from 11 cm to 15 cm. One circular hearth is sherd-lined and has a flat stone in the bottom; it is 24 cm in diameter and 10 cm deep.

Only one outdoor hearth was found; it is located in the plaza, 2 m northeast of Room 3. This hearth is circular, originally formed by six upright waterworn cobbles, of which five remain; it has a flat cobble set in the bottom. The cobbles project some 5 cm above the surface of the ground and presumably projected somewhat more above the surface of the plaza, although the latter could not be located with assurance in this area. It is 30 cm in diameter and about 25 cm deep.

A deflector wall is a low, usually L-shaped wall of adobe and cobbles or sandstone slabs, one leg of which is connected to the right side of the doorway (as one enters the room) and the other leg of which (the deflector portion) extends between the doorway and the hearth. The deflector portion of the wall is located 47–68 cm inside the doorway, is 55–60 cm long, and stands to a height of 25–32 cm. The deflector wall of Room 16 is unique in that it is U-shaped, with the upper ends of the U connected to either side of the doorway. The arm on the left side is about 7 cm lower than the arm on the right side. Four rooms have deflector walls inside them.

Deflector walls are also located outside rooms in two examples. In one case, the L-shaped wall is connected to the left side of the doorway; in the other, it is connected to the right side. Both are of about the same size as the interior deflector walls and were apparently constructed to keep sand and other debris from blowing directly into the rooms.

[*Editor: Gerald refers to the features appended to the interiors of some of the doorways at the Davis Ranch Site (e.g., Rooms 3, 6, 10, and 16) as deflectors. Such installations were first noted in the Kayenta region by Fewkes (1911:15). Ambler and others (1964:24–25, Figure 9) dubbed them "entryboxes," although they were first formally described by Lindsay and others (1968:7–8). Dean (1969:27–28) offers the following regarding entryboxes:*

> *In rooms with lateral entries, a firepit is set into the floor about two feet inside the doorway. To lessen the blast of air through the doorway, a masonry or stone slab deflector was placed at the edge of the firepit nearest the door. The deflector was joined to the doorway by the entrybox. One form of entrybox consists of two wing walls connecting each side of the deflector with the corresponding jambs of the doorway. These wing walls may be of masonry, or more commonly, of upright slabs. In other instances only one side of the deflector is joined to the doorway, leaving one side open.*

According to Lindsay (1969:185), although entryboxes are considered a diagnostic trait of the Tsegi phase (AD 1250–1300), they initially appeared in the Kayenta region circa AD 1225. More recent work has shown, however, that the earliest, most securely dated examples were built between AD 1050 and 1070 (based on dendrochronology). This evidence comes from AZ I:1:17(ASM), a site near the south rim of the Grand Canyon (Sullivan 1986:67–68, 102–104, 127–128, 347–352, Figures 4.6, 4.22, 4.23, 4.29, 4.30, Table 4.33). Jeffrey S. Dean (personal communication 2013) indicates that entryboxes appeared in the core of the Kayenta region by about AD 1100, and that by AD 1200 they were ubiquitous in Kayenta sites.

Entryboxes occur in both pit houses and surface structures and are common in southeastern Utah (in the Navajo Mountain and Paiute Mesa areas) and northeastern Arizona (in the Klethla Valley and Tsegi Canyon as well as parts of Black Mesa) (Lyons 2003:33–34). Entryboxes have been recorded at very few sites south of the Hopi Mesas, all of which date after AD 1250. Aside from the Davis Ranch Site, examples include Homol'ovi IV (AZ J:14:13[ASM]; Lyons 2001:432), Horse Camp Mill (Site 616, LA 10983; McGimsey 1980:78–79, Figures 22, 26), Techado Spring Pueblo (LA6010; Smith et al. 2009), the Haby Ranch Site (AZ BB:3:1[AF], AZ BB:3:16[ASM]; Gerald 1957a), Reeve Ruin (Di Peso 1958a), José Solas Ruin (Di Peso 1953:134, Plates 45b, 45c, Figure 12; Lyons 2004a), and the Goat Hill Site (AZ CC:1:28[ASM]; Woodson 1995:96, Figures 31, 34; 1999:67, 76).

Rooms 3, 6, and 10 at the Davis Ranch Site are outfitted with L-shaped entryboxes, and Room 16 exhibits a U-shaped entrybox. Room 3 also has a feature appended to the exterior of its doorway, as does Room 16. These resemble L-shaped entryboxes. Dual entryboxes (interior and exterior) are rare in northern Arizona (e.g., Hewitt and Brisbin 1989:418–421, Figure 141). More common than this arrangement are square or rectangular entryboxes that straddle the doorway, with half of the box inside the room and half outside (e.g., Geib 1985:74–80, Figures 18, 19; Hewitt and Brisbin 1989:411–413, Figure 136).]

The only evidence of a mealing bin was found in Room 6. Similar features are found at AZ W:10:51(ASM) in the Point of Pines region (Wendorf 1950:29), Kinishba (AZ V:4:1[ASM]; Cummings 1940:28, 30), the Webb Ranch Site (76 Ranch Site; Duffen 1937), and numerous other sites. [*Editor: Mealing bins were introduced to central and southern Arizona by immigrants from the Kayenta region (Adams 1994, 2010).*]

Houseblock I

Houseblock I (figures 3.15, 3.16) was built over a period of time as population increased or changing social organization made more rooms desirable. The earliest units constructed in this cluster consist of two isolated rooms (Rooms 5 and 9) and a two-room structure (Rooms 7 and 11). It is impossible to determine which of these units was built first, although it may be suggested that the single-room units were outgrowths of the adobe-walled pit houses and predate the contiguous-walled unit (Rooms 7 and 11). With the addition of Room 4, which makes use of the walls of Rooms 5 and 11, the advantages of contiguous rooms and shared walls were utilized, and the growth of the houseblock commenced. Rooms 3 and 10 were added next, the latter connecting the previously unrelated Room 9 to the growing house cluster. This was followed by the construction of Room 6 (to use the irregular space between Rooms 5 and 9), and last of all Room 8 was added to Room 6.

The above history of the growth of the houseblock, based on wall abutment and corner bonding, is supplemented by other architectural data. Two of the earlier units, Rooms 5 and 9, are relatively small and lack both doorways and deflectors (Room 5 has a possible but not very convincing doorway in the southwest wall). The remaining two rooms of the earlier units, Rooms 7 and 11, which were constructed at the same time, have doorways and slab-lined hearths but lack deflectors. Room 4 is similar to Rooms 5 and 9 in that it lacks a doorway and deflector, and is similar to Room 9 in that it lacks

FIGURE 3.15 Houseblock I from the north. Photograph D/70 by Rex E. Gerald. Courtesy of the Amerind Foundation Inc., Dragoon, Arizona.

a hearth (Room 5 was not excavated completely, so the presence of a hearth there cannot be ruled out). The use of sandstone slabs in the northwest and northeast walls of Room 4 suggests an attempt to reproduce the masonry practices of the Reeve Ruin occupants. The next two rooms to be added to the houseblock, Room 3 and Room 10, are quite similar in that both have doorways, deflector walls, and similarly placed circular hearths. Room 6, next in the order of construction, is similar to Rooms 3 and 10 regarding the presence of a doorway, an interior deflector, and a hearth. Room 8, the last to be built, is again similar to Rooms 5 and 9 in that it lacks a doorway, a deflector, and a hearth.

These rooms may be classified functionally as living rooms and storage rooms on the presumption that hearths would be used in living rooms but would not be necessary in storage rooms. Rooms 3, 6, 7, 11, and 10 may thus be classified as living rooms and Rooms 4, 8, and 9 as storage rooms. Room 5 cannot be classified under this system because it was not excavated completely. In the section that follows, individual rooms are described. Room descriptions are presented in order by room number.

Room 3

Located at the north corner of Houseblock I, Room 3 (figures 3.17, 3.18) is a rectangular room that adjoins Room 7 on the southwest wall and Room 4 on the southeast wall. Only the northwest and the northeast walls were added to Houseblock I

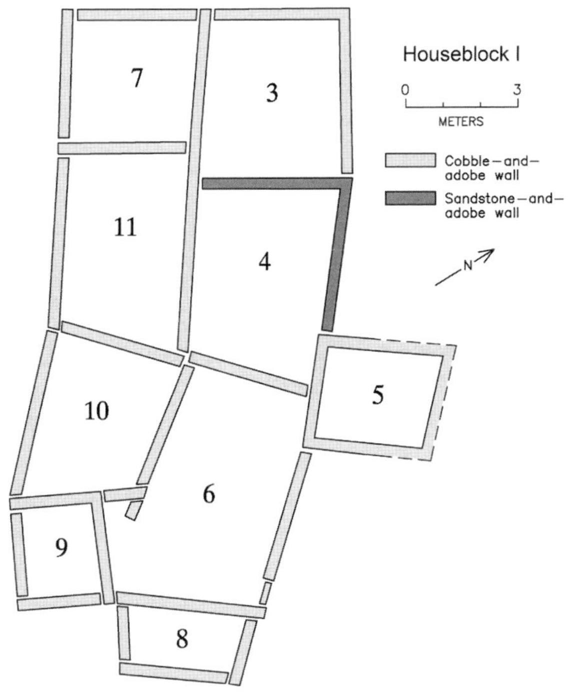

FIGURE 3.16 Plan of Houseblock I indicating wall bonds and abutments. Drawing by Ronald J. Beckwith based on Rex E. Gerald's field map and notes.

to construct this room. A pit house (House 3) is located 30 cm under the north corner of the room and probably accounts for the greater depth here of the Room 3 wall foundations. The subfloor material in this corner contains much ash and charcoal. Sterile soil was reached at a depth of 70 cm below the floor in the northwest one-third of the room.

Orientation and Size. Room 3 is oriented with its long axis running northwest-southeast and faces northeast; it is 4.10 m long × 3.40 m wide.

Floor. Soft and uneven in the north quarter, as well as in isolated portions of the remainder of the room, the floor is best preserved in the southwest half, where patches of brown plaster are found.

Floor Features. A single hearth is located between the center of the room and the doorway. It is a circular depression 27 cm in diameter and 11 cm deep and is plastered with adobe. There is a rim 1–2 cm high about the perimeter. It is filled with white ash.

The doorway of Room 3 is elaborated by the addition of two L-shaped deflector walls, one inside and the other outside the room. The interior deflector wall is connected to the right side of the doorway

FIGURE 3.17 Room 3. Photograph D/58 by Rex E. Gerald. Courtesy of the Amerind Foundation Inc., Dragoon, Arizona.

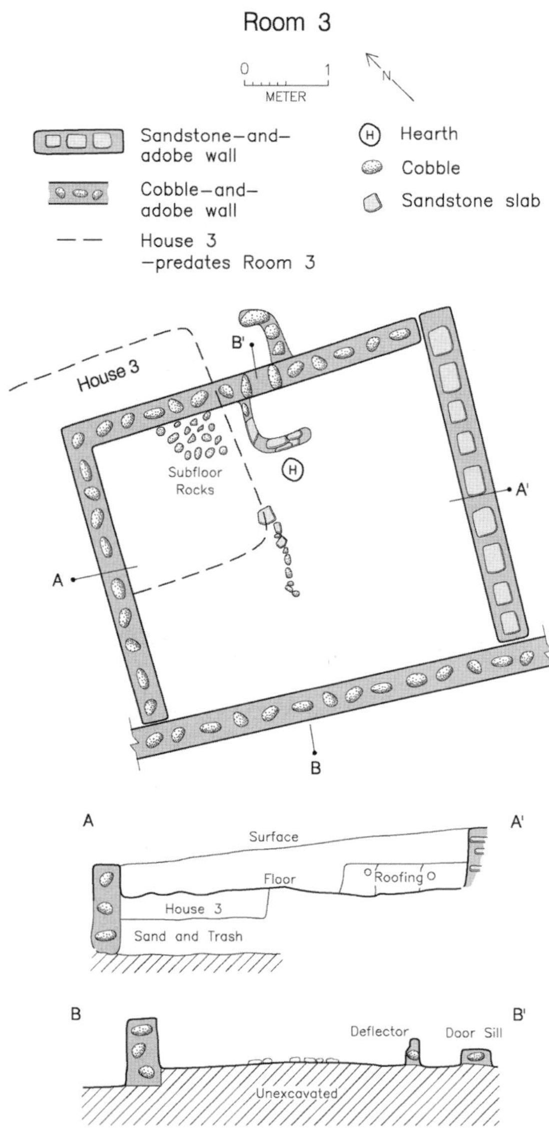

FIGURE 3.18 Plan of Room 3. Drawing by Ronald J. Beckwith based on Rex E. Gerald's field map and notes.

(as one enters) and extends 50 cm into the room before turning to the left to parallel the wall for 60 cm, thus coming directly between the hearth and the doorway. This deflector wall is built of sandstone slabs and a few cobbles, forming a wall standing to a height of about 30 cm. The exterior deflector wall is connected to the opposite side of the doorway, extends out 50 cm, and then crosses in front of the doorway for 30 cm. It is composed of adobe and a few cobbles and stands about 25 cm high.

Walls. The northwest and northeast walls are joined with a bonded corner. The southwest and southeast walls abut walls constructed for Rooms 7 and 4. The northwest and the northeast walls are both constructed of cobbles and adobe. The northeast wall is 25–30 cm thick and stands from 40 cm to 55 cm above the floor. The northwest wall is 30 cm thick and stands from 40 cm to 60 cm above the floor. At the north corner, where the two walls are bonded, the base of the wall is 70 cm below the floor; the base is not so deep in other areas. The lower portions of the walls in this corner contain the same ash and charcoal found in the subfloor, suggesting that the adobe for the walls was mixed in the trench dug for the wall bases.

Plaster adheres to the southwest and the southeast walls in some places. The surfaces of both walls were apparently smoothed by filling depressions with adobe plaster up to a thickness of 8.0 cm before the final coat of plaster was applied. The final coat is reddish-brown in color and is 0.2 cm thick on the southwest wall and as much as 1.0 cm thick on the southeast wall.

The doorway is located near the center of the northeast wall. It is 30 cm wide and has a sill of cobbles set in adobe 18 cm above the floor. The sides of the doorway are formed of elongated cobbles placed on end.

Roofing. Burned adobe, grass, and wood were found mixed with large amounts of unburned adobe near the floor in the southwest half of the room. Fragments of a burned log 10 cm in diameter (tree-ring sample 1 specimen group; see appendix A) were found in the northwest central part of the room about 30 cm above the floor. Adobe roofing material was found above and below this log. Charred grass was found on the log.

Artifacts. Fill: D/23 straw and wood, D/24 straw, D/s12 mano. Floor: D/26 concretion, D/32 projectile point, D/33 pigment, D/34 stone pendant, D/s7 mano. In wall at south corner: D/155 grooved abrader.

FIGURE 3.19 Room 4. Photograph D/71 by Rex E. Gerald. Courtesy of the Amerind Foundation Inc., Dragoon, Arizona.

Room 4

The second room from the north end of Houseblock I, on the southeast side, Room 4 (figures 3.19, 3.20) was built after Rooms 5, 7, and 11 were in place and used walls originally constructed for Rooms 5 and 11. Room 3 abuts it on the northeast, and Room 6 lies to the southwest. Sterile gravel was reached at 60 cm below the floor in a subfloor test, except in the east corner of the room, where the floor of House 9 is located 85–90 cm below the room floor.

Orientation and Size. Its long axis runs northeast-southwest and it measures 4.40 × 3.50 m.

Floor. Although the floor is relatively well preserved, it is soft and difficult to find in some areas. Two layers of plaster are present. The upper layer is reddish-brown and 1.5 cm thick. The lower layer is brown and of undetermined thickness.

Floor Features. A single posthole, 15 cm in diameter and 60 cm deep, is located in the center of the room.

Walls. The southwest wall and the southern quarter of the northeast wall are described under Rooms 5, 7, and 11. The southeast wall, which abuts both the southwest and the northeast walls, is composed of adobe and a few cobbles, stands 52 cm above the floor, and is 23–27 cm thick. The northern three-fourths of the northeast wall, which

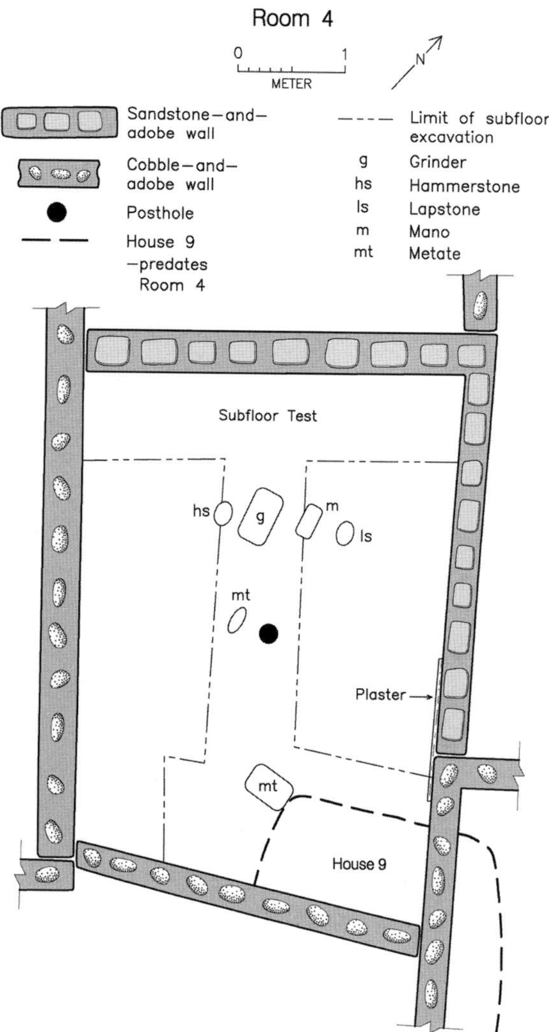

FIGURE 3.20 Plan of Room 4. Drawing by Ronald J. Beckwith based on Rex E. Gerald's field map and notes.

is built of rough courses of sandstone slabs set in adobe mortar, is 26 cm thick, stands 65 cm above the floor, and abuts the west corner of Room 5 on the south; it is bonded to the northwest wall at the north corner. The northwest wall is made primarily of adobe, although it does have a single course of sandstone slabs 57 cm above the floor and several other pieces of sandstone in lower parts of the wall near the north corner. This wall abuts the southwest wall and is 67 cm high and 35 cm thick.

Plaster is preserved on all the walls and is coved to join the floor on all but the northeast wall. Only a small, badly eroded patch of plaster is found on the southwest wall. The northwest wall retains a 0.5 cm thick layer of reddish-brown plaster on the lower quarter of its west end and under this is a layer of brown plaster 3.0 cm in thickness. The lower portion of the northeast wall bears a layer of reddish-brown plaster that is 0.8–1.2 cm thick. The southeast wall retains 1.0–1.8 cm thick layers of plaster near each end. No doorway was found.

Roofing. Charcoal fragments were found in the fill and roofing adobe was found near the floor.

Artifacts. Fill: D/s29 mano, D/s30 grinding slab. Floor: D/78 stone mirror; D/156a, D/156b concretions; D/156c unworked shell; D/156d bone awl; D/236 miniature vessel; D/s44, D/s45 metates; D/s47 mano; D/s48 lapstone; D/s49 grinding slab; D/s50 hammerstone. Subfloor test: D/157a palette; D/157b, D/157c, D/157d unworked shells; D/157e shell bead; D/157f, D/157h, D/157j, D/157n scrapers; D/157g, D/157i indeterminate flake tools; D/157k core; D/157l debitage; D/157m knife.

Room 5

Based on wall abutments, Room 5, which was not excavated completely, is one of the earliest in Houseblock I. Rooms 6 and 4 adjoin this room on the southwest wall. Sterile soil was reached 10 cm below the floor, except in the extreme southwest portion of the room, which overlies House 9. The floor of House 9 was encountered 60 cm below the floor of Room 5.

Orientation and Size. Room 5's long axis is oriented northeast-southwest, and it measures 2.70 × 2.40 m.

Floor. Although plaster remains in spots, the floor is uneven and broken up.

Floor Features. None were found, but the room was not excavated completely.

Walls. The northwest wall, which is constructed of adobe and cobbles, has a course of cobbles through most of the wall at a level 40 cm above the floor. This wall is 25–30 cm thick and stands 55–60 cm above the floor. The northeast wall, which has upright cobbles set in adobe as a basal course, is 35 cm thick and stands 26 cm above the floor. The southeast wall is composed of upright cobbles and boulders set in adobe; it is 27 cm thick and stands 40 cm above the floor. The southwest wall is of upright cobbles and adobe; it is 30 cm thick and stands 40 cm above the floor. The east and south corners are bonded; the other corners were not tested for abutments. No plaster was found on any of the walls; visible near the base of all walls, however, is a layer of adobe 1–5 cm thick, added to smooth the wall surface.

There may have been a doorway located near the center of the poorly preserved southwest wall. Its presence is suggested by an upright cobble set crosswise in the wall, similar to those utilized in doorways in some of the other rooms. The possibility that the upright cobble indicates a doorway must be tempered by the fact that the wall is constructed of upright cobbles and adobe. This ostensible doorway is about 30 cm wide and has a possible sill 20 cm above the floor.

Artifacts. Fill: D/42 bone awl, D/s83 mano, D/s84 grinding slab.

Room 6

One of the last rooms built in Houseblock I, Room 6 (figures 3.21, 3.22) is roughly rectangular in plan with an irregular projection at the south corner. House 7 was located under the northern two-thirds of the room. House 7 has one floor 50 cm below the floor of Room 6 and a second 75 cm below. At a depth of 90 cm below the floor of Room 6, the floor of House 9 was encountered. Caliche and lenses of sand and gravel were found at a depth of 1 m below Room 6's floor.

Orientation and Size. Room 6 is 5.50 m long × 3.35 m wide, and its long axis is oriented northeast-southwest.

Floor. Although soft in the northeast half of the room and in the center of the southwest half, the floor is well preserved. Roots and burrowing animals have cut through the floor in places.

Floor Features. Located between the center of the room and the doorway, the hearth was partially destroyed before being recognized. It is oval in shape, 38 × 48 cm, and 25 cm deep. Its long axis parallels that of the room. It is built directly against two large sandstone slabs in the deflector, which form the northeast side of the pit, has two small sandstone slabs plastered into the northwest side, and is plastered on the southwest and southeast sides.

The L-shaped deflector wall is connected to the right side of the doorway (as one enters). It extends 70 cm into the room, and the portion that crosses between the doorway and the hearth is 65 cm long. Constructed of sandstone slabs and adobe mortar, the deflector wall stands 35 cm above the floor.

Between 50 cm and 1.20 m from the east corner and plastered to the northeast wall are two large sandstone slabs, placed end to end, near the room's east corner. A third sandstone slab is set at right angles to the north end of these two, and a slab of basalt is embedded flat in the floor, 25 cm below floor level, in the angle between the slabs. The other two sides of the rectangle, of which these slabs form one-half, are missing, but the arrangement of the sandstone and basalt slabs suggests quite strongly that this was once a mealing bin. If these four slabs do represent about half of a mealing bin, as seems probable, the complete bin would measure 50 × 75 cm and would have been located about 50–60 cm from the southeast wall of the room. Neither the metate nor the adobe bed upon which it would have rested was found in the bin, the metate having been removed and the bin destroyed at the time of, or shortly after, the abandonment of the room.

Two postholes are located on the long axis of the room and divide it into equal thirds. The northern posthole is 13 cm in diameter and more than 30 cm deep; the southern one is 18 cm in diameter and 75 cm deep.

Walls. The northwest and southwest walls are described under Rooms 4 and 9, and the northern portion of the northeast wall under Room 5. The southeast wall is constructed of adobe and has a few sandstone slabs in the lower portion and a band of cobbles set in adobe in the upper portion. It stands 61 cm above the floor and is 24–26 cm thick. This wall is abutted by the south end of the northeast wall and abuts the northeast wall of Room 9 on the west end. The southern five-sixths of the northeast wall was erected during the construction

FIGURE 3.21 Room 6. Photograph D/98 by Rex E. Gerald. Courtesy of the Amerind Foundation Inc., Dragoon, Arizona.

of this room. It is made of cobbles and adobe, is 20–25 cm thick except near the south end, where a short section is apparently only 15 cm thick, and stands 30 cm above the floor. This wall abuts the south corner of Room 5. The southwest wall, the construction of which is discussed under Rooms 9 and 10, has a 90 cm offset in the southern one-third. A short wall, built as a continuation of the northeast wall of Room 10, extends partway across the offset. This short adobe wall abuts the southeast wall of Room 10 at the east corner.

There is a small patch of plaster on the lower part of the northwest and southwest walls at the west corner; this plaster is coved to join the floor. One other small patch of plaster is preserved on the short adobe wall and extends partway across the offset in the southwest wall.

The doorway is located near the center of the northeast wall and opens onto the plaza. The doorway is 30 cm wide and is faced with sandstone slabs: the northern slab is still in place, but the southern slab has fallen. The sandstone-slab sill is 10 cm above the floor. On the plaza floor outside the doorway is a sandstone slab, 61 × 45 × 10 cm, that appears to have served as a step.

Roofing. A juniper post was removed from the southern posthole in this room, and another juniper post was found in the northern posthole. [*Editor: Both were submitted as part of the group of specimens labeled tree-ring sample 2 (see appendix A).*] Near the

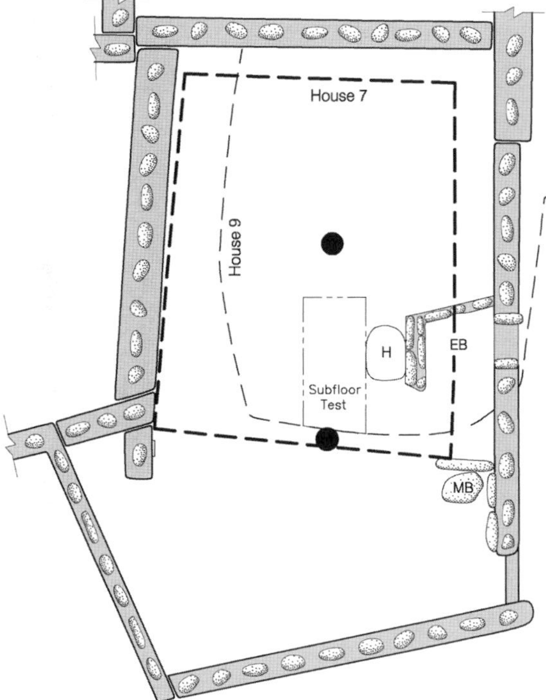

FIGURE 3.22 Plan of Room 6. Drawing by Ronald J. Beckwith based on Rex E. Gerald's field map and notes.

center of the northwest wall and parallel to it, near the floor, a 78 cm long section of a beam was found that had been burned in three places. [*Editor: This specimen is also part of the tree-ring sample 2 group.*] These burned spots are 28 cm and 32 cm apart and appear to have been caused by the burning of rafters that were laid across this beam. The beam is 10 cm in diameter but originally was larger.

Artifacts. Surface: D/s31 mano. Entryway: D/158 shell tinkler. Fill: D/s97 hammerstone, D/s101 metate. Entry floor: D/s92 mano blank. Subfloor in south half: D/s98 mano, D/s99 mano fragment, D/s100 chopper.

Room 7

Located at the west corner of Houseblock I, Room 7 (figure 3.23) shares its southeast wall with Room 11 and its northeast wall with Room 3. Sterile soil was reached at 30 cm below the floor.

Orientation and Size. Room 7 is oriented with its long axis running northeast-southwest, and it measures 3.2 × 3.0 m.

Floor. Relatively well preserved in the northeast half of the room, the floor is badly disturbed and difficult to locate in the southwest half of the room. The floor plaster is coved to join the wall plaster in places along the northeast wall.

Floor Features. Located between the center of the room and the doorway, the hearth was destroyed before the roof and walls collapsed. However, the impressions in the floor and the single piece of sandstone remaining in place indicate that it was a slab-lined firebox, 35 × 35 cm square and 15 cm deep. The depression is filled with white ash.

Walls. Room 7 and its neighbor to the southeast, Room 11, were built at the same time and are two of the four oldest rooms in Houseblock I, based on wall abutments. All walls are constructed of cobbles and adobe with the addition, in the northwest wall, of a few sandstone blocks. These walls are all about 30 cm in thickness and stand 53 cm above the floor at the west corner and 78 cm above the floor at the east corner. The northwest and southeast walls are about 15 cm wider at the floor than they are at the top. The northwest and southeast walls abut the northeast wall. The southwest wall abuts the southeast wall and is abutted by the northwest wall.

Plaster is preserved on large areas of the northeast and southeast walls and in one small patch on the southwest wall. Two layers of reddish-brown plaster are discernible on the south half of the northeast wall. The top layer is 0.1–0.2 cm thick and the bottom layer is 0.3–0.5 cm thick. The lower one-third of the southeast wall also bears two layers of

FIGURE 3.23 Room 7. Photograph D/18 by Rex E. Gerald. Courtesy of the Amerind Foundation Inc., Dragoon, Arizona.

reddish-brown plaster. The top layer is 0.1–0.2 cm thick and the lower layer is 1.8–4.5 cm thick. The plaster on the southwest wall is too eroded for measurement.

The doorway, just north of the center of the southwest wall, gives access to the plaza. It is 42 cm wide and has an adobe-and-cobble sill that is 25 cm above the floor. The sides of the doorway are constructed of cobbles and adobe.

Roofing. A fragment of a beam 25 cm long and 10 cm in diameter, surrounded by burned adobe, was found 22 cm above the hearth (tree-ring sample 3 specimens; see appendix A).

Artifacts. Fill: D/64 scraper, D/65 shaft smoother/straightener, D/79 knife. Floor: D/66 bone awl, D/80 biface, D/s32 mano, D/s33 metate. Floor 1: D/s90 metate. In northwest wall: D/s34 metate.

Room 8

One of the latest rooms, if not the last, built in Houseblock I, Room 8 (figures 3.24, 3.25) is located on the extreme southeast corner of the houseblock. It is trapezoidal in shape, with the base being the northwest wall, which is shared with Room 6. Sterile soil was reached at 45 cm below the floor.

Orientation and Size. Room 8 measures 2.50 × 1.40 m, and its long axis runs northeast-southwest.

Floor. Fairly soft, the floor is made of adobe. It is about 2 cm thick in places.

Floor Features. None were found.

Walls. All but the northwest wall were originally built for this room. The northeast wall is constructed of basalt cobbles and sandstone slabs set in adobe. Its base is about 40 cm below floor level. A portion

FIGURE 3.24 Room 8. Photograph D/24 by Rex E. Gerald. Courtesy of the Amerind Foundation Inc., Dragoon, Arizona.

of a flat metate was found in this wall, which stands about 20 cm above the floor and is 22 cm thick. The southeast wall is made of cobbles set in adobe mortar; it stands only 5 cm above the floor and is 22–26 cm thick. The southwest wall is also constructed of adobe and cobbles; it stands 10 cm above the floor and is 22 cm thick. The northeast wall abuts the southeast wall of Room 6 and is abutted by the southeast wall of Room 8. The southwest wall abuts both the northeast wall of Room 9 and the southeast wall of Room 8. Neither wall plaster nor a doorway was found.

Roofing. No evidence was found.

Artifacts. Floor fill: D/s102 slab. In northeast wall: D/s116 metate.

Room 9

Almost square in plan, Room 9 (figure 3.26) is located at the south corner of Houseblock I. It is one of the earliest rooms in the houseblock and is adjoined on the northwest by Room 10 and on the northeast by Room 6. Sterile sand and gravel were reached at a depth of 38 cm below Floor 2, in parts of the subfloor test. A borrow pit was located under the northwest wall. [*Editor: In the trench in front of Room 9, Gerald recovered two tree-ring specimens submitted as sample group 8 (see appendix A).*]

Orientation and Size. Room 9 is 2.35 m long and 2.13 m wide, with the longer dimension oriented northwest-southeast.

Floor. Two floors in good condition were found in this room. The upper, Floor 1, is composed of a 2 cm thick layer of adobe plaster. Floor 2 is also made of adobe, although of undetermined thickness.

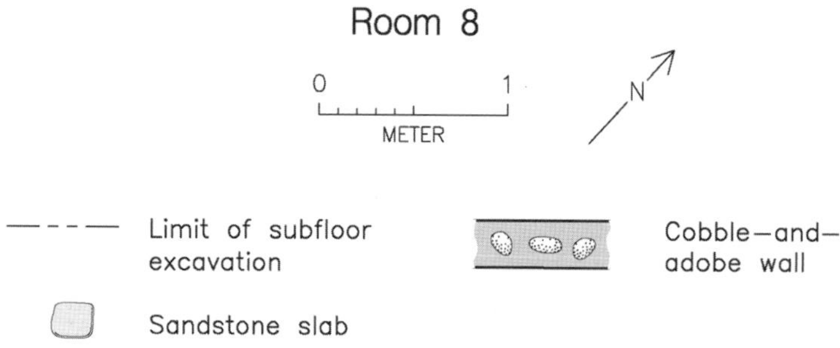

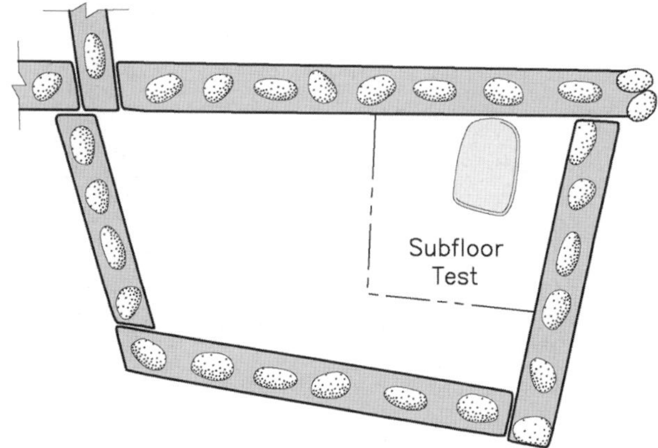

FIGURE 3.25 Plan of Room 8. Drawing by Ronald J. Beckwith based on Rex E. Gerald's field map and notes.

Floor Features. Five postholes, which range in diameter from 11.0 cm to 13.5 cm, are located near each of the four corners and near the center of the room. These postholes are not located uniformly in relation to the corners, suggesting that the corner postholes were not utilized for roof supports. The center post may have served as a supplementary roof support, although that would not seem necessary in such a small room.

Walls. All of Room 9's walls are constructed of cobbles and adobe, the northwest and northeast walls apparently having higher proportions of adobe than the other two. The northwest and northeast walls are joined by a bonded corner. A few flat cobbles, laid horizontally, are visible in the upper portions of the remnants of these two walls. The northwest wall is 25 cm thick and stands 25–35 cm above Floor 1. The northeast wall is 17 cm thick and stands 22 cm above Floor 1 at the south end and is 20 cm thick and stands 55 cm above Floor 1 at the north end. The southwest and southeast walls appear to contain a higher proportion of cobbles than the other walls, but this may only be characteristic of the lower parts of the walls. The upper parts of these walls are mostly eroded away and the lower portions of the northeast and northwest walls were not exposed. The southwest wall, which abuts both the northwest and the southeast walls, is 35–47 cm thick and stands 5 cm above Floor 1 at the south end and 20 cm above Floor 1 at the north end. The southeast wall, which abuts the northeast wall, is 26 cm thick and stands 25 cm above Floor 1. Traces of brown plaster were found on the northwest and northeast walls.

Roofing. No evidence was found.

Artifacts. Fill: D/81 knife. Floor: D/82 shaft smoother/straightener, D/s121 metate, D/s36 mano. Floor 1 northeast posthole: D/160 pigment. Subfloor test: D/161 pigment.

FIGURE 3.26 Room 9. Photograph D/23 by Rex E. Gerald. Courtesy of the Amerind Foundation Inc., Dragoon, Arizona.

Room 10

Located near the center of the south side of Houseblock I, Room 10 (figures 3.27, 3.28) is the second unit from the east end in this row of rooms. It was built between Rooms 11 and 9 by the addition of two walls to enclose the area between them. It takes the shape of a trapezoid with a curved base. The adjoining rooms are Room 11 on the northwest, Room 6 on the northeast, and Room 9 on the southeast. Sterile sand and gravel were found at a depth of 40 cm below the floor, in the east corner of the room.

Orientation and Size. This room measures roughly 3.03 × 3.70 m.

Floor. Well-preserved plaster covers part of the floor, but the majority of the surface is soft and poorly defined.

Floor Features. A circular hearth is located between the center of the room and the doorway. It is lined with sherds set in adobe plaster except where the cobbles in the deflector form part of the perimeter; a flat cobble forms the bottom of the hearth. It is 25 cm in diameter and 10 cm deep.

An L-shaped deflector wall is connected to the right side of the doorway (as one enters). It extends 45 cm into the room, then turns left for 75 cm to parallel the wall and pass between the doorway and the hearth. This deflector wall is made of adobe except for two cobbles, backed with adobe, that face and form part of this feature.

Four postholes were located in the soft floor of this room. One is northeast of the center, and the others are in the north, east, and south quarters of the room near the corners. The central posthole is 22 cm in diameter, the north posthole is 25 cm in diameter, the east posthole is 20 cm in diameter, and the south posthole is 15 cm in diameter. [*Editor: Only the central posthole appears on the plan.*]

FIGURE 3.27 Room 10. Photograph D/22 by Rex E. Gerald. Courtesy of the Amerind Foundation Inc., Dragoon, Arizona.

Walls. The northwest and southeast walls, with the exception of a portion of the east corner, are described under Rooms 11 and 9, respectively. The southwest wall, which is slightly curved and in which the doorway is located, is composed of cobbles and boulders held in place by adobe. It is 30–35 cm thick throughout most of its length but has an added buttress on the outside at the north end, where the total thickness is 50 cm. Its height above the floor is 20 cm at the south end and 40 cm at the north end. The northeast wall is composed of adobe and cobbles; it is 38–40 cm thick and stands 55 cm above the floor. This wall utilizes the stub of the southwest wall of House 7 as a footing. The southwest wall abuts both the northwest and the southeast walls; the northeast wall abuts the southeast wall of Room 4 and is built against the east end of the southeast wall of Room 11 on the north. The northwest wall of Room 9, which forms the southeast wall of this room, has been extended 1 m to the northeast, where it is abutted by the south end of the northeast wall of Room 10. This extension wall is 25 cm thick and stands 55 cm above the floor; it is constructed of a poor grade of adobe and a few stones.

Plaster is preserved in the north corner, where two layers are visible: a thin reddish-brown upper layer and a thick brown lower layer.

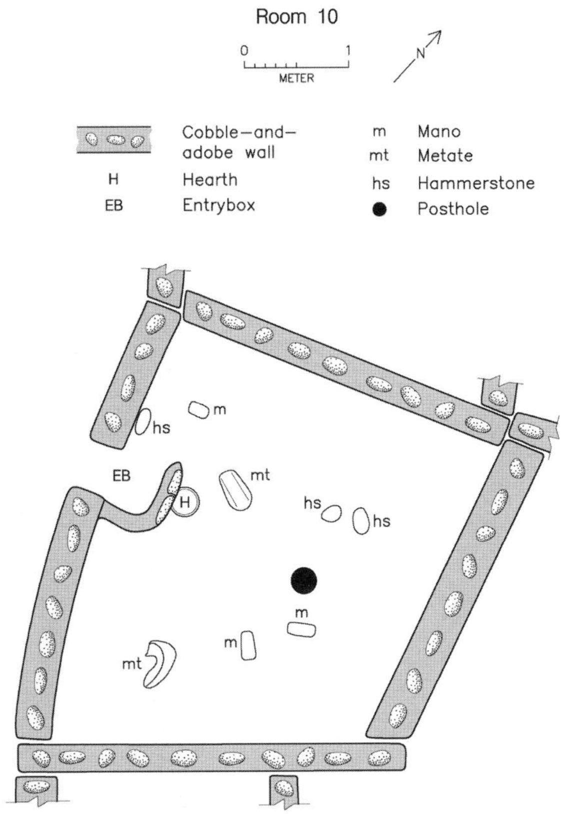

FIGURE 3.28 Plan of Room 10. Drawing by Ronald J. Beckwith based on Rex E. Gerald's field map and notes.

The curved wall on the southwest side contains the doorway, located one-third of the way from the north end. It is 45 cm wide and has an adobe sill 10 cm above the floor.

Roofing. Several fragments of burned roofing material were found on the floor and in the fill just above the floor. Three fragments of logs (tree-ring sample 4 specimens; see appendix A) were on or near the floor. Unfortunately, all were too small and too scattered to give much information on the roofing beyond the fact that roofing beams, which these are presumed to be, ranged from 6.5 cm to 10.5 cm in diameter. In addition, several fragments of burned cane were found in the fill near the floor.

Artifacts. Fill: D/83 perforated sherd disk, D/84 cane, D/s28 metate, D/s40 mano, D/s41 stone ball. Floor: D/85 knife; D/s21, D/s22, D/s23 manos; D/s24, D/s25, D/s26 hammerstones; D/s27 metate. In southwest wall: D/s111 metate.

Room 11

The second room from the northwest end of House-block I on the southwest side, Room 11 (figures 3.29, 3.30) is trapezoidal in shape. The top of the trapezoid, which is slightly curved, forms the outer (southwest) wall of the room. Adjoining rooms are Room 7 on the northwest, Room 4 and a bit of Room 3 on the northeast, and Room 10 on the southeast. Sterile soil was reached 25 cm below floor level.

Orientation and Size. This room measures roughly 3.00 × 4.40 m, and its long axis runs northwest-southeast.

Floor. Poorly preserved in the southwest quarter and broken in portions of the remainder of the room, the floor is covered with reddish-brown plaster in places.

Floor Features. Located between the center of the room and the doorway, the hearth is rectangular in shape, 35 × 40 cm. Its long axis is parallel to that of the room, and it is 23 cm deep, from floor level. A flat, vesicular basalt cobble forms the bottom of the hearth, and there are indications that it was once lined with sandstone slabs; they now remain only on the southeast and part of the northeast sides. The slabs extend 5 cm above floor level.

A single possible posthole, 17 cm in diameter and 30 cm deep, is located near the center of the north quarter of the room. Several fragments of leather, of apparent machine manufacture, and a hackberry seed found in this hole suggest that it may, instead, be an animal burrow.

Walls. The northwest wall of this room is described under Room 7. The northeast wall is a continuation of the northeast wall of Room 7 and stands 72 cm in height throughout most of its length; it is 30 cm thick and is constructed of cobbles and adobe. The southeast wall, also built of cobbles and adobe, stands about 50 cm above the floor and is 25 cm thick. The southwest wall is made of a high proportion of cobbles and boulders (up to 30 × 32 × 15 cm in size) set in adobe mortar. It is 50–60 cm thick and

FIGURE 3.29 Room 11. Photograph D/20 by Rex E. Gerald. Courtesy of the Amerind Foundation Inc., Dragoon, Arizona.

stands 40 cm above the floor. The southern end of this wall and the adjacent end of the abutting southwest wall of Room 10 are reinforced with a 20 cm thick addition of cobbles and adobe. This addition, which is about 1 m long, may have served as a buttress to prevent the corners of the rooms from separating. The northwest wall abuts the northeast wall and is abutted by the southwest wall; the southeast wall is abutted by the northeast wall and abuts the southwest wall.

The plaster preserved in the north corner of the room ranges in thickness from 0.2 cm to 2.0 cm. This plaster is coved to join the floor.

The doorway is located in the center of the southwest wall. It is 47 cm wide and has a cobble-and-adobe sill that is 2–9 cm above the floor.

Roofing. A single fragment of charcoal, about 5 cm in diameter and 7 cm long, was found on the floor near the center of the room (tree-ring sample 5; see appendix A).

Artifacts. Fill: D/s37 worked stone. Posthole: D/88 leather fragments, D/103 hackberry seeds.

Houseblock II

[*Editor: Houseblock II consists of a row of six pueblo rooms (Rooms 16–21) oriented northeast-southwest; a room (Room 33) adjacent to one of the central rooms on the northwest side; the possible remains of another*

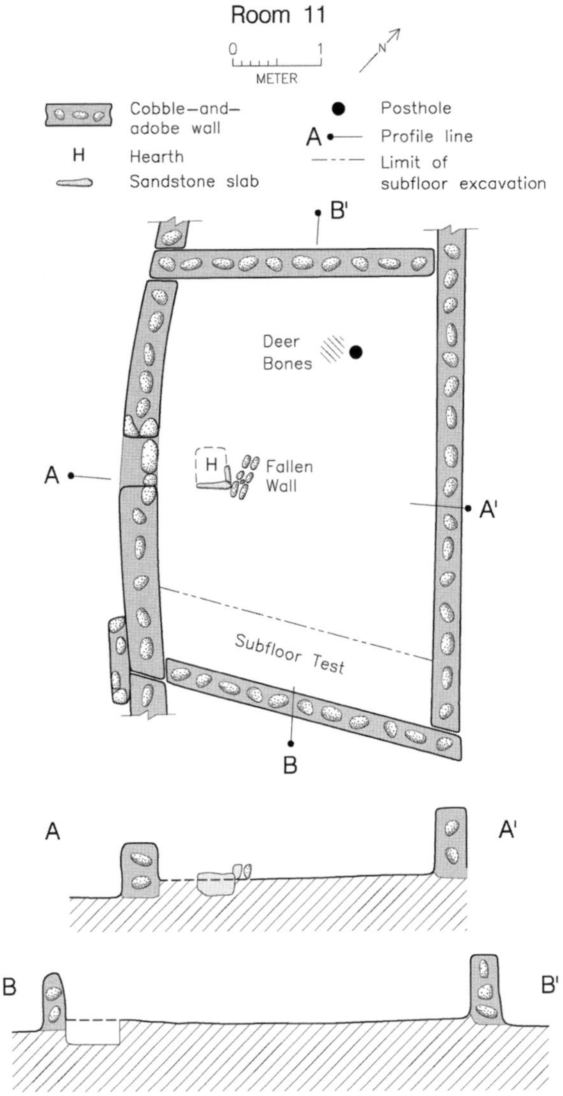

FIGURE 3.30 Plan of Room 11. Drawing by Ronald J. Beckwith based on Rex E. Gerald's field map and notes.

room (Room 35) adjacent to Room 33; Room 15, which is appended to the compound wall; and "Room" 14, a courtyard-like space between Rooms 15 and 16.] The southeast walls of Rooms 16–21 are built on the south edge of the terrace and form the southeast side of the compound. The northwest wall of these rooms is built in a relatively straight line, while the southeast wall is distinctly offset at Rooms 20 and 21. The northeastern four rooms are fairly uniform in size, and their northwest and southeast walls are built in straight lines. The same can be said for the southwestern two rooms (Rooms 20 and 21), but they are much narrower in a northwest-southeast direction, the southeast wall being offset 2 m to the northwest from the corner of the northeastern group of rooms.

None of the rooms of Houseblock II were completely excavated, and only two were tested extensively. The remaining rooms were trenched along the southeast wall in order to determine the extent of the pueblo and to facilitate mapping the site. As a result, the description of these rooms is brief and incomplete.

Room 14

[*Editor: A search of Gerald's papers failed to yield a written description of Room 14. This apparently unroofed space, about 3.00 × 5.00 m in area, was created by the continuation of the northwest wall of Room 15, the continuation of the northwest wall of Room 16, and a wall joining these two, running roughly parallel to the northeast wall of Room 15. A field photograph (figure 3.31), an associated photo log entry, and the master site map indicate that Gerald recovered one or more reconstructible plain ware jars along the northeast wall, between the midpoint of the wall and the southeast corner of Room 14. The log entry for photo D/93 reads "clustered plain jars by wall N of Rm. 16," and the map bears a circle in this area within Room 14 that is labeled "jars." Catalog numbers apparently were never assigned and the object or objects in figure 3.31 were not encountered during the reanalysis. Gerald records the following artifacts as having been recovered from the fill of Room 14: Ds/59 metate; Ds/60, 61, 62 pebble choppers; Ds/63 mano. The provenience designation used for some of these was that associated with a trench within what was later called Room 14: T24E 20–21S. Gerald's sherd totals for Room 14 are listed under T23–27E 20–24S.*]

Room 15

Located in the east corner of the plaza, Room 15 is opposite Room 16. Its northwest wall forms a portion

FIGURE 3.31 Room 14. The vessel or vessels in the photograph were not encountered during the reanalysis. Photograph D/93 by Rex E. Gerald. Courtesy of the Amerind Foundation Inc., Dragoon, Arizona.

of the perimeter wall of the compound. It is rectangular in shape. This room was outlined by trenches.

Orientation and Size. Room 15 measures 3.00 m long × 2.12 m wide, and its long axis runs northeast-southwest.

Floor. Room 15's floor is poorly preserved.

Floor Features. None were found.

Walls. The walls are so poorly preserved that it is impossible to ascertain the nature of their construction. They are recognizable only by an occasional cobble set in very sandy adobe. It is probable that this structure is a poorly constructed adobe-and-cobble-walled pueblo room that was abandoned and partially removed before the site was abandoned by the occupants. Another possibility that would account for the paucity of adobe and cobbles in the walls is that the structure was a ramada with only a low wall of sandy adobe around it; however, no postholes were located. None of the walls of this room stood more than 20 cm above the floor level, and they ranged in thickness as follows: northwest wall, 38 cm; northeast, 28 cm; southeast, 50 cm; and southwest, 35 cm. No other architectural features were observed in this room.

Roofing. No evidence was found.

Artifacts. Fill: D/s114 mano blank.

Room 16

The northeasternmost of the rooms of this houseblock, Room 16 (figures 3.32, 3.33) is adjoined on the southwest by Room 17. It was trenched along the northwest, northeast, and southeast walls. Relatively little trash was found under the floor of Room 16, and sterile red clay was reached at a depth of 25 cm below the floor.

Orientation and Size. This room measures 4.45 × 3.55 m, and its long axis runs northeast-southwest.

Floor. Composed of adobe that is hard in some places and soft in others, the floor is coved at the walls on the northwest and northeast.

FIGURE 3.32 Room 16. Photograph D/148 by Rex E. Gerald. Courtesy of the Amerind Foundation Inc., Dragoon, Arizona.

Floor Features. In the portion of this room that was excavated, two hearths were located. One is in the expected location, between the center of the room and the doorway. It is square with rounded corners, 30 × 30 cm, lined with adobe plaster, and filled with white ash. The second hearth is a plastered circular depression, 25 cm in diameter and 20 cm deep. It is located in the center of the north quarter of the room and is also filled with white ash.

Located between the doorway and the hearth, the deflector is connected to the right side of the doorway (as one enters) by an adobe wall and to the left side of the doorway by an adobe and basalt cobble wall that appears to have been added later, probably to better protect the fire from the draft entering through the doorway. The portion that runs parallel to the room's northwest wall, facing the square hearth, is 46 cm inside the doorway and 52 cm long. It consists of a single squared block of tuff, 50 × 18 cm, which stands 25 cm above the floor. The wall connected to the right side of the doorway is 22 cm high, and the wall connected to the left side of the doorway is 18 cm high.

Another deflector wall is located outside and connected to the right side of the doorway (as one enters). It is constructed of sandstone slabs and basalt cobbles set in adobe, extends out 30 cm from the doorway, and runs parallel to the room wall for 70 cm.

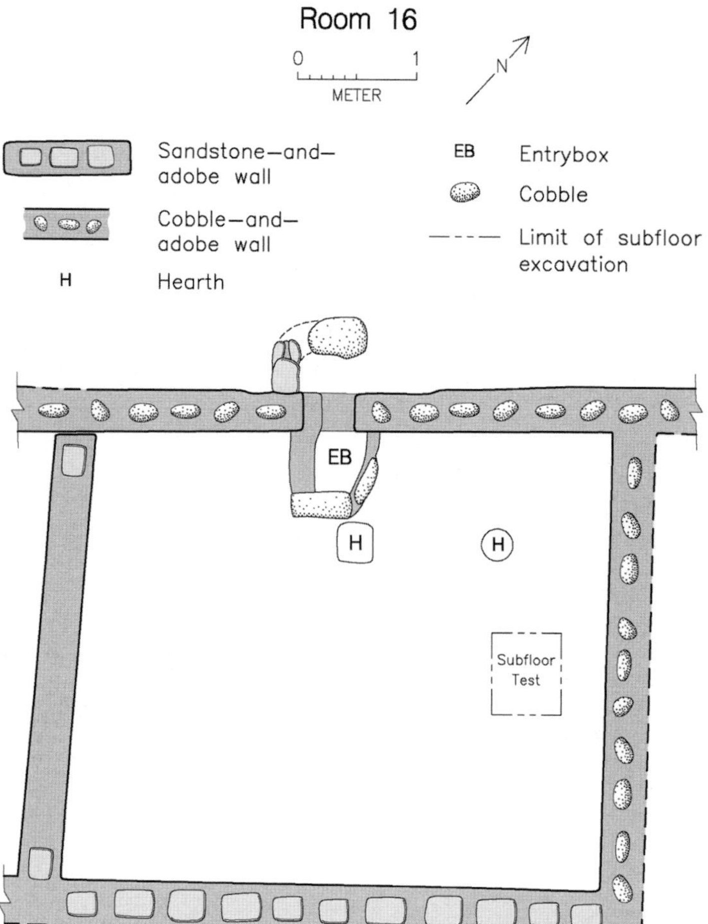

FIGURE 3.33 Plan of Room 16. Drawing by Ronald J. Beckwith based on Rex E. Gerald's field map and notes.

Walls. The adobe used in the walls of this room seems to be harder than that used in Houseblock I. The northwest wall, constructed of cobbles and adobe, is 27–37 cm thick and stands 80 cm above the floor. The northeast wall, also made of cobbles and adobe, is 35 cm thick and stands 40 cm above the floor on the south end and 65 cm above the floor on the north end. The southeast wall was constructed of cobbles and adobe, with the addition of some sandstone slabs; it is 40 cm thick and stands 60 cm above the floor. The southwest wall, which was exposed at the south and west corners only, is constructed of sandstone slabs set in adobe; it is 33 cm thick and stands 60 cm above the floor on the south end and 80 cm above the floor on the north end. Wall abutments were not determined.

The southwest wall bears a 0.5 cm thick layer of brown plaster over most of the surface that was exposed by excavation. Most of the stones in the southeast wall were covered with plaster. The northeast and northwest walls retain plaster in spots.

The doorway is in the center of the northwest wall and gives access to the plaza. It is 30 cm wide for the first 20 cm above the sill and is widened by an offset on the right side (as one enters) to a width of 45 cm. The sill is 15 cm above the floor.

Roofing. The floor was covered with hard chunks of adobe. Some charcoal fragments were found near the floor.

Artifacts. Floor: D/106a knife, D/106b debitage, D/s118 mano.

Room 17

The second room from the northeast end of the houseblock, Room 17 (figure 3.34) is adjacent to Rooms 16 and 18 on the northeast and southwest,

FIGURE 3.34 Room 17. Photograph D/147 by Rex E. Gerald. Courtesy of the Amerind Foundation Inc., Dragoon, Arizona.

respectively. It is rectangular in plan. The southeast wall was exposed for its full length, the northeast and southwest walls only where the trench along the southeast wall crossed them, and the northwest wall only in places at the surface.

Orientation and Size. Room 17 is 4.20 m long and 3.50 m wide. It is oriented with its long axis parallel the long axis of the houseblock.

Floor. In the area excavated, the floor is soft and difficult to follow.

Floor Features. None were exposed.

Walls. The northeast wall is described under Room 16; it stands 55 cm above floor level in Room 17. The southeast wall is constructed of adobe and some cobbles; it stands 50 cm above the floor. Its thickness is not known. The southwest wall is also made of adobe and cobbles; it stands 33 cm above the floor and is 35 cm thick. Wall abutments are not known. All three walls that were exposed by excavation were covered with relatively well-preserved brown plaster. No doorway was found.

Roofing. Adobe chunks were found near the floor.

Artifacts. Floor: D/s133 knife.

Room 18

The third room from the northeast end of the houseblock, Room 18 (figure 3.35) is adjacent to Rooms 17 and 19 on the northeast and southwest, respectively. It is rectangular in shape. Only the southeast and portions of the northeast and southwest walls were exposed by excavation.

Orientation and Size. Measuring 5.30 m long × 3.38 m wide, its long axis is parallel to that of the houseblock.

Floor. Room 18's floor is soft and difficult to delineate.

Floor Features. None were found.

Walls. The northeast wall is described under Room 17; it stands 35 cm above the floor. The southwest wall is constructed of cobbles set in adobe and stands 32 cm above the floor. The northwest wall is

FIGURE 3.35 Room 18. Photograph D/146 by Rex E. Gerald. Courtesy of the Amerind Foundation Inc., Dragoon, Arizona.

made of adobe and cobbles; it is 35 cm thick and stands about 40 cm above the floor. Brown plaster is preserved on the portions of all three walls exposed by excavation. No doorway was found.

Roofing. No evidence was found.

Artifacts. None were found.

Room 19

The fourth room from the northeast end of Houseblock II, Room 19 (figure 3.36) is adjacent to Rooms 18, 20, and 33 on the northeast, southwest, and northwest, respectively. It is rectangular in shape. More than half of this room was excavated; the northeast wall was not completely exposed.

Orientation and Size. Measuring 5.05 m long and 3.70 m wide, its long axis parallels that of the houseblock.

Floor. Room 19's floor is soft and poorly preserved.

Floor Features. None were found.

Walls. All four walls are of adobe-and-cobble construction; in addition, the eastern quarter of the southeast wall contains some sandstone slabs in adobe. The northeast wall is described under Room 18; it stands 26 cm above the floor. The southeast wall is 42 cm thick and stands 26 cm above the floor. The southwest and northwest walls are 32 cm thick and stand about 30 cm above the floor. Patches

FIGURE 3.36 Room 19. Photograph D/145 by Rex E. Gerald. Courtesy of the Amerind Foundation Inc., Dragoon, Arizona.

of brown plaster are preserved on both walls near the east corner. No doorway was found.

Roofing. No evidence was found.

Artifacts. Fill: D/s64 hammerstone, D/s87 grooved abrader.

Room 20

The fifth room from the northeast end of Houseblock II, Room 20 (figure 3.37) is rectangular in plan and narrower than Room 19, which it adjoins on the northeast. Its northwest wall, facing the plaza, is aligned with the corresponding walls of Room 21, which adjoins it on the southwest. Room 20 was apparently built after Room 19. All of the southeast wall and portions of the other three walls of Room 20 were exposed by excavation.

Orientation and Size. Measuring 5.65 m long and 2.30 m wide, its long axis is parallel to that of the houseblock.

Floor. Soft and poorly preserved, Room 20's floor is 11 cm lower than the floor of Room 19.

Floor Features. None were found.

Walls. All were constructed of adobe and cobbles; in addition, the southeast wall contains many sandstone slabs set in adobe. All the walls are poorly preserved. The southeast wall is 38 cm thick, the southwest is 35 cm thick, and the northwest is 25 cm thick. All stand 20–25 cm above the floor. Neither wall plaster nor a doorway was found.

Artifacts. None were found.

FIGURE 3.37 Room 20. Photograph D/144 by Rex E. Gerald. Courtesy of the Amerind Foundation Inc., Dragoon, Arizona.

Room 21

The sixth and southwesternmost room in Houseblock II, Room 21 (figure 3.38) adjoins Room 20 to the northeast. The western corner of this room is approximately 2 m from Room 47 in Houseblock VI. All four walls of this room were located, but the northwest wall was not exposed for its full length.

Orientation and Size. Measuring 5.50 × 3.35 m, its long axis parallels that of the houseblock.

Floor. Soft and poorly defined, the floor of Room 21 is about 5 cm lower than the floor of Room 20.

Floor Features. None were found.

Walls. All are poorly preserved and are constructed of sandy adobe and cobbles except the southeast wall, which contains many sandstone slabs. The southeast wall is 35 cm thick, the southwest is 20 cm thick, and the northwest is 22 cm thick. None of them stand more than 25 cm above the floor. The northwest wall is so soft and poorly preserved at the west corner that it is discernible only in cross section. Neither wall plaster nor a doorway was found.

Roofing. No evidence was found.

Artifacts. Fill: D/107 maul, D/s65 chopper.

Room 33

Adjoining and located to the northwest of Room 19, Room 33 is rectangular in shape. The northeast and southeast walls were not exposed in the single trench dug through the room.

Orientation and Size. Room 33 measures about 4.75 × 4.40 m, and its long axis parallels that of the houseblock. [*Editor: Gerald's field notes indicate a room*

FIGURE 3.38 Room 21. Photograph D/143 by Rex E. Gerald. Courtesy of the Amerind Foundation Inc., Dragoon, Arizona.

width of 4.75 m and some versions of the site map corroborate this, showing the northeast wall of Room 33 as a continuation of the northeast wall of Room 19. However, the same annotated map that indicates the vessels recovered from Room 14 seen in figure 3.31 shows a northeast wall for Room 33 only about 3 m from the southwest wall. A partially legible note reads "Burned Plaster down . . ." next to an arrow pointing to this wall. In addition, on the annotated map, the continuation of the northeast wall of Room 19 is crossed out, making Room 33 only about 3 m wide. Site maps in Gerald's (1975:Figures 3, 5, 8) dissertation also show Room 33 to be closer to 3 m rather than nearly 5 m in width.]

Floor. Room 33's floor is well preserved near the west corner only.

Floor Features. None were exposed.

Walls. Both walls are constructed of adobe and cobbles; both are poorly preserved and difficult to follow. The southwest wall is 20 cm thick, and the northwest wall is 22 cm thick.

Artifacts. Fill: D/s134 debitage, D/s136 chopper, D/s138 unworked stone. Floor: D/s132 tabular tool.

Room 35

[*Editor: A search of Gerald's papers failed to yield a written description of Room 35; however, the annotated map discussed above identifies the space northwest of Room 33 as Room 35 and sherds stamped with*

Room 35 proveniences were encountered during the reanalysis. Most artifacts considered here to have come from the space designated Room 35 were stamped or otherwise identified as having been recovered from "T. Ft. Rm-33" (trench in front of Room 33). Gerald considered the northwest wall of Room 33 to be the southeast wall of Room 35. The only other architectural feature bounding this space, as indicated by Gerald's maps, is a cobble-and-adobe wall fragment less than 1 m in length (extending from the southwest wall of Room 33) that might have formed part of the southwest wall of Room 35. Gerald records the following as having been recovered from Room 35 (trench in front of Room 33): D/100, a unifacially worked flake.]

Houseblock VI

Room 47

[*Editor: A search of Gerald's papers failed to yield a written description of Room 47. It is the southernmost room in Houseblock VI. It has walls constructed of cobbles and adobe and is approximately 5.00 × 3.50 m in area. Gerald lists sherd totals for this room under the grid coordinates of two trenches: T5W 44S and T3–5W 43S.*]

Houseblock VII

Room 37

During the pueblo occupation of the Davis Ranch Site, the northwest side of the plaza was walled by a northeast-southwest trending row of about 17 rooms, to judge from surface indications. This houseblock reached to within 2 m of the west corner of Houseblock II on the south. Again, judging from surface indications, it appears to extend to and join the northeast wall surrounding the plaza on the north. Only one rectangular room, Room 37 (figure 3.39), located near the center of this houseblock, was outlined by excavation. It appears to be adjoined on the southeast by a room of similar size, shape, and orientation, and on the northwest by a slightly smaller room of similar shape, which is oriented such that its long axis parallels that of the houseblock.

Orientation and Size. Room 37 measures 3.20 × 5.20 m, and its long axis runs northeast-southwest, perpendicular to that of the houseblock.

Floor. In all parts of the area excavated, the floor was soft and difficult to locate.

Floor Features. None were found.

Walls. The walls are all of adobe-and-cobble construction, and all stand to a height of about 25–30 cm above the floor.

Roofing. No evidence remained.

Artifacts. Only pottery was recovered during the limited excavation in this room.

Room 45

[*Editor: A search of Gerald's papers failed to yield a written description of Room 45. This room is located nearly in the middle of Houseblock VII and has cobble-and-adobe walls. It is nearly square, measuring >3.00 × <3.00 m. Gerald lists sherd totals for this room under the grid coordinates of a trench: T22W 1S.*]

Rooms Associated with the Compound Wall

Room 2

Rectangular in shape and located near the center of the northeast compound wall, the northeast wall of Room 2 (figure 3.40; see also figure 3.2) forms part of the perimeter wall. No adjoining rooms were located to the southeast, southwest, or northeast, and no tests were made on the northwest. Sterile gravel and caliche underlie Room 2 within 15 cm of the floor in all areas except the eastern quarter, where the floor of House 5 is located 20 cm below, and the floor of House 8 is located 61 cm below.

Orientation and Size. Room 2 is 4.60 m long and 3.38 m wide; its long axis is parallel to the perimeter wall.

Floor. Hard and well preserved in almost all areas, the floor is covered with reddish-brown plaster in places. Plaster of this kind is found only in rooms

FIGURE 3.39 Room 37. Photograph D/142 by Rex E. Gerald. Courtesy of the Amerind Foundation Inc., Dragoon, Arizona.

that have burned and is probably the result of oxidation of the iron in the adobe.

Floor Features. Located between the center of the room and the southwest wall, Hearth 1 is made of adobe plaster with a low rim around the southeastern half of its perimeter. It is oval in shape, 40 × 48 cm, and 15 cm deep; it is oriented with its long axis parallel to that of the room. Hearth 2 is against the northeast wall just north of its center. It is made of adobe plaster and cobbles, with its northwest rim raised about 5 cm above the floor. Its northeast side is formed by the wall. It is rectangular in shape, 47 × 40 cm, and 15 cm deep. It is oriented with its long axis parallel to that of the room. Both hearths contain white ash.

A shallow floor pit, 80 cm × 1.05 m and 15 cm deep, is located in the western quarter of the room. The side and bottom of the pit are smooth but unplastered. There is no artifact association to indicate its function, and the few sherds in the pit are of the same types as those found in the fill and on the floor of the room.

The largest of the 12 postholes is located in the center of the room and is 30 cm in diameter and 25 cm deep. The second-largest posthole is located near the center of the northeast wall and is 20 cm in diameter and 22 cm deep. The remaining 10 postholes, most of which are located in the corners and along the walls, range in diameter from 8 cm to 15 cm and in depth from 11 cm to 16 cm.

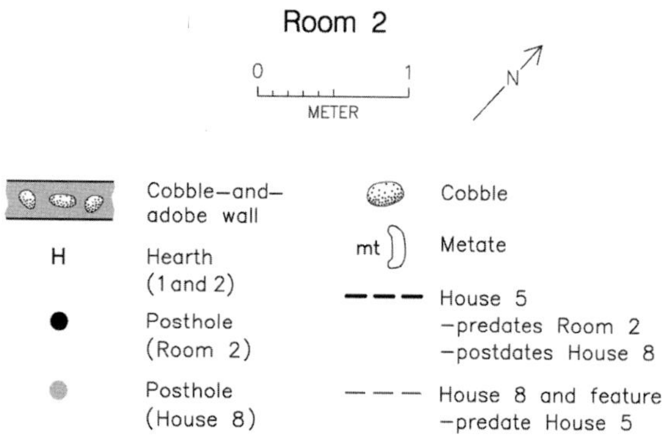

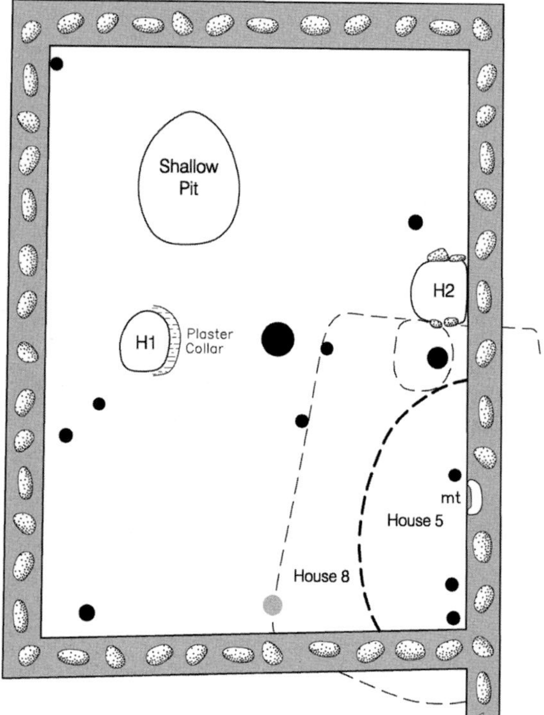

FIGURE 3.40 Plan of Room 2. Drawing by Ronald J. Beckwith based on Rex E. Gerald's field map and notes.

Walls. All four walls are constructed of cobbles held in place by adobe. The basal course is made of cobbles set on end. The single example of a Type II metate was found set into the basal course of the northeast wall, with the grinding surface facing into the room. The portions of the walls still standing range in height from 47 cm to 65 cm above the floor and in thickness from 27 cm to 35 cm. An estimate of the total height of the original walls may be obtained by adding the height of the wall stub of the northeast wall to the height of a toppled section of the same wall that is preserved where it fell. The stub stands 55–60 cm above the floor, and the fallen section measures 1.40–1.60 m, suggesting that the original wall stood between 1.95 m and 2.20 m in height. This wall, which forms a part of the perimeter wall of the compound, is similar in all respects to the other walls of Room 2. No evidence of plaster is preserved on any of the walls.

There is no evidence of a doorway. The standing height of the wall stubs suggests that either there was no doorway, entrance being gained through the roof, or that the door sill was very high, some 47 cm or more above the floor.

Roofing. Burned fragments of wood and reeds were found near the floor.

Artifacts. Fill: D/16 scraper. Floor: D/153a grooved abrader; D/153b miniature vessel; D/153d, D/153h, D/153i, D/153k knives; D/153e, D/153f, D/153g debitage; D/153j, D/153l scrapers; D/154a bone awl; D/154b shell bracelet; D/154c reed; D/154d, D/154e projectile point fragments; D/154f, D/154g projectile points; D/154h stone pendant. In northeast wall: D/s120 metate.

Room 36

The existence of this room is open to question, since it was only tested in one area and is suggested only by two poor walls of sandy adobe and a few cobbles, along with a section of the perimeter wall of the compound. This room is located against the perimeter wall, east and a bit north of, but not adjoining, Room 5. If this is in fact a room, it must have been abandoned before the end of the pueblo occupation, because Puddle Pit 1 is located near its northwestern edge. Artifacts from this room are a stone vessel (D/111) and a mano fragment (D/s113).

Room 48

[*Editor: This room is never mentioned in Gerald's manuscript or field notes. It appears on his final site map curated by the Amerind Foundation but is not numbered on any version yet located, including those in his dissertation (Gerald 1975:Figures 3, 5, 8). The room's southwestern wall is made of sandstone slabs and adobe. Sandstone-and-adobe wall stubs project from the south and west corners of the room toward the northeast wall of the compound, which consists of cobbles and adobe. Gerald posited that these walls continued northeastward to meet the compound wall (the northeast wall of the room), enclosing a space approximately 3.00 × 5.00 m in area.*]

Other Rooms

Room 34

[*Editor: A search of Gerald's papers failed to yield a written description of Room 34, an apparently unroofed space about 3.75 × 4.50 m in area defined by three cobble-and-adobe walls: the southwest wall of Room 36, the northeast wall of Room 5, and a wall that connects these two rooms. Gerald tallied sherds recovered from this space under the heading associated with a trench: T13–17S 8–12E. Room 34 also yielded a flaked stone drill, D/109.*]

Room 46

[*Editor: A search of Gerald's papers failed to yield a written description of Room 46. It is somewhat isolated within the compound, north of Houseblock I. Room 46's west wall, however, extends past the corner where it meets its south wall, perhaps indicating the former presence of an adjacent, now stone-robbed room to the south. Room 46 was investigated during Gerald's 1965 return to the site to obtain additional pollen samples. It does not appear on his sherd chart, despite the fact that ceramics were recovered. These were examined as part of the reanalysis. Gerald's (1975) site map indicates that Room 46 measured circa 3.00 × 3.50 m in area.*]

Artifacts. Fill: D/s135 debitage, D/s137 unclassified stone artifact, D/s139 unworked stone. Floor: D/s130, D/s131 tabular tools.

Plaza

In all areas in which tests were made in the plaza, the floor was at approximately the same level as the floors of nearby rooms. The fill that has accumulated over the plaza floor in areas away from the pueblo rooms and the compound wall ranges in depth from 15 cm to 30 cm in the areas tested. It consists of sand and silt, with the amount of admixed trash varying from area to area.

Other Features

Pit Ovens

Filled with fire-fractured rocks and trash that show signs of thermal alteration, none of the pit ovens are plastered.

Pit Oven 1. Located at the north corner of House 4, Pit Oven 1 is oval in shape, 2.00 × 1.00 m. It extends 95 cm below the present surface and 50 cm below the floor of House 4. The sides of the pit are slightly undercut on the northwest end, and the bottom is relatively flat. Both sides and bottom are formed of gravel and cobbles, as well as adobe that has been burned to a depth of 1.5 cm. There is no evidence that the pit was plastered. The pit was filled with fire-fractured stones and trash, including burned beans (?) and corn (?) (D/4). This pit oven postdates House 4.

Pit Oven 2. Three meters northeast of House 4, Pit Oven 2 is circular in outline, 1.00 m in diameter, and has a dish-shaped bottom that extends about 30 cm below the present surface. It contains fire-fractured rocks.

Pit Oven 3. Located 10.50 m north of House 1, Pit Oven 3 is oval in shape. It measures 1.20 × 0.65 m and extends about 45 cm below the present surface. It is filled with fire-fractured stones and a single mano (D/s117).

Discussion. The presence of beans and corn in one pit oven suggests that all these pits were used for cooking. Other vegetable foods were probably cooked in the pits, but evidence as to species was not recovered. Sherds found in them fit best in the Aravaipa (Sosa) phase.

Puddle Pits

These features are depressions that have resulted from the mixing of clayey soil and water to produce

FIGURE 3.41 Puddle Pit 1. Photograph D/154 by Rex E. Gerald. Courtesy of the Amerind Foundation Inc., Dragoon, Arizona.

adobe. A layer of adobe left in the pit, following its use, hardens with exposure and, unless it is disturbed, remains until it is covered and preserved.

Puddle Pit 1. Located in Room 36, Puddle Pit 1 (figure 3.41) is oval; the lower portions of its sides and bottom are covered with adobe. Its dimensions are 75 × 95 cm. It extends 65 cm below the present surface and 50 cm below the surface in use at the time it was dug. There is no evidence of burning. No artifacts were found.

Puddle Pit 2. Located 40 cm west of Room 10, Puddle Pit 2 (figure 3.42) is similar to Puddle Pit 1 in every respect except size. It is 90 cm long and 85 cm wide and extends 30 cm below the present surface. A flake scraper (D/184) and a mano (D/s119) were found in it.

Discussion. These pits are probably the equivalent of the "caliche mixing bowls" found in the Civano period sites of the Phoenix area (Hayden 1957), although caliche, readily available just below the surface, was not used at the Davis Ranch Site. The location of Puddle Pit 1 inside an abandoned Romero (late Reeve) phase room and the location of Puddle Pit 2 beside a Redfield (early Reeve) phase room suggest that these pits date to the Redfield and Romero phases (Reeve phase). [*Editor: The ceramics recovered from Puddle Pit 2 are consistent with this temporal assignment.*]

FIGURE 3.42 Puddle Pit 2. Photograph D/153 by Rex E. Gerald. Courtesy of the Amerind Foundation Inc., Dragoon, Arizona.

Borrow Pit

Located under the northwest wall of Room 9 and extending 80 cm below Floor 2 of that room is a borrow pit. It contained boulders as large as 40 × 40 × 40 cm.

HOUSEBLOCKS III, IV, AND V

Houseblock III

The designation Houseblock III was originally intended to apply to a group of four rooms located on a higher terrace 100 m northeast of the pueblo compound at the Davis Ranch Site (figure 3.43). The designation has been extended to include three nearby isolated rooms and a two-room structure. This group of rectilinear buildings is spread over an area 45 × 30 m. The surface manifestations of all of these buildings, except for a portion of the four-room structure, are double rows of cobbles, 30–40 cm wide, that protrude above the surface of the ground and outline the rooms. [*Editor: Gerald originally believed that the four-room structure referred to above was a six-room structure. Thus, in some tables, data are reported for "Rooms 29 and 30" (later designated Room 29) and "Rooms 31 and 32" (later designated Room 31).*]

FIGURE 3.43 Houseblock III from the east. Room 23 is in the foreground, on the right. Photograph D/110 by Rex E. Gerald. Courtesy of the Amerind Foundation Inc., Dragoon, Arizona.

Room 22

The fill of Room 22 (figure 3.44) consists of a few stones and red adobe, indistinguishable from the underlying, undisturbed, sterile soil. It is located 6 m to the southeast of Room 23. The northeast walls of the two rooms are aligned.

Orientation and Size. Measuring 7.10 × 3.35 m, its long axis is oriented at right angles to that of Room 23; that is to say, northwest-southeast.

Floor. No floor could be located in the test excavation near the center of the southwest wall.

Floor Features. None were found.

Walls. They range in width from 30 cm to 35 cm and stand 20 cm above their bases. There is a possible doorway, 75 cm wide, near the center of the southwest wall.

Roofing. No evidence was found.

Artifacts. None were found.

Room 23

Six meters to the northwest, its northwest wall aligned with the common northwest wall of Rooms 27, 28, and 29, Room 23 (see figure 3.43) was not tested, but the double row of cobbles protruding above the surface made it possible to map its outline.

Orientation and Size. Room 23 is 7.05 m long by 3.40 m wide, and its long axis runs northeast-southwest.

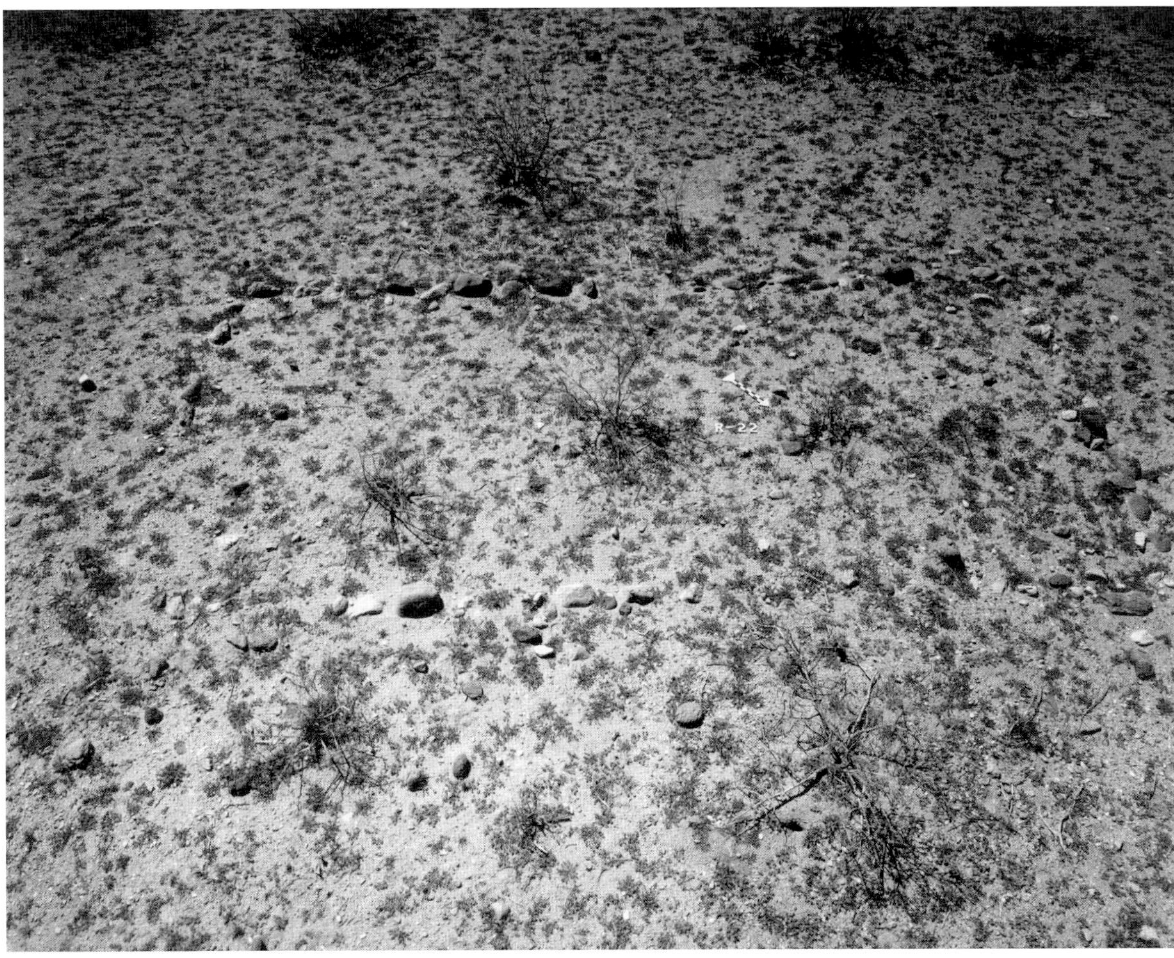

FIGURE 3.44 Room 22. Photograph D/109 by Rex E. Gerald. Courtesy of the Amerind Foundation Inc., Dragoon, Arizona.

Walls. They range from 25 to 30 cm in width. The absence of cobbles near the center of the southeast wall suggests that a doorway, 1.00 m wide, may have been located there.

Artifacts. None were found.

Rooms 24 and 25

These rooms are 6.6 m southwest of Room 26. This two-room structure is oriented such that its northwest wall is aligned with the northwest wall of Room 26 (figures 3.45, 3.46).

Orientation and Size. The entire structure measures 14.85 × 3.95 m. Room 24, the southeastern room, is 7.05 m long and 3.35 m wide. Room 25, the northwestern room, is 7.00 m long and 3.22 m wide. Their long axes run northwest-southeast.

Floor. No evidence of a floor was found in the trench dug through the center on Room 25's short axis.

Walls. The walls are constructed of double rows of cobbles set in the reddish adobe that underlies this entire houseblock; they range from 30 cm to 35 cm in width and stand 20–25 cm above their bases. No evidence of a doorway was found, even though trenches were dug around the walls of the room.

Artifacts. None were found.

FIGURE 3.45 Room 24. Photograph D/113 by Rex E. Gerald. Courtesy of the Amerind Foundation Inc., Dragoon, Arizona.

Room 26

The northwest wall of Room 26 parallels the southeast wall of Room 31. The southwest wall of Room 26 is almost aligned with the corresponding wall of Room 31, being only 30–35 cm northeast of an alignment. A trench was dug around all four walls.

Orientation and Size. Room 26 measures 6.60 × 3.20 m, and its long axis runs northeast-southwest.

Floor. No evidence of a floor was found.

Walls. Its walls range in width from 28 cm to 33 cm. No doorway was found.

Artifacts. None were found.

Rooms 27 and 28

The adjoining Rooms 27 and 28 (figures 3.47, 3.48) make up approximately one-third of the floor area of a four-room building. They form the center of a mound, which is about 50 cm higher than the surrounding rooms and the ground surface. Apparently, these two rooms were intentionally filled with cobbles and adobe.

Orientation and Size. The four-room building covers an area 8.90 × 11.40 m. Rooms 27 and 28 measure 3.00 × 3.50 m and 3.00 × 3.25 m, respectively, and their long axes run northeast-southwest.

Floor. Both rooms had well-plastered floors.

Walls. Composed of cobble and adobe, the walls of these rooms are 30–40 cm thick and stand 75 cm

FIGURE 3.46 Room 25. Photograph D/157 by Rex E. Gerald. Courtesy of the Amerind Foundation Inc., Dragoon, Arizona.

above the floor. They are well preserved and well plastered.

Artifacts. None found.

Room 29

Rooms 28 and 31 are adjacent to Room 29, to the northeast.

Orientation and Size. Room 29 measures 8.10 m long and 3.35 m wide. Its long axis runs at right angles to the long axes of the other rooms in this four-room building.

Floor. No evidence of a floor was found.

Walls. The southwest wall, which is 40 cm wide, is 75 cm high at the northwest end and 25 cm high at the southeast end. The other walls, which are all exterior walls, range in height from 75 cm at the west corner to 25 cm at the north, east, and south corners.

Artifacts. None were found.

Room 31

This is a large room adjacent to Rooms 27 and 28 to the southwest.

Orientation and Size. Room 27 measures 4.90 × 6.90 m; its long axis parallels the long axes of Rooms 27 and 28.

Floor. No evidence of a floor was found.

Walls. The northwest wall of this room is 30 cm thick and stands 75 cm high. The southeast wall is

FIGURE 3.47 Rooms 27 and 28. Photograph D/155 by Rex E. Gerald. Courtesy of the Amerind Foundation Inc., Dragoon, Arizona.

FIGURE 3.48 Room 27 fill. Photograph D/156 by Rex E. Gerald. Courtesy of the Amerind Foundation Inc., Dragoon, Arizona.

40 cm wide, as are all the exterior walls of this group of rooms, and stands only 25 cm above the floor. The northeast wall, which is 40 cm wide, and the southwest wall, which is an exterior wall, both slope from a height of 75 cm on their northwest ends to 25 cm on their southeast ends.

Discussion

The regularity of size and the placement of the rooms in this houseblock suggest that they were all built with a preconceived plan during a brief period of construction. The paucity of floors, hearths, and other features in any of the rooms, except Rooms 27 and 28, which had floors only, indicates that these buildings were never completed or occupied.

The fact that Rooms 27 and 28 contained gravel and cobbles in greater concentration than was present in the walls suggest that they were intentionally filled. Other rooms in the same structure did not contain gravel and cobbles in nearly this quantity. The subfloor 1 fill in House 7 is similar to that in Rooms 27 and 28, but it lacks the reddish adobe found in these rooms.

Intentionally filled rooms or adobe-walled enclosures have been reported at other sites in southern Arizona, such as Martinez Hill (AZ BB:13:3[ASM]; Gabel 1931:27–29) and the University Indian Ruin (AZ BB:9:33[ASM]) near Tucson (Hayden 1957:68), Jackrabbit Ruin (AZ DD:1:6[ASM]) near Sells (Scantling 1940:18–21), and Pueblo Grande (AZ U:9:1[ASM]) in Phoenix, as well as in western Mexico (Lister 1955:17, Map 6). It is possible that Rooms 27 and 28 were the first rooms to be filled as an intended artificial mound and that the mound was never completed.

No artifacts other than sherds were found on the surface or in the excavations in this area. Of the 188 sherds recovered, 139 came from the fill of Room 28, while the remainder came from six of the seven tested rooms. Room 26, which was trenched around the perimeter, produced no sherds. The pottery types represented by these sherds fit into the Redfield and Romero phases (Reeve phase) as they are manifested at the Davis Ranch Site.

Other Features

Borrow Pit. Beginning about 5 m north of the four-room structure (Rooms 27, 28, 29, and 31) is a borrow pit, which is 20–25 m in diameter and 40 cm deep at the center. A small test pit in this depression revealed reddish adobe immediately under the grass roots and extending down at least a meter. Gravel and cobbles, which cover the slopes of the terrace, presumably would be reached if the test were deepened.

Gravel Line. In the area between Rooms 22 and 26 and extending to the south-southeast is a vaguely discernable line of gravel 24 m long and about 1 m wide. This line of gravel, which was not tested, may be part of an uncompleted wall, although it runs through the plaza rather than around it or around the rooms; it is not aligned with, nor is it parallel to, the buildings in this area.

Houseblock IV

Consisting of tumbled rows of cobbles that cover a rectangular area 3.65 × 2.75 m, the long axis of Houseblock IV (figure 3.49) runs east-northeast by west-southwest. It is situated on the west slope of the terrace on which the main site is located and is 3 m west of the pueblo compound wall near its west corner. There are three rooms in Houseblock IV: Room 38 forms the eastern half of the structure and measures 2.18 × 1.50 m; Room 39 makes up the northern portion of the western half of the houseblock and measures 1.62 × 1.05 m; and Room 40 constitutes the southern portion of the western half, measuring 1.68 × 0.98 m. None of the walls stand more than two cobbles high, and none of the cobbles are mortared in place with adobe. Postholes were not found in association with these stones, as they were with those of the stone-and-pole enclosure. Distinct floors were not found in any of these rooms, although they are presumed to have been near the bases of the walls, which are 5–10 cm below the present surface. Subfloor testing of this houseblock uncovered caliche-cemented gravel immediately below the floor level.

FIGURE 3.49 Houseblock IV. Photograph D/140 by Rex E. Gerald. Courtesy of the Amerind Foundation Inc., Dragoon, Arizona.

The ceramics from these rooms are consistent with occupation during the Redfield and Romero phases (Reeve phase), but their small size suggests that they reached the houseblock as sherds rather than as whole vessels. They may have been in the adobe used in the walls or roof, or they may have drifted down the slope from the pueblo rooms nearby.

Houseblock V

Consisting of four rooms (Rooms 41–44), Houseblock V (figure 3.50) is located on the west slope of the terrace on which the main part of the site is situated. It is 3 m west of Room 37 (hence outside the compound wall) and is 16 m south of Houseblock IV. As in Houseblock IV, the walls of Houseblock V consist of lines of loose cobbles, the floors are not definable, and there are no postholes in association with the cobbles. The rooms are not rectilinear in plan but rather suggest the appearance of a honeycomb. The entire structure measures 5.60 × 4.60 m, and its long axis runs northeast-southwest. Although none of the rooms are regular in plan, two dimensions are given for each to convey an idea of size. The easternmost room, Room 41, measures about 1.50 × 1.50 m; the east-central room (Room 42) is 1.40 × 1.60 m; the southeastern room (Room 43) is 1.10 × 1.20 m; and the westernmost room (Room 44) is 3.20 × 2.60 m. No hearths or other floor features were located. Because of the scarcity of stones in some areas, it can only be assumed that doorways once connected Room 41 with Rooms 42 and 44. Caliche and gravel were reached at a depth of 20 cm below the putative floor level.

Artifacts from this houseblock consist of a projectile point (D/144) and a scraper (D/115) from the fill of Room 44, debitage (D/113) from the fill

FIGURE 3.50 Houseblock V. Photograph D/141 by Rex E. Gerald. Courtesy of the Amerind Foundation Inc., Dragoon, Arizona.

of Room 41, and an iron nail (D/112) from a pothunter's hole in Room 40. As in the case of Houseblock IV, the ceramics recovered are all relatively small and appear not to belong to the period of this houseblock's occupation.

STONE-AND-POLE ENCLOSURE

The latest architectural feature at the Davis Ranch Site is a surface enclosure of aligned cobbles and small boulders set beside or around small postholes, which are spaced between 20 cm and 70 cm apart. The enclosure is in the shape of a seven-sided polygon, 34.00 × 27.00 m, and is divided into two roughly equal parts (see figure 1.5). The rock-and-post alignment that divides the enclosure extends from one side to within 4.00 m of an angle in the opposite side, where it terminates in a small square 1.50 m long on each side. The stones of this enclosure range in size from 15 × 20 × 10 cm to 20 × 40 × 25 cm. The postholes range from 10 cm to 15 cm in diameter and from 15 cm to 20 cm in depth. Approximately 25.00 m of the perimeter of this enclosure was explored for postholes, and 50 were located. [*Editor: D/172, tree-ring sample 9 (see appendix A), was recovered from a posthole in the vicinity of 11E 11S. Its grid coordinates strongly suggest that it is a sample taken from one of the postholes near the east corner of the stone-and-pole enclosure.*]

The surface position of the stones and the lack of associated dwellings (unless Houseblocks IV and V are accepted as being of this period) or artifacts make it impossible to determine the cultural relationship of this enclosure. It is possible, however, from evidence of superposition, to say with assurance that the enclosure is later than the prehistoric phases. [*Editor: The stone-and-pole enclosure, indicated in dark blue in figure 1.5, overlies a considerable portion of the pueblo, including the northern portion of Houseblock I, the northeastern compound wall, Room 48, Room 46, and the plaza.*]

Even in the absence of factual evidence for the interpretation of this structure, it may still be illuminating to speculate on its cultural relations on the basis of circumstantial evidence. First, given its stratigraphic position, which indicates post-Romero (Reeve) phase construction, it is quite possible that this enclosure belongs to the historic era, since the Romero (late Reeve) phase represents one of the latest prehistoric phases known in this area. A second possibility, based on the size and construction of the enclosure, is that the enclosure may have served as a palisade around an Indian village (possibly the Sobaipuri village of Cusac), the remains of which have disappeared. A third possibility is that the structure served as a corral for livestock for Spanish or American cavalry details, as a corral for a station on the stage route that passed over the site, or for the Ronquillo family who lived near the site within the memory of a local man still living (1957). The final possibility, based on construction alone, is that the structure enclosed an Indian garden of the type seen within recent years at Zuni (Hodge 1939:Plate opposite p. 106). There is no compelling evidence to confirm any one of the suggested uses. The author is inclined to believe that the enclosure was a corral for livestock, as outlined above.

SUMMARY AND DISCUSSION

The architectural features found at the Davis Ranch Site have been divided into eight classes for descriptive purposes: round houses, pit houses, the kiva, surface rooms that constitute the pueblo, Houseblock III, Houseblock IV, Houseblock V, and the stone-and-pole enclosure. Each of these classes, except the pit houses, has been assigned to a temporal interval on the basis of stratigraphic position and, except for the historic era (Embudo phase) features, pottery type associations.

The round houses and the irregular or subrectangular shaped pit houses, the latter with lateral entryways, represent the Early Agricultural period and the Hohokam Colonial and Sedentary periods (Davis phase), respectively. The rectangular pit houses without extended entryways are habitation structures of the Aravaipa (Sosa) phase. The pueblo (Houseblocks I, II, VI, and VII; the rooms associated with the compound wall; and Rooms 34 and 46) and the kiva can be placed in the Redfield and Romero phases (Reeve phase). [*Editor: As discussed above, a better argument can be made for assigning the kiva to the Aravaipa phase.*] Finally, the historic era (Embudo phase) is represented by Houseblocks IV and V and the stone-and-pole enclosure.

The change in dwelling type between the Hohokam Colonial and Sedentary periods (Davis phase) and the Aravaipa (Sosa) phase is relatively minor. The change from the Aravaipa (Sosa) phase to the Redfield and Romero phases (Reeve phase), however, is marked by the introduction of a form of architecture previously unknown in this part of the Southwest. That only a short period of time elapsed is indicated by the remodeling of House 7, inhabited first during the Aravaipa (Sosa) phase, to conform more closely to the architectural style of the Redfield and Romero (Reeve) phase occupation. This rather abrupt change in architectural types at the Davis Ranch Site suggests that a foreign culture was responsible for the rapid transformation; migration is indicated. The change in structures between the Redfield and Romero phases (Reeve phase) and the historic era (Embudo phase) is again dramatic. The pueblo compound had fallen to ruin before the historic era structures and the stone-and-pole enclosure were built, and both show, by their method of construction, that a culture distinct from that responsible for the Redfield and Romero phases (Reeve phase) was responsible.

4

Burial Practices

Two methods of disposing of the dead, inhumation and cremation, were practiced at the Davis Ranch Site. Inhumation is of two types, flexed and extended supine (table 4.1). Cremations are all of the pit type.

INHUMATIONS

[*Editor: The following discussion is based on the number of individuals identified by Barnes (appendix B). Aside from one isolated interment (Burial 10), the human burials associated with the late Classic period occupation of the site occur in three clusters: one inside the kiva (10 individuals, Burials 1, 2, 3, 4, 5, 6, 6a, 7, 7a, and 8), one located to the south of the pit house hamlet (two individuals, Burials 9 and 11), and one in the Northeast Trash (five individuals, Burials 12, 12a, 13, 14, and 15). The isolated burial is northwest of the pit house hamlet but nearly equidistant from the southern cluster and the Northeast Trash cluster.*]

Inhumations Recovered from the Kiva

Burial 1

Located in kiva fill, near the center of the northwest bench, the bottom of the burial pit is 1.25 m below the present surface and 45 cm below the top of the bench. The burial pit was dug into adobe roofing material in the fill of the kiva and also into the northwest bench, where a 1.50 m section of the edge was cut back 45 cm. The pit outline was not discernible in vertical or horizontal planes above the level of the bench. The fill around and above this burial consisted of trash, roofing adobe, and water- and wind-deposited sand and silt. Burial 1 was interred after the kiva was abandoned and the roof had fallen in, and after Burial 8 had been interred on the floor of the kiva immediately below.

Position. The body, from which the skull was missing, was placed in an extended, supine position with the legs parallel, the left arm at the side, and the right hand over the pubic area (figure 4.1). The skull, had it been present, would have been oriented to the west-southwest (243° from true north). The overall body length was estimated at 1.55 m.

Burial Offerings. D/30a and D/30b, two unworked shell fragments, and D/36, a projectile point found in the fill near the skeleton, may have been offerings.

[*Editor: Barnes (appendix B) identifies this individual as an adult female, 45–50 years old.*]

Burial 2

The burial pit could not be detected. The partially flexed legs rested on the edge of the northwest bench, 85 cm below the surface, and the badly disintegrated trunk and skull rested on fill above the floor, 1.00 m

TABLE 4.1 Attributes of Davis Ranch Site inhumations

	Burial no.														
Attribute	1	2	3	4	5	6	7	8	9	10	11	12	13	14	15
Interred															
In trash	X	X	X			X	X								X
On sterile, in trash				X				X			X		X		
In pit, in sterile					X				X	X				X	
On sterile and covered with adobe												X			
Body position															
Flexed/prone					X										
Flexed/supine									X		X			X	
Flexed/right side		X		X				X		X		X			
Extended/supine	X		X			X									
Unknown							X								X
Orientation (pelvis to skull)	WSW	ENE	SSW	N	NW	ESE	?	NW	ESE	W	?	S		SE	?
Age[a]															
Infant							X				X				X
Child					X				X					X	
Adult	X	X	X	X		X		X		X		X	X		
Offerings	?			X	X			X	X	X	X	X	X	X	X

[a]Gerald's age data; cf. Barnes (appendix B)

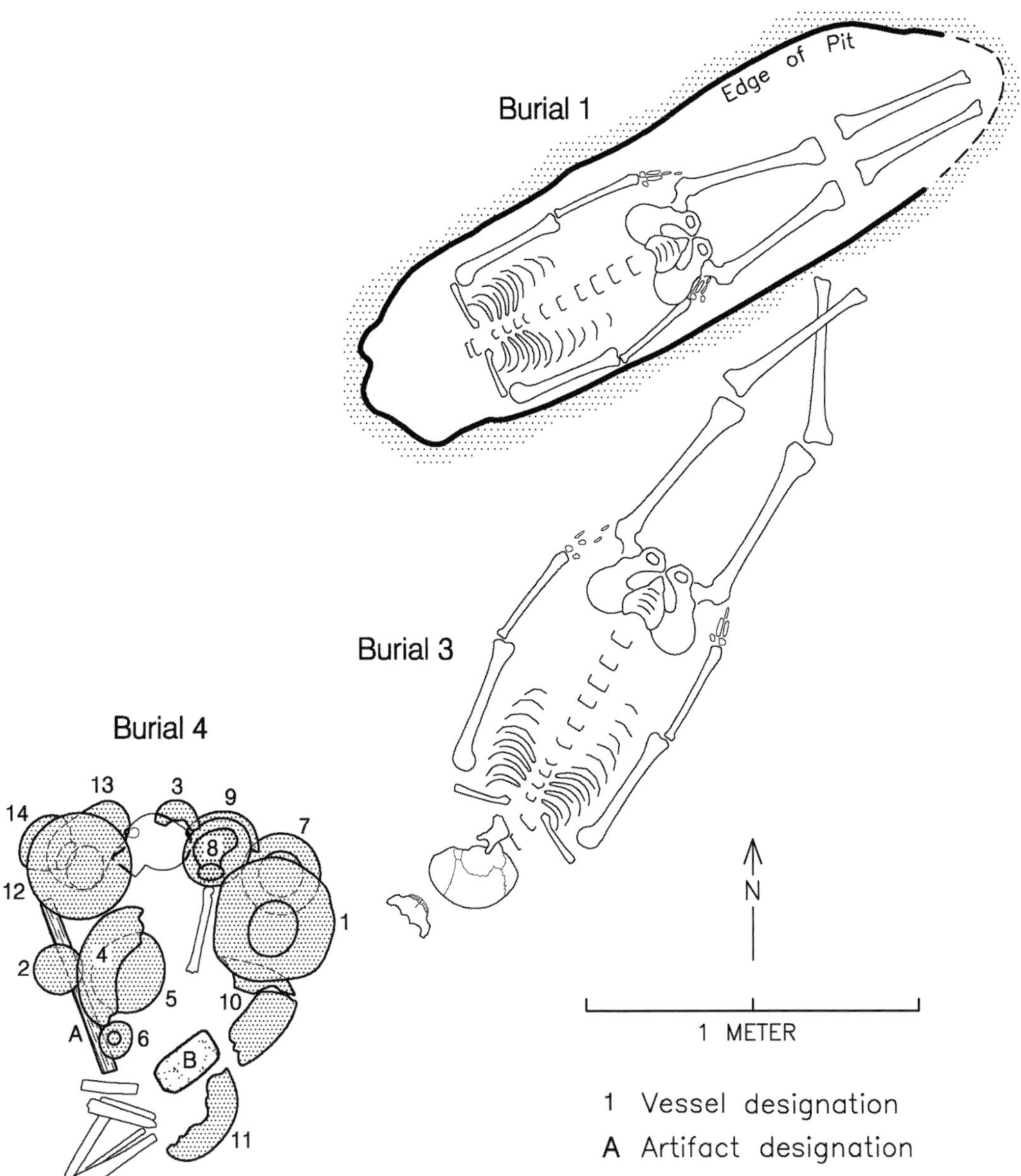

FIGURE 4.1 Plan view of Burials 1, 3, and 4. Burial 4 associated vessels: (1) Gila Polychrome jar, D/192; (2) Gila Polychrome [*Editor: This vessel is now classified as Gila Polychrome: Salmon Variety*] bowl, D/193; (3) Gila Polychrome bowl, D/194; (4) Davis Plain [*Editor: Belford Plain*] jar, D/195; (5) Gila Polychrome [*Editor: Cliff Polychrome*] bowl, D/196; (6) Salt Red: Davis Variety [*Editor: Belford Red*] bowl, D/197; (7) Davis Plain [*Editor: Belford Plain*] jar, D/198; (8) Davis Plain [*Editor: Belford Plain*] boot-shaped jar, D/199; (9) Gila Polychrome [*Editor: Phoenix Polychrome*] bowl, D/200; (10) Gila Polychrome bowl, D/201; (11) Gila Polychrome [*Editor: Cliff Polychrome*] bowl, D/202; (12) Gila Polychrome bowl, D/203; (13) Davis Plain [*Editor: Belford Plain*] boot-shaped jar, D/204; (14) Gila Polychrome [*Editor: Cliff Polychrome*] bowl, D/205. A is an antler baton (?), D/206. B is a mano, D/s39. Drawing by Ronald J. Beckwith based on Rex E. Gerald's field map and notes.

below the surface (see figure 3.12). This burial was surrounded by trash and water- and wind-deposited silt and sand. Burial 2 was interred after the kiva had been abandoned, the roof had collapsed, and the north corner had been filled with trash and other debris to within about 85 cm of the present surface. This burial is not superimposed directly above Burial 8, which rests on the kiva floor, but it would have been difficult to inter the latter remains without disturbing the legs of Burial 2.

Position. Burial 2 was partially flexed, on the right side, with the upper legs forming an obtuse angle with the trunk and the lower legs parallel to the axis of the trunk. The position of the skull and arms could not be determined because of their disintegrated condition. The trunk-skull orientation was to the east-northeast (ca. 66° from true north).

Burial Offerings. None were found.

[*Editor: Barnes (appendix B) identifies this individual as an adult female, 40–45 years old.*]

Burial 3

Located in the fill of the kiva, in the center of the west quarter, Burial 3 was found in a red sandy layer, 1.10 m below the surface. No pit was discernible. Burial 3 was interred after the kiva had been abandoned, the roof had collapsed, and the depression had been filled to within 1.10 m of the present surface. Burials 4 and 1 were near Burial 3, but they were not placed in direct superposition and therefore cannot be related in this manner. However, it may be worth noting that Burial 4 was interred at a much lower level than Burial 3, and Burial 2 was interred at about the same level.

Position. Burial 3 was extended, supine, with the knees spread and the left ankle crossed over the right ankle (see figure 4.1). The arms were by the sides. The skull was turned to face the left, and the maxilla was found about 30 cm above the forehead, where it and fragments of vertebrae had probably been carried by burrowing animals. This skeleton was about 1.60 m long, from skull to feet. It was oriented with the skull to the south-southwest (198° from true north).

Burial Offerings. None were found.

[*Editor: Barnes (appendix B) identifies this individual as an adult male, 25–27 years old.*]

Burial 4

Located on the floor of the kiva, in the west corner, Burial 4 is 1.60 m below the present surface. It was 60 cm below the surface of the sandy red layer on which Burial 3 rested and through which the excavation for Burial 4 was dug. Trash, adobe, and sand surrounded and covered the body. Burial 4 was interred on the floor of the kiva, after it had been abandoned and after the roof had collapsed. A sandy, red, water- and wind-deposited stratum had accumulated in the west corner of the kiva before the excavation was made for this burial. The outline of the pit was noted 60 cm above the kiva floor and 1.00 m below the surface. No burials were superimposed above Burial 4.

Position. Burial 4 was flexed, on the right side, with the knees at right angles to the trunk and the heels drawn up near the pelvis (see figure 4.1; see also Di Peso 1958a:Plate 14b). The right forearm was at right angles to the trunk, and the elbow was in front of the body; the right hand was near an antler baton (?), D/206. The left upper arm was above and in line with the trunk, and the lower arm was drawn up so that the hand was near the jaw. The trunk was oriented so that the skull was to the north (358° from true north).

Burial Offerings. Burial 4 was almost completely covered with burial offerings, mostly upright pottery vessels, so that only the knees, parts of the lower legs, and the top of the skull were visible before removal of the offerings. Fourteen pottery vessels were removed from around and on the body. They include eight Gila Polychrome bowls, D/193 [*Editor: This vessel is now classified as Gila Polychrome: Salmon Variety (Lyons 2012b).*], D/194, D/196 [*Editor: Cliff Polychrome (Lyons 2004b)*], D/200 [*Editor: Phoenix Polychrome (Lyons and Neuzil 2006; Neuzil and Lyons 2006)*], D/201, D/202 [*Editor: Cliff Polychrome*], D/203, D/205 [*Editor: Cliff Polychrome*]; one Gila Polychrome jar, D/192;

two Davis Plain [*Editor: Belford Plain; see chapter 6*] jars, D/195, D/198; two Davis Plain [*Editor: Belford Plain*] boot-shaped jars, D/199, D/204; and one Salt Red: Davis Variety [*Editor: Belford Red; see chapter 6*] bowl, D/197. In addition to pottery, there were the following artifacts: near the right hand, an antler baton (?), D/206; in vessel D/196, a projectile point (D/67); in vessel D/204, a shell ring (D/68) and some charred seeds and wood (D/72); in vessel D/199, more charred seeds and wood (D/73) and a small shell bracelet (D/104); in the fill around the body, three stone pendants (D/87, D/71, D/235), four shell beads (D/102), white pigment (D/69), a shell pendant (D/70), and a mano (D/s39).

[*Editor: Barnes (appendix B) identifies this individual as an adolescent, 16–17 years old.*]

Burial 5

Located in the south corner, in a pit dug into the edge of the bench of the kiva, the pit for this burial extends 1.46 m below the present surface (that is, to within 30 cm of the floor of the kiva), is roughly spherical in plan, and 65–66 cm in diameter (see figure 3.12). The north corner of the rectangular area separating the platform from the southwest bench was partially removed during the excavation of this pit. The fill above and around this burial consisted of trash and sand. Burial 5 was interred after the kiva had been abandoned and had filled with debris at least to the level of the bench, or 90 cm above the floor. This depth of fill had accumulated in other parts of the kiva only after the roof had collapsed, and that is the presumed situation here.

Position. Burial 5 was flexed, face down, with the arms and legs flexed closely to the body. The skull was forced down into the pit, the forehead resting against the northwest edge. The skull was oriented to the northwest (about 330° from true north).

Burial Offerings. Two pottery vessels were found with the body; D/207, a Gila Polychrome bowl, was placed upright on the right side of the body, and D/208, a Salt Red: Davis Variety [*Editor: Belford Red*] bowl, was placed upright on top of the body.

[*Editor: Barnes (appendix B) identifies this individual as an adolescent, 12–14 years old.*]

Burial 6

Located in the fill of the kiva, with the head and left shoulder placed in the ventilator opening, the skull of Burial 6 was 20 cm above the floor of the kiva, or 1.40 m below the present surface (figure 4.2). The feet were 30 cm above the kiva floor, or 1.30 m below the present surface. The burial pit was excavated through trash, silt, sand, and some roofing adobe; the same materials were used to fill the grave. Burial 6 was placed in the kiva after at least 30 cm, and probably 60 cm, of fill had accumulated. Burial 7 was scattered around and above Burial 6 and appears to have been a later interment; the exact location of the Burial 7 interment could not be determined.

Position. Burial 6 was extended, supine. The right arm was at the side. The upper left arm was across the upper chest and the lower left arm extended down across the lower chest and abdomen, an unusual position. The trunk was bent slightly to the left, apparently as the result of an attempt to force the body around the corner of the ventilator opening. The skull was tilted up until it almost rested on its crown. The skeleton, as exposed, measured 1.5 m, from skull to feet. The pelvis-to-skull orientation was to the east-southeast (102° from true north).

Burial Offerings. None were found.

[*Editor: Barnes (appendix B) recognizes the remains of two individuals. She identifies individual 6a as an adult female, 35–39 years old, and individual 6b as an infant, 18–30 months old.*]

Burial 7

In the kiva fill, near the west side of the ventilator opening and distributed over an area about 70 cm in diameter and from 20 cm to 60 cm above the kiva floor, the poorly preserved bones of this infant were strewn above as well as between and around the legs of Burial 6 (see figure 4.2). The fill above and around this burial is general kiva fill composed of trash, roofing adobe, sand, and silt. This burial was scattered from the level of Burial 6 to a level some

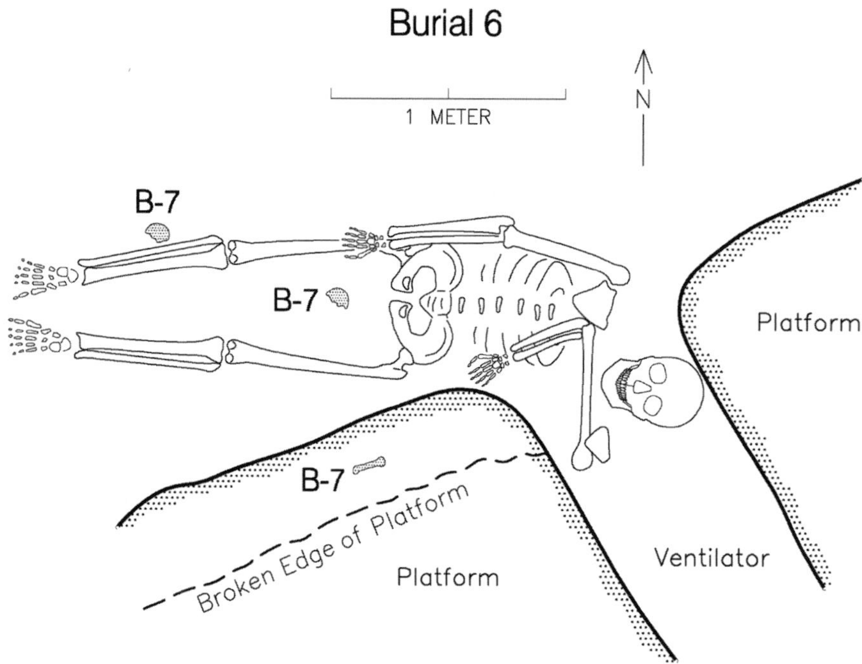

FIGURE 4.2 Plan view of Burials 6 and 7. Drawing by Ronald J. Beckwith based on Rex E. Gerald's field map and notes.

30–40 cm above it, but in the absence of articulated bones, it is impossible to say whether Burial 7 was interred contemporaneously with, earlier than, or later than Burial 6.

Position. Not determined.

Burial Offerings. None were found.

[*Editor: Barnes (appendix B) recognizes the remains of two individuals. She identifies individual 7a as an infant, about 6 months old, and individual 7b as an infant older than 12 months.*]

Burial 8

Located near the floor of the kiva, in a pit excavated through the edge of the northwest bench, near its center, the pit for this burial removed a section of bench about 1.00 m long and 45 cm wide and penetrated some 5 cm below the floor of the kiva in places (figure 4.3). Some of this section of the bench edge was occupied by a roof-support post that was partially removed when the burial pit was dug. The fill around and above the burial was composed of trash, sand, silt, adobe, and cobbles and gravel from the edge of the bench. Burial 8 was interred in the kiva after it had been abandoned and filled to the level of the bench, otherwise there would have been no reason for digging in the hard cobble and caliche sterile earth that formed the bench. The roof must have collapsed before the time of the burial, because Burial 1, which was located directly above this burial, was placed in a pit dug into adobe roofing material.

Position. Burial 8 was flexed, on the right side, with the legs drawn up against the trunk and the arms extended. The right arm was slightly behind the trunk, and the left arm was just in front of the trunk and extended between the legs. The feet were poorly preserved as were the hands, except for portions of the left hand, which was found in and under a Davis Plain jar (D/212) placed against the back of the skeleton. A boulder, 40 × 25 × 20 cm in size, rested on the abdomen and lower chest. The skull was orientated to the east (85° from true north).

Burial Offerings. Four pottery vessels were placed behind the body. They included two Gila Polychrome bowls: D/209, behind the pelvis, and D/210, behind the skull; a Davis Plain [*Editor: Belford Plain*] bowl, D/211, placed beside or under a Gila Polychrome bowl, D/210; and D/212, an inverted Davis Plain [*Editor: Belford Plain*] jar behind

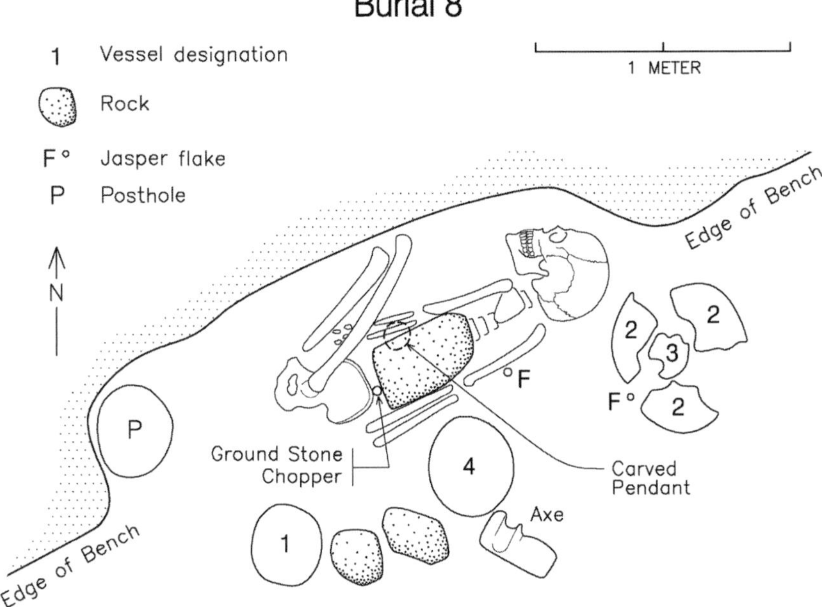

FIGURE 4.3 Plan view of Burial 8. Burial 8 associated vessels: (1) Gila Polychrome bowl, D/209; (2) Gila Polychrome bowl, D/210; (3) Davis Plain [*Editor*: *Belford Plain*] bowl, D/211; (4) Davis Plain [*Editor*: *Belford Plain*] jar, D/212. Drawing by Ronald J. Beckwith based on Rex E. Gerald's field map and notes.

the lower thoracic region. In addition, there was a lump of molded pigment (D/96) and a stone pendant (D/100d) in front of the skeleton, in the abdominal region, and a bow-and-arrow-making kit behind the skeleton, extending from the lumbar to the skull region. This kit consisted of an axe (D/100a), a grooved abrader (D/100b), a lump of pigment (D/100e), two cores (D/100c, D/100x), two scrapers (D/100f, D/100g), two knives (D/100h, D/100k), and much debitage (D/100i, D/100j, D/100l, D/100m, D/100n, D/100o, D/100p, D/100q, D/100r, D/100s, D/100t, D/100u, D/100v, D/100w).

[*Editor: Barnes (appendix B) identifies this individual as an adult male, 35–39 years old. The 10 individuals in the kiva (recovered as six single and two multiple interments) were buried after the kiva was decommissioned and its roof collapsed, during the Romero phase. Unlike the stratigraphically early burials outside or beneath the kiva, none inside the kiva were associated with Maverick Mountain Series pottery. Although no master profiles of the kiva's fill have been located, based on stratigraphic clues derived from partial profiles, photographs, and field notes, it is possible to definitively place all but two of the interments (Burials 6 and 7; Individuals 6a, 6b, 7a, and 7b) in stratigraphic order.*

The keys to disentangling the temporal relationships among these burials are fourfold: (1) the deposits in the kiva (based on depth measurements associated with different strata and corroborating field photographs) slant significantly downward from northeast to southwest, with the deepest (i.e., highest peak elevation) accumulations of fill in the east and north corners of the structure and the shallowest (i.e., lowest peak elevation) accumulations in the south and west corners; (2) Gerald was able to observe direct superposition of some burials; (3) Gerald was able to determine the stratum (these were defined by depositional and compositional characteristics, i.e., they were not arbitrary units) within and the elevation at which most of the burial pits became visible; and (4) Gerald was able to place the digging of a number of burial pits in time relative to the deposition of a distinctive red, sandy adobe in the west corner of the kiva.

The pronounced slant of the stratigraphy (likely reflecting a plane created by the partially collapsed roof, with one end resting on or near the floor and the other end still attached to a wall or walls) means that fill accumulated most quickly in the east corner, followed in decreasing depth by the north corner, the south corner, and the west corner. Burials were not placed in the east corner, however. Burials 2, 5, 6, 6a, 7, 7a, and 8 were placed in the parts of the kiva that filled up more quickly (the south and north corners) than the location chosen for Burials 3 and 4 (the west corner). Burial 1 straddles the north and west corners. These data alone suggest that Burials 3 and 4 should postdate burials 2, 5, 6, 6a, 7, 7a, and 8.

Gerald documented the fact that Burial 1 clearly overlay Burial 2 and that Burial 2 was superimposed over Burial 8. The pits for Burials 3 and 4 cut through the distinctive red, sandy adobe stratum, which makes them roughly coeval with or later than Burial 1. Although Burial 5 could not be placed precisely relative to the red, sandy adobe stratum (due to the slant of the strata), its pit was not visible above the level of the bench, and it was dug into a trash stratum that underlay the red, sandy adobe stratum. In addition, despite being located in the last quadrant of the kiva to fill up, the pit for Burial 4 was initiated at least 10 cm higher (in the red, sandy adobe stratum) than that of Burial 5.

Compiling all these clues leads to the conclusion that Burial 8 was the first to be interred in the kiva, followed by 2 and 5, which are roughly coeval. Next was Burial 1. The last two interred were Burials 3 and 4. Burials 6, 6a, 7, and 7a could not be placed with certainty relative to the others, although most evidence suggests these interments predate Burials 3 and 4. The stratigraphic relationships discussed here are addressed in the context of ceramic dating in chapter 7.]

Inhumations South of the Pit House Hamlet

Burial 9

Located in a pit dug about 20 cm into sterile cobbles and clay, partially underlying the outside wall of the kiva, at the south corner, it was 1.20 m below the present surface (see figure 3.12). The grave furnishings, which rested directly under the walls, at the corner, extended from about 20 cm below the walls up to the adobe that formed their foundations. The fill around and above the burial was trash, sand, and silt. The orientation of the pit and the placement of the offerings, partway under the wall foundations, indicate quite strongly that this burial predates the construction of the kiva.

Position. Burial 9 was flexed and supine, with the arms and legs folded closely over the body. The skull faced up, and the pelvis-to-skull orientation was to the east-southeast (119° from true north).

Burial Offerings. Three pottery vessels were placed upright to the left of the skull. They included a small Gila Polychrome bowl (D/214) that rested upright, on top of, and formed a lid for a Tucson Polychrome jar (D/215), and a Redington Plain Smudged [*Editor: Belford Burnished; see chapter 6*] bowl (D/213).

[*Editor: Barnes (appendix B) identifies this individual as child, 3.0–3.5 years old.*]

Burial 11

Located 50 cm outside the Romero (late Reeve) phase perimeter wall and 3.00 m south of the kiva, the burial was interred in trash, about 30 cm below the present surface. No stratigraphy was discerned.

Position. The body was badly disintegrated but appeared to be flexed and supine. Its orientation was not noted.

Burial Offerings. One broken Davis Plain [*Editor: Belford Plain*] jar (not cataloged) was set over the body.

[*Editor: Barnes (appendix B) identifies this individual as a newborn. One of the interments (Burial 9) in the southern cluster, a child interred with a Tucson Polychrome jar and a Gila Polychrome bowl, predates the construction of the kiva and thus most likely dates to the Aravaipa (Sosa) phase, when the immigrants first arrived. The other (Burial 11), located only about 3 m south of the first, cannot be placed in time based on stratigraphy or ceramic associations; it may date to the Aravaipa (Sosa) phase or the Redfield (early Reeve) phase. Its location, however, at the southern end of the area demarcated by the arc of Kayenta pit houses (and near Burial 9) may be an indicator that it dates to the earliest portion of the immigrant occupation.*]

Inhumations in the Northeast Trash

Burial 12

Located in the Northeast Trash (20E 37N) under 80 cm of trash, the burial rested on sterile clay and cobbles and was covered with a 5 cm thick layer of adobe. No pit could be delineated in the overlying trash. Because of the adobe cap over the body, it would not have been necessary for the trash mound to have been there originally, but it is also possible that the burial was dug through the trash above.

Position. Burial 12 was flexed, on the right side, with knees drawn up to the chest, heels drawn up to the pelvis, and the upper left arm at the side. The right arm and lower left arm were not located because of disintegration. The pelvis-to-head orientation was to the south (171° from true north).

Burial Offerings. One pottery vessel, a Davis Plain [*Editor: Belford Plain*] jar (D/225), was found with this burial, placed behind the body in the pelvic area.

[*Editor: Barnes (appendix B) recognizes the remains of two individuals. She identifies individual 12a as a child, 11–12 years old, and individual 12b as an infant, 6–12 months old.*]

Burial 13

Located in the Northeast Trash (18E 37N), at a depth of 80 cm below the present surface, the burial rested on sterile deposits. The outline of the burial pit was not discernible in the overlying trash; however, some trash must have been present to cover the burial at the time of interment.

Position. The only skeletal element present was a skull.

Burial Offerings. Six pottery vessels were placed on one side of this skull. They included one Gila Black-on-red bowl (D/229), a Davis Plain: Sobaipuri Coil Rim Variety [*Editor: Belford Plain*] jar (D/227), a Davis Plain [*Editor: Belford Plain*] jar (D/230), a Redington Plain Smudged [*Editor: Belford Burnished*] bowl (D/228), and two Sosa Plain bowls (D/226, 231). Near the skull were three shell beads (D/189a).

[*Editor: Barnes (appendix B) identifies this individual as an adult.*]

Burial 14

Located in the Northeast Trash (15E 36N), the pit was 1.10 × 1.25 m and dug 30–35 cm into sterile deposits (1.10 m below the present surface). The fill over and around the body was trash. The fill above the body consisted of trash with some gravel and clay.

Position. Burial 14 was flexed and supine, with the face turned to the left and the legs, which were flexed to slightly less than a 90° angle with the trunk, turned to the right. The arms and feet were not located; all vertebrae and ribs were disturbed by burrowing animals. The skull was orientated to the southeast (136° from true north).

Burial Offerings. One Gila Polychrome bowl (D/232) was placed in an upright position on the right side of the body.

[*Editor: Barnes (appendix B) identifies this individual as a child, 4–5 years old.*]

Burial 15

Scattered over a square meter in the Northeast Trash (17E 35N) and ranging in depth from 40 cm to 60 cm below the present surface, the burial is presumed to have been interred after 40–60 cm of trash had accumulated. No definite burial site or evidence of a pit was located in the trash. It was located over House 6 and is therefore later than that structure.

Position. This burial's position could not be determined.

Burial Offerings. A Gila Polychrome bowl (D/233) was found in the immediate vicinity of the burial and is assumed to have been interred with the body.

[*Editor: Barnes (appendix B) identifies this individual as a newborn. The Northeast Trash is the refuse deposit generated initially by the occupants of the pit houses and later by those who inhabited the pueblo. Stratigraphic data are inadequate for determining the ages of these burials relative to each other or the site's late Classic period features. It is important to note, however, that none associated with painted pottery*

(Burials 13, 14, and 15) yielded Maverick Mountain Series vessels. As a group, these three inhumations likely postdate Burials 9 and 11 and thus date to the initial occupation of Houseblock I or later. Ceramic stylistic data discussed in chapter 7 suggest that Burial 13 dates to the Aravaipa or Redfield phase, Burial 14 to the Redfield or Romero phase, and Burial 15 to the Romero phase. Gerald raises the possibility that Burial 12 (12a and 12b, per Barnes) may have been interred at a time when the refuse deposit in the Northeast Trash area was shallow. This would suggest interment early in the Aravaipa phase.]

Isolated Inhumation

Burial 10

Located in a pit dug through the floor of House 5, this burial underlies the east corner of Room 2 as well as the perimeter wall of the Romero (late Reeve) phase pueblo. The pit was dug 83 cm into sterile deposits below the floor of House 5 and 1.45 m below the present surface. The fill of the pit and the area above it contained trash, cobbles, sand, and silt. The pit for this burial was excavated through the floor of House 5, presumably after that house had been abandoned. Room 2 and the compound perimeter wall of the Romero (late Reeve) phase pueblo were built after the burial was in place.

Position. Burial 10 was flexed, on the right side, with the legs drawn up near the trunk, the upper left arm by the side, and the lower left arm bent up toward the face (figure 4.4). The pelvis-to-skull orientation was to the west (264° from true north).

Burial Offerings. Nine pottery vessels were arranged behind the skeleton, between the skull and the feet. They included three Tucson Polychrome jars, D/216 placed bottom-up near the lumbar region, D/217 placed upright near the pelvis, and D/219 placed upright behind the thorax; two Davis Plain [*Editor: Belford Plain*] bowls, D/218 placed near the pelvis, and D/223 placed at the feet; one Davis Plain [*Editor: Belford Plain*] jar, D/221 placed near the skull; one Gila Polychrome bowl, D/220 placed bottom-up over D/221; one Salt Smudged: Davis Variety [*Editor: Belford Red Smudged; see chapter 6*] bowl, D/222 placed on its side against the cervical vertebrae, thorax, and skull; and one Dragoon Red bowl, D/224 placed on its side at the feet. In addition, there were two sherd disks (D/188a, b), a stone pendant (D/188c), a shell bracelet (D/188d), 32 stone tesserae from a mosaic (D/188e), and a cucurbit (?) seed (D/188f).

[*Editor: Barnes (appendix B) identifies this individual as an adult female, 24–25 years old. This burial underlies the Romero (late Reeve) phase compound wall and therefore may date to the Redfield (early Reeve) phase or the Aravaipa (Sosa) phase pit house occupation. It more likely belongs with the pit house occupation, however, as it is one of only two burials to yield Maverick Mountain Series vessels (three Tucson Polychrome jars).*]

CREMATIONS

Cremation 1

Located on the flat top of the terrace about 40.0 m northeast of the pueblo, and some 9.5 m north of House 1 (52E 5N), the half dozen or so calcined bone fragments and burial offerings designated Cremation 1 were placed in a slight depression about 20 cm below the present surface, in relatively clean sand and silt.

Burial Offerings

Scattered within a radius of about 25 cm were a stone disk (D/141a), a stone vessel (D/141b), a shell pendant (D/141c), a palette (D/141d), and pigment (D/141e).

Cremation 2

Located near Cremation 1, about 8 m north of House 1 (52E 4N), the few fragments of calcined bone and offerings labeled Cremation 2 were interred in a small depression some 20 cm below the present surface. The poorly delineated pit appeared to be about 30 cm in diameter. The fill around and

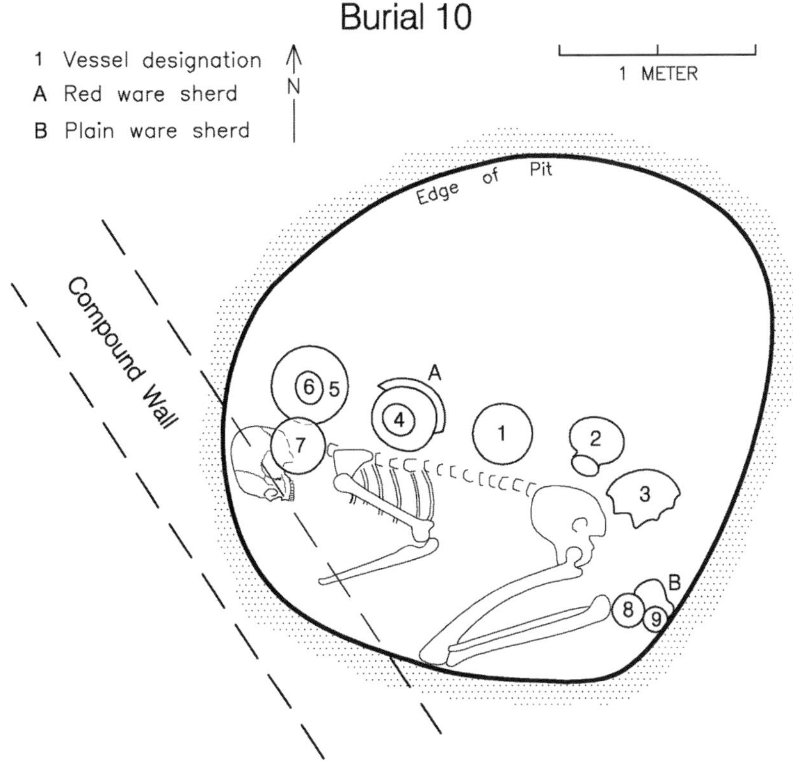

FIGURE 4.4 Plan view of Burial 10. Burial 10 associated vessels: (1) Tucson Polychrome jar, D/216; (2) Tucson Polychrome jar, D/217; (3) Davis Plain [*Editor: Belford Plain*] bowl, D/218; (4) Tucson Polychrome jar, D/219; (5) Gila Polychrome bowl, D/220; (6) Davis Plain [*Editor: Belford Plain*] jar, D/221; (7) Salt Smudged: Davis Variety [*Editor: Belford Red Smudged*] bowl, D/222; (8) Davis Plain [*Editor: Belford Plain*] bowl, D/223; (9) Dragoon Red bowl, D/224. Drawing by Ronald J. Beckwith based on Rex E. Gerald's field map and notes.

above the cremation consisted of clean gravel and cobbles with sand and silt.

Burial Offerings

In the immediate vicinity of the calcined bone were pigment (D/142a) and a Tres Alamos Red-on-brown [*Editor: Santa Cruz Red-on-buff: Aravaipa Variety; see chapter 6*] scoop (D/142b).

Cremation 3

Located in the vicinity of Cremations 1 and 2, 5.5 m north of House 1 (49E 4N), the bone and stone bowls making up Cremation 3 were found in a restricted area approximately 20 cm below the present surface. Part of this cremation lay about 10 cm above the disturbed remains of House 10.

Burial Offerings

Two stone vessels (D/143a, b) were found with this cremation.

SUMMARY AND CONCLUSION

Fifteen inhumations and three cremations were found at the Davis Ranch Site. The latter are all pit cremations with a few associated offerings, all assignable to the Hohokam Colonial or Sedentary period (Davis phase). [*Editor: Among the inhumations, there are three interment patterns based on body position and the presence or absence of associated artifacts (table 4.1). The dominant pattern in the sample for which body position was discernable is flexed inhumation with funerary objects (*n = *8; Burials 4, 5, 8, 9, 10, 11, 14, and Individual 12a). This mode of treating the dead began in the Aravaipa phase and persisted into the Romero phase. Three Romero phase inhumations (Burials 1 and 3 and Individual 6a) were extended, supine burials interred without funerary objects (assuming that the items discussed above as having been found with Burial 1 do not represent a purposeful association, as the individual was interred in trash). One Romero phase inhumation (Burial 2) was flexed and buried without associated objects.*

The presence of nine late Classic period flexed burials distinguishes the Davis Ranch Site from contemporary sites in the San Pedro Valley, where the dead either were cremated or buried supine and extended. Flexed inhumation was dominant in the Kayenta region during the thirteenth century AD, immediately before it was depopulated (Beals et al. 1945:Map 6, Plates 16–18; Colton 1939:52–59; Kidder and Guernsey 1919:66–70, 90, Plates 23b, 24, 25; Lindsay 1969:386; Spurr 2013), and the presence of this practice at the Davis Ranch Site supports the inference that the settlement was established and occupied by immigrants from the Kayenta region and/or their descendants.]

5

Artifacts

[Editor: This chapter was altered in order to add clarity and consistency to descriptions of types and individual specimens; update typological terminology, taxonomic nomenclature, and known distributional patterns; and include information regarding objects recovered as part of Gerald's 1965 fieldwork. Sometimes, as in the case of the flaked-stone artifacts, substantial revisions were required. Some of these revisions entailed input from specialists, who are acknowledged below. Gerald devoted a section of the original version of this chapter to "ceramic artifacts" (worked sherds, clay coils, a figurine, etc.). That section has been moved to chapter 6.]

STONE

Metates

"Metate," as used here, refers to the stationary stone upon which grain or other foods were ground by means of a smaller, upper stone that was rubbed back and forth (figures 5.1, 5.2, table 5.1). The rubbing motion, except in the case of basin metates, was reciprocal (cf. Woodbury 1954:50–51). "Grinding surface" refers to the part of the metate actually worn by use in grinding. Types of grinding surfaces have been used to define metate types.

Four basic types of metates were found at the Davis Ranch Site. The grinding surface of Type I is trough shaped, with a concave bottom and straight, parallel sides, and extends from one end of the stone to the other (i.e., both ends of the trough are open). All of the relatively complete specimens are unshaped, or only slightly shaped, waterworn boulders. The fragmentary metates have been shaped to a much greater degree. This likely reflects the use of more easily worked materials (andesite and tuff). In this regard, it is interesting to note that the troughs of the metates made of the softer stones are deeper than those of the metates made of the harder stones. It is impossible to determine whether this difference is due to the original shaping of the stone or to use. Fragmentary and broken metates of this type do not appear to be worn out, though it is possible that they were broken and discarded for this reason. On the other hand, it seems quite possible that they were broken when the people who used them abandoned the site, or that they were broken by a marauding group trying to discourage the occupation of the site. Five of the seven specimens of this type were found in Redfield or Romero (Reeve) phase associations, and the remaining two were found in the fill of pre-Redfield (pre-Reeve) phase houses, in the immediate vicinity of Redfield and/or Romero (Reeve) phase dwellings from which they may have come.

The grinding surface of the Type II metate is similar to that characteristic of Type I, except that one end of the trough is closed. When the closed

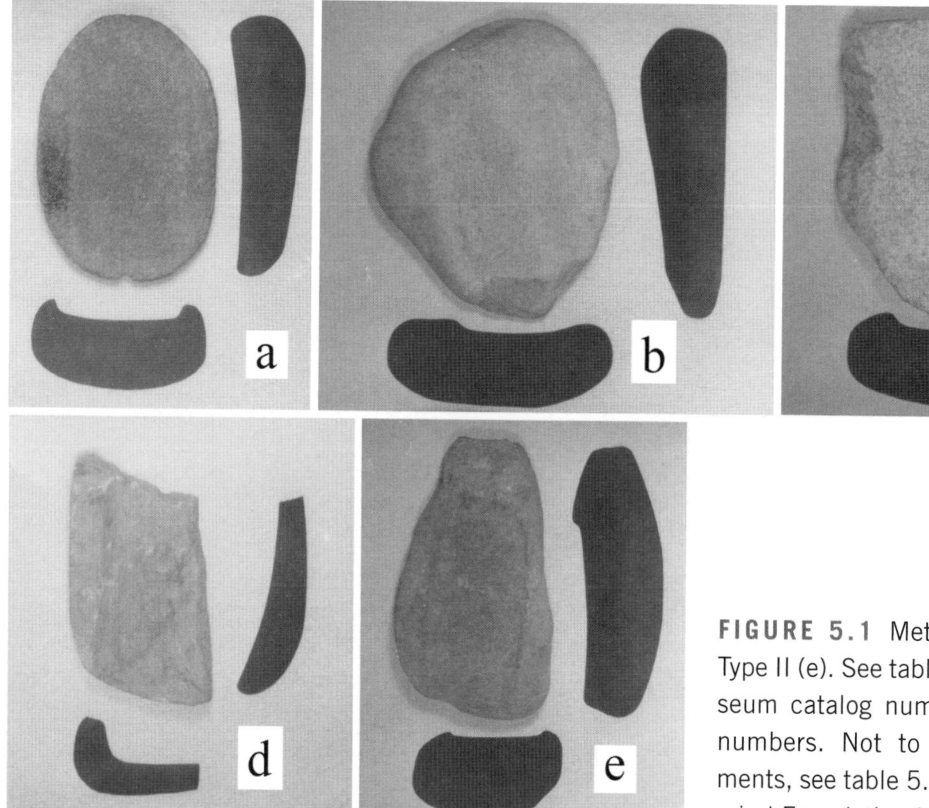

FIGURE 5.1 Metates: Type I (a–d) and Type II (e). See table D.1 for Amerind Museum catalog numbers and photograph numbers. Not to scale. For measurements, see table 5.1. Courtesy of the Amerind Foundation Inc., Dragoon, Arizona.

end of the trough is raised until the rough and irregular lower surface reaches a relatively stable position, the upper end is 6–7 cm above the floor, the trough forms an angle of about 19° with the floor, and the irregular surface that forms the closed end of the trough is in a position to support a mano. In this respect, this metate is roughly comparable to the "Utah type" metate with the specially prepared mano rest at the closed end of the trough (Woodbury 1954:50–52, Figure 16a, b). That it was built into the basal course of a Romero (late Reeve) phase wall suggests that the type belongs to an earlier occupation; otherwise this unbroken specimen probably would not have been reused as a wall stone.

The Type III metate is characterized by a slightly concave grinding surface pecked into one entire surface of an ovoid-to-rectanguloid boulder. The "depth" measurement, referring to the grinding surface concavity, was measured from an imaginary line projected transversely across the grinding surface at the point of greatest concavity. None of the fragmentary specimens have been modified to any extent on the non-grinding surfaces, but the one complete specimen has been shaped on all surfaces and conforms closely to the flat metate type from the Jeddito area described by Woodbury (1954:54). The major difference is that the grinding surface of this specimen is not "approximately flat from side to side" (Woodbury 1954:54) but is concave to a depth of 1.10 cm. Unfortunately, Woodbury does not publish comparable data. None of these specimens, other than the one mentioned above, show great wear. The use of two Type III metate fragments in the construction of the walls of Redfield (early Reeve) phase rooms and the presence of one fragment on the floor of a Hohokam Colonial or Sedentary period (Davis phase) house indicates quite strongly that the unshaped Type III metate belongs to the

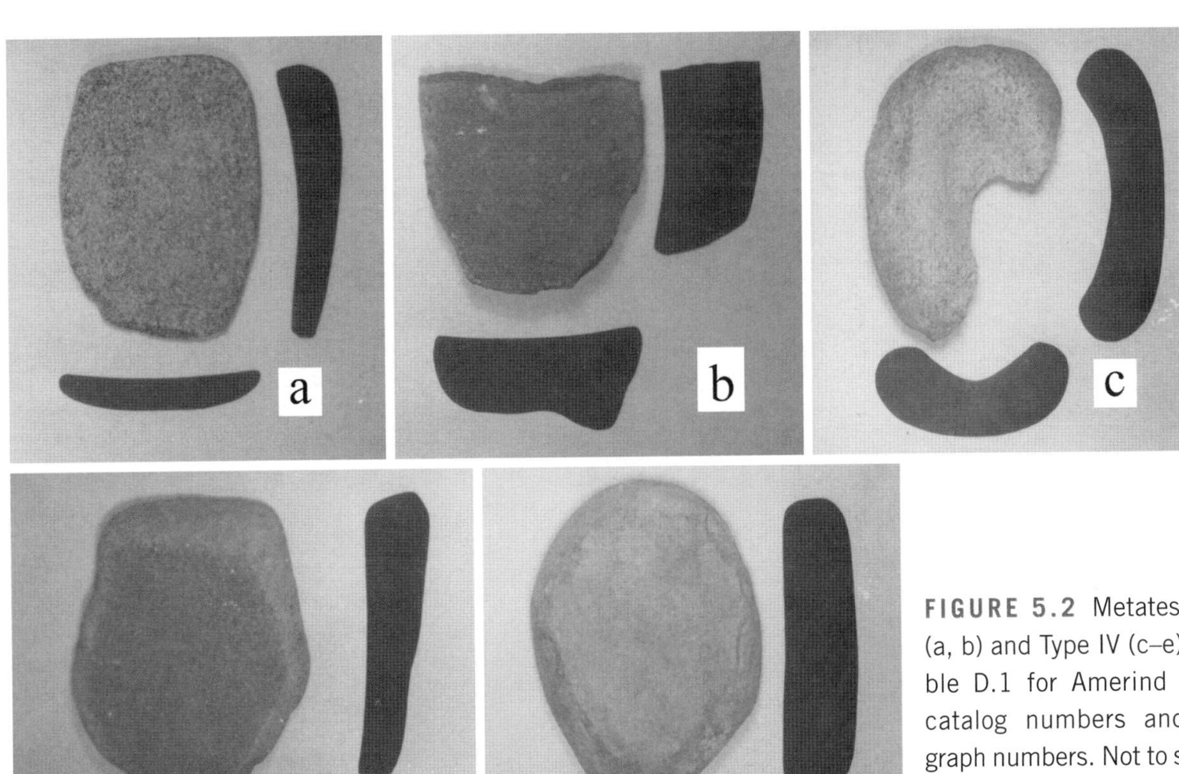

FIGURE 5.2 Metates: Type III (a, b) and Type IV (c–e). See table D.1 for Amerind Museum catalog numbers and photograph numbers. Not to scale. For measurements, see table 5.1. Courtesy of the Amerind Foundation Inc., Dragoon, Arizona.

pre-Redfield (pre-Reeve) phase occupation of Davis Ranch Site. The single fragment from the trench in front of Room 7 may have been mixed with the Redfield and Romero (Reeve) phase trash in the plaza, or it may have fallen from the disintegrating wall of the room. Only the complete specimen, shaped on all surfaces, is in indisputable Redfield (early Reeve) phase association, and therefore it probably represents a distinct type.

Type IV includes stationary grinding implements frequently called "basin metates," in so far as this term refers to grinding implements on which the motion employed was of a rotary nature rather than reciprocal. Several stages of wear are represented on these specimens—one has a depression worn only 0.2 cm deep, another has one 0.6 cm deep, and the third's is 6.4 cm deep. The distribution of basin metates at the Davis Ranch Site suggests that the type was in use both before and during the Redfield and Romero phases (Reeve phase). It is possible that this type of stationary grinding surface functioned particularly well for the preparation of seeds and that it continued to be used by the occupants of the site for that purpose. This type of grinding implement has been utilized since Cochise Culture times (Sayles and Antevs 1941:28).

Summary and Discussion

Nearly half of the metates found at the Davis Ranch Site are Type I, which are assigned to the Redfield and Romero phases (Reeve phase) (table 5.2). The Type III metate encompasses the next largest proportion of the metates recovered and is associated with the Hohokam Colonial and Sedentary periods (Davis phase) and the Redfield and Romero phases (Reeve phase). Type IV metates were apparently used both before and during the Redfield and Romero phases (Reeve phase) (one was used

TABLE 5.1 Characteristics of metates from the Davis Ranch Site

		Body			Basin					
Type	Cat. no.	Length	Width	Thickness	Length	Width	Depth	Material	Provenience	Figure
I	D/s28	40.0	27.8	13.2	38.5	20.0	4.0	Vesicular basalt	Room 10 fill	5.1a
	D/s33	41.5	34.2	14.0	29.0	17.0	1.4	Granite	Room 7 floor, NW corner	5.1b
	D/s44	45.2	31.0	12.0	43.0	17.0	2.6	Granite	Room 4 floor, SW center	5.1c
	D/s63	20.0+	15.5+	7.6+			7.5+	Andesite	Room 14 fill	
	D/s70	31.5+	18.0+	10.5			9.0	Andesite	House 4 fill	5.1d
	D/s91	34.0+	38.0	16.0	33.0+	20.0	17.0	Rhyolite	House 7 10 cm above Floor 1	
	D/s101	36.0+	15.0+	19.0+			8.0+	Tuff	Room 6 fill	
II	D/s120	46.5	25.5	15.5	32.0	14.0	1.8	Vesicular basalt	Room 2 SE wall, basal course	5.1e
III	D/s45	34.2	25.0	6.8			1.0	Gabbro	Room 4 floor	5.2a
	D/s110	25.0+	27.5+	11.5+			0.6	Vesicular basalt	Trench in front of Room 7	
	D/s111	22.0+	28.5+	11.4		25.0+		Tuff	Room 10 W wall, S side of doorway	
	D/s116	27.0+	27.6	13.0		27.0		Vesicular basalt	Room 8 E wall, N end	5.2b
	D/s121	24.0+	24.8	8.7	22.0+	20.5	0.1	Vesicular basalt	House 9 floor, E center	
IV	D/s27	44.0+	29.5	13.7	32.0	16.0	6.4	Granite	Room 10 floor, SW corner	5.2c
	D/s34	33.3	25.9	8.1	27.0	21.0	0.6	Rhyolite	Room 7 N wall	5.2d
	D/s90	39.5	30.0	12.0	32.0	23.0	0.2	Andesite	House 7 Floor 1, center	5.2e

Note: All measurements are in cm.

TABLE 5.2 Metate type distribution by time period at the Davis Ranch Site

Phase(s) or period(s)	Metate type				
	I	II	III	IV	Total
Redfield or Romero (Reeve) phase	7	0	2	2	11
Aravaipa (Sosa) phase	0	0	0	0	0
Colonial or Sedentary period (Davis phase)	0	0	1	0	1
Unplaced	0	1	2	1	4
Total	**7**	**1**	**5**	**3**	**16**

as construction material in a Redfield [early Reeve] phase room wall). The single Type II metate was used as a Romero (late Reeve) phase wall stone and therefore probably belongs to the Hohokam Colonial or Sedentary period (Davis phase), the Aravaipa (Sosa) phase, or the Redfield (early Reeve) phase.

There is no obvious preference of material for metates, if this small sample is representative. Type I metates are made of five different materials, with andesite and granite represented by two each. The Type II metate is vesicular basalt, while Type III metates are of three different materials: vesicular basalt, tuff, and gabbro. The Type IV basin metates are granite, rhyolite, and andesite.

According to Bartlett (1933) and Woodbury (1954:58–59), the trough metate is the earlier type in the Southwest, being supplemented in Pueblo II times and replaced in Pueblo III times by the flat metate. Trough metates continued to be used in a few areas in northern Arizona and New Mexico into Pueblo III, particularly at Pinedale Ruin (AZ P:12:2[ASM]), Aztec Ruins (LA 45), and Pueblo Bonito (LA 225) (Woodbury 1954:59).

The open trough metate on an unshaped boulder seemingly was the preferred type in southeastern Arizona during Pueblo III and Pueblo IV (Di Peso 1951a:130–131, 1956:463, 1958a:117, Figure 18, Plates 37, 74a; Gladwin 1957:325; Haury 1945:127; Mills and Mills 1940–1949:68, 1955:53–54; Pierson 1962:50, Plate 10a; Steen 1962:25, Plate 13b; Tuthill 1947:77, Plate 30). Flat metates were a minor type at the late prehistoric sites of Babocomari Village and Paloparado (ARIZONA:DD:8:1[AF], AZ DD:8:2[ASM]; Di Peso 1951a:132–133, 1956:466) and are the dominant type at one historic site (Di Peso 1953:161–162).

[*Editor: Four of the five metates recovered from Reeve Ruin are flat (Di Peso 1958a:17, Figure 18, Plate 74b). One was recovered from José Solas Ruin as well (Di Peso 1953:134; see Lyons 2004a). Flat metates largely replaced other forms on the Colorado Plateau by the Pueblo IV period; they were the dominant type used during the Tsegi phase (AD 1250–1300) in the Kayenta region (Anderson 1969:186; Woodbury 1954:58). Di Peso (1958b) pointed to flat metates as a key marker (as well as thin, multifaceted manos with finger grips; see Manos, below) of the presence at Reeve Ruin of immigrants from north of the Mogollon Rim. Adams (1994:218, 2002:126–127, 2010) later documented the introduction of the same grinding technology to Point of Pines by Kayenta immigrants.*]

Grinding Slabs

Grinding slabs are relatively flat stones that have been used for grinding on a portion of one or more surfaces (figure 5.3a–g, table 5.3). A more specialized function for these tools is not known.

Almost all of the Type I grinding slabs were cobbles with one or both faces used for grinding. Three had a portion of one convex surface smoothed by abrading; the remainder of the stone is unmodified. All three have been broken or have large percussion flake scars along one edge. It is not impossible that the smallest of these was used as a mano, though such use was not extensive.

Three specimens are too small to have been used as a metate, yet each exhibits a slightly concave grinding surface. Two are made of slightly used manos,

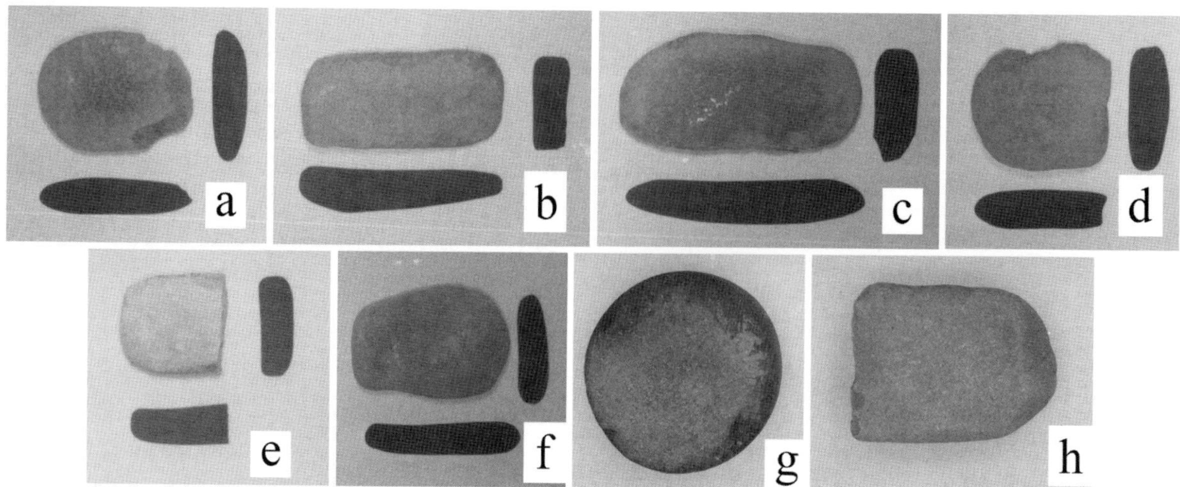

FIGURE 5.3 Grinding slabs: Type I (a–f) and Type II (g) and lapstone (h). See table D.1 for Amerind Museum catalog numbers and photograph numbers. Not to scale. For measurements, see table 5.3 (grinding stones) and text (lapstone). Courtesy of the Amerind Foundation Inc., Dragoon, Arizona.

TABLE 5.3 Characteristics of grinding slabs from the Davis Ranch Site

Type	Catalog no.	Length	Width	Thickness	Material	Provenience	Figure
I	D/s16	22.2	16.2	5.0	Basalt	Trench in front of Room 10	5.3a
	D/s18	26.8	12.4	5.6	Rhyolite	Plaza in front of Room 9	5.3b
	D/s30	34.7	16.3	5.6	Dacite	Room 4 fill	5.3c
	D/s49	23.4	20.5	6.3	Vesicular basalt	Room 4 floor, N center	5.3d
	D/s54	20.6+	11.0+	3.6	Andesite	Plaza in front of Room 16	
	D/s55	12.0+	11.5	4.4	Basalt	Plaza in front of Room 16	5.3e
	D/s84	15.5+	13.0	5.9	Vesicular basalt	Room 5 fill	
	D/s96	24.5	17.0	5.5	Basalt	House 7 fill	5.3f
II	D/164	16.2	16.4	5.8	Andesite	House 6 floor level over Pit 1	5.3g

Note: All measurements are in cm.

and one is an otherwise unmodified flat cobble. One bears a red stain on the grinding surface, suggesting that it, and possibly the others, was employed for paint grinding and/or mixing. Two examples of this type are flat, waterworn cobbles. Each has a concave grinding surface on one face and a convex grinding surface on the other. In addition, one specimen has been pecked and chipped on the edges and ends. All Type I grinding slabs are from Redfield or Romero (Reeve) phase proveniences.

Type II is represented by a disk well shaped on all surfaces and used on one face as a small, basin-shaped, stationary grinding stone. The pit formed by grinding is 4.5–10.1 cm in diameter and ranges from 0.7 cm to 0.8 cm in depth.

Summary and Discussion

The grinding slabs found at the Davis Ranch Site are all of relatively unspecialized types. Type I convex grinding slabs are not represented in material from the Jeddito area (Woodbury 1954). A similar type of object, called an anvil, is reported from Snaketown (Sayles 1937:104, Plate 41a), where it is said to occur in all phases, though the chart on Plate 41 lists only Sacaton phase occurrences. No similar objects are known from the desert area, unless the stone anvils reported from Babocomari Village (Di Peso 1951a:146) and Quiburi (Di Peso 1953:174–175; cf. Gerald 1968; Masse 1981; Seymour 1989) served like functions, although no grinding surfaces are mentioned as being present on these specimens. Anvils are apparently not found in Mogollon sites or at least have not been described (Wheat 1955). Concave grinding slabs are probably similar to the "grinding slabs" reported by Woodbury (1954:113, Figure 23g, j), but the depressions exhibited by the Davis Ranch Site specimens are not as well defined. Similar artifacts, called "miscellaneous metates," were found at Snaketown in Gila Butte (one specimen) and Sacaton (five specimens) phase contexts (Sayles 1937:104–105, Plate 50). Concave grinding slabs are also reported from the Younger Deposits at Ventana Cave (AZ Z:12:5[ASM]; Haury 1950:306, Figure 69b–d).

Grinding Stone

D/s68 is a large, irregular andesite boulder, 43.0 cm long, 40.0 cm wide, and 28.0 cm thick. Its flat surface bears a grinding depression 27.0 cm long, 10.0 cm wide, and 0.5 cm deep. It appears to have been used to grind stone into shape and was recovered from the fill of the kiva.

Lapstone

D/s48 is a flattened quartzite pebble, 9.9 cm long, 7.5 cm wide, and 3.2 cm thick, bearing numerous elongated scratches and peck marks near the center of one face (figure 5.3h). This stone was apparently used as a base upon which a substance such as leather was chopped or cut. Both large faces have been used for rubbing. One end bears an ancient break, the sharp edges of which have been dulled through use as a pecking or pounding instrument. It was recovered from the northeast corner of the floor of Room 4.

Slabs

Type I is a large slab of poorly cemented sandstone, which was probably quarried from the outcrop on the edge of the terrace just below the site (figure 5.4a, table 5.4). It was probably pecked into its rectanguloid shape and may have served as a door or as a hatch cover.

Type II is a class of small stone slabs that have been shaped by percussion flaking and by pecking (figure 5.4b). They are all of the general shape of manos, and one was found on the plaza floor with a group of manos. However, it is larger than any of the manos recorded and has not been pecked along the face to flatten it for use on a metate as have the indisputable mano blanks. The two fragmentary slabs have flattened faces that would have functioned on a metate, but both specimens were broken before wear facets developed.

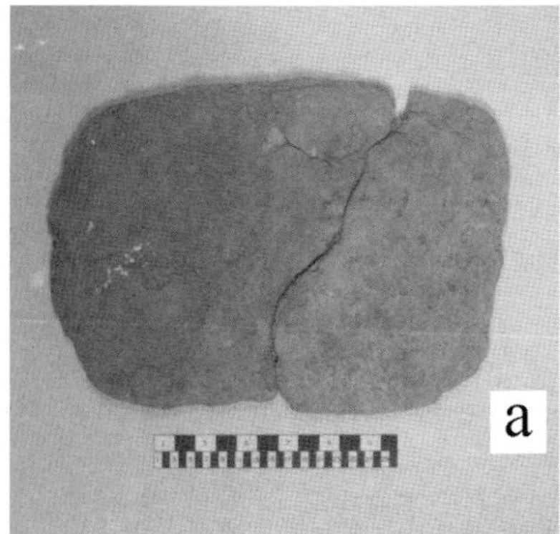

FIGURE 5.4 Stone slabs: Type I (a) and Type II (b). See table D.1 for Amerind Museum catalog numbers and photograph numbers. Not to scale. For measurements, see table 5.4. Courtesy of the Amerind Foundation Inc., Dragoon, Arizona.

TABLE 5.4 Characteristics of stone slabs from the Davis Ranch Site

Type	Catalog no.	Length	Width	Thickness	Material	Provenience	Figure
I	D/s102	55.0	37.5	9.0	Sandstone	Room 8 floor fill	5.4a
II	D/s15	9.5+	11.2	1.3	Quartzite	T 12S 18–20E	
	D/s38	12.7+	11.4	2.6	Sandstone	Kiva fill	
	D/s57	29.5	13.0	4.5	Andesite	Plaza in front of Room 16	5.4b

Note: All measurements are in cm.

Manos

A "mano" has been defined as a tabular piece of stone held in the hands and moved back and forth (in a reciprocal motion) on a metate for grinding (figures 5.5, 5.6a–i, table 5.5; Woodbury 1954:66). This definition seems adequate to describe the manos found at the Davis Ranch Site, though an occasional mano is loaf-shaped rather than tabular. Rubbing stones, which were used with a rotary motion, are excluded from this class and are described below.

In the following descriptions, "grinding surface" is used to refer to that portion of the stone that is normally in contact with the metate during the grinding operation. The grinding surface is always on one or both of the larger faces of the stone, although in the case of manos used with a trough metate, the grinding surface also extends partway over the adjacent portions of the ends of the mano. "Edges" and "ends" respectively refer to the longitudinal and transverse borders of the stone adjoining the grinding surface(s). The center portions of the edges occasionally have shallow pecked grooves, which are called "finger grips" (Woodbury 1954:66; see also Bartlett 1933:11–12, Figure 6d; Kidder 1932:70, Figure 44) since they are believed to have aided in holding or lifting the mano.

Forty-nine manos are represented in the material recovered from the Davis Ranch Site. These have been divided into two main classes, those used on trough metates (Type I) and those used on flat metates (Type II). These groups are each subdivided based on the general shape of the mano and whether it has been used on one or both faces. Additional groups encompass unclassifiable mano fragments and mano blanks.

The Type IA mano was made from relatively flat cobbles pecked to a flat surface on one side only. The ends of some have been pecked to shape but most have been shaped by use. The grinding surface is

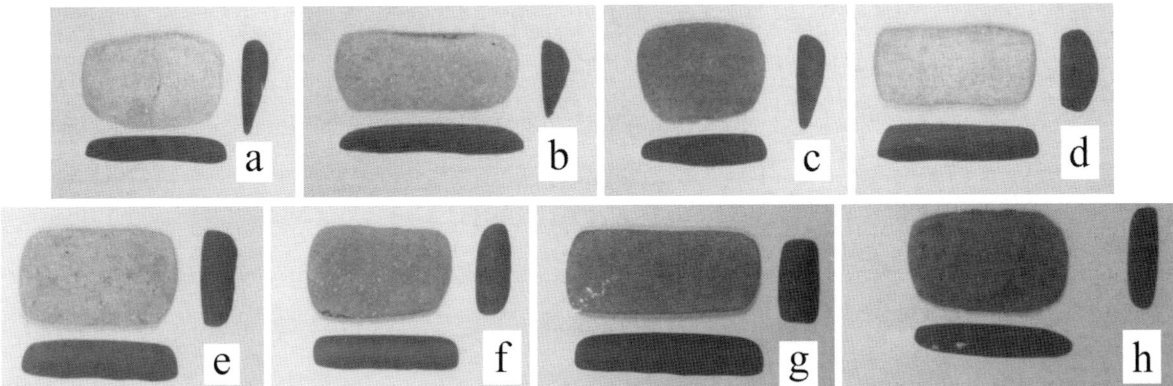

FIGURE 5.5 Manos: Type IA (a–c), Type IB (d–f), Type IC (g), and Type ID (h). See table D.1 for Amerind Museum catalog numbers and photograph numbers. Not to scale. For measurements, see table 5.5. Courtesy of the Amerind Foundation Inc., Dragoon, Arizona.

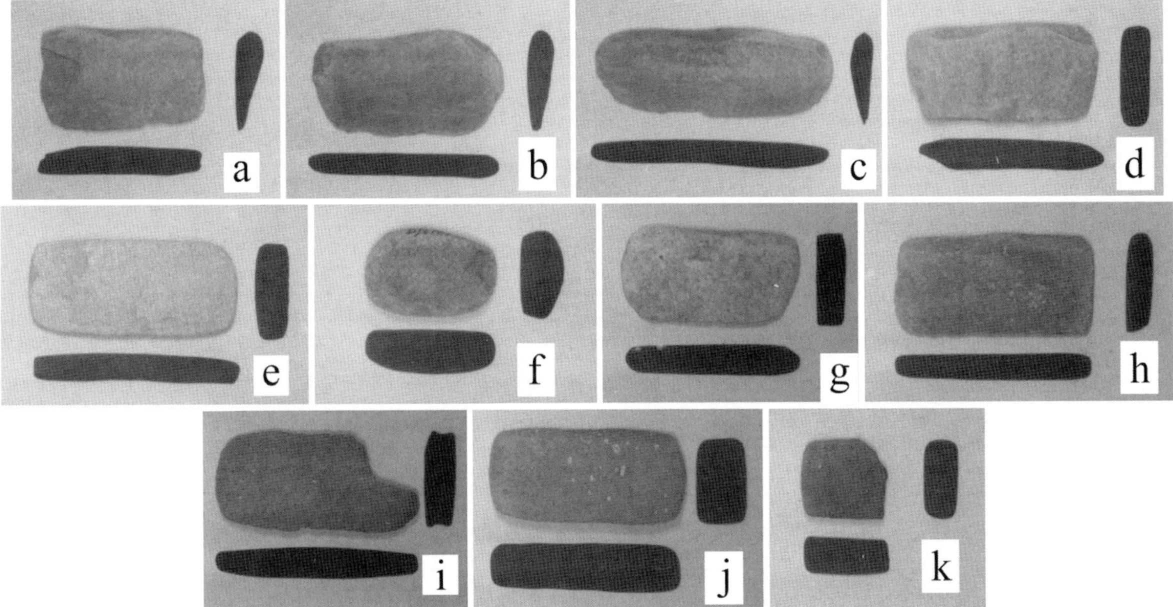

FIGURE 5.6 Manos: Type IIA (a–c), Type IIB (d, e), Type IIC (f), and Type IID (g–i); mano blank (j); and bifacial mano or rubbing stone (k). See table D.1 for Amerind Museum catalog numbers and photograph numbers. Not to scale. For measurements, see tables 5.5, 5.7 (manos and mano blank) and text (bifacial mano or rubbing stone). Courtesy of the Amerind Foundation Inc., Dragoon, Arizona.

slightly convex and extends partway up the ends as a result of rubbing against the sides of the trough. This type is triangular in cross section, probably as a result of the application of pressure to the rear of the mano during the downward stroke (Bartlett 1933:15–16). Five of these specimens manifest evidence of having been shaped on the non-grinding surfaces. This shaping ranges from what appears to be merely a roughening of the thicker edge, presumably to facilitate the raising of the lower edge of the mano on the downward stroke, to the pecking and smoothing of part or all of all surfaces. None of the

TABLE 5.5 Characteristics of manos from the Davis Ranch Site

Type	Catalog no.	Length	Width	Thickness	Material	Provenience	Figure
IA	D/s7	16.5	10.2	2.8	Andesite	Room 3 floor	
	D/s40	17.6	11.2	3.1	Sandstone	Room 10 fill	
	D/s42	18.5	11.6	3.4	Andesite	Kiva foot drum fill	5.5a
	D/s51	18.9	8.0	3.3	Sandstone	Plaza in front of Room 16	5.5b
	D/s52	19.0	11.0	3.8	Andesite	Plaza in front of Room 16	
	D/s98	9.9+	10.3	3.6	Andesite	Room 6 subfloor test	
	D/s104	16.6	11.1	3.6	Vesicular basalt	House 5 fill	5.5c
	D/s118	15.9	10.0	3.0	Vesicular basalt	Room 16 floor	
IB	D/s5	11.6+	10.3	6.3	Sandstone	T11N 13E surface	
	D/s12	20.5	9.4	4.7	Rhyolite	Room 3 fill	5.5d
	D/s21	17.5	10.4	4.3	Vesicular basalt	Room 10 floor, NW corner	5.5e
	D/s29	23.1	10.9	6.7	Vesicular basalt	Room 4 fill	
	D/s58	17.0	10.8	4.7	Vesicular basalt	Plaza in front of Room 16	5.5f
	D/s71	13.0+	9.8	4.5	Vesicular basalt	House 4 fill	
	D/s103	12.5+	8.6	3.0	Vesicular basalt	House 2 fill	
	D/s108	16.7	11.5	3.5	Granite	Trench in front of Room 2	
	D/s117	15.4+	10.6	4.8	Vesicular basalt	Pit Oven 3	
IC	D/s22	26.2	11.0	5.4	Vesicular basalt	Room 10 floor, S center	5.5g
ID	D/s8	11.1+	10.4	3.2	Vesicular basalt	T32N 12W surface	
	D/s72	16.6	10.1	4.0	Vesicular basalt	NE Trash	5.5h
IIA	D/s19	17.7	10.9	2.4	Schist	Trench in front of Room 9	5.6a
	D/s83	21.4	11.5	2.1	Schist	Room 5 fill	5.6b
	D/s124	24.8	9.2	2.5	Schist	Trench in front of Room 9	5.6c
IIB	D/s11	22.3+	10.8	5.0	Vesicular basalt	Surface	

(continued)

TABLE 5.5 *(continued)*

Type	Catalog no.	Length	Width	Thickness	Material	Provenience	Figure
	D/s20	24.1	12.1	4.9	Schist	Trench in front of Room 9	5.6d
	D/s36	16.5+	10.5	5.5	Porphyritic basalt	Room 9 floor	
	D/s47	24.3	10.8	3.2	Andesite	Room 4 floor, NE corner	5.6e
	D/s93	19.4+	10.6	3.1	Breccia	House 7 fill	
	D/s115	21.2	10.9	2.3	Granite	House 5 floor, E of hearth	
	D/s119	6.1+	4.9+	4.5	Vesicular basalt	Puddle Pit 2	
IIC	D/s107	13.0	8.5	4.3	Granite	Plaza in front of Room 2	5.6f
IID	D/s3	15.0+	11.4	3.4	Andesite	T10N 46E, 15 cm below surface	
	D/s4	21.3	11.2	4.0	Andesite	T10N 7E, 30 cm below surface	5.6g
	D/s23	25.7	11.4	5.1	Vesicular basalt	Room 10 floor, SE center	
	D/s31	19.9	12.1	3.7	Andesite	Room 6 surface	
	D/s32	19.7	9.7	2.5	Schist	Room 7 floor, NW corner	5.6h
	D/s39	24.4	13.0	5.1	Vesicular basalt	Burial 4	
	D/s53	24.5	11.2	4.6	Vesicular basalt	Plaza in front of Room 16	5.6i
	D/s59	13.6	9.5	3.5	Andesite	Room 14 fill	
	D/s109	11.7+	9.6+	3.4	Vesicular basalt	Trench in front of Room 2	
	D/s112	10.6+	11.1	5.1	Granite	House 7 Floor 2, NE corner	

Note: All measurements are in cm.

Type IA manos have finger grips. One specimen (D/s52) has a flattened upper surface that may have been used occasionally for grinding. In the center of this surface is a small pit that may have been used for cracking nuts or grains prior to grinding, the pit presumably holding the nut or grain between the stones until it was fractured, rather than allowing it to slide out from between two smooth surfaces. The presence of six of the eight Type IA manos in Redfield or Romero (Reeve) phase associations suggests that Type IA manos were in use during these phases.

Type IB manos are rectanguloid in shape and have convex edges and ends. Two specimens are relatively unmodified cobbles, and the remainder were pecked and ground to shape on one or more of the non-grinding surfaces. The grinding surface of each specimen is convex and extends partway up the end as a result of wear on the sides of the metate trough. One mano of this type (D/s5) has been ground smooth on one edge, and another (D/s12) has been pecked on one edge, possibly to facilitate the lifting of the advancing edge of the mano on the down stroke. None of the other specimens have finger grips of any sort. Type IB manos occur in Redfield or Romero (Reeve) phase associations in six cases, Aravaipa (Sosa) phase association in one case, Hohokam Colonial or Sedentary period (Davis phase) in one case, and unplaced association in one case, suggesting that the type was used primarily during the Redfield and Romero phases (Reeve phase).

The Type IC mano is distinguished from Type IB by its greater length and greater wear on the ends, which suggest that this type was used in wider and deeper trough metates than was Type IB. The grinding surface is convex and extends up over the ends of the mano. Both edges have been squared by pecking, and the top has been smoothed somewhat. This specimen is too long to have been used on any of the complete metates found at the Davis Ranch Site. The wear on the ends indicated that it was used on a metate as deep as the fragmentary specimens of metate Type I. The location of this find suggests use during the Redfield (early Reeve) phase.

Each of the two specimens of Type ID is a relatively flat stone with a convex grinding surface on both of its two larger faces. The edges have been pecked to a slightly convex surface, and the ends, which are also slightly convex, have been shaped almost entirely by their contact with the sides of the metate trough. The occurrence of one specimen of this type in the Northeast Trash suggests that the type was in use during the Aravaipa (Sosa) phase.

The oval stones from which Type IIA manos were made were apparently flat, waterworn cobbles. The ends of one specimen were broken off before it was employed as a mano; otherwise, the original stone is unmodified except on the grinding surface. The grinding surface is convex on both axes, though the convexity of the transverse axis is much greater and approaches the type of grinding surface described by Woodbury (1954:73) for his "manos with two adjoining grinding surfaces." In none of these specimens, however, is the grinding surface faceted as distinctly as those described by Woodbury. Type IIA manos were probably in use during the Redfield and Romero phases (Reeve phase).

Type IIB manos are characterized by a single, slightly convex grinding surface that does not curve up on the ends. In outline, the type is usually rectanguloid, though ovoid examples do occur. The degree of shaping varies from the pecking and smoothing of the grinding surface only to the pecking and smoothing of all surfaces. An intermediate degree of shaping, in which the edges and ends as well as the grinding surface are shaped, is most common. One specimen has pecked finger grips in both edges; one specimen has a pecked finger grip in one edge and a natural depression in the opposite edge; and the upper surface of one was used as a grinding slab. Five of the seven manos of this type were found in Redfield or Romero (Reeve) phase associations, suggesting it was most popular during this period.

The Type IIC specimen is separated from those of Type IIB because of its small size. It was formerly classed as a unifacial rubbing stone until an examination of the grinding surface showed that it had been used for reciprocal rather than rotary grinding. This cobble has been flattened by pecking and grinding on one edge, and the ends bear evidence of hard usage as a hammerstone. The grinding surface is slightly convex and is rounded up slightly on the side near the flattened edge, possibly as a result of wear from the down stroke when the leading edge—in this case the unflattened edge—was raised to allow the grain to be caught under the mano, if modern Hopi practices are comparable (Bartlett 1933:15). In this case, the flattened side could not be interpreted as the equivalent of a finger grip. This specimen occurred in a Redfield or Romero (Reeve) phase context.

The Type IID mano is rectangular and is characterized by opposed, slightly convex grinding surfaces. All of these manos have been shaped by pecking on all surfaces; many have been smoothed by grinding also. One specimen has pecked finger grips on both edges and one grinding surface bears two wear facets (the "adjoining grinding surfaces" of Woodbury [1954:73]). Six of these manos were found in Redfield or Romero (Reeve) phase deposits, one was recovered from a Aravaipa (Sosa) phase context, and two are unplaced. This suggests that Type IID manos were used primarily during the Redfield and Romero phases (Reeve phase).

Five mano fragments were too small to be classified as to type (table 5.6). Only one fragment is of a bifacial, wedge shape not represented by more complete specimens. The others are fragments of unifacial, block-shaped manos.

Two mano blanks are shaped on all surfaces by pecking, but a grinding surface has not yet been started (figure 5.6j, table 5.7). These are block-shaped mano blanks. The third specimen is an unaltered vesicular basalt cobble that was found on the plaza floor in front of Room 16 with a group of manos. The size, shape, and provenience of this specimen suggest that it may have been a mano blank.

Bifacial Mano or Rubbing Stone

D/s105 is a small rectanguloid block of vesicular basalt, 6.3 cm wide, 2.9 cm thick, and originally more

TABLE 5.6 Characteristics of mano fragments from the Davis Ranch Site

Catalog no.	Length	Width	Thickness	Material	Provenience
D/s77	9.0+	6.9	5.5	Granite	NE Trash
D/s78	5.1+	8.5	3.8	Vesicular basalt	NE Trash
D/s99	12.1+	11.2	4.3	Andesite	Room 6 subfloor test
D/s113	14.6+	10.5	3.2	Granite	Room 36 fill
D/s127	10.0+	10.7	4.4	Rhyolite	Kiva fill

Note: All measurements are in cm.

TABLE 5.7 Characteristics of mano blanks from the Davis Ranch Site

Catalog no.	Length	Width	Thickness	Material	Provenience	Figure
D/s56	19.8	14.4	5.4	Vesicular basalt	Plaza in front of Room 16	
D/s92	25.1	11.4	6.8	Vesicular basalt	Room 6 entryway floor	5.6j
D/s114	20.5	12.1	5.6	Andesite	Room 15 fill	

Note: All measurements are in cm.

than 7.4 cm long (figure 5.6k). It is pecked and ground on all surfaces except the fractured end, and all of its ground surfaces are convex. It was recovered from the fill of House 5.

Summary and Discussion

Of the 49 manos recovered at the Davis Ranch Site, 20 were placed in Type I and 21 in Type II. Eighteen of the 20 manos of Type I, those used on a trough metate, are unifacial. Woodbury (1954:67–68) found that the majority of the manos used on trough metates in the Jeddito area are also unifacial and suggested that bifacial manos were not used with greater frequency because to do so would result in faster wear on the mano ends, thus reducing efficiency. His argument is well borne out at the Davis Ranch Site. Type II manos, those used on flat metates, show a strikingly different proportion of unifacial and bifacial types—11 are unifacial and 10 are bifacial.

Finger grips are found on three manos (10% of the Redfield and/or Romero [Reeve] phase manos), all Type II, of which two are unifacial and one is bifacial. The Type II unifacial manos were found on the surface and in the fill of House 7; the Type II bifacial specimen was found on the plaza floor in front of Room 16. Thus, the only association of manos with finger grips is with the Redfield or Romero (Reeve) phase.

[*Editor: Manos with finger grips are an important marker of northern immigrants (Valado 1999). Di Peso (1958b:13) called attention to this fact in his brief article on the Reeve Ruin where 24% of the manos exhibit finger grips (Di Peso 1958a). Finger grips date as early as Basketmaker III or early Pueblo I on the Colorado Plateau and peaked in popularity during the Pueblo III and Pueblo IV periods (Woodbury 1954:67–78, 81, 83, Table 8). Tsegi phase manos in the Kayenta region frequently exhibit this trait (Anderson 1969:187–188; Lindsay 1969:272), which is said to be lacking among Hohokam manos (Haury 1976:282; Sayles 1937:116; Woodbury 1954:83).*]

Twenty-nine of the 41 manos assignable to a type were in use during the Redfield or Romero (Reeve) phase based on provenience and associated materials (table 5.8). Of these 29, 13 are Type I and 16 are Type II. Two Type I manos and one Type II are assigned to the Aravaipa (Sosa) phase; a similar group is assigned to the Hohokam Colonial and Sedentary periods (Davis phase). Six manos are unplaced as to phase.

Rubbing Stones

Rubbing stones are grinding tools held in the hand and used for rubbing on a stationary stone with a rotary motion (figure 5.7, table 5.9). The Type I specimen is a small cobble that has possibly been used on a flat metate. The grinding surface is convex and the cobble is otherwise unshaped. It differs from Type IIB manos for use on a flat metate in being smaller and triangular in shape, and in having been used with a rotary motion. This specimen has been assigned to the Aravaipa (Sosa) phase.

TABLE 5.8 Mano type distribution by time period at the Davis Ranch Site

	Mano type								
Phase(s) or period(s)	IA	IB	IC	ID	IIA	IIB	IIC	IID	Total
Redfield or Romero (Reeve) phase	6	6	1	0	3	5	1	7	29
Aravaipa (Sosa) phase	0	1	0	1	0	0	0	1	3
Colonial or Sedentary period (Davis phase)	1	1	0	0	0	1	0	0	3
Unplaced	1	1	0	1	0	1	0	2	6
Total	**8**	**9**	**1**	**2**	**3**	**7**	**1**	**10**	**41**

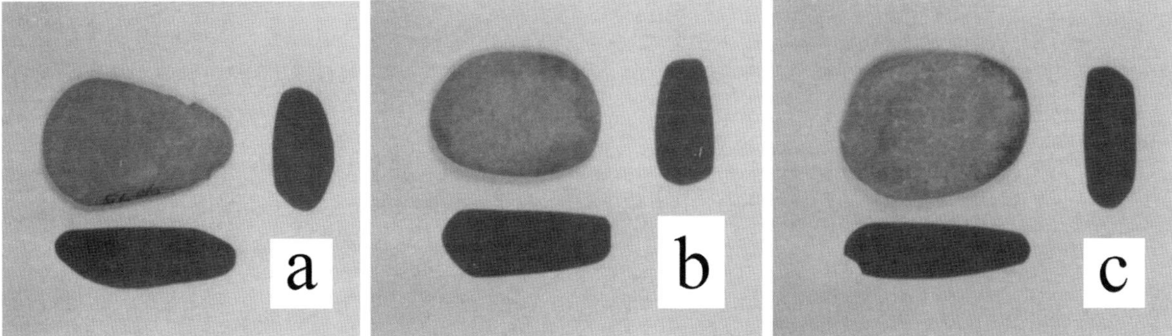

FIGURE 5.7 Rubbing stones: Type I (a) and Type II (b, c). See table D.1 for Amerind Museum catalog numbers and photograph numbers. Not to scale. For measurements, see table 5.9. Courtesy of the Amerind Foundation Inc., Dragoon, Arizona.

TABLE 5.9 Characteristics of rubbing stones from the Davis Ranch Site

Type	Catalog no.	Length	Width	Thickness	Material	Provenience	Figure
I	D/s75	13.7	9.2	4.0	Vesicular basalt	NE Trash	5.7a
II	D/s17	10.8	8.1	4.3	Granite	T23E 10S fill	5.7b
	D/s74	12.7	9.1	3.9	Mica schist	House 6 Pit 1	
	D/s76	9.2+	7.8+	3.3	Basalt	NE Trash	5.7c

Note: All measurements are in cm.

Bifacial Type II rubbing stones may be distinguished from Types ID and IID manos by their small size, irregular shape, opposed but non-parallel grinding surfaces, and use in rotary motion grinding. These are small cobbles whose two larger faces have been flattened somewhat. Their edges and ends show evidence of having been used as hammerstones. Two of these specimens occurred in Aravaipa (Sosa) phase associations and one in Redfield or Romero (Reeve) phase association.

Hammerstones

Hammerstones are cobbles with one or more surfaces battered from use as a pounding tool (figure 5.8, table 5.10). Ten of the hammerstones are from Redfield and Romero (Reeve) phase associations and three are from Aravaipa (Sosa) phase contexts.

Type I hammerstones are waterworn stones bearing numerous flake scars, the sharp edges of which have been battered by pecking and/or hammering without evidence of other use. Any or all of these pounders may have been used with the two mortars found at the site, but since none was found in association with them, it seems preferable to reserve the term "pestle" for the more specialized tool in accordance with the views expressed by Woodbury (1954:95). Four are of such a size and shape as to allow their use in one hand (Type IA), but the others are too large and heavy to be manipulated easily with one hand (Type IB). Type II hammerstones are waterworn pebbles, the ends, edges, and protruding corners of which are battered, and in some cases chipped from use; one or more sides have been smoothed as a result of rubbing action.

[*Editor: A number of the objects identified here as hammerstones are likely better classified as peckingstones,*

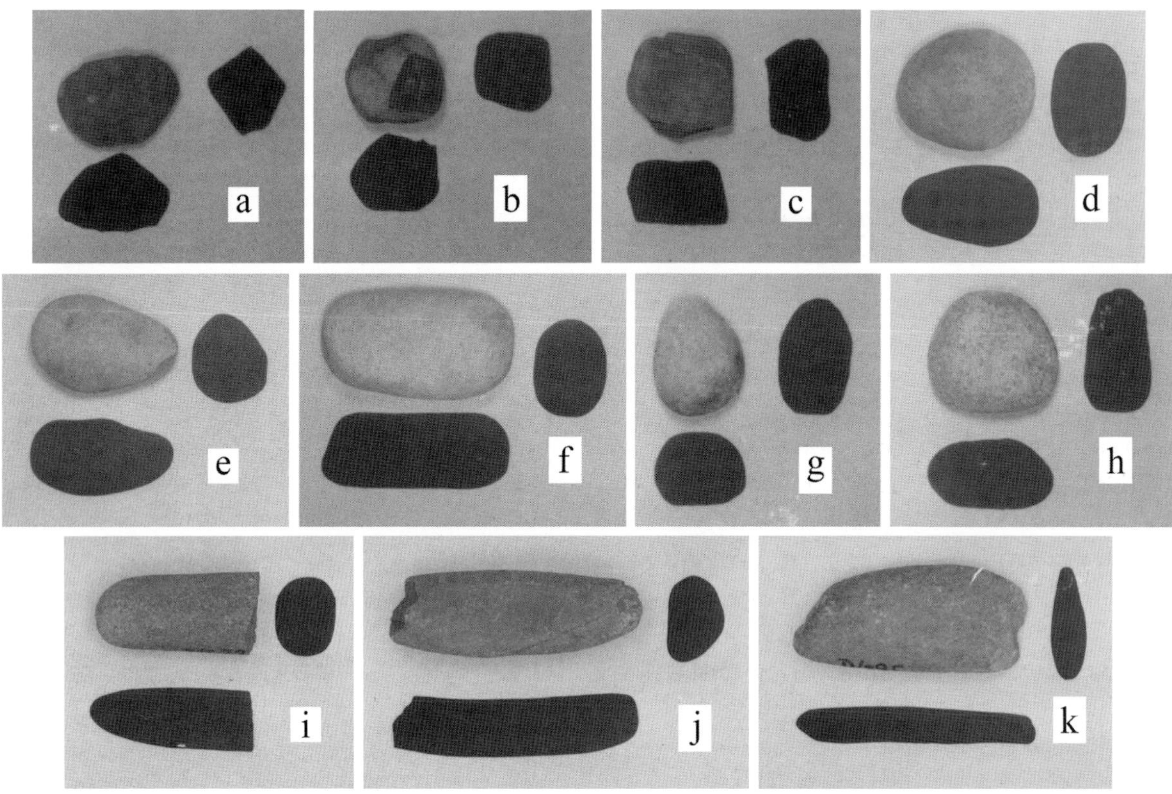

FIGURE 5.8 Hammerstones: Type IA (a–c), Type IB (d–f), and Type II (g–k). See table D.1 for Amerind Museum catalog numbers and photograph numbers. Not to scale. For measurements, see table 5.10. Courtesy of the Amerind Foundation Inc., Dragoon, Arizona.

TABLE 5.10 Characteristics of hammerstones from the Davis Ranch Site

Type	Catalog no.	Length	Width	Thickness	Material	Provenience	Figure
IA	D/s89	10.5	8.4	6.6	Basalt	T31S 8E	5.8a
	D/s94	8.0	7.6	6.1	Basalt	House 7 fill	5.8b
	D/s97	10.4	9.8	8.0	Andesite	Room 6 fill	
	D/s122	9.3	9.3	6.0	Quartzite	T31–32S 7E	5.8c
IB	D/s24	18.8	15.7	10.6	Granite	Room 10 floor, N center	5.8d
	D/s25	16.8	10.8	9.7	Andesite	Room 10 floor, NE center	5.8e
	D/s26	22.0	11.8	8.5	Granite	Room 10 floor, N of entry	5.8f
	D/s73	22.5	10.6	9.3	Vesicular basalt	NE Trash	
II	D/s50	9.9	7.9	6.4	Granite	Room 4 floor, NW corner	5.8g
	D/s64	11.8	10.8	6.6	Granite	Room 19 fill	5.8h
	D/s79	8.5+	4.1	3.1	Quartzite	NE Trash	5.8i
	D/s80	14.5	4.8	3.2	Basalt	NE Trash	5.8j
	D/s95	11.7	5.4	1.9	Gabbro	House 7 fill	5.8k

Note: All measurements are in cm.

tools used to shape manos and metates and to refresh their grinding surfaces. As noted by Adams (2014:156–158), hammerstones and peckingstones are often difficult to separate as they are used in similar percussive activities, resulting in similar use-wear.]

Mortars

Two vesicular basalt boulder mortars were found at the Davis Ranch Site. Neither specimen has been shaped except to form the depression. One mortar, D/s43, was found in a Romero (late Reeve) phase deposit (the fill of the kiva). The other, D/s10, is unplaced in terms of phase (T38E 0, surface; figure 5.9a). D/s43 is 42.0 cm long, 34.0 cm wide, and 32.0 cm tall, with a depression 16.0 × 19.0 cm and 3.7 cm deep. D/s10 is 36.0 cm long, 34.5 cm wide, and 19.0 cm tall, with a depression 12.5 × 13.0 cm and 2.5 cm deep.

Pestle

D/s86 is cylindrical tool, 25.0 cm long, made of porphyritic basalt (figure 5.9b). It is pecked and smoothed on all surfaces. The larger end (7.1–9.1 cm in diameter) is rounded and shows signs of use, while the smaller end (6.3–7.3 cm in diameter) is flattened and shows no evidence of having been used. Having been recovered from the trench in front of Room 21, it is of Redfield or Romero (Reeve) phase association.

Abrading Tools

[*Editor: Woodbury (1954:98, 101; see also Adams 2002:79–91, 2014:81–101) has called attention to the confusing nature of the terminology used to refer to this class of objects. Woodbury and others make a basic distinction between "flat" (i.e., ungrooved) and grooved abraders. Woodbury further subdivides the latter category into simple grooved abraders and shaft smoothers. The distinction between the two reflects the degree of intentional shaping exhibited. Simple grooved abraders are irregular in form, showing little or no intentional shaping, whereas shaft smoothers have been pecked and/or ground to an oval, rectangular, or subrectangular outline and often exhibit shaping on multiple surfaces.*

The term "shaft smoother" is problematic as well. Although Kidder (1932:76–82), Toulouse (1939), and others have separated shaft smoothers (coarse-grained, abrasive material) from shaft straighteners (fine-grained, nonabrasive material) based on raw material texture, Woodbury (1954:101) argues that the line between abrasive and nonabrasive is arbitrarily drawn, and that most implements classified as shaft smoothers or shaft straighteners are suitable for use in both smoothing (sand can be used as the abrasive agent in the groove of a fine-grained tool) and straightening (heat can be applied to any tool, regardless of texture, to facilitate straightening) (see Cosner 1951). Woodbury prefers "shaft smoother" over "shaft straightener" based on the established use of the latter term to refer to perforated bone, antler, or wood objects also known as shaft-wrenches

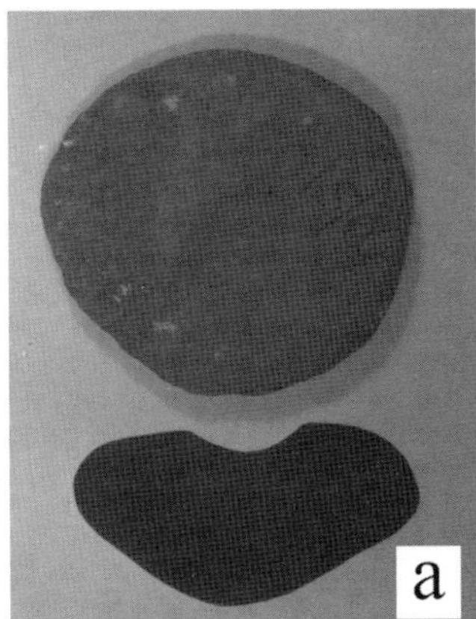

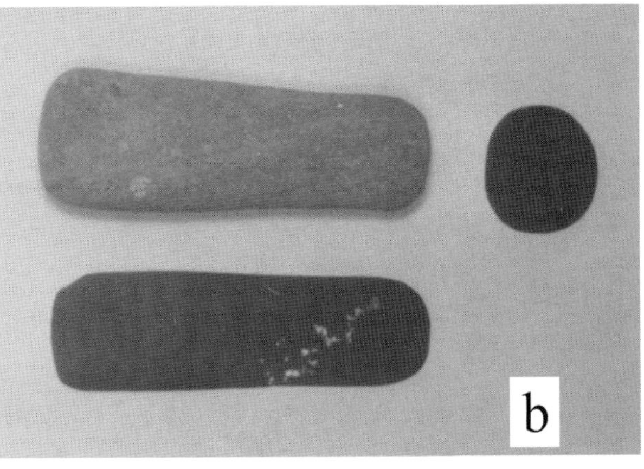

FIGURE 5.9 Mortar (a) and pestle (b). See table D.1 for Amerind Museum catalog numbers and photograph numbers. Not to scale. Measurements in text. Courtesy of the Amerind Foundation Inc., Dragoon, Arizona.

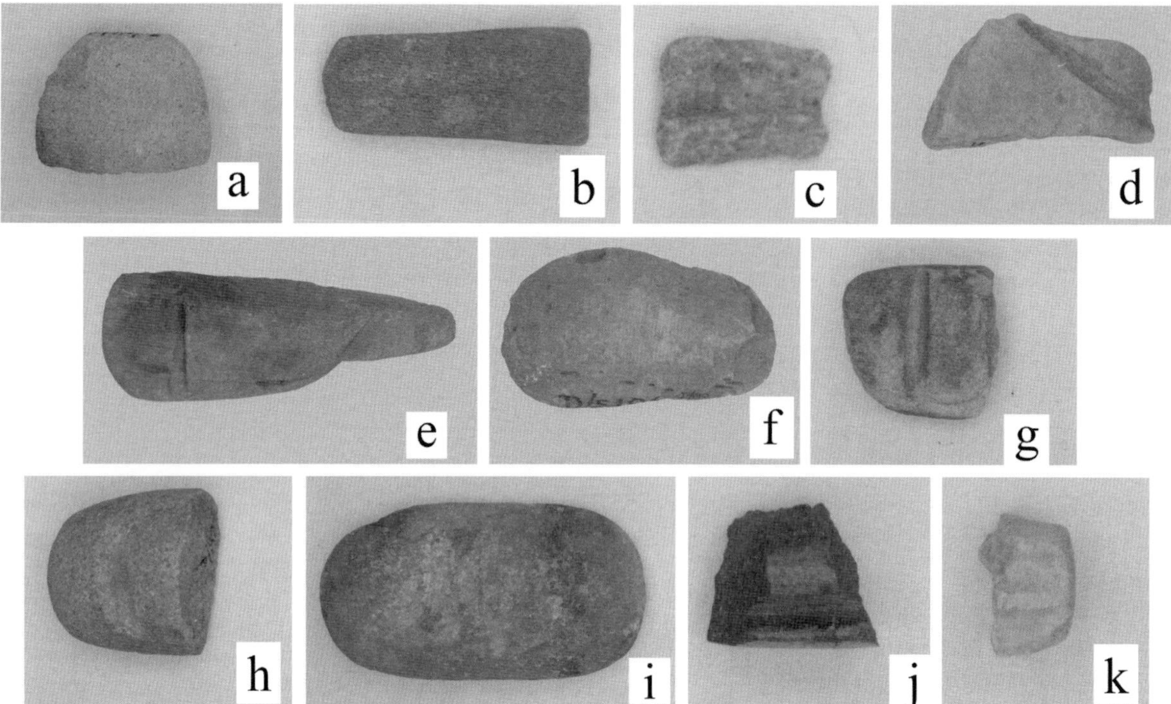

FIGURE 5.10 Flat abrader (a); simple grooved abraders: Type I (b–d) and Type II (e, f); and shaft smoothers/straighteners: Type I (g–i) and Type II (j, k). See table D.1 for Amerind Museum catalog numbers and photograph numbers. Not to scale. For measurements, see text (flat abrader), table 5.11 (simple grooved abraders), and table 5.12 (shaft smoothers/straighteners). Courtesy of the Amerind Foundation Inc., Dragoon, Arizona.

(cf. Adams 2002:84–88, 2014:91–95). The term "shaft smoother/straightener" is used here.]

Flat Abrader

D/121a, recovered from the floor of House 4, is sandstone and has been shaped on all of its unbroken surfaces (figure 5.10a). It is 4.2 cm long, 3.2 cm wide, and 1.1 cm thick. It has two large, flat faces and a convex side that rounds into the flat end. None of the surfaces bear discernible striations, though a small patch of red pigment is present on one face.

Simple Grooved Abraders

Type I simple grooved abraders are tabular pieces of abrasive stone that have been grooved longitudinally and are only slightly shaped or are otherwise unshaped on all surfaces (figure 5.10b–d, table 5.11). The single groove varies in width and depth but tends to be shallow. One specimen has been ground on the sides and another has apparently been chipped or battered into shape on one end. Grooves are U-shaped in cross section, and in most cases the bottom of the groove is not flat longitudinally but may be irregular, concave, or convex.

Type II simple grooved abraders (figure 5.10e, f) are elongated, waterworn pebbles of irregular shape, modified only by the cutting of a single groove in the upper surface and by secondary functions. The groove of one specimen is highly polished. The position of the groove was apparently determined in part by a desire to have the groove on the upper surface of the stone when it was in a stable position. The ends have been used for pecking or pounding, and the upper face of one of these specimens has been used to a slight extent in the area near the groove as an abrading stone.

TABLE 5.11 Characteristics of simple grooved abraders from the Davis Ranch Site

	Catalog	Artifact			Groove					
Type	no.	Length	Width	Thickness	Length	Width	Thickness	Material	Provenience	Figure
I	D/100b	10.2	4.4	1.8				Sandstone	Burial 8	5.10b
	D/153a	5.8	4.5	1.2	5.6	1.1	0.4	Pumice	Room 2 floor	5.10c
	D/162	6.0+	5.0	1.6	4.8+	0.4	0.1	Sandstone	Trench in front of Room 9	
	D/s87	11.5	6.4+	4.2		1.3	0.6	Sandstone	Room 19 fill	5.10d
II	D/155	15.7	5.6	2.9	4.6	1.0	0.4	Schist	Room 3 wall, SE corner	5.10e
	D/190	13.8	8.1	5.2	3.0	1.7	0.4	Vesicular basalt	Trench in front of Room 2	5.10f

Note: All measurements are in cm.

Although the Type II simple grooved abraders exhibit very little evidence of intentional alteration aside from their grooves, the pebbles chosen for this use are similar in both outline and cross section to the finished forms of the intentionally shaped shaft smoothers/straighteners described below. All simple grooved abraders were found in Redfield and Romero (Reeve) phase associations.

Shaft Smoothers/Straighteners

Shaft smoothers/straighteners are loaf-shaped stones of a variety of materials having two grooves of rounded cross section and of a size to accommodate slender shafts of wood or cane, for abrasion and/or for heat straightening (figure 5.10g–k, table 5.12). Type I encompasses transversely grooved shaft smoothers/straighteners. All three have or had two parallel grooves and a flattened lower surface; none of the grooves is highly polished. In two cases, the groove bears red pigment. One specimen is shaped on all surfaces, the second apparently has been shaped on one surface other than the grinding surface, and the third, a waterworn cobble, has been shaped on the grinding surface only. The grinding surfaces on all three have been shaped by pecking to a flat plane. The ends of the complete specimen bear marks as though it was occasionally used as a peckingstone. The flattened lower surfaces of two specimens may have been used for grinding. All Type I shaft smoothers/straighteners were found in Redfield or Romero (Reeve) phase associations.

Type II shaft smoothers/straighteners are longitudinally grooved and shaped overall. Each is flattened on its lower surface, with two grooves on the upper surface running the length of the stone. The grooves of the micaceous schist specimen are highly polished in the portions accessible to a rounded shaft, while the deeper portion of the groove still exhibits longitudinal striations resulting from the shaping procedure. The grooves are slightly polished, but the material probably will not take a high polish. Both specimens of this type were found in Redfield or Romero (Reeve) phase associations.

Summary and Discussion

If the flattened bottom surfaces of some Type I shaft smoothers/straighteners were used for grinding, this would not be a unique situation. Similar specimens have been found at Babocomari Village (Di Peso 1951a:174, Types 1 and 2), Tres Alamos (Amerind Museum collection), Reeve Ruin (Di Peso 1958a:113–114, Figure 17, Plate 71c), and Paloparado (Di Peso 1956:496–497). The attribution of a grinding function to the lower surfaces of these tools is reinforced by finding red pigment in the crevices on two specimens from the Davis Ranch Site, one from Babocomari Village, five from Tres Alamos, and four from Paloparado (see also Rinaldo 1974a:86). This combination of grinding and straightening functions in one tool suggests that red pigment was used on the shaft that was straightened, possibly as decoration on an arrow shaft.

All the simple grooved abraders and all of the shaft smoothers/straighteners were found in Redfield or Romero (Reeve) phase contexts. This is consistent with previous analyses of the distributions of these artifact types (Haury 1945:139, 1976:285–286; Toulouse 1939; Woodbury 1954:104, 110–111 [*Editor: see also Adams 2002:88–91, 2014:92–93*]).

[*Editor: Haury (1945:139) and Di Peso (1958a:113–114) specifically attribute the much longer history of grooved abraders north of the Mogollon Rim and their abrupt appearance in central and southern Arizona to the movement of people from north to south. Both use the term "Salado" to label these immigrants, but it is important to note that simple grooved abraders date as early as Basketmaker III or Pueblo I in the Kayenta region. In addition, both simple grooved abraders and shaft smoother/straighteners regularly occur in Kayenta region deposits of the Pueblo III and Pueblo IV periods (e.g., Anderson 1969:189–190, Figure 111 upper left and upper right; Beals et al. 1945:79, Figure 16n; Fewkes 1898:731, Plate 169a, b, 1904:103; Guernsey 1931:Plate 28; Hough 1903:322, 338, 343, Plate 55; Woodbury 1954:103, 106–108, 110–111). Simple grooved abraders and shaft smoothers/straighteners like those described above have been recovered from deposits of roughly equivalent age at Reeve Ruin (Di Peso*

TABLE 5.12 Characteristics of shaft smoothers/straighteners from the Davis Ranch Site

Type	Catalog no.	Artifact			Groove(s)			Material	Provenience	Figure
		Length	Width	Thickness	Length	Width	Thickness			
I	D/76		6.7	3.3	5.6	1.5	0.6	Sandstone	Kiva fill	5.10g
	D/82	6.7+	6.3	4.6	4.5	1.6	0.5	Sandstone	Room 9 floor, center of S wall	5.10h
	D/86	15.3	7.8	3.6	4.9	1.6	0.4	Sandstone	Trench in front of Room 10	5.10i
					4.8	1.2	0.5			
II	D/62	4.5+	3.3+	4.2	4.5+	1.0	0.7	Micaceous schist	Kiva level 3	5.10j
	D/65	2.3+	3.1+	3.4	2.3+	1.0	0.4	Andesite	Room 7 fill	5.10k
					2.3+	0.9	0.4			

Note: All measurements are in cm.

1958a:113–114, Figure 17, Plate 71), Tres Alamos (Tuthill 1947:75–76, Plate 26), Babocomari Village (Di Peso 1951a:173–176, Plate 65), and Paloparado (Di Peso 1956:496–497, Figures 72, 78, Plate 131).]

Axe

Nomenclature used in this section is adapted from Kidder (1932:45) by Woodbury (1954:25–26). A single three-quarter-groove axe, D/100a, is represented in the Davis Ranch Site collection (figure 5.11a). Made of dacite, it is 12.9 cm long, 5.9 cm wide, and 3.8 cm thick. It was recovered from Burial 8 with what appears to be a bow-and-arrow-making kit.

The axe has been regrooved; two three-quarter grooves are present. A cross section of the bit near the groove resembles a flattened oval. A large chip has been knocked out of the inner half of the edge. The poll is relatively flat though still convex and is pitted as though from use as a hammerstone. The face of the poll has been removed by the pecking of the secondary groove in the same direction as the first. This groove is unpolished and apparently unworn, while the primary groove, which is located in the more normal position, about one-third of the way from the poll end toward the bit, is polished, possibly from wear, over portions of the remaining inner one-third. The edge of this primary groove nearest the bit has been removed by pecking but is not polished. There is a slight amount of pecking in the vicinity of the flake scar on the bit as though this axe was in the process of being resharpened. There is no evidence of a wedge channel on the inner side. [*Editor: A wedge channel (Haury 1945:131) or "wedge groove" (Adams 2002:168, Figure 7.5b; see also Fulton 1934a:22, Plate 19a, 1938:16–17, Plate 21a; Fulton and Tuthill 1940:28, Plate 17b, c) is a small, linear depression carved into the inner side of an axe head, in the area where the handle attaches. This depression is designed to hold a wooden peg or wedge inserted between the axe head and the handle, tightening and securing the handle's grip on the head.*]

Mauls

D/107 and D/163 are diorite three-quarter-groove axes reused as mauls (figure 5.11b, c). D/107, re-

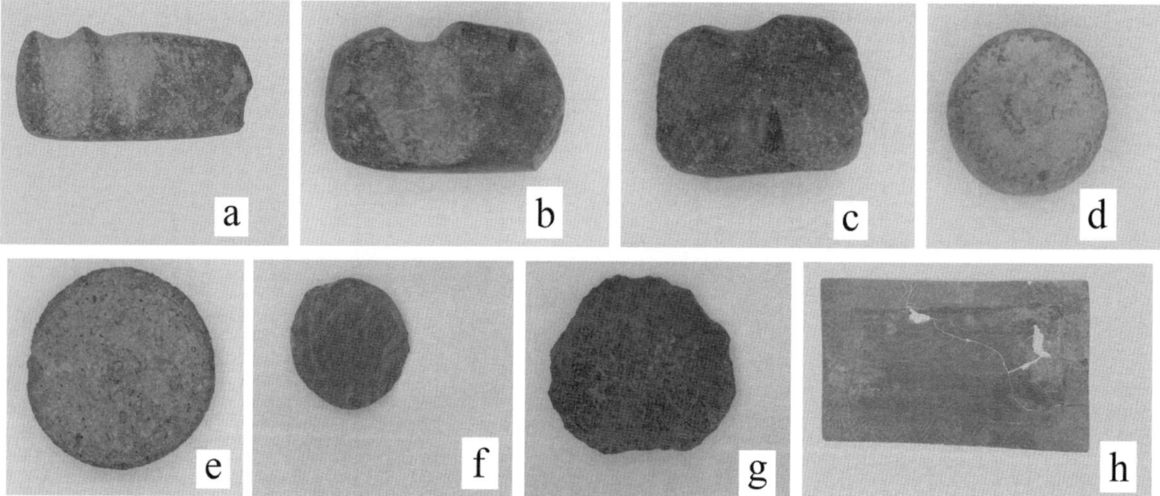

FIGURE 5.11 Axe (a); mauls (b, c); stone disks: Type I (d, e) and Type II (f, g); and palette (h). See table D.1 for Amerind Museum catalog numbers and photograph numbers. Not to scale. For measurements, see text (axe and mauls), table 5.13 (stone disks), and table 5.14 (palette). Courtesy of the Amerind Foundation Inc., Dragoon, Arizona.

covered from the fill of Room 21, is 10.9 cm long, 6.6 cm wide, and 5.5 cm thick. Its groove is 3.0 cm wide and 0.7 cm deep. D/163, found outside the compound wall at T19–25E 18–20S, is 7.6 cm long, 5.6 cm wide, and 5.1 cm thick. Its groove is 2.5 cm wide and 0.4 cm deep. The larger tool, D/107, is more nearly rectangular in cross section than the smaller. The groove of one maul is polished. Neither bears a wedge channel and neither had been regrooved.

Disks

There are two plain disks, Type I (figure 5.11d, e). These were apparently pecked and ground on the edges until almost perfectly round. The upper and lower surfaces have been flattened somewhat and bear a pecked depression in the center of both surfaces. They are assigned to the Hohokam Colonial and Sedentary periods (Davis phase) and the Aravaipa (Sosa) phase.

Two of these specimens are pitted disks, Type II (figure 5.11f, g, table 5.13). One has been ground to shape around half of the perimeter; the other has been chipped to shape. One specimen is assigned to the Aravaipa (Sosa) phase and one is unplaced.

[*Editor: Adams (2014:98–100, 206, 229–231) discusses a number of recorded and inferred uses for unperforated stone disks. Similar objects were used as lids for ceramic vessels, as floor polishers, and as projectiles in a traditional Zuni game (Culin 1907:726–727).*]

Palettes

[*Editor: Gerald's descriptions of "palettes" and a "proto-palette" follow the conventions of the 1950s, including the nomenclature introduced by Haury (1937b). In the discussion that follows, updated information regarding the probable function(s) of these objects and the temporal placement of the Davis Ranch Site specimens is presented.*]

The only complete palette recovered (D/141d) is made from a large sheet of schist (figure 5.11h, table 5.14). The bottom of the specimen is unmodified except by the original splitting of the stone, while the edges and ends have been ground smooth and the upper surface has been excavated, leaving an incised border around the perimeter. The incised design is that of a zigzag line going all the way around the border; the resulting triangles are hatched, and the hatching in adjacent triangles is at right angles. The grinding surface, which is smoothed in the center but is not depressed, is 0.1 cm below the raised border.

Two corner fragments of schist palettes both have raised borders. One specimen (D/157a) has deeply sawed notches in the upper outside corner of the border, an unsmoothed bottom, and a scored, poorly finished grinding surface. The second fragment (D/118) is smoothed and polished on all unfractured surfaces. The outside upper corner of the border bears a number of shallow, irregularly spaced, incised notches, and the upper face of the border exhibits two parallel incised lines, which may have gone all the way around the perimeter of the palette.

TABLE 5.13 Characteristics of stone disks from the Davis Ranch Site

Type	Catalog no.	Diameter	Thickness	Material	Provenience	Figure
I	D/141a	6.7	3.9	Rhyolite	Cremation 1	5.11d
	D/173a	12.2	4.6	Vesicular basalt	T64N 1W to 40N 13W	5.11e
II	D/57	3.7	0.4	Schist	Surface	5.11f
	D/170f	6.8	0.6	Rhyolite	NE Trash	5.11g

Note: All measurements are in cm.

TABLE 5.14 Characteristics of palettes from the Davis Ranch Site

Catalog no.	Artifact Length	Artifact Width	Artifact Thickness	Border width	Material	Provenience	Figure
D/118	2.2+	2.1+	0.6	1.2	Schist	House 3 fill	
D/141d	19.3	11.6	0.5	1.9	Schist	Cremation 1	5.11h
D/157a	5.3+	2.8+	0.4	1.0	Schist	Room 4 subfloor test	

Note: All measurements are in cm.

Discussion

[*Editor: White's (2004) study of Hohokam palettes addressed function as well as spatial and temporal variability in form and decoration. He has also introduced a revised nomenclature for the description and discussion of this class of objects. White concludes that most specimens identified as palettes were not used in the preparation of paints, but rather were employed in mortuary ritual involving the melting of lead compounds, as previously suggested by Haury (1976:288; see also Hawley 1937).*

White's nomenclature, which replaces Haury's (1937b), reflects the inference that these objects were not typically used to make paints. White suggests that archaeologists refer to the objects currently known as Hohokam palettes by using the term "tablet." In addition, he asserts that the area of the artifact formerly referred to as the "grinding surface" should be called the "basin." Based on patterns described by White (see also Haury 1937b, 1976), D/141d dates to the Sedentary period (given the motifs incised along its borders), and D/118 and D/157a date to the Colonial period (given the notches they exhibit).

White (2004:Table 6.2a) reports 21 tablets from Tres Alamos and seven from the K.E.G. Site, both in the San Pedro Valley. All of these have been assigned to the Sedentary period by White. Additional, fragmentary examples have been recovered from Second Canyon Ruin (AZ BB:11:20[ASM]; Franklin 1980:151–152, Figure 40). Franklin describes these as typical of the Hohokam Colonial period.]

Protopalette

D/144b, recovered from the fill of the kiva, is a thin slab of schist with one smoothed edge and grinding depressions on both faces that are partially covered with red pigment. It was originally more than 6.9 cm long and more than 6.1 cm wide. It is 0.8 cm thick.

Tabular Tools

[*Editor: Gerald classified five objects as "hoes," following then-current convention (Di Peso 1958a:110–111, Figure 16, Plate 69; Haury 1945:134–136, Figure 79, 1950:258–260, Figure 49; Jackson and Van Valkenburgh 1954:28, Photo 34; Tuthill 1947:75, Plate 27). By the 1960s, such artifacts were referred to as "mescal knives" or "agave knives" (Franklin 1980:148–150, Figure 39; Pierson 1962:50–52, Plate 10d, e; Steen 1962:25, Plate 10c; Teague 1981:225, 227, Figure 135; Windmiller 1972:13, 1974:14, 25, 36, Figures 6f, g, 11a–d). Some researchers attribute this change in archaeological terminology to Hayden's (1957:142–146) observation that many so-called hoes lack use-wear transverse to the apparent working edge and instead exhibit wear parallel to the edge, as if employed in slicing or sawing. Steen's (1962:25) remark that these objects are most abundant in areas within or near the current range of agave likely played a part as well.*

By the 1970s, the term "tabular knife" was also regularly applied to this class of objects (Bayham 1976:

FIGURE 5.12 Tabular tools: Type II (a, b), Type IIIA (c, d), and Type IIIB (e). See table D.1 for Amerind Museum catalog numbers and photograph numbers. Not to scale. For measurements, see table 5.15. Courtesy of the Amerind Foundation Inc., Dragoon, Arizona.

224–225, Plate 22a; Doyel 1974:79–81, 1977:18, 53, 56, Figure 28, 1978:38, 61, 106, 127, 146, 168, 178, 188–189, Figures 11, 40, 44, 53; McGuire 1975:70–73, Figure 45; Teague 1980:299–300, 305, Figure 151). Work over the last 30 years has increasingly resulted in support for the inference that tabular knives (or tabular tools) were used to harvest and/or process agave (Bernard-Shaw 1983, 1988, 1990; Bowen 1993; Doyel 1974:81; Fish et al. 1992; Greenwald 1988:179–183; Huntington 1986:265).

Ten objects are classified here as tabular tools (figure 5.12, table 5.15). The more inclusive word "tool" is used, reflecting the likelihood that the "tabular knife" category includes objects used for scraping as well as slicing (see below). In addition to the five Gerald previously referred to as hoes, three fragments and two additional complete tabular tool specimens have been identified. One of the fragments and two of the complete specimens were recovered during the 1965 excavations. The others were previously classified as flake knives.

Type I tabular tools are roughly semilunar (or nearly triangular) in outline. Each exhibits a straight working edge. Both specimens have been retouched along one side to create a blunted edge suitable for gripping. It appears that the working edge of one (D/s85) may originally have been created as a result of grinding. This edge has also been retouched or resharpened via flaking. Most of the retouch (resharpening?) scars were driven from one face, although a few originated from the opposite face. The working edge of the other specimen (D/s130) is not retouched, although small flake scars likely resulting from use are present. Both objects were manufactured from rhyolite flakes. The flat surfaces of D/s85 exhibit traces of red pigment but lack clearly identifiable traces of use as a nether stone.

Type II tabular tools, both of which were made from pieces of rhyolite, exhibit the same outline shape characteristic of Type I. The working edges of Type II specimens, however, are convex. One specimen (D/186b) has been bifacially flaked along most of its perimeter, creating a

TABLE 5.15 Characteristics of tabular tools from the Davis Ranch Site

Type	Catalog no.	Length	Width	Thickness	Material	Provenience	Figure
I	D/s130	14.9	10.7	1.6	Rhyolite	Room 46 floor	
	D/s85	9.9	6.2	0.9	Rhyolite	Between Rooms 15 and 16	
II	D/186b	10.1	6.6	0.8	Rhyolite	T21–22W 31–32S	5.12a
	D/s13	6.7	4.2	0.6	Rhyolite	Kiva fill	5.12b
IIIA	D/144a	10.4+	9.4	0.6	Schist	Kiva fill	5.12c
	D/s2	13.5	6.0	1.5	Schist	T1S 30–46E	5.12d
IIIB	D/187	9.4	7.0	0.7	Basalt	T15W 12–13N	5.12e
IV	D/s131	12.7	8.7	1.2	Schist	Room 46 floor	

Note: All measurements are in cm.

sharp working edge opposite a blunt edge suitable for gripping. Most of one face of this object is covered with red pigment and bears striations. Both traces suggest that this face was used for pigment grinding. The opposite face exhibits a depressed area, created as a result of grinding, which measures 3.5 × 4.7 cm and about 0.5 mm in depth. The depression bears numerous striations and a small, red stain similar in color to the red pigment adhering to the other face of the tool.

Although D/s13 has a semilunar outline, achieved through flaking around most of its perimeter, it may be a reworked fragment of a larger tabular tool. Its convex working edge is bifacially flaked. Retouch has sharpened most of the edge. One portion, however, has been blunted. The opposite, straight edge appears to have been originally created by snapping. It has been dulled via flaking and perhaps some grinding. Both instances of dulling were likely intended to facilitate gripping the tool.

Type IIIA tabular tools are subrectangular in outline and exhibit straight or slightly convex working edges. D/s2 is made of schist and is flaked along much of its perimeter. Its retouched working edge (one of the two longer edges) is marked by numerous flake scars that are likely the result of use. The edge opposite the working edge has been blunted via flaking, creating a surface suitable for holding. D/144a, also made of schist, is a fragment of a larger tool. Its working edge has been created through grinding. The opposite edge and a portion of one of the adjacent edges have been blunted via bifacial flaking. The working edge bears flake scars likely resulting from use rather than sharpening or resharpening.

The single specimen of Type IIIB (D/187) is a flat, subrectangular, fine-grained basalt tool with a working edge formed by grinding along one of the long sides. A series of carefully made, narrow, and closely spaced notches was cut into the working edge, creating fine serrations. Subsequent use has dulled and rounded the serrations. There is also one small chip out of this edge, and the entire tool had been snapped in half. Just below each end of the long side opposite the cutting edge is a broad, shallow notch. This edge and both ends of this specimen have been dulled, as a result of flaking. The two broad notches exhibited by this tool were likely designed to facilitate hafting.

The single Type IV tabular tool (D/s131) has an outline shape approaching that of a teardrop and a convex working edge. The working edge is along the widest portion of the tool (the bottom of the teardrop) and was created as a result of flaking and grinding. A dark polish is evident on both flat surfaces, extending 1.0 cm (maximum) from the working edge on one and 1.5 cm (maximum) on the other. Both of these surfaces also exhibit red pigment. The sides of this object have been blunted by flake removals and the same is true of the top. The edges of the sides and the top exhibit rounding, perhaps as a result of hafting or being gripped during use. The remnant of a very large step-fracture is present on one of the surfaces, near the top. This fracture created a ledge that would have facilitated gripping and/or hafting, and its edge exhibits rounding and polish.

Two tabular tool fragments were recovered. D/s132, found on the floor of Room 33, is a very thin, subtriangular piece from near the convex working edge of a larger rhyolite tool. It is 5.3 cm long, 3.5 cm wide, and 0.5 cm thick. The portion of the working edge present has been chipped and ground to make it sharp. There is some edge rounding and polish (which extends a maximum of 0.4 cm back from the edge) likely related to use.

D/144h, recovered from the fill of the kiva, is a nearly rectangular portion of a larger rhyolite tool that had either a straight or a convex working edge. It is 8.6 cm long, 2.9 cm wide, and 1.0 cm thick. The part of the working edge present (one of the longer sides) is not retouched. Flake scars resulting from use are present, however. The flat edge opposite the working edge appears to have been produced when the larger tool was snapped. Subsequently, a few small flakes were driven off a portion of this flat surface, toward the working edge. Perhaps this represents secondary shaping of the fragmentary tool for continued use or reuse.]

Discussion

[*Editor: Implements similar in shape to the Type IIIB tabular tool, both hafted and unhafted, have been recovered from many sites in southern Arizona (Di Peso 1958a:110–111, Plate 69; Franklin 1980:148–149, Figure 39; Haury 1945:135, Figure 79; Hayden 1957: 142–146, Plate 28e, f; Hough 1930:8, Plate 7; McGuire 1975:70, Figure 45a, b; Pierson 1962:50–52, Plate 10d; Steen 1962:25, Plate 10c).*]

The Amerind Museum has in its collections a hafted implement (No. 132 in the general catalog) quite similar to this that came from a cave in Redfield Canyon, a few miles northeast of the Davis Ranch Site. This specimen is hafted in the manner of an axe with a small stick twisted twice about the stone, utilizing the notches, and both ends of the stick tied together with bark to form a handle. The handle is burned so its entire length cannot be determined, but the 26 cm long portion remaining is apparently too flexible for the tool to have served efficiently as a chopping implement, though the edge has been chipped in a few places as though from use. [*Editor: It is important to note that some hafted tabular tools lack notches (e.g., Hohmann and Eshbaugh 1988:100, Figure 46).*

Ethnographic work among the Chiricahua Apache, Havasupai, Mescalero Apache, Tohono O'odham, Hualapai, Western Apache, and Yavapai (Castetter et al. 1938; Ferg 2003; Gifford 1932; Mekeel 1935; Spier 1928), interviews with Tipai individuals (Rogers 1939: 50–51), and an ethnoarchaeological study among the Otomí of central Mexico (Parsons and Parsons 1985, 1990) have resulted in a model of the types of activities and tools associated with harvesting agave for food and processing its leaves to extract fiber. Key activities include severing leaves, detaching lateral spines and distal thorns from them, and removing the epidermis and pulp to expose the fibers. Slicing, chopping, and scraping activities such as these have implications for tool design related to choice of material, edge angle, and edge shape.

Historically, many native southwestern and Great Basin groups employed the "mescal knife," or "mescal hatchet," a hafted slicing and/or chopping tool with a blade made of scavenged metal, in leaf removal (Baldwin 1944; Ferg 2003; Harrington 1930:119–120, Figure 11). The Otomí use a specially designed, metal-bladed implement called a "tajadera" *(Parsons and Parsons 1990:28, 152, Figures 21, 22). Stone tools, hafted or unhafted, were also used for this purpose by many of these same groups, including the Havasupai, Tohono O'odham, Western Apache, and Yavapai (Castetter et al. 1938:28, 48–49, 52; Ferg 2003:36; Gifford 1932:225; Mekeel 1935:48–53; Spier 1928:105).*

Ethnographic analogs for agave fiber extraction via planing are available. Among the Tipai, scraper planes (also known as "pulping planes"; Fish et al. 1992:84, Figure 7.13) were employed for this purpose (Rogers 1939:50–51, Plate 11c; see also Kowta 1969:54; Rogers 1929). Experimental archaeology offers corroborating evidence (Bernard-Shaw 1990; Fish et. al 1992:84; Hester and Heizer 1972; Salls 1985).

The Otomí of central Mexico use a hafted scraping tool with a metal blade to extract maguey fiber (Parsons and Parsons 1990:148–149, Figure 14, Plates 89, 90). There is evidence to suggest, however, that such tools formerly had stone blades among the Otomí as well as the Aztecs (Montell 1937:312, Figure 6; Parsons and Parsons 1990:300). Stone scrapers the same shape as those referred to as agave knives in the Southwest are frequently recovered in the archaeological sites of central Mexico, where they have been linked to fiber production and are referred to as "azadas" *(Brumfiel 1976:102–103; Parsons and Parsons 1990:299–302, 361, Figure 38).*

Seven of the 10 tabular tools were found in Redfield or Romero (Reeve) phase deposits. The other three cannot be placed chronologically. The recovery of so many tabular tools, presumably designed for agave procurement and processing, from late Classic period contexts is odd. A recent synthesis presented by Clark, Diehl, and others (2012) shows—based on the distribution and dating of rockpile fields, agave remains identified in flotation samples, and tabular tools—that agave production peaked in the San Pedro Valley during the late Sedentary period and the early Classic period. The results reported in this same study suggest very little, if any, production of agave during the late Classic period. In fact, agave is absent from all of the 76 analyzed flotation samples taken from late Classic period contexts, within 21 sites, that yielded food remains. Taken together, these facts, along with evidence that two of the Davis Ranch Site tabular tools appear to have been reused for pigment processing, suggest that the presence of these objects in late Classic period deposits reflects scavenging of tools manufactured and originally used by the site's Colonial and/or Sedentary period inhabitants.]

Stone Vessels

Type I stone vessels are round (figure 5.13a–c, table 5.16). Two with rounded sides are classified as Type IA. They were shaped by pecking and grinding but are not polished, and each has a vertical-walled and concave-bottomed depression pecked into one of its flattened surfaces. The rim of one is rounded, while the other's is relatively sharp. Neither vessel is flat enough on the bottom to prevent its rocking back and forth when tipped, but their low centers of gravity due to their thick bottoms tends to hold them upright. The fragmentary specimen (D/141b) was apparently intentionally broken and placed with Cremation 1.

Type IB vessels are cylindrical. The complete, reconstructed specimen (D/143b), found in association with Cremation 3, is a short cylinder with a slightly convex bottom that is rounded where it joins the sides. The rim is thick, almost flat, and bears a groove in the center. One portion of the rim bears a crudely incised crosshatch/diamond design; no evidence of this design is found on other rim fragments. The diameter of the depression decreases slightly toward the bottom, which is concave. This vessel was shaped by pecking and grinding but was not polished. It apparently went through the crematory fire, as some of the pieces are cracked and distorted.

The fragmentary specimen of this type is a small section with a flat bottom and slightly flaring side connected by an abrupt but not sharp corner. The side and bottom are relatively smooth though not polished, while the depression's surface still bears pecking marks. The side is incised with diamond crosshatching.

Type II is a shallow, block-shaped vessel that has been shaped by pecking (figure 5.13d). Only one surface is smooth; it is weathered more than the other surfaces and therefore the texture may be a result of natural processes. The bottom is relatively flat on its long axis and convex on its short axis. The shallow, oval depression is rough and shows little evidence of having been used.

Each of the Type III vessels is unique in form (figure 5.13e, f). D/170g is a fragment of an apparently large, well-finished, relatively shallow vessel. The side and bottom are both slightly convex and are roughly paralleled by the side and bottom of the depression. The rim is rounded inward to a relatively sharp edge. D/191 may be a fragment of an effigy vessel, though it is too incomplete to be certain. The

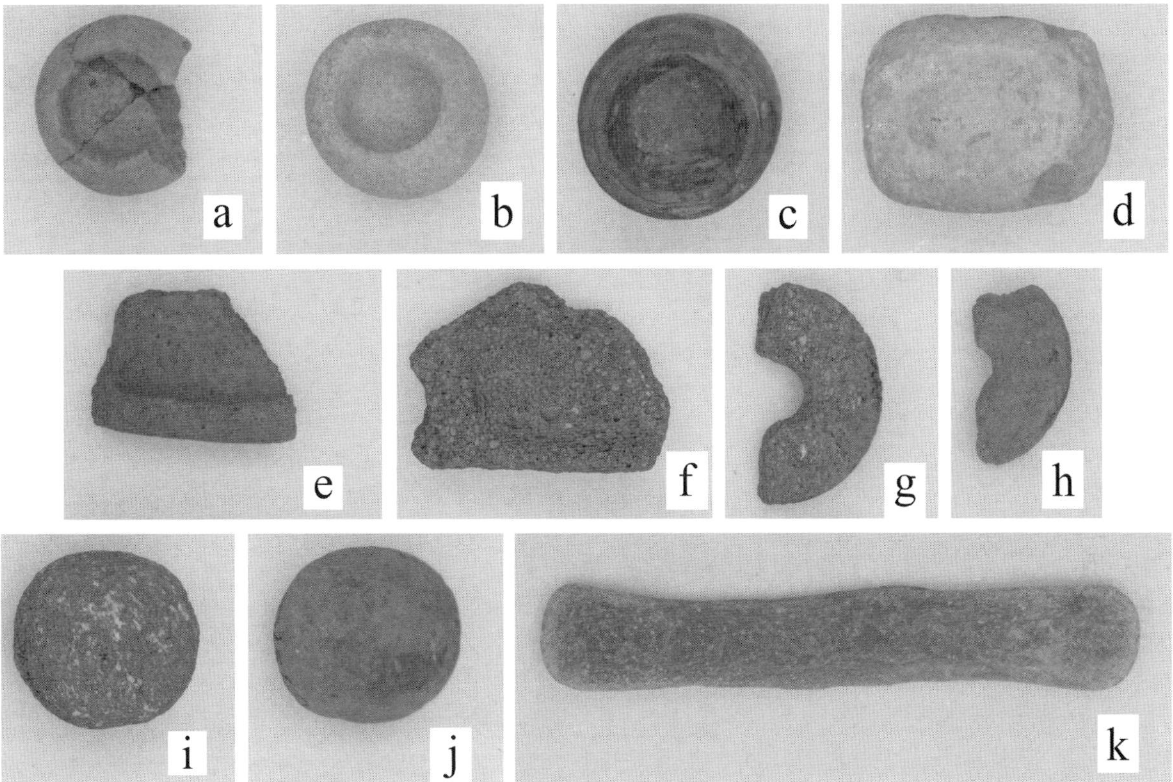

FIGURE 5.13 Stone vessels: Type IA (a, b), Type IB (c), Type II (d), and Type III (e, f); stone rings (g, h); stone balls (i, j); and unclassified stone artifact (k). See table D.1 for Amerind Museum catalog numbers and photograph numbers. Not to scale. For stone vessel measurements, see table 5.16. Other measurements in text. Courtesy of the Amerind Foundation Inc., Dragoon, Arizona.

projecting corner is formed by a straight side and a concave end. The stone's vesicles are large, but the unfractured surfaces are relatively smooth, and the convex bottom is rounded up to join the side and end. The bottom of the depression appears to have been slightly concave but is rounded up to join the side and end so there is no break between bottom and sides or end. The rim is rounded.

[*Editor: Shallow, rectanguloid or ovoid vessels, most often made of vesicular basalt, have been referred to as "stone trays" (Adams 2002:221–223; Ferg 1997, 1998). Many have carefully shaped projections at their corners or ends, and these been labeled "knobbed stone trays." The Type III vessels described above are pieces of stone trays, and D/191 is a corner fragment of a knobbed tray. Available evidence, based on use-wear analysis, residues, and associations, indicates that these objects were used as mortars for stone-on-stone grinding using pestles (Adams 2006, 2015; Ferg 1998). Some of this grinding involved red pigments. Although Ferg (1998) reports examples from a number of sites postdating AD 1200, Adams's (2015:Table 3.28) study of the temporal distribution of stone trays strongly suggests that these objects are diagnostic of the Early Agricultural period (ca. 2100 BC–AD 50) and the Early Ceramic period (Agua Caliente phase, ca. AD 50–500). Nearly 90% of the stone trays in Adams's comparative sample, from 16 Tucson Basin sites from the Early Agricultural period through the late Classic period, were recovered from Early Agricultural period contexts (82% of these were assignable to the Cienega and late San Pedro phases). The remainder were found in Early Ceramic period deposits. It is*

TABLE 5.16 Characteristics of stone vessels from the Davis Ranch Site

Type	Catalog no.	Body			Wall thickness	Basin			Material	Provenience	Figure
		Length	Width	Height		Length	Width	Depth			
IA	D/141b	7.1		4.7	2.7	4.3		2.2	Vesicular basalt	Cremation 1	5.13a
	D/143a	7.2		4.4	1.5	4.2		2.6	Andesite	Cremation 3	5.13b
IB	D/143b	9.0		5.6	1.5	6.1		4.5	Sandstone	Cremation 3	5.13c
	D/180				2.2				Sandstone	T1S 54–61E	
II	D/111	12.5	9.8	6.8		7.3	5.5	1.4	Tuff	Room 36 fill	5.13d
III	D/170g				1.5				Vesicular basalt	NE Trash	5.13e
	D/191				3.4				Vesicular basalt	House 6 Pit 1	5.13f

Note: All measurements are in cm.

reasonable to suggest that specimens found in later contexts, such as those discussed by Ferg (1998), represent objects that had been scavenged from earlier deposits.]

Stone Rings

These specimens were apparently shaped by pecking and grinding, thus forming relatively flat upper and lower surfaces and, in cross section, somewhat flattened circumferential surfaces (figure 5.13g, h). The perforations were made by pecking from both sides. The smallest diameter of the perforation is in both cases near the center of the disk, but not in the exact center.

D/170d is 10.2 cm in diameter, 3.5 cm thick, and has a perforation 2.8 cm in diameter. D/170e had a diameter of more than 3.7 cm, a perforation in excess of 1.6 cm in diameter, and is 2.8 cm thick. Both were made from vesicular basalt and were recovered from the Northeast Trash. The larger specimen is ground smooth on all surfaces, including the perforation, while the smaller specimen is relatively roughly finished.

[*Editor: Adams (2014:207–210) distinguishes between stone rings and "donut stones." She defines the former as objects with central perforations larger in diameter than half the overall diameter of the object. A donut stone, therefore, is characterized by a small central perforation relative to its overall diameter. Adams reports a lack of systematic study of stone rings and donut stones and the presence of diverse traces of use on those she has examined. Nonetheless, she suggests these objects may have been employed in shelling corn, as weights on digging sticks, to smooth and bend wooden tool handles, and/or as chunkee stones (targets in a version of the widespread hoop-and-pole game; see Culin 1907:490, 510, 521).*]

Polishing Stone

In spite of the numerous stone-polished sherds recovered at the Davis Ranch Site, only a single possible polishing stone was recovered. D/s66, found in the Northeast Trash, is a flattened oval basalt pebble, the major faces of which have been used for rubbing. The striations on these faces cross the pebble in a direction parallel to the transverse axis and suggest that the stone may have been used for abrading rather than polishing. It measures more than 5.7 cm in length, 5.6 cm in width, and 2.3 cm in thickness.

Stone Balls

Two stone balls were found at the Davis Ranch Site (figure 5.13i, j). One, D/s41, has been pecked from a porphyritic basalt pebble, while the other, D/s69, is a slightly modified basalt pebble. D/s69, which was recovered from T41N 13W, may have been used for rubbing. Its diameter ranges from 5.2 cm to 6.0 cm. D/s41 may possibly have been a hammerstone, though the overall distribution of the pecking suggests intentional rounding. Its diameter varies from 5.6 cm to 6.6 cm, and it was found in the fill of Room 10.

[*Editor: Based on ethnographic data, Adams (2014:198–201) suggests that pre-Hispanic stone balls may have been used as gaming pieces, club heads, noise-making stones ("thunder stones"), and racing stones (kickballs). She provides approximate size ranges for gaming pieces (3–4 cm in diameter), kickballs (5–7 cm), and thunder stones (7–10 cm). The specimens from the Davis Ranch Site fall into the middle range.*]

Unclassified Stone Artifacts

D/116 is a long, thin, waterworn, spatulate cobble of schist recovered from the fill of House 2 (figure 5.13k). It is 14.9 cm long, 2.6 cm wide, and 0.5 cm thick. Its ends shows more evidence of wear than its sides. D/s137, found in the fill of Room 46, is similar in shape and material but does not show the same kind of wear. It is 4.5 cm long, 2.3 cm wide, and 0.7 cm thick.

Stone Pendants

Eight stone pendants were recovered (figure 5.14a–h, table 5.17). Approximately half of an incised schist ornament, D/100d, was found in front of Burial 8. The ovoid stone was broken lengthwise through the perforation, which was placed at one end and was drilled from both sides. Both surfaces of the stone have been smoothed by grinding; one face is incised with seven sets of parallel zigzag lines across the short axis. The edge bears about three sawed notches per centimeter except on the end bearing the perforation. Another pendant, D/188c, is a long slate pebble that has been perforated near one end by drilling from both sides. A splinter split off one of the upper corners and passed through the perforation. The small size of the perforation (about 0.1 cm in diameter) and the fresh appearance of its surface suggest that the stone was broken in the process of manufacture. All unbroken surfaces appear to be those of a waterworn pebble.

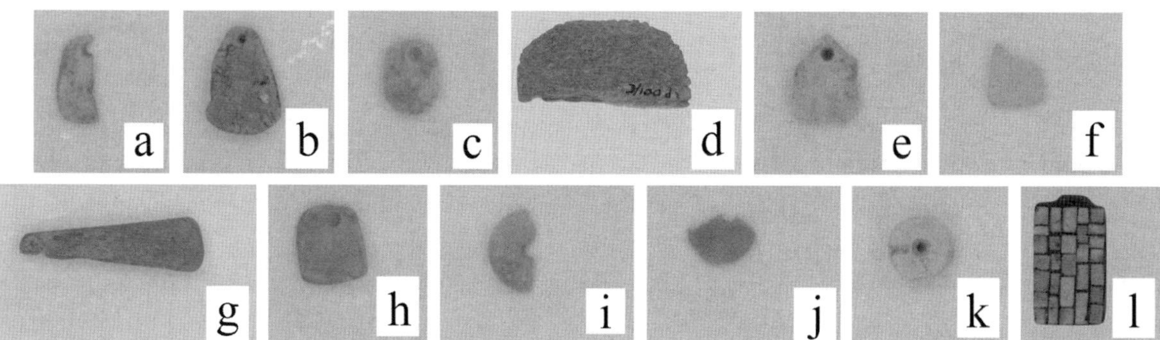

FIGURE 5.14 Stone pendants (a–h), stone beads (i–k), and tesserae (l). See table D.1 for Amerind Museum catalog numbers and photograph numbers. Not to scale. For measurements, see table 5.17 (stone pendants), table 5.18 (stone beads), and text (tesserae). Courtesy of the Amerind Foundation Inc., Dragoon, Arizona.

TABLE 5.17 Characteristics of stone pendants from the Davis Ranch Site

Catalog no.	Length	Width	Thickness	Perforation diameter	Material	Provenience	Figure
D/34	2.0	0.6+	0.2	0.1	Turquoise	Room 3 floor	5.14a
D/71	2.0	1.5	0.1		Turquoise	Burial 4	5.14b
D/87	1.0	0.7	0.2	0.2	Turquoise	Burial 4	5.14c
D/100d	5.6	2.6+	0.4	0.4	Schist	Burial 8	5.14d
D/154h	1.1+	0.9+	0.2	0.1	Turquoise	Room 2 floor	5.14e
D/171v	0.6+	0.6	0.1		Turquoise	Surface	5.14f
D/188c	5.2	1.5	0.6		Schist	Burial 10	5.14g
D/235	1.2	0.8	0.2	0.2	Turquoise	Burial 4 near head	5.14h

Note: All measurements are in cm.

All of the turquoise pendants recovered at the Davis Ranch Site are flat pieces of stone; three have biconical perforations, one was perforated from one side only, and the perforation was broken off one. No two pendants are of the same shape. Two grades of turquoise are readily discernible, one of a pale blue color with no matrix and the second of a sky blue with small to large amounts of white and brown matrix scattered through the stone.

Stone Beads

Two beads, D/54a and D/92, are circular disks with biconical perforations in their centers (figure 5.14i, k, table 5.18). The faces of these beads are flat, and their perimeters are at right angles to their faces. The third bead, D/54b, is also thin; however, its perimeter is rounded in cross section instead of flattened (figure 5.14j). The biconical perforation is slightly off center.

Tesserae

Thirty-two turquoise mosaic overlay pieces, D/188e, were found in the fill around and above Burial 10 and probably all belong to a single mosaic originally placed with it (figure 5.14l). There was no evidence of the backing material nor was there conclusive evidence of the placement of the specimen, though the largest concentration of pieces was in the chest area. The burial was badly disturbed by burrowing animals. All of these pieces are rectangular and well polished; seven have one or more edges beveled toward one face. If fitted closely together, these tesserae would make a mosaic about 2.3 × 3.5 cm in size. Individual pieces range in length from 0.4 cm to 1.0 cm and in width from 0.3 cm to 0.4 cm. Each is about 0.1 cm thick.

[*Editor: A number of burials from the Kayenta region were accompanied by similar objects. Unlike the typical Hohokam turquoise mosaic, which was sometimes applied to a shell bracelet or most often a shell carved into the form of a toad or a raptorial bird, turquoise mosaics from Kayenta sites were usually applied to wood or lignite backing and are square or rectangular in shape (Jernigan 1978). Such pendants have been recovered from RB 568 (Crotty 1983:32–33, Figure16) and Inscription House (Ward 1975:30). Cummings (1910:34–36) reports ear ornaments of similar shape and size (on a wood backing) from Betatakin (AZ D:6:7[ASM]). Hodge (1921:18–19, 26, Plates 1e, f, 2c, c') discusses additional examples from Hawikku and their continued use by Zunis during the historic era. Comparable objects have been recovered from pre-Hispanic Hopi sites as well and have been worn by Hopis in recent times (Fewkes 1904:86–87; Hough 1918:272, Plate 27.2).*]

Stone Mirror

This flat, rectanguloid stone, D/78, has been ground to varying degrees on all surfaces, but only one large face has been polished sufficiently to reflect sunlight (figure 5.15a). The mirror surface is slightly convex

TABLE 5.18 Characteristics of stone beads from the Davis Ranch Site

Catalog no.	Diameter	Thickness	Perforation diameter	Material	Provenience	Figure
D/54a	1.1	0.2	0.2	Turquoise	Surface	5.14i
D/54b	0.7+	0.1	0.2	Turquoise	Surface	5.14j
D/92	0.9	0.4	0.2	Turquoise	Kiva ventilator	5.14k

Note: All measurements are in cm.

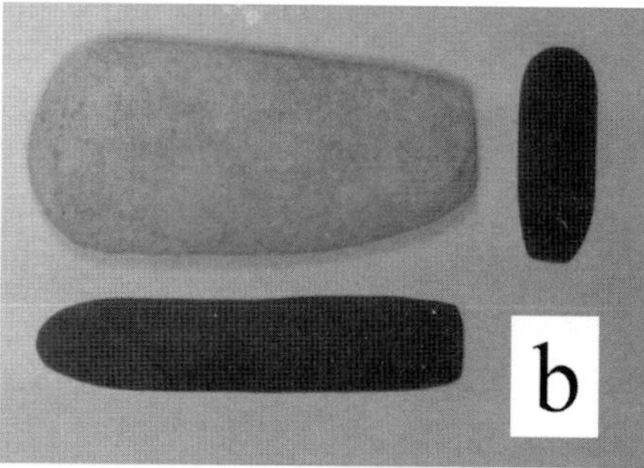

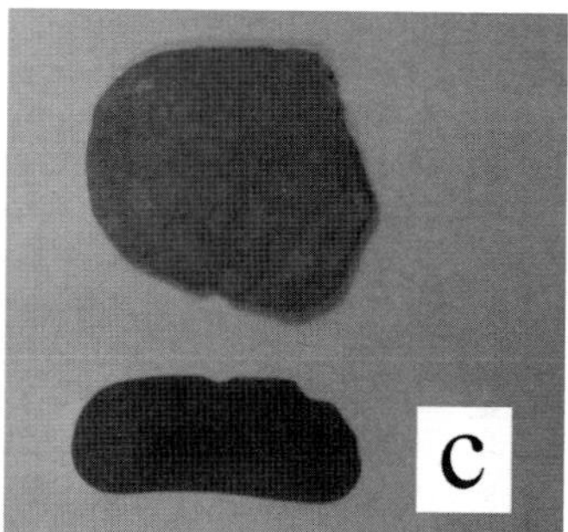

FIGURE 5.15 Stone mirror (a) and worked stone (b, c). See table D.1 for Amerind Museum catalog numbers and photograph numbers. Not to scale. All measurements in text. Courtesy of the Amerind Foundation Inc., Dragoon, Arizona.

as are the sides. The back has been ground flat on the edges, but the center of the base bears a natural depression. Recovered from the floor of Room 4, D/78 is made of hematite. It is 4.1 cm long, 4.0 cm wide, and 0.8 cm thick.

Worked Stone

This category includes two objects. D/s37 is an andesite cobble that has been flattened by pecking on one end and one side (figure 5.15b). There are no wear facets on the stone, and its provenience, the fill of Room 11, offers no clue to its function. It is 32.2 cm long, 15.1 cm wide, and 6.9 cm thick.

D/s67 is a waterworn, ovoid, vesicular basalt cobble recovered from the Northeast Trash (figure 5.15c). It is 20.5 cm long, 17.8 cm wide, and 3.3 cm thick. It bears a groove 2.0 cm wide and as much as 0.5 cm deep pecked across one large face and one edge.

Projectile Points

[*Editor: Alan Ferg of the Arizona State Museum, Marie-Blanche Roudaut, then of Tierra Right of Way Services Inc., and James M. Vint of Desert Archaeology Inc. examined 19 of the 20 projectile points described here (figures 5.16–5.19, table 5.19). One point (D/171l) is missing and could only be classified based on a photograph. There was overwhelming but not total agreement in the classification of these points by the Editor and these experts. The largest number of points was assigned to the Pueblo Side Notched Cluster. Others were typed as Bull Creek, Cienega, Concave Base Triangular, Huachuca (Sobaipuri), and San Pedro points. Three specimens were too small and fragmentary to classify. Points are discussed here in chronological order, based on their production/initial use dates rather than their recovery contexts at the Davis Ranch Site.*

D/93a is a San Pedro point (Sayles 1941:Plate 16), Type I, made from dacite. Its base is complete, the tip of the blade has been broken off, and one side of the blade is damaged.

Three specimens were identified as Cienega points (Huckell 1988; Sliva 2005:95–98, Figure 3.16), Type II. One (D/3b) is a Cienega Short point. There is a break at the base of the point, and one of its tangs has been snapped off. D/32 is a Cienega Stemmed point, broken at the tip and missing a portion of one of its tangs. The third (D/154g) is a Cienega Long point with a broken blade.

Justice (2002:289–319) has defined the Pueblo Side Notched type cluster (Type III), which includes two generalized categories—Concave Base Pueblo Side Notched (Type IIIA) and Straight Base Pueblo Side Notched (Type IIIB)—as well as a number of specific types with additional, distinctive features (Ridge Ruin Side Notched, Point of Pines Side Notched, Walnut

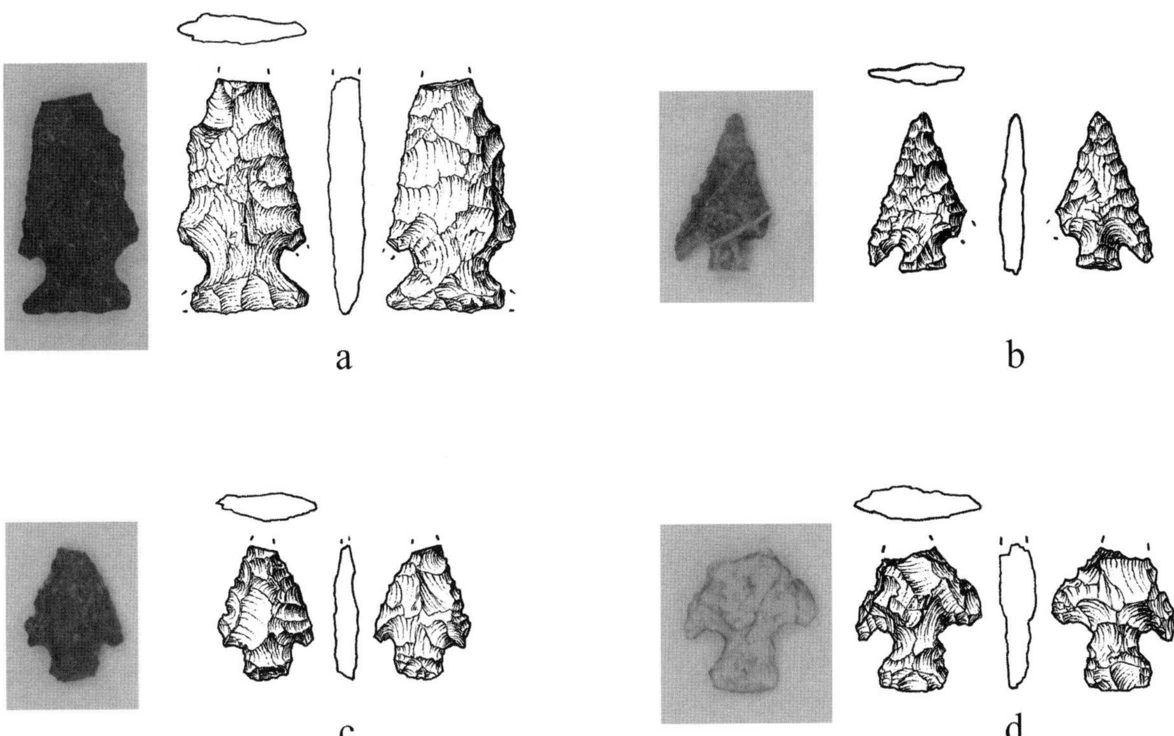

FIGURE 5.16 Early Agricultural period projectile points: San Pedro (a), Cienega Short (b), Cienega Stemmed (c), and Cienega Long (d). See table D.1 for Amerind Museum catalog numbers and photograph numbers. Not to scale. For measurements, see table 5.19. Drawings by Allen Denoyer. Photographs courtesy of the Amerind Foundation Inc., Dragoon, Arizona.

Canyon Side Notched, Gatlin Side Notched, Citrus Side Notched, Snaketown Side Notched, White Mountain Side Notched, Buck Taylor Notched, and Awatovi Side Notched). His clusters are designed to reflect similarities in shape and age, as well as spatial distributions (Justice 2002:1). Justice's (2002:302) definitions of Concave Base Pueblo Side Notched and Straight Base Pueblo Side Notched match Hoffman's (1997:210–214) description of Salado Side Notched. The Pueblo Side Notched Cluster includes points with an isosceles triangle outline shape, straight blade edges, and small, narrow notches placed perpendicular to the vertical axis of the blade. Pueblo Side Notched points appeared after AD 1150 and became common across the Southwest after AD 1300. Their spatial distribution is bounded by the Colorado River, Paquimé (CHIHUAHUA:D:9:1[AF], CH D:9:1[ASM]), Gila Bend, and the Pecos River. All five specimens in the Davis Ranch Site assemblage are obsidian. Three are complete. One is a basal fragment (D/114), and the tip of another (D/67) had broken off but was recovered.

Roudaut classified four specimens as Bull Creek points (Holmer and Weder 1980), Type IV. Justice (2002:261–274) places Bull Creek points in his Western Triangular Cluster, along with Cottonwood Triangular, Cohonina, and Sobaipuri points (Sobaipuri points are better referred to as Huachuca points; Seymour 2009, 2011:90–95, Figures 4.1, 4.6). He describes this group as being characterized by an isosceles triangle outline shape and the absence of notches. He notes, however, that points in this cluster are difficult to distinguish from preforms for Pueblo Side Notched points (Justice 2002: 261, 269).

Bull Creek points date between AD 1050 and 1300 and are most common in southern Utah and northern Arizona, in Fremont and Kayenta sites (Holmer and

TABLE 5.19 Characteristics of projectile points from the Davis Ranch Site

Type	Catalog no.	Length	Width	Thickness	Material	Provenience	Figure
I	D/93a	4.5+	2.5+	0.5	Dacite	Kiva stratitest level 5	5.16a
II	D/3b	2.4	1.5+	0.4	Jasper	Pit Oven 1, 30 cm below surface	5.16b
	D/32	2.1+	1.5+	0.4	Jasper	Room 3 floor	5.16c
	D/154g	2.2+	2.0	0.6	Chert	Room 2 floor	5.16d
IIIA	D/14	1.6	1.0	0.3	Obsidian	Surface	5.17a
	D/67	2.4	1.0	0.2	Obsidian	Burial 4 vessel 5	5.17b
	D/114	0.7+	1.2	0.2	Obsidian	Room 44 fill	5.17c
IIIB	D/36	1.5	1.0	0.2	Obsidian	Burial 1 level 2	5.17d
	D/75	1.8	1.0	0.3	Obsidian	Kiva fill	5.17e
IV	D/93b	2.0+	1.4	0.5	Obsidian	Kiva stratitest level 5	5.18a
	D/129b	2.4	1.2	0.3	Obsidian	House 5 floor	5.18b
	D/154f	1.7	1.2	0.3	Obsidian	Room 2 floor	5.18c
	D/171j	1.3	1.1	0.3	Obsidian	Surface	5.18d
V	D/13	2.3	1.4	0.3	Chalcedony	Surface	5.19a
	D/171l	1.4+	1.2	0.3	Jasper	Surface	5.19b
VI	D/171i	1.7	1.1	0.3	Chert	Surface	5.19c
	D/171m	1.3	0.6+	0.2	Jasper	Surface	5.19d

Note: All measurements are in cm.

Weder 1980; Justice 2002:268–270). The southernmost possible occurrences in Justice's survey were recovered from Canyon Creek Ruin (AZ V:2:1[ASM]). Geib (1996:107–108) distinguishes between "long" (longer than 4.5 cm) and "short" (less than 4.0 cm in length) Bull Creek points. He argues, based on robust spatial patterning, that long Bull Creek points are associated with Fremont groups and that short Bull Creek points are associated with Kayenta groups. None of the Type IV points could be classified as long Bull Creek points.

Two of the Davis Ranch Site specimens (D/93b and D/171j) have straight bases, and two (D/129b and D/154f) have concave bases. Those with straight bases do not fit the Bull Creek type definition (Holmer and Weder 1980; see also Justice 2002:268–270) and are perhaps better classified as Cottonwood Triangular or as preforms. One of the concave-base points (D/129b) exhibits ears and compares favorably with Bull Creek specimens, although the lateral margins of its blade are perhaps a bit too convex. All four specimens from the Davis Ranch Site were made from obsidian. All but one (D/93b) are complete. The incomplete specimen is broken at the tip.

Two points, D/13 and D/171l, are classified as Concave Base Triangular (Type V) (Loendorf and Rice 2004:56–57, Figure 7j; Sliva 1997:55). These are unnotched and triangular and lack the deeply concave ("U-shaped") base of Huachuca points (see below). Instead,

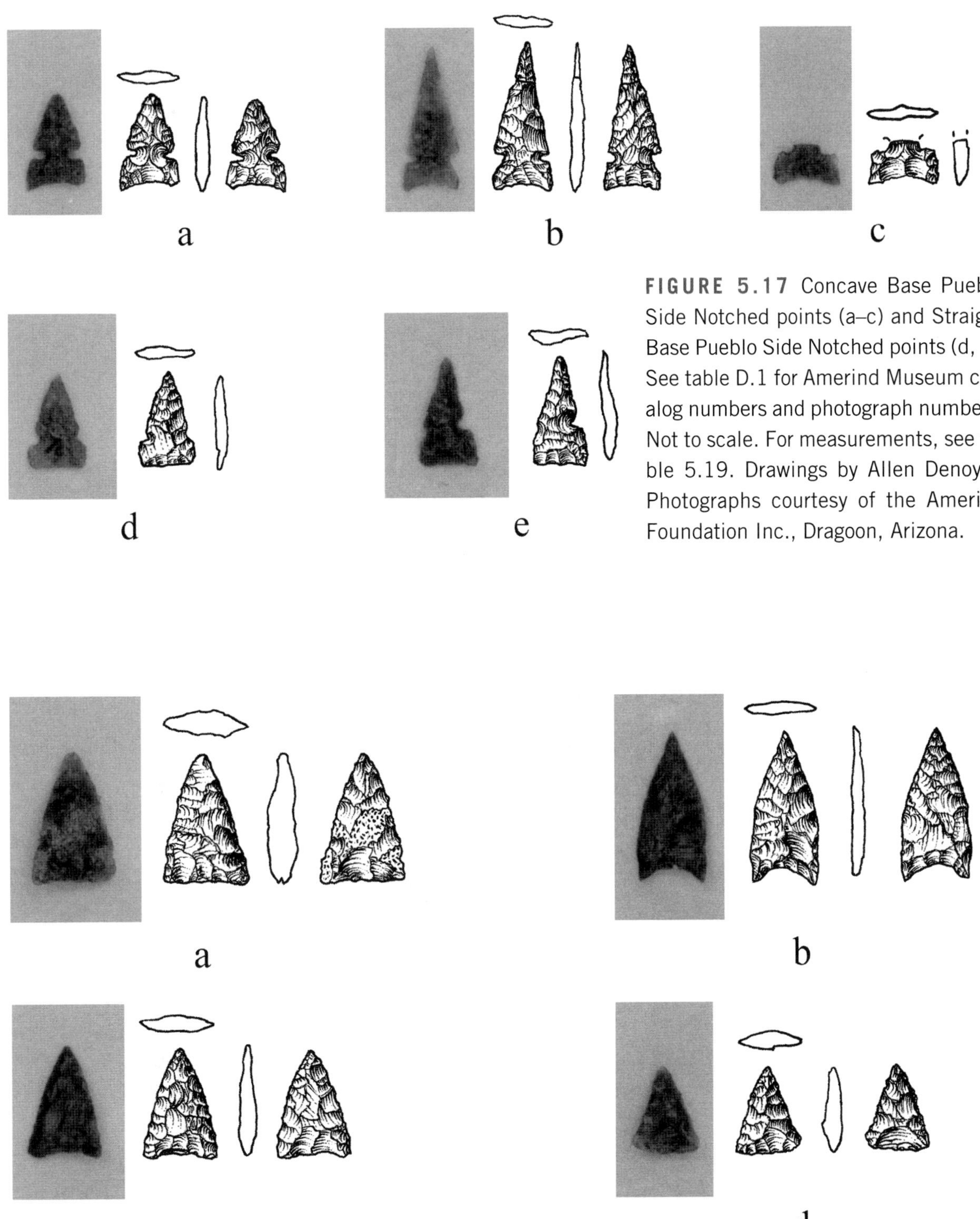

FIGURE 5.17 Concave Base Pueblo Side Notched points (a–c) and Straight Base Pueblo Side Notched points (d, e). See table D.1 for Amerind Museum catalog numbers and photograph numbers. Not to scale. For measurements, see table 5.19. Drawings by Allen Denoyer. Photographs courtesy of the Amerind Foundation Inc., Dragoon, Arizona.

FIGURE 5.18 Bull Creek points (?). See table D.1 for Amerind Museum catalog numbers and photograph numbers. Not to scale. For measurements, see table 5.19. Drawings by Allen Denoyer. Photographs courtesy of the Amerind Foundation Inc., Dragoon, Arizona.

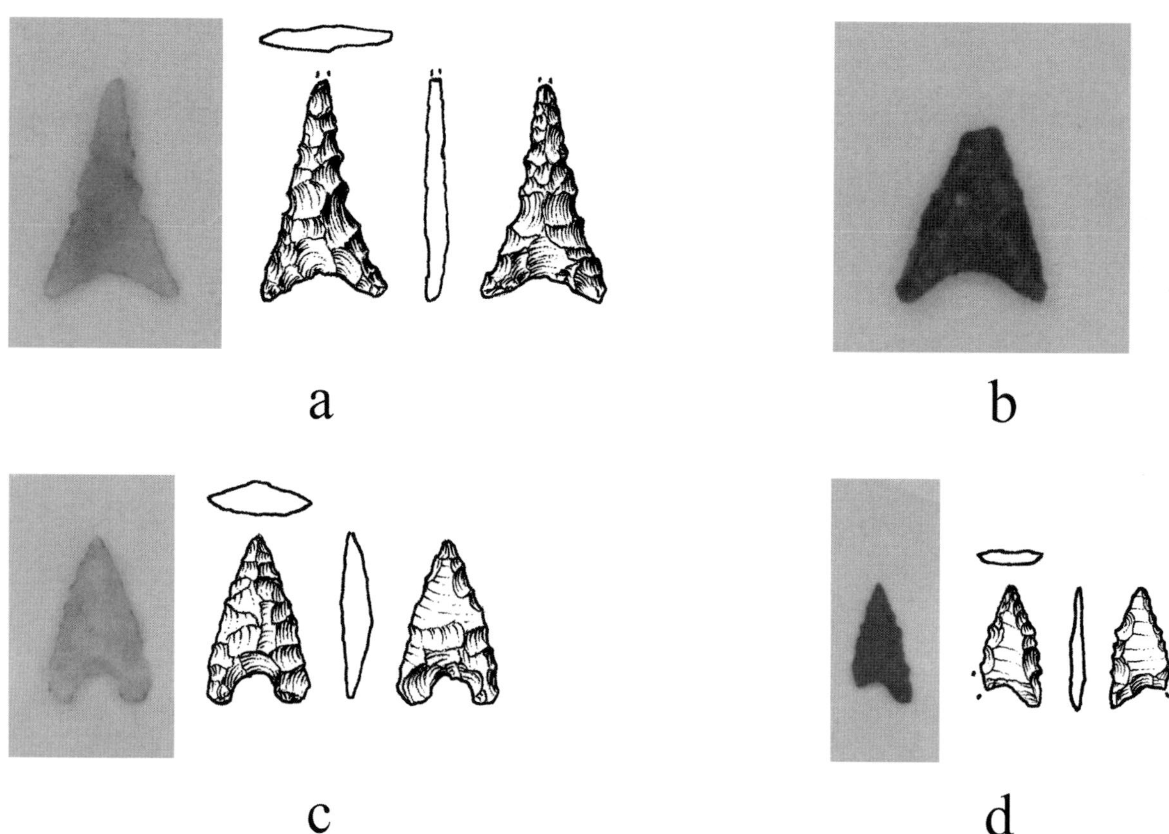

FIGURE 5.19 Concave Base Triangular points (a, b) and Huachuca points (c, d). See table D.1 for Amerind Museum catalog numbers and photograph numbers. Not to scale. For measurements, see table 5.19. Drawings by Allen Denoyer. Photographs courtesy of the Amerind Foundation Inc., Dragoon, Arizona.

their basal concavities take the form of a crescent or a "V." Whereas Bull Creek points are also triangular and lack notches, their basal concavities are rarely as deep as those exhibited by D/13 and D/171l. In addition, the blade of D/13 has concave lateral margins. This is apparently not a characteristic of Bull Creek points. According to Sliva (1997:55), Concave Base Triangular points date to the period AD 1150–1350 in central Arizona and between AD 1000 and 1450 on the Colorado Plateau.

As noted above, Justice (2002:261, 272–274, Figure 32) includes Sobaipuri (Huachuca) points (Type VI) in his Western Triangular Cluster, along with Cottonwood Triangular, Bull Creek, and Cohonina points. Sobaipuri points are named for the Piman speakers who inhabited southeastern Arizona at Spanish contact and were eventually absorbed by other O'odham groups (Masse 1981). Sobaipuri (Huachuca) points have been the focus of controversy over the years, with some researchers claiming secure Classic period associations (e.g., Ravesloot and Whittlesey 1987:96). Others, however, are confident that protohistoric Piman points can be distinguished based on their very deeply concave bases and their lack of hafting notches (e.g., Loendorf and Rice 2004:60).

Justice (2002:272) uses serration as a key trait (along with a deeply indented base and the absence of notches), and serrated blades are common among specimens recovered from most sites located east of the Tohono O'odham Reservation (e.g., Brew and Huckell 1987; Doyel 1977:Figure 39; Franklin 1980:Figure 46; Mabry 1999; Teague 1980). Brew and Huckell (1987), citing

Germeshausen (1972:Plate 19–20), Haury (1950:274, Figure 56n–p, q, s), and Shenk and Teague (1975:80, Figure 52), suggest that Tohono O'odham (and perhaps Akimel O'odham) points are similar in shape to Sobaipuri points but thicker and without serrations (see also Huckell and Huckell 1982:87, Figure 8c). More recently, Loendorf and Rice (2004:59–60) have reported that in some point assemblages from sites on Gila River Indian Community lands, serration is very rare (2%). They note, however, that serrated points account for as much as 30% of other assemblages. Both of the points identified here as Sobaipuri exhibit serrated blades, and each was recovered from the surface of the site.

The three unclassified point fragments are all obsidian. D/154d, from the floor of Room 2, is 1.3 cm long, 1.3 cm wide, and 0.3 cm thick. D/154e, also from the floor of Room 2, is 1.6 cm long, 1.1 cm wide, and 0.3 cm thick. Found on the surface of the site, D/171k is 1.8 cm long, 1.2 cm wide, and 0.3 cm thick.]

Drills

One complete chert biface, D/3a, might be classified as a drill because of its thick cross section and narrow, tapering width, although it bears no obvious evidence that it has been used as a drill (figure 5.20a). D/3a, found in Pit Oven 1 (30 cm below surface), is 2.9 cm long, 1.4 cm wide, and 0.5 cm thick. D/109, made from jasper, is fragmentary and exhibits edge-rounding and small step-fractures consistent with use as a drill (figure 5.20b). It is 2.6 cm long, 1.0 cm wide, and 0.4 cm thick. It was found in the fill of Room 34.

Knives

[*Editor: Twenty-one flake tools having at least one working edge forming an acute angle were classified as knives (figure 5.21, table 5.20).*] Sixteen of these flakes, Type I, have not been retouched. The impression conveyed by these artifacts is that any handy flake was utilized. Another four flakes have only been shaped by edge retouching and are placed in Type II. Only a single knife exhibits further working by means of unifacial thinning, Type III.

Scrapers

[*Editor: Twenty flake tools, each with a steeper working edge angle in comparison to the knives, were classified as scrapers (figure 5.22, table 5.21). Most exhibit more intentional shaping than the objects classified as knives.*

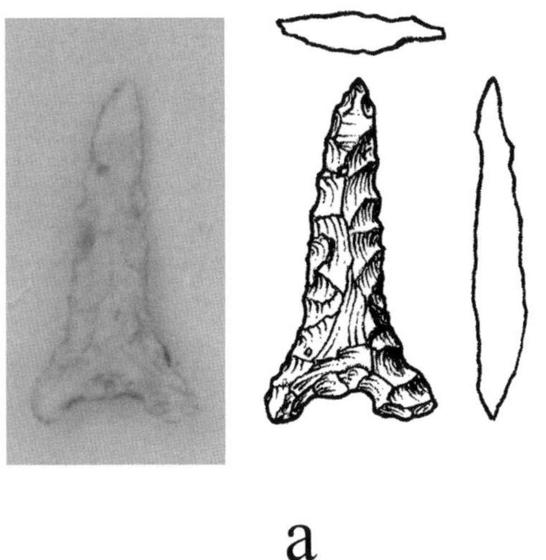

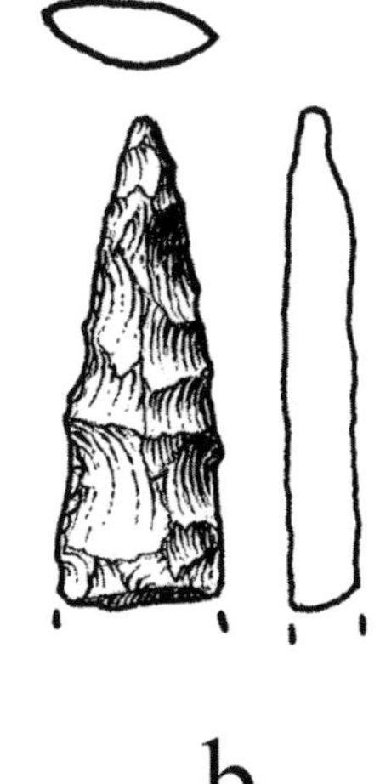

FIGURE 5.20 Drills. See table D.1 for Amerind Museum catalog numbers and photograph numbers. Not to scale. Measurements in text. Drawings by Allen Denoyer. Photographs courtesy of the Amerind Foundation Inc., Dragoon, Arizona.

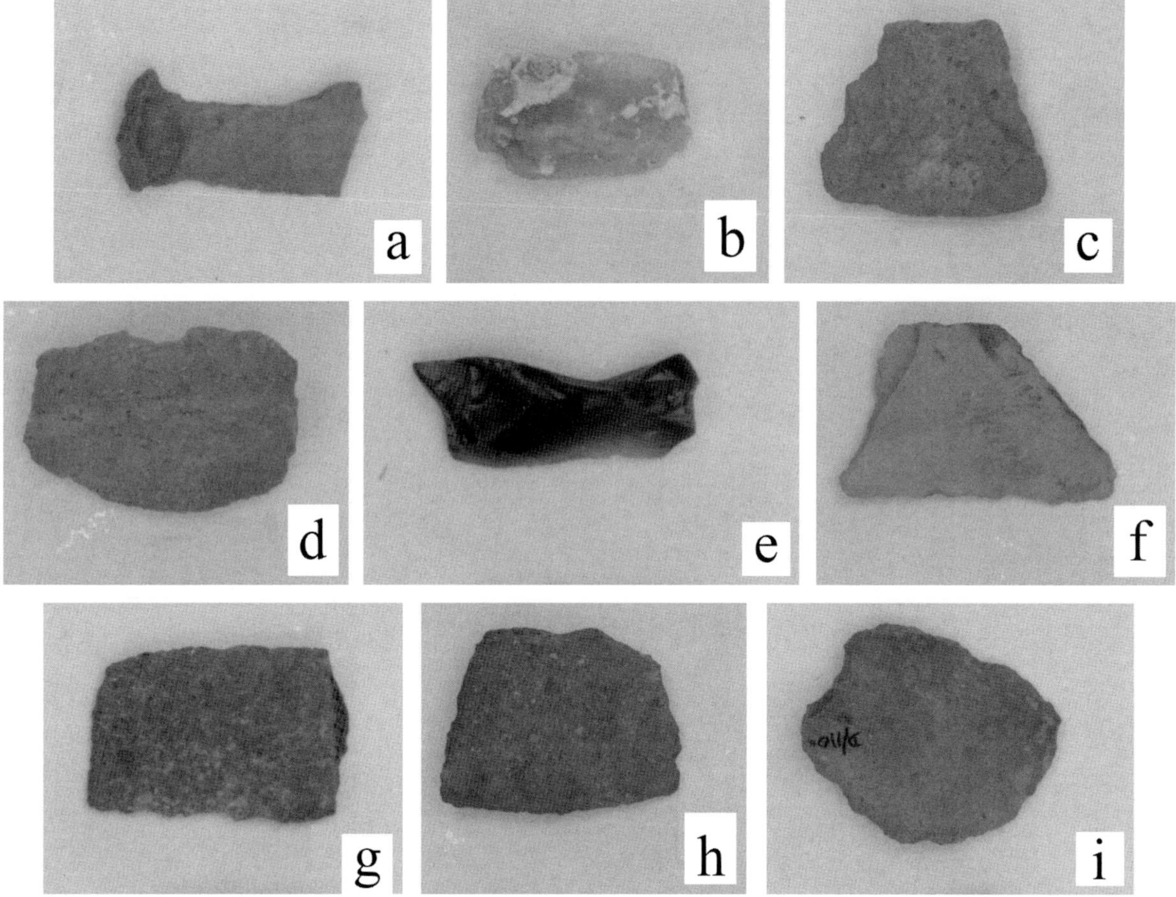

FIGURE 5.21 Flaked stone knives: Type I (a–e), Type II (f–h), and Type III (i). See table D.1 for Amerind Museum catalog numbers and photograph numbers. Not to scale. For measurements, see table 5.20. Courtesy of the Amerind Foundation Inc., Dragoon, Arizona.

Only two are unretouched flakes, Type I. The six Type II scrapers are shaped by edge retouch only. Type III scrapers, four specimens, are unifacially thinned. The largest category, with eight specimens, is Type IV: bifacially thinned scrapers.]

Unclassified Biface

The midsection of a knife or large projectile point, D/80 has a thin, lenticular cross section (figure 5.23a). Found on the floor of Room 7, it is made from chert and is 2.8 cm long, 2.6 cm wide, and 0.6 cm thick.

Preform

D/170c, found in the Northeast Trash, is a complete but unfinished artifact of red rhyolite (figure 5.23b). Bifacially flaked to a rough, leaf-shaped outline and a diamond-shaped cross section, it is 6.2 cm long, 3.3 cm wide, and 2.0 cm thick.

Choppers

Nine specimens are classed in a common category as choppers because they are larger and more crudely made than artifacts commonly called knives

TABLE 5.20 Characteristics of flaked stone knives from the Davis Ranch Site

Type	Catalog no.	Length	Width	Thickness	Material	Provenience	Figure
I	D/37	4.3+	2.0	1.0	Jasper	Kiva level 3	5.21a
	D/51	3.5+	2.0	0.6	Chalcedony	Kiva level 2	5.21b
	D/79	4.4	4.5	0.9	Chert	Room 7 fill	
	D/81	6.8	4.0	0.7	Jasper	Room 9 fill	
	D/85	2.8+	3.8	0.9	Chert	Room 10 floor	
	D/100h	3.6	2.9	1.0	Jasper	Burial 8	
	D/100k	3.9	3.1	1.3	Chert	Burial 8	
	D/106a	5.0	3.3	0.8	Chert	Room 16 floor	
	D/144c	4.2	4.9	1.2	Andesite	Kiva fill	5.21c
	D/144e	5.4	3.8	1.1	Andesite	Kiva fill	5.21d
	D/144f	4.3	3.8	0.9	Chert	Kiva fill	
	D/146c	4.3	2.3	0.7	Chert	Kiva levels 3–5	
	D/153h	3.6	1.5	0.9	Obsidian	Room 2 floor	5.21e
	D/153i	3.1	2.2	0.5	Obsidian	Room 2 floor	
	D/153k	2.0	1.1	0.5	Obsidian	Room 2 floor	
	D/157m	3.5	1.7	0.7	Obsidian	Room 4 subfloor test	
II	D/144d	5.1	3.1	0.8	Chert	Kiva fill	5.21f
	D/146b	4.7	3.1	0.8	Dacite	Kiva levels 3–5	5.21g
	D/153d	5.0	3.7	1.1	Andesite	Room 2 floor	5.21h
	D/s133	4.0	2.3	0.9	Jasper	Room 17 floor	
III	D/110	6.0	5.1	1.5	Andesite	Room 35	5.21i

Note: All measurements are in cm.

(figure 5.24, table 5.22). The four Type I choppers all bear chipped edges that expand rapidly above to form thick blades. A single core chopper is classified as Type II.

Type III is a group of flat cobbles or pebbles that have been used for grinding to a limited extent on one or both flat surfaces and that have had one or more flakes removed from one or both ends. Except for the flake scars and grinding surfaces, three of these tools are unmodified cobbles. The fourth has been pecked and smoothed on one edge and one end. Only one has been used sufficiently to have blunted flake scars on one end. Two specimens have edges that may have been used to chop relatively soft materials since the edges show only slight wear. The others do not have enough flakes removed to form sharp edges. Six of these tools are associated with Redfield or Romero (Reeve) phase deposits, one dates to the Aravaipa (Sosa) phase, and two are unplaced.

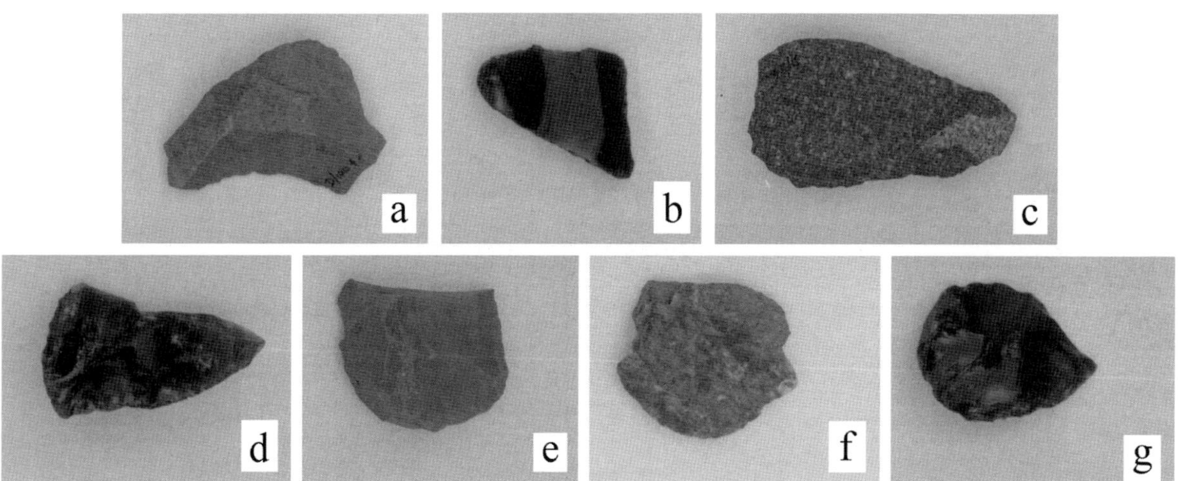

FIGURE 5.22 Flaked stone scrapers: Type I (a), Type II (b), Type III (c), and Type IV (d–g). See table D.1 for Amerind Museum catalog numbers and photograph numbers. Not to scale. For measurements, see table 5.21. Courtesy of the Amerind Foundation Inc., Dragoon, Arizona.

TABLE 5.21 Characteristics of flaked stone scrapers from the Davis Ranch Site

Type	Catalog no.	Length	Width	Thickness	Material	Provenience	Figure
I	D/100f	5.8	4.0	1.6	Andesite	Burial 8	5.22a
	D/157h	2.9	1.9	0.6	Obsidian	Room 4 subfloor test	
II	D/16	6.5	5.3	1.8	Chert	Room 2 fill	
	D/100g	5.0	3.8	2.5	Quartzite	Burial 8	
	D/153j	3.3	2.0	0.7	Obsidian	Room 2 floor	5.22b
	D/153l	2.8	2.5	0.6	Obsidian	Room 2 floor	
	D/157f	4.3	2.2	1.1	Obsidian	Room 4 subfloor test	
	D/157j	3.7	1.9	1.0	Obsidian	Room 4 subfloor test	
III	D/56	8.0	4.5	1.1	Porphyritic basalt	Surface	5.22c
	D/115	5.2	3.6	2.1	Chert	Room 44 fill	
	D/157n	3.4	2.1	1.0	Obsidian	Room 4 subfloor test	
	D/s35	5.1	4.6	0.9	Chert	T1S 54–61E	
IV	D/49	4.0	2.4	0.9	Obsidian	Kiva level 2	5.22d
	D/64	2.8+	3.2	1.6	Chert	Room 7 fill	5.22e
	D/144i	6.8	4.6	3.3	Basalt	Kiva fill	
	D/144j	6.7	5.5	2.0	Jasper	Kiva fill	5.22f
	D/144k	6.3	5.7	2.2	Basalt	Kiva fill	
	D/170b	4.5	3.0	1.3	Chert	NE Trash	
	D/176	3.2	2.5	1.6	Jasper	T11N 16–17E	
	D/184	3.2	2.4	0.8	Obsidian	Puddle Pit 2 fill	5.22g

Note: All measurements are in cm.

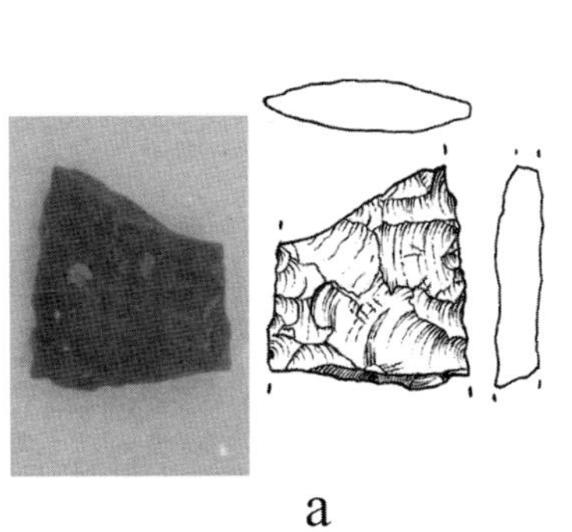

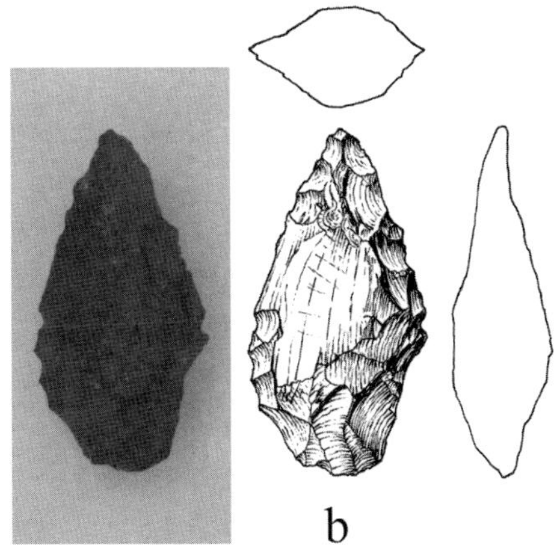

FIGURE 5.23 Unclassified biface (a) and preform (b). See table D.1 for Amerind Museum catalog numbers and photograph numbers. Not to scale. Measurements in text. Drawings by Allen Denoyer. Photographs courtesy of the Amerind Foundation Inc., Dragoon, Arizona.

FIGURE 5.24 Flaked stone choppers: Type I (a–d) and Type III (e–g). See table D.1 for Amerind Museum catalog numbers and photograph numbers. Not to scale. For measurements, see table 5.22. Courtesy of the Amerind Foundation Inc., Dragoon, Arizona.

TABLE 5.22 Characteristics of flaked stone choppers from the Davis Ranch Site

Type	Catalog no.	Length	Width	Thickness	Material	Provenience	Figure
I	D/s14	7.9	6.8	4.5	Porphyritic basalt	Kiva fill	5.24a
	D/s65	10.6	6.1	1.6	Schist	Room 21 fill	5.24b
	D/s81	8.1	7.2	3.0	Quartzite	NE Trash	5.24c
	D/s100	7.6	6.6	5.4	Quartzite	Room 6 subfloor test	5.24d
II	D/s136	6.2	4.4	4.2	Andesite	Room 33 fill	
III	D/s6	16.9	12.1	3.6	Basalt	T1S 39E surface	5.24e
	D/s60	14.8	8.3	2.9	Basalt	Room 14 fill	5.24f
	D/s61	13.0	9.9	3.1	Basalt	Room 14 fill	5.24g
	D/s62	13.4	10.8	2.4	Basalt	Room 14 fill	

Note: All measurements are in cm.

Indeterminate Flake Tools

[Editor: Two primary decortication flakes of obsidian, both recovered from the Room 4 subfloor test, are classified as indeterminate flake tools. D/157i was thinned by a single linear flake, and tiny pressure flakes have been removed from the tip and part of one edge. A larger, but still small, flake was removed from the tip, but whether as a result of use or thinning is uncertain. It is 3.5 cm long, 1.3 cm wide, and 0.9 cm thick. Its shape suggests that it may have been a burin. D/157g, which is 3.2 cm long, 2.5 cm wide, and 0.7 cm thick, is merely thinned unifacially.]

Debitage

[Editor: Twenty-eight apparently unused stone flakes are present in the collection (figure 5.25, table 5.23). Fourteen were found with the utilized flakes and other artifacts in the possible bow-and-arrow-making kit with Burial 8. Most of these flakes were struck from the same jasper core as were many of the flake tools described elsewhere.]

Cores

Eight stones bearing numerous flake scars on their surfaces were found at the Davis Ranch Site (figure 5.26, table 5.24). None show evidence of having been used as choppers, scrapers, et cetera, nor do any of them bear prepared striking platforms. Two are from a possible bow-and-arrow-making kit associated with Burial 8.

Pigments

Each of the eight samples of red hematite pigment (Type I) is relatively homogeneous, but among the different collections, there is a range from a dark red, fine-grained material to a buff-colored, sandy material (figure 5.27a–g, table 5.25). Only two examples (D/170j and part of D/183) appear to be fragments of molded loaves of pigment; the others are apparently natural lumps of red ocher. Some of the latter have grinding facets on them where pigment has been removed. Two pieces of malachite (Type II) are unworked, and three bear grinding facets

FIGURE 5.25 Flaked stone debitage. See table D.1 for Amerind Museum catalog numbers and photograph numbers. Not to scale. For measurements, see table 5.23. Courtesy of the Amerind Foundation Inc., Dragoon, Arizona.

TABLE 5.23 Characteristics of flaked stone debitage from the Davis Ranch Site

Catalog no.	Length	Width	Thickness	Material	Provenience	Figure
D/100i	4.9	3.6	1.3	Chert	Burial 8	5.25a
D/100j	5.1	3.8	1.7	Chert	Burial 8	
D/100l	3.7	2.0	0.7	Jasper	Burial 8	5.25b
D/100m	3.3	3.1	1.2	Jasper	Burial 8	
D/100n	2.3	1.7	1.5	Chert	Burial 8	
D/100o	3.5	2.5	1.4	Jasper	Burial 8	
D/100p	2.3	2.4	0.7	Jasper	Burial 8	
D/100q	3.9	2.7	0.9	Jasper	Burial 8	
D/100r	3.3	2.1	0.6	Jasper	Burial 8	
D/100s	3.1	2.6	0.8	Jasper	Burial 8	5.25c
D/100t	3.8	3.2	0.8	Jasper	Burial 8	5.25d
D/100u	2.4	2.1	0.7	Jasper	Burial 8	
D/100v	1.9	1.7	1.2	Jasper	Burial 8	
D/100w	2.1	1.7	0.3	Obsidian	Burial 8	5.25e
D/106b	4.8	3.1	1.0	Chert	Room 16 floor	
D/113	1.4	1.3	0.3	Obsidian	Room 41 fill	
D/137b	7.0	4.8	1.2	Jasper	House 8 fill	
D/144g	1.9+	2.5	0.5	Jasper	Kiva fill	5.25f
D/147	3.8	2.6	0.8	Andesite	Kiva levels 6–8	
D/149	5.2	3.5	0.8	Chert	Kiva stratitest level 6	
D/153e	4.1	3.2	0.8	Quartzite	Room 2 floor	5.25g
D/153f	2.2	1.8	0.3	Jasper	Room 2 floor	
D/153g	3.0	2.0	0.9	Obsidian	Room 2 floor	
D/157l	2.8	1.8	0.5	Obsidian	Room 4 subfloor test	
D/186a	4.8+	3.8	1.7	Quartzite	T21–22W 31–32S	5.25h
D/s129	6.4	3.5	1.6	Andesite	Kiva fill	
D/s134	1.5	2.5	0.4	Obsidian	Room 33 fill	
D/s135	3.8	3.0	1.1	Andesite	Room 46 fill	

FIGURE 5.26 Flaked stone cores. See table D.1 for Amerind Museum catalog numbers and photograph numbers. Not to scale. For measurements, see table 5.24. Courtesy of the Amerind Foundation Inc., Dragoon, Arizona.

TABLE 5.24 Characteristics of flaked stone cores from the Davis Ranch Site

Catalog no.	Length	Width	Thickness	Material	Provenience	Figure
D/100c	4.8	4.0	3.1	Basalt	Burial 8	5.26a
D/100x	9.0	6.2	4.7	Chert	Burial 8	5.26b
D/146a	5.4	4.5	3.7	Diorite	Kiva levels 3–5	5.26c
D/157k	4.0	2.0	1.0	Obsidian	Room 4 subfloor test	
D/s82	5.7	4.6	4.0	Chert	NE Trash	5.26d
D/s123	9.6	9.4	4.8	Jasper	T31–32S 7E	5.26e
D/s125	8.2	6.8	4.9	Chert	T21–22W 31–32S	5.26f
D/s126	4.1	3.7	2.5	Jasper	T21–22W 31–32S	5.26g

Note: All measurements are in cm.

(figure 5.27h–k). All specimens are small, the total collection weighing less than an ounce. Two batches of yellow ocher (Type III) with a white matrix were found (figure 5.27l). Neither batch has grinding facets where material was removed for making paint; one sample (D/141e) was found in association with a palette (D/141d) in a cremation.

All examples of white or tannish pigment (Type IV) show evidence of having been molded into lumps (figure 5.27m–p). Two specimens (D/1 and D/69) effervesced when treated with muriatic acid, which suggests that they may contain calcite; another (D/134) may be relatively pure kaolin. Several fragments of a buff-colored material (D/96)

FIGURE 5.27 Pigments: Type I (a–g), Type II (h–k), Type III (l), Type IV (m–p), Type V (q). See table D.1 for Amerind Museum catalog numbers and photograph numbers. Not to scale. For measurements, see table 5.25. Courtesy of the Amerind Foundation Inc., Dragoon, Arizona.

have numerous sandy-looking inclusions. The surfaces of these fragments are broken by many fissures as though the material had been molded into a lump while damp and had cracked upon drying. This material did not effervesce when treated with acid.

A single specimen of specular iron was found (figure 5.27q). This black pigment (Type V) has a small grinding facet on one end.

Quartz Crystals

Of the four quartz crystals recovered, two have been chipped on one end, probably from use; one has been split lengthwise (figure 5.28a–d, table 5.26). A third has been rounded on all edges, possibly from water rolling, and one has a cleavage fracture on one end and is round on other edges.

TABLE 5.25 Characteristics of pigments from the Davis Ranch Site

Type	Catalog no.	Length	Width	Thickness	Material	Provenience	Figure
I	D/8	11.5	6.4	5.1	Hematite	T1S 30–46E	
	D/91				Hematite	T16S 24–25E	
	D/100e	2.5	0.8	0.4	Hematite	Burial 8	5.27a
	D/142a	7.1	2.8	2.3	Hematite	Cremation 2	5.27b
	D/152	6.9	5.1	2.6	Hematite	Kiva foot drum	5.27c
	D/159	3.0	2.6	1.5	Hematite	Trench in front of Room 7	5.27d
		1.5	1.3	0.3			
		1.5	0.8	0.4			
	D/170j	6.0–7.8	3.9–5.6	3.3–3.7	Hematite	NE Trash	5.27e
	D/183	3.1–4.3	2.4–3.3	1.5–2.3	Hematite	T19S 23–25E	5.27f, g
II	D/33	1.9	1.1	0.8	Malachite	Room 3 floor	5.27h
	D/35	1.4	0.9	0.7	Malachite	Trench in front of Room 3	5.27i
	D/52	3.3	2.0	0.8	Malachite	Kiva fill	5.27j
	D/129a	1.5+	0.4	0.4	Malachite	House 5 floor	5.27k
	D/171u	1.5	1.2	0.8	Malachite	Surface	
III	D/141e	5.3	3.8	3.2	Yellow ochre	Cremation 1	
	D/161	5.0	3.6	2.9	Yellow ochre	Room 9 subfloor test	5.27l
IV	D/1	2.0–2.6	1.5–2.0	0.9–1.3	Unidentified	T10N 4–20E	5.27m
	D/69	4.0	4.0	2.8	Unidentified	Burial 4	5.27n
	D/96				Unidentified	Burial 8	5.27o
	D/134	2.6–3.3	2.0	0.9–1.5	Kaolin?	House 7 fill	5.27p
V	D/160	4.0	1.9	1.4	Specular iron	Room 9 Floor 1, NE posthole	5.27q

Note: All measurements are in cm.

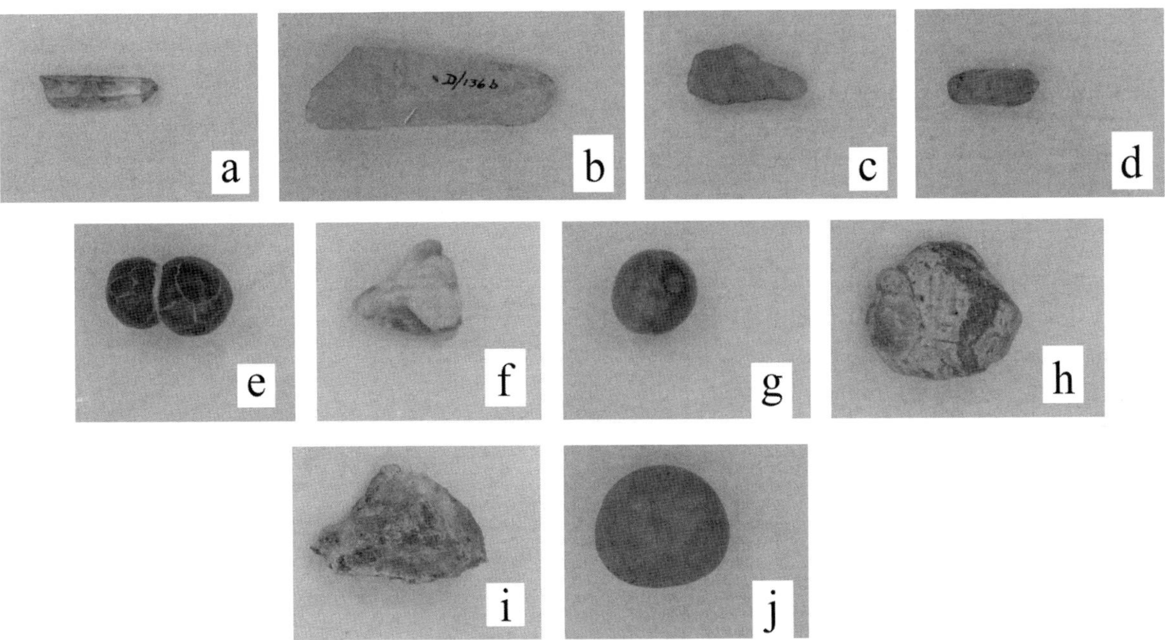

FIGURE 5.28 Quartz crystals (a–d), concretions (e–g), miscellaneous unworked stones (h, i), and possible lightning stone (j). See table D.1 for Amerind Museum catalog numbers and photograph numbers. Not to scale. For measurements, see table 5.26 (quartz crystals), table 5.27 (concretions), table 5.28 (miscellaneous unworked stones), and text (possible lightning stone). Courtesy of the Amerind Foundation Inc., Dragoon, Arizona.

TABLE 5.26 Characteristics of quartz crystals from the Davis Ranch Site

Catalog no.	Length	Width	Thickness	Provenience	Figure
D/93c	2.3	0.5	0.6	Kiva stratitest level 5	5.28a
D/136b	6.7+	2.2	1.6	House 7, 0–10 cm above Floor 2	5.28b
D/171a	2.4	1.1	0.8	Surface	5.28c
D/171b	1.9	0.9	0.7	Surface	5.28d

Note: All measurements are in cm.

Concretions

One of the three specimens, D/26, is a botryoidal concretion of two lobes, each of which is covered with roughly hexagonal shrinkage cracks (figure 5.28e, table 5.27). The second, D/156b, is a small ovoid agate pebble, well smoothed overall (figure 5.28g). Approximately half of the surface is highly polished and of a slightly darker color. The third example, D/156a, is a waterworn fragment of a chalcedony concretion (figure 5.28f).

Miscellaneous Unworked Stones

These stones are classed together only because of their uncommon characteristics (figure 5.28h, i, table 5.28). Like the concretions, two may have been

TABLE 5.27 Characteristics of concretions from the Davis Ranch Site

Catalog no.	Length	Width	Thickness	Provenience	Figure
D/26	3.8	2.3	2.1	Room 3 floor	5.28e
D/156a	2.2	2.1	1.4	Room 4 floor	5.28f
D/156b	1.5 (diameter)			Room 4 floor	5.28g

Note: All measurements are in cm.

TABLE 5.28 Characteristics of miscellaneous unworked stones from the Davis Ranch Site

Catalog no.	Length	Width	Thickness	Material	Provenience	Figure
D/135	4.2	3.7	2.2	Epidote?	House 7 subfloor 1 fill	5.28h
D/139	5.3	3.7	2.0	Quartz	House 9 fill	5.28i
D/s138	2.4	2.2	1.1+	Phyllite	Room 33 fill	
D/s139	3.1+	2.8+	0.9+	Micaceous schist	Room 46 fill	

Note: All measurements are in cm.

ceremonial objects or were picked up because of their unusual color or shape. D/135 is a rounded natural pebble with one flat surface; it has a streak of epidote surrounded by a white matrix. D/139 is a flake of malachite-stained quartz; one surface is a fresh break. [*Editor: D/s138 is a chunk of phyllite, a material used as temper by pottery producers at sites near the confluence of the San Pedro River and Aravaipa Creek (where it crops out), and D/s139 is piece of micaceous schist.*]

Lightning Stone?

[*Editor: A quartzite pebble (D/151), 3.3 cm long, 2.8 cm wide, and 2.3 cm thick, was recovered from one of the loom-anchor holes (G-4) in the floor of the kiva (figure 5.28j). Its context suggests it had a ceremonial use. Jeancon (1923:68, Plate 59b) and Kidder (1932:93–94) have described similar though formally shaped objects in use among the historic Pueblo peoples of the Rio Grande Valley. Jeancon (1923:68) refers to them as "firestones" and reports their use by the people of Santa Clara and San Ildefonso: "At one time during the rain ceremonies the drum is beaten to represent the thunder and the white quartz pieces are rubbed together. This rubbing produces an incandescent glow which resembles lightning." Objects identified as lightning stones or "possible lightning stones" have also been recovered from kivas and other pit structures at Acoma (Dittert 1959:158) and in the Ackmen-Lowry area (Martin 1939:404–405, Figure 112).*]

BONE AND ANTLER

Awls

Awl classification is based on Kidder (1932:211). Type I awls have the head of the bone left intact and the shaft tapered to a point (figure 5.29a–c, table 5.29). Two are deer ulnae (D/40, D/108), and one is a deer metapodial with the proximal end removed (D/156d). Four fragmentary specimens probably belong to the latter category.

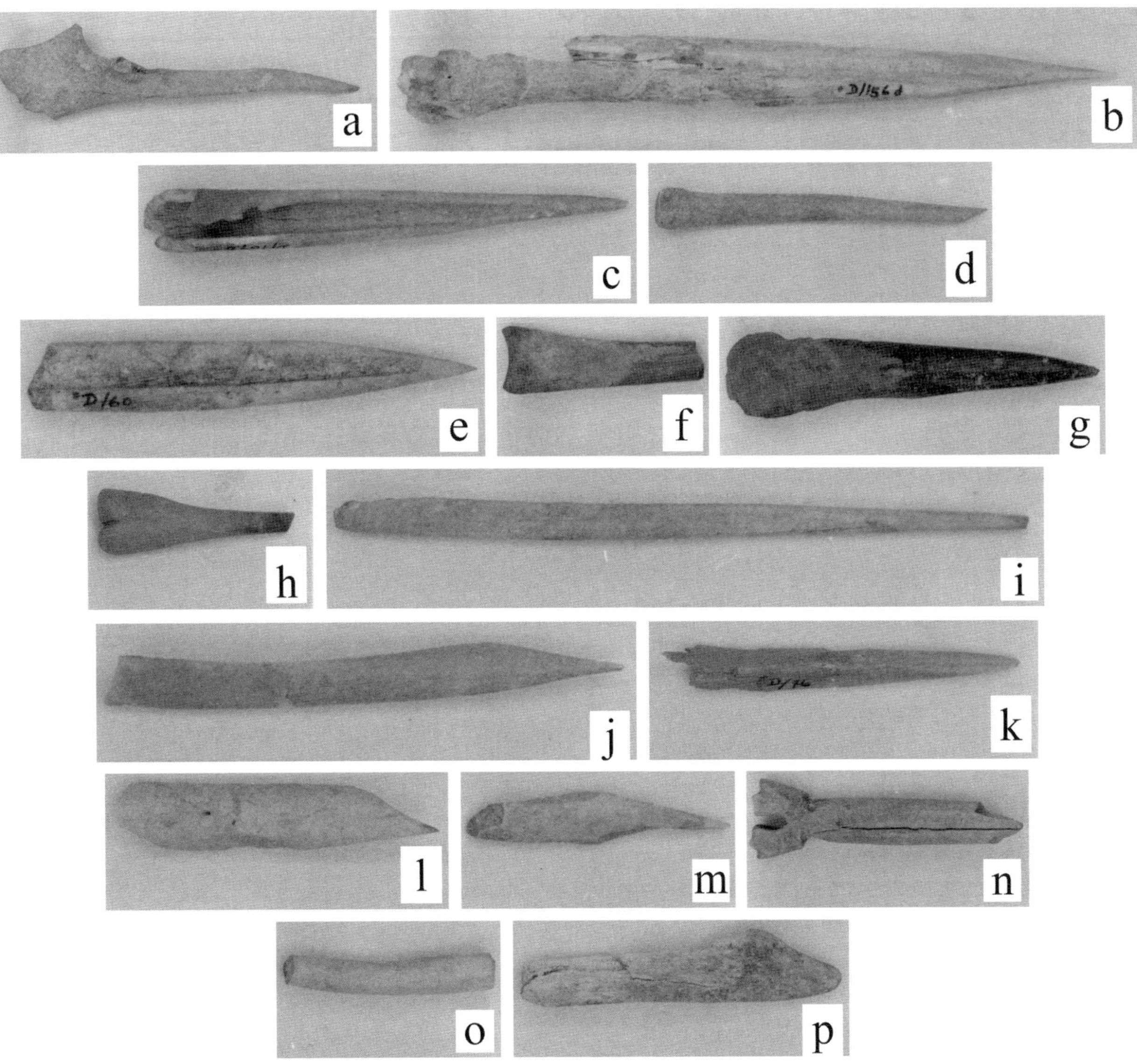

FIGURE 5.29 Bone awls (a–m), bone handle (n), bone tube (o), and worked antler (p). See table D.1 for Amerind Museum catalog numbers and photograph numbers. Not to scale. For bone awl measurements, see table 5.29. Other measurements in text. Courtesy of the Amerind Foundation Inc., Dragoon, Arizona.

Type II awls have a split head and pointed shaft (figure 5.29d–g). Two are made from deer metapodials, each with the distal end split, the proximal end removed, and the shaft pointed (D/89, D/131a). A fragmentary example with the head broken off (D/60) is probably this type. The fourth Type II awl is a split long bone with its distal end removed and its shaft pointed (D/45).

The head of the Type III awl is partly worked down (figure 5.29h). The distal end of a long bone has been modified by deepening the groove exposed when the epiphysis became detached. The distal end was ground down, the proximal end removed, and the shaft sharpened. The Type IV awl is a split long bone with the head almost wholly removed (figure 5.29i). Splinter awls are Type V (figure 5.29j–m). They are

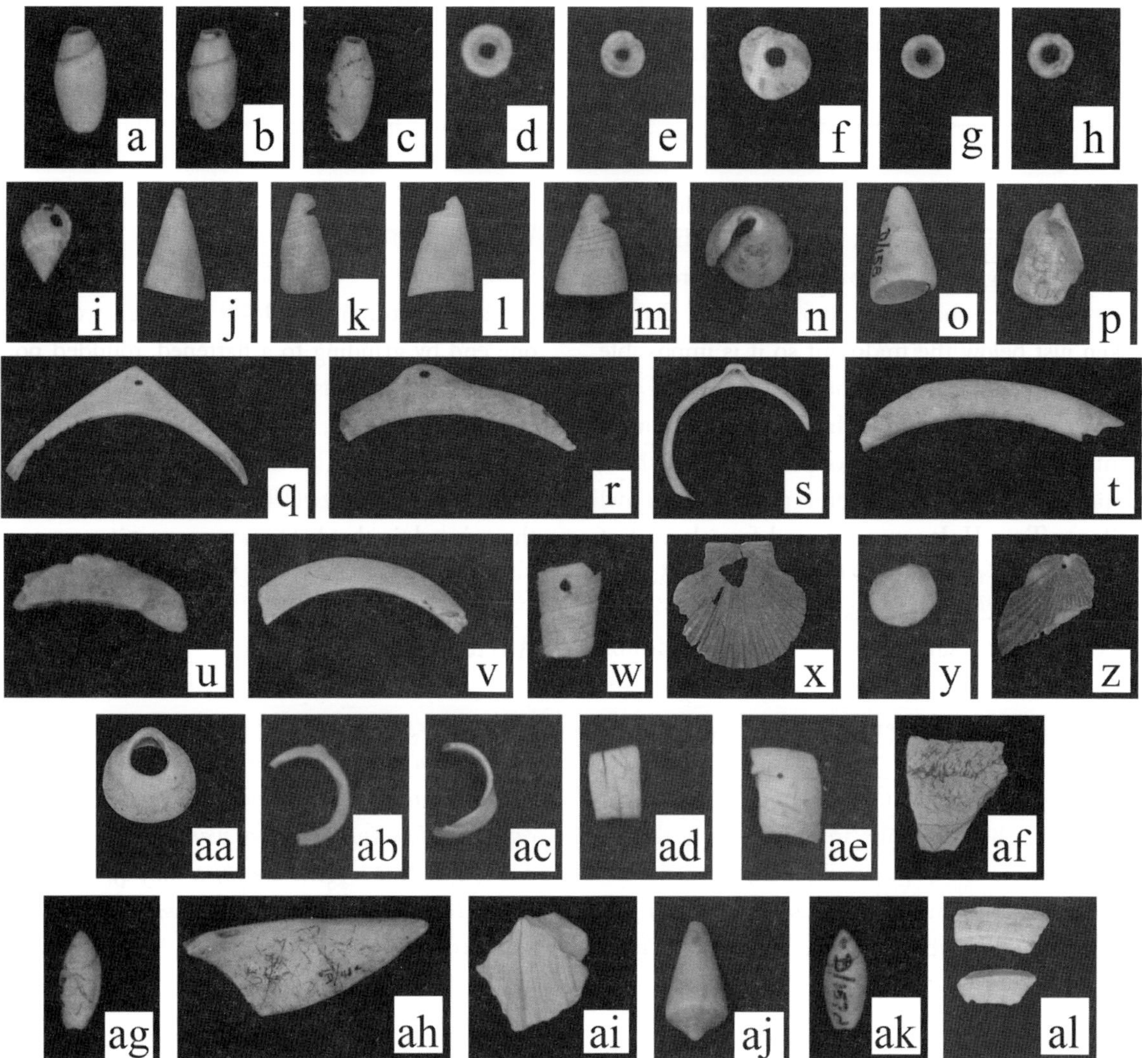

FIGURE 5.31 Shell beads (a–i), tinklers (j–p), bracelets (q–v), pendants (w–aa), rings (ab–ae), and unworked shell (af–al). See table D.1 for Amerind Museum catalog numbers and photograph numbers. Not to scale. For measurements, see table 5.30 (beads), table 5.31 (tinklers), table 5.32 (bracelets), table 5.33 (pendants), table 5.34 (rings), and table 5.35 (unworked shell). Courtesy of the Amerind Foundation Inc., Dragoon, Arizona.

SHELL

[*Editor: In 1957, George P. Kanakoff, then curator of paleontology at the Los Angeles County Museum, made the species identifications used here by Gerald. Arthur W. Vokes and Erika Heacock reanalyzed the entire shell assemblage, producing a report included in this volume as appendix C.*]

Beads

Type I, truncated, shell beads were ground to remove the spire, thus making it possible to string them (figure 5.31a–c, table 5.30). Disk beads, Type II, are with one exception of a relatively uniform size (figure 5.31d–h). The exception (D/157e) is saucer shaped—that is, concavo-convex in form—roughly

TABLE 5.30 Characteristics of shell beads from the Davis Ranch Site

Type	Catalog no.	Length	Diameter	Thickness	Perforation diameter	Species	*n*	Provenience	Figure
I	D/53b	1.4	0.7			*Olivella dama* Mawe	1	Kiva fill	5.31a
	D/98b	1.5	0.8			*Olivella dama* Mawe	1	Kiva ventilator	5.31b
	D/166c	1.4	0.7			*Olivella dama* Mawe	1	Stratitest level 1	5.31c
II	D/102		0.5	0.1	0.2	Unidentified	4	Burial 4	
	D/130a		0.5	0.2	0.1	*Olivella* sp.	1	House 6 fill	5.31d
	D/131d		0.4	0.1	0.1	Unidentified	1	House 6 floor	5.31e
	D/157e		1.2	0.1	0.3	Nacre	1	Room 4 subfloor test	5.31f
	D/189a		0.4	0.1	0.2	Unidentified	3	Burial 13	5.31g, h
III	D/166d	1.0	0.6			*Nassarius iodes* Dall	1	Stratitest 1 level 1	5.31i

Note: All measurements are in cm.

oval in outline, and made from a fragment of mother-of-pearl (figure 5.31f). The perforation is biconical.

A single example of a whole shell bead, D/166d, is classified as Type III (figure 5.31i). It was modified only by having a hole broken through it near the lip.

Tinklers

The spires of each of the Type I tinklers have been removed, leaving a conical whorl (figure 5.31j–n, table 5.31). Each has been perforated near the apex and close to the lip by a sawed groove at an approximate right angle to the axis of the cone. These shells, described by Kidder (1932:190) as "pinkish . . . with wavy, longitudinal red-brown markings," have been eroded, exposing a white layer below the original surface. A comparison with specimens from Paloparado reveals that the "Bead Pendant Type 1A-Conus shell (Base removed)" (Di Peso 1956:92) is identical to those from the Davis Ranch Site, except that many of the Paloparado specimens retain patches of the red-brown marked surface. This may be the result of different soil conditions at the two sites or of the use of dead, beach-worn shells by the Davis Ranch Site's occupants.

Type II tinklers are perhaps unfinished (figure 5.31o, p). Their spires have been removed but have not been perforated. It is possible that they were suspended by some other method, such as passing a knotted cord through the natural slit. The interior of one specimen (D/168a) is covered with sand and small shells cemented in place with a white substance. This, with the weathered condition of the surface and the lack of colored layers on the shell, suggests that this specimen and possibly the others may have been obtained from beach deposits rather than from the sea where they could be collected alive and fresh. The shells adhering to D/168a are *Barleeia acuta* Carpenter, *Dentalium dalli* Pilsbury and Sharp, *Halistylus subpupoides* Tryon, and *Teinostoma* cf. *polita* A. Adams.

Bracelets

The majority of the *Glycymeris* shell bracelets found at the Davis Ranch Site are of the thin, narrow sort described by Haury (1937c:142, Plate 157) as the earlier type at Snaketown (figure 5.31q–s, table 5.32). These specimens are slightly thicker than the Snaketown specimens. Only one specimen is complete enough to allow an interior diameter measurement, which is 4.3 cm. Of the seven fragments bearing umbos, only one is ground to an angle; three are perforated, one as a result of the shaping process and two as a result of drilling. One fragment has a hole drilled about halfway through it near one end;

TABLE 5.31 Characteristics of shell tinklers from the Davis Ranch Site

Type	Catalog no.	Length	Diameter	Species	Provenience	Figure
I	D/41	2.6	1.6	*Conus recurvus* Broderip	Kiva fill	5.31j
	D/53a	2.0	1.2	*Conus recurvus* Broderip	Kiva fill	5.31k
	D/55	2.0+	1.5	*Conus* cf. *purpurascens* Broderip	Surface	5.31l
	D/132	2.1	2.5	*Conus recurvus* Broderip	House 6 Pit 1	5.31m
	D/165	2.0	1.6	*Conus recurvus* Broderip	Kiva fill	5.31n
II	D/158	2.4	1.5	*Conus regularis* Sowerby	Room 6 entry fill	5.31o
	D/168a	2.3	1.6	*Conus purpurascens* Broderip	Stratitest 1 level 4	5.31p

Note: All measurements are in cm.

TABLE 5.32 Characteristics of shell bracelets from the Davis Ranch Site

Type	Catalog no.	Width	Thickness	Species	Provenience	Figure
I	D/17	0.4	0.5	*Glycymeris maculata* Broderip	T10N 0–7E	
	D/28	1.5	0.5	*Glycymeris maculata* Broderip	Kiva level 3	
	D/104	0.5	0.3	*Glycymeris maculata* Broderip	Burial 4 Vessel 8	5.31q
	D/122	0.3	0.3	*Glycymeris maculata* Broderip	House 4 fill	
	D/124	0.5	0.5	*Glycymeris maculata* Broderip	House 4 fill	
	D/126	0.5	0.5	*Glycymeris maculata* Broderip	House 4 floor	
	D/127	0.3	0.4	*Glycymeris maculata* Broderip	House 4 Pit 2	
	D/130b	0.4	0.5	*Glycymeris maculata* Broderip	House 6 fill	
	D/131b	0.4	0.4	*Glycymeris maculata* Broderip	House 6 floor	
	D/131c	0.3	0.4	*Glycymeris maculata* Broderip	House 6 floor	
	D/154b	0.4	0.4	*Glycymeris maculata* Broderip	Room 2 floor	
	D/166a	0.6	0.5	*Glycymeris maculata* Broderip	Stratitest 1 level 1	
	D/169a	0.5	0.6	*Glycymeris maculata* Broderip	NE Trash	5.31r
	D/171c	0.3	0.6	*Glycymeris maculata* Broderip	Surface	
	D/171d	0.3	0.4	*Glycymeris maculata* Broderip	Surface	
	D/177	0.4	0.4	*Glycymeris maculata* Broderip	T60E 14–15N	
	D/188d	0.4	0.1	*Glycymeris maculata* Broderip	Burial 10	5.31s
II	D/6	0.8	0.7	*Glycymeris maculata* Broderip	T1S 40–46E	
	D/94	0.6	0.7	*Glycymeris maculata* Broderip	Kiva floor	5.31t
	D/150	0.7	0.7	*Glycymeris multicostata* Sowerby	Kiva platform	5.31u
	D/166b	0.6	0.5	*Glycymeris maculata* Broderip	Stratitest 1 level 1	
III	D/43	1.1	0.5	*Glycymeris maculata* Broderip	House 1 floor	5.31v

Note: All measurements are in cm.

it may have been intended to function as a needle or a pendant (D/131b).

There are four Type II shell bracelets of medium width, all fragmentary (figure 5.31t, u). A single specimen, D/43, is classified as Type III. It is thick enough to be classed with the heavy band type described by Haury (1937c:142, 1945:154) and attributed to the later phases at Snaketown and the Classic period in the Gila-Salt area (figure 5.31v). Bracelets like these were found on the upper arms of burials at Paloparado and are called "armlets" by Di Peso (1956:97).

Pendants

Type I pendants are whole shells, only modified by providing a hole for suspension (figure 5.31w–z, table 5.33). Both *Pecten* [*Editor*: Euvola] pendants

TABLE 5.33 Characteristics of shell pendants from the Davis Ranch Site

Type	Catalog no.	Length	Width	Thickness	Perforation diameter	Species	Provenience	Figure
I	D/5	1.9+	1.3	1.3		*Turritella tigrina* Kiener	T1S 40–46E	5.31w
	D/141c	5.4	5.8		1.0	*Pecten vogdesi* Arnold	Cremation 1	5.31x
	D/171f	1.2	1.1	0.1	0.2	*Glycymeris subob-soleta* Carpenter	Surface	5.31y
	D/179	4.5+	3.1+	0.2	0.2	*Pecten vogdesi* Arnold	T17E 12S	5.31z
II	D/70	4.2	4.1	1.2	0.2	*Glycymeris macu-lata* Broderip	Burial 4	5.31aa

Note: All measurements are in cm.

were perforated at the beak, one apparently by breaking and the other by drilling. A triangular area over 1 cm on a side was broken out of the first specimen. This object subsequently was burned in a crematory fire. The second, fragmentary specimen has a drilled perforation. The *Glycymeris* shell was perforated at the beak by grinding until a breach was made. The fragmentary *Turritella* pendant had a hole broken through its lip.

The single Type II pendant, D/70, is a bivalve with a large central perforation (figure 5.31aa). The suspension hole was formed first by grinding at the umbo, then enlarged by drilling. The central perforation was apparently drilled and then enlarged by abrading.

Rings

D/15, a small *Glycymeris* shell, has been ground in the same manner as in making bracelets, and the umbo has been emphasized by grinding away the sloping edges, thus leaving a low, rectangular protuberance (figure 5.31ab, table 5.34). The *Conus* (identified by Gerald) rings were made by cutting a section from the large part of the shell after removing the spire, according to Haury (1945:156; figure 5.31ac–ae). One specimen, D/68, is incised with a running, rectilinear spiral design.

Unworked Shell

These whole and fragmentary shells show little or no shaping (figure 5.31af–al, table 5.35). The bivalves include four pieces from the hinge area, and all have broken rather than cut or ground edges. Six are fragments that may have been discarded because of their small size; the other four pieces are large enough to have been made into pendants, beads, et cetera. The univalves have not been modified in any way. The *Conus* has been eroded until almost none of the surface spiral markings are visible. This supports the suggestion offered above that these shells were collected from beach deposits rather than as fresh, living shells.

METAL

Skillet

Part of the bowl and most of the handle of a cast iron skillet of relatively recent vintage, D/171y, was

TABLE 5.34 Characteristics of shell rings from the Davis Ranch Site

Catalog no.	Diameter	Width	Species	Provenience	Figure
D/15	1.6	0.4	*Glycymeris subobsoleta* Carpenter	T1S 35E	5.31ab
D/47	2.1	0.9	*Conus* sp.	Kiva fill	5.31ac
D/48b		0.1	*Conus* sp.	Kiva fill	5.31ad
D/68		2.0	*Conus* sp.	Burial 4 Vessel 13	5.31ae

Note: All measurements are in cm.

TABLE 5.35 Unworked shell from the Davis Ranch Site

Catalog no.	*n*	Species	Provenience	Figure
D/18	1	*Laevicardium elatum* Sowerby	Kiva fill	
D/30a, b	2	*Glycymeris maculata* Broderip	Burial 1 level 4	5.31af
D/31	1	*Olivella dama* Mawe	Kiva fill	5.31ag
D/48a	1	*Laevicardium elatum* Sowerby	Kiva fill	5.31ah
D/105	1	*Laevicardium elatum* Sowerby	Kiva fill	
D/136c	1	*Tivela stultorum* Mawe	House 7 Floor 2	5.31ai
D/156c	1	*Olivella dama* Mawe	Room 4 floor	
D/157b	1	*Conus regularis* Sowerby	Room 4 subfloor test	5.31aj
D/157c, d	2	*Olivella dama* Mawe	Room 4 subfloor test	5.31ak
D/167	1	*Modiolus* sp. (probably *M. capax* Conrad)	Stratitest 1 level 2	5.31al
D/169c	1	*Anodonta* cf. *californiensis* Lea	NE Trash	
D/170a	1	*Glycymeris multicostata* Sowerby	NE Trash	
D/171e	1	Unidentified	Surface	

recovered from the surface of the site. The tip of the handle is missing, but enough remains to indicate it was perforated for hanging. Near the point where the handle attaches to the bowl is the number 8, which in present practice indicates the diameter (in inches) of the bowl of the skillet (20.3 cm). The bowl is 4.0 cm deep, and its walls range in thickness from 0.2 cm to 0.4 cm. The handle, which is broader near the tip than near the bowl, ranges from 2.1 cm to more than 3.4 cm in width and in thickness from 0.7 cm near the tip to 0.9 cm near the bowl. This artifact may have reached the site through pothunters who have occasionally visited the site or through the Ronquillo family who lived in a small house about 50 m to the south.

Nail

A cut iron nail, D/112, of the type in use in the United States from 1840 or 1860 onward (Gerald 1957b:193) was found during the subfloor testing of Room 40 in a pothunter's pit. The nail is 6.4 cm long, 0.2–0.6 cm wide, and 0.4 cm thick. The head measures 0.7 × 0.7 cm.

Sheet Iron

A strip of sheet iron, which was broken after excavation, has straight sides except for one small filed notch, and the ends are torn as though the strip had been bent back and forth until it broke. This specimen, D/39a, b, is apparently a portion of a metal band of the general type used to secure heavy wooden boxes. It is 6.8 cm long, 1.5 cm wide, 0.1 cm thick, and was recovered from the upper 40 cm of fill in the kiva.

Harmonica

One end of a harmonica frame with four slots and vibrators, D/171h, was found on the surface of the site. The frame is of a white metal, and the vibrators are of a yellow, brass-like metal. It measures 4.70 cm long, 4.30 cm wide, and 0.20 cm thick. The vibrators are attached alternately to opposite sides of the frame by iron rivets. The frame is slightly wider at the unbroken end than it is at the broken end (3.90 cm), and the slot at the unbroken end is slightly longer (2.70 cm) than the slot at the other end (2.55 cm), all of which suggests that this fragment is from the bass end of the instrument.

Cartridge Cases

Two center-fire cartridge cases, D/171w and D/171x, were found on the surface of the site. The cap has been removed from D/171w. It measures 4.6 cm long, and its diameter ranges from 1.5 cm to 1.7 cm. The slug-end is flattened and cracked, and a triangular strip 1.2 cm wide × 2.4 cm long has been cut out of one side. This casing probably carried a .50-caliber slug. D/171x is a modern .30-06 casing that may have been dropped within the year. It is 6.3 cm long, and its diameter varies from 0.9 cm to 1.2 cm. The markings on its base read "Super X 30-06 SPRG."

Unidentified Fragments

Three badly corroded fragments of iron recovered from the upper 30 cm of kiva fill, D/59, were of indeterminable shape, but all belong to the same piece. One end of the largest fragment appears to remain in its original form, from which a cross section of the specimen may be obtained. This less-corroded end suggests that the specimen is a portion of the edge of a flat plate with a thickened, rounded rim. The heavier portion is 0.4 cm thick and extends 1.5 cm in from the edge; the metal is 0.2 cm thick away from this rim section. The cross-sectional view would indicate that the thickening is equal on each side of the 0.2 cm thick plate, but the remainder of the specimen suggests that the thickening is all on one side.

GLASS

Bottle Sherds

Three fragments of hand-blown green glass bottles were picked up (table 5.36). A restorable bottle base is 6.4 cm in diameter and has an indentation of the type commonly seen in champagne bottles, 2.3 cm deep. Fragments of brown glass with white corrosion of the surface are too small to give much information about the size and shape of the complete specimen. One fragment of an orifice has a thickened band extending 2.5 cm down from the lip. A fragment of blue glass contains several small air bubbles and has been cast in a mold that imparted two design elements. One is a circle with a raised perimeter and a raised dot in the center, and the other is deep crosshatching.

TABLE 5.36 Characteristics of glass bottle fragments from the Davis Ranch Site

Catalog no.	Diameter	Thickness	Color	Provenience
D/171n	6.4	—	Green	Surface
D/171o	—	0.4	Green	Surface
D/171p	—	0.5	Brown	Surface
D/171q	—	0.7	Brown	Surface
D/171r	—	0.3	Brown	Surface
D/171s	—	0.3	Brown	Surface
D/171t	—	0.7	Blue	Surface
D/185	—	0.5	Green	T20W 35–36S surface

Note: All measurements are in cm.

TABLE 5.37 Characteristics of leather fragments from the Davis Ranch Site

Catalog no.	Length	Width	Thickness	Provenience
D/88	8.0	6.3	0.2	Room 11 NE corner, animal burrow in floor
	7.5	0.8	0.2	
	5.5	2.9	0.2	
	4.8	0.6	0.2	
	3.5	0.7	0.2	

Note: All measurements are in cm.

PERISHABLE MATERIAL

Leather

Five fragments of leather, D/88, were found in an apparent animal burrow in the northeast corner of Room 11 (table 5.37). This hole is 30 cm deep and has vertical sides. Two fragments appear to be from the edge of a shoe sole because they bear holes that are connected by depressions caused by stitches. The holes are long and narrow, and their long axis forms a slight angle with the stitch depressions. In addition, part of the central portion of the sole has been cut away, leaving a smooth, straight-edged cut with an occasional pointed projection where the blade deviated. The remainder of the central portion has apparently been removed by tearing. Another section of the fragment bears what appear to be rodent teeth marks. Two other leather fragments are apparently from the shoe sole though they bear no holes or stitch depressions. The fifth piece is apparently a length of a leather thong. The larger piece of shoe sole has no indications of stitching on one side, and it probably was originally wider.

TABLE 5.38 Macrobotanical materials from the Davis Ranch Site and field identifications

Catalog no.	Description	Provenience
D/4	Charred corn and mesquite beans (?)	Pit Oven 1
D/23	Burned straw or wood	Room 3 fill
D/24	Burned straw (?)	Room 3 fill
D/72	Charred seeds and wood	Burial 4 Vessel 13
D/73	Charred seeds and wood	Burial 4 Vessel 8
D/77	Charred corncobs	Kiva fill
D/84	Charred cane fragments	Room 10 fill, roofing
D/101	Decayed wood	Kiva Posthole 1
D/103	Hackberry seeds	Room 11 floor
D/133	Burned cane	House 6 Pit 2
D/154c	Burned cane	Room 2 floor
D/172	Wood fragment	T11E 11S posthole
D/188f	Cucurbit (?) seed	Burial 10
D/189b	Hackberry seeds	Burial 13

Note: Information in this table is derived from catalog cards.

Plant Remains

[*Editor: Plant remains identified in the field as corncobs, hackberry and possibly cucurbit seeds, cane, grass, wood, and possibly mesquite beans were sent to Hugh C. Cutler of the Missouri Botanical Garden for detailed analysis (table 5.38). A letter from Cutler to Gerald in El Paso, dated August 5, 1965, states that the analysis was completed "some time ago" and that a report would be forthcoming. Unfortunately, no such report has been located.*]

6

Pottery Types

[*Editor: This chapter consists of portions of two incomplete chapters written by Rex Gerald. The bulk of the original text was meant to constitute a report on the pottery recovered from the Davis Ranch Site and consisted entirely of type descriptions based on unworked potsherds and vessels. Most type descriptions included some treatment of vessel form and size. Text describing ceramic objects such as worked sherds, miniature vessels, a portion of an effigy vessel, and a figurine fragment was originally included in Gerald's chapter reporting on his analyses of the non-ceramic artifacts.*

Decorated pottery is discussed first, by ware or series and type, in descending order of abundance. Next, utility wares and types are addressed, following the same frequency-based sequence. Red ware has been included with plain ware and corrugated pottery in the utility ware category. The ware, series, and type names employed represent current usage, with the exception of some formal and informal taxa created by Gerald and Di Peso. A reanalysis of the Roosevelt Red Ware, Maverick Mountain Series pottery, and perforated plates is presented in chapter 7.

Discrepancies were noted upon comparison of type totals that appeared in Gerald's table (appendix E) with those found in the draft version of the manuscript. The table seemingly reflects an attempt by Gerald to refine his typological assignments. For example, Gila Polychrome was reduced by 108 sherds, and other Roosevelt Red Ware type frequencies—Pinto Polychrome, Tonto Polychrome, Gila Black-on-red, Gila White Slip, and Gila Polychrome (Pink Variant)—increased by a total of 108 sherds. I feel confident in my choice to use the totals in appendix E as this is the only dataset that provides comprehensive provenience information along with typological assignments. I assume that Gerald had not yet updated the totals in the manuscript to match his master table (appendix E). Two other minor differences between the manuscript and the table were discovered. Three sherds appear in the table under the rubric "unidentified polychrome," yet they are not described in the manuscript. One sherd of Kinishba Polychrome is mentioned in the manuscript but does not appear in the table. Finally, I located and described six partially reconstructible vessels identified and/or assembled but not cataloged by Gerald (D/237, D/238, D/239, D/240, D/241, and D/242).]

DECORATED WARES, SERIES, AND TYPES

Roosevelt Red Ware

Gila Polychrome

The Gila Polychrome (Colton and Hargrave 1937: 88–90) assemblage includes 8,404 sherds and 16 vessels (figure 6.1, table 6.1). [*Editor: Gerald's draft manuscript indicated the recovery of 8,512 sherds of*

FIGURE 6.1 Gila Polychrome bowl (D/232) from Burial 14. For measurements, see table 6.1. Photograph by Jannelle Weakly.

Gila Polychrome. I have classified three of Gerald's whole or reconstructible Gila Polychrome vessels as Cliff Polychrome (Lyons 2004b), one as Gila Polychrome: Salmon Variety (see Gila Polychrome [Pink Variant], below), and one as Phoenix Polychrome (Lyons and Neuzil 2006; Neuzil and Lyons 2006). I also located three partially reconstructible Roosevelt Red Ware bowls identified but not cataloged by Gerald. Two are Gila Polychrome (D/237 and D/239), and one is Cliff Polychrome (D/238).]

Gila Polychrome is by far the most numerous decorated type represented at the Davis Ranch Site. It occurs in assemblages of all phases but was not produced during the Hohokam Colonial or Sedentary periods (Davis phase). The few sherds found in Colonial or Sedentary period associations probably were introduced by rodent activity. Gila Polychrome represents about 40% of the decorated sherds of the Aravaipa (Sosa) phase and about 85% of the decorated sherds of the Redfield and Romero phases (Reeve phase). [*Editor: Included among the sherds assigned by Gerald to Gila Polychrome are specimens of Cliff Polychrome, Phoenix Polychrome, and Nine Mile Polychrome (Lyons and Neuzil 2006; Neuzil and Lyons 2006). Currently accepted dates for these types are Gila Polychrome, AD 1300–1450; Cliff Polychrome, AD 1360–1450; Phoenix and Nine Mile Polychrome, AD 1375–1450 (Lyons 2013a).*]

Gila White Slip

The Gila White Slip (Di Peso 1958a:99) sample consists of 374 sherds. [*Editor: Gerald's draft manuscript reported 365 sherds of Gila White Slip. Reexamination resulted in the conclusion that many of these Roosevelt Red Ware sherds bore traces of black, organic pigment that had burned out, likely as a result of firing accidents.*]

Most specimens of Gila White Slip are probably unpainted sherds of Gila Polychrome vessels. These sherds are listed separately because an unpainted variety of Gila Polychrome was recognized and described by Di Peso at Reeve Ruin. [*Editor: Some of the sherds of Gila White Slip in the Reeve Ruin collection exhibit traces of black, organic paint, like those recovered from the Davis Ranch Site. Others may be unpainted portions of Gila Polychrome vessels. It is possible, based on the available fragments, that two large Roosevelt Red Ware bowls found at Reeve Ruin lacked interior black paint entirely.*] The nearest approximation of this type in whole vessels from the Davis

TABLE 6.1 Characteristics of Roosevelt Red Ware vessels from the Davis Ranch Site

Type	Form	Cat. no.	Max. diameter	Orifice diameter	Height	Wall thickness	Provenience	Comments/ revised type	Figure
Gila Black-on-red	Bowl	D/229	19.7	17.7	9.9	0.6	Burial 13		6.2
Gila Polychrome	Bowl	D/193	19.5	16.7	9.5	0.3	Burial 4	Gila Polychrome: Salmon Variety	7.22b
		D/194	15.5	13.1	8.2	0.4	Burial 4		7.22c
		D/196	23.9	21.1	14.3	0.5	Burial 4	Cliff Polychrome	7.22d
		D/200	20.9	17.8	11.0	0.5	Burial 4	Phoenix Polychrome	7.22e
		D/201	31.5	29.0	16.2	0.5	Burial 4		7.22f
		D/202	35.4	31.0	16.0	0.7	Burial 4	Cliff Polychrome	7.22g
		D/203	27.3	25.4	14.1	0.4	Burial 4		7.22h
		D/205	26.9	23.1	13.8	0.5	Burial 4	Cliff Polychrome	7.22i
		D/207	17.5	16.5	8.6	0.5	Burial 5		7.21c
		D/209	17.9	15.5	10.1	0.6	Burial 8		7.21a
		D/210	29.3	26.5	14.5	0.5	Burial 8		7.21b
		D/214	10.8	9.6	5.4	0.3	Burial 9	Cover for D/215	7.20a
		D/220	21.1	19.8	9.8	0.6	Burial 10		7.20b
		D/232	20.2	17.0	12.5	0.5	Burial 14		6.1
		D/233	24.7	22.2	13.3	0.6	Burial 15		7.20c
		D/237	24.0	24.0	11.5	0.6	Kiva floor		7.28d
		D/238	36.0	33.0		0.6	Trench in front of Room 21	Cliff Polychrome	7.37a
		D/239	30.0	27.0		0.6	Room 16 fill		7.36c
	Jar	D/192	37.0	15.7	14.7	0.4	Burial 4		7.22a

Note: All measurements are in cm.

Ranch Site is a Gila Polychrome bowl (D/232) with two black bands, one wide and one narrow, near the rim; the remainder of the bowl interior apparently is undecorated (see figure 6.1). Gila White Slip sherds were found in Redfield and Romero (Reeve) phase contexts almost exclusively.

Tonto Polychrome

The Tonto Polychrome (Colton and Hargrave 1937:90–91) assemblage includes 202 sherds. [*Editor: The total number of Tonto Polychrome sherds reported in Gerald's draft manuscript is 192.*] Tonto Polychrome, the fourth most numerous decorated pottery type, is confined almost entirely to the Redfield and Romero phases (Reeve phase). [*Editor: The currently accepted dates for Tonto Polychrome are AD 1340–1450 (Lyons 2013a).*] Tonto Polychrome at the Davis Ranch Site occurs in jar form in 87% of the sherds. Decoration is almost always on the exterior of bowls, though interior decoration also occurs frequently as well. Overall design layout is difficult to discern from sherds, but almost all seem to bear, on their exteriors, portions of broad horizontal or oblique bands of black-on-white design. Bowl interiors usually also bear a broad white band around the rim on which black designs are executed; the remainder of the interior is slipped red. [*Editor: Here, Gerald refers to portions of Nine Mile Polychrome vessels (Lyons and Neuzil 2006; Neuzil and Lyons 2006), although they are not nearly as common in the assemblage as one would assume based on his use of the word "usually" (see chapter 7).*] A few bowls bear Gila Polychrome decoration on the interior; that is, the entire interior is slipped white and covered with black designs. No sherds bearing red designs on white slip were found; this type occurs occasionally at Los Muertos (Haury 1945:65–66) and on the Verde River (personal observation at Mercer Ruin, AZ O:14:1[ASM]). [*Editor: This type is now known as Los Muertos Polychrome (Lyons 2004b:366, 2013a; Lyons and Neuzil 2006; Neuzil and Lyons 2006) and recognized as one of the latest types in the Roosevelt Red Ware sequence. Its absence from the Davis Ranch Site assemblage is not unexpected.*]

Design elements are almost all rectilinear in form: lines, triangles, pendant triangles, ticked lines, rectilinear scrolls, and squares with dotted centers. Curvilinear motifs include scrolls attached to triangles and the "bird-wing." The edges of bands are occasionally bordered by black lines covering the white slip and part of the red slip rather than by white slip. Paste is usually black at the core and contains abundant, light-colored sand temper. One bowl sherd recovered from the fill of House 7 exhibits an exterior surface treatment similar to that characteristic of Tularosa Fillet Rim (Rinaldo 1952:65). [*Editor: The interior decoration of this partial vessel is unusual. It is a variety of Nine Mile Polychrome that exhibits the usual band of black-on-white decoration at the rim but also a fragment of what is likely a large black-on-white motif surrounded by red slip and pendant from the rim band. I know of only one other published example of this treatment, a bowl from the Curtis Site, AZ CC:2:3(ASM) (Lister and Lister 1978:Figure 45, bottom row, right).*]

Gila Black-on-red

The Gila Black-on-red (Wendorf 1950:123–124) sample consists of 155 sherds and one vessel (figure 6.2). [*Editor: Gerald's draft manuscript indicates the presence of 154 sherds of Gila Black-on-red.*] Gila Black-on-red is the seventh most numerous decorated pottery type found at the Davis Ranch Site. Sherds of this type are found in all phase contexts but are most numerous in those assigned to the Aravaipa (Sosa) phase, during which the type is believed to have been introduced to the site. [*Editor: The currently accepted dates for Gila Black-on-red are AD 1300–1450 (Lyons 2013a).*] This type occurs mainly in bowl form (88% of the sherds are of bowls), jar sherds being relatively rare. This is the opposite of Tucson Polychrome and Tucson Black-on-red.

Gila Black-on-red at the Davis Ranch Site exhibits a greater range of surface color than the described type, some sherds having the appearance of Awatovi Black-on-orange (Watson Smith, personal communication 1957) but with what appears to be local paste. [*Editor: Here Gerald very likely*

FIGURE 6.2 Gila Black-on-red bowl (D/229) from Burial 13. For measurements, see table 6.1. Photograph by Jannelle Weakly.

refers to Jeddito Black-on-orange, the dominant black-on-orange type found at Awat'ovi (Smith 1971:352–441).] Twenty-four sherds appear to be intrusive to the site because of their temper and paste. These are relatively equally divided between Redfield and Romero (Reeve) phase and Aravaipa (Sosa) phase contexts; one sherd was recovered from a Hohokam Colonial or Sedentary period (Davis phase) context. [*Editor: The majority of the material Gerald classified as Gila Black-on-red has been re-typed as Maverick Mountain Black-on-red and Tucson Black-on-red. Gila Black-on-red remains a poorly described type and has long been troublesome to researchers (see the discussion of Tucson Black-on-red, below).*]

Pinto Polychrome

The Pinto Polychrome (Colton and Hargrave 1937:87–88) assemblage includes 110 sherds. [*Editor: Gerald's draft manuscript indicates the presence of 24 sherds.*] Pinto Polychrome is poorly represented at the Davis Ranch Site, and of the few sherds placed in this class, less than half of them conform in all respects to the type description. The majority are of the variety of Gila Polychrome lacking the rim band and having the design extend up to the rim, which is said to occur in southeastern Arizona (Haury 1949:137). [*Editor: Here, Gerald appears to be referring to what has been called Pinto-Gila Polychrome A (Lyons 2012b).*] The type occurs in Aravaipa (Sosa) phase associations mainly, and in Redfield and Romero (Reeve) phase associations to a lesser extent. [*Editor: The currently accepted dates for Pinto Polychrome are AD 1280–1330 (Mills and Herr 1999).*]

Gila Polychrome (Pink Variant)

The Gila Polychrome (Pink Variant) (Di Peso 1958a:100) sample consists of 17 sherds. [*Editor: Gerald's draft manuscript indicates 16 sherds were present. This type is now known as Gila Polychrome: Salmon Variety (Lyons 2012b).*] Gila Polychrome (Pink Variant) is a form of Gila Polychrome having a decidedly pink slip in place of the normally white or cream slip. It occurs sporadically in Aravaipa (Sosa) and Redfield and Romero (Reeve) phase associations. [*Editor: Discussions of the salmon varieties of Pinto Polychrome and Gila Polychrome have been offered by Haury (1931:70–71, 1934:135), Lindsay and Jennings (1968:9), and Crown (1994:17). As noted by Haury (1931:70–71), salmon variety Roosevelt Red Ware polychrome bowls were produced in two ways. Some have unslipped interiors, and others bear a pink interior slip.*]

Gila-Tucson Polychrome

This is a new type, defined on the basis of four sherds. These sherds are from three different bowls. Two bowls have Gila Polychrome style decoration on the interior and Tucson Polychrome style decoration on the exterior. They occur in Redfield and Romero (Reeve) phase associations. [*Editor: At the Davis Ranch Site, three rim sherds and a body sherd from a single vessel of this type exhibit Cliff Polychrome interior decoration and exterior decoration characteristic of Tucson Polychrome (figure 6.3). This manifestation is now referred to as Cliff Polychrome: Tucson Variety (Lyons 2013a). The second vessel Gerald placed in this class is represented by a Gila Polychrome bowl rim sherd with black exterior painted decoration. The third vessel, represented by a bowl body sherd, is something quite different: the interior decoration is like that of Tucson Black-on-red, and the exterior bears black painted designs on white slip. Di Peso (1958a:100) named Pinto-Tucson Polychrome based on six sherds recovered from Reeve Ruin. Some exhibit Tucson Polychrome exterior design and Pinto Polychrome interior decoration. Others bear Gila Polychrome interior decoration and Tucson Polychrome exterior designs. Franklin (1980:66) reports similar material at the nearby Second Canyon Ruin (see also Lindsay and Jennings 1968:12). An additional specimen (Gila Polychrome interior, Tucson Polychrome exterior) was recently encountered during a study of uncataloged sherds from Kinishba that are now curated by the Arizona State Museum (Lyons 2013a).*]

Maverick Mountain Series

[*Editor: The Maverick Mountain Series was named in 1955, appearing in Colton's (1955:8) first comprehensive checklist of the region's pottery types, and was mentioned in Morris's (1957:31) master's thesis on AZ W:10:50B at Point of Pines. The series, as it was first conceived, included five types: Maverick Mountain Black-on-red, Maverick Mountain Polychrome, Nantack Polychrome, Prieto Polychrome, and Tucson Polychrome. The first formal type definitions, for Tucson Polychrome and Tucson Black-on-red, were published in 1957 and 1958. The other types, however, have only been described recently and somewhat informally (Lindsay 1987, 1992; Lyons 2004d, 2012b, 2013a). Danson (1957), based on work with material from the University Indian Ruin and Point of Pines, fleshed out and provided interpretive context for Clarke's (1933:66, Plate 36, 1935:55, Plate 26) brief description of Tucson Polychrome (named Martinez Hill Polychrome by Gabel [1931:43, 52–53]). Di Peso (1958a:103) soon afterward described Tucson Black-on-red based on material found at the Reeve Ruin. Most of the Maverick Mountain Series pottery encountered by Gerald could be accommodated by then-current conceptions of Tucson Polychrome, Tucson Black-on-red, and Tucson Polychrome (Hachured Variant) (Di Peso 1958a:103).*]

Tucson Polychrome

The Tucson Polychrome (Clarke 1935:55, Plate 26) assemblage includes 184 sherds and four vessels (figure 6.4, table 6.2). [*Editor: (See also Clarke 1933:*

FIGURE 6.3 Cliff Polychrome: Tucson Variety partially reconstructible bowl (Kiva Decorated Vessel 12): (a) interior, (b) exterior. Photographs by Patrick D. Lyons.

66, Plate 36). Di Peso (1958a:103; see also Rinaldo 1974b:151), based on material from Reeve Ruin, named a Tucson Polychrome (Hachured Variant). Gerald's manuscript implies and his sherd groupings indicate that he recognized but did not analytically separate this variant. The hatched specimens would today be typed as Maverick Mountain Polychrome (Lindsay 1992).] Tucson Polychrome is the fifth most popular decorated type at the Davis Ranch Site. Forty percent of the sherds are bowls and the remainder are jars. Decoration is confined to the exteriors of bowls (a few sherds with interior decoration are not definitely this type) and is almost always composed of large wide lines in black outlined in narrow white lines and laid out in rectilinear patterns of scrolls often terminating in stepped elements, triangles, and

FIGURE 6.4 Tucson Polychrome jars: D/215 (a) from Burial 9 and D/216 (b), D/217 (c), and D/219 (d) from Burial 10. Not to scale. For measurements, see table 6.2. Photographs by Jannelle Weakly.

TABLE 6.2 Characteristics of Maverick Mountain Series vessels from the Davis Ranch Site

Type	Form	Catalog no.	Maximum diameter	Orifice diameter	Height	Wall thickness	Provenience	Comments	Figure
Tucson Polychrome	Jar	D/215	16.8	8.8	13.2	0.5	Burial 9	D/214 was on top, upright as a cover	6.4a
		D/216	20.6	10.1	15.4	0.5	Burial 10		6.4b
		D/217	19.7	9.9	16.7	0.5	Burial 10		6.4c
		D/219	18.2	9.6	14.1	0.5	Burial 10		6.4d

Note: All measurements are in cm.

vertical, horizontal, and oblique lines. Solid elements are almost the exclusive form; triangles are sometimes outlined in such a manner that there is seldom massing of black greater than the width of the lines; hatching is very rare, appearing only on sherds believed to represent a transitional type between the Kayenta-Maverick Mountain Polychrome and Tucson Polychrome as represented at Point of Pines (Danson 1957). The four vessels of this type occur in Aravaipa (Sosa) phase burials. Tucson Polychrome is present in all phases but most strongly represented in the Aravaipa (Sosa) phase. [*Editor: The currently accepted dates for Tucson Polychrome and Tucson Black-on-red are AD 1300–1400 (Lindsay 1992).*]

Tucson Black-on-red

The Tucson Black-on-red (Clarke 1935:55, Plate 25 [*Editor: Here, Clarke refers to Middle Gila Black-on-red.*]; Di Peso 1958a:103) sample consists of 175 sherds [*Editor: (see also Clarke 1933:65–66, Plate 35)*]. Tucson Black-on-red, the sixth most popular decorated type, is a companion of Tucson Polychrome and is distinguishable from the latter by the absence of the narrow white lines bordering the black lines. [*Editor: Franklin (1980:65–66) notes that the white paint used to outline black Tucson Polychrome motifs is very easily eroded, leaving no visible trace. Nonetheless, bichrome whole vessels in excellent condition attest to the reality of Tucson Black-on-red as a useful type.*] The same design elements and design layout are found, and there are also a few samples of thin black lines and of hatching, but these are rare. [*Editor: Today, the hatched specimens would be identified as Maverick Mountain Black-on-red.*] This type is also found in all phases, but as with Tucson Polychrome, it is believed to belong to the Aravaipa (Sosa) phase primarily with a continuation into the Redfield and Romero phases (Reeve phase).

[*Editor: By citing Clarke (1935), Gerald is calling attention to the fact that much of the material formerly classified as Gila Black-on-red or Middle Gila Black-on-red is actually Tucson Black-on-red or Maverick Mountain Black-on-red. There is also the matter of Upper Gila Black-on-red (Clarke 1933:55–56, Plate 26, 1935:46–47, Plate 18), which Di Peso (1958a:98–99) includes in Gila Black-on-red. Di Peso's discussion of Gila Black-on-red indicates identification based on carbon paint. Danson (1957:228), however, suggests an iron-bearing paint was used to produce Tucson Polychrome (and by extension, presumably, Tucson Black-on-red). Franklin's (1980:65) oxidation tests instead indicate Tucson Polychrome (and by extension, Tucson Black-on-red) exhibits a manganese-bearing paint (see also Wilson 1998a:206). Lindsay's (1992) later review of Tucson Polychrome does not address paint composition. Recent examination of specimens from the Sulphur Springs Valley, the San Pedro Valley, Point of Pines, and the Tucson and Safford Basins (including the University Indian Ruin) has resulted in the observation that the "black" mineral paint characteristic of the type ranges in color from a deep black to brown and that some even has a purplish cast. All three colors are evident in the sample of Tucson Polychrome and Tucson Black-on-red recovered from San Pedro Valley sites by Archaeology Southwest (Lyons 2012b). Brownish-black paint, however, is dominant among specimens from the Davis Ranch Site and from the San Pedro Valley as a whole.*]

Middle Gila Buff Ware

[*Editor: Following Wallace (2001), I refer to the group of red-on-buff pottery types that exhibit "micaceous schist" (Pinal Schist; Miksa 2001) temper as "Middle Gila Buff Ware." These types are also known by the term "Hohokam Buff Ware" (Colton and Hargrave 1937; Whittlesey and Heckman 2000:95). Like Wallace, I prefer the term that refers to the area where these types were produced, as local "Hohokam" buff ware traditions were established in other regions, including the San Pedro Valley, the Safford Basin, the Gila Bend area, and some would argue, the Tucson Basin. Middle Gila Buff Ware types were originally defined by Winifred and Harold Gladwin (1933:25–27) and Emil Haury (1937a), and later refined by Haury (1945, 1976; see also Crown 1981). Based on a numerical seriation of attributes exhibited by specimens from the Grewe Site (AZ AA:2:2[ASM]) in the middle Gila River Valley, Wallace (2001, 2004) has recently subdivided some types. Although none of the specimens from the Amerind Foundation collection have been subjected to provenance analysis, a sample of sherds Gerald identified as Gila Butte Red-on-buff, Santa Cruz Red-on-buff, and Sacaton Red-on-buff were compared with type sherds curated by ASM. Based on macroscopic observations and examination using a 10-power hand lens, the Middle Gila Buff Ware sherds recovered from the Davis Ranch Site are indistinguishable from specimens found at Snaketown.*]

Santa Cruz Red-on-buff

The Santa Cruz Red-on-buff (Gladwin and Gladwin 1933:8–14; Haury 1937a:179–185) assemblage includes 236 sherds. [*Editor: Gerald's draft manuscript indicates 237 sherds were present.*] Santa Cruz Red-on-buff is the second most numerous decorated type found at the Davis Ranch Site, and though there are sherds of this type in assemblages representing all phases, there is a noticeably higher frequency in the Hohokam Colonial and Sedentary period (Davis phase) deposits than those attributable to later phases. It seems probable that this pottery type was in use during the Colonial period and that scattered sherds reached the later occupation areas by being included in adobe wall and roofing material. [*Editor: The currently accepted dates for Santa Cruz Red-on-buff are AD 850–950 (Craig 2001).*]

Sacaton Red-on-buff

The Sacaton Red-on-buff (Gladwin and Gladwin 1933:16–21; Haury 1937a:171–178) sample consists of 108 sherds. [*Editor: Gerald's draft manuscript indicates 112 sherds were present.*] Sacaton Red-on-buff sherds do not form a high proportion of the decorated ware of any phase, but they occur with greatest frequency during the Hohokam Colonial and Sedentary periods (Davis phase) and the Aravaipa (Sosa) phase. The scattered sherds in later associations were most likely redeposited. [*Editor: The currently accepted dates for Sacaton Red-on-buff are AD 950–1150 (Craig 2001).*]

Gila Butte Red-on-buff

The Gila Butte Red-on-buff (Haury 1937a:185–189) assemblage includes 11 sherds. [*Editor: Gerald's draft manuscript indicates nine sherds were present.*] Gila Butte Red-on-buff sherds occurred in assemblages of all phases, but the greatest concentration is found in Hohokam Colonial and Sedentary period (Davis phase) contexts. [*Editor: The currently accepted dates for Gila Butte Red-on-buff are AD 750–850 (Craig 2001).*]

Casa Grande Red-on-buff

One sherd of Casa Grande Red-on-buff (Gladwin and Gladwin 1933:22–24; Haury 1945:51–62) was recovered. This specimen was found in the fill of a Hohokam Colonial or Sedentary period (Davis phase) house, but the presence of Redfield and Romero (Reeve) phase structures nearby make it extremely dubious that the phase association is valid. [*Editor: Casa Grande Red-on-buff is a marker of the early Hohokam Classic period, the Soho phase, and persists at least through part of the succeeding Civano phase (Haury 1945). A start date of AD 1150 is currently accepted, but an end date is difficult to establish. This type seems to have been replaced by Roosevelt Red Ware types that were produced until circa AD 1450, suggesting production of Casa Grande Red-on-buff ceased sometime between 1350 and 1400.*]

Tucson Basin Brown Ware

[*Editor: The term "Tucson Basin Brown Ware" is used here to refer to the red-on-brown types, black-on-brown subtypes, and polychrome types made in the Tucson Basin. Heckman (2000a) has presented the most recent historical treatment of Tucson Basin Brown Ware typology, tracing the first formal type descriptions to Isabel Kelly's manuscript on the 1937–1938 work at the Hodges Ruin (AZ AA:12:18[ASM]; see Kelly et al. 1978). The typology has been debated, expanded, and revised by a number of researchers over time (e.g., Danson 1957; Deaver 1984; Greenleaf 1975; Heckman and Whittlesey 1999; Heidke 1995, 2000; Wallace 1986). The painted designs characteristic of Tucson Basin Brown Ware largely match those exhibited by Middle Gila Buff Ware types, such that Cañada del Oro Red-on-brown is the analog of Gila Butte Red-on-buff, Rillito Red-on-brown parallels Santa Cruz Red-on-buff, Rincon Red-on-brown is reminiscent of Sacaton Red-on-buff, and Tanque Verde Red-on-brown bears the same decorations as Casa Grande Red-on-buff (and San Carlos Red-on-brown).*]

Rillito Red-on-brown (Micaceous)

The sample of Rillito Red-on-brown with micaceous paste (Di Peso 1956:355; cf. Kelly 1938; Kelly et al. 1978:29–39) consists of 114 sherds. [*Editor: Gerald's draft manuscript indicates 115 sherds were present.*] Rillito Red-on-brown with micaceous paste is the ninth most abundant pottery type at the Davis Ranch Site. It occurs in all phases but is relatively rare in Redfield and Romero (Reeve) phase assemblages. The type occurs in highest proportion in the Hohokam Colonial and Sedentary periods (Davis phase) and in a slightly lower proportion in the Aravaipa (Sosa) phase. It is believed to have been in use during both of these intervals. [*Editor: Currently accepted dates for Rillito Red-on-brown are AD 850–950 (Swartz 2008). Although none of these sherds have been subjected to provenance analysis, recent petrographic work with specimens recovered from the San Pedro Valley by Archaeology Southwest resulted in the discovery that Tucson Basin Brown Ware and Tucson Basin Brown Ware–like pottery was produced in the area surrounding the Davis Ranch Site. Production areas include the Aravaipa Creek-San Pedro River confluence and the stretch of the valley between Benson and Mammoth (Lyons 2012b). In some cases, the "mica" or "schist" temper previously identified as characteristic of San Pedro Valley pottery (e.g., Franklin 1980:73–75, 99–104) has turned out, upon inspection by geologists, to be phyllite, which crops out in the vicinity of the San Pedro-Aravaipa confluence. Mica is typically found in vessels produced in the vicinity of the Davis Ranch Site. These facts together suggest that some specimens of the "micaceous" Tucson Basin Brown Ware types reported by Gerald (see also Franklin 1980) are local, San Pedro Valley products. That said, based on macroscopic observations and examination with the aid of a 10-power hand lens, a sample of sherds identified as Rillito Red-on-brown, Rincon Red-on-brown, and Tanque Verde Red-on-brown by Gerald was found to be indistinguishable from type sherds recovered from the Hodges Ruin curated at ASM. A sample of Gerald's Pantano Red-on-brown was similarly compared with type specimens from University Indian Ruin, and no significant differences were apparent.*]

Rincon Red-on-brown

The Rincon Red-on-brown (Kelly 1938; Kelly et al. 1978:39–48) assemblage includes 58 sherds. [*Editor: Gerald's draft manuscript indicates 59 sherds were present.*] Rincon Red-on-brown occurred in its highest proportion in Hohokam Colonial and Sedentary period (Davis phase) associations. Sporadic sherds also were found in later phase associations. [*Editor: The currently accepted dates for Rincon Red-on-brown are AD 950–1150 (Swartz 2008).*]

Rillito Red-on-brown (Non-micaceous)

The sample of Rillito Red-on-brown with a non-micaceous paste (Di Peso 1956:355; cf. Kelly 1938; Kelly et al. 1978:29–39) consists of 36 sherds. [*Editor: Gerald's draft manuscript indicates 34 sherds were present.*] Rillito Red-on-brown with a non-micaceous paste is poorly represented at this site. It occurs in its highest proportion in the Hohokam Colonial and Sedentary periods (Davis phase), the interval during which it is believed to have been in use. The scarcity or lack of the type in other phases suggests that it reached the site during the Colonial period (Davis phase) only. [*Editor: See the discussion following the description of Rillito Red-on-brown (Micaceous), above.*]

Pantano Red-on-brown

Twenty sherds were classified as Pantano Red-on-brown (Danson 1957:224–226). This type occurred in its highest proportions in Hohokam Colonial and Sedentary period (Davis phase) associations, although it also occurred in very small proportions in later phases. [*Editor: Pantano Red-on-brown was defined based on material from the University Indian Ruin. Danson (1957:220–226) described it as being distinguished from Tanque Verde Red-on-brown mainly on the basis of temper. Pantano Red-on-brown is tempered with abundant micaceous material and Tanque Verde Red-on-brown is not (see also Kelly et al. 1978:4, Table 1.1). Hayden (1957:117–118, Plate 23) reported stratigraphic evidence of the replacement of Tanque Verde Red-on-brown by Pantano Red-on-brown. Hayden and Danson assign Pantano Red-on-brown a date range of AD 1300–1450 and treat the abundance of the type as an indicator of the Tucson phase. See the discussion following the description of Rillito Red-on-brown (micaceous), above.*]

Tanque Verde Red-on-brown

The Tanque Verde Red-on-brown (Kelly 1938; Kelly et al. 1978:48–59) assemblage includes 31 sherds. [*Editor: Gerald's draft manuscript indicates 33 sherds were present.*] Tanque Verde Red-on-brown was found in greatest proportions in Hohokam Colonial and Sedentary period (Davis phase) associations but also occurred in later phases. [*Editor: The currently accepted dates for Tanque Verde Red-on-brown are AD 1150 to post-1400 (Henderson 1993; Marmaduke and Henderson 1995:82; Martynec 1993).*]

Cañada del Oro Red-on-brown

Two sherds were identified as Cañada del Oro Red-on-brown (Kelly 1938; Kelly et al. 1978:22–29). One was found in a Hohokam Colonial or Sedentary period (Davis phase) association and one in a Romero (late Reeve) phase association. [*Editor: The currently accepted dates for Cañada del Oro Red-on-brown are AD 750–850 (Swartz 2008).*]

Dragoon Series

[*Editor: The Dragoon Series was first described by Fulton and Tuthill (Fulton 1934a, 1934b, 1938; Fulton and Tuthill 1940; Tuthill 1947) based on material recovered from Texas Canyon, the Gleeson Site, and Tres Alamos. Five red-on-brown and/or red-on-white types were eventually named: Dragoon Red-on-brown, Cascabel Red-on-brown, Tres Alamos Red-on-brown, Deep Well Red-on-brown, and Benson Red-on-brown. Although some researchers have argued that the Dragoon Series and the San Simon Series (discussed below) are indistinguishable, suggesting that the "Dragoon Culture" should be considered part of the San Simon Branch, others point to important differences between these groups of types (Heckman 2000d:45; Franklin 1980:55–57; Masse 1980b:96–112; see also chapter 1). According to Heckman (2000c:70; 2000d:61), San Simon Series vessels are characterized by "well-polished surfaces; hard, dense paste; and well-bonded paints and slips," whereas Dragoon Series vessels exhibit "thicker, granular slips; a softer, lighter paste; and thinner, less dense paint." He adds that Dragoon Series pottery displays more curvilinear motifs (reminiscent of Middle Gila Buff Ware and Tucson Basin Brown Ware), whereas San Simon Series motifs are more typical of the painted pottery of the Mogollon highlands. Another marker of close affinity between Dragoon Series pottery and the painted types of the Hohokam tradition, according to Heckman (2000d:61), is the fact that jars (including shouldered jars) and flare-rimmed bowls are common among Dragoon Series vessels.*

Masse (1980b:96–112) and Heckman (2000d:45) have noted inconsistencies inherent in the typology, which emphasizes the presence and color of slip over the style of painted design exhibited by a sherd or vessel. Masse suggests collapsing and eliminating types in order to remedy the aforementioned problem and to reflect the fact that many painted design styles crosscut the Dragoon and San Simon Series.

Masse argues that the type Dragoon Red-on-brown, as originally defined, was a catchall and that its use should be discontinued. He also lumps the inappropriately named Tres Alamos Red-on-brown (a red-on-white type) under the rubric of Cerros Red-on-white (a type in the San Simon Series; Sayles 1945). He equates Cascabel Red-on-brown with Galiuro Red-on-brown (a San Simon Series type) and chooses to use Galiuro Red-on-brown, based on temporal priority. Finally, he relegates Deep Well Red-on-brown to the status of a variety of Galiuro Red-on-brown and argues that Benson Red-on-brown (which is actually a red-on-white type) should be considered a variety of Cerros Red-on-white.

Heckman (2000d; see also Heckman and Whittlesey 2000), like Masse, offers revisions that emphasize the essential similarities among the painted decorations exhibited by vessels in the Dragoon Series and the San Simon Series. Heckman's approach to the problem is somewhat different than Masse's, however, in that he only applies San Simon Series type names to specimens that exhibit technological attributes associated with the San Simon Series. For sherds exhibiting technological attributes characteristic of the Dragoon Series, Heckman (2000d; see also Heckman and Whittlesey 2000; Whittlesey et al. 1994) suggests substituting descriptive stylistic categories (broad-line design, fine-line design, and elaborated design) for the type names offered by Fulton and Tuthill. The effect is the same. Dragoon Series vessels with broad-line designs are considered stylistically similar to and treated as roughly contemporaneous with Dos Cabezas Red-on-brown. Dragoon Series specimens bearing fine-line designs are considered stylistic and temporal analogs of Galiuro Red-on-brown, and Dragoon Series sherds and vessels exhibiting elaborated designs are equated temporally and stylistically with Encinas Red-on-brown. Presumably, Dragoon Series red-on-white specimens would be dealt with in the same fashion as vessels and sherds of Cerros Red-on-white (see San Simon Series, below). Such specimens could be referred to by the styles they exhibit: fine-line (Galiuro) or elaborated (Encinas).

Colton's (1955:6, 1965:8, 29–30) approach to the Dragoon Series involved lumping it, along with the San Simon Series, under the rubric of the San Pedro Series of Mogollon Brown Ware, and later also under the heading of the San Pedro Series of Pimeria Brown Ware. In addition, he included Sobaipuri Plain (Di Peso's [1953:147–153] Sobaipuri Plainware), Sobaipuri Red (Di Peso's [1953:157–159] Sobaipuri Redware), and Whetstone Plain (Di Peso's [1953:154–156] Whetstone Plainware) in his various versions of the San Pedro Series. Colton's revisions do not represent improvements. His grouping strategy does nothing to address the typological fuzziness that plagues the Dragoon Series. Furthermore, the grouping of Sobaipuri Red, Sobaipuri Plain, and Whetstone Plain with the San Simon Series and Dragoon Series types implies cultural continuity between the makers of the late types and the early types in his San Pedro Series. Direct continuity between the makers of the so-called Sobaipuri types (Di Peso 1953) and the pre-Hispanic inhabitants of the San Pedro is very unlikely (Gerald 1968; Masse 1981), and links between the makers of Whetstone Plain (the Sobaipuri) and ancient groups remain a focus of intense research and debate (Lyons 2004a; Lyons et al. 2014).

Heckman (2000d:43) places the Dragoon Series (or as he refers to it, the Dragoon Tradition) between AD 700 and 1100, apparently based on associated intrusives recovered by the Amerind Foundation from the Gleeson Site and Tres Alamos (Fulton and Tuthill 1940; Tuthill 1947). According to Heckman and Whittlesey (2000), in southeastern Arizona, broad-line designs are characteristic of the period AD 650–750, whereas fine-line and elaborated designs are associated with the periods AD 750–950 and 950–1400, respectively. It is important to note, however, that the best available evidence suggests types in the San Simon Series were not produced after AD 1200. Likewise, Heckman's (2000d) analysis of associations between Dragoon Series types and intrusive types at Tres Alamos (Tuthill 1947) suggests that Dragoon Series types were not produced after AD 1150.]

Cascabel Red-on-brown

The Cascabel Red-on-brown (Tuthill 1947:50–51) sample consists of 122 sherds. Cascabel Red-on-brown is the eighth most numerous decorated pottery type found at the Davis Ranch Site. It is one of the main decorated types of the Hohokam Colonial and Sedentary periods (Davis phase) and occurs in decreasing proportions in later phases. The type probably was not in use during the Redfield or Romero phases (Reeve phase) but is believed to have still been used in small quantities during the Aravaipa (Sosa) phase. Unfortunately no whole vessels were found and sherds, though they occur in sealed assemblages, are slim evidence to use in assigning phase associations.

[Editor: In an undated note left among the sherds typed as Cascabel Red-on-brown, Gerald indicated that, in his view, this type encompassed both Deep Well Red-on-brown and Benson Red-on-brown. Adding to the confusion associated with the Dragoon Series types is the fact that, per Gloria J. Fenner, the published type descriptions for Deep Well and Benson Red-on-brown (Tuthill 1947:53–54) are switched; that is, the description for Deep Well Red-on-brown appears under the heading for Benson Red-on-brown, and vice versa.]

Dragoon Red-on-brown

The Dragoon Red-on-brown (Fulton and Tuthill 1940:40–44; Tuthill 1947:54) assemblage includes 92 sherds. [*Editor: Gerald's draft manuscript indicates 93 sherds were present.*] Dragoon Red-on-brown is one of the relatively minor types of decorated pottery at the Davis Ranch Site and occurs in all phases, though the majority probably belongs to the Hohokam Colonial and Sedentary periods (Davis phase) and the Aravaipa (Sosa) phase; it occurs in its highest proportions in the Aravaipa (Sosa) phase.

Tres Alamos Red-on-brown

The Tres Alamos Red-on-brown (Tuthill 1947:51–53) sample consists of 49 sherds and one vessel (figure 6.5). The field designation for this type was Davis Red-on-white, a name that was meant to replace Tuthill's because it is a red-on-white type, not a red-on-brown type. Because of the scarcity of sherds and whole vessels, however, it is not profitable to redefine the type at this time. Tres Alamos Red-on-brown is found in all phases at the Davis Ranch Site but is relatively strongly represented in the Hohokam Colonial and Sedentary periods (Davis phase) only, the interval during which the type is believed to have been used. The single restorable vessel is an oblong dish (D/142b) 19.3 cm long, 10.8 cm wide, and 6.2 cm tall. It was found in association with Cremation 2. Its average wall thickness is 0.6 cm, and its decoration is reminiscent of Rillito Red-on-brown. [*Editor: The single vessel Gerald identified as Tres Alamos Red-on-brown has been reclassified as a Santa Cruz Red-on-buff: Aravaipa Variety scoop (Wallace 1996).*]

San Simon Series

[Editor: The San Simon Series was defined by Sayles (1945) based on his work in the San Simon Valley, which defined the San Simon Branch of the Mogollon. The San Simon Series, as originally described, includes four red-on-brown types (Dos Cabezas, Pinaleño, Galiuro, and Encinas Red-on-brown) and one red-on-white type (Cerros Red-on-white).

Sayles's San Simon Series typology, consisting of categories defined on the basis of painted style and line width (and in the case of Cerros Red-on-white, the presence of white slip), has been critiqued and revised by Whittlesey and others (1994:68–74) and Heckman (2000c). Pinaleño Red-on-brown, as originally described (Sayles 1945:42), was used to refer to specimens bearing painted designs characteristic of both Dos Cabezas and Galiuro Red-on-brown. One of the key attributes used by Sayles to separate these types was line width. Because Pinaleño Red-on-brown grades into both Dos Cabezas Red-on-brown (at the broad end of the line-width continuum) and Galiuro Red-on-brown (at the narrow end), Whittlesey and others (1994:68) and Heckman (2000c:63) argue that the use of Pinaleño Red-on-brown as a typological category should be discontinued. Instead, they recommend typing sherds and vessels previously assigned to Pinaleño Red-on-brown as either Dos Cabezas or Galiuro Red-on-brown. This results in a tripartite red-on-brown sequence from simple broad-line rectilinear designs, to simple fine-line rectilinear designs, to elaborated designs composed of rectilinear and/or curvilinear motifs (Heckman 2000c:69–70, Table 1).

Heckman (2000c:69) has also addressed Cerros Red-on-white, noting that specimens assigned to this type display painted designs characteristic of either Galiuro Red-on-brown or Encinas Red-on-brown. He recommends that researchers note which style is present (Galiuro or Encinas), as this distinction can have temporal significance.]

Encinas Red-on-brown

The Encinas Red-on-brown (Sayles 1945:43) assemblage includes 49 sherds. This type occurs

FIGURE 6.5 Santa Cruz Red-on-buff: Aravaipa Variety scoop (D/142b) from Cremation 2: (a) interior, (b) exterior. Measurements in text. Photographs by Jannelle Weakly.

in all phases but in its highest proportions in the Hohokam Colonial and Sedentary periods (Davis phase) and its second highest in the Aravaipa (Sosa) phase; it is relatively rare in the Redfield and Romero phases (Reeve phase). [*Editor: Heckman (2000c:Table 1) assigns Encinas Red-on-brown a date range of AD 950–1200.*]

Dos Cabezas Red-on-brown

[*Editor: In his manuscript, Gerald refers to seven sherds using the term "Broadline Red-on-brown." The sherds in the collection so identified include six jar fragments, five of which are very likely from the same vessel, and a single bowl body sherd. I have classified these as Dos Cabezas Red-on-brown. Although Heckman (2000c:67) indicates that San Simon Series jars only occur rarely, as in Cerros Red-on-white and Encinas Red-on-brown, the ASM sherd type collection includes a large Dos Cabezas Red-on-brown jar sherd (rim and neck) recovered from the Westfall Ruin (AZ BB:16:1[ASM]; AZ BB:16:2[AF]).*] This is a well-finished pottery having a moderately dense paste, a polished face, and rectilinear decoration in broad, red lines. This type occurs with greatest frequency in the Aravaipa (Sosa) phase, though it also occurs in Redfield and Romero (Reeve) phase associations. [*Editor: Heckman (2000c:Table 1) assigns Dos Cabezas Red-on-brown a date range of AD 650–800.*]

Cerros Red-on-white

Four sherds were classified as Cerros Red-on-white (Sayles 1945:43). [*Editor: Gerald's draft manuscript indicates three sherds were present.*] Two of these were found in indisputable Hohokam Colonial or Sedentary period (Davis phase) associations, and one was found in the area of an Aravaipa (Sosa) phase dwelling. [*Editor: Heckman (2000c:Table 1) assigns Cerros Red-on-white a date range of AD 800–1000.*]

San Carlos Red-on-white

This new type is defined on the basis of 26 sherds. [*Editor: Gerald's draft manuscript indicates 27 sherds were present. Gerald placed slipped specimens of San Carlos Red-on-brown with lighter surface colors in a new category: San Carlos Red-on-white. His partial type description, based in large part on 10 whole vessels from upper Tonto Creek, curated at the Amerind Museum (Catalog Nos. T161, T163, T164, T166, T167, T168, T170–173), is presented below.*

Recent analysis of assemblages from the San Pedro Valley (Lyons 2012a) has resulted in the observation that two color groupings are indeed evident among sherds of San Carlos Red-on-brown. Fully oxidized and unaltered portions of unslipped vessel surfaces are Munsell Color (1994) light reddish-brown (5YR 6/4) or light brown (7.5YR 6/3, 7.5YR 6/4). Vessels that appear to be slipped are very pale brown (10YR 8/2), pinkish-white (7.5YR 8/2), or pink (7.5YR 7/3).

Most who have written about San Carlos Red-on-brown have suggested that it is slipped (e.g., Brandes 1957:52–54; Hawley 1936:109, 1950b:109; Olson 1959:115–117; Smith 1977). The color contrast between the cores and the surfaces of vessels exhibiting lighter-toned exteriors (very pale brown, pinkish-white, pink [Munsell Color 1994]) suggests the presence of a slip. Haury (see Ferg 1982; see also Smith 1977; Vickrey 1939) hypothesized that early San Carlos Red-on-brown is characterized by a "creamy," buff-colored slip and delicate linework, while later expressions of the type exhibit a slip that is not buff in color (presumably the same color as the unsmudged core) and coarser linework, as well as thicker vessel walls and less intensive polishing.]

Type Description

This type is the same as San Carlos Brown in terms of construction, core color, firing atmosphere, temper, core texture, and fracture. [*Editor: San Carlos Brown is a problematic category discussed below, under the heading of Plain Ware.*]

Surface Finish. Treatment: scraped, slipped with fugitive white slip that ranges in color from light gray (10YR 7/1 and 7/2) to pinkish-gray (7.5YR 7/2); Texture: well polished, interior often has lustrous finish, paste or temper contains minute flakes of mica, which often cause minute spalls to flake from the surface.

Surface Color. Interior: same as San Carlos Brown; Exterior: covered with white slip described above.

Wall Thickness. Range 3.0–6.0 mm; mean 4.5 mm; greatest range in one sherd 2.0 mm.

Forms. The following is based on 10 whole vessels from upper Tonto Creek in the Amerind Museum collection, as the vessels recovered from the Davis Ranch Site are all bowls of indeterminate subform. Bowls: unrestricted form of simple contour in the shape of a sphere cut below the equator and having a simple direct or slightly thinned rim; unrestricted form of simple contour in the shape of an upright oval and cut below the equator and having a simple direct or thinned rim (some of these have been flattened at the bottom); unrestricted form of simple contour in the shape of an upright oval cut at the equator and having vertical extensions above the equator of the oval and a simple direct rim; unrestricted form of simple contour in the shape of an ellipse with its long axis horizontal, cut below the equator, and having a simple thinned rim. Jars: independent, restricted vessel of inflected contour having the shape of an ellipse with its long axis horizontal and a simple direct rim; dependent, restricted vessel of composite contour, lower portion in the shape of an ellipse with the long axis cut below the equator and upper portion rising in a concave contour to a direct, unthickened rim that forms an end point and a point of vertical tangency. Pitcher: dependent restricted vessel of composite contour; lower portion in the shape of a sphere cut below the equator and upper portion rising in a concave contour to a point of vertical tangency from which a slightly flared unthickened rim originates; a flattened coil handle is attached vertically to the concave portion of the vessel wall.

Rims. IA3, IIIA3, IB3 (Colton 1953:43–44, Figure 10; Colton and Hargrave 1937:9–11, Figure 2).

Paint. Weak red (10R 4/4, 7.5R 4/4) and very dusky red (10R 2/2). Paint can be rubbed off with a dry cloth.

Decoration and Styles of Design. Design layout: band on exteriors of vessels, occasionally two bands. Design elements: medium-width lines; solid triangles; concentric chevrons; curvilinear, rectangular, and triangular scrolls; ticking. Design motifs: interlocking rectangular scrolls terminating in solid triangles; solid triangles pendant to a line; solid triangles with single, double, and triple hooks; solid triangles with curvilinear and rectangular scrolls; solid triangles with ticking on one side; triangles with crosshatching.

Comparisons. San Carlos Red-on-brown lacks the white slip. Tanque Verde Red-on-brown is a thicker type and is not highly polished on the interior.

Range. Tonto Creek to Safford area is the central area, but the ware is widely traded; for example, to Point of Pines, the Kuykendall Site (ARIZONA:FF:2:1[AF]; AZ FF:2:2[ASM]), and Tres Alamos.

Remarks. San Carlos Red-on-white is usually found with Gila Polychrome. Only one site, ARIZONA:BB:2:2(AF), an adobe-and-cobble compound, has yielded San Carlos Red-on-white but no Gila, Pinto, or Tonto Polychromes. [*Editor: The site referred to above is also designated AZ BB:2:2(ASM) and is known as Big Ditch. Alice Carpenter, the celebrated avocational archaeologist from Oracle, Arizona, used this name to label a large pre-Classic Hohokam village near the confluence of the San Pedro River and Aravaipa Creek (Carpenter 1996:322–326; Gregonis and Masse 1996). This site was later the focus of field school excavations by the Arizona College of Technology (now the Aravaipa Campus of Central Arizona College; Carpenter 1996:338n60; Masse 1980a; Masse et al. 2014). See also the discussion of San Carlos Red, below.*]

San Carlos Red-on-brown

Six sherds were identified as San Carlos Red-on-brown (Hawley 1950b:109). [*Editor: San Carlos Red-on-brown is a pottery type that is somewhat poorly understood in terms of its typological relationships, geographical and cultural historical origin(s), areal distribution, dating, production locations, and technological and stylistic variability. As it is here, San Carlos Red-on-brown is often considered a type without a ware or a series. However, Wood (1987:41–42) placed it under his "Salt-Gila Buffware" rubric along with the Middle Gila Buff Ware types of the Phoenix Basin, and Foster (1994:139–140) mentions a "San Carlos Series" that includes San Carlos Red-on-brown and San Carlos Red.*

The areas that have yielded the highest percentages of this type include the Safford Basin (Brown 1973; Gregory 1995b; Johnson and Wasley 1966; Lyons 2004d) and the lower San Pedro Valley (Franklin 1980:73–75; Lyons 2012b; Masse 1980a:222, 1980b:169). San Carlos Red-on-brown has also been recovered from sites in the Globe-Miami area, the Phoenix Basin, the Tucson Basin, the Tonto Basin, the Dripping Springs Valley, and the Point of Pines region (Doyel 1978; Foster 1994; Olson 1959; Smith 1979; Wallace 1995).

Work with assemblages from the Safford Basin and the San Pedro Valley has revealed distinctive tempering materials in the San Carlos Red-on-brown sherds and vessels recovered from these two regions. Thus, the type has been split into varieties named for suspected production locations, San Carlos Red-on-brown: Safford Variety (Lyons 2004d) and San Carlos Red-on-brown: Aravaipa Variety (Lyons 2012b).

Masse (1982:86) first offered the hypothesis that Hohokam-style buff ware types and San Carlos Red-on-brown were produced in the San Pedro Valley, at the mouth of Aravaipa Creek (see also Franklin 1980:101,

103; Masse et al. 2014; Wallace 1995, 1996, 2003). This inference was based on the concentration at sites near the San Pedro River/Aravaipa Creek confluence of Hohokam-style buff ware types and San Carlos Red-on-brown sherds and vessels tempered with crushed phyllite. Wallace (1996) later noted the close proximity of these sites to phyllite outcrops and phyllite-bearing sands found near the San Pedro/Aravaipa confluence.

San Carlos Red-on-brown vessels recovered from the Safford Basin, in contrast, are tempered with red, angular fragments that appear to be sand-tempered sherds (Lyons 2004c). Those lacking sherd temper are tempered with granitic sand. Apparently, sherd-tempered San Carlos Red-on-brown has not been recorded elsewhere, suggesting this is a Safford Basin phenomenon and an indicator of local production.

Wallace (1995:76) reports the presence of locally produced San Carlos Red-on-brown in the Tonto Basin, made with sand temper derived from the Pinto Petrofacies or the Meddler Petrofacies (see also Wood 1987:41–42). A fourth possible production area is the Globe-Miami area, where Doyel (1978:36–37, 98) found a variety of tempers represented. One tempering material, fine quartz sand, is apparently consistent with local manufacture (cf. Hawley 1936:109).

Type descriptions for San Carlos Red-on-brown all make reference to interior smudging and the style of painted decoration that appears on vessel exteriors (all vessel forms). This design style is the same as that displayed by Tanque Verde Red-on-brown and Casa Grande Red-on-buff (Haury 1945:55–63; Kelly et al. 1978:59). Most descriptions of this type also mention its relatively thin walls (those who have offered data on the subject report a range between 4.0 mm and 6.5 mm) and lustrous polish on vessel interiors and exteriors. Type descriptions differ, however, in terms of the tempering materials reported and whether or not the author suggests the type is slipped.

Kelly and others' (1978:59) discussion of the similarities and differences among San Carlos Red-on-brown, Tanque Verde Red-on-brown, and Casa Grande Red-on-buff emphasizes three points: (1) all three types bear a related design style that represents something of a break with pre-Classic Hohokam conventions; (2) Tanque Verde Red-on-brown and San Carlos Red-on-brown are more similar to each other than either is to Casa Grande Red-on-buff; and (3) the strong similarity in design style suggests a common origin for these types, with the best evidence pointing to San Carlos Red-on-brown as the latest of the three to have been introduced.

Tanque Verde Red-on-brown and San Carlos Red-on-brown are well polished, whereas Casa Grande Red-on-buff is not polished. Additionally, San Carlos Red-on-brown and Tanque Verde Red-on-brown are very frequently recovered in bowl form (although bowls of the former are quite a bit shallower than those of the latter), and these bowls most often exhibit interior smudging. The smudging of San Carlos Red-on-brown is much darker, however, and the interior rim-pendant designs characteristic of Tanque Verde Red-on-brown are absent. Casa Grande Red-on-buff bowls are extremely rare.]

This type is represented by one sherd from the Aravaipa (Sosa) phase and three from the Redfield or Romero (Reeve) phase. Two sherds were not assigned to a phase. This pottery type is said to be later than San Carlos Red-on-white (Emil Haury, personal communication 1957), and this seems to be the case at the Davis Ranch Site. [*Editor: Here, Gerald refers to a June 1957 conversation with Haury documented by notes found among the Davis Ranch Site sherds typed as San Carlos Red-on-white and San Carlos Red-on-brown.*] Both types occurred almost exclusively in the Redfield and Romero phases (Reeve phase), but there is a suggestion that San Carlos Red-on-white, which occurred on the floor of House 7, is slightly earlier than San Carlos Red-on-brown, which was found in Redfield and Romero (Reeve) phase pueblo rooms.

[*Editor: Researchers have proposed different date ranges for San Carlos Red-on-brown over time, but based on recent advances in desert dendrochronology (Dean et al. 1996) and the Safford Basin ceramic associations reported by Lyons (2004c), it seems that Franklin's (1980:90, Table 11) argument for the span AD 1250–1400 seems the most secure. Breternitz's (1966:94) proposed dates for the type, AD 1275–1400, are based on its association with Gila Polychrome and Tonto Polychrome at Gila Pueblo and its presence in*

Maverick Mountain phase deposits at Point of Pines. However, Franklin (1980:90) reports that San Carlos Red-on-brown was recovered from the Whiptail Ruin (AZ BB:10:3[ASM]), which yielded tree-ring dates suggesting construction in the late AD 1230s and mid-1240s and apparently lacks significant Tucson phase (post-AD 1300) deposits (Dean et al. 1996:19).

Hypothetical start dates in the AD 1100s used by some researchers are based on weak evidence and reflect problems with the original definition of the Bylas phase, of which San Carlos Red-on-brown is a key marker (see Clark et al. 2004; Lyons 2004d; Neily et al. 1993; cf. Johnson and Wasley 1966). In an attempt to break the type into early and late varieties, based on an examination of 88 whole San Carlos Red-on-brown vessels from more than 20 sites, Smith (1977) found it difficult to identify consistent temporal trends in linework, vessel wall thickness, and polish. It is unclear, however, if his sample was chosen in such a way as to allow robust chronological inferences to be drawn.]

Mimbres Black-on-white

Sixteen sherds of Mimbres Black-on-white (Cosgrove and Cosgrove 1932) were recovered (figure 6.6). [*Editor: See also Anyon and LeBlanc (1984), Brody and Swentzell (1996), Shafer (2003), and Shafer and Brewington (1995). Gerald's manuscript reports 16 sherds of this type, but I located 18, 12 of which are fragments of a partially reconstructible bowl.*]

The majority of the Mimbres Black-on-white sherds occurred in or near House 1, an Aravaipa (Sosa) phase structure, and a minority occurred in Hohokam Colonial or Sedentary period (Davis phase) houses. All of the sherds bear geometric painted designs. [*Editor: Twelve of these sherds are from a single transitional Style I/Style II (AD 875–900) bowl discussed in chapter 7. The other sherds, all body fragments, appear to be pieces of six different bowls. Three are Style III (AD 1000–1140/1150), one is Style II (AD 900–980), and two are Style II or Style III (AD 900–1140/1150) (Roger Anyon and Darrell Creel, personal communication 2012).*]

Tsegi Orange Ware

Tusayan-like Polychrome

Eight sherds were assigned to this category. [*Editor: Gerald's draft manuscript indicates seven sherds were present.*] This is an orange pottery decorated with broad red lines outlined in black. The paste is black with white inclusions; it is not as dense as that of the Kayenta-like Polychrome sherd paste described below. Harold S. Colton notes that these sherds resemble Tusayan Polychrome (H. Colton to R. Gerald, letter, September 19, 1957, Archives, Amerind Museum, Dragoon), and Edward B. Danson feels that some of them resemble Nantack Polychrome, a similar type from Point of Pines (E. Danson to R. Gerald, letter, September 13, 1957, Archives, Amerind Museum, Dragoon). One sherd occurred in an Aravaipa (Sosa) phase context, and one occurred in a Romero (late Reeve) phase association. The others are unplaced.

[*Editor: These seven sherds likely represent fragments of two jars (three sherds from one vessel and four from the other) of Tusayan Polychrome made using materials local to southern Arizona (see figure 7.3e). The appropriate label for these specimens is Nantack Polychrome A, the Maverick Mountain Series type analogous to Tusayan Polychrome. Although late Tsegi Orange Ware made in northern Arizona is typically tempered with roughly equal amounts of quartz sand and crushed sherds, these jars appear to lack sherd temper and bear multimineralic sand temper. The latter includes mica, which is characteristic of pottery made in the Cascabel area (Lyons 2012b).*]

Kayenta-like Polychrome

Six sherds were assigned to this category. Two were examined by Colton, Danson, and David A. Breternitz at the Museum of Northern Arizona, and their conclusions are in general that design is similar to Kayenta Polychrome and to the Point of Pines variant, Maverick Mountain Polychrome, but the paste and temper are different (H. Colton to R. Gerald, letter, September 19, 1957, Archives, Amerind Museum, Dragoon). There is also a certain resemblance

FIGURE 6.6 Mimbres Black-on-white sherds. Upper row, Style III, left to right: House 4 floor, Room 44 fill, T26E 0–10N. Middle row, Style II or Style III, left to right: House 5 fill, T10N 36–45E. Bottom row, Style II: Room 7 fill. Photograph by Patrick D. Lyons.

to Tucson Polychrome as it is found at Point of Pines according to Danson (E. Danson to R. Gerald, letter, September 13, 1957, Archives, Amerind Museum, Dragoon). The paste is black and dense; the temper is light-colored angular particles with some rounded sand grains. Surfaces are scraped and smooth but not particularly well polished. Decoration is broad black lines and triangles outlined with white, and black hachured triangles outlined in white, on red. All sherds appear to be from jars. These sherds occurred only in Redfield or Romero (Reeve) phase associations.

[*Editor: Five of these six sherds most likely represent fragments of one jar and the sixth a piece of a second jar (see figure 7.3c). The temper of these specimens is unlike that associated with late Tsegi Orange Ware types and is very similar if not identical to that seen in the sherds Gerald classified as "Tusayan-like Polychrome." These are vessels of Kiet Siel Polychrome made using materials local to southern Arizona, and the proper name for such specimens of Maverick Mountain Series pottery is Maverick Mountain Polychrome. Gerald suggests they are similar in decoration to Kayenta Polychrome (which would make them Nantack Polychrome B). However, Kayenta Polychrome is a four-color type characterized by an unslipped orange surface and red, black, and white paint. These jars exhibit black and white paint on a red slip. Danson's suggestion that they resemble Tucson Polychrome makes sense, as Maverick Mountain Polychrome and Tucson Polychrome display the same color scheme. These two types are distinguished, in jar form, by the presence or absence of hatching. Maverick Mountain Polychrome exhibits hatched elements, whereas Tucson Polychrome does not.*]

El Paso Polychrome

Two sherds are tentatively identified as El Paso Polychrome (Stallings 1931) by Stanley Stubbs (S. Stubbs to R. Gerald, letter, September 19, 1957, Archives, Amerind Museum, Dragoon). One sherd was found in a Romero (late Reeve) phase association and one in an Aravaipa (Sosa) phase association. [*Editor: El Paso Polychrome is currently thought to postdate AD 1000 and was made at least as late as AD 1450 (Burgett 2006).*]

Trincheras Series

Nogales Purple-on-red

One sherd of Nogales Purple-on-red (Di Peso 1956:361) was found on the surface, and one was found in the fill of House 3. This suggests, very tenuously, an Aravaipa (Sosa) phase association. [*Editor: This type name is now recognized as a synonym for Trincheras Purple-on-red as defined by Withers (1941:36–40, 1973:37–43; see also Brand 1935; Clarke 1935:57; Gladwin and Gladwin 1929; Hawley 1936:59, 1950b:59; Heckman 2000e:75; Sauer and Brand 1931). Hawley (1936:59) attributes the label Nogales Purple-on-red to Byron Cummings but provides neither a citation nor a reference.*]

White Mountain Red Ware

Kinishba Polychrome

One sherd of Kinishba Polychrome (Cummings 1940:87, Plates 26, 27) was identified (figure 6.7). [*Editor: First noted by Hough (1903:293–294, 1930:20) at Tundastusa (AZ P:16:3[ASM]) and Grasshopper Pueblo, by Haury (1934:135–137, Figure 25b) at Canyon Creek Ruin, and by Baldwin (1934:71) at Kinishba, this type was not formally named or described until Baldwin's 1938 publication.*

During the 1930s, 1940s, and 1950s, researchers assumed that Kinishba Polychrome was produced at Kinishba, that the type was a variant of Fourmile Polychrome, and that it dated circa AD 1350/1375–1400/1425 based on associations with Fourmile Polychrome, Jeddito Black-on-yellow, and early Zuni Glaze Ware types (Baldwin 1938, 1939, 1941; Cummings 1940; Second Southwestern Ceramic Seminar 1959). Baldwin (1938) placed Kinishba Polychrome in White Mountain Red Ware (as defined by Colton and Hargrave in 1937), suggesting that the clearest indication of an origin for the type was the presence of, at Kinishba (in the sherd collection) and at Grasshopper Pueblo, bowls with Kinishba Polychrome interior treatment (black and red painted designs on a tan or yellow background) and exterior decoration characteristic of Fourmile Polychrome (thick black lines and thin white lines on a red background). He posits that the use of black and red on yellow was a product of "influence" from the Hopi Mesas.

FIGURE 6.7 Kinishba Polychrome bowl rim sherd from the floor of House 8. Photograph by Patrick D. Lyons.

Triadan (1997, 2013; Triadan et al. 2002) has recently shown that Kinishba Polychrome was not produced at Kinishba but at sites north of the Mogollon Rim, most likely in the Silver Creek drainage. Although she has documented some local production of White Mountain Red Ware at the site, she has also demonstrated that most vessels of these types were brought to Kinishba from the same sites (and places nearby) where Kinishba Polychrome was made. Based on current knowledge of tree-ring dates associated with Fourmile Polychrome (Mills and Herr 1999), Kinishba Polychrome is assumed to date circa AD 1330–1390 (Lyons 2013a).]

Davis Black-on-red

This new type is described based on one partially reconstructible vessel comprising 56 sherds and two

FIGURE 6.8 Davis Black-on-red jar (D/242) from the foot drum/sipapu in the kiva. Photograph by Patrick D. Lyons.

sherds from other vessels (figure 6.8). The partial jar (D/242) is of a thin (0.4–0.5 cm) variety of Davis Plain with a smudged interior that has been decorated on the exterior with a number of lines of a thin black paint. The line widths range from 3 mm to 12 mm and form no recognizable pattern. A series of five lines are pendant from the rim in one area and cross the body of the vessel at a slight angle to the vertical. Body sherds sometimes bear a series of roughly parallel lines and one or more curved lines in a group. The sherds comprising the partial vessel were recovered from the foot drum/sipapu (Feature E) and the floor of the kiva. One sherd not from this vessel was found near the floor of Room 7, and another was recovered from the floor of Room 46. The type was in use during the Redfield and/or Romero (Reeve) phase.

PLAIN WARE TYPES

[*Editor: Gerald described 15 different plain ware types in his manuscript. Seven types or varieties are introduced as new categories. They include Davis Plain, Davis Plain: Sobaipuri Coil Rim Variety, Sandy Perforated, Sosa Perforated, Sosa Plain, Redington Plain, and Redington Plain Smudged. Gerald's type descriptions vary in their completeness, but most of the taxa listed above can easily be correlated with types introduced by Di Peso (1958a) in his Reeve Ruin report.*]

Davis Plain

This new type is described based on 22,851 sherds and 14 vessels (figures 6.9–6.11, table 6.3). [*Editor:*

FIGURE 6.9 Davis Plain globular jars: D/195 (a) and D/198 (b) from Burial 4, D/221 (c) from Burial 10, D/225 (d) from Burial 12, and D/230 (e) from Burial 13. Not to scale. For measurements, see table 6.3. Photographs by Jannelle Weakly.

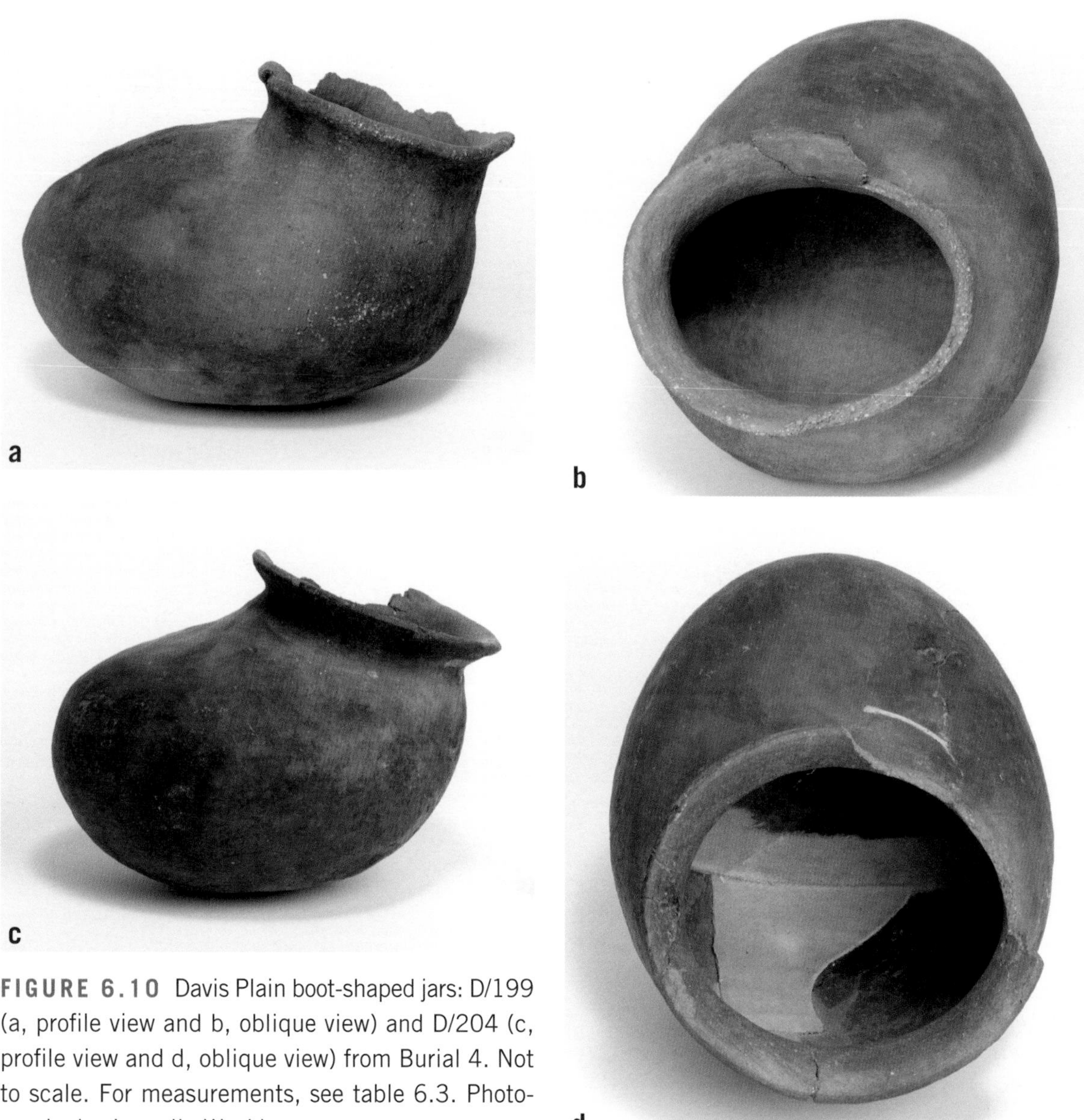

FIGURE 6.10 Davis Plain boot-shaped jars: D/199 (a, profile view and b, oblique view) and D/204 (c, profile view and d, oblique view) from Burial 4. Not to scale. For measurements, see table 6.3. Photographs by Jannelle Weakly.

Gerald's manuscript indicates 10 vessels of this type, and catalog cards document 13 vessels classified as Davis Plain. A fourteenth vessel, D/241, was not cataloged but was identified as Davis Plain by Gerald. He discusses one of these 14 vessels, D/236, separately, in a section below devoted to miniature vessels. Although he did not classify the other four miniature vessels (D/97, D/140, D/153b, and D/182) as Davis Plain, he describes three as having paste "similar to" or "the same as" that used to produce Davis Plain, and he indicates that the fourth (D/182) is "made of Davis Plain paste."

The written description of Davis Plain left by Gerald and a comparison of specimens of this type with examples of Belford Plain (Di Peso 1958a:90–91) indicate that these categories should be merged. Gerald's own discussion of Belford Perforated Rim (below) represents strong corroborating evidence that he considered Davis Plain and Belford Plain to be indistinguishable. Based

a

b

c

FIGURE 6.11 Davis Plain bowls: D/211 (a) from Burial 8 and D/218 (b) and D/223 (c) from Burial 10. Not to scale. For measurements, see table 6.3. Photographs by Jannelle Weakly.

on the rules of priority (Colton 1953:51–58; Colton and Hargrave 1935), the term Davis Plain should be retired and Belford Plain retained. Sherds and vessels similar to those assigned to this category have been identified as Cliff Plain (Nelson and LeBlanc 1986:127–133).]

Type Description

Construction. This type is coiled and scraped. Most vessels show the effects of hand smoothing after the scraping process had been completed. The area of the orifice of most jars has been polished, to a minor extent at least, on the interior. Plates are occasionally relatively well polished on their interiors, though individual polishing strokes are still visible.

Core Color. Pieces that are not completely oxidized most commonly range in color from very dark gray (N3/) to dark gray (N4/). Sherds that are nearly completely oxidized range from dark reddish-gray (5YR 4/2) to reddish-brown (5YR 5/3, 5YR 5/4) and red (2.5YR 5/6).

Firing Atmosphere. Oxidizing atmosphere but core not completely oxidized.

Temper. Shape: rounded; Material: sand; Color: predominantly of light color; Quantity: abundant.

Core Texture. Very coarse (1.0–2.0 mm).

Fracture. Friable.

Surface Finish. Treatment: scraped and hand-smoothed in most cases, not slipped; Texture: hand-smoothed but granular in most cases, interiors of orifices of jars polished, interiors of plates sometimes polished, dull finish.

Surface Color. Interior (jars): dark gray (5YR 4/1; N4/) through very dark gray (N3/) to black (N2/) in most examples; some range to the colors

living in diaspora—the Salado phenomenon—was the web of relationships through which objects and ideas such as the culinary shoe-pot moved into Arizona from Mesoamerica.]

Davis Plain: Sobaipuri Coil Rim Variety

This new variety is described based on 61 sherds and one vessel (figure 6.12). [*Editor: See the discussion of Belford Perforated Rim, below; see also Lyons (2004a).*] Davis Plain: Sobaipuri Coil Rim Variety is a subcategory of Davis Plain that, because of the importance of the rim form as a Sobaipuri pottery type diagnostic (Di Peso 1953:149–150), has been tabulated separately. The Sobaipuri rim coil first appeared at the Davis Ranch Site during the Aravaipa (Sosa) phase and continued into the Redfield and Romero phases (Reeve phase), where it is present on 0.2% of the plain wares. In the pure Redfield and Romero (Reeve) phase contexts at Reeve Ruin, 0.8% of the plain ware exhibits this rim form. [*Editor: At the Davis Ranch Site, all but one of the sherds in this category are definitely fragments of perforated plates, which could have been classified as Belford Perforated Rim (Di Peso 1958a:92–94). The remaining sherd is from a plate that may or may not have been perforated. If unperforated, this plate could have been classified as Belford Sobaipuri Plain (Di Peso 1958a:95–96). The significance of the Sobaipuri rim coil, despite its name, relates to evidence of Kayenta immigrants at the Davis Ranch Site, not cultural continuity between ancient groups and the Sobaipuri (contra Di Peso 1953, 1981). The single whole vessel in this category, D/227, is a jar recovered from Burial 13. Its maximum diameter is 15.2 cm, its orifice diameter is 10.2 cm, it is 11.1 cm tall, and its average wall thickness is 0.6 cm.*]

Babocomari Plain

This pottery type, represented by 3,641 sherds, is identical, as far as it is possible to tell from macroscopic examination, to the described type from Babocomari Village (Di Peso 1951a:109–123). [*Editor: Gerald's draft manuscript indicates 3,640 sherds were present.*] Babocomari Plain is probably a variation of Gila Plain (Di Peso 1951a:119), which it resembles in the smooth exterior finish and the finger- or

FIGURE 6.12 Davis Plain: Sobaipuri Coil Rim jar (D/227) from Burial 13. Measurements in text. Photograph by Mathew A. Devitt.

anvil-marked interiors of jars and in the high mica content of the paste. It differs from Gila Plain in having larger mica flakes and thicker vessel walls and in not having polishing striations (Colton and Hargrave 1937:174–175).

Babocomari Plain and Davis Plain are the two most numerous plain ware types found at the Davis Ranch Site, and their relative popularity, as measured by sherd counts, in the various phases is believed to reflect culture changes. Babocomari Plain is the earlier of the two types and constitutes as much as 77% of the plain ware of the Hohokam Colonial and Sedentary periods (Davis phase), 16%–36% of that of the Aravaipa (Sosa) phase, and up to 2.7% of that of the Redfield and Romero phases (Reeve phase). No Babocomari Plain was recovered at Reeve Ruin. Therefore, we may say with confidence that this type is not a part of the culture of the intrusive people who brought the Redfield and Romero (Reeve) phase complex to the San Pedro Valley. This information suggests that the type is an indigenous ware that died out, or at least became much less popular, during the Redfield and Romero phases (Reeve phase) at the Davis Ranch Site.

Babocomari Plain occurred in 170 of the 195 pottery samples taken from the Davis Ranch Site and, as would be suspected, was associated, in one or another of these samples, with every other pottery type found at the site. The absence of this type at the Reeve Ruin, just across the San Pedro River, and the higher percentages of this type in the earliest cultural deposits at the Davis Ranch Site suggest that Babocomari Plain should date to the Hohokam Colonial and Sedentary periods (Davis phase) and the Aravaipa (Sosa) phase but not the Redfield and Romero phases (Reeve phase).

Redington Plain

This new type is described based on 636 sherds. [*Editor: Gerald's choice of the descriptor "plain" is a misnomer, as this is a type mainly distinguished (especially from Davis Plain) by its polished surface. Redington Plain also differs from Davis Plain in being dominated by bowls (see below). Based on the written description of this type left by Gerald and a comparison of specimens of Redington Plain with examples of Belford Burnished (Di Peso 1958a:92), Redington Plain appears to represent Belford Burnished without smudging. Sherds and vessels similar to those assigned to this category have been identified as Cliff Plain (Nelson and LeBlanc 1986:127–133). It is also worth noting that Gerald originally typed D/226 and D/231 as Redington Plain and then later identified them as the type specimens of Sosa Plain (see below).*]

Type Description

Construction. This type is coiled and scraped.

Core Color. Most specimens exhibit cores that are black (5YR 2/1), very dark gray (N3/), dark gray (N4/), or gray (5YR 6/1), ranging to dark reddish-gray (5YR 4/2) and pinkish-gray (7.5YR 6/2).

Firing Atmosphere. Fired in an oxidizing atmosphere, but cores are not completely oxidized except in the case of sherds exposed to fire after having been broken.

Temper. Shape: rounded; Color: mostly light but some dark; Material: sand; Quantity: moderate to abundant.

Core Texture. Medium (0.2–0.5 mm).

Fracture. Friable.

Surface Finish. Treatment: scraped; Slip: none; Texture: polished on both exterior and interior surfaces, jars better polished on exteriors than interiors; Other Surface Features: fissures between coils sometimes discernible on exteriors of bowls.

Surface Color. Interior: light reddish-brown (5YR 6/4), reddish-gray (5YR 5/2), and dark gray (10YR 4/1) predominantly, ranging to light brown (7.5YR 6/4), pinkish-gray (7.5YR 6/2), weak red (2.5YR 4/2), and dark brown (7.5YR 3/2); Exterior: dark reddish-gray (5YR 4/2) and light brownish-gray (10YR 6/2) most common, ranging to weak red (2.5YR 4/2) and brown (7.5YR 5/2); Fire Clouds: common.

Wall Thickness. Bowls: range 4.0–9.0 mm, mean 5.4 mm, range in one vessel 3.0 mm; Jars:

range 4.0–7.0 mm, mean 6.0 mm (small sample), range in one sherd 2.0 mm.

Forms. Deep bowls (90% of rim sherds), wide-mouthed jars (10% of rim sherds). Bowls: independent, restricted vessel of inflected contour, in the shape of an ellipse with the long axis horizontal and cut above the equator (predominant form); restricted vessel of simple contour, in the shape of an ellipse with its long axis horizontal, cut above the equator (minor form); unrestricted vessel of simple contour, in the shape of an ellipse with its long axis horizontal and cut below the equator (rare form). Jars: independent, restricted vessels of inflected contour; specific shape unknown.

Rims. Bowls: IA2, IA3, IB2, IB3, IB10 (rare); Jars: IB2, IB3, IA2, IA3 (Colton 1953:43–44, Figure 10; Colton and Hargrave 1937:9–11, Figure 2).

Paint. None.

Decoration. None.

Comparisons. Davis Plain vessel walls are thicker, its surfaces are unpolished, and jar forms predominate. Babocomari Plain has finger marks inside, high mica content in paste, and a higher proportion of jar forms. Gila Plain is a thinner type, the mica content of the paste is much higher, and independent, restricted bowls of inflected contour do not occur. San Carlos Brown is a thinner type, much better polished, and the interiors of vessels are always smudged.

Range. Unknown.

[*Editor: Gerald does not address this type's chronology and gives no indication of intrasite spatial patterning associated with Redington Plain.*]

Gila Plain

The assemblage of Gila Plain (Colton and Hargrave 1937:174–175; Gladwin and Gladwin 1933:25–27; Haury 1937a:205–211, 1945:101–106) includes 428 sherds. The Gila Plain from the Davis Ranch Site is similar in most respects to that described in the above references. Most of the jar rim sherds, which constitute 56% of the rim sherds recovered, appear to have come from independent, restricted jars of inflected contour of the type illustrated by Haury (1945:Figure 63a, b) for the Classic period. Other jar rim forms represented are similar to those illustrated for the Sacaton phase (Haury 1937a:Figure 99f, k), the Santa Cruz phase (Haury 1937a:Figure 101b), and the Estrella phase (Haury 1937a:Figure 102e). The last two groups of forms are rare.

Two types of bowls are represented. One is a restricted form of simple contour in the shape of an ellipse with the long axis horizontal and cut above the equator, similar in shape to the heavy-walled Santa Cruz phase vessel illustrated by Haury (1937a:Figure 100d) but not having the heavy walls. This form constitutes 33% of the rim sherds recovered. An unrestricted bowl form of simple contour, similar to one illustrated by Haury (1937a:Figure 99c), is represented by 11% of the rim sherds.

[*Editor: Gerald does not provide any indication of intrasite spatial patterning associated with this type. As Gila Plain was in use through the entire Hohokam sequence, it is of no use in chronological analyses.*]

Redington Plain Smudged

This new type is described based on 355 sherds and two vessels (figure 6.13). [*Editor: Gerald's draft manuscript indicates 356 sherds were present. The written description of this type left by Gerald and a comparison of specimens of Redington Plain Smudged with examples of Belford Burnished (Di Peso 1958a:92) indicate that these categories should be merged. Based on the rules of priority (Colton 1953:51–58; Colton and Hargrave 1935), the term Redington Plain Smudged should be retired and Belford Burnished retained. Sherds and vessels similar to those assigned to this category have been identified as Cliff Plain (Nelson and LeBlanc 1986:127–133).*]

Type Description

This type is the same as Redington Plain, except that the interior of each vessel is smudged. No unrestricted bowls of simple contour were found.

a

b

FIGURE 6.13 Redington Plain Smudged bowls: D/213 (a) from Burial 9 and D/228 (b) from Burial 13. Not to scale. Measurements in text. Photographs by Jannelle Weakly.

Restricted bowls of simple contour and independent, restricted bowls of inflected contour were represented by 95% of the rim sherds, and jars were represented by only 5% of the rim sherds.

[*Editor: Gerald does not address this type's chronology and gives no indication of intrasite spatial patterning associated with Redington Plain Smudged. Two vessels of this type, both bowls, were recovered. D/213, associated with Burial 9, has a maximum diameter of 18.7 cm, an orifice diameter of 17.2 cm, is 9.9 cm tall, and its average wall thickness is 0.6 cm. D/228, associated with Burial 13, measures 20.0 cm at its widest point, has an orifice 18.3 cm in diameter, is 9.7 cm tall, and has an average wall thickness of 0.6 cm.*]

Belford Perforated Rim

The sample of Belford Perforated Rim (Di Peso 1958a:92–94) consists of 300 sherds. [*Editor: In table E.34, Gerald indicates 239 sherds of Belford Perforated Rim and 61 sherds of Belford Perforated Rim (Sobaipuri Coil Rim) were present. This is one of only five places in the manuscript's ceramics chapter where Gerald made specific reference to Di Peso's report on Reeve Ruin, which was itself in manuscript form at the time. Another important citation appears in Gerald's discussion of Salt Red: Davis Variety (see below).*]

Belford Perforated Rim is a variety of Belford Plain and, as it is manifest at the Davis Ranch Site, is also, as far as it is possible to determine without a petrographic analysis, identical to Davis Plain in paste and finish. The sherd count is based on perforated rim sherds only and therefore undoubtedly gives a false impression of the proportion of Belford Perforated Rim to other pottery types, but the perforations are the only feature that distinguish this type from Davis Plain.

Belford Perforated Rim occurs in only one general form, a shallow bowl. The shape of all of the vessels represented, as far as it is possible to tell from sherds, is that of an upright oval cut below the equator. Six varieties of this basic shape are recognized on the basis of rim treatment and a flaring of the rim area. An unrestricted form of simple contour and direct rim constitutes 30.7% of the total sherds of this type; a similar form with a rim coil (a coil of clay at the rim that has been obliterated on the interior of the vessel but not on the exterior) constitutes 7.0% of the total; another similar form with a broad, flattened rim coil, the Sobaipuri rim coil (Di Peso 1953:149–150), constitutes 8.7% of the total. An unrestricted form of inflected contour also occurs. It exhibits direct rims (29.7% of the total sherds of this type), Sobaipuri rim coils (11.7% of the total), and bead rims (10.0% of the total). [*Editor: Di Peso's*

(1958a:Plate 59.3) term "bead rim," used here by Gerald, refers to a narrow, rounded ridge running along the exterior of the vessel, just below the lip, similar in appearance to the reinforced portion of a rubber tire that fits within the rim of a wheel, or a weld joining two pieces of metal together.] A variety of the first form mentioned above, the unrestricted form of simple contour and direct rim, makes up the remaining 2.2% of the sherds—this is a variety in which the coils of clay are partially but not completely obliterated on the exterior surface. The vessels having Sobaipuri rim coils are usually perforated through the rim coil.

Belford Perforated Rim first appeared during the Aravaipa (Sosa) phase and continued on into the Redfield and Romero phases (Reeve phase). The type is never numerous and occurs in no particular assemblage of artifacts as far as has been recognized. [*Editor: The rim coil was a focus for Gerald because this trait became central to Di Peso's (1953, 1981) argument for cultural continuity across "the gap" between the pre-Hispanic era and the Spanish period in southern Arizona (see Lyons 2004a). However, currently available information indicates that folded rims resulting in "rim coils" were introduced to southern Arizona on two separate occasions: (1) circa AD 1275–1300 by immigrants from the Kayenta and Tusayan regions and (2) during the Spanish period by Yuman speakers or the Spanish (Cable 1990; Deaver 1990; Masse 1981:37–38; Waters 1982a, 1982b).*

This feature occurs regularly on perforated plates and late plain gray and plain yellow jars in the Kayenta and Tusayan regions (e.g., Colton 1956:Ware 7A, Type 2; Gifford and Smith 1978:47, Figure 17b, 20b, 21a, 26). It has also been noted among late Classic period plain ware vessels at sites in the San Pedro Valley and the Cliff phase sites of the Mimbres Valley (Nelson and LeBlanc 1986:133, Figure 7.6c).

The rim coil is a regular feature of Patayan III Yuman pottery, which has traditionally been dated to post-AD 1500 (Waters 1982a:280, 291–293, Figure 7.1, 1982b:568–569). Schaefer (1994), however, based on more recently obtained chronometric and geomorphological data, has argued that this period began between AD 1650 and 1700. Thus, it is likely that Yuman-speaking groups began producing rim-coiled pottery in the late seventeenth century or perhaps the early eighteenth century.

This same trait is characteristic of eighteenth- and nineteenth-century Tohono O'odham pottery (Lyons 2004a:Table 1; see also Fontana et al. 1962:103–105). It is absent, however, from all protohistoric Piman (Sobaipuri) sites in the San Pedro and Santa Cruz Valleys known to predate AD 1700 (Lyons 2004a:Table 2; see also Masse 1981:37–38). Assuming that Cable (1990; see also Deaver 1990; Masse 1990) is correct regarding the ages of three ceramic complexes found on the Ak-Chin Indian Reservation (in association with European artifacts), the earliest protohistoric rim-coiled pottery in southern Arizona dates between AD 1550 and 1625. The radiocarbon dates associated with the Ak-Chin sites are problematic, however, due to their wide calibrated age ranges (Cable 1990:23.8–23.9; Woodson 2002:251). Cable argues that the protohistoric inhabitants of Ak-Chin, located near the confluence of the Gila River and Santa Cruz Wash, were most likely Piman speakers (Akimel O'odham or Tohono O'odham) who made pottery reminiscent of neighboring Yuman speakers. In support of this hypothesis, he presents documentary evidence that Yuman speakers and Piman speakers commonly inhabited multiethnic communities along the Gila and in adjacent regions. In addition, he discusses instances of cultural traits crossing the linguistic boundary between these groups.

If Schaefer (1994) is correct in his reassessment of the dating of Patayan III, and by extension, rim-coiled pottery, the Ak-Chin sites represent something of a temporal anomaly, as they yielded "Patayan III-like" pottery ostensibly made before AD 1650, during the Patayan II period (assuming Cable's sequence is sound).

Masse (1981:37–38), instead, suggests that "the use of a rim coil is a Spanish promulgated trait." Possible supporting evidence is provided by Di Peso (1981:116), who reports the recovery of rim-coiled pottery from Ojinaga, eastern Chihuahua, in apparent association with the remains of the Presidio de la Junta de los Ríos, established in 1760 (Gerald 1968:28, 37). Also relevant to this discussion is the presence of Colorado Buff at the San Diego presidio (Waters 1982a:291). Although Waters

(1982b:569) does not specifically state if the specimens he observed exhibit rim coils, such treatment is characteristic of this type.

If Schaefer is correct and Cable's sequence is incorrect, Masse's (1981) model of the rim coil as a "Spanish-promulgated trait" garners additional support. The trait's wide geographic distribution and apparently rapid spread during the AD 1700s suggest a single entity (e.g., Spanish colonial authorities) affected the indigenous ceramic traditions of southern California, southern Arizona, and eastern Chihuahua. Regardless of whether the rim coil can be attributed to Yumans or the Spanish, currently available data strongly suggest this trait was not characteristic of the protohistoric Sobaipuri ceramic tradition. The significance of perforated plates, as an indicator of the presence of Kayenta immigrants in the southern Southwest (Lyons and Lindsay 2006), is discussed in more detail in chapters 7 and 8.]

Sacaton Buff

The Sacaton Buff (Haury 1937a:178–179) assemblage includes 117 sherds. This category is a catchall class in which all undecorated buff sherds having Snaketown-type paste have been lumped. [*Editor: Here, Gerald means sherds having paste characteristics similar to Middle Gila Buff Ware.*] Some sherds are nearer to Santa Cruz Buff (Haury 1937a:185) in color, but none of them approach the thinness of Santa Cruz Buff.

Sacaton Buff occurs most frequently in Hohokam Colonial and Sedentary period (Davis phase) and Aravaipa (Sosa) phase contexts and is relatively rare in Redfield and Romero (Reeve) phase contexts at the Davis Ranch Site. That it was not in use during the latter phases is further indicated by the complete absence of the type at Reeve Ruin.

San Carlos Brown

The San Carlos Brown (Di Peso 1951a:216; Tuthill 1947:59) sample consists of 59 sherds. [*Editor: Gerald's draft manuscript indicates 69 sherds were present. San Carlos Brown is a name introduced but not defined by Tuthill (1947:59). Di Peso (1951a:216) later used the term, seemingly discussing material he eventually referred to as San Carlos Brown Smudged (Di Peso 1956:343–344) and San Carlos Smudged (Di Peso 1958a:148). Gregonis (1996:227; see also Heidke 1995:393–394) has used a related category, "San Carlos-style Plain." She also uses the term "San Carlos Plain" (Gregonis 1996:227), which she distinguishes from San Carlos Red based on the absence of red slip. She notes, however, that Henry Wallace, upon inspecting sherds identified as San Carlos Plain, concluded that some of these were sherds of San Carlos Red with "underoxizided slip" (Gregonis 1996:227).*

Although Di Peso, Gerald, and others have suggested that there is a thin, unslipped, polished brown ware type that is similar to and accompanies San Carlos Red-on-brown and/or San Carlos Red, the results of a recent examination of relevant sherds from the Davis Ranch Site indicate that sherds placed in this category are dominated by unpainted fragments of San Carlos Red-on-brown vessels and pieces of San Carlos Red vessels with discolored slip.]

Type Description

Construction. This type is coiled and scraped.

Core Color. The smudge blackening usually penetrates two-thirds or more of the distance from the interior surface to the exterior and ranges in color from black (N2/) to very dark gray (N3/) and dark gray (N4/). The thin portion of the core between the smudge-penetrated area and the exterior surface ranges in color from light reddish-brown (5YR 6/4) to pale brown (10YR 6/3). The cores of sherds from which the smudge has been burned out exhibit these same colors.

Firing Atmosphere. Oxidizing atmosphere (exterior) and reducing atmosphere (interior).

Temper. Shape: angular rounded; Color: mostly light; Material: crushed schist and sand; Quantity: moderate.

Core Texture. Coarse (0.5–1.0 mm).

Fracture. Dense.

Surface Finish. Treatment: scraped, not slipped; Texture: well polished, interior often has a lustrous finish, paste or temper contains minute flakes of mica that often causes minute spalls to flake from the surface.

Surface Color. Interior: smudged and burnished and therefore very dark gray (N3/) to black (N2/). Exterior: reddish-brown (5YR 4/3; 5YR 5/3; 5YR 5/4; 2.5YR 5/4) predominantly, ranging to dusky red (10R 3/2) and light brown (7.5YR 6/4). Fire clouds are common and range in color from gray (N5/) to black (N2/).

Wall Thickness. Range 2.0–6.0 mm; mean 4.2 mm; greatest range in one sherd 1.5 mm.

Forms. Bowls only: unrestricted form of simple contour in the shape of a sphere cut below the equator and having a direct rim. Bowls having independent, restricted form, an inflected contour, and the shape of an ellipse with its long axis horizontal cut above the equator occur occasionally, but none were found at the Davis Ranch Site. The Amerind Museum curates one such vessel from the Tonto Basin. Asymmetrical vessels that are elliptical-orificed versions of the unrestricted form mentioned above also occur in the Amerind Museum's collection from the Tonto Basin. Vickrey (1962) mentions other shapes for the closely related type, "San Carlos Red" [*Editor: see San Carlos Red, below*], which may also occur in San Carlos Brown, but none are available for description at present; these forms include globular pitchers with medium-length necks and variably shaped canteens.

Rims. IA3 almost exclusively, IA2, IA4, and IB3 rare (Colton 1953:43–44, Figure 10; Colton and Hargrave 1937:9–11, Figure 2).

Paint. None.

Decoration. None.

Comparisons. San Carlos Brown is thinner, of finer texture, and better polished than any other plain ware in southern Arizona. Sherds of Tularosa Fillet Rim [*Editor: see below*] are somewhat similar but are usually thicker, not as well polished on the interior, of coarser texture, and, when the rim is present, bear rim fillets. Forestdale Smudged (Haury 1940) is similar in thinness, shape, and finish to San Carlos Brown but lacks the extremely high luster noted on the interior. The paste of Forestdale Smudged is much more friable and contains a higher proportion of sand. San Carlos Red is identical to San Carlos Brown, but it has a red to brown slip.

Range. Apparently most common in the area from Globe to Safford and traded to Point of Pines, Babocomari Village, and the Roosevelt Lake area.

Remarks. Some San Carlos Brown from the Globe area now in the Arizona State Museum collection contains larger quantities of schist than is found in the Davis Ranch Site collection. This tempering material is often visible on the interior and exterior surfaces though the surfaces are well polished. Restored vessels from the Tonto Basin and now in the Amerind Museum's collection do not show this quality as frequently.

Sosa Plain

This new type is described based on 37 sherds and two vessels (figure 6.14). [*Editor: See the discussion of Redington Plain, above.*]

Type Description

Construction. This type is coiled and scraped.

Core Color. Gray (N5/) to dark gray (N4/) normally, light reddish-brown (5YR 6/4) when completely oxidized.

Firing Atmosphere. Oxidizing, but core not normally oxidized.

Temper. Shape: rounded; Color: mostly dark; Material: fine sand containing finely divided gold mica; Quantity: sparse.

Core Texture. Fine (0.1–0.2 mm).

Fracture. Friable.

Surface Finish. Treatment: usually scraped, not slipped, plate exteriors occasionally are hand-smoothed; Texture: interiors of bowls and plates are polished, exteriors of plates are usually hand-smoothed or scraped, exteriors of bowls are polished; Other Features: polished surfaces manifest many minute flecks of gold mica (less discernible on unpolished surfaces).

FIGURE 6.14 Sosa Plain bowls: D/226 (a) and D/231 (b, exterior and c, interior) from Burial 13. Not to scale. Measurements in text. Photographs by Jannelle Weakly.

Surface Color. Light reddish-brown (5YR 6/4) almost exclusively, ranging to pinkish-gray (7.5YR 7/2). Fire clouds are common on the exterior surfaces of bowls and plates but very rare on interior surfaces.

Wall Thickness. Range 4.0–11.0 mm; mean 5.8 mm; greatest range in a single sherd 3.0 mm.

Forms. Plates (unperforated), deep bowls, everted-rim bowls. Plates: unrestricted vessels of simple contour, in the shape of an upright oval cut below the equator. Deep bowls: restricted vessel of simple contour, in the shape of an ellipse with its long axis horizontal, cut above the equator. Everted-rim bowls: independent, restricted vessel of inflected contour, in the shape of an ellipse with the long axis horizontal and cut above the equator (rare form).

Rims. IA3 most common, IIIA3 rare (Colton 1953:43–44, Figure 10; Colton and Hargrave 1937:9–11, Figure 2).

Paint. None.

Comparisons. The paste of Sosa Plain is finer than that of Davis Plain, Redington Plain, Babocomari Plain, and Sandy Paste Perforated and contains less mica and larger particles thereof than Gila Plain.

Remarks. Sosa Plain occurs in the Aravaipa (Sosa) phase, as well as the Redfield and Romero phases (Reeve phase). [*Editor: The two vessels of this type, both bowls, were recovered from Burial 13. D/226 has a maximum diameter of 26.8 cm, an orifice diameter of 25.2 cm, is 15.4 cm tall, and its average wall thickness is 0.5 cm. D/231 measures 22.0 cm at its widest point, has an orifice 20.0 cm in diameter, is 10.5 tall, and its walls average 0.7 cm in thickness.*]

Whetstone Plain

The Whetstone Plain (Di Peso 1953:154–156) sample consists of 42 sherds. [*Editor: Di Peso (1953:*

147–159) defined three wares that he believed were made by the Sobaipuri: "Sobaipuri Plainware," "Whetstone Plainware," and "Sobaipuri Redware." However, based on more recent work in the San Pedro and Santa Cruz Valleys, Whetstone Plain (now treated as a type) is the only one of the three that can convincingly be associated with the Sobaipuri (Lyons 2004a; Masse 1981).]

Whetstone Plain was found at the Davis Ranch Site in only one locality, on the edge of the second terrace, about midway between the pueblo and Houseblock III. The nearest dwellings are of the Hohokam Colonial or Sedentary period (Davis phase), and these are too far away to have much bearing on the cultural affiliations of these sherds. The only statement to be made concerning phase association is that Whetstone Plain sherds were not found in the relatively large samples representing the Aravaipa (Sosa) phase or the Redfield and Romero phases (Reeve phase). Whether or not they belong to the Hohokam Colonial or Sedentary period (Davis phase) cannot be said as definitely because of the small sample of sherds from this phase.

Gila Plain Smudged

This type, represented by 35 sherds, is a part of Gila Plain as described by Haury (1937a:206), who says of surface color, "bowl interiors frequently blackened." The smudged variety seems to be a minor companion of the unsmudged variety wherever it occurs at the Davis Ranch Site. It is retained as a separate category, however, because it is a recognizable variety and because, as far as I am aware, no one has made an extensive study of its temporal and spatial distribution. There is a suggestion, to be derived from Haury (1945:102), that smudging, other than that caused by use, does not occur in Classic period Gila Plain. Perhaps Gila Plain Smudged does not occur in Classic period sites of the Gila-Salt area, but it does occur at Reeve Ruin and the Davis Ranch Site in phases that appear to be contemporary with or later than the Classic period.

Wingfield Plain

The Wingfield Plain (Colton 1941:46) assemblage includes 16 sherds. This type was found scattered throughout the site, with no concentration, and therefore cannot be assigned to any particular phase. Wingfield Plain did not occur at Reeve Ruin and therefore probably does not belong to the equivalent phase at the Davis Ranch Site. [*Editor: Colton distinguished Wingfield Plain from Gila Plain based on the "very, very coarse mica schist temper" that characterizes the former. The sherds Gerald typed as Wingfield Plain would have been classified as "plain brown, coarse phyllite temper" by Lyons (2012b) and appear to represent fragments of vessels made near the confluence of the San Pedro River and Aravaipa Creek.*]

Sosa Perforated

This new type is defined on the basis of 11 sherds from the Davis Ranch Site, 47 sherds and 1 vessel from San Salvador de Baicatcan, and 4 sherds from Reeve Ruin. [*Editor: San Salvador de Baicatcan was a protohistoric settlement occupied by the Sobaipuri, the Piman speakers who inhabited the region at Spanish contact, left the San Pedro Valley in the late 1700s, and were absorbed by other O'odham groups (Masse 1981). Di Peso (1953) erroneously identified as San Salvador de Baicatcan the site also called José Solas Ruin and the Solas Ranch Site (Lyons 2004a). Although the site became the linchpin of Di Peso's chronological and cultural sequence linking the ancient and historic inhabitants of the San Pedro Valley, Amerind personnel excavated only one room there. As a result of more recent work with the existing collection from José Solas Ruin and its associated records, as well as new fieldwork in 2000 (Clark and Lyons 2012), the site has been identified as a Kayenta immigrant enclave much like the Davis Ranch Site and Reeve Ruin; that is, it is not a Sobaipuri settlement. The perforated plates found at José Solas Ruin, typed by Gerald as Sosa Perforated, are key markers of immigrants from the north (Lyons and Lindsay 2006).*]

Type Description

This type is the same as Sosa Plain in terms of construction, core color, surface color, wall thickness, firing atmosphere, temper, core texture, fracture, comparison, range, and remarks.

Surface Finish. Treatment: exteriors usually scraped, occasionally hand-smoothed, not slipped; Texture: interiors polished, exteriors hand-smoothed or scraped; Other Features: polished surfaces manifest numerous flecks of gold mica (less discernible on unpolished surfaces).

Forms. Plate forms the same as Sosa Plain but have perforations, about 2.0 mm in diameter, located 1.8–2.8 cm from the rim and 2.4–3.5 cm apart.

Rims. IIA3, IA3 (Colton 1953:43–44, Figure 10; Colton and Hargrave 1937:9–11, Figure 2).

Paint. None.

Sandy Paste Perforated

This new type is described based on four sherds. Sandy Paste Perforated is another pottery type made in the form of the perforated plate or bowl as described for Belford Perforated but is represented by too few sherds to allow a full description. These sherds indicate a form identical to that described for Sosa Perforated. The paste is porous and of a sandy texture, and the temper includes much mica and ranges up to medium texture. The surface color is a dark gray, though this may be the result of secondary firing, as the paste is light brown in color. The distribution of this type is unknown.

RED WARE TYPES

Salt Red: Davis Variety

This new variety of Salt Red (Schroeder 1940:113, 183–186, 1952; see also Haury 1945:80–100) is described based on 891 sherds and three vessels (figure 6.15, table 6.4). [*Editor: Gerald's draft manuscript indicates 887 sherds were present. The written description of this type left by Gerald and a comparison of specimens of Salt Red: Davis Variety with examples of Belford Red (Di Peso 1958a:86, 104) indicate that these categories should be merged. In fact, in his manuscript, Gerald indicates that "Salt Red, Davis Variety is very similar to the Salt Red, Local Paste described for Reeve Ruin," and he cites Di Peso's then unpublished report. Based on the rules of priority (Colton 1953:51–58; Colton and Hargrave 1935), the term Salt Red: Davis Variety should be retired and Belford Red retained. Gerald originally listed only two vessels of this type. However, I located a third specimen, D/240, a partially reconstructible bowl he had classified as Salt Red: Davis Variety but did not catalog.*]

Type Description

Synonym. Previously included as part of Salt Red.

Named By. Schroeder (1940:113, 183–186, 1952; see also Haury 1945:80–100); new variety.

Construction. Coiled and scraped. [*Editor: The fact that this taxon includes pottery thinned by scraping, rather than via paddle and anvil, strongly suggests that it is not, in fact, similar to material classified as Salt Red by Schroeder (1940:185).*]

Core Color. Dark gray (N4/) to very dark gray (N3/).

Firing Atmosphere. Oxidizing atmosphere but core not oxidized.

Temper. Shape: rounded; Color: light; Material: sand; Quantity: moderate.

Core Texture. Very coarse (1.0–2.0 mm).

Fracture. Friable.

Surface Finish. Treatment: scraped, exteriors and interiors of bowls slipped, jar exteriors slipped, jar interiors slipped at the rim; Texture: polished, with tool marks still visible but not forming a pattern.

Surface Color. Slipped Surfaces: red (10R 5/6; 7.5R 5/6) and weak red (7.5R 5/4; 10R 4/4); Unslipped Surfaces: light red (2.5YR 6/6), red (2.5YR 5/6), reddish-brown (2.5YR 5/4), and light reddish-brown (5YR 6/4). Fire clouds are common.

Wall Thickness. Range 3.0–7.0 mm; mean 5.1 mm; range in one sherd 3.0 mm.

FIGURE 6.15 Salt Red: Davis Variety bowls: D/197 (a) from Burial 4, D/208 (b) from Burial 5, and D/240 (c, interior and d, exterior close-up of largest sherd) from House 7 Floor 2. Not to scale. For measurements, see table 6.4. Photographs by Jannelle Weakly.

Forms. Deep bowls (incurved and recurved bowls as represented by Haury [1945:Figure 54r, u]) and wide-mouthed jars. Relatively few of the forms represented at Los Muertos are found at the Davis Ranch Site. Incurved Bowls: restricted vessels of simple contour, in the shape of an ellipse with its long axis horizontal and cut above the equator; Recurved Bowls: independent, restricted vessels of inflected contour, in the shape of an ellipse with the long axis horizontal and cut above the equator; Wide-Mouthed Jars: independent, restricted vessels of inflected contour, in the shape of an ellipse with the long axis horizontal.

Rims. IA3, IB3, IB6, IIB3 (Colton 1953:43–44, Figure 10; Colton and Hargrave 1937:9–11, Figure 2). Bowls: direct 39.4%, recurved 24.3%, recurved thinned 21.2%; Jars: turned out 15.1%.

Paint. None.

Comparison. This variety is similar to Salt Red of the Gila-Salt area (Schroeder 1952:322). It is not always as highly polished and usually lacks a shattering fracture. Specimens examined by Schroeder were identified as "Salt Red" and "Salt Red, hammered." Regarding one specimen, he noted, "paint [*Editor: presumably, slip*], paste, and rim form do not fit any of the Gila-Salt types in this combination" (A. Schroeder to R. Gerald, letter, September 16, 1957, Archives, Amerind Museum, Dragoon). As one is not able to distinguish clearly between the paste and slip of the "Salt Red" and the other type noted by Schroeder, they are classified as Salt Red: Davis Variety on the basis of the distinct forms of rims and vessels. [*Editor: Schroeder called attention to*

TABLE 6.4 Characteristics of Salt Red: Davis Variety (Belford Red) vessels from the Davis Ranch Site

Form	Catalog no.	Maximum diameter	Orifice diameter	Height	Wall thickness	Provenience	Comments	Figure
Bowl	D/197	14.2	10.7	7.9	0.4	Burial 4		6.15a
	D/208	36.1	32.0	19.4	0.5	Burial 5		6.15b
	D/240	29.0	27.0		0.6	House 7 Floor 2	Partially reconstructible	6.15c, d

Note: All measurements are in cm.

the distinctive recurved bowl form exhibited by almost half of the specimens of this type, writing:

> *As for the recurved rim . . . , I do not know of a described redware in southern Arizona exhibiting this particular rim form. It appears to have been similar to rim forms encountered in Sacaton Red-on-buff, which is too early for redware associations to have borrowed from it. It is not found on Gila Red, Salt Red, Valshni Red, Sells Red, or any of the others I know. It does not occur on the lower Colorado River or in the Verde Valley. There are somewhat similar rims in Turkey Hill Red of the Flagstaff area, but not the same. The paste and temper is quite different from your sample. This leaves one area—Point of Pines. You might check types from there for possible derivation. Perhaps this form is localized in your area (A. Schroeder to R. Gerald, letter, September 14, 1957, Archives, Amerind Museum, Dragoon).*]

Gila Red from the Davis Ranch Site is a thinner ware and has much mica in the paste; polishing striations are often visible also. Sells Red has thickened rims, polishing striations, and unrestricted bowl forms.

Range. Salt Red: Davis Variety is known only from Reeve Ruin and the Davis Ranch Site.

Remarks. This pottery type is identified as a variety of Salt Red because it most closely resembles that type and is not distinct enough to warrant a new name. [*Editor: Rather than indicating a link to Hohokam traditions, via Salt Red, this type represents another marker of immigrants from northern Arizona, and their descendants, living among local groups in central and southern Arizona. Belford Red (including Salt Red: Davis Variety) is a type made by the coil-and-scrape method and basically represents Roosevelt Red Ware without white slip and black paint (Di Peso 1958a:86). Similar sherds and vessels have been classified as Phoenix Red (Abbott and Gregory 1988; Brunson 1989:158–159; also known as "unnamed red ware," see Crown 1981:113), Cliff Red (Nelson and LeBlanc 1986:134–135), and Kinishba Red (Wendorf 1950:42–43; cf. Lyons 2013a).*]

Dragoon Red

The Dragoon Red (Fulton and Tuthill 1940:45) sample consists of 369 sherds and one vessel (figure 6.16). [*Editor: Gerald's draft manuscript indicates 367 sherds were present.*] Dragoon Red occurs most frequently in Hohokam Colonial and Sedentary period (Davis phase) associations and less frequently in others. The few sherds found in Redfield and Romero (Reeve) phase contexts are believed to be accidents. No Dragoon Red was found at the Reeve Ruin. [*Editor: Fulton and Tuthill describe this type as having the same paste as Dragoon Red-on-brown, but with bowl interiors and exteriors slipped red. The whole vessel, D/224, is a bowl recovered from Burial 10, which dates no earlier than the Aravaipa phase (see chapter 7). Its maximum diameter is 7.5 cm, its orifice diameter is 7.0 cm, it is 3.4 cm tall, and its average wall thickness is 0.5 cm.*]

FIGURE 6.16 Dragoon Red bowl (D/224) from Burial 10. Measurements in text. Photograph by Jannelle Weakly.

Salt Smudged: Davis Variety

This new variety of Salt Smudged (Haury 1945:80–100; Schroeder 1940:186) is described based on 199 sherds and one vessel (figure 6.17). [*Editor: Gerald's draft manuscript indicates 187 sherds were present.*] It is identical to Salt Red: Davis Variety, except that the interior surfaces of vessels of this variety are smudged. [*Editor: The written description of this type left by Gerald and a comparison of specimens of Salt Smudged: Davis Variety with examples of Belford Red Smudged (Di Peso 1958a:86, 104–105) indicate that these categories should be merged. Based on the rules of priority (Colton 1953:51–58; Colton and Hargrave 1935), the term Salt Smudged: Davis Variety should be retired and Belford Red Smudged retained. The single vessel, D222, is a bowl recovered from Burial 10. Its maximum diameter is 16.8 cm, its orifice diameter is 15.8 cm, it is 9.1 cm tall, and it has an average wall thickness of 0.5 cm.*]

Gila Red

The Gila Red (Gladwin and Gladwin 1930:12–15; Haury 1945:80–100; Schroeder 1940:113, 183–184, 1952) assemblage includes 155 sherds. [*Editor: Gerald's draft manuscript indicates 163 sherds were present.*] Only 10 rim sherds are present, and of these, five are fragments of squared-rim jars, four are fragments of outcurved-rim bowls, and one is of a plate or shallow bowl. Three sherds are portions of vessel bottoms bearing mold impressions similar to forms at Los Muertos (Haury 1945:Figure 57). Gila Red seems to have been introduced to the site during the Redfield (early Reeve) phase.

Dragoon Red Smudged

This new variety of Dragoon Red (Fulton and Tuthill 1940:45) is described on the basis of 70 sherds. [*Editor: Gerald's draft manuscript indicates 69 sherds were present.*] Dragoon Red Smudged is simply a smudged variety of Dragoon Red and occurs in the same associations.

San Carlos Red

The San Carlos Red (Vickrey 1962) sample consists of 61 sherds [*Editor: Gerald's draft manuscript*

FIGURE 6.17 Salt Smudged: Davis Variety bowl (D/222) from Burial 10. Measurements in text. Photograph by Jannelle Weakly.

indicates 65 sherds were present. When Gerald was preparing his manuscript, the only available description of San Carlos Red was Vickrey's brief treatment of the type, based on specimens from Besh-Ba-Gowah (AZ V:9:11[ASM]). Vickrey's description was included in the 1954 prepublication version of Steen's (1962) report on the 1940 excavations at the Upper Ruin (AZ U:8:48[ASM]) at Tonto National Monument, as well as the published version. Given the lack of a published description, Gerald decided to provide detailed information on sherds from the Davis Ranch Site.]

Type Description

This type is the same as San Carlos Brown in terms of construction, core color, firing atmosphere, temper, core texture, fracture, wall thickness, forms, and rims.

Surface Finish. Treatment: scraped, slipped (slip thickness ca. 50–150 microns); Texture: well polished, interior often has a lustrous finish, paste or temper contains minute flakes of mica.

Surface Color. Interior: same as San Carlos Brown; Exterior: red (10R 5/6), dusky red (10R 3/4), and reddish-brown (7.5R 4/4, 2.5YR 4/4, 2.5YR 5/4).

Paint. None.

Comparison. San Carlos Red is thinner and better polished than any other type of red ware known at present. It is distinguishable from San Carlos Brown by the presence of a slip on the exterior surface.

Range. Tonto Basin to Safford seems to be the center of distribution, with trade sherds found at Point of Pines, in the Phoenix area, and south to Tucson and Babocomari Village.

Remarks. San Carlos Red is a companion type of Gila Polychrome but apparently came into existence slightly earlier, at least at one site, ARIZONA:BB:2:2(AF), the lower Flieger Site [*Editor: see comments, below*], and did not exist as long as Gila Polychrome. Only one sherd of this type manifests schist temper on the surfaces as is characteristic of some of the San Carlos Red from the Gila Valley near San Carlos.

[*Editor: The Flieger name had become associated with sites at the Aravaipa–San Pedro confluence by 1953, based on the ASM site card for Big Ditch (AZ BB:2:2[ASM]) (see also Lyons 2010). In 1952, 1953, and 1954, Harvey L. Johnson, an avocational archaeologist from Tucson, Arizona, excavated portions of sites that would bear the name Flieger (Johnson 1957;*

Smith 1959). In 1957, Di Peso and Johnson recorded Flieger Site A (ARIZONA:BB:2:1[AF]), Site B (ARIZONA:BB:2:2[AF]), and Site C (ARIZONA:BB:2:3[AF]). The Amerind Foundation's sites A and C are locus 3 and locus 1, respectively, of what is today referred to as the Flieger Ruin (AZ BB:2:7[ASM]). Site B is currently known as Big Ditch (AZ BB:2:2[ASM]) and was later excavated by the Arizona College of Technology (now the Aravaipa Campus of Central Arizona College) field school (Carpenter 1996:322–326, 338n60; Gregonis and Masse 1996; Masse 1980a; Masse et al. 2014). In 1958, the designation ARIZONA:BB:2:1(AF) was mistakenly assigned a second time. The site recorded by the Amerind Foundation in 1958 is a shallow rockshelter located along a tributary of Aravaipa Canyon.

San Carlos Red is problematic in the same ways as San Carlos Red-on-brown (see above), a type with which it is sometimes grouped (e.g., Foster 1994:139–140). The typological relationships, geographical and cultural origins, areal distribution, dating, and production locations of San Carlos Red currently are inadequately understood.

Researchers began referring to the type in print during the 1940s, but a formal type description was not published until 1962 (Vickrey 1962). Type descriptions (Doyel 1978:56; Franklin 1980:73–75; Kelly et al. 1978:67–69; Vickrey 1962) and discussions of the type emphasize the following distinctive characteristics: thin walls (in the range of 3–5 mm for bowls), highly polished interior and exterior surfaces, interior smudging, and variable exterior surface color (ranging from maroon to tan to black fire clouds on the same vessel). Vickrey (1962) and Franklin (1980) address temper, with the former reporting mica or micaceous schist and the latter documenting ground schist inclusions that Miksa and others (2003) have identified as phyllite.

At Los Morteros (AZ AA:12:57[ASM]), Heidke (1995:326, 336, 426–427, Table 5.2) notes the presence of San Carlos Red and a class of pottery he calls "imitation" San Carlos Red. Similarly, at Gibbon Springs (AZ BB:9:50[ASM]), Gregonis (1996:183, 226) reports San Carlos Red and "San Carlos-style" red. Heidke (1995) suggests, based on their crushed phyllite temper, that San Carlos Red specimens found at Los Morteros were made outside the Tucson Basin, whereas he implies that those identified as "imitation" San Carlos may have been produced locally. Gregonis (1996:226–227) documents the presence of crushed phyllite temper in the sherds she identifies as San Carlos Red, but reports having lumped them with specimens of San Carlos-style red. The latter were tempered with sand containing fine mica particles.

Based on the data discussed above and the observation that Safford Basin assemblages exhibit a thin-walled, well-polished, smudged (interior) and red-slipped (exterior) type (Lyons 2004d), San Carlos Red seems to have been made in a number of places, and formal varieties based on distinguishing characteristics might be proposed. San Pedro Valley specimens typed as San Carlos Red exhibit phyllite temper similar to that displayed by San Carlos Red-on-brown: Aravaipa Variety, but the inclusions in the former are usually much finer (Lyons 2012a, 2012b).]

Gila Smudged

The Gila Smudged (Haury 1945:80–100; Schroder 1940:113, 184–185) assemblage includes 43 sherds. All of the nine rim sherds of this type are fragments of bowls. Three are pieces of direct-rim bowls (Haury 1945:Figure 55g, m), and six are portions of outcurved-rim bowls (Haury 1945:Figure 55f, n). Gila Smudged occurs in association with Gila Red.

Wingfield Red

Eight sherds were classified as Wingfield Red (Di Peso 1956:350). This is a red-slipped variety of Wingfield Plain (Colton 1941:46) that was first recognized by Di Peso. The few sherds of this type that occurred in associations that can be dated are placed in the Aravaipa (Sosa), Redfield (early Reeve), and Romero (late Reeve) phases. [*Editor: Di Peso (1956:350) indicates that vessels of this variety of Wingfield Plain bear slip only on their exteriors. However, at least one bowl rim sherd in Gerald's sample is slipped red on both surfaces. Today, sherds assigned by Gerald to Wingfield Red would be referred to as Aravaipa Red based on their temper, which includes abundant, relatively large chunks of phyllite (Lyons 2012a, 2012b).*]

Unidentified Red #1

This pottery, represented by 32 sherds, is much better polished than the majority of the Davis Variety of Salt Red and has a reddish instead of a black core. [*Editor: Gerald's draft manuscript indicates 33 sherds were present.*] The only vessel form represented is that of a shallow bowl having a direct rim. Schroeder (A. Schroeder to R. Gerald, letter, September 16, 1957, Archives, Amerind Museum, Dragoon) remarked that it is similar to Salt Red except for the "hammered" marks and that he had included the type in Salt Red in his work in the Phoenix area. Emil Haury (personal communication 1957) suggested that it may be a variety of Sells Red that lacks the thickened rim and polishing striations. In this connection it is worth mentioning that one of 15 sherds of this pottery, recovered from an excavated room in a compound overlying a Hohokam village at the Flieger Site (ARIZONA:BB:2:2[AF]), bore polishing striations in a narrow strip parallel to the rim and in the area below the rim at right angles to the rim.

Unidentified red #1 occurred most frequently in Hohokam Colonial and Sedentary period (Davis phase) and Aravaipa (Sosa) phase associations at the Davis Ranch Site. At the Flieger Site, similar pottery was found in a room of an adobe-walled compound in association with Pinedale Polychrome, San Carlos Red-on-white and Red-on-brown, Tanque Verde Red-on-brown, Sacaton Red-on-buff, Gila Butte Red-on-buff, Cañada del Oro Red-on-brown, Rincon Red-on-brown, Santa Cruz Red-on-buff, Casa Grande Red-on-buff, Babocomari Plain, San Carlos Brown, an unidentified dull red, and a polished, smudged plain ware similar to Redington Plain. Gila and Tucson Polychromes were absent from the room and the site. Unidentified red #1 is therefore probably of a time period antedating Gila Polychrome, at least in part, and contemporaneous with the San Carlos types. [*Editor: This category seems to include specimens of more than one type. Some appear to be identical to sherds of San Francisco Red: Peppersauce Variety (Masse 1980a, 1980b; Masse et al. 2014) curated at the Arizona State Museum (this type is also known as Peppersauce Red; see Franklin 1980:72–73; Hammack 1971:16).*]

Unidentified Red #2

This is a fine-textured, brown-paste pottery that bears a slip that tends to lose its luster readily. It is represented by 35 sherds. [*Editor: Gerald's draft manuscript indicates 37 sherds were present.*] Schroeder (A. Schroeder to R. Gerald, letter, September 16, 1957, Archives, Amerind Museum, Dragoon) has suggested that the paste is similar to that utilized in Gila Polychrome from the Elfrida area of southeastern Arizona. [*Editor: This category, like unidentified red #1, appears to be a mixed bag. Some specimens resemble sherds from unpainted portions of Roosevelt Red Ware vessels and others seem to be fire-clouded sherds from vessels of Belford Red Smudged.*]

CORRUGATED TYPES

[*Editor: With the exception of Tularosa Fillet Rim, Gerald eschewed formally named and described types for the pottery he placed in the corrugated category. Instead, he applied informal, descriptive terms.*]

Late Indented Corrugated

Late indented corrugated, represented by 134 sherds, is similar to Point of Pines Indented Corrugated, as described and illustrated by Breternitz and others (1957:Figure 3a), except that the indentations are not as regular on most sherds. [*Editor: Gerald's draft manuscript indicates 135 sherds were present.*] This pottery type occurs throughout the Davis Ranch Site in minor portions and is not numerous in any phase. Point of Pines Indented Corrugated came into use in the Point of Pines area about AD 1200 and continued as a popular utility ware type until the area was abandoned by puebloan peoples about AD 1450 (Breternitz et al. 1957:Figure 2). It is presumed that the pottery type was being imported to the Davis Ranch Site during this time period. [*Editor: Although none of these specimens were subjected to provenance analysis, corrugated pottery was manufactured in the San Pedro Valley (Lyons 2012b). Thus, there is no reason to assume these fragments derive from vessels that were "imported."*]

Late Plain Corrugated

Late plain corrugated, represented by 104 sherds, is similar to Point of Pines Plain Corrugated, as illustrated and described by Breternitz and others (1957:Figure 3b). [*Editor: Gerald's draft manuscript indicates 84 sherds were present.*] This type occurs throughout the site in minor proportions and is not numerous in any one phase. It is presumed to be contemporaneous with Point of Pines Plain Corrugated, which dates from about AD 1200 to 1450.

Neck Corrugated

All 40 neck corrugated sherds are similar in corrugated surface finish to late indented corrugated. [*Editor: Gerald's draft manuscript indicates 39 sherds were present.*] They were found in sherd assemblages of all phases at the Davis Ranch Site.

Obliterated Corrugated

Sixteen sherds of obliterated corrugated were recovered in sherd assemblages associated with all phases at the Davis Ranch Site. These sherds are similar to Point of Pines Obliterated Corrugated, as described by Breternitz and others (1957:Figure 3e) and as seen at Point of Pines by the writer.

Early Indented Corrugated, Smudged Interior

Early indented corrugated, smudged interior, represented by nine sherds, is similar to Reserve Indented Corrugated, Smudged Interior Variety as defined by Rinaldo and Bluhm (1956:159–161) and illustrated by Breternitz and others (1957:Figure 3i), except that the Davis Ranch Site specimens are thinner than the Reserve variety and more closely resemble those seen at Point of Pines. The Davis Ranch Site sherds range from 4.5 mm to 7.0 mm in thickness and average 5.4 mm; the greatest range in a single specimen is 3.0 mm as opposed to a range of 4.0 mm to 10.0 mm and an average of 7.0 mm for Reserve Indented Corrugated, Smudged Interior Variety (Rinaldo and Bluhm 1956:159). The average number of corrugations per 2 cm is relatively close in the two samples: 5.3 for Reserve Indented Corrugated, Smudged Interior and 5.4 for early indented, smudged interior. The number of indentations per 2 cm is somewhat different: 3.0 for Reserve Indented Corrugated, Smudged Interior and 3.8 for early indented, smudged interior.

It seems probable that Reserve Indented Corrugated, Smudged Interior Variety and early indented corrugated, smudged interior are derived from a common archetype (Taylor 1948:116, 120) and that the differences are due to conscious selection on the basis of the recognized temporal shift at Point of Pines from a thin, finely corrugated ware to the thick, coarsely corrugated ware. Early indented corrugated, smudged interior is found in sherd assemblages of the Aravaipa (Sosa) phase as well as the Redfield and Romero phases (Reeve phase) at the Davis Ranch Site.

Red-Slipped, Neck Corrugated

All of the eight sherds of this type appear to be jar fragments (no rim sherds are present), and all are smudged. All are quite similar and could be from the same vessel, although they come from several different areas. The only similar sherd from another site in the Amerind Museum collections is from Nine Mile Ruin (ARIZONA:CC:15:1[AF]). This type occurs most frequently in Redfield and/or Romero (Reeve) phase associations.

Neck Corrugated Gray Ware

A single sherd of neck corrugated gray ware was recovered in level 3 of the stratitest in the kiva.

Tularosa Fillet Rim

The single sherd representing this pottery type was found in what is presumed to be a Romero (late Reeve) phase association. The sherd conforms to the type description (Wendorf 1950:121) but appears to be more crudely made, characteristic of the later phases at Point of Pines. [*Editor: This sherd was not subjected to provenance analysis. However, based on examination with a 10-power hand lens, its temper is similar to material known to have been produced at Point of Pines.*]

INDETERMINATE WARE

Slipped Brown

These 33 sherds of smudged and unsmudged bowls and jars were found scattered throughout the site and, consequently, cannot be assigned to a phase with any degree of assurance. [*Editor: Gerald's draft manuscript indicates 28 sherds were present. This category, like unidentified red #1 and #2, seems to represent a catchall for specimens difficult to assign to a ware or a type. Some sherds appear to be fragments of Belford Burnished and Belford Red Smudged vessels.*]

Stucco Ware?

A single sherd of a reddish-brown pottery with a few fragments of slightly darker clay adhering to the exterior surface and a smudged interior was found in association with Pit Oven 1. This sherd is not similar to Colorado River stucco ware [*Editor: Here, Gerald refers to Lower Colorado Buff Ware (Schroeder 1958; see also Waters 1982a).*] but appears to be a specimen of Davis Plain with about 0.1 mm of the same paste adhering to the surface in spots.

CERAMIC ARTIFACTS

Effigy Vessel Fragment

The single sherd of an effigy vessel (D/181) is made of a paste very similar to that utilized in the buff wares of the Gila-Salt area; in addition, there are traces of red painted lines that would appear to be within the range of Sacaton Red-on-buff in color and design (figure 6.18). Positive identification as to pottery type must be based on sounder evidence than this, however. This sherd appears to be from the middle portion of the neck of a cylindrical vessel upon which have been applied two breast-shaped knobs of clay; below, in what would be the abdominal region, is a hand with five fingers incised in the plastic clay. The traces of paint remaining do not appear to have represented physical features but rather a geometric design. The vessel was probably hand-modeled to judge from the irregularities of both the interior and exterior surfaces.

[*Editor: The paste of this specimen, recovered from T12S 18–20E, is consistent with material known to have been manufactured in the middle Gila region. Similar Middle Gila Buff Ware (Haury 1937a:Plate 184; see also Pilles and Danson 1974:3) and San Carlos Red-on-brown (Lyons 2012b:Figure 4.10) effigy vessels have been reported.*]

Figurine

This specimen (D/145) has a flattened coil body with an enlarged, flattened area for a head (figure 6.19). Unfortunately, that portion of the head above the

FIGURE 6.18 Middle Gila Buff Ware effigy vessel fragment (D/181). Measurements in text. Photograph by Patrick D. Lyons.

FIGURE 6.19 Babe-in-cradle figurine (D/145) from the fill of the kiva. Measurements in text. Photograph by Patrick D. Lyons.

mouth is missing, as is the lower part of the body. The mouth is formed by a punched slit. The only other possible tool mark is a slight groove on the right side, separating the head from the body. This figurine is similar to one reported by Kidder and Guernsey (1919:Figure 62) from the Marsh Pass area and dated to the Pueblo II or III period of the Kayenta Branch, or about AD 1000–1300.

[*Editor: This is a specimen of what later came to be called "babe-in-cradle figurines" (Morss 1954:38–42; see also Lyons 2003:24–25). Such objects, like perforated plates, are important indicators of ancient immigrants from the Kayenta region. This specimen has not been subjected to provenance analysis, but its paste is consistent with local manufacture. It is 3.5 cm long, 2.5 cm wide, and 1.1 cm thick. It was recovered from the fill of the kiva.*]

Miniature Vessels

[*Editor: Five miniature vessels were recovered. Four are fragmentary and one is complete (figure 6.20, table 6.5).*] The complete vessel (D/97) is a sphere of clay with a cylindrical hole punched into one side, apparently by a finger or thumb, while the clay was still plastic. It is made of the same clay utilized in the manufacture of Davis Plain [*Editor: Belford Plain*].

D/140 was crudely made by the modeling technique. [*Editor: It is a recurved bowl form with fingernail indentations running as a line of arcs perpendicular to and just below the rim on its exterior surface. The paste is similar in color to that associated with Belford Plain, though it seems to be untempered.*]

D/153b is a jar that has a high shoulder from which the upper portion curves inward and upward to the rim, which, though missing, appears to have been on a vertical part of the neck. Hand-molded, the paste is similar to that utilized in Davis Plain. [*Editor: Belford Plain. This vessel is nearly 30% complete.*]

D/182 is a fragment that includes part of the bowl and the handle of what appears to be a ladle. The handle is a simple coil attached to the base of the bowl and projecting straight out from it. The vessel may have stood on tripod or tetrapod legs, as two rough areas on the bottom of the bowl seem to mark the spots where legs were attached. This vessel is also made of Davis Plain paste [*Editor: Belford Plain*]. It was also hand-modeled.

[*Editor: The fourth fragmentary vessel (D/236) is a flat-bottomed bowl with nearly vertical walls. Like the others, it exhibits paste like that characteristic of*

FIGURE 6.20 Miniature vessels: D/97 (a) from the fill of the kiva, D/140 (b) from the floor of House 9, D/153b (c) from the floor of Room 2, D/182 (d, side and e, underside) from the fill of Room 34, and D/236 (f) from the floor of Room 4. For measurements, see table 6.5. Photographs by Patrick D. Lyons.

TABLE 6.5 Characteristics of miniature vessels from the Davis Ranch Site

Catalog no.	Maximum diameter	Orifice diameter	Height	Wall thickness	Provenience	Comments	Figure
D/97	4.1	1.8	3.3	1.0	Kiva fill		6.20a
D/140			4.1	0.7	House 9 floor		6.20b
D/153b			4.5	0.5	Room 2 floor		6.20c
D/182			3.7+	1.0	Room 34 fill	6.8 cm long	6.20d, e
D/236		3.4	2.5	0.4	Room 4 floor		6.20f

Note: All measurements are in cm.

Belford Plain. It consists of seven conjoining sherds and an eighth matching rim fragment. Together, these pieces account for nearly 80% of the vessel.]

Appliqué (?)

One piece of what appears to be ceramic coil appliqué, D/2, was recovered from T10N 14–20E (figure 6.21). No recognizable design can be reconstructed from the fragment, nor is there indisputable evidence that the flattened back was ever attached to anything. The coils range in diameter from 0.5 cm to 1.0 cm. [*Editor: This artifact consists of at least two and perhaps more conjoined coils. The entire object is 5.4 cm long, 3.5 cm wide, and 1.2 cm thick.*]

FIGURE 6.21 Possible appliqué element (D/2). Measurements in text. Photograph by Patrick D. Lyons.

Coils

Two fragmentary coils of fired clay were found. D/138 is curved, crudely finished, of coarse paste, and may be a fragment of a Davis Plain miniature vessel or figurine. It has a diameter of 1.0 cm and was found on the floor of House 4. D/121b is a straight coil of light-colored, fine-textured clay similar to that used in Sosa Plain, with a rough extension along one side as though it had once been the heavily beaded rim of a vessel. Recovered from House 8, stratitest level 3 (floor), it is 0.9 cm in diameter.

Perforated Sherd Disks

None of these objects are perfectly round, nor is there evidence that great care was exercised in their manufacture (figure 6.22a–f, table 6.6). All were made from sherds by chipping and grinding. All perforations are near the center, and all are biconically drilled. These artifacts probably functioned as spindle whorls. [*Editor: Inconsistencies within and between Gerald's draft manuscript and the catalog cards for the perforated sherd disks make it impossible to precisely reconstruct the original typological assignments for these objects. As a result, the typological data presented in table 6.6 reflect the results of the reanalysis.*]

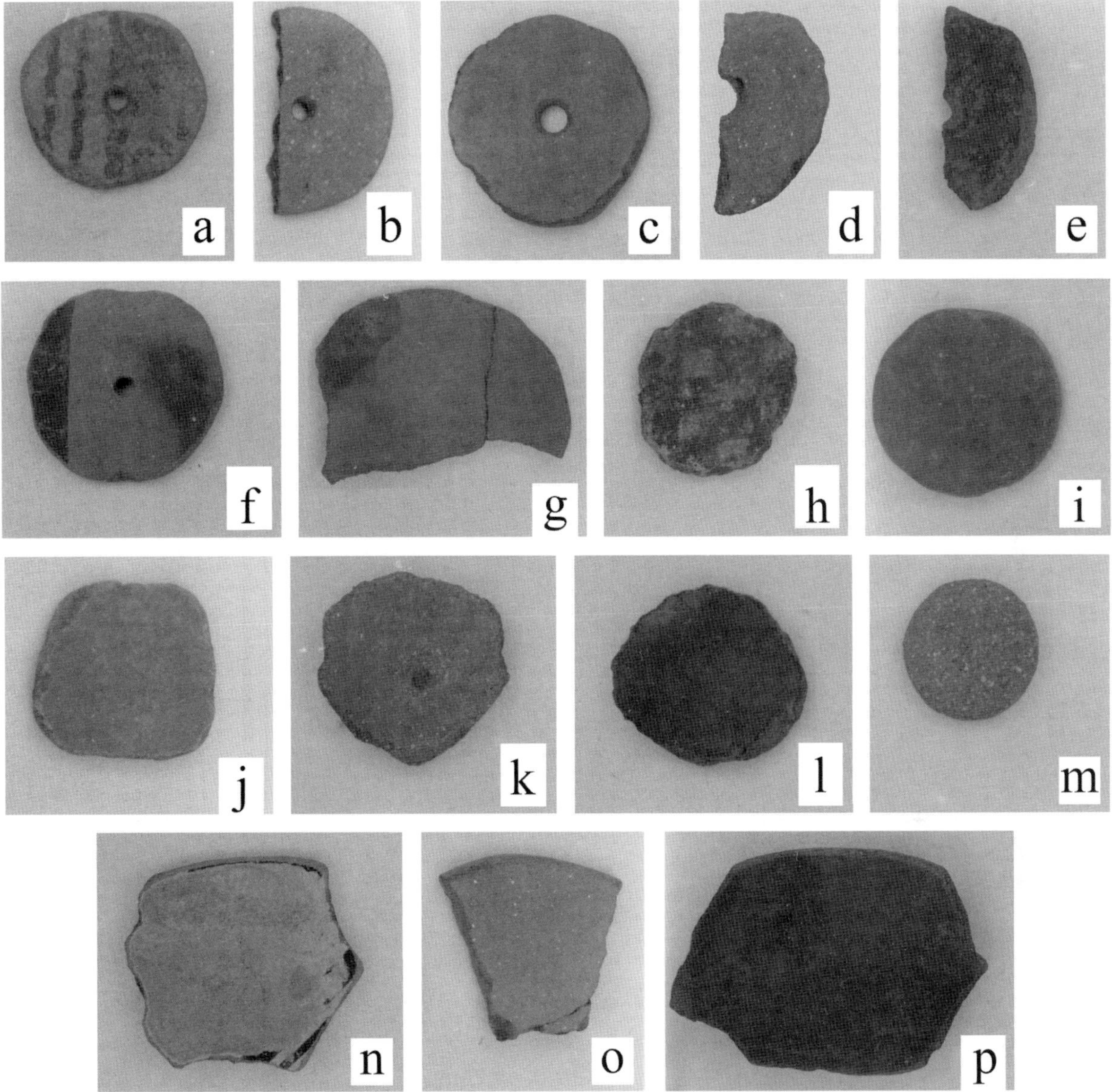

FIGURE 6.22 Perforated sherd disks (a–f), sherd disks (g–m), and worked sherds (n–p). See table D.1 for Amerind Museum catalog numbers and photograph numbers. Not to scale. For measurements, see tables 6.6–6.8. Courtesy of the Amerind Foundation Inc., Dragoon, Arizona.

Sherd Disks

Sherd disks may be described in much the same terms as perforated sherd disks, though there is a greater range in the degree of shaping (figure 6.22g–m, table 6.7). One sherd disk might be termed rectangular with rounded corners while another is ground to within 0.1 cm of a perfect circle. Only two examples of drilling are found. One of them is near the center of a sherd, perhaps indicating the object is an unfinished perforated sherd disk or spindle whorl. The other has a conical drill hole on one edge. An attempt had apparently been made to perforate the sherd but because of breakage or some other reason,

TABLE 6.6 Characteristics of perforated sherd disks from the Davis Ranch Site

Catalog no.	Diameter	Thickness	Perforation diameter	Type	Provenience	Figure
D/19	3.2	0.7	0.5	Belford Plain	T10N 21–26E	
D/21	3.2	0.3	0.5	Rillito Red-on-brown	T10N 36–45E	6.22a
D/83	5.5	0.6	0.6	indeterminate	Room 10 fill	6.22b
D/119b		0.7		Babocomari Plain	House 3 fill	
D/120	6.0	0.5	0.8	Belford Red	House 4 fill	6.22c
D/128		0.7		Babocomari Plain	House 5 floor	
D/137a		0.8		Babocomari Plain	House 8 fill	6.22d
D/148	4.7	0.7	0.5	indeterminate Roosevelt Red Ware polychrome	Kiva stratitest level 5	6.22e
D/170h		0.8	0.8	Belford Plain	NE Trash	
D/170i	4.8	0.5	0.4	Tucson Black-on-red	NE Trash	6.22f
D/252	3.3	0.6	0.9	indeterminate	T10S 23–25E level 2	

Note: All measurements are in cm.

the perforation was never completed and the sherd was subsequently made into a disk. [*Editor: Inconsistencies within and between Gerald's draft manuscript and the catalog cards for the sherd disks make it impossible to precisely reconstruct the original typological assignments for these objects. As a result, the typological data presented in table 6.7 reflect the results of the reanalysis.*]

Worked Sherds

The distinction between worked sherds and fragmentary sherd disks is admittedly arbitrary in a few cases. Worked sherds are those that have one ground edge that does not appear to be an arc of a circle or, if the edge does appear to form an arc, the diameter of the resulting circle would be much greater than the range for sherd disks (figures 6.22n–p, 6.23, table 6.8). All of these sherds have one ground edge, and from the few striations visible, it appears that most of these edges have been subjected to longitudinal abrasion. [*Editor: Striations are parallel to the wall of the vessel.*]

[*Editor: Five worked sherds, D/63, D/125b, D/178, D/243, and D/244, may be scrapers used to thin pottery. Such objects are referred to using the term* "kajepe" *in Tewa (Guthe 1925:27, Plate 11; Herr 1993:349, Figure 199–202; Oppelt 1984:3). Each of the specimens in question exhibits a rounded, abraded edge that would have been suitable for scraping the insides of pottery vessel walls during the manufacturing process. D/243 exhibits an interesting area of discoloration on its interior surface: a dark area roughly the size and shape of a thumb, in the exact location where a thumb would rest if the object were in use as a scraper (see figure 6.23b, left).*]

D/166e is a fragment of a horizontal section from the neck-body juncture of a Tucson Black-on-red jar. The upper and lower surfaces have been ground smooth (parallel to the rim) and are beveled toward the interior (figure 6.23c, d). The larger worked sherd

TABLE 6.7 Characteristics of sherd disks from the Davis Ranch Site

Catalog no.	Diameter	Thickness	Type	Provenience	Figure
D/9	3.9	0.7	Belford Burnished	T1S 14–20E	
D/10	7.0	0.3	Belford Plain	T1S 14–20E	6.22g
D/12	3.2	0.6	Belford Plain	Surface	
D/20	3.2	0.5	Belford Red Smudged	T10N 21–26E	
D/22	6.0	0.7	indeterminate	Kiva fill	
D/58	3.3	0.4	Babocomari Polychrome	Kiva level 3	6.22h
D/99	4.2	0.5	Belford Red	Kiva floor	6.22i
D/117	3.8	0.6	Belford Red	House 2 fill	6.22j
D/119a		0.5	San Carlos brown	House 3 fill	
D/125a		0.5	Belford Plain	House 4 Pit 2	
D/136a	4.4	0.9	indeterminate Dragoon Series	House 7 Floor 2	6.22k
D/175	4.5	0.6	Belford Plain	T15N 25–26E	6.22l
D/188a	2.8	0.7	indeterminate	Burial 10	6.22m
D/188b	4.2	0.4	Babocomari Plain	Burial 10	
D/247	8.5	0.8	Gila Polychrome or later	Kiva stratitest level 5	
D/248	5.5	0.5	indeterminate Roosevelt Red Ware	Kiva stratitest level 4	
D/249	5.8	0.7	indeterminate Roosevelt Red Ware	T23E 11–15S	

Note: All measurements are in cm.

of which this is a fragment may have functioned as a pot support. [*Editor: Three additional specimens are, like D/166e, portions of jar rims that have been ground at the lip and seem to be pot rests (figures 6.23e–h, 6.24, table 6.9). The first consists of a rim sherd and a neck sherd, from a Roosevelt Red Ware polychrome jar of indeterminate type (Gila-configuration neck), that conjoin (D/245). Both sherds are ground on the edge opposite the lip as well, indicating an attempt to improve stability. The second example is also a fragment of a Roosevelt Red Ware polychrome jar of indeterminate type. The third is Decorated Partially Reconstructible Vessel 85 from the kiva (see chapter 7), a Roosevelt Red Ware polychrome jar of indeterminate type (the neck decoration is almost certainly Gila configuration). It consists of six rim sherds: one from T8S 23–25E, level 4 refits one from T10S 23–25E, level 1, and they match one sherd each from the kiva fill; T8.5–9S 24–25E, level 2; kiva fill, level 3–5; and kiva fill, level 6–8.*

Excavations at the Davis Ranch Site by Archaeology Southwest (then the Center for Desert Archaeology) in 2000 produced an additional pot rest made from a Belford Red jar neck. The nearby José Solas Ruin yielded another locally produced red ware specimen that, like D/166e and D/245, was ground both at the rim and opposite (parallel to) the rim (Devitt and Lyons 2012). Objects identified as worked-sherd pot rests, like perforated plates and babe-in-cradle figurines, are indicators

FIGURE 6.23 Worked sherds. Possible pottery scrapers (a, b) and pot rests (c–h): D/178 (a), D/243 (b, left), D/244 (b, right), D/166e (c, exterior side view and d, lower edge), D/245 (e, exterior side view and f, upper/rim edge), and D/246 (g, exterior side view and h, upper/rim edge). For measurements, see table 6.8. Photographs by Patrick D. Lyons.

FIGURE 6.23 *(continued)*

TABLE 6.8 Characteristics of worked sherds from the Davis Ranch Site

Catalog no.	Length	Width	Thickness	Type	Provenience	Figure
D/11	4.8+	3.0+	0.5	Babocomari Plain	Pit Oven 1	
D/63	6.1	5.7	0.5	indeterminate Roosevelt Red Ware polychrome	Kiva level 3	6.22n
D/123	4.3+	4.3+	0.6	Babocomari Plain	House 4 fill	6.22o
D/125b	12.4+	8.5+	0.5	Babocomari Plain	House 4 Pit 2	6.22p
D/166e	10.2+	4.0	0.6	Tucson Black-on-red	Stratitest 1 level 1	6.23c, d
D/178	6.7+	4.0+	0.6	Belford Plain	T19E 16–18S	6.23a
D/243	9.3	6.4	0.5	indeterminate Roosevelt Red Ware	Kiva fill	6.23b, left
D/244	5.8	5.1	0.5	indeterminate Roosevelt Red Ware	Kiva fill	6.23b, right
D/245	12.5	7.2	0.6	indeterminate Roosevelt Red Ware polychrome	T15N 25–26E	6.23e, f
D/246	7.3	4.9	0.8	indeterminate Roosevelt Red Ware polychrome	Kiva fill	6.23g, h
D/250	4.7	2.7	0.7	indeterminate Roosevelt Red Ware	T1S 20–14E	
D/251	5.9	5.1	0.5	Gila Polychrome or later	T10S 23–25E level 2	
D/253	4.7	4.6	0.6	Tucson Polychrome	Kiva fill	

Note: All measurements are in cm. See also table 6.9.

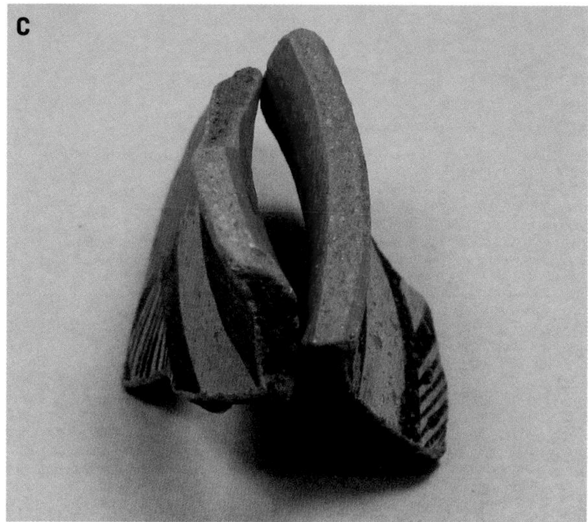

FIGURE 6.24 Worked sherd pot rest, Kiva Decorated Vessel 85: (a) exterior side view of all conjoining and matching sherds, (b) close-up of four fragments showing upper/rim edge, and (c) close-up of two fragments showing upper/rim edge. For measurements, see table 6.9. Photographs by Patrick D. Lyons.

TABLE 6.9 Characteristics of fragments that conjoin and match to form Decorated Partially Reconstructible Vessel 85 from the kiva

Length	Width	Thickness	Provenience	Comments
11.4	5.0	0.8	T8S 23–25E level 4	Dimensions reflect conjoin with sherd below
			T10S 23–25E level 1	See above
7.5	5.7	0.7	Kiva fill	
6.0	5.3	0.7	T8.5–9S 24–25E level 2	
9.5	8.1	0.7	Kiva levels 3–5	
5.1	4.6	0.7	Kiva levels 6–8	

Note: All measurements are in cm.

of ancient immigrants from northern Arizona (Devitt 2006; Devitt and Lyons 2012).

The five other objects classified as worked sherds include two identified by Gerald (D/11 and D/123) and three identified as a result of the reanalysis (D/250, D/251, and D/253). D/11 is either unfinished or is a fragment of a larger worked sherd. Modification to a portion of the object has created a roughly rounded edge. D/123 appears to be a portion of a large worked-sherd disk. D/250 and D/251 have been modified around their entire perimeters. D/250 has been flaked and ground into a subrectangular shape, and D/251 has been flaked into a subtriangular or teardrop shape. D/253 is worked (flaked and ground) on one edge only. It is trapezial in shape.]

7

Roosevelt Red Ware, Maverick Mountain Series Pottery, and Perforated Plates from the Davis Ranch Site

Patrick D. Lyons

The analysis reported in this chapter focused on those painted whole vessels, partially reconstructible vessels, and sherds recovered from Aravaipa (AD 1250/1275–1300/1325), Redfield (AD 1300/1325–1350/1375), and Romero (AD 1350/1375–1425/1450) phase contexts at the Davis Ranch Site that are still curated by the Amerind Museum and could be located (n = 5,672; table 7.1). The perforated plate sherds from the site were also reexamined. The painted sherds from the site had been stored in more than 40 boxes, primarily sorted based on Gerald's conceptions of types (based on what was known as of 1958), and sometimes vessel form (bowls versus jars) and vessel part (bodies versus rims) rather than provenience. The perforated plate sherds were stored in the same manner, with most in three boxes. After re-sorting the sherds and laying them out in trays by context, we embarked on an ambitious search for mends and matches in order to identify as many vessels as possible. The immediate goals were to produce more meaningful counts than usually result from ceramic studies and to obtain as much stylistic information as possible so that intrasite chronological patterns might be discerned. The ultimate goals were threefold: to better document evidence supporting the inference that the Davis Ranch Site was a Kayenta enclave, to use the assemblage from the site to test temporal patterns in Roosevelt Red Ware perceived at the level of the San Pedro Valley and at a regional scale, and to search for additional evidence linking Kayenta immigrants with the production of Roosevelt Red Ware (Crown 1994; Lyons 2003, 2004a, 2004b, 2012b, 2013a; Lyons and Clark 2012; Lyons and Lindsay 2006).

TABLE 7.1 Number of painted specimens in the sample (based on conjoins and matches) versus sherd count (each whole or partially reconstructible vessel counted as one specimen or sherd)

Context	Specimen count	Sherd count	% Reduction
Rooms	1,582	2,250	29.69
Houses	498	679	26.66
Kiva	1,857	2,428	23.52
Northeast Trash	123	175	29.71
Other	117	140	16.43
Total	**4,177**	**5,672**	**26.36**

The main decorated pottery dataset used here includes all Roosevelt Red Ware and Maverick Mountain Series specimens (whole or partially reconstructible vessels and sherds; n = 3,145) that could be linked to their proveniences (table 7.2). Painted wares derived largely or exclusively from pre-Classic contexts, including Middle Gila Buff Ware, Tucson

Basin Brown Ware, Dragoon Series types, San Simon Series types, and Mimbres Black-on-white, are discussed in chapter 6 and only briefly addressed in this chapter.

Gerald's Roosevelt Red Ware assemblage, based on the counts he provided, included 9,266 sherds and 17 whole or partially reconstructible vessels (see chapter 6 and appendix E). The sample discussed here numbers 3,208 specimens (34.62%). Likewise, Gerald's Maverick Mountain Series assemblage includes 359 sherds and 4 whole vessels, whereas the sample I report on includes only 224 specimens (62.39%). Three factors account for these differences in quantity: totals were reduced an average of 26% due to conjoins and matches being counted in aggregate, as vessels, rather than as the number of sherds that conjoined and/or matched (see table 7.1); assemblages derived from trenches that did not intersect architectural units or other features were cursorily reexamined but not systematically documented or included in quantitative analyses; and sherds and vessels from the kiva were treated differently from those recovered from other contexts.

The sheer number of objects recovered from the kiva, including 5,450 Roosevelt Red Ware sherds and 63 Maverick Mountain Series sherds (see tables E.24, E.25), the varying ways in which kiva recovery contexts were recorded (table 7.3), and the desire to isolate the best sample with which to investigate change over time led to a primary focus on the stratigraphic column (that is, stratitest levels 1–8), level 9 (which extended out from the sides of the stratigraphic column), and the kiva floor and floor features. Although all other kiva contexts were examined systematically for refits and matches (and many were found and recorded), only those sherds that formed parts of (i.e., conjoined or matched) vessels derived from the stratigraphic column, level 9, the floor, or the floor features are represented in table 7.2 and quantitative analyses.

Sherds recovered from trenches within rooms were incorporated into the sample and treated as having been derived from general room fill. A relatively small number of sherds (n = 287) bear provenience stamps that are illegible. These are overwhelmingly (84%) specimens of indeterminate Roosevelt Red Ware polychrome types and are not considered further. Perforated plates, which are discussed later in the chapter, are represented by 344 sherds. Of these, 185 combine through conjoins and matches to make up 51 partially reconstructible vessels.

THE DECORATED CERAMIC ASSEMBLAGE

The decorated ceramic assemblage subjected to reanalysis is overwhelmingly dominated by Roosevelt Red Ware (93%). Maverick Mountain Series types account for the second largest proportion (nearly 7%), and traces of the following are present: indeterminate decorated (n = 6), Mimbres Black-on-white (n = 5), Dragoon Series or San Simon Series pottery (n = 2), Babocomari Polychrome (n = 1), "Davis Black-on-red" (n = 1), indeterminate red-on-brown (n = 1), Kinishba Polychrome (n = 1), and San Carlos Red-on-brown: Aravaipa Variety (n = 1). In the sections that immediately follow, the typological conventions used in the analysis are reviewed and site-level spatial patterns related to chronology are explored.

Roosevelt Red Ware

Because I have proposed a number of revisions to the typology of Roosevelt Red Ware (Lyons 2004b, 2012b, 2013a; Lyons and Clark 2012; Lyons and Neuzil 2006; Lyons, Hill, and Clark 2011; Neuzil and Lyons 2006), here I provide a discussion of my approach to Roosevelt Red Ware types and their chronology (table 7.4). The types Pinto, Gila, and Tonto Polychrome are retained, though with modifications in the usage of the last two based on decorative configuration; that is, the nature of interaction between red and white slips on different portions of the vessel. Bowl interior surfaces are privileged in classification, resulting in type names such as Gila

TABLE 7.2 Typological overview of the reanalyzed portion of the Davis Ranch Site painted ceramics assemblage

Ware or ware-level category and/ or type or type-level category	Houseblock I		Houseblock II		Houseblock VI		Houseblock VII		Compound-wall-associated rooms and other rooms		Houseblock III		Houseblock IV		Houseblock V	
	n	%	*n*	%	*n*	%	*n*	%	*n*	%	*n*	%	*n*	%	*n*	%
Roosevelt Red Ware																
Cliff Black-on-red	0	0.00	0	0.00	0	0.00	0	0.00	0	0.00	0	0.00	0	0.00	1	1.35
Cliff Polychrome or Nine Mile Polychrome	13	1.86	2	0.67	0	0.00	0	0.00	13	2.80	0	0.00	0	0.00	0	0.00
Cliff Polychrome	19	2.72	16	5.33	0	0.00	0	0.00	13	2.80	1	25.00	1	5.88	0	0.00
Cliff Polychrome: Salmon Variety	1	0.14	0	0.00	0	0.00	0	0.00	0	0.00	0	0.00	0	0.00	0	0.00
Cliff Polychrome: Tonto Variety	1	0.14	0	0.33	0	0.00	0	0.00	0	0.00	0	0.00	0	0.00	0	0.00
Cliff Polychrome: Tucson Variety	0	0.00	0	0.00	0	0.00	0	0.00	0	0.00	0	0.00	0	0.00	0	0.00
Gila Black-on-red	0	0.00	0	0.00	0	0.00	0	0.00	0	0.00	0	0.00	0	0.00	0	0.00
Gila Polychrome	76	10.87	25	8.33	4	50.00	1	6.25	66	14.22	1	25.00	0	0.00	3	4.05
Gila Polychrome or later	85	12.16	62	20.67	2	25.00	4	25.00	90	19.40	0	0.00	1	5.88	5	6.76
Gila Polychrome or later (salmon variety)	0	0.00	0	0.00	0	0.00	0	0.00	0	0.00	0	0.00	0	0.00	0	0.00
Gila Polychrome, no banding line	2	0.29	0	0.00	0	0.00	0	0.00	2	0.43	0	0.00	0	0.00	0	0.00
Gila Polychrome: Gila Variety	0	0.00	0	0.00	0	0.00	0	0.00	0	0.00	0	0.00	0	0.00	0	0.00
Gila Polychrome: Salmon Variety	0	0.00	0	0.00	0	0.00	0	0.00	0	0.00	0	0.00	0	0.00	0	0.00
Gila Polychrome: Tonto Variety	0	0.00	0	0.00	0	0.00	0	0.00	0	0.00	0	0.00	0	0.00	0	0.00
indeterminate Roosevelt Red Ware black-on-red	1	0.14	0	0.00	0	0.00	1	6.25	2	0.43	0	0.00	0	0.00	0	0.00
indeterminate Roosevelt Red Ware polychrome	439	62.80	162	54.00	2	25.00	5	31.25	255	54.96	1	25.00	15	88.24	53	71.62
indeterminate Roosevelt Red Ware (salmon variety)	3	0.43	2	0.67	0	0.00	0	0.00	1	0.22	0	0.00	0	0.00	0	0.00
Nine Mile Polychrome	2	0.29	0	0.00	0	0.00	0	0.00	1	0.22	0	0.00	0	0.00	0	0.00
Nine Mile Polychrome: Safford Variety	0	0.00	0	0.00	0	0.00	0	0.00	0	0.00	0	0.00	0	0.00	0	0.00
Nine Mile Polychrome: Tonto Variety	1	0.14	0	0.00	0	0.00	0	0.00	0	0.00	0	0.00	0	0.00	0	0.00
Phoenix Polychrome	0	0.00	0	0.00	0	0.00	0	0.00	0	0.00	0	0.00	0	0.00	0	0.00

Pinto Black-on-red	1	0.14	0	0.00	0	0.00	0	0.00	0	0.00	0	0.00	0	0.00	0	0.00
Pinto Polychrome	5	0.72	2	0.67	0	0.00	1	6.25	2	0.43	0	0.00	0	0.00	0	0.00
Pinto Polychrome: Salmon Variety	0	0.00	1	0.33	0	0.00	0	0.00	0	0.00	0	0.00	0	0.00	0	0.00
Tonto Polychrome	9	1.29	3	1.00	0	0.00	2	12.50	13	2.80	0	0.00	0	0.00	0	0.00
Whiteriver Polychrome	4	0.57	2	0.67	0	0.00	0	0.00	0	0.00	0	0.00	0	0.00	0	0.00
Subtotal	*662*	*94.71*	*278*	*92.67*	*8*	*100*	*14*	*87.50*	*458*	*98.71*	*3*	*75.00*	*17*	*100*	*62*	*83.78*
Maverick Mountain Series																
indeterminate Maverick Mountain series	3	0.43	4	1.33	0	0.00	0	0.00	0	0.00	0	0.00	0	0.00	3	4.05
indeterminate Maverick Mountain Series black-on-red	4	0.57	0	0.00	0	0.00	1	6.25	0	0.00	0	0.00	0	0.00	0	0.00
indeterminate Maverick Mountain Series, Roosevelt Red Ware exterior	0	0.00	0	0.00	0	0.00	0	0.00	0	0.00	0	0.00	0	0.00	0	0.00
Maverick Mountain Black-on-red	8	1.14	1	0.33	0	0.00	0	0.00	1	0.22	1	25.00	0	0.00	3	4.05
Maverick Mountain Polychrome	0	0.00	0	0.00	0	0.00	0	0.00	1	0.22	0	0.00	0	0.00	0	0.00
Nantack Polychrome A (Tusayan Polychrome analog)	0	0.00	0	0.00	0	0.00	0	0.00	0	0.00	0	0.00	0	0.00	0	0.00
Tucson Black-on-red	5	0.72	4	1.33	0	0.00	0	0.00	0	0.00	0	0.00	0	0.00	2	2.70
Tucson Black-on-red or Tucson Polychrome	2	0.29	2	0.67	0	0.00	0	0.00	1	0.22	0	0.00	0	0.00	0	0.00
Tucson Polychrome	13	1.86	10	3.33	0	0.00	1	6.25	3	0.65	0	0.00	0	0.00	3	4.05
Subtotal	*35*	*5.01*	*21*	*7.00*	*0*	*0.00*	*2*	*12.50*	*6*	*1.29*	*1*	*25.00*	*0*	*0.00*	*11*	*14.86*
Babocomari Polychrome	0	0.00	0	0.00	0	0.00	0	0.00	0	0.00	0	0.00	0	0.00	0	0.00
Subtotal	*0*	*0.00*	*0*	*0.00*	*0*	*0.00*	*0*	*0.00*	*0*	*0.00*	*0*	*0.00*	*0*	*0.00*	*0*	*0.00*
Davis Black-on-red	0	0.00	0	0.00	0	0.00	0	0.00	0	0.00	0	0.00	0	0.00	0	0.00
Subtotal	*0*	*0.00*	*0*	*0.00*	*0*	*0.00*	*0*	*0.00*	*0*	*0.00*	*0*	*0.00*	*0*	*0.00*	*0*	*0.00*
Dragoon or San Simon Series	0	0.00	0	0.00	0	0.00	0	0.00	0	0.00	0	0.00	0	0.00	0	0.00
Subtotal	*0*	*0.00*	*0*	*0.00*	*0*	*0.00*	*0*	*0.00*	*0*	*0.00*	*0*	*0.00*	*0*	*0.00*	*0*	*0.00*
indeterminate decorated	1	0.14	1	0.33	0	0.00	0	0.00	0	0.00	0	0.00	0	0.00	0	0.00
Subtotal	*1*	*0.14*	*1*	*0.33*	*0*	*0.00*	*0*	*0.00*	*0*	*0.00*	*0*	*0.00*	*0*	*0.00*	*0*	*0.00*
indeterminate red-on-brown	0	0.00	0	0.00	0	0.00	0	0.00	0	0.00	0	0.00	0	0.00	0	0.00
Subtotal	*0*	*0.00*	*0*	*0.00*	*0*	*0.00*	*0*	*0.00*	*0*	*0.00*	*0*	*0.00*	*0*	*0.00*	*0*	*0.00*

(continued)

TABLE 7.2 *(continued)*

Ware or ware-level category and/ or type or type-level category	Houseblock I		Houseblock II		Houseblock VI		Houseblock VII		Compound-wall-associated rooms and other rooms		Houseblock III		Houseblock IV		Houseblock V	
	n	%	*n*	%	*n*	%	*n*	%	*n*	%	*n*	%	*n*	%	*n*	%
Kinishba Polychrome	0	0.00	0	0.00	0	0.00	0	0.00	0	0.00	0	0.00	0	0.00	0	0.00
Subtotal	*0*	*0.00*	*0*	*0.00*	*0*	*0.00*	*0*	*0.00*	*0*	*0.00*	*0*	*0.00*	*0*	*0.00*	*0*	*0.00*
Mimbres Black-on-white	1	0.14	0	0.00	0	0.00	0	0.00	0	0.00	0	0.00	0	0.00	1	1.35
Subtotal	*1*	*0.14*	*0*	*0.00*	*0*	*0.00*	*0*	*0.00*	*0*	*0.00*	*0*	*0.00*	*0*	*0.00*	*1*	*1.35*
San Carlos Red-on-brown	0	0.00	0	0.00	0	0.00	0	0.00	0	0.00	0	0.00	0	0.00	0	0.00
Subtotal	*0*	*0.00*	*0*	*0.00*	*0*	*0.00*	*0*	*0.00*	*0*	*0.00*	*0*	*0.00*	*0*	*0.00*	*0*	*0.00*
Total	**699**	**100**	**300**	**100**	**8**	**100**	**16**	**100**	**464**	**100**	**4**	**100**	**17**	**100**	**74**	**100**

Ware or ware-level category and/ or type or type-level category	Houses		Kiva		Northeast Trash		Stratitest 1		Other contexts		Subtotal		Unknown provenience (sherds with illegible provenience stamps)		Total	
	n	%	*n*	%	*n*	%	*n*	%	*n*	%	*n*	%	*n*	%	*n*	%
Roosevelt Red Ware																
Cliff Black-on-red	0	0.00	1	0.12	0	0.00	0	0.00	0	0.00	2	0.06	0	0.00	2	0.06
Cliff Polychrome or Nine Mile Polychrome	6	1.20	25	2.97	1	0.81	0	0.00	1	1.82	61	1.93	4	1.39	65	1.88
Cliff Polychrome	8	1.61	20	2.37	2	1.63	1	1.61	1	1.82	82	2.59	0	0.00	82	2.38
Cliff Polychrome: Salmon Variety	0	0.00	0	0.00	0	0.00	0	0.00	0	0.00	1	0.03	0	0.00	1	0.03
Cliff Polychrome: Tonto Variety	0	0.00	0	0.00	0	0.00	0	0.00	0	0.00	2	0.06	0	0.00	2	0.06
Cliff Polychrome: Tucson Variety	0	0.00	1	0.12	0	0.00	0	0.00	0	0.00	1	0.03	0	0.00	1	0.03
Gila Black-on-red	4	0.80	1	0.12	4	3.25	1	1.61	1	1.82	11	0.35	0	0.00	11	0.32
Gila Polychrome	46	9.24	70	8.30	8	6.50	4	6.45	6	10.91	310	9.80	12	4.18	322	9.33
Gila Polychrome or later	51	10.24	190	22.54	7	5.69	10	16.13	7	12.73	514	16.25	24	8.36	538	15.59
Gila Polychrome or later (salmon variety)	0	0.00	2	0.24	0	0.00	0	0.00	0	0.00	2	0.06	0	0.00	2	0.06

Gila Polychrome, no banding line	3	0.60	2	0.24	0	0.00	0	0.00	0	0.00	9	0.28	1	0.35	10	0.29
Gila Polychrome: Gila Variety	1	0.20	0	0.00	0	0.00	0	0.00	0	0.00	1	0.03	0	0.00	1	0.03
Gila Polychrome: Salmon Variety	2	0.40	0	0.00	1	0.81	0	0.00	0	0.00	3	0.09	0	0.00	3	0.09
Gila Polychrome: Tonto Variety	1	0.20	0	0.00	0	0.00	0	0.00	0	0.00	1	0.03	0	0.00	1	0.03
indeterminate Roosevelt Red Ware black-on-red	2	0.40	2	0.24	5	4.07	1	1.61	0	0.00	14	0.44	1	0.35	15	0.43
indeterminate Roosevelt Red Ware polychrome	282	56.63	495	58.72	43	34.96	33	53.23	29	52.73	1814	57.35	241	83.97	2055	59.57
indeterminate Roosevelt Red Ware (salmon variety)	1	0.20	0	0.00	0	0.00	0	0.00	0	0.00	7	0.22	0	0.00	7	0.20
Nine Mile Polychrome	0	0.00	0	0.00	0	0.00	0	0.00	0	0.00	3	0.09	0	0.00	3	0.09
Nine Mile Polychrome: Safford Variety	1	0.20	0	0.00	0	0.00	0	0.00	0	0.00	1	0.03	0	0.00	1	0.03
Nine Mile Polychrome: Tonto Variety	0	0.00	0	0.00	0	0.00	0	0.00	0	0.00	1	0.03	0	0.00	1	0.03
Phoenix Polychrome	2	0.40	2	0.24	0	0.00	0	0.00	0	0.00	4	0.13	0	0.00	4	0.12
Pinto Black-on-red	2	0.40	0	0.00	0	0.00	0	0.00	0	0.00	3	0.09	0	0.00	3	0.09
Pinto Polychrome	9	1.81	3	0.36	3	2.44	0	0.00	1	1.82	26	0.82	0	0.00	26	0.75
Pinto Polychrome: Salmon Variety	1	0.20	0	0.00	1	0.81	0	0.00	0	0.00	3	0.09	0	0.00	3	0.09
Tonto Polychrome	1	0.20	10	1.19	1	0.81	0	0.00	0	0.00	39	1.23	0	0.00	39	1.13
Whiteriver Polychrome	0	0.00	3	0.36	0	0.00	0	0.00	0	0.00	9	0.28	1	0.35	10	0.29
Subtotal	*423*	*84.94*	*827*	*98.10*	*76*	*61.79*	*50*	*80.65*	*46*	*83.64*	*2924*	*92.44*	*284*	*98.95*	*3208*	*92.99*
Maverick Mountain Series																
indeterminate Maverick Mountain Series	11	2.21	0	0.00	1	0.81	0	0.00	1	1.82	23	0.73	0	0.00	23	0.67
indeterminate Maverick Mountain series black-on-red	0	0.00	0	0.00	0	0.00	0	0.00	0	0.00	5	0.16	0	0.00	5	0.14
indeterminate Maverick Mountain Series, Roosevelt Red Ware exterior	0	0.00	0	0.00	1	0.81	0	0.00	0	0.00	1	0.03	0	0.00	1	0.03
Maverick Mountain Black-on-red	11	2.21	4	0.47	7	5.69	1	1.61	0	0.00	37	1.17	0	0.00	37	1.07
Maverick Mountain Polychrome	0	0.00	0	0.00	0	0.00	0	0.00	0	0.00	1	0.03	0	0.00	1	0.03
Nantack Polychrome A (Tusayan Polychrome analog)	0	0.00	0	0.00	1	0.81	0	0.00	0	0.00	1	0.03	0	0.00	1	0.03

(continued)

TABLE 7.2 *(continued)*

Ware or ware-level category and/ or type or type-level category	Houses		Kiva		Northeast Trash		Stratitest 1		Other contexts		Subtotal		Unknown provenience (sherds with illegible provenience stamps)		Total	
	n	%	*n*	%	*n*	%	*n*	%	*n*	%	*n*	%	*n*	%	*n*	%
Tucson Black-on-red	8	1.61	0	0.00	9	7.32	4	6.45	0	0.00	32	1.01	0	0.00	32	0.93
Tucson Black-on-red or Tucson Polychrome	5	1.00	1	0.12	4	3.25	0	0.00	0	0.00	15	0.47	0	0.00	15	0.43
Tucson Polychrome	32	6.43	7	0.83	23	18.70	6	9.68	8	14.55	106	3.35	3	1.05	109	3.16
Subtotal	*67*	*13.45*	*12*	*1.42*	*46*	*37.40*	*11*	*17.74*	*9*	*16.36*	*221*	*6.99*	*3*	*1.05*	*224*	*6.49*
Babocomari Polychrome	0	0.00	1	0.12	0	0.00	0	0.00	0	0.00	1	0.03	0	0.00	1	0.03
Subtotal	*0*	*0.00*	*1*	*0.12*	*0*	*0.00*	*0*	*0.00*	*0*	*0.00*	*1*	*0.03*	*0*	*0.00*	*1*	*0.03*
Davis Black-on-red	0	0.00	1	0.12	0	0.00	0	0.00	0	0.00	1	0.03	0	0.00	1	0.03
Subtotal	*0*	*0.00*	*1*	*0.12*	*0*	*0.00*	*0*	*0.00*	*0*	*0.00*	*1*	*0.03*	*0*	*0.00*	*1*	*0.03*
Dragoon or San Simon Series	1	0.20	1	0.12	0	0.00	0	0.00	0	0.00	2	0.06	0	0.00	2	0.06
Subtotal	*1*	*0.20*	*1*	*0.12*	*0*	*0.00*	*0*	*0.00*	*0*	*0.00*	*2*	*0.06*	*0*	*0.00*	*2*	*0.06*
indeterminate decorated	1	0.20	1	0.12	1	0.81	1	1.61	0	0.00	6	0.19	0	0.00	6	0.17
Subtotal	*1*	*0.20*	*1*	*0.12*	*1*	*0.81*	*1*	*1.61*	*0*	*0.00*	*6*	*0.19*	*0*	*0.00*	*6*	*0.17*
indeterminate red-on-brown	1	0.20	0	0.00	0	0.00	0	0.00	0	0.00	1	0.03	0	0.00	1	0.03
Subtotal	*1*	*0.20*	*0*	*0.00*	*0*	*0.00*	*0*	*0.00*	*0*	*0.00*	*1*	*0.03*	*0*	*0.00*	*1*	*0.03*
Kinishba Polychrome	1	0.20	0	0.00	0	0.00	0	0.00	0	0.00	1	0.03	0	0.00	1	0.03
Subtotal	*1*	*0.20*	*0*	*0.00*	*0*	*0.00*	*0*	*0.00*	*0*	*0.00*	*1*	*0.03*	*0*	*0.00*	*1*	*0.03*
Mimbres Black-on-white	3	0.60	0	0.00	0	0.00	0	0.00	0	0.00	5	0.16	0	0.00	5	0.14
Subtotal	*3*	*0.60*	*0*	*0.00*	*0*	*0.00*	*0*	*0.00*	*0*	*0.00*	*5*	*0.16*	*0*	*0.00*	*5*	*0.14*
San Carlos Red-on-brown	1	0.20	0	0.00	0	0.00	0	0.00	0	0.00	1	0.03	0	0.00	1	0.03
Subtotal	*1*	*0.20*	*0*	*0.00*	*0*	*0.00*	*0*	*0.00*	*0*	*0.00*	*1*	*0.03*	*0*	*0.00*	*1*	*0.03*
Total	**498**	**100**	**843**	**100**	**123**	**100**	**62**	**100**	**55**	**100**	**3163**	**100**	**287**	**100**	**3450**	**100**

Note: Frequencies have been reduced by sherd conjoins and matches (e.g., a vessel comprising 10 sherds is represented in this table by a "1"; see table 7.1). Whole vessels recovered by Rex Gerald are also included here.

TABLE 7.3 Provenience designations used in the recovery of pottery from the kiva

Provenience	Description or comment
Kiva fill	General fill
Kiva stratitest level 1	0–20 cm
Kiva stratitest level 2	20–40 cm
Kiva stratitest level 3	40–60 cm
Kiva stratitest level 4	60–80 cm
Kiva stratitest level 5	80–100 cm
Kiva stratitest level 6	100–120 cm
Kiva stratitest level 7	120–140 cm
Kiva stratitest level 8	140–160 cm
Kiva level 9	150–160 cm
Kiva level 3–5	40–100 cm
Kiva level 6–8	100–160 cm
Kiva floor	Floor contact
Structure 1 fill	The kiva was originally designated Structure 1
Kiva SW compartment	Enclosed area created by constricting the platform
Feature A (ventilator)	Floor feature
Feature D (hearth)	Floor feature
Feature E (foot drum)	Floor feature
Feature F (subfloor pit)	Floor feature
T8S 23–25E	Trench that intersects the kiva
T8.5–9S 24–25E L1	Trench that intersects the kiva
T8.5–9S 24–25E L2	Trench that intersects the kiva
T8.5–9S 24–25E L3	Trench that intersects the kiva
T8.5–9S 24–25E L4	Trench that intersects the kiva
T10S 23–25E L1	Trench that intersects the kiva
T10S 23–25E L2	Trench that intersects the kiva
T10S 23–25E L3	Trench that intersects the kiva
T12S 18–20E	Trench that intersects the kiva
T23E 10S	Trench that intersects the kiva
T23E 11–15S	Trench that intersects the kiva
T23E 11–16S	Trench that intersects the kiva
T23E 14–15S	Trench that intersects the kiva
T26E 7–16S	Trench that intersects the kiva
T26E 10S	Trench that intersects the kiva
T26E 10–16S	Trench that intersects the kiva
T26E 11–15S	Trench that intersects the kiva

TABLE 7.4 Roosevelt Red Ware types, dates (all are AD), summary descriptions, and references

Type (date)	Summary description	Reference(s)
Los Muertos Polychrome (1390–1450)	bowls, jars, mugs; red used as paint (alongside black paint) on white slip	Lyons and Neuzil 2006; Neuzil and Lyons 2006
Dinwiddie Polychrome (1390–1450)	recurved bowls only; exterior: decoration like Gila or Tonto Polychrome jars; interior: smudged	Lyons and Neuzil 2006; Neuzil and Lyons 2006
Cliff White-on-red (1390–1450)	recurved bowls only; exterior: white paint on red slip; interior: smudged	Lyons and Neuzil 2006; Mills and Mills 1972; Neuzil and Lyons 2006
Phoenix Polychrome (1375–1450)	recurved bowls only; exterior: decoration like Gila or Tonto Polychrome jars; interior: slipped red	Lyons and Neuzil 2006; Neuzil and Lyons 2006
Nine Mile Polychrome (1375–1450)	recurved bowls only; exterior: decoration like Gila or Tonto Polychrome jars; interior: slipped red except for band of black paint on white slip near rim except in the case of Nine Mile Polychrome: Safford Variety, which exhibits Tonto-configuration decoration pendant from the band of painted decoration at the rim	Lyons and Neuzil 2006; Neuzil and Lyons 2006
Whiteriver Polychrome (1360–1450)	incurved and hemispherical bowls only; exterior: decoration like Gila or Tonto Polychrome jars; interior: slipped red	Lyons 2013a
Cliff Polychrome[a,b] (1360–1450)	recurved bowls only; interior: two black-on-white design fields (one at rim and one below) separated by banding line; exterior: slipped red[c]	Harlow 1968; Lyons 2004b
Cliff Black-on-red (1360–1450)	recurved bowls only; interior: two black-on-red design fields (one at rim and one below) separated by banding line; exterior: slipped red	Arizona State Museum Collections
Tonto Polychrome (1340–1450)	jars, bowls, mugs, ladles; bowl interior: panels or meandering ribbons of black paint on white slip surrounded by red slip; bowl exterior: slipped red[c]; jar exterior: (1) single design field comprised by panels or meandering ribbons of black paint on white slip surrounded by red slip, (2) separate design fields for neck and body, each comprised by panels or ribbons of black paint on white slip surrounded by red slip, or (3) separate design fields for neck and body: one comprised by panels or ribbons of black paint on white slip surrounded by red slip, the other consisting of horizontal band of white slip with black paint	Colton and Hargrave 1937:90–91; Gladwin and Gladwin 1930:8–9; Haury 1945:63–80

Gila Polychrome[a,b,d] (1300–1450)	bowls, jars; bowl interior: black paint on white slip (usually wide, black, banding line at rim); bowl exterior: slipped red[c]; jar exterior: (1) single horizontal band of white slip and black paint, jar base (below black-on-white zone) slipped red, or (2) multiple, horizontal stripes of white slip and black paint separated by stripes of red slip	Colton and Hargrave 1937:88–90; Gladwin and Gladwin 1930:6–7; Haury 1945:63–80
Gila Black-on-red[e] (1300–1450)	bowls, jars; bowl interior: black paint on red slip (usually wide, black, banding line at rim); bowl exterior: slipped red; jar exterior: black paint on red slip	Wendorf 1950:123–124
Pinto Polychrome[a,b,d] (1280–1330)	bowls only; interior: black paint on white slip (lacks wide, black, banding line at rim); exterior: slipped red	Colton and Hargrave 1937:87–88; Gladwin and Gladwin 1930:4–5
Pinto Black-on-red[e] (1280–1330)	bowls only; interior: black paint on red slip (lacks wide, black, banding line at rim); exterior: slipped red	Gifford 1980:36–37

[a]Includes "salmon varieties," e.g., Pinto Polychrome: Salmon Variety, Gila Polychrome: Salmon Variety (Di Peso 1958a:100; Haury 1931:70–71, 1934:135; Lindsay and Jennings 1968:9; Lyons 2012b). Salmon variety vessels (all bowls) exhibit a pink interior surface. Most have been slipped with a pink-firing rather than a white-firing clay, although some appear to be unslipped, i.e., the interior surface is the oxidized color of the clay used to build the vessel. In both cases, the color of the interior contrasts with the red slip applied to the exterior.

[b]Includes "Tucson varieties," e.g., Gila Polychrome: Tucson Variety (also known as Pinto-Tucson Polychrome and Gila-Tucson Polychrome; see Di Peso 1958a:100; Franklin 1980:66; Gerald 1958; Lindsay and Jennings 1968:12). Such vessels (all bowls) exhibit Roosevelt Red Ware technology (including black, carbon paint) and decoration on the inside and Maverick Mountain Series technology and decoration (specifically, that associated with Tucson Polychrome—solid geometric elements in brownish, mineral paint outlined in white; see Lindsay 1992) on the outside.

[c]Bowl exteriors may be slipped red and lack painted decoration or, instead, may bear decoration characteristic of Gila Polychrome (e.g., Cliff Polychrome: Gila Variety) or Tonto Polychrome (e.g., Cliff Polychrome: Tonto Variety) jars.

[d]Some Gila and Pinto Polychrome bowls bear banded (rather than radial) interior designs similar to those seen on the exteriors of Gila Polychrome jars. Such vessels sometimes exhibit a circular, unpainted area of red slip in the center of the design field. More rarely, black, painted decoration is applied to this area of red slip. In cases such as the latter, the vessel's layout often consists of concentric bands of black painted decoration (some on white slip and some on red slip).

[e]Maverick Mountain Black-on-red is often mistakenly identified as Pinto or Gila Black-on-red.

Polychrome: Tonto Variety (Gila configuration interior and Tonto configuration exterior) or Tonto Polychrome: Gila Variety (Tonto configuration interior and Gila configuration exterior). Bowls with no interior painted decoration are classified based on exterior decoration and vessel form.

Though not labeled with formal variety names, Pinto Polychrome and Gila Polychrome bowls exhibiting central, circular, red-slipped areas on their interior surfaces are identified thus: "Pinto Polychrome, red center" and "Gila Polychrome, red center." Likewise, bowls bearing painted decoration characteristic of Gila Polychrome but lacking a banding line are identified as "Gila Polychrome, no banding line." Tonto Polychrome jars with multiple rather than single design fields (i.e., separate neck and body decorations) are informally identified here as "Tonto Polychrome (Gila neck, Tonto body)" or "Tonto Polychrome (Tonto neck, Gila body)."

Recently Defined Types

Cliff Polychrome (Lyons 2004b; see also Harlow 1968) occurs only in recurved bowl form and is distinguished from Gila Polychrome by the presence of two interior design fields—one at the rim and the other on the bottom and walls—separated by a thick banding line (figure 7.1a). Cliff Polychrome bowls may bear exterior painted decoration. Nine Mile Polychrome (Lyons and Neuzil 2006; Neuzil and Lyons 2006) is similar to Cliff Polychrome. Both occur only as recurved bowls and exhibit a banded field of black-on-white painted decoration on the interior surface, at the rim. Nine Mile differs from Cliff in that the remainder of the interior surface of the former is typically slipped red and bears no painted decoration (figure 7.1b). Nine Mile Polychrome bowl exteriors usually bear Gila- or Tonto-configuration decoration. A new variety of Nine Mile Polychrome is described below, based on a partially reconstructible vessel from the Davis Ranch Site and whole specimens from other sites.

Phoenix Polychrome (Lyons and Neuzil 2006; Neuzil and Lyons 2006) lacks black-on-white interior decoration; the entire interior is slipped red (figure 7.1c). Only occurring in the form of recurved bowls, Phoenix Polychrome vessels exhibit either Gila- or Tonto-configuration exterior decoration. Recurved Roosevelt Red Ware bowls exhibiting Gila- or Tonto-configuration exterior decoration and smudged interiors are referred to as Dinwiddie Polychrome. Los Muertos Polychrome (figure 7.1d) is distinguished by the use of red paint alongside black paint on white-slipped surfaces and occurs in a variety of bowl and jar forms (Crown 1981:146–147, 1994:88; Haury 1945:65–66).

Cliff White-on-red is characterized by a red-slipped exterior, a smudged interior, and white painted decoration on top of the red slip (Mills and Mills 1972:46–47). The type occurs primarily in the form of recurved bowls and is distinguished from Tularosa, Gila, and Salado White-on-red based on technological traits and painted decoration. Whiteriver Polychrome (Lyons 2013a) is named in reference to the Kinishba area (the name Kinishba Polychrome was already taken) and is used as a label for hemispherical to slightly incurved Roosevelt Red Ware bowls with red-slipped but unpainted interior surfaces and Gila- or Tonto-configuration exterior decoration (figure 7.1e).

Roosevelt Red Ware Seriation

Based on an analysis of surface collections and excavated assemblages from an area bounded by the Little Colorado River to the north, Paquimé to the south, the Agua Fria drainage to the west, and the Cliff Valley of New Mexico to the east, the newly defined Roosevelt Red Ware types appear to form a sequence, from oldest to youngest, in the following order: (1) Cliff Polychrome and Whiteriver Polychrome (ca. AD 1360–1450); (2) Nine Mile Polychrome and Phoenix Polychrome (ca. AD 1375–1450); and (3) Cliff White-on-red, Dinwiddie Polychrome, and Los Muertos Polychrome (ca. AD 1390–1450).

Each of these types, except Cliff Polychrome and Whiteriver Polychrome, has an areal distribution much smaller than that associated with Gila and Tonto Polychrome (Lyons 2013a). Phoenix

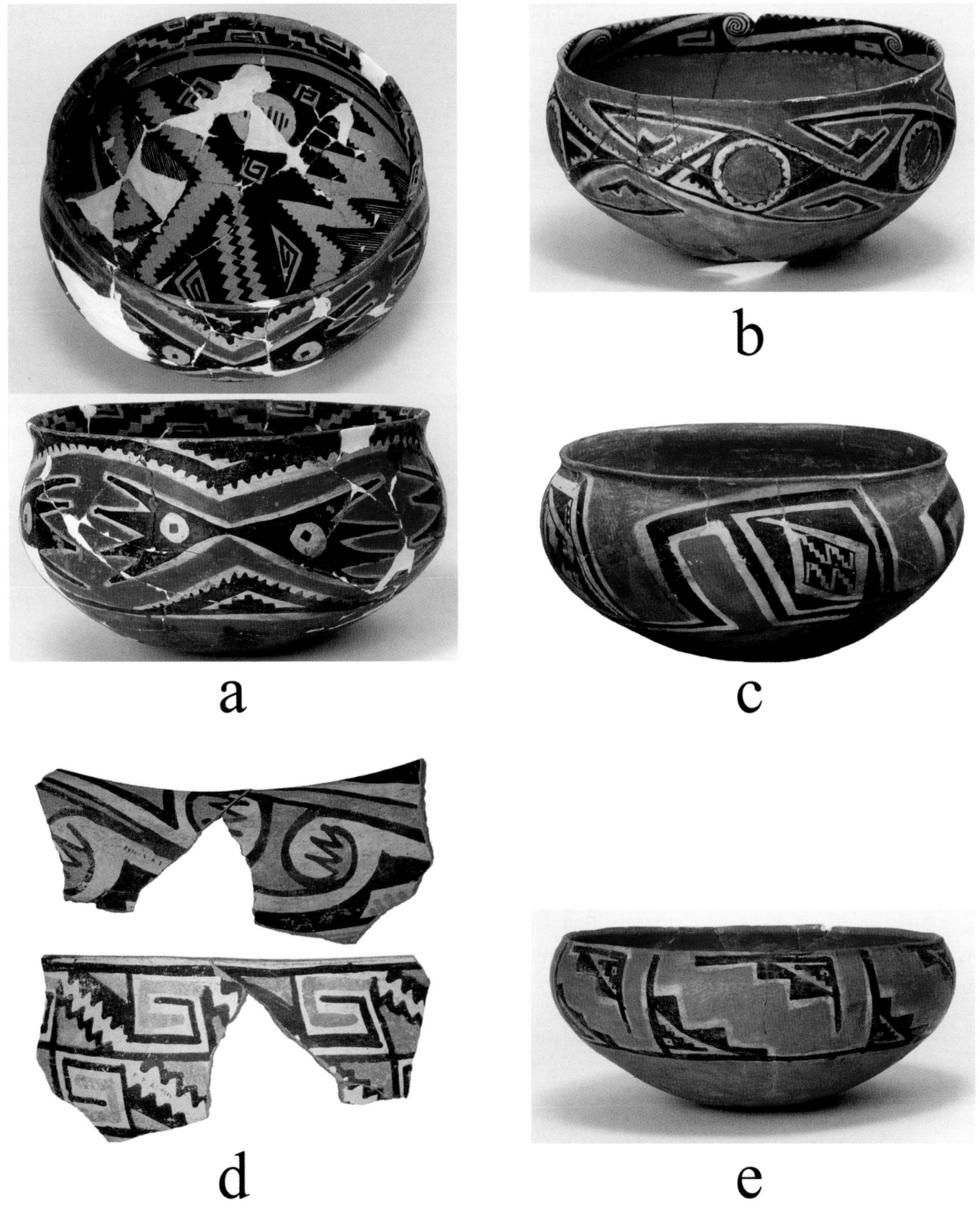

FIGURE 7.1 Late Roosevelt Red Ware types: (a) Cliff Polychrome, Catalog No. 23705; (b) Nine Mile Polychrome, A-33402; (c) Phoenix Polychrome, 443; (d) Los Muertos Polychrome, 2011-687-1; (e) Whiteriver Polychrome, A-33395. Phoenix Polychrome specimen (c) recovered from the Nine Mile site (AZ CC:15:1[AF]); all others from Kinishba (AZ V:4:1[ASM]). Maximum diameters: (a) 40.0 cm, (b) 36.0 cm, (c) 37.8 cm, (e) 41.0 cm. Photographs by Jannelle Weakly (a, b, d, e) and Patrick D. Lyons (c), courtesy of the Arizona State Museum, University of Arizona (a, b, d, e) and Eastern Arizona College, Thatcher (c).

and Nine Mile Polychrome together cover the largest area, spanning the mostly non-overlapping distributions of Los Muertos Polychrome, to the west, and Dinwiddie Polychrome and Cliff White-on-red, to the east (to date, Fourmile Ruin, AZ P:12:4[ASM], is the only site where Los Muertos Polychrome and Dinwiddie Polychrome are known to occur together). This spatial pattern seems to reflect chronology, in that the more widespread types, Phoenix and Nine Mile Polychrome, are earlier than those with much more restricted distributions: Los Muertos Polychrome, Dinwiddie Polychrome, and Cliff White-on-red.

Although Nine Mile Polychrome and Phoenix Polychrome mostly occur in the same places, Nine Mile Polychrome is more common in the east and Phoenix Polychrome is more common in the west. Similarly, Whiteriver Polychrome is widespread—occurring as far west as Bloody Basin and at least as far east as Safford, and from Chevelon Ruin to the north to Reeve Ruin and the Davis Ranch Site to the south—but the type is most abundant in sites in the northeastern portion of its distribution, including Kinishba and Fourmile Ruin.

Spatial patterns are also evident at the local level. In some site clusters, Cliff Polychrome, for example, may be present at many or even most sites, whereas only a few have yielded specimens of one or more of the newly defined types discussed here. In the San Pedro Valley, although many sites have yielded large quantities of Cliff Polychrome and some Whiteriver Polychrome, Nine Mile and Phoenix Polychrome are rare, and when they occur, they are seen only in small numbers. Two conjoining body sherds from the Davis Ranch Site may represent a single specimen of Dinwiddie Polychrome, the only possible example of this type yet documented in the valley. Analysis of stratified trash in the kiva at the Davis Ranch Site (discussed below) corroborates the seriation-based inferences that Cliff Polychrome was introduced after Gila and Tonto Polychrome, and that Nine Mile and Phoenix Polychrome appeared after Cliff Polychrome became abundant.

In the nearby Globe highlands, at Besh-Ba-Gowah, Cliff Polychrome and Whiteriver Polychrome are present among the whole vessels, but Nine Mile, Phoenix, and Los Muertos Polychrome are absent. In addition to Cliff and Whiteriver Polychrome, Gila Pueblo (AZ V:9:52[ASM]) yielded Nine Mile and Los Muertos Polychrome. Although Cliff Polychrome occurs in the very large Roosevelt Red Ware whole vessel assemblage from Grasshopper Pueblo (consisting of more than 240 specimens), Nine Mile, Phoenix, and Los Muertos Polychrome do not.

Assigning an Absolute Date Range to Cliff Polychrome and Whiteriver Polychrome

Cliff Polychrome is found in sites and specific contexts with tree-ring dates between the AD 1350s and 1380s. Examples include Sherwood Ranch Ruin (AZ Q:11:48[ASM]), in the Little Colorado Valley, the University Indian Ruin, in the Tucson Basin, a number of sites in the Cliff and Mimbres Valleys of New Mexico, and Paquimé (Lyons 2004b). This type is also abundant in sites and contexts with archaeomagnetic and radiocarbon dates spanning the period AD 1350–1450, including Las Colinas (AZ T:12:10[ASM]), Escalante Ruin (AZ U:15:3[ASM]), El Polvorón (AZ U:15:59[ASM]), Las Fosas (AZ U:15:19[ASM]), Dutch Canal Ruin (AZ T:12:62[ASM]), and Pueblo Salado (AZ T:12:47[ASM]).

Cliff Polychrome is absent from some sites that have yielded vessels bearing Tonto-configuration decoration, such as Canyon Creek Ruin, and is rare relative to Tonto-configuration vessels in other assemblages such as those from Grasshopper Pueblo and Besh-Ba-Gowah. Grasshopper is especially important here, as Riggs (2001:115–116, 147) places the beginning of population dispersion and the process of abandonment between AD 1330 and 1345, with limited construction post-1350 and dwindling occupation, ending circa 1390. This is consistent with the presence at Grasshopper of two partial vessels of Awatovi Black-on-yellow (ca. AD 1300/1325–1375/1385) and the apparent absence of Jeddito

Black-on-yellow (ca. AD 1375–1700) and Sikyatki Polychrome (ca. AD 1385–1700). Regarding the dating of Whiteriver Polychrome, it is important to note the absence of this type from Grasshopper, where Cliff Polychrome is rare, and the presence of both Whiteriver Polychrome and Cliff Polychrome at Besh-Ba-Gowah. Given these facts, relevant to the genesis of these types, and their presence in the latest Roosevelt Red Ware assemblages available for analysis, a date range of AD 1360–1450 is suggested.

Dating Post-Cliff Polychrome Types

Work with archival materials and existing museum collections has resulted in the discovery of associations between post-Cliff Polychrome types and others securely dated post-AD 1370, post-1385, and post-1400. For example, based on the Woodburys' unpublished notes on material recovered from Hawikku by Hodge, it has been possible to determine that Phoenix and Nine Mile Polychrome and Cliff White-on-red were present. Nine Mile Polychrome was recovered from a room floor in association with Kechipawan Polychrome (a post-AD 1370 type) and below a floor bearing Matsaki Polychrome (a post-AD 1400 type). Other specific associations at Zuni have not yet been ferreted out, but more general data provided by Smith and others (1966) and Bushnell (1955) are instructive.

At Hawikku, Roosevelt Red Ware was found in cremations alongside Pinnawa Red-on-white (ca. AD 1350–1450), Kechipawan Polychrome (ca. AD 1370–1500), and Matsaki Polychrome (ca. AD 1400–1680) (Smith et al. 1966:190). At Kechipawan, Roosevelt Red Ware was recovered from cremations with Pinnawa Glaze-on-white (AD 1350–1500), Kechipawan Polychrome, and Matsaki Brown-on-buff (AD 1400–1680) (Bushnell 1955:659–662). Schachner's (2006) analysis of stratigraphic data from Zuni Pueblo and Hawikku suggests that Roosevelt Red Ware first appeared there circa AD 1375–1400. Knowing, based on seriation and stratigraphy, that Phoenix and Nine Mile Polychrome appeared after Cliff Polychrome, and given the recovery of Nine Mile Polychrome in a context at Hawikku dating circa AD 1370–1400, it seems reasonable to use AD 1375 as a start date for both Phoenix and Nine Mile Polychrome. Because these types, like Cliff and Whiteriver Polychrome, continue to occur in the latest Roosevelt Red Ware assemblages in the region, an end date of AD 1450 is proposed.

Los Muertos Polychrome is encountered only at the latest sites within a region. In the Phoenix Basin, it was recovered from Los Muertos (the type's eponym), Las Colinas, Pueblo Salado, and Pueblo Grande. In the Globe highlands, it is only known to occur at Gila Pueblo. In many settlement clusters, Jeddito Black-on-yellow and Sikyatki Polychrome occur at many of the same sites that have yielded Los Muertos Polychrome. This is true of the Tonto Basin, at the Schoolhouse Point (AZ U:8:24[ASM]), Cline Terrace (AZ U:4:33[ASM]), and VIV (AZ U:3:1[ASM]) platform mound sites; Polles Mesa Pueblo (AZ O:10:13[ASM]); a number of sites in the Perry Mesa area (Wilcox and Holmlund 2007); the Dugan Site (AZ O:13:4[ASU]), in the Bloody Basin; and Mercer Ruin, in the upper Lower Verde Valley.

Based on my recent analysis of the whole vessel assemblage from Fourmile Ruin (now curated by the Museum of Peoples and Cultures at Brigham Young University; see Harris 2009), in the Silver Creek drainage, the association between Los Muertos Polychrome and Sikyatki Polychrome holds there as well. Sites in the Phoenix Basin and the Santa Cruz Flats–Picacho District with high frequencies of Los Muertos Polychrome have produced some of the latest archaeomagnetic and radiocarbon dates in the southern Southwest (Ahlstrom et al. 1995; Ciolek-Torrello et al. 1988; Eighmy and Doyel 1987; Henderson and Martynec 1993). These indicate occupation well into the AD 1400s. Based on these patterns, especially the strong association with Sikyatki Polychrome, a reasonable date range for Los Muertos Polychrome is circa AD 1390–1450.

Dinwiddie Polychrome has a very limited spatial distribution and, like Los Muertos Polychrome, is typically found at the latest occupied sites in a given settlement cluster. This is true of the Curtis Site (AZ CC:2:3[ASM]) in the Safford Basin, for example, and the latest sites in the Sulphur Springs and upper Gila Valleys. Also like Los Muertos Polychrome, sites yielding Dinwiddie Polychrome often have Jeddito Black-on-yellow and/or Sikyatki Polychrome in their assemblages. These include AZ W:10:47(ASM) and AZ W:10:50B(ASM) at Point of Pines, and Fourmile Ruin. The type is also present at Hawikku. A suggested date range for Dinwiddie Polychrome, based on these data, is circa AD 1390–1450.

Cliff White-on-red's spatial distribution mirrors that of Dinwiddie Polychrome, with a few exceptions, such as Table Rock Pueblo (AZ Q:7:5[ASM]), suggesting a similar date range. At Table Rock Pueblo, some of the white-on-red pottery described by Martin and Rinaldo (1960:208–210) is Cliff White-on-red, though some is probably the unnamed white-on-red found at Hawikku and discussed by Woodbury and Woodbury (1966). Table Rock also yielded a small amount of Sikyatki Polychrome and Matsaki Buff Ware. Martin and Rinaldo (1960; see also Duff 2002) place the white-on-red pottery in the latest complex of types used at Table Rock. Also important in dating Cliff White-on-red is its presence in the latest occupied sites in the upper Gila Valley, including Kwilleylekia (LA 4937), with two tree-ring cutting dates of AD 1380. All available evidence points to the period circa AD 1390–1450 as a reasonable date range for this type.

Typological Breakdown

Nearly two-thirds of the specimens in the Roosevelt Red Ware assemblage from the Davis Ranch Site were classified as indeterminate Roosevelt Red Ware polychrome (75% of these are bowls, 24% are jars, and the rest are indeterminate as to vessel form), and almost 20% were assigned to the category "Gila Polychrome or later," meaning they might be portions of Gila Polychrome bowls or bowls of any of the later types with white-slipped interiors (e.g., Cliff Polychrome, Gila Polychrome with no banding line; see table 7.2).

Sherds and partially reconstructible vessels assignable to a formal typological category are dominated by Gila Polychrome, which accounts for more than 10% of the assemblage, followed in order of decreasing frequency by Cliff Polychrome, Cliff or Nine Mile Polychrome (a mixed typological category), Tonto Polychrome, Pinto Polychrome, and others. It is important to note the presence, at the Davis Ranch Site, of specimens of Whiteriver Polychrome, which seems to have appeared at about the same time as Cliff Polychrome (ca. AD 1360), as well as Phoenix and Nine Mile Polychrome, which were introduced after Cliff Polychrome (ca. AD 1375) (Lyons 2012b, 2013a). One specimen from the site may represent Dinwiddie Polychrome, a type that appears to postdate AD 1390, suggesting an end to the occupation in the last quarter of the fourteenth century (figure 7.2). It is not listed in table 7.2, however. The possible Dinwiddie Polychrome specimen consists of two conjoinable body fragments recovered from deposits within the kiva (Kiva fill and Kiva level 6–8) that were not included in the full reanalysis. As discussed above, assemblages from these deposits were searched for conjoins and matches with sherds from the kiva's stratigraphic column, but nonconjoining and nonmatching sherds were not recorded or incorporated into quantitative comparisons.

Maverick Mountain Series

The Maverick Mountain Series assemblage from the Davis Ranch Site is dominated by Tucson Polychrome (51%; n = 114), with the following types or mixed typological categories also present, listed in descending order of frequency: Maverick Mountain Black-on-red, Tucson Black-on-red, indeterminate Maverick Mountain Series, Tucson Black-on-red or Tucson Polychrome, indeterminate Maverick Mountain Series black-on-red, indeterminate Maverick Mountain Series with Roosevelt Red Ware exterior decoration, Maverick Mountain Polychrome, and Nantack Polychrome A (analog of Tusayan Polychrome; figure 7.3). Nantack Polychrome B (analog of Kayenta Polychrome) and Prieto Polychrome

FIGURE 7.2 Possible Dinwiddie Polychrome bowl fragment recovered from the Davis Ranch Site, Kiva Decorated Vessel 112: (a) exterior, (b) interior. Photographs by Patrick D. Lyons.

are absent from the Amerind Foundation collection and also the assemblage recovered by the Center for Desert Archaeology (now Archaeology Southwest) in 2000.

Seriation and stratigraphic evidence at Point of Pines and elsewhere indicate that Maverick Mountain Black-on-red, Maverick Mountain Polychrome, Prieto Polychrome, and Nantack Polychrome appeared before Tucson Polychrome and Tucson Black-on-red and that Tucson Polychrome and Tucson Black-on-red outlasted the other types. Breternitz (1966:85, 87, 98) dates Maverick Mountain Polychrome and Nantack Polychrome between AD 1265 and 1290 and places Tucson Polychrome after AD 1300 with no suggested end date. Because assemblages that include these types indicate temporal overlap, and because such assemblages often contain Gila Polychrome, I use AD 1265–1325 as a range for most Maverick Mountain Series types and, following Lindsay (1992), place Tucson Polychrome (and Tucson Black-on-red) between AD 1300 and 1400. Because Nantack Polychrome has been recovered from contexts dating well after AD 1325, I use an end date of 1400 for this type as well (Di Peso et al. 1974:147; Lyons 2004b).

SPATIAL PATTERNING

The spatial distribution of Maverick Mountain Series types (which were manufactured less often as Roosevelt Red Ware production increased through time) is consistent with the model of the Davis Ranch Site's development based on architecture (see tables F.1–F.8; see also table 7.2). The contexts with the highest percentages of Maverick Mountain

FIGURE 7.3 Maverick Mountain Series types recovered from the Davis Ranch Site: (a) partially reconstructible Tucson Polychrome jar, Northeast Trash Decorated Vessel 4; (b) partially reconstructible Maverick Mountain Black-on-red jar, Kiva Decorated Vessel 13; (c) partially reconstructible Maverick Mountain Polychrome jar, Kiva Decorated Vessel 146; (d) partially reconstructible Maverick Mountain Polychrome jar, Kiva Decorated Vessel 148; (e) matching sherds from a Nantack Polychrome A jar, Kiva Decorated Vessel 147. Photographs by Patrick D. Lyons.

Series types (as a proportion of the total number of decorated sherds recovered) cluster in the eastern portion of the area associated with the bulk of the late Classic period occupation, east of the wall separating Houseblock I and the kiva and north of the kiva (figure 7.4).

Two high-density transects are evident when Maverick Mountain Series types are measured in terms of the proportion of the site's Maverick Mountain Series assemblage present in each context (figure 7.5). One transect runs roughly east-west, from House 1 to Room 44 (in Houseblock V), and another runs roughly north-south, from the Northeast Trash to the kiva. These linear concentrations mark what should be the earliest portions of the site's Classic period (Aravaipa phase) occupation, including Houses 1, 2, 3, and 7, the kiva, and the Northeast Trash. Plotting the percentages of early Maverick Mountain Series types (Maverick Mountain Black-on-red, Maverick Mountain Polychrome, and Nantack Polychrome) produces a similar pattern but with a much narrower east-west transect.

The western end of the east-west transect extends well beyond the westernmost Aravaipa phase pit house, to the Houseblock V area (Rooms 42 and 44). However, Gerald (chapter 3) notes a lack of clearly defined floors in these rooms and hypothesizes that the sherds he recovered, based on their small size, represent trash from an earlier component. This area, which is situated near the western edge of the rise upon which the site rests, above the San Pedro River, was tested by the Center for Desert Archaeology precisely because it seemed to represent a secondary trash accumulation rather than de facto refuse (Clark and Lyons 2012:Figure 3.56). Based on percentages alone, the east-west transect might extend as far eastward as Houseblock III, specifically Room 28, but only two decorated specimens were recovered from this structure, one of which is Maverick Mountain Black-on-red. Furthermore, Gerald concludes that this room and Room 27 were intentionally filled with trash from elsewhere. Ceramics that accumulated in the fills of Houses 4 and 5, after these Colonial period (AD 750–950) pit structures (located near the middle of the north-south transect and just north of the arc of Aravaipa phase pit houses) fell into disuse, clearly indicate the presence of a nearby Aravaipa phase occupation.

Very few Pinto Polychrome (including Pinto Polychrome: Salmon Variety) and Pinto Black-on-red specimens were recovered from the site (*n* = 32). Their spatial distribution largely matches that of all Maverick Mountain Series types and the early types in the series; that is, the highest percentages of these types occur in a north-south transect running from the Northeast Trash to the kiva, as well as in and around Houseblock I (including House 7) (figures 7.6, 7.7). Notably, Pinto Polychrome was recovered from the floors of Rooms 3, 16, and 37, as well as House 2, both floors of House 7 (also the fill between these floors), and the floor of the kiva.

Late Roosevelt Red Ware types display a different distribution; these types are concentrated to the west and south relative to the peak densities of Maverick Mountain Series types and Pinto Polychrome (figures 7.8, 7.9). Only 39 specimens of Tonto Polychrome were identified, and 10 of these were recovered from the kiva. The only pit house to yield Tonto Polychrome is House 3 (one sherd from the fill), and this type is poorly represented in the Northeast Trash and adjacent contexts (the northern end of the north-south transect marked by high frequencies of early types). Structures with Tonto Polychrome on their floors include Rooms 2, 3, and the kiva. Plotting the 149 specimens of known provenience classified as Cliff Polychrome (*n* = 86), Cliff Black-on-red (*n* = 2), and Cliff or Nine Mile Polychrome (*n* = 61) creates a similar but higher-resolution picture of late deposits, indicating the late accumulation of trash in the kiva, Room 2, and parts of Houseblock I (figures 7.10, 7.11). Phoenix Polychrome (*n* = 4) and Nine Mile Polychrome (*n* = 5) are rare at the site but occur in trash deposits identified as having accumulated relatively late in the site's occupation (see Seriation of Trash Deposits, below) (figure 7.12).

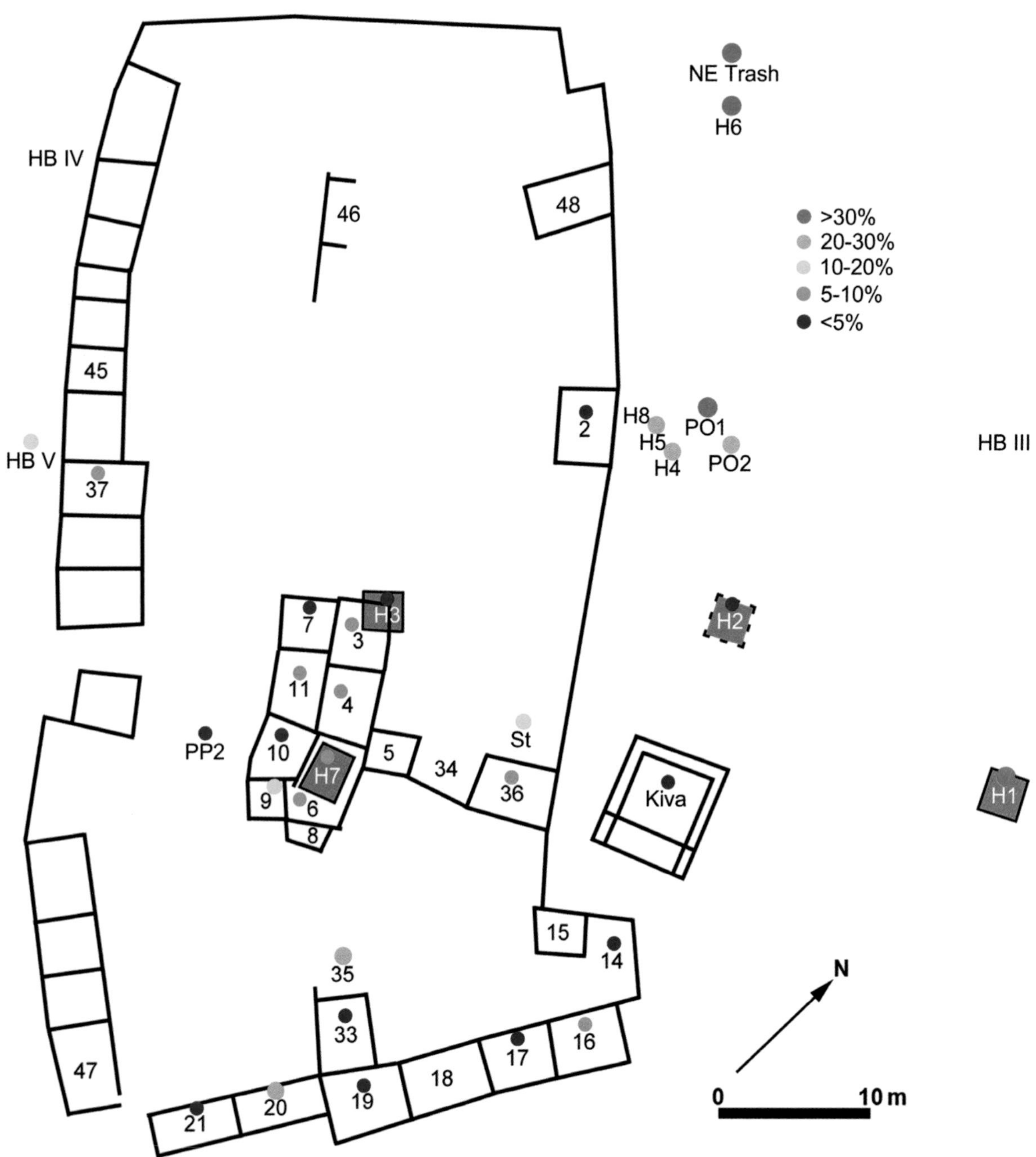

FIGURE 7.4 Distribution of Maverick Mountain Series types at the Davis Ranch Site. Percentages are based on the total number of decorated sherds in each context. Data from Room 45 and Room 28 are not plotted, as the assemblage from each included only two sherds.

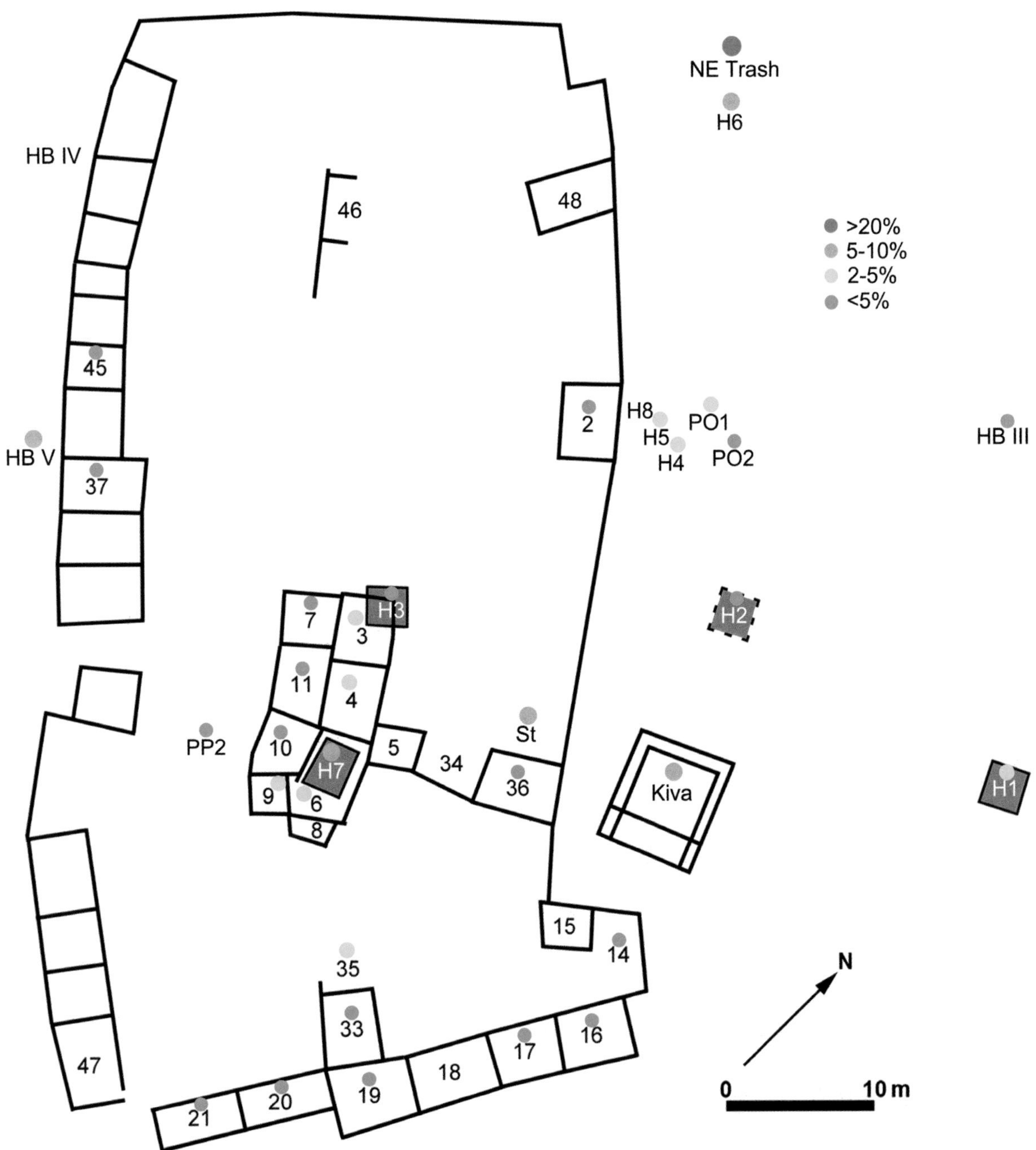

FIGURE 7.5 Distribution of Maverick Mountain Series types at the Davis Ranch Site. Percentages are based on the proportion of the site's Maverick Mountain Series assemblage present in each context.

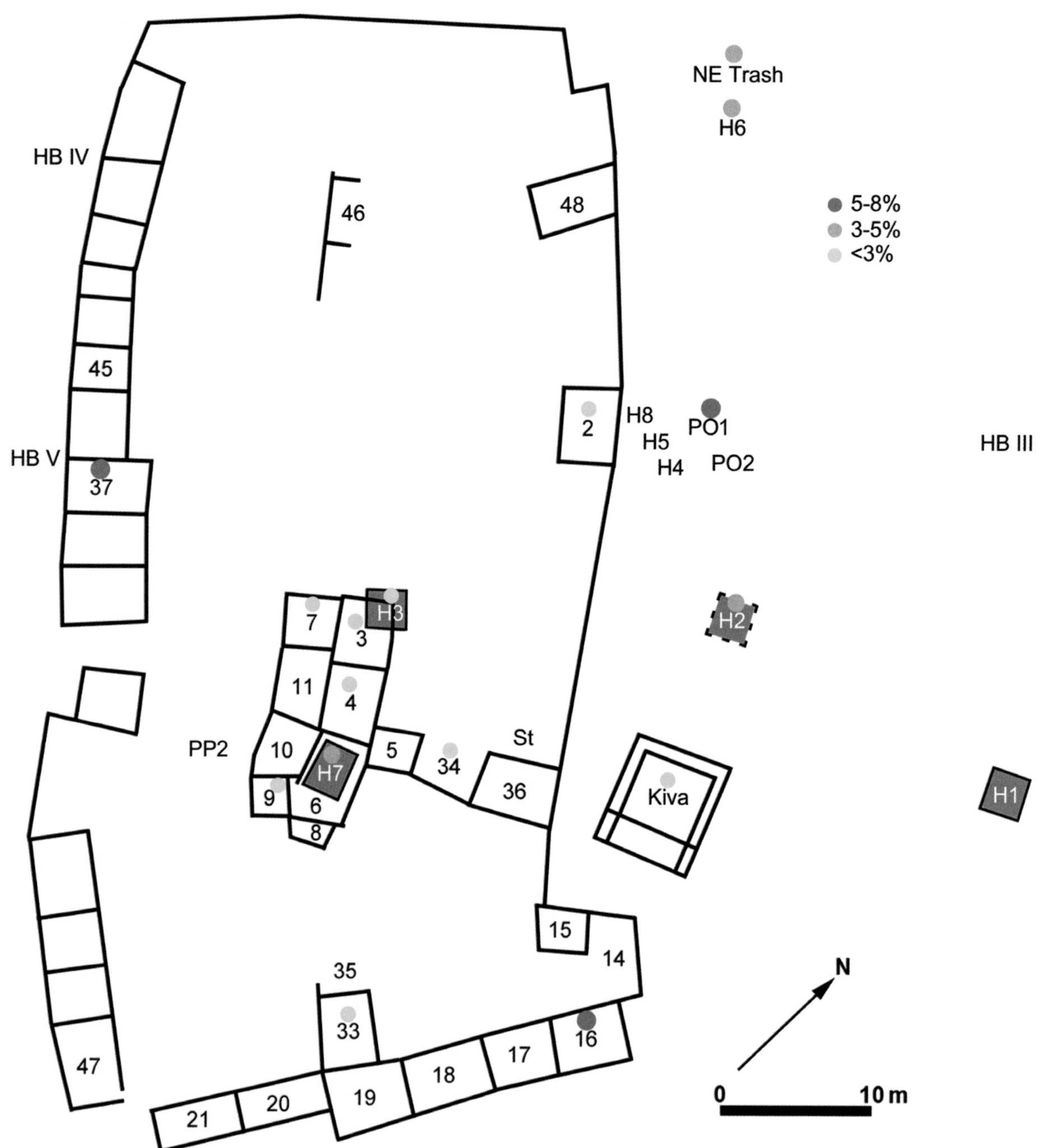

FIGURE 7.6 Distribution of Pinto Polychrome (including Pinto Polychrome: Salmon Variety) and Pinto Black-on-red at the Davis Ranch Site. Percentages are based on the total number of decorated sherds in each context.

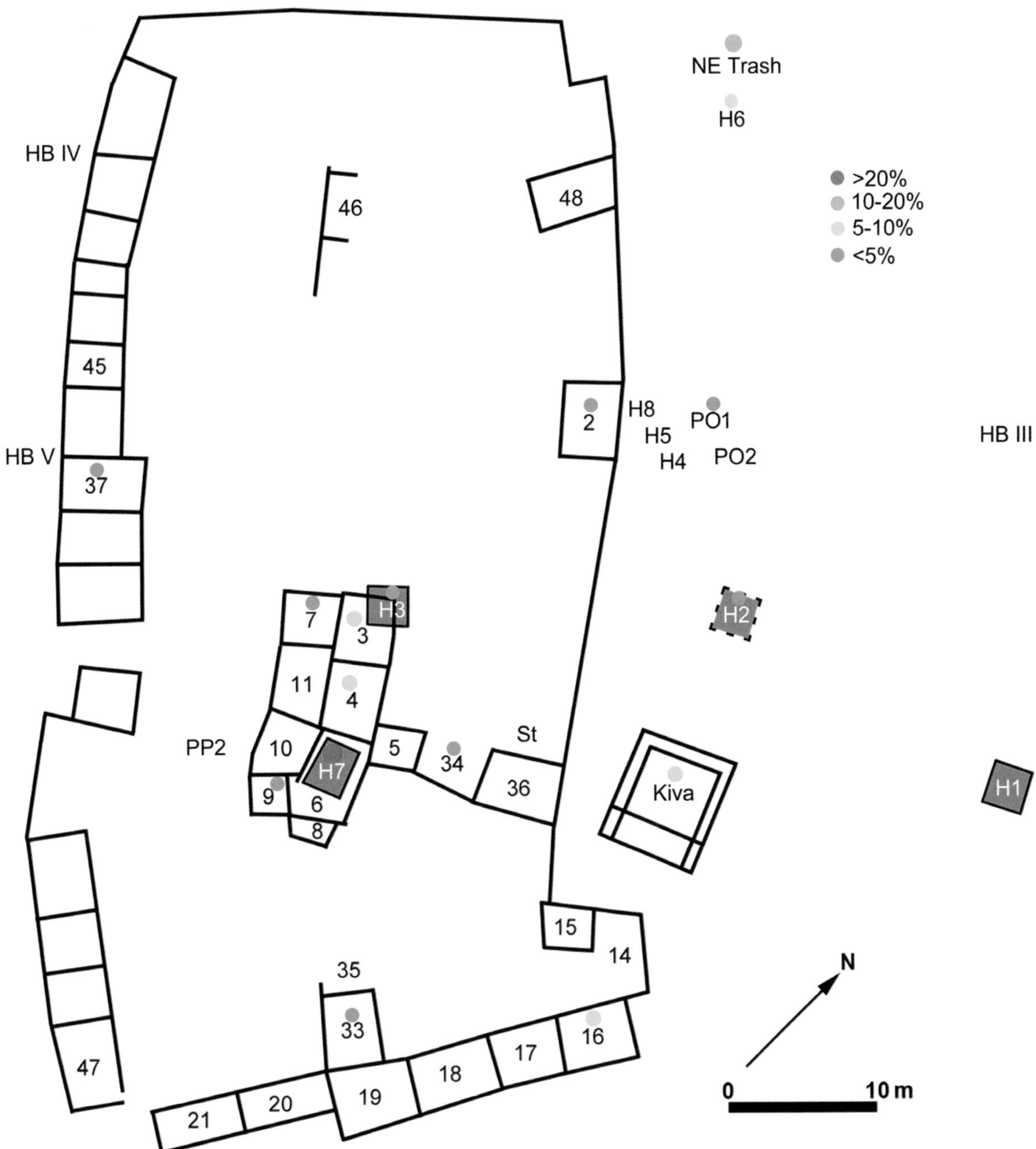

FIGURE 7.7 Distribution of Pinto Polychrome (including Pinto Polychrome: Salmon Variety) and Pinto Black-on-red at the Davis Ranch Site. Percentages are based on the proportion of the site's Pinto Polychrome and Pinto Black-on-red assemblage present in each context.

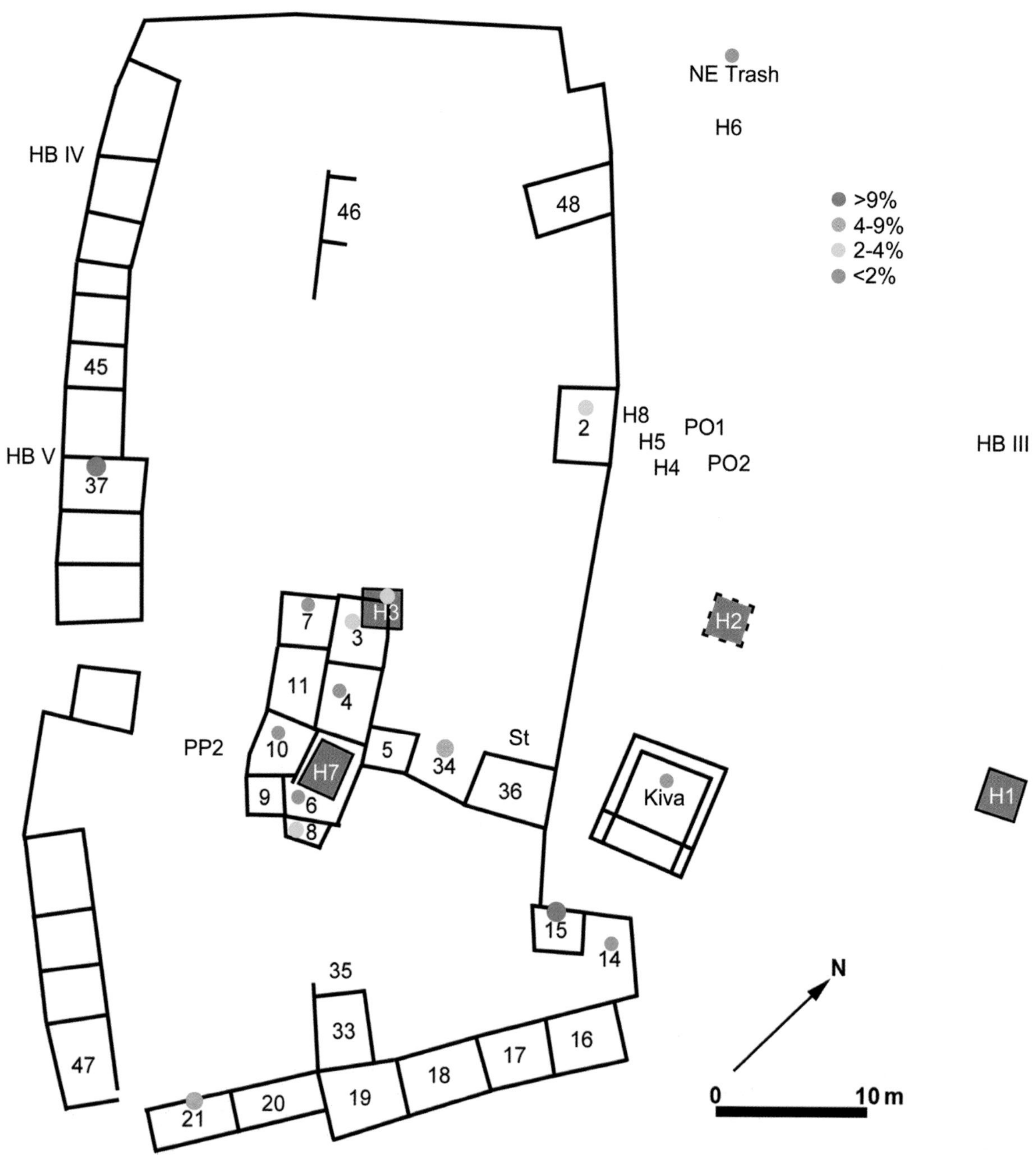

FIGURE 7.8 Distribution of Tonto Polychrome at the Davis Ranch Site. Percentages are based on the total number of decorated sherds in each context.

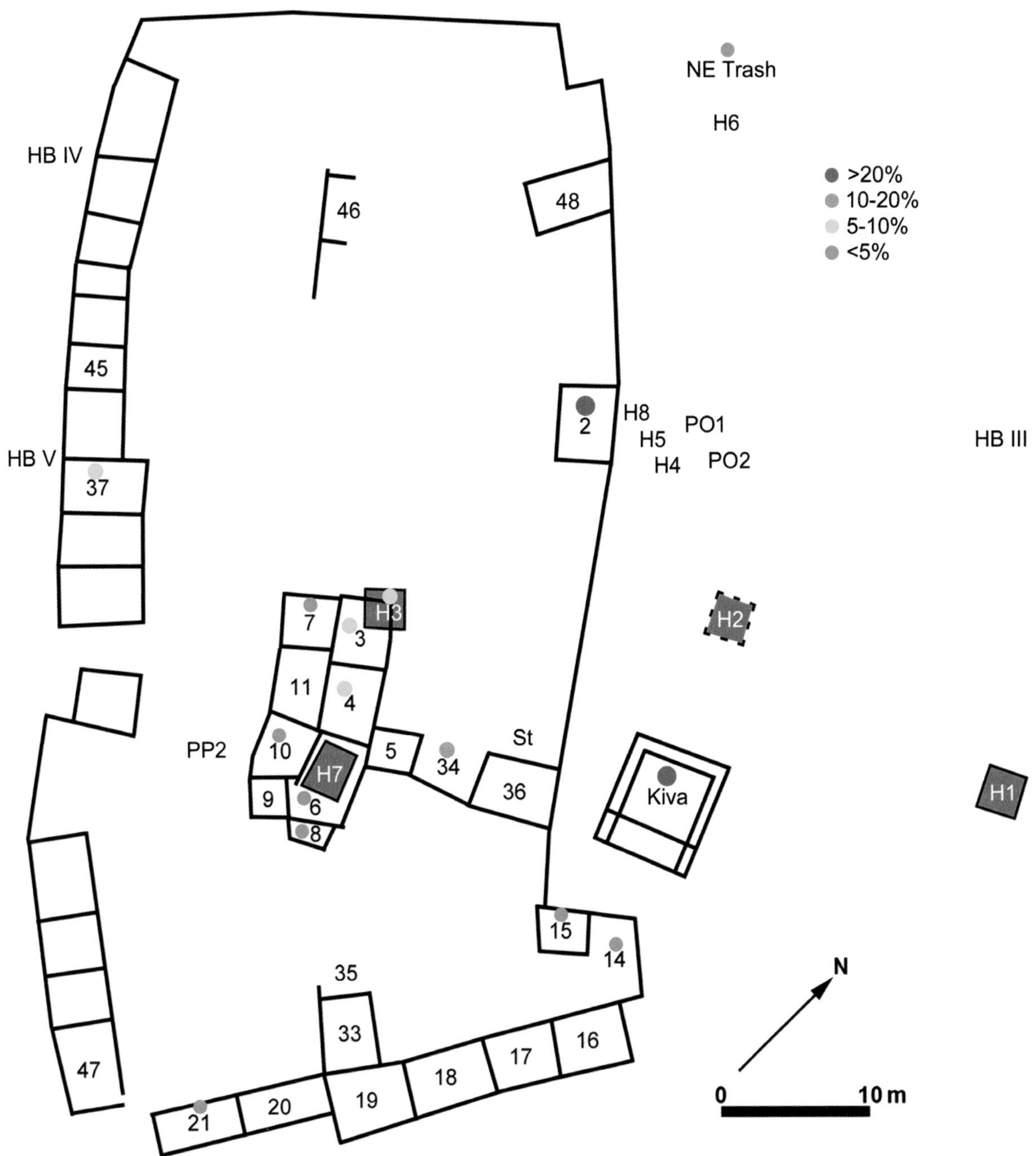

FIGURE 7.9 Distribution of Tonto Polychrome at the Davis Ranch Site. Percentages are based on the proportion of the site's Tonto Polychrome assemblage present in each context.

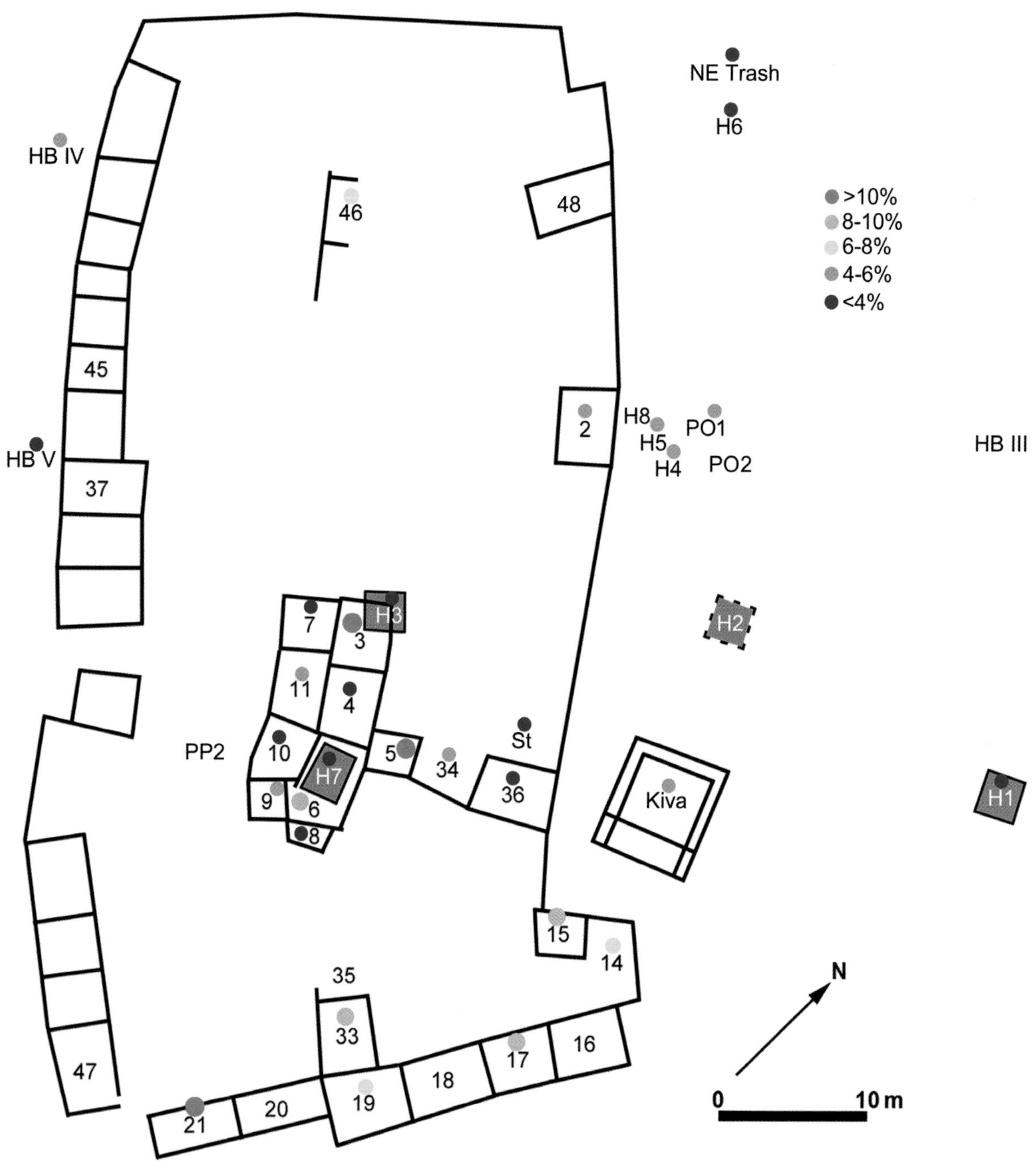

FIGURE 7.10 Distribution of Cliff Polychrome and Cliff or Nine Mile Polychrome at the Davis Ranch Site. Percentages are based on the total number of decorated sherds in each context. Data from Room 28 are not plotted, as the assemblage included only two sherds.

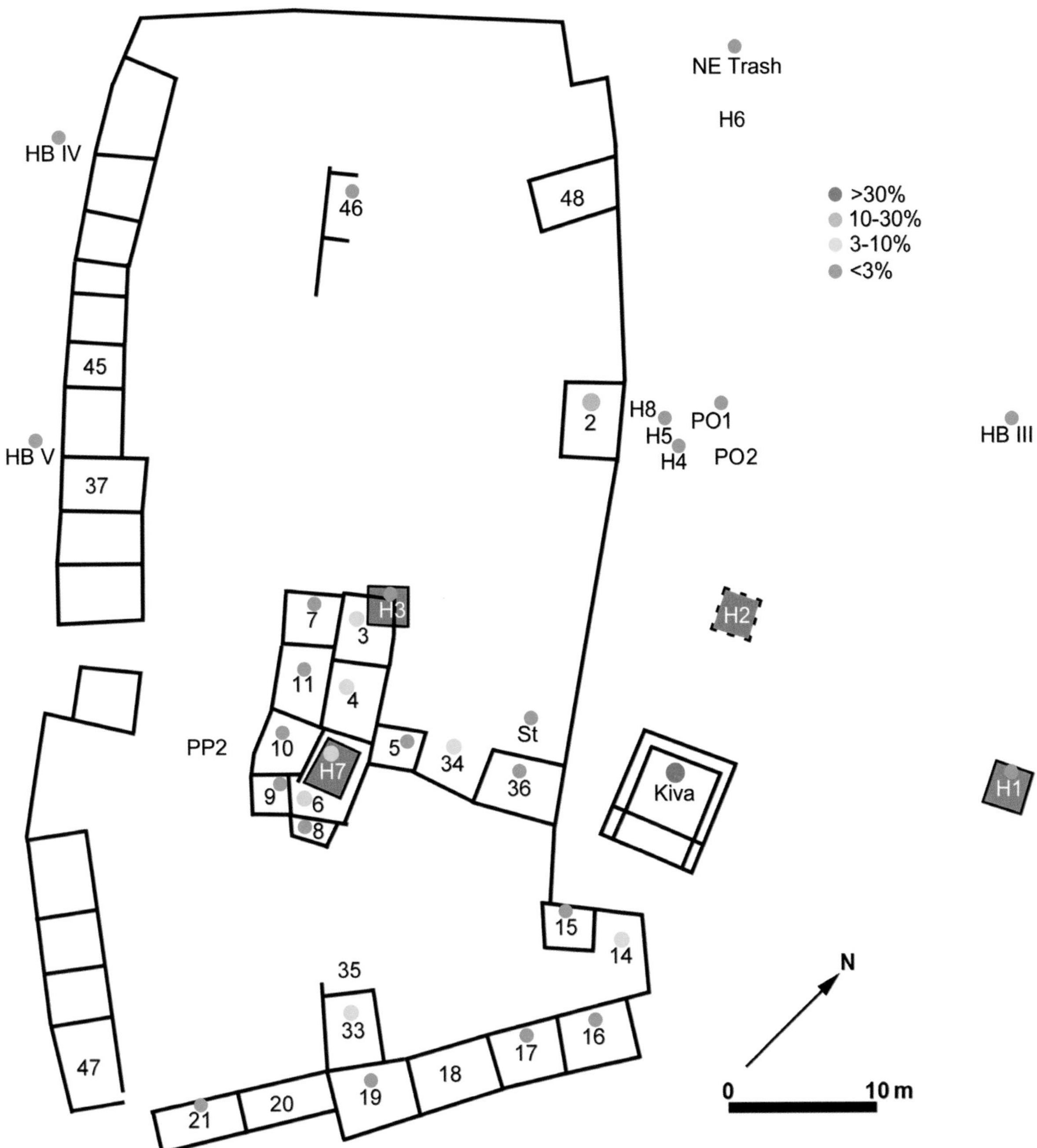

FIGURE 7.11 Distribution of Cliff Polychrome and Cliff or Nine Mile Polychrome at the Davis Ranch Site. Percentages are based on the proportion of the site's Cliff Polychrome and Cliff or Nine Mile Polychrome assemblage present in each context.

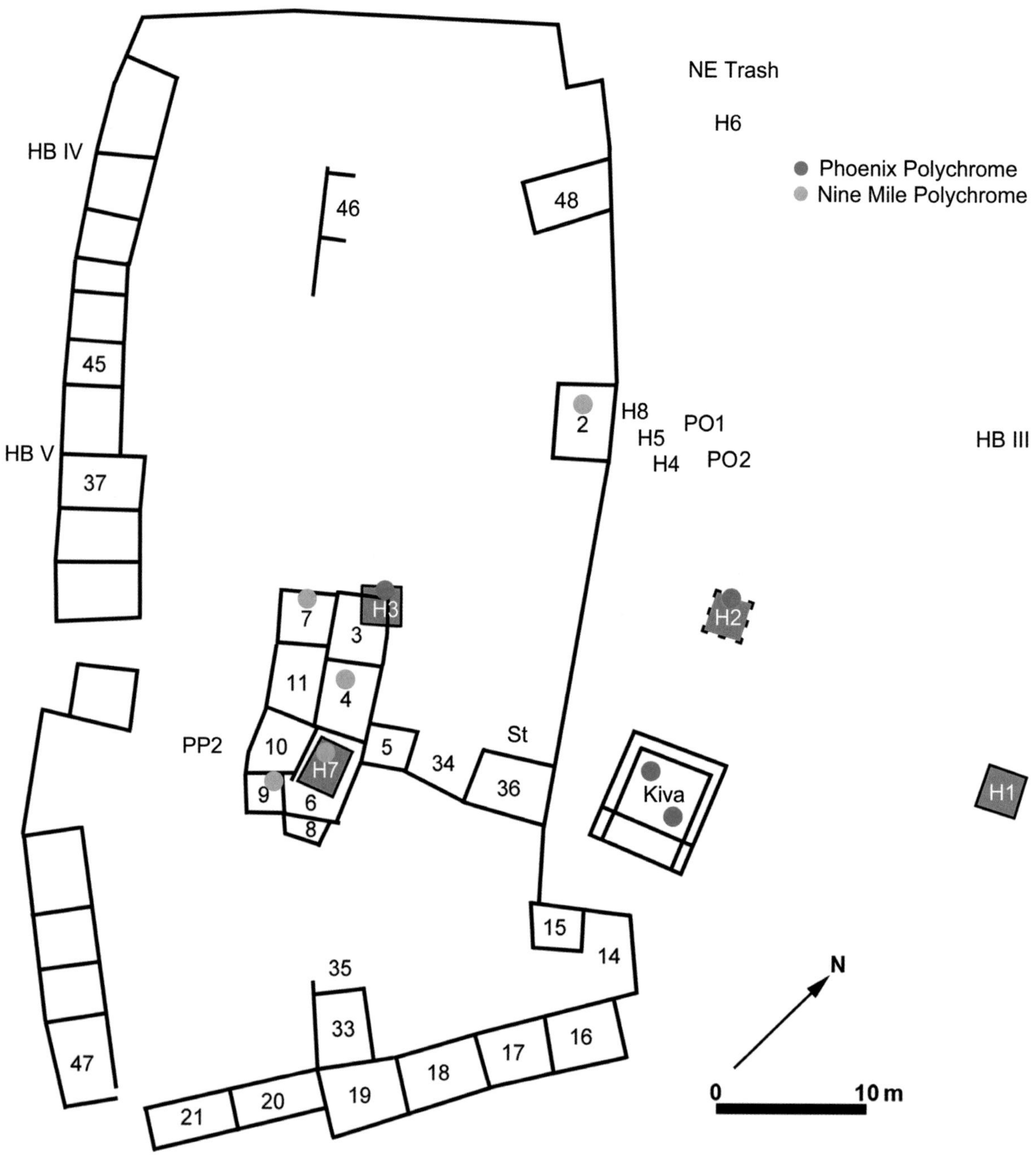

FIGURE 7.12 Distribution of Phoenix Polychrome (n = 4) and Nine Mile Polychrome (n = 5) at the Davis Ranch Site.

Seriation of Trash Deposits

The 10 structures or loci with the highest sherd frequencies, all more than 500 (per Gerald's original counts), can be grouped based on when they began to accumulate late Classic period trash. These contexts sort into two groups, based on percentages of Roosevelt Red Ware and Maverick Mountain Series pottery (table 7.5). The first group (n = 2) is characterized by high percentages (34.88% and 37.40%) of Maverick Mountain Series pottery, and members of the second group (n = 8) exhibit extremely high percentages (equal to or greater than 90%) of Roosevelt Red Ware. The same grouping is evident upon comparing assemblages based on the percentage of early Roosevelt Red Ware types (Pinto Black-on-red and Pinto Polychrome) present (table 7.6). The contexts having yielded high frequencies of Maverick Mountain Series pottery and early Roosevelt Red Ware types, House 6 and the Northeast Trash, began to accumulate refuse during the Aravaipa phase. The others began to accumulate trash during either the Redfield phase or the Romero phase.

House 7, which produced a Roosevelt Red Ware assemblage that placed it in the second group (97.21% of the decorated pottery recovered), underlies Room 6. Based on wall bonds and abutments, Rooms 4, 7, and 10 (all members of the second group) were all constructed before Room 6, and a portion of Room 10 overlies House 7. The use of House 7 as a habitation structure appears to overlap with the use of Room 4 as a storage structure and Room 7 as a habitation structure. These House-block I stratigraphic data and other clues suggest that the assemblage recovered from House 7 should have begun accumulating refuse after deposition began in House 6 and the Northeast Trash, and before the initial deposition of trash in the other contexts exhibiting high percentages of Roosevelt Red Ware (Rooms 2, 4, 6, 7, 10, 14, and the kiva).

TABLE 7.5 Percentages of Roosevelt Red Ware and Maverick Mountain Series pottery (based on the reanalysis) in the samples recovered from the 10 Classic period contexts that yielded the highest sherd frequencies

	Roosevelt Red Ware		Maverick Mountain Series		
Context	*n*	%	*n*	%	Total (all painted pottery) (*n*)
NE Trash	76	61.79	46	37.40	123
House 6	27	62.79	15	34.88	43
Room 6	63	90.00	7	10.00	70
Room 7	89	93.68	4	4.21	95
Room 4	115	95.83	5	4.17	120
Room 14	78	96.30	3	3.70	81
House 7	209	97.21	6	2.79	215
Room 10	133	97.79	3	2.21	136
Kiva	827	98.10	12	1.42	843
Room 2	297	99.00	3	1.00	300

TABLE 7.6 Percentage of Pinto Black-on-red and Pinto Polychrome (based on the reanalysis) in the samples recovered from the 10 Classic period contexts that yielded the highest sherd frequencies

Context	Pinto Black-on-red and Pinto Polychrome (*n*)	Roosevelt Red Ware (*n*)	Pinto Black-on-red and Pinto Polychrome (%)
House 6	2	27	7.41
NE Trash	4	76	5.26
House 7	4	209	1.91
Room 4	2	115	1.74
Room 7	1	89	1.12
Kiva	3	827	0.36
Room 2	1	297	0.34
Room 6	0	63	0.00
Room 14	0	78	0.00
Room 10	0	133	0.00

When the frequencies (derived from the reanalysis) of five temporally sensitive types or sets of related types are considered (in descending order, by latest start date: Nine Mile and Phoenix Polychrome, Cliff Polychrome and Cliff or Nine Mile Polychrome, Tonto Polychrome, Pinto Black-on-red and Pinto Polychrome, early Maverick Mountain Series types), a pattern is evident (figure 7.13, table 7.7). Although many of the samples used in this seriation are small, the assemblages from House 6 and the Northeast Trash fall at the early end of the sequence and those from the kiva and Room 2 are clearly identifiable as contexts that began to acquire refuse nearer to the late end of the sequence. These results are consistent with those based on the comparisons discussed above, which employed larger samples (see tables 7.5, 7.6).

The limited data available for the seriation suggest that the assemblages from House 7, Room 4, and Room 7 began to accumulate after those from House 6 and the Northeast Trash but before those from the kiva and Room 2. Likewise, the assemblages from Rooms 6, 10, and 14 seemingly began to accumulate after those from the kiva and Room 2. This makes sense, in that late trash deposition in rooms would be expected after the construction of the wall between Rooms 36 and 15 that separated the kiva from the pueblo.

Four seriation groups can thus be identified. Group A, those spaces that began to acquire Classic period trash earliest, are identifiable based on their high percentages of early Maverick Mountain Series types (Maverick Mountain Black-on-red and Maverick Mountain Polychrome) and early Roosevelt Red Ware types (Pinto Black-on-red and Pinto Polychrome) (figure 7.14). These are House 6 and the overlying Northeast Trash. Types with start dates before AD 1300 account for at least 75% of each of the seriation samples recovered from these spaces (see table 7.7). House 6, of course, is inferred to have been built and occupied during the Early Agricultural period.

Group B, next in the seriation, includes House 7, Room 4, and Room 7. The assemblages from these

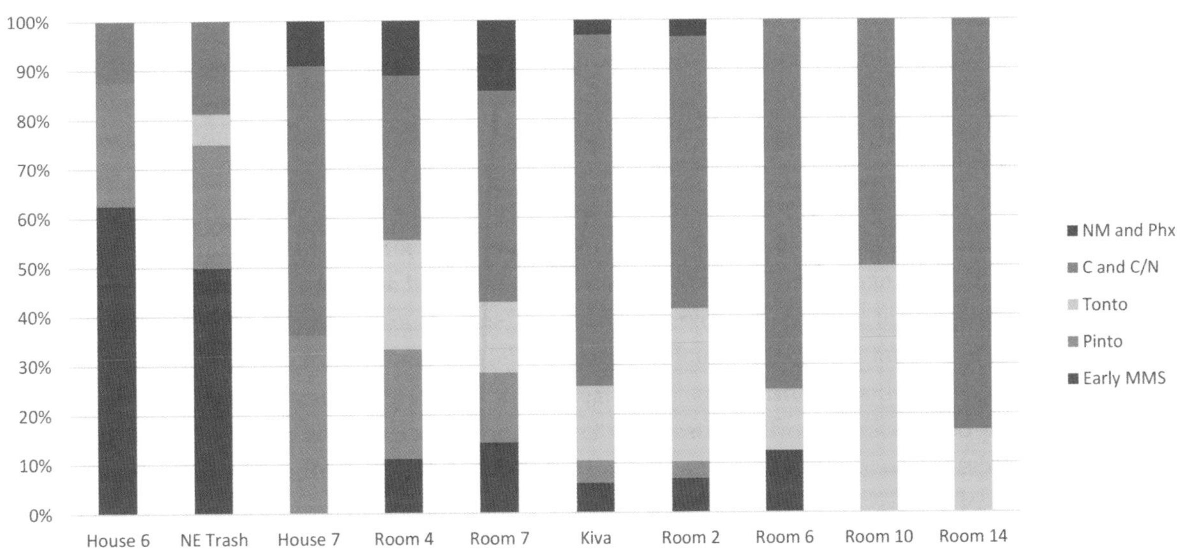

FIGURE 7.13 Seriation of Classic period trash deposits at the Davis Ranch Site based on proportions of Nine Mile and Phoenix Polychrome (NM and Phx), Cliff and Cliff or Nine Mile Polychrome (C and C/N), Tonto Polychrome (Tonto), Pinto Polychrome and Pinto Black-on-red (Pinto), and early Maverick Mountain Series types (Early MMS) (see table 7.7).

TABLE 7.7 Seriation of the 10 Classic period structures or loci that yielded the highest sherd frequencies

	Early Maverick Mountain Series		Pinto Polychrome		Tonto Polychrome		Cliff Polychrome and Cliff or Nine Mile Polychrome		Nine Mile and Phoenix Polychrome		Total
Context	*n*	%	*n*	%	*n*	%	*n*	%	*n*	%	(*n*)
House 6	5	62.50	2	25.00	0	0.00	1	12.50	0	0.00	8
Northeast Trash	8	50.00	4	25.00	1	6.25	3	18.75	0	0.00	16
House 7	0	0.00	4	36.36	0	0.00	6	54.55	1	9.09	11
Room 4	1	11.11	2	22.22	2	22.22	3	33.33	1	11.11	9
Room 7	1	14.29	1	14.29	1	14.29	3	42.86	1	14.29	7
Kiva	4	6.06	3	4.55	10	15.15	47	71.21	2	3.03	66
Room 2	2	6.90	1	3.45	9	31.03	16	55.17	1	3.45	29
Room 6	1	12.50	0	0.00	1	12.50	6	75.00	0	0.00	8
Room 10	0	0.00	0	0.00	1	50.00	1	50.00	0	0.00	2
Room 14	0	0.00	0	0.00	1	16.67	5	83.33	0	0.00	6

specimens of Tanque Verde Red-on-brown (*n* = 31) and "Pantano Red-on-brown" (*n* = 20). By way of comparison, Colonial period painted types, including Santa Cruz Red-on-buff (*n* = 236), Rillito Red-on-brown (*n* = 150), Gila Butte Red-on-buff (*n* = 11), and Cañada del Oro Red-on-brown (*n* = 2), total nearly 400 specimens. Sedentary period specimens are concentrated in the area discussed above, bounded by the Northeast Trash and the kiva and running along the arc of Kayenta pit houses, which is distinguished by concentrations of other early ceramic types (e.g., Maverick Mountain Series, Pinto Polychrome, Pinto Black-on-red).

House 3 and Room 3

Unfortunately, House 3 was excavated largely as one recovery unit. Very few sherds were labeled as having come from the floor, and Gerald presents the results of his typological analysis of the material from the house as if it represents fill entirely. He notes (see chapter 3) that construction of the walls of Room 3 caused significant disturbance to House 3 and suggests that the material used to construct parts of Room 3's walls was derived from the fill and floor of House 3. Furthermore, as in the case of the pit structures discussed above, House 3 is only partially overlain by Room 3. This means that materials recovered from some portions of House 3's fill likely accumulated much later than the Aravaipa phase, to which it has been assigned, based on its stratigraphic position and the overall spatial patterns evident in the site's architectural units.

Counterintuitive ceramic data from House 3 and Room 3 make sense in the context of this knowledge (table 7.8). Room 3, the younger stratigraphic unit, yielded more than twice as much Maverick Mountain Series pottery (as a percentage) as House 3. Similarly, Room 3's assemblage boasts more than twice as much Pinto Polychrome (as a percentage) than House 3's assemblage, and Phoenix Polychrome was present in the fill of House 3 but is not in the collection recovered from Room 3. That said, Cliff Polychrome and Cliff or Nine Mile Polychrome specimens were more than twice as common in Room 3 than House 3 (based on percentages), and Room 3 yielded more Tonto Polychrome than House 3.

House 7 and Room 6

The ceramic data from House 7 and Room 6 are much more consistent with what one would expect from superimposed structures, likely due to the fact that the older architectural unit is completely sealed by the younger (figure 7.15, table 7.9). There is a steady decrease in early types (early Maverick Mountain Series types and Pinto Polychrome) and a concomitant increase in late types (Gila Polychrome and Gila Polychrome or later, Tonto Polychrome, Cliff Polychrome and Cliff or Nine Mile Polychrome, and Nine Mile Polychrome) from the bottom of the stratigraphic column (House 7 Floor 2) to the top (Room 6 fill). This provided an excellent opportunity to evaluate Crown's (1994:79–89) Roosevelt Red Ware stylistic seriation.

House 7 and Room 6 yielded 25 partially reconstructible Roosevelt Red Ware vessels (comprising 180 sherds) bearing enough diagnostic traits to be classified according to Crown's (1994) styles and stages (subdivisions of styles). Some specimens could not, however, be placed in a single stage and instead were assigned to an aggregate category, such as Pinedale Style: Stage 1 or 2. Although the sample sizes are quite small, the results of this exercise are remarkably consistent with Crown's seriation (figure 7.16, table 7.10).

The assemblage includes examples of styles from the early end and the middle of the sequence, from Pinedale Style: Stage 1 through Pinedale Style: Stage 5. The sample from the lowest (oldest) stratigraphic unit, below the upper floor (Floor 1) of House 7, includes two specimens bearing Pinedale Style: Stage 1 (figure 7.17). The middle unit, from the upper floor of House 7 to just below the floor of Room 6, produced 16 specimens representing Pinedale Style: Stage 1 or 2 through Pinedale Style: Stage 5 (figure 7.18), and the uppermost unit, the floor and fill of Room 6, yielded 7 specimens with decorations ranging from Pinedale Style: Stage 2, 3, or 4 to Pinedale Style: Stage 5 (figure 7.19).

TABLE 7.8 Ceramic typological data from House 3 and Room 3 (Room 3 is superimposed on House 3)

	House 3		Room 3	
Ware or ware-level category and/or type or type-level category	*n*	%	*n*	%
Roosevelt Red Ware				
Cliff Black-on-red	0	0.00	0	0.00
Cliff Polychrome or Nine Mile Polychrome	0	0.00	1	1.72
Cliff Polychrome	2	2.56	3	5.17
Cliff Polychrome: Salmon Variety	0	0.00	0	0.00
Cliff Polychrome: Tonto Variety	0	0.00	0	0.00
Cliff Polychrome: Tucson Variety	0	0.00	0	0.00
Gila Black-on-red	0	0.00	0	0.00
Gila Polychrome	8	10.26	2	3.45
Gila Polychrome or later	9	11.54	9	15.52
Gila Polychrome or later (salmon variety)	0	0.00	0	0.00
Gila Polychrome, no banding line	1	1.28	0	0.00
Gila Polychrome: Gila Variety	0	0.00	0	0.00
Gila Polychrome: Salmon Variety	1	1.28	0	0.00
Gila Polychrome: Tonto Variety	0	0.00	0	0.00
indeterminate Roosevelt Red Ware black-on-red	1	1.28	0	0.00
indeterminate Roosevelt Red Ware polychrome	49	62.82	33	56.90
indeterminate Roosevelt Red Ware (salmon variety)	0	0.00	0	0.00
Nine Mile Polychrome	0	0.00	0	0.00
Nine Mile Polychrome: Safford Variety	0	0.00	0	0.00
Nine Mile Polychrome: Tonto Variety	0	0.00	0	0.00
Phoenix Polychrome	1	1.28	0	0.00
Pinto Black-on-red	0	0.00	0	0.00
Pinto Polychrome	1	1.28	2	3.45
Pinto Polychrome: Salmon Variety	0	0.00	0	0.00
Tonto Polychrome	1	1.28	2	3.45
Whiteriver Polychrome	0	0.00	0	0.00
Subtotal	*74*	*94.87*	*52*	*89.66*

(*continued*)

TABLE 7.8 *(continued)*

Ware or ware-level category and/or type or type-level category	House 3 *n*	House 3 %	Room 3 *n*	Room 3 %
Maverick Mountain Series				
indeterminate Maverick Mountain Series	0	0.00	1	1.72
indeterminate Maverick Mountain Series black-on-red	0	0.00	1	1.72
indeterminate Maverick Mountain Series, Roosevelt Red Ware exterior	0	0.00	0	0.00
Maverick Mountain Black-on-red	0	0.00	3	5.17
Maverick Mountain Polychrome	0	0.00	0	0.00
Nantack Polychrome A (Tusayan Polychrome analog)	0	0.00	0	0.00
Tucson Black-on-red	0	0.00	1	1.72
Tucson Black-on-red (no slip)	0	0.00	0	0.00
Tucson Black-on-red or Tucson Polychrome	0	0.00	0	0.00
Tucson Polychrome	3	3.85	0	0.00
Subtotal	*3*	*3.85*	*6*	*10.34*
Babocomari Polychrome	0	0.00	0	0.00
Subtotal	*0*	*0.00*	*0*	*0.00*
Davis Black-on-red	0	0.00	0	0.00
Subtotal	*0*	*0.00*	*0*	*0.00*
Dragoon or San Simon Series	0	0.00	0	0.00
Subtotal	*0*	*0.00*	*0*	*0.00*
indeterminate decorated	0	0.00	0	0.00
Subtotal	*0*	*0.00*	*0*	*0.00*
indeterminate red-on-brown	0	0.00	0	0.00
Subtotal	*0*	*0.00*	*0*	*0.00*
Kinishba Polychrome	0	0.00	0	0.00
Subtotal	*0*	*0.00*	*0*	*0.00*
Mimbres Black-on-white	0	0.00	0	0.00
Subtotal	*0*	*0.00*	*0*	*0.00*
San Carlos Red-on-brown	1	1.28	0	0.00
Subtotal	*1*	*1.28*	*0*	*0.00*
Total	**78**	**100.00**	**58**	**100.00**

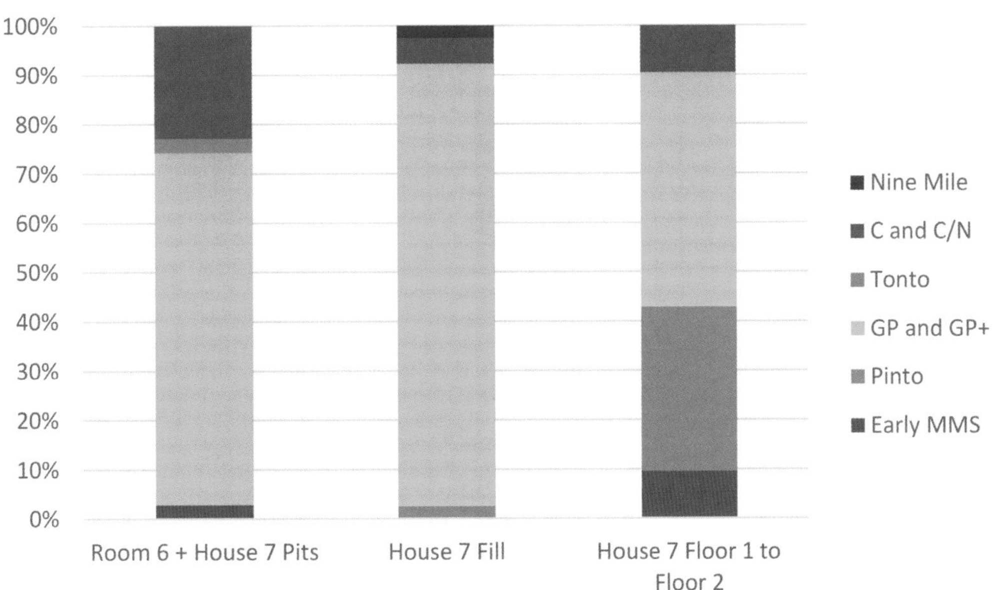

FIGURE 7.15 Proportions of temporally sensitive pottery types recovered from the House 7-Room 6 stratigraphic sequence: early Maverick Mountain Series types (Early MMS), Pinto Black-on-red and Pinto Polychrome (Pinto), Gila Polychrome and Gila Polychrome or later (GP and GP+), Tonto Polychrome (Tonto), Cliff Polychrome and Cliff or Nine Mile Polychrome (C and C/N), and Nine Mile Polychrome (Nine Mile). Room 6 is superimposed on House 7 (see table 7.9).

TABLE 7.9 Trends in the distribution of temporally sensitive pottery types across strata in House 7 and Room 6 (Room 6 is superimposed on House 7)

Temporally sensitive pottery type(s)	Room 6		House 7 pits intruding fill		House 7 fill		House 7 Floor 1 and floor features		House 7 Subfloor		House 7 Floor 2	
	n	%	*n*	%	*n*	%	*n*	%	*n*	%	*n*	%
Early Maverick Mountain Series	1	5.00	0	0.00	0	0.00	0	0.00	1	20.00	1	25.00
Pinto Polychrome and Pinto Black-on-red	0	0.00	0	0.00	1	2.56	3	25.00	2	40.00	2	50.00
Gila Polychrome and Gila Polychrome or later	12	60.00	13	86.67	35	89.74	7	58.33	2	40.00	1	25.00
Tonto Polychrome	1	5.00	0	0.00	0	0.00	0	0.00	0	0.00	0	0.00
Cliff Polychrome and Cliff or Nine Mile Polychrome	6	30.00	2	13.33	2	5.13	2	16.67	0	0.00	0	0.00
Nine Mile Polychrome	0	0.00	0	0.00	1	2.56	0	0.00	0	0.00	0	0.00
Total	**20**	**100**	**15**	**100**	**39**	**100**	**12**	**100**	**5**	**100**	**4**	**100**

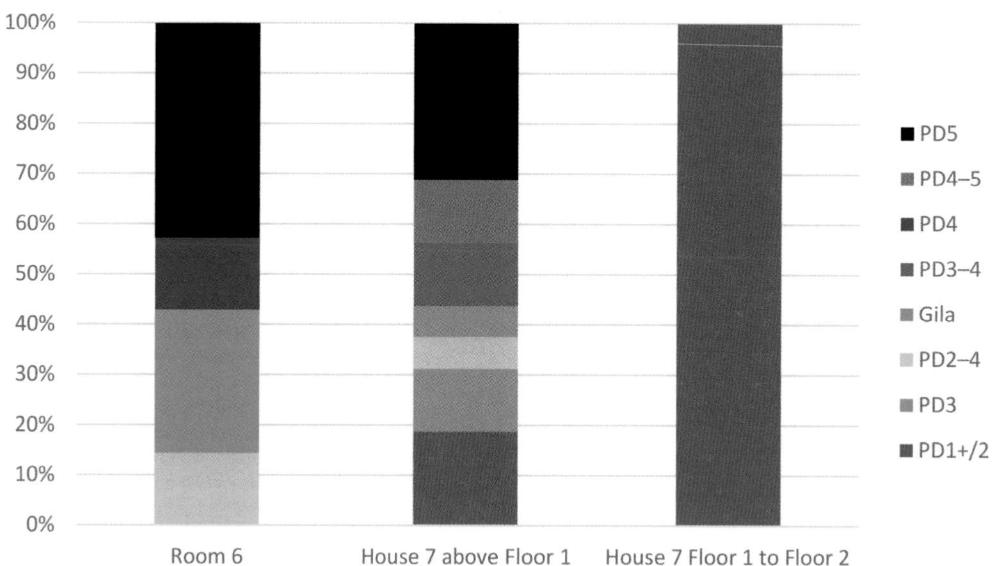

FIGURE 7.16 Stratigraphic trends in styles and stages exhibited by partially reconstructible Roosevelt Red Ware vessels from House 7 and Room 6: Pinedale Style: Stage 1 and Stage 1 or Stage 2 (PD1+/2); Pinedale Style: Stage 3 (PD3); Pinedale Style: Stage 2, or Stage 3, or Stage 4 (PD2–4); Gila Style (Gila); Pinedale Style: Stage 3 or Stage 4 (PD3–4); Pinedale Style: Stage 4 (PD4); Pinedale Style: Stage 4 or Stage 5 (PD4–5); Pinedale Style: Stage 5 (PD5). The stratigraphic units indicated are Room 6 floor and fill (Room 6); Upper floor (Floor 1) of House 7 to the floor of Room 6 (House 7 above Floor 1); and House 7, under Floor 1 (House 7 Floor 1 to Floor 2). Room 6 is superimposed on House 7 (see table 7.10).

Stratigraphic Relationships Among and Ceramic Seriation of Burials

Burials at the Davis Ranch Site occur in three clusters and as one isolated feature (see figure 1.5; see also figures in chapter 8). The cluster with the largest number of burials (six single and two multiple interments; 10 individuals) is contained by the kiva. The second cluster, comprising four individuals, is northwest of the kiva, in the Northeast Trash. The third consists of two individuals. One, Burial 9, underlies the southern corner of the kiva, and the other, Burial 11, is south of the kiva. The isolated interment, Burial 10, is overlain by Room 2.

Unfortunately, there is a dearth of direct stratigraphic evidence with which to assign many of the burials to individual periods in a chronological sequence. That said, most of the burials in the kiva, all of which date to the Romero phase, can be placed in time relative to one another. In addition, Burials 9 and 10 must predate the architectural units that overlay them. Ceramic associations also shed some light on relative chronology (table 7.11).

Burial 9 is the earliest interment that can be securely placed in a chronological sequence (table 7.12). It is associated with the Aravaipa phase occupation of the Kayenta pit houses and predates the construction of the kiva. Burial 9 yielded two painted vessels: a Tucson Polychrome jar (D/215) and a Gila Polychrome bowl (D/214) decorated with a Roosevelt Style: Stage 1 design (the third of four styles or stages thereof at the early end of the Roosevelt Red Ware sequence) (figure 7.20a). Burial 11, south of Burial 9 and a few meters south of the kiva, was not disturbed by the construction of the nearby compound wall, and Gerald did not

TABLE 7.10 Stratigraphic test of Crown's (1994) Roosevelt Red Ware stylistic seriation using partially reconstructible vessels from House 7 and Room 6

Stratigraphic contexts	Vessel designation	Style	Stage
Room 6 floor and fill	Room 6 Vessel 1	Pinedale	5
	Room 6 Vessel 2	Pinedale	2–4
	Room 6 Vessel 3	Pinedale	5
	Room 6 Vessel 4	Gila	—
	Room 6 Vessel 5	Pinedale	5
	Room 6 Vessel 10	Gila	—
	Room 6 Vessel 11	Pinedale	4
Upper floor (Floor 1) of House 7 to floor of Room 6	House 7 Vessel 2	Pinedale	5
	House 7 Vessel 3	Pinedale	3–4
	House 7 Vessel 5	Pinedale	3
	House 7 Vessel 8	Pinedale	5
	House 7 Vessel 9	Pinedale	1–2
	House 7 Vessel 10	Pinedale	5
	House 7 Vessel 11	Pinedale	3
	House 7 Vessel 13	Pinedale	5
	House 7 Vessel 15	Pinedale	4–5
	House 7 Vessel 16	Pinedale	4–5
	House 7 Vessel 17	Pinedale	3–4
	House 7 Vessel 20	Pinedale	5
	House 7 Vessel 21	Pinedale	1
	House 7 Vessel 23	Pinedale	2–4
	House 7 Vessel 24	Pinedale	1
	House 7 Vessel 25	Gila	—
House 7, under Floor 1	House 7 Vessel 1	Pinedale	1
	House 7 Vessel 28	Pinedale	1

FIGURE 7.17 Partially reconstructible Roosevelt Red Ware vessels from below Floor 1 in House 7: (a) House 7 Decorated Vessel 1, a Gila Polychrome bowl bearing Pinedale Style: Stage 1 painted decoration; (b) House 7 Decorated Vessel 28, a Roosevelt Red Ware black-on-red bowl of indeterminate type bearing Pinedale Style: Stage 1 painted decoration. Photographs by Patrick D. Lyons.

FIGURE 7.18 Partially reconstructible Roosevelt Red Ware vessels from between Floor 1 of House 7 and the floor of Room 6: (a) House 7 Decorated Vessel 24, a Pinto Polychrome bowl bearing Pinedale Style: Stage 1 painted decoration; (b) House 7 Decorated Vessel 11, a Gila Polychrome: Gila Variety bowl bearing Pinedale Style: Stage 3 painted decoration, interior; (c) House 7 Decorated Vessel 11, exterior; (d) House 7 Decorated Vessel 10, a Gila Polychrome (no banding line) bowl bearing Pinedale Style: Stage 5 painted decoration; (e) House 7 Decorated Vessel 2, a Cliff Polychrome bowl bearing Pinedale Style: Stage 5 painted decoration. Photographs by Patrick D. Lyons.

FIGURE 7.19 Partially reconstructible Roosevelt Red Ware vessels from the fill of Room 6: (a) Room 6 Decorated Vessel 1, a Cliff Polychrome bowl bearing Pinedale Style: Stage 5 painted decoration; (b) Room 6 Decorated Vessel 3, a Gila Polychrome jar bearing Pinedale Style: Stage 5 painted decoration. Photographs by Patrick D. Lyons.

TABLE 7.11 Typological and stylistic classification of painted pottery associated with Classic period burials

Burial no.	Location	Catalog no.	Ware	Type	Form	Style	Stage
4	Kiva	D/192	Roosevelt Red Ware	Gila Polychrome	jar	Pinedale	5
		D/193	Roosevelt Red Ware	Gila Polychrome: Salmon Variety	bowl	Pinedale	5
		D/194	Roosevelt Red Ware	Gila Polychrome	bowl	Gila	—
		D/196	Roosevelt Red Ware	Cliff Polychrome	bowl	Pinedale	4
		D/200	Roosevelt Red Ware	Phoenix Polychrome	bowl	Roosevelt	3
		D/201	Roosevelt Red Ware	Gila Polychrome	bowl	Pinedale	5
		D/202	Roosevelt Red Ware	Cliff Polychrome	bowl	Pinedale	5
		D/203	Roosevelt Red Ware	Gila Polychrome	bowl	Roosevelt	3
		D/205	Roosevelt Red Ware	Cliff Polychrome	bowl	Pinedale	5
5	Kiva	D/207	Roosevelt Red Ware	Gila Polychrome	bowl	Gila	—
8	Kiva	D/209	Roosevelt Red Ware	Gila Polychrome	bowl	Pinedale	5
		D/210	Roosevelt Red Ware	Gila Polychrome	bowl	Pinedale	5
9	Under kiva	D/214	Roosevelt Red Ware	Gila Polychrome	bowl	Roosevelt	1
		D/215	Maverick Mountain Series	Tucson Polychrome	jar	—	—
10	Under Room 2	D/216	Maverick Mountain Series	Tucson Polychrome	jar	—	—
		D/217	Maverick Mountain Series	Tucson Polychrome	jar	—	—
		D/219	Maverick Mountain Series	Tucson Polychrome	jar	—	—
		D/220	Roosevelt Red Ware	Gila Polychrome	bowl	Pinedale	4
13	Northeast Trash	D/229	Roosevelt Red Ware	Gila Black-on-red	bowl	Gila	—
14	Northeast Trash	D/232	Roosevelt Red Ware	Gila Polychrome	bowl	?	?
15	Northeast Trash	D/233	Roosevelt Red Ware	Gila Polychrome	bowl	Roosevelt	4

TABLE 7.12 Phase assignments for Davis Ranch Site burials based on stratigraphic position and ceramic associations

Burial no.	Phase(s)	Comment(s)
1	Romero	Interred in kiva decommissioned during the Romero phase
2	Romero	Interred in kiva decommissioned during the Romero phase
3	Romero	Interred in kiva decommissioned during the Romero phase
4	Romero	Interred in kiva decommissioned during the Romero phase
5	Romero	Interred in kiva decommissioned during the Romero phase
6	Romero	Interred in kiva decommissioned during the Romero phase
7	Romero	Interred in kiva decommissioned during the Romero phase
8	Romero	Interred in kiva decommissioned during the Romero phase
9	Aravaipa	Underlies kiva built during the Aravaipa phase or the Redfield phase
10	Aravaipa, early Redfield, or middle Redfield	Underlies Room 2, built during the late Redfield phase
11	Aravaipa?	Placed based on proximity to Burial 9
12	Aravaipa?	May predate significant Aravaipa phase trash deposition
13	Aravaipa or Redfield	No associated Maverick Mountain Series pottery; placed based on style of associated Roosevelt Red Ware vessel
14	Redfield or Romero	Interred in trash; no associated Maverick Mountain Series pottery
15	Romero	Associated Roosevelt Red Ware vessel is the latest specimen on site, based on the style of its painted decoration

provide any indication of stratigraphic correlations suggesting whether the wall predated the burial or vice versa. Furthermore, Burial 11 was not associated with any painted pottery vessels, precluding a placement based on ceramic evidence. Its location, however, at the southern end of the area demarcated by the arc of Kayenta pit houses (and near Burial 9), may be an indicator that it dates to the earliest portion of the immigrant occupation.

Burial 10 could date to the Kayenta pit house occupation (the Aravaipa phase) or the interval when Houseblock I was occupied, but before the construction of Room 2 and thus before the compound wall was built. The painted pottery associated with Burial 10 includes three Tucson Polychrome jars (D/216, D/217, D/219) and a Gila Polychrome bowl (D/220). The latter bears decoration classified as Pinedale Style: Stage 4 (the third of four styles or stages thereof in the middle of the stylistic sequence) (figure 7.20b). Based on the associated pottery, this burial likely dates a bit later than Burial 9.

The burials that yielded painted pottery in the Northeast Trash and inside the kiva lack Maverick Mountain Series vessels and therefore should postdate Burial 9 and Burial 10, which were associated with Tucson Polychrome jars. Of course, the burials inside the kiva must postdate Burial 9, which underlies the kiva. The Roosevelt Red Ware vessels associated with Burials 5 and 8, in the kiva, and Burial 13, in the Northeast Trash, bear Gila Style

a

b

c

FIGURE 7.20 Roosevelt Red Ware vessels recovered from Burials 9, 10, and 15: (a) Gila Polychrome bowl (D/214, from Burial 9) bearing Roosevelt Style: Stage 1 painted decoration, (b) Gila Polychrome bowl (D/220, from Burial 10) bearing Pinedale Style: Stage 4 painted decoration, (c) Gila Polychrome bowl (D/233, from Burial 15) bearing Roosevelt Style: Stage 4 painted decoration. For measurements, see table 6.1. Photographs by Jannelle Weakly.

and Pinedale Style: Stage 5 decorations, placing them in the middle of the stylistic sequence. Therefore, from a stylistic perspective, Burials 5, 8, and 13 are later than Burial 9 and of similar age to or later than Burial 10. Because other lines of evidence indicate that Room 2 was built during the Redfield phase, before burials began to be placed in the kiva, Burial 10 (which underlies Room 2) must have been interred before Burials 5 and 8 (see chapter 8).

The latest interments at the site, based on ceramic style, are Burial 4, inside the kiva, and Burial 15, in the Northeast Trash. Burial 4 yielded two vessels bearing Roosevelt Style: Stage 3 decorations, and Burial 15 was associated with a vessel painted in Roosevelt Style: Stage 4 (figure 7.20c). These are two of the latest stylistic nodes in the sequence.

Burial 12 and Burial 14, both recovered from the Northeast Trash, could not be placed relative to the others on the basis of ceramic data. The only pottery vessel associated with Burial 12 was a specimen of Belford Plain (D/225). Although Burial 14 was interred with a Gila Polychrome bowl (D/232), the fragments recovered were not diagnostic as to style or stage (see figure 6.1). Because Gerald indicates that Burial 12 may predate significant trash deposition (see chapter 4), it has been placed, tentatively, in the Aravaipa phase, roughly contemporaneous with Burials 9 and 11. Gerald's description of the fill of Burial 14 suggests it was laid to rest after a considerable amount of trash had accumulated. Thus, it is considered, tentatively, to date to the Redfield phase or the Romero phase.

Burials in the Kiva

As discussed in chapter 4, 10 individuals (recovered as six single and two multiple interments) were buried in the kiva after it was decommissioned and its roof collapsed. Although no comprehensive profiles of the kiva deposits have survived, based on stratigraphic clues derived from partial profiles, photographs, and field notes, it is possible to definitively place all but two of the interments in stratigraphic order. Burial 8 was the first to be interred in the kiva, followed by 2 and 5, which are roughly coeval. Next was Burial 1. The last two interred were Burials 3 and 4. Burials 6 and 7, which included two individuals each, could not be placed with certainty relative to the others, although most evidence suggests these interments predate Burials 3 and 4.

Inside the kiva, only Burials 4, 5, and 8 were associated with painted pottery vessels (table 7.13). Burial 9, discussed above, is the earliest in the kiva area, having been partially disturbed by and thus predating the kiva's construction. Funerary objects as-

TABLE 7.13 Painted vessels associated with burials recovered from within and near the kiva, in stratigraphic order by burial (Burial 4 was the latest interment in the sequence)

Burial no.	Catalog no.	Ware	Type	Form	Style	Stage
4	D/200	Roosevelt Red Ware	Phoenix Polychrome	bowl	Roosevelt	3
	D/203	Roosevelt Red Ware	Gila Polychrome	bowl	Roosevelt	3
	D/192	Roosevelt Red Ware	Gila Polychrome	jar	Pinedale	5
	D/193	Roosevelt Red Ware	Gila Polychrome: Salmon Variety	bowl	Pinedale	5
	D/201	Roosevelt Red Ware	Gila Polychrome	bowl	Pinedale	5
	D/202	Roosevelt Red Ware	Cliff Polychrome	bowl	Pinedale	5
	D/205	Roosevelt Red Ware	Cliff Polychrome	bowl	Pinedale	5
	D/196	Roosevelt Red Ware	Cliff Polychrome	bowl	Pinedale	4
	D/194	Roosevelt Red Ware	Gila Polychrome	bowl	Gila	—
5	D/207	Roosevelt Red Ware	Gila Polychrome	bowl	Gila	—
8	D/209	Roosevelt Red Ware	Gila Polychrome	bowl	Pinedale	5
	D/210	Roosevelt Red Ware	Gila Polychrome	bowl	Pinedale	5
9	D/214	Roosevelt Red Ware	Gila Polychrome	bowl	Roosevelt	1
	D/215	Maverick Mountain Series	Tucson Polychrome	jar	—	—

Note: Vessels from each burial are sorted by style and stage based on Crown (1994).

FIGURE 7.21 Roosevelt Red Ware vessels recovered from Burials 8 and 5: (a) Gila Polychrome bowl (D/209) from Burial 8 bearing Pinedale Style: Stage 5 painted decoration, (b) Gila Polychrome bowl (D/210) from Burial 8 bearing Pinedale Style: Stage 5 painted decoration, (c) Gila Polychrome bowl (D/207) from Burial 5 bearing Gila Style painted decoration. For measurements, see table 6.1. Photographs by Jannelle Weakly.

sociated with Burial 9 included two painted vessels: a Gila Polychrome bowl (Roosevelt Style: Stage 1) and a Tucson Polychrome jar. Burial 8, the next oldest, stratigraphically speaking, was associated with two painted vessels, both Gila Polychrome bowls (both Pinedale Style: Stage 5) (figure 7.21a, b). Burial 5, next in the sequence, was interred with a single painted vessel, a Gila Polychrome bowl (Gila Style) (figure 7.21c). The latest interment, Burial 4, was accompanied by nine painted vessels: four Gila Polychrome bowls (one Roosevelt Style: Stage 3, two Pinedale Style: Stage 5, and one Gila Style), three Cliff Polychrome bowls (two Pinedale Style: Stage 5 and one Pinedale Style: Stage 4), one Phoenix Polychrome bowl (Roosevelt Style: Stage 3), and one Gila Polychrome jar (Pinedale Style: Stage 5) (figure 7.22). The stratigraphic distribution of types just discussed is entirely consistent with the recently proposed seriation of old and new Roosevelt Red Ware types (Lyons 2004b, 2012b, 2013a; Lyons and Clark 2012; Lyons and Neuzil 2006; Lyons, Hill, and Clark 2011; Neuzil and Lyons 2006; see also the discussion of rim sherds from the kiva, below). Furthermore, the stratigraphic distribution of styles, as in the case of House 7 and Room 6, conforms to Crown's (1994) proposed Roosevelt Red Ware stylistic sequence.

FIGURE 7.22 Roosevelt Red Ware vessels recovered from Burial 4: (a) Gila Polychrome jar (D/192) bearing Pinedale Style: Stage 5 painted decoration, (b) Gila Polychrome: Salmon Variety bowl (D/193) bearing Pinedale Style: Stage 5 painted decoration, (c) Gila Polychrome bowl (D/194) bearing Gila Style painted decoration, (d) Cliff Polychrome bowl (D/196) bearing Pinedale Style: Stage 4 painted decoration, (e) Phoenix Polychrome bowl (D/200) bearing Roosevelt Style: Stage 3 painted decoration, (f) Gila Polychrome bowl (D/201) bearing Pinedale Style: Stage 5 painted decoration, (g) Cliff Polychrome bowl (D/202) bearing Pinedale Style: Stage 5 painted decoration, (h) Gila Polychrome bowl (D/203) bearing Roosevelt Style: Stage 3 painted decoration, (i) Cliff Polychrome bowl (D/205) bearing Pinedale Style: Stage 5 painted decoration. For measurements, see table 6.1. Photographs by Jannelle Weakly.

FIGURE 7.22 *(continued)*

THE PERFORATED PLATE ASSEMBLAGE

As noted above, the Amerind Museum collections from the Davis Ranch Site include 344 perforated plate sherds, 185 (54%) of which combine, through conjoins and matches, to make up 51 partially reconstructible vessels (figure 7.23, tables 7.14, 7.15; see also tables F.9, F.10). These sherds had been sorted and boxed according to Gerald's conception of types and varieties, including Belford Perforated Rim (a variety of Belford Plain), Sobaipuri Coil Rim (a variety of Belford Plain/Davis Plain; see chapter 6), Sosa Perforated (new type; see chapter 6), and Sandy Paste Perforated (new type; see chapter 6). Sosa Perforated sherds were physically contained within a portion of a subdivided box. The label associated with this subdivision reads "Fine Paste Perforated." Belford Perforated Rim sherds without rim coils were further sorted into the following categories: direct rim, bead rim, and flare rim. Many conjoins and matches across types, varieties, and rim forms were documented, however, undermining the utility of these categories (see table F.9).

Forty of the 51 partially reconstructible perforated plates were complete enough for maximum diameter to be measured (see table F.9). The smallest diameter recorded is 24.00 cm, the largest

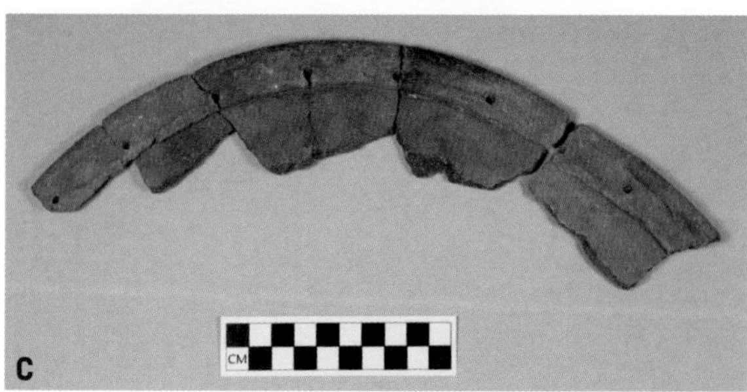

FIGURE 7.23 Partially reconstructible perforated plates: (a) Perforated Plate Vessel 1, from the kiva; (b) Perforated Plate Vessel 4, consisting of fragments recovered from Room 8, House 7, Room 21, and the trenches in front of Rooms 6 and 9; (c) Perforated Plate Vessel 14, from the kiva; (d) Perforated Plate Vessel 35, from the kiva. Photographs by Patrick D. Lyons.

TABLE 7.14 Perforated plate sherds counted individually and grouped by recovery context

Architectural unit or locus	Structure or locus	*n*	%
Houses	House 1	1	0.29
	House 2	3	0.87
	House 3	3	0.87
	House 4	3	0.87
	House 6	1	0.29
	House 7	2	0.58
Kiva		206	59.88
Northeast Trash		9	2.62
Puddle Pit 2		1	0.29
Houseblock I	Room 3	2	0.58
	Trench in front of Room 3	1	0.29
	Room 4	4	1.16
	Room 4 subfloor	4	1.16
	Room 5	1	0.29
	Room 6	10	2.91
	Trench in front of Room 6	2	0.58
	Room 7	3	0.87
	Room 8	12	3.49
	Trench in front of Room 8	1	0.29
	Room 9	1	0.29
	Trench in front of Room 9	1	0.29
	Room 10	4	1.16
	Room 11	1	0.29
Houseblock II	Room 14	5	1.45
	Room 15	1	0.29
	Room 17	1	0.29
	Room 18	2	0.58
	Room 21	1	0.29
	Room 33	2	0.58
	Room 35	2	0.58

(*continued*)

TABLE 7.14 *(continued)*

Architectural unit or locus	Structure or locus	*n*	%
Houseblock III	Room 25	1	0.29
Houseblock V	Room 44	2	0.58
Houseblock VII	Room 37	1	0.29
Other rooms	Room 2	6	1.74
	Room 34	10	2.91
	Room 36	4	1.16
	Room 46	2	0.58
Stratitest 1		3	0.87
Surface		2	0.58
Trenches		23	6.69
Total		**344**	**100.00**

TABLE 7.15 Perforated plate sherds and partially reconstructible vessels (PRVs) grouped by recovery context

Architectural unit or locus	Structure or locus	Unmatched sherds	PRVs[a]	Total	%
Houses	House 1	1	0	1	0.48
	House 2	1	1	2	0.95
	House 3	1	1	2	0.95
	House 4	3	0	3	1.43
	House 6	1	0	1	0.48
	House 7	1	0	1	0.48
Kiva		86	34	120	57.14
Northeast Trash		7	1	8	3.81
Puddle Pit 2		1	0	1	0.48
Houseblock I	Room 3	1	0	1	0.48
	Trench in front of Room 3	1	0	1	0.48
	Room 4	1	2	3	1.43

(continued)

TABLE 7.15 *(continued)*

Architectural unit or locus	Structure or locus	Unmatched sherds	PRVs[a]	Total	%
	Room 4 subfloor	1	1	2	0.95
	Room 5	1	0	1	0.48
	Room 6	1	2	3	1.43
	Room 7	3	0	3	1.43
	Room 8	1	1	2	0.95
	Trench in front of Room 8	1	0	1	0.48
	Room 9	1	0	1	0.48
	Room 10	4	0	4	1.90
	Room 11	1	0	1	0.48
Houseblock II	Room 14	3	1	4	1.90
	Room 15	1	0	1	0.48
	Room 18	1	0	1	0.48
	Room 33	2	0	2	0.95
	Room 35	2	0	2	0.95
Houseblock III	Room 25	1	0	1	0.48
Houseblock V	Room 44	0	1	1	0.48
Houseblock VII	Room 37	1	0	1	0.48
Other rooms	Room 2	4	1	5	2.38
	Room 34	5	2	7	3.33
	Room 36	2	1	3	1.43
	Room 46	2	0	2	0.95
Stratitest 1		1	1	2	0.95
Surface		1	0	1	0.48
Trenches		14	1	15	7.14
Total		**159**	**51**	**210**	**100.00**

Note: In most cases, the recovery context listed for a PRV indicates the location where the majority of fragments were found (see table F.9). In three cases, a PRV consisted of one fragment recovered from a trench and another from an architectural unit, and the recovery context listed is the architectural unit.

[a]Partially reconstructible vessels

is 58.00 cm, the mean is 36.65 cm, and the mode is 34.00 cm. The distribution of diameters is positively skewed, with 95% of the values falling between the minimum of 24.00 cm and a maximum of 46.00 cm. By way of comparison, Christenson's (1994:Figure 4-2) sample of 33 perforated plates from Black Mesa, largely dating circa AD 1050–1150, exhibits a mean diameter of 25.33 cm and a mode of 22.00 cm, with 97% measuring between a minimum of 14.00 cm and a maximum of 36.00 cm.

Red Pigment

Fourteen of the 51 partially reconstructible perforated plate vessels and seven of the 159 perforated plate sherds that do not form parts of reconstructible vessels exhibit traces of unfired red pigment in the form of fingerprints and smudges (on their exteriors, interiors, or both surfaces), as if a potter had gripped them with slip-covered hands (figure 7.24). This phenomenon also has been observed in the assemblages from José Solas Ruin and Point of Pines Pueblo (AZ W:10:50[ASM]). Unfired red pigment is present on two reconstructible plate specimens (one perforated and one unperforated) recovered from José Solas Ruin by Di Peso. A fragment of a second perforated specimen bearing similar traces was recovered as a result of Archaeology Southwest's excavations at the site (Lyons 2004a). Four different fragmentary perforated plates found on the floor and in the fill of the D-shaped kiva at Point of Pines Ruin have red pigment adhering to them. These findings and other evidence support the inference that perforated plates were used as base molds in pottery production and as potters' turntables (Christenson 1991, 1994; Crotty 1983:30, 57–59; Hargrave 1931:119; Haury 1931:68–69, 1945:111–112; Hough 1903:337; Lyons and Lindsay 2006).

Spatial Patterns

Perforated plate sherds and/or partially reconstructible perforated plate vessels were recovered from 23 of the 43 rooms investigated, all four of the Aravaipa phase pit houses, the kiva, the Northeast Trash, and a number of other contexts. Whether measured in terms of the total number of sherds or as partially reconstructible vessels (with each group of matching and/or conjoining sherds counted as one) plus unmatched and unconjoined sherds, the majority of perforated plates were recovered from the kiva (see

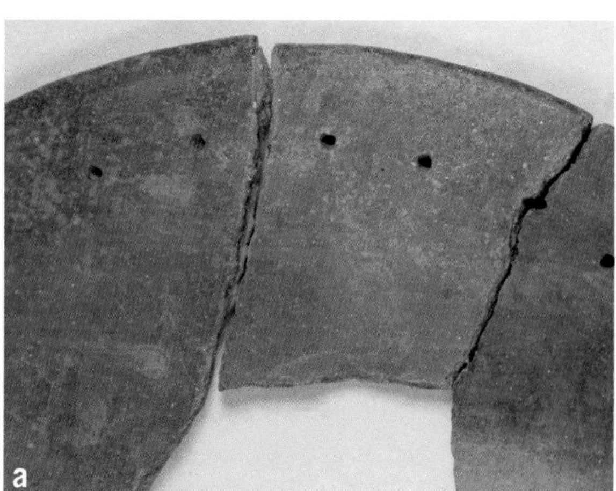

FIGURE 7.24 Traces of red slip on perforated plates: (a) close-up of interior of Perforated Plate Vessel 1, from the kiva; (b) exterior of Perforated Plate Vessel 47, from Room 4. Photographs by Patrick D. Lyons.

tables 7.14, 7.15). The most important fact observed, however, is that *at least* 80% of the specimens (regardless of counting method) were recovered from deposits postdating the initial occupation by immigrants from the Kayenta region. This means that perforated plates were commonly made, used, and discarded during the period when Roosevelt Red Ware was being produced at the site (evidence of on-site pottery production is addressed below and in chapter 8).

STRUCTURE-BY-STRUCTURE ANALYSIS

In this section, the decorated ceramic assemblage and perforated plates recovered from each structure are examined in depth, especially in the case of partially reconstructible vessels and refits and matches that link different structures. Data are presented mostly in chronological order. Comparable information about the assemblages from extramural areas (including the Northeast Trash and Stratitest 1) and isolated features is presented in the following section.

Early Agricultural Period Pit House: House 6

House 6, like House 4 and House 5 (discussed below), exhibits a high percentage of Maverick Mountain Series pottery, nearly 35%. This seems to be a product of location, since House 6 is situated in the Northeast Trash, an area used for refuse disposal by the Aravaipa phase Kayenta inhabitants of the site. Three partially reconstructible decorated vessels, consisting of six sherds total, were recovered from House 6 (table 7.16).

Pre-Classic Pit Houses: Houses 4, 5, and 8

The decorated assemblages from Houses 4 and 5 are distinctive in that both exhibit high percentages of Maverick Mountain Series pottery (nearly 30%; see table F.1). This makes sense, however, in the context of larger, site-level patterns, in that these collapsed structures were depressions located between the Aravaipa phase Kayenta pit houses (Houses 1, 2, 3, and 7) discussed below and the Northeast Trash (which is dominated by Aravaipa phase refuse). House 4 and House 5 were likely situated on the southern end of the sheet trash deposited by the inhabitants of Houses 1, 2, 3, and 7.

House 4 yielded three partially reconstructible decorated vessels, comprising eight sherds (see table 7.16). One of these, a Tucson Black-on-red jar (Vessel 1) includes a sherd from House 6, adding support to the notion that pieces of broken Aravaipa phase vessels made their way into Houses 4 and 5 during the movement of refuse from the arc of Aravaipa phase pit houses to the area bounded by Houses 4 and 5, on the south, and the Northeast Trash, on the north.

Four partially reconstructible decorated vessels were found in House 5, consisting of a total of 16 sherds (see table 7.16). One of these, a Cliff or Nine Mile Polychrome bowl (Vessel 4), is composed of one sherd each from House 5 and House 8. House 8, which was largely destroyed by the later construction of House 5, yielded very little in the way of Classic period ceramic material. One sherd from a Kinishba Polychrome bowl, however, was recovered from this structure. Clearly this sherd, as well as the portion of the Cliff or Nine Mile Polychrome bowl just discussed, must relate to the Classic period occupation of the site.

Aravaipa Phase Pit Houses: House 1

The decorated assemblage from House 1, like those from all the Aravaipa phase houses (Houses 1, 2, 3, and 7), is dominated by Roosevelt Red Ware (see table F.1). That said, of the structures of this type and age, it exhibits the smallest proportion of Roosevelt Red Ware, nearly 54%. Roosevelt Red Ware

TABLE 7.16 Decorated partially reconstructible vessels (PRVs) recovered from the pit houses and subjected to reanalysis

House no.	Decorated PRV no.	Ware	Type	Vessel form	Sherd count	Comment(s)
1	1	Maverick Mountain Series	Tucson Polychrome	bowl	6	1 T1S 46–30E rim refits 3 floor bodies and matches 1 floor rim and 1 fill body
	2	Roosevelt Red Ware	indeterminate polychrome	bowl	7	6 floor bodies refit, 1 matches
	3	Maverick Mountain Series	Tucson Polychrome	bowl	2	1 fill rim matches 1 floor body
	4	Maverick Mountain Series	Tucson Polychrome	bowl	5	1 fill body refits 1 floor body and matches 2 floor bodies, which refit, and 1 fill body
	5		Mimbres Black-on-white	bowl	12	1 fill rim refits 2 T1S 46–30E bodies and matches: 1 floor rim that refits 1 floor body, 2 fill bodies, and 4 T1S 46–30E bodies; and 1 T1S 46–30E rim
	6	Maverick Mountain Series	indeterminate	jar	2	2 fill rims refit
	7	Roosevelt Red Ware	indeterminate polychrome	bowl	2	2 fill bodies refit
	8	Roosevelt Red Ware	indeterminate polychrome	bowl	3	3 fill bodies refit
2	1	Roosevelt Red Ware	Gila Black-on-red	jar	2	2 fill bodies match
3	1	Roosevelt Red Ware	Gila Polychrome	bowl	4	1 rim and 3 bodies refit
	2	Roosevelt Red Ware	Gila Polychrome	bowl	4	2 rims and 2 bodies refit
	3	Roosevelt Red Ware	Pinto Polychrome	bowl	5	2 bodies refit and match 2 rims and 1 body
	4	Roosevelt Red Ware	Cliff Polychrome	bowl	6	2 rims and 1 neck refit and match 2 necks and 1 body
	5	Roosevelt Red Ware	indeterminate polychrome	bowl	2	2 bodies refit
	6	Roosevelt Red Ware	Tonto Polychrome	jar	2	2 bodies refit
4	1[a]	Maverick Mountain Series	Tucson Black-on-red	jar	4	2 fill necks refit and match 1 fill neck and 1 House 6 stratitest level 1 neck
	2	Maverick Mountain Series	Tucson Black-on-red	bowl	2	2 fill bodies refit
	3	Roosevelt Red Ware	indeterminate polychrome	jar	2	2 fill necks refit
5	1	Maverick Mountain Series	Tucson Polychrome	jar	6	4 fill bodies refit and match 2 fill rims that refit
	2	Maverick Mountain Series	Tucson Black-on-red	jar	2	2 fill rims refits

	3	Roosevelt Red Ware	indeterminate polychrome	jar	6	3 fill necks refit and match 2 fill necks and 1 fill rim
	4[a]	Roosevelt Red Ware	Cliff or Nine Mile Polychrome	bowl	2	1 fill rim refits 1 House 8 fill rim; indeterminate polychrome exterior decoration
6	1	Maverick Mountain Series	Tucson Black-on-red	jar	2	1 stratitest level 1 neck and 1 body match
	2	Maverick Mountain Series	Tucson Polychrome	jar	2	2 stratitest level 1 body sherds match
	3	Roosevelt Red Ware	indeterminate polychrome	bowl	2	2 stratitest level 2 bodies refit
7	1	Roosevelt Red Ware	Gila Polychrome	bowl	19	2 subfloor rims refit and match: 1 Floor 2 rim that refits 2 Pit 4 bodies and 1 Floor 2 body, 2 subfloor bodies that refit, 1 subfloor rim, 1 Pit 4 body, 1 body stamped "H-7," 1 stratitest level 3 body, 4 Floor 2 bodies, and 3 subfloor bodies
	2	Roosevelt Red Ware	Cliff Polychrome	bowl	34	all Fire Pit 3: 2 rims, 1 neck, and 6 bodies refit and match: 1 rim; 2 rims that refit; 5 bodies, 2 of which refit and 3 of which refit; 6 bodies (each is one of three pairs that refit); and 11 bodies
	3	Roosevelt Red Ware	Gila Polychrome	bowl	3	1 Pits 1 and 2 rim and 1 body refit 1 fill body
	4	Roosevelt Red Ware	Gila Polychrome	bowl	2	1 Pits 1 and 2 rim and 1 body refit
	5	Roosevelt Red Ware	Gila Polychrome	bowl	3	2 Pits 1 and 2 rims refit and match 1 body
	6	Roosevelt Red Ware	Cliff Polychrome	bowl	2	1 Pits 1 and 2 rim matches 1 neck
	7	Roosevelt Red Ware	Cliff Polychrome	bowl	3	3 Pits 1 and 2 rims match
	8	Roosevelt Red Ware	Nine Mile Polychrome: Safford Variety	bowl	4	1 fill rim and 3 bodies refit
	9[a]	Roosevelt Red Ware	indeterminate polychrome	bowl	4	1 fill body refits 1 Room 6 fill body and matches 2 fill bodies; Nine Mile, Whiteriver, or Phoenix Polychrome
	10	Roosevelt Red Ware	Gila Polychrome, no banding line	bowl	5	3 fill rims and 2 bodies refit
	11[a]	Roosevelt Red Ware	Gila Polychrome: Gila Variety	bowl	11	2 fill rims and 7 bodies refit and match 1 Pits 1 and 2 rim and 1 Room 10 fill rim

(*continued*)

TABLE 7.16 *(continued)*

House no.	Decorated PRV no.	Ware	Type	Vessel form	Sherd count	Comment(s)
	12	Roosevelt Red Ware	Gila Polychrome	bowl	5	4 fill rims and 1 body refit
	13	Roosevelt Red Ware	Gila Polychrome	jar	4	3 fill necks and 1 body refit
	14	Roosevelt Red Ware	Gila Polychrome	bowl	2	2 fill rims refit
	15	Roosevelt Red Ware	Gila Polychrome or later	bowl	3	3 fill bodies match
	16	Roosevelt Red Ware	Gila Polychrome or later	bowl	3	3 fill bodies match
	17	Roosevelt Red Ware	Gila Polychrome or later	bowl	2	2 fill bodies match
	18	Roosevelt Red Ware	Gila Polychrome or later	bowl	2	2 fill bodies refit
	19	Roosevelt Red Ware	indeterminate polychrome	bowl	3	3 fill bodies match
	20	Roosevelt Red Ware	indeterminate polychrome	bowl	5	3 fill bodies refit and match 1 fill body and 1 Pits 1 and 2 body
	21	Roosevelt Red Ware	indeterminate polychrome	jar	2	2 Fire Pit 3 bodies match
	22	Roosevelt Red Ware	indeterminate polychrome	bowl	4	2 Fire Pit 4 bodies refit and match 2 bodies
	23	Roosevelt Red Ware	indeterminate polychrome	jar	2	2 Floor 1 bodies refit
	24	Roosevelt Red Ware	Pinto Polychrome	bowl	2	1 Floor 1 rim refits 1 fill rim
	25	Roosevelt Red Ware	indeterminate polychrome	bowl	2	2 Floor 1 rims match
	26	Maverick Mountain Series	Maverick Mountain Black-on-red	bowl	2	1 Floor 2 body matches 1 subfloor body
	27	Roosevelt Red Ware	Gila Black-on-red	bowl	2	2 Floor 2 bodies refit
	28	Roosevelt Red Ware	indeterminate black-on-red	bowl	3	1 Floor 2 body refits 1 subfloor body and matches 1 Floor 2 body
	29	Maverick Mountain Series	Maverick Mountain Black-on-red	jar	2	1 subfloor body matches 1 Fire Pit 3 body
	30	Maverick Mountain Series	Tucson Polychrome	jar	2	2 subfloor bodies refit
Total					**236**	

[a]Vessel composed of fragments from two structures

accounts for more than 90% of the other decorated assemblages.

Eight partially reconstructible decorated vessels were identified, comprising 39 sherds (see table 7.16). Three of these, which include pieces found in contact with the floor, are Tucson Polychrome bowls (figure 7.25). Another from floor contact is a Roosevelt Red Ware polychrome bowl of indeterminate type, but quite likely represents a specimen of Pinto Polychrome (figure 7.26a). This assemblage is consistent with the assignment of this structure to the Aravaipa phase. The fifth partial vessel, a Mimbres Black-on-white bowl (figure 7.26b), fragments of which were recovered from the floor, is something of an anomaly and probably represents reuse of a pre-Classic object by the site's Classic period inhabitants. Roger Anyon and Darrell Creel (personal communication 2012) indicate this specimen is transitional between Style I and Style II and assign it a date of circa AD 875–900.

House 2

House 2 yielded a single partially reconstructible decorated vessel, fragments of a Gila Black-on-red jar recovered from the fill, and a single partially reconstructible perforated plate, also found in the fill (see tables 7.16, F.9).

House 3

Six partially reconstructible decorated vessels, accounting for a total of 23 sherds, were found in House 3 (figure 7.26c; see table 7.16). Because Room 3 was essentially dug as a single recovery unit, contextual data for these vessels are unavailable. The partially reconstructible perforated plate represented in part by two sherds from House 3 also includes a fragment from the floor of Room 3, which overlies House 3 (see table F.9).

FIGURE 7.25 Partially reconstructible Tucson Polychrome bowls from House 1: (a) House 1 Decorated Vessel 1, (b) House 1 Decorated Vessel 3, (c) House 1 Decorated Vessel 4. Photographs by Patrick D. Lyons.

FIGURE 7.26 Partially reconstructible vessels from House 1 and House 3: (a) House 1 Decorated Vessel 2, a Roosevelt Red Ware polychrome bowl of indeterminate type; (b) House 1 Decorated Vessel 5, a Mimbres Black-on-white bowl; (c) House 3 Decorated Vessel 3, a Pinto Polychrome bowl. Photographs by Patrick D. Lyons.

House 7

No less than 30 partially reconstructible decorated vessels were retrieved from House 7 (see table 7.16). These comprise 142 sherds. One of these, Vessel 2, a Cliff Polychrome bowl found in Fire Pit 3, is composed of 34 fragments (see figure 7.18e). Another, Vessel 1, a Gila Polychrome bowl, is represented by 19 sherds (see figure 7.17a).

As discussed above, in the section devoted to superimposed structures, the stratigraphic sequence preserved in House 7 and Room 6, which overlies it, track important trends through time lending support to seriation-based revisions to Roosevelt Red Ware typology and also the Roosevelt Red Ware stylistic seriation proposed by Crown (1994). The clear typological/chronological patterns in the overall decorated assemblage (sherds and partially reconstructible vessels) are equally evident when only the partially reconstructible vessels are considered (see table 7.16). Maverick Mountain Series vessels are present below but not above the upper floor (Floor 1), and, likewise, although there is no Cliff Polychrome below Floor 1, it is present in overlying strata.

Perhaps the most significant find among the partially reconstructible vessels from House 7 is one I have labeled an example of Nine Mile Polychrome: Safford Variety (figure 7.27). The type specimen is curated by the University of Colorado Museum of Natural History (Catalog No. 9643) and reportedly was "obtained" by Earl Morris "from a site on the east side of the Gila River, about 3 miles above Safford, Arizona, summer of 1926" (Lister and Lister 1978:91, Figure 45 bottom row, right). The description "east side of the Gila River" does not make much sense, however, unless the location indicated is three miles above Solomon (rather than Safford), where the Gila River turns from a northeast-southwest course to one that runs from southeast to northwest (from Solomon to the San Carlos Reservoir). The site from which this vessel was most likely recovered, then, is that known as the Curtis Site (a.k.a., Buena Vista Ruin, the Solomonsville Site; AZ CC:2:3[ASM]). Additional catalog information supplied by Stephen H. Lekson (personal communication 2009) indicates that this vessel was indeed recovered from "the Curtis Ranch."

Nine Mile Polychrome (Lyons 2013a; Lyons and Neuzil 2006; Neuzil and Lyons 2006) is similar to Cliff Polychrome. Both occur only as recurved bowls and exhibit a banded field of black-on-white painted decoration on the interior surface, at the rim. Nine Mile differs from Cliff in that the remainder of the interior surface of the former is slipped red and bears no painted decoration. Nine Mile Polychrome bowl exteriors usually bear Gila- or Tonto-configuration decoration. The Safford Variety, named based on the specimen discussed above, as well as others seen in sherd collections and as whole vessels in private collections, is distinguished from the established variety by the presence of Tonto-configuration painted decoration pendant from the design field at the rim rather than an unadorned field of red slip below the design field at the rim. The specimen from House 7 (Vessel 8) bears Tonto-configuration painted decoration on its exterior surface as well. In addition, it exhibits surface treatment on its exterior similar to that characteristic of Tularosa Fillet Rim: four indented corrugated coils (slipped red) are present below the rim, at the point of inflection.

Also notable is the fact that two partially reconstructible decorated vessels link House 7 with other structures. Vessel 9, a Roosevelt Red Ware polychrome bowl of indeterminate type (very likely Nine Mile Polychrome or Whiteriver Polychrome) includes sherds from House 7 and Room 6. Vessel 11, a Gila Polychrome: Gila Variety bowl, is made up of sherds from House 7 and Room 10 (see figure 7.18b, c).

The Kiva

As noted above, although all kiva contexts were examined for refits and matches (and many were found and recorded), the primary foci of the analysis were the stratigraphic column (stratitest levels

FIGURE 7.27 Partially reconstructible bowl of Nine Mile Polychrome: Safford Variety, House 7 Decorated Vessel 8: (a) interior, (b) exterior. Photographs by Patrick D. Lyons.

1–8), level 9 (which extended out from the sides of the stratigraphic column to the walls of the kiva), the floor, and the floor features. Specimens recovered from contexts other than these were not included in the full reanalysis, but assemblages from these deposits were searched for conjoins and matches with sherds from the kiva's stratigraphic column, level 9, the floor, and the floor features. Such conjoins and matches are reflected in the data tables.

A total of 2,428 decorated vessel fragments and vessels from the kiva (and Burial 9, underlying it) were ultimately examined and recorded (see table 7.1). Included were 1,694 sherds not identified as portions of partially reconstructible vessels, 149 partially reconstructible vessels comprising 720 sherds (table 7.17), and 14 whole reconstructible vessels recovered by Gerald. These represent all specimens (i.e., all sherds, regardless of vessel part, and all partially reconstructible vessels) recovered from the stratigraphic column, level 9, the floor, and the floor features; the whole painted vessels from the burials; and all rim sherds and partially reconstructible vessels from the general fill, the recovery units designated kiva levels 3–5 (fill adjacent to levels 3, 4, and 5 in the stratigraphic column) and kiva levels 6–8 (fill adjacent to levels 6, 7, and 8 in the stratigraphic column), and the trenches that fell within the area defined by the kiva.

Data in table 7.2 reflect only those sherds and partially reconstructible or whole vessels (each counted as one specimen) recovered from the stratigraphic column, level 9, the floor, the floor features, and the burials that yielded painted pottery (tables 7.18–7.21). Roosevelt Red Ware accounts for more than 98% of this sample, with 60% classified as indeterminate Roosevelt Red Ware polychrome. Among specimens assignable to a more diagnostic type-level category, nearly one-quarter were identified as Gila Polychrome or later, and nearly 9% were classified as Gila Polychrome (figures 7.28, 7.29).

TABLE 7.17 Decorated partially reconstructible vessels (PRVs) recovered from the kiva and subjected to reanalysis

Decorated PRV no. or catalog no.	Ware	Type	Vessel form	Sherd count	From stratigraphic column, level 9, floor, or floor feature(s)	Used in stratigraphic analysis of RRW[a]	Comment(s)
1	Roosevelt Red Ware	Whiteriver Polychrome	bowl	10	X		2 stratitest level 4 rims refit and refit 1 body and match: 2 rims that refit (stratitest level 3, T10S 23–25E L2), 2 bodies that refit (stratitest level 1, stratitest level 2), 1 level 6–8 rim, 1 stratitest level 4 body, and 1 Trench in front of Room 3 body
2	Roosevelt Red Ware	Gila Polychrome	bowl	6	X	X	2 stratitest level 5 rims refit and match 3 bodies that refit and match 1 other body
3	Roosevelt Red Ware	Gila Polychrome	bowl	16	X		2 stratitest level 6 rims refit 4 bodies and refit 5 stratitest level 7 rims and 5 bodies
4	Roosevelt Red Ware	Gila Polychrome	bowl	8	X	X	3 stratitest level 6 rims refit and refit 5 bodies
5	Roosevelt Red Ware	Cliff Polychrome	bowl	18	X	X	5 stratitest level 6 bodies refit and match: 10 stratitest level 5 bodies that refit, 1 stratitest level 6 rim and 1 level 6–8 body that refit, and 1 stratitest level 5 body
6	Roosevelt Red Ware	Gila Polychrome	bowl	2	X	X	1 stratitest level 7 rim refits 1 stratitest level 8 body; child painter
7	Roosevelt Red Ware	Gila Polychrome	bowl	4	X	X	1 rim each from level 9 and the ventilator refit and match 2 bodies, 1 each from the same proveniences
8	Roosevelt Red Ware	Gila Polychrome, no banding line	bowl	5	X	X	1 level 9 rim refits 1 body and 1 neck, and they all match 1 rim and 1 body that refit
9	Roosevelt Red Ware	Whiteriver Polychrome	bowl	14	X	X	2 level 9 rims and 5 bodies refit and refit 1 ventilator neck and match: 1 level 3–5 body, 3 level 6–8 bodies that refit, 1 T19S 20E body, and 1 fill body
10	Roosevelt Red Ware	Gila Polychrome	bowl	6	X	X	1 floor rim and 2 bodies refit and match 2 bodies and 1 level 9 rim
11	Roosevelt Red Ware	Pinto Polychrome	bowl	30	X	X	3 ventilator rims and 2 bodies refit and refit 1 level 9 body and 1 level 9 rim and match: 1 ventilator rim and 1 level 9 body that refit, 4 ventilator bodies that refit and refit 1 level 9 rim and 1 body from the foot drum, 5 ventilator bodies that refit, 2 ventilator bodies that refit, 1 level 9 body and 1 ventilator body that refit, 4 ventilator bodies, and 2 level 9 bodies

(continued)

TABLE 7.17 *(continued)*

Decorated PRV no. or catalog no.	Ware	Type	Vessel form	Sherd count	From stratigraphic column, level 9, floor, or floor feature(s)	Used in stratigraphic analysis of RRW[a]	Comment(s)
12	Roosevelt Red Ware	Cliff Polychrome: Tucson Variety	bowl	4	X	X	2 fill rims refit and match 1 ventilator rim and 1 T10S 23–25E L1 body
13	Maverick Mountain Series	Maverick Mountain Black-on-red	jar	13	X		3 foot drum rims refit and refit 5 necks and match 4 rims that refit and refit 1 neck
14	Roosevelt Red Ware	Gila Polychrome, no banding line	bowl	4	X	X	1 subfloor pit rim refits 1 body and two bodies match; child painter
15	Roosevelt Red Ware	Gila Polychrome	jar	13	X	X	2 fill rims refit and refit 1 stratitest level 4 rim and 1 fill neck and match: 1 T10S 23–25E L3 rim that refits 1 T10S 23–25E L2 rim and 3 L2 necks, 1 stratitest level 5 rim that refits 1 stratitest level 4 neck, and 1 stratitest level 4 neck and 1 fill neck
16	Roosevelt Red Ware	Gila Polychrome	jar	9	X	X	all match: 2 fill rims, 5 fill bodies, 1 T23E 10S body, and 1 stratitest level 4 neck
17	Roosevelt Red Ware	indeterminate RRW polychrome	jar	4	X	X	1 stratitest level 5 rim and neck refit and match 1 stratitest level 5 rim and 1 fill neck
18	Roosevelt Red Ware	Tonto Polychrome	jar	8	X	X	2 stratitest level 5 bodies refit and match: 1 stratitest level 4 body and 1 T23E 11–15S body that refit, 2 stratitest level 5 necks, and 2 stratitest level 5 bodies
19	Roosevelt Red Ware	indeterminate RRW polychrome	jar	4	X	X	2 stratitest level 5 bodies refit and match 2 bodies that refit
20	Roosevelt Red Ware	indeterminate RRW polychrome	jar	9	X	X	1 stratitest level 6 neck refits 2 bodies and matches 1 neck that refits 2 bodies, 1 neck, and 2 bodies
21	Roosevelt Red Ware	Gila Polychrome	jar	19	X	X	1 T26E 7–16S neck refits 1 fill neck, 1 stratitest level 5 neck, 1 level 6–8 neck, 1 stratitest level 5 body, and 2 stratitest level 6 bodies, and matches: 2 T10S 23–25E L3 necks that refit and refit 1 level 6–8 neck; 2 level 6–8 bodies that refit and refit 2 fill bodies, 1 T23E 11–16S neck, 1 level 6–8 body, 1 stratitest level 5 body, 1 T10S 23–25E L1 body, and 1 body of unknown provenience
22	Roosevelt Red Ware	indeterminate RRW polychrome	jar	9	X	X	1 fill rim refits 1 stratitest level 6 neck and matches 2 fill rims that refit, 3 fill necks, 1 Structure 1 fill neck, and 1 fill rim

23	Roosevelt Red Ware	Gila Polychrome	bowl	14	X	X	all refit: 3 level 6–8 rims, 2 fill rims, 1 stratitest level 4 rim, 1 stratitest level 6 rim, 4 stratitest level 5 bodies, and 3 stratitest level 6 bodies
24	Roosevelt Red Ware	Gila Polychrome	jar	9	X	X	1 fill neck refits 1 fill body and matches 2 fill necks, 1 fill body and 1 stratitest level 7 body that refit, 2 fill bodies, and 1 level 6–8 body
25	Roosevelt Red Ware	Gila Polychrome	oval bowl	7			all refit: 3 fill rims and 4 bodies
26	Roosevelt Red Ware	Gila Polychrome	jar	15			1 level 6–8 rim refits 2 fill rims and 2 fill necks and matches 2 level 6–8 necks and 1 body that refit, 2 level 6–8 bodies that refit, 1 level 6–8 neck, 2 fill bodies, and 2 level 6–8 bodies
27	Roosevelt Red Ware	Gila Polychrome	jar	11			1 T23E 11–15S rim refits 2 T23E 11–15S necks and 2 fill necks and matches 2 fill rims and 2 fill necks that refit, 1 T26E 7–16S neck, and 1 26E 10–16S neck
28	Roosevelt Red Ware	indeterminate RRW polychrome	jar	3			1 fill rim matches 1 fill neck and 1 T26E 7–16S neck
29	Roosevelt Red Ware	indeterminate RRW polychrome	jar	2			1 fill body and 1 T23E 11–15S body refit
30	Roosevelt Red Ware	indeterminate RRW polychrome	jar	3			2 T23E 11–15S bodies refit and match 1 body
31	Roosevelt Red Ware	Cliff Polychrome	bowl	7			1 fill rim refits 1 level 6–8 rim and matches 1 fill rim and 2 fill necks that refit, 1 fill rim, and 1 level 6–8 neck
32	Roosevelt Red Ware	Cliff Polychrome	bowl	8			2 T20E 17–20S rims refit and refit 2 fill rims and match 2 fill rims that refit, 1 fill rim, and 1 T10S 23–25E L1 neck
33	Roosevelt Red Ware	Cliff Polychrome	bowl	4			1 Structure 1 fill rim refits 1 T26E 16S rim and matches 1 T10S 23–25E L2 rim and 1 T8.5–9S 24–25 E L4 rim
34	Roosevelt Red Ware	Gila Polychrome	bowl	6			1 fill rim refits 1 Structure 1 fill rim and 1 fill body and matches 2 fill rims that refit and 1 fill rim
35	Roosevelt Red Ware	Gila Polychrome	bowl	4			2 fill rims and 2 level 6–8 rims refit
36	Roosevelt Red Ware	Cliff or Nine Mile Polychrome	bowl	4			1 T8.5–9S 24–25E L2 rim and 1 26E 7–16S rim refit and match 1 T8.5–9S 24–25E L4 rim and 1 T23E 11–15S rim
37	Roosevelt Red Ware	Gila Polychrome	bowl	2			2 level 6–8 rims refit
38	Roosevelt Red Ware	Gila Polychrome	bowl	2			2 T10S 23–25E L3 rims refit
39	Roosevelt Red Ware	Gila Polychrome	bowl	3			3 level 6–8 rims refit

(*continued*)

TABLE 7.17 *(continued)*

Decorated PRV no. or catalog no.	Ware	Type	Vessel form	Sherd count	From stratigraphic column, level 9, floor, or floor feature(s)	Used in stratigraphic analysis of RRW[a]	Comment(s)
40	Roosevelt Red Ware	Gila Polychrome	bowl	4			1 T10S 23–25E L2 rim refits 1 House 2 fill rim and matches 1 level 6–8 rim and 1 T8.5–9S 24–25E L1 rim
41	Roosevelt Red Ware	Gila Polychrome	bowl	4			4 T26E 11–15S rims refit
42	Roosevelt Red Ware	Gila Polychrome	bowl	6			2 fill rims refit and refit 2 bodies and match 1 T8.5–9S 24–25E L1 rim that refits 1 Structure 1 fill rim
43	Roosevelt Red Ware	Cliff Polychrome	bowl	3	X	X	2 fill rims and 1 stratitest level 5 rim match
44	Roosevelt Red Ware	Cliff Polychrome	bowl	3			1 level 6–8 rim refits 1 level 6–8 neck and matches 1 fill neck
45	Roosevelt Red Ware	Cliff Polychrome	bowl	2			2 fill rims match
46	Roosevelt Red Ware	Cliff Polychrome: Tonto Variety	bowl	2			2 level 6–8 necks match
47	Roosevelt Red Ware	Gila Polychrome	bowl	2			1 T10S 23–25E rim refits 1 neck
48	Roosevelt Red Ware	Gila Polychrome	bowl	2			2 level 6–8 rims refit
49	Roosevelt Red Ware	Gila Polychrome	bowl	2			2 T8S 23–25E L4 rims refit
50	Roosevelt Red Ware	Gila Polychrome	bowl	3			2 T10S 23–25E L2 rims refit; 1 matches
51	Roosevelt Red Ware	Gila Polychrome	bowl	2			2 level 3–5 rims refit
52	Roosevelt Red Ware	Gila Polychrome	bowl	2			2 level 6–8 rims refit
53	Roosevelt Red Ware	Gila Polychrome	bowl	2			2 fill rims match
54	Roosevelt Red Ware	Gila Polychrome	bowl	2			2 fill rims match
55/56	Roosevelt Red Ware	Cliff Polychrome	bowl	4			1 T10S 23–25E rim refits 1 Structure 1 fill rim and match 2 T8.5–9S 24–25E L3 rims
57	Roosevelt Red Ware	Cliff or Nine Mile Polychrome	bowl	3			1 fill rim refits 1 level 3–5 rim and matches 1 fill rim; indeterminate polychrome exterior decoration
58	Roosevelt Red Ware	Cliff or Nine Mile Polychrome	bowl	3			2 fill necks refit, 1 neck matches; indeterminate polychrome exterior decoration
59	Roosevelt Red Ware	Gila Polychrome	bowl	3			2 fill rims match and match 1 body
60	Roosevelt Red Ware	Cliff Polychrome	bowl	6			2 fill rims refit and match 2 rims that refit and 2 necks

61	Roosevelt Red Ware	Cliff Polychrome	bowl	4	2 fill rims match and match 2 necks
62	Roosevelt Red Ware	Gila Polychrome	bowl	3	1 fill rim and 1 T8.5–9S 24–25E L3 rim refit and match 1 T23E 10S rim; all have rim ticks
63	Roosevelt Red Ware	Gila Polychrome or later	bowl	4	1 fill body refits 1 T23E 10 S body and matches 1 T26E 7–16S body and 1 T23E 10S body; indeterminate polychrome exterior decoration
64	Roosevelt Red Ware	Gila Polychrome: Gila Variety	bowl	2	1 level 6–8 rim matches 1 T26E 10–16S body
65	Roosevelt Red Ware	Whiteriver Polychrome: Gila Variety	bowl	6	2 level 6–8 rims refit and refit 1 level 6–8 body and match 1 8.5–9S 24–25E rim and 1 level 6–8 body that refit and 1 body with no known provenience
66	Roosevelt Red Ware	White River Polychrome	bowl	2	1 fill rim matches 1 level 3–5 rim; probably Gila Variety
67	Roosevelt Red Ware	White River Polychrome	bowl	2	1 fill rim matches 1 body
68	Roosevelt Red Ware	Nine Mile Polychrome	bowl	2	2 T26E 10–16S necks match
69	Roosevelt Red Ware	Gila Polychrome, no banding line	bowl	3	all match: 1 T23E 11–15S rim, 1 T23E 14–15S rim, and 1 level 6–8 rim
70	Roosevelt Red Ware	Gila Polychrome, no banding line	bowl	5	all match: 3 T26E 16 S rims, 1 fill rim, and 1 level 3–5 rim
71	Roosevelt Red Ware	Cliff Black-on-red	bowl	2	1 fill rim matches 1 rim of unknown provenience
72	Roosevelt Red Ware	Phoenix Polychrome	bowl	2	2 T23E 10S rims refit; indeterminate polychrome exterior decoration
73	Roosevelt Red Ware	Nine Mile Polychrome	bowl	2	2 fill necks match
74	Roosevelt Red Ware	indeterminate RRW polychrome	bowl	2	2 fill bodies refit; red-slipped interior, indeterminate polychrome exterior decoration
75	Roosevelt Red Ware	Gila Polychrome, no banding line	bowl	10	1 level 3–5 rim refits 3 T10S 23–25E L2 rims and matches 1 fill rim, 2 T10S 23–25E L2 rims, 1 T26E 7–16S rim, 1 T10S 23E rim, and 1 T11–15S 23E rim
76	Roosevelt Red Ware	Whiteriver Polychrome	bowl	3	3 fill rims match

(continued)

TABLE 7.17 *(continued)*

Decorated PRV no. or catalog no.	Ware	Type	Vessel form	Sherd count	From stratigraphic column, level 9, floor, or floor feature(s)	Used in stratigraphic analysis of RRW[a]	Comment(s)
77	Roosevelt Red Ware	Pinto Polychrome	bowl	2			2 fill rims match
78	Roosevelt Red Ware	indeterminate RRW polychrome	bowl	3			1 fill rim refits 1 fill neck and 1 T8.5–9S 24–25E L2 rim
79	Roosevelt Red Ware	Gila Polychrome or later	oval bowl	2	X	X	1 stratitest level 4 indeterminate part refits 1 body; scoop wear
80	Roosevelt Red Ware	Phoenix Polychrome	bowl	3	X	X	2 stratitest level 5 rims refit and match 1 rim from T10S 23–25E L3
81	Roosevelt Red Ware	Tonto Polychrome	jar	2			1 T23E 10S body refits 1 T10S 23–25E L2 body
82	Roosevelt Red Ware	indeterminate RRW polychrome	jar	3			1 fill rim matches 1 fill neck and 1 Structure 1 fill rim
83	Roosevelt Red Ware	Tonto Polychrome	jar	17			4 fill rims refit and refit 5 fill necks and 2 level 6–8 necks and match 1 fill body that refits 1 T23E 11–16S neck, 2 fill necks that refit, 1 fill body, and 1 level 6–8 body
84	Roosevelt Red Ware	indeterminate RRW polychrome	jar	9	X	X	1 level 6–8 rim refits 3 level 6–8 necks and matches 1 T8.5–9S 24–25E L2 rim that refits 1 T10S 23–25E L2 rim, 1 stratitest level 4 rim, 1 T8.5–9S 24–25E L2 rim, and 1 fill neck
85	Roosevelt Red Ware	indeterminate RRW polychrome	jar	6			1 T8S 23–25E L4 rim refits 1 T10S 23–25E L1 rim and matches 1 fill rim, 1 T8.5–9S 24–25E L2 rim, 1 level 3–5 rim, and 1 level 6–8 rim; all ground on lip, like pot rest fragments
87	Roosevelt Red Ware	Gila Black-on-red	bowl	6	X	X	all bodies that refit: 1 stratitest level 1, 1 T10S 23–25E L1, 1 T10S 23–25E L2, 1 level 6–8, 1 T10S 23–25E L3, and 1 fill
88	Roosevelt Red Ware	Cliff Polychrome	bowl	3			1 T10S 23–25E L2 rim matches 2 necks: 1 T10S 23–25E L2 and 1 T8.5–9S 24–25E L4
89	Roosevelt Red Ware	Cliff or Nine Mile Polychrome	bowl	2			2 T10S 23–25E L2 rims refit
90	Roosevelt Red Ware	Cliff Polychrome	bowl	2	X	X	1 stratitest level 5 rim matches 1 fill neck
91	Roosevelt Red Ware	Cliff Polychrome	bowl	2			2 fill rims match
92	Roosevelt Red Ware	Cliff Polychrome	bowl	2			1 fill rim matches 1 level 6–8 rim

93	Roosevelt Red Ware	Cliff Polychrome	bowl	2			1 fill rim matches 1 T26E 7–16S rim
94	Roosevelt Red Ware	Cliff Polychrome	bowl	3			3 fill rims match
95	Roosevelt Red Ware	Cliff Polychrome	bowl	4			1 T8.5–9S 24–25E L2 rim matches 1 fill neck and 2 fill rims
96	Roosevelt Red Ware	Cliff Polychrome	bowl	6			1 fill rim refits 1 T10S 23–25E L2 rim and matches 3 fill rims and 1 fill neck that refit
97	Roosevelt Red Ware	Cliff Polychrome	bowl	3			all match: 1 fill rim, 1 fill neck, and 1 T20E 10–16S neck
98	Roosevelt Red Ware	Cliff or Nine Mile Polychrome	bowl	5			3 fill rims refit and refit 1 fill neck and refit 1 T23E 11–15S neck
99	Roosevelt Red Ware	Cliff Polychrome	bowl	2			2 fill necks match
100	Roosevelt Red Ware	Cliff Polychrome	bowl	2			1 level 6–8 rim refits 1 level 3–5 neck
101	Roosevelt Red Ware	Cliff Polychrome	bowl	2			2 fill rims match
102	Roosevelt Red Ware	Cliff Polychrome	bowl	2			1 fill rim matches 1 level 6–8 rim
103/107	Roosevelt Red Ware	Cliff Polychrome	bowl	2			3 fill rims refit and match 1 T10S 23–25E rim and 1 T23E 10S rim
104	Roosevelt Red Ware	Cliff Polychrome	bowl	2			1 T8.5–9S 24–25E L2 rim matches 1 T28E 10S rim
105	Roosevelt Red Ware	Cliff Polychrome	bowl	2			2 fill rims refit
106	Roosevelt Red Ware	Cliff Polychrome	bowl	2			2 fill rims refit
108	Roosevelt Red Ware	Cliff or Nine Mile Polychrome	bowl	2			2 fill rims refit
109	Roosevelt Red Ware	Gila Polychrome	bowl	2			2 level 3–5 rims match
110	Roosevelt Red Ware	Gila Polychrome	bowl	2	X		1 stratitest level 6 rim refits 1 stratitest level 7 rim
111	Roosevelt Red Ware	Cliff Polychrome	bowl	2	X	X	1 level 6–8 rim refits 1 stratitest level 5 rim
112	Roosevelt Red Ware	Dinwiddie Polychrome?	bowl?	2			1 level 6–8 body refits 1 fill body
113	Roosevelt Red Ware	indeterminate RRW polychrome	bowl	5	X	X	2 stratitest level 1 rims and 1 neck refit and match 1 neck and 1 body
114	Roosevelt Red Ware	Cliff Polychrome	bowl	2	X	X	1 stratitest level 4 rim refits 1 neck
115	Roosevelt Red Ware	Gila Polychrome or later	bowl	7	X	X	4 stratitest level 4 bodies refit and match 2 bodies that refit and 1 body
116	Roosevelt Red Ware	Gila Polychrome or later	bowl	3	X	X	2 stratitest level 4 bodies refit; 1 matches

(continued)

TABLE 7.17 *(continued)*

Decorated PRV no. or catalog no.	Ware	Type	Vessel form	Sherd count	From stratigraphic column, level 9, floor, or floor feature(s)	Used in stratigraphic analysis of RRW[a]	Comment(s)
117	Roosevelt Red Ware	Gila Polychrome or later	bowl	3	X	X	3 stratitest level 4 bodies refit
118	Roosevelt Red Ware	Gila Polychrome	bowl	2	X	X	2 stratitest level 5 rims refit
119	Roosevelt Red Ware	Gila Polychrome	bowl	2	X	X	2 stratitest level 5 rims match
120	Roosevelt Red Ware	Gila Polychrome	bowl	2	X	X	2 stratitest level 5 rims match
121	Roosevelt Red Ware	Cliff or Nine Mile Polychrome	bowl	2	X	X	2 stratitest level 5 rims refit
122	Roosevelt Red Ware	Gila Polychrome	bowl	2	X	X	1 stratitest level 5 rim refits 1 body
123	Roosevelt Red Ware	Gila Polychrome	bowl	3	X	X	2 stratitest level 5 rims refit; 1 matches
124	Roosevelt Red Ware	indeterminate RRW polychrome	bowl	2	X	X	1 stratitest level 5 rim refits 1 body
125	Roosevelt Red Ware	Gila Polychrome	bowl	2	X	X	2 stratitest level 5 rims refit
126	Roosevelt Red Ware	Cliff Polychrome	bowl	2	X	X	2 stratitest level 5 necks refit
127	Roosevelt Red Ware	indeterminate RRW polychrome	bowl	2	X	X	2 stratitest level 5 bodies refit
128	Roosevelt Red Ware	Gila Polychrome or later	bowl	3	X	X	3 stratitest level 4 bodies refit
129	Roosevelt Red Ware	Gila Polychrome	bowl	2	X	X	2 stratitest level 4 rims match
130	Roosevelt Red Ware	indeterminate RRW polychrome	bowl	2	X	X	2 stratitest level 3 bodies refit
131	Roosevelt Red Ware	Gila Polychrome or later	bowl	2	X	X	2 stratitest level 1 bodies match; indeterminate exterior polychrome decoration
132	Roosevelt Red Ware	Gila Polychrome or later	bowl	2	X	X	2 stratitest level 5 bodies refit
133	Roosevelt Red Ware	Gila Polychrome	bowl	2	X	X	2 stratitest level 6 rims match
134	Roosevelt Red Ware	Gila Polychrome or later	bowl	2	X	X	2 stratitest level 6 bodies refit

135	Roosevelt Red Ware	Gila Polychrome or later	bowl	2	X	X	2 stratitest level 6 bodies refit
136	Roosevelt Red Ware	indeterminate RRW polychrome	bowl	2	X	X	2 stratitest level 6 bodies refit
137	Roosevelt Red Ware	Gila Polychrome	bowl	2	X	X	2 stratitest level 7 rims refit
138	Roosevelt Red Ware	Cliff Polychrome	bowl	3	X	X	2 stratitest level 7 rims and 1 neck refit
139	Roosevelt Red Ware	Gila Polychrome	bowl	3	X	X	2 stratitest level 8 rims and 1 body refit
140	Roosevelt Red Ware	Gila Polychrome or later	bowl	3	X	X	3 level 9 bodies match
141	Roosevelt Red Ware	Gila Polychrome or later	bowl	2	X	X	2 ventilator bodies refit
142	Roosevelt Red Ware	Gila Polychrome or later	bowl	3	X	X	3 subfloor pit bodies match; black-on-red exterior decoration
143	Roosevelt Red Ware	indeterminate RRW polychrome	jar	2	X	X	2 stratitest level 4 rims refit
144	Roosevelt Red Ware	Tonto Polychrome	jar	2	X	X	2 stratitest level 5 necks match
145	Roosevelt Red Ware	Tonto Polychrome	jar	2	X	X	2 stratitest level 5 necks match
146	Maverick Mountain Series	Maverick Mountain Polychrome	jar	5			1 fill body matches 1 T23E 11–15S neck, 1 surface rim, and 1 T12S 13–20E neck which refits 1 T17E 12S body
147	Maverick Mountain Series	Nantack Poly-chrome A	jar	4			all match: 1 level 6–8 neck, 1 T1S 20–14E neck, and 2 T1S 20–14E bodies
148	Maverick Mountain Series	Maverick Mountain Polychrome	jar	3			3 SW compartment rims refit
149	Roosevelt Red Ware	indeterminate RRW polychrome	jar	3			2 T8.5–9S 24–25E L2 rims refit and match 1 T8.5–9S 24–25E L3 rim
150	Roosevelt Red Ware	indeterminate RRW polychrome	jar	3			3 T8.5–9S 24–25E L2 necks refit
D/237	Roosevelt Red Ware	Gila Polychrome	bowl	4	X	X	2 floor rims refit and 2 bodies all refit
D/242		"Davis Black-on-red"	jar	67	X		1 foot drum rim refits 3 necks and 35 bodies and matches 1 neck that refits 5 bodies, and 20 bodies
Total				**720**			

[a]Roosevelt Red Ware

TABLE 7.18 Sherds from the stratigraphic column (stratitest levels 1–8), level 9, the floor, and the floor features of the kiva

Ware or ware-level category and/or type or type-level category	Stratitest level 1	Stratitest level 2	Stratitest level 3	Stratitest level 4	Stratitest level 5
Roosevelt Red Ware					
Cliff Black-on-red	0	0	0	0	0
Cliff Polychrome or Nine Mile Polychrome	1	3	2	2	10
Cliff Polychrome	0	1	0	5	3
Cliff Polychrome: Salmon Variety	0	0	0	0	0
Cliff Polychrome: Tonto Variety	0	0	0	0	0
Cliff Polychrome: Tucson Variety	0	0	0	0	0
Gila Black-on-red	0	0	0	0	0
Gila Polychrome	0	5	4	6	7
Gila Polychrome or later	2	7	9	44	62
Gila Polychrome or later (Salmon Variety)	0	1	0	0	0
Gila Polychrome, no banding line	0	0	0	0	0
Gila Polychrome: Gila Variety	0	0	0	0	0
Gila Polychrome: Salmon Variety	0	0	0	0	0
Gila Polychrome: Tonto Variety	0	0	0	0	0
indeterminate Roosevelt Red Ware black-on-red	1	0	0	0	1
indeterminate Roosevelt Red Ware polychrome	37	26	24	89	175
indeterminate Roosevelt Red Ware (Salmon Variety)	0	0	0	0	0
Nine Mile Polychrome	0	0	0	0	0
Nine Mile Polychrome: Safford Variety	0	0	0	0	0
Nine Mile Polychrome: Tonto Variety	0	0	0	0	0
Phoenix Polychrome	0	0	0	0	0
Pinto Black-on-red	0	0	0	0	0
Pinto Polychrome	0	0	0	0	0
Pinto Polychrome: Salmon Variety	0	0	0	0	0
Tonto Polychrome	0	1	0	2	2
Whiteriver Polychrome	1	0	0	0	0
Subtotal	*42*	*44*	*39*	*148*	*260*

Stratitest level 6	Stratitest level 7	Stratitest level 8	Stratitest level 9	Floor	Foot drum	Hearth	Subfloor pit	Ventilator	**Total**
0	0	0	0	0	0	0	1	0	**1**
1	1	1	1	0	0	0	0	2	**24**
0	0	0	0	0	0	0	1	0	**10**
0	0	0	0	0	0	0	0	0	**0**
0	0	0	0	0	0	0	0	0	**0**
0	0	0	0	0	0	0	0	0	**0**
0	0	0	0	0	0	0	0	0	**0**
3	5	4	3	0	0	1	0	0	**38**
18	13	3	11	1	1	0	1	6	**178**
0	0	0	0	0	0	0	0	0	**1**
0	0	0	0	0	0	0	0	0	**0**
0	0	0	0	0	0	0	0	0	**0**
0	0	0	0	0	0	0	0	0	**0**
0	0	0	0	0	0	0	0	0	**0**
0	0	0	0	0	0	0	0	0	**2**
64	24	12	11	6	1	2	2	11	**484**
0	0	0	0	0	0	0	0	0	**0**
0	0	0	0	0	0	0	0	0	**0**
0	0	0	0	0	0	0	0	0	**0**
0	0	0	0	0	0	0	0	0	**0**
0	0	0	0	0	0	0	0	0	**0**
0	0	0	0	0	0	0	0	0	**0**
0	0	0	2	0	0	0	0	0	**2**
0	0	0	0	0	0	0	0	0	**0**
0	1	0	0	0	0	0	0	1	**7**
0	0	0	0	0	0	0	0	0	**1**
86	*44*	*20*	*28*	*7*	*2*	*3*	*5*	*20*	***748***

(*continued*)

TABLE 7.18 *(continued)*

Ware or ware-level category and/or type or type-level category	Stratitest level 1	Stratitest level 2	Stratitest level 3	Stratitest level 4	Stratitest level 5
Maverick Mountain Series					
indeterminate Maverick Mountain Series	0	0	0	0	0
indeterminate Maverick Mountain Series black-on-red	0	0	0	0	0
indeterminate Maverick Mountain Series, Roosevelt Red Ware exterior	0	0	0	0	0
Maverick Mountain Black-on-red	0	0	0	2	1
Maverick Mountain Polychrome	0	0	0	0	0
Nantack Polychrome A (Tusayan Polychrome Analog)	0	0	0	0	0
Tucson Black-on-red	0	0	0	0	0
Tucson Black-on-red (no slip)	0	0	0	0	0
Tucson Black-on-red or Tucson Polychrome	0	0	1	0	0
Tucson Polychrome	0	0	1	0	0
Subtotal	*0*	*0*	*2*	*2*	*1*
Babocomari Polychrome	0	0	1	0	0
Subtotal	*0*	*0*	*1*	*0*	*0*
Davis Black-on-red	0	0	0	0	0
Subtotal	*0*	*0*	*0*	*0*	*0*
Dragoon or San Simon Series	0	0	0	0	0
Subtotal	*0*	*0*	*0*	*0*	*0*
indeterminate decorated	0	0	0	0	1
Subtotal	*0*	*0*	*0*	*0*	*1*
indeterminate red-on-brown	0	0	0	0	0
Subtotal	*0*	*0*	*0*	*0*	*0*
Kinishba Polychrome	0	0	0	0	0
Subtotal	*0*	*0*	*0*	*0*	*0*
Mimbres Black-on-white	0	0	0	0	0
Subtotal	*0*	*0*	*0*	*0*	*0*
San Carlos Red-on-brown	0	0	0	0	0
Subtotal	*0*	*0*	*0*	*0*	*0*
Total	**42**	**44**	**42**	**150**	**262**

Stratitest level 6	Stratitest level 7	Stratitest level 8	Stratitest level 9	Floor	Foot drum	Hearth	Subfloor pit	Ventilator	**Total**
0	0	0	0	0	0	0	0	0	**0**
0	0	0	0	0	0	0	0	0	**0**
0	0	0	0	0	0	0	0	0	**0**
0	0	0	0	0	0	0	0	0	**3**
0	0	0	0	0	0	0	0	0	**0**
0	0	0	0	0	0	0	0	0	**0**
0	0	0	0	0	0	0	0	0	**0**
0	0	0	0	0	0	0	0	0	**0**
0	0	0	0	0	0	0	0	0	**1**
0	1	2	1	0	0	0	0	1	**6**
0	*1*	*2*	*1*	*0*	*0*	*0*	*0*	*1*	***10***
0	0	0	0	0	0	0	0	0	**1**
0	*0*	*0*	*0*	*0*	*0*	*0*	*0*	*0*	***1***
0	0	0	0	0	0	0	0	0	**0**
0	*0*	*0*	*0*	*0*	*0*	*0*	*0*	*0*	***0***
0	0	0	0	0	0	0	0	1	**1**
0	*0*	*0*	*0*	*0*	*0*	*0*	*0*	*1*	***1***
0	0	0	0	0	0	0	0	0	**1**
0	*0*	*0*	*0*	*0*	*0*	*0*	*0*	*0*	***1***
0	0	0	0	0	0	0	0	0	**0**
0	*0*	*0*	*0*	*0*	*0*	*0*	*0*	*0*	***0***
0	0	0	0	0	0	0	0	0	**0**
0	*0*	*0*	*0*	*0*	*0*	*0*	*0*	*0*	***0***
0	0	0	0	0	0	0	0	0	**0**
0	*0*	*0*	*0*	*0*	*0*	*0*	*0*	*0*	***0***
0	0	0	0	0	0	0	0	0	**0**
0	*0*	*0*	*0*	*0*	*0*	*0*	*0*	*0*	***0***
86	**45**	**22**	**29**	**7**	**2**	**3**	**5**	**22**	**761**

TABLE 7.20 Roosevelt Red Ware partially reconstructible vessels (PRVs), from the kiva, with fragments recovered from multiple stratitest levels

Kiva decorated PRV no.	Type	Form	Stratitest levels represented
1	Whiteriver Polychrome	bowl	1, 2, 3, 4
3	Gila Polychrome	bowl	6, 7
5	Cliff Polychrome	bowl	5, 6
6	Gila Polychrome	bowl	7, 8
15	Gila Polychrome	jar	4, 5
18	Tonto Polychrome	jar	4, 5
21	Gila Polychrome	jar	5, 6
23	Gila Polychrome	bowl	4, 5, 6
110	Gila Polychrome	bowl	6, 7

TABLE 7.21 Whole, reconstructible, and partially reconstructible painted vessels, from within and beneath the kiva, recovered and recorded by Rex Gerald, by context

Ware or ware-level category and/or type or type-level category	Burial 4	Burial 5	Burial 8	Burial 9	Burial subtotal	Level 9, floor, and floor features	**Total**
Roosevelt Red Ware							
Cliff Black-on-red	0	0	0	0	0	0	**0**
Cliff Polychrome or Nine Mile Polychrome	0	0	0	0	0	0	**0**
Cliff Polychrome	3	0	0	0	3	0	**3**
Cliff Polychrome: Salmon Variety	0	0	0	0	0	0	**0**
Cliff Polychrome: Tonto Variety	0	0	0	0	0	0	**0**
Cliff Polychrome: Tucson Variety	0	0	0	0	0	0	**0**
Gila Black-on-red	0	0	0	0	0	0	**0**
Gila Polychrome	4	1	2	1	8	1	**9**
Gila Polychrome or later	0	0	0	0	0	0	**0**
Gila Polychrome or later (Salmon Variety)	1	0	0	0	1	0	**1**

(continued)

TABLE 7.21 *(continued)*

Ware or ware-level category and/or type or type-level category	Burial 4	Burial 5	Burial 8	Burial 9	Burial subtotal	Level 9, floor, and floor features	**Total**
Gila Polychrome, no banding line	0	0	0	0	0	0	**0**
Gila Polychrome: Gila Variety	0	0	0	0	0	0	**0**
Gila Polychrome: Salmon Variety	0	0	0	0	0	0	**0**
Gila Polychrome: Tonto Variety	0	0	0	0	0	0	**0**
indeterminate Roosevelt Red Ware black-on-red	0	0	0	0	0	0	**0**
indeterminate Roosevelt Red Ware polychrome	0	0	0	0	0	0	**0**
indeterminate Roosevelt Red Ware (Salmon Variety)	0	0	0	0	0	0	**0**
Nine Mile Polychrome	0	0	0	0	0	0	**0**
Nine Mile Polychrome: Safford Variety	0	0	0	0	0	0	**0**
Nine Mile Polychrome: Tonto Variety	0	0	0	0	0	0	**0**
Phoenix Polychrome	1	0	0	0	1	0	**1**
Pinto Black-on-red	0	0	0	0	0	0	**0**
Pinto Polychrome	0	0	0	0	0	0	**0**
Pinto Polychrome: Salmon Variety	0	0	0	0	0	0	**0**
Tonto Polychrome	0	0	0	0	0	0	**0**
Whiteriver Polychrome	0	0	0	0	0	0	**0**
Subtotal	*9*	*1*	*2*	*1*	*13*	*1*	***14***
Maverick Mountain Series							
indeterminate Maverick Mountain Series	0	0	0	0	0	0	**0**
indeterminate Maverick Mountain Series black-on-red	0	0	0	0	0	0	**0**

(continued)

TABLE 7.21 (*continued*)

Ware or ware-level category and/or type or type-level category	Burial 4	Burial 5	Burial 8	Burial 9	Burial subtotal	Level 9, floor, and floor features	**Total**
indeterminate Maverick Mountain Series, Roosevelt Red Ware exterior	0	0	0	0	0	0	**0**
Maverick Mountain Black-on-red	0	0	0	0	0	0	**0**
Maverick Mountain Polychrome	0	0	0	0	0	0	**0**
Nantack Polychrome A (Tusayan Polychrome analog)	0	0	0	0	0	0	**0**
Tucson Black-on-red	0	0	0	0	0	0	**0**
Tucson Black-on-red (no slip)	0	0	0	0	0	0	**0**
Tucson Black-on-red or Tucson Polychrome	0	0	0	0	0	0	**0**
Tucson Polychrome	0	0	0	1	1	0	**1**
Subtotal	*0*	*0*	*0*	*1*	*1*	*0*	***1***
Babocomari Polychrome	0	0	0	0	0	0	**0**
Subtotal	*0*	*0*	*0*	*0*	*0*	*0*	***0***
Davis Black-on-red	0	0	0	0	0	1	**1**
Subtotal	*0*	*0*	*0*	*0*	*0*	*1*	***1***
Dragoon or San Simon Series	0	0	0	0	0	0	**0**
Subtotal	*0*	*0*	*0*	*0*	*0*	*0*	***0***
indeterminate decorated	0	0	0	0	0	0	**0**
Subtotal	*0*	*0*	*0*	*0*	*0*	*0*	***0***
indeterminate red-on-brown	0	0	0	0	0	0	**0**
Subtotal	*0*	*0*	*0*	*0*	*0*	*0*	***0***
Kinishba Polychrome	0	0	0	0	0	0	**0**
Subtotal	*0*	*0*	*0*	*0*	*0*	*0*	***0***
Mimbres Black-on-white	0	0	0	0	0	0	**0**
Subtotal	*0*	*0*	*0*	*0*	*0*	*0*	***0***
San Carlos Red-on-brown	0	0	0	0	0	0	**0**
Subtotal	*0*	*0*	*0*	*0*	*0*	*0*	***0***
Total	**9**	**1**	**2**	**2**	**14**	**2**	**16**

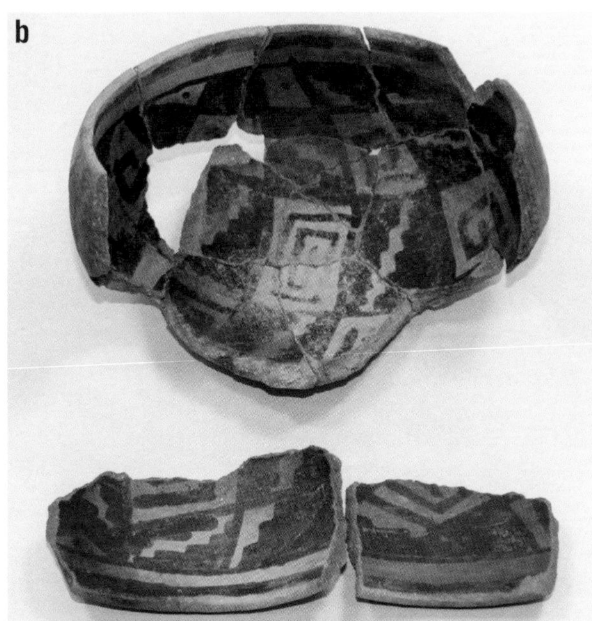

FIGURE 7.28 Partially reconstructible Gila Polychrome bowls from the kiva: (a) Decorated Vessel 3, (b) Decorated Vessel 23, (c) Decorated Vessel 25, (d) D/237. For D/237 measurements, see table 6.1. Photographs by Patrick D. Lyons.

FIGURE 7.29 Partially reconstructible Gila Polychrome jars from the kiva: (a) Decorated Vessel 15, (b) Decorated Vessel 21, (c) Decorated Vessel 26, (d) Decorated Vessel 27. Photographs by Patrick D. Lyons (a–c) and Samantha G. Fladd (d).

Smaller percentages of the sample (accounting for between 1% and 3%) were identified, in decreasing order of frequency, as Cliff or Nine Mile Polychrome, Cliff Polychrome (figure 7.30a), and Tonto Polychrome (figure 7.30b). Traces of Phoenix and Whiteriver Polychrome are present (figure 7.31a, b), as well as Pinto Polychrome (figure 7.31c). As a group, the start dates for these types span the period from the late AD 1200s to the late 1300s. As discussed above, a possible specimen of the post-AD 1390 type Dinwiddie Polychrome was also recovered.

The Maverick Mountain Series sample from these contexts is dominated by Tucson Polychrome, which accounts for nearly 60%. One-third was identified as Maverick Mountain Black-on-red. Single specimens of each of the following round out the sample: indeterminate decorated, Davis Black-on-red, and Dragoon or San Simon Series.

Stratigraphic patterns are evident in the Roosevelt Red Ware sample, although additional discussion of units of analysis is required before these trends can be addressed. Gerald used a wide variety of recovery units that can be combined analytically in many ways (see table 7.3). Stratitest levels 1–8, as a group, represent a logical focus for the investigation of temporal trends. However, the search for conjoins

FIGURE 7.30 Partially reconstructible vessels from the kiva: (a) Decorated Vessel 5, Cliff Polychrome bowl; (b) Decorated Vessel 83, Tonto Polychrome jar. Photographs by Patrick D. Lyons.

FIGURE 7.31 Partially reconstructible vessels from the kiva: (a) Decorated Vessel 1, Whiteriver Polychrome bowl; (b) Decorated Vessel 9, Whiteriver Polychrome bowl; (c) Decorated Vessel 11, Pinto Polychrome bowl. Photographs by Patrick D. Lyons.

TABLE 7.26 Roosevelt Red Ware partially reconstructible vessels (PRVs) from the kiva, with fragments recovered from level 9, the floor, and floor features

Kiva decorated PRV no.	Type	Form	Recovery units represented
7	Gila Polychrome	bowl	Level 9, Ventilator
9	Whiteriver Polychrome	bowl	Level 9, Ventilator
10	Gila Polychrome	bowl	Level 9, Floor
11	Pinto Polychrome	bowl	Level 9, Foot drum, Ventilator

Polychrome. Sherd size hinders the separation of these two types, and data in table 7.25 show that this is clearly an issue affecting the sample from the kiva.

Kiva level 9, the floor, and the floor features, in some sense, represent one behaviorally meaningful unit, in that many partially reconstructible vessels include sherds from two or more of these contexts (tables 7.26, 7.27). Although level 9, the floor, and the floor features as a group are not strictly comparable to the levels of the stratigraphic column, there is some value in including the data from them in additional quantitative comparisons. Because level 9 (150–160 cm, outside the stratigraphic column) overlaps stratitest level 8 (140–160 cm in the stratigraphic column), and because stratitest levels 7 and 8 are already treated as a single analytical unit, I have grouped data from stratitest levels 7 and 8, level 9, the floor, and the floor features in table 7.28. The increase over time in Cliff Polychrome and Cliff or Nine Mile Polychrome holds under this grouping scheme.

There is additional value in considering level 9, the floor, and the floor features as a unit, in that Cliff Polychrome and Whiteriver Polychrome are present, yet no definitive Nine Mile Polychrome was recovered and Phoenix Polychrome is absent. These facts lend further support to the seriation-based revisions of Roosevelt Red Ware discussed above. It is fortunate that observable patterns in these data remain, given the amount of churning of deposits that likely accompanied the use of the kiva as a cemetery.

In addition to the decorated pottery just discussed, the kiva yielded 34 of the 51 partially reconstructible perforated plates identified (see tables 7.15, F.9). One of these, Vessel 23, consists of a sherd from Room 17 and two from the kiva. Another, Vessel 29, is made up of eight sherds from the kiva and one from Room 18.

TABLE 7.27 Roosevelt Red Ware rim sherds, neck sherds, and partially reconstructible vessels recovered from level 9, the floor, and the floor features of the kiva

Type	*n*	%
Cliff Black-on-red	1	4.17
Cliff Polychrome and Cliff or Nine Mile Polychrome	5	20.83
Gila Black-on-red	0	0.00
Gila Polychrome	9	37.50
Gila Polychrome or later	0	0.00
indeterminate Roosevelt Red Ware black-on-red	0	0.00
indeterminate Roosevelt Red Ware polychrome	5	20.83
Phoenix Polychrome	0	0.00
Pinto Polychrome	3	12.50
Tonto Polychrome	0	0.00
Whiteriver Polychrome	1	4.17
Total	**24**	**100.00**

TABLE 7.28 Roosevelt Red Ware rim sherds, neck sherds, and partially reconstructible vessels recovered from the stratigraphic column, as well as level 9, the floor, and the floor features of the kiva

	Stratitest levels 1–3		Stratitest levels 4–6		Stratitest levels 7–8, level 9, floor, and floor features		**Total**
Type(s)	*n*	%	*n*	%	*n*	%	**(*n*)**
Cliff Black-on-red	0	0.00	0	0.00	1	2.13	**1**
Cliff Polychrome and Cliff or Nine Mile Polychrome	7	26.92	27	23.89	9	19.15	**43**
Gila Black-on-red	1	3.85	0	0.00	0	0.00	**1**
Gila Polychrome	9	34.62	30	26.55	18	38.30	**57**
Gila Polychrome or later	0	0.00	1	0.88	0	0.00	**1**
indeterminate Roosevelt Red Ware black-on-red	0	0.00	1	0.88	0	0.00	**1**
indeterminate Roosevelt Red Ware polychrome	8	30.77	48	42.48	14	29.79	**70**
Phoenix Polychrome	0	0.00	1	0.88	0	0.00	**1**
Pinto Polychrome	0	0.00	0	0.00	3	6.38	**3**
Tonto Polychrome	0	0.00	5	4.42	1	2.13	**6**
Whiteriver Polychrome	1	3.85	0	0.00	1	2.13	**2**
Total	**26**	**100.00**	**113**	**100.00**	**47**	**100.00**	**186**

Note: Specimens recovered from stratitest levels 7 and 8 are grouped with those from level 9, the floor, and the floor features.

Houseblock I: Rooms 3–11

As discussed above, the pueblo (Houseblocks I, II, VI, and VII and Rooms 2, 34, 36, 46, and 48) is inferred to predate Houseblocks IV and V. All of the Pinto Polychrome (n = 11) and Pinto Black-on-red (n = 1) specimens (sherds and partially reconstructible vessels) recovered from surface architecture were found in pueblo contexts (see tables 7.2, F.2–F.5). In addition, the pueblo yielded nearly three-quarters of the early Maverick Mountain Series specimens (n = 15) found in surface structures. Another 20% of the Maverick Mountain Series specimens from surface architecture were recovered from Houseblock V, but as previously indicated, these most likely represent trash generated by people living in the pueblo.

Houseblock I is inferred to have been the first of the pueblo room blocks built at the Davis Ranch Site and also the first unit of surface architecture to be used as a trash dump. Nearly half of the Pinto Polychrome specimens from surface structures were found in this group of rooms, as were more than half of the Maverick Mountain Series specimens and the single Pinto Black-on-red specimen. These ceramic patterns are not unexpected, given the apparent evolution of Houseblock I out of the underlying Classic period pit structures, House 3 and House 7.

Nineteen partially reconstructible vessels in the Davis Ranch Site decorated pottery assemblage are composed of fragments recovered from two or more structures. Eleven of these were recovered from Houseblock I contexts (n = 9; table 7.29) and one of the underlying pit houses, House 7 (n = 2). The partially reconstructible vessels from the pit structures are discussed above. In table 7.29, the partially reconstructible vessels and other notable finds from Houseblock I are addressed.

Room 3

Eight partially reconstructible decorated vessels comprising 28 sherds were identified in the assemblage from Room 3 (see table 7.29). One of these, Vessel 2, an indeterminate Roosevelt Red Ware polychrome jar, includes sherds from adjacent Room 4. Vessel 2 and three others (Vessels 3, 7, and 8) are composed of sherds from both Room 3 and the trench in front of Room 3.

Room 4

As discussed above, Room 4 was identified as a member of Group B, the second-earliest set of architectural units or features to be used as trash dumps, based on a seriation of assemblages from the 10 Classic period structures or loci with the highest sherd frequencies (all more than 500 sherds). Room 4 yielded 11 partially reconstructible decorated vessels represented by 92 sherds (see table 7.29). Four specimens are particularly noteworthy. Vessel 1 is a partially reconstructible Nine Mile Polychrome: Tonto Variety bowl (figure 7.33a, b). Vessel 2 is a partially reconstructible Gila Polychrome bowl comprising 50 sherds (figure 7.33c). Another partially reconstructible Gila Polychrome bowl, Vessel 3, is composed of sherds from Room 4 and the adjacent Room 6 (figure 7.33d). Vessel 4, a partially reconstructible Gila Polychrome bowl with no banding line, includes sherds from Room 4 and the fill of House 7. A partially reconstructible decorated vessel that links Room 4, Room 5, and House 3 is discussed below in the section devoted to Room 5.

Room 4 contexts yielded three partially reconstructible perforated plates (see table F.9). Vessels 47 and 50 were found in fill deposits and Vessel 46 was recovered from below the floor of the structure. Vessel 47 comprises two conjoining sherds, one from Room 4 and the other from a trench to the east of Room 2 and north of House 2 (T26E 0–9N).

Room 5

Room 5 yielded six partially reconstructible decorated vessels, comprising 28 sherds (see table 7.29). Two of these, Vessels 1 and 2, are Cliff Polychrome bowls. Vessel 2 is a specimen of Cliff Polychrome: Tonto Variety. Vessel 6, a partially reconstructible Tonto Polychrome jar, consists of a rim from the fill of Room 5, a neck sherd from the fill of Room 4, and a neck sherd from House 3.

TABLE 7.29 Decorated partially reconstructible vessels (PRVs) recovered from the rooms and subjected to reanalysis

Houseblock no.	Room no.	Decorated PRV or catalog no.	Ware	Type	Vessel form	Sherd count	Comment(s)
I	3	1	Roosevelt Red Ware	Gila Polychrome	bowl	6	4 floor bodies refit and match 2 rims
		2[a]	Roosevelt Red Ware	indeterminate polychrome	jar	4	2 trench in front bodies refit 1 neck and match 1 Room 4 stratitest level 4 body
		3	Roosevelt Red Ware	Gila Polychrome	bowl	7	2 trench in front rims match and match 5 bodies that refit
		4	Maverick Mountain Series	Maverick Mountain Black-on-red	bowl	2	2 floor bodies match
		5	Roosevelt Red Ware	Cliff Polychrome	bowl	2	2 floor rims refit
		6	Roosevelt Red Ware	Tonto Polychrome	jar	3	2 fill necks refit and match 1 neck
		7	Roosevelt Red Ware	Cliff Polychrome	bowl	2	1 trench in front rim refits 1 neck
		8	Roosevelt Red Ware	indeterminate polychrome	jar	2	2 trench in front bodies refit
	4	1	Roosevelt Red Ware	Nine Mile Polychrome: Tonto Variety	bowl	12	1 stratitest level 4 neck refits 1 body and matches 5 stratitest level 4 bodies and 1 neck that refit, 2 stratitest level 4 bodies, 1 stratitest level 4 rim, and 1 fill body
		2	Roosevelt Red Ware	Gila Polychrome	bowl	50	4 floor rims and 26 floor bodies refit and match 1 stratitest level 4 rim that refits 3 stratitest level 4 bodies, 3 floor bodies that refit, 2 floor bodies that refit, 4 floor bodies that refit, 2 floor bodies that refit, 4 floor bodies, and 1 stratitest level 4 body
		3[a]	Roosevelt Red Ware	Gila Polychrome	bowl	10	4 stratitest level 4 rims and 4 bodies refit and match 1 Room 6 fill rim and 1 Room 6 fill body

	4[a]	Roosevelt Red Ware	Gila Polychrome, no banding line	bowl	2	1 fill rim matches 1 House 7 fill rim
	5	Roosevelt Red Ware	indeterminate polychrome	jar	2	2 fill bodies refit
	6	Roosevelt Red Ware	Gila Polychrome or later	bowl	4	3 floor bodies refit and match 1 body
	7	Roosevelt Red Ware	indeterminate polychrome	bowl	3	2 stratitest level 4 bodies refit and match 1 body
	8	Roosevelt Red Ware	indeterminate polychrome	bowl	2	2 stratitest level 4 bodies refit
	9	Roosevelt Red Ware	indeterminate polychrome	jar	2	1 stratitest level 4 body refits 1 stratitest level 1 body
	10	Maverick Mountain Series	Tucson Black-on-red	jar	2	2 subfloor bodies match
	11	Maverick Mountain Series	Tucson Polychrome	bowl	3	3 subfloor bodies match
5	1	Roosevelt Red Ware	Cliff Polychrome	bowl	12	2 fill rims and 6 bodies refit and match 2 rims and 2 bodies
	2	Roosevelt Red Ware	Cliff Polychrome: Tonto Variety	bowl	2	2 fill rims match
	3	Roosevelt Red Ware	indeterminate polychrome	bowl	2	2 fill bodies refit
	4	Roosevelt Red Ware	indeterminate polychrome	bowl	7	7 fill bodies match
	5	Roosevelt Red Ware	indeterminate polychrome	jar	2	2 fill bodies refit

(*continued*)

TABLE 7.29 *(continued)*

Houseblock no.	Room no.	Decorated PRV or catalog no.	Ware	Type	Vessel form	Sherd count	Comment(s)
		6[a]	Roosevelt Red Ware	Tonto Polychrome	jar	3	1 fill rim matches 1 Room 4 fill neck that refits 1 House 3 neck
	6	1[a]	Roosevelt Red Ware	Cliff Polychrome	bowl	13	2 stratitest level 1 rims refit 1 fill rim and match 1 fill rim, 2 fill bodies, 3 fill bodies that refit, 1 stratitest level 1 rim, 1 trench in front body, 1 fill body, and 1 Room 4 fill body
		2[a]	Roosevelt Red Ware	Cliff Polychrome	bowl	17	2 fill rims refit and match 1 fill neck, 13 fill bodies, and 1 Room 4 stratitest level 4 neck
		3[a]	Roosevelt Red Ware	Gila Polychrome	jar	28	1 Room 4 fill rim refits 1 Room 6 fill rim and matches 6 Room 6 fill bodies, 1 neck, and 1 rim, 6 Room 4 fill bodies and 3 Room 4 fill necks, all of which refit; 2 Room 4 fill bodies; 1 Room 4 fill neck; 1 Room 4 fill rim; 2 Room 6 fill bodies; 1 Room 6 fill neck; 1 Room 6 stratitest level 3 neck; and 1 Room 6 body
		4	Roosevelt Red Ware	Gila Polychrome or later	bowl	3	1 stratitest level 1 body matches 1 stratitest level 2 body and 1 trench in front body
		5	Roosevelt Red Ware	indeterminate polychrome	jar	2	2 stratitest level 3 bodies refit
		6	Maverick Mountain Series	Tucson Black-on-red	jar	2	2 fill necks refit
		7	Roosevelt Red Ware	Cliff Polychrome	bowl	2	1 fill rim and 1 neck refit
		8	Roosevelt Red Ware	Gila Polychrome	bowl	2	2 fill rims refit
		9	Roosevelt Red Ware	Gila Polychrome	bowl	2	2 fill rims refit

	10	Roosevelt Red Ware	Gila Polychrome or later	bowl	3	2 fill bodies and 1 stratitest level 3 body refit
	11	Roosevelt Red Ware	indeterminate polychrome	jar	2	2 fill bodies refit
	12	Roosevelt Red Ware	indeterminate polychrome	bowl	2	2 stratitest level 1 bodies match
7	1	Roosevelt Red Ware	Gila Polychrome	bowl	11	2 floor rims and 9 bodies refit
	2	Roosevelt Red Ware	Gila Polychrome	bowl	5	2 floor rims, 2 floor bodies, and 1 stratitest level 2 body refit
	3[a]	Roosevelt Red Ware	Whiteriver Polychrome	bowl	3	1 fill rim refits 1 Room 4 stratitest level 2 rim and matches 1 Room 11 trench in front rim
	4	Roosevelt Red Ware	Gila Polychrome	jar	70	16 floor rims, 12 necks, and 12 bodies refit and match: 1 floor neck, 1 fill neck, 3 floor bodies, 1 fill body, and 1 stratitest level 2 body, which all refit; 2 floor bodies that refit; 2 floor bodies that refit; 2 floor bodies that refit; 12 floor bodies; 3 floor necks; 1 fill body; and 1 neck of indeterminate provenience
	5	Roosevelt Red Ware	Gila Polychrome	jar	4	1 floor neck, 2 floor bodies, and 1 fill body refit
	6	Roosevelt Red Ware	indeterminate polychrome	jar	4	2 floor bodies refit and match 1 floor body and 1 fill body
	7[a]	Roosevelt Red Ware	Gila Polychrome	jar	11	2 trench in front necks refit 2 bodies and match 3 trench in front necks, 2 trench in front bodies that refit, 1 trench in front body, and 1 Room 11 stratitest level 3 body

(continued)

TABLE 7.29 *(continued)*

Houseblock no.	Room no.	Decorated PRV or catalog no.	Ware	Type	Vessel form	Sherd count	Comment(s)
		8	Roosevelt Red Ware	Gila Polychrome	jar	16	9 floor bodies refit and refit 1 stratitest level 2 body and match: 1 trench in front neck and 1 body, which refit; 3 trench in front necks; and 1 floor body
		9	Roosevelt Red Ware	Nine Mile Polychrome: Tonto Variety	bowl	10	2 stratitest level 2 rims, 1 stratitest level 1 rim, 1 fill rim and 6 stratitest level 2 bodies refit
		10	Roosevelt Red Ware	Gila Polychrome or later	bowl	2	2 fill bodies match
		11	Roosevelt Red Ware	indeterminate polychrome	jar	4	2 floor bodies refit and 2 floor bodies match
	8	1	Roosevelt Red Ware	Gila Polychrome	bowl	3	1 trench in front rim and 2 bodies refit
		2	Roosevelt Red Ware	indeterminate polychrome	jar	4	4 subfloor necks match
	9	1	Roosevelt Red Ware	Gila Polychrome	bowl	8	4 trench in front rims and 2 bodies refit and match 2 bodies that refit
		2	Maverick Mountain Series	Maverick Mountain Black-on-red	jar	5	2 subfloor necks and 2 bodies refit and match 1 body
		3	Roosevelt Red Ware	Gila Polychrome	jar	19	1 fill neck refits 3 fill bodies and 2 trench in front bodies and matches: 1 trench in front rim that refits 1 neck, 3 fill bodies that refit, 2 trench in front bodies that refit, and 6 trench in front bodies
		4	Roosevelt Red Ware	Cliff or Nine Mile Polychrome	bowl	2	1 fill rim and 1 fill neck match

	5	Roosevelt Red Ware	indeterminate polychrome	jar	3	1 fill rim and 2 bodies match
	6	Roosevelt Red Ware	Gila Polychrome or later	bowl	2	2 subfloor bodies match
10	1	Roosevelt Red Ware	Gila Polychrome	bowl	10	4 fill rims and 2 bodies refit and match 2 rims that refit and 2 bodies
	2	Roosevelt Red Ware	Gila Polychrome or later	bowl	6	2 fill bodies refit and match 3 fill bodies that refit and 1 floor body
	3	Roosevelt Red Ware	Gila Polychrome or later	bowl	2	1 floor body matches 1 fill body
	4	Roosevelt Red Ware	indeterminate black-on-red	bowl	3	2 fill rims match and match 1 floor body
	5	Roosevelt Red Ware	indeterminate polychrome	jar	5	3 floor bodies refit and match 2 fill necks that refit
	6	Roosevelt Red Ware	Gila Polychrome	bowl	2	1 fill rim refits 1 fill body
	7	Roosevelt Red Ware	Gila Polychrome	bowl	2	1 fill rim refits 1 fill body
	8	Roosevelt Red Ware	Gila Polychrome or later	bowl	3	3 fill bodies match; indeterminate exterior polychrome decoration
	9	Roosevelt Red Ware	Tonto Polychrome	jar	2	2 fill necks refit
	10	Roosevelt Red Ware	Whiteriver Polychrome	bowl	2	1 fill rim matches 1 stratitest level 2 rim
	11	Roosevelt Red Ware	Gila Polychrome	bowl	3	2 floor rims and 1 body refit
	12	Roosevelt Red Ware	Gila Polychrome or later	bowl	2	2 stratitest level 3 bodies refit
	13	Roosevelt Red Ware	indeterminate polychrome	jar	2	2 stratitest level 3 necks match

(continued)

TABLE 7.29 *(continued)*

Houseblock no.	Room no.	Decorated PRV or catalog no.	Ware	Type	Vessel form	Sherd count	Comment(s)
		14	Roosevelt Red Ware	Gila Polychrome or later	bowl	4	4 trench in front bodies refit
	11	1	Roosevelt Red Ware	Gila Polychrome	bowl	8	1 trench in front rim matches 2 bodies that refit and 5 bodies
		2	Roosevelt Red Ware	indeterminate polychrome	jar	2	2 trench in front necks refit
II	14	1[a]	Roosevelt Red Ware	Cliff Polychrome	bowl	19	2 T24E 20–21S rims, 2 necks, and 1 body refit and match: 1 T24E 20–21S rim; 1 Room 17 fill rim and 1 neck, which refit; 1 T24E 20–21S rim; 1 T24E 20–21S rim and 1 neck that refit; 1 T24E neck; 1 Room 14 fill body; 2 T24E 20–21S bodies; 1 Room 15 fill body; and 3 Room 17 fill bodies
		2	Roosevelt Red Ware	Whiteriver Polychrome	bowl	3	1 T24E 20–21S rim and 1 Room 14 fill body refit and match 1 T24E 20–21S body
		3[a]	Roosevelt Red Ware	Gila Polychrome	jar	8	2 T24E 20–21S necks refit and match: 2 Room 14 fill necks that refit; 1 Room 14 fill neck; and 1 rim, 1 neck, and 1 body, all from Room 15 fill
		4	Roosevelt Red Ware	indeterminate polychrome	bowl	2	2 fill bodies refit
		5	Roosevelt Red Ware	indeterminate polychrome	jar	2	2 fill bodies refit

	6	Roosevelt Red Ware	indeterminate polychrome	bowl	2	2 1 T24E 20–21S bodies refit
15	1	Roosevelt Red Ware	Tonto Polychrome	jar	3	2 fill necks refit and 1 matches
16	1	Roosevelt Red Ware	Gila Polychrome or later	bowl	2	2 floor bodies refit
	2	Roosevelt Red Ware	Gila Polychrome or later	bowl	2	1 fill body refits 1 stratitest level 2 body
	D/239	Roosevelt Red Ware	Gila Polychrome	bowl	9	3 fill rims and 6 bodies refit
17	1[a]	Roosevelt Red Ware	Gila Polychrome	bowl	5	2 floor rims and 2 bodies refit and match 1 body from T24E, 20–21S (Room 14)
	2	Roosevelt Red Ware	Gila Polychrome or later	bowl	2	2 fill bodies match
	3	Roosevelt Red Ware	Gila Polychrome or later	bowl	2	2 floor bodies match
19	1[a]	Roosevelt Red Ware	indeterminate polychrome	jar	7	2 fill bodies, 1 neck, and 1 rim match and match 2 Room 35 fill bodies and 1 Room 33 trench in front (Room 35) neck
	2	Roosevelt Red Ware	Gila Polychrome or later	bowl	2	2 fill bodies match
	3	Roosevelt Red Ware	Gila Polychrome or later	bowl	2	2 fill bodies refit
	4	Roosevelt Red Ware	indeterminate polychrome	jar	2	2 fill rims refit
20	1	Roosevelt Red Ware	Gila Polychrome	bowl	2	1 fill rim matches 1 body
21	1	Maverick Mountain Series	Tucson Black-on-red	bowl	2	2 fill bodies match

(*continued*)

TABLE 7.29 *(continued)*

Houseblock no.	Room no.	Decorated PRV or catalog no.	Ware	Type	Vessel form	Sherd count	Comment(s)
		2	Roosevelt Red Ware	indeterminate polychrome	jar	2	2 trench in front bodies refit
		3	Roosevelt Red Ware	indeterminate polychrome	jar	2	2 trench in front bodies refit and match 1 body
		4	Roosevelt Red Ware	indeterminate polychrome	jar	2	2 fill bodies refit
		D/238	Roosevelt Red Ware	Cliff Polychrome	bowl	3	1 trench in front rim refits 2 bodies
	33	1	Roosevelt Red Ware	Gila Polychrome	bowl	5	1 fill rim and 3 bodies refit and match 1 body
		2	Maverick Mountain Series	Tucson Black-on-red	bowl	2	2 fill bodies match
		3	Roosevelt Red Ware	Gila Polychrome or later	bowl	2	2 fill bodies refit
		4	Roosevelt Red Ware	Gila Polychrome or later	bowl	8	8 fill bodies refit
		5	Roosevelt Red Ware	Gila Polychrome or later	bowl	7	6 fill bodies refit and match 1 body
		6	Roosevelt Red Ware	Gila Polychrome or later	bowl	2	2 fill bodies match
		7	Roosevelt Red Ware	indeterminate polychrome	bowl	2	2 fill bodies refit
		8	Roosevelt Red Ware	indeterminate polychrome	jar	3	3 fill bodies match

		9	Roosevelt Red Ware	indeterminate polychrome	jar	2	2 fill necks match
		10	Roosevelt Red Ware	indeterminate polychrome	jar	2	2 fill bodies match
		11	Roosevelt Red Ware	indeterminate polychrome	jar	3	3 fill necks match
	35	1	Roosevelt Red Ware	Gila Polychrome	bowl	3	1 Room 33 trench in front rim and 2 bodies refit
		2	Roosevelt Red Ware	Gila Polychrome	bowl	3	2 Room 33 trench in front rims and 1 body refit
		3	Maverick Mountain Series	Maverick Mountain Black-on-red	jar	5	1 Room 33 trench in front rim matches 4 bodies, which refit, and 1 body
		4[a]	Roosevelt Red Ware	Gila Polychrome	jar	34	1 Room 33 trench in front rim, 4 necks, and 4 bodies refit and match: 1 Room 33 trench in front neck, 10 bodies, and 1 Room 33 fill body, which refit; 5 Room 33 trench in front bodies, which refit; 1 Room 33 trench in front rim, 2 necks, and 3 bodies; 1 Room 33 fill neck; and 1 Room 33 fill body
		5	Maverick Mountain Series	Tucson Black-on-red	jar	2	2 Room 35 trench in front bodies refit
		6	Maverick Mountain Series	Tucson Black-on-red	bowl	3	3 Room 35 fill bodies refit; hatched design like Maverick Mountain Polychrome, but exterior decoration only, like Tucson Polychrome
III	28	1[a]	Roosevelt Red Ware	Cliff Polychrome	bowl	11	2 fill rims, 2 necks and 4 bodies refit and match 3 Room 27 fill bodies, which refit; probably Gila Style exterior polychrome decoration
		2	Maverick Mountain Series	Maverick Mountain Black-on-red	jar	4	2 fill bodies refit and match 2 bodies
V	44	1	Roosevelt Red Ware	indeterminate polychrome	jar	3	1 fill rim refits 1 subfloor rim and matches 1 fill neck

(*continued*)

TABLE 7.29 *(continued)*

Houseblock no.	Room no.	Decorated PRV or catalog no.	Ware	Type	Vessel form	Sherd count	Comment(s)
		2	Roosevelt Red Ware	indeterminate polychrome	bowl	2	2 fill bodies refit
VI	47	1	Roosevelt Red Ware	Gila Polychrome or later	bowl	2	2 T3–5W 43S bodies refit
		2	Roosevelt Red Ware	indeterminate polychrome	jar	3	1 T44S 5W neck refits 1 body and matches 1 body
VII	45	1	Maverick Mountain Series	Tucson Polychrome	bowl	7	3 T22W 1S rims refit and match 1 rim and 3 bodies
n/a	2	1	Roosevelt Red Ware	Gila Polychrome	bowl	6	2 fill rims and 4 bodies refit
		2	Roosevelt Red Ware	Gila Polychrome	bowl	5	2 floor rims and 2 bodies refit and match 1 Room 2 rim; no framing line
		3	Roosevelt Red Ware	indeterminate polychrome	bowl	8	1 fill rim, 1 fill body, and 1 T10N 10–11E body refit and match: 1 fill rim and 2 T10N 10–11E bodies that refit, 1 fill rim, and 1 T10N 10–11E body; miniature; interior abraded away; Gila Variety exterior
		4	Roosevelt Red Ware	Cliff Polychrome	bowl	6	3 fill necks and 3 bodies refit
		5	Roosevelt Red Ware	Nine Mile Polychrome	bowl	5	4 fill necks and 1 T10N 10–11E neck match
		6	Roosevelt Red Ware	indeterminate polychrome	jar	6	3 fill necks refit and match 1 neck and 2 bodies
		7	Roosevelt Red Ware	indeterminate polychrome	jar	4	1 fill neck and 2 bodies refit and match 1 neck

	8	Roosevelt Red Ware	indeterminate polychrome	jar	5	4 floor bodies refit and match 1 body
	9	Roosevelt Red Ware	Cliff Polychrome	bowl	2	1 fill rim matches 1 neck; indeterminate exterior polychrome decoration
	10	Roosevelt Red Ware	Cliff Polychrome	bowl	2	1 fill rim matches 1 T10N 10–11E neck
	11	Roosevelt Red Ware	Gila Polychrome	bowl	2	1 fill rim refits 1 body
	12	Roosevelt Red Ware	Gila Polychrome	bowl	2	1 fill rim refits 1 body
	13	Roosevelt Red Ware	Gila Polychrome	bowl	3	1 fill rim matches 1 T10N 10–11E rim, which refits 1 T10N 10–11E body
	14	Roosevelt Red Ware	Gila Polychrome or later	bowl	2	2 fill bodies refit
	15	Roosevelt Red Ware	Gila Polychrome or later	bowl	2	2 fill bodies refit
	16	Roosevelt Red Ware	Gila Polychrome or later	bowl	2	2 fill bodies match
	17	Roosevelt Red Ware	indeterminate polychrome	bowl	2	2 fill bodies refit; red-slipped interior; indeterminate polychrome exterior decoration
	18	Roosevelt Red Ware	indeterminate polychrome	jar	3	3 fill bodies refit
	19	Roosevelt Red Ware	indeterminate polychrome	jar	2	1 fill rim matches 1 strip test 5–9N 8–14E rim
	20	Roosevelt Red Ware	indeterminate polychrome	jar	3	3 fill necks refit
	21	Roosevelt Red Ware	Gila Polychrome or later	bowl	3	3 floor bodies refit
	22	Roosevelt Red Ware	Gila Polychrome or later	bowl	3	3 floor bodies refit

(*continued*)

TABLE 7.29 *(continued)*

Houseblock no.	Room no.	Decorated PRV or catalog no.	Ware	Type	Vessel form	Sherd count	Comment(s)
		23	Roosevelt Red Ware	Gila Polychrome or later	bowl	2	2 floor bodies refit
		24	Roosevelt Red Ware	indeterminate polychrome	jar	2	2 floor bodies match
		25	Roosevelt Red Ware	Tonto Polychrome	jar	2	2 floor bodies refit
		26	Roosevelt Red Ware	Tonto Polychrome	jar	2	2 floor bodies refit
		27	Roosevelt Red Ware	Tonto Polychrome	jar	3	1 floor neck and 2 bodies refit
		28	Roosevelt Red Ware	Tonto Polychrome	jar	6	2 floor bodies and 1 neck refit and match 2 necks and 1 body
		29	Roosevelt Red Ware	indeterminate polychrome	jar	2	2 fill bodies refit
n/a	34	1	Roosevelt Red Ware	Gila Polychrome	bowl	6	4 fill rims and 2 bodies refit
		2	Roosevelt Red Ware	Cliff Polychrome	bowl	8	2 fill rims and 2 bodies refit and match 2 bodies that refit and 2 bodies
		3	Roosevelt Red Ware	Tonto Polychrome	jar	5	2 fill necks refit and match 3 bodies
		4	Roosevelt Red Ware	Tonto Polychrome	jar	10	7 fill bodies match and match 2 necks that refit and 1 neck
		5	Roosevelt Red Ware	Cliff or Nine Mile Polychrome	bowl	2	1 fill rim refits 1 neck

		6	Roosevelt Red Ware	Cliff Polychrome	bowl	2	2 fill rims match
		7	Roosevelt Red Ware	Gila Polychrome	bowl	2	2 fill rims refit
		8	Roosevelt Red Ware	Gila Polychrome	bowl	2	2 fill rims match
		9	Roosevelt Red Ware	Gila Polychrome	bowl	2	2 fill rims refit
		10	Roosevelt Red Ware	Gila Polychrome or later	bowl	3	3 fill bodies refit
		11	Roosevelt Red Ware	indeterminate polychrome	bowl	4	4 fill bodies match
n/a	36	1	Roosevelt Red Ware	Cliff Polychrome	bowl	2	1 T13S 12–16E rim matches 1 neck
		2	Roosevelt Red Ware	Gila Polychrome or later	bowl	2	2 T13S 12–16E bodies match
		3	Roosevelt Red Ware	Gila Polychrome or later	bowl	2	2 T13S 12–16E bodies refit
		4	Roosevelt Red Ware	indeterminate polychrome	bowl	3	3 T13S 12–16E bodies refit
		5	Roosevelt Red Ware	indeterminate polychrome	jar	2	2 T13S 12–16E bodies refit
n/a	46	1	Roosevelt Red Ware	Gila Polychrome or later	bowl	2	2 floor bodies refit
Total						**833**	

[a]Vessel composed of fragments from two or more structures

FIGURE 7.33 Partially reconstructible vessels from Room 4: (a) interior of Decorated Vessel 1, Nine Mile Polychrome bowl; (b) exterior of Decorated Vessel 1; (c) Decorated Vessel 2, Gila Polychrome bowl; (d) Decorated Vessel 3, Gila Polychrome bowl. Photographs by Patrick D. Lyons.

FIGURE 7.33 *(continued)*

Room 6

As discussed above, Room 6 is critical for understanding the Davis Ranch Site and for testing models of Roosevelt Red Ware typological and stylistic trends over time. This is because it represents the upper portion of a long stratigraphic sequence, the lower portion of which includes the House 7 deposits, and because it is part of the second-to-last group (Group C, Subgroup 2) of architectural units or features to be used as trash dumps, based on the seriation of the 10 largest Classic period assemblages from the site.

Twelve partially reconstructible decorated vessels were recovered from Room 6, comprising 78 sherds (see table 7.29). Three of these merit discussion. Vessel 1, a Cliff Polychrome bowl represented by 13 sherds, is composed of 12 fragments from Room 6 and one from adjacent Room 4. Vessel 2, another Cliff Polychrome bowl, consists of 17 sherds, one of which was found in Room 4. Not surprisingly, Room 4 also yielded half of the 28 sherds that make up Vessel 3 from Room 6, a Gila Polychrome jar (see figure 7.19b). A partially reconstructible decorated vessel that links Room 6 to House 7 is discussed above in the section devoted to House 7. Two partially reconstructible perforated plates, Vessels 5 and 6, were found in Room 6 (see table F.9).

Room 7

Room 7, along with Room 4, was identified as a member of Group B, the second-earliest set of architectural units or features to be used as trash dumps, based on a seriation of assemblages from the 10 Classic period structures or loci with the highest sherd frequencies. Clearly, however, it continued to receive refuse into the late AD 1300s. This room yielded 11 partially reconstructible decorated vessels, comprising 140 sherds (see table 7.29). Vessel 3, a Whiteriver Polychrome bowl, links Room 7 with adjacent Rooms 4 and 11 (figure 7.34a). Vessel 7, a Gila Polychrome jar, also links Room 7 to Room 11 (figure 7.34b). Vessel 4, another Gila Polychrome jar, is composed of 70 sherds (figure 7.34c–f), and Vessel 9 is a specimen of Nine Mile Polychrome: Tonto Variety (figure 7.34g, h).

Room 8

Seven sherds recovered from Room 8 represent two partially reconstructible decorated vessels, a Gila Polychrome bowl and a Roosevelt Red Ware polychrome jar of indeterminate type (see table 7.29). One partially reconstructible perforated plate, Vessel 4, was found in this room (see figure 7.23b, table F.9). This vessel consists of 16 sherds: 11 from Room 8, two from the trench in front of Room 6, and one each from the fill of House 7, the trench in front of Room 9, and the fill of Room 21. This spatial pattern suggests that the vessel was used by an inhabitant of Houseblock II, and that, when broken, most sherds were tossed into adjacent portions of the southern end of Houseblock I.

Room 9

Six partially reconstructible decorated vessels were recovered from Room 9 (see table 7.29). These account for a total of 39 sherds. One of these, Vessel 3, is a Gila Polychrome jar represented by 19 sherds (figure 7.35a). Another notable find in the Room 9 assemblage is a sherd of Nine Mile Polychrome.

Room 10

As discussed above, Room 10 was identified as a member of Group D, one of the two latest spaces to accumulate trash, based on the seriation of the 10 largest Classic period assemblages from the site. Room 10 yielded 14 partially reconstructible decorated vessels, which comprise 48 sherds (see table 7.29). One of these, Vessel 1, is a Gila Polychrome bowl represented by 10 sherds (figure 7.35b). Another, Vessel 10, is a specimen of Whiteriver Polychrome. A partially reconstructible decorated vessel that links Room 10 to House 7 is discussed above in the section devoted to House 7.

Room 11

Ten sherds from Room 11 are fragments of two partially reconstructible vessels (see table 7.29). Vessel 1 is a Gila Polychrome bowl represented by eight sherds, and Vessel 2 is a Roosevelt Red Ware polychrome jar of indeterminate type comprising two sherds.

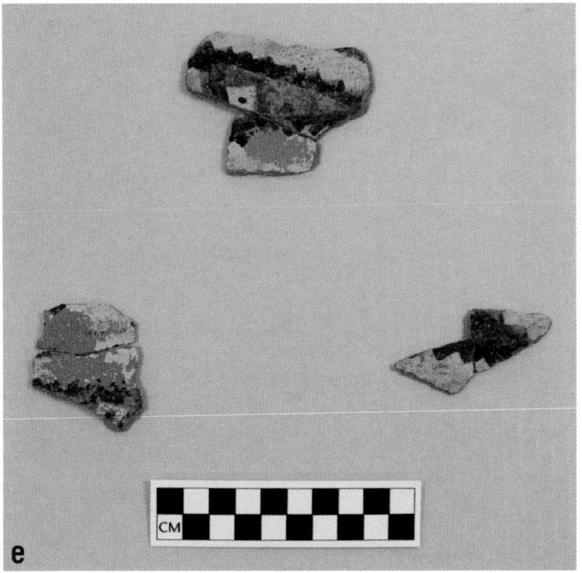

FIGURE 7.34 Partially reconstructible vessels from Room 7: (a) Decorated Vessel 3, a Whiteriver Polychrome bowl; (b) Decorated Vessel 7, Gila Polychrome jar; (c–f) Decorated Vessel 4, Gila Polychrome jar; (g) interior of Decorated Vessel 9, Nine Mile Polychrome: Tonto Variety bowl; (h) exterior of Decorated Vessel 9. Photographs by Patrick D. Lyons.

FIGURE 7.34 *(continued)*

FIGURE 7.35 Partially reconstructible vessels from Rooms 9 and 10: (a) Decorated Vessel 3 from Room 9, Gila Polychrome jar; (b) Decorated Vessel 1 from Room 10, Gila Polychrome bowl. Photographs by Patrick D. Lyons.

Houseblock II: Rooms 14–21, 33, and 35

As discussed above, 23 partially reconstructible vessels in the Davis Ranch Site decorated pottery assemblage are composed of fragments recovered from two or more structures or areas. Five of these were recovered from Houseblock II contexts, two from Room 14 and one each from Rooms 17, 19, and 35.

Room 14

This room, like Room 10 (in Houseblock I), was identified as a member of Group D, one of the two latest spaces to accumulate trash, based on the seriation of the 10 largest Classic period assemblages from the site. Six partially reconstructible decorated vessels, comprising 36 sherds, were recovered from Room 14 (see table 7.29). These include a Cliff Polychrome bowl (Vessel 1) represented by 19 sherds (figure 7.36a), a Whiteriver Polychrome bowl (Vessel 2), and a Gila Polychrome jar (Vessel 3) composed of nine sherds (figure 7.36b). Vessel 1 includes five sherds found in Room 17 and one recovered from Room 15. Three sherds forming part of Vessel 3 were recovered from Room 15. One partially reconstructible perforated plate, Vessel 48, was also found in Room 14 (see table F.9).

Room 15

A single partially reconstructible decorated vessel, a fragmentary Tonto Polychrome jar consisting of three sherds, was recovered from this room (see table 7.29).

Room 16

Three partially reconstructible decorated vessels were found in Room 16, accounting for 13 sherds (see table 7.29). One of these, a Gila Polychrome bowl represented by nine sherds (D/239), was reconstructed by Gerald (figure 7.36c). The Room 16 area is one of only two spaces in Houseblock II to have yielded Pinto Polychrome, the other being Room 33. One sherd was found in the trench in front of Room 16, and one sherd of Pinto Polychrome: Salmon Variety was recovered from the room's floor.

Room 17

Nine sherds from Room 17 represent fragments of three partially reconstructible decorated vessels (see table 7.29). Vessel 1, a Gila Polychrome bowl consisting of five sherds, includes a sherd recovered from Room 14 (figure 7.36d).

Room 19

Room 19 yielded four partially reconstructible decorated vessels comprising 13 sherds (see table 7.29). One of these, Vessel 1, is a Roosevelt Red Ware polychrome jar of indeterminate type (but most likely Gila Polychrome) represented by seven sherds. Two fragments of this vessel were found in Room 35.

Room 20

A single partially reconstructible decorated vessel, a fragmentary Gila Polychrome bowl consisting of two sherds, was recovered from this room (see table 7.29).

Room 21

Five partially reconstructible decorated vessels, comprising 11 sherds, were recovered from this room (see table 7.29). One of these, a Cliff Polychrome bowl represented by three sherds (D/238), was reconstructed by Gerald (figure 7.37a).

Room 33

The Room 33 decorated ceramic assemblage includes 11 partially reconstructible vessels comprising 38 sherds (see table 7.29). One of these, Vessel 1, is a fragmentary Gila Polychrome bowl represented by five sherds (figure 7.37b). Room 33, as discussed above, is one of only two spaces in Houseblock II to have yielded Pinto Polychrome. A single sherd of this type was recovered from the room's fill.

Room 35

Six partially reconstructible vessels, represented by 50 sherds, were recovered from Room 35 (see table 7.29). Vessel 4, a Gila Polychrome jar, consists of 34 sherds (figure 7.37c). Three sherds of this vessel were found in adjacent Room 33. Vessel 6 is a rare example of Tucson Black-on-red. It is a bowl slipped

FIGURE 7.36 Partially reconstructible vessels from Rooms 14, 16, and 17: (a) Decorated Vessel 1 from Room 14, Cliff Polychrome bowl; (b) Decorated Vessel 3 from Room 14, Gila Polychrome jar; (c) D/239, Gila Polychrome bowl from Room 16; (d) Decorated Vessel 1 from Room 17, Gila Polychrome bowl. Photographs by Patrick D. Lyons (a, b, and d) and Jannelle Weakly (c).

FIGURE 7.37 Partially reconstructible vessels from Rooms 21, 33, and 35: (a) D/238, Cliff Polychrome bowl from Room 21; (b) Decorated Vessel 1 from Room 33, Gila Polychrome bowl; (c) Decorated Vessel 4 from Room 35, Gila Polychrome jar; (d) Decorated Vessel 6 from Room 35, Tucson Black-on-red bowl bearing hatched painted decoration. Photographs by Patrick D. Lyons (b–d) and Jannelle Weakly (a).

entirely red on the interior, and it bears painted decoration on the exterior, as specimens of this type should. However, the painted decoration is in the style typical of Maverick Mountain Black-on-red and Maverick Mountain Polychrome, in that hachure was used (figure 7.37d).

Houseblock VI: Room 47

Room 47 yielded two partially reconstructible decorated vessels, comprising five sherds (see table 7.29). One is a fragmentary bowl of Gila Polychrome or a later type. The other is a Roosevelt Red Ware polychrome jar of indeterminate type.

Houseblock VII: Rooms 37 and 45

No partially reconstructible decorated or perforated plate vessels were found in Room 37. Room 45 yielded a single partially reconstructible vessel, a Tucson Polychrome bowl represented by seven sherds (figure 7.38a; see table 7.29).

Rooms 2, 34, 36, and 46

Twenty-nine partially reconstructible decorated vessels, represented by 97 sherds, were recovered from Room 2 (see table 7.29). One of these, Vessel 5, is a fragmentary Nine Mile Polychrome bowl consisting of five sherds (figure 7.38b, c). Room 2 yielded the most specimens of Tonto Polychrome of any surface structure. Five sherds and four partially reconstructible vessels (Vessels 25, 26, 27, and 28) of this type are present in the Room 2 assemblage. Only 39 total specimens (sherds and partially reconstructible vessels) were recovered from the site as a whole, and 26 of these were from surface structures. Not surprisingly, Room 2 was assigned, based on the seriation of the 10 largest Classic period assemblages from the site, to seriation Group C, Subgroup 2. It, along with Room 6, is a member of the second-to-last set of architectural units or features in the seriation to be used as trash dumps. Room 2 also yielded a single partially reconstructible perforated plate, Vessel 51 (see table F.9).

Forty-six sherds found in Room 34 represent 11 partially reconstructible decorated vessels (see table 7.29). Two of these, Vessels 3 (five sherds) and 4 (ten sherds), are fragmentary Tonto Polychrome jars (figure 7.38d, e). Two partially reconstructible perforated plates, Vessels 9 (three sherds) and 10 (two sherds), were also recovered from Room 34 (see table F.9). Room 36 yielded five partially reconstructible decorated vessels comprising 11 sherds and a single partially reconstructible perforated plate, Vessel 43 (see tables 7.29, F.9). Two sherds recovered from Room 46 represent a partially reconstructible bowl of Gila Polychrome or a later type.

Houseblock III: Rooms 27 and 28

Two partially reconstructible vessels were recovered from Houseblock III. One, a fragmentary Cliff Polychrome bowl with indeterminate (but likely Gila-configuration) exterior decoration, is represented by 11 sherds (see table 7.29). Eight of these were found in Room 28 and three were found in Room 27 (figure 7.39a, b). The other, also from Room 28, consists of four sherds from a Maverick Mountain Black-on-red jar.

Houseblock V: Rooms 41–44

Houseblock V yielded two partially reconstructible decorated vessels comprising five sherds (see table 7.29). Both were found in Room 44. A single partially reconstructible perforated plate, Vessel 44, was also recovered from Room 44 (see table F.9).

OTHER FEATURES AND AREAS

Compared to the pit structures, the houseblocks, and all other areas of the site with appreciable sample sizes, the decorated assemblage from the Northeast

FIGURE 7.38 Partially reconstructible vessels from Rooms 45, 2, and 34: (a) Decorated Vessel 1 from Room 45, Tucson Polychrome bowl; (b) interior of Decorated Vessel 5 from Room 2, Nine Mile Polychrome bowl; (c) exterior of Decorated Vessel 5 from Room 2; (d) Decorated Vessel 3 from Room 34, Tonto Polychrome jar; (e) Decorated Vessel 4 from Room 34, Tonto Polychrome jar. Photographs by Patrick D. Lyons.

FIGURE 7.38 *(continued)*

FIGURE 7.39 Partially reconstructible vessels from Room 28 and the Northeast Trash: (a) interior of Vessel 1 from Room 28, Cliff Polychrome bowl; (b) exterior of Decorated Vessel 1 from Room 28; (c) interior of Decorated Vessel 2 from the Northeast Trash, Pinto Polychrome: Salmon Variety bowl with exterior red slip applied in the manner of some specimens of Tsegi Orange Ware types; (d) exterior of Decorated Vessel 2 from the Northeast Trash. Photographs by Patrick D. Lyons.

Trash boasted, by far, the highest proportion of Maverick Mountain Series specimens (nearly 38%). The Northeast Trash yielded 19 partially reconstructible decorated vessels, comprising 71 sherds, and eight of these are Maverick Mountain Series specimens (Vessels 4, 5, and 7–12; table 7.30). Five of these are Tucson Polychrome (four jars and one bowl), two are Maverick Mountain Black-on-red (both bowls), and one is Tucson Black-on-red (a jar). Vessel 4, one of the Tucson Polychrome jars, is represented by 12 sherds (see figure 7.3a). Vessel 2, a Pinto Polychrome: Salmon Variety bowl, comprising 12 sherds, bears exterior decoration sometimes displayed by Tsegi Orange Ware types (Beals et al. 1945:129, Figure 53d, h; Colton 1956); red slip has been applied in a wide band beginning at the lip and ending a few centimeters short of the base, leaving a circular area unslipped (figure 7.39c, d). This is another important indicator of the northern origin of Roosevelt Red Ware. A partially reconstructible perforated plate, Vessel 11, was also recovered from the Northeast Trash (see table F.9).

Pit Oven 1, which cuts into and thus postdates House 4, yielded four partially reconstructible decorated vessels comprising nine sherds (see table 7.30). Two are fragmentary Tucson Polychrome bowls, another represents portions of a Tucson Polychrome jar, and the fourth is part of a Gila Black-on-red bowl. The typological mix here is what would be expected if this assemblage represented trash associated with the Aravaipa phase deposition of refuse in the area between the arc of Kayenta pit houses and the Northeast Trash.

Fifteen sherds recovered from Puddle Pit 2, located 40 cm west of Room 10, represent three partially reconstructible vessels (see table 7.30). Two of these, Vessels 1 (seven sherds) and 2 (six sherds), are fragmentary Gila Polychrome bowls (figure 7.40). Vessel 3 (two sherds) is a portion of a Roosevelt Red Ware polychrome bowl of indeterminate type.

Stratitest 1, located just north of Room 36 and inside the eastern compound wall, yielded four partially reconstructible decorated bowls represented by 10 sherds (see table 7.30). Two are fragmentary vessels of Gila Polychrome or a later Roosevelt Red Ware type, one is a Roosevelt Red Ware polychrome of indeterminate type, and the fourth is a specimen of Tucson Polychrome. Partially reconstructible perforated plate Vessel 42 was also recovered from Stratitest 1 (see table F.9).

SUMMARY AND CONCLUSIONS

The reanalysis addressed 5,672 painted vessel fragments and vessels, reduced to 4,177 specimens (whole vessels, partially reconstructible vessels, and nonconjoining and unmatched sherds), as well as 344 perforated plate sherds, reduced to 210 specimens. The reanalyzed sample of decorated pottery, dominated by Roosevelt Red Ware, was used to explore spatial and temporal patterns useful for understanding the Davis Ranch Site and for refining ceramic chronology on a regional scale.

Spatial patterns with chronological implications lent strong support to inferences based on architecture regarding the growth and development of the site during the Classic period (see chapter 3). These patterns also illuminated the order in which different structures fell into disuse and became trash dumps. The earliest identifiable Classic period occupation consists of Houses 1, 2, 3, and 7 (all pit houses) and the kiva, built and used during the late AD 1200s and/or the early 1300s. Refuse associated with this interval is concentrated in the area bounded by the kiva and the area called the Northeast Trash and also along a transect following the arc of houses just listed.

Houseblock I, which, with Houseblocks II, VI, and VII and Rooms 2, 34, 36, 46, and 48, is part of the pueblo, seems to have evolved directly out of Houses 3 and 7 (Gerald 1975:91–93). Refuse associated with the occupation of Houseblock I seems to have been deposited in the same general areas used for discard during the occupation of the Classic period pit houses. Early on, refuse accumulated in the pit houses, the Northeast Trash, and intervening spaces. Later, but still during the early AD 1300s,

TABLE 7.30 Decorated partially reconstructible vessels (PRVs) recovered from the Northeast Trash, Pit Oven 1, Puddle Pit 2, and Stratitest 1 and subjected to reanalysis

Area or feature	Decorated PRV or catalog no.	Ware	Type	Vessel form	Sherd count	Comment(s)
NE Trash	1	Roosevelt Red Ware	Gila Polychrome	bowl	5	1 rim and 4 bodies refit
	2	Roosevelt Red Ware	Pinto Polychrome: Salmon Variety	bowl	12	1 rim and 11 bodies refit; exterior use of red slip is in the style of Kiet Siel Polychrome
	3	Roosevelt Red Ware	Gila Polychrome: Salmon Variety	bowl	6	1 rim, 2 necks, and 1 body refit and match 2 bodies
	4	Maverick Mountain Series	Tucson Polychrome	jar	12	2 necks and 10 bodies refit
	5	Maverick Mountain Series	Maverick Mountain Black-on-red	bowl	2	1 rim and 1 body match
	6	Roosevelt Red Ware	Gila Black-on-red	bowl	2	2 rims match
	7	Maverick Mountain Series	Maverick Mountain Black-on-red	bowl	3	2 bodies refit and match 1 body
	8	Maverick Mountain Series	Tucson Black-on-red	jar	2	1 rim and 1 neck match
	9	Maverick Mountain Series	Tucson Polychrome	bowl	3	1 rim and 1 body refit and match 1 rim
	10	Maverick Mountain Series	Tucson Polychrome	jar	4	4 bodies refit
	11	Maverick Mountain Series	Tucson Polychrome	jar	2	2 bodies refit
	12	Maverick Mountain Series	Tucson Polychrome	jar	2	1 neck and 1 body match
	13	Roosevelt Red Ware	Gila Black-on-red	jar	2	1 NE Trash neck and 1 strip test 5–9N 8–14E body match
	14	Roosevelt Red Ware	Gila Black-on-red	bowl	3	2 rims and 1 body refit

	15	Roosevelt Red Ware	Gila Polychrome or later	bowl	2	2 bodies match
	16	Roosevelt Red Ware	indeterminate polychrome	bowl	3	3 bodies match
	17	Roosevelt Red Ware	indeterminate polychrome	jar	2	2 bodies refit
	18	Roosevelt Red Ware	indeterminate polychrome	jar	2	2 bodies match
	19	Roosevelt Red Ware	Pinto Polychrome	bowl	2	2 rims refit
Pit Oven 1	1	Maverick Mountain Series	Tucson Polychrome	bowl	2	1 rim and 1 body match
	2	Maverick Mountain Series	Tucson Polychrome	jar	3	3 bodies match
	3	Maverick Mountain Series	Tucson Polychrome	bowl	2	2 bodies refit
	4	Roosevelt Red Ware	Gila Black-on-red	bowl	2	2 rims refit
Puddle Pit 2	1	Roosevelt Red Ware	Gila Polychrome	bowl	7	1 rim and 1 body refit and match 5 bodies that refit
	2	Roosevelt Red Ware	Gila Polychrome	bowl	6	1 rim and 5 bodies match
	3	Roosevelt Red Ware	indeterminate polychrome	bowl	2	2 bodies refit
Stratitest 1	1	Roosevelt Red Ware	Gila Polychrome or later	bowl	3	2 level 1 bodies refit and match 1 body
	2	Roosevelt Red Ware	indeterminate polychrome	bowl	2	2 level 1 bodies refit
	3	Maverick Mountain Series	Tucson Polychrome	bowl	3	2 level 2 rims and 1 body refit
	4	Roosevelt Red Ware	Gila Polychrome or later	bowl	2	2 level 2 bodies refit
Total					**105**	

FIGURE 7.40 Partially reconstructible vessels from Puddle Pit 2: (a) Decorated Vessel 1, Gila Polychrome bowl; (b) Decorated Vessel 2, Gila Polychrome bowl. Photographs by Patrick D. Lyons.

based on the amount of Pinto Polychrome recovered from them, two of the earliest constructed rooms in Houseblock I (Room 4 and Room 7) became trash dumps.

The compound wall separating the pueblo from the kiva is abutted to both Room 2 and Room 15 (Gerald 1975:93, Figure 3). The prodigious quantity of trash dumped in the kiva is likely a good indicator that this structure was decommissioned well before the compound wall was erected, as this feature would have severely curtailed movement between the pueblo and areas to the east, such as the kiva depression. The transition of the kiva from a context for ritual activity to refuse receptacle and cemetery must have occurred during the mid-AD 1300s, based on the presence of multiple specimens (both sherds and partially reconstructible vessels) of Cliff Polychrome on its floor and within its floor features, including the sealed subfloor pit, which yielded Cliff Polychrome and Cliff Black-on-red. A partially reconstructible Whiteriver Polychrome bowl was also recovered from level 9 (seven conjoining sherds), the ventilator (one sherd that conjoins the seven from level 9), and other kiva contexts (six additional sherds). After the compound wall was constructed, trash deposition shifted from the kiva to spaces in the pueblo, such as Rooms 2 and 6, and then Rooms 10 and 14. Presumably, this refuse was generated by people living in Houseblocks II, VI, and VII.

Stratigraphic trends in the assemblages recovered from superimposed structures House 7 and Room 6, as well as that recovered from the kiva, lend support to the stylistic seriation of Roosevelt Red Ware presented by Crown (1994) and the typological and chronological refinements to Roosevelt Red Ware that I have proposed (Lyons 2004b, 2012b, 2013a; Lyons and Clark 2012; Lyons and Neuzil 2006; Lyons, Hill, and Clark 2011; Neuzil and Lyons 2006). Just as researchers have long been able to achieve relatively precise temporal ordering of sites and deposits based on differing amounts of White Mountain Red Ware types, we may now do so by considering variability in frequencies of Cliff Polychrome, Whiteriver Polychrome, Phoenix Polychrome, Nine Mile Polychrome, Los Muertos Polychrome, Dinwiddie Polychrome, and Cliff White-on-red. We now have greater potential to improve our ability to understand ancient demography and social dynamics on a variety of scales, from the individual river valley to the region as a whole (Hill et al. 2004, 2015; Lyons, Hill, and Clark 2011).

In addition to the Classic period decorated assemblage, attention was focused on the site's perforated plates, a key indicator of Kayenta immigrants (Lyons and Lindsay 2006). Fifty-one partially reconstructible vessels of this form were identified, and in the process, Gerald's 1958 (see chapter 6) plain ware typology, based on rim form and paste, was shown to be of limited value given numerous conjoins across "type" boundaries. Much more importantly, examination of these objects resulted in the observation of many more examples of a previously documented phenomenon: traces of red pigment likely indicating the handling of these objects by potters engaged in the manufacture of Roosevelt Red Ware. Indeed, all available evidence points to the use of perforated plates as base molds and potters' turntables (Christenson 1991, 1994; Lyons and Lindsay 2006). More than 80% of the perforated plates from the site are from deposits postdating the initial Classic period pit house occupation; that is, the overwhelming majority were in use during the period when Roosevelt Red Ware dominated the painted pottery assemblage, strongly linking Kayenta immigrants and their descendants to Roosevelt Red Ware production.

Evidence recovered by Gerald (chapters 5 and 6), including clay coils, a clay appliqué element, shaped-sherd scrapers, pigments useful in pottery decoration, pigment-stained ground stone, and misfired Roosevelt Red Ware ("Gila White Slip") points to on-site pottery production during the Classic period. Schoenwetter's palynological study documenting the presence of Rocky Mountain beeweed, an exotic plant likely used in the production of organic paint for pottery decoration, is also relevant here (appendix J).

More recent work by the Center for Desert Archaeology (CDA; now Archaeology Southwest) at 29 Classic period sites in the lower San Pedro Valley has produced strong support for the inference that Maverick Mountain Series types, perforated plates, and Roosevelt Red Ware were produced at the Davis Ranch Site and nearby sites in the Cascabel District and the adjacent San Manuel District (Clark and Lyons, eds. 2012; figure 7.41). The results of a large-scale petrographic analysis indicate that all of the Roosevelt Red Ware and Maverick Mountain Series pottery found in the Cascabel and San Manuel Districts was produced locally and that potters in the Cascabel and San Manuel Districts also made nearly all of the Maverick Mountain Series pottery found in the Aravaipa and Dudleyville Districts to the north (Lyons 2012b). Furthermore, more than 40% of the Roosevelt Red Ware found at sites in the Dudleyville District and more than 70% of the Roosevelt Red Ware recovered from sites in the Aravaipa District was produced in the Cascabel and/or San Manuel Districts. Finally, 32 of the 35 perforated plates found during the CDA excavations were recovered from the Davis Ranch Site ($n = 11$), the Reeve Ruin ($n = 17$), and other sites in the Cascabel District. All 20 that could be linked to a petrofacies based on temper analysis were identified as having been produced in the Cascabel District ($n = 10$), the San Manuel District ($n = 3$), or one of the two (most likely the former; $n = 7$).

The reanalysis reported here illuminates other links between Kayenta immigrants and the production of Roosevelt Red Ware; for example, hybrid vessels combining aspects of Roosevelt Red Ware and Maverick Mountain Series/Tsegi Orange Ware style and technology. These include bowls with interior decoration typical of Roosevelt Red Ware and exterior painted decoration characteristic of Tucson Polychrome. Another example would be the partially reconstructible Pinto Polychrome: Salmon Variety

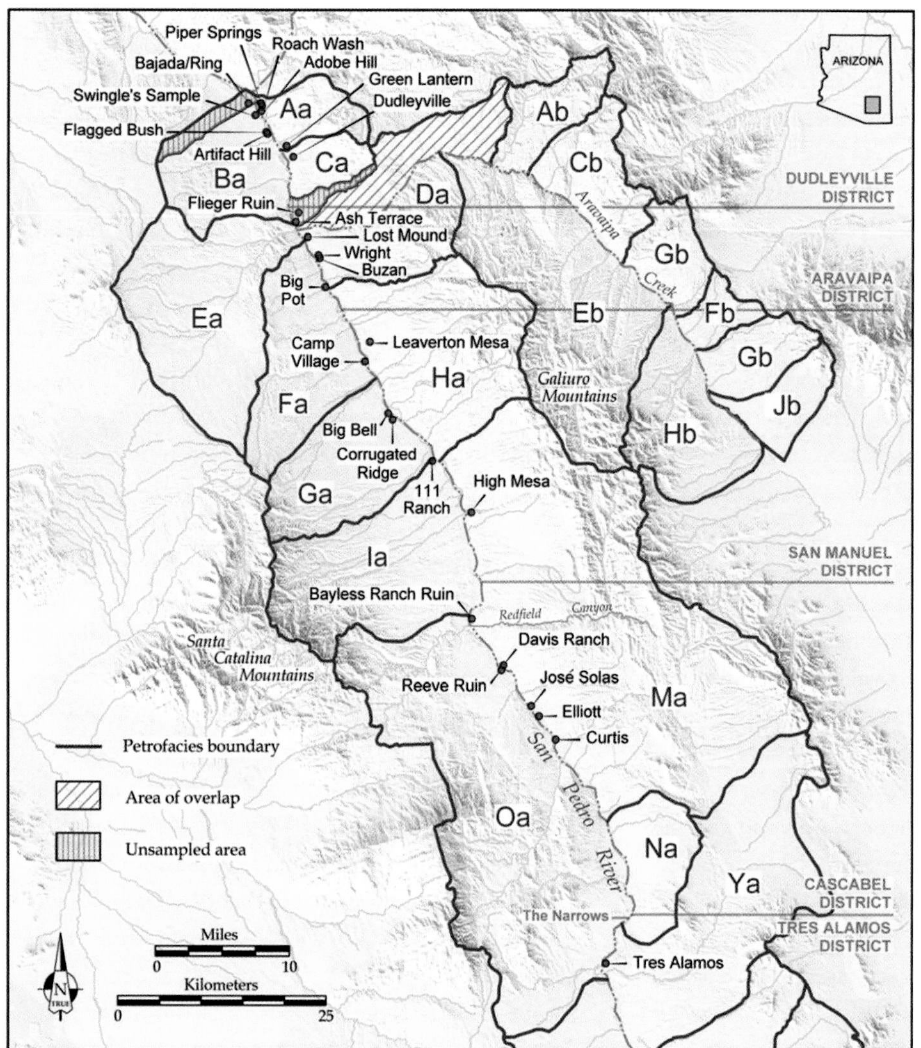

FIGURE 7.41 Archaeological districts, sites, and petrofacies in the lower San Pedro Valley. Map produced by Catherine Gilman.

bowl that bears exterior decoration like that sometimes exhibited by specimens of a number of Tsegi Orange Ware types Tusayan Polychrome and Kayenta Polychrome.

In the chapter that follows, these and other aspects of the ceramic assemblage are revisited, and the evidence recovered from the Davis Ranch Site by Rex Gerald is given special attention in a review of what is currently known and inferred regarding ceramic chronology, production, and consumption; population dynamics; socioeconomics; and the politics of identity during the late Classic period in the lower San Pedro Valley. In addition, patterns observed in the lower San Pedro are juxtaposed with data derived from adjacent areas where late pre-Hispanic influxes of northern immigrants have been inferred.

8

The Significance of the Davis Ranch Site

Jeffery J. Clark and Patrick D. Lyons

In previous chapters, Rex Gerald's excavations at the Davis Ranch Site are placed in the historical context of archaeological knowledge and practice during the 1950s in the U.S. Southwest, the results of his fieldwork and analyses are reported, and a reanalysis of a portion of the site's ceramic assemblage is presented. Unfortunately, Gerald's 1958 manuscript lacks a concluding chapter that amalgamates the information he gathered in a brief, integrated summary.

This chapter is meant to serve that purpose and to do a bit more. We begin by revisiting, as Gerald likely would have, the questions that structured his research. We then summarize and synthesize the results of his excavations and analyses. We conclude by placing the Davis Ranch Site in the larger context of current knowledge about the lower San Pedro Valley and the Salado phenomenon in the southern U.S. Southwest. Throughout, we maintain a focus on the abundant and robust evidence that the Davis Ranch Site was both a Kayenta enclave and a Roosevelt Red Ware production center, and we emphasize the strong and enduring connection between groups of Kayenta origin or descent and the Salado phenomenon.

ANSWERING GERALD'S RESEARCH QUESTIONS

Rex Gerald excavated the Davis Ranch Site with three research questions in mind (see chapter 2):

1. What was the stratigraphic (i.e., temporal) relationship between local red-on-brown types and Roosevelt Red Ware?
2. Was there evidence of a protohistoric Sobaipuri occupation, specifically the settlement called Cusac, shown in the approximate location of the Davis Ranch Site on early Spanish maps (see Di Peso 1953:54)?
3. Were there temporal and regional variants of Gila Polychrome, the dominant Roosevelt Red Ware type?

Relevant to the first question, Roosevelt Red Ware was found to postdate nearly all of the local red-on-brown types, including those in the Dragoon Series, the San Simon Series, and Tucson Basin Brown Ware. The vast majority of the red-on-brown and red-on-buff pottery was associated with the late pre-Classic (Gerald's Davis phase) pit house settlement underlying the pueblo (Houseblocks I, II, VI, and VII and Rooms 2, 34, 36, 46, and 48; see figure 1.5). The pueblo dates to Gerald's Reeve phase, which corresponds to the Redfield and early Romero phases in the current chronological scheme that subdivides the Classic period in the lower San Pedro Valley into four phases (figure 8.1). The decorated ceramic assemblages recovered from the pueblo and the kiva are dominated by Roosevelt Red Ware.

As for the second question, Gerald found very little evidence of a protohistoric Sobaipuri presence at the site. He recovered two Sobaipuri projectile

Date (AD)	Hohokam Period[a]	Phoenix Basin Phase[a]	Tucson Basin Phase[b]	San Pedro Valley Phase[c]	San Pedro Valley Phase Revised[d]
1700			(Tohono O'odham)	Embudo	
					(Sobaipuri)
1600	(Protohistoric)	(Protohistoric)	?	?	
1500					?
				Reeve	Romero
1400		Civano	Tucson		
	Classic				Redfield
1300				Sosa	Aravaipa
		Soho	Tanque Verde		Soza
1200					
1100	Sedentary	Sacaton	Rincon		
1000				Davis	
900	Colonial	Santa Cruz	Rillito		
800		Gila Butte	Cañada del Oro		

[a]Henderson 2002; Wallace et al. 1995; [b]Thiel and Diehl 2006; [c]Gerald 1958, 1975; [d]Clark and Lyons, eds. 2012

FIGURE 8.1 San Pedro Valley phase sequence and chronology.

points from the surface and identified 42 sherds as Whetstone Plain, a type securely linked to the Sobaipuri (Masse 1981). Most of this material was found between the pueblo and Houseblock III and was not associated with architecture or other features. It is possible that a small and ephemeral Sobaipuri component was missed by Gerald in this area, considering how difficult we now know such occupations are to find. However, a protohistoric period village such as Cusac, consisting of "20 houses and 70 people" according to Manje (1954:80), was not identified.

A total of 61 sherds of what Gerald described as Davis Plain: Sobaipuri Coil Rim Variety was also recovered. At the time of the excavations, "Sobaipuri" rim coils were considered diagnostic of the protohistoric period (Di Peso 1953, 1958a; see chapter 6). However, rim coils are also a hallmark of Kayenta pottery brought southward by immigrants during the thirteenth century AD, and the trait was apparently reintroduced to the southern U.S. Southwest by Yuman speakers or Spaniards during the eighteenth century (Lyons 2004a). Reexamination of these sherds shows that all but one are fragments of perforated plates, Kayenta pottery-making tools (Lyons and Lindsay 2006). The sole exception is a plate that may or may not have been perforated. With respect to paste, these sherds are identical to the dominant utility ware (Davis Plain, a.k.a., Belford Plain) used in the pueblo during the fourteenth century. The rim coil appeared at the site during the late thirteenth century AD and was present until the end of the prehistoric occupation, circa AD 1400. Thus, rather than a protohistoric marker, rim coils represent further evidence of a Kayenta presence.

The informally built Houseblocks IV and V, to the west of the pueblo, and the post-and-upright-cobble enclosure overlying the pueblo could not be dated by ceramics. However, based on the presence of metal and glass trash at the site and the absence of protohistoric ceramics near these structures, Gerald inferred that they probably dated to the late historic era. The enclosure overlying the pueblo was thought to be a corral.

Gerald never resolved his third research question, typing nearly all of the nearly 9,000 Roosevelt Red Ware bowl sherds he recovered as Gila Polychrome. He did, however, identify more than 100 bowl sherds as Pinto Polychrome, including transitional specimens that today would be called Pinto-Gila Polychrome or Gila Polychrome with no banding line. This suggests that Kayenta groups first arrived at the Davis Ranch Site during the Aravaipa phase, before Gila Polychrome was widely produced.

The reanalysis of ceramics reported on in chapter 7, which builds on studies completed as part of the Center for Desert Archaeology's (CDA, now Archaeology Southwest) San Pedro Preservation Project (Lyons 2004b, 2012b), addresses head-on temporal and spatial variability in Roosevelt Red Ware. The strong stratigraphic trends observed at the Davis Ranch Site lend support to the Roosevelt Red Ware typology used here (Lyons 2004b, 2012b, 2013a; Lyons and Clark 2012; Lyons and Neuzil 2006; Lyons, Hill, and Clark 2011; Neuzil and Lyons 2006) and strengthen the conclusion that this new system is useful in refining ceramic chronology. These same data reinforce the validity of Crown's (1994) Roosevelt Red Ware stylistic seriation.

Using the new Roosevelt Red Ware typology and the dates associated with the new types present (as well as those that are absent), it can be demonstrated that the Davis Ranch Site was occupied at least as late as the AD 1370s and that it was depopulated by circa 1400. Cliff Polychrome, which dates circa AD 1360–1450, accounts for 2.68% (n = 86) of the site's Roosevelt Red Ware assemblage used in the quantitative analysis (all sherds, regardless of vessel part) and Cliff Black-on-red accounts for 0.06% (n = 2). However, when only rim and neck sherds, whole vessels, and partially reconstructible vessels are considered (n = 773), the proportion represented by Cliff Polychrome and Cliff Black-on-red together rises to 11.38%. Because Cliff Polychrome and other late Roosevelt Red Ware types can only be identified on the basis of rim or neck sherds, this is the preferred method of quantification and comparison (Lyons 2004b, 2012b; Lyons, Hill, and

Clark 2011). Adding rim and neck sherds identified as Cliff or Nine Mile Polychrome (n = 61), most of which are probably Cliff Polychrome (see chapter 7), the percentage rises to 19.27. Nine Mile Polychrome (n = 5) and Phoenix Polychrome (n = 4), which date circa AD 1375–1450, are also present and together account for 1.16% of the Roosevelt Red Ware rims, necks, and vessels. Two conjoining body sherds from the site may represent a single specimen of Dinwiddie Polychrome, which dates circa AD 1390–1450. This is the only possible example of this type yet documented in the lower San Pedro Valley. Los Muertos Polychrome and Cliff White-on-red, which date circa AD 1390–1450, are absent from the Davis Ranch Site assemblage and have not yet been observed at any site in the San Pedro Valley (Lyons 2012b, 2013a).

Di Peso (1958a:Figure 12) reports that 32.4% of the Roosevelt Red Ware *bowls* at Reeve Ruin are recurved; this means that 22.6% of the Roosevelt Red Ware *vessels* at Reeve are recurved bowls (how many of these would be typed as Nine Mile or Phoenix Polychrome is unknown). Adding three specimens of Gila Polychrome with no banding line—but with recurved rims—to the count of Cliff Polychrome, Nine Mile Polychrome, and Phoenix Polychrome specimens discussed above, the total number of Roosevelt Red Ware bowls with recurved rims from the Davis Ranch Site is 161 (20.83%). The small difference between the sites in terms of recurved bowl percentage likely reflects significant overlap in occupation dates. Thus, the argument put forth in Gerald's (1975) PhD dissertation, based on environmental data, for sequential occupation of the sites (during the Classic period)—with the Davis Ranch Site as the earlier of the two—is not supported.

SUMMARY AND SYNTHESIS OF GERALD'S EXCAVATION RESULTS

Gerald divided the occupational sequence at the Davis Ranch Site into four phases. Contexts that predated AD 1250 were assigned to the Davis phase. This poorly defined interval includes structures currently believed to date to the Early Agricultural period, a component unrecognized by Gerald, as well as late pre-Classic pit houses. As discussed below, ceramics at the site may also indicate the presence of as yet undocumented early Classic period pit houses.

Gerald's Sosa phase (not to be confused with the recently defined Soza phase) is roughly coterminous with the Aravaipa phase (see figure 8.1), and he assigned the Kayenta pit house settlement to this interval. The pueblo and the kiva were assigned to the Reeve phase (Redfield and early Romero phases). However, the layout and architectural evolution of the site suggest that the kiva at the Davis Ranch Site was constructed during the Aravaipa phase, earlier than Gerald had placed it.

The poorly dated Houseblocks IV and V, as well as the stone-and-pole enclosure overlying the pueblo, were assigned by Gerald to the ill-defined Embudo phase. Although these structures obviously postdate the precontact occupation, little more can be determined about the date of their use. A post-1840 date is likely, however, considering the historic material found at the site, including a cut iron nail, and the relatively late establishment of permanent Mexican and Anglo settlements in the area.

In the sections that follow, we summarize and synthesize Gerald's results. We have organized the discussion chronologically, from the earliest to the latest identifiable pre-Hispanic component at the Davis Ranch Site.

Early Agricultural Period (San Pedro and Cienega Phases; 1200 BC–AD 50)

Gerald considered the possibility that Houses 6 and 10 (figure 8.2; see figure 1.5) were granaries, and stratigraphic evidence showed that the former predated his Sosa phase (the Aravaipa phase). However, they are more likely part of an Early Agricultural period occupation dating to the San Pedro (1200–800 BC) and Cienega (800 BC–AD 50) phases. Both pit

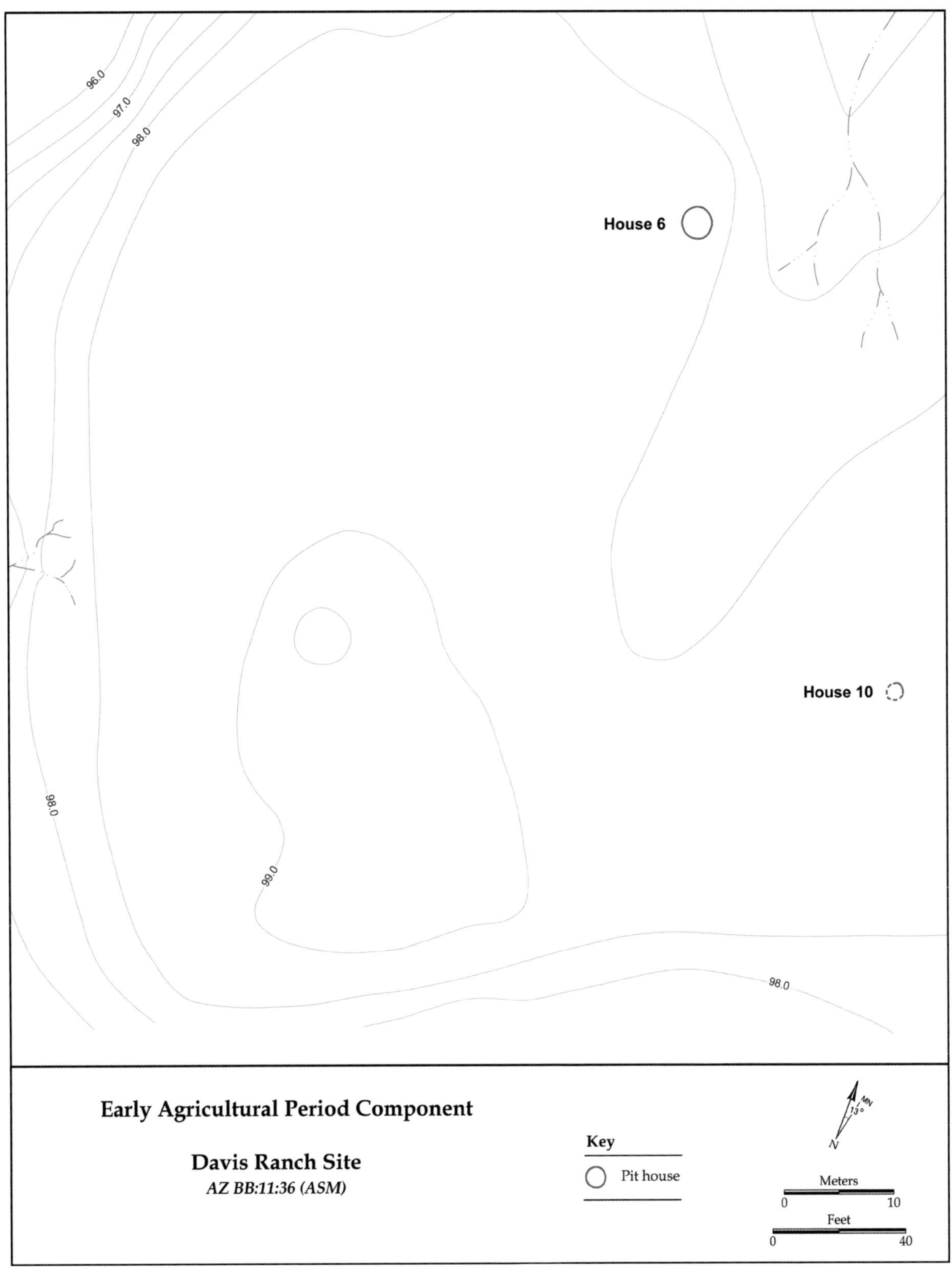

FIGURE 8.2 Early Agricultural period component at the Davis Ranch Site. Map produced by Catherine Gilman.

structures are small and circular in shape, consistent with Early Agricultural period houses found in the Tucson Basin, along the Santa Cruz River (Gregory 2001; Mabry et al. 1997). Both also lack hearths.

Although the upper fills of both structures contained ceramics, none were clearly associated with their occupations. The disturbed or secondary burial (Burial 15) overlying House 6 is well above the floor and associated with a Gila Polychrome bowl. The recovery of three Cienega projectile points and one San Pedro projectile point from the excavations (all were redeposited in later contexts; see chapter 5) further supports the presence of an Early Agricultural component at the site. Also relevant here is a fragment of a knobbed stone tray (D/191) recovered from a pit in the floor of House 6. Such objects are known to occur in Cienega phase contexts in the Tucson Basin and the Cienega Valley (Ferg 1998).

Houses 6 and 10 represent the most convincing evidence of an Early Agricultural component in the lower San Pedro Valley to date. More such houses may be located in the substantial and uninvestigated pre-Classic artifact scatter to the east of the pueblo. Artifacts diagnostic of this period also have been recovered from Big Ditch (Masse et al. 2014), near the Aravaipa confluence, and Tres Alamos (Clark and Lyons 2012:77–81). Several excavated pit structures at Tres Alamos are morphologically similar to Early Agricultural period and Early Ceramic period (AD 150–700) structures, but these are not discussed in the report (Tuthill 1947; see Clark and Lyons 2012:Figure 3.3).

Considering the similar hydrological regimes (modest and manageable precontact period flows) and geomorphological settings (broad swaths of arable floodplain) of the middle Santa Cruz River and lower San Pedro River, extensive Early Agricultural period settlements likely await discovery in the latter valley, especially in optimal areas where water would have flowed perennially. The floodplain in the vicinity of the Davis Ranch Site may have been one such area.

Late Pre-Classic (AD 850–1150)

Four pit houses (Houses 4, 5, 8, and 9) excavated by Gerald date to the Colonial period and/or the Sedentary period (figure 8.3; see figure 1.5). Three secondary cremations to the east of these structures are also associated with this component. Because three of the pit houses are stratigraphically related, only two of them could have been occupied contemporaneously.

Although construction details are not evenly preserved, the four houses are similar in shape (subrectangular/oval) and, in the case of House 4, roof support arrangement (two supports along the long axis) to Hohokam houses-in-pits. The floor grooves and interior postholes in House 4 are also characteristic of Hohokam houses-in-pits.

A strong connection to groups in the Phoenix Basin is also evident in the preponderance of Middle Gila Buff Ware in the pre-Classic decorated assemblage (see chapter 6). Although traces of Gila Butte Red-on-buff and Cañada del Oro Red-on-brown are present, the assemblage is dominated by Santa Cruz Red-on-buff with some Sacaton Red-on-buff, suggesting that the pit house settlement was occupied for the most part during the tenth and the early eleventh centuries. This inference is corroborated by the presence of apparently locally produced versions of Tucson Basin Brown Ware types (Lyons 2012b). Among these, Rillito Red-on-brown is about twice as abundant as Rincon Red-on-brown. Sherds of Dragoon Series red-on-brown types are almost equal in frequency to fragments of Tucson Basin Brown Ware vessels, and limited quantities of San Simon Series ceramics are also present.

Three palettes, characteristic of the Hohokam Colonial and Sedentary periods, were recovered from the Davis Ranch Site. One was associated with a cremation and another was found below the floor of House 4 (see chapter 5). The third was redeposited in the fill of a Kayenta pit house (House 3; see below).

The size of the late pre-Classic pit house component can only be estimated. Gerald may have

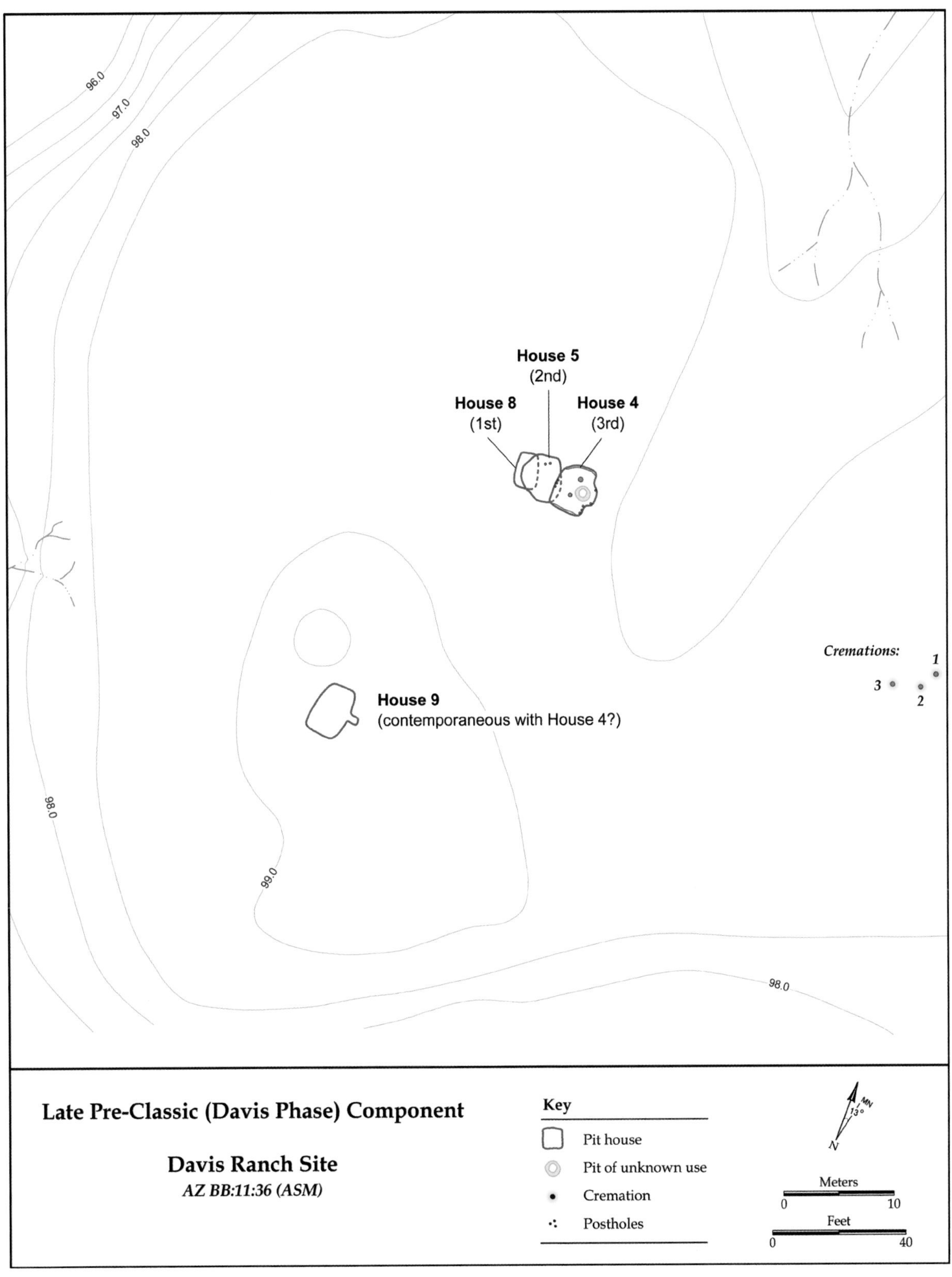

FIGURE 8.3 Late pre-Classic (Davis phase) component at the Davis Ranch Site. Map produced by Catherine Gilman.

excavated only a small portion of the settlement, as indicated by the scatter of pre-Classic artifacts that extends at least 150 m east of the pueblo to the adjacent historic cemetery (Clark and Lyons 2012:159–162). The eastward-facing pit houses excavated by Gerald and the cluster of cremations farther east may be part of a courtyard group. This courtyard group may in turn be a portion of a hamlet, considering the size of the artifact scatter. However, the absence of a ballcourt suggests that this settlement was not a large village. The nearest ballcourt that would have served this settlement is at the Soza Wash site (AZ BB:11:18[ASM]), several kilometers to the south.

Soza Phase (AD 1175/1200–1250/1275)?

There is no architecture at the Davis Ranch Site that conclusively demonstrates occupational continuity between the Hohokam pit house component and the initial Kayenta component that was established during the late thirteenth or the early fourteenth century AD. However, a small settlement occupied by locals during the twelfth and early thirteenth centuries AD (Soza phase) may have been present, as indicated by the recovery of a limited quantity of locally produced Tanque Verde Red-on-brown (including Gerald's Pantano Red-on-brown) and a single sherd of Casa Grande Red-on-buff.

Elsewhere in the lower San Pedro Valley, there was a shift from a few large pit house villages to numerous small farmsteads and hamlets during the late eleventh and twelfth centuries AD (Clark, Hill et al. 2012:358–359; Wallace and Doelle 2001:Figure 10.10). This shift coincided with the decline in the use of ballcourts, the abatement of Middle Gila Buff Ware exchange, and the waning of the ideology associated with both. If a small settlement occupied by locals was present when the Kayenta immigrants arrived at the Davis Ranch Site, this may explain the enigmatic Houseblock III (which Gerald [1975:193] inferred was a great house that was never completed), as well as the dominant use of local wall-construction techniques (rock-reinforced adobe), in the pueblo that otherwise has many ancestral puebloan characteristics (see figure 1.5).

Houseblock III is a cluster of nine rooms formally arranged around a courtyard or a small plaza. Only two of these rooms had floors, and floor features were entirely absent. The artifact scatter around Houseblock III was very sparse, and no middens were present. The available evidence suggests that construction was never completed and that this component was never used. This is intriguing, considering the amount of planning involved in its layout and the labor expended in the initial building activities.

Room 27 and Room 28, in the largest Houseblock III unit, were partially filled with adobe and cobbles, presumably from the borrow pit immediately to the northwest. This building (which also includes Rooms 29 and 31) is roughly the size and shape of a typical platform mound built in late thirteenth-century settlements farther north along the lower San Pedro River. Rooms 27 and 28 may have been cells in the process of being filled to erect a mound. If Houseblock III was intended to be a platform mound and an associated compound built by a local group, then the arrival of Kayenta immigrants with a different ideology may have caused them to abandon its construction. Evidence counter to this reconstruction is the apparent absence of a compound wall, although such a feature could have been planned as a later construction stage that never ensued. A similar hypothesis has been presented based on evidence for the construction and abandonment of a "proto-platform mound" at Redington Ruin (AZ BB:11:1[ASM]) and local groups moving in with immigrants at nearby Bayless Ranch Ruin (AZ BB:11:2[ASM]) (Clark, Hill et al. 2012:377–378). North of Bayless Ranch Ruin, at least one definitive platform mound was constructed in nearly every major Classic period settlement in the lower valley.

The small ceramic assemblage from the nine rooms in Houseblock III comprises only 188 specimens, and 74% of these were recovered from Room 28. Gerald typed 174 of these as plain ware

(159 Davis Plain, 14 Babocomari Plain, and one Redington Plain), two as red ware (one Gila Red and one Salt Red: Davis Variety), and one as Belford Perforated. He also identified four specimens as Gila Polychrome, four as Gila Black-on-red, and one each as Tucson Black-on-red, Sacaton Red-on-buff, and Rincon Red-on-buff. During the reanalysis, the two specimens from Rooms 27 and 28 identified by Gerald as Gila Polychrome were found to be fragments of a partially reconstructible Cliff Polychrome bowl comprising 11 sherds. The four specimens of Gila Black-on-red he listed as having been recovered from Room 28 represent a fragment of a Maverick Mountain Black-on-red jar, and the single specimen of Tucson Black-on-red he reported was not relocated.

This assemblage is clearly dominated by Classic period types with production dates spanning the Aravaipa, Redfield, and Romero phases. Limited contextual data, however, prevent any meaningful integration of the ceramic data with the architectural information. Only Rooms 27 and 28 had clearly identifiable, prepared floors, and all of the ceramic specimens discussed here were assigned to fill contexts. It is unclear, however, which might represent intentional filling of Rooms 27 and 28 versus refuse introduced after construction was abandoned.

Gerald (1975:193) infers that Houseblock III is a Reeve (Redfield and Romero) phase construction, postdating the decommissioning of the kiva. Considering that the pueblo, the only residential occupation comparable to Houseblock III, dates to this period, this alternative may be the best conclusion.

Aravaipa Phase (AD 1250/1275–1300/1325)

The inference that, during the late Classic period, the Davis Ranch Site was a Kayenta enclave is strengthened considerably by a close examination of the data in this report. The first compelling piece of evidence is the presence of a late thirteenth- and/or early fourteenth-century AD pit house component beneath and in the vicinity of the pueblo, represented by Houses 1, 2, 3, and 7 (figure 8.4; see figure 1.5; Lyons 2003:73–74, 97, 2004a; Lyons and Lindsay 2006; Lyons, Clark, and Hill 2011:185, Figure 8.4; see also Clark and Lyons 2012:159–163, Figure 3.56).

These structures are distinct, both morphologically and in terms of construction technique, from those associated with the late pre-Classic pit house component. House 7 overlies one of the largest and perhaps latest pre-Classic structures (House 9; see figure 3.22). House 1 was outfitted with an entrybox (Lindsay et al. 1968:Figure 204; Lyons 2004a), and the lower floor of House 7 exhibits a rectangular, slab-lined firebox typically associated with Ancestral Pueblo habitations.

In most cases, the fills and even the floors of the Kayenta pit structures yielded temporally mixed ceramic assemblages spanning the late pre-Classic through late Classic periods, suggesting that they became receptacles for primary refuse and redeposited trash. However, perforated plates, a reliable indicator of a Kayenta presence (Lyons and Lindsay 2006), were recovered from the floor of House 2 and the lower floor of House 7. Locally produced Maverick Mountain Series ceramics, pottery produced in accordance with the technological and stylistic canons of the Kayenta region, were also found on or near the floors of Houses 1 and 2 and the lower floor of House 7. The ceramic assemblage from the Northeast Trash, the area with the highest percentage of Maverick Mountain Series pottery at the site (nearly 40%), marks this locus as the main area initially used for refuse disposal by the immigrants.

This Kayenta occupation predates the construction of the pueblo, as indicated by the superpositioning of this building over Houses 3 and 7, although there may have been some occupational overlap before the construction of Rooms 3 and 6 (see below; see figures 1.5, 3.18, 3.22). The four Kayenta pit houses at the Davis Ranch Site suggest that no more than four nuclear families formed the founding immigrant group. Whether several local families were already present is an intriguing question. If

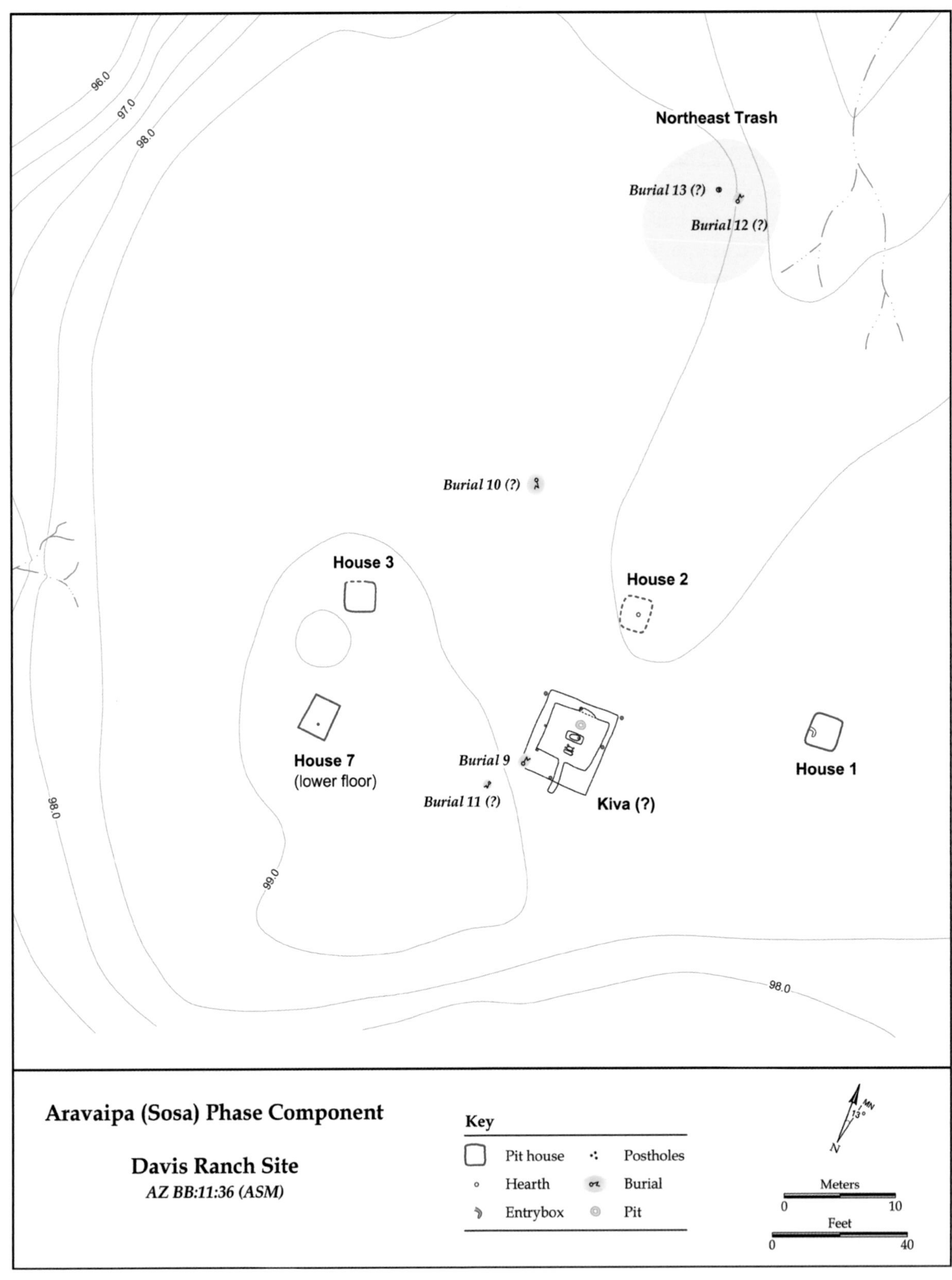

FIGURE 8.4 Aravaipa (Sosa) phase component at the Davis Ranch Site. Map produced by Catherine Gilman.

Houseblock III does, indeed, represent an aborted Aravaipa phase platform mound, the arrival of the first Kayenta immigrants may have halted its construction.

The Kayenta pit houses were arranged in an arc around the kiva, and the two that have intact hearths and whose orientation can be determined appear to face the kiva. This layout supports the inference that the kiva was built during the Aravaipa phase, overlapping with the pit house component, predating or contemporaneous with the earliest surface masonry construction episodes. The construction of the kiva was a significant labor investment and may have marked the decision by its builders to settle permanently and to attract other Kayenta immigrant groups to the region.

Ceramic Evidence for the Aravaipa Phase at the Davis Ranch Site

The Aravaipa phase is defined as a 25–75-year interval during which the Kayenta arrived in the San Pedro Valley and before the widespread production and distribution of Roosevelt Red Ware, particularly Gila Polychrome (Clark and Lyons 2012:104–106; Clark, Hill et al. 2012:368–384). Decorated ceramic assemblages from Aravaipa phase contexts should be dominated by Maverick Mountain Series types (and possibly Pinto Polychrome) with little or no Gila Polychrome present.

Behaviorally, the Aravaipa phase is characterized as an interval of tension between local groups and immigrants, with the former aggregating and building small platform mound villages. Shortly after their arrival, the immigrants began locally producing their homeland decorated ceramic tradition, the Maverick Mountain Series. In response, local groups revived their Hohokam-influenced painted pottery tradition, producing San Carlos Red-on-brown. Hence decorated ceramics reflected ethnic boundaries.

As transformative as the Aravaipa phase was, it is difficult to isolate pure Aravaipa phase ceramic assemblages at the Davis Ranch Site. For example, as noted above, the group of decorated pottery types associated with the Kayenta pit houses is temporally mixed. The absence of discrete contexts with an Aravaipa phase ceramic signature could, at first glance, be considered problematic and might even beg a reconsideration of the definition or at least the duration of the phase. In this context, it is important to consider three factors: the nature of the recovery units used by Gerald and his crew, assemblage formation processes related to discard as opposed to use, and large-scale spatial patterns in the distribution of wares and types.

The basic recovery units Gerald employed were fill, floor, subfloor, and feature. When he broke fill into levels, arbitrary subdivisions were used (e.g., 20 cm). Unfortunately, some loci particularly useful for addressing the late Classic period pit house occupation, such as the Northeast Trash, were excavated as single recovery units; that is, there was no subdivision of deposits into strata or arbitrary levels. This is problematic because the refuse generated by the inhabitants of the Aravaipa phase pit houses most likely was deposited in the Northeast Trash (see chapter 7). Indeed, the trash recovered from Houses 1, 2, 3, and 7 should date to the period when these structures were no longer in use as habitations. Such considerations are less critical in identifying architectural evidence of a Colonial/Sedentary period occupation (a span of 300 years), but the Aravaipa phase is conceived as having lasted less than half as long, perhaps as little as 25 years.

Gerald's typological conventions (e.g., lumping what would now be called Maverick Mountain Polychrome with Tucson Polychrome and Maverick Mountain Black-on-red with Tucson Black-on-red), inconsistent quantification procedures (i.e., sometimes counting partially reconstructible vessels as one specimen and sometimes including the number of sherds in totals), and other factors have obscured the nature of the early Maverick Mountain Series assemblage at the Davis Ranch Site (see chapter 6), hampering discussions of the Aravaipa phase and the contrast between local groups producing and using San Carlos Red-on-brown vessels and immigrants making and consuming Maverick Mountain

Series vessels. That said, Gerald reports 359 sherds and four vessels of Maverick Mountain Series types. The sample subjected to reanalysis and reported on in chapter 7 includes 224 specimens (62%). The difference in frequency is due mainly to reduction based on conjoins and matches (partially reconstructible vessels) but also the fact that specimens from some contexts (e.g., kiva trenches, multiple-level kiva fill units such as kiva level 3–5, trenches that fell outside architectural units or other key loci, and the surface of the site) were not included in the full quantitative analysis. Maverick Mountain Series types, including early types, are present in the assemblages from each of these contexts.

Types with pre-AD 1300 start dates (Maverick Mountain Black-on-red, Maverick Mountain Polychrome, and Nantack Polychrome) account for nearly 18% of the reanalyzed Maverick Mountain Series sample. More than 20% of the Maverick Mountain Series pottery from the reanalyzed sample and more than 20% of the specimens of early types in the sample were recovered from the Northeast Trash, identifying it, along with House 6 and House 7, as one of the earliest loci to accumulate late Classic period refuse (see chapter 7). More than 30% of the reanalyzed Maverick Mountain Series sample, and nearly 30% of the early types in the sample, were found in the pit houses—including Houses 6, 5, and 4—in and near the Northeast Trash (see figure 1.5).

A closer look at the assemblages from the Kayenta pit houses is instructive. Although House 3 was excavated in such a way that fill and floor artifacts cannot be distinguished consistently, House 1, House 2, and Floor 2 of House 7 yielded important data bearing on this issue. Four Classic period ceramic specimens were recovered from the floor of House 1, as were two sherds from a redeposited, partially reconstructible Mimbres Black-on-white bowl. The Classic period specimens include three partially reconstructible Tucson Polychrome bowls and one partially reconstructible Roosevelt Red Ware polychrome bowl lacking a rim (Vessel 2). This stylistically early specimen (Pinedale Style: Stage 1; the earliest category in Crown's [1994] Roosevelt Red Ware stylistic seriation) is most likely a vessel of Pinto Polychrome. Gerald, however, identified it as Gila Polychrome.

The floor of House 2 yielded three late Classic period sherds: an indeterminate Maverick Mountain Series bowl body, an indeterminate Roosevelt Red Ware polychrome bowl body (too small to permit any assessment of style; Gerald classified it as Gila Polychrome), and a Pinto Polychrome bowl rim. The lower floor (Floor 2) of House 7 produced seven specimens each of Maverick Mountain Series and Roosevelt Red Ware types. Those classified as Maverick Mountain Series include three Tucson Black-on-red sherds, two sherds of either Tucson Black-on-red or Tucson Polychrome, and one specimen each of Maverick Mountain Black-on-red (two matching sherds) and Tucson Polychrome. Those identified as Roosevelt Red Ware include two polychrome bowl body sherds of indeterminate type, one Pinto Polychrome: Salmon Variety bowl rim sherd, one Pinto Black-on-red bowl body sherd, one black-on-red specimen of indeterminate type (comprising two conjoining sherds and one matching body sherd; Vessel 28), one Gila Black-on-red specimen (consisting of two bowl body sherds that conjoin; Vessel 27), and a partially reconstructible Gila Polychrome bowl (comprising 19 sherds; Vessel 1). Although Vessel 27 is too small to assign to a style category, Vessel 28 and Vessel 1 are both decorated in Pinedale Style: Stage 1.

In summary, the only Kayenta pit house with Gila Polychrome on its floor is House 7, very likely the latest occupied, as its use seems to overlap with that of the early rooms in Houseblock I. Significantly, this single Gila Polychrome specimen bears a decoration classified as one of the earliest painted designs applied to Roosevelt Red Ware. More than 70% of the vessels in Crown's (1994:Figure 5.43) whole vessel sample exhibiting decoration of this style and stage were Pinto Polychrome vessels. Thus, despite the mixed nature of the ceramic assemblages from these structures, the available evidence strongly suggests that the latest material deposited dates to the late Aravaipa phase or the early Redfield phase.

Considering the temporal placement of the kiva in the context of these facts, it is important to note that Burial 9, a flexed child inhumation, is situated below this ceremonial structure and predates it. Among the funerary objects is a Gila Polychrome bowl bearing a Roosevelt Style: Stage 1 painted decoration. This is one of four styles or stages at the early end of the Roosevelt Red Ware sequence (Crown 1994:78–90). This evidence indicates that the kiva was constructed near the end of the Aravaipa phase, shortly after AD 1300.

How the initial settlement at nearby Reeve Ruin relates to that of the Davis Ranch Site is difficult to ascertain, considering the fact that the Reeve Ruin ceramic assemblage has not been reanalyzed. The bedrock outcrop where Reeve Ruin is situated would have made the construction of pit houses extremely difficult, and ephemeral surface structures would have been removed by subsequent construction. The initial room blocks at both sites are comparable in size and layout and may have been built close in time. Pinto Polychrome, Pinto Black-on-red, Maverick Mountain Polychrome, Maverick Mountain Black-on-red, and Tularosa Black-on-white, all predating Gila Polychrome, are present at Reeve Ruin in limited quantities, raising the possibility of a small Aravaipa phase occupation. Reeve Ruin is in a defensible location, unlike the Davis Ranch Site, but similar to the Goat Hill Site (AZ CC:1:28[ASM]), a late thirteenth-century AD Kayenta enclave in the Safford Basin (Woodson 1995, 1999).

Redfield Phase (AD 1300/1325–1350/1375) and Romero Phase (AD 1350/1375–1425/1450)

The Redfield and Romero phases are approximately equivalent to Gerald's Reeve phase (see figure 8.1). During the Redfield phase, much of the pueblo was built and Gila Polychrome dominated the decorated assemblage not only at this site, but throughout the lower San Pedro Valley. Occupation continued into the Romero phase, as indicated by the presence of Cliff Polychrome in significant quantities. However, the available evidence suggests that the Davis Ranch Site was depopulated by AD 1400, when the last substantial precontact settlements in the lower San Pedro were concentrated between the Aravaipa and Gila confluences (Clark, Hill et al. 2012:399–402; Lyons 2004b).

Pueblo Construction Sequence

A seamless transition can be traced from the Kayenta pit house component through the construction episodes associated with the pueblo. Houseblock I, the most intensively excavated building at the site, was the first surface masonry component constructed and formed the core room block of the settlement. Bond-abut sequences suggest either five or six building episodes.

Five rooms that were built in the first two episodes avoided nearby Kayenta pit houses (Houses 3 and 7). These may have remained in use while the initial surface structures were built (figure 8.5a, b; see figure 3.16). House 3 fell out of use by the third construction episode, partially covered by a masonry room. However, House 7 probably remained in use after Houseblock I was almost entirely constructed. House 7 had two prepared floors (one superimposed over the other), indicating an extended use-life. The ceramic assemblage from the lower floor (Floor 2) is discussed above, and the pottery recovered from the upper floor dates to the Redfield phase. This pit house was encompassed by the irregularly shaped Room 6 during the fourth Houseblock I building episode (figure 8.6a, b). This atypical room, outfitted with a slab-lined mealing bin, was apparently built as a replacement for House 7 with the intention of maintaining the same orientation of the underlying pit house, aligned with the kiva, while connecting with the other rooms in Houseblock I that were aligned slightly more to the west. The final construction episode in Houseblock I added a small room onto the southern end of this building. Three L-shaped entryboxes and two slab-lined fireboxes are associated with Houseblock I habitation rooms. Of note, all the entryboxes are associated with circular

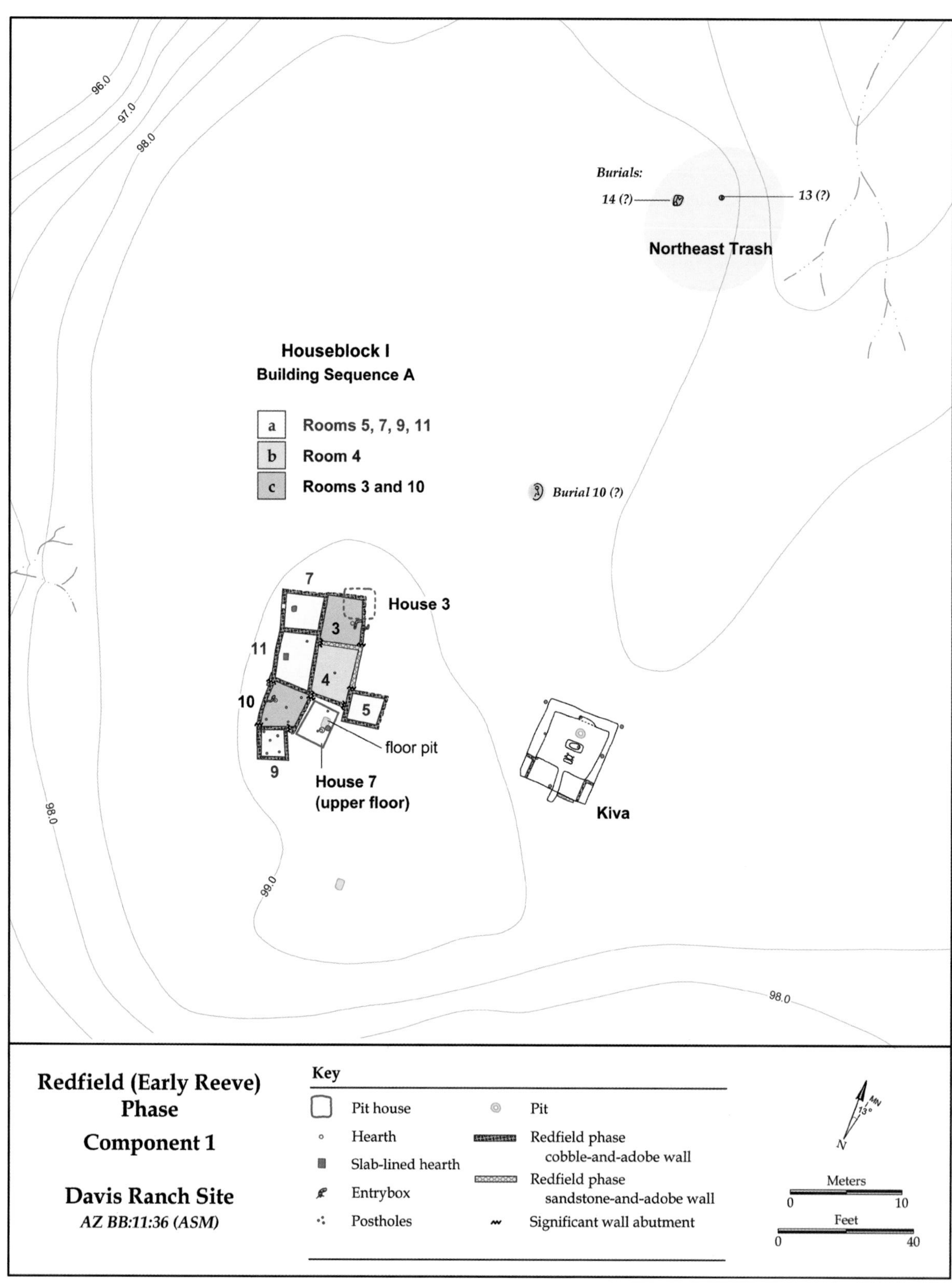

FIGURE 8.5A Redfield (early Reeve) phase component 1 at the Davis Ranch Site. Map produced by Catherine Gilman.

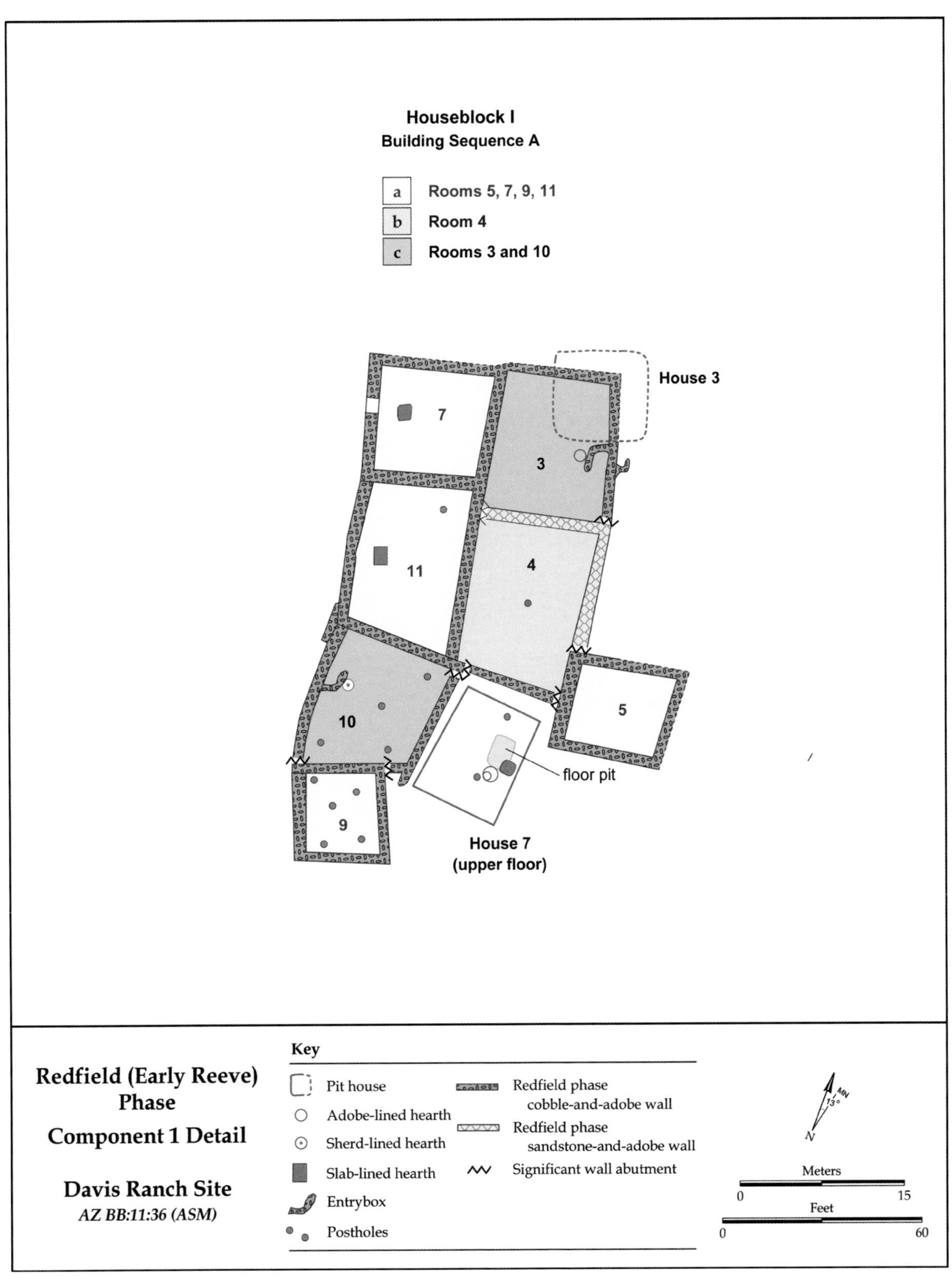

FIGURE 8.5B Redfield (early Reeve) phase component 1 at the Davis Ranch Site (detail). Map produced by Catherine Gilman.

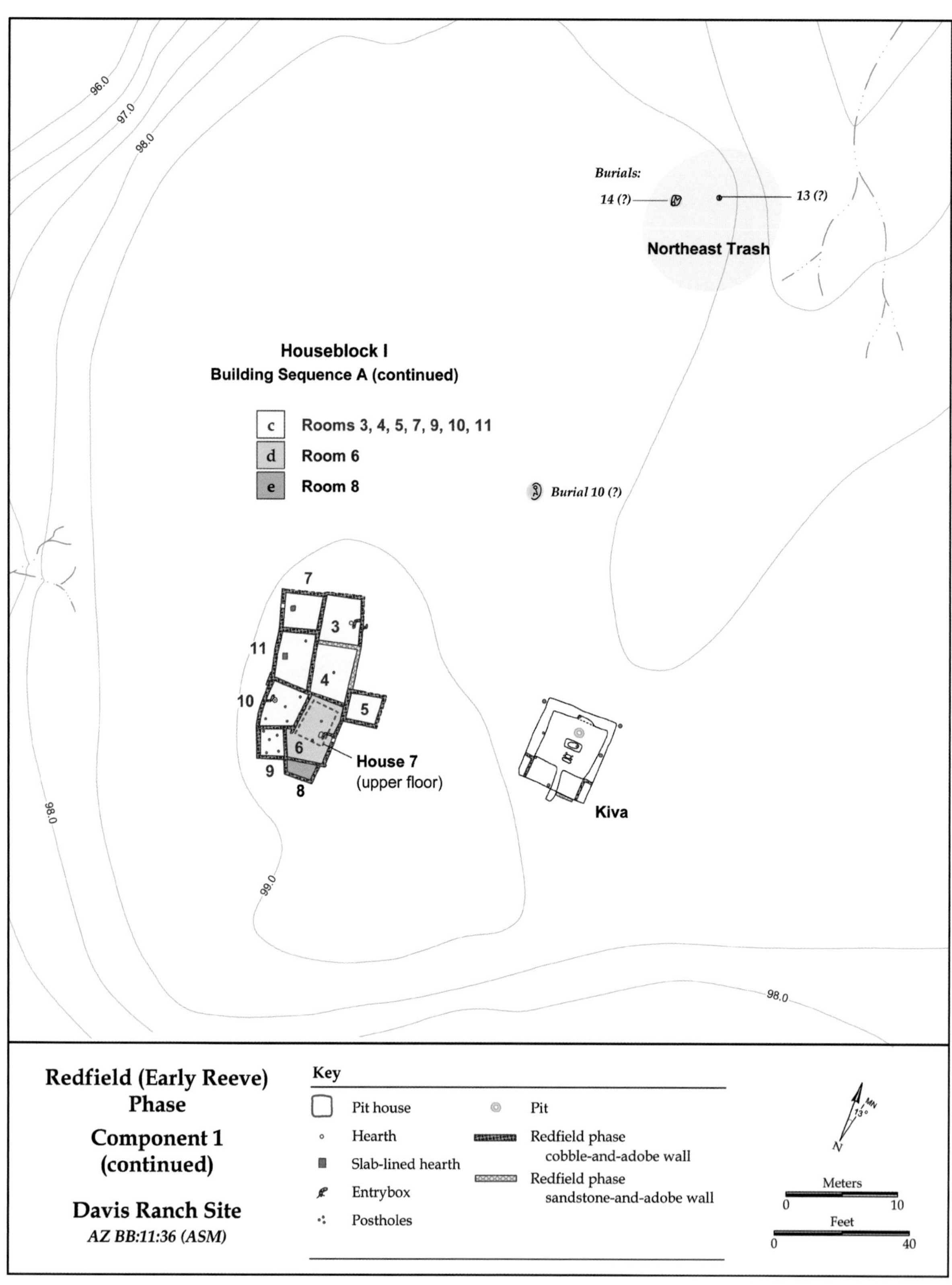

FIGURE 8.6A Redfield (early Reeve) phase component 1 (continued) at the Davis Ranch Site. Map produced by Catherine Gilman.

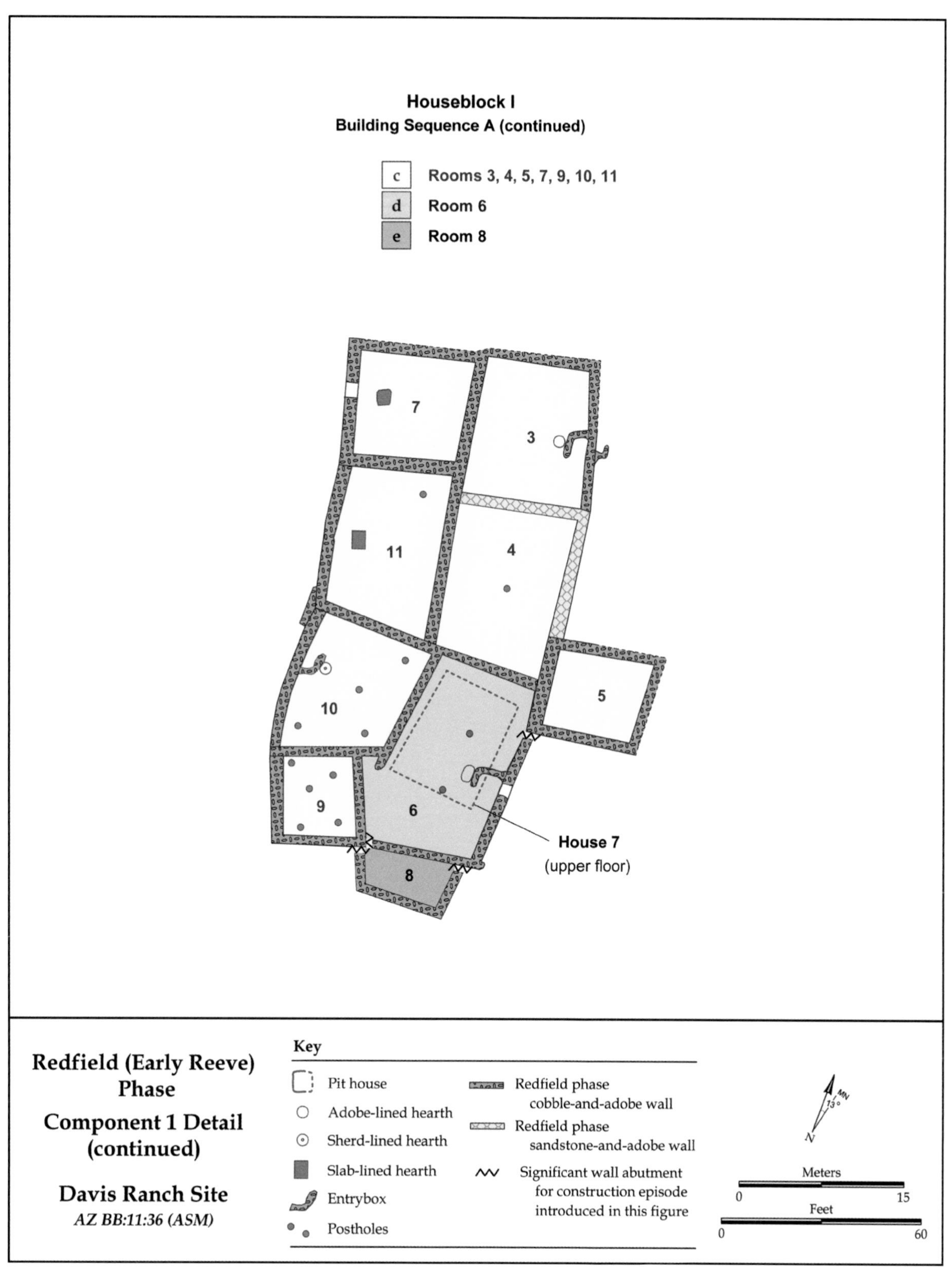

FIGURE 8.6B Redfield (early Reeve) phase component 1 (continued) at the Davis Ranch Site (detail). Map produced by Catherine Gilman.

or oval, earthen or plastered hearths, and the rooms with slab-lined hearths do not have entryboxes.

Although the lack of intensive excavation precludes a detailed reconstruction, Houseblock II seemingly was built next, forming the southeast corner of the final compound configuration (figure 8.7a, b). Additional rooms were added to the western end of Houseblock II in a subsequent construction episode. The easternmost room in Houseblock II (Room 16) had a hearth, an interior U-shaped entrybox, and an L-shaped exterior deflector.

Room 2, an isolated structure to the northeast of Houseblock I, may also have been constructed at this time. Room 2, which had both an oval, adobe-lined hearth and a rectangular hearth lined with cobbles and adobe, and Room 16 are the only rooms outside of Houseblock I with documented floor features. However, the rooms in Houseblock II were only trenched, and only three of the 16 rooms in Houseblocks VI and VII were investigated.

The construction sequence for the northern, western, and eastern portions of the final compound remains unclear. One plausible scenario has the southern four rooms of Houseblock VI constructed first, nearly enclosing a small plaza area to the south of Houseblock I (figure 8.8). Houseblock VII, the northern compound wall, and the compound wall segment and northernmost room in Houseblock VI likely were then constructed using a different alignment, perhaps in one or two substantial construction episodes. The eastern compound wall, most likely built after Houseblock I, changes alignment to accommodate Room 2. This strongly suggests that Room 2 predates the enclosing wall. Room 36 seems to have been built at the same time as the portion of the eastern compound wall that terminates to form that room's east corner. Room 34 apparently was constructed at the same time as Room 36. Room 48 postdates the eastern compound wall.

It is important to note that, from the point where it extends beyond the east corner of Room 36 to the point where it abuts Room 15, the eastern compound wall changes direction slightly. The change of direction and the abutment indicate that this segment of the eastern compound wall postdates both Room 36 and Room 15. At this point, the kiva would have been isolated from residential space, and Houseblock I would have been completely enclosed with the compound. Room 46 and ill-defined remnants of room walls in the northern portion of the compound cannot be placed in a construction sequence.

Finally, Houseblock III may represent the last precontact construction at the site, near the end of the fourteenth century AD (see figure 1.5), considering its unfinished condition and the lack of associated refuse (for an alternative interpretation see the discussion of the Soza phase, above). This interpretation is consistent with the recovery of a partially reconstructible Cliff Polychrome bowl from Rooms 27 and 28. However, the intentional filling of these two rooms with soil and rubble, apparently from a large borrow pit to the northwest, suggests the initial stages of platform mound construction. Platform mounds are not associated with Kayenta groups, and even local groups were not building mounds at this late date. Hence, the temporal placement and function of this building remain unresolved.

Based on this reconstruction, a continuous occupation can be traced from the initial Kayenta pit house settlement to the depopulation of the pueblo circa AD 1400. Houseblock I and Room 2, as well as the kiva, may have been constructed and occupied by the founding families who built and occupied the Aravaipa phase pit houses. Other houseblocks, especially VI and VII, probably represent influxes of new groups. Based on the total number of rooms and an occupation duration of a century or slightly longer, the maximum population of the Davis Ranch Site was no more than 75 people and probably closer to 50, depending on the number of contemporaneously occupied habitation structures (Hill et al. 2004).

The Kiva

Details of the kiva's construction and similarities to structures in northeastern Arizona, particularly those used by the Hopi, are discussed at length in chapter 3. The size, platform, benches, ventilator-deflector

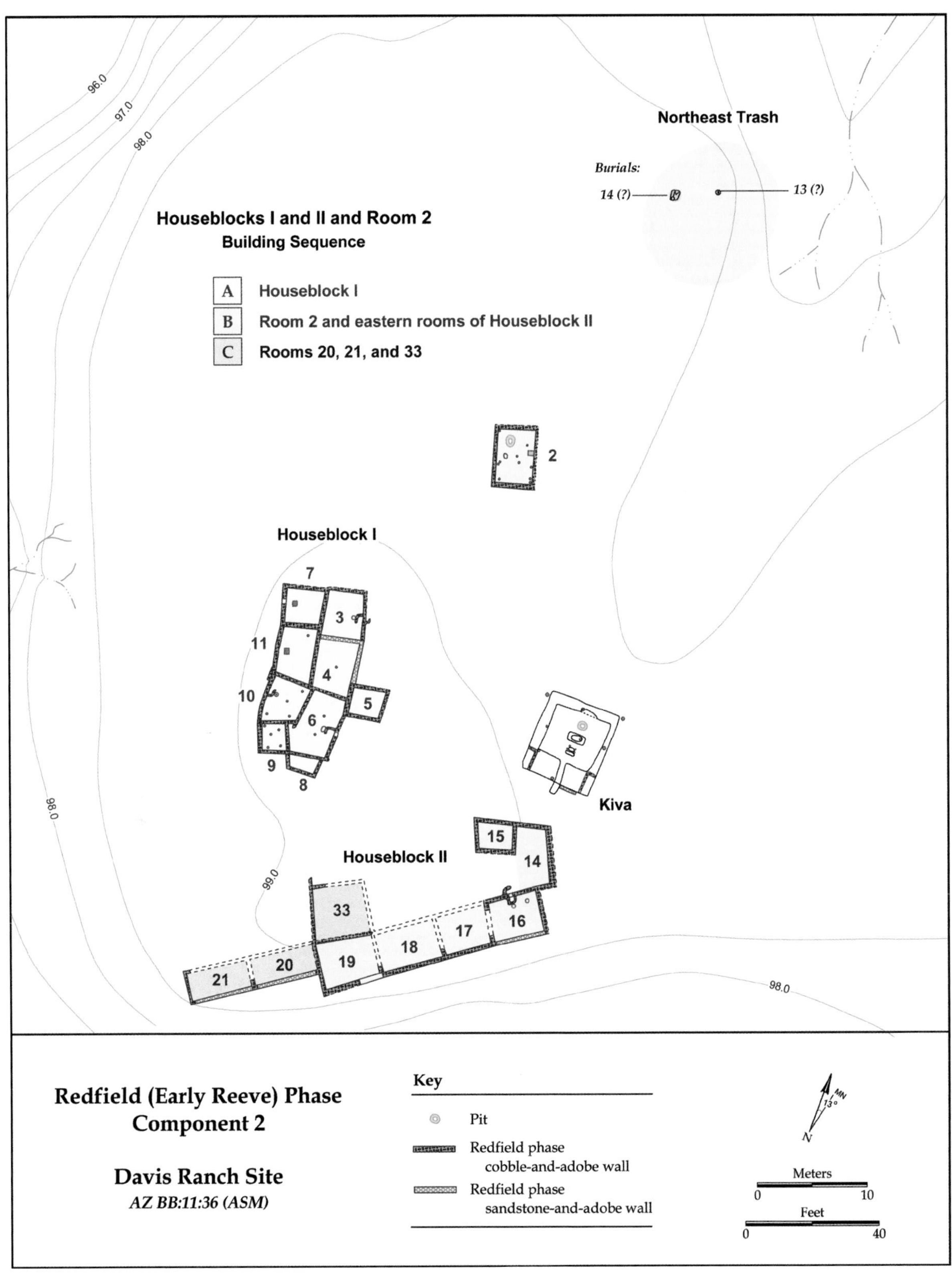

FIGURE 8.7A Redfield (early Reeve) phase component 2 at the Davis Ranch Site. Map produced by Catherine Gilman.

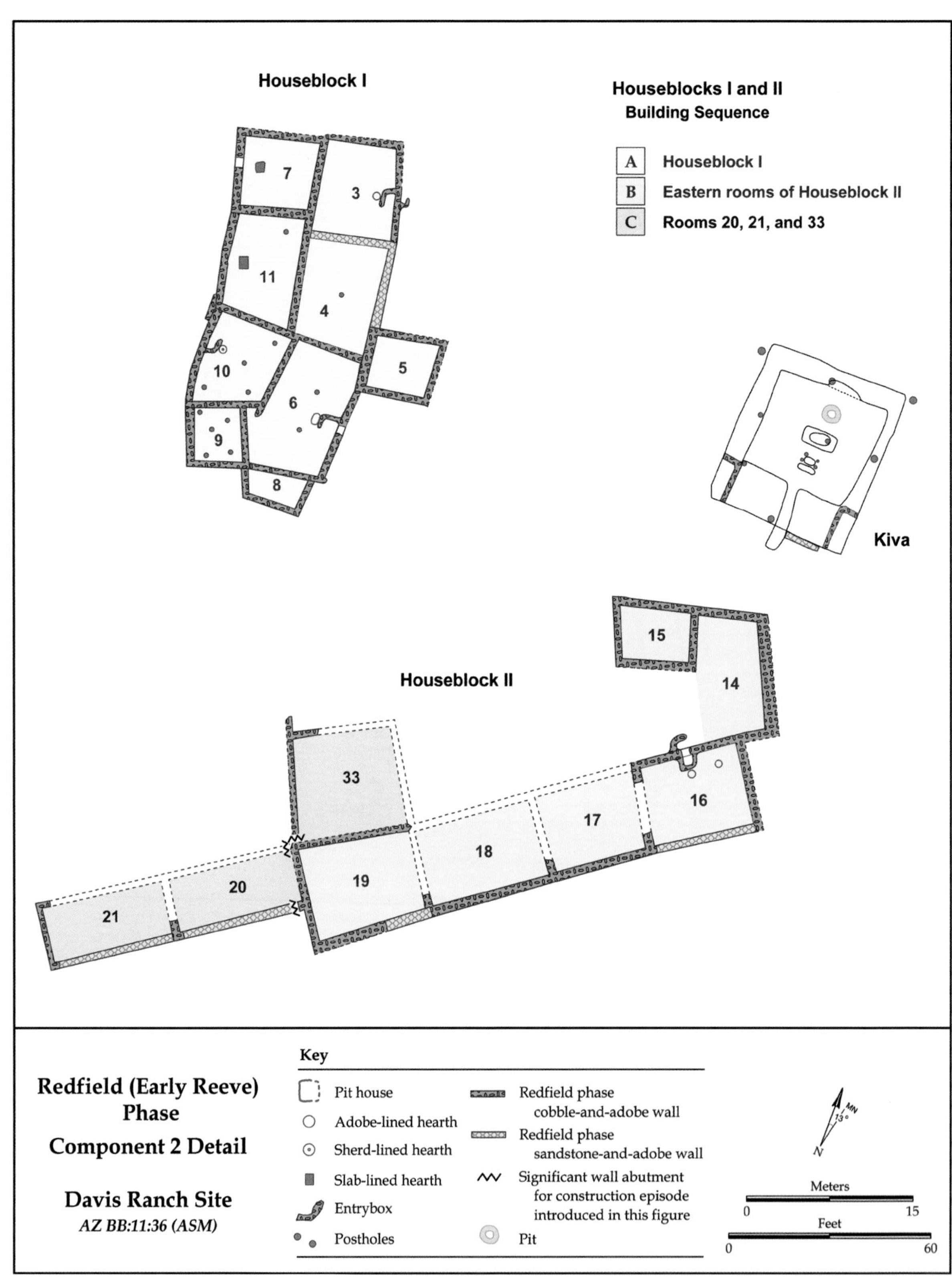

FIGURE 8.7B Redfield (early Reeve) phase component 2 at the Davis Ranch Site (detail). Map produced by Catherine Gilman.

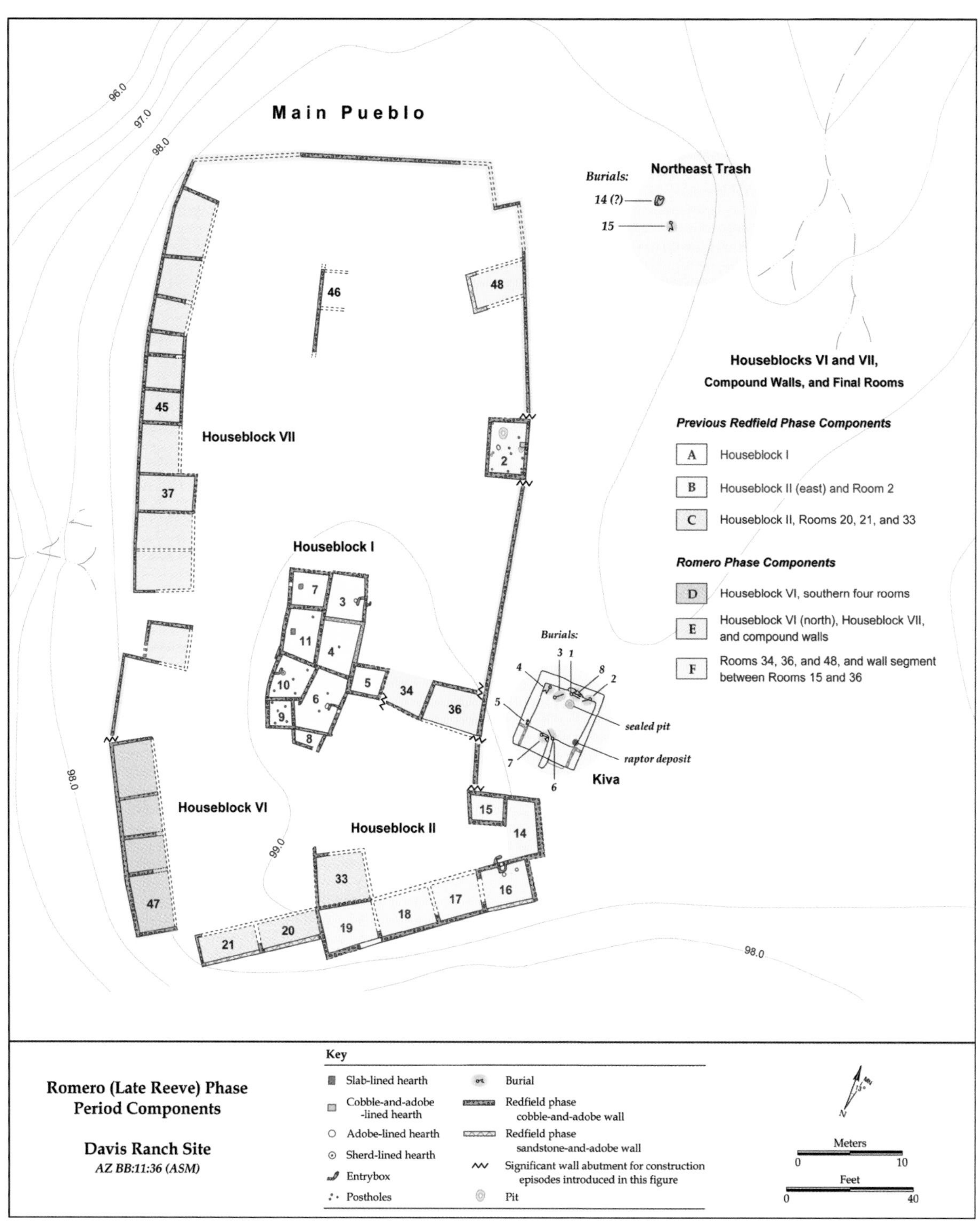

FIGURE 8.8 Romero (late Reeve) phase component at the Davis Ranch Site. Map produced by Catherine Gilman.

complex, loom-anchor holes, and foot drum leave little doubt as to either the use or the origin of this ceremonial structure.

One interesting detail revealed in the report but not apparent from the published photograph is that the large pit behind the foot drum (see figure 3.13) was carefully sealed. The existence of this feature, sufficiently large to hold an average-sized man, was suggested by faint cracks in the floor plaster. Based on ethnographic analogy (Ellis 1952), Gerald interprets this sealed pit as the location of a dedicatory ceremony (associated with a newly built or a remodeled kiva), like that recorded at Jemez, in which a man hidden below the floor speaks to members of the community gathered in the kiva. The pit is then secretly filled and all traces are obliterated. Although the pit in the Davis Ranch Site kiva may have been used in the manner described above, it must have been sealed after AD 1360, as its contents included, among other fourteenth-century ceramic specimens, one rim sherd each of Cliff Black-on-red and Cliff Polychrome.

As discussed above, the kiva was probably built during the late Aravaipa or early Redfield phase, close to the time when the founding Kayenta families decided to establish a permanent residence at the site. Perhaps more interesting than the kiva's construction and use was its ultimate fate, as revealed in the stratigraphy of its fill. After its last use as a ceremonial structure, the kiva was exposed to the elements sufficiently long for 15 cm of sandy wind- and water-deposited fill to accumulate on the floor while the walls and the roof were still intact. A cluster of more than 80 associated bones and bone fragments from at least four raptors was deposited in the east corner of the kiva, presumably as an act of ritual closure and decommissioning. At least 3 red-tailed hawk and/or Swainson's hawk individuals are represented by a complete cranium, 22 cranial fragments, 44 foot bones, 7 leg bones, and 6 wing bones. A tarsometatarsus from a common black hawk was also identified (see chapter 3, appendix I). A similar deposit, primarily comprising elements of 15 wings from 9 different raptors, was found in a possible kiva at José Solas Ruin (Clark and Lyons 2012:92–93; Lyons 2004a; Vint 2000). Comparable assemblages, likely representing worn-out ritual objects, or "ceremonial trash," have been recovered from several Kayenta and Tusayan kivas in northern Arizona (e.g., McKusick 2001; Mills, Van Keuren et al. 1999; Olsen 1978; Strand 1998; Walker 1995, 1999).

The roof of the kiva and portions of its walls subsequently collapsed. The remaining depression was used both as a trash dump and a burial area for the inhabitants of the pueblo for an extended interval, nearly filling the concavity. More than half of the Roosevelt Red Ware recovered from the lower levels assignable to a type is Gila Polychrome, and Cliff Polychrome and Cliff Black-on-red were found on the floor and in the floor features, indicating that the structure fell out of use during the Romero phase. Increasing amounts of Cliff Polychrome occur in the upper levels.

Although the last use of the kiva cannot be linked to a specific construction episode within the pueblo, the large amount of trash in the depression and evidence for time depth in the ceramic sequence represented in the fill suggest that the site was occupied long after the kiva was decommissioned. The last use of the kiva as a religious structure may have coincided with the construction of the compound wall that isolated it. Afterward, the enclosed plaza created by this wall probably served as the main locale for ritual activities, especially feasting (Lyons and Clark 2012; Mills 2007). Regardless of the precise timing, it is clear that the first Kayenta immigrants perpetuated northern ceremonial architecture and, presumably, related traditions in their new homeland. However, within a few generations, these traditions seemingly were replaced by new ones.

Burial Practices

Gerald recovered the remains of 18 individuals interred during the Classic period (see figure 1.5, chapter 4, and appendix B). As discussed above, Burial 9 was placed in the area of the kiva prior to its construction. Five individuals were laid to rest in the Northeast Trash, one underlies Room 2 and the eastern compound wall, and one was placed just outside this wall. Ten individuals were buried in the kiva fill after this structure was decommissioned. Classic period burials outside the kiva could be dated based on associated vessels of Roosevelt Red Ware, Maverick Mountain Series types, or Davis Plain (Belford Plain). Although the site's Classic period inhabitants treated their dead in a variety of ways, none were cremated. This stands in stark contrast to nearby Second Canyon Compound, several kilometers to the north, where cremation was the dominant mode of interment employed by local groups (Franklin 1980).

Crosscutting age and sex, half of the interred individuals (n = 9) were interred in partially or tightly flexed positions: beneath the kiva and Room 2, outside the eastern compound wall, in the Northeast Trash, and in the kiva fill. Five of the flexed burials were lying on their right sides, three were flexed and supine, and one individual was flexed, face down. All but one was associated with at least one ceramic vessel. Burial 4, in the kiva, was interred with nine Roosevelt Red Ware vessels, five other vessels, and numerous non-ceramic objects, including an antler baton.

In addition, three extended supine adult burials were interred in the kiva. None of these individuals were associated with obvious funerary objects, perhaps suggesting low status and/or non-Kayenta origins. In addition to the atypical body placement of these individuals, one was missing its cranium and thus may have met a violent end. The only artifacts in the vicinity of this individual were two pieces of unworked shell and a projectile point. It is possible that the point had been embedded in the body, although Gerald did not make this inference.

To our knowledge, this is the only late precontact site in southern Arizona where flexed inhumation was so prevalent as a burial practice. Tightly and partially flexed inhumation either on the right or left side was the dominant burial practice in the Kayenta region during the thirteenth century AD, immediately before the area was depopulated (Beals et al. 1945:Map 6, Plates 16–18; Colton 1939:52–59; Kidder and Guernsey 1919:66–70, 90, Plates 23b, 24, 25; Lindsay 1969:386; Spurr 2013). The evidence from the Davis Ranch Site indicates that Kayenta burial practices persisted long after migration. Undisturbed burials have not been recovered from Reeve Ruin, the Goat Hill Site, or any other Kayenta enclave in southern Arizona.

Ceramics

The presence of locally made Maverick Mountain Series vessels, pottery derived directly from ceramic traditions in the Kayenta homeland, has been discussed above (Lindsay 1987, 1992; Lyons 2003, 2012b, 2013a; Lyons and Lindsay 2006). Gerald recovered a substantial quantity of Maverick Mountain Series pottery, between 350 and 500 sherds, depending on whether most of the Gila Black-on-red he reports is actually mistyped Maverick Mountain Black-on-red or Tucson Black-on-red (see chapter 6). However, this sample pales in comparison to the more than 9,000 sherds of Roosevelt Red Ware recovered.

Decorated vessels, because of their high physical and contextual visibility, often convey social messages that can be copied, although invisible elements of technology and complex and relational aspects of decoration, such as layout and symmetry, are not easily emulated (Carr 1995a, 1995b; Clark 2001; Lyons 2003, 2014; Stark et al. 1998). Utilitarian pottery, an artifact class with relatively low purposeful messaging potential due to its low physical and contextual visibility, also sheds light on the origin of the site's inhabitants.

Locally manufactured Davis Plain (Belford Plain), represented by nearly 23,000 sherds and 14 vessels, dominates the Redfield/Romero phase ceramic assemblage. This same type is also dominant at Reeve Ruin. Belford Plain and related types and varieties (Redington Plain Smudged, a.k.a., Belford Burnished; Salt Red: Davis Variety, a.k.a., Belford Red) were manufactured using the coil-and-scrape technique characteristic of Ancestral Pueblo groups. This can be contrasted with the paddle-and-anvil method used by most groups in southern Arizona. Late Belford Plain bowls were made in the same form as Cliff Polychrome. A Davis Plain babe-in-cradle figurine fragment, found in the fill of the kiva, is another strong indicator of a Kayenta presence (Lyons 2003:24–25; Morss 1954:38–42).

Belford Red (Di Peso 1958a:104) is slipped red and polished inside and out. It basically represents Roosevelt Red Ware without white slip and black paint (Di Peso 1958a:86). It was made in vessel forms characteristic of Roosevelt Red Ware and the Maverick Mountain Series (see, e.g., Colton 1965:8–9), and the red slip utilized is the same as that exhibited by the former. Similar material has been recovered from sites in the Cliff and Mimbres Valleys of New Mexico (Nelson and LeBlanc 1986; Wilson 1998a, 1998b) and the Phoenix Basin in Arizona (see Crown 1981). In the Cliff Valley and the Mimbres Valley, it goes by the name "Cliff Red," and in the Phoenix Basin, "Phoenix Red" (Abbott and Gregory 1988:19–22; Brunson 1989:159). Some vessels identified as Kinishba Red (Wendorf 1950:42–43) are likely part of this same horizon. Belford Red Smudged (Di Peso 1958a:104–105) is Belford Red with a smudged interior, and both types seem to represent pottery made and used by Kayenta groups in diaspora across the southern Southwest (see below).

Gerald recorded a total of 314 perforated plate rim sherds, all from Classic period contexts. The reanalysis reported in chapter 7 resulted in the recording of 344 such specimens. As noted there, 185 of these fragments combine, through conjoins and matches, to produce 51 partially reconstructible vessels, leaving 159 sherds unmatched and unconjoined. Although considered a reliable marker of Kayenta occupation, as discussed in detail elsewhere (Lyons and Lindsay 2006), perforated plates are not abundant even in enclaves, such as the Davis Ranch Site. Indeed, when their frequency (n = 344) is considered using a standardized count (per 1,000 Classic period sherds), as we did when examining results from the sites in the CDA sample from the lower San Pedro Valley (Clark and Hill 2012), the value for the Davis Ranch Site, based on Gerald's sherd counts for all Classic period types (n = 35,638), is 9.65. This standardized count rises, of course, if sherds smaller than 5 cm^2 (0.78 in^2) are eliminated from the total number of sherds (as we did in the CDA analyses). Gerald did not tabulate sherd size data, and the only measure of this variable in the reanalysis dataset comes from the stratigraphic column, floor, and floor features of the kiva, where 3.64% of sherds were smaller than 4 cm^2 (0.62 in^2). Reducing the total number of sherds from the entire assemblage accordingly (i.e., by 1,297) produces a standardized count of 10.02. This figure is quite similar to that (10.50) computed for CDA test excavation units at the Davis Ranch Site.

By comparison, the standardized count of perforated plates for Reeve Ruin, based on CDA's work at the site, is 14.42. Using Di Peso's (1958a) data for Reeve Ruin, we compute a standardized count of 13.65. The modest standardized counts from these enclaves are consistent with the specialized use of perforated plates in ceramic production (see below) as opposed to more commonplace domestic activities such as food processing and consumption. Nonetheless, perforated plates are nearly absent from sites to the north, in the lower San Pedro Valley, that were occupied largely by local groups (Clark, Hill et al. 2012:Figure 6.18).

Less than 300 corrugated sherds were recovered from the Davis Ranch Site, with late indented corrugated (ca. AD 1200–1450) the most abundant type. These sherds are distributed across the site with little evidence of spatial clustering. The paucity of corrugated pottery at the site is consistent with the results of the CDA test excavations in the lower San Pedro Valley. High percentages of corrugated pottery were found to be linked with immigrants from the Mogollon highlands and the Safford Basin who preceded the Kayenta (Clark, Hill et al. 2012:363–368). Corrugated pottery is also rare at Reeve Ruin (Di Peso 1958a) and the Goat Hill Site (Woodson 1999).

Finally, more than 3,600 sherds of Babocomari Plain were recovered from the site, making it the second most abundant utility type after Belford Plain. According to Gerald, in addition to high mica content, Babocomari Plain can be distinguished from

Belford Plain by paddle-and-anvil construction (see chapter 6). Gerald describes Babocomari Plain as essentially a variant of Gila Plain, and thus it represents the local ceramic manufacturing tradition. More than 75% of the utilitarian ceramic assemblage from the late pre-Classic pit house component consists of Babocomari Plain, as expected. Indeed, nearly 30% of the sherds Gerald identified as Babocomari Plain were recovered from contexts known to be early based on stratigraphy and decorated ceramics, including House 4, House 5, House 6, and the Northeast Trash (see figure 1.5).

Gerald points out that this type also accounts for between 16% and 36% of the Aravaipa phase utilitarian assemblage. An examination of Gerald's sherd data indicates that nearly 15% of the Babocomari Plain he identified was recovered from the floor and fill of the kiva (n = 543), deposits that date to the late Redfield and early Romero phases (ca. AD 1360–1400). The distribution of Babocomari Plain in Classic period deposits could indicate the presence of local groups when the first Kayenta immigrants arrived. Likewise, Babocomari Plain in Redfield and Romero phase deposits might be interpreted as evidence of the continued presence of local groups practicing Hohokam pottery making traditions or exchange relationships with groups occupying other sites.

However, a cursory examination of sherds identified by Gerald as Babocomari Plain and Belford Plain (including specimens from the kiva) resulted in the conclusion that these types grade into one another; that is, differences in surface smoothness and the amount of mica in the paste are insufficient to consistently separate them, absent visible traces of paddle-and-anvil thinning. This is especially true of bowl sherds. Detailed reanalysis of the utility ware assemblage from the Davis Ranch Site, which was beyond the scope of the project that resulted in this volume, is required before the spatial distribution and behavioral implications of Babocomari Plain can be evaluated. It is important to note, in this context, that Babocomari Plain is entirely absent from the Reeve Ruin assemblage.

Other Artifacts

Close scrutiny of other artifacts recovered by Gerald reveals additional evidence that the Davis Ranch Site was a Kayenta enclave. For example, four of the nine Classic period projectile points recovered from the excavations were classified as Bull Creek points by Marie-Blanche Roudaut (see chapter 5). A reexamination by Lyons resulted in the opinion that only one of these points meets all the elements of the Bull Creek type definition (Geib 1996:107–108; Holmer and Weder 1980; Justice 2002:268–270), and two are more likely preforms or specimens of the longer-lived and more geographically widespread Cottonwood Triangular type (which is common in the Kayenta region). Bull Creek points are most common in northern Arizona and southern Utah, a region that includes the Kayenta homeland, during the AD 1050–1300 interval. If even one of the four Davis Ranch specimens is correctly classified, it would be the first example of a Bull Creek point identified in southern Arizona to date.

Of note, all nine Classic period points were made from obsidian, whereas the four Early Agricultural period and two protohistoric period points recovered from the site were made from other, presumably local, raw materials. No tool-grade source of obsidian exists in the San Pedro Valley. Sourcing of obsidian recovered from CDA test units at the Davis Ranch Site and Reeve Ruin, via X-ray fluorescence (XRF), show that this material was obtained exclusively from upper Gila Valley sources, with nearly all of it coming from the large Mule Creek source (Clark et al. 2014:252–256). Recent work has identified a probable Kayenta enclave at the 3-Up Site (LA 150373), the only large fourteenth-century AD settlement identified to date in the immediate vicinity of the primary Mule Creek deposit (Huntley et al. 2010).

Another marker of the Kayenta is pecked finger grips on manos (Bartlett 1933:11–12, Figure 6d; Di Peso 1958b:13; Valado 1999; Woodbury 1954:66; see also Kidder 1932:70, Figure 44). Finger grips date as early as the Basketmaker III period in northern Arizona and reached their peak popularity in the Kayenta homeland during the thirteenth century AD (Woodbury 1954:67–78, 81, 83, Table 8). Finger grips have yet to be identified on manos recovered from pre-Classic contexts in southern Arizona (Haury 1976:282; Sayles 1937:116; Woodbury 1954:83). Of the 41 nearly complete manos recovered from the Davis Ranch Site, 29 could be assigned to the Redfield or Romero phases (see chapter 5). Finger grips were found on three of these (10% of the assemblage), and none were found on the manos associated with the pre-Classic occupation of the site. At Reeve Ruin, 24% of the manos had finger grips.

Only 65 marine shell artifacts are present in the sample from Gerald's excavations, including 18 *Glycymeris* bracelet fragments, 10 objects made from *Conus* valves (including five tinklers), and six unworked or unfinished *Laevicardium* specimens (see appendix C). Fifteen whole-shell and disk beads, four whole-shell pendants, and four ring-pendants were also recovered. Although finished artifacts dominate the assemblage, limited evidence for on-site manufacture is present. This meager collection (only 1.6 specimens per 1,000 sherds; see table E.34) is comparable to that recovered from CDA test units at the Davis Ranch Site (only one specimen) and is lower than the Cascabel District average (3.9 specimens per 1,000 sherds), although the latter calculation only includes sherds larger than 5 cm^2 (Clark, Hill et al. 2012:Table 6.3). Marine shell was rare in Classic period mortuary contexts at the Davis Ranch Site, and most of this material was associated with a single inhumation in the kiva (Burial 4).

Much of the marine shell is difficult to sort temporally because it was recovered from surface and fill contexts (see appendix C). However, marine shell was nearly absent from the Aravaipa phase Kayenta pit houses, suggesting that the early immigrants had little access to this material. Access increased during the subsequent Redfield and Romero phases, after the immigrants had settled in and established contacts with local groups. The proportion of *Glycymeris* bracelets decreased during the Romero phase, while *Conus* specimens (tinklers and a ring-pendant) increased in frequency. Half of the *Conus* specimens were found in the fill of the kiva and may represent ceremonial trash. The preference for gastropods over bivalves identified in the small marine shell collection recovered from CDA test units at sites in the immigrant-dominated Cascabel District (Clark, Hill et al. 2012:393–396) was not replicated in Gerald's sample. However, gastropods still account for a relatively large fraction of the Classic period assemblage from Gerald's excavations, with a gastropod:bivalve ratio of 0.65.

Although Gerald did not systematically report on the animal bones he recovered, William Burt (1961; and appendix G, herein; see also appendices H, I) published a brief article on the faunal remains from the Davis Ranch Site. As expected, food animals such as jackrabbit, cottontail, and deer make up the bulk of the material. The presence of ocelot and possibly jaguar was considered unusual since the site is at the very northern limit of their ranges.

Perhaps the most interesting finds, however, were the avian remains, especially those from the raptor deposit in the kiva, discussed above. The overall assemblage from the Classic period included elements from at least nine different raptor species: golden eagle, Cooper's hawk, Harris's hawk, northern harrier, prairie falcon, peregrine falcon, common black hawk, red-tailed hawk and/or Swainson's hawk, and great horned owl. The falcon and harrier bones as well as elements from between 8 and 14 different hawks were recovered from the kiva fill. In addition to raptors, between one and two heron, dove, quail, duck, goose, kingfisher, roadrunner, raven, and robin individuals were represented at the site. Neither Gerald nor Burt had the benefit of comparative data from other San Pedro Valley sites other than Reeve Ruin (Burt and Storer 1958; see also Gerald 1975), but currently available information indicates that the late Classic period inhabitants of the Davis Ranch Site made more extensive use of avifauna than local groups (Clark, Diehl et al. 2012).

Finally, pollen from Rocky Mountain beeweed (*Cleome serrulata*) was identified in samples from multiple contexts at both the Davis Ranch Site and Reeve Ruin (appendix J; see also Schoenwetter 1965a). Rocky Mountain beeweed does not occur naturally south of the Mogollon Rim. To our knowledge, the only two sites where this pollen has been identified in southern Arizona are Reeve Ruin and the Davis Ranch Site. This finding, which sheds light on both cultural origins and ceramic production (see below), was not mentioned in Gerald's (1975) dissertation, despite the pivotal role that pollen analysis played in his conclusions about the relative dating of these sites and environmental conditions during their occupation. Beeweed and similar plants were commonly used during the historic era by Pueblo potters (Colton 1953:20; Shepard 1956:33; Stewart and Adams 1999), and presumably by Ancestral Pueblo groups (Stewart and Adams 1999; Stewart et al. 2002), as a source of black carbon paint.

Roosevelt Red Ware Production

Rex Gerald addressed neither evidence of the local production of Roosevelt Red Ware at the Davis Ranch Site nor its implications, given the likely origin of the producers. Nonetheless, the collections that resulted from Gerald's excavations are among the most important resources available for investigating the link between Kayenta immigrants and the development and spread of the Salado phenomenon. Put simply, because the Salado phenomenon is largely defined by the distribution of Roosevelt Red Ware, documenting production and consumption patterns associated with these pottery types is critical to any explanation of the larger processes of change they represent. Gerald's work yielded invaluable data bearing on these issues that can only be appreciated properly in the context of what is known today—in particular, the results of CDA's San Pedro Preservation Project and related research (Clark and Lyons, eds. 2012; Clark et al. 2013, 2014; Hill et al. 2004, 2015; Lyons 2004a; Lyons and Clark 2012; Lyons and Lindsay 2006; Neuzil 2008).

As noted in chapter 7, clay coils, a clay appliqué element, shaped-sherd scrapers, pigments useful in pottery decoration, and pigment-stained ground stone point to on-site pottery production during the Classic period. Also relevant is a Roosevelt Red Ware phenomenon called "Gila White Slip," (see chapter 6) present in substantial quantities (377 sherds) at the Davis Ranch Site and not found elsewhere in the region except at Reeve Ruin. This "type" represents firing mistakes: Gila Polychrome bowls bearing only subtle traces of painted decoration because the black carbon paint used to apply it was accidentally burned out. Assuming that such misfired products did not travel far from where they were made, their presence indicates that Roosevelt Red Ware vessels were being fired at the Davis Ranch Site (and Reeve Ruin). Rocky Mountain beeweed, as mentioned above, was present at the Davis Ranch Site as well as Reeve Ruin and could have been used to produce the black carbon paint characteristic of Roosevelt Red Ware.

Additional evidence consistent with Roosevelt Red Ware production at the Davis Ranch Site includes the significant quantity of perforated plates recovered by Gerald (these are also abundant at Reeve Ruin). These objects were used as base molds or potters' turntables (Lyons 2003; Lyons and Lindsay 2006). Fourteen of the 51 partially reconstructible perforated plate vessels and seven of the 159 perforated plate sherds from the Davis Ranch Site bear traces of unfired red pigment similar in color to the slip used to make Roosevelt Red Ware vessels (see chapter 7). These residues are often in the form of fingerprints or smudges as if a potter had gripped them with slip-covered fingers.

The reanalysis reported here illuminated other links between Kayenta immigrants and the production of Roosevelt Red Ware, including hybrid vessels combining aspects of Roosevelt Red Ware and Maverick Mountain Series/Tsegi Orange Ware style and technology. These include bowls with interior decoration typical of Roosevelt Red Ware and exterior painted decoration characteristic of Tucson Polychrome ("Gila-Tucson Polychrome"; see chapter 6). Another example would be the partially reconstructible Pinto Polychrome: Salmon Variety bowl that bears distinctive exterior decoration: red slip applied in a manner sometimes seen on specimens of a number of Tsegi Orange Ware types (see figure 7.39c, d).

The results of petrographic analyses of sand temper conducted as part of CDA's San Pedro Preservation Project (discussed below) and the abundance of Roosevelt Red Ware at the Davis Ranch Site and Reeve Ruin strongly suggest the inhabitants of these enclaves were the principal producers in the lower valley (Lyons 2012b). All the lines of evidence just discussed establish a clear link between Kayenta immigrants and their descendants and the manufacture of the ware that defines the Salado phenomenon. In the following section, we situate the data from the Davis Ranch Site in the context of what is currently known about the archaeology of the lower San Pedro Valley.

THE DAVIS RANCH SITE AND THE ARCHAEOLOGY OF THE LOWER SAN PEDRO VALLEY

The Davis Ranch Site is one of only five or six intensively excavated Classic period sites in the lower San Pedro Valley (figure 8.9). Two of the other sites, Tres Alamos and Reeve Ruin, were also excavated by the Amerind Foundation (Di Peso 1958a; Tuthill 1947). Second Canyon Compound was excavated in 1969 and 1970 by the Arizona Highway Salvage program of the Arizona State Museum. This work was supervised by Laurens Hammack and later published by Hayward Franklin (1980). Finally, Twin Hawks (AZ BB:6:20[ASM]), in the upper bajada of the lower San Pedro Valley, was excavated by Dudley Meade during the early 1970s as part of a Central Arizona College field school (Luchetta 2005). Bayless Ranch Ruin may have been intensively excavated as well, but the extent of the fieldwork conducted is difficult to determine based on the brief report in William Duffen's (1936b) master's thesis.

Much less work has focused on earlier and later time periods in the lower valley. Pre-Classic pit house components were investigated both at Tres Alamos and Second Canyon Compound. During the mid-1930s, Duffen excavated an unknown number of features at Redington Ruin, a large ballcourt village near Bayless Ranch Ruin, and the Amerind Foundation spent three weeks in 1948 excavating the K.E.G. Site, another ballcourt village at the south end of the lower valley (Di Peso 1951b).

The most intensive efforts to address the valley's pre-Classic occupation were conducted as part of the Peppersauce Wash Project, a segment of the highway salvage undertaking that resulted in the investigation of Second Canyon Compound. Alder Wash Ruin (AZ BB:6:9[ASM]) and two nearby pit house farmsteads, Una Cholla (AZ BB:6:18[ASM]) and Dos Bisnagas (AZ BB:6:6[ASM]), were excavated (Hammack 1971; Masse 1980b). Alder Wash Ruin includes both a pit house hamlet, dating primarily to the tenth and eleventh centuries AD, and a late protohistoric period (ca. AD 1650–1700) Sobaipuri component. Finally, Big Ditch, a large ballcourt village in the northern part of the lower valley, was investigated for several seasons during the 1970s under the auspices of a Central Arizona College field school after the excavations at Twin Hawks were completed (Masse et al. 2014).

Nearly all of the collections from the intensively investigated sites have been analyzed, and unpublished manuscripts or at least preliminary excavation reports are available for each. Luchetta (2005) reported on Meade's work at Twin Hawks, analyzing the collections and summarizing his field notes. The extensive Peppersauce Wash Project manuscript is nearly complete and available for use in the Arizona State Museum's Library and Archives but remains unpublished. Until now, the Davis Ranch Site was the only site intensively excavated by the Amerind Foundation that had not been published. This is an impressive record, considering those of many academic institutions conducting excavations in the U.S. Southwest at the scale of the Amerind Foundation.

The San Pedro Preservation Project

All of the intensive fieldwork discussed above preceded CDA's preservation archaeology program. The

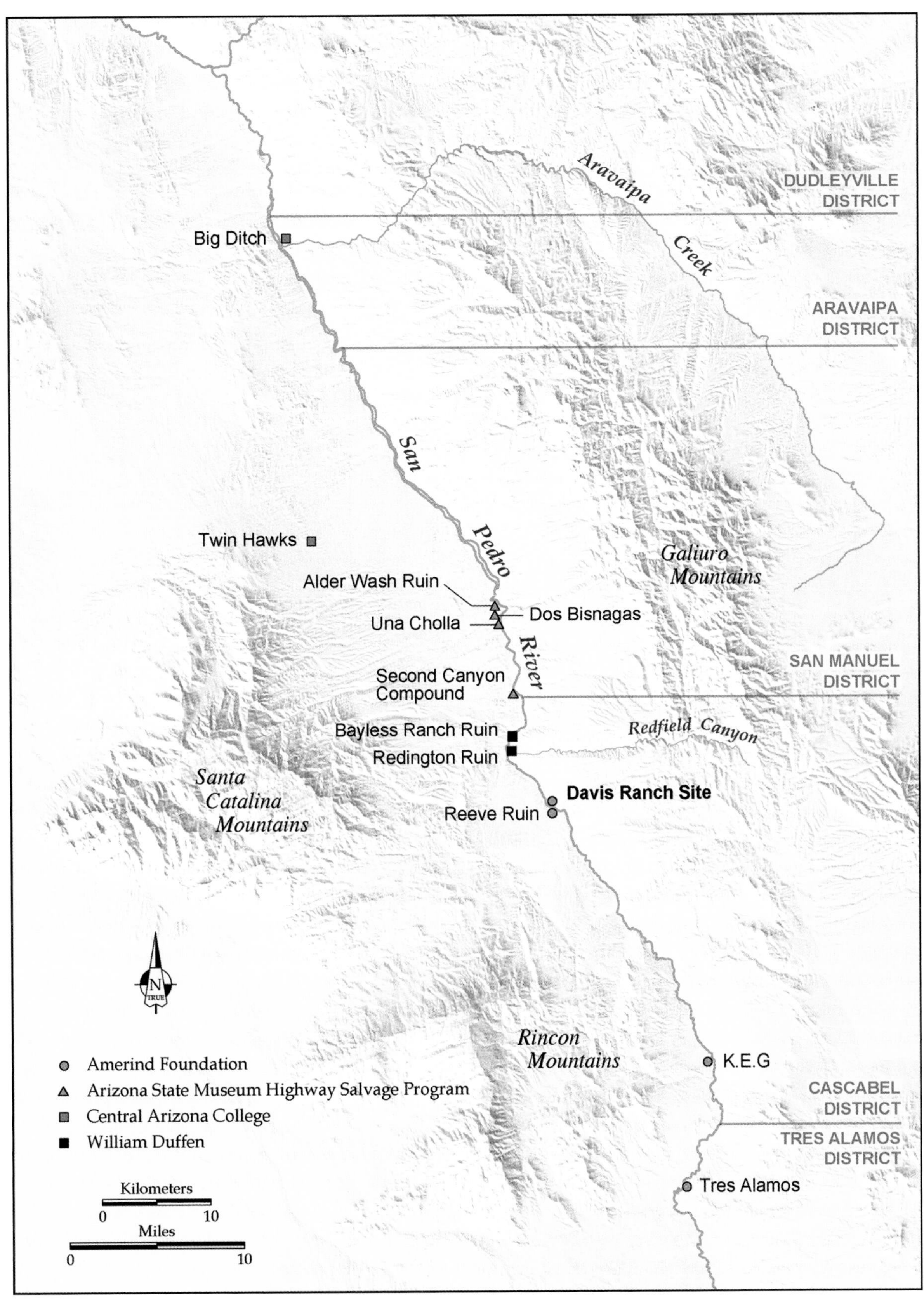

FIGURE 8.9 Sites in the lower San Pedro Valley intensively excavated before Archaeology Southwest's San Pedro Preservation Project (1990–2001). Map produced by Catherine Gilman.

fieldwork component of this endeavor began in the early 1990s and continued through the early 2000s (Clark and Lyons, eds. 2012). This included a survey of many of the Pleistocene terrace segments near the floodplain, from the Gila confluence to Cascabel. Coverage south of Cascabel to Tres Alamos was more sporadic. During the course of the survey, 5,518 ha (13,636 acres) were covered, 442 new sites (primarily dry farming fields and associated small architectural components) were recorded, and 46 known sites (primarily pit house and Classic period villages with surface architecture) were revisited (Doelle et al. 2012). Based on knowledge gained through the survey, 29 Classic period sites were selected for test excavations, with a focus on middens and other trash deposits that maximized artifact and ecosample return while minimizing adverse impacts (figure 8.10). All three sites intensively investigated by the Amerind Foundation, including the Davis Ranch Site, were tested using modern recovery techniques as part of this project. In 2000, CDA crews excavated six 1 × 2 m units at the Davis Ranch Site (Clark and Lyons 2012:162–163, Figure 3.56). Three were located south of Houseblock II, two between Houseblocks IV and V, and one west of Houseblock VI (see figure 1.5).

The test excavations resulted in a refined chronology for the lower San Pedro Valley that subdivided the previously bipartite (early and late) Classic period (ca. AD 1200–1450) into four phases (see figure 8.1; Clark, Hill et al. 2012). Particularly important was the recognition of Cliff Polychrome as a late Roosevelt Red Ware type (Lyons 2004b). Patterns in architecture and artifact assemblages also led us to subdivide the lower San Pedro into four Classic period districts, with a fifth district represented by Tres Alamos and surrounding sites in the northern upper valley (see figure 8.10). Particularly important are the fertile Aravaipa District, occupied by local groups who were heavily influenced by the Phoenix Basin Hohokam, and the Cascabel District to the south, which exhibits abundant and robust evidence of Kayenta immigrants, especially at the Davis Ranch Site and Reeve Ruin. Between the Aravaipa and Cascabel Districts is the San Manuel District, which was occupied predominately by local groups, but its inhabitants most likely included both Mogollon and Kayenta immigrants.

THE SALADO PHENOMENON IN THE LOWER SAN PEDRO VALLEY

The lower San Pedro Valley was an ideal place to study the Salado phenomenon. The area is relatively circumscribed by semiarid desert and mountains, and at least a portion of nearly every Classic period site is preserved and accessible. As part of the San Pedro Preservation project, trash deposits at the vast majority of these sites, including Reeve Ruin and the Davis Ranch Site, were tested and resulting collections were analyzed using standardized techniques. Finally, strong archaeological patterns emerged that could be used to tackle more complicated and fragmented archaeological records in other valleys.

Because of the valley's relatively intact cultural landscape and the strong material culture patterns that emerged, the lower San Pedro case study forms the keystone of our conception of the Salado phenomenon on a regional scale (Clark, Hill et al. 2012). We have used the lower San Pedro case study as a "gold standard" when comparing and contrasting contemporaneous developments in adjacent areas from which considerably less is known because of modern development and limited investigation (Clark et al. 2013; Hill et al. 2004, 2015; Huntley et al. 2016; Lyons and Clark 2012; Neuzil 2008).

As the fieldwork, analysis, and write-up components of the San Pedro Preservation Project were completed over the course of 20 years, Reeve Ruin and the Davis Ranch Site became increasingly important in our reconstruction of the Salado phenomenon, not only in the lower San Pedro Valley, but throughout the southern U.S. Southwest. Key to this reconstruction was establishing the origin of the valley's late Classic period "Western Pueblo" (see Di Peso 1958a) immigrants as the Kayenta region of northeastern Arizona and southeastern

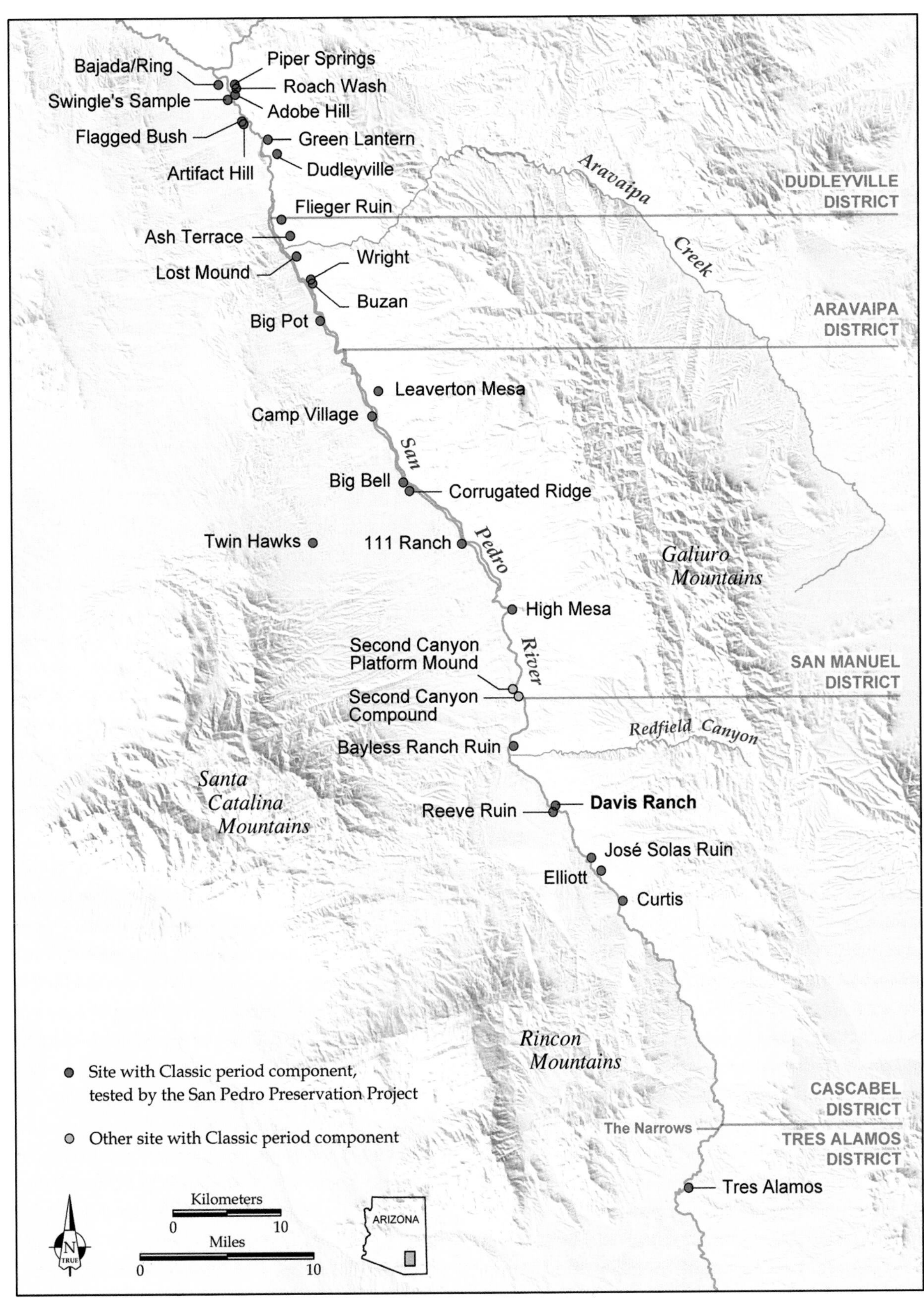

FIGURE 8.10 Sites in the lower San Pedro Valley with Classic period components. Map produced by Catherine Gilman.

Utah (Lindsay 1987; Lyons 2003; Lyons and Lindsay 2006), defining the Salado phenomenon as a transcendent and inclusive ideology reflected in the iconography of Roosevelt Red Ware (Clark et al. 2013; Crown 1994; Lyons and Clark 2012; Mills et al. 2013), and demonstrating the fundamental role these immigrants played in developing and propagating this ideology as the first producers of Roosevelt Red Ware (Lyons 2003; Lyons and Clark 2012). This model closely follows Crown's (1994) but places more emphasis on the role of the Kayenta in the development and spread of Salado ideology.

Western Pueblo or Kayenta?

Drawing on Erik Reed's (1948) seminal work, Di Peso (1958a:13–14, 16, Figure 4, part 2) differentiated the Western Pueblo archaeological complex from the Salado concept, associating kivas, mealing bins, contiguous masonry room construction, semi-flexed burial, perforated plates, rim coiling, and the "Gila-Tucson Polychrome art tradition" with Western Pueblo groups. At the time, the term "Salado" was applied to the ancient inhabitants of the Roosevelt Lake area in the Tonto Basin, who were said to have moved southward and westward over time. It had been observed that the Salado built large villages and made Gila Polychrome, a type that exhibited strong northern influence and perhaps indicated immigration (Gladwin and Gladwin 1930, 1934, 1935; Hawley 1928; Schmidt 1927, 1928), but no sites in the purported Salado heartland had yet been excavated and published. Thus, with the exception of Gila Polychrome, a link between Western Pueblo and Salado was not indicated.

One of the most important inferences about the Davis Ranch Site and Reeve Ruin, and one strongly supported by this volume, is that both were enclaves established in the late thirteenth century AD by Kayenta immigrants from northeastern Arizona (Lindsay 1987; see also Clark and Laumbach 2011; Clark and Lyons, eds. 2012; Lyons 2003, 2004a; Lyons and Lindsay 2006). This is a substantial refinement of Di Peso's (1958a; see also Willey et al. 1956) Western Pueblo, site-unit intrusion model, pinpointing the origin of the newcomers.

The Reeve Ruin excavations were painstakingly reported by Di Peso (1958a). Because the data are so well published and the evidence for migration is so compelling, few archaeologists currently disagree with the interpretation that this site was founded by Ancestral Pueblo immigrants, specifically groups from the Kayenta region. Another widely accepted enclave is the Goat Hill Site on the southern margin of the Safford Basin (Woodson 1995, 1999). The Maverick Mountain phase occupation at Point of Pines Pueblo constitutes a third example (Haury 1958).

Prior to the publication of this volume, the Davis Ranch Site generally has been accepted as an enclave because of its proximity to Reeve Ruin, the photograph of its kiva in Di Peso's (1958a:Plate 5) Reeve Ruin report (see also figure 3.11), and bits and pieces of information that have come to light since 1957. However, in the absence of a published report, archaeologists were forced to accept the word of the few people familiar with the data. This volume rectifies the situation and, we believe, presents a case for a Kayenta settlement that is even more compelling than that of Reeve Ruin.

At least six enculturative markers (i.e., perforated plates, locally made Maverick Mountain Series vessels, entryboxes, the kiva, a babe-in-cradle figurine, and one or more Bull Creek projectile points) associated with Kayenta groups were documented at the Davis Ranch Site. In addition to these indicators that point specifically to the Kayenta region as the provenance of the builders and inhabitants of the site, a long list of more generic markers of Ancestral Pueblo groups that include the people of the Kayenta region was observed: room-block architecture, walls made of shaped and coursed sandstone, slab-lined hearths, a mealing bin, locally produced pottery made using the coil-and-scrape technique, shaped-sherd pottery scrapers, evidence of the use of beeweed (see appendix J), shaped-sherd pot rests, manos with finger grips, bifacial manos, a faceted mano, flat metates, and flexed human burials. The

TABLE 8.1 Sites having yielded evidence suggesting co-residence by local groups and Kayenta immigrants and/or their descendants

Site name	Site no.	Region	Reference(s)
76 Ranch Ruin	AZ BB:8:1(ASM)	Aravaipa Valley	Duffen 1936a, 1937; Duffen and Hartmann 1997
Fort Grant Pueblo	AZ CC:5:8(ASM)	Aravaipa Valley	Neuzil 2008
Haby Pueblo	AZ BB:3:16(ASM)	Aravaipa Valley	Gerald 1957a; Neuzil 2008
Pueblo Devol	AZ W:14:18(BLM)	Bonita Creek	Welch 1995
Dinwiddie Site	LA 106003	Cliff Valley	Huntley et al. 2016; Mills and Mills 1972
Ormand Village	LA 5793	Cliff Valley	Wallace 1998
Besh-Ba-Gowah	AZ V:9:11(ASM)	Globe-Miami	Hohmann et al. 1992; Lyons 2003:73; Lyons and Lindsay 2006
Gila Pueblo	AZ V:9:52(ASM)	Globe-Miami	Lyons 2003:73; Lyons and Lindsay 2006; McGregor 1965:423
Hilltop House	AZ V:9:68(ASM)	Globe-Miami	Lyons 2003:73; Lyons and Lindsay 2006
Carter Ranch Site	no site number	Hay Hollow Valley	Longacre 1970; Lyons 1999b; Martin et al. 1964
Broken K Pueblo	AZ Q:5:28(ASM)	Hay Hollow Valley	Hill 1970; Lyons 1999b; Martin et al. 1967
Las Colinas	AZ T:12:10(ASM)	Lower Salt Valley	Hill et al. 2015; Lyons 2004e; Lyons, Hill, and Clark 2011
Los Muertos	AZ U:9:56(ASM)	Lower Salt Valley	Haury 1945; Lyons 2004e; Lyons, Hill, and Clark 2011
Bajada/Ring Site	AZ BB:1:6(ASM)	Lower San Pedro Valley	Clark and Lyons, eds. 2012
Bayless Ranch Ruin	AZ BB:11:2(ASM)	Lower San Pedro Valley	Clark and Lyons, eds. 2012; Duffen 1936b
José Solas Ruin	AZ BB:11:90(ASM)	Lower San Pedro Valley	Lyons 2004a
Swingle's Sample	AZ BB:1:22(ASM)	Lower San Pedro Valley	Clark and Lyons, eds. 2012
Horse Camp Mill Site	LA 10983	Mariana Mesa	McGimsey 1980
Techado Spring Pueblo	LA 6010	Mariana Mesa	Smith et al. 2009
3-Up Site	LA 150373	Mule Creek	Huntley et al. 2010

(continued)

TABLE 8.1 *(continued)*

Site name	Site no.	Region	Reference(s)
Dutch Ruin	LA 8706	Redrock Valley	Fortenberry and Bennett 1968; Lekson 2002
Curtis Site	AZ CC:2:3(ASM)	Safford Basin	Mills and Mills 1978; Neuzil 2008
Marijilda Site	AZ CC:5:6(ASM)	Safford Basin	Neuzil 2008
Spear Ranch Site	AZ CC:1:11(ASM)	Safford Basin	Neuzil 2008
Kuykendall Site	AZ FF:2:2(ASM)	Sulphur Springs Valley	Mills and Mills 1969a, 1969b
Keystone Ruin	AZ U:8:480(ASM)	Tonto Basin	Lyons 2013b; Lyons and Lindsay 2006
Lower Ruin, Tonto National Monument	AZ U:8:47(ASM)	Tonto Basin	Lyons 2013b; Pierson 1962
Schoolhouse Point Mesa complex	AZ U:8:450(ASM)	Tonto Basin	Lindauer 1997; Lyons 2013b; Lyons and Lindsay 2006
Schoolhouse Point Mesa complex	AZ U:8:454(ASM)	Tonto Basin	Clark 2001; Lindauer 1997; Lyons 2013b; Lyons and Lindsay 2006
Schoolhouse Point Mesa Mound	AZ U:8:24(ASM)	Tonto Basin	Lindauer 1996; Lyons 2013b; Lyons and Lindsay 2006
Upper Ruin, Tonto National Monument	AZ U:8:48(ASM)	Tonto Basin	Lyons 2013b; Steen 1962
University Indian Ruin	AZ BB:9:33(ASM)	Tucson Basin	Hayden 1957
Rillito Fan Site	AZ AA:12:788(ASM)	Tucson Basin	Craig 2011; Wöcherl 2007

had heavily favored the local majority. Part of the trans-cultural appeal of Salado ideology may have been the important role played by the plumed or horned serpent that was at least indirectly associated with the Mesoamerican Quetzalcoatl or Kulkulkan (also Paalölöqangw and Kolowisi among the Hopi and Zuni, respectively). Quetzalcoatl/Kulkulkan may have served a similar high-level integrative role in Mesoamerica (Boone 2003; Sharer and Traxler 2006:582–583).

CONCLUDING REMARKS

Although written more than 60 years ago, Rex Gerald's report on the Amerind Foundation's excavations at the Davis Ranch Site, finally brought to light in this volume, is a treasure trove of information. Gerald's data attest to the high quality of his fieldwork, especially considering the era during which it was conducted. Gerald's report must be the centerpiece of any reconstruction of processes unfolding during the Classic period in the lower San Pedro Valley.

First and foremost, this volume provides detailed information on the establishment and development of the fourteenth-century AD Kayenta immigrant settlement at the site that can now be compared and contrasted with data from the well-documented enclave at nearby Reeve Ruin. It also provides compelling evidence that these immigrants and their descendants were the principal producers of the Roosevelt Red Ware vessels that circulated throughout the lower San Pedro Valley. Gerald's results, interpreted through the lens of more recent research, represent a crucial link between the Kayenta community in diaspora and the development of Salado ideology reflected in Roosevelt Red Ware iconography.

Gerald's excavations also shed light on the pre-Classic occupation of the Davis Ranch Site. Of particular importance is the recent identification of a small Early Agricultural period component. If the San Pedro Valley is analogous to the neighboring Santa Cruz Valley, much more evidence of occupation during this interval awaits discovery in the floodplain and on adjacent terraces. Finally, it is our hope that readers of this volume come to accept one of the key tenets of preservation archaeology: that museum collections are invaluable sources of information, allowing researchers to ask old questions in new ways and to ask questions that previous generations of researchers never imagined could be addressed.

APPENDIX A

Dendrochronology

Jeffrey S. Dean

Tree-ring samples (nine field numbers) from the 1957 excavations at the Davis Ranch Site were submitted to the Laboratory of Tree-Ring Research. All material was examined in 1957 by an unknown technician and again in 2004 by the author (table A.1). These samples represented 24 separate trees. The collection was dominated by *Populus* sp. (probably floodplain cottonwoods; 10 samples). Two samples were *Prosopis* (mesquite), and one was identified in 1957 as *Sapindus* (soapberry). None of these nonconiferous samples are datable. Apart from the general problems with these species, most of the samples have too few rings or are too rotten to produce any results.

Juniper is the most common coniferous species from the site, but none of the five samples have enough rings or sufficient ring-width variability to allow dating. The two samples identified as *Pinus* are likely some other large pine species rather than ponderosa. Three Douglas fir samples have too few rings and too little sensitivity to be dated. It may be significant that all three of these samples come from the same provenience, the floor of Room 10.

diameter of 36.00 mm. Age based on recent fusion of vertebral epiphyseal rings, clavicle epiphyses, and pubic symphysis fragment.

Burial 11: Newborn

Fragments of skull, both mandibular halves, fragments of ribs, vertebral neural arches, right clavicle, and one metacarpal mixed with animal bone fragments. Age based on sizes and fibrous nature of bones and 44.00 mm diaphyseal length of clavicle.

Burial 12a: Child, 11–12 Years Old; Burial 12b: Infant, 6–12 Months Old

Fragments of skull and loose teeth with fragments of vertebrae, ribs, upper and lower limbs. Small infant right humerus and metatarsal. Child's age based on dental development and infant's age estimated on sizes of bones. Child's teeth show protostylid pits on lower first molars and occlusal pit caries on lower first molar.

Burial 13: Adult

Skull fragments only.

Burial 14: Child, 4–5 Years Old

Fragments of skull, ribs, vertebral neural arch, long bones, one metacarpal, right clavicle, and several loose teeth. Age based on dental development and 79.00 mm diaphyseal length of clavicle.

Burial 15: Newborn

Left frontal and skull fragments, rib, and metatarsal mixed with animal bone fragments. Age based on sizes and fibrous nature of bones.

CREMATIONS

Cremation 1: Adult

Small amount of whitish gray fragments of skull, humerus, ulna, and radius with one white long bone fragment of adult size.

Cremation 2: Adult

Small amount of white and yellowed fragments of occipital, mandible, distal femur, and long bones of adult size.

Cremation 3: Adult Male

Small amount of whitish gray fragments of mandible, femur, and radius of adult size. Sex based on large mandibular condyle.

APPENDIX C

The Davis Ranch Site Shell Assemblage

Arthur W. Vokes and Erika Heacock

The excavations at the Davis Ranch Site by Rex Gerald in the spring of 1957 produced a shell assemblage of 119 pieces that is estimated to represent approximately 67 individual items. The majority of this material, which is predominately ornamental in nature, is fragmented and was from non-mortuary contexts, although several specimens were associated with one cremation and four inhumations. The occupation of the site is primarily attributed to the Aravaipa (AD 1250/1275–1300/1325), Redfield (AD 1300/1325–1350/1375), and Romero (AD 1350/1375–1425/1450) phases of the late Classic period, although there is evidence of smaller Early Agricultural period and late pre-Classic components. Various lines of evidence indicate that the Classic period occupation is associated with a late intrusion of people from the Kayenta region (Clark, Hill et al. 2012:371).

METHODOLOGY

Although Gerald had prepared a short descriptive report on the shell assemblage, using species identifications supplied by George P. Kanakoff, typological refinements since the 1950s warranted a new analysis. The assemblage was subjected to detailed study involving the creation of a descriptive record, including digital images and measurements obtained with a digital vernier caliper (recorded to the nearest 0.01 mm). Notes on technologies employed in the manufacturing process, form, decorative motifs, and condition were also recorded. Finally, whenever possible, an estimate of the relative completeness of each specimen was made. For unworked fragments, this assessment is the percentage of the original valve that remains. For purposes of analysis, fragments that could be refitted were considered to be single occurrences, with the number of pieces recorded in the notes. Specimens were generally considered to be complete if a full set of linear measurements could be obtained.

The artifact classification structure employed during this analysis is largely based on the system presented by Haury for the material from Snaketown (Haury 1937c, 1976). The shell nomenclature used and the biological determinations were made in accordance with Keen's (1971) *Sea Shells of Tropical West America*, with additional information obtained from Abbott's (1974) *American Seashells*. The taxonomic identifications were checked against the World Register of Marine Species (WoRMS 2018) to ensure that the names of the identified taxa conform to current standards. Only one freshwater pelecypod was identified in the assemblage: *Anodonta californiensis*, a gracile bivalve that was widely distributed prior to the impoundment of many rivers and streams during the twentieth century (Myers 2009).

Definitions of terms related to the structural elements of shell can be found in the glossaries available in most malacology guides. Figures that illustrate these elements and their associated nomenclature have been published previously by the senior author (Vokes 1984, 1986).

GENERA AND SPECIES

There were two general sources of shell available to the prehistoric inhabitants of southern Arizona: the marine communities of the west coast of California and the Gulf of California and freshwater mollusks that were endemic to the streams and rivers of the region. Table C.1 summarizes the species of mollusks identified in the assemblage. Nine marine and one freshwater genera were identified. By far, the most common is *Glycymeris*, with 26 specimens, followed by *Conus* (*n* = 10), *Olivella* (*n* = 7), and *Laevicardium* (*n* = 6).

Archaeologists analyzing shell in the Southwest benefit from a natural division of oceanic environments that occurs off the western coast of the Baja Peninsula, where the cold northern California current collides with the warm, Panamic current that sweeps up the west coast of Central America and Mexico. The differences in these ecological environments have produced biotic communities where many molluscan species reside in only one region or have a limited distribution and frequency in one zone relative to the other. As a result, the marine material in southwestern sites can be divided, with some success, into species and genera native to the Gulf of California and those that originate off the California coast. The source of the marine shell in the Davis Ranch Site assemblage appears to have been the Gulf of California, the northernmost finger of the tropical Panamic province.

The dominance of *Glycymeris* in the sample is not surprising, as it is consistently prominent in Hohokam assemblages in the form of shell bracelets. The species identified in the assemblage, *Glycymeris gigantea*, is restricted to the warmer waters off the western coasts of Central America, which include the Gulf of California, where they occur in some abundance today.

Laevicardium elatum is the only species present in this assemblage that is found in both biotic communities. Its northern range extends into the area near San Pedro, California (Abbott 1974:486). However, it does not appear to be as prevalent in the colder waters off the California coast as it is in the gulf region (Keen 1971:160). Additionally, archaeological evidence indicates it was not extensively used by the aboriginal populations of southern California (Gifford 1947). It would therefore appear more likely that *Laevicardium* recovered from sites in the southern portion of the U.S. Southwest originated in the Gulf of California, where it is relatively common and is known to have been extensively used by the prehistoric populations of the region (Bowen 1972, 1976:43; McGuire and Villalpando 1993).

The species *Euvola vogdesi* is endemic to the warm waters of the Gulf of California. However, a related species, *Leopecten diegensis*, that occurs in the deep water off the San Pedro area of southern California is similar in shape. *Euvola vogdesi* can be distinguished by the presence of a faint radiating ridge running between the main ribbings of the flattened left-hand valve. Both specimens in the sample are confirmed to be *Euvola vogdesi*.

The second most common genus in the assemblage and the most prominent gastropod is *Conus*, with 10 individual specimens. This genus is very diverse, but virtually all of the species are endemic to tropical climates. All of the *Conus* in the assemblage were lacking diagnostic features, so species could not be determined.

Olivella is represented by seven individuals, with all but one identified as *Olivella dama*, a species common in the intertidal regions of the upper Gulf of California. The one unidentified specimen has been bleached white, thus removing the diagnostic coloration of *Olivella dama*. However, the shape of the callus and overall shape of the shell is consistent with this species.

The remaining marine shells are of genera represented within the sample by one or two occurrences

TABLE C.1 Shell species represented in Gerald's assemblage from the Davis Ranch Site

Species	MNI[a]	NISP[b]	Biotic province
Marine			
Pelecypods			
Glycymeris			
Glycymeris sp.	7	7	Panamic community
Glycymeris gigantea	19	19	Panamic community
Laevicardium elatum	6	6	Panamic and Californian communities
Euvola vogdesi	2	6	Panamic community
Dosinia ponderosa	1	1	Panamic community
Gastropods			
Olivella			
Olivella sp.	1	1	
Olivella dama	6	6	Panamic community
Conus sp.	10	10	Panamic community
Oliva sp.	1	1	Panamic community
Turritella leucostoma	1	1	Panamic community
Nassarius moestus	1	1	Panamic community
Unidentified	4	4	
Unidentified nacreous	1	1	
Unidentified marine shell	5	5	
Freshwater/Terrestrial			
Pelecypods			
Anodonta californiensis	2	50	Freshwater
Total	**67**	**119**	

[a]Number of Identified Specimens (counted)

[b]Minimum Number of Individuals (estimated)

and are thought to originated in the Gulf of California. The species that were identified, *Turritella leucostoma*, *Nassarius moestus*, and *Dosinia ponderosa*, are all found in the Gulf of California.

The second general source for shell would have been the freshwater rivers and streams that cross the desert regions of the Southwest. *Anodonta californiensis* is the only freshwater shell in the Davis Ranch Site assemblage. It is a comparatively large, although very gracile, bivalve that was endemic to most of the permanent watercourses in Arizona prior to the development and impoundment of rivers that occurred early in the last century (Bequaert and Miller 1973:220–223; Myers 2009). This species is commonly recovered in considerable quantities in prehistoric sites of the Phoenix Basin and along the Salt River, where the number of specimens recovered at some settlements has led to the conclusion that some prehistoric populations may have employed this shellfish as a food resource as well as a raw material for the local artisans (Haury 1976:308; Howard 1987:77; Vokes 1988a:373). Excavations in historic middens investigated by the Tucson Urban Renewal Project indicate that some local groups exploited this resource as a dietary element during the nineteenth century (Bequaert and Miller 1973:221; Lister and Lister 1989:Figure 3.35, bottom). However, the 50 fragments in the Davis Ranch Site assemblage are thought to represent only two specimens, indicating that this resource was used very rarely. The most likely source of these specimens is the nearby San Pedro River, which should have provided a relatively reliable local population of this freshwater shellfish. Its scarcity at the Davis Ranch Site likely reflects a cultural choice.

ARTIFACT FORMS, MANUFACTURING EVIDENCE, AND FRAGMENTARY MATERIAL

The collection of 67 artifacts (table C.2) includes numerous finished artifact forms, several specimens in the manufacturing process, whole unworked valves representing raw material, and both worked and unworked fragments.

Finished Artifacts

Finished artifacts are specimens that have completed the manufacturing process and are sufficiently intact to permit identification of the resulting form. These include bracelets, beads, pendants, and ring-pendants.

Bracelets

Bracelets are the most numerous finished artifact form in the collection, with a total of 18 bands or band fragments present (table C.3). All but one are plain, in that the bands, although often ground smooth, are not embellished beyond what was necessary to finish the basic form. The one exception is a carved band depicting a rattlesnake. All of the bracelets were made from *Glycymeris* valves, with all but three identified as of *Glycymeris gigantea*, which is the largest species in the genus. The remaining specimens are too fragmentary for species assignment.

Plain bracelets account for more than 46% of the finished shell ornaments in the collection, if beads are counted by context, and nearly 40% if beads are counted as individual specimens. Portions of the hinge, or dorsal margin, are retained on nine specimens, while the ventral and side portions are present on eight pieces. The shell's beak is present in eight cases. Five of these specimens are unperforated, while the beaks of the remaining three have been ground down to breach the shell wall to create a perforation. Officer (1978:116–117) suggests that bracelets with these secondary perforations through the umbo/beak were pendants. However, the senior author and others have subsequently noted that many of the bands found in situ around the arms of individuals in mortuary contexts were similarly perforated. A more likely explanation is provided by Haury (1976:313), who suggested that umbos were perforated so that small objects, such as feathers, could to be attached as tassels.

Of the eight segments that incorporate the umbo, two retain the natural form of the shell's beak, while the remaining specimens are shaped in some manner; three are tabular (figure C.1a), one is pointed, and one is reduced to a rounded dome (figure C.1b). The umbo of the final specimen was largely ground down and essentially obliterated.

By definition, the exterior face of a plain bracelet is not embellished with decorative elements; however, this does not mean that the surface was necessarily left in its natural state. Many were ground smooth

TABLE C.2 Finished artifacts, manufacturing evidence, and fragmentary material in Gerald's shell assemblage from the Davis Ranch Site

Artifact form, manufacturing evidence, or fragmentary material category	Genera					
	Marine					
	Pelecypods				Gastropods	
	Glycymeris	*Laevicardium*	*Euvola*	*Dosinia*	*Olivella*	*Conus*
Finished artifact form						
Bracelets						
Plain	17					
Carved snake	1					
Beads						
Whole-shell	1				3	
Disk						
Pendants						
Whole-shell			2			
Perforated whole-shell	1					
Tinkler						5
Ring-pendants						
Plain	1					2
Incised						
Manufacturing evidence						
Artifacts in process						
Tinkler						2
Needle pendant in process	3					
Reworked bracelet fragment	1					
Raw material						
Cut-shell segment, blank		1				
Whole valves					4	1
Fragmentary material						
Worked fragments, unknown form		1		1		
Unworked fragments	1	4				
Total	**26**	**6**	**2**	**1**	**7**	**10**

[a]Minimum Number of Individuals

Genera							Total (MNI[a])
Marine				Unidentified nacreous	Unidentified shell	Freshwater	
Gastropods						Pelecypods	
Turritella	*Oliva*	*Nassarius*	Unidentified			Anodonta	
							17
							1
		1					**5**
			4	1	5		**10**
1							**3**
							1
							5
							3
	1						**1**
							2
							3
							1
							1
							5
							2
						2	**7**
1	**1**	**1**	**4**	**1**	**5**	**2**	**67**

TABLE C.3 Shell bracelets in Gerald's assemblage from the Davis Ranch Site

Bracelet type	Catalog no.	Species	Length	Width	Thickness	% Complete	Burned	Context
Plain bracelet	D/6	*Glycymeris* sp.	46.08	6.96	4.63	20	No	T1S 40–46E
	D/17	*Glycymeris gigantea*	34.98	3.90	4.30	20	No	T10N 0–7E
	D/28	*Glycymeris gigantea*	34.07	5.46	5.12	15	Yes	Kiva stratitest level 3
	D/43	*Glycymeris gigantea*	54.19	7.92	8.12	25	No	House 1 floor
	D/94	*Glycymeris gigantea*	49.45	6.35	7.09	20	No	Kiva floor
	D/104	*Glycymeris gigantea*	46.41	4.25	3.15	30	No	Burial 4 Vessel 8
	D/124	*Glycymeris gigantea*	38.83	5.16	5.34	15	No	House 4 fill
	D/126	*Glycymeris gigantea*	50.10	4.36	5.35	30	No	House 4 floor
	D/130b	*Glycymeris gigantea*	42.46	3.75	4.76	30	No	House 6 fill
	D/131c	*Glycymeris* sp.	23.28	3.17	3.80	5	No	House 6 floor
	D/154b	*Glycymeris gigantea*	33.94	3.76	3.97	15	No	Room 2 floor
	D/166a	*Glycymeris gigantea*	45.69	4.96	5.32	30	No	Stratitest 1 level 1
	D/166b	*Glycymeris gigantea*	37.29	7.52	5.29	15	Partly	Stratitest 1 level 1
	D/169a	*Glycymeris gigantea*	44.98	4.64	5.72	20	No	NE Trash
	D/171c	*Glycymeris* sp.	28.32	4.10	4.94	10	No	Surface
	D/171d	*Glycymeris gigantea*	37.58	3.56	2.95	20	No	Surface
	D/188d	*Glycymeris gigantea*	50.27	5.04	3.98	55	No	Burial 10
Decorated bracelet, carved band	D/150	*Glycymeris gigantea*	28.31	8.63	6.39	5	No	Kiva platform

Note: All measurements are in mm.

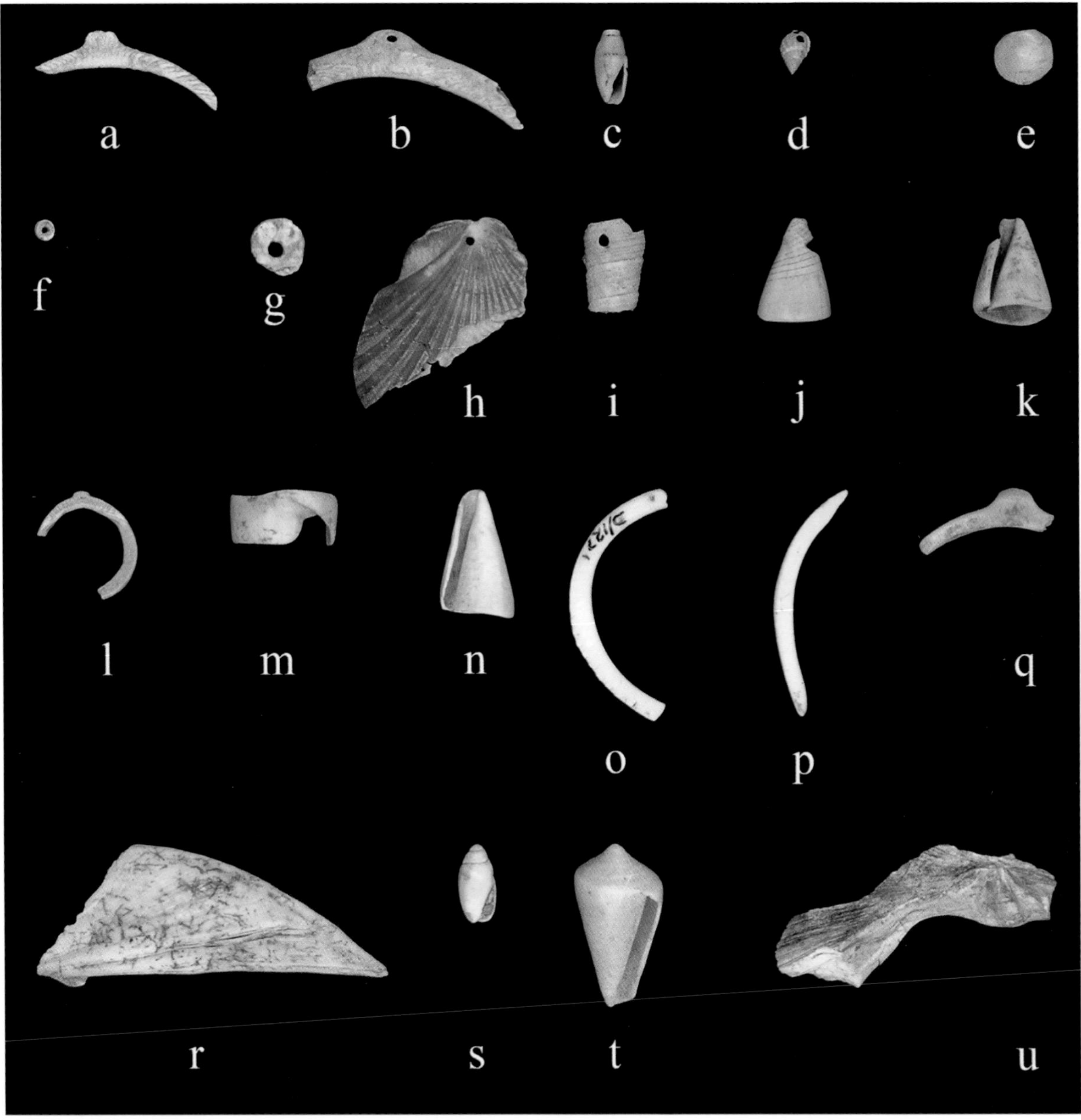

FIGURE C.1 Selected shell artifacts reflecting diversity of material at the Davis Ranch Site: (a) D/171d, (b) D/169a, (c) D/166c, (d) D/166d, (e) D/171f, (f) D/131d, (g) D/157e, (h) D/179, (i) D/5, (j) D/132, (k) D/165, (l) D/15, (m) D/47, (n) D/158, (o) D/127, (p) D/131, (q) D/122, (r) D/48a, (s) D/157c, (t) D/157b, (u) D/105. Length of D/48a (r) is 71.12 mm. Photographs by Arthur W. Vokes.

and polished. The exterior faces of six bands (35% of the plain bracelets) appear to have been left completely natural, with no grinding present. The surfaces of the 11 additional bands (65%) were ground to some extent, with nine reduced to a vertical face. The upper portion of the exterior surface of one band retained its natural slope in profile while the lower marginal edge was reduced to a nearly vertical face. One other band has been ground down and reduced to a round profile.

There is a considerable range in band width, from a minimum of 3.17 mm to a maximum of 7.92 mm (average 4.99 mm). The bracelets exhibit a somewhat greater range in band thickness, with a minimum of 2.95 mm, a maximum of 8.12 mm, and a mean of 4.93 mm.

The one decorated bracelet is represented by a small segment (about 5%) of the dorsal edge that incorporates one side of the hinge. The umbo/beak area has been broken away and worn down, leaving the taxodontic plate and the adjacent outer face of the shell. The exterior face that remains is ground and carved, with indications of a notch near the break along the dorsal side portion of the shell. This section is carved to represent the tail of a rattlesnake, with four rattles indicated. This suggests the non-dorsal band segments were carved to depict a snake's body, which would have encircled the arm of the wearer.

Beads

Aside from bracelets, beads are the most common artifact form in the assemblage when considered as individual items. Fifteen specimens are present (table C.4).

There are five beads that were created by simply perforating the valve to create a hole for suspension; otherwise, the craftsperson relied on the shell's natural form and coloration to provide the decorative elements that might appeal to the individual. There are three different methods of suspension represented in the recovered sample, and while each is distinct, none involved modification of the shell beyond what is required to suspend it from a cord. The method employed in three cases entailed grinding the apex of the spire away so that a cord could pass through the shell along its columellar axis. The product of this method is often referred to in the literature as a spire-lopped bead. All of the beads in the Davis Ranch Site assemblage modified in this manner are *Olivella* shells, which range in length from 13.04 mm to 14.57 mm (figure C.1c).

The second method involves punching a hole through the back of the body whorl of a gastropod in line with the aperture, which allows the bead to be directly suspended below a cord. There is one example in the assemblage, a bead fashioned from a *Nassarius moestus* valve (figure C.1d). It is intact and measures 9.94 mm in length and 5.66 mm in width.

The third technique entailed perforating the umbo area of a small, possibly juvenile, *Glycymeris* valve (figure C.1e), creating a hole above the taxodontic plate. A cord could then be looped around the hinge for suspension. The bead produced this way measures 10.49 mm long (from perforation to ventral edge) and is 12.16 mm wide.

The largest number of individual beads are disk forms that were made from unidentified marine shell (figure C.1f), five of which appear to have been fashioned out of the side walls of univalves, and one was made of a nacreous shell that lacks any cortex or other identifying attribute. Mortuary contexts account for seven of the 10 disk beads, with Burial 4 containing five beads, all made from unidentified white marine shell.

The nine non-nacreous disk beads have a mean thickness of 2.16 mm. They range in diameter from 3.67 mm to 5.92 mm, with a mean of 4.27 mm. The beads fashioned from the side walls of univalves have a characteristic concave-convex profile, while the unidentified marine shell beads have a wedge-shaped profile.

The largest disk bead is complete and was fashioned from a nacreous marine shell (figure C.1g). Its surfaces lack any cortex and there are no diagnostic features that would distinguish between the possible marine candidates, although it is clearly not made from the gracile freshwater *Anodonta*. The perimeter of the bead is uneven, and the disk's surface undulates slightly so that it has an essentially concave-convex profile. The bead, although quite large in diameter (11.96 mm), is relatively thin, with a maximum thickness of 0.88 mm. The perforation is centered and is essentially uniconical in form.

Pendants

There are nine shell pendants present (table C.5). These include four whole-shell pendants and five tinklers.

TABLE C.4 Shell beads in Gerald's assemblage from the Davis Ranch Site

Bead type	Catalog no.	Species	Length	Width	Thickness	% Complete	Burned	Context
Whole-shell bead	D/53b	*Olivella* sp.	13.04	6.46	5.61	100	No	Kiva fill
	D/98b	*Olivella dama*	14.57	7.96	7.23	100	No	Kiva ventilator shaft
	D/166c	*Olivella dama*	14.35	7.04	6.13	100	No	Stratitest 1 level 1
	D/166d	*Nassarius moestus*	9.94	5.66	5.27	100	No	Stratitest 1 level 1
	D/171f	*Glycymeris* sp.	10.49	12.16	4.46	100	No	Surface
Disk bead	D/102	Unidentified marine shell	4.81	4.29	2.84	100	No	Burial 4
	D/102	Unidentified marine shell	5.92	5.45	2.84	100	No	Burial 4
	D/102	Unidentified marine shell	4.40	4.36	1.99	100	No	Burial 4
	D/102	Unidentified marine shell	4.14	4.03	1.27	100	No	Burial 4
	D/102	Unidentified marine shell	4.50	4.15	2.39	100	No	Burial 4
	D/130a	Unidentified marine univalve	3.91	3.68	1.34	100	No	House 6 fill
	D/131d	Unidentified marine univalve	4.08	3.94	2.52	100	No	House 6 floor
	D/157e	Unidentified marine nacreous	11.96	10.76	0.88	100	No	Room 4 subfloor
	D/189a	Unidentified marine univalve	3.73	3.67	2.04	100	No	Burial 13
	D/189a	Unidentified marine univalve	3.89	3.87	2.19	100	No	Burial 13

Note: All measurements are in mm.

TABLE C.5 Shell pendants in Gerald's assemblage from the Davis Ranch Site

Pendant type	Catalog no.	Species	Length	Width	Thickness	% Complete	Burned	Context
Whole-shell pendant	D/5	*Turritella leucostoma*	17.88	12.56	12.53	?	No	T1S 46–40E
	D/70	*Glycymeris* sp.	41.74	41.19	12.14	100	No	Burial 4
	D/141c	*Euvola vogdesi*	53.61	57.22	2.14	90	Yes	Cremation 1
	D/179	*Euvola vogdesi*	36.41	37.38	2.05	60	No	T17E 12S
Tinkler	D/41	*Conus* sp.	24.77	15.48	13.75	85	No	Kiva fill
	D/53a	*Conus* sp.	20.62	11.29	3.71	25	No	Kiva fill
	D/55	*Conus* sp.	20.34	14.81	4.12	25	No	Surface
	D/132	*Conus* sp.	19.59	15.09	7.64	45	No	House 6 Pit 1
	D/165	*Conus* sp.	20.11	15.96	15.35	100	No	Kiva fill

Note: All measurements are in mm.

TABLE C.6 Shell ring-pendants in Gerald's assemblage from the Davis Ranch Site

Ring-pendant type	Catalog no.	Species	Length	Width	Thickness	% Complete	Burned	Context
Plain ring-pendant	D/15	*Glycymeris* sp.	21.52	3.38	2.70	70	No	T1S 35E fill
	D/47	*Conus* sp.	21.78	10.55	4.16	55	No	Kiva stratitest level 1
	D/48b	*Conus* sp.	7.83	10.72	2.08	20	No	Kiva stratitest level 2
Decorated ring-pendant, incised band	D/68	*Oliva* sp.	14.50	11.52	2.37	20	No	Burial 4 Vessel 13

Note: All measurements are in mm.

Two whole-shell pendants were fashioned from *Euvola vogdesi* valves, and the others are a *Turritella leucostoma* shell and a *Glycymeris* valve. The first two employ the flat, left-hand side of the shell, which is relatively common in earlier Hohokam assemblages. These are perforated by drilling a hole through the umbo, just behind the hinge area. One of the *Euvola* specimens is almost fully reconstructible (90% of the valve) but was badly burned as it was part of a crematory offering (Cremation 1). The other *vogdesi* pendant (figure C.1h) was recovered from a trench near the compound wall. This specimen represents 60% of the valve, and it retained its natural, reddish coloration.

The whole-shell pendant made from a *Turritella* valve (figure C.1i) was fashioned by punching a hole through the shell wall and reaming out the resulting hole. This perforation aligns with the aperture so that the bulk of this shell would have been suspended below the cord. This pendant comprises two intact whorls with the rest of the spire broken away. It was recovered from a trench. While much of the specimen is missing, it is clear that the original valve was quite large, with the widest portion of the remnant being 12.55 mm in diameter.

The remaining whole-shell pendant, recovered from Burial 4, is fashioned from a medium-sized *Glycymeris* shell. It is somewhat unusual as it has two distinct perforations: one that penetrates the valve's beak area and another through the back of the shell. The latter is a large central perforation cut through the lower umbo/upper back, with the resulting hole reamed out. The perforation in the back has a maximum diameter of 16.66 mm. The smaller suspension hole is located in the beak area, which was ground back at an angle to the valve's margin. It appears to have been formed by drilling or reaming the hole out to create a uniconical perforation. The edge of the perforation appears to have been worn smooth and polished. The taxodontic plate adjacent to the umbo perforation is also worn with a shallow notch that appears to be polished from use abrasion.

Five shell tinklers are present: three are from the fill of the kiva, one is from a pit in House 6, and the other is from the site's surface. All are made from *Conus* valves (figure C.1j, k). In each case, the entire spire has been removed, down to the shoulder, leaving a residual shelf around the interior edge of the cone. The suspension hole was achieved by cutting a groove across the columellar axis of the shell, near the anterior end of the body whorl. The lengths of the cones range from 19.59 mm to 24.77 mm, with an average of 21.09 mm.

Ring-Pendants

Four ring-pendants were recovered (table C.6). Three are plain bands, with one manufactured from a small *Glycymeris* valve. The other two are each fashioned from the posterior portion of the body whorl of a *Conus* shell. The fourth specimen is a ring-pendant created from the upper body of an *Oliva* valve that has been decorated with an incised design.

The *Glycymeris* band (figure C.1l) represents roughly two-thirds of the circumference of the original valve. The exterior face of the band is ground back to create a very sharply defined vertical face, with the umbo/beak area ground to form a small, but well defined, unperforated, tabular extension projecting out from the surface. The interior is rounded and smooth. The band is 3.38 mm in width and has a thickness of 2.70 mm, with an interior diameter of 16.02 mm.

The other two plain bands were each fashioned from the upper, or posterior, portion of the body whorl of a *Conus* valve (figure C.1m). The larger of the two is a segment that represents roughly half of the original band, with the remaining segment incorporating the front of the body whorl and the back portion of the aperture and the outer lip. The upper and lower edges have been ground and are beveled out from the interior to the exterior face, creating a smooth edge that has no lipping present. The second specimen is a smaller fragment that also incorporates a portion of the upper body whorl, but the interior edge, adjacent to the shoulder, has an inner lip. The two bands are similar in width, with the first being 10.55 mm wide and the other measuring 10.72 mm. The thicknesses are variable in that the first band incorporates the overlapping area of the aperture, with a maximum measurement of 4.16 mm, and the other band is 2.08 mm thick.

The single decorated ring-pendant is an incised band segment made from the upper (posterior) portion of a medium-sized *Oliva* valve, roughly the size of *Oliva spicata* or *Oliva porphyria*. The "upper" edge is thicker and appears to be from the area adjacent to the suture area. The wider edge is from the middle of the body whorl. The band is quite wide, measuring 11.52 mm, and has an incised design across the face. The design is a series of lines that form a running zigzag pattern that appears to have encircled the band. The central element seems to be continuous, while the flanking elements are linear bands that parallel the central element and converge with it. A single, deep hole is visible on the exterior surface, but this appears to be a natural worm hole. The inner face is well polished with both the upper and lower edges beveled inward from the exterior surface.

Manufacturing Evidence

Evidence reflecting local efforts to supply shell ornaments is found in two forms: ornaments in the process of being produced and whole valves that represent the raw material from which the ornaments were fashioned. However, there are no examples of manufacturing debris in the assemblage. A total of 11 specimens relating to local manufacturing were identified (table C.7).

Artifacts in Process

Six of the artifacts recovered appear to have been in the manufacturing process when they were lost or discarded. Two are examples of *Conus* shells that were being fashioned into tinklers, while the rest are segments of bracelets that were being remodeled into needle pendants or some other form.

Two specimens represent unfinished tinklers. In both instances (figure C.1n), the spire has been completely removed, leaving only a residual lip in the area of the shoulder. However, in neither case has the base of the cone been perforated for suspension.

Three segments from fragmentary finished bracelets that were in the process of being reworked into needle-shaped pendants were recovered. All of these pieces incorporate portions of the side and ventral margin of the original bracelet, with the largest extending all the way around to the dorsal edge. This last piece is a large section of a narrow-styled plain bracelet that represents as much as 40% of the original band (figure C.1o). The end at the side-dorsal area is ground and partly rounded, with part of the break still present. Immediately adjacent to this terminus is a partially drilled depression representing an initial effort to perforate the fragmentary segment and thereby create a suspension hole. The opposite end of the shaft ends with some limited high-point grinding, which gives it a squared terminus with rounded edges. The margin edge appears to have some limited grinding that many have been an initial step toward tapering this end to a more pointed terminus.

The other two band segments incorporate less of the original bracelet and are in varying stages of the remodeling process. The first of these segments (figure C.1p) has one end that is rounded and tapered to a flattened face, in which a faint, partially drilled depression is present. This appears to be the initial step in creating a suspension perforation. The opposite end of the shaft is ground to a fairly sharp point. The sides of the shaft are tapered for roughly 8.00 mm prior to the tip. Overall, the band has a maximum width of 4.07 mm and a thickness of 3.79 mm. The other specimen is a large section of a narrow-styled plain bracelet that is remodeled into an awl or is in the early stages of being reshaped into a needle pendant. The section begins with the side margin and wraps around to the midline area of the ventral margin, thus representing as much as 25% of the original band. One end of the shaft tapers to a fairly sharp point, while the opposite end terminates with a recent break. There is no evidence of a perforation, but this may well have been lost with the break. The pointed tip does not exhibit any wear that might be

TABLE C.7 Evidence for on-site shell artifact manufacturing at the Davis Ranch Site

Type of evidence	Catalog no.	Species	Length	Width	Thickness	% Complete	Burned	Context
Tinklers in process of manufacture	D/158	*Conus* sp.	23.91	14.82	13.93	100	No	Room 6 entryway fill
	D/168a	*Conus* sp.	23.11	16.13	8.74	45	No	Stratitest 1 level 4
Needle pendants in process	D/127	*Glycymeris gigantea*	45.72	2.95	4.15	100	No	House 4 Pit 2
	D/131b	*Glycymeris gigantea*	45.57	4.07	3.79	100	No	House 6 floor
	D/177	*Glycymeris gigantea*	44.51	4.86	4.83	80	No	T60E 14–15N
Reworked bracelet segment, unknown form	D/122	*Glycymeris* sp.	28.45	3.06	3.96	10	No	House 4 fill
Raw material, carved shell	D/48a	*Laevicardium elatum*	71.12	26.88	6.08	70	No	Kiva stratitest level 2
Raw material, whole marine shells	D/31	*Olivella dama*	16.48	7.22	6.45	100	No	Kiva stratitest level 4
	D/156c	*Olivella dama*	15.36	7.14	6.22	100	No	Room 4 floor
	D/157b	*Conus* sp.	34.66	18.01	16.24	100	No	Room 4 subfloor
	D/157c	*Olivella dama*	15.74	7.51	6.43	100	No	Room 4 subfloor
	D/157d	*Olivella dama*	14.21	6.20	5.52	100	No	Room 4 subfloor

Note: All measurements are in mm.

associated with its use as an awl, so it is included here as an unfinished pendant.

A fragment of a plain *Glycymeris* bracelet was in the process of being reworked, but its intended function is unclear (figure C.1q). This segment is from the dorsal margin of a fairly small, narrow bracelet (3.06 mm wide and 3.96 mm thick). The section includes the umbo/beak area, which is ground and reduced to an unperforated, polished tabular extension. The end of the band adjacent to the umbo terminates in a rough break, while the other end has been rounded by grinding; however, the end is not entirely finished, as the original break is still evident.

Raw Material

One segment from a *Laevicardium* valve (figure C.1r) that incorporates most of the anterior side panel and part of the adjoining back area was recovered. The piece is triangular in shape with one edge formed by the valve's natural margin. The shorter of the other edges is a rough, unmodified break that extends up from the lateral tooth across the side panel to the ribbing on the back. The edge that parallels the ribs is shaped by a groove-and-snap cut with the resulting edge extensively ground and rounded; however, there are still some vestiges of the original cut groove present. Since this does not appear to be discarded waste, as the edge is fairly well finished, it is thought to be a roughly shaped piece of raw material.

Five complete, unmodified valves are present, including four *Olivella dama* shells and one *Conus* valve. The *Olivella* (figure C.1s) range in length from 14.21 mm to 16.48 mm. These valves are in good condition with some vestiges of their natural coloration present. The surface of the *Conus* (figure C.1t) shell exhibits some weathering but is otherwise in relatively good condition and measures 34.66 mm in length.

Fragmentary Material

Pieces of shell that are either worked but are too incomplete to be classified or lack evidence of having been worked are relatively common in many assemblages (table C.8). These remnants may be fragments of finished ornaments, by-products of local manufacturing activities, or the product of accidental breakage of whole unworked shells.

Worked Fragments

There are two fragments that are modified to some degree but lack features that might provide insight into the original form of the artifact. One is a long and narrow segment of the dorsal margin of a massive *Laevicardium* valve that includes the cardinal tooth and portions of one of the lateral teeth (figure C.1u). The dorsal edge is ground back and flattened to form a sinuous surface that extends from the cardinal tooth, which is unmodified, to the lateral tooth, which is broken away.

The other worked fragment is a blocky segment from the middle back of a *Dosinia ponderosa* valve, a shell that is not commonly found in assemblages in southern Arizona and was not otherwise represented in the assemblage. All edges are rough, unmodified breaks, but the exterior surface is extensively scored from abrasion. This fragment measures 30.03 × 27.50 mm, with a thickness of 5.30 mm.

Unworked Fragments

There are seven unworked fragments representing three different genera, including four *Laevicardium*, one *Glycymeris*, and two occurrences of *Anodonta*. All of the *Laevicardium* pieces were quite small, with unmodified broken edges. The one piece of *Glycymeris* is from the upper back and is also quite small.

The two occurrences of *Anodonta* incorporate multiple layer fragments of this very gracile shell. One is from the lower back of the original shell, while the other is too fragmentary to tell what portion is represented. The presence of unworked specimens of *Anodonta californiensis* is not all that surprising since the species is known to have thrived in the San Pedro River during the historic era (Myers 2009:45–46). It does not appear to have been exploited as a food resource by the local inhabitants, as these are the only occurrences in the collection.

TABLE C.8 Fragmentary shell in Gerald's assemblage from the Davis Ranch Site

Type of fragment	Catalog no.	Species	Length	Width	Thickness	% Complete	Burned	Context
Worked fragments, unknown form	D/30a	*Dosinia ponderosa*	30.03	27.50	5.30	10	No	Burial 1 level 4
	D/105	*Laevicardium elatum*	59.77	20.09	10.68	5	Yes	Kiva fill
Unworked fragments	D/18	*Laevicardium elatum*	41.51	13.02	5.91	1	No	Kiva fill
	D/30b	*Glycymeris gigantea*	32.22	16.89	2.43	15	No	Burial 1 level 4
	D/136c	*Laevicardium elatum*	28.21	25.21	9.19	1	No	House 7 Floor 2
	D/167	*Anodonta californiensis*	19.14	8.78	1.41	20	No	Stratitest 1 level 2
	D/169c	*Anodonta californiensis*	0.00	0.00	0.00	5	No	NE Trash
	D/170a	*Laevicardium elatum*	24.61	11.03	3.30	1	No	NE Trash
	D/171e	*Laevicardium elatum*	17.67	9.97	1.94	1	No	Surface

Note: All measurements are in mm.

DISCUSSION

The shell assemblage collected by Gerald principally comprises finished ornaments, which represent more than two-thirds of the total specimens. Bracelets are the most common form in the sample, accounting for nearly 40% of the finished pieces. Other forms include different styles of beads (which account for nearly one-third of the individual specimens), naturalistic pendants, and ring-pendants made from *Glycymeris*, *Conus*, and *Oliva* valves. Evidence of local craft production is manifest in 12 pieces representing nearly 18% of the assemblage. Manufacturing activity appears to have been primarily focused on remodeling pieces of broken bracelets (four pieces) and fashioning tinklers (two specimens). Only one piece of *Laevicardium* appears to reflect possible carving of shell at the site, with the remaining material being whole, unmodified *Olivella* and *Conus* valves.

The assemblage is thought to reflect a multi-component occupation, spanning the interval from the Early Agricultural period to the early Romero phase of the late Classic period, with possible later ephemeral uses of the site. Shell artifacts appear to be largely related to the late Classic period occupation of the Aravaipa, Redfield, and Romero phases, with some material derived from an earlier, late pre-Classic occupation. Although there is a postulated Early Agricultural period component, this occupation may not be reflected in the shell assemblage.

Temporal Summary

The possible Early Agricultural period occupation is represented by Houses 6 and 10. The latter structure did not produce any shell material. House 6 did, but its association with the Early Agricultural period use of the structure is doubtful. Located in the area Gerald refers to as the Northeast Trash, House 6 is overlain by refuse deposited during the site's late Classic period occupation. The shell material recovered from House 6 (table C.9) appears to be related to this later, overlying trash. Excavations at Early Agricultural period sites (Vargas 2000; Vokes 1996a, 1998, 2001a, 2005) indicate that shell assemblages of this age are predominately made up of various styles of beads and whole-shell and geometric pendants. The sample recovered from House 6 includes disk beads, bracelets, a needle pendant in the process of being refashioned from a bracelet segment, and a shell tinkler. While the disk beads could be associated with the Early Agricultural period, the rest of the material represents forms usually not attributed to this interval. Near this house is an inhumation, Burial 13, which also produced a few disk beads that are similar in form, size, and character to the beads recovered from the house. The associated ceramics indicate that this individual was interred during the Aravaipa or Redfield phase, which indirectly supports the idea that the fill of the house is intrusive from the overlying trash deposit, although it is unclear what the association is between the trash fill within the house and the burial.

A later occupation of the site is attributed to the late pre-Classic portion of the Hohokam sequence, with a number of pit structures thought to have been occupied at this time. Only one of these, however, House 4, produced any shell: four bracelet segments, two of which were in the process of being reworked, one into a needle pendant and the other into an unknown form. This high percentage of bracelet-related artifacts is consistent with Colonial and Sedentary period occupations elsewhere (Vokes 1988b, 1989a, 1989b, 1989c), where bracelets can represent as much as 70% of the shell assemblage. Cremation 1 appears to be a Colonial or Sedentary period burial, in that the deposit has a whole-shell pendant made from the left-handed valve of a *Euvola vogdesi* shell, which is a form that became quite popular in the Hohokam region at that time (Nelson 1981, 1991; Woodward 1931). Also present in this cremation are other non-shell artifacts, such as a palette, which corroborate this temporal assignment.

The occupation of the settlement during the Aravaipa phase is initially represented by four houses (Houses 1, 2, 3, and 7) that are dispersed in a shallow

TABLE C.9 Summary of Gerald's Davis Ranch Site shell assemblage by context

Context group	Context	Deposition phase(s) or period(s)	Artifact type	Species	NISP[a]	MNI[b]
Surface	Surface	Unknown	Whole-shell bead	*Glycymeris* sp.	1	1
			Tinkler	*Conus* sp.	1	1
			Plain bracelet	*Glycymeris* sp.	1	1
			Plain bracelet	*Glycymeris gigantea*	1	1
			Unworked fragment	*Laevicardium elatum*	1	1
Stratitest 1	Stratitest 1 level 1	Unknown	Whole-shell bead	*Olivella dama*	1	1
			Whole-shell bead	*Nassarius moestus*	1	1
			Plain bracelet	*Glycymeris gigantea*	1	1
			Plain bracelet	*Glycymeris gigantea*	1	1
	Stratitest 1 level 2	Unknown	Unworked fragment	*Anodonta californiensis*	5	1
	Stratitest 1 level 4	Unknown	Tinkler in process	*Conus* sp.	1	1
Trenches	T1S 35E	Unknown	Plain ring-pendant	*Glycymeris* sp.	1	1
	T1S 46–30E	Unknown	Whole-shell pendant	*Turritella leucostoma*	1	1
			Plain bracelet	*Glycymeris* sp.	1	1
	T17E 12S	Unknown	Whole-shell pendant	*Euvola vogdesi*	1	1
	T60E 14–15N	Unknown	Needle pendant in process	*Glycymeris gigantea*	1	1
	T10N 0–7E	Unknown	Plain bracelet	*Glycymeris gigantea*	1	1
NE Trash	NE Trash	Aravaipa to Redfield	Plain bracelet	*Glycymeris gigantea*	1	1
			Unworked fragment	*Laevicardium elatum*	1	1
			Unworked fragment	*Anodonta californiensis*	45	1
Inhumations	Burial 1 level 4	Romero	Worked fragment, unknown form	*Dosinia ponderosa*	1	1
			Unworked fragment	*Glycymeris gigantea*	1	1

(continued)

TABLE C.9 *(continued)*

Context group	Context	Deposition phase(s) or period(s)	Artifact type	Species	NISP[a]	MNI[b]
	Burial 4	Romero	Disk bead	Unidentified marine shell	5	5
			Whole-shell pendant	*Glycymeris* sp.	1	1
	Burial 4 Vessel 8		Plain bracelet	*Glycymeris gigantea*	1	1
	Burial 4 Vessel 13		Incised ring-pendant	*Oliva* sp.	1	1
	Burial 10	Aravaipa/Redfield	Plain bracelet	*Glycymeris gigantea*	1	1
	Burial 13	Aravaipa/Redfield	Disk bead	Unidentified marine univalve	2	2
Cremations	Cremation 1	Colonial/Sedentary	Whole-shell pendant	*Euvola vogdesi*	5	1
Pit Houses	House 1 floor	Aravaipa/Redfield	Plain bracelet	*Glycymeris gigantea*	1	1
	House 4 fill	Colonial/Sedentary through Redfield	Plain bracelet	*Glycymeris gigantea*	1	1
		Colonial/Sedentary through Redfield	Reworked bracelet segment	*Glycymeris* sp.	1	1
	House 4 floor	Colonial/Sedentary	Plain bracelet	*Glycymeris gigantea*	1	1
	House 4 Pit 2	Colonial/Sedentary	Needle pendant in process	*Glycymeris gigantea*	1	1
	House 6 fill	Colonial/Sedentary through Redfield	Disk bead	Unidentified marine univalve	1	1
			Plain bracelet	*Glycymeris gigantea*	1	1
	House 6 floor	Colonial/Sedentary through Redfield	Disk bead	Unidentified marine univalve	1	1
			Plain bracelet	*Glycymeris* sp.	1	1
			Needle pendant in process	*Glycymeris gigantea*	1	1
	House 6 Pit 1	Colonial/Sedentary through Redfield	Tinkler	*Conus* sp.	1	1
	House 7 Floor 2	Aravaipa/Redfield	Unworked fragment	*Laevicardium elatum*	1	1

Genera							
Marine						Freshwater	
Gastropods				Unidentified	Unidentified	Pelecypods	**Total**
Turritella	*Oliva*	*Nassarius*	Unidentified	nacreous	shell	*Anodonta*	**(MNI[a])**
1		1				1	**17**
						1	**3**
			2				**12**
				1			**7**
							14
1		*1*	*2*	*1*		*2*	***53***
	1		2		5		**13**
							1
	1		*2*		*5*		***14***
1	**1**	**1**	**4**	**1**	**5**	**2**	**67**

TABLE C.11 Comparison by artifact type of shell recovered from non-mortuary and mortuary contexts at the Davis Ranch Site

	Artifact assemblage					
	Finished artifacts					
	Beads		Pendants			
Contexts	Whole-shell	Disk	Whole-shell	Tinklers	Bracelets	Ring-pendants
Non-mortuary contexts						
Non-feature contexts[a]	3		2	1	6	1
NE Trash					1	
Pit houses		2		1	5	
Rooms		1			1	
Kiva	2			3	3	2
Subtotal	*5*	*3*	*2*	*5*	*16*	*3*
Mortuary contexts						
Inhumations		7	1		2	1
Cremations			1			
Subtotal		*7*	*2*		*2*	*1*
Total	**5**	**10**	**4**	**5**	**18**	**4**

[a]Includes surface, Stratitest 1, and trenches

	Artifact assemblage						
	Manufacturing evidence						
	Objects in process		Raw material		Fragments		
	Tinklers	Reworked bracelets	Cut shell	Whole valve	Worked	Unworked	**Total**
	1	1				2	**17**
						2	**3**
		3				1	**12**
	1			4			**7**
			1	1	1	1	**14**
	2	*4*	*1*	*5*	*1*	*6*	***53***
					1	1	**13**
							1
					1	*1*	***14***
	2	**4**	**1**	**5**	**2**	**7**	**67**

TABLE C.12 Shell artifacts recovered from various sites with components coeval with the Davis Ranch Site

Region, site, temporal interval(s), and contexts	Artifact form — Finished artifacts — Beads — Natural			
	Whole shell		Tubular	
	Count	*Occ.*[a]	Count	*Occ.*[a]
San Pedro Valley				
Davis Ranch Site				
Romero phase	2	*2*	—	—
Aravaipa phase/Redfield phase	—	—	—	—
Colonial/Sedentary through Redfield phase	—	—	—	—
Colonial/Sedentary through Aravaipa phase	—	—	—	—
Colonial/Sedentary	—	—	—	—
Unknown	3	*2*	—	—
Subtotal	5	*4*	—	—
Reeve Ruin				
Aravaipa phase through Romero phase	5	*4*	—	—
Second Canyon Ruin				
Aravaipa and Redfield phases	9	*7*		
Soza phase	3	*3*	—	—
Other and unknown	11	*7*	1	*1*
Ash Terrace				
Locus 1 (Aravaipa through Romero phases)	5	*3*	—	—
Locus 2 (Soza phase)	9	*7*	—	—
Eastern Tucson Basin				
Whiptail Ruin				
Tanque Verde phase	22	*7*	—	—
Gibbon Springs Site				
Tanque Verde phase	6	*4*	—	—

Artifact form						
Finished artifacts						
Pendants						
Cut	Needle/ crescent (reworked bracelet)		Ring-bead/pendant			
Other/unknown form		Bracelets	*Glycymeris*/ bivalve	*Conus*/ *Oliva*	Other	Utilitarian, awl/punch
—	—	5	—	3	—	—
—	—	3	—	—	—	—
—	—	3	—	—	—	—
—	—	—	—	—	—	—
—	—	1	—	—	—	—
—	—	6	1		—	—
—	—	18	1	3	—	—
—	—	7	—	—	—	—
—	1	29	1	2	1	—
—	—	18	1	—	—	—
1	—	46	4	2	—	—
—	—	4	1	2	—	—
—	3	22	2	—	—	—
—	1	60	16	—	1	2

(*continued*)

TABLE C.12 (*continued*)

Region, site, temporal interval(s), and contexts	Artifact form			
	Finished artifacts			
	Pendants			
	Natural		Cut	
	Whole shell	Tinkler	Zoomorphic	Geometric
Tanque Verde phase	2	1	1	1
University Indian Ruin				
Tucson and Tanque Verde phases	6	4	4	3
Southern Tucson Basin				
Zanardelli Site				
Tucson phase	3	3	—	—
Transitional	—	1	—	—
Tanque Verde phase	2	2	3	2
Classic period	1	8	1	—
Western Tucson Basin				
Yuma Wash Site (Classic period)				
Non-mortuary	26	35	17	5
Mortuary	20	—	7	4
Rabid Ruin				
Tucson and Tanque Verde phases	1	3	5	—

Artifact form						
Finished artifacts						
Pendants						
Cut	Needle/ crescent (reworked bracelet)	Bracelets	Ring-bead/pendant		Other	Utilitarian, awl/punch
Other/unknown form			*Glycymeris*/ bivalve	*Conus*/ *Oliva*		
—	—	13	2	—	—	1
—	1	36	4	5	1	—
1	—	30	2	3	—	—
—	—	5	1	—	—	—
—	5	62	5	8	—	3
—	—	64	3	2	—	2
4	—	126	34	6	15	—
1	—	45	5	2	—	—
—	—	23	1	3	—	—

(*continued*)

TABLE C.12 *(continued)*

Region, site, temporal interval(s), and contexts	Artifact form — Manufacturing evidence — Artifacts in process		
	Other forms	Bracelet or ring-bead/pendant	Remodeling finished fragments
San Pedro Valley			
Davis Ranch Site			
Romero phase	2	—	—
Aravaipa phase/Redfield phase	—	—	—
Colonial/Sedentary through Redfield phase	—	—	2
Colonial/Sedentary through Aravaipa phase	—	—	—
Colonial/Sedentary	—	—	1
Unknown	1	—	1
Subtotal	3	—	4
Reeve Ruin			
Aravaipa phase through Romero phase	1	—	—
Second Canyon Ruin			
Aravaipa and Redfield phases	—	—	1
Soza phase	2	—	—
Other and unknown	1	4	1
Ash Terrace			
Locus 1 (Aravaipa through Romero phases)	1	—	—
Locus 2 (Soza phase)	1	2	1
Eastern Tucson Basin			
Whiptail Ruin			
Tanque Verde phase	—	—	—
Gibbon Springs Site			
Tanque Verde phase	—	—	—

	Artifact form			
	Manufacturing evidence			
		Total (MNI[c])		
Debris/waste/ by-product	Whole/ reconstructible valves	Count	*Occ.*[b]	Reference(s)
				This report
—	2	25	*21*	
—	—	5	*4*	
—	—	8	*8*	
—	3	4	*3*	
—	—	3	*3*	
—	—	15	*14*	
—	5	58	*51*	
				Di Peso 1958a
—	5	22	*21*	
				Franklin 1980; Heacock and Vokes 2013
1	—	57	*52*	
—	—	26	*26*	
—	—	90	*78*	
				Heacock and Vokes 2013
—	1	17	*14*	
—	6	77	*61*	
				Gregonis 2011
—	—	119	*100*	
				Vokes 1993, 1996b
1	3	31	*29*	

(*continued*)

TABLE C.12 *(continued)*

Region, site, temporal interval(s), and contexts	Artifact form		
	Manufacturing evidence		
	Artifacts in process		
	Other forms	Bracelet or ring-bead/pendant	Remodeling finished fragments
University Indian Ruin			
Tucson and Tanque Verde phases	2	2	—
Southern Tucson Basin			
Zanardelli Site			
Tucson phase	3	1	—
Transitional	1	—	—
Tanque Verde phase	3	—	2
Classic period	3	1	1
Western Tucson Basin			
Yuma Wash Site (Classic period)			
Non-mortuary	29	99	1
Mortuary	—	8	—
Rabid Ruin			
Tucson and Tanque Verde phases	1	3	—

[a]Occurrence by type is the number of features and non-feature deposits with this type of bead

[b]Total occurrences sum all deposits of bead together, regardless of type (not total of bead type occurrences)

[c]Minimum Number of Individuals

Artifact form				
Manufacturing evidence				
		Total (MNI[c])		
Debris/waste/ by-product	Whole/ reconstructible valves	Count	*Occ.*[b]	Reference(s)
				Hayden 1957; Heacock and Vokes 2013
1	10	806	*86*	
				Boggess et al. 2003; Urban 2003; Vokes 2009d, 2011; Wright and Gerald 1950
—	—	691	*62*	
—	—	173	*15*	
—	2	127	*125*	
—	—	101	*97*	
				Vokes 1997, 2001b, 2008, 2009a, 2009b, 2009c, 2016
46	325	1,225	*934*	
1	52	14,020	*279*	
				Heacock and Vokes 2013; Huckell 1976
1	5	7,168	*90*	

TABLE C.13 Shell genera recovered from various Classic period sites with components coeval with the Davis Ranch Site

	Genera							
	Marine							
	Pelecypods							
Region, site, and temporal interval(s)[a]	*Glycymeris*	*Anadara*	*Laevicardium*	*Trachycardium*	*Trigoniocardium*	*Euvola*	*Argopecten*	*Pteria/Pinctada*
San Pedro Valley								
Davis Ranch Site								
Romero phase	7	—	3	—	—	—	—	—
Aravaipa phase/ Redfield phase	3	—	2	—	—	—	—	—
Colonial/Sedentary through Redfield phase	5	—	—	—	—	—	—	—
Colonial/Sedentary through Aravaipa phase	—	—	—	—	—	—	—	—
Colonial/Sedentary	2	—	—	—	—	1	—	—
Unknown	9	—	1	—	—	1	—	—
Subtotal	26	—	6	—	—	2	—	—
Reeve Ruin								
Aravaipa through Romero phases	11	—	1	—	—	—	2	—
Second Canyon Ruin								
Aravaipa and Redfield phases	36	—	2	—	—	—	2	1
Soza phase	20	—	1	—	—	—	—	—
Other and unknown	58	—	6	—	—	—	1	—
Ash Terrace								
Locus 1 (Aravaipa through Romero phases)	7	—	3	—	—	1	—	—

Genera										
Marine										
Pelecypods										
Spon-dylus	*Chama*	*Spon-dylus/ Chama*	*Hinnites*	*Chione*	*Proto-thaca*	*Cardita*	*Dosinia*	*Pinna*	*Mytella*	Uniden-tified
—	—	—	—	—	—	—	1	—	—	—
—	—	—	—	—	—	—	—	—	—	—
—	—	—	—	—	—	—	—	—	—	—
—	—	—	—	—	—	—	—	—	—	—
—	—	—	—	—	—	—	—	—	—	—
—	—	—	—	—	—	—	—	—	—	—
—	—	—	—	—	—	—	1	—	—	—
—	—	—	—	—	—	—	—	—	—	—
—	—	—	—	—	—	—	—	—	—	—
—	—	—	—	—	—	—	—	—	—	—
1	—	1	—	—	—	—	—	—	—	—
—	—	—	—	—	—	—	—	—	—	—

(*continued*)

TABLE C.13 *(continued)*

	Genera							
	Marine							
	Pelecypods							
Region, site, and temporal interval(s)[a]	*Glycymeris*	*Anadara*	*Laevicardium*	*Trachycardium*	*Trigoniocardium*	*Euvola*	*Argopecten*	*Pteria/Pinctada*
Locus 2 (Soza phase)	38	—	22	—	—	—	1	—
Eastern Tucson Basin								
Whiptail Ruin								
Tanque Verde phase	117	—	27	—	—	1	—	—
Gibbon Springs Site								
Tanque Verde phase	33	—	7	1	—	—	—	—
University Indian Ruin								
Tucson and Tanque Verde phases	54	—	1	—	—	4	1	2
Southern Tucson Basin								
Zanardelli Site								
Tucson phase	38	—	9	1	—	—	1	—
Transition	30	—	1	—	—	—	—	—
Tanque Verde phase	99	—	13	—	—	—	1	—
Classic period	76	—	10	1	—	1	1	—
Western Tucson Basin								
Yuma Wash Site (Classic period)								
Tucson and Tanque Verde phases	1,410	1	220	3	1	9	34	1
Rabid Ruin								
Tucson and Tanque Verde phases	498	—	19	1	—	—	1	—

Genera										
Marine										
Pelecypods										
Spondylus	*Chama*	*Spondylus/ Chama*	*Hinnites*	*Chione*	*Protothaca*	*Cardita*	*Dosinia*	*Pinna*	*Mytella*	Unidentified
—	—	—	—	—	—	—	—	—	—	3
—	—	—	—	—	—	—	—	—	—	—
—	—	—	—	—	—	—	1	—	1	1
—	—	—	—	—	—	—	—	—	—	—
—	—	—	—	—	—	—	—	—	—	—
—	—	1	—	—	—	—	—	—	—	—
—	—	—	—	—	—	—	—	—	—	6
—	—	—	—	—	—	—	—	—	—	3
3	—	87	1	6	3	1	1	1	—	53
—	—	7	—	1	—	—	1	—	—	8

(*continued*)

TABLE C.13 (*continued*)

Region, site, and temporal interval(s)[a]	Genera							
	Marine							
	Gastropods							
	Olivella	*Conus*	*Nassarius*	*Cerithidea*	*Cerithium*	*Columbella*	*Turritella*	*Agaronia*
San Pedro Valley								
Davis Ranch Site								
Romero phase	4	6	—	—	—	—	—	—
Aravaipa phase/ Redfield phase	—	—	—	—	—	—	—	—
Colonial/Sedentary through Redfield phase	—	—	—	—	—	—	—	—
Colonial/Sedentary through Aravaipa phase	2	1	—	—	—	—	—	—
Colonial/Sedentary	—	1	—	—	—	—	—	—
Unknown	1	2	1	—	—	—	1	—
Subtotal	7	10	1	—	—	—	1	—
Reeve Ruin								
Aravaipa phase through Romero phase	6	1	—	—	—	—	1	—
Second Canyon Ruin								
Aravaipa and Redfield phases	7	8	—	1	—	—	—	—
Soza phase	3	2	1	—	—	—	—	—
Other and unknown	9	4	2	—	—	—	—	—
Ash Terrace								
Locus 1 (Aravaipa through Romero phases)	1	4	2	—	—	—	—	—

Genera									
Marine									
Gastropods									
Oliva	*Trivia*	*Theodoxus*	*Polinces*	*Nerita*	*Crucibulum*	*Hipponix*	*Cypraea*	*Crepi-patella*	*Murex*
1	—	—	—	—	—	—	—	—	—
—	—	—	—	—	—	—	—	—	—
—	—	—	—	—	—	—	—	—	—
—	—	—	—	—	—	—	—	—	—
—	—	—	—	—	—	—	—	—	—
—	—	—	—	—	—	—	—	—	—
1	—	—	—	—	—	—	—	—	—
—	—	—	—	—	—	—	—	—	—
1	—	1	—	—	—	—	—	—	—
—	—	—	—	—	—	—	—	—	—
1	—	—	—	—	—	—	—	—	—
—	—	1	—	—	—	—	—	—	—

(continued)

TABLE C.13 *(continued)*

Region, site, and temporal interval(s)[a]	Genera							
	Marine							
	Gastropods							
	Olivella	*Conus*	*Nassarius*	*Cerithidea*	*Cerithium*	*Columbella*	*Turritella*	*Agaronia*
Locus 2 (Soza phase)	13	11	2	—	—	1	—	—
Eastern Tucson Basin								
Whiptail Ruin								
Tanque Verde phase	4	4	1	—	—	—	—	—
Gibbon Springs Site								
Tanque Verde phase	—	1	—	—	—	—	—	—
University Indian Ruin								
Tucson and Tanque Verde phases	2	20	—	—	—	—	1	—
Southern Tucson Basin								
Zanardelli Site								
Tucson phase	2	4	—	—	—	—	1	—
Transition	—	2	136	—	—	—	—	—
Tanque Verde phase	8	11	—	—	—	—	—	—
Classic period	4	9	—	—	—	—	—	—
Western Tucson Basin								
Yuma Wash Site (Classic period)								
Tucson and Tanque Verde phases	804	97	1,435	29	10	60	7	1
Rabid Ruin								
Tucson and Tanque Verde phases	674	7	16	—	—	—	1	—

Genera									
Marine									
Gastropods									
Oliva	*Trivia*	*Theodoxus*	*Polinces*	*Nerita*	*Crucibulum*	*Hipponix*	*Cypraea*	*Crepi-patella*	*Murex*
1	—	2	—	—	1	—	—	—	—
—	—	—	—	—	—	—	—	—	—
—	—	—	—	—	—	—	—	—	—
—	—	—	—	—	—	—	—	—	—
—	—	2	—	1	—	—	—	—	—
—	—	—	—	—	—	—	—	—	—
—	—	—	—	—	—	—	—	—	—
2	—	—	—	—	—	—	—	—	—
5	3	21	1	—	2	2	1	1	1
635	—	—	—	—	—	—	—	—	—

(continued)

TABLE C.13 *(continued)*

Region, site, and temporal interval(s)[a]	Genera			
	Marine			
	Gastropods			
	Melongena	*Strombus*	Vermetidae	*Haliotis*
San Pedro Valley				
Davis Ranch Site				
Romero phase	—	—	—	—
Aravaipa phase/Redfield phase	—	—	—	—
Colonial/Sedentary through Redfield phase	—	—	—	—
Colonial/Sedentary through Aravaipa phase	—	—	—	—
Colonial/Sedentary	—	—	—	—
Unknown	—	—	—	—
Subtotal	—	—	—	—
Reeve Ruin				
Aravaipa phase through Romero phase	—	—	—	—
Second Canyon Ruin				
Aravaipa and Redfield phases	—	1	—	—
Soza phase	—	—	—	—
Other and unknown	—	—	1	—
Ash Terrace				
Locus 1 (Aravaipa through Romero phases)	—	—	—	—
Locus 2 (Soza phase)	—	—	—	—

Genera					
Marine			Freshwater		
Gastropods			Pelecypods		
Unidentified	Unidentified nacreous	Unidentified shell	*Anodonta*	Unidentified	**Total**
—	—	5	—	—	**27**
2	—	—	1	—	**8**
2	—	—	—	—	**7**
—	1	—	—	—	**4**
—	—	—	—	—	**4**
—	—	—	1	—	**17**
4	1	5	2	—	**67**
—	—	—	—	—	**22**
—	—	2	1	—	**63**
—	—	—	—	—	**27**
9	—	—	2	2	**97**
—	—	2	4	—	**25**
1	—	8	9	—	**113**

(*continued*)

TABLE C.13 *(continued)*

Region, site, and temporal interval(s)[a]	Genera			
	Marine			
	Gastropods			
	Melongena	*Strombus*	Vermetidae	*Haliotis*
Eastern Tucson Basin				
Whiptail Ruin				
Tanque Verde phase	—	—	—	—
Gibbon Springs Site				
Tanque Verde phase	—	—	—	—
University Indian Ruin				
Tucson and Tanque Verde phases	1	—	—	1
Southern Tucson Basin				
Zanardelli Site				
Tucson phase	—	—	—	—
Transition	—	—	2	1
Tanque Verde phase	1	—	1	—
Classic period	—	—	—	1
Western Tucson Basin				
Yuma Wash Site (Classic period)				
Tucson and Tanque Verde phases	—	2	3	1
Rabid Ruin				
Tucson and Tanque Verde phases	—	—	—	—

[a]For references, see table C.12

Genera					
Marine			Freshwater		
Gastropods	Unidentified nacreous	Unidentified shell	Pelecypods		
Unidentified			*Anodonta*	Unidentified	**Total**
—	—	5	3	—	**162**
3	—	—	1	—	**49**
—	—	720	—	—	**807**
2	1	632	12	—	**706**
—	—	3	1	—	**177**
2	—	1	7	—	**150**
—	—	2	4	—	**114**
20	—	8,002	109	2	**12,454**
2	1	5,349	14	—	**7,237**

for this type of shell by the intrusive Kayenta population. This shift has been observed elsewhere (Vokes 1984) and likely reflects a broader pattern: the relative decline of bracelets and an increase in the simpler forms of pendants and beads. A parallel development is the rise in popularity of small whole-shell beads fashioned from small bivalves, often utilizing small *Glycymeris* valves (Vokes 1995:571, 2001c:399). This style of bead is represented in the Davis Ranch Site assemblage by a single specimen but is also reported in the Reeve Ruin collection, where specimens were classified as bead-pendants (Di Peso 1958a:141), and other assemblages in the San Pedro Valley comparative sample. However, they do not appear to be all that common, which contrasts with some assemblages from the northwestern portion of the Tucson Basin, such as that from Rabid Ruin, which yielded 457 *Glycymeris* beads (Heacock and Vokes 2013) and the Yuma Wash Site, which produced 923 (Vokes 1997, 2001b, 2008, 2009a, 2009b, 2009c, 2016).

Brainerd-Robinson (Brainerd 1951; Robinson 1951) similarity coefficient matrices have been calculated for both the artifact forms and the genera employed in an effort to clarify the relationships among these different assemblages. The sample was drawn from the sites identified in the comparative tables (tables C.12, C.13, C.14, and C.16), with the results presented in table C.15 for artifact types and table C.17 for genera present. The scores indicate that the assemblages from settlements within the San Pedro Valley are generally similar to one another, and as a group they are most similar to those from the eastern part of the Tucson Basin, the Zanardelli Site (AZ BB:13:1[ASM]), and the Marana Platform Mound Site (AZ AA:12:251[ASM]).

In terms of genera, the assemblage from Reeve Ruin is most similar to that from the Davis Ranch Site. The same set of scores indicate, however, that the Davis Ranch Site assemblage is most similar to that from Ash Terrace. This is somewhat surprising, as this is the one settlement represented among the excavated sites where the inhabitants (local groups) are thought to have shunned the influence of immigrants (Clark, Hill et al. 2012:380). Based on artifact forms, the Davis Ranch Site's assemblage is most similar to that from University Indian Ruin, and the Reeve Ruin assemblage is most similar to that from the Gibbon Springs Site (Vokes 1993, 1996b). The two eastern Tucson Basin sites just mentioned yielded substantial amounts of corrugated ceramics thought to reflect a close relationship with the Soza phase sites in the San Manuel District of the San Pedro Valley. Thus, the relatively high Brainerd-Robinson similarity values between these areas can be seen as supporting the assertion of economic and possibly social contacts via Redington Pass. Indeed, the populations in the eastern Tucson Basin appear to have been more closely aligned with the San Pedro communities than with settlements in the western portion of the Tucson Basin. Settlements in the northwestern portion of the Tucson Basin, such as Yuma Wash, were perhaps more directly linked to the Hohokam of the Salt-Gila core region.

In their summation of the San Pedro Preservation project, Clark, Hill, and others (2012) conclude that the Kayenta immigrants who settled at Reeve Ruin and the Davis Ranch Site lacked their own links to the networks that supplied shell to the region and therefore were dependent on local populations for this material. This would account for the strong similarities between these sites and others in the drainage, and ultimately with sites in the adjoining portions of the Tucson Basin. Since local groups would have served as a filter, restricting the variety of forms available to the newcomers, it is not surprising that the collections from the immigrant enclaves so closely mirrored those from the more established communities, which maintained contacts with the Hohokam core areas to the northwest. The divergence of the assemblages from the Yuma Wash Site (Vokes 1997, 2001b, 2008, 2009a, 2009b, 2009c, 2016) and Rabid Ruin (Heacock and Vokes 2013; Huckell 1976) seems to reflect the large number of mortuary contexts investigated at these sites. These specialized ritual deposits are excavated with more refined techniques, resulting in the recovery of larger shell assemblages (Vokes and Adams 2016).

TABLE C.14 Data used to compute Brainerd-Robinson similarity coefficients for artifact forms from Classic period sites (see table C.12)

	Finished ornaments											Manufacturing evidence				
	Beads (by Occurrence)				Pendants				Ring-pendants			In-process artifacts				
Site name (contexts)	Whole shell	Barrel	Disk	Other cut	Whole shell	Tinklers	Carved	Bracelets	Bivalve	Uni-valve	Other	Bracelet/ ring-pendants	Other	Reworking finished fragments	Raw material/ debris	Total
Davis Ranch Site	4	0	4	0	4	5	0	18	1	3	0	0	3	4	5	51
Reeve Ruin	4	0	0	0	3	1	0	7	0	0	0	0	1	0	5	21
Second Canyon Ruin	18	1	5	3	2	8	7	93	6	2	1	4	3	2	1	156
Ash Terrace	10	7	6	0	0	8	9	26	3	2	0	2	2	1	7	83
University Indian Ruin	6	0	1	0	6	4	8	36	4	5	1	2	2	0	11	86
Gibbon Springs Site	4	0	0	0	2	1	2	13	2	0	1	0	0	0	4	29
Whiptail Ruin	7	3	3	1	0	2	7	60	15	0	3	0	0	0	0	101
Zanardelli Site	36	6	16	2	6	14	12	161	11	13	0	2	10	3	2	294
Yuma Wash Site (non-mortuary)	191	22	31	2	26	35	26	126	34	6	15	99	29	1	371	1,014
Yuma Wash Site (mortuary)	68	46	91	22	20	0	12	45	5	2	0	8	0	0	53	372
Yuma Wash Site (all)	259	68	122	24	46	35	38	171	39	8	15	107	29	1	424	1,386
Rabid Ruin	33	27	28	9	1	3	5	23	1	3	0	3	1	0	6	143

TABLE C.15 Brainerd-Robinson similarity coefficients for artifact forms from Classic period sites (see tables C.12, C.14)

Site name (contexts)	Davis Ranch Site	Reeve Ruin	Second Canyon Ruin	Ash Terrace	Zanardelli Site
Davis Ranch Site		136.7	119.7	145.3	133.8
Reeve Ruin	136.7		106.2	118.1	112.8
Second Canyon Ruin	119.7	106.2		134.7	180.6
Ash Terrace	145.3	118.1	134.7		141.3
Zanardelli Site	133.8	112.8	180.6	141.3	
Yuma Wash (non-mortuary)	89.3	127.6	89.8	106.3	92.6
Yuma Wash (mortuary)	89.7	100.0	76.8	110.9	81.6
Yuma Wash (all)	96.8	125.4	90.2	116.5	93.8
Rabid Ruin	84.5	85.6	90.0	118.5	94.5
University Indian Ruin	150.8	133.9	142.3	146.0	145.3
Gibbon Springs Site	130.5	142.4	141.4	132.0	142.0
Whiptail Ruin	98.3	84.2	163.8	113.5	154.4

Yuma Wash (non-mortuary)	Yuma Wash (mortuary)	Yuma Wash (all)	Rabid Ruin	University Indian Ruin	Gibbon Springs Site	Whiptail Ruin
89.3	89.7	96.8	84.5	150.8	130.5	98.3
127.6	100.0	125.4	85.6	133.9	142.4	84.2
89.8	76.8	90.2	90.0	142.3	141.4	163.8
106.3	110.9	116.5	118.5	146.0	132.0	113.5
92.6	81.6	93.8	94.5	145.3	142.0	154.4
	118.4	178.2	100.4	103.3	106.8	68.0
118.4		104.2	159.2	91.1	99.2	60.8
178.2	104.2		120.4	101.3	104.8	70.0
100.4	159.2	120.4		80.5	82.2	72.2
103.3	91.1	101.3	80.5		169.5	129.3
106.8	99.2	104.8	82.2	169.5		141.0
68.0	60.8	70.0	72.2	129.3	141.0	

TABLE C.16 Data used to compute Brainerd-Robinson similarity coefficients for genera from Classic period sites (see table C.13)

Site name	*Glycymeris*	*Laevicardium*	*Argopecten/ Euvola*	Other bivalves	*Olivella*	*Conus*	*Nassarius*	Other univalves	Total
Davis Ranch Site	26	6	2	1	7	10	1	2	55
Reeve Ruin	11	1	2	0	6	1	0	1	22
Second Canyon Ruin	114	9	3	3	19	14	3	5	170
Ash Terrace	45	25	2	0	14	15	4	6	111
University Indian Ruin	54	1	5	2	2	20	0	3	87
Gibbon Springs Site	33	7	0	3	0	1	0	0	44
Whiptail Ruin	117	27	1	0	4	4	1	0	154
Zanardelli Site	243	33	4	3	14	26	136	12	471
Yuma Wash Site	1,410	220	43	108	804	97	1,435	148	4,265
Rabid Ruin	498	19	1	10	1,309	7	16	1	1,861
Marana Platform Mound	263	141	4	1	15	30	1	15	470

TABLE C.17 Brainerd-Robinson similarity coefficients for shell genera from Classic period sites (see tables C.13, C.16)

Site name	Davis Ranch Site	Reeve Ruin	Second Canyon Ruin	Ash Terrace	University Indian Ruin	Gibbon Springs Site	Whiptail Ruin	Zanardelli Site	Yuma Wash Site	Rabid Ruin	Marana Platform Mound
Davis Ranch Site		152.7	160.4	169.7	155.6	124.5	129.3	137.2	122.7	84.8	144.4
Reeve Ruin	152.7		149.9	137.3	134.4	113.6	120.7	130.0	126.4	111.1	132.7
Second Canyon Ruin	160.4	149.9		143.4	160.3	152.9	157.8	141.3	118.3	81.8	150.0
Ash Terrace	169.7	137.3	143.4		125.5	117.5	129.2	126.3	122.5	83.8	153.8
University Indian Ruin	155.6	134.4	160.3	125.5		135.6	137.5	128.0	91.0	62.1	140.1
Gibbon Springs Site	124.5	113.6	152.9	117.5	135.6		186.3	122.8	86.0	57.3	148.7
Whiptail Ruin	129.3	120.7	157.8	129.2	137.5	186.3		130.7	88.2	63.0	159.0
Zanardelli Site	137.2	130.0	141.3	126.3	128.0	122.8	130.7		151.8	65.3	141.3
Yuma Wash Site	122.7	126.4	118.3	122.5	91.0	86.0	88.2	151.8		97.1	96.3
Rabid Ruin	84.8	111.1	81.8	83.8	62.1	57.3	63.0	65.3	97.1		63.8
Marana Platform Mound	144.4	132.7	150.0	153.8	140.1	148.7	159.0	141.3	96.3	63.8	

CONCLUSIONS

The excavations by Rex Gerald at the Davis Ranch Site produced a collection of shell artifacts representing an estimated 67 specimens. These are largely thought to be associated with a late Classic period influx of Kayenta immigrants who settled at this location and several others within the Cascabel District, although some of the assemblage predates the newcomers. Characteristics of the collection indicate that the intrusive population initially may have lacked direct contacts with sources of shell material but developed these relationships through interaction with local groups. Most of the material came to the site as finished ornaments, as manufacturing evidence is limited to remodeling of bracelet segments and a few unfinished *Conus* tinklers. Thus, it is not surprising that the assemblage is similar to those from neighboring communities in the San Pedro Valley and those from settlements in the eastern Tucson Basin.

APPENDIX D

Cross-Listing of Figure Numbers, Amerind Museum Photograph Numbers, and Catalog Numbers

Patrick D. Lyons

[*Editor: Figures 5.1–5.31 and 6.22 were created using images of groups of artifacts that had been arranged and photographed by Rex Gerald. In order to make the order of the images presented better match the sequence of artifact types discussed in the text, each of Gerald's images was disassembled and the components were recombined. The tables in this appendix cross-list figure numbers with Amerind Museum photograph numbers and Amerind Museum catalog numbers. Data in table D.1 are sorted by figure number. Data in table D.2 are sorted by catalog number. The objects in each photograph, except D/185, D/187, and D/188, were labeled with letters.*]

TABLE D.1 Cross-listing of figure numbers with Amerind Museum photograph numbers and catalog numbers, sorted by figure number

Figure no.	Amerind Museum photograph no.	Amerind Museum catalog no.
5.1a	D/158c	D/s28
5.1b	D/158a	D/s33
5.1c	D/158b	D/s44
5.1d	D/158d	D/s70
5.1e	D/159a	D/s120
5.2a	D/158e	D/s45
5.2b	D/158f	D/s116
5.2c	D/159c	D/s27
5.2d	D/159b	D/s34
5.2e	D/159d	D/s90
5.3a	D/161a	D/s16
5.3b	D/161d	D/s18
5.3c	D/161e	D/s30
5.3d	D/161b	D/s49
5.3e	D/161c	D/s55
5.3f	D/161f	D/s96
5.3g	D/168b	D/164
5.3h	D/166d	D/s48
5.4a	D/187	D/s102

(continued)

TABLE D.1 *(continued)*

Figure no.	Amerind Museum photograph no.	Amerind Museum catalog no.
5.4b	D/165e	D/s57
5.5a	D/162b	D/s42
5.5b	D/162c	D/s51
5.5c	D/162a	D/s104
5.5d	D/162f	D/s12
5.5e	D/162e	D/s21
5.5f	D/162d	D/s58
5.5g	D/162g	D/s22
5.5h	D/162h	D/s72
5.6a	D/163b	D/s19
5.6b	D/163a	D/s83
5.6c	D/163c	D/s124
5.6d	D/163e	D/s20
5.6e	D/163d	D/s47
5.6f	D/163f	D/s107
5.6g	D/163h	D/s4
5.6h	D/163g	D/s32
5.6i	D/163i	D/s53
5.6j	D/162i	D/s92
5.6k	D/164i	D/s105
5.7a	D/164a	D/s75
5.7b	D/164b	D/s17
5.7c	D/164c	D/s76
5.8a	D/164k	D/s89
5.8b	D/164l	D/s94
5.8c	D/164j	D/s122
5.8d	D/165b	D/s24
5.8e	D/165a	D/s25
5.8f	D/165c	D/s26
5.8g	D/164h	D/s50
5.8h	D/164g	D/s64
5.8i	D/166c	D/s79
5.8j	D/166a	D/s80
5.8k	D/166b	D/s95
5.9a	D/159f	D/s10
5.9b	D/165d	D/s86
5.10a	D/169f	D/121a
5.10b	D/167i	D/100b
5.10c	D/167h	D/153a
5.10d	D/167j	D/s87
5.10e	D/167d	D/155
5.10f	D/167e	D/190
5.10g	D/167a	D/76
5.10h	D/167b	D/82
5.10i	D/167c	D/86
5.10j	D/167g	D/62
5.10k	D/167f	D/65
5.11a	D/168f	D/100a
5.11b	D/168e	D/107
5.11c	D/168d	D/163
5.11d	D/168c	D/141a
5.11e	D/168a	D/173a
5.11f	D/169b	D/57
5.11g	D/169c	D/170f
5.11h	D/170i	D/141d
5.12a	D/171d	D/186b
5.12b	D/180d	D/s13

(continued)

TABLE D.1 *(continued)*

Figure no.	Amerind Museum photograph no.	Amerind Museum catalog no.
5.12c	D/171b	D/144a
5.12d	D/171c	D/s2
5.12e	D/171a	D/187
5.13a	D/170b	D/141b
5.13b	D/170a	D/143a
5.13c	D/170c	D/143b
5.13d	D/170e	D/111
5.13e	D/170d	D/170g
5.13f	D/170f	D/191
5.13g	D/170h	D/170d
5.13h	D/170g	D/170e
5.13i	D/166f	D/s41
5.13j	D/166e	D/s69
5.13k	D/169g	D/116
5.14a	D/179i	D/34
5.14b	D/179h	D/71
5.14c	D/179g	D/87
5.14d	D/169d	D/100d
5.14e	D/179f	D/154h
5.14f	D/179e	D/171v
5.14g	D/169e	D/188c
5.14h	D/179j	D/235
5.14i	D/179b	D/54a
5.14j	D/179c	D/54b
5.14k	D/179a	D/92
5.14l	D/179d	D/188e
5.15a	D/169a	D/78
5.15b	D/165f	D/s37
5.15c	D/159e	D/s67
5.16a	D/178s	D/93a
5.16b	D/178p	D/3b
5.16c	D/178q	D/32
5.16d	D/178r	D/154g
5.17a	D/178l	D/14
5.17b	D/178k	D/67
5.17c	D/178o	D/114
5.17d	D/178n	D/36
5.17e	D/178m	D/75
5.18a	D/178h	D/93b
5.18b	D/178b	D/129b
5.18c	D/178c	D/154f
5.18d	D/178g	D/171j
5.19a	D/178i	D/13
5.19b	D/178e	D/171l
5.19c	D/178d	D/171i
5.19d	D/178f	D/171m
5.20a	D/178j	D/3a
5.21a	D/181p	D/37
5.21b	D/180f	D/51
5.21c	D/180a	D/144c
5.21d	D/180e	D/144e
5.21e	D/181t	D/153h
5.21f	D/180c	D/144d
5.21g	D/181n	D/146b
5.21h	D/180b	D/153d
5.21i	D/181k	D/110
5.22a	D/181l	D/100f

(continued)

TABLE D.1 *(continued)*

Figure no.	Amerind Museum photograph no.	Amerind Museum catalog no.
5.22b	D/181u	D/153j
5.22c	D/180h	D/56
5.22d	D/180i	D/49
5.22e	D/180j	D/64
5.22f	D/171e	D/144j
5.22g	D/180g	D/184
5.23a	D/178t	D/80
5.23b	D/178a	D/170c
5.24a	D/171i	D/s14
5.24b	D/171g	D/s65
5.24c	D/171h	D/s81
5.24d	D/171f	D/s100
5.24e	D/164d	D/s6
5.24f	D/164f	D/s60
5.24g	D/164e	D/s61
5.25a	D/181h	D/100i
5.25b	D/181q	D/100l
5.25c	D/181j	D/100s
5.25d	D/181i	D/100t
5.25e	D/181s	D/100w
5.25f	D/181r	D/144g
5.25g	D/181o	D/153e
5.25h	D/181m	D/186a
5.26a	D/181g	D/100c
5.26b	D/181b	D/100x
5.26c	D/181d	D/146a
5.26d	D/181e	D/s82
5.26e	D/181a	D/s123
5.26f	D/181c	D/s125
5.26g	D/181f	D/s126
5.27a	D/186g	D/100e
5.27b	D/186c	D/142a
5.27c	D/186b	D/152
5.27d	D/186f	D/159
5.27e	D/186a	D/170j
5.27f	D/186d	D/183
5.27g	D/186e	D/183
5.27h	D/186o	D/33
5.27i	D/186p	D/35
5.27j	D/186n	D/52
5.27k	D/186q	D/129a
5.27l	D/186k	D/161
5.27m	D/186j	D/1
5.27n	D/186h	D/69
5.27o	D/186l	D/96
5.27p	D/186i	D/134
5.27q	D/186m	D/160
5.28a	D/172a	D/93c
5.28b	D/172d	D/136b
5.28c	D/172b	D/171a
5.28d	D/172c	D/171b
5.28e	D/172f	D/26
5.28f	D/172h	D/156a
5.28g	D/172e	D/156b
5.28h	D/172j	D/135
5.28i	D/172i	D/139
5.28j	D/172g	D/151

(continued)

TABLE D.1 *(continued)*

Figure no.	Amerind Museum photograph no.	Amerind Museum catalog no.
5.29a	D/184a	D/40
5.29b	D/184b	D/156d
5.29c	D/184c	D/169b
5.29d	D/184g	D/45
5.29e	D/184e	D/60
5.29f	D/184f	D/89
5.29g	D/184d	D/131a
5.29h	D/184h	D/74a
5.29i	D/184i	D/7
5.29j	D/184j	D/29
5.29k	D/184m	D/46
5.29l	D/184l	D/61
5.29m	D/184k	D/174
5.29n	D/184n	D/27
5.29o	D/184p	D/50
5.29p	D/184o	D/44
5.30	D/188	D/206
5.31a	D/185	D/53b
5.31b	D/185	D/98b
5.31c	D/185	D/166c
5.31d	D/185	D/130a
5.31e	D/185	D/131d
5.31f	D/185	D/157e
5.31g	D/185	D/189a
5.31h	D/185	D/189a
5.31i	D/185	D/166d
5.31j	D/185	D/41
5.31k	D/185	D/53a
5.31l	D/185	D/55
5.31m	D/185	D/132
5.31n	D/185	D/165
5.31o	D/185	D/158
5.31p	D/185	D/168a
5.31q	D/185	D/104
5.31r	D/185	D/169a
5.31s	D/185	D/188d
5.31t	D/185	D/94
5.31u	D/185	D/150
5.31v	D/185	D/43
5.31w	D/185	D/5
5.31x	D/185	D/141c
5.31y	D/185	D/171f
5.31z	D/185	D/179
5.31aa	D/185	D/70
5.31ab	D/185	D/15
5.31ac	D/185	D/47
5.31ad	D/185	D/48b
5.31ae	D/185	D/68
5.31af	D/185	D/30a, b
5.31ag	D/185	D/31
5.31ah	D/185	D/48a
5.31ai	D/185	D/136c
5.31aj	D/185	D/157b
5.31ak	D/185	D/157c, d
5.31al	D/185	D/167
6.22a	D/182c	D/21
6.22b	D/182f	D/83

(continued)

TABLE D.1 *(continued)*

Figure no.	Amerind Museum photograph no.	Amerind Museum catalog no.
6.22c	D/182a	D/120
6.22d	D/182e	D/137a
6.22e	D/182d	D/148
6.22f	D/182b	D/170i
6.22g	D/182o	D/10
6.22h	D/182k	D/58
6.22i	D/182g	D/99
6.22j	D/182l	D/117
6.22k	D/182i	D/136a
6.22l	D/182h	D/175
6.22m	D/182j	D/188a
6.22n	D/182n	D/63
6.22o	D/182p	D/123
6.22p	D/182m	D/125b

TABLE D.2 Cross-listing of figure numbers with Amerind Museum photograph numbers and catalog numbers, sorted by catalog number

Amerind Museum catalog no.	Figure no.	Amerind Museum photograph no.
D/1	5.27m	D/186j
D/3a	5.20a	D/178j
D/3b	5.16b	D/178p
D/5	5.31w	D/185
D/7	5.29i	D/184i
D/10	6.22g	D/182o
D/13	5.19a	D/178i
D/14	5.17a	D/178l
D/15	5.31ab	D/185
D/21	6.22a	D/182c
D/26	5.28e	D/172f
D/27	5.29n	D/184n
D/29	5.29j	D/184j
D/30a, b	5.31af	D/185
D/31	5.31ag	D/185
D/32	5.16c	D/178q
D/33	5.27h	D/186o
D/34	5.14a	D/179i
D/35	5.27i	D/186p
D/36	5.17d	D/178n
D/37	5.21a	D/181p
D/40	5.29a	D/184a
D/41	5.31j	D/185
D/43	5.31v	D/185
D/44	5.29p	D/184o
D/45	5.29d	D/184g
D/46	5.29k	D/184m
D/47	5.31ac	D/185
D/48a	5.31ah	D/185

(continued)

TABLE D.2 *(continued)*

Amerind Museum catalog no.	Figure no.	Amerind Museum photograph no.	Amerind Museum catalog no.	Figure no.	Amerind Museum photograph no.
D/48b	5.31ad	D/185	D/80	5.23a	D/178t
D/49	5.22d	D/180i	D/82	5.10h	D/167b
D/50	5.29o	D/184p	D/83	6.22b	D/182f
D/51	5.21b	D/180f	D/86	5.10i	D/167c
D/52	5.27j	D/186n	D/87	5.14c	D/179g
D/53a	5.31k	D/185	D/89	5.29f	D/184f
D/53b	5.31a	D/185	D/92	5.14k	D/179a
D/54a	5.14i	D/179b	D/93a	5.16a	D/178s
D/54b	5.14j	D/179c	D/93b	5.18a	D/178h
D/55	5.31l	D/185	D/93c	5.28a	D/172a
D/56	5.22c	D/180h	D/94	5.31t	D/185
D/57	5.11f	D/169b	D/96	5.27o	D/186l
D/58	6.22h	D/182k	D/98b	5.31b	D/185
D/60	5.29e	D/184e	D/99	6.22i	D/182g
D/61	5.29l	D/184l	D/100a	5.11a	D/168f
D/62	5.10j	D/167g	D/100b	5.10b	D/167i
D/63	6.22n	D/182n	D/100c	5.26a	D/181g
D/64	5.22e	D/180j	D/100d	5.14d	D/169d
D/65	5.10k	D/167f	D/100e	5.27a	D/186g
D/67	5.17b	D/178k	D/100f	5.22a	D/181l
D/68	5.31ae	D/185	D/100i	5.25a	D/181h
D/69	5.27n	D/186h	D/100l	5.25b	D/181q
D/70	5.31aa	D/185	D/100s	5.25c	D/181j
D/71	5.14b	D/179h	D/100t	5.25d	D/181i
D/74a	5.29h	D/184h	D/100w	5.25e	D/181s
D/75	5.17e	D/178m	D/100x	5.26b	D/181b
D/76	5.10g	D/167a	D/104	5.31q	D/185
D/78	5.15a	D/169a			

(continued)

TABLE D.2 *(continued)*

Amerind Museum catalog no.	Figure no.	Amerind Museum photograph no.	Amerind Museum catalog no.	Figure no.	Amerind Museum photograph no.
D/107	5.11b	D/168e	D/143a	5.13b	D/170a
D/110	5.21i	D/181k	D/143b	5.13c	D/170c
D/111	5.13d	D/170e	D/144a	5.12c	D/171b
D/114	5.17c	D/178o	D/144c	5.21c	D/180a
D/116	5.13k	D/169g	D/144d	5.21f	D/180c
D/117	6.22j	D/182l	D/144e	5.21d	D/180e
D/120	6.22c	D/182a	D/144g	5.25f	D/181r
D/121a	5.10a	D/169f	D/144j	5.22f	D/171e
D/123	6.22o	D/182p	D/146a	5.26c	D/181d
D/125b	6.22p	D/182m	D/146b	5.21g	D/181n
D/129a	5.27k	D/186q	D/148	6.22e	D/182d
D/129b	5.18b	D/178b	D/150	5.31u	D/185
D/130a	5.31d	D/185	D/151	5.28j	D/172g
D/131a	5.29g	D/184d	D/152	5.27c	D/186b
D/131d	5.31e	D/185	D/153a	5.10c	D/167h
D/132	5.31m	D/185	D/153d	5.21h	D/180b
D/134	5.27p	D/186i	D/153e	5.25g	D/181o
D/135	5.28h	D/172j	D/153h	5.21e	D/181t
D/136a	6.22k	D/182i	D/153j	5.22b	D/181u
D/136b	5.28b	D/172d	D/154f	5.18c	D/178c
D/136c	5.31ai	D/185	D/154g	5.16d	D/178r
D/137a	6.22d	D/182e	D/154h	5.14e	D/179f
D/139	5.28i	D/172i	D/155	5.10e	D/167d
D/141a	5.11d	D/168c	D/156a	5.28f	D/172h
D/141b	5.13a	D/170b	D/156b	5.28g	D/172e
D/141c	5.31x	D/185	D/156d	5.29b	D/184b
D/141d	5.11h	D/170i	D/157b	5.31aj	D/185
D/142a	5.27b	D/186c			

(continued)

TABLE D.2 *(continued)*

Amerind Museum catalog no.	Figure no.	Amerind Museum photograph no.	Amerind Museum catalog no.	Figure no.	Amerind Museum photograph no.
D/157c, d	5.31ak	D/185	D/171m	5.19d	D/178f
D/157e	5.31f	D/185	D/171v	5.14f	D/179e
D/158	5.31o	D/185	D/173a	5.11e	D/168a
D/159	5.27d	D/186f	D/174	5.29m	D/184k
D/160	5.27q	D/186m	D/175	6.22l	D/182h
D/161	5.27l	D/186k	D/179	5.31z	D/185
D/163	5.11c	D/168d	D/183	5.27f	D/186d
D/164	5.3g	D/168b	D/183	5.27g	D/186e
D/165	5.31n	D/185	D/184	5.22g	D/180g
D/166c	5.31c	D/185	D/186a	5.25h	D/181m
D/166d	5.31i	D/185	D/186b	5.12a	D/171d
D/167	5.31al	D/185	D/187	5.12e	D/171a
D/168a	5.31p	D/185	D/188a	6.22m	D/182j
D/169a	5.31r	D/185	D/188c	5.14g	D/169e
D/169b	5.29c	D/184c	D/188d	5.31s	D/185
D/170c	5.23b	D/178a	D/188e	5.14l	D/179d
D/170d	5.13g	D/170h	D/189a	5.31g	D/185
D/170e	5.13h	D/170g	D/189a	5.31h	D/185
D/170f	5.11g	D/169c	D/190	5.10f	D/167e
D/170g	5.13e	D/170d	D/191	5.13f	D/170f
D/170i	6.22f	D/182b	D/206	5.30	D/188
D/170j	5.27e	D/186a	D/235	5.14h	D/179j
D/171a	5.28c	D/172b	D/s2	5.12d	D/171c
D/171b	5.28d	D/172c	D/s4	5.6g	D/163h
D/171f	5.31y	D/185	D/s6	5.24e	D/164d
D/171i	5.19c	D/178d	D/s10	5.9a	D/159f
D/171j	5.18d	D/178g	D/s12	5.5d	D/162f
D/171l	5.19b	D/178e			

(continued)

TABLE D.2 *(continued)*

Amerind Museum catalog no.	Figure no.	Amerind Museum photograph no.	Amerind Museum catalog no.	Figure no.	Amerind Museum photograph no.
D/s13	5.12b	D/180d	D/s53	5.6i	D/163i
D/s14	5.24a	D/171i	D/s55	5.3e	D/161c
D/s16	5.3a	D/161a	D/s57	5.4b	D/165e
D/s17	5.7b	D/164b	D/s58	5.5f	D/162d
D/s18	5.3b	D/161d	D/s60	5.24f	D/164f
D/s19	5.6a	D/163b	D/s61	5.24g	D/164e
D/s20	5.6d	D/163e	D/s64	5.8h	D/164g
D/s21	5.5e	D/162e	D/s65	5.24b	D/171g
D/s22	5.5g	D/162g	D/s67	5.15c	D/159e
D/s24	5.8d	D/165b	D/s69	5.13j	D/166e
D/s25	5.8e	D/165a	D/s70	5.1d	D/158d
D/s26	5.8f	D/165c	D/s72	5.5h	D/162h
D/s27	5.2c	D/159c	D/s75	5.7a	D/164a
D/s28	5.1a	D/158c	D/s76	5.7c	D/164c
D/s30	5.3c	D/161e	D/s79	5.8i	D/166c
D/s32	5.6h	D/163g	D/s80	5.8j	D/166a
D/s33	5.1b	D/158a	D/s81	5.24c	D/171h
D/s34	5.2d	D/159b	D/s82	5.26d	D/181e
D/s37	5.15b	D/165f	D/s83	5.6b	D/163a
D/s41	5.13i	D/166f	D/s86	5.9b	D/165d
D/s42	5.5a	D/162b	D/s87	5.10d	D/167j
D/s44	5.1c	D/158b	D/s89	5.8a	D/164k
D/s45	5.2a	D/158e	D/s90	5.2e	D/159d
D/s47	5.6e	D/163d	D/s92	5.6j	D/162i
D/s48	5.3h	D/166d	D/s94	5.8b	D/164l
D/s49	5.3d	D/161b	D/s95	5.8k	D/166b
D/s50	5.8g	D/164h	D/s96	5.3f	D/161f
D/s51	5.5b	D/162c			

(continued)

TABLE D.2 (*continued*)

Amerind Museum catalog no.	Figure no.	Amerind Museum photograph no.
D/s100	5.24d	D/171f
D/s102	5.4a	D/187
D/s104	5.5c	D/162a
D/s105	5.6k	D/164i
D/s107	5.6f	D/163f
D/s116	5.2b	D/158f
D/s120	5.1e	D/159a
D/s122	5.8c	D/164j
D/s123	5.26e	D/181a
D/s124	5.6c	D/163c
D/s125	5.26f	D/181c
D/s126	5.26g	D/181f

APPENDIX E

Rex E. Gerald's 1958 Summary of the Ceramic Assemblage from the Davis Ranch Site by Ware, Type, and Context

[*Editor: The 34 tables in this appendix reproduce the data presented in Gerald's 4′ × 12′ table of Davis Ranch Site sherd counts and percentages by type and provenience.*]

TABLE E.1 Gerald's typological analysis of sherds from Houses 1 and 2 at the Davis Ranch Site

	House 1								House 2			
	Fill		Stratitest level 1		Stratitest level 2		Floor		Fill		Floor	
	n	%	*n*	%	*n*	%	*n*	%	*n*	%	*n*	%
Painted types												
Gila Polychrome	12	44.4	2	40.0	2	25.0	7	30.4	26	68.4	1	8.3
Gila Black-on-red	1	3.7	0	0.0	1	12.5	0	0.0	3	7.9	1	8.3
Pinto Polychrome	0	0.0	0	0.0	0	0.0	0	0.0	0	0.0	1	8.3
Gila Polychrome (Pink Variant)	0	0.0	0	0.0	0	0.0	0	0.0	0	0.0	0	0.0
Gila-Tucson Polychrome	0	0.0	0	0.0	0	0.0	0	0.0	0	0.0	0	0.0
Tucson Polychrome	4	14.8	0	0.0	2	25.0	7	30.4	1	2.6	0	0.0
Tucson Black-on-red	2	7.4	0	0.0	0	0.0	1	4.3	0	0.0	0	0.0
Tonto Polychrome	0	0.0	0	0.0	0	0.0	0	0.0	0	0.0	0	0.0
Dragoon Red-on-brown	0	0.0	0	0.0	0	0.0	0	0.0	0	0.0	1	8.3
Cascabel Red-on-brown	2	7.4	0	0.0	1	12.5	3	13.0	0	0.0	1	8.3
Davis Red-on-white	0	0.0	0	0.0	0	0.0	0	0.0	1	2.6	1	8.3
Tres Alamos Red-on-brown	0	0.0	0	0.0	0	0.0	0	0.0	0	0.0	0	0.0
Gila White Slip	0	0.0	0	0.0	0	0.0	0	0.0	0	0.0	0	0.0
Cañada del Oro Red-on-brown	0	0.0	0	0.0	0	0.0	0	0.0	0	0.0	0	0.0
Gila Butte Red-on-buff	0	0.0	0	0.0	0	0.0	0	0.0	0	0.0	0	0.0
Santa Cruz Red-on-buff	1	3.7	0	0.0	1	12.5	0	0.0	1	2.6	2	16.7
Sacaton Red-on-buff	1	3.7	0	0.0	0	0.0	0	0.0	1	2.6	3	25.0
Casa Grande Red-on-buff	0	0.0	0	0.0	0	0.0	0	0.0	0	0.0	0	0.0
Rillito Red-on-brown	0	0.0	2	40.0	0	0.0	0	0.0	0	0.0	0	0.0

(*continued*)

TABLE E.1 *(continued)*

	House 1								House 2			
	Fill		Stratitest level 1		Stratitest level 2		Floor		Fill		Floor	
	n	%	*n*	%	*n*	%	*n*	%	*n*	%	*n*	%
Rillito Red-on-brown (micaceous)	2	7.4	1	20.0	1	12.5	3	13.0	3	7.9	0	0.0
Rincon Red-on-brown	0	0.0	0	0.0	0	0.0	0	0.0	0	0.0	0	0.0
Pantano Red-on-brown	0	0.0	0	0.0	0	0.0	0	0.0	1	2.6	0	0.0
Tanque Verde Red-on-brown	0	0.0	0	0.0	0	0.0	0	0.0	1	2.6	0	0.0
Mimbres Black-on-white	2	7.4	0	0.0	0	0.0	2	8.7	0	0.0	0	0.0
Dos Cabezas Red-on-brown	0	0.0	0	0.0	0	0.0	0	0.0	0	0.0	0	0.0
Encinas Red-on-brown	0	0.0	0	0.0	0	0.0	0	0.0	0	0.0	1	8.3
Nogales Purple-on-red	0	0.0	0	0.0	0	0.0	0	0.0	0	0.0	0	0.0
Cerros Red-on-white	0	0.0	0	0.0	0	0.0	0	0.0	0	0.0	0	0.0
San Carlos Red-on-brown	0	0.0	0	0.0	0	0.0	0	0.0	0	0.0	0	0.0
San Carlos Red-on-white	0	0.0	0	0.0	0	0.0	0	0.0	0	0.0	0	0.0
El Paso Polychrome	0	0.0	0	0.0	0	0.0	0	0.0	0	0.0	0	0.0
Unidentified polychrome	0	0.0	0	0.0	0	0.0	0	0.0	0	0.0	0	0.0
Kayenta-like polychrome	0	0.0	0	0.0	0	0.0	0	0.0	0	0.0	0	0.0
Tusayan-like polychrome	0	0.0	0	0.0	0	0.0	0	0.0	0	0.0	0	0.0
Subtotal	*27*	*100.0*	*5*	*100.0*	*8*	*100.0*	*23*	*100.0*	*38*	*100.0*	*12*	*100.0*
Plain types												
Davis Plain	96	65.3	11	73.3	9	69.2	99	77.3	116	64.1	39	78.0
Davis Plain: Sobaipuri Coil Rim Variety	0	0.0	0	0.0	0	0.0	0	0.0	1	0.6	0	0.0
Belford Perforated Rim	1	0.7	0	0.0	0	0.0	0	0.0	3	1.7	0	0.0
Belford Perforated Rim (Sobaipuri Coil Rim)	0	0.0	0	0.0	0	0.0	0	0.0	0	0.0	0	0.0

Babocomari Plain	31	21.1	2	13.3	3	23.1	22	17.2	45	24.9	6	12.0
Redington Plain	6	4.1	1	6.7	0	0.0	2	1.6	6	3.3	3	6.0
Redington Smudged	4	2.7	0	0.0	0	0.0	1	0.8	3	1.7	0	0.0
Sacaton Buff	1	0.7	0	0.0	1	7.7	2	1.6	2	1.1	2	4.0
Gila Plain	8	5.4	1	6.7	0	0.0	2	1.6	1	0.6	0	0.0
Gila Smudged	0	0.0	0	0.0	0	0.0	0	0.0	1	0.6	0	0.0
San Carlos Brown	0	0.0	0	0.0	0	0.0	0	0.0	1	0.6	0	0.0
Slipped brown	0	0.0	0	0.0	0	0.0	0	0.0	1	0.6	0	0.0
Sosa Plain	0	0.0	0	0.0	0	0.0	0	0.0	1	0.6	0	0.0
Whetstone Plain	0	0.0	0	0.0	0	0.0	0	0.0	0	0.0	0	0.0
Wingfield Plain	0	0.0	0	0.0	0	0.0	0	0.0	0	0.0	0	0.0
Fingernail indented	0	0.0	0	0.0	0	0.0	0	0.0	0	0.0	0	0.0
Incised plain	0	0.0	0	0.0	0	0.0	0	0.0	0	0.0	0	0.0
Tularosa Fillet Rim	0	0.0	0	0.0	0	0.0	0	0.0	0	0.0	0	0.0
Neck corrugated gray ware	0	0.0	0	0.0	0	0.0	0	0.0	0	0.0	0	0.0
Stucco ware?	0	0.0	0	0.0	0	0.0	0	0.0	0	0.0	0	0.0
Sandy Paste Perforated	0	0.0	0	0.0	0	0.0	0	0.0	0	0.0	0	0.0
Sosa Perforated	0	0.0	0	0.0	0	0.0	0	0.0	0	0.0	0	0.0
Subtotal	*147*	*100.0*	*15*	*100.0*	*13*	*100.0*	*128*	*100.0*	*181*	*100.0*	*50*	*100.0*
Red ware types												
Salt Red: Davis Variety	7	70.0	0	0.0	0	0.0	3	50.0	1	16.7	0	0.0
Salt Smudged: Davis Variety	0	0.0	0	0.0	0	0.0	0	0.0	0	0.0	0	0.0
Dragoon Red	3	30.0	0	0.0	1	100.0	3	50.0	4	66.7	3	75.0
Dragoon Red Smudged	0	0.0	0	0.0	0	0.0	0	0.0	0	0.0	0	0.0
Gila Red	0	0.0	0	0.0	0	0.0	0	0.0	0	0.0	1	25.0

(*continued*)

TABLE E.1 *(continued)*

	House 1								House 2			
	Fill		Stratitest level 1		Stratitest level 2		Floor		Fill		Floor	
	n	%	*n*	%	*n*	%	*n*	%	*n*	%	*n*	%
Gila Smudged	0	0.0	0	0.0	0	0.0	0	0.0	1	16.7	0	0.0
San Carlos Red	0	0.0	0	0.0	0	0.0	0	0.0	0	0.0	0	0.0
Wingfield Red	0	0.0	0	0.0	0	0.0	0	0.0	0	0.0	0	0.0
Unidentified red #1	0	0.0	0	0.0	0	0.0	0	0.0	0	0.0	0	0.0
Unidentified red #2	0	0.0	0	0.0	0	0.0	0	0.0	0	0.0	0	0.0
Subtotal	*10*	*100.0*	*0*	*0.0*	*1*	*100.0*	*6*	*100.0*	*6*	*100.0*	*4*	*100.0*
Corrugated types												
Late plain corrugated	0	0.0	0	0.0	0	0.0	0	0.0	1	25.0	2	100.0
Late indented corrugated	1	100.0	0	0.0	0	0.0	0	0.0	2	50.0	0	0.0
Early indented corrugated, smudged interior	0	0.0	0	0.0	0	0.0	0	0.0	0	0.0	0	0.0
Obliterated corrugated	0	0.0	0	0.0	0	0.0	0	0.0	1	25.0	0	0.0
Neck corrugated	0	0.0	0	0.0	0	0.0	0	0.0	0	0.0	0	0.0
Red-slipped neck corrugated	0	0.0	0	0.0	0	0.0	0	0.0	0	0.0	0	0.0
Subtotal	*1*	*100.0*	*0*	*0.0*	*0*	*0.0*	*0*	*0.0*	*4*	*100.0*	*2*	*100.0*
Miscellaneous												
Porcelain	0	0.0	0	0.0	0	0.0	0	0.0	0	0.0	0	0.0
White glaze ware	0	0.0	0	0.0	0	0.0	0	0.0	0	0.0	0	0.0
Glass	0	0.0	0	0.0	0	0.0	0	0.0	0	0.0	0	0.0
Unidentified	1	100.0	0	0.0	1	100.0	0	0.0	1	100.0	1	100.0
Subtotal	*1*	*100.0*	*0*	*0.0*	*1*	*100.0*	*0*	*0.0*	*1*	*100.0*	*1*	*100.0*
Total	**186**		**20**		**23**		**157**		**230**		**69**	

TABLE E.2 Gerald's typological analysis of sherds from House 3 at the Davis Ranch Site

	House 3 fill	
	n	%
Painted types		
Gila Polychrome	78	74.3
Gila Black-on-red	1	1.0
Pinto Polychrome	1	1.0
Gila Polychrome (Pink Variant)	2	1.9
Gila-Tucson Polychrome	0	0.0
Tucson Polychrome	2	1.9
Tucson Black-on-red	1	1.0
Tonto Polychrome	4	3.8
Dragoon Red-on-brown	0	0.0
Cascabel Red-on-brown	1	1.0
Davis Red-on-white	2	1.9
Tres Alamos Red-on-brown	0	0.0
Gila White Slip	5	4.8
Cañada del Oro Red-on-brown	0	0.0
Gila Butte Red-on-buff	1	1.0
Santa Cruz Red-on-buff	3	2.9
Sacaton Red-on-buff	0	0.0
Casa Grande Red-on-buff	0	0.0
Rillito Red-on-brown	0	0.0
Rillito Red-on-brown (micaceous)	2	1.9
Rincon Red-on-brown	1	1.0
Pantano Red-on-brown	0	0.0
Tanque Verde Red-on-brown	0	0.0
Mimbres Black-on-white	0	0.0
Dos Cabezas Red-on-brown	0	0.0
Encinas Red-on-brown	0	0.0
Nogales Purple-on-red	1	1.0
Cerros Red-on-white	0	0.0
San Carlos Red-on-brown	0	0.0

(continued)

TABLE E.2 *(continued)*

	House 3 fill	
	n	%
San Carlos Red-on-white	0	0.0
El Paso Polychrome	0	0.0
Unidentified polychrome	0	0.0
Kayenta-like polychrome	0	0.0
Tusayan-like polychrome	0	0.0
Subtotal	*105*	*100.0*
Plain types		
Davis Plain	231	65.4
Davis Plain: Sobaipuri Coil Rim Variety	1	0.3
Belford Perforated Rim	3	0.8
Belford Perforated Rim (Sobaipuri Coil Rim)	0	0.0
Babocomari Plain	104	29.5
Redington Plain	8	2.3
Redington Smudged	2	0.6
Sacaton Buff	2	0.6
Gila Plain	2	0.6
Gila Smudged	0	0.0
San Carlos Brown	0	0.0
Slipped brown	0	0.0
Sosa Plain	0	0.0
Whetstone Plain	0	0.0
Wingfield Plain	0	0.0
Fingernail indented	0	0.0
Incised plain	0	0.0
Tularosa Fillet Rim	0	0.0
Neck corrugated gray ware	0	0.0
Stucco ware?	0	0.0
Sandy Paste Perforated	0	0.0

(continued)

TABLE E.2 *(continued)*

	House 3 fill	
	n	%
Sosa Perforated	0	0.0
Subtotal	*353*	*100.0*
Red ware types		
Salt Red: Davis Variety	3	20.0
Salt Smudged: Davis Variety	3	20.0
Dragoon Red	4	26.7
Dragoon Red Smudged	0	0.0
Gila Red	0	0.0
Gila Smudged	0	0.0
San Carlos Red	5	33.3
Wingfield Red	0	0.0
Unidentified red #1	0	0.0
Unidentified red #2	0	0.0
Subtotal	*15*	*100.0*
Corrugated types		
Late plain corrugated	2	28.6
Late indented corrugated	1	14.3
Early indented corrugated, smudged interior	0	0.0
Obliterated corrugated	3	42.9
Neck corrugated	1	14.3
Red-slipped neck corrugated	0	0.0
Subtotal	*7*	*100.0*
Miscellaneous		
Porcelain	0	0.0
White glaze ware	0	0.0
Glass	0	0.0
Unidentified	1	100.0
Subtotal	*1*	*100.0*
Total	**481**	

TABLE E.3 Gerald's typological analysis of sherds from House 4 at the Davis Ranch Site

	Fill		Stratitest level 1		Stratitest level 2		Stratitest level 3		Floor		Pit 1		Pit 2	
	n	%	*n*	%	*n*	%	*n*	%	*n*	%	*n*	%	*n*	%
Painted types														
Gila Polychrome	23	29.9	0	0.0	1	14.3	0	0.0	3	7.3	0	0.0	0	0.0
Gila Black-on-red	1	1.3	0	0.0	0	0.0	0	0.0	0	0.0	0	0.0	0	0.0
Pinto Polychrome	1	1.3	0	0.0	0	0.0	0	0.0	0	0.0	0	0.0	0	0.0
Gila Polychrome (Pink Variant)	0	0.0	0	0.0	0	0.0	0	0.0	0	0.0	0	0.0	0	0.0
Gila-Tucson Polychrome	0	0.0	0	0.0	0	0.0	0	0.0	0	0.0	0	0.0	0	0.0
Tucson Polychrome	4	5.2	0	0.0	0	0.0	0	0.0	0	0.0	0	0.0	0	0.0
Tucson Black-on-red	5	6.5	0	0.0	0	0.0	0	0.0	0	0.0	0	0.0	0	0.0
Tonto Polychrome	0	0.0	0	0.0	0	0.0	0	0.0	0	0.0	0	0.0	0	0.0
Dragoon Red-on-brown	6	7.8	2	40.0	0	0.0	1	20.0	6	14.6	0	0.0	0	0.0
Cascabel Red-on-brown	3	3.9	0	0.0	0	0.0	0	0.0	6	14.6	0	0.0	0	0.0
Davis Red-on-white	1	1.3	0	0.0	0	0.0	0	0.0	1	2.4	0	0.0	0	0.0
Tres Alamos Red-on-brown	0	0.0	0	0.0	0	0.0	0	0.0	0	0.0	0	0.0	0	0.0
Gila White Slip	0	0.0	0	0.0	0	0.0	0	0.0	0	0.0	0	0.0	0	0.0
Cañada del Oro Red-on-brown	0	0.0	0	0.0	0	0.0	0	0.0	0	0.0	0	0.0	0	0.0
Gila Butte Red-on-buff	0	0.0	0	0.0	0	0.0	0	0.0	0	0.0	0	0.0	0	0.0
Santa Cruz Red-on-buff	11	14.3	3	60.0	1	14.3	2	40.0	7	17.1	1	16.7	0	0.0
Sacaton Red-on-buff	6	7.8	0	0.0	1	14.3	1	20.0	2	4.9	0	0.0	0	0.0
Casa Grande Red-on-buff	1	1.3	0	0.0	0	0.0	0	0.0	0	0.0	0	0.0	0	0.0
Rillito Red-on-brown	0	0.0	0	0.0	0	0.0	0	0.0	2	4.9	2	33.3	0	0.0
Rillito Red-on-brown (micaceous)	7	9.1	0	0.0	2	28.6	0	0.0	5	12.2	2	33.3	0	0.0
Rincon Red-on-brown	3	3.9	0	0.0	0	0.0	0	0.0	3	7.3	1	16.7	0	0.0

Pantano Red-on-brown	2	2.6	0	0.0	0	0.0	0	0.0	0	0.0	0	0.0	0	0.0
Tanque Verde Red-on-brown	0	0.0	0	0.0	2	28.6	0	0.0	0	0.0	0	0.0	1	100.0
Mimbres Black-on-white	0	0.0	0	0.0	0	0.0	0	0.0	1	2.4	0	0.0	0	0.0
Dos Cabezas Red-on-brown	1	1.3	0	0.0	0	0.0	0	0.0	0	0.0	0	0.0	0	0.0
Encinas Red-on-brown	2	2.6	0	0.0	0	0.0	1	20.0	4	9.8	0	0.0	0	0.0
Nogales Purple-on-red	0	0.0	0	0.0	0	0.0	0	0.0	0	0.0	0	0.0	0	0.0
Cerros Red-on-white	0	0.0	0	0.0	0	0.0	0	0.0	0	0.0	0	0.0	0	0.0
San Carlos Red-on-brown	0	0.0	0	0.0	0	0.0	0	0.0	0	0.0	0	0.0	0	0.0
San Carlos Red-on-white	0	0.0	0	0.0	0	0.0	0	0.0	0	0.0	0	0.0	0	0.0
El Paso Polychrome	0	0.0	0	0.0	0	0.0	0	0.0	0	0.0	0	0.0	0	0.0
Unidentified polychrome	0	0.0	0	0.0	0	0.0	0	0.0	1	2.4	0	0.0	0	0.0
Kayenta-like polychrome	0	0.0	0	0.0	0	0.0	0	0.0	0	0.0	0	0.0	0	0.0
Tusayan-like polychrome	0	0.0	0	0.0	0	0.0	0	0.0	0	0.0	0	0.0	0	0.0
Subtotal	*77*	*100.0*	*5*	*100.0*	*7*	*100.0*	*5*	*100.0*	*41*	*100.0*	*6*	*100.0*	*1*	*100.0*
Plain types														
Davis Plain	197	35.7	20	40.0	18	46.2	6	20.0	64	29.2	1	20.0	16	18.8
Davis Plain: Sobaipuri Coil Rim Variety	0	0.0	0	0.0	0	0.0	0	0.0	0	0.0	0	0.0	0	0.0
Belford Perforated Rim	3	0.5	0	0.0	0	0.0	0	0.0	0	0.0	0	0.0	0	0.0
Belford Perforated Rim (Sobaipuri Coil Rim)	0	0.0	0	0.0	0	0.0	0	0.0	0	0.0	0	0.0	0	0.0
Babocomari Plain	310	56.2	22	44.0	14	35.9	20	66.7	145	66.2	4	80.0	65	76.5
Redington Plain	27	4.9	7	14.0	4	10.3	2	6.7	3	1.4	0	0.0	4	4.7
Redington Smudged	8	1.4	1	2.0	1	2.6	0	0.0	1	0.5	0	0.0	0	0.0
Sacaton Buff	1	0.2	0	0.0	1	2.6	1	3.3	4	1.8	0	0.0	0	0.0
Gila Plain	1	0.2	0	0.0	1	2.6	1	3.3	2	0.9	0	0.0	0	0.0
Gila Smudged	0	0.0	0	0.0	0	0.0	0	0.0	0	0.0	0	0.0	0	0.0

(continued)

TABLE E.3 *(continued)*

	Fill		Stratitest level 1		Stratitest level 2		Stratitest level 3		Floor		Pit 1		Pit 2	
	n	%	*n*	%	*n*	%	*n*	%	*n*	%	*n*	%	*n*	%
San Carlos Brown	3	0.5	0	0.0	0	0.0	0	0.0	0	0.0	0	0.0	0	0.0
Slipped brown	0	0.0	0	0.0	0	0.0	0	0.0	0	0.0	0	0.0	0	0.0
Sosa Plain	0	0.0	0	0.0	0	0.0	0	0.0	0	0.0	0	0.0	0	0.0
Whetstone Plain	0	0.0	0	0.0	0	0.0	0	0.0	0	0.0	0	0.0	0	0.0
Wingfield Plain	1	0.2	0	0.0	0	0.0	0	0.0	0	0.0	0	0.0	0	0.0
Fingernail indented	0	0.0	0	0.0	0	0.0	0	0.0	0	0.0	0	0.0	0	0.0
Incised plain	1	0.2	0	0.0	0	0.0	0	0.0	0	0.0	0	0.0	0	0.0
Tularosa Fillet Rim	0	0.0	0	0.0	0	0.0	0	0.0	0	0.0	0	0.0	0	0.0
Neck corrugated gray ware	0	0.0	0	0.0	0	0.0	0	0.0	0	0.0	0	0.0	0	0.0
Stucco ware?	0	0.0	0	0.0	0	0.0	0	0.0	0	0.0	0	0.0	0	0.0
Sandy Paste Perforated	0	0.0	0	0.0	0	0.0	0	0.0	0	0.0	0	0.0	0	0.0
Sosa Perforated	0	0.0	0	0.0	0	0.0	0	0.0	0	0.0	0	0.0	0	0.0
Subtotal	*552*	*100.0*	*50*	*100.0*	*39*	*100.0*	*30*	*100.0*	*219*	*100.0*	*5*	*100.0*	*85*	*100.0*
Red ware types														
Salt Red: Davis Variety	6	31.6	0	0.0	0	0.0	0	0.0	4	26.7	1	25.0	1	16.7
Salt Smudged: Davis Variety	1	5.3	0	0.0	0	0.0	0	0.0	0	0.0	0	0.0	0	0.0
Dragoon Red	8	42.1	0	0.0	1	100.0	1	100.0	10	66.7	0	0.0	2	33.3
Dragoon Red Smudged	2	10.5	1	100.0	0	0.0	0	0.0	0	0.0	0	0.0	0	0.0
Gila Red	0	0.0	0	0.0	0	0.0	0	0.0	0	0.0	0	0.0	0	0.0

Gila Smudged	0	0.0	0	0.0	0	0.0	0	0.0	0	0.0	0	0.0	3	50.0
San Carlos Red	1	5.3	0	0.0	0	0.0	0	0.0	0	0.0	1	25.0	0	0.0
Wingfield Red	0	0.0	0	0.0	0	0.0	0	0.0	0	0.0	0	0.0	0	0.0
Unidentified red #1	1	5.3	0	0.0	0	0.0	0	0.0	1	6.7	2	50.0	0	0.0
Unidentified red #2	0	0.0	0	0.0	0	0.0	0	0.0	0	0.0	0	0.0	0	0.0
Subtotal	*19*	*100.0*	*1*	*100.0*	*1*	*100.0*	*1*	*100.0*	*15*	*100.0*	*4*	*100.0*	*6*	*100.0*
Corrugated types														
Late plain corrugated	10	20.0	3	50.0	0	0.0	1	100.0	0	0.0	0	0.0	0	0.0
Late indented corrugated	11	22.0	3	50.0	2	100.0	0	0.0	1	100.0	0	0.0	0	0.0
Early indented corrugated, smudged interior	2	4.0	0	0.0	0	0.0	0	0.0	0	0.0	0	0.0	0	0.0
Obliterated corrugated	2	4.0	0	0.0	0	0.0	0	0.0	0	0.0	0	0.0	0	0.0
Neck corrugated	25	50.0	0	0.0	0	0.0	0	0.0	0	0.0	0	0.0	0	0.0
Red-slipped neck corrugated	0	0.0	0	0.0	0	0.0	0	0.0	0	0.0	0	0.0	0	0.0
Subtotal	*50*	*100.0*	*6*	*100.0*	*2*	*100.0*	*1*	*100.0*	*1*	*100.0*	*0*	*0.0*	*0*	*0.0*
Miscellaneous	0	0.0	0	0.0	0	0.0	0	0.0	0	0.0	0	0.0	0	0.0
Porcelain	0	0.0	0	0.0	0	0.0	0	0.0	0	0.0	0	0.0	0	0.0
White glaze ware	0	0.0	0	0.0	0	0.0	0	0.0	0	0.0	0	0.0	0	0.0
Glass	0	0.0	0	0.0	0	0.0	0	0.0	0	0.0	0	0.0	0	0.0
Unidentified	5	100.0	0	0.0	0	0.0	0	0.0	0	0.0	0	0.0	0	0.0
Subtotal	*5*	*100.0*	*0*	*0.0*	*0*	*0.0*	*0*	*0.0*	*0*	*0.0*	*0*	*0.0*	*0*	*0.0*
Total	**703**		**62**		**49**		**37**		**276**		**15**		**92**	

TABLE E.4 Gerald's typological analysis of sherds from House 5 at the Davis Ranch Site

	Fill		Floor	
	n	%	*n*	%
Painted types				
Gila Polychrome	12	22.6	2	15.4
Gila Black-on-red	2	3.8	0	0.0
Pinto Polychrome	0	0.0	0	0.0
Gila Polychrome (Pink Variant)	0	0.0	0	0.0
Gila-Tucson Polychrome	0	0.0	0	0.0
Tucson Polychrome	8	15.1	0	0.0
Tucson Black-on-red	0	0.0	0	0.0
Tonto Polychrome	0	0.0	0	0.0
Dragoon Red-on-brown	3	5.7	1	7.7
Cascabel Red-on-brown	3	5.7	1	7.7
Davis Red-on-white	2	3.8	1	7.7
Tres Alamos Red-on-brown	0	0.0	0	0.0
Gila White Slip	1	1.9	0	0.0
Cañada del Oro Red-on-brown	0	0.0	0	0.0
Gila Butte Red-on-buff	1	1.9	0	0.0
Santa Cruz Red-on-buff	9	17.0	5	38.5
Sacaton Red-on-buff	0	0.0	0	0.0
Casa Grande Red-on-buff	0	0.0	0	0.0
Rillito Red-on-brown	0	0.0	0	0.0
Rillito Red-on-brown (micaceous)	2	3.8	1	7.7
Rincon Red-on-brown	2	3.8	0	0.0
Pantano Red-on-brown	2	3.8	0	0.0
Tanque Verde Red-on-brown	2	3.8	1	7.7
Mimbres Black-on-white	1	1.9	0	0.0
Dos Cabezas Red-on-brown	0	0.0	0	0.0
Encinas Red-on-brown	3	5.7	0	0.0
Nogales Purple-on-red	0	0.0	0	0.0
Cerros Red-on-white	0	0.0	1	7.7
San Carlos Red-on-brown	0	0.0	0	0.0

(*continued*)

TABLE E.4 *(continued)*

	Fill		Floor	
	n	%	*n*	%
San Carlos Red-on-white	0	0.0	0	0.0
El Paso Polychrome	0	0.0	0	0.0
Unidentified polychrome	0	0.0	0	0.0
Kayenta-like polychrome	0	0.0	0	0.0
Tusayan-like polychrome	0	0.0	0	0.0
Subtotal	*53*	*100.0*	*13*	*100.0*
Plain types				
Davis Plain	137	55.0	20	30.3
Davis Plain: Sobaipuri Coil Rim Variety	0	0.0	0	0.0
Belford Perforated Rim	0	0.0	0	0.0
Belford Perforated Rim (Sobaipuri Coil Rim)	0	0.0	0	0.0
Babocomari Plain	82	32.9	44	66.7
Redington Plain	12	4.8	0	0.0
Redington Smudged	4	1.6	1	1.5
Sacaton Buff	0	0.0	1	1.5
Gila Plain	11	4.4	0	0.0
Gila Smudged	1	0.4	0	0.0
San Carlos Brown	1	0.4	0	0.0
Slipped brown	0	0.0	0	0.0
Sosa Plain	0	0.0	0	0.0
Whetstone Plain	0	0.0	0	0.0
Wingfield Plain	1	0.4	0	0.0
Fingernail indented	0	0.0	0	0.0
Incised plain	0	0.0	0	0.0
Tularosa Fillet Rim	0	0.0	0	0.0
Neck corrugated gray ware	0	0.0	0	0.0
Stucco ware?	0	0.0	0	0.0
Sandy Paste Perforated	0	0.0	0	0.0
Sosa Perforated	0	0.0	0	0.0
Subtotal	*249*	*100.0*	*66*	*100.0*

(continued)

TABLE E.4 *(continued)*

	Fill		Floor	
	n	%	*n*	%
Red ware types				
Salt Red: Davis Variety	5	50.0	0	0.0
Salt Smudged: Davis Variety	0	0.0	0	0.0
Dragoon Red	1	10.0	0	0.0
Dragoon Red Smudged	0	0.0	0	0.0
Gila Red	1	10.0	0	0.0
Gila Smudged	1	10.0	0	0.0
San Carlos Red	1	10.0	0	0.0
Wingfield Red	0	0.0	0	0.0
Unidentified red #1	1	10.0	1	100.0
Unidentified red #2	0	0.0	0	0.0
Subtotal	*10*	*100.0*	*1*	*100.0*
Corrugated types				
Late plain corrugated	0	0.0	1	100.0
Late indented corrugated	5	83.3	0	0.0
Early indented corrugated, smudged interior	0	0.0	0	0.0
Obliterated corrugated	1	16.7	0	0.0
Neck corrugated	0	0.0	0	0.0
Red-slipped neck corrugated	0	0.0	0	0.0
Subtotal	*6*	*100.0*	*1*	*100.0*
Miscellaneous				
Porcelain	0	0.0	0	0.0
White glaze ware	0	0.0	0	0.0
Glass	0	0.0	0	0.0
Unidentified	0	0.0	0	0.0
Subtotal	*0*	*0.0*	*0*	*0.0*
Total	**318**		**81**	

TABLE E.5 Gerald's typological analysis of sherds from House 6 at the Davis Ranch Site

	Fill		Stratitest level 1		Stratitest level 2		Stratitest level 3		Floor		Pit 1	
	n	%	*n*	%	*n*	%	*n*	%	*n*	%	*n*	%
Painted types												
Gila Polychrome	3	75.0	4	23.5	8	50.0	12	54.5	1	12.5	1	100.0
Gila Black-on-red	0	0.0	1	5.9	3	18.8	1	4.5	0	0.0	0	0.0
Pinto Polychrome	0	0.0	2	11.8	0	0.0	1	4.5	0	0.0	0	0.0
Gila Polychrome (Pink Variant)	0	0.0	0	0.0	0	0.0	0	0.0	0	0.0	0	0.0
Gila-Tucson Polychrome	0	0.0	0	0.0	0	0.0	0	0.0	0	0.0	0	0.0
Tucson Polychrome	1	25.0	1	5.9	0	0.0	3	13.6	0	0.0	0	0.0
Tucson Black-on-red	0	0.0	6	35.3	1	6.3	1	4.5	1	12.5	0	0.0
Tonto Polychrome	0	0.0	0	0.0	0	0.0	0	0.0	0	0.0	0	0.0
Dragoon Red-on-brown	0	0.0	0	0.0	0	0.0	1	4.5	0	0.0	0	0.0
Cascabel Red-on-brown	0	0.0	0	0.0	0	0.0	0	0.0	0	0.0	0	0.0
Davis Red-on-white	0	0.0	1	5.9	0	0.0	0	0.0	0	0.0	0	0.0
Tres Alamos Red-on-brown	0	0.0	0	0.0	0	0.0	0	0.0	0	0.0	0	0.0
Gila White Slip	0	0.0	0	0.0	0	0.0	0	0.0	0	0.0	0	0.0
Cañada del Oro Red-on-brown	0	0.0	0	0.0	0	0.0	0	0.0	0	0.0	0	0.0
Gila Butte Red-on-buff	0	0.0	0	0.0	0	0.0	0	0.0	0	0.0	0	0.0
Santa Cruz Red-on-buff	0	0.0	1	5.9	1	6.3	1	4.5	2	25.0	0	0.0
Sacaton Red-on-buff	0	0.0	0	0.0	0	0.0	0	0.0	0	0.0	0	0.0
Casa Grande Red-on-buff	0	0.0	0	0.0	0	0.0	0	0.0	0	0.0	0	0.0
Rillito Red-on-brown	0	0.0	0	0.0	0	0.0	0	0.0	0	0.0	0	0.0

(continued)

TABLE E.5 *(continued)*

	Fill		Stratitest level 1		Stratitest level 2		Stratitest level 3		Floor		Pit 1	
	n	%	*n*	%	*n*	%	*n*	%	*n*	%	*n*	%
Rillito Red-on-brown (micaceous)	0	0.0	1	5.9	0	0.0	2	9.1	2	25.0	0	0.0
Rincon Red-on-brown	0	0.0	0	0.0	0	0.0	0	0.0	0	0.0	0	0.0
Pantano Red-on-brown	0	0.0	0	0.0	0	0.0	0	0.0	1	12.5	0	0.0
Tanque Verde Red-on-brown	0	0.0	0	0.0	0	0.0	0	0.0	0	0.0	0	0.0
Mimbres Black-on-white	0	0.0	0	0.0	0	0.0	0	0.0	0	0.0	0	0.0
Dos Cabezas Red-on-brown	0	0.0	0	0.0	0	0.0	0	0.0	0	0.0	0	0.0
Encinas Red-on-brown	0	0.0	0	0.0	2	12.5	0	0.0	1	12.5	0	0.0
Nogales Purple-on-red	0	0.0	0	0.0	0	0.0	0	0.0	0	0.0	0	0.0
Cerros Red-on-white	0	0.0	0	0.0	0	0.0	0	0.0	0	0.0	0	0.0
San Carlos Red-on-brown	0	0.0	0	0.0	1	6.3	0	0.0	0	0.0	0	0.0
San Carlos Red-on-white	0	0.0	0	0.0	0	0.0	0	0.0	0	0.0	0	0.0
El Paso Polychrome	0	0.0	0	0.0	0	0.0	0	0.0	0	0.0	0	0.0
Unidentified polychrome	0	0.0	0	0.0	0	0.0	0	0.0	0	0.0	0	0.0
Kayenta-like polychrome	0	0.0	0	0.0	0	0.0	0	0.0	0	0.0	0	0.0
Tusayan-like polychrome	0	0.0	0	0.0	0	0.0	0	0.0	0	0.0	0	0.0
Subtotal	*4*	*100.0*	*17*	*100.0*	*16*	*100.0*	*22*	*100.0*	*8*	*100.0*	*1*	*100.0*
Plain types												
Davis Plain	12	66.7	69	77.5	49	70.0	101	55.2	40	62.5	8	88.9
Davis Plain: Sobaipuri Coil Rim Variety	0	0.0	1	1.1	0	0.0	0	0.0	0	0.0	0	0.0
Belford Perforated Rim	0	0.0	0	0.0	1	1.4	0	0.0	0	0.0	0	0.0
Belford Perforated Rim (Sobaipuri Coil Rim)	0	0.0	0	0.0	0	0.0	0	0.0	0	0.0	0	0.0
Babocomari Plain	4	22.2	11	12.4	11	15.7	61	33.3	14	21.9	0	0.0

Redington Plain	1	5.6	5	5.6	3	4.3	10	5.5	5	7.8	0	0.0
Redington Smudged	1	5.6	2	2.2	3	4.3	6	3.3	3	4.7	1	11.1
Sacaton Buff	0	0.0	1	1.1	2	2.9	0	0.0	1	1.6	0	0.0
Gila Plain	0	0.0	0	0.0	0	0.0	4	2.2	0	0.0	0	0.0
Gila Smudged	0	0.0	0	0.0	0	0.0	0	0.0	0	0.0	0	0.0
San Carlos Brown	0	0.0	0	0.0	1	1.4	0	0.0	0	0.0	0	0.0
Slipped brown	0	0.0	0	0.0	0	0.0	0	0.0	0	0.0	0	0.0
Sosa Plain	0	0.0	0	0.0	0	0.0	1	0.5	1	1.6	0	0.0
Whetstone Plain	0	0.0	0	0.0	0	0.0	0	0.0	0	0.0	0	0.0
Wingfield Plain	0	0.0	0	0.0	0	0.0	0	0.0	0	0.0	0	0.0
Fingernail indented	0	0.0	0	0.0	0	0.0	0	0.0	0	0.0	0	0.0
Incised plain	0	0.0	0	0.0	0	0.0	0	0.0	0	0.0	0	0.0
Tularosa Fillet Rim	0	0.0	0	0.0	0	0.0	0	0.0	0	0.0	0	0.0
Neck corrugated gray ware	0	0.0	0	0.0	0	0.0	0	0.0	0	0.0	0	0.0
Stucco ware?	0	0.0	0	0.0	0	0.0	0	0.0	0	0.0	0	0.0
Sandy Paste Perforated	0	0.0	0	0.0	0	0.0	0	0.0	0	0.0	0	0.0
Sosa Perforated	0	0.0	0	0.0	0	0.0	0	0.0	0	0.0	0	0.0
Subtotal	*18*	*100.0*	*89*	*100.0*	*70*	*100.0*	*183*	*100.0*	*64*	*100.0*	*9*	*100.0*
Red ware types												
Salt Red: Davis Variety	0	0.0	2	50.0	1	25.0	8	53.3	0	0.0	0	0.0
Salt Smudged: Davis Variety	0	0.0	1	25.0	0	0.0	0	0.0	0	0.0	0	0.0
Dragoon Red	0	0.0	1	25.0	3	75.0	5	33.3	1	16.7	0	0.0
Dragoon Red Smudged	0	0.0	0	0.0	0	0.0	1	6.7	0	0.0	0	0.0
Gila Red	0	0.0	0	0.0	0	0.0	0	0.0	0	0.0	0	0.0
Gila Smudged	1	50.0	0	0.0	0	0.0	0	0.0	3	50.0	0	0.0

(continued)

TABLE E.5 *(continued)*

	Fill		Stratitest level 1		Stratitest level 2		Stratitest level 3		Floor		Pit 1	
	n	%	*n*	%	*n*	%	*n*	%	*n*	%	*n*	%
San Carlos Red	0	0.0	0	0.0	0	0.0	0	0.0	0	0.0	0	0.0
Wingfield Red	0	0.0	0	0.0	0	0.0	0	0.0	0	0.0	0	0.0
Unidentified red #1	1	50.0	0	0.0	0	0.0	1	6.7	1	16.7	0	0.0
Unidentified red #2	0	0.0	0	0.0	0	0.0	0	0.0	1	16.7	0	0.0
Subtotal	*2*	*100.0*	*4*	*100.0*	*4*	*100.0*	*15*	*100.0*	*6*	*100.0*	*0*	*0.0*
Corrugated types												
Late plain corrugated	0	0.0	0	0.0	1	50.0	0	0.0	0	0.0	0	0.0
Late indented corrugated	0	0.0	0	0.0	1	50.0	1	50.0	1	100.0	0	0.0
Early indented corrugated, smudged interior	0	0.0	0	0.0	0	0.0	1	50.0	0	0.0	0	0.0
Obliterated corrugated	0	0.0	0	0.0	0	0.0	0	0.0	0	0.0	0	0.0
Neck corrugated	0	0.0	0	0.0	0	0.0	0	0.0	0	0.0	0	0.0
Red-slipped neck corrugated	0	0.0	0	0.0	0	0.0	0	0.0	0	0.0	0	0.0
Subtotal	*0*	*0.0*	*0*	*0.0*	*2*	*100.0*	*2*	*100.0*	*1*	*100.0*	*0*	*0.0*
Miscellaneous												
Porcelain	0	0.0	0	0.0	0	0.0	0	0.0	0	0.0	0	0.0
White glaze ware	0	0.0	0	0.0	0	0.0	0	0.0	0	0.0	0	0.0
Glass	0	0.0	0	0.0	0	0.0	0	0.0	0	0.0	0	0.0
Unidentified	0	0.0	1	100.0	0	0.0	2	100.0	0	0.0	0	0.0
Subtotal	*0*	*0.0*	*1*	*100.0*	*0*	*0.0*	*2*	*100.0*	*0*	*0.0*	*0*	*0.0*
Total	**24**		**111**		**92**		**224**		**79**		**10**	

TABLE E.6 Gerald's typological analysis of sherds from House 7 at the Davis Ranch Site

	Fill		Pits 1 and 2		Stratitest level 1		Stratitest level 2		Stratitest level 3	
	n	%	*n*	%	*n*	%	*n*	%	*n*	%
Painted types										
Gila Polychrome	118	79.2	49	92.5	3	100.0	2	25.0	12	80.0
Gila Black-on-red	1	0.7	0	0.0	0	0.0	1	12.5	0	0.0
Pinto Polychrome	7	4.7	0	0.0	0	0.0	0	0.0	1	6.7
Gila Polychrome (Pink Variant)	0	0.0	0	0.0	0	0.0	0	0.0	0	0.0
Gila-Tucson Polychrome	0	0.0	0	0.0	0	0.0	0	0.0	0	0.0
Tucson Polychrome	2	1.3	1	1.9	0	0.0	0	0.0	0	0.0
Tucson Black-on-red	3	2.0	0	0.0	0	0.0	0	0.0	0	0.0
Tonto Polychrome	4	2.7	0	0.0	0	0.0	0	0.0	1	6.7
Dragoon Red-on-brown	1	0.7	0	0.0	0	0.0	0	0.0	0	0.0
Cascabel Red-on-brown	0	0.0	1	1.9	0	0.0	3	37.5	0	0.0
Davis Red-on-white	0	0.0	0	0.0	0	0.0	0	0.0	0	0.0
Tres Alamos Red-on-brown	0	0.0	0	0.0	0	0.0	0	0.0	0	0.0
Gila White Slip	7	4.7	0	0.0	0	0.0	0	0.0	1	6.7
Cañada del Oro Red-on-brown	0	0.0	0	0.0	0	0.0	0	0.0	0	0.0
Gila Butte Red-on-buff	0	0.0	0	0.0	0	0.0	0	0.0	0	0.0
Santa Cruz Red-on-buff	3	2.0	1	1.9	0	0.0	0	0.0	0	0.0
Sacaton Red-on-buff	0	0.0	0	0.0	0	0.0	0	0.0	0	0.0
Casa Grande Red-on-buff	0	0.0	0	0.0	0	0.0	0	0.0	0	0.0
Rillito Red-on-brown	0	0.0	0	0.0	0	0.0	0	0.0	0	0.0

(continued)

TABLE E.6 *(continued)*

	Fill		Pits 1 and 2		Stratitest level 1		Stratitest level 2		Stratitest level 3	
	n	%	*n*	%	*n*	%	*n*	%	*n*	%
Rillito Red-on-brown (micaceous)	0	0.0	0	0.0	0	0.0	0	0.0	0	0.0
Rincon Red-on-brown	0	0.0	1	1.9	0	0.0	0	0.0	0	0.0
Pantano Red-on-brown	0	0.0	0	0.0	0	0.0	1	12.5	0	0.0
Tanque Verde Red-on-brown	2	1.3	0	0.0	0	0.0	0	0.0	0	0.0
Mimbres Black-on-white	0	0.0	0	0.0	0	0.0	0	0.0	0	0.0
Dos Cabezas Red-on-brown	0	0.0	0	0.0	0	0.0	0	0.0	0	0.0
Encinas Red-on-brown	0	0.0	0	0.0	0	0.0	1	12.5	0	0.0
Nogales Purple-on-red	0	0.0	0	0.0	0	0.0	0	0.0	0	0.0
Cerros Red-on-white	0	0.0	0	0.0	0	0.0	0	0.0	0	0.0
San Carlos Red-on-brown	0	0.0	0	0.0	0	0.0	0	0.0	0	0.0
San Carlos Red-on-white	1	0.7	0	0.0	0	0.0	0	0.0	0	0.0
El Paso Polychrome	0	0.0	0	0.0	0	0.0	0	0.0	0	0.0
Unidentified polychrome	0	0.0	0	0.0	0	0.0	0	0.0	0	0.0
Kayenta-like polychrome	0	0.0	0	0.0	0	0.0	0	0.0	0	0.0
Tusayan-like polychrome	0	0.0	0	0.0	0	0.0	0	0.0	0	0.0
Subtotal	*149*	*100.0*	*53*	*100.0*	*3*	*100.0*	*8*	*100.0*	*15*	*100.0*
Plain types										
Davis Plain	337	87.8	163	87.2	6	60.0	14	70.0	67	84.8
Davis Plain: Sobaipuri Coil Rim Variety	1	0.3	0	0.0	0	0.0	0	0.0	0	0.0
Belford Perforated Rim	0	0.0	0	0.0	0	0.0	0	0.0	0	0.0
Belford Perforated Rim (Sobaipuri Coil Rim)	0	0.0	0	0.0	0	0.0	0	0.0	0	0.0
Babocomari Plain	21	5.5	6	3.2	3	30.0	6	30.0	9	11.4

Redington Plain	4	1.0	4	2.1	0	0.0	0	0.0	2	2.5
Redington Smudged	3	0.8	2	1.1	1	10.0	0	0.0	0	0.0
Sacaton Buff	1	0.3	1	0.5	0	0.0	0	0.0	0	0.0
Gila Plain	14	3.6	8	4.3	0	0.0	0	0.0	1	1.3
Gila Smudged	1	0.3	0	0.0	0	0.0	0	0.0	0	0.0
San Carlos Brown	2	0.5	3	1.6	0	0.0	0	0.0	0	0.0
Slipped brown	0	0.0	0	0.0	0	0.0	0	0.0	0	0.0
Sosa Plain	0	0.0	0	0.0	0	0.0	0	0.0	0	0.0
Whetstone Plain	0	0.0	0	0.0	0	0.0	0	0.0	0	0.0
Wingfield Plain	0	0.0	0	0.0	0	0.0	0	0.0	0	0.0
Fingernail indented	0	0.0	0	0.0	0	0.0	0	0.0	0	0.0
Incised plain	0	0.0	0	0.0	0	0.0	0	0.0	0	0.0
Tularosa Fillet Rim	0	0.0	0	0.0	0	0.0	0	0.0	0	0.0
Neck corrugated gray ware	0	0.0	0	0.0	0	0.0	0	0.0	0	0.0
Stucco ware?	0	0.0	0	0.0	0	0.0	0	0.0	0	0.0
Sandy Paste Perforated	0	0.0	0	0.0	0	0.0	0	0.0	0	0.0
Sosa Perforated	0	0.0	0	0.0	0	0.0	0	0.0	0	0.0
Subtotal	*384*	*100.0*	*187*	*100.0*	*10*	*100.0*	*20*	*100.0*	*79*	*100.0*
Red ware types										
Salt Red: Davis Variety	17	39.5	4	50.0	1	100.0	0	0.0	7	70.0
Salt Smudged: Davis Variety	2	4.7	0	0.0	0	0.0	0	0.0	1	10.0
Dragoon Red	3	7.0	1	12.5	0	0.0	0	0.0	0	0.0
Dragoon Red Smudged	0	0.0	0	0.0	0	0.0	0	0.0	1	10.0
Gila Red	13	30.2	2	25.0	0	0.0	0	0.0	0	0.0
Gila Smudged	0	0.0	0	0.0	0	0.0	0	0.0	0	0.0

(*continued*)

TABLE E.6 *(continued)*

	Fill		Pits 1 and 2		Stratitest level 1		Stratitest level 2		Stratitest level 3	
	n	%	*n*	%	*n*	%	*n*	%	*n*	%
San Carlos Red	8	18.6	1	12.5	0	0.0	1	100.0	1	10.0
Wingfield Red	0	0.0	0	0.0	0	0.0	0	0.0	0	0.0
Unidentified red #1	0	0.0	0	0.0	0	0.0	0	0.0	0	0.0
Unidentified red #2	0	0.0	0	0.0	0	0.0	0	0.0	0	0.0
Subtotal	*43*	*100.0*	*8*	*100.0*	*1*	*100.0*	*1*	*100.0*	*10*	*100.0*
Corrugated types										
Late plain corrugated	1	25.0	1	100.0	0	0.0	0	0.0	0	0.0
Late indented corrugated	3	75.0	0	0.0	0	0.0	0	0.0	0	0.0
Early indented corrugated, smudged interior	0	0.0	0	0.0	0	0.0	0	0.0	0	0.0
Obliterated corrugated	0	0.0	0	0.0	0	0.0	0	0.0	0	0.0
Neck corrugated	0	0.0	0	0.0	0	0.0	0	0.0	0	0.0
Red-slipped neck corrugated	0	0.0	0	0.0	0	0.0	0	0.0	0	0.0
Subtotal	*4*	*100.0*	*1*	*100.0*	*0*	*0.0*	*0*	*0.0*	*0*	*0.0*
Miscellaneous										
Porcelain	0	0.0	0	0.0	0	0.0	0	0.0	0	0.0
White glaze ware	0	0.0	0	0.0	0	0.0	0	0.0	0	0.0
Glass	0	0.0	0	0.0	0	0.0	0	0.0	0	0.0
Unidentified	0	0.0	1	100.0	0	0.0	0	0.0	0	0.0
Subtotal	*0*	*0.0*	*1*	*100.0*	*0*	*0.0*	*0*	*0.0*	*0*	*0.0*
Total	**580**		**250**		**14**		**29**		**104**	

(continued)

	Floor 1		Fire Pit 2		Fire Pit 3		Fire Pit 4	
	n	%	*n*	%	*n*	%	*n*	%
Painted types								
Gila Polychrome	44	72.1	0	0.0	26	100.0	5	100.0
Gila Black-on-red	0	0.0	0	0.0	0	0.0	0	0.0
Pinto Polychrome	5	8.2	0	0.0	0	0.0	0	0.0
Gila Polychrome (Pink Variant)	0	0.0	0	0.0	0	0.0	0	0.0
Gila-Tucson Polychrome	0	0.0	0	0.0	0	0.0	0	0.0
Tucson Polychrome	0	0.0	0	0.0	0	0.0	0	0.0
Tucson Black-on-red	0	0.0	0	0.0	0	0.0	0	0.0
Tonto Polychrome	0	0.0	0	0.0	0	0.0	0	0.0
Dragoon Red-on-brown	1	1.6	0	0.0	0	0.0	0	0.0
Cascabel Red-on-brown	1	1.6	0	0.0	0	0.0	0	0.0
Davis Red-on-white	0	0.0	0	0.0	0	0.0	0	0.0
Tres Alamos Red-on-brown	0	0.0	0	0.0	0	0.0	0	0.0
Gila White Slip	1	1.6	0	0.0	0	0.0	0	0.0
Cañada del Oro Red-on-brown	0	0.0	0	0.0	0	0.0	0	0.0
Gila Butte Red-on-buff	0	0.0	0	0.0	0	0.0	0	0.0
Santa Cruz Red-on-buff	2	3.3	0	0.0	0	0.0	0	0.0
Sacaton Red-on-buff	0	0.0	0	0.0	0	0.0	0	0.0
Casa Grande Red-on-buff	0	0.0	0	0.0	0	0.0	0	0.0
Rillito Red-on-brown	0	0.0	0	0.0	0	0.0	0	0.0
Rillito Red-on-brown (micaceous)	0	0.0	0	0.0	0	0.0	0	0.0
Rincon Red-on-brown	1	1.6	0	0.0	0	0.0	0	0.0
Pantano Red-on-brown	0	0.0	0	0.0	0	0.0	0	0.0

(continued)

TABLE E.6 *(continued)*

	Floor 1		Fire Pit 2		Fire Pit 3		Fire Pit 4	
	n	%	*n*	%	*n*	%	*n*	%
Tanque Verde Red-on-brown	0	0.0	0	0.0	0	0.0	0	0.0
Mimbres Black-on-white	0	0.0	0	0.0	0	0.0	0	0.0
Dos Cabezas Red-on-brown	0	0.0	0	0.0	0	0.0	0	0.0
Encinas Red-on-brown	0	0.0	0	0.0	0	0.0	0	0.0
Nogales Purple-on-red	0	0.0	0	0.0	0	0.0	0	0.0
Cerros Red-on-white	0	0.0	0	0.0	0	0.0	0	0.0
San Carlos Red-on-brown	0	0.0	0	0.0	0	0.0	0	0.0
San Carlos Red-on-white	6	9.8	0	0.0	0	0.0	0	0.0
El Paso Polychrome	0	0.0	0	0.0	0	0.0	0	0.0
Unidentified polychrome	0	0.0	0	0.0	0	0.0	0	0.0
Kayenta-like polychrome	0	0.0	0	0.0	0	0.0	0	0.0
Tusayan-like polychrome	0	0.0	0	0.0	0	0.0	0	0.0
Subtotal	*61*	*100.0*	*0*	*0.0*	*26*	*100.0*	*5*	*100.0*
Plain types								
Davis Plain	199	89.2	14	100.0	27	87.1	2	100.0
Davis Plain: Sobaipuri Coil Rim Variety	0	0.0	0	0.0	0	0.0	0	0.0
Belford Perforated Rim	0	0.0	0	0.0	0	0.0	0	0.0
Belford Perforated Rim (Sobaipuri Coil Rim)	0	0.0	0	0.0	0	0.0	0	0.0
Babocomari Plain	5	2.2	0	0.0	2	6.5	0	0.0
Redington Plain	6	2.7	0	0.0	0	0.0	0	0.0
Redington Smudged	0	0.0	0	0.0	0	0.0	0	0.0

Sacaton Buff	0	0.0	0	0.0	0	0.0	0	0.0
Gila Plain	5	2.2	0	0.0	0	0.0	0	0.0
Gila Smudged	0	0.0	0	0.0	1	3.2	0	0.0
San Carlos Brown	7	3.1	0	0.0	1	3.2	0	0.0
Slipped brown	1	0.4	0	0.0	0	0.0	0	0.0
Sosa Plain	0	0.0	0	0.0	0	0.0	0	0.0
Whetstone Plain	0	0.0	0	0.0	0	0.0	0	0.0
Wingfield Plain	0	0.0	0	0.0	0	0.0	0	0.0
Fingernail indented	0	0.0	0	0.0	0	0.0	0	0.0
Incised plain	0	0.0	0	0.0	0	0.0	0	0.0
Tularosa Fillet Rim	0	0.0	0	0.0	0	0.0	0	0.0
Neck corrugated gray ware	0	0.0	0	0.0	0	0.0	0	0.0
Stucco ware?	0	0.0	0	0.0	0	0.0	0	0.0
Sandy Paste Perforated	0	0.0	0	0.0	0	0.0	0	0.0
Sosa Perforated	0	0.0	0	0.0	0	0.0	0	0.0
Subtotal	*223*	*100.0*	*14*	*100.0*	*31*	*100.0*	*2*	*100.0*
Red ware types								
Salt Red: Davis Variety	1	5.9	0	0.0	3	60.0	5	100.0
Salt Smudged: Davis Variety	0	0.0	0	0.0	0	0.0	0	0.0
Dragoon Red	0	0.0	0	0.0	0	0.0	0	0.0
Dragoon Red Smudged	0	0.0	0	0.0	0	0.0	0	0.0
Gila Red	9	52.9	1	100.0	0	0.0	0	0.0
Gila Smudged	1	5.9	0	0.0	2	40.0	0	0.0

(*continued*)

TABLE E.6 *(continued)*

	Floor 1		Fire Pit 2		Fire Pit 3		Fire Pit 4	
	n	%	*n*	%	*n*	%	*n*	%
San Carlos Red	6	35.3	0	0.0	0	0.0	0	0.0
Wingfield Red	0	0.0	0	0.0	0	0.0	0	0.0
Unidentified red #1	0	0.0	0	0.0	0	0.0	0	0.0
Unidentified red #2	0	0.0	0	0.0	0	0.0	0	0.0
Subtotal	*17*	*100.0*	*1*	*100.0*	*5*	*100.0*	*5*	*100.0*
Corrugated types								
Late plain corrugated	2	66.7	0	0.0	0	0.0	0	0.0
Late indented corrugated	1	33.3	0	0.0	0	0.0	0	0.0
Early indented corrugated, smudged interior	0	0.0	0	0.0	0	0.0	0	0.0
Obliterated corrugated	0	0.0	0	0.0	0	0.0	0	0.0
Neck corrugated	0	0.0	0	0.0	0	0.0	0	0.0
Red-slipped neck corrugated	0	0.0	0	0.0	0	0.0	0	0.0
Subtotal	*3*	*100.0*	*0*	*0.0*	*0*	*0.0*	*0*	*0.0*
Miscellaneous								
Porcelain	0	0.0	0	0.0	0	0.0	0	0.0
White glaze ware	0	0.0	0	0.0	0	0.0	0	0.0
Glass	0	0.0	0	0.0	0	0.0	0	0.0
Unidentified	0	0.0	0	0.0	3	100.0	0	0.0
Subtotal	*0*	*0.0*	*0*	*0.0*	*3*	*100.0*	*0*	*0.0*
Total	**304**		**15**		**65**		**12**	

(continued)

	Pit 4		Subfloor 1 fill		Floor 2	
	n	%	*n*	%	*n*	%
Painted types						
Gila Polychrome	3	75.0	20	57.1	6	18.2
Gila Black-on-red	0	0.0	3	8.6	6	18.2
Pinto Polychrome	0	0.0	0	0.0	0	0.0
Gila Polychrome (Pink Variant)	0	0.0	0	0.0	0	0.0
Gila-Tucson Polychrome	0	0.0	0	0.0	0	0.0
Tucson Polychrome	0	0.0	1	2.9	2	6.1
Tucson Black-on-red	0	0.0	1	2.9	4	12.1
Tonto Polychrome	0	0.0	0	0.0	0	0.0
Dragoon Red-on-brown	0	0.0	2	5.7	4	12.1
Cascabel Red-on-brown	0	0.0	1	2.9	1	3.0
Davis Red-on-white	0	0.0	1	2.9	0	0.0
Tres Alamos Red-on-brown	0	0.0	0	0.0	0	0.0
Gila White Slip	0	0.0	0	0.0	0	0.0
Cañada del Oro Red-on-brown	0	0.0	0	0.0	0	0.0
Gila Butte Red-on-buff	0	0.0	0	0.0	0	0.0
Santa Cruz Red-on-buff	0	0.0	4	11.4	4	12.1
Sacaton Red-on-buff	1	25.0	2	5.7	1	3.0
Casa Grande Red-on-buff	0	0.0	0	0.0	0	0.0
Rillito Red-on-brown	0	0.0	0	0.0	0	0.0
Rillito Red-on-brown (micaceous)	0	0.0	0	0.0	3	9.1

(*continued*)

TABLE E.6 *(continued)*

	Pit 4		Subfloor 1 fill		Floor 2	
	n	%	*n*	%	*n*	%
Rincon Red-on-brown	0	0.0	0	0.0	0	0.0
Pantano Red-on-brown	0	0.0	0	0.0	0	0.0
Tanque Verde Red-on-brown	0	0.0	0	0.0	0	0.0
Mimbres Black-on-white	0	0.0	0	0.0	0	0.0
Dos Cabezas Red-on-brown	0	0.0	0	0.0	0	0.0
Encinas Red-on-brown	0	0.0	0	0.0	2	6.1
Nogales Purple-on-red	0	0.0	0	0.0	0	0.0
Cerros Red-on-white	0	0.0	0	0.0	0	0.0
San Carlos Red-on-brown	0	0.0	0	0.0	0	0.0
San Carlos Red-on-white	0	0.0	0	0.0	0	0.0
El Paso Polychrome	0	0.0	0	0.0	0	0.0
Unidentified polychrome	0	0.0	0	0.0	0	0.0
Kayenta-like polychrome	0	0.0	0	0.0	0	0.0
Tusayan-like polychrome	0	0.0	0	0.0	0	0.0
Subtotal	*4*	*100.0*	*35*	*100.0*	*33*	*100.0*
Plain types						
Davis Plain	12	57.1	86	63.2	58	51.3
Davis Plain: Sobaipuri Coil Rim Variety	0	0.0	0	0.0	0	0.0
Belford Perforated Rim	0	0.0	0	0.0	1	0.9
Belford Perforated Rim (Sobaipuri Coil Rim)	0	0.0	0	0.0	0	0.0
Babocomari Plain	8	38.1	42	30.9	48	42.5
Redington Plain	1	4.8	3	2.2	1	0.9

Redington Smudged	0	0.0	3	2.2	0	0.0
Sacaton Buff	0	0.0	2	1.5	1	0.9
Gila Plain	0	0.0	0	0.0	3	2.7
Gila Smudged	0	0.0	0	0.0	1	0.9
San Carlos Brown	0	0.0	0	0.0	0	0.0
Slipped brown	0	0.0	0	0.0	0	0.0
Sosa Plain	0	0.0	0	0.0	0	0.0
Whetstone Plain	0	0.0	0	0.0	0	0.0
Wingfield Plain	0	0.0	0	0.0	0	0.0
Fingernail indented	0	0.0	0	0.0	0	0.0
Incised plain	0	0.0	0	0.0	0	0.0
Tularosa Fillet Rim	0	0.0	0	0.0	0	0.0
Neck corrugated gray ware	0	0.0	0	0.0	0	0.0
Stucco ware?	0	0.0	0	0.0	0	0.0
Sandy Paste Perforated	0	0.0	0	0.0	0	0.0
Sosa Perforated	0	0.0	0	0.0	0	0.0
Subtotal	*21*	*100.0*	*136*	*100.0*	*113*	*100.0*
Red ware types						
Salt Red: Davis Variety	7	100.0	21	84.0	29	93.5
Salt Smudged: Davis Variety	0	0.0	0	0.0	0	0.0
Dragoon Red	0	0.0	4	16.0	2	6.5
Dragoon Red Smudged	0	0.0	0	0.0	0	0.0
Gila Red	0	0.0	0	0.0	0	0.0
Gila Smudged	0	0.0	0	0.0	0	0.0
San Carlos Red	0	0.0	0	0.0	0	0.0

(*continued*)

TABLE E.6 *(continued)*

	Pit 4		Subfloor 1 fill		Floor 2	
	n	%	*n*	%	*n*	%
Wingfield Red	0	0.0	0	0.0	0	0.0
Unidentified red #1	0	0.0	0	0.0	0	0.0
Unidentified red #2	0	0.0	0	0.0	0	0.0
Subtotal	*7*	*100.0*	*25*	*100.0*	*31*	*100.0*
Corrugated types						
Late plain corrugated	0	0.0	0	0.0	2	100.0
Late indented corrugated	0	0.0	0	0.0	0	0.0
Early indented corrugated, smudged interior	0	0.0	0	0.0	0	0.0
Obliterated corrugated	0	0.0	0	0.0	0	0.0
Neck corrugated	0	0.0	0	0.0	0	0.0
Red-slipped neck corrugated	0	0.0	0	0.0	0	0.0
Subtotal	*0*	*0.0*	*0*	*0.0*	*2*	*100.0*
Miscellaneous						
Porcelain	0	0.0	0	0.0	0	0.0
White glaze ware	0	0.0	0	0.0	0	0.0
Glass	0	0.0	0	0.0	0	0.0
Unidentified	1	100.0	0	0.0	1	100.0
Subtotal	*1*	*100.0*	*0*	*0.0*	*1*	*100.0*
Total	**33**		**196**		**180**	

TABLE E.7 Gerald's typological analysis of sherds from House 8 at the Davis Ranch Site

	Fill		Stratitest level 1		Stratitest level 2		Stratitest level 3		Floor	
	n	%	*n*	%	*n*	%	*n*	%	*n*	%
Painted types										
Gila Polychrome	1	4.5	0	0.0	0	0.0	0	0.0	0	0.0
Gila Black-on-red	0	0.0	0	0.0	0	0.0	0	0.0	0	0.0
Pinto Polychrome	0	0.0	0	0.0	0	0.0	0	0.0	0	0.0
Gila Polychrome (Pink Variant)	0	0.0	0	0.0	0	0.0	0	0.0	0	0.0
Gila-Tucson Polychrome	0	0.0	0	0.0	0	0.0	0	0.0	0	0.0
Tucson Polychrome	0	0.0	0	0.0	0	0.0	0	0.0	0	0.0
Tucson Black-on-red	0	0.0	0	0.0	0	0.0	0	0.0	0	0.0
Tonto Polychrome	0	0.0	0	0.0	0	0.0	0	0.0	0	0.0
Dragoon Red-on-brown	1	4.5	0	0.0	0	0.0	1	12.5	0	0.0
Cascabel Red-on-brown	3	13.6	0	0.0	2	28.6	1	12.5	1	4.2
Davis Red-on-white	0	0.0	0	0.0	0	0.0	1	12.5	1	4.2
Tres Alamos Red-on-brown	0	0.0	0	0.0	0	0.0	0	0.0	0	0.0
Gila White Slip	0	0.0	0	0.0	0	0.0	0	0.0	0	0.0
Cañada del Oro Red-on-brown	1	4.5	0	0.0	0	0.0	0	0.0	0	0.0
Gila Butte Red-on-buff	1	4.5	0	0.0	0	0.0	1	12.5	0	0.0
Santa Cruz Red-on-buff	7	31.8	1	50.0	2	28.6	2	25.0	3	12.5
Sacaton Red-on-buff	3	13.6	1	50.0	0	0.0	0	0.0	2	8.3
Casa Grande Red-on-buff	0	0.0	0	0.0	0	0.0	0	0.0	0	0.0

(continued)

TABLE E.7 *(continued)*

	Fill		Stratitest level 1		Stratitest level 2		Stratitest level 3		Floor	
	n	%	*n*	%	*n*	%	*n*	%	*n*	%
Rillito Red-on-brown	0	0.0	0	0.0	0	0.0	0	0.0	1	4.2
Rillito Red-on-brown (micaceous)	1	4.5	0	0.0	1	14.3	1	12.5	1	4.2
Rincon Red-on-brown	1	4.5	0	0.0	0	0.0	0	0.0	10	41.7
Pantano Red-on-brown	0	0.0	0	0.0	0	0.0	0	0.0	3	12.5
Tanque Verde Red-on-brown	0	0.0	0	0.0	0	0.0	0	0.0	1	4.2
Mimbres Black-on-white	0	0.0	0	0.0	0	0.0	0	0.0	0	0.0
Dos Cabezas Red-on-brown	0	0.0	0	0.0	0	0.0	0	0.0	0	0.0
Encinas Red-on-brown	3	13.6	0	0.0	2	28.6	0	0.0	1	4.2
Nogales Purple-on-red	0	0.0	0	0.0	0	0.0	0	0.0	0	0.0
Cerros Red-on-white	0	0.0	0	0.0	0	0.0	1	12.5	0	0.0
San Carlos Red-on-brown	0	0.0	0	0.0	0	0.0	0	0.0	0	0.0
San Carlos Red-on-white	0	0.0	0	0.0	0	0.0	0	0.0	0	0.0
El Paso Polychrome	0	0.0	0	0.0	0	0.0	0	0.0	0	0.0
Unidentified polychrome	0	0.0	0	0.0	0	0.0	0	0.0	0	0.0
Kayenta-like polychrome	0	0.0	0	0.0	0	0.0	0	0.0	0	0.0
Tusayan-like polychrome	0	0.0	0	0.0	0	0.0	0	0.0	0	0.0
Subtotal	*22*	*100.0*	*2*	*100.0*	*7*	*100.0*	*8*	*100.0*	*24*	*100.0*
Plain types										
Davis Plain	62	63.3	3	15.8	19	37.3	11	21.2	38	29.0
Davis Plain: Sobaipuri Coil Rim Variety	0	0.0	0	0.0	0	0.0	0	0.0	0	0.0
Belford Perforated Rim	0	0.0	0	0.0	0	0.0	0	0.0	0	0.0
Belford Perforated Rim (Sobaipuri Coil Rim)	0	0.0	0	0.0	0	0.0	0	0.0	0	0.0

Babocomari Plain	13	13.3	16	84.2	27	52.9	37	71.2	64	48.9
Redington Plain	6	6.1	0	0.0	2	3.9	1	1.9	4	3.1
Redington Smudged	1	1.0	0	0.0	0	0.0	0	0.0	0	0.0
Sacaton Buff	6	6.1	0	0.0	0	0.0	0	0.0	17	13.0
Gila Plain	10	10.2	0	0.0	3	5.9	2	3.8	8	6.1
Gila Smudged	0	0.0	0	0.0	0	0.0	1	1.9	0	0.0
San Carlos Brown	0	0.0	0	0.0	0	0.0	0	0.0	0	0.0
Slipped brown	0	0.0	0	0.0	0	0.0	0	0.0	0	0.0
Sosa Plain	0	0.0	0	0.0	0	0.0	0	0.0	0	0.0
Whetstone Plain	0	0.0	0	0.0	0	0.0	0	0.0	0	0.0
Wingfield Plain	0	0.0	0	0.0	0	0.0	0	0.0	0	0.0
Fingernail indented	0	0.0	0	0.0	0	0.0	0	0.0	0	0.0
Incised plain	0	0.0	0	0.0	0	0.0	0	0.0	0	0.0
Tularosa Fillet Rim	0	0.0	0	0.0	0	0.0	0	0.0	0	0.0
Neck corrugated gray ware	0	0.0	0	0.0	0	0.0	0	0.0	0	0.0
Stucco ware?	0	0.0	0	0.0	0	0.0	0	0.0	0	0.0
Sandy Paste Perforated	0	0.0	0	0.0	0	0.0	0	0.0	0	0.0
Sosa Perforated	0	0.0	0	0.0	0	0.0	0	0.0	0	0.0
Subtotal	*98*	*100.0*	*19*	*100.0*	*51*	*100.0*	*52*	*100.0*	*131*	*100.0*
Red ware types										
Salt Red: Davis Variety	1	14.3	0	0.0	0	0.0	0	0.0	1	25.0
Salt Smudged: Davis Variety	0	0.0	0	0.0	0	0.0	0	0.0	0	0.0
Dragoon Red	3	42.9	0	0.0	0	0.0	0	0.0	1	25.0
Dragoon Red Smudged	0	0.0	0	0.0	0	0.0	0	0.0	0	0.0

(continued)

TABLE E.7 *(continued)*

	Fill		Stratitest level 1		Stratitest level 2		Stratitest level 3		Floor	
	n	%	*n*	%	*n*	%	*n*	%	*n*	%
Gila Red	0	0.0	0	0.0	0	0.0	0	0.0	2	50.0
Gila Smudged	0	0.0	0	0.0	0	0.0	0	0.0	0	0.0
San Carlos Red	0	0.0	0	0.0	0	0.0	0	0.0	0	0.0
Wingfield Red	1	14.3	0	0.0	0	0.0	0	0.0	0	0.0
Unidentified red #1	2	28.6	0	0.0	0	0.0	2	100.0	0	0.0
Unidentified red #2	0	0.0	0	0.0	0	0.0	0	0.0	0	0.0
Subtotal	*7*	*100.0*	*0*	*0.0*	*0*	*0.0*	*2*	*100.0*	*4*	*100.0*
Corrugated types										
Late plain corrugated	0	0.0	0	0.0	0	0.0	0	0.0	0	0.0
Late indented corrugated	0	0.0	0	0.0	0	0.0	0	0.0	0	0.0
Early indented corrugated, smudged interior	0	0.0	0	0.0	0	0.0	0	0.0	0	0.0
Obliterated corrugated	0	0.0	0	0.0	0	0.0	0	0.0	0	0.0
Neck corrugated	0	0.0	0	0.0	0	0.0	0	0.0	0	0.0
Red-slipped neck corrugated	0	0.0	0	0.0	0	0.0	0	0.0	0	0.0
Subtotal	*0*	*0.0*	*0*	*0.0*	*0*	*0.0*	*0*	*0.0*	*0*	*0.0*
Miscellaneous										
Porcelain	0	0.0	0	0.0	0	0.0	0	0.0	0	0.0
White glaze ware	0	0.0	0	0.0	0	0.0	0	0.0	0	0.0
Glass	0	0.0	0	0.0	0	0.0	0	0.0	0	0.0
Unidentified	0	0.0	0	0.0	0	0.0	0	0.0	1	100.0
Subtotal	*0*	*0.0*	*0*	*0.0*	*0*	*0.0*	*0*	*0.0*	*1*	*100.0*
Total	**127**		**21**		**58**		**62**		**160**	

TABLE E.8 Gerald's typological analysis of sherds from House 9 at the Davis Ranch Site

	Fill		Floor	
	n	%	*n*	%
Painted types				
Gila Polychrome	3	60.0	0	0.0
Gila Black-on-red	0	0.0	1	9.1
Pinto Polychrome	0	0.0	0	0.0
Gila Polychrome (Pink Variant)	0	0.0	0	0.0
Gila-Tucson Polychrome	0	0.0	0	0.0
Tucson Polychrome	1	20.0	1	9.1
Tucson Black-on-red	0	0.0	0	0.0
Tonto Polychrome	0	0.0	0	0.0
Dragoon Red-on-brown	0	0.0	0	0.0
Cascabel Red-on-brown	0	0.0	1	9.1
Davis Red-on-white	0	0.0	1	9.1
Tres Alamos Red-on-brown	0	0.0	0	0.0
Gila White Slip	0	0.0	0	0.0
Cañada del Oro Red-on-brown	0	0.0	0	0.0
Gila Butte Red-on-buff	0	0.0	0	0.0
Santa Cruz Red-on-buff	1	20.0	4	36.4
Sacaton Red-on-buff	0	0.0	0	0.0
Casa Grande Red-on-buff	0	0.0	0	0.0
Rillito Red-on-brown	0	0.0	0	0.0
Rillito Red-on-brown (micaceous)	0	0.0	2	18.2
Rincon Red-on-brown	0	0.0	0	0.0
Pantano Red-on-brown	0	0.0	0	0.0
Tanque Verde Red-on-brown	0	0.0	0	0.0
Mimbres Black-on-white	0	0.0	0	0.0
Dos Cabezas Red-on-brown	0	0.0	0	0.0
Encinas Red-on-brown	0	0.0	1	9.1
Nogales Purple-on-red	0	0.0	0	0.0
Cerros Red-on-white	0	0.0	0	0.0
San Carlos Red-on-brown	0	0.0	0	0.0

(*continued*)

TABLE E.8 *(continued)*

	Fill		Floor	
	n	%	*n*	%
San Carlos Red-on-white	0	0.0	0	0.0
El Paso Polychrome	0	0.0	0	0.0
Unidentified polychrome	0	0.0	0	0.0
Kayenta-like polychrome	0	0.0	0	0.0
Tusayan-like polychrome	0	0.0	0	0.0
Subtotal	*5*	*100.0*	*11*	*100.0*
Plain types				
Davis Plain	12	63.2	13	11.9
Davis Plain: Sobaipuri Coil Rim Variety	0	0.0	0	0.0
Belford Perforated Rim	0	0.0	0	0.0
Belford Perforated Rim (Sobaipuri Coil Rim)	0	0.0	0	0.0
Babocomari Plain	6	31.6	93	85.3
Redington Plain	0	0.0	1	0.9
Redington Smudged	0	0.0	0	0.0
Sacaton Buff	0	0.0	1	0.9
Gila Plain	1	5.3	0	0.0
Gila Smudged	0	0.0	0	0.0
San Carlos Brown	0	0.0	0	0.0
Slipped brown	0	0.0	0	0.0
Sosa Plain	0	0.0	0	0.0
Whetstone Plain	0	0.0	0	0.0
Wingfield Plain	0	0.0	0	0.0
Fingernail indented	0	0.0	1	0.9
Incised plain	0	0.0	0	0.0
Tularosa Fillet Rim	0	0.0	0	0.0
Neck corrugated gray ware	0	0.0	0	0.0
Stucco ware?	0	0.0	0	0.0
Sandy Paste Perforated	0	0.0	0	0.0

(continued)

TABLE E.8 *(continued)*

	Fill		Floor	
	n	%	*n*	%
Sosa Perforated	0	0.0	0	0.0
Subtotal	*19*	*100.0*	*109*	*100.0*
Red ware types				
Salt Red: Davis Variety	2	33.3	2	50.0
Salt Smudged: Davis Variety	1	16.7	0	0.0
Dragoon Red	0	0.0	2	50.0
Dragoon Red Smudged	3	50.0	0	0.0
Gila Red	0	0.0	0	0.0
Gila Smudged	0	0.0	0	0.0
San Carlos Red	0	0.0	0	0.0
Wingfield Red	0	0.0	0	0.0
Unidentified red #1	0	0.0	0	0.0
Unidentified red #2	0	0.0	0	0.0
Subtotal	*6*	*100.0*	*4*	*100.0*
Corrugated types				
Late plain corrugated	1	100.0	12	80.0
Late indented corrugated	0	0.0	3	20.0
Early indented corrugated, smudged interior	0	0.0	0	0.0
Obliterated corrugated	0	0.0	0	0.0
Neck corrugated	0	0.0	0	0.0
Red-slipped neck corrugated	0	0.0	0	0.0
Subtotal	*1*	*100.0*	*15*	*100.0*
Miscellaneous				
Porcelain	0	0.0	0	0.0
White glaze ware	0	0.0	0	0.0
Glass	0	0.0	0	0.0
Unidentified	0	0.0	1	100.0
Subtotal	*0*	*0.0*	*1*	*100.0*
Total	**31**		**140**	

TABLE E.9 Gerald's typological analysis of sherds from Rooms 2 and 3 at the Davis Ranch Site

	Room 2						Room 3					
	Fill		Floor		Pit		Fill		Floor		Trench in front	
	n	%	*n*	%	*n*	%	*n*	%	*n*	%	*n*	%
Painted types												
Gila Polychrome	238	93.7	110	84.0	3	60.0	22	75.9	39	73.6	29	87.9
Gila Black-on-red	2	0.8	1	0.8	0	0.0	0	0.0	1	1.9	0	0.0
Pinto Polychrome	2	0.8	1	0.8	0	0.0	0	0.0	3	5.7	0	0.0
Gila Polychrome (Pink Variant)	0	0.0	0	0.0	0	0.0	0	0.0	1	1.9	1	3.0
Gila-Tucson Polychrome	0	0.0	0	0.0	0	0.0	0	0.0	0	0.0	0	0.0
Tucson Polychrome	0	0.0	1	0.8	0	0.0	0	0.0	0	0.0	0	0.0
Tucson Black-on-red	2	0.8	0	0.0	0	0.0	1	3.4	1	1.9	0	0.0
Tonto Polychrome	2	0.8	9	6.9	0	0.0	2	6.9	2	3.8	1	3.0
Dragoon Red-on-brown	1	0.4	0	0.0	0	0.0	0	0.0	0	0.0	0	0.0
Cascabel Red-on-brown	0	0.0	0	0.0	1	20.0	0	0.0	1	1.9	0	0.0
Davis Red-on-white	1	0.4	1	0.8	1	20.0	1	3.4	0	0.0	0	0.0
Tres Alamos Red-on-brown	0	0.0	0	0.0	0	0.0	0	0.0	0	0.0	0	0.0
Gila White Slip	1	0.4	1	0.8	0	0.0	0	0.0	0	0.0	1	3.0
Cañada del Oro Red-on-brown	0	0.0	0	0.0	0	0.0	0	0.0	0	0.0	0	0.0
Gila Butte Red-on-buff	0	0.0	0	0.0	0	0.0	0	0.0	0	0.0	0	0.0
Santa Cruz Red-on-buff	1	0.4	6	4.6	0	0.0	1	3.4	1	1.9	0	0.0
Sacaton Red-on-buff	1	0.4	0	0.0	0	0.0	1	3.4	0	0.0	1	3.0
Casa Grande Red-on-buff	0	0.0	0	0.0	0	0.0	0	0.0	0	0.0	0	0.0
Rillito Red-on-brown	0	0.0	0	0.0	0	0.0	0	0.0	0	0.0	0	0.0
Rillito Red-on-brown (micaceous)	2	0.8	0	0.0	0	0.0	0	0.0	0	0.0	0	0.0

Rincon Red-on-brown	0	0.0	1	0.8	0	0.0	0	0.0	0	0.0	0	0.0
Pantano Red-on-brown	0	0.0	0	0.0	0	0.0	0	0.0	0	0.0	0	0.0
Tanque Verde Red-on-brown	1	0.4	0	0.0	0	0.0	0	0.0	0	0.0	0	0.0
Mimbres Black-on-white	0	0.0	0	0.0	0	0.0	0	0.0	0	0.0	0	0.0
Dos Cabezas Red-on-brown	0	0.0	0	0.0	0	0.0	0	0.0	0	0.0	0	0.0
Encinas Red-on-brown	0	0.0	0	0.0	0	0.0	0	0.0	0	0.0	0	0.0
Nogales Purple-on-red	0	0.0	0	0.0	0	0.0	0	0.0	0	0.0	0	0.0
Cerros Red-on-white	0	0.0	0	0.0	0	0.0	0	0.0	0	0.0	0	0.0
San Carlos Red-on-brown	0	0.0	0	0.0	0	0.0	0	0.0	1	1.9	0	0.0
San Carlos Red-on-white	0	0.0	0	0.0	0	0.0	1	3.4	3	5.7	0	0.0
El Paso Polychrome	0	0.0	0	0.0	0	0.0	0	0.0	0	0.0	0	0.0
Unidentified polychrome	0	0.0	0	0.0	0	0.0	0	0.0	0	0.0	0	0.0
Kayenta-like polychrome	0	0.0	0	0.0	0	0.0	0	0.0	0	0.0	0	0.0
Tusayan-like polychrome	0	0.0	0	0.0	0	0.0	0	0.0	0	0.0	0	0.0
Subtotal	*254*	*100.0*	*131*	*100.0*	*5*	*100.0*	*29*	*100.0*	*53*	*100.0*	*33*	*100.0*
Plain types												
Davis Plain	303	77.7	277	86.8	14	77.8	42	76.4	91	85.8	118	97.5
Davis Plain: Sobaipuri Coil Rim Variety	1	0.3	0	0.0	0	0.0	1	1.8	2	1.9	0	0.0
Belford Perforated Rim	5	1.3	0	0.0	0	0.0	1	1.8	1	0.9	1	0.8
Belford Perforated Rim (Sobaipuri Coil Rim)	0	0.0	0	0.0	0	0.0	1	1.8	0	0.0	0	0.0
Babocomari Plain	66	16.9	31	9.7	3	16.7	6	10.9	9	8.5	0	0.0
Redington Plain	5	1.3	4	1.3	0	0.0	0	0.0	0	0.0	2	1.7
Redington Smudged	3	0.8	2	0.6	0	0.0	0	0.0	0	0.0	0	0.0
Sacaton Buff	2	0.5	2	0.6	1	5.6	0	0.0	0	0.0	0	0.0
Gila Plain	3	0.8	3	0.9	0	0.0	3	5.5	3	2.8	0	0.0

(*continued*)

TABLE E.9 *(continued)*

	Room 2						Room 3					
	Fill		Floor		Pit		Fill		Floor		Trench in front	
	n	%	*n*	%	*n*	%	*n*	%	*n*	%	*n*	%
Gila Smudged	0	0.0	0	0.0	0	0.0	0	0.0	0	0.0	0	0.0
San Carlos Brown	1	0.3	0	0.0	0	0.0	0	0.0	0	0.0	0	0.0
Slipped brown	0	0.0	0	0.0	0	0.0	0	0.0	0	0.0	0	0.0
Sosa Plain	0	0.0	0	0.0	0	0.0	0	0.0	0	0.0	0	0.0
Whetstone Plain	0	0.0	0	0.0	0	0.0	0	0.0	0	0.0	0	0.0
Wingfield Plain	1	0.3	0	0.0	0	0.0	1	1.8	0	0.0	0	0.0
Fingernail indented	0	0.0	0	0.0	0	0.0	0	0.0	0	0.0	0	0.0
Incised plain	0	0.0	0	0.0	0	0.0	0	0.0	0	0.0	0	0.0
Tularosa Fillet Rim	0	0.0	0	0.0	0	0.0	0	0.0	0	0.0	0	0.0
Neck corrugated gray ware	0	0.0	0	0.0	0	0.0	0	0.0	0	0.0	0	0.0
Stucco ware?	0	0.0	0	0.0	0	0.0	0	0.0	0	0.0	0	0.0
Sandy Paste Perforated	0	0.0	0	0.0	0	0.0	0	0.0	0	0.0	0	0.0
Sosa Perforated	0	0.0	0	0.0	0	0.0	0	0.0	0	0.0	0	0.0
Subtotal	*390*	*100.0*	*319*	*100.0*	*18*	*100.0*	*55*	*100.0*	*106*	*100.0*	*121*	*100.0*
Red ware types												
Salt Red: Davis Variety	14	66.7	7	50.0	2	50.0	4	36.4	4	44.4	4	40.0
Salt Smudged: Davis Variety	1	4.8	0	0.0	1	25.0	1	9.1	3	33.3	0	0.0
Dragoon Red	1	4.8	4	28.6	1	25.0	2	18.2	1	11.1	2	20.0

Dragoon Red Smudged	1	4.8	0	0.0	0	0.0	1	9.1	1	11.1	3	30.0
Gila Red	2	9.5	2	14.3	0	0.0	0	0.0	0	0.0	0	0.0
Gila Smudged	1	4.8	0	0.0	0	0.0	0	0.0	0	0.0	0	0.0
San Carlos Red	0	0.0	0	0.0	0	0.0	2	18.2	0	0.0	0	0.0
Wingfield Red	1	4.8	0	0.0	0	0.0	0	0.0	0	0.0	0	0.0
Unidentified red #1	0	0.0	1	7.1	0	0.0	0	0.0	0	0.0	1	10.0
Unidentified red #2	0	0.0	0	0.0	0	0.0	1	9.1	0	0.0	0	0.0
Subtotal	*21*	*100.0*	*14*	*100.0*	*4*	*100.0*	*11*	*100.0*	*9*	*100.0*	*10*	*100.0*
Corrugated types												
Late plain corrugated	0	0.0	0	0.0	0	0.0	0	0.0	0	0.0	0	0.0
Late indented corrugated	1	33.3	0	0.0	0	0.0	0	0.0	0	0.0	0	0.0
Early indented corrugated, smudged interior	0	0.0	0	0.0	0	0.0	1	100.0	0	0.0	0	0.0
Obliterated corrugated	0	0.0	0	0.0	0	0.0	0	0.0	1	100.0	0	0.0
Neck corrugated	1	33.3	0	0.0	0	0.0	0	0.0	0	0.0	0	0.0
Red-slipped neck corrugated	1	33.3	0	0.0	0	0.0	0	0.0	0	0.0	0	0.0
Subtotal	*3*	*100.0*	*0*	*0.0*	*0*	*0.0*	*1*	*100.0*	*1*	*100.0*	*0*	*0.0*
Miscellaneous												
Porcelain	0	0.0	0	0.0	0	0.0	0	0.0	0	0.0	0	0.0
White glaze ware	0	0.0	0	0.0	0	0.0	0	0.0	0	0.0	0	0.0
Glass	0	0.0	0	0.0	0	0.0	0	0.0	0	0.0	0	0.0
Unidentified	0	0.0	0	0.0	0	0.0	0	0.0	0	0.0	0	0.0
Subtotal	*0*	*0.0*	*0*	*0.0*	*0*	*0.0*	*0*	*0.0*	*0*	*0.0*	*0*	*0.0*
Total	**668**		**464**		**27**		**96**		**169**		**164**	

TABLE E.10 Gerald's typological analysis of sherds from Room 4 at the Davis Ranch Site

	Fill		Stratitest level 1		Stratitest level 2		Stratitest level 3		Stratitest level 4		Floor		Subfloor		Trench in front	
	n	%	*n*	%	*n*	%	*n*	%	*n*	%	*n*	%	*n*	%	*n*	%
Painted types																
Gila Polychrome	33	82.5	22	71.0	10	76.9	12	80.0	69	84.1	59	96.7	13	56.5	3	100.0
Gila Black-on-red	0	0.0	1	3.2	0	0.0	1	6.7	1	1.2	0	0.0	0	0.0	0	0.0
Pinto Polychrome	1	2.5	1	3.2	0	0.0	0	0.0	0	0.0	0	0.0	0	0.0	0	0.0
Gila Polychrome (Pink Variant)	0	0.0	0	0.0	0	0.0	0	0.0	0	0.0	0	0.0	0	0.0	0	0.0
Gila-Tucson Polychrome	0	0.0	0	0.0	0	0.0	0	0.0	0	0.0	0	0.0	0	0.0	0	0.0
Tucson Polychrome	0	0.0	0	0.0	2	15.4	0	0.0	1	1.2	0	0.0	5	21.7	0	0.0
Tucson Black-on-red	0	0.0	0	0.0	0	0.0	0	0.0	0	0.0	0	0.0	0	0.0	0	0.0
Tonto Polychrome	4	10.0	0	0.0	0	0.0	0	0.0	8	9.8	0	0.0	0	0.0	0	0.0
Dragoon Red-on-brown	0	0.0	0	0.0	0	0.0	0	0.0	0	0.0	0	0.0	1	4.3	0	0.0
Cascabel Red-on-brown	0	0.0	1	3.2	1	7.7	0	0.0	0	0.0	0	0.0	1	4.3	0	0.0
Davis Red-on-white	0	0.0	0	0.0	0	0.0	0	0.0	0	0.0	0	0.0	0	0.0	0	0.0
Tres Alamos Red-on-brown	0	0.0	0	0.0	0	0.0	0	0.0	0	0.0	0	0.0	0	0.0	0	0.0
Gila White Slip	2	5.0	4	12.9	0	0.0	0	0.0	3	3.7	2	3.3	0	0.0	0	0.0
Cañada del Oro Red-on-brown	0	0.0	0	0.0	0	0.0	0	0.0	0	0.0	0	0.0	0	0.0	0	0.0
Gila Butte Red-on-buff	0	0.0	0	0.0	0	0.0	0	0.0	0	0.0	0	0.0	0	0.0	0	0.0
Santa Cruz Red-on-buff	0	0.0	0	0.0	0	0.0	2	13.3	0	0.0	0	0.0	2	8.7	0	0.0
Sacaton Red-on-buff	0	0.0	0	0.0	0	0.0	0	0.0	0	0.0	0	0.0	0	0.0	0	0.0
Casa Grande Red-on-buff	0	0.0	0	0.0	0	0.0	0	0.0	0	0.0	0	0.0	0	0.0	0	0.0
Rillito Red-on-brown	0	0.0	1	3.2	0	0.0	0	0.0	0	0.0	0	0.0	0	0.0	0	0.0

Rillito Red-on-brown (micaceous)	0	0.0	0	0.0	0	0.0	0	0.0	0	0.0	0	0.0	1	4.3	0	0.0
Rincon Red-on-brown	0	0.0	0	0.0	0	0.0	0	0.0	0	0.0	0	0.0	0	0.0	0	0.0
Pantano Red-on-brown	0	0.0	0	0.0	0	0.0	0	0.0	0	0.0	0	0.0	0	0.0	0	0.0
Tanque Verde Red-on-brown	0	0.0	1	3.2	0	0.0	0	0.0	0	0.0	0	0.0	0	0.0	0	0.0
Mimbres Black-on-white	0	0.0	0	0.0	0	0.0	0	0.0	0	0.0	0	0.0	0	0.0	0	0.0
Dos Cabezas Red-on-brown	0	0.0	0	0.0	0	0.0	0	0.0	0	0.0	0	0.0	0	0.0	0	0.0
Encinas Red-on-brown	0	0.0	0	0.0	0	0.0	0	0.0	0	0.0	0	0.0	0	0.0	0	0.0
Nogales Purple-on-red	0	0.0	0	0.0	0	0.0	0	0.0	0	0.0	0	0.0	0	0.0	0	0.0
Cerros Red-on-white	0	0.0	0	0.0	0	0.0	0	0.0	0	0.0	0	0.0	0	0.0	0	0.0
San Carlos Red-on-brown	0	0.0	0	0.0	0	0.0	0	0.0	0	0.0	0	0.0	0	0.0	0	0.0
San Carlos Red-on-white	0	0.0	0	0.0	0	0.0	0	0.0	0	0.0	0	0.0	0	0.0	0	0.0
El Paso Polychrome	0	0.0	0	0.0	0	0.0	0	0.0	0	0.0	0	0.0	0	0.0	0	0.0
Unidentified polychrome	0	0.0	0	0.0	0	0.0	0	0.0	0	0.0	0	0.0	0	0.0	0	0.0
Kayenta-like polychrome	0	0.0	0	0.0	0	0.0	0	0.0	0	0.0	0	0.0	0	0.0	0	0.0
Tusayan-like polychrome	0	0.0	0	0.0	0	0.0	0	0.0	0	0.0	0	0.0	0	0.0	0	0.0
Subtotal	*40*	*100.0*	*31*	*100.0*	*13*	*100.0*	*15*	*100.0*	*82*	*100.0*	*61*	*100.0*	*23*	*100.0*	*3*	*100.0*
Plain types																
Davis Plain	150	94.9	160	93.6	82	95.3	142	91.6	320	93.3	10	100.0	49	66.2	21	95.5
Davis Plain: Sobaipuri Coil Rim Variety	0	0.0	0	0.0	0	0.0	0	0.0	0	0.0	0	0.0	0	0.0	0	0.0
Belford Perforated Rim	0	0.0	0	0.0	0	0.0	0	0.0	1	0.3	0	0.0	4	5.4	1	4.5
Belford Perforated Rim (Sobaipuri Coil Rim)	0	0.0	0	0.0	1	1.2	0	0.0	0	0.0	0	0.0	0	0.0	0	0.0
Babocomari Plain	3	1.9	3	1.8	3	3.5	4	2.6	4	1.2	0	0.0	7	9.5	0	0.0
Redington Plain	0	0.0	2	1.2	0	0.0	1	0.6	6	1.7	0	0.0	2	2.7	0	0.0

(*continued*)

TABLE E.10 *(continued)*

	Fill		Stratitest level 1		Stratitest level 2		Stratitest level 3		Stratitest level 4		Floor		Subfloor		Trench in front	
	n	%	*n*	%	*n*	%	*n*	%	*n*	%	*n*	%	*n*	%	*n*	%
Redington Smudged	3	1.9	1	0.6	0	0.0	2	1.3	1	0.3	0	0.0	2	2.7	0	0.0
Sacaton Buff	0	0.0	0	0.0	0	0.0	0	0.0	0	0.0	0	0.0	0	0.0	0	0.0
Gila Plain	2	1.3	4	2.3	0	0.0	5	3.2	11	3.2	0	0.0	10	13.5	0	0.0
Gila Smudged	0	0.0	1	0.6	0	0.0	1	0.6	0	0.0	0	0.0	0	0.0	0	0.0
San Carlos Brown	0	0.0	0	0.0	0	0.0	0	0.0	0	0.0	0	0.0	0	0.0	0	0.0
Slipped brown	0	0.0	0	0.0	0	0.0	0	0.0	0	0.0	0	0.0	0	0.0	0	0.0
Sosa Plain	0	0.0	0	0.0	0	0.0	0	0.0	0	0.0	0	0.0	0	0.0	0	0.0
Whetstone Plain	0	0.0	0	0.0	0	0.0	0	0.0	0	0.0	0	0.0	0	0.0	0	0.0
Wingfield Plain	0	0.0	0	0.0	0	0.0	0	0.0	0	0.0	0	0.0	0	0.0	0	0.0
Fingernail indented	0	0.0	0	0.0	0	0.0	0	0.0	0	0.0	0	0.0	0	0.0	0	0.0
Incised plain	0	0.0	0	0.0	0	0.0	0	0.0	0	0.0	0	0.0	0	0.0	0	0.0
Tularosa Fillet Rim	0	0.0	0	0.0	0	0.0	0	0.0	0	0.0	0	0.0	0	0.0	0	0.0
Neck corrugated gray ware	0	0.0	0	0.0	0	0.0	0	0.0	0	0.0	0	0.0	0	0.0	0	0.0
Stucco ware?	0	0.0	0	0.0	0	0.0	0	0.0	0	0.0	0	0.0	0	0.0	0	0.0
Sandy Paste Perforated	0	0.0	0	0.0	0	0.0	0	0.0	0	0.0	0	0.0	0	0.0	0	0.0
Sosa Perforated	0	0.0	0	0.0	0	0.0	0	0.0	0	0.0	0	0.0	0	0.0	0	0.0
Subtotal	*158*	*100.0*	*171*	*100.0*	*86*	*100.0*	*155*	*100.0*	*343*	*100.0*	*10*	*100.0*	*74*	*100.0*	*22*	*100.0*
Red ware types																
Salt Red: Davis Variety	5	50.0	4	50.0	4	66.7	4	50.0	9	69.2	0	0.0	2	50.0	1	100.0
Salt Smudged: Davis Variety	4	40.0	2	25.0	2	33.3	1	12.5	1	7.7	0	0.0	0	0.0	0	0.0
Dragoon Red	0	0.0	0	0.0	0	0.0	0	0.0	0	0.0	0	0.0	0	0.0	0	0.0
Dragoon Red Smudged	0	0.0	0	0.0	0	0.0	1	12.5	1	7.7	0	0.0	1	25.0	0	0.0

Gila Red	0	0.0	1	12.5	0	0.0	2	25.0	1	7.7	0	0.0	1	25.0	0	0.0
Gila Smudged	0	0.0	0	0.0	0	0.0	0	0.0	0	0.0	0	0.0	0	0.0	0	0.0
San Carlos Red	0	0.0	1	12.5	0	0.0	0	0.0	1	7.7	0	0.0	0	0.0	0	0.0
Wingfield Red	0	0.0	0	0.0	0	0.0	0	0.0	0	0.0	0	0.0	0	0.0	0	0.0
Unidentified red #1	0	0.0	0	0.0	0	0.0	0	0.0	0	0.0	0	0.0	0	0.0	0	0.0
Unidentified red #2	1	10.0	0	0.0	0	0.0	0	0.0	0	0.0	0	0.0	0	0.0	0	0.0
Subtotal	*10*	*100.0*	*8*	*100.0*	*6*	*100.0*	*8*	*100.0*	*13*	*100.0*	*0*	*0.0*	*4*	*100.0*	*1*	*100.0*
Corrugated types																
Late plain corrugated	0	0.0	0	0.0	0	0.0	0	0.0	1	20.0	0	0.0	2	50.0	0	0.0
Late indented corrugated	2	100.0	0	0.0	1	50.0	1	50.0	3	60.0	0	0.0	2	50.0	0	0.0
Early indented corrugated, smudged interior	0	0.0	0	0.0	1	50.0	0	0.0	1	20.0	0	0.0	0	0.0	0	0.0
Obliterated corrugated	0	0.0	0	0.0	0	0.0	0	0.0	0	0.0	0	0.0	0	0.0	0	0.0
Neck corrugated	0	0.0	1	100.0	0	0.0	1	50.0	0	0.0	0	0.0	0	0.0	0	0.0
Red-slipped neck corrugated	0	0.0	0	0.0	0	0.0	0	0.0	0	0.0	0	0.0	0	0.0	0	0.0
Subtotal	*2*	*100.0*	*1*	*100.0*	*2*	*100.0*	*2*	*100.0*	*5*	*100.0*	*0*	*0.0*	*4*	*100.0*	*0*	*0.0*
Miscellaneous																
Porcelain	0	0.0	0	0.0	0	0.0	0	0.0	0	0.0	0	0.0	0	0.0	0	0.0
White glaze ware	0	0.0	0	0.0	0	0.0	0	0.0	0	0.0	0	0.0	0	0.0	0	0.0
Glass	0	0.0	0	0.0	0	0.0	0	0.0	0	0.0	0	0.0	0	0.0	0	0.0
Unidentified	1	100.0	1	100.0	0	0.0	0	0.0	0	0.0	0	0.0	0	0.0	0	0.0
Subtotal	*1*	*100.0*	*1*	*100.0*	*0*	*0.0*	*0*	*0.0*	*0*	*0.0*	*0*	*0.0*	*0*	*0.0*	*0*	*0.0*
Total	**211**		**212**		**107**		**180**		**443**		**71**		**105**		**26**	

TABLE E.11 Gerald's typological analysis of sherds from Rooms 5 and 6 at the Davis Ranch Site

	Room 5 Fill		Room 6									
			Fill		Stratitest level 1		Stratitest level 2		Stratitest level 3		Trench in front	
	n	%	*n*	%	*n*	%	*n*	%	*n*	%	*n*	%
Painted types												
Gila Polychrome	85	90.4	103	84.4	8	100.0	6	85.7	9	100.0	14	100.0
Gila Black-on-red	0	0.0	2	1.6	0	0.0	0	0.0	0	0.0	0	0.0
Pinto Polychrome	0	0.0	1	0.8	0	0.0	0	0.0	0	0.0	0	0.0
Gila Polychrome (Pink Variant)	0	0.0	0	0.0	0	0.0	0	0.0	0	0.0	0	0.0
Gila-Tucson Polychrome	0	0.0	0	0.0	0	0.0	0	0.0	0	0.0	0	0.0
Tucson Polychrome	0	0.0	0	0.0	0	0.0	0	0.0	0	0.0	0	0.0
Tucson Black-on-red	0	0.0	7	5.7	0	0.0	0	0.0	0	0.0	0	0.0
Tonto Polychrome	3	3.2	1	0.8	0	0.0	0	0.0	0	0.0	0	0.0
Dragoon Red-on-brown	0	0.0	1	0.8	0	0.0	0	0.0	0	0.0	0	0.0
Cascabel Red-on-brown	0	0.0	0	0.0	0	0.0	0	0.0	0	0.0	0	0.0
Davis Red-on-white	0	0.0	0	0.0	0	0.0	0	0.0	0	0.0	0	0.0
Tres Alamos Red-on-brown	0	0.0	0	0.0	0	0.0	0	0.0	0	0.0	0	0.0
Gila White Slip	6	6.4	4	3.3	0	0.0	0	0.0	0	0.0	0	0.0
Cañada del Oro Red-on-brown	0	0.0	0	0.0	0	0.0	0	0.0	0	0.0	0	0.0
Gila Butte Red-on-buff	0	0.0	0	0.0	0	0.0	0	0.0	0	0.0	0	0.0
Santa Cruz Red-on-buff	0	0.0	1	0.8	0	0.0	0	0.0	0	0.0	0	0.0
Sacaton Red-on-buff	0	0.0	0	0.0	0	0.0	1	14.3	0	0.0	0	0.0
Casa Grande Red-on-buff	0	0.0	0	0.0	0	0.0	0	0.0	0	0.0	0	0.0

Rillito Red-on-brown	0	0.0	0	0.0	0	0.0	0	0.0	0	0.0	0	0.0
Rillito Red-on-brown (micaceous)	0	0.0	0	0.0	0	0.0	0	0.0	0	0.0	0	0.0
Rincon Red-on-brown	0	0.0	0	0.0	0	0.0	0	0.0	0	0.0	0	0.0
Pantano Red-on-brown	0	0.0	0	0.0	0	0.0	0	0.0	0	0.0	0	0.0
Tanque Verde Red-on-brown	0	0.0	0	0.0	0	0.0	0	0.0	0	0.0	0	0.0
Mimbres Black-on-white	0	0.0	0	0.0	0	0.0	0	0.0	0	0.0	0	0.0
Dos Cabezas Red-on-brown	0	0.0	0	0.0	0	0.0	0	0.0	0	0.0	0	0.0
Encinas Red-on-brown	0	0.0	0	0.0	0	0.0	0	0.0	0	0.0	0	0.0
Nogales Purple-on-red	0	0.0	0	0.0	0	0.0	0	0.0	0	0.0	0	0.0
Cerros Red-on-white	0	0.0	0	0.0	0	0.0	0	0.0	0	0.0	0	0.0
San Carlos Red-on-brown	0	0.0	0	0.0	0	0.0	0	0.0	0	0.0	0	0.0
San Carlos Red-on-white	0	0.0	2	1.6	0	0.0	0	0.0	0	0.0	0	0.0
El Paso Polychrome	0	0.0	0	0.0	0	0.0	0	0.0	0	0.0	0	0.0
Unidentified polychrome	0	0.0	0	0.0	0	0.0	0	0.0	0	0.0	0	0.0
Kayenta-like polychrome	0	0.0	0	0.0	0	0.0	0	0.0	0	0.0	0	0.0
Tusayan-like polychrome	0	0.0	0	0.0	0	0.0	0	0.0	0	0.0	0	0.0
Subtotal	*94*	*100.0*	*122*	*100.0*	*8*	*100.0*	*7*	*100.0*	*9*	*100.0*	*14*	*100.0*
Plain types												
Davis Plain	284	89.9	391	94.0	18	72.0	27	93.1	85	94.4	60	87.0
Davis Plain: Sobaipuri Coil Rim Variety	1	0.3	1	0.2	0	0.0	0	0.0	0	0.0	0	0.0
Belford Perforated Rim	0	0.0	0	0.0	0	0.0	0	0.0	0	0.0	2	2.9
Belford Perforated Rim (Sobaipuri Coil Rim)	1	0.3	3	0.7	0	0.0	0	0.0	0	0.0	0	0.0
Babocomari Plain	24	7.6	8	1.9	4	16.0	2	6.9	1	1.1	5	7.2

(continued)

TABLE E.12 Gerald's typological analysis of sherds from Room 7 at the Davis Ranch Site

	Fill		Stratitest level 1		Stratitest level 2		Floor		Trench in front	
	n	%	*n*	%	*n*	%	*n*	%	*n*	%
Painted types										
Gila Polychrome	23	88.5	14	82.4	21	75.0	138	88.5	22	95.7
Gila Black-on-red	0	0.0	0	0.0	1	3.6	1	0.6	0	0.0
Pinto Polychrome	0	0.0	0	0.0	0	0.0	0	0.0	0	0.0
Gila Polychrome (Pink Variant)	0	0.0	0	0.0	0	0.0	0	0.0	0	0.0
Gila-Tucson Polychrome	0	0.0	0	0.0	0	0.0	0	0.0	0	0.0
Tucson Polychrome	0	0.0	0	0.0	0	0.0	1	0.6	0	0.0
Tucson Black-on-red	0	0.0	0	0.0	1	3.6	1	0.6	0	0.0
Tonto Polychrome	0	0.0	2	11.8	3	10.7	6	3.8	0	0.0
Dragoon Red-on-brown	0	0.0	0	0.0	0	0.0	0	0.0	0	0.0
Cascabel Red-on-brown	0	0.0	0	0.0	1	3.6	0	0.0	0	0.0
Davis Red-on-white	0	0.0	0	0.0	0	0.0	1	0.6	0	0.0
Tres Alamos Red-on-brown	0	0.0	0	0.0	0	0.0	1	0.6	0	0.0
Gila White Slip	1	3.8	0	0.0	0	0.0	2	1.3	0	0.0
Cañada del Oro Red-on-brown	0	0.0	0	0.0	0	0.0	0	0.0	0	0.0
Gila Butte Red-on-buff	0	0.0	0	0.0	0	0.0	0	0.0	0	0.0
Santa Cruz Red-on-buff	0	0.0	0	0.0	0	0.0	2	1.3	0	0.0
Sacaton Red-on-buff	0	0.0	0	0.0	0	0.0	0	0.0	0	0.0
Casa Grande Red-on-buff	0	0.0	0	0.0	0	0.0	0	0.0	0	0.0
Rillito Red-on-brown	0	0.0	0	0.0	0	0.0	0	0.0	0	0.0

Rillito Red-on-brown (micaceous)	0	0.0	0	0.0	1	3.6	1	0.6	0	0.0
Rincon Red-on-brown	0	0.0	0	0.0	0	0.0	0	0.0	0	0.0
Pantano Red-on-brown	0	0.0	0	0.0	0	0.0	0	0.0	0	0.0
Tanque Verde Red-on-brown	0	0.0	0	0.0	0	0.0	0	0.0	1	4.3
Mimbres Black-on-white	1	3.8	0	0.0	0	0.0	0	0.0	0	0.0
Dos Cabezas Red-on-brown	0	0.0	0	0.0	0	0.0	0	0.0	0	0.0
Encinas Red-on-brown	0	0.0	1	5.9	0	0.0	2	1.3	0	0.0
Nogales Purple-on-red	0	0.0	0	0.0	0	0.0	0	0.0	0	0.0
Cerros Red-on-white	0	0.0	0	0.0	0	0.0	0	0.0	0	0.0
San Carlos Red-on-brown	1	3.8	0	0.0	0	0.0	0	0.0	0	0.0
San Carlos Red-on-white	0	0.0	0	0.0	0	0.0	0	0.0	0	0.0
El Paso Polychrome	0	0.0	0	0.0	0	0.0	0	0.0	0	0.0
Unidentified polychrome	0	0.0	0	0.0	0	0.0	0	0.0	0	0.0
Kayenta-like polychrome	0	0.0	0	0.0	0	0.0	0	0.0	0	0.0
Tusayan-like polychrome	0	0.0	0	0.0	0	0.0	0	0.0	0	0.0
Subtotal	*26*	*100.0*	*17*	*100.0*	*28*	*100.0*	*156*	*100.0*	*23*	*100.0*
Plain types										
Davis Plain	93	86.1	63	88.7	143	86.7	227	83.8	36	97.3
Davis Plain: Sobaipuri Coil Rim Variety	0	0.0	1	1.4	0	0.0	1	0.4	0	0.0
Belford Perforated Rim	1	0.9	0	0.0	0	0.0	2	0.7	0	0.0
Belford Perforated Rim (Sobaipuri Coil Rim)	0	0.0	0	0.0	0	0.0	0	0.0	0	0.0
Babocomari Plain	9	8.3	7	9.9	16	9.7	30	11.1	0	0.0
Redington Plain	2	1.9	0	0.0	1	0.6	4	1.5	0	0.0

(continued)

TABLE E.12 *(continued)*

	Fill		Stratitest level 1		Stratitest level 2		Floor		Trench in front	
	n	%	*n*	%	*n*	%	*n*	%	*n*	%
Redington Smudged	3	2.8	0	0.0	0	0.0	0	0.0	0	0.0
Sacaton Buff	0	0.0	0	0.0	0	0.0	0	0.0	0	0.0
Gila Plain	0	0.0	0	0.0	4	2.4	4	1.5	0	0.0
Gila Smudged	0	0.0	0	0.0	1	0.6	2	0.7	0	0.0
San Carlos Brown	0	0.0	0	0.0	0	0.0	1	0.4	1	2.7
Slipped brown	0	0.0	0	0.0	0	0.0	0	0.0	0	0.0
Sosa Plain	0	0.0	0	0.0	0	0.0	0	0.0	0	0.0
Whetstone Plain	0	0.0	0	0.0	0	0.0	0	0.0	0	0.0
Wingfield Plain	0	0.0	0	0.0	0	0.0	0	0.0	0	0.0
Fingernail indented	0	0.0	0	0.0	0	0.0	0	0.0	0	0.0
Incised plain	0	0.0	0	0.0	0	0.0	0	0.0	0	0.0
Tularosa Fillet Rim	0	0.0	0	0.0	0	0.0	0	0.0	0	0.0
Neck corrugated gray ware	0	0.0	0	0.0	0	0.0	0	0.0	0	0.0
Stucco ware?	0	0.0	0	0.0	0	0.0	0	0.0	0	0.0
Sandy Paste Perforated	0	0.0	0	0.0	0	0.0	0	0.0	0	0.0
Sosa Perforated	0	0.0	0	0.0	0	0.0	0	0.0	0	0.0
Subtotal	*108*	*100.0*	*71*	*100.0*	*165*	*100.0*	*271*	*100.0*	*37*	*100.0*
Red ware types										
Salt Red: Davis Variety	0	0.0	4	80.0	2	40.0	10	52.6	0	0.0
Salt Smudged: Davis Variety	2	66.7	0	0.0	1	20.0	1	5.3	1	100.0

Dragoon Red	1	33.3	0	0.0	2	40.0	3	15.8	0	0.0
Dragoon Red Smudged	0	0.0	0	0.0	0	0.0	1	5.3	0	0.0
Gila Red	0	0.0	0	0.0	0	0.0	0	0.0	0	0.0
Gila Smudged	0	0.0	0	0.0	0	0.0	3	15.8	0	0.0
San Carlos Red	0	0.0	0	0.0	0	0.0	0	0.0	0	0.0
Wingfield Red	0	0.0	0	0.0	0	0.0	0	0.0	0	0.0
Unidentified red #1	0	0.0	1	20.0	0	0.0	1	5.3	0	0.0
Unidentified red #2	0	0.0	0	0.0	0	0.0	0	0.0	0	0.0
Subtotal	*3*	*100.0*	*5*	*100.0*	*5*	*100.0*	*19*	*100.0*	*1*	*100.0*
Corrugated types										
Late plain corrugated	0	0.0	0	0.0	0	0.0	0	0.0	0	0.0
Late indented corrugated	0	0.0	0	0.0	0	0.0	1	100.0	0	0.0
Early indented corrugated, smudged interior	0	0.0	0	0.0	0	0.0	0	0.0	0	0.0
Obliterated corrugated	0	0.0	0	0.0	0	0.0	0	0.0	0	0.0
Neck corrugated	0	0.0	0	0.0	0	0.0	0	0.0	0	0.0
Red-slipped neck corrugated	0	0.0	0	0.0	0	0.0	0	0.0	0	0.0
Subtotal	*0*	*0.0*	*0*	*0.0*	*0*	*0.0*	*1*	*100.0*	*0*	*0.0*
Miscellaneous										
Porcelain	0	0.0	0	0.0	0	0.0	0	0.0	0	0.0
White glaze ware	0	0.0	0	0.0	0	0.0	0	0.0	0	0.0
Glass	0	0.0	0	0.0	0	0.0	0	0.0	0	0.0
Unidentified	0	0.0	0	0.0	0	0.0	1	100.0	0	0.0
Subtotal	*0*	*0.0*	*0*	*0.0*	*0*	*0.0*	*1*	*100.0*	*0*	*0.0*
Total	**137**		**93**		**198**		**448**		**61**	

TABLE E.13 Gerald's typological analysis of sherds from Room 8 at the Davis Ranch Site

	Fill		Subfloor		Trench in front	
	n	%	*n*	%	*n*	%
Painted types						
Gila Polychrome	4	66.7	11	100.0	15	88.2
Gila Black-on-red	0	0.0	0	0.0	0	0.0
Pinto Polychrome	0	0.0	0	0.0	0	0.0
Gila Polychrome (Pink Variant)	0	0.0	0	0.0	0	0.0
Gila-Tucson Polychrome	0	0.0	0	0.0	0	0.0
Tucson Polychrome	0	0.0	0	0.0	0	0.0
Tucson Black-on-red	0	0.0	0	0.0	0	0.0
Tonto Polychrome	2	33.3	0	0.0	0	0.0
Dragoon Red-on-brown	0	0.0	0	0.0	0	0.0
Cascabel Red-on-brown	0	0.0	0	0.0	0	0.0
Davis Red-on-white	0	0.0	0	0.0	0	0.0
Tres Alamos Red-on-brown	0	0.0	0	0.0	0	0.0
Gila White Slip	0	0.0	0	0.0	2	11.8
Cañada del Oro Red-on-brown	0	0.0	0	0.0	0	0.0
Gila Butte Red-on-buff	0	0.0	0	0.0	0	0.0
Santa Cruz Red-on-buff	0	0.0	0	0.0	0	0.0
Sacaton Red-on-buff	0	0.0	0	0.0	0	0.0
Casa Grande Red-on-buff	0	0.0	0	0.0	0	0.0
Rillito Red-on-brown	0	0.0	0	0.0	0	0.0
Rillito Red-on-brown (micaceous)	0	0.0	0	0.0	0	0.0
Rincon Red-on-brown	0	0.0	0	0.0	0	0.0
Pantano Red-on-brown	0	0.0	0	0.0	0	0.0
Tanque Verde Red-on-brown	0	0.0	0	0.0	0	0.0
Mimbres Black-on-white	0	0.0	0	0.0	0	0.0
Dos Cabezas Red-on-brown	0	0.0	0	0.0	0	0.0
Encinas Red-on-brown	0	0.0	0	0.0	0	0.0
Nogales Purple-on-red	0	0.0	0	0.0	0	0.0
Cerros Red-on-white	0	0.0	0	0.0	0	0.0
San Carlos Red-on-brown	0	0.0	0	0.0	0	0.0

(*continued*)

TABLE E.13 *(continued)*

	Fill		Subfloor		Trench in front	
	n	%	*n*	%	*n*	%
San Carlos Red-on-white	0	0.0	0	0.0	0	0.0
El Paso Polychrome	0	0.0	0	0.0	0	0.0
Unidentified polychrome	0	0.0	0	0.0	0	0.0
Kayenta-like polychrome	0	0.0	0	0.0	0	0.0
Tusayan-like polychrome	0	0.0	0	0.0	0	0.0
Subtotal	*6*	*100.0*	*11*	*100.0*	*17*	*100.0*
Plain types						
Davis Plain	27	71.05	49	87.5	33	86.8
Davis Plain: Sobaipuri Coil Rim Variety	0	0.0	0	0.0	0	0.0
Belford Perforated Rim	9	23.7	0	0.0	1	2.6
Belford Perforated Rim (Sobaipuri Coil Rim)	0	0.0	0	0.0	0	0.0
Babocomari Plain	0	0.0	0	0.0	3	7.9
Redington Plain	0	0.0	2	3.6	0	0.0
Redington Smudged	0	0.0	0	0.0	0	0.0
Sacaton Buff	0	0.0	0	0.0	0	0.0
Gila Plain	0	0.0	4	7.1	1	2.6
Gila Smudged	1	2.6	1	1.8	0	0.0
San Carlos Brown	0	0.0	0	0.0	0	0.0
Slipped brown	1	2.6	0	0.0	0	0.0
Sosa Plain	0	0.0	0	0.0	0	0.0
Whetstone Plain	0	0.0	0	0.0	0	0.0
Wingfield Plain	0	0.0	0	0.0	0	0.0
Fingernail indented	0	0.0	0	0.0	0	0.0
Incised plain	0	0.0	0	0.0	0	0.0
Tularosa Fillet Rim	0	0.0	0	0.0	0	0.0
Neck corrugated gray ware	0	0.0	0	0.0	0	0.0
Stucco ware?	0	0.0	0	0.0	0	0.0
Sandy Paste Perforated	0	0.0	0	0.0	0	0.0
Sosa Perforated	0	0.0	0	0.0	0	0.0
Subtotal	*38*	*100.0*	*56*	*100.0*	*38*	*100.0*

(continued)

TABLE E.13 (*continued*)

	Fill		Subfloor		Trench in front	
	n	%	*n*	%	*n*	%
Red ware types						
Salt Red: Davis Variety	0	0.0	1	20.0	0	0.0
Salt Smudged: Davis Variety	0	0.0	0	0.0	0	0.0
Dragoon Red	0	0.0	1	20.0	0	0.0
Dragoon Red Smudged	0	0.0	0	0.0	1	50.0
Gila Red	0	0.0	2	40.0	1	50.0
Gila Smudged	0	0.0	1	20.0	0	0.0
San Carlos Red	0	0.0	0	0.0	0	0.0
Wingfield Red	0	0.0	0	0.0	0	0.0
Unidentified red #1	0	0.0	0	0.0	0	0.0
Unidentified red #2	0	0.0	0	0.0	0	0.0
Subtotal	*0*	*0.0*	*5*	*100.0*	*2*	*100.0*
Corrugated types						
Late plain corrugated	0	0.0	0	0.0	0	0.0
Late indented corrugated	0	0.0	0	0.0	0	0.0
Early indented corrugated, smudged interior	0	0.0	0	0.0	0	0.0
Obliterated corrugated	0	0.0	0	0.0	0	0.0
Neck corrugated	0	0.0	0	0.0	0	0.0
Red-slipped neck corrugated	0	0.0	0	0.0	0	0.0
Subtotal	*0*	*0.0*	*0*	*0.0*	*0*	*0.0*
Miscellaneous						
Porcelain	0	0.0	0	0.0	0	0.0
White glaze ware	0	0.0	0	0.0	0	0.0
Glass	0	0.0	0	0.0	0	0.0
Unidentified	0	0.0	0	0.0	0	0.0
Subtotal	*0*	*0.0*	*0*	*0.0*	*0*	*0.0*
Total	**44**		**72**		**57**	

TABLE E.14 Gerald's typological analysis of sherds from Room 9 at the Davis Ranch Site

	Fill		Floor 1		Floor 1 NE posthole		Floor 2		Subfloor		Trench in front	
	n	%	*n*	%	*n*	%	*n*	%	*n*	%	*n*	%
Painted types												
Gila Polychrome	19	82.6	1	25.0	1	100.0	3	100.0	3	42.9	36	80.0
Gila Black-on-red	1	4.3	0	0.0	0	0.0	0	0.0	2	28.6	0	0.0
Pinto Polychrome	0	0.0	0	0.0	0	0.0	0	0.0	0	0.0	1	2.2
Gila Polychrome (Pink Variant)	0	0.0	0	0.0	0	0.0	0	0.0	0	0.0	0	0.0
Gila-Tucson Polychrome	0	0.0	0	0.0	0	0.0	0	0.0	0	0.0	0	0.0
Tucson Polychrome	0	0.0	0	0.0	0	0.0	0	0.0	0	0.0	2	4.4
Tucson Black-on-red	1	4.3	1	25.0	0	0.0	0	0.0	2	28.6	0	0.0
Tonto Polychrome	1	4.3	0	0.0	0	0.0	0	0.0	0	0.0	0	0.0
Dragoon Red-on-brown	0	0.0	0	0.0	0	0.0	0	0.0	0	0.0	0	0.0
Cascabel Red-on-brown	1	4.3	0	0.0	0	0.0	0	0.0	0	0.0	0	0.0
Davis Red-on-white	0	0.0	0	0.0	0	0.0	0	0.0	0	0.0	0	0.0
Tres Alamos Red-on-brown	0	0.0	0	0.0	0	0.0	0	0.0	0	0.0	0	0.0
Gila White Slip	0	0.0	0	0.0	0	0.0	0	0.0	0	0.0	3	6.7
Cañada del Oro Red-on-brown	0	0.0	0	0.0	0	0.0	0	0.0	0	0.0	0	0.0
Gila Butte Red-on-buff	0	0.0	0	0.0	0	0.0	0	0.0	0	0.0	0	0.0
Santa Cruz Red-on-buff	0	0.0	0	0.0	0	0.0	0	0.0	0	0.0	1	2.2
Sacaton Red-on-buff	0	0.0	1	25.0	0	0.0	0	0.0	0	0.0	0	0.0
Casa Grande Red-on-buff	0	0.0	0	0.0	0	0.0	0	0.0	0	0.0	0	0.0
Rillito Red-on-brown	0	0.0	0	0.0	0	0.0	0	0.0	0	0.0	0	0.0

(*continued*)

TABLE E.14 *(continued)*

	Fill		Floor 1		Floor 1 NE posthole		Floor 2		Subfloor		Trench in front	
	n	%	*n*	%	*n*	%	*n*	%	*n*	%	*n*	%
Rillito Red-on-brown (micaceous)	0	0.0	1	25.0	0	0.0	0	0.0	0	0.0	0	0.0
Rincon Red-on-brown	0	0.0	0	0.0	0	0.0	0	0.0	0	0.0	0	0.0
Pantano Red-on-brown	0	0.0	0	0.0	0	0.0	0	0.0	0	0.0	0	0.0
Tanque Verde Red-on-brown	0	0.0	0	0.0	0	0.0	0	0.0	0	0.0	0	0.0
Mimbres Black-on-white	0	0.0	0	0.0	0	0.0	0	0.0	0	0.0	0	0.0
Dos Cabezas Red-on-brown	0	0.0	0	0.0	0	0.0	0	0.0	0	0.0	0	0.0
Encinas Red-on-brown	0	0.0	0	0.0	0	0.0	0	0.0	0	0.0	0	0.0
Nogales Purple-on-red	0	0.0	0	0.0	0	0.0	0	0.0	0	0.0	0	0.0
Cerros Red-on-white	0	0.0	0	0.0	0	0.0	0	0.0	0	0.0	0	0.0
San Carlos Red-on-brown	0	0.0	0	0.0	0	0.0	0	0.0	0	0.0	0	0.0
San Carlos Red-on-white	0	0.0	0	0.0	0	0.0	0	0.0	0	0.0	2	4.4
El Paso Polychrome	0	0.0	0	0.0	0	0.0	0	0.0	0	0.0	0	0.0
Unidentified polychrome	0	0.0	0	0.0	0	0.0	0	0.0	0	0.0	0	0.0
Kayenta-like polychrome	0	0.0	0	0.0	0	0.0	0	0.0	0	0.0	0	0.0
Tusayan-like polychrome	0	0.0	0	0.0	0	0.0	0	0.0	0	0.0	0	0.0
Subtotal	*23*	*100.0*	*4*	*100.0*	*1*	*100.0*	*3*	*100.0*	*7*	*100.0*	*45*	*100.0*
Plain types												
Davis Plain	49	94.2	6	100.0	11	100.0	8	100.0	30	85.7	91	91.0
Davis Plain: Sobaipuri Coil Rim Variety	0	0.0	0	0.0	0	0.0	0	0.0	0	0.0	0	0.0
Belford Perforated Rim	0	0.0	0	0.0	0	0.0	0	0.0	0	0.0	1	1.0
Belford Perforated Rim (Sobaipuri Coil Rim)	1	1.9	0	0.0	0	0.0	0	0.0	0	0.0	0	0.0
Babocomari Plain	1	1.9	0	0.0	0	0.0	0	0.0	1	2.9	1	1.0

Redington Plain	0	0.0	0	0.0	0	0.0	0	0.0	2	5.7	3	3.0
Redington Smudged	0	0.0	0	0.0	0	0.0	0	0.0	2	5.7	4	4.0
Sacaton Buff	0	0.0	0	0.0	0	0.0	0	0.0	0	0.0	0	0.0
Gila Plain	0	0.0	0	0.0	0	0.0	0	0.0	0	0.0	0	0.0
Gila Smudged	0	0.0	0	0.0	0	0.0	0	0.0	0	0.0	0	0.0
San Carlos Brown	1	1.9	0	0.0	0	0.0	0	0.0	0	0.0	0	0.0
Slipped brown	0	0.0	0	0.0	0	0.0	0	0.0	0	0.0	0	0.0
Sosa Plain	0	0.0	0	0.0	0	0.0	0	0.0	0	0.0	0	0.0
Whetstone Plain	0	0.0	0	0.0	0	0.0	0	0.0	0	0.0	0	0.0
Wingfield Plain	0	0.0	0	0.0	0	0.0	0	0.0	0	0.0	0	0.0
Fingernail indented	0	0.0	0	0.0	0	0.0	0	0.0	0	0.0	0	0.0
Incised plain	0	0.0	0	0.0	0	0.0	0	0.0	0	0.0	0	0.0
Tularosa Fillet Rim	0	0.0	0	0.0	0	0.0	0	0.0	0	0.0	0	0.0
Neck corrugated gray ware	0	0.0	0	0.0	0	0.0	0	0.0	0	0.0	0	0.0
Stucco ware?	0	0.0	0	0.0	0	0.0	0	0.0	0	0.0	0	0.0
Sandy Paste Perforated	0	0.0	0	0.0	0	0.0	0	0.0	0	0.0	0	0.0
Sosa Perforated	0	0.0	0	0.0	0	0.0	0	0.0	0	0.0	0	0.0
Subtotal	*52*	*100.0*	*6*	*100.0*	*11*	*100.0*	*8*	*100.0*	*35*	*100.0*	*100*	*100.0*
Red ware types												
Salt Red: Davis Variety	5	45.5	1	100.0	0	0.0	0	0.0	1	33.3	1	50.0
Salt Smudged: Davis Variety	0	0.0	0	0.0	0	0.0	0	0.0	0	0.0	1	50.0
Dragoon Red	3	27.3	0	0.0	0	0.0	0	0.0	0	0.0	0	0.0
Dragoon Red Smudged	0	0.0	0	0.0	0	0.0	0	0.0	0	0.0	0	0.0
Gila Red	3	27.3	0	0.0	0	0.0	0	0.0	1	33.3	0	0.0

(continued)

TABLE E.15 *(continued)*

	Fill		Stratitest level 1		Stratitest level 2		Stratitest level 3		Floor		Trench in front	
	n	%	*n*	%	*n*	%	*n*	%	*n*	%	*n*	%
Rillito Red-on-brown (micaceous)	0	0.0	0	0.0	0	0.0	0	0.0	0	0.0	0	0.0
Rincon Red-on-brown	0	0.0	0	0.0	0	0.0	0	0.0	0	0.0	0	0.0
Pantano Red-on-brown	0	0.0	0	0.0	0	0.0	0	0.0	0	0.0	0	0.0
Tanque Verde Red-on-brown	0	0.0	0	0.0	0	0.0	0	0.0	0	0.0	0	0.0
Mimbres Black-on-white	0	0.0	0	0.0	0	0.0	0	0.0	0	0.0	0	0.0
Dos Cabezas Red-on-brown	0	0.0	0	0.0	0	0.0	0	0.0	0	0.0	0	0.0
Encinas Red-on-brown	0	0.0	0	0.0	0	0.0	0	0.0	0	0.0	0	0.0
Nogales Purple-on-red	0	0.0	0	0.0	0	0.0	0	0.0	0	0.0	0	0.0
Cerros Red-on-white	0	0.0	0	0.0	0	0.0	0	0.0	0	0.0	0	0.0
San Carlos Red-on-brown	0	0.0	0	0.0	0	0.0	0	0.0	0	0.0	0	0.0
San Carlos Red-on-white	0	0.0	0	0.0	0	0.0	0	0.0	0	0.0	0	0.0
El Paso Polychrome	0	0.0	0	0.0	0	0.0	0	0.0	0	0.0	0	0.0
Unidentified polychrome	0	0.0	0	0.0	0	0.0	0	0.0	0	0.0	0	0.0
Kayenta-like polychrome	0	0.0	0	0.0	0	0.0	0	0.0	0	0.0	0	0.0
Tusayan-like polychrome	0	0.0	0	0.0	0	0.0	0	0.0	0	0.0	0	0.0
Subtotal	*106*	*100.0*	*4*	*100.0*	*6*	*100.0*	*33*	*100.0*	*40*	*100.0*	*21*	*100.0*
Plain types												
Davis Plain	207	90.8	21	91.3	9	81.8	64	94.1	97	90.7	38	97.4
Davis Plain: Sobaipuri Coil Rim Variety	0	0.0	0	0.0	0	0.0	1	1.5	1	0.9	1	2.6
Belford Perforated Rim	4	1.8	0	0.0	0	0.0	0	0.0	0	0.0	0	0.0
Belford Perforated Rim (Sobaipuri Coil Rim)	0	0.0	1	4.3	0	0.0	0	0.0	0	0.0	0	0.0
Babocomari Plain	10	4.4	1	4.3	1	9.1	1	1.5	0	0.0	0	0.0

Redington Plain	3	1.3	0	0.0	1	9.1	0	0.0	4	3.7	0	0.0
Redington Smudged	3	1.3	0	0.0	0	0.0	1	1.5	2	1.9	0	0.0
Sacaton Buff	0	0.0	0	0.0	0	0.0	0	0.0	0	0.0	0	0.0
Gila Plain	1	0.4	0	0.0	0	0.0	1	1.5	3	2.8	0	0.0
Gila Smudged	0	0.0	0	0.0	0	0.0	0	0.0	0	0.0	0	0.0
San Carlos Brown	0	0.0	0	0.0	0	0.0	0	0.0	0	0.0	0	0.0
Slipped brown	0	0.0	0	0.0	0	0.0	0	0.0	0	0.0	0	0.0
Sosa Plain	0	0.0	0	0.0	0	0.0	0	0.0	0	0.0	0	0.0
Whetstone Plain	0	0.0	0	0.0	0	0.0	0	0.0	0	0.0	0	0.0
Wingfield Plain	0	0.0	0	0.0	0	0.0	0	0.0	0	0.0	0	0.0
Fingernail indented	0	0.0	0	0.0	0	0.0	0	0.0	0	0.0	0	0.0
Incised plain	0	0.0	0	0.0	0	0.0	0	0.0	0	0.0	0	0.0
Tularosa Fillet Rim	0	0.0	0	0.0	0	0.0	0	0.0	0	0.0	0	0.0
Neck corrugated gray ware	0	0.0	0	0.0	0	0.0	0	0.0	0	0.0	0	0.0
Stucco ware?	0	0.0	0	0.0	0	0.0	0	0.0	0	0.0	0	0.0
Sandy Paste Perforated	0	0.0	0	0.0	0	0.0	0	0.0	0	0.0	0	0.0
Sosa Perforated	0	0.0	0	0.0	0	0.0	0	0.0	0	0.0	0	0.0
Subtotal	*228*	*100.0*	*23*	*100.0*	*11*	*100.0*	*68*	*100.0*	*107*	*100.0*	*39*	*100.0*
Red ware types												
Salt Red: Davis Variety	12	52.2	0	0.0	0	0.0	1	100.0	4	80.0	0	0.0
Salt Smudged: Davis Variety	4	17.4	0	0.0	0	0.0	0	0.0	0	0.0	0	0.0
Dragoon Red	5	21.7	0	0.0	0	0.0	0	0.0	1	20.0	3	60.0
Dragoon Red Smudged	0	0.0	0	0.0	0	0.0	0	0.0	0	0.0	0	0.0
Gila Red	1	4.3	0	0.0	0	0.0	0	0.0	0	0.0	0	0.0

(continued)

TABLE E.15 *(continued)*

	Fill		Stratitest level 1		Stratitest level 2		Stratitest level 3		Floor		Trench in front	
	n	%	*n*	%	*n*	%	*n*	%	*n*	%	*n*	%
Gila Smudged	0	0.0	0	0.0	0	0.0	0	0.0	0	0.0	0	0.0
San Carlos Red	0	0.0	0	0.0	0	0.0	0	0.0	0	0.0	2	40.0
Wingfield Red	0	0.0	0	0.0	0	0.0	0	0.0	0	0.0	0	0.0
Unidentified red #1	0	0.0	0	0.0	0	0.0	0	0.0	0	0.0	0	0.0
Unidentified red #2	1	4.3	0	0.0	0	0.0	0	0.0	0	0.0	0	0.0
Subtotal	*23*	*100.0*	*0*	*0.0*	*0*	*0.0*	*1*	*100.0*	*5*	*100.0*	*5*	*100.0*
Corrugated types												
Late plain corrugated	1	100.0	0	0.0	0	0.0	0	0.0	0	0.0	0	0.0
Late indented corrugated	0	0.0	0	0.0	0	0.0	1	100.0	0	0.0	0	0.0
Early indented corrugated, smudged interior	0	0.0	0	0.0	0	0.0	0	0.0	0	0.0	0	0.0
Obliterated corrugated	0	0.0	0	0.0	0	0.0	0	0.0	0	0.0	0	0.0
Neck corrugated	0	0.0	0	0.0	0	0.0	0	0.0	0	0.0	0	0.0
Red-slipped neck corrugated	0	0.0	0	0.0	0	0.0	0	0.0	0	0.0	0	0.0
Subtotal	*1*	*100.0*	*0*	*0.0*	*0*	*0.0*	*1*	*100.0*	*0*	*0.0*	*0*	*0.0*
Miscellaneous												
Porcelain	0	0.0	0	0.0	0	0.0	0	0.0	0	0.0	0	0.0
White glaze ware	0	0.0	0	0.0	0	0.0	0	0.0	0	0.0	0	0.0
Glass	0	0.0	0	0.0	0	0.0	0	0.0	0	0.0	0	0.0
Unidentified	1	100.0	0	0.0	0	0.0	1	100.0	1	100.0	0	0.0
Subtotal	*1*	*100.0*	*0*	*0.0*	*0*	*0.0*	*1*	*100.0*	*1*	*100.0*	*0*	*0.0*
Total	**359**		**27**		**17**		**104**		**153**		**65**	

TABLE E.16 Gerald's typological analysis of sherds from Room 11 at the Davis Ranch Site

	Fill		Stratitest level 1		Stratitest level 2		Stratitest level 3		Floor		Trench in front	
	n	%	*n*	%	*n*	%	*n*	%	*n*	%	*n*	%
Painted types												
Gila Polychrome	21	80.8	3	60.0	4	57.1	5	55.6	9	100.0	17	89.5
Gila Black-on-red	0	0.0	0	0.0	0	0.0	0	0.0	0	0.0	0	0.0
Pinto Polychrome	0	0.0	0	0.0	0	0.0	0	0.0	0	0.0	0	0.0
Gila Polychrome (Pink Variant)	0	0.0	0	0.0	0	0.0	0	0.0	0	0.0	0	0.0
Gila-Tucson Polychrome	0	0.0	0	0.0	0	0.0	0	0.0	0	0.0	0	0.0
Tucson Polychrome	0	0.0	0	0.0	0	0.0	0	0.0	0	0.0	0	0.0
Tucson Black-on-red	0	0.0	1	20.0	1	14.3	0	0.0	0	0.0	0	0.0
Tonto Polychrome	0	0.0	0	0.0	0	0.0	0	0.0	0	0.0	0	0.0
Dragoon Red-on-brown	0	0.0	0	0.0	0	0.0	0	0.0	0	0.0	0	0.0
Cascabel Red-on-brown	0	0.0	0	0.0	0	0.0	0	0.0	0	0.0	0	0.0
Davis Red-on-white	1	3.8	0	0.0	0	0.0	0	0.0	0	0.0	0	0.0
Tres Alamos Red-on-brown	0	0.0	0	0.0	0	0.0	0	0.0	0	0.0	0	0.0
Gila White Slip	0	0.0	0	0.0	0	0.0	0	0.0	0	0.0	1	5.3
Cañada del Oro Red-on-brown	0	0.0	0	0.0	0	0.0	0	0.0	0	0.0	0	0.0
Gila Butte Red-on-buff	0	0.0	0	0.0	0	0.0	2	22.2	0	0.0	0	0.0
Santa Cruz Red-on-buff	0	0.0	1	20.0	0	0.0	1	11.1	0	0.0	1	5.3
Sacaton Red-on-buff	1	3.8	0	0.0	0	0.0	0	0.0	0	0.0	0	0.0
Casa Grande Red-on-buff	0	0.0	0	0.0	0	0.0	0	0.0	0	0.0	0	0.0

(continued)

TABLE E.16 *(continued)*

	Fill		Stratitest level 1		Stratitest level 2		Stratitest level 3		Floor		Trench in front	
	n	%	*n*	%	*n*	%	*n*	%	*n*	%	*n*	%
Rillito Red-on-brown	0	0.0	0	0.0	0	0.0	0	0.0	0	0.0	0	0.0
Rillito Red-on-brown (micaceous)	1	3.8	0	0.0	0	0.0	0	0.0	0	0.0	0	0.0
Rincon Red-on-brown	0	0.0	0	0.0	0	0.0	0	0.0	0	0.0	0	0.0
Pantano Red-on-brown	0	0.0	0	0.0	1	14.3	0	0.0	0	0.0	0	0.0
Tanque Verde Red-on-brown	0	0.0	0	0.0	0	0.0	0	0.0	0	0.0	0	0.0
Mimbres Black-on-white	0	0.0	0	0.0	0	0.0	0	0.0	0	0.0	0	0.0
Dos Cabezas Red-on-brown	0	0.0	0	0.0	0	0.0	0	0.0	0	0.0	0	0.0
Encinas Red-on-brown	2	7.7	0	0.0	1	14.3	1	11.1	0	0.0	0	0.0
Nogales Purple-on-red	0	0.0	0	0.0	0	0.0	0	0.0	0	0.0	0	0.0
Cerros Red-on-white	0	0.0	0	0.0	0	0.0	0	0.0	0	0.0	0	0.0
San Carlos Red-on-brown	0	0.0	0	0.0	0	0.0	0	0.0	0	0.0	0	0.0
San Carlos Red-on-white	0	0.0	0	0.0	0	0.0	0	0.0	0	0.0	0	0.0
El Paso Polychrome	0	0.0	0	0.0	0	0.0	0	0.0	0	0.0	0	0.0
Unidentified polychrome	0	0.0	0	0.0	0	0.0	0	0.0	0	0.0	0	0.0
Kayenta-like polychrome	0	0.0	0	0.0	0	0.0	0	0.0	0	0.0	0	0.0
Tusayan-like polychrome	0	0.0	0	0.0	0	0.0	0	0.0	0	0.0	0	0.0
Subtotal	*26*	*100.0*	*5*	*100.0*	*7*	*100.0*	*9*	*100.0*	*9*	*100.0*	*19*	*100.0*
Plain types												
Davis Plain	94	91.3	24	75.0	33	76.7	123	93.2	22	81.5	14	73.7
Davis Plain: Sobaipuri Coil Rim Variety	0	0.0	0	0.0	0	0.0	0	0.0	0	0.0	0	0.0
Belford Perforated Rim	1	1.0	0	0.0	0	0.0	0	0.0	0	0.0	0	0.0
Belford Perforated Rim (Sobaipuri Coil Rim)	0	0.0	0	0.0	0	0.0	0	0.0	0	0.0	0	0.0

Babocomari Plain	5	4.9	7	21.9	10	23.3	7	5.3	5	18.5	2	10.5
Redington Plain	0	0.0	0	0.0	0	0.0	1	0.8	0	0.0	2	10.5
Redington Smudged	1	1.0	0	0.0	0	0.0	1	0.8	0	0.0	1	5.3
Sacaton Buff	0	0.0	0	0.0	0	0.0	0	0.0	0	0.0	0	0.0
Gila Plain	1	1.0	1	3.1	0	0.0	0	0.0	0	0.0	0	0.0
Gila Smudged	1	1.0	0	0.0	0	0.0	0	0.0	0	0.0	0	0.0
San Carlos Brown	0	0.0	0	0.0	0	0.0	0	0.0	0	0.0	0	0.0
Slipped brown	0	0.0	0	0.0	0	0.0	0	0.0	0	0.0	0	0.0
Sosa Plain	0	0.0	0	0.0	0	0.0	0	0.0	0	0.0	0	0.0
Whetstone Plain	0	0.0	0	0.0	0	0.0	0	0.0	0	0.0	0	0.0
Wingfield Plain	0	0.0	0	0.0	0	0.0	0	0.0	0	0.0	0	0.0
Fingernail indented	0	0.0	0	0.0	0	0.0	0	0.0	0	0.0	0	0.0
Incised plain	0	0.0	0	0.0	0	0.0	0	0.0	0	0.0	0	0.0
Tularosa Fillet Rim	0	0.0	0	0.0	0	0.0	0	0.0	0	0.0	0	0.0
Neck corrugated gray ware	0	0.0	0	0.0	0	0.0	0	0.0	0	0.0	0	0.0
Stucco ware?	0	0.0	0	0.0	0	0.0	0	0.0	0	0.0	0	0.0
Sandy Paste Perforated	0	0.0	0	0.0	0	0.0	0	0.0	0	0.0	0	0.0
Sosa Perforated	0	0.0	0	0.0	0	0.0	0	0.0	0	0.0	0	0.0
Subtotal	*103*	*100.0*	*32*	*100.0*	*43*	*100.0*	*132*	*100.0*	*27*	*100.0*	*19*	*100.0*
Red ware types												
Salt Red: Davis Variety	2	28.6	1	50.0	0	0.0	2	33.3	1	33.3	2	66.7
Salt Smudged: Davis Variety	0	0.0	0	0.0	0	0.0	1	16.7	0	0.0	0	0.0
Dragoon Red	1	14.3	1	50.0	0	0.0	1	16.7	2	66.7	1	33.3
Dragoon Red Smudged	0	0.0	0	0.0	0	0.0	0	0.0	0	0.0	0	0.0

(*continued*)

TABLE E.16 *(continued)*

	Fill		Stratitest level 1		Stratitest level 2		Stratitest level 3		Floor		Trench in front	
	n	%	*n*	%	*n*	%	*n*	%	*n*	%	*n*	%
Gila Red	2	28.6	0	0.0	1	50.0	0	0.0	0	0.0	0	0.0
Gila Smudged	0	0.0	0	0.0	0	0.0	0	0.0	0	0.0	0	0.0
San Carlos Red	1	14.3	0	0.0	1	50.0	1	16.7	0	0.0	0	0.0
Wingfield Red	0	0.0	0	0.0	0	0.0	0	0.0	0	0.0	0	0.0
Unidentified red #1	0	0.0	0	0.0	0	0.0	1	16.7	0	0.0	0	0.0
Unidentified red #2	1	14.3	0	0.0	0	0.0	0	0.0	0	0.0	0	0.0
Subtotal	*7*	*100.0*	*2*	*100.0*	*2*	*100.0*	*6*	*100.0*	*3*	*100.0*	*3*	*100.0*
Corrugated types												
Late plain corrugated	0	0.0	0	0.0	0	0.0	0	0.0	0	0.0	0	0.0
Late indented corrugated	0	0.0	0	0.0	0	0.0	0	0.0	0	0.0	0	0.0
Early indented corrugated, smudged interior	0	0.0	0	0.0	0	0.0	0	0.0	0	0.0	0	0.0
Obliterated corrugated	0	0.0	0	0.0	0	0.0	0	0.0	0	0.0	0	0.0
Neck corrugated	0	0.0	0	0.0	0	0.0	0	0.0	0	0.0	1	100.0
Red-slipped neck corrugated	0	0.0	0	0.0	0	0.0	0	0.0	0	0.0	0	0.0
Subtotal	*0*	*0.0*	*0*	*0.0*	*0*	*0.0*	*0*	*0.0*	*0*	*0.0*	*1*	*100.0*
Miscellaneous												
Porcelain	0	0.0	0	0.0	0	0.0	0	0.0	0	0.0	0	0.0
White glaze ware	0	0.0	0	0.0	0	0.0	0	0.0	0	0.0	0	0.0
Glass	0	0.0	0	0.0	0	0.0	0	0.0	0	0.0	0	0.0
Unidentified	1	100.0	0	0.0	0	0.0	1	100.0	0	0.0	0	0.0
Subtotal	*1*	*100.0*	*0*	*0.0*	*0*	*0.0*	*1*	*100.0*	*0*	*0.0*	*0*	*0.0*
Total	**137**		**39**		**52**		**148**		**39**		**42**	

TABLE E.17 Gerald's typological analysis of sherds from Room 15 at the Davis Ranch Site

	Room 15 fill	
	n	%
Painted types		
Gila Polychrome	13	81.3
Gila Black-on-red	0	0.0
Pinto Polychrome	0	0.0
Gila Polychrome (Pink Variant)	0	0.0
Gila-Tucson Polychrome	0	0.0
Tucson Polychrome	0	0.0
Tucson Black-on-red	0	0.0
Tonto Polychrome	1	6.3
Dragoon Red-on-brown	0	0.0
Cascabel Red-on-brown	0	0.0
Davis Red-on-white	0	0.0
Tres Alamos Red-on-brown	0	0.0
Gila White Slip	0	0.0
Cañada del Oro Red-on-brown	0	0.0
Gila Butte Red-on-buff	0	0.0
Santa Cruz Red-on-buff	1	6.3
Sacaton Red-on-buff	0	0.0
Casa Grande Red-on-buff	0	0.0
Rillito Red-on-brown	0	0.0
Rillito Red-on-brown (micaceous)	0	0.0
Rincon Red-on-brown	0	0.0
Pantano Red-on-brown	0	0.0
Tanque Verde Red-on-brown	0	0.0
Mimbres Black-on-white	0	0.0
Dos Cabezas Red-on-brown	0	0.0
Encinas Red-on-brown	1	6.3

(*continued*)

TABLE E.17 *(continued)*

	Room 15 fill	
	n	%
Nogales Purple-on-red	0	0.0
Cerros Red-on-white	0	0.0
San Carlos Red-on-brown	0	0.0
San Carlos Red-on-white	0	0.0
El Paso Polychrome	0	0.0
Unidentified polychrome	0	0.0
Kayenta-like polychrome	0	0.0
Tusayan-like polychrome	0	0.0
Subtotal	*16*	*100.0*
Plain types		
Davis Plain	28	87.5
Davis Plain: Sobaipuri Coil Rim Variety	0	0.0
Belford Perforated Rim	0	0.0
Belford Perforated Rim (Sobaipuri Coil Rim)	0	0.0
Babocomari Plain	2	6.3
Redington Plain	1	3.1
Redington Smudged	1	3.1
Sacaton Buff	0	0.0
Gila Plain	0	0.0
Gila Smudged	0	0.0
San Carlos Brown	0	0.0
Slipped brown	0	0.0
Sosa Plain	0	0.0
Whetstone Plain	0	0.0
Wingfield Plain	0	0.0
Fingernail indented	0	0.0
Incised plain	0	0.0
Tularosa Fillet Rim	0	0.0
Neck corrugated gray ware	0	0.0
Stucco ware?	0	0.0

(continued)

TABLE E.17 *(continued)*

	Room 15 fill	
	n	%
Sandy Paste Perforated	0	0.0
Sosa Perforated	0	0.0
Subtotal	*32*	*100.0*
Red ware types		
Salt Red: Davis Variety	0	0.0
Salt Smudged: Davis Variety	4	100.0
Dragoon Red	0	0.0
Dragoon Red Smudged	0	0.0
Gila Red	0	0.0
Gila Smudged	0	0.0
San Carlos Red	0	0.0
Wingfield Red	0	0.0
Unidentified red #1	0	0.0
Unidentified red #2	0	0.0
Subtotal	*4*	*100.0*
Corrugated types		
Late plain corrugated	0	0.0
Late indented corrugated	0	0.0
Early indented corrugated, smudged interior	0	0.0
Obliterated corrugated	0	0.0
Neck corrugated	0	0.0
Red-slipped neck corrugated	0	0.0
Subtotal	*0*	*0.0*
Miscellaneous		
Porcelain	0	0.0
White glaze ware	0	0.0
Glass	0	0.0
Unidentified	0	0.0
Subtotal	*0*	*0.0*
Total	**52**	

TABLE E.18 Gerald's typological analysis of sherds from Room 16 at the Davis Ranch Site

	Fill		Stratitest Level 1		Stratitest Level 2		Stratitest Level 3		Floor		Subfloor		Trench in Front	
	n	%	*n*	%	*n*	%	*n*	%	*n*	%	*n*	%	*n*	%
Painted types														
Gila Polychrome	7	70.0	1	25.0	3	42.9	1	20.0	12	80.0	0	0.0	2	40.0
Gila Black-on-red	0	0.0	0	0.0	0	0.0	0	0.0	2	13.3	0	0.0	0	0.0
Pinto Polychrome	0	0.0	0	0.0	0	0.0	0	0.0	0	0.0	0	0.0	1	20.0
Gila Polychrome (Pink Variant)	0	0.0	0	0.0	0	0.0	0	0.0	0	0.0	0	0.0	0	0.0
Gila-Tucson Polychrome	0	0.0	0	0.0	0	0.0	0	0.0	0	0.0	0	0.0	0	0.0
Tucson Polychrome	1	10.0	0	0.0	0	0.0	0	0.0	0	0.0	0	0.0	1	20.0
Tucson Black-on-red	0	0.0	0	0.0	1	14.3	0	0.0	0	0.0	0	0.0	0	0.0
Tonto Polychrome	0	0.0	0	0.0	0	0.0	0	0.0	0	0.0	0	0.0	0	0.0
Dragoon Red-on-brown	0	0.0	0	0.0	0	0.0	0	0.0	0	0.0	0	0.0	1	20.0
Cascabel Red-on-brown	0	0.0	0	0.0	0	0.0	0	0.0	0	0.0	0	0.0	0	0.0
Davis Red-on-white	0	0.0	1	25.0	0	0.0	0	0.0	0	0.0	0	0.0	0	0.0
Tres Alamos Red-on-brown	0	0.0	0	0.0	0	0.0	0	0.0	0	0.0	0	0.0	0	0.0
Gila White Slip	0	0.0	0	0.0	0	0.0	0	0.0	1	6.7	0	0.0	0	0.0
Cañada del Oro Red-on-brown	0	0.0	0	0.0	0	0.0	0	0.0	0	0.0	0	0.0	0	0.0
Gila Butte Red-on-buff	0	0.0	0	0.0	0	0.0	0	0.0	0	0.0	0	0.0	0	0.0
Santa Cruz Red-on-buff	0	0.0	0	0.0	1	14.3	2	40.0	0	0.0	0	0.0	0	0.0
Sacaton Red-on-buff	1	10.0	0	0.0	0	0.0	0	0.0	0	0.0	0	0.0	0	0.0
Casa Grande Red-on-buff	0	0.0	0	0.0	0	0.0	0	0.0	0	0.0	0	0.0	0	0.0
Rillito Red-on-brown	0	0.0	1	25.0	1	14.3	1	20.0	0	0.0	0	0.0	0	0.0

Rillito Red-on-brown (micaceous)	0	0.0	1	25.0	1	14.3	1	20.0	0	0.0	0	0.0	0	0.0
Rincon Red-on-brown	1	10.0	0	0.0	0	0.0	0	0.0	0	0.0	0	0.0	0	0.0
Pantano Red-on-brown	0	0.0	0	0.0	0	0.0	0	0.0	0	0.0	0	0.0	0	0.0
Tanque Verde Red-on-brown	0	0.0	0	0.0	0	0.0	0	0.0	0	0.0	0	0.0	0	0.0
Mimbres Black-on-white	0	0.0	0	0.0	0	0.0	0	0.0	0	0.0	0	0.0	0	0.0
Dos Cabezas Red-on-brown	0	0.0	0	0.0	0	0.0	0	0.0	0	0.0	0	0.0	0	0.0
Encinas Red-on-brown	0	0.0	0	0.0	0	0.0	0	0.0	0	0.0	0	0.0	0	0.0
Nogales Purple-on-red	0	0.0	0	0.0	0	0.0	0	0.0	0	0.0	0	0.0	0	0.0
Cerros Red-on-white	0	0.0	0	0.0	0	0.0	0	0.0	0	0.0	0	0.0	0	0.0
San Carlos Red-on-brown	0	0.0	0	0.0	0	0.0	0	0.0	0	0.0	0	0.0	0	0.0
San Carlos Red-on-white	0	0.0	0	0.0	0	0.0	0	0.0	0	0.0	0	0.0	0	0.0
El Paso Polychrome	0	0.0	0	0.0	0	0.0	0	0.0	0	0.0	0	0.0	0	0.0
Unidentified polychrome	0	0.0	0	0.0	0	0.0	0	0.0	0	0.0	0	0.0	0	0.0
Kayenta-like polychrome	0	0.0	0	0.0	0	0.0	0	0.0	0	0.0	0	0.0	0	0.0
Tusayan-like polychrome	0	0.0	0	0.0	0	0.0	0	0.0	0	0.0	0	0.0	0	0.0
Subtotal	*10*	*100.0*	*4*	*100.0*	*7*	*100.0*	*5*	*100.0*	*15*	*100.0*	*0*	*0.0*	*5*	*100.0*
Plain types														
Davis Plain	17	68.0	12	85.7	32	78.0	56	76.7	166	97.6	3	100.0	60	93.8
Davis Plain: Sobaipuri Coil Rim Variety	0	0.0	0	0.0	0	0.0	0	0.0	0	0.0	0	0.0	0	0.0
Belford Perforated Rim	0	0.0	0	0.0	0	0.0	0	0.0	0	0.0	0	0.0	0	0.0
Belford Perforated Rim (Sobaipuri Coil Rim)	0	0.0	0	0.0	0	0.0	0	0.0	1	0.6	0	0.0	0	0.0
Babocomari Plain	5	20.0	0	0.0	3	7.3	10	13.7	3	1.8	0	0.0	3	4.7
Redington Plain	0	0.0	2	14.3	0	0.0	5	6.8	0	0.0	0	0.0	0	0.0
Redington Smudged	2	8.0	0	0.0	1	2.4	1	1.4	0	0.0	0	0.0	0	0.0

(*continued*)

TABLE E.18 *(continued)*

	Fill		Stratitest Level 1		Stratitest Level 2		Stratitest Level 3		Floor		Subfloor		Trench in Front	
	n	%	*n*	%	*n*	%	*n*	%	*n*	%	*n*	%	*n*	%
Sacaton Buff	1	4.0	0	0.0	1	2.4	1	1.4	0	0.0	0	0.0	1	1.6
Gila Plain	0	0.0	0	0.0	3	7.3	0	0.0	0	0.0	0	0.0	0	0.0
Gila Smudged	0	0.0	0	0.0	0	0.0	0	0.0	0	0.0	0	0.0	0	0.0
San Carlos Brown	0	0.0	0	0.0	0	0.0	0	0.0	0	0.0	0	0.0	0	0.0
Slipped brown	0	0.0	0	0.0	0	0.0	0	0.0	0	0.0	0	0.0	0	0.0
Sosa Plain	0	0.0	0	0.0	0	0.0	0	0.0	0	0.0	0	0.0	0	0.0
Whetstone Plain	0	0.0	0	0.0	0	0.0	0	0.0	0	0.0	0	0.0	0	0.0
Wingfield Plain	0	0.0	0	0.0	1	2.4	0	0.0	0	0.0	0	0.0	0	0.0
Fingernail indented	0	0.0	0	0.0	0	0.0	0	0.0	0	0.0	0	0.0	0	0.0
Incised plain	0	0.0	0	0.0	0	0.0	0	0.0	0	0.0	0	0.0	0	0.0
Tularosa Fillet Rim	0	0.0	0	0.0	0	0.0	0	0.0	0	0.0	0	0.0	0	0.0
Neck corrugated gray ware	0	0.0	0	0.0	0	0.0	0	0.0	0	0.0	0	0.0	0	0.0
Stucco ware?	0	0.0	0	0.0	0	0.0	0	0.0	0	0.0	0	0.0	0	0.0
Sandy Paste Perforated	0	0.0	0	0.0	0	0.0	0	0.0	0	0.0	0	0.0	0	0.0
Sosa Perforated	0	0.0	0	0.0	0	0.0	0	0.0	0	0.0	0	0.0	0	0.0
Subtotal	*25*	*100.0*	*14*	*100.0*	*41*	*100.0*	*73*	*100.0*	*170*	*100.0*	*3*	*100.0*	*64*	*100.0*
Red ware types														
Salt Red: Davis Variety	2	66.7	2	50.0	3	75.0	1	33.3	0	0.0	0	0.0	1	50.0
Salt Smudged: Davis Variety	0	0.0	0	0.0	0	0.0	0	0.0	0	0.0	0	0.0	0	0.0
Dragoon Red	0	0.0	2	50.0	1	25.0	2	66.7	1	100.0	0	0.0	0	0.0

Dragoon Red Smudged	0	0.0	0	0.0	0	0.0	0	0.0	0	0.0	0	0.0	0	0.0
Gila Red	0	0.0	0	0.0	0	0.0	0	0.0	0	0.0	0	0.0	1	50.0
Gila Smudged	0	0.0	0	0.0	0	0.0	0	0.0	0	0.0	0	0.0	0	0.0
San Carlos Red	0	0.0	0	0.0	0	0.0	0	0.0	0	0.0	0	0.0	0	0.0
Wingfield Red	0	0.0	0	0.0	0	0.0	0	0.0	0	0.0	0	0.0	0	0.0
Unidentified red #1	0	0.0	0	0.0	0	0.0	0	0.0	0	0.0	0	0.0	0	0.0
Unidentified red #2	1	33.3	0	0.0	0	0.0	0	0.0	0	0.0	0	0.0	0	0.0
Subtotal	*3*	*100.0*	*4*	*100.0*	*4*	*100.0*	*3*	*100.0*	*1*	*100.0*	*0*	*0.0*	*2*	*100.0*
Corrugated types														
Late plain corrugated	0	0.0	0	0.0	0	0.0	0	0.0	0	0.0	0	0.0	0	0.0
Late indented corrugated	0	0.0	0	0.0	0	0.0	0	0.0	0	0.0	0	0.0	0	0.0
Early indented corrugated, smudged interior	0	0.0	0	0.0	0	0.0	0	0.0	0	0.0	0	0.0	0	0.0
Obliterated corrugated	0	0.0	0	0.0	0	0.0	0	0.0	0	0.0	0	0.0	0	0.0
Neck corrugated	0	0.0	0	0.0	0	0.0	0	0.0	0	0.0	0	0.0	0	0.0
Red-slipped neck corrugated	0	0.0	0	0.0	0	0.0	0	0.0	0	0.0	0	0.0	0	0.0
Subtotal	*0*	*0.0*	*0*	*0.0*	*0*	*0.0*	*0*	*0.0*	*0*	*0.0*	*0*	*0.0*	*0*	*0.0*
Miscellaneous														
Porcelain	0	0.0	0	0.0	0	0.0	0	0.0	0	0.0	0	0.0	0	0.0
White glaze ware	0	0.0	0	0.0	0	0.0	0	0.0	0	0.0	0	0.0	0	0.0
Glass	0	0.0	0	0.0	0	0.0	0	0.0	0	0.0	0	0.0	0	0.0
Unidentified	0	0.0	0	0.0	0	0.0	0	0.0	0	0.0	0	0.0	0	0.0
Subtotal	*0*	*0.0*	*0*	*0.0*	*0*	*0.0*	*0*	*0.0*	*0*	*0.0*	*0*	*0.0*	*0*	*0.0*
Total	**38**		**22**		**52**		**81**		**186**		**3**		**71**	

TABLE E.19 Gerald's typological analysis of sherds from Rooms 17, 18, 19, 20, and 21 at the Davis Ranch Site

	Room 17 Fill		Room 18 Fill		Room 19 Fill		Room 20 Fill		Room 21 Fill		Room 21 Trench in front	
	n	%	*n*	%	*n*	%	*n*	%	*n*	%	*n*	%
Painted types												
Gila Polychrome	18	100.0	1	100.0	52	92.9	7	87.5	19	82.6	9	100.0
Gila Black-on-red	0	0.0	0	0.0	0	0.0	0	0.0	0	0.0	0	0.0
Pinto Polychrome	0	0.0	0	0.0	0	0.0	0	0.0	0	0.0	0	0.0
Gila Polychrome (Pink Variant)	0	0.0	0	0.0	0	0.0	0	0.0	0	0.0	0	0.0
Gila-Tucson Polychrome	0	0.0	0	0.0	0	0.0	0	0.0	0	0.0	0	0.0
Tucson Polychrome	0	0.0	0	0.0	0	0.0	0	0.0	0	0.0	0	0.0
Tucson Black-on-red	0	0.0	0	0.0	0	0.0	0	0.0	2	8.7	0	0.0
Tonto Polychrome	0	0.0	0	0.0	1	1.8	1	12.5	2	8.7	0	0.0
Dragoon Red-on-brown	0	0.0	0	0.0	0	0.0	0	0.0	0	0.0	0	0.0
Cascabel Red-on-brown	0	0.0	0	0.0	0	0.0	0	0.0	0	0.0	0	0.0
Davis Red-on-white	0	0.0	0	0.0	0	0.0	0	0.0	0	0.0	0	0.0
Tres Alamos Red-on-brown	0	0.0	0	0.0	0	0.0	0	0.0	0	0.0	0	0.0
Gila White Slip	0	0.0	0	0.0	1	1.8	0	0.0	0	0.0	0	0.0
Cañada del Oro Red-on-brown	0	0.0	0	0.0	0	0.0	0	0.0	0	0.0	0	0.0
Gila Butte Red-on-buff	0	0.0	0	0.0	0	0.0	0	0.0	0	0.0	0	0.0
Santa Cruz Red-on-buff	0	0.0	0	0.0	0	0.0	0	0.0	0	0.0	0	0.0
Sacaton Red-on-buff	0	0.0	0	0.0	0	0.0	0	0.0	0	0.0	0	0.0
Casa Grande Red-on-buff	0	0.0	0	0.0	0	0.0	0	0.0	0	0.0	0	0.0
Rillito Red-on-brown	0	0.0	0	0.0	0	0.0	0	0.0	0	0.0	0	0.0
Rillito Red-on-brown (micaceous)	0	0.0	0	0.0	0	0.0	0	0.0	0	0.0	0	0.0

Rincon Red-on-brown	0	0.0	0	0.0	1	1.8	0	0.0	0	0.0	0	0.0
Pantano Red-on-brown	0	0.0	0	0.0	0	0.0	0	0.0	0	0.0	0	0.0
Tanque Verde Red-on-brown	0	0.0	0	0.0	1	1.8	0	0.0	0	0.0	0	0.0
Mimbres Black-on-white	0	0.0	0	0.0	0	0.0	0	0.0	0	0.0	0	0.0
Dos Cabezas Red-on-brown	0	0.0	0	0.0	0	0.0	0	0.0	0	0.0	0	0.0
Encinas Red-on-brown	0	0.0	0	0.0	0	0.0	0	0.0	0	0.0	0	0.0
Nogales Purple-on-red	0	0.0	0	0.0	0	0.0	0	0.0	0	0.0	0	0.0
Cerros Red-on-white	0	0.0	0	0.0	0	0.0	0	0.0	0	0.0	0	0.0
San Carlos Red-on-brown	0	0.0	0	0.0	0	0.0	0	0.0	0	0.0	0	0.0
San Carlos Red-on-white	0	0.0	0	0.0	0	0.0	0	0.0	0	0.0	0	0.0
El Paso Polychrome	0	0.0	0	0.0	0	0.0	0	0.0	0	0.0	0	0.0
Unidentified polychrome	0	0.0	0	0.0	0	0.0	0	0.0	0	0.0	0	0.0
Kayenta-like polychrome	0	0.0	0	0.0	0	0.0	0	0.0	0	0.0	0	0.0
Tusayan-like polychrome	0	0.0	0	0.0	0	0.0	0	0.0	0	0.0	0	0.0
Subtotal	*18*	*100.0*	*1*	*100.0*	*56*	*100.0*	*8*	*100.0*	*23*	*100.0*	*9*	*100.0*
Plain types												
Davis Plain	23	76.7	18	90.0	136	92.5	42	85.7	75	89.3	48	100.0
Davis Plain: Sobaipuri Coil Rim Variety	0	0.0	0	0.0	0	0.0	0	0.0	0	0.0	0	0.0
Belford Perforated Rim	0	0.0	0	0.0	0	0.0	0	0.0	1	1.2	0	0.0
Belford Perforated Rim (Sobaipuri Coil Rim)	0	0.0	0	0.0	0	0.0	0	0.0	0	0.0	0	0.0
Babocomari Plain	7	23.3	1	5.0	1	0.7	0	0.0	0	0.0	0	0.0
Redington Plain	0	0.0	1	5.0	1	0.7	1	2.0	1	1.2	0	0.0
Redington Smudged	0	0.0	0	0.0	2	1.4	1	2.0	6	7.1	0	0.0
Sacaton Buff	0	0.0	0	0.0	0	0.0	0	0.0	0	0.0	0	0.0
Gila Plain	0	0.0	0	0.0	5	3.4	5	10.2	0	0.0	0	0.0

(continued)

TABLE E.19 *(continued)*

	Room 17 Fill		Room 18 Fill		Room 19 Fill		Room 20 Fill		Room 21			
									Fill		Trench in front	
	n	%	*n*	%	*n*	%	*n*	%	*n*	%	*n*	%
Gila Smudged	0	0.0	0	0.0	0	0.0	0	0.0	1	1.2	0	0.0
San Carlos Brown	0	0.0	0	0.0	2	1.4	0	0.0	0	0.0	0	0.0
Slipped brown	0	0.0	0	0.0	0	0.0	0	0.0	0	0.0	0	0.0
Sosa Plain	0	0.0	0	0.0	0	0.0	0	0.0	0	0.0	0	0.0
Whetstone Plain	0	0.0	0	0.0	0	0.0	0	0.0	0	0.0	0	0.0
Wingfield Plain	0	0.0	0	0.0	0	0.0	0	0.0	0	0.0	0	0.0
Fingernail indented	0	0.0	0	0.0	0	0.0	0	0.0	0	0.0	0	0.0
Incised plain	0	0.0	0	0.0	0	0.0	0	0.0	0	0.0	0	0.0
Tularosa Fillet Rim	0	0.0	0	0.0	0	0.0	0	0.0	0	0.0	0	0.0
Neck corrugated gray ware	0	0.0	0	0.0	0	0.0	0	0.0	0	0.0	0	0.0
Stucco ware?	0	0.0	0	0.0	0	0.0	0	0.0	0	0.0	0	0.0
Sandy Paste Perforated	0	0.0	0	0.0	0	0.0	0	0.0	0	0.0	0	0.0
Sosa Perforated	0	0.0	0	0.0	0	0.0	0	0.0	0	0.0	0	0.0
Subtotal	*30*	*100.0*	*20*	*100.0*	*147*	*100.0*	*49*	*100.0*	*84*	*100.0*	*48*	*100.0*
Red ware types												
Salt Red: Davis Variety	2	100.0	0	0.0	4	44.4	4	0.0	8	80.0	1	50.0
Salt Smudged: Davis Variety	0	0.0	0	0.0	2	22.2	2	0.0	1	10.0	0	0.0
Dragoon Red	0	0.0	0	0.0	2	22.2	2	0.0	0	0.0	0	0.0

Dragoon Red Smudged	0	0.0	0	0.0	1	11.1	1	0.0	1	10.0	0	0.0
Gila Red	0	0.0	0	0.0	0	0.0	0	0.0	0	0.0	0	0.0
Gila Smudged	0	0.0	0	0.0	0	0.0	0	0.0	0	0.0	0	0.0
San Carlos Red	0	0.0	0	0.0	0	0.0	0	0.0	0	0.0	0	0.0
Wingfield Red	0	0.0	0	0.0	0	0.0	0	0.0	0	0.0	0	0.0
Unidentified red #1	0	0.0	0	0.0	0	0.0	0	0.0	0	0.0	0	0.0
Unidentified red #2	0	0.0	0	0.0	0	0.0	0	0.0	0	0.0	1	50.0
Subtotal	*2*	*100.0*	*0*	*0.0*	*9*	*100.0*	*9*	*0.0*	*10*	*100.0*	*2*	*100.0*
Corrugated types												
Late plain corrugated	0	0.0	0	0.0	0	0.0	0	0.0	0	0.0	0	0.0
Late indented corrugated	1	100.0	0	0.0	0	0.0	0	0.0	0	0.0	0	0.0
Early indented corrugated, smudged interior	0	0.0	0	0.0	0	0.0	0	0.0	0	0.0	0	0.0
Obliterated corrugated	0	0.0	0	0.0	0	0.0	0	0.0	0	0.0	0	0.0
Neck corrugated	0	0.0	0	0.0	1	100.0	1	0.0	0	0.0	0	0.0
Red-slipped neck corrugated	0	0.0	0	0.0	0	0.0	0	0.0	0	0.0	0	0.0
Subtotal	*1*	*100.0*	*0*	*0.0*	*1*	*100.0*	*1*	*0.0*	*0*	*0.0*	*0*	*0.0*
Miscellaneous												
Porcelain	0	0.0	0	0.0	0	0.0	0	0.0	0	0.0	0	0.0
White glaze ware	0	0.0	0	0.0	0	0.0	0	0.0	0	0.0	0	0.0
Glass	0	0.0	0	0.0	0	0.0	0	0.0	0	0.0	0	0.0
Unidentified	0	0.0	0	0.0	3	100.0	3	0.0	0	0.0	0	0.0
Subtotal	*0*	*0.0*	*0*	*0.0*	*3*	*100.0*	*3*	*0.0*	*0*	*0.0*	*0*	*0.0*
Total	**51**		**21**		**216**		**70**		**117**		**59**	

TABLE E.20 Gerald's typological analysis of sherds from Rooms 22, 25, 27, 28, 29, and 30 at the Davis Ranch Site

	Room 22 fill		Room 25 fill		Room 27 fill		Room 28 fill		Rooms 29 and 30 fill	
	n	%	*n*	%	*n*	%	*n*	%	*n*	%
Painted types										
Gila Polychrome	0	0.0	2	100.0	1	100.0	1	14.3	0	0.0
Gila Black-on-red	0	0.0	0	0.0	0	0.0	4	57.1	0	0.0
Pinto Polychrome	0	0.0	0	0.0	0	0.0	0	0.0	0	0.0
Gila Polychrome (Pink Variant)	0	0.0	0	0.0	0	0.0	0	0.0	0	0.0
Gila-Tucson Polychrome	0	0.0	0	0.0	0	0.0	0	0.0	0	0.0
Tucson Polychrome	0	0.0	0	0.0	0	0.0	0	0.0	0	0.0
Tucson Black-on-red	0	0.0	0	0.0	0	0.0	1	14.3	0	0.0
Tonto Polychrome	0	0.0	0	0.0	0	0.0	0	0.0	0	0.0
Dragoon Red-on-brown	0	0.0	0	0.0	0	0.0	0	0.0	0	0.0
Cascabel Red-on-brown	0	0.0	0	0.0	0	0.0	0	0.0	0	0.0
Davis Red-on-white	0	0.0	0	0.0	0	0.0	0	0.0	0	0.0
Tres Alamos Red-on-brown	0	0.0	0	0.0	0	0.0	0	0.0	0	0.0
Gila White Slip	0	0.0	0	0.0	0	0.0	0	0.0	0	0.0
Cañada del Oro Red-on-brown	0	0.0	0	0.0	0	0.0	0	0.0	0	0.0
Gila Butte Red-on-buff	0	0.0	0	0.0	0	0.0	0	0.0	0	0.0
Santa Cruz Red-on-buff	0	0.0	0	0.0	0	0.0	0	0.0	0	0.0
Sacaton Red-on-buff	0	0.0	0	0.0	0	0.0	1	14.3	0	0.0
Casa Grande Red-on-buff	0	0.0	0	0.0	0	0.0	0	0.0	0	0.0
Rillito Red-on-brown	0	0.0	0	0.0	0	0.0	0	0.0	0	0.0

Rillito Red-on-brown (micaceous)	0	0.0	0	0.0	0	0.0	0	0.0	0	0.0
Rincon Red-on-brown	0	0.0	0	0.0	0	0.0	0	0.0	0	0.0
Pantano Red-on-brown	0	0.0	0	0.0	0	0.0	0	0.0	0	0.0
Tanque Verde Red-on-brown	0	0.0	0	0.0	0	0.0	0	0.0	0	0.0
Mimbres Black-on-white	0	0.0	0	0.0	0	0.0	0	0.0	0	0.0
Dos Cabezas Red-on-brown	0	0.0	0	0.0	0	0.0	0	0.0	0	0.0
Encinas Red-on-brown	0	0.0	0	0.0	0	0.0	0	0.0	0	0.0
Nogales Purple-on-red	0	0.0	0	0.0	0	0.0	0	0.0	0	0.0
Cerros Red-on-white	0	0.0	0	0.0	0	0.0	0	0.0	0	0.0
San Carlos Red-on-brown	0	0.0	0	0.0	0	0.0	0	0.0	0	0.0
San Carlos Red-on-white	0	0.0	0	0.0	0	0.0	0	0.0	0	0.0
El Paso Polychrome	0	0.0	0	0.0	0	0.0	0	0.0	0	0.0
Unidentified polychrome	0	0.0	0	0.0	0	0.0	0	0.0	0	0.0
Kayenta-like polychrome	0	0.0	0	0.0	0	0.0	0	0.0	0	0.0
Tusayan-like polychrome	0	0.0	0	0.0	0	0.0	0	0.0	0	0.0
Subtotal	*0*	*0.0*	*2*	*100.0*	*1*	*100.0*	*7*	*100.0*	*0*	*0.0*
Plain types										
Davis Plain	3	75.0	4	36.4	13	100.0	128	97.7	9	56.3
Davis Plain: Sobaipuri Coil Rim Variety	0	0.0	0	0.0	0	0.0	1	0.8	0	0.0
Belford Perforated Rim	0	0.0	1	9.1	0	0.0	0	0.0	0	0.0
Belford Perforated Rim (Sobaipuri Coil Rim)	0	0.0	0	0.0	0	0.0	0	0.0	0	0.0
Babocomari Plain	1	25.0	6	54.5	0	0.0	1	0.8	7	43.8
Redington Plain	0	0.0	0	0.0	0	0.0	1	0.8	0	0.0

(continued)

TABLE E.20 *(continued)*

	Room 22 fill		Room 25 fill		Room 27 fill		Room 28 fill		Rooms 29 and 30 fill	
	n	%	*n*	%	*n*	%	*n*	%	*n*	%
Redington Smudged	0	0.0	0	0.0	0	0.0	0	0.0	0	0.0
Sacaton Buff	0	0.0	0	0.0	0	0.0	0	0.0	0	0.0
Gila Plain	0	0.0	0	0.0	0	0.0	0	0.0	0	0.0
Gila Smudged	0	0.0	0	0.0	0	0.0	0	0.0	0	0.0
San Carlos Brown	0	0.0	0	0.0	0	0.0	0	0.0	0	0.0
Slipped brown	0	0.0	0	0.0	0	0.0	0	0.0	0	0.0
Sosa Plain	0	0.0	0	0.0	0	0.0	0	0.0	0	0.0
Whetstone Plain	0	0.0	0	0.0	0	0.0	0	0.0	0	0.0
Wingfield Plain	0	0.0	0	0.0	0	0.0	0	0.0	0	0.0
Fingernail indented	0	0.0	0	0.0	0	0.0	0	0.0	0	0.0
Incised plain	0	0.0	0	0.0	0	0.0	0	0.0	0	0.0
Tularosa Fillet Rim	0	0.0	0	0.0	0	0.0	0	0.0	0	0.0
Neck corrugated gray ware	0	0.0	0	0.0	0	0.0	0	0.0	0	0.0
Stucco ware?	0	0.0	0	0.0	0	0.0	0	0.0	0	0.0
Sandy Paste Perforated	0	0.0	0	0.0	0	0.0	0	0.0	0	0.0
Sosa Perforated	0	0.0	0	0.0	0	0.0	0	0.0	0	0.0
Subtotal	*4*	*100.0*	*11*	*100.0*	*13*	*100.0*	*131*	*100.0*	*16*	*100.0*
Red ware types										
Salt Red: Davis Variety	0	0.0	0	0.0	0	0.0	0	0.0	1	100.0
Salt Smudged: Davis Variety	0	0.0	0	0.0	0	0.0	0	0.0	0	0.0

Dragoon Red	0	0.0	0	0.0	0	0.0	0	0.0	0	0.0
Dragoon Red Smudged	0	0.0	0	0.0	0	0.0	0	0.0	0	0.0
Gila Red	0	0.0	0	0.0	0	0.0	1	100.0	0	0.0
Gila Smudged	0	0.0	0	0.0	0	0.0	0	0.0	0	0.0
San Carlos Red	0	0.0	0	0.0	0	0.0	0	0.0	0	0.0
Wingfield Red	0	0.0	0	0.0	0	0.0	0	0.0	0	0.0
Unidentified red #1	0	0.0	0	0.0	0	0.0	0	0.0	0	0.0
Unidentified red #2	0	0.0	0	0.0	0	0.0	0	0.0	0	0.0
Subtotal	*0*	*0.0*	*0*	*0.0*	*0*	*0.0*	*1*	*100.0*	*1*	*100.0*
Corrugated types										
Late plain corrugated	0	0.0	0	0.0	0	0.0	0	0.0	0	0.0
Late indented corrugated	0	0.0	0	0.0	0	0.0	0	0.0	0	0.0
Early indented corrugated, smudged interior	0	0.0	0	0.0	0	0.0	0	0.0	0	0.0
Obliterated corrugated	0	0.0	0	0.0	0	0.0	0	0.0	0	0.0
Neck corrugated	0	0.0	0	0.0	0	0.0	0	0.0	0	0.0
Red-slipped neck corrugated	0	0.0	0	0.0	0	0.0	0	0.0	0	0.0
Subtotal	*0*	*0.0*	*0*	*0.0*	*0*	*0.0*	*0*	*0.0*	*0*	*0.0*
Miscellaneous										
Porcelain	0	0.0	0	0.0	0	0.0	0	0.0	0	0.0
White glaze ware	0	0.0	0	0.0	0	0.0	0	0.0	0	0.0
Glass	0	0.0	0	0.0	0	0.0	0	0.0	0	0.0
Unidentified	0	0.0	0	0.0	0	0.0	0	0.0	0	0.0
Subtotal	*0*	*0.0*	*0*	*0.0*	*0*	*0.0*	*0*	*0.0*	*0*	*0.0*
Total	**4**		**13**		**14**		**139**		**17**	

TABLE E.21 Gerald's typological analysis of sherds from Rooms 31, 32, 33, 36, and 37 at the Davis Ranch Site

	Rooms 31 and 32 Fill		Room 33				Room 36 Fill		Room 37			
			Fill		Trench in front				Fill		Floor	
	n	%	*n*	%	*n*	%	*n*	%	*n*	%	*n*	%
Painted types												
Gila Polychrome	0	0.0	61	100.0	55	85.9	16	80.0	7	53.8	3	33.3
Gila Black-on-red	0	0.0	0	0.0	2	3.1	0	0.0	1	7.7	0	0.0
Pinto Polychrome	0	0.0	0	0.0	0	0.0	0	0.0	0	0.0	1	11.1
Gila Polychrome (Pink Variant)	0	0.0	0	0.0	0	0.0	0	0.0	0	0.0	0	0.0
Gila-Tucson Polychrome	0	0.0	0	0.0	0	0.0	0	0.0	0	0.0	0	0.0
Tucson Polychrome	0	0.0	0	0.0	0	0.0	1	5.0	0	0.0	0	0.0
Tucson Black-on-red	0	0.0	0	0.0	5	7.8	0	0.0	0	0.0	0	0.0
Tonto Polychrome	0	0.0	0	0.0	0	0.0	0	0.0	2	15.4	0	0.0
Dragoon Red-on-brown	0	0.0	0	0.0	0	0.0	1	5.0	0	0.0	0	0.0
Cascabel Red-on-brown	0	0.0	0	0.0	0	0.0	1	5.0	1	7.7	0	0.0
Davis Red-on-white	0	0.0	0	0.0	0	0.0	0	0.0	0	0.0	0	0.0
Tres Alamos Red-on-brown	0	0.0	0	0.0	0	0.0	0	0.0	0	0.0	0	0.0
Gila White Slip	0	0.0	0	0.0	0	0.0	1	5.0	0	0.0	0	0.0
Cañada del Oro Red-on-brown	0	0.0	0	0.0	0	0.0	0	0.0	0	0.0	0	0.0
Gila Butte Red-on-buff	0	0.0	0	0.0	0	0.0	0	0.0	0	0.0	0	0.0
Santa Cruz Red-on-buff	0	0.0	0	0.0	0	0.0	0	0.0	0	0.0	4	44.4
Sacaton Red-on-buff	0	0.0	0	0.0	1	1.6	0	0.0	0	0.0	1	11.1
Casa Grande Red-on-buff	0	0.0	0	0.0	0	0.0	0	0.0	0	0.0	0	0.0
Rillito Red-on-brown	0	0.0	0	0.0	0	0.0	0	0.0	0	0.0	0	0.0
Rillito Red-on-brown (micaceous)	0	0.0	0	0.0	0	0.0	0	0.0	0	0.0	0	0.0

Rincon Red-on-brown	1	100.0	0	0.0	1	1.6	0	0.0	0	0.0	0	0.0
Pantano Red-on-brown	0	0.0	0	0.0	0	0.0	0	0.0	0	0.0	0	0.0
Tanque Verde Red-on-brown	0	0.0	0	0.0	0	0.0	0	0.0	0	0.0	0	0.0
Mimbres Black-on-white	0	0.0	0	0.0	0	0.0	0	0.0	0	0.0	0	0.0
Dos Cabezas Red-on-brown	0	0.0	0	0.0	0	0.0	0	0.0	0	0.0	0	0.0
Encinas Red-on-brown	0	0.0	0	0.0	0	0.0	0	0.0	1	7.7	0	0.0
Nogales Purple-on-red	0	0.0	0	0.0	0	0.0	0	0.0	0	0.0	0	0.0
Cerros Red-on-white	0	0.0	0	0.0	0	0.0	0	0.0	0	0.0	0	0.0
San Carlos Red-on-brown	0	0.0	0	0.0	0	0.0	0	0.0	1	7.7	0	0.0
San Carlos Red-on-white	0	0.0	0	0.0	0	0.0	0	0.0	0	0.0	0	0.0
El Paso Polychrome	0	0.0	0	0.0	0	0.0	0	0.0	0	0.0	0	0.0
Unidentified polychrome	0	0.0	0	0.0	0	0.0	0	0.0	0	0.0	0	0.0
Kayenta-like polychrome	0	0.0	0	0.0	0	0.0	0	0.0	0	0.0	0	0.0
Tusayan-like polychrome	0	0.0	0	0.0	0	0.0	0	0.0	0	0.0	0	0.0
Subtotal	*1*	*100.0*	*61*	*100.0*	*64*	*100.0*	*20*	*100.0*	*13*	*100.0*	*9*	*100.0*
Plain types												
Davis Plain	0	0.0	107	89.2	108	93.9	50	84.7	89	92.7	21	84.0
Davis Plain: Sobaipuri Coil Rim Variety	0	0.0	0	0.0	1	0.9	0	0.0	0	0.0	0	0.0
Belford Perforated Rim	0	0.0	0	0.0	1	0.9	3	5.1	1	1.0	0	0.0
Belford Perforated Rim (Sobaipuri Coil Rim)	0	0.0	0	0.0	0	0.0	0	0.0	0	0.0	0	0.0
Babocomari Plain	0	0.0	3	2.5	0	0.0	4	6.8	2	2.1	2	8.0
Redington Plain	0	0.0	8	6.7	4	3.5	0	0.0	1	1.0	0	0.0
Redington Smudged	0	0.0	2	1.7	0	0.0	1	1.7	2	2.1	0	0.0
Sacaton Buff	0	0.0	0	0.0	0	0.0	0	0.0	0	0.0	1	4.0

(*continued*)

TABLE E.21 *(continued)*

	Rooms 31 and 32 Fill		Room 33 Fill		Room 33 Trench in front		Room 36 Fill		Room 37 Fill		Room 37 Floor	
	n	%	*n*	%	*n*	%	*n*	%	*n*	%	*n*	%
Gila Plain	0	0.0	0	0.0	0	0.0	1	1.7	1	1.0	1	4.0
Gila Smudged	0	0.0	0	0.0	0	0.0	0	0.0	0	0.0	0	0.0
San Carlos Brown	0	0.0	0	0.0	0	0.0	0	0.0	0	0.0	0	0.0
Slipped brown	0	0.0	0	0.0	0	0.0	0	0.0	0	0.0	0	0.0
Sosa Plain	0	0.0	0	0.0	0	0.0	0	0.0	0	0.0	0	0.0
Whetstone Plain	0	0.0	0	0.0	0	0.0	0	0.0	0	0.0	0	0.0
Wingfield Plain	0	0.0	0	0.0	0	0.0	0	0.0	0	0.0	0	0.0
Fingernail indented	0	0.0	0	0.0	0	0.0	0	0.0	0	0.0	0	0.0
Incised plain	0	0.0	0	0.0	0	0.0	0	0.0	0	0.0	0	0.0
Tularosa Fillet Rim	0	0.0	0	0.0	1	0.9	0	0.0	0	0.0	0	0.0
Neck corrugated gray ware	0	0.0	0	0.0	0	0.0	0	0.0	0	0.0	0	0.0
Stucco ware?	0	0.0	0	0.0	0	0.0	0	0.0	0	0.0	0	0.0
Sandy Paste Perforated	0	0.0	0	0.0	0	0.0	0	0.0	0	0.0	0	0.0
Sosa Perforated	0	0.0	0	0.0	0	0.0	0	0.0	0	0.0	0	0.0
Subtotal	*0*	*0.0*	*120*	*100.0*	*115*	*100.0*	*59*	*100.0*	*96*	*100.0*	*25*	*100.0*
Red ware types												
Salt Red: Davis Variety	0	0.0	3	33.3	4	66.7	1	100.0	5	100.0	3	75.0
Salt Smudged: Davis Variety	0	0.0	0	0.0	0	0.0	0	0.0	0	0.0	0	0.0
Dragoon Red	0	0.0	1	11.1	2	33.3	0	0.0	0	0.0	1	25.0

Dragoon Red Smudged	0	0.0	0	0.0	0	0.0	0	0.0	0	0.0	0	0.0
Gila Red	0	0.0	3	33.3	0	0.0	0	0.0	0	0.0	0	0.0
Gila Smudged	0	0.0	0	0.0	0	0.0	0	0.0	0	0.0	0	0.0
San Carlos Red	0	0.0	1	11.1	0	0.0	0	0.0	0	0.0	0	0.0
Wingfield Red	0	0.0	0	0.0	0	0.0	0	0.0	0	0.0	0	0.0
Unidentified red #1	0	0.0	0	0.0	0	0.0	0	0.0	0	0.0	0	0.0
Unidentified red #2	0	0.0	1	11.1	0	0.0	0	0.0	0	0.0	0	0.0
Subtotal	*0*	*0.0*	*9*	*100.0*	*6*	*100.0*	*1*	*100.0*	*5*	*100.0*	*4*	*100.0*
Corrugated types												
Late plain corrugated	0	0.0	0	0.0	0	0.0	0	0.0	0	0.0	0	0.0
Late indented corrugated	0	0.0	3	100.0	1	100.0	0	0.0	2	100.0	0	0.0
Early indented corrugated, smudged interior	0	0.0	0	0.0	0	0.0	0	0.0	0	0.0	0	0.0
Obliterated corrugated	0	0.0	0	0.0	0	0.0	0	0.0	0	0.0	0	0.0
Neck corrugated	0	0.0	0	0.0	0	0.0	0	0.0	0	0.0	0	0.0
Red-slipped neck corrugated	0	0.0	0	0.0	0	0.0	0	0.0	0	0.0	0	0.0
Subtotal	*0*	*0.0*	*3*	*100.0*	*1*	*100.0*	*0*	*0.0*	*2*	*100.0*	*0*	*0.0*
Miscellaneous												
Porcelain	0	0.0	0	0.0	0	0.0	0	0.0	0	0.0	0	0.0
White glaze ware	0	0.0	0	0.0	0	0.0	0	0.0	0	0.0	0	0.0
Glass	0	0.0	0	0.0	0	0.0	0	0.0	0	0.0	0	0.0
Unidentified	0	0.0	1	100.0	0	0.0	0	0.0	0	0.0	0	0.0
Subtotal	*0*	*0.0*	*1*	*100.0*	*0*	*0.0*	*0*	*0.0*	*0*	*0.0*	*0*	*0.0*
Total	**1**		**194**		**186**		**80**		**116**		**38**	

TABLE E.22 Gerald's typological analysis of sherds from Rooms 38–40, 41, 42, and 44 at the Davis Ranch Site

	Rooms 38–40 Fill		Room 40 Subfloor		Room 41 Fill		Room 42 Fill		Room 44			
									Fill		Subfloor	
	n	%	*n*	%	*n*	%	*n*	%	*n*	%	*n*	%
Painted types												
Gila Polychrome	13	92.9	9	100.0	13	100.0	6	85.7	25	64.1	14	82.4
Gila Black-on-red	0	0.0	0	0.0	0	0.0	0	0.0	5	12.8	0	0.0
Pinto Polychrome	0	0.0	0	0.0	0	0.0	0	0.0	0	0.0	0	0.0
Gila Polychrome (Pink Variant)	0	0.0	0	0.0	0	0.0	0	0.0	0	0.0	0	0.0
Gila-Tucson Polychrome	0	0.0	0	0.0	0	0.0	0	0.0	0	0.0	0	0.0
Tucson Polychrome	0	0.0	0	0.0	0	0.0	0	0.0	1	2.6	2	11.8
Tucson Black-on-red	0	0.0	0	0.0	0	0.0	0	0.0	4	10.3	0	0.0
Tonto Polychrome	0	0.0	0	0.0	0	0.0	0	0.0	0	0.0	0	0.0
Dragoon Red-on-brown	1	7.1	0	0.0	0	0.0	0	0.0	0	0.0	0	0.0
Cascabel Red-on-brown	0	0.0	0	0.0	0	0.0	0	0.0	0	0.0	0	0.0
Davis Red-on-white	0	0.0	0	0.0	0	0.0	0	0.0	0	0.0	0	0.0
Tres Alamos Red-on-brown	0	0.0	0	0.0	0	0.0	0	0.0	0	0.0	0	0.0
Gila White Slip	0	0.0	0	0.0	0	0.0	1	14.3	1	2.6	1	5.9
Cañada del Oro Red-on-brown	0	0.0	0	0.0	0	0.0	0	0.0	0	0.0	0	0.0
Gila Butte Red-on-buff	0	0.0	0	0.0	0	0.0	0	0.0	0	0.0	0	0.0
Santa Cruz Red-on-buff	0	0.0	0	0.0	0	0.0	0	0.0	0	0.0	0	0.0
Sacaton Red-on-buff	0	0.0	0	0.0	0	0.0	0	0.0	1	2.6	0	0.0
Casa Grande Red-on-buff	0	0.0	0	0.0	0	0.0	0	0.0	0	0.0	0	0.0
Rillito Red-on-brown	0	0.0	0	0.0	0	0.0	0	0.0	1	2.6	0	0.0
Rillito Red-on-brown (micaceous)	0	0.0	0	0.0	0	0.0	0	0.0	0	0.0	0	0.0

Rincon Red-on-brown	0	0.0	0	0.0	0	0.0	0	0.0	0	0.0	0	0.0
Pantano Red-on-brown	0	0.0	0	0.0	0	0.0	0	0.0	0	0.0	0	0.0
Tanque Verde Red-on-brown	0	0.0	0	0.0	0	0.0	0	0.0	0	0.0	0	0.0
Mimbres Black-on-white	0	0.0	0	0.0	0	0.0	0	0.0	1	2.6	0	0.0
Dos Cabezas Red-on-brown	0	0.0	0	0.0	0	0.0	0	0.0	0	0.0	0	0.0
Encinas Red-on-brown	0	0.0	0	0.0	0	0.0	0	0.0	0	0.0	0	0.0
Nogales Purple-on-red	0	0.0	0	0.0	0	0.0	0	0.0	0	0.0	0	0.0
Cerros Red-on-white	0	0.0	0	0.0	0	0.0	0	0.0	0	0.0	0	0.0
San Carlos Red-on-brown	0	0.0	0	0.0	0	0.0	0	0.0	0	0.0	0	0.0
San Carlos Red-on-white	0	0.0	0	0.0	0	0.0	0	0.0	0	0.0	0	0.0
El Paso Polychrome	0	0.0	0	0.0	0	0.0	0	0.0	0	0.0	0	0.0
Unidentified polychrome	0	0.0	0	0.0	0	0.0	0	0.0	0	0.0	0	0.0
Kayenta-like polychrome	0	0.0	0	0.0	0	0.0	0	0.0	0	0.0	0	0.0
Tusayan-like polychrome	0	0.0	0	0.0	0	0.0	0	0.0	0	0.0	0	0.0
Subtotal	*14*	*100.0*	*9*	*100.0*	*13*	*100.0*	*7*	*100.0*	*39*	*100.0*	*17*	*100.0*
Plain types												
Davis Plain	48	96.0	1	50.0	37	97.4	10	83.3	128	93.4	43	84.3
Davis Plain: Sobaipuri Coil Rim Variety	0	0.0	0	0.0	0	0.0	0	0.0	0	0.0	0	0.0
Belford Perforated Rim	0	0.0	0	0.0	0	0.0	0	0.0	1	0.7	1	2.0
Belford Perforated Rim (Sobaipuri Coil Rim)	0	0.0	0	0.0	0	0.0	0	0.0	0	0.0	0	0.0
Babocomari Plain	0	0.0	0	0.0	0	0.0	1	8.3	5	3.6	5	9.8
Redington Plain	0	0.0	1	50.0	1	2.6	1	8.3	1	0.7	0	0.0
Redington Smudged	1	2.0	0	0.0	0	0.0	0	0.0	2	1.5	1	2.0
Sacaton Buff	0	0.0	0	0.0	0	0.0	0	0.0	0	0.0	0	0.0
Gila Plain	1	2.0	0	0.0	0	0.0	0	0.0	0	0.0	1	2.0

(continued)

TABLE E.22 *(continued)*

	Rooms 38–40 Fill		Room 40 Subfloor		Room 41 Fill		Room 42 Fill		Room 44 Fill		Room 44 Subfloor	
	n	%	*n*	%	*n*	%	*n*	%	*n*	%	*n*	%
Gila Smudged	0	0.0	0	0.0	0	0.0	0	0.0	0	0.0	0	0.0
San Carlos Brown	0	0.0	0	0.0	0	0.0	0	0.0	0	0.0	0	0.0
Slipped brown	0	0.0	0	0.0	0	0.0	0	0.0	0	0.0	0	0.0
Sosa Plain	0	0.0	0	0.0	0	0.0	0	0.0	0	0.0	0	0.0
Whetstone Plain	0	0.0	0	0.0	0	0.0	0	0.0	0	0.0	0	0.0
Wingfield Plain	0	0.0	0	0.0	0	0.0	0	0.0	0	0.0	0	0.0
Fingernail indented	0	0.0	0	0.0	0	0.0	0	0.0	0	0.0	0	0.0
Incised plain	0	0.0	0	0.0	0	0.0	0	0.0	0	0.0	0	0.0
Tularosa Fillet Rim	0	0.0	0	0.0	0	0.0	0	0.0	0	0.0	0	0.0
Neck corrugated gray ware	0	0.0	0	0.0	0	0.0	0	0.0	0	0.0	0	0.0
Stucco ware?	0	0.0	0	0.0	0	0.0	0	0.0	0	0.0	0	0.0
Sandy Paste Perforated	0	0.0	0	0.0	0	0.0	0	0.0	0	0.0	0	0.0
Sosa Perforated	0	0.0	0	0.0	0	0.0	0	0.0	0	0.0	0	0.0
Subtotal	*50*	*100.0*	*2*	*100.0*	*38*	*100.0*	*12*	*100.0*	*137*	*100.0*	*51*	*100.0*
Red ware types												
Salt Red: Davis Variety	4	80.0	0	0.0	2	100.0	0	0.0	2	25.0	0	0.0
Salt Smudged: Davis Variety	0	0.0	0	0.0	0	0.0	0	0.0	1	12.5	0	0.0
Dragoon Red	1	20.0	0	0.0	0	0.0	0	0.0	2	25.0	5	71.4
Dragoon Red Smudged	0	0.0	0	0.0	0	0.0	0	0.0	1	12.5	0	0.0

Gila Red	0	0.0	0	0.0	0	0.0	0	0.0	0	0.0	2	28.6
Gila Smudged	0	0.0	0	0.0	0	0.0	0	0.0	1	12.5	0	0.0
San Carlos Red	0	0.0	0	0.0	0	0.0	0	0.0	0	0.0	0	0.0
Wingfield Red	0	0.0	0	0.0	0	0.0	0	0.0	0	0.0	0	0.0
Unidentified red #1	0	0.0	0	0.0	0	0.0	0	0.0	0	0.0	0	0.0
Unidentified red #2	0	0.0	0	0.0	0	0.0	0	0.0	1	12.5	0	0.0
Subtotal	*5*	*100.0*	*0*	*0.0*	*2*	*100.0*	*0*	*0.0*	*8*	*100.0*	*7*	*100.0*
Corrugated types												
Late plain corrugated	0	0.0	0	0.0	0	0.0	0	0.0	0	0.0	2	100.0
Late indented corrugated	0	0.0	0	0.0	0	0.0	0	0.0	0	0.0	0	0.0
Early indented corrugated, smudged interior	0	0.0	0	0.0	0	0.0	0	0.0	0	0.0	0	0.0
Obliterated corrugated	0	0.0	0	0.0	0	0.0	0	0.0	0	0.0	0	0.0
Neck corrugated	0	0.0	0	0.0	0	0.0	0	0.0	0	0.0	0	0.0
Red-slipped neck corrugated	0	0.0	0	0.0	0	0.0	0	0.0	0	0.0	0	0.0
Subtotal	*0*	*0.0*	*0*	*0.0*	*0*	*0.0*	*0*	*0.0*	*0*	*0.0*	*2*	*100.0*
Miscellaneous												
Porcelain	0	0.0	0	0.0	0	0.0	0	0.0	0	0.0	0	0.0
White glaze ware	0	0.0	0	0.0	0	0.0	0	0.0	0	0.0	0	0.0
Glass	0	0.0	0	0.0	0	0.0	0	0.0	0	0.0	0	0.0
Unidentified	0	0.0	0	0.0	0	0.0	0	0.0	0	0.0	0	0.0
Subtotal	*0*	*0.0*	*0*	*0.0*	*0*	*0.0*	*0*	*0.0*	*0*	*0.0*	*0*	*0.0*
Total	**69**		**11**		**53**		**19**		**184**		**77**	

TABLE E.23 Gerald's typological analysis of sherds from Room 45 at the Davis Ranch Site

	Room 45 fill	
	n	%
Painted types		
Gila Polychrome	3	30.0
Gila Black-on-red	0	0.0
Pinto Polychrome	0	0.0
Gila Polychrome (Pink Variant)	0	0.0
Gila-Tucson Polychrome	0	0.0
Tucson Polychrome	4	40.0
Tucson Black-on-red	3	30.0
Tonto Polychrome	0	0.0
Dragoon Red-on-brown	0	0.0
Cascabel Red-on-brown	0	0.0
Davis Red-on-white	0	0.0
Tres Alamos Red-on-brown	0	0.0
Gila White Slip	0	0.0
Cañada del Oro Red-on-brown	0	0.0
Gila Butte Red-on-buff	0	0.0
Santa Cruz Red-on-buff	0	0.0
Sacaton Red-on-buff	0	0.0
Casa Grande Red-on-buff	0	0.0
Rillito Red-on-brown	0	0.0
Rillito Red-on-brown (micaceous)	0	0.0
Rincon Red-on-brown	0	0.0
Pantano Red-on-brown	0	0.0
Tanque Verde Red-on-brown	0	0.0
Mimbres Black-on-white	0	0.0
Dos Cabezas Red-on-brown	0	0.0
Encinas Red-on-brown	0	0.0
Nogales Purple-on-red	0	0.0

(*continued*)

TABLE E.23 *(continued)*

	Room 45 fill	
	n	%
Cerros Red-on-white	0	0.0
San Carlos Red-on-brown	0	0.0
San Carlos Red-on-white	0	0.0
El Paso Polychrome	0	0.0
Unidentified polychrome	0	0.0
Kayenta-like polychrome	0	0.0
Tusayan-like polychrome	0	0.0
Subtotal	*10*	*100.0*
Plain types		
Davis Plain	22	88.0
Davis Plain: Sobaipuri Coil Rim Variety	0	0.0
Belford Perforated Rim	0	0.0
Belford Perforated Rim (Sobaipuri Coil Rim)	0	0.0
Babocomari Plain	2	8.0
Redington Plain	1	4.0
Redington Smudged	0	0.0
Sacaton Buff	0	0.0
Gila Plain	0	0.0
Gila Smudged	0	0.0
San Carlos Brown	0	0.0
Slipped brown	0	0.0
Sosa Plain	0	0.0
Whetstone Plain	0	0.0
Wingfield Plain	0	0.0
Fingernail indented	0	0.0
Incised plain	0	0.0
Tularosa Fillet Rim	0	0.0
Neck corrugated gray ware	0	0.0

(continued)

TABLE E.23 *(continued)*

	Room 45 fill	
	n	%
Stucco ware?	0	0.0
Sandy Paste Perforated	0	0.0
Sosa Perforated	0	0.0
Subtotal	*25*	*100.0*
Red ware types		
Salt Red: Davis Variety	0	0.0
Salt Smudged: Davis Variety	0	0.0
Dragoon Red	0	0.0
Dragoon Red Smudged	0	0.0
Gila Red	1	50.0
Gila Smudged	0	0.0
San Carlos Red	0	0.0
Wingfield Red	0	0.0
Unidentified red #1	0	0.0
Unidentified red #2	1	50.0
Subtotal	*2*	*100.0*
Corrugated types		
Late plain corrugated	0	0.0
Late indented corrugated	1	100.0
Early indented corrugated, smudged interior	0	0.0
Obliterated corrugated	0	0.0
Neck corrugated	0	0.0
Red-slipped neck corrugated	0	0.0
Subtotal	*1*	*100.0*
Miscellaneous		
Porcelain	0	0.0
White glaze ware	0	0.0
Glass	0	0.0
Unidentified	0	0.0
Subtotal	*0*	*0.0*
Total	**38**	

TABLE E.24 Gerald's typological analysis of sherds from the fill of the kiva at the Davis Ranch Site

	General fill		Levels 3–5 (40–100 cm)		Levels 6–8 (100–160 cm)		Southwest compartment		Stratit-est level 1 (0–20 cm)		Stratit-est level 2 (20–40 cm)	
	n	%	*n*	%	*n*	%	*n*	%	*n*	%	*n*	%
Painted types												
Gila Polychrome	3,502	87.6	153	89.5	377	89.5	42	85.7	33	82.5	40	81.6
Gila Black-on-red	27	0.7	1	0.6	1	0.2	1	2.0	2	5.0	1	2.0
Pinto Polychrome	30	0.8	2	1.2	4	1.0	0	0.0	0	0.0	0	0.0
Gila Polychrome (Pink Variant)	4	0.1	0	0.0	0	0.0	1	2.0	0	0.0	1	2.0
Gila-Tucson Polychrome	2	0.1	0	0.0	0	0.0	0	0.0	0	0.0	0	0.0
Tucson Polychrome	20	0.5	3	1.8	2	0.5	0	0.0	0	0.0	0	0.0
Tucson Black-on-red	21	0.5	2	1.2	2	0.5	0	0.0	0	0.0	0	0.0
Tonto Polychrome	65	1.6	2	1.2	7	1.7	0	0.0	0	0.0	1	2.0
Dragoon Red-on-brown	9	0.2	0	0.0	0	0.0	0	0.0	0	0.0	1	2.0
Cascabel Red-on-brown	21	0.5	0	0.0	1	0.2	0	0.0	1	2.5	0	0.0
Davis Red-on-white	3	0.1	0	0.0	0	0.0	0	0.0	0	0.0	0	0.0
Tres Alamos Red-on-brown	0	0.0	0	0.0	0	0.0	0	0.0	0	0.0	0	0.0
Gila White Slip	198	5.0	6	3.5	18	4.3	4	8.2	4	10.0	3	6.1
Cañada del Oro Red-on-brown	1	0.0	0	0.0	0	0.0	0	0.0	0	0.0	0	0.0
Gila Butte Red-on-buff	2	0.1	0	0.0	0	0.0	0	0.0	0	0.0	0	0.0
Santa Cruz Red-on-buff	31	0.8	1	0.6	3	0.7	0	0.0	0	0.0	1	2.0
Sacaton Red-on-buff	18	0.5	0	0.0	2	0.5	0	0.0	0	0.0	0	0.0
Casa Grande Red-on-buff	0	0.0	0	0.0	0	0.0	0	0.0	0	0.0	0	0.0
Rillito Red-on-brown	4	0.1	0	0.0	0	0.0	0	0.0	0	0.0	0	0.0

(continued)

TABLE E.24 *(continued)*

	General fill		Levels 3–5 (40–100 cm)		Levels 6–8 (100–160 cm)		Southwest compartment		Stratit-est level 1 (0–20 cm)		Stratit-est level 2 (20–40 cm)	
	n	%	*n*	%	*n*	%	*n*	%	*n*	%	*n*	%
Rillito Red-on-brown (micaceous)	13	0.3	0	0.0	2	0.5	0	0.0	0	0.0	0	0.0
Rincon Red-on-brown	7	0.2	0	0.0	0	0.0	1	2.0	0	0.0	0	0.0
Pantano Red-on-brown	3	0.1	1	0.6	0	0.0	0	0.0	0	0.0	0	0.0
Tanque Verde Red-on-brown	5	0.1	0	0.0	0	0.0	0	0.0	0	0.0	0	0.0
Mimbres Black-on-white	1	0.0	0	0.0	0	0.0	0	0.0	0	0.0	0	0.0
Dos Cabezas Red-on-brown	0	0.0	0	0.0	0	0.0	0	0.0	0	0.0	0	0.0
Encinas Red-on-brown	3	0.1	0	0.0	0	0.0	0	0.0	0	0.0	0	0.0
Nogales Purple-on-red	0	0.0	0	0.0	0	0.0	0	0.0	0	0.0	0	0.0
Cerros Red-on-white	0	0.0	0	0.0	0	0.0	0	0.0	0	0.0	0	0.0
San Carlos Red-on-brown	0	0.0	0	0.0	0	0.0	0	0.0	0	0.0	0	0.0
San Carlos Red-on-white	7	0.2	0	0.0	1	0.2	0	0.0	0	0.0	1	2.0
El Paso Polychrome	0	0.0	0	0.0	0	0.0	0	0.0	0	0.0	0	0.0
Unidentified polychrome	0	0.0	0	0.0	0	0.0	0	0.0	0	0.0	0	0.0
Kayenta-like polychrome	2	0.1	0	0.0	0	0.0	0	0.0	0	0.0	0	0.0
Tusayan-like polychrome	0	0.0	0	0.0	1	0.2	0	0.0	0	0.0	0	0.0
Subtotal	*3,999*	*100.0*	*171*	*100.0*	*421*	*100.0*	*49*	*100.0*	*40*	*100.0*	*49*	*100.0*
Plain types												
Davis Plain	6,355	87.5	252	88.4	617	88.8	71	78.9	76	84.4	58	92.1

Davis Plain: Sobaipuri Coil Rim Variety	16	0.2	1	0.4	2	0.3	0	0.0	0	0.0	0	0.0
Belford Perforated Rim	100	1.4	6	2.1	8	1.2	4	4.4	1	1.1	0	0.0
Belford Perforated Rim (Sobaipuri Coil Rim)	28	0.4	0	0.0	6	0.9	0	0.0	0	0.0	0	0.0
Babocomari Plain	399	5.5	13	4.6	21	3.0	12	13.3	6	6.7	5	7.9
Redington Plain	123	1.7	5	1.8	16	2.3	1	1.1	3	3.3	0	0.0
Redington Smudged	98	1.3	3	1.1	15	2.2	2	2.2	2	2.2	0	0.0
Sacaton Buff	10	0.1	0	0.0	0	0.0	0	0.0	0	0.0	0	0.0
Gila Plain	71	1.0	2	0.7	3	0.4	0	0.0	2	2.2	0	0.0
Gila Smudged	3	0.0	1	0.4	0	0.0	0	0.0	0	0.0	0	0.0
San Carlos Brown	12	0.2	0	0.0	1	0.1	0	0.0	0	0.0	0	0.0
Slipped brown	12	0.2	0	0.0	0	0.0	0	0.0	0	0.0	0	0.0
Sosa Plain	24	0.3	2	0.7	0	0.0	0	0.0	0	0.0	0	0.0
Whetstone Plain	0	0.0	0	0.0	0	0.0	0	0.0	0	0.0	0	0.0
Wingfield Plain	2	0.0	0	0.0	1	0.1	0	0.0	0	0.0	0	0.0
Fingernail indented	0	0.0	0	0.0	0	0.0	0	0.0	0	0.0	0	0.0
Incised plain	0	0.0	0	0.0	0	0.0	0	0.0	0	0.0	0	0.0
Tularosa Fillet Rim	0	0.0	0	0.0	0	0.0	0	0.0	0	0.0	0	0.0
Neck corrugated gray ware	0	0.0	0	0.0	0	0.0	0	0.0	0	0.0	0	0.0
Stucco ware?	0	0.0	0	0.0	0	0.0	0	0.0	0	0.0	0	0.0
Sandy Paste Perforated	0	0.0	0	0.0	4	0.6	0	0.0	0	0.0	0	0.0
Sosa Perforated	10	0.1	0	0.0	1	0.1	0	0.0	0	0.0	0	0.0
Subtotal	*7,263*	*100.0*	*285*	*100.0*	*695*	*100.0*	*90*	*100.0*	*90*	*100.0*	*63*	*100.0*

(*continued*)

TABLE E.24 *(continued)*

	General fill		Levels 3–5 (40–100 cm)		Levels 6–8 (100–160 cm)		Southwest compartment		Stratit-est level 1 (0–20 cm)		Stratit-est level 2 (20–40 cm)	
	n	%	*n*	%	*n*	%	*n*	%	*n*	%	*n*	%
Red ware types												
Salt Red: Davis Variety	235	47.3	9	40.9	22	36.7	1	50.0	3	75.0	3	100.0
Salt Smudged: Davis Variety	67	13.5	5	22.7	18	30.0	0	0.0	0	0.0	0	0.0
Dragoon Red	100	20.1	5	22.7	9	15.0	0	0.0	1	25.0	0	0.0
Dragoon Red Smudged	22	4.4	1	4.5	2	3.3	0	0.0	0	0.0	0	0.0
Gila Red	37	7.4	2	9.1	7	11.7	1	50.0	0	0.0	0	0.0
Gila Smudged	8	1.6	0	0.0	0	0.0	0	0.0	0	0.0	0	0.0
San Carlos Red	9	1.8	0	0.0	0	0.0	0	0.0	0	0.0	0	0.0
Wingfield Red	1	0.2	0	0.0	0	0.0	0	0.0	0	0.0	0	0.0
Unidentified red #1	3	0.6	0	0.0	0	0.0	0	0.0	0	0.0	0	0.0
Unidentified red #2	15	3.0	0	0.0	2	3.3	0	0.0	0	0.0	0	0.0
Subtotal	*497*	*100.0*	*22*	*100.0*	*60*	*100.0*	*2*	*100.0*	*4*	*100.0*	*3*	*100.0*
Corrugated types												
Late plain corrugated	11	35.5	0	0.0	0	0.0	0	0.0	0	0.0	0	0.0
Late indented corrugated	16	51.6	0	0.0	1	50.0	1	100.0	0	0.0	1	100.0
Early indented corrugated, smudged interior	0	0.0	0	0.0	0	0.0	0	0.0	0	0.0	0	0.0
Obliterated corrugated	1	3.2	0	0.0	0	0.0	0	0.0	0	0.0	0	0.0
Neck corrugated	2	6.5	0	0.0	1	50.0	0	0.0	0	0.0	0	0.0

Red-slipped neck corrugated	1	3.2	0	0.0	0	0.0	0	0.0	0	0.0	0	0.0
Subtotal	*31*	*100.0*	*0*	*0.0*	*2*	*100.0*	*1*	*100.0*	*0*	*0.0*	*1*	*100.0*
Miscellaneous												
Porcelain	0	0.0	0	0.0	0	0.0	0	0.0	0	0.0	0	0.0
White glaze ware	0	0.0	0	0.0	0	0.0	0	0.0	0	0.0	0	0.0
Glass	0	0.0	0	0.0	0	0.0	0	0.0	0	0.0	0	0.0
Unidentified	40	100.0	0	0.0	2	100.0	0	0.0	0	0.0	0	0.0
Subtotal	*40*	*100.0*	*0*	*0.0*	*2*	*100.0*	*0*	*0.0*	*0*	*0.0*	*0*	*0.0*
Total	**11,830**		**478**		**1,180**		**142**		**134**		**116**	

	Stratitest level 3 (40–60 cm)		Stratitest level 4 (60–80 cm)		Stratitest level 5 (80–100 cm)		Stratitest level 6 (100–120 cm)		Stratitest level 7 (120–140 cm)		Stratitest level 8 (140–160 cm)	
	n	%	*n*	%	*n*	%	*n*	%	*n*	%	*n*	%
Painted types												
Gila Polychrome	31	72.1	169	82.0	284	91.6	145	94.8	58	92.1	20	69.0
Gila Black-on-red	0	0.0	2	1.0	1	0.3	0	0.0	0	0.0	0	0.0
Pinto Polychrome	0	0.0	0	0.0	2	0.6	0	0.0	0	0.0	1	3.4
Gila Polychrome (Pink Variant)	0	0.0	0	0.0	0	0.0	0	0.0	0	0.0	0	0.0
Gila-Tucson Polychrome	0	0.0	0	0.0	0	0.0	0	0.0	0	0.0	0	0.0
Tucson Polychrome	2	4.7	0	0.0	0	0.0	0	0.0	0	0.0	0	0.0
Tucson Black-on-red	1	2.3	1	0.5	0	0.0	0	0.0	1	1.6	0	0.0
Tonto Polychrome	1	2.3	11	5.3	11	3.5	1	0.7	1	1.6	0	0.0
Dragoon Red-on-brown	0	0.0	0	0.0	0	0.0	0	0.0	0	0.0	0	0.0

(continued)

TABLE E.24 *(continued)*

	Stratitest level 3 (40–60 cm)		Stratitest level 4 (60–80 cm)		Stratitest level 5 (80–100 cm)		Stratitest level 6 (100–120 cm)		Stratitest level 7 (120–140 cm)		Stratitest level 8 (140–160 cm)	
	n	%	*n*	%	*n*	%	*n*	%	*n*	%	*n*	%
Cascabel Red-on-brown	0	0.0	1	0.5	1	0.3	0	0.0	0	0.0	0	0.0
Davis Red-on-white	1	2.3	0	0.0	0	0.0	0	0.0	0	0.0	0	0.0
Tres Alamos Red-on-brown	0	0.0	0	0.0	0	0.0	0	0.0	0	0.0	0	0.0
Gila White Slip	6	14.0	18	8.7	8	2.6	6	3.9	3	4.8	5	17.2
Cañada del Oro Red-on-brown	0	0.0	0	0.0	0	0.0	0	0.0	0	0.0	0	0.0
Gila Butte Red-on-buff	0	0.0	0	0.0	0	0.0	0	0.0	0	0.0	0	0.0
Santa Cruz Red-on-buff	0	0.0	1	0.5	2	0.6	0	0.0	0	0.0	0	0.0
Sacaton Red-on-buff	0	0.0	1	0.5	1	0.3	0	0.0	0	0.0	1	3.4
Casa Grande Red-on-buff	0	0.0	0	0.0	0	0.0	0	0.0	0	0.0	0	0.0
Rillito Red-on-brown	0	0.0	0	0.0	0	0.0	0	0.0	0	0.0	1	3.4
Rillito Red-on-brown (micaceous)	0	0.0	1	0.5	0	0.0	1	0.7	0	0.0	0	0.0
Rincon Red-on-brown	0	0.0	0	0.0	0	0.0	0	0.0	0	0.0	1	3.4
Pantano Red-on-brown	0	0.0	0	0.0	0	0.0	0	0.0	0	0.0	0	0.0
Tanque Verde Red-on-brown	0	0.0	0	0.0	0	0.0	0	0.0	0	0.0	0	0.0
Mimbres Black-on-white	0	0.0	0	0.0	0	0.0	0	0.0	0	0.0	0	0.0
Dos Cabezas Red-on-brown	1	2.3	0	0.0	0	0.0	0	0.0	0	0.0	0	0.0
Encinas Red-on-brown	0	0.0	0	0.0	0	0.0	0	0.0	0	0.0	0	0.0
Nogales Purple-on-red	0	0.0	0	0.0	0	0.0	0	0.0	0	0.0	0	0.0
Cerros Red-on-white	0	0.0	0	0.0	0	0.0	0	0.0	0	0.0	0	0.0

San Carlos Red-on-brown	0	0.0	0	0.0	0	0.0	0	0.0	0	0.0	0	0.0
San Carlos Red-on-white	0	0.0	0	0.0	0	0.0	0	0.0	0	0.0	0	0.0
El Paso Polychrome	0	0.0	1	0.5	0	0.0	0	0.0	0	0.0	0	0.0
Unidentified polychrome	0	0.0	0	0.0	0	0.0	0	0.0	0	0.0	0	0.0
Kayenta-like polychrome	0	0.0	0	0.0	0	0.0	0	0.0	0	0.0	0	0.0
Tusayan-like polychrome	0	0.0	0	0.0	0	0.0	0	0.0	0	0.0	0	0.0
Subtotal	*43*	*100.0*	*206*	*100.0*	*310*	*100.0*	*153*	*100.0*	*63*	*100.0*	*29*	*100.0*
Plain types												
Davis Plain	84	81.6	462	93.3	492	91.8	224	98.7	90	90.9	65	82.3
Davis Plain: Sobaipuri Coil Rim Variety	1	1.0	2	0.4	0	0.0	0	0.0	0	0.0	0	0.0
Belford Perforated Rim	1	1.0	7	1.4	7	1.3	0	0.0	1	1.0	0	0.0
Belford Perforated Rim (Sobaipuri Coil Rim)	0	0.0	3	0.6	1	0.2	0	0.0	0	0.0	0	0.0
Babocomari Plain	7	6.8	7	1.4	11	2.1	3	1.3	1	1.0	14	17.7
Redington Plain	9	8.7	8	1.6	11	2.1	0	0.0	5	5.1	0	0.0
Redington Smudged	0	0.0	5	1.0	12	2.2	0	0.0	1	1.0	0	0.0
Sacaton Buff	0	0.0	0	0.0	0	0.0	0	0.0	0	0.0	0	0.0
Gila Plain	0	0.0	0	0.0	0	0.0	0	0.0	1	1.0	0	0.0
Gila Smudged	0	0.0	0	0.0	1	0.2	0	0.0	0	0.0	0	0.0
San Carlos Brown	0	0.0	0	0.0	0	0.0	0	0.0	0	0.0	0	0.0
Slipped brown	0	0.0	1	0.2	0	0.0	0	0.0	0	0.0	0	0.0
Sosa Plain	0	0.0	0	0.0	1	0.2	0	0.0	0	0.0	0	0.0

(continued)

TABLE E.24 *(continued)*

	Stratitest level 3 (40–60 cm)		Stratitest level 4 (60–80 cm)		Stratitest level 5 (80–100 cm)		Stratitest level 6 (100–120 cm)		Stratitest level 7 (120–140 cm)		Stratitest level 8 (140–160 cm)	
	n	%	*n*	%	*n*	%	*n*	%	*n*	%	*n*	%
Whetstone Plain	0	0.0	0	0.0	0	0.0	0	0.0	0	0.0	0	0.0
Wingfield Plain	0	0.0	0	0.0	0	0.0	0	0.0	0	0.0	0	0.0
Fingernail indented	0	0.0	0	0.0	0	0.0	0	0.0	0	0.0	0	0.0
Incised plain	0	0.0	0	0.0	0	0.0	0	0.0	0	0.0	0	0.0
Tularosa Fillet Rim	0	0.0	0	0.0	0	0.0	0	0.0	0	0.0	0	0.0
Neck corrugated gray ware	1	1.0	0	0.0	0	0.0	0	0.0	0	0.0	0	0.0
Stucco ware?	0	0.0	0	0.0	0	0.0	0	0.0	0	0.0	0	0.0
Sandy Paste Perforated	0	0.0	0	0.0	0	0.0	0	0.0	0	0.0	0	0.0
Sosa Perforated	0	0.0	0	0.0	0	0.0	0	0.0	0	0.0	0	0.0
Subtotal	*103*	*100.0*	*495*	*100.0*	*536*	*100.0*	*227*	*100.0*	*99*	*100.0*	*79*	*100.0*
Red ware types												
Salt Red: Davis Variety	6	75.0	19	65.5	22	53.7	15	65.2	3	50.0	2	66.7
Salt Smudged: Davis Variety	0	0.0	6	20.7	9	22.0	1	4.3	0	0.0	0	0.0
Dragoon Red	0	0.0	4	13.8	6	14.6	3	13.0	1	16.7	1	33.3
Dragoon Red Smudged	0	0.0	0	0.0	2	4.9	1	4.3	0	0.0	0	0.0
Gila Red	1	12.5	0	0.0	2	4.9	3	13.0	2	33.3	0	0.0
Gila Smudged	0	0.0	0	0.0	0	0.0	0	0.0	0	0.0	0	0.0
San Carlos Red	0	0.0	0	0.0	0	0.0	0	0.0	0	0.0	0	0.0
Wingfield Red	1	12.5	0	0.0	0	0.0	0	0.0	0	0.0	0	0.0

Unidentified red #1	0	0.0	0	0.0	0	0.0	0	0.0	0	0.0	0	0.0
Unidentified red #2	0	0.0	0	0.0	0	0.0	0	0.0	0	0.0	0	0.0
Subtotal	*8*	*100.0*	*29*	*100.0*	*41*	*100.0*	*23*	*100.0*	*6*	*100.0*	*3*	*100.0*
Corrugated types												
Late plain corrugated	0	0.0	0	0.0	0	0.0	0	0.0	0	0.0	0	0.0
Late indented corrugated	0	0.0	1	100.0	4	100.0	0	0.0	0	0.0	1	100.0
Early indented corrugated, smudged interior	0	0.0	0	0.0	0	0.0	0	0.0	0	0.0	0	0.0
Obliterated corrugated	0	0.0	0	0.0	0	0.0	0	0.0	0	0.0	0	0.0
Neck corrugated	0	0.0	0	0.0	0	0.0	0	0.0	0	0.0	0	0.0
Red-slipped neck corrugated	0	0.0	0	0.0	0	0.0	0	0.0	0	0.0	0	0.0
Subtotal	*0*	*0.0*	*1*	*100.0*	*4*	*100.0*	*0*	*0.0*	*0*	*0.0*	*1*	*100.0*
Miscellaneous												
Porcelain	0	0.0	0	0.0	0	0.0	0	0.0	0	0.0	0	0.0
White glaze ware	0	0.0	0	0.0	0	0.0	0	0.0	0	0.0	0	0.0
Glass	0	0.0	0	0.0	0	0.0	0	0.0	0	0.0	0	0.0
Unidentified	0	0.0	1	100.0	2	100.0	0	0.0	0	0.0	0	0.0
Subtotal	*0*	*0.0*	*1*	*100.0*	*2*	*100.0*	*0*	*0.0*	*0*	*0.0*	*0*	*0.0*
Total	**154**		**732**		**893**		**403**		**168**		**112**	

TABLE E.25 Gerald's typological analysis of sherds from the floor and the floor features of the kiva at the Davis Ranch Site

	Stratitest level 9 (150–160 cm)		Floor contact		Ventilator (Feature A)		Fire Pit (Feature D)		Foot drum (Feature E)		Subfloor Pit (Feature F)	
	n	%	*n*	%	*n*	%	*n*	%	*n*	%	*n*	%
Painted types												
Gila Polychrome	58	84.1	5	38.5	47	94.0	3	75.0	5	5.8	9	56.3
Gila Black-on-red	0	0.0	0	0.0	0	0.0	0	0.0	1	1.2	1	6.3
Pinto Polychrome	2	2.9	0	0.0	1	2.0	0	0.0	0	0.0	0	0.0
Gila Polychrome (Pink Variant)	0	0.0	0	0.0	0	0.0	0	0.0	0	0.0	0	0.0
Gila-Tucson Polychrome	0	0.0	0	0.0	0	0.0	0	0.0	0	0.0	0	0.0
Tucson Polychrome	1	1.4	0	0.0	1	2.0	0	0.0	0	0.0	0	0.0
Tucson Black-on-red	0	0.0	1	7.7	0	0.0	0	0.0	0	0.0	5	31.3
Tonto Polychrome	0	0.0	0	0.0	0	0.0	0	0.0	0	0.0	0	0.0
Dragoon Red-on-brown	0	0.0	0	0.0	0	0.0	0	0.0	0	0.0	0	0.0
Cascabel Red-on-brown	4	5.8	0	0.0	0	0.0	0	0.0	0	0.0	1	6.3
Davis Red-on-white	0	0.0	0	0.0	1	2.0	0	0.0	0	0.0	0	0.0
Tres Alamos Red-on-brown	0	0.0	6	46.2	0	0.0	0	0.0	51	59.3	0	0.0
Gila White Slip	1	1.4	1	7.7	0	0.0	0	0.0	0	0.0	0	0.0
Cañada del Oro Red-on-brown	0	0.0	0	0.0	0	0.0	0	0.0	0	0.0	0	0.0
Gila Butte Red-on-buff	0	0.0	0	0.0	0	0.0	0	0.0	0	0.0	0	0.0
Santa Cruz Red-on-buff	1	1.4	0	0.0	0	0.0	0	0.0	1	1.2	0	0.0
Sacaton Red-on-buff	0	0.0	0	0.0	0	0.0	0	0.0	0	0.0	0	0.0
Casa Grande Red-on-buff	0	0.0	0	0.0	0	0.0	0	0.0	0	0.0	0	0.0

Rillito Red-on-brown	0	0.0	0	0.0	0	0.0	0	0.0	0	0.0	0	0.0
Rillito Red-on-brown (micaceous)	1	1.4	0	0.0	0	0.0	0	0.0	0	0.0	0	0.0
Rincon Red-on-brown	1	1.4	0	0.0	0	0.0	0	0.0	0	0.0	0	0.0
Pantano Red-on-brown	0	0.0	0	0.0	0	0.0	0	0.0	0	0.0	0	0.0
Tanque Verde Red-on-brown	0	0.0	0	0.0	0	0.0	0	0.0	0	0.0	0	0.0
Mimbres Black-on-white	0	0.0	0	0.0	0	0.0	0	0.0	0	0.0	0	0.0
Dos Cabezas Red-on-brown	0	0.0	0	0.0	0	0.0	0	0.0	0	0.0	0	0.0
Encinas Red-on-brown	0	0.0	0	0.0	0	0.0	0	0.0	0	0.0	0	0.0
Nogales Purple-on-red	0	0.0	0	0.0	0	0.0	0	0.0	0	0.0	0	0.0
San Carlos Red-on-brown	0	0.0	0	0.0	0	0.0	0	0.0	0	0.0	0	0.0
San Carlos Red-on-white	0	0.0	0	0.0	0	0.0	1	25.0	0	0.0	0	0.0
El Paso Polychrome	0	0.0	0	0.0	0	0.0	0	0.0	0	0.0	0	0.0
Unidentified polychrome	0	0.0	0	0.0	0	0.0	0	0.0	0	0.0	0	0.0
Kayenta-like polychrome	0	0.0	0	0.0	0	0.0	0	0.0	0	0.0	0	0.0
Tusayan-like polychrome	0	0.0	0	0.0	0	0.0	0	0.0	0	0.0	0	0.0
Subtotal	*69*	*100.0*	*13*	*100.0*	*50*	*100.0*	*4*	*100.0*	*58*	*67.4*	*16*	*100.0*
Plain types												
Davis Plain	223	79.4	43	91.5	91	83.5	13	92.9	72	91.1	53	91.4
Davis Plain: Sobaipuri Coil Rim Variety	0	0.0	0	0.0	0	0.0	0	0.0	0	0.0	0	0.0
Belford Perforated Rim	2	0.7	1	2.1	9	8.3	0	0.0	1	1.3	0	0.0
Belford Perforated Rim (Sobaipuri Coil Rim)	0	0.0	0	0.0	0	0.0	0	0.0	0	0.0	0	0.0
Babocomari Plain	32	11.4	1	2.1	5	4.6	1	7.1	5	6.3	0	0.0
Redington Plain	11	3.9	0	0.0	1	0.9	0	0.0	0	0.0	3	5.2

(continued)

TABLE E.25 *(continued)*

	Stratitest level 9 (150–160 cm)		Floor contact		Ventilator (Feature A)		Fire Pit (Feature D)		Foot drum (Feature E)		Subfloor Pit (Feature F)	
	n	%	*n*	%	*n*	%	*n*	%	*n*	%	*n*	%
Redington Smudged	3	1.1	2	4.3	2	1.8	0	0.0	0	0.0	1	1.7
Sacaton Buff	2	0.7	0	0.0	0	0.0	0	0.0	0	0.0	0	0.0
Gila Plain	4	1.4	0	0.0	1	0.9	0	0.0	1	1.3	1	1.7
Gila Smudged	0	0.0	0	0.0	0	0.0	0	0.0	0	0.0	0	0.0
San Carlos Brown	0	0.0	0	0.0	0	0.0	0	0.0	0	0.0	0	0.0
Slipped brown	4	1.4	0	0.0	0	0.0	0	0.0	0	0.0	0	0.0
Sosa Plain	0	0.0	0	0.0	0	0.0	0	0.0	0	0.0	0	0.0
Whetstone Plain	0	0.0	0	0.0	0	0.0	0	0.0	0	0.0	0	0.0
Wingfield Plain	0	0.0	0	0.0	0	0.0	0	0.0	0	0.0	0	0.0
Fingernail indented	0	0.0	0	0.0	0	0.0	0	0.0	0	0.0	0	0.0
Incised plain	0	0.0	0	0.0	0	0.0	0	0.0	0	0.0	0	0.0
Tularosa Fillet Rim	0	0.0	0	0.0	0	0.0	0	0.0	0	0.0	0	0.0
Neck corrugated gray ware	0	0.0	0	0.0	0	0.0	0	0.0	0	0.0	0	0.0
Stucco ware?	0	0.0	0	0.0	0	0.0	0	0.0	0	0.0	0	0.0
Sandy Paste Perforated	0	0.0	0	0.0	0	0.0	0	0.0	0	0.0	0	0.0
Sosa Perforated	0	0.0	0	0.0	0	0.0	0	0.0	0	0.0	0	0.0
Subtotal	*281*	*100.0*	*47*	*100.0*	*109*	*100.0*	*14*	*100.0*	*79*	*100.0*	*58*	*100.0*
Red ware types												
Salt Red: Davis Variety	11	50.0	3	75.0	2	40.0	1	100.0	0	0.0	5	83.3

Salt Smudged: Davis Variety	0	0.0	1	25.0	1	20.0	0	0.0	0	0.0	0	0.0
Dragoon Red	6	27.3	0	0.0	0	0.0	0	0.0	0	0.0	1	16.7
Dragoon Red Smudged	0	0.0	0	0.0	0	0.0	0	0.0	0	0.0	0	0.0
Gila Red	5	22.7	0	0.0	2	40.0	0	0.0	0	0.0	0	0.0
Gila Smudged	0	0.0	0	0.0	0	0.0	0	0.0	0	0.0	0	0.0
San Carlos Red	0	0.0	0	0.0	0	0.0	0	0.0	0	0.0	0	0.0
Wingfield Red	0	0.0	0	0.0	0	0.0	0	0.0	0	0.0	0	0.0
Unidentified red #1	0	0.0	0	0.0	0	0.0	0	0.0	0	0.0	0	0.0
Unidentified red #2	0	0.0	0	0.0	0	0.0	0	0.0	0	0.0	0	0.0
Subtotal	*22*	*100.0*	*4*	*100.0*	*5*	*100.0*	*1*	*100.0*	*0*	*0.0*	*6*	*100.0*
Corrugated types												
Late plain corrugated	1	100.0	0	0.0	0	0.0	0	0.0	0	0.0	0	0.0
Late indented corrugated	0	0.0	0	0.0	1	100.0	0	0.0	0	0.0	0	0.0
Early indented corrugated, smudged interior	0	0.0	0	0.0	0	0.0	0	0.0	0	0.0	0	0.0
Obliterated corrugated	0	0.0	0	0.0	0	0.0	0	0.0	0	0.0	0	0.0
Neck corrugated	0	0.0	0	0.0	0	0.0	0	0.0	0	0.0	0	0.0
Red-slipped neck corrugated	0	0.0	0	0.0	0	0.0	0	0.0	0	0.0	0	0.0
Subtotal	*1*	*100.0*	*0*	*0.0*	*1*	*100.0*	*0*	*0.0*	*0*	*0.0*	*0*	*0.0*
Miscellaneous												
Porcelain	0	0.0	0	0.0	0	0.0	0	0.0	0	0.0	0	0.0
White glaze ware	0	0.0	0	0.0	0	0.0	0	0.0	0	0.0	0	0.0
Unidentified	1	100.0	0	0.0	0	0.0	0	0.0	0	0.0	0	0.0
Subtotal	*1*	*100.0*	*0*	*0.0*	*0*	*0.0*	*0*	*0.0*	*0*	*0.0*	*0*	*0.0*
Total	**374**		**64**		**165**		**19**		**137**		**80**	

TABLE E.26 Gerald's typological analysis of sherds from the surface, the Northeast Trash, and Stratitest 1 at the Davis Ranch Site

	Surface		Northeast Trash		Stratitest 1									
					Level 1 (0–25 cm)		Level 2 (25–50 cm)		Level 3 (50–75 cm)		Level 4 (75–100 cm)		Level 5 (100–125 cm)	
	n	%	*n*	%	*n*	%	*n*	%	*n*	%	*n*	%	*n*	%
Painted types														
Gila Polychrome	103	63.2	72	32.4	26	72.2	13	34.2	5	21.7	4	44.4	1	50.0
Gila Black-on-red	2	1.2	25	11.3	0	0.0	0	0.0	0	0.0	0	0.0	0	0.0
Pinto Polychrome	1	0.6	6	2.7	1	2.8	0	0.0	0	0.0	0	0.0	0	0.0
Gila Polychrome (Pink Variant)	0	0.0	4	1.8	0	0.0	0	0.0	0	0.0	0	0.0	0	0.0
Gila-Tucson Polychrome	0	0.0	0	0.0	0	0.0	0	0.0	0	0.0	0	0.0	0	0.0
Tucson Polychrome	9	5.5	25	11.3	2	5.6	2	5.3	2	8.7	1	11.1	1	50.0
Tucson Black-on-red	10	6.1	21	9.5	2	5.6	3	7.9	0	0.0	0	0.0	0	0.0
Tonto Polychrome	3	1.8	1	0.5	1	2.8	1	2.6	1	4.3	0	0.0	0	0.0
Dragoon Red-on-brown	4	2.5	5	2.3	1	2.8	4	10.5	1	4.3	1	11.1	0	0.0
Cascabel Red-on-brown	1	0.6	3	1.4	0	0.0	7	18.4	2	8.7	0	0.0	0	0.0
Davis Red-on-white	2	1.2	2	0.9	0	0.0	0	0.0	1	4.3	1	11.1	0	0.0
Tres Alamos Red-on-brown	0	0.0	0	0.0	0	0.0	0	0.0	0	0.0	0	0.0	0	0.0
Gila White Slip	5	3.1	3	1.4	0	0.0	1	2.6	2	8.7	0	0.0	0	0.0
Cañada del Oro Red-on-brown	0	0.0	0	0.0	0	0.0	0	0.0	0	0.0	0	0.0	0	0.0
Gila Butte Red-on-buff	0	0.0	1	0.5	1	2.8	0	0.0	1	4.3	0	0.0	0	0.0
Santa Cruz Red-on-buff	3	1.8	17	7.7	0	0.0	4	10.5	5	21.7	1	11.1	0	0.0
Sacaton Red-on-buff	7	4.3	12	5.4	0	0.0	0	0.0	1	4.3	0	0.0	0	0.0
Casa Grande Red-on-buff	0	0.0	0	0.0	0	0.0	0	0.0	0	0.0	0	0.0	0	0.0
Rillito Red-on-brown	3	1.8	4	1.8	0	0.0	0	0.0	0	0.0	0	0.0	0	0.0
Rillito Red-on-brown (micaceous)	1	0.6	8	3.6	2	5.6	3	7.9	2	8.7	0	0.0	0	0.0

Rincon Red-on-brown	0	0.0	4	1.8	0	0.0	0	0.0	0	0.0	0	0.0	0	0.0
Pantano Red-on-brown	1	0.6	1	0.5	0	0.0	0	0.0	0	0.0	0	0.0	0	0.0
Tanque Verde Red-on-brown	1	0.6	0	0.0	0	0.0	0	0.0	0	0.0	1	11.1	0	0.0
Mimbres Black-on-white	0	0.0	0	0.0	0	0.0	0	0.0	0	0.0	0	0.0	0	0.0
Dos Cabezas Red-on-brown	1	0.6	2	0.9	0	0.0	0	0.0	0	0.0	0	0.0	0	0.0
Encinas Red-on-brown	1	0.6	4	1.8	0	0.0	0	0.0	0	0.0	0	0.0	0	0.0
Nogales Purple-on-red	1	0.6	0	0.0	0	0.0	0	0.0	0	0.0	0	0.0	0	0.0
Cerros Red-on-white	1	0.6	0	0.0	0	0.0	0	0.0	0	0.0	0	0.0	0	0.0
San Carlos Red-on-brown	1	0.6	0	0.0	0	0.0	0	0.0	0	0.0	0	0.0	0	0.0
San Carlos Red-on-white	0	0.0	0	0.0	0	0.0	0	0.0	0	0.0	0	0.0	0	0.0
El Paso Polychrome	0	0.0	1	0.5	0	0.0	0	0.0	0	0.0	0	0.0	0	0.0
Unidentified polychrome	0	0.0	0	0.0	0	0.0	0	0.0	0	0.0	0	0.0	0	0.0
Kayenta-like polychrome	2	1.2	0	0.0	0	0.0	0	0.0	0	0.0	0	0.0	0	0.0
Tusayan-like polychrome	0	0.0	1	0.5	0	0.0	0	0.0	0	0.0	0	0.0	0	0.0
Subtotal	*163*	*100.0*	*222*	*100.0*	*36*	*100.0*	*38*	*100.0*	*23*	*100.0*	*9*	*100.0*	*2*	*100.0*
Plain types														
Davis Plain	242	80.4	758	71.0	117	90.0	95	62.5	47	51.1	22	53.7	9	56.3
Davis Plain: Sobaipuri Coil Rim Variety	1	0.3	4	0.4	0	0.0	0	0.0	0	0.0	0	0.0	0	0.0
Belford Perforated Rim	4	1.3	5	0.5	2	1.5	0	0.0	0	0.0	0	0.0	0	0.0
Belford Perforated Rim (Sobaipuri Coil Rim)	0	0.0	0	0.0	0	0.0	0	0.0	0	0.0	0	0.0	0	0.0
Babocomari Plain	10	3.3	173	16.2	8	6.2	49	32.2	44	47.8	12	29.3	4	25.0
Redington Plain	32	10.6	55	5.2	3	2.3	1	0.7	1	1.1	4	9.8	1	6.3
Redington Smudged	7	2.3	27	2.5	0	0.0	3	2.0	0	0.0	0	0.0	1	6.3
Sacaton Buff	1	0.3	10	0.9	0	0.0	0	0.0	0	0.0	1	2.4	0	0.0

(continued)

TABLE E.26 *(continued)*

	Surface		Northeast Trash		Stratitest 1									
					Level 1 (0–25 cm)		Level 2 (25–50 cm)		Level 3 (50–75 cm)		Level 4 (75–100 cm)		Level 5 (100–125 cm)	
	n	%	*n*	%	*n*	%	*n*	%	*n*	%	*n*	%	*n*	%
Gila Plain	3	1.0	15	1.4	0	0.0	2	1.3	0	0.0	2	4.9	1	6.3
Gila Smudged	0	0.0	6	0.6	0	0.0	1	0.7	0	0.0	0	0.0	0	0.0
San Carlos Brown	1	0.3	8	0.7	0	0.0	0	0.0	0	0.0	0	0.0	0	0.0
Slipped brown	0	0.0	0	0.0	0	0.0	1	0.7	0	0.0	0	0.0	0	0.0
Sosa Plain	0	0.0	4	0.4	0	0.0	0	0.0	0	0.0	0	0.0	0	0.0
Whetstone Plain	0	0.0	0	0.0	0	0.0	0	0.0	0	0.0	0	0.0	0	0.0
Wingfield Plain	0	0.0	2	0.2	0	0.0	0	0.0	0	0.0	0	0.0	0	0.0
Fingernail indented	0	0.0	0	0.0	0	0.0	0	0.0	0	0.0	0	0.0	0	0.0
Incised plain	0	0.0	0	0.0	0	0.0	0	0.0	0	0.0	0	0.0	0	0.0
Tularosa Fillet Rim	0	0.0	0	0.0	0	0.0	0	0.0	0	0.0	0	0.0	0	0.0
Neck corrugated gray ware	0	0.0	0	0.0	0	0.0	0	0.0	0	0.0	0	0.0	0	0.0
Stucco ware?	0	0.0	0	0.0	0	0.0	0	0.0	0	0.0	0	0.0	0	0.0
Sandy Paste Perforated	0	0.0	0	0.0	0	0.0	0	0.0	0	0.0	0	0.0	0	0.0
Sosa Perforated	0	0.0	0	0.0	0	0.0	0	0.0	0	0.0	0	0.0	0	0.0
Subtotal	*301*	*100.0*	*1,067*	*100.0*	*130*	*100.0*	*152*	*100.0*	*92*	*100.0*	*41*	*100.0*	*16*	*100.0*
Red ware types														
Salt Red: Davis Variety	6	19.4	24	43.6	4	44.4	2	28.6	0	0.0	3	100.0	0	0.0
Salt Smudged: Davis Variety	2	6.5	3	5.5	0	0.0	0	0.0	0	0.0	0	0.0	0	0.0
Dragoon Red	18	58.1	17	30.9	3	33.3	3	42.9	3	100.0	0	0.0	0	0.0

Dragoon Red Smudged	0	0.0	0	0.0	0	0.0	1	14.3	0	0.0	0	0.0	0	0.0
Gila Red	0	0.0	3	5.5	0	0.0	0	0.0	0	0.0	0	0.0	1	33.3
Gila Smudged	2	6.5	4	7.3	1	11.1	1	14.3	0	0.0	0	0.0	1	33.3
San Carlos Red	3	9.7	0	0.0	0	0.0	0	0.0	0	0.0	0	0.0	0	0.0
Wingfield Red	0	0.0	0	0.0	1	11.1	0	0.0	0	0.0	0	0.0	0	0.0
Unidentified red #1	0	0.0	3	5.5	0	0.0	0	0.0	0	0.0	0	0.0	0	0.0
Unidentified red #2	0	0.0	1	1.8	0	0.0	0	0.0	0	0.0	0	0.0	1	33.3
Subtotal	*31*	*100.0*	*55*	*100.0*	*9*	*100.0*	*7*	*100.0*	*3*	*100.0*	*3*	*100.0*	*3*	*100.0*
Corrugated types														
Late plain corrugated	2	16.7	11	44.0	0	0.0	0	0.0	0	0.0	0	0.0	0	0.0
Late indented corrugated	3	25.0	10	40.0	0	0.0	1	100.0	0	0.0	0	0.0	0	0.0
Early indented corrugated, smudged interior	0	0.0	2	8.0	0	0.0	0	0.0	0	0.0	0	0.0	0	0.0
Obliterated corrugated	4	33.3	1	4.0	0	0.0	0	0.0	0	0.0	0	0.0	0	0.0
Neck corrugated	1	8.3	1	4.0	0	0.0	0	0.0	0	0.0	0	0.0	0	0.0
Red-slipped neck corrugated	2	16.7	0	0.0	1	100.0	0	0.0	0	0.0	0	0.0	0	0.0
Subtotal	*12*	*100.0*	*25*	*100.0*	*1*	*100.0*	*1*	*100.0*	*0*	*0.0*	*0*	*0.0*	*0*	*0.0*
Miscellaneous														
Porcelain	2	20.0	0	0.0	0	0.0	0	0.0	0	0.0	0	0.0	0	0.0
White glaze ware	4	40.0	0	0.0	0	0.0	0	0.0	0	0.0	0	0.0	0	0.0
Glass	1	10.0	0	0.0	0	0.0	0	0.0	0	0.0	0	0.0	0	0.0
Unidentified	3	30.0	5	100.0	0	0.0	0	0.0	0	0.0	0	0.0	0	0.0
Subtotal	*10*	*100.0*	*5*	*100.0*	*0*	*0.0*	*0*	*0.0*	*0*	*0.0*	*0*	*0.0*	*0*	*0.0*
Total	**517**		**1,374**		**176**		**198**		**118**		**53**		**21**	

TABLE E.27 Gerald's typological analysis of sherds from the cremations, the Ballcourt Test, Puddle Pit 2, and the Pit Ovens at the Davis Ranch Site

	Cremation 2		Cremation 3		Ballcourt Test		Puddle Pit 2		Pit Oven 1		Pit Oven 2		Pit Oven 3	
	n	%	*n*	%	*n*	%	*n*	%	*n*	%	*n*	%	*n*	%
Painted types														
Gila Polychrome	1	25.0	2	16.7	3	60.0	40	97.6	7	21.9	3	60.0	0	0.0
Gila Black-on-red	0	0.0	0	0.0	0	0.0	0	0.0	2	6.3	0	0.0	0	0.0
Pinto Polychrome	0	0.0	0	0.0	0	0.0	0	0.0	3	9.4	0	0.0	0	0.0
Gila Polychrome (Pink Variant)	0	0.0	0	0.0	0	0.0	0	0.0	0	0.0	0	0.0	0	0.0
Gila-Tucson Polychrome	0	0.0	0	0.0	0	0.0	0	0.0	0	0.0	0	0.0	0	0.0
Tucson Polychrome	0	0.0	0	0.0	0	0.0	1	2.4	10	31.3	0	0.0	0	0.0
Tucson Black-on-red	0	0.0	0	0.0	0	0.0	0	0.0	0	0.0	1	20.0	0	0.0
Tonto Polychrome	0	0.0	0	0.0	0	0.0	0	0.0	1	3.1	0	0.0	0	0.0
Dragoon Red-on-brown	1	25.0	4	33.3	0	0.0	0	0.0	1	3.1	0	0.0	0	0.0
Cascabel Red-on-brown	0	0.0	1	8.3	1	20.0	0	0.0	0	0.0	0	0.0	0	0.0
Davis Red-on-white	0	0.0	3	25.0	0	0.0	0	0.0	1	3.1	0	0.0	0	0.0
Tres Alamos Red-on-brown	0	0.0	0	0.0	0	0.0	0	0.0	0	0.0	0	0.0	0	0.0
Gila White Slip	0	0.0	0	0.0	0	0.0	0	0.0	1	3.1	0	0.0	0	0.0
Cañada del Oro Red-on-brown	0	0.0	0	0.0	0	0.0	0	0.0	0	0.0	0	0.0	0	0.0
Gila Butte Red-on-buff	0	0.0	0	0.0	0	0.0	0	0.0	0	0.0	0	0.0	0	0.0
Santa Cruz Red-on-buff	2	50.0	1	8.3	0	0.0	0	0.0	3	9.4	0	0.0	1	33.3
Sacaton Red-on-buff	0	0.0	1	8.3	1	20.0	0	0.0	0	0.0	0	0.0	1	33.3
Casa Grande Red-on-buff	0	0.0	0	0.0	0	0.0	0	0.0	0	0.0	0	0.0	0	0.0
Rillito Red-on-brown	0	0.0	0	0.0	0	0.0	0	0.0	0	0.0	0	0.0	0	0.0

Rillito Red-on-brown (micaceous)	0	0.0	0	0.0	0	0.0	0	0.0	0	0.0	0	0.0	0	0.0
Rincon Red-on-brown	0	0.0	0	0.0	0	0.0	0	0.0	1	3.1	0	0.0	0	0.0
Pantano Red-on-brown	0	0.0	0	0.0	0	0.0	0	0.0	1	3.1	0	0.0	0	0.0
Tanque Verde Red-on-brown	0	0.0	0	0.0	0	0.0	0	0.0	1	3.1	1	20.0	0	0.0
Mimbres Black-on-white	0	0.0	0	0.0	0	0.0	0	0.0	0	0.0	0	0.0	0	0.0
Dos Cabezas Red-on-brown	0	0.0	0	0.0	0	0.0	0	0.0	0	0.0	0	0.0	0	0.0
Encinas Red-on-brown	0	0.0	0	0.0	0	0.0	0	0.0	0	0.0	0	0.0	1	33.3
Nogales Purple-on-red	0	0.0	0	0.0	0	0.0	0	0.0	0	0.0	0	0.0	0	0.0
Cerros Red-on-white	0	0.0	0	0.0	0	0.0	0	0.0	0	0.0	0	0.0	0	0.0
San Carlos Red-on-brown	0	0.0	0	0.0	0	0.0	0	0.0	0	0.0	0	0.0	0	0.0
San Carlos Red-on-white	0	0.0	0	0.0	0	0.0	0	0.0	0	0.0	0	0.0	0	0.0
El Paso Polychrome	0	0.0	0	0.0	0	0.0	0	0.0	0	0.0	0	0.0	0	0.0
Unidentified polychrome	0	0.0	0	0.0	0	0.0	0	0.0	0	0.0	0	0.0	0	0.0
Kayenta-like polychrome	0	0.0	0	0.0	0	0.0	0	0.0	0	0.0	0	0.0	0	0.0
Tusayan-like polychrome	0	0.0	0	0.0	0	0.0	0	0.0	0	0.0	0	0.0	0	0.0
Subtotal	*4*	*100.0*	*12*	*100.0*	*5*	*100.0*	*41*	*100.0*	*32*	*100.0*	*5*	*100.0*	*3*	*100.0*
Plain types														
Davis Plain	5	22.7	16	47.1	17	45.9	69	97.2	109	62.6	9	24.3	10	30.3
Davis Plain: Sobaipuri Coil Rim Variety	0	0.0	0	0.0	0	0.0	0	0.0	0	0.0	0	0.0	0	0.0
Belford Perforated Rim	0	0.0	0	0.0	0	0.0	0	0.0	0	0.0	0	0.0	0	0.0
Belford Perforated Rim (Sobaipuri Coil Rim)	0	0.0	0	0.0	0	0.0	1	1.4	0	0.0	0	0.0	0	0.0
Babocomari Plain	15	68.2	15	44.1	13	35.1	0	0.0	45	25.9	18	48.6	15	45.5
Redington Plain	0	0.0	0	0.0	2	5.4	1	1.4	9	5.2	4	10.8	1	3.0

(*continued*)

TABLE E.27 *(continued)*

	Cremation 2		Cremation 3		Ballcourt Test		Puddle Pit 2		Pit Oven 1		Pit Oven 2		Pit Oven 3	
	n	%	*n*	%	*n*	%	*n*	%	*n*	%	*n*	%	*n*	%
Redington Smudged	0	0.0	0	0.0	2	5.4	0	0.0	7	4.0	0	0.0	0	0.0
Sacaton Buff	1	4.5	3	8.8	0	0.0	0	0.0	0	0.0	0	0.0	0	0.0
Gila Plain	1	4.5	0	0.0	3	8.1	0	0.0	2	1.1	3	8.1	7	21.2
Gila Smudged	0	0.0	0	0.0	0	0.0	0	0.0	0	0.0	0	0.0	0	0.0
San Carlos Brown	0	0.0	0	0.0	0	0.0	0	0.0	1	0.6	0	0.0	0	0.0
Slipped brown	0	0.0	0	0.0	0	0.0	0	0.0	0	0.0	0	0.0	0	0.0
Sosa Plain	0	0.0	0	0.0	0	0.0	0	0.0	0	0.0	0	0.0	0	0.0
Whetstone Plain	0	0.0	0	0.0	0	0.0	0	0.0	0	0.0	0	0.0	0	0.0
Wingfield Plain	0	0.0	0	0.0	0	0.0	0	0.0	0	0.0	0	0.0	0	0.0
Fingernail indented	0	0.0	0	0.0	0	0.0	0	0.0	0	0.0	0	0.0	0	0.0
Incised plain	0	0.0	0	0.0	0	0.0	0	0.0	0	0.0	0	0.0	0	0.0
Tularosa Fillet Rim	0	0.0	0	0.0	0	0.0	0	0.0	0	0.0	0	0.0	0	0.0
Neck corrugated gray ware	0	0.0	0	0.0	0	0.0	0	0.0	0	0.0	0	0.0	0	0.0
Stucco ware?	0	0.0	0	0.0	0	0.0	0	0.0	1	0.6	0	0.0	0	0.0
Sandy Paste Perforated	0	0.0	0	0.0	0	0.0	0	0.0	0	0.0	0	0.0	0	0.0
Sosa Perforated	0	0.0	0	0.0	0	0.0	0	0.0	0	0.0	0	0.0	0	0.0
Subtotal	*22*	*100.0*	*34*	*100.0*	*37*	*100.0*	*71*	*100.0*	*174*	*100.0*	*34*	*91.9*	*33*	*100.0*
Red ware types														
Salt Red: Davis Variety	0	0.0	0	0.0	2	40.0	0	0.0	3	23.1	3	75.0	0	0.0
Salt Smudged: Davis Variety	0	0.0	1	50.0	1	20.0	0	0.0	0	0.0	0	0.0	0	0.0

Dragoon Red	0	0.0	1	50.0	1	20.0	0	0.0	7	53.8	0	0.0	1	100.0
Dragoon Red Smudged	0	0.0	0	0.0	0	0.0	0	0.0	0	0.0	0	0.0	0	0.0
Gila Red	0	0.0	0	0.0	1	20.0	0	0.0	0	0.0	0	0.0	0	0.0
Gila Smudged	0	0.0	0	0.0	0	0.0	0	0.0	0	0.0	0	0.0	0	0.0
San Carlos Red	0	0.0	0	0.0	0	0.0	0	0.0	3	23.1	0	0.0	0	0.0
Wingfield Red	0	0.0	0	0.0	0	0.0	0	0.0	0	0.0	0	0.0	0	0.0
Unidentified red #1	0	0.0	0	0.0	0	0.0	0	0.0	0	0.0	1	25.0	0	0.0
Unidentified red #2	0	0.0	0	0.0	0	0.0	0	0.0	0	0.0	0	0.0	0	0.0
Subtotal	*0*	*0.0*	*2*	*100.0*	*5*	*100.0*	*0*	*0.0*	*13*	*100.0*	*4*	*100.0*	*1*	*100.0*
Corrugated types														
Late plain corrugated	0	0.0	0	0.0	0	0.0	0	0.0	3	50.0	10	71.4	0	0.0
Late indented corrugated	0	0.0	0	0.0	0	0.0	1	100.0	3	50.0	4	28.6	0	0.0
Early indented corrugated, smudged interior	0	0.0	0	0.0	0	0.0	0	0.0	0	0.0	0	0.0	0	0.0
Obliterated corrugated	0	0.0	0	0.0	0	0.0	0	0.0	0	0.0	0	0.0	0	0.0
Neck corrugated	0	0.0	0	0.0	0	0.0	0	0.0	0	0.0	0	0.0	0	0.0
Red-slipped neck corrugated	0	0.0	0	0.0	0	0.0	0	0.0	0	0.0	0	0.0	0	0.0
Subtotal	*0*	*0.0*	*0*	*0.0*	*0*	*0.0*	*1*	*100.0*	*6*	*100.0*	*14*	*100.0*	*0*	*0.0*
Miscellaneous														
Porcelain	0	0.0	0	0.0	0	0.0	0	0.0	0	0.0	0	0.0	0	0.0
White glaze ware	0	0.0	0	0.0	0	0.0	0	0.0	0	0.0	0	0.0	0	0.0
Glass	0	0.0	0	0.0	0	0.0	0	0.0	0	0.0	0	0.0	0	0.0
Unidentified	0	0.0	0	0.0	0	0.0	0	0.0	5	100.0	1	100.0	0	0.0
Subtotal	*0*	*0.0*	*0*	*0.0*	*0*	*0.0*	*0*	*0.0*	*5*	*100.0*	*1*	*100.0*	*0*	*0.0*
Total	**26**		**48**		**47**		**113**		**230**		**58**		**37**	

TABLE E.28 Gerald's typological analysis of sherds from strip tests and miscellaneous trenches at the Davis Ranch Site

	Strip tests				Miscellaneous trenches					
	6S-0		5–9N 8–14E		15W 12–13N		1S 20–14E		10N 14–20E	
	n	%	*n*	%	*n*	%	*n*	%	*n*	%
Painted types										
Gila Polychrome	5	100.0	25	65.8	6	75.0	56	62.2	2	8.7
Gila Black-on-red	0	0.0	1	2.6	0	0.0	5	5.6	2	8.7
Pinto Polychrome	0	0.0	1	2.6	0	0.0	1	1.1	0	0.0
Gila Polychrome (Pink Variant)	0	0.0	0	0.0	0	0.0	0	0.0	0	0.0
Gila-Tucson Polychrome	0	0.0	0	0.0	0	0.0	0	0.0	0	0.0
Tucson Polychrome	0	0.0	0	0.0	0	0.0	4	4.4	1	4.3
Tucson Black-on-red	0	0.0	1	2.6	0	0.0	5	5.6	1	4.3
Tonto Polychrome	0	0.0	1	2.6	2	25.0	0	0.0	0	0.0
Dragoon Red-on-brown	0	0.0	0	0.0	0	0.0	0	0.0	6	26.1
Cascabel Red-on-brown	0	0.0	0	0.0	0	0.0	1	1.1	2	8.7
Davis Red-on-white	0	0.0	0	0.0	0	0.0	0	0.0	0	0.0
Tres Alamos Red-on-brown	0	0.0	0	0.0	0	0.0	0	0.0	0	0.0
Gila White Slip	0	0.0	1	2.6	0	0.0	0	0.0	0	0.0
Cañada del Oro Red-on-brown	0	0.0	0	0.0	0	0.0	0	0.0	0	0.0
Gila Butte Red-on-buff	0	0.0	0	0.0	0	0.0	0	0.0	0	0.0
Santa Cruz Red-on-buff	0	0.0	2	5.3	0	0.0	6	6.7	2	8.7
Sacaton Red-on-buff	0	0.0	1	2.6	0	0.0	1	1.1	2	8.7
Casa Grande Red-on-buff	0	0.0	0	0.0	0	0.0	0	0.0	0	0.0

Rillito Red-on-brown	0	0.0	1	2.6	0	0.0	1	1.1	0	0.0
Rillito Red-on-brown (micaceous)	0	0.0	1	2.6	0	0.0	1	1.1	4	17.4
Rincon Red-on-brown	0	0.0	2	5.3	0	0.0	0	0.0	1	4.3
Pantano Red-on-brown	0	0.0	0	0.0	0	0.0	1	1.1	0	0.0
Tanque Verde Red-on-brown	0	0.0	1	2.6	0	0.0	2	2.2	0	0.0
Mimbres Black-on-white	0	0.0	0	0.0	0	0.0	0	0.0	0	0.0
Dos Cabezas Red-on-brown	0	0.0	0	0.0	0	0.0	0	0.0	0	0.0
Encinas Red-on-brown	0	0.0	0	0.0	0	0.0	2	2.2	0	0.0
Nogales Purple-on-red	0	0.0	0	0.0	0	0.0	0	0.0	0	0.0
Cerros Red-on-white	0	0.0	0	0.0	0	0.0	0	0.0	0	0.0
San Carlos Red-on-brown	0	0.0	0	0.0	0	0.0	0	0.0	0	0.0
San Carlos Red-on-white	0	0.0	0	0.0	0	0.0	0	0.0	0	0.0
El Paso Polychrome	0	0.0	0	0.0	0	0.0	0	0.0	0	0.0
Unidentified polychrome	0	0.0	0	0.0	0	0.0	0	0.0	0	0.0
Kayenta-like polychrome	0	0.0	0	0.0	0	0.0	0	0.0	0	0.0
Tusayan-like polychrome	0	0.0	0	0.0	0	0.0	4	4.4	0	0.0
Subtotal	*5*	*100.0*	*38*	*100.0*	*8*	*100.0*	*90*	*100.0*	*23*	*100.0*
Plain types										
Davis Plain	8	100.0	71	68.9	45	90.0	355	90.1	97	71.3
Davis Plain: Sobaipuri Coil Rim Variety	0	0.0	0	0.0	0	0.0	3	0.8	2	1.5
Belford Perforated Rim	0	0.0	0	0.0	0	0.0	2	0.5	1	0.7
Belford Perforated Rim (Sobaipuri Coil Rim)	0	0.0	0	0.0	0	0.0	0	0.0	0	0.0
Babocomari Plain	0	0.0	28	27.2	4	8.0	18	4.6	21	15.4

(*continued*)

TABLE E.28 *(continued)*

	Strip tests				Miscellaneous trenches					
	6S-0		5–9N 8–14E		15W 12–13N		1S 20–14E		10N 14–20E	
	n	%	*n*	%	*n*	%	*n*	%	*n*	%
Redington Plain	0	0.0	2	1.9	0	0.0	2	0.5	7	5.1
Redington Smudged	0	0.0	0	0.0	1	2.0	7	1.8	0	0.0
Sacaton Buff	0	0.0	1	1.0	0	0.0	0	0.0	0	0.0
Gila Plain	0	0.0	1	1.0	0	0.0	5	1.3	7	5.1
Gila Smudged	0	0.0	0	0.0	0	0.0	0	0.0	1	0.7
San Carlos Brown	0	0.0	0	0.0	0	0.0	0	0.0	0	0.0
Slipped brown	0	0.0	0	0.0	0	0.0	2	0.5	0	0.0
Sosa Plain	0	0.0	0	0.0	0	0.0	0	0.0	0	0.0
Whetstone Plain	0	0.0	0	0.0	0	0.0	0	0.0	0	0.0
Wingfield Plain	0	0.0	0	0.0	0	0.0	0	0.0	0	0.0
Fingernail indented	0	0.0	0	0.0	0	0.0	0	0.0	0	0.0
Incised plain	0	0.0	0	0.0	0	0.0	0	0.0	0	0.0
Tularosa Fillet Rim	0	0.0	0	0.0	0	0.0	0	0.0	0	0.0
Neck corrugated gray ware	0	0.0	0	0.0	0	0.0	0	0.0	0	0.0
Stucco ware?	0	0.0	0	0.0	0	0.0	0	0.0	0	0.0
Sandy Paste Perforated	0	0.0	0	0.0	0	0.0	0	0.0	0	0.0
Sosa Perforated	0	0.0	0	0.0	0	0.0	0	0.0	0	0.0
Subtotal	*8*	*100.0*	*103*	*100.0*	*50*	*100.0*	*394*	*100.0*	*136*	*100.0*
Red ware types										
Salt Red: Davis Variety	0	0.0	1	12.5	0	0.0	10	34.5	2	33.3
Salt Smudged: Davis Variety	0	0.0	0	0.0	0	0.0	5	17.2	0	0.0

Dragoon Red	0	0.0	6	75.0	0	0.0	9	31.0	2	33.3
Dragoon Red Smudged	0	0.0	0	0.0	1	100.0	1	3.4	0	0.0
Gila Red	0	0.0	1	12.5	0	0.0	0	0.0	2	33.3
Gila Smudged	0	0.0	0	0.0	0	0.0	0	0.0	0	0.0
San Carlos Red	0	0.0	0	0.0	0	0.0	3	10.3	0	0.0
Wingfield Red	0	0.0	0	0.0	0	0.0	1	3.4	0	0.0
Unidentified red #1	0	0.0	0	0.0	0	0.0	0	0.0	0	0.0
Unidentified red #2	0	0.0	0	0.0	0	0.0	0	0.0	0	0.0
Subtotal	*0*	*0.0*	*8*	*100.0*	*1*	*100.0*	*29*	*100.0*	*6*	*100.0*
Corrugated types										
Late plain corrugated	0	0.0	1	100.0	0	0.0	2	66.7	1	33.3
Late indented corrugated	0	0.0	0	0.0	0	0.0	0	0.0	0	0.0
Early indented corrugated, smudged interior	0	0.0	0	0.0	0	0.0	0	0.0	1	33.3
Obliterated corrugated	0	0.0	0	0.0	0	0.0	0	0.0	0	0.0
Neck corrugated	0	0.0	0	0.0	0	0.0	0	0.0	1	33.3
Red-slipped neck corrugated	0	0.0	0	0.0	0	0.0	1	33.3	0	0.0
Subtotal	*0*	*0.0*	*1*	*100.0*	*0*	*0.0*	*3*	*100.0*	*3*	*100.0*
Miscellaneous										
Porcelain	0	0.0	0	0.0	0	0.0	0	0.0	0	0.0
White glaze ware	0	0.0	0	0.0	0	0.0	0	0.0	0	0.0
Glass	0	0.0	0	0.0	0	0.0	0	0.0	0	0.0
Unidentified	0	0.0	2	100.0	0	0.0	1	100.0	0	0.0
Subtotal	*0*	*0.0*	*2*	*100.0*	*0*	*0.0*	*1*	*100.0*	*0*	*0.0*
Total	**13**		**152**		**59**		**517**		**168**	

TABLE E.29 Gerald's typological analysis of sherds from north/east trenches at the Davis Ranch Site

	6N					
	7E		8–10E		7N 12E	
	n	%	*n*	%	*n*	%
Painted types						
Gila Polychrome	2	33.3	10	83.3	2	100.0
Gila Black-on-red	0	0.0	1	8.3	0	0.0
Pinto Polychrome	0	0.0	1	8.3	0	0.0
Gila Polychrome (Pink Variant)	0	0.0	0	0.0	0	0.0
Gila-Tucson Polychrome	0	0.0	0	0.0	0	0.0
Tucson Polychrome	1	16.7	0	0.0	0	0.0
Tucson Black-on-red	1	16.7	0	0.0	0	0.0
Tonto Polychrome	0	0.0	0	0.0	0	0.0
Dragoon Red-on-brown	0	0.0	0	0.0	0	0.0
Cascabel Red-on-brown	0	0.0	0	0.0	0	0.0
Davis Red-on-white	0	0.0	0	0.0	0	0.0
Tres Alamos Red-on-brown	0	0.0	0	0.0	0	0.0
Gila White Slip	0	0.0	0	0.0	0	0.0
Cañada del Oro Red-on-brown	0	0.0	0	0.0	0	0.0
Gila Butte Red-on-buff	0	0.0	0	0.0	0	0.0
Santa Cruz Red-on-buff	0	0.0	0	0.0	0	0.0
Sacaton Red-on-buff	0	0.0	0	0.0	0	0.0
Casa Grande Red-on-buff	0	0.0	0	0.0	0	0.0
Rillito Red-on-brown	1	16.7	0	0.0	0	0.0
Rillito Red-on-brown (micaceous)	0	0.0	0	0.0	0	0.0
Rincon Red-on-brown	1	16.7	0	0.0	0	0.0
Pantano Red-on-brown	0	0.0	0	0.0	0	0.0
Tanque Verde Red-on-brown	0	0.0	0	0.0	0	0.0
Mimbres Black-on-white	0	0.0	0	0.0	0	0.0
Dos Cabezas Red-on-brown	0	0.0	0	0.0	0	0.0
Encinas Red-on-brown	0	0.0	0	0.0	0	0.0
Nogales Purple-on-red	0	0.0	0	0.0	0	0.0
Cerros Red-on-white	0	0.0	0	0.0	0	0.0
San Carlos Red-on-brown	0	0.0	0	0.0	0	0.0

10N								11N 16–17E		15–16N 25–28E	
0–7E		21–26E		31–35E		36–45E					
n	%	*n*	%	*n*	%	*n*	%	*n*	%	*n*	%
30	85.7	12	42.9	0	0.0	6	21.4	1	3.4	19	52.8
0	0.0	2	7.1	0	0.0	2	7.1	1	3.4	0	0.0
0	0.0	1	3.6	0	0.0	0	0.0	0	0.0	1	2.8
1	2.9	0	0.0	0	0.0	1	3.6	0	0.0	1	2.8
1	2.9	0	0.0	0	0.0	0	0.0	0	0.0	0	0.0
0	0.0	2	7.1	0	0.0	1	3.6	0	0.0	2	5.6
0	0.0	3	10.7	0	0.0	2	7.1	0	0.0	5	13.9
1	2.9	0	0.0	0	0.0	0	0.0	0	0.0	0	0.0
1	2.9	0	0.0	0	0.0	3	10.7	1	3.4	1	2.8
0	0.0	0	0.0	0	0.0	1	3.6	5	17.2	0	0.0
0	0.0	0	0.0	0	0.0	1	3.6	0	0.0	0	0.0
0	0.0	0	0.0	0	0.0	0	0.0	0	0.0	0	0.0
0	0.0	0	0.0	0	0.0	0	0.0	0	0.0	1	2.8
0	0.0	0	0.0	0	0.0	0	0.0	0	0.0	0	0.0
0	0.0	0	0.0	0	0.0	0	0.0	0	0.0	0	0.0
0	0.0	0	0.0	0	0.0	2	7.1	10	34.5	2	5.6
0	0.0	0	0.0	0	0.0	2	7.1	3	10.3	1	2.8
0	0.0	0	0.0	0	0.0	0	0.0	0	0.0	0	0.0
0	0.0	2	7.1	0	0.0	1	3.6	0	0.0	0	0.0
0	0.0	2	7.1	0	0.0	2	7.1	1	3.4	0	0.0
0	0.0	0	0.0	0	0.0	2	7.1	4	13.8	2	5.6
0	0.0	0	0.0	0	0.0	0	0.0	1	3.4	0	0.0
1	2.9	1	3.6	0	0.0	0	0.0	1	3.4	1	2.8
0	0.0	0	0.0	0	0.0	1	3.6	0	0.0	0	0.0
0	0.0	1	3.6	0	0.0	0	0.0	0	0.0	0	0.0
0	0.0	1	3.6	0	0.0	1	3.6	1	3.4	0	0.0
0	0.0	0	0.0	0	0.0	0	0.0	0	0.0	0	0.0
0	0.0	0	0.0	0	0.0	0	0.0	0	0.0	0	0.0
0	0.0	1	3.6	0	0.0	0	0.0	0	0.0	0	0.0

(continued)

TABLE E.29 *(continued)*

	6N					
	7E		8–10E		7N 12E	
	n	%	*n*	%	*n*	%
San Carlos Red-on-white	0	0.0	0	0.0	0	0.0
El Paso Polychrome	0	0.0	0	0.0	0	0.0
Unidentified polychrome	0	0.0	0	0.0	0	0.0
Kayenta-like polychrome	0	0.0	0	0.0	0	0.0
Tusayan-like polychrome	0	0.0	0	0.0	0	0.0
Subtotal	*6*	*100.0*	*12*	*100.0*	*2*	*100.0*
Plain types						
Davis Plain	28	93.3	12	37.5	37	100.0
Davis Plain: Sobaipuri Coil Rim Variety	0	0.0	0	0.0	0	0.0
Belford Perforated Rim	0	0.0	0	0.0	0	0.0
Belford Perforated Rim (Sobaipuri Coil Rim)	0	0.0	0	0.0	0	0.0
Babocomari Plain	2	6.7	19	59.4	0	0.0
Redington Plain	0	0.0	1	3.1	0	0.0
Redington Smudged	0	0.0	0	0.0	0	0.0
Sacaton Buff	0	0.0	0	0.0	0	0.0
Gila Plain	0	0.0	0	0.0	0	0.0
Gila Smudged	0	0.0	0	0.0	0	0.0
San Carlos Brown	0	0.0	0	0.0	0	0.0
Slipped brown	0	0.0	0	0.0	0	0.0
Sosa Plain	0	0.0	0	0.0	0	0.0
Whetstone Plain	0	0.0	0	0.0	0	0.0
Wingfield Plain	0	0.0	0	0.0	0	0.0
Fingernail indented	0	0.0	0	0.0	0	0.0
Incised plain	0	0.0	0	0.0	0	0.0
Tularosa Fillet Rim	0	0.0	0	0.0	0	0.0
Neck corrugated gray ware	0	0.0	0	0.0	0	0.0
Stucco ware?	0	0.0	0	0.0	0	0.0
Sandy Paste Perforated	0	0.0	0	0.0	0	0.0
Sosa Perforated	0	0.0	0	0.0	0	0.0
Subtotal	*30*	*100.0*	*32*	*100.0*	*37*	*100.0*

10N								11N 16–17E		15–16N 25–28E	
0–7E		21–26E		31–35E		36–45E					
n	%	*n*	%	*n*	%	*n*	%	*n*	%	*n*	%
0	0.0	0	0.0	0	0.0	0	0.0	0	0.0	0	0.0
0	0.0	0	0.0	0	0.0	0	0.0	0	0.0	0	0.0
0	0.0	0	0.0	0	0.0	0	0.0	0	0.0	0	0.0
0	0.0	0	0.0	0	0.0	0	0.0	0	0.0	0	0.0
0	0.0	0	0.0	0	0.0	0	0.0	0	0.0	0	0.0
35	*100.0*	*28*	*100.0*	*0*	*0.0*	*28*	*100.0*	*29*	*100.0*	*36*	*100.0*
47	46.1	54	50.9	6	85.7	20	18.3	14	20.6	163	81.1
0	0.0	0	0.0	0	0.0	0	0.0	1	1.5	1	0.5
1	1.0	0	0.0	0	0.0	0	0.0	0	0.0	0	0.0
0	0.0	0	0.0	0	0.0	0	0.0	0	0.0	0	0.0
36	35.3	42	39.6	0	0.0	70	64.2	31	45.6	26	12.9
4	3.9	4	3.8	0	0.0	4	3.7	3	4.4	6	3.0
2	2.0	1	0.9	1	14.3	0	0.0	0	0.0	1	0.5
1	1.0	0	0.0	0	0.0	4	3.7	4	5.9	0	0.0
9	8.8	4	3.8	0	0.0	11	10.1	14	20.6	3	1.5
1	1.0	0	0.0	0	0.0	0	0.0	1	1.5	0	0.0
0	0.0	1	0.9	0	0.0	0	0.0	0	0.0	0	0.0
0	0.0	0	0.0	0	0.0	0	0.0	0	0.0	0	0.0
0	0.0	0	0.0	0	0.0	0	0.0	0	0.0	1	0.5
0	0.0	0	0.0	0	0.0	0	0.0	0	0.0	0	0.0
1	1.0	0	0.0	0	0.0	0	0.0	0	0.0	0	0.0
0	0.0	0	0.0	0	0.0	0	0.0	0	0.0	0	0.0
0	0.0	0	0.0	0	0.0	0	0.0	0	0.0	0	0.0
0	0.0	0	0.0	0	0.0	0	0.0	0	0.0	0	0.0
0	0.0	0	0.0	0	0.0	0	0.0	0	0.0	0	0.0
0	0.0	0	0.0	0	0.0	0	0.0	0	0.0	0	0.0
0	0.0	0	0.0	0	0.0	0	0.0	0	0.0	0	0.0
0	0.0	0	0.0	0	0.0	0	0.0	0	0.0	0	0.0
102	*100.0*	*106*	*100.0*	*7*	*100.0*	*109*	*100.0*	*68*	*100.0*	*201*	*100.0*

(*continued*)

TABLE E.29 *(continued)*

	6N					
	7E		8–10E		7N 12E	
	n	%	*n*	%	*n*	%
Red ware types						
Salt Red: Davis Variety	1	50.0	0	0.0	0	0.0
Salt Smudged: Davis Variety	0	0.0	0	0.0	0	0.0
Dragoon Red	1	50.0	0	0.0	0	0.0
Dragoon Red Smudged	0	0.0	0	0.0	0	0.0
Gila Red	0	0.0	0	0.0	0	0.0
Gila Smudged	0	0.0	0	0.0	0	0.0
San Carlos Red	0	0.0	0	0.0	0	0.0
Wingfield Red	0	0.0	0	0.0	0	0.0
Unidentified red #1	0	0.0	0	0.0	0	0.0
Unidentified red #2	0	0.0	0	0.0	0	0.0
Subtotal	*2*	*100.0*	*0*	*0.0*	*0*	*0.0*
Corrugated types						
Late plain corrugated	0	0.0	0	0.0	0	0.0
Late indented corrugated	0	0.0	1	100.0	0	0.0
Early indented corrugated, smudged interior	0	0.0	0	0.0	0	0.0
Obliterated corrugated	0	0.0	0	0.0	0	0.0
Neck corrugated	0	0.0	0	0.0	0	0.0
Red-slipped neck corrugated	0	0.0	0	0.0	0	0.0
Subtotal	*0*	*0.0*	*1*	*100.0*	*0*	*0.0*
Miscellaneous						
Porcelain	0	0.0	0	0.0	0	0.0
White glaze ware	0	0.0	0	0.0	0	0.0
Glass	0	0.0	0	0.0	0	0.0
Unidentified	0	0.0	0	0.0	0	0.0
Subtotal	*0*	*0.0*	*0*	*0.0*	*0*	*0.0*
Total	**38**		**45**		**39**	

10N								11N 16–17E		15–16N 25–28E	
0–7E		21–26E		31–35E		36–45E					
n	%	*n*	%	*n*	%	*n*	%	*n*	%	*n*	%
6	60.0	4	50.0	0	0.0	3	50.0	2	25.0	14	66.7
3	30.0	0	0.0	0	0.0	0	0.0	2	25.0	2	9.5
1	10.0	4	50.0	0	0.0	2	33.3	1	12.5	2	9.5
0	0.0	0	0.0	0	0.0	0	0.0	0	0.0	0	0.0
0	0.0	0	0.0	1	50.0	0	0.0	1	12.5	1	4.8
0	0.0	0	0.0	1	50.0	0	0.0	1	12.5	1	4.8
0	0.0	0	0.0	0	0.0	0	0.0	0	0.0	0	0.0
0	0.0	0	0.0	0	0.0	0	0.0	0	0.0	0	0.0
0	0.0	0	0.0	0	0.0	1	16.7	1	12.5	0	0.0
0	0.0	0	0.0	0	0.0	0	0.0	0	0.0	1	4.8
10	*100.0*	*8*	*100.0*	*2*	*100.0*	*6*	*100.0*	*8*	*100.0*	*21*	*100.0*
0	0.0	3	27.3	0	0.0	0	0.0	1	33.3	7	87.5
1	100.0	7	63.6	0	0.0	1	100.0	2	66.7	1	12.5
0	0.0	0	0.0	0	0.0	0	0.0	0	0.0	0	0.0
0	0.0	1	9.1	0	0.0	0	0.0	0	0.0	0	0.0
0	0.0	0	0.0	0	0.0	0	0.0	0	0.0	0	0.0
0	0.0	0	0.0	0	0.0	0	0.0	0	0.0	0	0.0
1	*100.0*	*11*	*100.0*	*0*	*0.0*	*1*	*100.0*	*3*	*100.0*	*8*	*100.0*
0	0.0	0	0.0	0	0.0	0	0.0	0	0.0	0	0.0
0	0.0	0	0.0	0	0.0	0	0.0	0	0.0	0	0.0
0	0.0	0	0.0	0	0.0	0	0.0	0	0.0	0	0.0
0	0.0	0	0.0	0	0.0	0	0.0	0	0.0	0	0.0
0	*0.0*	*0*	*0.0*	*0*	*0.0*	*0*	*0.0*	*0*	*0.0*	*0*	*0.0*
148		**153**		**9**		**144**		**108**		**266**	

TABLE E.30 Gerald's typological analysis of sherds from east/north trenches at the Davis Ranch Site

	26E 0–10N		35E 0–9N		44E 16–17N	
	n	%	*n*	%	*n*	%
Painted types						
Gila Polychrome	22	62.9	0	0.0	0	0.0
Gila Black-on-red	1	2.9	0	0.0	0	0.0
Pinto Polychrome	0	0.0	0	0.0	0	0.0
Gila Polychrome (Pink Variant)	0	0.0	0	0.0	0	0.0
Gila-Tucson Polychrome	0	0.0	0	0.0	0	0.0
Tucson Polychrome	1	2.9	0	0.0	0	0.0
Tucson Black-on-red	3	8.6	0	0.0	0	0.0
Tonto Polychrome	0	0.0	0	0.0	0	0.0
Dragoon Red-on-brown	1	2.9	0	0.0	0	0.0
Cascabel Red-on-brown	1	2.9	0	0.0	1	12.5
Davis Red-on-white	0	0.0	0	0.0	3	37.5
Tres Alamos Red-on-brown	0	0.0	0	0.0	0	0.0
Gila White Slip	0	0.0	0	0.0	0	0.0
Cañada del Oro Red-on-brown	0	0.0	0	0.0	0	0.0
Gila Butte Red-on-buff	0	0.0	0	0.0	0	0.0
Santa Cruz Red-on-buff	0	0.0	0	0.0	2	25.0
Sacaton Red-on-buff	4	11.4	0	0.0	2	25.0
Casa Grande Red-on-buff	0	0.0	0	0.0	0	0.0
Rillito Red-on-brown	0	0.0	0	0.0	0	0.0
Rillito Red-on-brown (micaceous)	0	0.0	0	0.0	0	0.0
Rincon Red-on-brown	0	0.0	0	0.0	0	0.0
Pantano Red-on-brown	0	0.0	0	0.0	0	0.0
Tanque Verde Red-on-brown	1	2.9	0	0.0	0	0.0
Mimbres Black-on-white	1	2.9	0	0.0	0	0.0
Dos Cabezas Red-on-brown	0	0.0	0	0.0	0	0.0
Encinas Red-on-brown	0	0.0	0	0.0	0	0.0
Nogales Purple-on-red	0	0.0	0	0.0	0	0.0
Cerros Red-on-white	0	0.0	0	0.0	0	0.0
San Carlos Red-on-brown	0	0.0	0	0.0	0	0.0

46E 4–9N		53E 5–8N		55E 16–17N		60E 14–15N		62E 9–10N	
n	%	*n*	%	*n*	%	*n*	%	*n*	%
5	55.6	1	6.7	0	0.0	0	0.0	1	33.3
0	0.0	0	0.0	0	0.0	0	0.0	0	0.0
0	0.0	0	0.0	0	0.0	0	0.0	0	0.0
0	0.0	0	0.0	0	0.0	0	0.0	0	0.0
0	0.0	0	0.0	0	0.0	0	0.0	0	0.0
0	0.0	0	0.0	0	0.0	0	0.0	0	0.0
1	11.1	1	6.7	0	0.0	0	0.0	0	0.0
0	0.0	0	0.0	0	0.0	0	0.0	0	0.0
0	0.0	3	20.0	0	0.0	0	0.0	0	0.0
1	11.1	5	33.3	0	0.0	0	0.0	1	33.3
0	0.0	2	13.3	0	0.0	0	0.0	1	33.3
0	0.0	0	0.0	0	0.0	0	0.0	0	0.0
0	0.0	0	0.0	0	0.0	0	0.0	0	0.0
0	0.0	0	0.0	0	0.0	0	0.0	0	0.0
0	0.0	0	0.0	0	0.0	0	0.0	0	0.0
1	11.1	2	13.3	0	0.0	0	0.0	0	0.0
0	0.0	0	0.0	0	0.0	0	0.0	0	0.0
0	0.0	0	0.0	0	0.0	0	0.0	0	0.0
0	0.0	0	0.0	0	0.0	0	0.0	0	0.0
0	0.0	0	0.0	0	0.0	1	100.0	0	0.0
1	11.1	1	6.7	0	0.0	0	0.0	0	0.0
0	0.0	0	0.0	0	0.0	0	0.0	0	0.0
0	0.0	0	0.0	0	0.0	0	0.0	0	0.0
0	0.0	0	0.0	0	0.0	0	0.0	0	0.0
0	0.0	0	0.0	0	0.0	0	0.0	0	0.0
0	0.0	0	0.0	0	0.0	0	0.0	0	0.0
0	0.0	0	0.0	0	0.0	0	0.0	0	0.0
0	0.0	0	0.0	0	0.0	0	0.0	0	0.0
0	0.0	0	0.0	0	0.0	0	0.0	0	0.0

(*continued*)

TABLE E.30 *(continued)*

	26E 0–10N		35E 0–9N		44E 16–17N	
	n	%	*n*	%	*n*	%
San Carlos Red-on-white	0	0.0	0	0.0	0	0.0
El Paso Polychrome	0	0.0	0	0.0	0	0.0
Unidentified polychrome	0	0.0	0	0.0	0	0.0
Kayenta-like polychrome	0	0.0	0	0.0	0	0.0
Tusayan-like polychrome	0	0.0	0	0.0	0	0.0
Subtotal	*35*	*100.0*	*0*	*0.0*	*8*	*100.0*
Plain types						
Davis Plain	232	80.3	2	40.0	14	37.8
Davis Plain: Sobaipuri Coil Rim Variety	0	0.0	0	0.0	0	0.0
Belford Perforated Rim	1	0.3	0	0.0	0	0.0
Belford Perforated Rim (Sobaipuri Coil Rim)	0	0.0	0	0.0	0	0.0
Babocomari Plain	45	15.6	1	20.0	20	54.1
Redington Plain	4	1.4	0	0.0	0	0.0
Redington Smudged	4	1.4	0	0.0	0	0.0
Sacaton Buff	0	0.0	1	20.0	1	2.7
Gila Plain	2	0.7	0	0.0	2	5.4
Gila Smudged	0	0.0	1	20.0	0	0.0
San Carlos Brown	0	0.0	0	0.0	0	0.0
Slipped brown	0	0.0	0	0.0	0	0.0
Sosa Plain	0	0.0	0	0.0	0	0.0
Whetstone Plain	0	0.0	0	0.0	0	0.0
Wingfield Plain	1	0.3	0	0.0	0	0.0
Fingernail indented	0	0.0	0	0.0	0	0.0
Incised plain	0	0.0	0	0.0	0	0.0
Tularosa Fillet Rim	0	0.0	0	0.0	0	0.0
Neck corrugated gray ware	0	0.0	0	0.0	0	0.0
Stucco ware?	0	0.0	0	0.0	0	0.0
Sandy Paste Perforated	0	0.0	0	0.0	0	0.0
Sosa Perforated	0	0.0	0	0.0	0	0.0
Subtotal	*289*	*100.0*	*5*	*100.0*	*37*	*100.0*

46E 4–9N		53E 5–8N		55E 16–17N		60E 14–15N		62E 9–10N	
n	%	*n*	%	*n*	%	*n*	%	*n*	%
0	0.0	0	0.0	0	0.0	0	0.0	0	0.0
0	0.0	0	0.0	0	0.0	0	0.0	0	0.0
0	0.0	0	0.0	0	0.0	0	0.0	0	0.0
0	0.0	0	0.0	0	0.0	0	0.0	0	0.0
0	0.0	0	0.0	0	0.0	0	0.0	0	0.0
9	*100.0*	*15*	*100.0*	*0*	*0.0*	*1*	*100.0*	*3*	*100.0*
26	48.1	25	26.3	5	10.6	1	3.8	15	65.2
0	0.0	0	0.0	0	0.0	0	0.0	0	0.0
0	0.0	0	0.0	0	0.0	0	0.0	0	0.0
0	0.0	0	0.0	0	0.0	0	0.0	0	0.0
19	35.2	69	72.6	0	0.0	22	84.6	8	34.8
3	5.6	0	0.0	0	0.0	0	0.0	0	0.0
2	3.7	0	0.0	0	0.0	0	0.0	0	0.0
2	3.7	0	0.0	0	0.0	3	11.5	0	0.0
1	1.9	1	1.1	0	0.0	0	0.0	0	0.0
0	0.0	0	0.0	0	0.0	0	0.0	0	0.0
1	1.9	0	0.0	0	0.0	0	0.0	0	0.0
0	0.0	0	0.0	0	0.0	0	0.0	0	0.0
0	0.0	0	0.0	0	0.0	0	0.0	0	0.0
0	0.0	0	0.0	42	89.4	0	0.0	0	0.0
0	0.0	0	0.0	0	0.0	0	0.0	0	0.0
0	0.0	0	0.0	0	0.0	0	0.0	0	0.0
0	0.0	0	0.0	0	0.0	0	0.0	0	0.0
0	0.0	0	0.0	0	0.0	0	0.0	0	0.0
0	0.0	0	0.0	0	0.0	0	0.0	0	0.0
0	0.0	0	0.0	0	0.0	0	0.0	0	0.0
0	0.0	0	0.0	0	0.0	0	0.0	0	0.0
0	0.0	0	0.0	0	0.0	0	0.0	0	0.0
54	*100.0*	*95*	*100.0*	*47*	*100.0*	*26*	*100.0*	*23*	*100.0*

(*continued*)

TABLE E.30 *(continued)*

	26E 0–10N		35E 0–9N		44E 16–17N	
	n	%	*n*	%	*n*	%
Red ware types						
Salt Red: Davis Variety	7	58.3	0	0.0	1	50.0
Salt Smudged: Davis Variety	1	8.3	0	0.0	0	0.0
Dragoon Red	4	33.3	0	0.0	1	50.0
Dragoon Red Smudged	0	0.0	0	0.0	0	0.0
Gila Red	0	0.0	0	0.0	0	0.0
Gila Smudged	0	0.0	0	0.0	0	0.0
San Carlos Red	0	0.0	0	0.0	0	0.0
Wingfield Red	0	0.0	0	0.0	0	0.0
Unidentified red #1	0	0.0	1	100.0	0	0.0
Unidentified red #2	0	0.0	0	0.0	0	0.0
Subtotal	*12*	*100.0*	*1*	*100.0*	*2*	*100.0*
Corrugated types						
Late plain corrugated	1	33.3	0	0.0	0	0.0
Late indented corrugated	2	66.7	0	0.0	0	0.0
Early indented corrugated, smudged interior	0	0.0	0	0.0	0	0.0
Obliterated corrugated	0	0.0	0	0.0	0	0.0
Neck corrugated	0	0.0	0	0.0	0	0.0
Red-slipped neck corrugated	0	0.0	0	0.0	0	0.0
Subtotal	*3*	*100.0*	*0*	*0.0*	*0*	*0.0*
Miscellaneous						
Porcelain	0	0.0	0	0.0	0	0.0
White glaze ware	0	0.0	0	0.0	0	0.0
Glass	0	0.0	0	0.0	0	0.0
Unidentified	2	100.0	0	0.0	0	0.0
Subtotal	*2*	*100.0*	*0*	*0.0*	*0*	*0.0*
Total	**341**		**6**		**47**	

46E 4–9N		53E 5–8N		55E 16–17N		60E 14–15N		62E 9–10N	
n	%	*n*	%	*n*	%	*n*	%	*n*	%
1	100.0	0	0.0	0	0.0	0	0.0	0	0.0
0	0.0	0	0.0	0	0.0	0	0.0	0	0.0
0	0.0	0	0.0	0	0.0	0	0.0	0	0.0
0	0.0	0	0.0	0	0.0	0	0.0	0	0.0
0	0.0	0	0.0	0	0.0	0	0.0	0	0.0
0	0.0	0	0.0	0	0.0	0	0.0	0	0.0
0	0.0	0	0.0	0	0.0	0	0.0	0	0.0
0	0.0	0	0.0	0	0.0	0	0.0	0	0.0
0	0.0	0	0.0	0	0.0	0	0.0	0	0.0
0	0.0	0	0.0	0	0.0	0	0.0	0	0.0
1	*100.0*	*0*	*0.0*	*0*	*0.0*	*0*	*0.0*	*0*	*0.0*
0	0.0	0	0.0	0	0.0	0	0.0	0	0.0
0	0.0	0	0.0	0	0.0	0	0.0	0	0.0
0	0.0	0	0.0	0	0.0	0	0.0	0	0.0
0	0.0	0	0.0	0	0.0	0	0.0	0	0.0
0	0.0	0	0.0	0	0.0	0	0.0	0	0.0
1	100.0	0	0.0	0	0.0	0	0.0	0	0.0
1	*100.0*	*0*	*0.0*	*0*	*0.0*	*0*	*0.0*	*0*	*0.0*
0	0.0	0	0.0	0	0.0	0	0.0	0	0.0
0	0.0	0	0.0	0	0.0	0	0.0	0	0.0
0	0.0	0	0.0	0	0.0	0	0.0	0	0.0
1	100.0	0	0.0	0	0.0	1	100.0	0	0.0
1	*100.0*	*0*	*0.0*	*0*	*0.0*	*1*	*100.0*	*0*	*0.0*
66		**110**		**47**		**28**		**26**	

TABLE E.31 Gerald's typological analysis of sherds from east/south trenches at the Davis Ranch Site

	17E 12S		19E 16–18S		19–25E 18–20S		23–27E 20–24S		37E 11–14S		46E 6–8S	
	n	%	*n*	%	*n*	%	*n*	%	*n*	%	*n*	%
Painted types												
Gila Polychrome	2	20.0	89	84.0	143	81.3	111	89.5	6	75.0	1	100.0
Gila Black-on-red	0	0.0	1	0.9	2	1.1	0	0.0	0	0.0	0	0.0
Pinto Polychrome	2	20.0	2	1.9	3	1.7	0	0.0	0	0.0	0	0.0
Gila Polychrome (Pink Variant)	0	0.0	0	0.0	0	0.0	0	0.0	0	0.0	0	0.0
Gila-Tucson Polychrome	0	0.0	0	0.0	0	0.0	0	0.0	0	0.0	0	0.0
Tucson Polychrome	0	0.0	1	0.9	8	4.5	2	1.6	0	0.0	0	0.0
Tucson Black-on-red	0	0.0	3	2.8	4	2.3	2	1.6	0	0.0	0	0.0
Tonto Polychrome	0	0.0	0	0.0	3	1.7	4	3.2	0	0.0	0	0.0
Dragoon Red-on-brown	1	10.0	1	0.9	1	0.6	0	0.0	0	0.0	0	0.0
Cascabel Red-on-brown	1	10.0	3	2.8	1	0.6	0	0.0	0	0.0	0	0.0
Davis Red-on-white	0	0.0	1	0.9	1	0.6	1	0.8	0	0.0	0	0.0
Tres Alamos Red-on-brown	0	0.0	0	0.0	0	0.0	0	0.0	0	0.0	0	0.0
Gila White Slip	0	0.0	2	1.9	1	0.6	0	0.0	1	12.5	0	0.0
Cañada del Oro Red-on-brown	0	0.0	0	0.0	0	0.0	0	0.0	0	0.0	0	0.0
Gila Butte Red-on-buff	0	0.0	0	0.0	0	0.0	0	0.0	0	0.0	0	0.0
Santa Cruz Red-on-buff	1	10.0	0	0.0	2	1.1	1	0.8	0	0.0	0	0.0
Sacaton Red-on-buff	1	10.0	0	0.0	2	1.1	2	1.6	1	12.5	0	0.0
Casa Grande Red-on-buff	0	0.0	0	0.0	0	0.0	0	0.0	0	0.0	0	0.0
Rillito Red-on-brown	0	0.0	2	1.9	1	0.6	1	0.8	0	0.0	0	0.0

Rillito Red-on-brown (micaceous)	0	0.0	1	0.9	1	0.6	0	0.0	0	0.0	0	0.0
Rincon Red-on-brown	0	0.0	0	0.0	0	0.0	0	0.0	0	0.0	0	0.0
Pantano Red-on-brown	0	0.0	0	0.0	0	0.0	0	0.0	0	0.0	0	0.0
Tanque Verde Red-on-brown	0	0.0	0	0.0	0	0.0	0	0.0	0	0.0	0	0.0
Mimbres Black-on-white	0	0.0	0	0.0	0	0.0	0	0.0	0	0.0	0	0.0
Dos Cabezas Red-on-brown	0	0.0	0	0.0	0	0.0	0	0.0	0	0.0	0	0.0
Encinas Red-on-brown	0	0.0	0	0.0	1	0.6	0	0.0	0	0.0	0	0.0
Nogales Purple-on-red	0	0.0	0	0.0	0	0.0	0	0.0	0	0.0	0	0.0
Cerros Red-on-white	0	0.0	0	0.0	0	0.0	0	0.0	0	0.0	0	0.0
San Carlos Red-on-brown	0	0.0	0	0.0	0	0.0	0	0.0	0	0.0	0	0.0
San Carlos Red-on-white	0	0.0	0	0.0	1	0.6	0	0.0	0	0.0	0	0.0
El Paso Polychrome	0	0.0	0	0.0	0	0.0	0	0.0	0	0.0	0	0.0
Unidentified polychrome	1	10.0	0	0.0	0	0.0	0	0.0	0	0.0	0	0.0
Kayenta-like polychrome	1	10.0	0	0.0	0	0.0	0	0.0	0	0.0	0	0.0
Tusayan-like polychrome	0	0.0	0	0.0	1	0.6	0	0.0	0	0.0	0	0.0
Subtotal	*10*	*100.0*	*106*	*100.0*	*176*	*100.0*	*124*	*100.0*	*8*	*100.0*	*1*	*100.0*
Plain types												
Davis Plain	12	48.0	186	81.6	646	88.9	488	89.7	23	74.2	19	76.0
Davis Plain: Sobaipuri Coil Rim Variety	0	0.0	1	0.4	4	0.6	1	0.2	0	0.0	0	0.0
Belford Perforated Rim	0	0.0	1	0.4	3	0.4	3	0.6	0	0.0	0	0.0
Belford Perforated Rim (Sobaipuri Coil Rim)	0	0.0	2	0.9	0	0.0	1	0.2	0	0.0	0	0.0
Babocomari Plain	11	44.0	20	8.8	26	3.6	31	5.7	5	16.1	6	24.0
Redington Plain	0	0.0	5	2.2	15	2.1	10	1.8	0	0.0	0	0.0

(continued)

TABLE E.31 *(continued)*

	17E 12S		19E 16–18S		19–25E 18–20S		23–27E 20–24S		37E 11–14S		46E 6–8S	
	n	%	*n*	%	*n*	%	*n*	%	*n*	%	*n*	%
Redington Smudged	1	4.0	0	0.0	8	1.1	2	0.4	3	9.7	0	0.0
Sacaton Buff	0	0.0	1	0.4	0	0.0	2	0.4	0	0.0	0	0.0
Gila Plain	1	4.0	6	2.6	16	2.2	3	0.6	0	0.0	0	0.0
Gila Smudged	0	0.0	0	0.0	1	0.1	1	0.2	0	0.0	0	0.0
San Carlos Brown	0	0.0	2	0.9	2	0.3	0	0.0	0	0.0	0	0.0
Slipped brown	0	0.0	3	1.3	5	0.7	1	0.2	0	0.0	0	0.0
Sosa Plain	0	0.0	0	0.0	0	0.0	0	0.0	0	0.0	0	0.0
Whetstone Plain	0	0.0	0	0.0	0	0.0	0	0.0	0	0.0	0	0.0
Wingfield Plain	0	0.0	1	0.4	0	0.0	1	0.2	0	0.0	0	0.0
Fingernail indented	0	0.0	0	0.0	1	0.1	0	0.0	0	0.0	0	0.0
Incised plain	0	0.0	0	0.0	0	0.0	0	0.0	0	0.0	0	0.0
Tularosa Fillet Rim	0	0.0	0	0.0	0	0.0	0	0.0	0	0.0	0	0.0
Neck corrugated gray ware	0	0.0	0	0.0	0	0.0	0	0.0	0	0.0	0	0.0
Stucco ware?	0	0.0	0	0.0	0	0.0	0	0.0	0	0.0	0	0.0
Sandy Paste Perforated	0	0.0	0	0.0	0	0.0	0	0.0	0	0.0	0	0.0
Sosa Perforated	0	0.0	0	0.0	0	0.0	0	0.0	0	0.0	0	0.0
Subtotal	*25*	*100.0*	*228*	*100.0*	*727*	*100.0*	*544*	*100.0*	*31*	*100.0*	*25*	*100.0*
Red ware types												
Salt Red: Davis Variety	0	0.0	5	33.3	18	30.5	13	50.0	2	100.0	0	0.0
Salt Smudged: Davis Variety	0	0.0	4	26.7	10	16.9	3	11.5	0	0.0	0	0.0

Dragoon Red	0	0.0	0	0.0	4	6.8	3	11.5	0	0.0	1	50.0
Dragoon Red Smudged	0	0.0	2	13.3	3	5.1	3	11.5	0	0.0	1	50.0
Gila Red	0	0.0	0	0.0	16	27.1	2	7.7	0	0.0	0	0.0
Gila Smudged	0	0.0	0	0.0	1	1.7	0	0.0	0	0.0	0	0.0
San Carlos Red	0	0.0	1	6.7	3	5.1	1	3.8	0	0.0	0	0.0
Wingfield Red	0	0.0	0	0.0	1	1.7	0	0.0	0	0.0	0	0.0
Unidentified red #1	0	0.0	0	0.0	2	3.4	1	3.8	0	0.0	0	0.0
Unidentified red #2	0	0.0	3	20.0	1	1.7	0	0.0	0	0.0	0	0.0
Subtotal	*0*	*0.0*	*15*	*100.0*	*59*	*100.0*	*26*	*100.0*	*2*	*100.0*	*2*	*100.0*
Corrugated types												
Late plain corrugated	0	0.0	0	0.0	0	0.0	1	33.3	0	0.0	0	0.0
Late indented corrugated	0	0.0	0	0.0	2	40.0	2	66.7	0	0.0	0	0.0
Early indented corrugated, smudged interior	0	0.0	0	0.0	0	0.0	0	0.0	0	0.0	0	0.0
Obliterated corrugated	0	0.0	0	0.0	1	20.0	0	0.0	0	0.0	0	0.0
Neck corrugated	0	0.0	0	0.0	1	20.0	0	0.0	0	0.0	0	0.0
Red-slipped neck corrugated	0	0.0	0	0.0	1	20.0	0	0.0	0	0.0	0	0.0
Subtotal	*0*	*0.0*	*0*	*0.0*	*5*	*100.0*	*3*	*100.0*	*0*	*0.0*	*0*	*0.0*
Miscellaneous												
Porcelain	0	0.0	0	0.0	0	0.0	0	0.0	0	0.0	0	0.0
White glaze ware	0	0.0	0	0.0	0	0.0	0	0.0	0	0.0	0	0.0
Glass	0	0.0	0	0.0	0	0.0	0	0.0	0	0.0	0	0.0
Unidentified	1	100.0	0	0.0	1	100.0	4	100.0	0	0.0	2	100.0
Subtotal	*1*	*100.0*	*0*	*0.0*	*1*	*100.0*	*4*	*100.0*	*0*	*0.0*	*2*	*100.0*
Total	**36**		**349**		**968**		**701**		**41**		**30**	

TABLE E.32 Gerald's typological analysis of sherds from west/south trenches at the Davis Ranch Site

	3–5W 43S		5W 44S		20W 35–36S		20–22W 11–12S	
	n	%	*n*	%	*n*	%	*n*	%
Painted types								
Gila Polychrome	5	100.0	7	100.0	31	79.5	35	81.4
Gila Black-on-red	0	0.0	0	0.0	1	2.6	3	7.0
Pinto Polychrome	0	0.0	0	0.0	1	2.6	4	9.3
Gila Polychrome (Pink Variant)	0	0.0	0	0.0	0	0.0	0	0.0
Gila-Tucson Polychrome	0	0.0	0	0.0	0	0.0	0	0.0
Tucson Polychrome	0	0.0	0	0.0	0	0.0	1	2.3
Tucson Black-on-red	0	0.0	0	0.0	1	2.6	0	0.0
Tonto Polychrome	0	0.0	0	0.0	5	12.8	0	0.0
Dragoon Red-on-brown	0	0.0	0	0.0	0	0.0	0	0.0
Cascabel Red-on-brown	0	0.0	0	0.0	0	0.0	0	0.0
Davis Red-on-white	0	0.0	0	0.0	0	0.0	0	0.0
Tres Alamos Red-on-brown	0	0.0	0	0.0	0	0.0	0	0.0
Gila White Slip	0	0.0	0	0.0	0	0.0	0	0.0
Cañada del Oro Red-on-brown	0	0.0	0	0.0	0	0.0	0	0.0
Gila Butte Red-on-buff	0	0.0	0	0.0	0	0.0	0	0.0
Santa Cruz Red-on-buff	0	0.0	0	0.0	0	0.0	0	0.0
Sacaton Red-on-buff	0	0.0	0	0.0	0	0.0	0	0.0
Casa Grande Red-on-buff	0	0.0	0	0.0	0	0.0	0	0.0
Rillito Red-on-brown	0	0.0	0	0.0	0	0.0	0	0.0

Rillito Red-on-brown (micaceous)	0	0.0	0	0.0	0	0.0	0	0.0
Rincon Red-on-brown	0	0.0	0	0.0	0	0.0	0	0.0
Pantano Red-on-brown	0	0.0	0	0.0	0	0.0	0	0.0
Tanque Verde Red-on-brown	0	0.0	0	0.0	0	0.0	0	0.0
Mimbres Black-on-white	0	0.0	0	0.0	0	0.0	0	0.0
Dos Cabezas Red-on-brown	0	0.0	0	0.0	0	0.0	0	0.0
Encinas Red-on-brown	0	0.0	0	0.0	0	0.0	0	0.0
Nogales Purple-on-red	0	0.0	0	0.0	0	0.0	0	0.0
Cerros Red-on-white	0	0.0	0	0.0	0	0.0	0	0.0
San Carlos Red-on-brown	0	0.0	0	0.0	0	0.0	0	0.0
San Carlos Red-on-white	0	0.0	0	0.0	0	0.0	0	0.0
El Paso Polychrome	0	0.0	0	0.0	0	0.0	0	0.0
Unidentified polychrome	0	0.0	0	0.0	0	0.0	0	0.0
Kayenta-like polychrome	0	0.0	0	0.0	0	0.0	0	0.0
Tusayan-like polychrome	0	0.0	0	0.0	0	0.0	0	0.0
Subtotal	*5*	*100.0*	*7*	*100.0*	*39*	*100.0*	*43*	*100.0*
Plain types								
Davis Plain	14	93.3	14	100.0	53	93.0	164	87.7
Davis Plain: Sobaipuri Coil Rim Variety	0	0.0	0	0.0	0	0.0	1	0.5
Belford Perforated Rim	0	0.0	0	0.0	1	1.8	1	0.5
Belford Perforated Rim (Sobaipuri Coil Rim)	0	0.0	0	0.0	0	0.0	0	0.0
Babocomari Plain	0	0.0	0	0.0	1	1.8	4	2.1
Redington Plain	0	0.0	0	0.0	1	1.8	5	2.7

(continued)

TABLE E.32 *(continued)*

	3–5W 43S		5W 44S		20W 35–36S		20–22W 11–12S	
	n	%	*n*	%	*n*	%	*n*	%
Redington Smudged	0	0.0	0	0.0	0	0.0	3	1.6
Sacaton Buff	0	0.0	0	0.0	0	0.0	2	1.1
Gila Plain	1	6.7	0	0.0	1	1.8	7	3.7
Gila Smudged	0	0.0	0	0.0	0	0.0	0	0.0
San Carlos Brown	0	0.0	0	0.0	0	0.0	0	0.0
Slipped brown	0	0.0	0	0.0	0	0.0	0	0.0
Sosa Plain	0	0.0	0	0.0	0	0.0	0	0.0
Whetstone Plain	0	0.0	0	0.0	0	0.0	0	0.0
Wingfield Plain	0	0.0	0	0.0	0	0.0	0	0.0
Fingernail indented	0	0.0	0	0.0	0	0.0	0	0.0
Incised plain	0	0.0	0	0.0	0	0.0	0	0.0
Tularosa Fillet Rim	0	0.0	0	0.0	0	0.0	0	0.0
Neck corrugated gray ware	0	0.0	0	0.0	0	0.0	0	0.0
Stucco ware?	0	0.0	0	0.0	0	0.0	0	0.0
Sandy Paste Perforated	0	0.0	0	0.0	0	0.0	0	0.0
Sosa Perforated	0	0.0	0	0.0	0	0.0	0	0.0
Subtotal	*15*	*100.0*	*14*	*100.0*	*57*	*100.0*	*187*	*100.0*
Red ware types								
Salt Red: Davis Variety	1	100.0	3	75.0	6	60.0	9	56.3
Salt Smudged: Davis Variety	0	0.0	0	0.0	1	10.0	2	12.5

Dragoon Red	0	0.0	0	0.0	3	30.0	1	6.3
Dragoon Red Smudged	0	0.0	1	25.0	0	0.0	1	6.3
Gila Red	0	0.0	0	0.0	0	0.0	1	6.3
Gila Smudged	0	0.0	0	0.0	0	0.0	1	6.3
San Carlos Red	0	0.0	0	0.0	0	0.0	0	0.0
Wingfield Red	0	0.0	0	0.0	0	0.0	0	0.0
Unidentified red #1	0	0.0	0	0.0	0	0.0	0	0.0
Unidentified red #2	0	0.0	0	0.0	0	0.0	1	6.3
Subtotal	*1*	*100.0*	*4*	*100.0*	*10*	*100.0*	*16*	*100.0*
Corrugated types								
Late plain corrugated	0	0.0	0	0.0	0	0.0	0	0.0
Late indented corrugated	0	0.0	0	0.0	0	0.0	1	50.0
Early indented corrugated, smudged interior	0	0.0	0	0.0	0	0.0	0	0.0
Obliterated corrugated	0	0.0	0	0.0	0	0.0	0	0.0
Neck corrugated	0	0.0	0	0.0	0	0.0	1	50.0
Red-slipped neck corrugated	0	0.0	0	0.0	0	0.0	0	0.0
Subtotal	*0*	*0.0*	*0*	*0.0*	*0*	*0.0*	*2*	*100.0*
Miscellaneous								
Porcelain	0	0.0	0	0.0	0	0.0	0	0.0
White glaze ware	0	0.0	0	0.0	0	0.0	0	0.0
Glass	0	0.0	0	0.0	0	0.0	0	0.0
Unidentified	0	0.0	0	0.0	0	0.0	0	0.0
Subtotal	*0*	*0.0*	*0*	*0.0*	*0*	*0.0*	*0*	*0.0*
Total	**21**		**25**		**106**		**248**	

TABLE E.33 Gerald's typological analysis of sherds from south/east trenches at the Davis Ranch Site

	1S					
	24–26E		31–46E		54–61E	
	n	%	*n*	%	*n*	%
Painted types						
Gila Polychrome	8	42.1	14	26.4	2	40.0
Gila Black-on-red	4	21.1	0	0.0	0	0.0
Pinto Polychrome	1	5.3	0	0.0	0	0.0
Gila Polychrome (Pink Variant)	0	0.0	0	0.0	0	0.0
Gila-Tucson Polychrome	0	0.0	0	0.0	0	0.0
Tucson Polychrome	1	5.3	4	7.5	0	0.0
Tucson Black-on-red	1	5.3	0	0.0	1	20.0
Tonto Polychrome	0	0.0	0	0.0	0	0.0
Dragoon Red-on-brown	1	5.3	1	1.9	0	0.0
Cascabel Red-on-brown	0	0.0	7	13.2	0	0.0
Davis Red-on-white	0	0.0	2	3.8	1	20.0
Tres Alamos Red-on-brown	0	0.0	0	0.0	0	0.0
Gila White Slip	0	0.0	0	0.0	0	0.0
Cañada del Oro Red-on-brown	0	0.0	0	0.0	0	0.0
Gila Butte Red-on-buff	0	0.0	0	0.0	0	0.0
Santa Cruz Red-on-buff	2	10.5	6	11.3	0	0.0
Sacaton Red-on-buff	0	0.0	3	5.7	1	20.0
Casa Grande Red-on-buff	0	0.0	0	0.0	0	0.0
Rillito Red-on-brown	0	0.0	2	3.8	0	0.0
Rillito Red-on-brown (micaceous)	1	5.3	7	13.2	0	0.0
Rincon Red-on-brown	0	0.0	1	1.9	0	0.0
Pantano Red-on-brown	0	0.0	0	0.0	0	0.0
Tanque Verde Red-on-brown	0	0.0	0	0.0	0	0.0
Mimbres Black-on-white	0	0.0	5	9.4	0	0.0
Dos Cabezas Red-on-brown	0	0.0	0	0.0	0	0.0
Encinas Red-on-brown	0	0.0	0	0.0	0	0.0
Nogales Purple-on-red	0	0.0	0	0.0	0	0.0

11S 13–14E		12S 18–20E		13S 12–16E		13–17S 8–12E		16S 23–26E	
n	%	*n*	%	*n*	%	*n*	%	*n*	%
2	40.0	22	53.7	24	75.0	99	79.2	7	53.8
1	20.0	3	7.3	1	3.1	0	0.0	1	7.7
0	0.0	5	12.2	0	0.0	1	0.8	0	0.0
0	0.0	0	0.0	0	0.0	0	0.0	0	0.0
0	0.0	0	0.0	0	0.0	0	0.0	0	0.0
0	0.0	4	9.8	2	6.3	0	0.0	3	23.1
0	0.0	4	9.8	0	0.0	0	0.0	0	0.0
0	0.0	0	0.0	0	0.0	14	11.2	0	0.0
0	0.0	0	0.0	2	6.3	0	0.0	0	0.0
0	0.0	1	2.4	1	3.1	0	0.0	0	0.0
0	0.0	0	0.0	0	0.0	0	0.0	0	0.0
0	0.0	0	0.0	0	0.0	0	0.0	0	0.0
1	20.0	0	0.0	0	0.0	11	8.8	1	7.7
0	0.0	0	0.0	0	0.0	0	0.0	0	0.0
0	0.0	0	0.0	0	0.0	0	0.0	0	0.0
1	20.0	0	0.0	1	3.1	0	0.0	0	0.0
0	0.0	0	0.0	0	0.0	0	0.0	0	0.0
0	0.0	0	0.0	0	0.0	0	0.0	0	0.0
0	0.0	0	0.0	0	0.0	0	0.0	0	0.0
0	0.0	0	0.0	1	3.1	0	0.0	1	7.7
0	0.0	0	0.0	0	0.0	0	0.0	0	0.0
0	0.0	0	0.0	0	0.0	0	0.0	0	0.0
0	0.0	0	0.0	0	0.0	0	0.0	0	0.0
0	0.0	0	0.0	0	0.0	0	0.0	0	0.0
0	0.0	0	0.0	0	0.0	0	0.0	0	0.0
0	0.0	0	0.0	0	0.0	0	0.0	0	0.0
0	0.0	0	0.0	0	0.0	0	0.0	0	0.0

(*continued*)

TABLE E.33 (continued)

	1S					
	24–26E		31–46E		54–61E	
	n	%	*n*	%	*n*	%
Cerros Red-on-white	0	0.0	1	1.9	0	0.0
San Carlos Red-on-brown	0	0.0	0	0.0	0	0.0
San Carlos Red-on-white	0	0.0	0	0.0	0	0.0
El Paso Polychrome	0	0.0	0	0.0	0	0.0
Unidentified polychrome	0	0.0	0	0.0	0	0.0
Kayenta-like polychrome	0	0.0	0	0.0	0	0.0
Tusayan-like polychrome	0	0.0	0	0.0	0	0.0
Subtotal	*19*	*100.0*	*53*	*100.0*	*5*	*100.0*
Plain types						
Davis Plain	27	64.3	84	26.2	15	48.4
Davis Plain: Sobaipuri Coil Rim Variety	0	0.0	0	0.0	0	0.0
Belford Perforated Rim	0	0.0	4	1.2	0	0.0
Belford Perforated Rim (Sobaipuri Coil Rim)	0	0.0	0	0.0	0	0.0
Babocomari Plain	11	26.2	202	62.9	11	35.5
Redington Plain	2	4.8	4	1.2	3	9.7
Redington Smudged	1	2.4	4	1.2	0	0.0
Sacaton Buff	0	0.0	6	1.9	0	0.0
Gila Plain	1	2.4	15	4.7	2	6.5
Gila Smudged	0	0.0	1	0.3	0	0.0
San Carlos Brown	0	0.0	0	0.0	0	0.0
Slipped brown	0	0.0	0	0.0	0	0.0
Sosa Plain	0	0.0	0	0.0	0	0.0
Whetstone Plain	0	0.0	0	0.0	0	0.0
Wingfield Plain	0	0.0	1	0.3	0	0.0
Fingernail indented	0	0.0	0	0.0	0	0.0
Incised plain	0	0.0	0	0.0	0	0.0
Tularosa Fillet Rim	0	0.0	0	0.0	0	0.0
Neck corrugated gray ware	0	0.0	0	0.0	0	0.0
Stucco ware?	0	0.0	0	0.0	0	0.0

11S 13–14E		12S 18–20E		13S 12–16E		13–17S 8–12E		16S 23–26E	
n	%	*n*	%	*n*	%	*n*	%	*n*	%
0	0.0	0	0.0	0	0.0	0	0.0	0	0.0
0	0.0	0	0.0	0	0.0	0	0.0	0	0.0
0	0.0	0	0.0	0	0.0	0	0.0	0	0.0
0	0.0	0	0.0	0	0.0	0	0.0	0	0.0
0	0.0	0	0.0	0	0.0	0	0.0	0	0.0
0	0.0	1	2.4	0	0.0	0	0.0	0	0.0
0	0.0	1	2.4	0	0.0	0	0.0	0	0.0
5	*100.0*	*41*	*100.0*	*32*	*100.0*	*125*	*100.0*	*13*	*100.0*
17	77.3	188	86.2	49	64.5	283	90.4	11	61.1
0	0.0	1	0.5	0	0.0	0	0.0	0	0.0
0	0.0	3	1.4	0	0.0	2	0.6	0	0.0
0	0.0	0	0.0	2	2.6	8	2.6	0	0.0
3	13.6	16	7.3	23	30.3	12	3.8	6	33.3
0	0.0	2	0.9	1	1.3	2	0.6	0	0.0
2	9.1	1	0.5	0	0.0	1	0.3	0	0.0
0	0.0	0	0.0	0	0.0	0	0.0	0	0.0
0	0.0	5	2.3	0	0.0	5	1.6	1	5.6
0	0.0	0	0.0	0	0.0	0	0.0	0	0.0
0	0.0	0	0.0	1	1.3	0	0.0	0	0.0
0	0.0	0	0.0	0	0.0	0	0.0	0	0.0
0	0.0	2	0.9	0	0.0	0	0.0	0	0.0
0	0.0	0	0.0	0	0.0	0	0.0	0	0.0
0	0.0	0	0.0	0	0.0	0	0.0	0	0.0
0	0.0	0	0.0	0	0.0	0	0.0	0	0.0
0	0.0	0	0.0	0	0.0	0	0.0	0	0.0
0	0.0	0	0.0	0	0.0	0	0.0	0	0.0
0	0.0	0	0.0	0	0.0	0	0.0	0	0.0
0	0.0	0	0.0	0	0.0	0	0.0	0	0.0

(*continued*)

TABLE E.33 *(continued)*

	1S					
	24–26E		31–46E		54–61E	
	n	%	*n*	%	*n*	%
Sandy Paste Perforated	0	0.0	0	0.0	0	0.0
Sosa Perforated	0	0.0	0	0.0	0	0.0
Subtotal	*42*	*100.0*	*321*	*100.0*	*31*	*100.0*
Red ware types						
Salt Red: Davis Variety	5	83.3	4	66.7	0	0.0
Salt Smudged: Davis Variety	0	0.0	1	16.7	0	0.0
Dragoon Red	1	16.7	1	16.7	1	100.0
Dragoon Red Smudged	0	0.0	0	0.0	0	0.0
Gila Red	0	0.0	0	0.0	0	0.0
Gila Smudged	0	0.0	0	0.0	0	0.0
San Carlos Red	0	0.0	0	0.0	0	0.0
Wingfield Red	0	0.0	0	0.0	0	0.0
Unidentified red #1	0	0.0	0	0.0	0	0.0
Unidentified red #2	0	0.0	0	0.0	0	0.0
Subtotal	*6*	*100.0*	*6*	*100.0*	*1*	*100.0*
Corrugated types						
Late plain corrugated	0	0.0	1	100.0	0	0.0
Late indented corrugated	0	0.0	0	0.0	0	0.0
Early indented corrugated, smudged interior	0	0.0	0	0.0	0	0.0
Obliterated corrugated	0	0.0	0	0.0	0	0.0
Neck corrugated	0	0.0	0	0.0	0	0.0
Red-slipped neck corrugated	0	0.0	0	0.0	0	0.0
Subtotal	*0*	*0.0*	*1*	*100.0*	*0*	*0.0*
Miscellaneous						
Porcelain	0	0.0	0	0.0	0	0.0
White glaze ware	0	0.0	0	0.0	0	0.0
Glass	0	0.0	0	0.0	0	0.0
Unidentified	0	0.0	4	100.0	0	0.0
Subtotal	*0*	*0.0*	*4*	*100.0*	*0*	*0.0*
Total	**67**		**385**		**37**	

11S 13–14E		12S 18–20E		13S 12–16E		13–17S 8–12E		16S 23–26E	
n	%	*n*	%	*n*	%	*n*	%	*n*	%
0	0.0	0	0.0	0	0.0	0	0.0	0	0.0
0	0.0	0	0.0	0	0.0	0	0.0	0	0.0
22	*100.0*	*218*	*100.0*	*76*	*100.0*	*313*	*100.0*	*18*	*100.0*
0	0.0	5	38.5	4	80.0	27	84.4	0	0.0
0	0.0	0	0.0	0	0.0	0	0.0	0	0.0
0	0.0	1	7.7	0	0.0	3	9.4	0	0.0
0	0.0	0	0.0	0	0.0	2	6.3	0	0.0
0	0.0	4	30.8	0	0.0	0	0.0	0	0.0
0	0.0	3	23.1	0	0.0	0	0.0	0	0.0
0	0.0	0	0.0	0	0.0	0	0.0	1	100.0
0	0.0	0	0.0	1	20.0	0	0.0	0	0.0
0	0.0	0	0.0	0	0.0	0	0.0	0	0.0
0	0.0	0	0.0	0	0.0	0	0.0	0	0.0
0	*0.0*	*13*	*100.0*	*5*	*100.0*	*32*	*100.0*	*1*	*100.0*
0	0.0	0	0.0	0	0.0	1	100.0	0	0.0
0	0.0	1	100.0	1	100.0	0	0.0	0	0.0
0	0.0	0	0.0	0	0.0	0	0.0	0	0.0
0	0.0	0	0.0	0	0.0	0	0.0	0	0.0
0	0.0	0	0.0	0	0.0	0	0.0	0	0.0
0	0.0	0	0.0	0	0.0	0	0.0	0	0.0
0	*0.0*	*1*	*100.0*	*1*	*100.0*	*1*	*100.0*	*0*	*0.0*
0	0.0	0	0.0	0	0.0	0	0.0	0	0.0
0	0.0	0	0.0	0	0.0	0	0.0	0	0.0
0	0.0	0	0.0	0	0.0	0	0.0	0	0.0
0	0.0	0	0.0	0	0.0	0	0.0	0	0.0
0	*0.0*	*0*	*0.0*	*0*	*0.0*	*0*	*0.0*	*0*	*0.0*
27		**273**		**114**		**471**		**32**	

(*continued*)

TABLE E.33 *(continued)*

	19S 18E		21S 14–19E		31S 8E		31–32S 7E	
	n	%	*n*	%	*n*	%	*n*	%
Painted types								
Gila Polychrome	0	0.0	4	66.7	3	100.0	8	61.5
Gila Black-on-red	0	0.0	0	0.0	0	0.0	1	7.7
Pinto Polychrome	0	0.0	0	0.0	0	0.0	0	0.0
Gila Polychrome (Pink Variant)	0	0.0	0	0.0	0	0.0	0	0.0
Gila-Tucson Polychrome	0	0.0	0	0.0	0	0.0	0	0.0
Tucson Polychrome	0	0.0	0	0.0	0	0.0	1	7.7
Tucson Black-on-red	0	0.0	0	0.0	0	0.0	2	15.4
Tonto Polychrome	0	0.0	0	0.0	0	0.0	0	0.0
Dragoon Red-on-brown	0	0.0	0	0.0	0	0.0	0	0.0
Cascabel Red-on-brown	0	0.0	0	0.0	0	0.0	0	0.0
Davis Red-on-white	0	0.0	0	0.0	0	0.0	0	0.0
Tres Alamos Red-on-brown	0	0.0	0	0.0	0	0.0	0	0.0
Gila White Slip	0	0.0	0	0.0	0	0.0	0	0.0
Cañada del Oro Red-on-brown	0	0.0	0	0.0	0	0.0	0	0.0
Gila Butte Red-on-buff	0	0.0	0	0.0	0	0.0	0	0.0
Santa Cruz Red-on-buff	0	0.0	0	0.0	0	0.0	0	0.0
Sacaton Red-on-buff	0	0.0	0	0.0	0	0.0	0	0.0
Casa Grande Red-on-buff	0	0.0	0	0.0	0	0.0	0	0.0
Rillito Red-on-brown	0	0.0	0	0.0	0	0.0	0	0.0
Rillito Red-on-brown (micaceous)	0	0.0	1	16.7	0	0.0	0	0.0
Rincon Red-on-brown	0	0.0	0	0.0	0	0.0	0	0.0
Pantano Red-on-brown	0	0.0	0	0.0	0	0.0	0	0.0
Tanque Verde Red-on-brown	0	0.0	0	0.0	0	0.0	0	0.0
Mimbres Black-on-white	0	0.0	0	0.0	0	0.0	0	0.0
Dos Cabezas Red-on-brown	0	0.0	0	0.0	0	0.0	1	7.7
Encinas Red-on-brown	0	0.0	1	16.7	0	0.0	0	0.0
Nogales Purple-on-red	0	0.0	0	0.0	0	0.0	0	0.0
Cerros Red-on-white	0	0.0	0	0.0	0	0.0	0	0.0

(continued)

TABLE E.33 *(continued)*

	19S 18E		21S 14–19E		31S 8E		31–32S 7E	
	n	%	*n*	%	*n*	%	*n*	%
San Carlos Red-on-brown	0	0.0	0	0.0	0	0.0	0	0.0
San Carlos Red-on-white	0	0.0	0	0.0	0	0.0	0	0.0
El Paso Polychrome	0	0.0	0	0.0	0	0.0	0	0.0
Unidentified polychrome	0	0.0	0	0.0	0	0.0	0	0.0
Kayenta-like polychrome	0	0.0	0	0.0	0	0.0	0	0.0
Tusayan-like polychrome	0	0.0	0	0.0	0	0.0	0	0.0
Subtotal	*0*	*0.0*	*6*	*100.0*	*3*	*100.0*	*13*	*100.0*
Plain types								
Davis Plain	25	100.0	47	79.7	9	75.0	39	84.8
Davis Plain: Sobaipuri Coil Rim Variety	0	0.0	2	3.4	0	0.0	0	0.0
Belford Perforated Rim	0	0.0	0	0.0	0	0.0	1	2.2
Belford Perforated Rim (Sobaipuri Coil Rim)	0	0.0	0	0.0	0	0.0	0	0.0
Babocomari Plain	0	0.0	7	11.9	1	8.3	0	0.0
Redington Plain	0	0.0	0	0.0	0	0.0	2	4.3
Redington Smudged	0	0.0	2	3.4	1	8.3	2	4.3
Sacaton Buff	0	0.0	0	0.0	0	0.0	0	0.0
Gila Plain	0	0.0	1	1.7	0	0.0	2	4.3
Gila Smudged	0	0.0	0	0.0	0	0.0	0	0.0
San Carlos Brown	0	0.0	0	0.0	1	8.3	0	0.0
Slipped brown	0	0.0	0	0.0	0	0.0	0	0.0
Sosa Plain	0	0.0	0	0.0	0	0.0	0	0.0
Whetstone Plain	0	0.0	0	0.0	0	0.0	0	0.0
Wingfield Plain	0	0.0	0	0.0	0	0.0	0	0.0
Fingernail indented	0	0.0	0	0.0	0	0.0	0	0.0
Incised plain	0	0.0	0	0.0	0	0.0	0	0.0
Tularosa Fillet Rim	0	0.0	0	0.0	0	0.0	0	0.0
Neck corrugated gray ware	0	0.0	0	0.0	0	0.0	0	0.0
Stucco ware?	0	0.0	0	0.0	0	0.0	0	0.0
Sandy Paste Perforated	0	0.0	0	0.0	0	0.0	0	0.0

(continued)

TABLE E.33 *(continued)*

	19S 18E		21S 14–19E		31S 8E		31–32S 7E	
	n	%	*n*	%	*n*	%	*n*	%
Sosa Perforated	0	0.0	0	0.0	0	0.0	0	0.0
Subtotal	*25*	*100.0*	*59*	*100.0*	*12*	*100.0*	*46*	*100.0*
Red ware types								
Salt Red: Davis Variety	0	0.0	1	50.0	2	100.0	1	16.7
Salt Smudged: Davis Variety	0	0.0	1	50.0	0	0.0	2	33.3
Dragoon Red	0	0.0	0	0.0	0	0.0	0	0.0
Dragoon Red Smudged	0	0.0	0	0.0	0	0.0	1	16.7
Gila Red	0	0.0	0	0.0	0	0.0	1	16.7
Gila Smudged	0	0.0	0	0.0	0	0.0	0	0.0
San Carlos Red	0	0.0	0	0.0	0	0.0	0	0.0
Wingfield Red	0	0.0	0	0.0	0	0.0	0	0.0
Unidentified red #1	0	0.0	0	0.0	0	0.0	1	16.7
Unidentified red #2	0	0.0	0	0.0	0	0.0	0	0.0
Subtotal	*0*	*0.0*	*2*	*100.0*	*2*	*100.0*	*6*	*100.0*
Corrugated types								
Late plain corrugated	0	0.0	0	0.0	0	0.0	0	0.0
Late indented corrugated	0	0.0	0	0.0	0	0.0	1	100.0
Early indented corrugated, smudged interior	0	0.0	0	0.0	0	0.0	0	0.0
Obliterated corrugated	0	0.0	0	0.0	0	0.0	0	0.0
Neck corrugated	0	0.0	0	0.0	0	0.0	0	0.0
Red-slipped neck corrugated	0	0.0	0	0.0	0	0.0	0	0.0
Subtotal	*0*	*0.0*	*0*	*0.0*	*0*	*0.0*	*1*	*100.0*
Miscellaneous								
Porcelain	0	0.0	0	0.0	0	0.0	0	0.0
White glaze ware	0	0.0	0	0.0	0	0.0	0	0.0
Glass	0	0.0	0	0.0	0	0.0	0	0.0
Unidentified	0	0.0	0	0.0	0	0.0	0	0.0
Subtotal	*0*	*0.0*	*0*	*0.0*	*0*	*0.0*	*0*	*0.0*
Total	**25**		**67**		**17**		**66**	

TABLE E.34 Gerald's typological analysis of sherds from Davis Ranch Site: totals by type

	n	%
Painted types		
Gila Polychrome	8,404	78.6
Gila Black-on-red	155	1.4
Pinto Polychrome	110	1.0
Gila Polychrome (Pink Variant)	17	0.2
Gila-Tucson Polychrome	4	0.0
Tucson Polychrome	184	1.7
Tucson Black-on-red	175	1.6
Tonto Polychrome	202	1.9
Dragoon Red-on-brown	92	0.9
Cascabel Red-on-brown	122	1.1
Davis Red-on-white	49	0.5
Tres Alamos Red-on-brown	58	0.5
Gila White Slip	374	3.5
Cañada del Oro Red-on-brown	2	0.0
Gila Butte Red-on-buff	11	0.1
Santa Cruz Red-on-buff	236	2.2
Sacaton Red-on-buff	108	1.0
Casa Grande Red-on-buff	1	0.0
Rillito Red-on-brown	36	0.3
Rillito Red-on-brown (micaceous)	114	1.1
Rincon Red-on-brown	58	0.5
Pantano Red-on-brown	20	0.2
Tanque Verde Red-on-brown	31	0.3
Mimbres Black-on-white	16	0.1
Dos Cabezas Red-on-brown	7	0.1
Encinas Red-on-brown	49	0.5
Nogales Purple-on-red	2	0.0

(*continued*)

TABLE E.34 *(continued)*

	n	%
Cerros Red-on-white	4	0.0
San Carlos Red-on-brown	6	0.1
San Carlos Red-on-white	26	0.2
El Paso Polychrome	2	0.0
Unidentified polychrome	2	0.0
Kayenta-like polychrome	6	0.1
Tusayan-like polychrome	8	0.1
Subtotal	*10,691*	*100.0*
Plain types		
Davis Plain	22,851	79.8
Davis Plain: Sobaipuri Coil Rim Variety	61	0.2
Belford Perforated Rim	239	0.8
Belford Perforated Rim (Sobaipuri Coil Rim)	61	0.2
Babocomari Plain	3,641	12.7
Redington Plain	636	2.2
Redington Smudged	355	1.2
Sacaton Buff	117	0.4
Gila Plain	428	1.5
Gila Smudged	35	0.1
San Carlos Brown	59	0.2
Slipped brown	33	0.1
Sosa Plain	37	0.1
Whetstone Plain	42	0.1
Wingfield Plain	16	0.1
Fingernail indented	2	0.0
Incised plain	1	0.0
Tularosa Fillet Rim	1	0.0
Neck corrugated gray ware	1	0.0
Stucco ware?	1	0.0

(continued)

TABLE E.34 *(continued)*

	n	%
Sandy Paste Perforated	4	0.0
Sosa Perforated	11	0.0
Subtotal	*28,632*	*100.0*
Red ware types		
Salt Red: Davis Variety	891	47.8
Salt Smudged: Davis Variety	199	10.7
Dragoon Red	369	19.8
Dragoon Red Smudged	70	3.8
Gila Red	155	8.3
Gila Smudged	43	2.3
San Carlos Red	61	3.3
Wingfield Red	8	0.4
Unidentified red #1	32	1.7
Unidentified red #2	35	1.9
Subtotal	*1,863*	*100.0*
Corrugated types		
Late plain corrugated	104	33.4
Late indented corrugated	134	43.1
Early indented corrugated, smudged interior	9	2.9
Obliterated corrugated	16	5.1
Neck corrugated	40	12.9
Red-slipped neck corrugated	8	2.6
Subtotal	*311*	*100.0*
Miscellaneous		
Porcelain	2	1.6
White glaze ware	4	3.1
Glass	1	0.8
Unidentified	121	94.5
Subtotal	*128*	*100.0*
Total	**41,625**	

APPENDIX F

Additional Ceramic Data Tables Generated as a Result of the Reanalysis

Patrick D. Lyons

TABLE F.1 Painted ceramics recovered from the pit houses and subjected to reanalysis

	House 1		House 2	
Ware or ware-level category and/or type or type-level category	Fill	Floor	Fill	Floor
Roosevelt Red Ware				
Cliff Black-on-red	0	0	0	0
Cliff Polychrome or Nine Mile Polychrome	0	0	0	0
Cliff Polychrome	1	0	0	0
Cliff Polychrome: Salmon Variety	0	0	0	0
Cliff Polychrome: Tonto Variety	0	0	0	0
Cliff Polychrome: Tucson Variety	0	0	0	0
Gila Black-on-red	0	0	2	0
Gila Polychrome	0	0	6	0
Gila Polychrome or later	1	0	1	0
Gila Polychrome or later (salmon variety)	0	0	0	0
Gila Polychrome, no banding line	0	0	0	0
Gila Polychrome: Gila Variety	0	0	0	0
Gila Polychrome: Salmon Variety	0	0	0	0
Gila Polychrome: Tonto Variety	0	0	0	0
indeterminate Roosevelt Red Ware black-on-red	0	0	0	0
indeterminate Roosevelt Red Ware polychrome	11	1	18	1
indeterminate Roosevelt Red Ware (salmon variety)	0	0	0	0
Nine Mile Polychrome	0	0	0	0
Nine Mile Polychrome: Safford Variety	0	0	0	0
Nine Mile Polychrome: Tonto Variety	0	0	0	0
Phoenix Polychrome	0	0	1	0
Pinto Black-on-red	0	0	0	0
Pinto Polychrome	0	0	0	1
Pinto Polychrome: Salmon Variety	0	0	0	0
Tonto Polychrome	0	0	0	0
Whiteriver Polychrome	0	0	0	0
Subtotal	*13*	*1*	*28*	*2*

House 3	House 4		House 5			House 6		
Fill	Fill	Floor	Fill	Floor	Burial 10	Fill	Floor	Pit 1
0	0	0	0	0	0	0	0	0
0	1	1	2	0	0	0	0	0
2	0	0	0	0	0	1	0	0
0	0	0	0	0	0	0	0	0
0	0	0	0	0	0	0	0	0
0	0	0	0	0	0	0	0	0
0	0	0	0	0	0	0	0	0
8	3	0	1	0	1	3	0	0
9	1	0	2	0	0	3	0	0
0	0	0	0	0	0	0	0	0
1	0	0	1	0	0	0	0	0
0	0	0	0	0	0	0	0	0
1	1	0	0	0	0	0	0	0
0	0	0	0	0	0	0	0	0
1	0	0	0	0	0	0	0	0
49	15	2	15	2	3	18	1	1
0	0	0	0	0	0	0	0	0
0	0	0	0	0	0	0	0	0
0	0	0	0	0	0	0	0	0
0	0	0	0	0	0	0	0	0
1	0	0	0	0	0	0	0	0
0	0	0	0	0	0	1	0	0
1	0	0	0	0	0	1	0	0
0	0	0	0	0	0	0	0	0
1	0	0	0	0	0	0	0	0
0	0	0	0	0	0	0	0	0
74	*21*	*3*	*21*	*2*	*4*	*27*	*1*	*1*

(*continued*)

TABLE F.1 *(continued)*

Ware or ware-level category and/or type or type-level category	House 1		House 2	
	Fill	Floor	Fill	Floor
Maverick Mountain Series				
indeterminate Maverick Mountain Series	2	0	0	1
indeterminate Maverick Mountain Series black-on-red	0	0	0	0
indeterminate Maverick Mountain Series, Roosevelt Red Ware exterior	0	0	0	0
Maverick Mountain Black-on-red	2	1	0	0
Maverick Mountain Polychrome	0	0	0	0
Nantack Polychrome A (Tusayan Polychrome analog)	0	0	0	0
Tucson Black-on-red	0	0	0	0
Tucson Black-on-red (no slip)	0	0	0	0
Tucson Black-on-red or Tucson Polychrome	0	0	0	0
Tucson Polychrome	1	4	0	0
Subtotal	*5*	*5*	*0*	*1*
Babocomari Polychrome	0	0	0	0
Subtotal	*0*	*0*	*0*	*0*
Davis Black-on-red	0	0	0	0
Subtotal	*0*	*0*	*0*	*0*
Dragoon or San Simon Series	0	0	0	0
Subtotal	*0*	*0*	*0*	*0*
indeterminate decorated	0	0	0	0
Subtotal	*0*	*0*	*0*	*0*
indeterminate red-on-brown	1	0	0	0
Subtotal	*1*	*0*	*0*	*0*
Kinishba Polychrome	0	0	0	0
Subtotal	*0*	*0*	*0*	*0*
Mimbres Black-on-white	1	0	0	0
Subtotal	*1*	*0*	*0*	*0*
San Carlos Red-on-brown	0	0	0	0
Subtotal	*0*	*0*	*0*	*0*
Total	**20**	**6**	**28**	**3**

House 3	House 4		House 5			House 6		
Fill	Fill	Floor	Fill	Floor	Burial 10	Fill	Floor	Pit 1
0	1	0	2	0	0	1	1	0
0	0	0	0	0	0	0	0	0
0	0	0	0	0	0	0	0	0
0	0	0	1	0	0	5	0	0
0	0	0	0	0	0	0	0	0
0	0	0	0	0	0	0	0	0
1	2	0	0	0	0	1	0	0
0	0	0	0	0	0	0	0	0
0	0	0	0	0	0	3	0	0
2	6	1	5	0	3	5	0	0
3	*9*	*1*	*8*	*0*	*3*	*15*	*1*	*0*
0	0	0	0	0	0	0	0	0
0	*0*	*0*	*0*	*0*	*0*	*0*	*0*	*0*
0	0	0	0	0	0	0	0	0
0	*0*	*0*	*0*	*0*	*0*	*0*	*0*	*0*
0	0	0	0	0	0	0	0	0
0	*0*	*0*	*0*	*0*	*0*	*0*	*0*	*0*
0	0	0	0	0	0	1	0	0
0	*0*	*0*	*0*	*0*	*0*	*1*	*0*	*0*
0	0	0	0	0	0	0	0	0
0	*0*	*0*	*0*	*0*	*0*	*0*	*0*	*0*
0	0	0	0	0	0	0	0	0
0	*0*	*0*	*0*	*0*	*0*	*0*	*0*	*0*
0	0	1	1	0	0	0	0	0
0	*0*	*1*	*1*	*0*	*0*	*0*	*0*	*0*
1	0	0	0	0	0	0	0	0
1	*0*	*0*	*0*	*0*	*0*	*0*	*0*	*0*
78	**30**	**5**	**30**	**2**	**7**	**43**	**2**	**1**

(*continued*)

TABLE F.1 *(continued)*

Ware or ware-level category and/or type or type-level category	House 7	
	Pits 1 and 2	Fill
Roosevelt Red Ware		
Cliff Black-on-red	0	0
Cliff Polychrome or Nine Mile Polychrome	0	1
Cliff Polychrome	2	1
Cliff Polychrome: Salmon Variety	0	0
Cliff Polychrome: Tonto Variety	0	0
Cliff Polychrome: Tucson Variety	0	0
Gila Black-on-red	0	1
Gila Polychrome	5	16
Gila Polychrome or later	8	19
Gila Polychrome or later (salmon variety)	0	0
Gila Polychrome, no banding line	0	1
Gila Polychrome: Gila Variety	0	1
Gila Polychrome: Salmon Variety	0	0
Gila Polychrome: Tonto Variety	0	1
indeterminate Roosevelt Red Ware black-on-red	0	0
indeterminate Roosevelt Red Ware polychrome	23	83
indeterminate Roosevelt Red Ware (salmon variety)	0	0
Nine Mile Polychrome	0	0
Nine Mile Polychrome: Safford Variety	0	1
Nine Mile Polychrome: Tonto Variety	0	0
Phoenix Polychrome	0	0
Pinto Black-on-red	0	0
Pinto Polychrome	0	1
Pinto Polychrome: Salmon Variety	0	0
Tonto Polychrome	0	0
Whiteriver Polychrome	0	0
Subtotal	*38*	*126*

House 7					House 8	
Fire Pit 3	Fire Pit 4	Floor 1	Subfloor	Floor 2	Floor	**Total**
0	0	0	0	0	0	**0**
0	0	1	0	0	0	**6**
1	0	0	0	0	0	**8**
0	0	0	0	0	0	**0**
0	0	0	0	0	0	**0**
0	0	0	0	0	0	**0**
0	0	0	0	1	0	**4**
0	0	2	0	1	0	**46**
0	0	5	2	0	0	**51**
0	0	0	0	0	0	**0**
0	0	0	0	0	0	**3**
0	0	0	0	0	0	**1**
0	0	0	0	0	0	**2**
0	0	0	0	0	0	**1**
0	0	0	0	1	0	**2**
1	2	30	4	2	0	**282**
0	0	0	1	0	0	**1**
0	0	0	0	0	0	**0**
0	0	0	0	0	0	**1**
0	0	0	0	0	0	**0**
0	0	0	0	0	0	**2**
0	0	0	0	1	0	**2**
0	0	3	2	0	0	**9**
0	0	0	0	1	0	**1**
0	0	0	0	0	0	**1**
0	0	0	0	0	0	**0**
2	*2*	*41*	*9*	*7*	*0*	***423***

(*continued*)

TABLE F.1 *(continued)*

Ware or ware-level category and/or type or type-level category	House 7	
	Pits 1 and 2	Fill
Maverick Mountain Series		
indeterminate Maverick Mountain Series	0	3
indeterminate Maverick Mountain Series black-on-red	0	0
indeterminate Maverick Mountain Series, Roosevelt Red Ware exterior	0	0
Maverick Mountain Black-on-red	0	0
Maverick Mountain Polychrome	0	0
Nantack Polychrome A (Tusayan Polychrome analog)	0	0
Tucson Black-on-red	0	0
Tucson Black-on-red (no slip)	0	0
Tucson Black-on-red or Tucson Polychrome	0	0
Tucson Polychrome	1	2
Subtotal	*1*	*5*
Babocomari Polychrome	0	0
Subtotal	*0*	*0*
Davis Black-on-red	0	0
Subtotal	*0*	*0*
Dragoon or San Simon Series	0	0
Subtotal	*0*	*0*
indeterminate decorated	0	0
Subtotal	*0*	*0*
indeterminate red-on-brown	0	0
Subtotal	*0*	*0*
Kinishba Polychrome	0	0
Subtotal	*0*	*0*
Mimbres Black-on-white	0	0
Subtotal	*0*	*0*
San Carlos Red-on-brown	0	0
Subtotal	*0*	*0*
Total	**39**	**131**

House 7					House 8	
Fire Pit 3	Fire Pit 4	Floor 1	Subfloor	Floor 2	Floor	**Total**
0	0	0	0	0	0	**11**
0	0	0	0	0	0	**0**
0	0	0	0	0	0	**0**
0	0	0	1	1	0	**11**
0	0	0	0	0	0	**0**
0	0	0	0	0	0	**0**
0	0	0	1	3	0	**7**
0	0	0	0	0	0	**0**
0	0	0	0	2	0	**5**
0	0	0	1	1	0	**33**
0	*0*	*0*	*3*	*7*	*0*	***67***
0	0	0	0	0	0	**0**
0	*0*	*0*	*0*	*0*	*0*	***0***
0	0	0	0	0	0	**0**
0	*0*	*0*	*0*	*0*	*0*	***0***
0	0	0	0	1	0	**1**
0	*0*	*0*	*0*	*1*	*0*	***1***
0	0	0	0	0	0	**1**
0	*0*	*0*	*0*	*0*	*0*	***1***
0	0	0	0	0	0	**1**
0	*0*	*0*	*0*	*0*	*0*	***1***
0	0	0	0	0	1	**1**
0	*0*	*0*	*0*	*0*	*1*	***1***
0	0	0	0	0	0	**3**
0	*0*	*0*	*0*	*0*	*0*	***3***
0	0	0	0	0	0	**1**
0	*0*	*0*	*0*	*0*	*0*	***1***
2	**2**	**41**	**12**	**15**	**1**	**498**

TABLE F.2 Painted ceramics recovered from Houseblock I rooms and subjected to reanalysis

	Room 3		
Ware or ware-level category and/or type or type-level category	Fill	Floor	Trench in front
Roosevelt Red Ware			
Cliff Black-on-red	0	0	0
Cliff Polychrome or Nine Mile Polychrome	0	1	1
Cliff Polychrome	0	3	2
Cliff Polychrome: Salmon Variety	0	0	1
Cliff Polychrome: Tonto Variety	0	0	0
Cliff Polychrome: Tucson Variety	0	0	0
Gila Black-on-red	0	0	0
Gila Polychrome	1	1	2
Gila Polychrome or later	5	4	1
Gila Polychrome or later (salmon variety)	0	0	0
Gila Polychrome, no banding line	0	0	0
Gila Polychrome: Gila Variety	0	0	0
Gila Polychrome: Salmon Variety	0	0	0
Gila Polychrome: Tonto Variety	0	0	0
indeterminate Roosevelt Red Ware black-on-red	0	0	0
indeterminate Roosevelt Red Ware polychrome	11	22	8
indeterminate Roosevelt Red Ware (salmon variety)	0	0	0
Nine Mile Polychrome	0	0	0
Nine Mile Polychrome: Safford Variety	0	0	0
Nine Mile Polychrome: Tonto Variety	0	0	0
Phoenix Polychrome	0	0	0
Pinto Black-on-red	0	0	0
Pinto Polychrome	0	2	0
Pinto Polychrome: Salmon Variety	0	0	0
Tonto Polychrome	1	1	0
Whiteriver Polychrome	0	0	0
Subtotal	*18*	*34*	*15*

Room 4					Room 6		Room 7		
Fill	Floor	Subfloor	Trench in front	Room 5 Fill	Fill	Trench in front	Fill	Floor	Trench in front
0	0	0	0	0	0	0	0	0	0
2	0	0	0	0	3	1	0	1	0
1	0	2	0	3	3	0	2	0	1
0	0	0	0	0	0	0	0	0	0
0	0	0	0	1	0	0	0	0	0
0	0	0	0	0	0	0	0	0	0
0	0	0	0	0	0	0	0	0	0
12	1	4	1	2	6	2	3	9	2
7	1	2	0	6	6	4	6	1	1
0	0	0	0	0	0	0	0	0	0
1	0	0	0	0	1	0	0	0	0
0	0	0	0	0	0	0	0	0	0
0	0	0	0	0	0	0	0	0	0
0	0	0	0	0	0	0	0	0	0
0	0	0	0	0	0	0	0	0	0
85	0	5	2	23	41	5	33	29	4
0	0	0	0	0	2	0	1	0	0
0	0	0	0	0	0	0	1	0	0
0	0	0	0	0	0	0	0	0	0
1	0	0	0	0	0	0	0	0	0
0	0	0	0	0	0	0	0	0	0
0	0	0	0	0	0	0	1	0	0
2	0	0	0	0	0	0	0	0	0
0	0	0	0	0	0	0	0	0	0
2	0	0	0	1	1	0	1	0	0
0	0	0	0	0	0	0	1	0	0
113	*2*	*13*	*3*	*36*	*63*	*12*	*49*	*40*	*8*

(*continued*)

TABLE F.2 *(continued)*

Ware or ware-level category and/or type or type-level category	Room 3		
	Fill	Floor	Trench in front
Maverick Mountain Series			
indeterminate Maverick Mountain Series	0	1	0
indeterminate Maverick Mountain Series black-on-red	1	0	0
indeterminate Maverick Mountain Series, Roosevelt Red Ware exterior	0	0	0
Maverick Mountain Black-on-red	0	3	0
Maverick Mountain Polychrome	0	0	0
Nantack Polychrome A (Tusayan Polychrome analog)	0	0	0
Tucson Black-on-red	0	1	0
Tucson Black-on-red (no slip)	0	0	0
Tucson Black-on-red or Tucson Polychrome	0	0	0
Tucson Polychrome	0	0	0
Subtotal	*1*	*5*	*0*
Babocomari Polychrome	0	0	0
Subtotal	*0*	*0*	*0*
Davis Black-on-red	0	0	0
Subtotal	*0*	*0*	*0*
Dragoon or San Simon Series	0	0	0
Subtotal	*0*	*0*	*0*
indeterminate decorated	0	0	0
Subtotal	*0*	*0*	*0*
indeterminate red-on-brown	0	0	0
Subtotal	*0*	*0*	*0*
Kinishba Polychrome	0	0	0
Subtotal	*0*	*0*	*0*
Mimbres Black-on-white	0	0	0
Subtotal	*0*	*0*	*0*
San Carlos Red-on-brown	0	0	0
Subtotal	*0*	*0*	*0*
Total	**19**	**39**	**15**

Room 4					Room 6		Room 7		
Fill	Floor	Subfloor	Trench in front	Room 5 Fill	Fill	Trench in front	Fill	Floor	Trench in front
0	0	0	0	0	1	0	0	1	0
1	0	0	0	0	0	0	0	0	0
0	0	0	0	0	0	0	0	0	0
1	0	0	0	0	1	0	0	1	0
0	0	0	0	0	0	0	0	0	0
0	0	0	0	0	0	0	0	0	0
0	0	1	0	0	2	0	1	0	0
0	0	0	0	0	0	0	0	0	0
0	0	0	0	0	0	0	0	0	0
3	0	1	0	0	3	0	0	1	0
5	*0*	*2*	*0*	*0*	*7*	*0*	*1*	*3*	*0*
0	0	0	0	0	0	0	0	0	0
0	*0*	*0*	*0*	*0*	*0*	*0*	*0*	*0*	*0*
0	0	0	0	0	0	0	0	0	0
0	*0*	*0*	*0*	*0*	*0*	*0*	*0*	*0*	*0*
0	0	0	0	0	0	0	0	0	0
0	*0*	*0*	*0*	*0*	*0*	*0*	*0*	*0*	*0*
0	0	0	0	0	0	0	1	0	0
0	*0*	*0*	*0*	*0*	*0*	*0*	*1*	*0*	*0*
0	0	0	0	0	0	0	0	0	0
0	*0*	*0*	*0*	*0*	*0*	*0*	*0*	*0*	*0*
0	0	0	0	0	0	0	0	0	0
0	*0*	*0*	*0*	*0*	*0*	*0*	*0*	*0*	*0*
0	0	0	0	0	0	0	1	0	0
0	*0*	*0*	*0*	*0*	*0*	*0*	*1*	*0*	*0*
0	0	0	0	0	0	0	0	0	0
0	*0*	*0*	*0*	*0*	*0*	*0*	*0*	*0*	*0*
118	**2**	**15**	**3**	**36**	**70**	**12**	**52**	**43**	**8**

(*continued*)

TABLE F.2 (*continued*)

Ware or ware-level category and/or type or type-level category	Room 8			
	Fill	Floor	Subfloor	Trench in front
Roosevelt Red Ware				
Cliff Black-on-red	0	0	0	0
Cliff Polychrome or Nine Mile Polychrome	0	0	0	1
Cliff Polychrome	0	0	0	0
Cliff Polychrome: Salmon Variety	0	0	0	0
Cliff Polychrome: Tonto Variety	0	0	0	0
Cliff Polychrome: Tucson Variety	0	0	0	0
Gila Black-on-red	0	0	0	0
Gila Polychrome	1	0	0	3
Gila Polychrome or later	0	0	2	4
Gila Polychrome or later (salmon variety)	0	0	0	0
Gila Polychrome, no banding line	0	0	0	0
Gila Polychrome: Gila Variety	0	0	0	0
Gila Polychrome: Salmon Variety	0	0	0	0
Gila Polychrome: Tonto Variety	0	0	0	0
indeterminate Roosevelt Red Ware black-on-red	0	0	0	0
indeterminate Roosevelt Red Ware polychrome	4	1	6	10
indeterminate Roosevelt Red Ware (salmon variety)	0	0	0	0
Nine Mile Polychrome	0	0	0	0
Nine Mile Polychrome: Safford Variety	0	0	0	0
Nine Mile Polychrome: Tonto Variety	0	0	0	0
Phoenix Polychrome	0	0	0	0
Pinto Black-on-red	0	0	0	0
Pinto Polychrome	0	0	0	0
Pinto Polychrome: Salmon Variety	0	0	0	0
Tonto Polychrome	1	0	0	0
Whiteriver Polychrome	0	0	0	0
Subtotal	*6*	*1*	*8*	*18*

Room 9				Room 10			Room 11			
Fill	Floor	Subfloor	Trench in front	Fill	Floor	Trench in front	Fill	Floor	Trench in front	**Total**
0	0	0	0	0	0	0	0	0	0	**0**
1	0	0	1	0	0	0	1	0	0	**13**
0	0	0	0	1	0	0	1	0	0	**19**
0	0	0	0	0	0	0	0	0	0	**1**
0	0	0	0	0	0	0	0	0	0	**1**
0	0	0	0	0	0	0	0	0	0	**0**
0	0	0	0	0	0	0	0	0	0	**0**
2	0	0	5	11	3	2	2	0	1	**76**
1	1	1	4	15	3	5	4	0	1	**85**
0	0	0	0	0	0	0	0	0	0	**0**
0	0	0	0	0	0	0	0	0	0	**2**
0	0	0	0	0	0	0	0	0	0	**0**
0	0	0	0	0	0	0	0	0	0	**0**
0	0	0	0	0	0	0	0	0	0	**0**
0	0	0	0	1	0	0	0	0	0	**1**
6	1	1	10	73	22	11	17	3	6	**439**
0	0	0	0	0	0	0	0	0	0	**3**
1	0	0	0	0	0	0	0	0	0	**2**
0	0	0	0	0	0	0	0	0	0	**0**
0	0	0	0	0	0	0	0	0	0	**1**
0	0	0	0	0	0	0	0	0	0	**0**
0	0	0	0	0	0	0	0	0	0	**1**
0	0	0	1	0	0	0	0	0	0	**5**
0	0	0	0	0	0	0	0	0	0	**0**
0	0	0	0	1	0	0	0	0	0	**9**
0	0	0	0	2	1	0	0	0	0	**4**
11	*2*	*2*	*21*	*104*	*29*	*18*	*25*	*3*	*8*	***662***

(*continued*)

TABLE F.2 *(continued)*

Ware or ware-level category and/or type or type-level category	Room 8			
	Fill	Floor	Subfloor	Trench in front
Maverick Mountain Series				
indeterminate Maverick Mountain Series	0	0	0	0
indeterminate Maverick Mountain Series black-on-red	0	0	0	0
indeterminate Maverick Mountain Series, Roosevelt Red Ware exterior	0	0	0	0
Maverick Mountain Black-on-red	0	0	0	0
Maverick Mountain Polychrome	0	0	0	0
Nantack Polychrome A (Tusayan Polychrome analog)	0	0	0	0
Tucson Black-on-red	0	0	0	0
Tucson Black-on-red (no slip)	0	0	0	0
Tucson Black-on-red or Tucson Polychrome	0	0	0	0
Tucson Polychrome	0	0	0	0
Subtotal	*0*	*0*	*0*	*0*
Babocomari Polychrome	0	0	0	0
Subtotal	*0*	*0*	*0*	*0*
Davis Black-on-red	0	0	0	0
Subtotal	*0*	*0*	*0*	*0*
Dragoon or San Simon Series	0	0	0	0
Subtotal	*0*	*0*	*0*	*0*
indeterminate decorated	0	0	0	0
Subtotal	*0*	*0*	*0*	*0*
indeterminate red-on-brown	0	0	0	0
Subtotal	*0*	*0*	*0*	*0*
Kinishba Polychrome	0	0	0	0
Subtotal	*0*	*0*	*0*	*0*
Mimbres Black-on-white	0	0	0	0
Subtotal	*0*	*0*	*0*	*0*
San Carlos Red-on-brown	0	0	0	0
Subtotal	*0*	*0*	*0*	*0*
Total	**6**	**1**	**8**	**18**

Room 9				Room 10			Room 11			
Fill	Floor	Subfloor	Trench in front	Fill	Floor	Trench in front	Fill	Floor	Trench in front	**Total**
0	0	0	0	0	0	0	0	0	0	**3**
1	0	0	0	1	0	0	0	0	0	**4**
0	0	0	0	0	0	0	0	0	0	**0**
0	0	1	0	0	0	0	1	0	0	**8**
0	0	0	0	0	0	0	0	0	0	**0**
0	0	0	0	0	0	0	0	0	0	**0**
0	0	0	0	0	0	0	0	0	0	**5**
0	0	0	0	0	0	0	0	0	0	**0**
0	0	0	0	2	0	0	0	0	0	**2**
0	1	0	2	0	0	0	2	0	0	**13**
1	*1*	*1*	*2*	*3*	*0*	*0*	*3*	*0*	*0*	***35***
0	0	0	0	0	0	0	0	0	0	**0**
0	*0*	*0*	*0*	*0*	*0*	*0*	*0*	*0*	*0*	***0***
0	0	0	0	0	0	0	0	0	0	**0**
0	*0*	*0*	*0*	*0*	*0*	*0*	*0*	*0*	*0*	***0***
0	0	0	0	0	0	0	0	0	0	**0**
0	*0*	*0*	*0*	*0*	*0*	*0*	*0*	*0*	*0*	***0***
0	0	0	0	0	0	0	0	0	0	**1**
0	*0*	*0*	*0*	*0*	*0*	*0*	*0*	*0*	*0*	***1***
0	0	0	0	0	0	0	0	0	0	**0**
0	*0*	*0*	*0*	*0*	*0*	*0*	*0*	*0*	*0*	***0***
0	0	0	0	0	0	0	0	0	0	**0**
0	*0*	*0*	*0*	*0*	*0*	*0*	*0*	*0*	*0*	***0***
0	0	0	0	0	0	0	0	0	0	**1**
0	*0*	*0*	*0*	*0*	*0*	*0*	*0*	*0*	*0*	***1***
0	0	0	0	0	0	0	0	0	0	**0**
0	*0*	*0*	*0*	*0*	*0*	*0*	*0*	*0*	*0*	***0***
12	**3**	**3**	**23**	**107**	**29**	**18**	**28**	**3**	**8**	**699**

TABLE F.3 Painted ceramics recovered from Houseblock II rooms and subjected to reanalysis

Ware or ware-level category and/or type or type-level category	Room 14 Fill	Room 15 Fill	Room 16 Fill	Room 16 Floor	Room 16 Trench in front
Roosevelt Red Ware					
Cliff Black-on-red	0	0	0	0	0
Cliff Polychrome or Nine Mile Polychrome	0	0	0	0	0
Cliff Polychrome	4	1	0	1	0
Cliff Polychrome: Salmon Variety	0	0	0	0	0
Cliff Polychrome: Tonto Variety	1	0	0	0	0
Cliff Polychrome: Tucson Variety	0	0	0	0	0
Gila Black-on-red	0	0	0	0	0
Gila Polychrome	6	1	1	0	0
Gila Polychrome or later	15	1	1	2	1
Gila Polychrome or later (salmon variety)	0	0	0	0	0
Gila Polychrome, no banding line	0	0	0	0	0
Gila Polychrome: Gila Variety	0	0	0	0	0
Gila Polychrome: Salmon Variety	0	0	0	0	0
Gila Polychrome: Tonto Variety	0	0	0	0	0
indeterminate Roosevelt Red Ware black-on-red	0	0	0	0	0
indeterminate Roosevelt Red Ware polychrome	49	7	8	7	1
indeterminate Roosevelt Red Ware (salmon variety)	0	0	0	0	0
Nine Mile Polychrome	0	0	0	0	0
Nine Mile Polychrome: Safford Variety	0	0	0	0	0
Nine Mile Polychrome: Tonto Variety	0	0	0	0	0
Phoenix Polychrome	0	0	0	0	0
Pinto Black-on-red	0	0	0	0	0
Pinto Polychrome	0	0	0	0	1
Pinto Polychrome: Salmon Variety	0	0	0	1	0
Tonto Polychrome	1	1	0	0	0
Whiteriver Polychrome	2	0	0	0	0
Subtotal	*78*	*11*	*10*	*11*	*3*

Room 17					Room 21				
Fill	Floor	Room 18 Fill	Room 19 Fill	Room 20 Fill	Fill	Trench in front	Room 33 fill	Room 35 fill	**Total**
0	0	0	0	0	0	0	0	0	**0**
0	0	0	0	0	0	0	2	0	**2**
1	1	0	2	0	1	2	3	0	**16**
0	0	0	0	0	0	0	0	0	**0**
0	0	0	0	0	0	0	0	0	**1**
0	0	0	0	0	0	0	0	0	**0**
0	0	0	0	0	0	0	0	0	**0**
0	2	0	3	1	2	0	4	5	**25**
4	2	2	9	4	1	0	14	6	**62**
0	0	0	0	0	0	0	0	0	**0**
0	0	0	0	0	0	0	0	0	**0**
0	0	0	0	0	0	0	0	0	**0**
0	0	0	0	0	0	0	0	0	**0**
0	0	0	0	0	0	0	0	0	**0**
0	0	0	0	0	0	0	0	0	**0**
8	5	0	13	5	10	3	34	12	**162**
0	0	0	0	0	1	0	0	1	**2**
0	0	0	0	0	0	0	0	0	**0**
0	0	0	0	0	0	0	0	0	**0**
0	0	0	0	0	0	0	0	0	**0**
0	0	0	0	0	0	0	0	0	**0**
0	0	0	0	0	0	0	0	0	**0**
0	0	0	0	0	0	0	1	0	**2**
0	0	0	0	0	0	0	0	0	**1**
0	0	0	0	0	1	0	0	0	**3**
0	0	0	0	0	0	0	0	0	**2**
13	*10*	*2*	*27*	*10*	*16*	*5*	*58*	*24*	***278***

(*continued*)

TABLE F.3 *(continued)*

Ware or ware-level category and/or type or type-level category	Room 14 Fill	Room 15 Fill	Room 16 Fill	Room 16 Floor	Room 16 Trench in front
Maverick Mountain Series					
indeterminate Maverick Mountain Series	1	0	0	0	0
indeterminate Maverick Mountain Series black-on-red	0	0	0	0	0
indeterminate Maverick Mountain Series, Roosevelt Red Ware exterior	0	0	0	0	0
Maverick Mountain Black-on-red	0	0	0	0	0
Maverick Mountain Polychrome	0	0	0	0	0
Nantack Polychrome A (Tusayan Polychrome analog)	0	0	0	0	0
Tucson Black-on-red	0	0	0	0	0
Tucson Black-on-red (no slip)	0	0	0	0	0
Tucson Black-on-red or Tucson Polychrome	1	0	0	0	0
Tucson Polychrome	1	0	1	0	1
Subtotal	*3*	*0*	*1*	*0*	*1*
Babocomari Polychrome	0	0	0	0	0
Subtotal	*0*	*0*	*0*	*0*	*0*
Davis Black-on-red	0	0	0	0	0
Subtotal	*0*	*0*	*0*	*0*	*0*
Dragoon or San Simon Series	0	0	0	0	0
Subtotal	*0*	*0*	*0*	*0*	*0*
indeterminate decorated	0	0	0	0	0
Subtotal	*0*	*0*	*0*	*0*	*0*
indeterminate red-on-brown	0	0	0	0	0
Subtotal	*0*	*0*	*0*	*0*	*0*
Kinishba Polychrome	0	0	0	0	0
Subtotal	*0*	*0*	*0*	*0*	*0*
Mimbres Black-on-white	0	0	0	0	0
Subtotal	*0*	*0*	*0*	*0*	*0*
San Carlos Red-on-brown	0	0	0	0	0
Subtotal	*0*	*0*	*0*	*0*	*0*
Total	**81**	**11**	**11**	**11**	**4**

Room 17		Room 18	Room 19	Room 20	Room 21		Room 33	Room 35	
Fill	Floor	Fill	Fill	Fill	Fill	Trench in front	fill	fill	**Total**
0	0	0	1	2	0	0	0	0	**4**
0	0	0	0	0	0	0	0	0	**0**
0	0	0	0	0	0	0	0	0	**0**
0	0	0	0	0	0	0	0	1	**1**
0	0	0	0	0	0	0	0	0	**0**
0	0	0	0	0	0	0	0	0	**0**
0	0	0	0	0	1	0	1	2	**4**
0	0	0	0	0	0	0	0	0	**0**
0	0	0	0	0	0	0	0	1	**2**
0	1	0	0	2	0	0	0	4	**10**
0	*1*	*0*	*1*	*4*	*1*	*0*	*1*	*8*	***21***
0	0	0	0	0	0	0	0	0	**0**
0	*0*	*0*	*0*	*0*	*0*	*0*	*0*	*0*	***0***
0	0	0	0	0	0	0	0	0	**0**
0	*0*	*0*	*0*	*0*	*0*	*0*	*0*	*0*	***0***
0	0	0	0	0	0	0	0	0	**0**
0	*0*	*0*	*0*	*0*	*0*	*0*	*0*	*0*	***0***
0	0	0	0	1	0	0	0	0	**1**
0	*0*	*0*	*0*	*1*	*0*	*0*	*0*	*0*	***1***
0	0	0	0	0	0	0	0	0	**0**
0	*0*	*0*	*0*	*0*	*0*	*0*	*0*	*0*	***0***
0	0	0	0	0	0	0	0	0	**0**
0	*0*	*0*	*0*	*0*	*0*	*0*	*0*	*0*	***0***
0	0	0	0	0	0	0	0	0	**0**
0	*0*	*0*	*0*	*0*	*0*	*0*	*0*	*0*	***0***
0	0	0	0	0	0	0	0	0	**0**
0	*0*	*0*	*0*	*0*	*0*	*0*	*0*	*0*	***0***
13	**11**	**2**	**28**	**15**	**17**	**5**	**59**	**32**	**300**

TABLE F.4 Painted ceramics recovered from Houseblocks VI and VII and subjected to reanalysis

	Houseblock VI		Houseblock VII							
			Room 37							
Ware or ware-level category and/or type or type-level category	Room 47		Floor	Fill	Subtotal		Room 45		Total	
	n	%	*n*	*n*	*n*	%	*n*	%	*n*	%
Roosevelt Red Ware										
Cliff Black-on-red	0	0.00	0	0	0	0.00	0	0.00	0	0.00
Cliff Polychrome or Nine Mile Polychrome	0	0.00	0	0	0	0.00	0	0.00	0	0.00
Cliff Polychrome	0	0.00	0	0	0	0.00	0	0.00	0	0.00
Cliff Polychrome: Salmon Variety	0	0.00	0	0	0	0.00	0	0.00	0	0.00
Cliff Polychrome: Tonto Variety	0	0.00	0	0	0	0.00	0	0.00	0	0.00
Cliff Polychrome: Tucson Variety	0	0.00	0	0	0	0.00	0	0.00	0	0.00
Gila Black-on-red	0	0.00	0	0	0	0.00	0	0.00	0	0.00
Gila Polychrome	4	50.00	0	1	1	7.14	0	0.00	1	6.25
Gila Polychrome or later	2	25.00	0	4	4	28.57	0	0.00	4	25.00
Gila Polychrome or later (salmon variety)	0	0.00	0	0	0	0.00	0	0.00	0	0.00
Gila Polychrome, no banding line	0	0.00	0	0	0	0.00	0	0.00	0	0.00
Gila Polychrome: Gila Variety	0	0.00	0	0	0	0.00	0	0.00	0	0.00
Gila Polychrome: Salmon Variety	0	0.00	0	0	0	0.00	0	0.00	0	0.00
Gila Polychrome: Tonto Variety	0	0.00	0	0	0	0.00	0	0.00	0	0.00
indeterminate Roosevelt Red Ware black-on-red	0	0.00	0	1	1	7.14	0	0.00	1	6.25
indeterminate Roosevelt Red Ware polychrome	2	25.00	0	4	4	28.57	1	50.00	5	31.25
indeterminate Roosevelt Red Ware (salmon variety)	0	0.00	0	0	0	0.00	0	0.00	0	0.00

Nine Mile Polychrome	0	0.00	0	0	0	0.00	0	0.00	0	0.00
Nine Mile Polychrome: Safford Variety	0	0.00	0	0	0	0.00	0	0.00	0	0.00
Nine Mile Polychrome: Tonto Variety	0	0.00	0	0	0	0.00	0	0.00	0	0.00
Phoenix Polychrome	0	0.00	0	0	0	0.00	0	0.00	0	0.00
Pinto Black-on-red	0	0.00	0	0	0	0.00	0	0.00	0	0.00
Pinto Polychrome	0	0.00	1	0	1	7.14	0	0.00	1	6.25
Pinto Polychrome: Salmon Variety	0	0.00	0	0	0	0.00	0	0.00	0	0.00
Tonto Polychrome	0	0.00	0	2	2	14.29	0	0.00	2	12.50
Whiteriver Polychrome	0	0.00	0	0	0	0.00	0	0.00	0	0.00
Subtotal	*8*	*100.00*	*1*	*12*	*13*	*92.86*	*1*	*50.00*	*14*	*87.50*
Maverick Mountain Series										
indeterminate Maverick Mountain Series	0	0.00	0	0	0	0.00	0	0.00	0	0.00
indeterminate Maverick Mountain Series black-on-red	0	0.00	1	0	1	7.14	0	0.00	1	6.25
indeterminate Maverick Mountain Series, Roosevelt Red Ware exterior	0	0.00	0	0	0	0.00	0	0.00	0	0.00
Maverick Mountain Black-on-red	0	0.00	0	0	0	0.00	0	0.00	0	0.00
Maverick Mountain Polychrome	0	0.00	0	0	0	0.00	0	0.00	0	0.00
Nantack Polychrome A (Tusayan Polychrome analog)	0	0.00	0	0	0	0.00	0	0.00	0	0.00
Tucson Black-on-red	0	0.00	0	0	0	0.00	0	0.00	0	0.00
Tucson Black-on-red (no slip)	0	0.00	0	0	0	0.00	0	0.00	0	0.00
Tucson Black-on-red or Tucson Polychrome	0	0.00	0	0	0	0.00	0	0.00	0	0.00
Tucson Polychrome	0	0.00	0	0	0	0.00	1	50.00	1	6.25
Subtotal	*0*	*0.00*	*1*	*0*	*1*	*7.14*	*1*	*50.00*	*2*	*12.50*

(*continued*)

TABLE F.4 *(continued)*

Ware or ware-level category and/or type or type-level category	Houseblock VI		Houseblock VII							Total	
			Room 37								
	Room 47		Floor	Fill	Subtotal		Room 45				
	n	%	*n*	*n*	*n*	%	*n*	%		*n*	%
Babocomari Polychrome	0	0.00	0	0	0	0.00	0	0.00		0	0.00
Subtotal	*0*	*0.00*	*0*	*0*	*0*	*0.00*	*0*	*0.00*		*0*	*0.00*
Davis Black-on-red	0	0.00	0	0	0	0.00	0	0.00		0	0.00
Subtotal	*0*	*0.00*	*0*	*0*	*0*	*0.00*	*0*	*0.00*		*0*	*0.00*
Dragoon or San Simon Series	0	0.00	0	0	0	0.00	0	0.00		0	0.00
Subtotal	*0*	*0.00*	*0*	*0*	*0*	*0.00*	*0*	*0.00*		*0*	*0.00*
indeterminate decorated	0	0.00	0	0	0	0.00	0	0.00		0	0.00
Subtotal	*0*	*0.00*	*0*	*0*	*0*	*0.00*	*0*	*0.00*		*0*	*0.00*
indeterminate red-on-brown	0	0.00	0	0	0	0.00	0	0.00		0	0.00
Subtotal	*0*	*0.00*	*0*	*0*	*0*	*0.00*	*0*	*0.00*		*0*	*0.00*
Kinishba Polychrome	0	0.00	0	0	0	0.00	0	0.00		0	0.00
Subtotal	*0*	*0.00*	*0*	*0*	*0*	*0.00*	*0*	*0.00*		*0*	*0.00*
Mimbres Black-on-white	0	0.00	0	0	0	0.00	0	0.00		0	0.00
Subtotal	*0*	*0.00*	*0*	*0*	*0*	*0.00*	*0*	*0.00*		*0*	*0.00*
San Carlos Red-on-brown	0	0.00	0	0	0	0.00	0	0.00		0	0.00
Subtotal	*0*	*0.00*	*0*	*0*	*0*	*0.00*	*0*	*0.00*		*0*	*0.00*
Total	**8**	**100.00**	**2**	**12**	**14**	**100.00**	**2**	**100.00**		**16**	**100.00**

TABLE F.5 Painted ceramics recovered from Rooms 2, 34, 36, and 46 and subjected to reanalysis

Ware or ware-level category and/or type or type-level category	Room 2					Room 34 Fill		Room 36			
	Fill (*n*)	Floor (*n*)	Strip test south of Room 2 (*n*)	Subtotal *n*	Subtotal %	*n*	%	Fill (*n*)	Trench in front (*n*)	Subtotal *n*	Subtotal %
Roosevelt Red Ware											
Cliff Black-on-red	0	0	0	0	0.00	0	0.00	0	0	0	0.00
Cliff Polychrome or Nine Mile Polychrome	7	0	2	9	2.93	3	3.41	0	0	0	0.00
Cliff Polychrome	8	1	0	9	2.93	2	2.27	1	0	1	2.63
Cliff Polychrome: Salmon Variety	0	0	0	0	0.00	0	0.00	0	0	0	0.00
Cliff Polychrome: Tonto Variety	0	0	0	0	0.00	0	0.00	0	0	0	0.00
Cliff Polychrome: Tucson Variety	0	0	0	0	0.00	0	0.00	0	0	0	
Gila Black-on-red	0	0	0	0	0.00	0	0.00	0	0	0	0.00
Gila Polychrome	33	6	0	39	12.70	19	21.59	3	1	4	10.53
Gila Polychrome or later	34	16	1	51	16.61	20	22.73	12	0	12	31.58
Gila Polychrome or later (salmon variety)	0	0	0	0	0.00	0	0.00	0	0	0	
Gila Polychrome, no banding line	2	0	0	2	0.65	0	0.00	0	0	0	0.00
Gila Polychrome: Gila Variety	0	0	0	0	0.00	0	0.00	0	0	0	0.00
Gila Polychrome: Salmon Variety	0	0	0	0	0.00	0	0.00	0	0	0	0.00
Gila Polychrome: Tonto Variety	0	0	0	0	0.00	0	0.00	0	0	0	0.00
indeterminate Roosevelt Red Ware black-on-red	1	0	0	1	0.33	0	0.00	1	0	1	2.63
indeterminate Roosevelt Red Ware polychrome	126	51	4	181	58.96	39	44.32	17	0	17	44.74
indeterminate Roosevelt Red Ware (salmon variety)	0	1	0	1	0.33	0	0.00	0	0	0	0.00

(continued)

TABLE F.5 *(continued)*

Ware or ware-level category and/or type or type-level category	Room 2					Room 34 Fill		Room 36			
	Fill (*n*)	Floor (*n*)	Strip test south of Room 2 (*n*)	Subtotal *n*	Subtotal %	*n*	%	Fill (*n*)	Trench in front (*n*)	Subtotal *n*	Subtotal %
Nine Mile Polychrome	1	0	0	1	0.33	0	0.00	0	0	0	0.00
Nine Mile Polychrome: Safford Variety	0	0	0	0	0.00	0	0.00	0	0	0	0.00
Nine Mile Polychrome: Tonto Variety	0	0	0	0	0.00	0	0.00	0	0	0	0.00
Phoenix Polychrome	0	0	0	0	0.00	0	0.00	0	0	0	0.00
Pinto Black-on-red	0	0	0	0	0.00	0	0.00	0	0	0	0.00
Pinto Polychrome	1	0	0	1	0.33	1	1.14	0	0	0	0.00
Pinto Polychrome: Salmon Variety	0	0	0	0	0.00	0	0.00	0	0	0	0.00
Tonto Polychrome	2	7	0	9	2.93	4	4.55	0	0	0	0.00
Whiteriver Polychrome	0	0	0	0	0.00	0	0.00	0	0	0	0.00
Subtotal	*215*	*82*	*7*	*304*	*99.02*	*88*	*100.00*	*34*	*1*	*35*	*92.11*
Maverick Mountain Series											
indeterminate Maverick Mountain Series	0	0	0	0	0.00	0	0.00	0	0	0	0.00
indeterminate Maverick Mountain Series black-on-red	0	0	0	0	0.00	0	0.00	0	0	0	0.00
indeterminate Maverick Mountain Series, Roosevelt Red Ware exterior	0	0	0	0	0.00	0	0.00	0	0	0	0.00
Maverick Mountain Black-on-red	1	0	0	1	0.33	0	0.00	0	0	0	0.00
Maverick Mountain Polychrome	1	0	0	1	0.33	0	0.00	0	0	0	0.00
Nantack Polychrome A (Tusayan Polychrome analog)	0	0	0	0	0.00	0	0.00	0	0	0	0.00

Tucson Black-on-red	0	0	0	0	0.00	0	0.00	0	0	0	0.00
Tucson Black-on-red (no slip)	0	0	0	0	0.00	0	0.00	0	0	0	0.00
Tucson Black-on-red or Tucson Polychrome	0	1	0	1	0.33	0	0.00	0	0	0	0.00
Tucson Polychrome	0	0	0	0	0.00	0	0.00	3	0	3	7.89
Subtotal	*2*	*1*	*0*	*3*	*0.98*	*0*	*0.00*	*3*	*0*	*3*	*7.89*
Babocomari Polychrome	0	0	0	0	0.00	0	0.00	0	0	0	0.00
Subtotal	*0*	*0*	*0*	*0*	*0.00*	*0*	*0.00*	*0*	*0*	*0*	*0.00*
Davis Black-on-red	0	0	0	0	0.00	0	0.00	0	0	0	0.00
Subtotal	*0*	*0*	*0*	*0*	*0.00*	*0*	*0.00*	*0*	*0*	*0*	*0.00*
Dragoon or San Simon Series	0	0	0	0	0.00	0	0.00	0	0	0	0.00
Subtotal	*0*	*0*	*0*	*0*	*0.00*	*0*	*0.00*	*0*	*0*	*0*	*0.00*
indeterminate decorated	0	0	0	0	0.00	0	0.00	0	0	0	0.00
Subtotal	*0*	*0*	*0*	*0*	*0.00*	*0*	*0.00*	*0*	*0*	*0*	*0.00*
indeterminate red-on-brown	0	0	0	0	0.00	0	0.00	0	0	0	0.00
Subtotal	*0*	*0*	*0*	*0*	*0.00*	*0*	*0.00*	*0*	*0*	*0*	*0.00*
Kinishba Polychrome	0	0	0	0	0.00	0	0.00	0	0	0	0.00
Subtotal	*0*	*0*	*0*	*0*	*0.00*	*0*	*0.00*	*0*	*0*	*0*	*0.00*
Mimbres Black-on-white	0	0	0	0	0.00	0	0.00	0	0	0	0.00
Subtotal	*0*	*0*	*0*	*0*	*0.00*	*0*	*0.00*	*0*	*0*	*0*	*0.00*
San Carlos Red-on-brown	0	0	0	0	0.00	0	0.00	0	0	0	0.00
Subtotal	*0*	*0*	*0*	*0*	*0.00*	*0*	*0.00*	*0*	*0*	*0*	*0.00*
Total	**217**	**83**	**7**	**307**	**100.00**	**88**	**100.00**	**37**	**1**	**38**	**100.00**

(*continued*)

TABLE F.5 *(continued)*

	Room 46 fill		Total	
	n	%	*n*	%
Roosevelt Red Ware				
Cliff Black-on-red	0	0.00	0	0.00
Cliff Polychrome or Nine Mile Polychrome	1	3.23	13	2.80
Cliff Polychrome	1	3.23	13	2.80
Cliff Polychrome: Salmon Variety	0	0.00	0	0.00
Cliff Polychrome: Tonto Variety	0	0.00	0	0.00
Cliff Polychrome: Tucson Variety	0	0.00	0	0.00
Gila Black-on-red	0	0.00	0	0.00
Gila Polychrome	4	12.90	66	14.22
Gila Polychrome or later	7	22.58	90	19.40
Gila Polychrome or later (salmon variety)	0	0.00	0	0.00
Gila Polychrome, no banding line	0	0.00	2	0.43
Gila Polychrome: Gila Variety	0	0.00	0	0.00
Gila Polychrome: Salmon Variety	0	0.00	0	0.00
Gila Polychrome: Tonto Variety	0	0.00	0	0.00
indeterminate Roosevelt Red Ware black-on-red	0	0.00	2	0.43
indeterminate Roosevelt Red Ware polychrome	18	58.06	255	54.96
indeterminate Roosevelt Red Ware (salmon variety)	0	0.00	1	0.22
Nine Mile Polychrome	0	0.00	1	0.22
Nine Mile Polychrome: Safford Variety	0	0.00	0	0.00

Nine Mile Polychrome: Tonto Variety	0	0.00	0	0.00
Phoenix Polychrome	0	0.00	0	0.00
Pinto Black-on-red	0	0.00	0	0.00
Pinto Polychrome	0	0.00	2	0.43
Pinto Polychrome: Salmon Variety	0	0.00	0	0.00
Tonto Polychrome	0	0.00	13	2.80
Whiteriver Polychrome	0	0.00	0	0.00
Subtotal	*31*	*100.00*	*458*	*98.71*
Maverick Mountain Series				
indeterminate Maverick Mountain Series	0	0.00	0	0.00
indeterminate Maverick Mountain Series black-on-red	0	0.00	0	0.00
indeterminate Maverick Mountain Series, Roosevelt Red Ware exterior	0	0.00	0	0.00
Maverick Mountain Black-on-red	0	0.00	1	0.22
Maverick Mountain Polychrome	0	0.00	1	0.22
Nantack Polychrome A (Tusayan Polychrome analog)	0	0.00	0	0.00
Tucson Black-on-red	0	0.00	0	0.00
Tucson Black-on-red (no slip)	0	0.00	0	0.00
Tucson Black-on-red or Tucson Polychrome	0	0.00	1	0.22
Tucson Polychrome	0	0.00	3	0.65
Subtotal	*0*	*0.00*	*6*	*1.29*

(continued)

TABLE F.5 *(continued)*

	Room 46 fill		Total	
	n	%	*n*	%
Babocomari Polychrome	0	0.00	0	0.00
Subtotal	*0*	*0.00*	*0*	*0.00*
Davis Black-on-red	0	0.00	0	0.00
Subtotal	*0*	*0.00*	*0*	*0.00*
Dragoon or San Simon Series	0	0.00	0	0.00
Subtotal	*0*	*0.00*	*0*	*0.00*
indeterminate decorated	0	0.00	0	0.00
Subtotal	*0*	*0.00*	*0*	*0.00*
indeterminate red-on-brown	0	0.00	0	0.00
Subtotal	*0*	*0.00*	*0*	*0.00*
Kinishba Polychrome	0	0.00	0	0.00
Subtotal	*0*	*0.00*	*0*	*0.00*
Mimbres Black-on-white	0	0.00	0	0.00
Subtotal	*0*	*0.00*	*0*	*0.00*
San Carlos Red-on-brown	0	0.00	0	0.00
Subtotal	*0*	*0.00*	*0*	*0.00*
Total	**31**	**100.00**	**464**	**100.00**

TABLE F.6 Painted ceramics recovered from Houseblocks III and IV and subjected to reanalysis

Ware or ware-level category and/or type or type-level category	Houseblock III						Houseblock IV					
	Room 25		Room 28		Total		Rooms 38–40		Room 40		Total	
	n	%	*n*	%	*n*	%	*n*	%	*n*	%	*n*	%
Roosevelt Red Ware												
Cliff Black-on-red	0	0.00	0	0.00	0	0.00	0	0.00	0	0.00	0	0.00
Cliff Polychrome or Nine Mile Polychrome	0	0.00	0	0.00	0	0.00	0	0.00	0	0.00	0	0.00
Cliff Polychrome	0	0.00	1	50.00	1	25.00	1	11.11	0	0.00	1	5.88
Cliff Polychrome: Salmon Variety	0	0.00	0	0.00	0	0.00	0	0.00	0	0.00	0	0.00
Cliff Polychrome: Tonto Variety	0	0.00	0	0.00	0	0.00	0	0.00	0	0.00	0	0.00
Cliff Polychrome: Tucson Variety	0	0.00	0	0.00	0	0.00	0	0.00	0	0.00	0	0.00
Gila Black-on-red	0	0.00	0	0.00	0	0.00	0	0.00	0	0.00	0	0.00
Gila Polychrome	1	50.00	0	0.00	1	25.00	0	0.00	0	0.00	0	0.00
Gila Polychrome or later	0	0.00	0	0.00	0	0.00	0	0.00	1	12.50	1	5.88
Gila Polychrome or later (salmon variety)	0	0.00	0	0.00	0	0.00	0	0.00	0	0.00	0	0.00
Gila Polychrome, no banding line	0	0.00	0	0.00	0	0.00	0	0.00	0	0.00	0	0.00
Gila Polychrome: Gila Variety	0	0.00	0	0.00	0	0.00	0	0.00	0	0.00	0	0.00
Gila Polychrome: Salmon Variety	0	0.00	0	0.00	0	0.00	0	0.00	0	0.00	0	0.00
Gila Polychrome: Tonto Variety	0	0.00	0	0.00	0	0.00	0	0.00	0	0.00	0	0.00
indeterminate Roosevelt Red Ware black-on-red	0	0.00	0	0.00	0	0.00	0	0.00	0	0.00	0	0.00
indeterminate Roosevelt Red Ware polychrome	1	50.00	0	0.00	1	25.00	8	88.89	7	87.50	15	88.24

(continued)

TABLE F.6 *(continued)*

Ware or ware-level category and/or type or type-level category	Houseblock III						Houseblock IV					
	Room 25		Room 28		Total		Rooms 38–40		Room 40		Total	
	n	%	*n*	%	*n*	%	*n*	%	*n*	%	*n*	%
indeterminate Roosevelt Red Ware (salmon variety)	0	0.00	0	0.00	0	0.00	0	0.00	0	0.00	0	0.00
Nine Mile Polychrome	0	0.00	0	0.00	0	0.00	0	0.00	0	0.00	0	0.00
Nine Mile Polychrome: Safford Variety	0	0.00	0	0.00	0	0.00	0	0.00	0	0.00	0	0.00
Nine Mile Polychrome: Tonto Variety	0	0.00	0	0.00	0	0.00	0	0.00	0	0.00	0	0.00
Phoenix Polychrome	0	0.00	0	0.00	0	0.00	0	0.00	0	0.00	0	0.00
Pinto Black-on-red	0	0.00	0	0.00	0	0.00	0	0.00	0	0.00	0	0.00
Pinto Polychrome	0	0.00	0	0.00	0	0.00	0	0.00	0	0.00	0	0.00
Pinto Polychrome: Salmon Variety	0	0.00	0	0.00	0	0.00	0	0.00	0	0.00	0	0.00
Tonto Polychrome	0	0.00	0	0.00	0	0.00	0	0.00	0	0.00	0	0.00
Whiteriver Polychrome	0	0.00	0	0.00	0	0.00	0	0.00	0	0.00	0	0.00
Subtotal	*2*	*100.00*	*1*	*50.00*	*3*	*75.00*	*9*	*100.00*	*8*	*100.00*	*17*	*100.00*
Maverick Mountain Series												
indeterminate Maverick Mountain Series	0	0.00	0	0.00	0	0.00	0	0.00	0	0.00	0	0.00
indeterminate Maverick Mountain Series black-on-red	0	0.00	0	0.00	0	0.00	0	0.00	0	0.00	0	0.00
indeterminate Maverick Mountain Series, Roosevelt Red Ware exterior	0	0.00	0	0.00	0	0.00	0	0.00	0	0.00	0	0.00
Maverick Mountain Black-on-red	0	0.00	1	50.00	1	25.00	0	0.00	0	0.00	0	0.00
Maverick Mountain Polychrome	0	0.00	0	0.00	0	0.00	0	0.00	0	0.00	0	0.00
Nantack Polychrome A (Tusayan Polychrome analog)	0	0.00	0	0.00	0	0.00	0	0.00	0	0.00	0	0.00

Tucson Black-on-red	0	0.00	0	0.00	0	0.00	0	0.00	0	0.00	0	0.00
Tucson Black-on-red (no slip)	0	0.00	0	0.00	0	0.00	0	0.00	0	0.00	0	0.00
Tucson Black-on-red or Tucson Polychrome	0	0.00	0	0.00	0	0.00	0	0.00	0	0.00	0	0.00
Tucson Polychrome	0	0.00	0	0.00	0	0.00	0	0.00	0	0.00	0	0.00
Subtotal	*0*	*0.00*	*1*	*50.00*	*1*	*25.00*	*0*	*0.00*	*0*	*0.00*	*0*	*0.00*
Babocomari Polychrome	0	0.00	0	0.00	0	0.00	0	0.00	0	0.00	0	0.00
Subtotal	*0*	*0.00*	*0*	*0.00*	*0*	*0.00*	*0*	*0.00*	*0*	*0.00*	*0*	*0.00*
Davis Black-on-red	0	0.00	0	0.00	0	0.00	0	0.00	0	0.00	0	0.00
Subtotal	*0*	*0.00*	*0*	*0.00*	*0*	*0.00*	*0*	*0.00*	*0*	*0.00*	*0*	*0.00*
Dragoon or San Simon Series	0	0.00	0	0.00	0	0.00	0	0.00	0	0.00	0	0.00
Subtotal	*0*	*0.00*	*0*	*0.00*	*0*	*0.00*	*0*	*0.00*	*0*	*0.00*	*0*	*0.00*
indeterminate decorated	0	0.00	0	0.00	0	0.00	0	0.00	0	0.00	0	0.00
Subtotal	*0*	*0.00*	*0*	*0.00*	*0*	*0.00*	*0*	*0.00*	*0*	*0.00*	*0*	*0.00*
indeterminate red-on-brown	0	0.00	0	0.00	0	0.00	0	0.00	0	0.00	0	0.00
Subtotal	*0*	*0.00*	*0*	*0.00*	*0*	*0.00*	*0*	*0.00*	*0*	*0.00*	*0*	*0.00*
Kinishba Polychrome	0	0.00	0	0.00	0	0.00	0	0.00	0	0.00	0	0.00
Subtotal	*0*	*0.00*	*0*	*0.00*	*0*	*0.00*	*0*	*0.00*	*0*	*0.00*	*0*	*0.00*
Mimbres Black-on-white	0	0.00	0	0.00	0	0.00	0	0.00	0	0.00	0	0.00
Subtotal	*0*	*0.00*	*0*	*0.00*	*0*	*0.00*	*0*	*0.00*	*0*	*0.00*	*0*	*0.00*
San Carlos Red-on-brown	0	0.00	0	0.00	0	0.00	0	0.00	0	0.00	0	0.00
Subtotal	*0*	*0.00*	*0*	*0.00*	*0*	*0.00*	*0*	*0.00*	*0*	*0.00*	*0*	*0.00*
Total	**2**	**100.00**	**2**	**100.00**	**4**	**100.00**	**9**	**100.00**	**8**	**100.00**	**17**	**100.00**

TABLE F.7 *(continued)*

Ware or ware-level category and/or type or type-level category	Rooms 41–44		Room 41		Room 42		Room 44				Total	
							Fill	Subfloor	Subtotal			
	n	%	*n*	%	*n*	%	(*n*)	(*n*)	*n*	%	*n*	%
Tucson Black-on-red or Tucson Polychrome	0	0.00	0	0.00	0	0.00	0	0	0	0.00	0	0.00
Tucson Polychrome	0	0.00	0	0.00	1	12.50	0	2	2	3.92	3	4.05
Subtotal	*0*	*0.00*	*0*	*0.00*	*1*	*12.50*	*8*	*2*	*10*	*19.61*	*11*	*14.86*
Babocomari Polychrome	0	0.00	0	0.00	0	0.00	0	0	0	0.00	0	0.00
Subtotal	*0*	*0.00*	*0*	*0.00*	*0*	*0.00*	*0*	*0*	*0*	*0.00*	*0*	*0.00*
Davis Black-on-red	0	0.00	0	0.00	0	0.00	0	0	0	0.00	0	0.00
Subtotal	*0*	*0.00*	*0*	*0.00*	*0*	*0.00*	*0*	*0*	*0*	*0.00*	*0*	*0.00*
Dragoon or San Simon Series	0	0.00	0	0.00	0	0.00	0	0	0	0.00	0	0.00
Subtotal	*0*	*0.00*	*0*	*0.00*	*0*	*0.00*	*0*	*0*	*0*	*0.00*	*0*	*0.00*
indeterminate decorated	0	0.00	0	0.00	0	0.00	0	0	0	0.00	0	0.00
Subtotal	*0*	*0.00*	*0*	*0.00*	*0*	*0.00*	*0*	*0*	*0*	*0.00*	*0*	*0.00*
indeterminate red-on-brown	0	0.00	0	0.00	0	0.00	0	0	0	0.00	0	0.00
Subtotal	*0*	*0.00*	*0*	*0.00*	*0*	*0.00*	*0*	*0*	*0*	*0.00*	*0*	*0.00*
Kinishba Polychrome	0	0.00	0	0.00	0	0.00	0	0	0	0.00	0	0.00
Subtotal	*0*	*0.00*	*0*	*0.00*	*0*	*0.00*	*0*	*0*	*0*	*0.00*	*0*	*0.00*
Mimbres Black-on-white	0	0.00	0	0.00	0	0.00	1	0	1	1.96	1	1.35
Subtotal	*0*	*0.00*	*0*	*0.00*	*0*	*0.00*	*1*	*0*	*1*	*1.96*	*1*	*1.35*
San Carlos Red-on-brown	0	0.00	0	0.00	0	0.00	0	0	0	0.00	0	0.00
Subtotal	*0*	*0.00*	*0*	*0.00*	*0*	*0.00*	*0*	*0*	*0*	*0.00*	*0*	*0.00*
Total	**3**	**100.00**	**12**	**100.00**	**8**	**100.00**	**35**	**16**	**51**	**100.00**	**74**	**100.00**

TABLE F.8 Painted ceramics recovered from the Ballcourt Test, Cremation 2, Pit Ovens, and Puddle Pit 2 and subjected to reanalysis

Ware or ware-level category and/or type or type-level category	Ballcourt Test		Cremation 2		Pit Oven 1		Pit Oven 2		Puddle Pit 2		Total	
	n	%	*n*	%	*n*	%	*n*	%	*n*	%	*n*	%
Roosevelt Red Ware												
Cliff Black-on-red	0	0.00	0	0.00	0	0.00	0	0.00	0	0.00	0	0.00
Cliff Polychrome or Nine Mile Polychrome	0	0.00	0	0.00	1	5.00	0	0.00	0	0.00	1	1.82
Cliff Polychrome	1	33.33	0	0.00	0	0.00	0	0.00	0	0.00	1	1.82
Cliff Polychrome: Salmon Variety	0	0.00	0	0.00	0	0.00	0	0.00	0	0.00	0	0.00
Cliff Polychrome: Tonto Variety	0	0.00	0	0.00	0	0.00	0	0.00	0	0.00	0	0.00
Cliff Polychrome: Tucson Variety	0	0.00	0	0.00	0	0.00	0	0.00	0	0.00	0	0.00
Gila Black-on-red	0	0.00	0	0.00	1	5.00	0	0.00	0	0.00	1	1.82
Gila Polychrome	1	33.33	0	0.00	2	10.00	0	0.00	3	11.11	6	10.91
Gila Polychrome or later	0	0.00	0	0.00	3	15.00	1	25.00	3	11.11	7	12.73
Gila Polychrome or later (salmon variety)	0	0.00	0	0.00	0	0.00	0	0.00	0	0.00	0	0.00
Gila Polychrome, no banding line	0	0.00	0	0.00	0	0.00	0	0.00	0	0.00	0	0.00
Gila Polychrome: Gila Variety	0	0.00	0	0.00	0	0.00	0	0.00	0	0.00	0	0.00
Gila Polychrome: Salmon Variety	0	0.00	0	0.00	0	0.00	0	0.00	0	0.00	0	0.00
Gila Polychrome: Tonto Variety	0	0.00	0	0.00	0	0.00	0	0.00	0	0.00	0	0.00
indeterminate Roosevelt Red Ware black-on-red	0	0.00	0	0.00	0	0.00	0	0.00	0	0.00	0	0.00
indeterminate Roosevelt Red Ware polychrome	1	33.33	1	100.00	5	25.00	2	50.00	20	74.07	29	52.73

(continued)

TABLE F.8 *(continued)*

Ware or ware-level category and/or type or type-level category	Ballcourt Test		Cremation 2		Pit Oven 1		Pit Oven 2		Puddle Pit 2		Total	
	n	%	*n*	%	*n*	%	*n*	%	*n*	%	*n*	%
indeterminate Roosevelt Red Ware (salmon variety)	0	0.00	0	0.00	0	0.00	0	0.00	0	0.00	0	0.00
Nine Mile Polychrome	0	0.00	0	0.00	0	0.00	0	0.00	0	0.00	0	0.00
Nine Mile Polychrome: Safford Variety	0	0.00	0	0.00	0	0.00	0	0.00	0	0.00	0	0.00
Nine Mile Polychrome: Tonto Variety	0	0.00	0	0.00	0	0.00	0	0.00	0	0.00	0	0.00
Phoenix Polychrome	0	0.00	0	0.00	0	0.00	0	0.00	0	0.00	0	0.00
Pinto Black-on-red	0	0.00	0	0.00	0	0.00	0	0.00	0	0.00	0	0.00
Pinto Polychrome	0	0.00	0	0.00	1	5.00	0	0.00	0	0.00	1	1.82
Pinto Polychrome: Salmon Variety	0	0.00	0	0.00	0	0.00	0	0.00	0	0.00	0	0.00
Tonto Polychrome	0	0.00	0	0.00	0	0.00	0	0.00	0	0.00	0	0.00
Whiteriver Polychrome	0	0.00	0	0.00	0	0.00	0	0.00	0	0.00	0	0.00
Subtotal	*3*	*100.00*	*1*	*100.00*	*13*	*65.00*	*3*	*75.00*	*26*	*96.30*	*46*	*83.64*
Maverick Mountain Series												
indeterminate Maverick Mountain Series	0	0.00	0	0.00	1	5.00	0	0.00	0	0.00	1	1.82
indeterminate Maverick Mountain Series black-on-red	0	0.00	0	0.00	0	0.00	0	0.00	0	0.00	0	0.00
indeterminate Maverick Mountain Series, Roosevelt Red Ware exterior	0	0.00	0	0.00	0	0.00	0	0.00	0	0.00	0	0.00
Maverick Mountain Black-on-red	0	0.00	0	0.00	0	0.00	0	0.00	0	0.00	0	0.00
Maverick Mountain Polychrome	0	0.00	0	0.00	0	0.00	0	0.00	0	0.00	0	0.00

Nantack Polychrome A (Tusayan Polychrome analog)	0	0.00	0	0.00	0	0.00	0	0.00	0	0.00	0	0.00
Tucson Black-on-red	0	0.00	0	0.00	0	0.00	0	0.00	0	0.00	0	0.00
Tucson Black-on-red (no slip)	0	0.00	0	0.00	0	0.00	0	0.00	0	0.00	0	0.00
Tucson Black-on-red or Tucson Polychrome	0	0.00	0	0.00	0	0.00	0	0.00	0	0.00	0	0.00
Tucson Polychrome	0	0.00	0	0.00	6	30.00	1	25.00	1	3.70	8	14.55
Subtotal	*0*	*0.00*	*0*	*0.00*	*7*	*35.00*	*1*	*25.00*	*1*	*3.70*	*9*	*16.36*
Babocomari Polychrome	0	0.00	0	0.00	0	0.00	0	0.00	0	0.00	0	0.00
Subtotal	*0*	*0.00*	*0*	*0.00*	*0*	*0.00*	*0*	*0.00*	*0*	*0.00*	*0*	*0.00*
Davis Black-on-red	0	0.00	0	0.00	0	0.00	0	0.00	0	0.00	0	0.00
Subtotal	*0*	*0.00*	*0*	*0.00*	*0*	*0.00*	*0*	*0.00*	*0*	*0.00*	*0*	*0.00*
Dragoon or San Simon Series	0	0.00	0	0.00	0	0.00	0	0.00	0	0.00	0	0.00
Subtotal	*0*	*0.00*	*0*	*0.00*	*0*	*0.00*	*0*	*0.00*	*0*	*0.00*	*0*	*0.00*
indeterminate decorated	0	0.00	0	0.00	0	0.00	0	0.00	0	0.00	0	0.00
Subtotal	*0*	*0.00*	*0*	*0.00*	*0*	*0.00*	*0*	*0.00*	*0*	*0.00*	*0*	*0.00*
indeterminate red-on-brown	0	0.00	0	0.00	0	0.00	0	0.00	0	0.00	0	0.00
Subtotal	*0*	*0.00*	*0*	*0.00*	*0*	*0.00*	*0*	*0.00*	*0*	*0.00*	*0*	*0.00*
Kinishba Polychrome	0	0.00	0	0.00	0	0.00	0	0.00	0	0.00	0	0.00
Subtotal	*0*	*0.00*	*0*	*0.00*	*0*	*0.00*	*0*	*0.00*	*0*	*0.00*	*0*	*0.00*
Mimbres Black-on-white	0	0.00	0	0.00	0	0.00	0	0.00	0	0.00	0	0.00
Subtotal	*0*	*0.00*	*0*	*0.00*	*0*	*0.00*	*0*	*0.00*	*0*	*0.00*	*0*	*0.00*
San Carlos Red-on-brown	0	0.00	0	0.00	0	0.00	0	0.00	0	0.00	0	0.00
Subtotal	*0*	*0.00*	*0*	*0.00*	*0*	*0.00*	*0*	*0.00*	*0*	*0.00*	*0*	*0.00*
Total	**3**	**100.00**	**1**	**100.00**	**20**	**100.00**	**4**	**100.00**	**27**	**100.00**	**55**	**100.00**

TABLE F.9 Partially reconstructible perforated plate vessels

Perforated plate PRV[a] no.	Provenience	Gerald's type or variety	Gerald's rim form	Rim diameter (cm)	Comment(s)
1	Kiva stratitest level 4	Belford Perforated Rim	Flare	26	First five refit; 6th matches
	Kiva fill (T10S 23–25E L2)	Belford Perforated Rim	Flare		
	Kiva fill (T10S 23–25E L2)	Belford Perforated Rim	Flare		
	Kiva fill (T10S 23–25E L2)	Belford Perforated Rim	Bead		
	Kiva fill (T10S 23–25E L2)	Belford Perforated Rim	Direct		
	Kiva fill	Belford Perforated Rim	Bead		
2	Kiva fill	Belford Perforated Rim	Flare	40	First three refit; 4th matches
	Kiva stratitest level 4	Belford Perforated Rim	Flare		
	Kiva fill	Belford Perforated Rim	Flare		
	Kiva fill	Belford Perforated Rim	Flare		
3	Kiva fill	Belford Perforated Rim	Flare	30	Refit
	Kiva fill	Belford Perforated Rim	Flare		
4	Room 8 fill	Belford Perforated Rim	Bead	42	First four refit; 5th–11th refit; 12th and 13th refit; others match
	Trench in front of Room 6	Belford Perforated Rim	Direct		
	Room 8 fill	Belford Perforated Rim	Bead		
	Room 8 fill	Belford Perforated Rim	Bead		
	Room 8 fill	Belford Perforated Rim	Flare		
	Room 8 fill	Belford Perforated Rim	Bead		
	Room 8 fill	Belford Perforated Rim	Bead		
	Room 8 fill	Belford Perforated Rim	Bead		
	House 7 fill	Belford Perforated Rim	Bead		

(continued)

TABLE F.9 (*continued*)

Perforated plate PRV[a] no.	Provenience	Gerald's type or variety	Gerald's rim form	Rim diameter (cm)	Comment(s)
	Trench in front of Room 6	Belford Perforated Rim	Bead		
	Room 8 fill	Belford Perforated Rim	Bead		
	Room 8 fill	Belford Perforated Rim	Flare		
	Room 8 fill	Belford Perforated Rim	Direct		
	Room 8 fill	Belford Perforated Rim	Flare		
	Room 21 fill	Belford Perforated Rim	Bead		
	Trench in front of Room 9	Belford Perforated Rim	Bead		
5	Room 6 fill	Sobaipuri Coil Rim		36	All refit
	Room 6 fill	Sobaipuri Coil Rim			
	Room 6 fill	Sobaipuri Coil Rim			
	Room 6 fill	Sobaipuri Coil Rim			
	Room 6 fill	Sobaipuri Coil Rim			
	Room 6 fill	Sobaipuri Coil Rim			
6	Room 6 fill	Sobaipuri Coil Rim		34	All refit
	Room 6 fill	Sobaipuri Coil Rim			
	Room 6 fill	Sobaipuri Coil Rim			
7	Kiva fill	Sosa Perforated		36	All match
	Kiva fill	Sosa Perforated			
	Kiva fill	Sosa Perforated			
	Kiva fill	Sosa Perforated			
	Kiva fill	Sosa Perforated			
	Surface	Belford Perforated Rim	Direct		
	Kiva fill	Sosa Perforated			
	Kiva fill	Sosa Perforated			
8	Kiva fill	Sosa Perforated			Refit
	Kiva fill	Sosa Perforated			

(*continued*)

TABLE F.9 *(continued)*

Perforated plate PRV[a] no.	Provenience	Gerald's type or variety	Gerald's rim form	Rim diameter (cm)	Comment(s)
9	Room 34 fill	Sobaipuri Coil Rim		40	All match
	Room 34 fill	Sobaipuri Coil Rim			
	Room 34 fill	Sobaipuri Coil Rim			
10	Room 34 fill	Sobaipuri Coil Rim			Match
	Room 34 fill	Belford Perforated Rim	Flare		
11	Northeast Trash	Belford Perforated Rim	Bead	46	Refit
	Northeast Trash	Belford Perforated Rim	Bead		
12	T1S 46–30E	Belford Perforated Rim	Bead	30	All refit
	T1S 46–30E	Belford Perforated Rim	Bead		
	T1S 46–30E	Belford Perforated Rim	Bead		
	T1S 46–30E	Belford Perforated Rim	Bead		
13	Kiva level 6–8	Sobaipuri Coil Rim		34	First two refit; 3rd matches
	Kiva level 6–8	Sobaipuri Coil Rim			
	Kiva level 6–8	Sobaipuri Coil Rim			
14	Kiva level 6–8	Sobaipuri Coil Rim		34	First five refit; 6th matches
	Kiva fill (T10S 23–25E L2)	Sobaipuri Coil Rim			
	Kiva fill	Sobaipuri Coil Rim			
	Kiva fill	Sobaipuri Coil Rim			
	Kiva fill (T10S 23–25E L2)	Sobaipuri Coil Rim			
	Kiva fill	Sobaipuri Coil Rim			
15	T19E 16–18S	Sobaipuri Coil Rim			Match
	Kiva fill	Sobaipuri Coil Rim			
16	Kiva fill	Sobaipuri Coil Rim		44	All refit
	Kiva fill	Sobaipuri Coil Rim			
	Kiva fill	Sobaipuri Coil Rim			

(continued)

TABLE F.9 (*continued*)

Perforated plate PRV[a] no.	Provenience	Gerald's type or variety	Gerald's rim form	Rim diameter (cm)	Comment(s)
	Kiva fill	Sobaipuri Coil Rim			
	Kiva fill	Sobaipuri Coil Rim			
	Kiva fill	Sobaipuri Coil Rim			
17	Kiva fill	Sobaipuri Coil Rim		58	All match
	Kiva fill	Sobaipuri Coil Rim			
	Kiva fill	Sobaipuri Coil Rim			
18	T26E 16S	Sobaipuri Coil Rim		46	All match
	T26E 16S	Sobaipuri Coil Rim			
	Kiva fill	Sobaipuri Coil Rim			
	Kiva fill	Sobaipuri Coil Rim			
	Kiva fill	Sobaipuri Coil Rim			
19	Kiva level 6–8	Belford Perforated Rim	Bead	42	Refit
	Kiva fill (T10S 23–25E L2)	Belford Perforated Rim	Bead		
20	Kiva fill	Sobaipuri Coil Rim		54	Match
	Kiva level 6–8	Sobaipuri Coil Rim			
21	Kiva fill (T10S 23–25E L2)	Belford Perforated Rim	Bead	40	First two refit; last two match
	Kiva fill (T10S 23–25E L2)	Belford Perforated Rim	Bead		
	Kiva fill	Belford Perforated Rim	Bead		
	Kiva level 3–5	Belford Perforated Rim	Bead		
22	T19E 16–18S	Sobaipuri Coil Rim		24	Match
	Kiva fill	Sobaipuri Coil Rim			
23	Kiva stratitest level 4	Belford Perforated Rim	Flare	34	All match
	Kiva stratitest level 4	Belford Perforated Rim	Flare		
	Room 17 floor	Belford Perforated Rim	Bead		
24	Kiva stratitest level 5	Sobaipuri Coil Rim			Match
	Kiva level 6–8	Sobaipuri Coil Rim			

(*continued*)

TABLE F.9 *(continued)*

Perforated plate PRV[a] no.	Provenience	Gerald's type or variety	Gerald's rim form	Rim diameter (cm)	Comment(s)
25	Kiva fill	Belford Perforated Rim	Direct		Match
	Kiva fill	Belford Perforated Rim	Direct		
26	Kiva fill	Belford Perforated Rim	Direct	34	First two refit; last two refit
	Kiva fill	Belford Perforated Rim	Direct		
	Kiva fill (T10S 23–25E L2)	Belford Perforated Rim	Direct		
	Kiva fill (T10S 23–25E L2)	Belford Perforated Rim	Direct		
27	Kiva fill	Belford Perforated Rim	Bead	40	All match
	Kiva fill	Belford Perforated Rim	Bead		
	Kiva fill (T10S 23–25E L2)	Belford Perforated Rim	Bead		
28	Kiva fill (T8.5–9S 24–25E L4)	Belford Perforated Rim	Direct	32	First two refit; last two refit
	Kiva fill (T8.5–9S 24–25E L3)	Belford Perforated Rim	Direct		
	Kiva fill	Belford Perforated Rim	Flare		
	Kiva fill	Belford Perforated Rim	Direct		
29	Kiva fill (T8.5–9S 24–25E L4)	Belford Perforated Rim	Direct	38	First three refit; 4th and 5th refit; others match
	Kiva fill (T8S 23–25E L3)	Belford Perforated Rim	Flare		
	Kiva fill (T8.5–9S 24–25E L4)	Belford Perforated Rim	Bead		
	Kiva fill (T26E 7–16S)	Belford Perforated Rim	Direct		
	Kiva fill	Belford Perforated Rim	Flare		
	Kiva level 6–8	Belford Perforated Rim	Direct		
	Kiva fill (T8S 23–25E L3)	Belford Perforated Rim	Flare		

(continued)

TABLE F.9 *(continued)*

Perforated plate PRV[a] no.	Provenience	Gerald's type or variety	Gerald's rim form	Rim diameter (cm)	Comment(s)
	Kiva fill (T8.5–9S 24–25E L3)	Belford Perforated Rim	Flare		
	Room 18 fill	Belford Perforated Rim	Bead		
30	Kiva stratitest level 6	Belford Perforated Rim	Direct	40	First two refit; last two refit
	Kiva stratitest level 5	Belford Perforated Rim	Flare		
	Kiva fill (T10S 23–25E L2)	Belford Perforated Rim	Flare		
	Kiva fill (T10S 23–25E L1)	Belford Perforated Rim	Direct		
31	Kiva fill	Belford Perforated Rim	Direct	26	Match
	Kiva fill	Belford Perforated Rim	Flare		
32	Kiva fill	Belford Perforated Rim	Bead	34	Refit
	Kiva level 6–8	Belford Perforated Rim	Bead		
33	Kiva fill (T8S 23–25E L3)	Belford Perforated Rim	Bead	30	Refit
	Kiva fill (T8.5–9S 24–25E L4)	Belford Perforated Rim	Bead		
34	Kiva fill (T8.5–9S 24–25E L3)	Belford Perforated Rim	Direct		Refit
	Kiva fill (T8.5–9S 24–25E L4)	Belford Perforated Rim	Direct		
35	Kiva Feature A (ventilator)	Belford Perforated Rim	Direct	36	Third and 4th refit; 5th and 6th refit; 9th and 10th refit; others match
	Kiva Feature A (ventilator)	Belford Perforated Rim	Direct		
	Kiva Feature A (ventilator)	Belford Perforated Rim	Direct		
	Kiva level 9	Belford Perforated Rim	Direct		

(continued)

TABLE F.9 *(continued)*

Perforated plate PRV[a] no.	Provenience	Gerald's type or variety	Gerald's rim form	Rim diameter (cm)	Comment(s)
	Kiva Feature A (ventilator)	Belford Perforated Rim	Direct		
	Kiva Feature A (ventilator)	Belford Perforated Rim	Direct		
	Kiva Feature A (ventilator)	Belford Perforated Rim	Direct		
	Kiva Feature A (ventilator)	Belford Perforated Rim	Direct		
	Kiva level 9	Belford Perforated Rim	Direct		
	Kiva Feature A (ventilator)	Belford Perforated Rim	Direct		
	Kiva Feature A (ventilator)	Belford Perforated Rim	Direct		
36	Kiva fill (T23E 10S)	Belford Perforated Rim	Flare		Match
	Kiva fill (T23E 11–15S)	Belford Perforated Rim	Flare		
37	Kiva fill	Belford Perforated Rim	Direct	36	All match
	Kiva fill	Belford Perforated Rim	Direct		
	Kiva stratitest level 5	Belford Perforated Rim	Direct		
38	Kiva level 3–5	Sandy Paste Perforated			All match
	Kiva level 6–8	Sandy Paste Perforated			
	Kiva level 6–8	Sandy Paste Perforated			
	Kiva level 6–8	Sandy Paste Perforated			
	Kiva fill	Belford Perforated Rim	Direct		
39	Kiva fill	Belford Perforated Rim	Bead	40	Third and 4th refit; others match
	Kiva fill (T26E 10–16S)	Belford Perforated Rim	Bead		
	Kiva fill (T26E 10–16S)	Belford Perforated Rim	Bead		
	Kiva fill	Belford Perforated Rim	Bead		
40	Kiva fill (T26E 7–16S)	Belford Perforated Rim	Flare	36	All match

(continued)

TABLE F.9 *(continued)*

Perforated plate PRV[a] no.	Provenience	Gerald's type or variety	Gerald's rim form	Rim diameter (cm)	Comment(s)
	Kiva fill	Belford Perforated Rim	Bead		
	Kiva fill	Belford Perforated Rim	Bead		
	Kiva fill	Belford Perforated Rim	Flare		
41	Kiva fill	Sosa Perforated			All match
	Kiva fill	Sosa Perforated			
42	Stratitest 1 level 1	Belford Perforated Rim	Direct		Refit
	Stratitest 1 level 1	Belford Perforated Rim	Direct		
43	Room 36 fill	Belford Perforated Rim	Flare	34	Refit
	Room 36 fill	Belford Perforated Rim	Bead		
44	Room 44 subfloor	Belford Perforated Rim	Direct	32	Match
	Room 44 fill	Belford Perforated Rim	Direct		
45	House 3 fill	Belford Perforated Rim	Direct	42	All match
	House 3 fill	Belford Perforated Rim	Flare		
	Room 3 floor	Belford Perforated Rim	Direct		
46	Room 4 subfloor	Belford Perforated Rim	Bead	30	All match
	Room 4 subfloor	Belford Perforated Rim	Bead		
	Room 4 subfloor	Belford Perforated Rim	Direct		
47	T26E 0–9N	Belford Perforated Rim	Bead	40	Refit
	Room 4 stratitest level 4	Belford Perforated Rim	Bead		
48	Room 14 fill	Belford Perforated Rim	Flare	34	Refit
	Room 14 fill	Belford Perforated Rim	Flare		
49	House 2 fill	Belford Perforated Rim	Flare		Match
	House 2 fill	Belford Perforated Rim	Flare		
50	Room 4 stratitest level 2	Sobaipuri Coil Rim		36	Refit
	Room 4 stratitest level 2	Sobaipuri Coil Rim			
51	Room 2 fill	Belford Perforated Rim	Flare	26	Match
	Room 2 floor	Belford Perforated Rim	Flare		

[a]Partially reconstructible vessel

TABLE F.10 Unmatched perforated plate sherds sorted by provenience, Gerald's type or variety, and rim form

Provenience	Gerald's type or variety	Gerald's rim form	*n*
House 1 fill	Belford Perforated Rim	Direct	1
House 2 floor	Belford Perforated Rim	Direct	1
House 3 fill	Belford Perforated Rim	Direct	1
House 4 fill	Belford Perforated Rim	Direct	1
House 4 fill	Belford Perforated Rim	Flare	2
House 6 stratitest level 2	Belford Perforated Rim	Direct	1
House 7 floor 2	Belford Perforated Rim	Direct	1
Kiva fill	Belford Perforated Rim	Bead	3
Kiva fill	Belford Perforated Rim	Direct	10
Kiva fill	Belford Perforated Rim	Flare	15
Kiva fill	Sobaipuri Coil Rim		6
Kiva SW compartment	Belford Perforated Rim	Direct	3
Kiva SW compartment	Belford Perforated Rim	Flare	1
Kiva stratitest level 3	Belford Perforated Rim	Flare	1
Kiva level 3–5	Belford Perforated Rim	Direct	2
Kiva level 3–5	Belford Perforated Rim	Flare	3
Kiva stratitest level 4	Belford Perforated Rim	Direct	1
Kiva stratitest level 4	Belford Perforated Rim	Flare	2
Kiva stratitest level 4	Sobaipuri Coil Rim		3
Kiva stratitest level 5	Belford Perforated Rim	Bead	1
Kiva stratitest level 5	Belford Perforated Rim	Flare	2
Kiva level 6–8	Belford Perforated Rim	Direct	2
Kiva level 6–8	Belford Perforated Rim	Flare	3
Kiva level 6–8	Sobaipuri Coil Rim		1
Kiva level 6–8	Sosa Perforated		1
Kiva stratitest level 7	Belford Perforated Rim	Flare	1
Kiva stratitest level 8	Belford Perforated Rim	Direct	1
Kiva fill (T10S 23–25E L1)	Belford Perforated Rim	Direct	2

(*continued*)

TABLE F.10 *(continued)*

Provenience	Gerald's type or variety	Gerald's rim form	*n*
Kiva fill (T10S 23–25E L2)	Belford Perforated Rim	Direct	2
Kiva fill (T10S 23–25E L2)	Belford Perforated Rim	Flare	3
Kiva fill (T10S 23–25E L3)	Belford Perforated Rim	Bead	1
Kiva fill (T10S 23–25E L3)	Belford Perforated Rim	Direct	1
Kiva fill (T23E 11–15S)	Belford Perforated Rim	Bead	1
Kiva fill (T23E 11–15S)	Belford Perforated Rim	Direct	1
Kiva fill (T23E 11–16S)	Belford Perforated Rim	Flare	1
Kiva fill (T26E 10–16S)	Sobaipuri Coil Rim		1
Kiva fill (T26E 10–16S)	Sosa Perforated		1
Kiva fill (T26E 7–16S)	Belford Perforated Rim	Bead	1
Kiva fill (T26E 7–16S)	Belford Perforated Rim	Flare	1
Kiva fill (T27E 8–15S)	Belford Perforated Rim	Direct	1
Kiva fill (T8S 23–25E L3)	Belford Perforated Rim	Flare	1
Kiva fill (T8S 23–25E L4)	Belford Perforated Rim	Flare	1
Kiva fill (T8.5–9S 24–25E L2)	Belford Perforated Rim	Direct	1
Kiva fill (T8.5–9S 24–25E L2)	Belford Perforated Rim	Flare	1
Kiva fill (T8.5–9S 24–25E)	Belford Perforated Rim	Bead	1
Kiva floor	Belford Perforated Rim	Flare	1
Kiva Feature A (ventilator)	Belford Perforated Rim	Direct	1
Northeast Trash	Belford Perforated Rim	Bead	2
Northeast Trash	Belford Perforated Rim	Direct	2
Northeast Trash	Belford Perforated Rim	Flare	3
Puddle Pit 2	Sobaipuri Coil Rim		1
Room 2	Belford Perforated Rim	Direct	1
Room 2	Belford Perforated Rim	Flare	1
Room 2 (T10N 10–11E)	Belford Perforated Rim	Direct	1
Room 2 (T10N 10–11E)	Belford Perforated Rim	Flare	1
Room 3	Sobaipuri Coil Rim		1
Trench in front of Room 3	Belford Perforated Rim	Direct	1

(*continued*)

TABLE F.10 *(continued)*

Provenience	Gerald's type or variety	Gerald's rim form	*n*
Room 4 fill	Sobaipuri Coil Rim		1
Room 4 subfloor	Belford Perforated Rim	?	1
Room 5 fill	Sobaipuri Coil Rim		1
Room 6 fill	Sobaipuri Coil Rim		1
Room 7 fill	Belford Perforated Rim	Flare	1
Room 7 floor	Belford Perforated Rim	?	1
Room 7 floor	Belford Perforated Rim	Flare	1
Room 8 fill	Belford Perforated Rim	Direct	1
Trench in front of Room 8	Belford Perforated Rim	Direct	1
Room 9 fill	Sobaipuri Coil Rim		1
Room 10 fill	Belford Perforated Rim	Bead	1
Room 10 fill	Belford Perforated Rim	Direct	2
Room 10 stratitest level 4	Sobaipuri Coil Rim		1
Room 11 fill	Belford Perforated Rim	Flare	1
Room 14 fill	Belford Perforated Rim	Direct	1
Room 14 (T24E 20–21S)	Belford Perforated Rim	Direct	1
Room 14 (T24E 20–21S)	Sobaipuri Coil Rim		1
Room 15 floor	Sobaipuri Coil Rim		1
Room 18 fill	Belford Perforated Rim	Direct	1
Room 25 fill	Belford Perforated Rim	?	1
Room 33 floor	Belford Perforated Rim	?	1
Room 33 floor	Belford Perforated Rim	Direct	1
Room 34 fill	Belford Perforated Rim	Bead	1
Room 34 fill	Sobaipuri Coil Rim		4
Room 35 (trench in front of Room 33)	Belford Perforated Rim	Direct	1
Room 35 (trench in front of Room 33)	Belford Perforated Rim	Flare	1
Room 36 fill	Belford Perforated Rim	Bead	1
Room 36 (T13S 12–16E)	Sobaipuri Coil Rim		1
Room 37 fill	Belford Perforated Rim	Direct	1

(continued)

TABLE F.10 *(continued)*

Provenience	Gerald's type or variety	Gerald's rim form	*n*
Room 46 floor	Belford Perforated Rim	Direct	1
Room 46 floor	Sobaipuri Coil Rim		1
Surface	Belford Perforated Rim	Direct	1
Stratitest 1 level 1	Belford Perforated Rim	Flare	1
T1S 20–14E	Belford Perforated Rim	?	1
T1S 20–14E	Belford Perforated Rim	Direct	1
T8S 12–16E	Sobaipuri Coil Rim		1
T10S 14–20E	Belford Perforated Rim	Flare	1
T12S 18–20E	Belford Perforated Rim	Direct	2
T12S 18–20E	Belford Perforated Rim	Flare	1
T13S 0–11E	Sobaipuri Coil Rim		1
T19E 8–18S	Belford Perforated Rim	Flare	1
T20E 17–20S	Belford Perforated Rim	Flare	1
T26E 16S	Sobaipuri Coil Rim		2
T10N 0–7E	Belford Perforated Rim	?	1
T21–22W 31–32S	Belford Perforated Rim	Flare	1
Total			**159**

APPENDIX G

A Fauna from an Indian Site Near Redington, Arizona[1]

William H. Burt

Members of the Amerind Foundation, under the direction of Dr. Charles C. Di Peso, recently excavated an Indian village site on the San Pedro River, near Redington, Arizona (Davis Site, Arizona:BB:11:7). Although the date has not been established, occupancy of the site probably preceded the Spanish contact period. A relatively large mammalian fauna (21 species of wild mammals) is represented in the bone material recovered. Only five species were recorded from the Reeve Ruin Site across the river (Di Peso, The Amerind Foundation, Publ. No. 8, 1958). The reasons for this discrepancy are not clear.

As is to be expected, most of the bone elements represent food animals. Jackrabbits (*Lepus*), cottontails (*Sylvilagus*), and deer (*Odocoileus*) make up the bulk of the material (table G.1). The remainder, each represented by eight or less bone elements, includes 15 species of wild mammals, some of which may be accidentals or intrusions that have little or nothing to do with the particular Indian culture. Pocket mice (*Perognathus*) and kangaroo rats (*Dipodomys*) might fit this category.

1. Burt, William H., A Fauna from an Indian Site near Redington, Arizona, *Journal of Mammalogy*, 1961, Vol. 42, No. 1, pp. 115–116, reprinted by permission of the American Society of Mammalogists, established in 1919 for the purpose of promoting interest in the study of mammals.

The absence of certain kinds of mammals that might have been utilized by the Indians may be of some interest. We do not know whether these kinds were absent in the area at the time, were there but not utilized by the Indians, or whether their remains were not preserved (or found). In this group are: bear, coati, skunks, badger, gray fox, tree squirrels, porcupine, and peccary.

Judging from the remains present, the ecology of the area was probably similar to what we now find there. The white-tailed deer and eastern cottontail indicate a wooded area similar to that found on the lower slopes of the adjacent mountains today. Jackrabbits, mule deer, pronghorn, and prairie dog all would indicate open plains conditions that probably prevailed in the San Pedro River Valley. The raccoon and especially the beaver would indicate a continuous flow of water in the river.

From the distributional or zoogeographic point of view, the presence of the ocelot (*Felis pardalis*), and possibly the jaguar, is of some interest. This is near the northern limit of the range of the species and it is now very rare or absent in the area.

If abundance of remains is any indication of abundance of animals, then it would appear that the little white-tailed deer (*O. v. couesi*) was much more prevalent than the mule deer (*O. hemionus*); the blacktail jackrabbit (*Lepus californicus*) was more in evidence than the antelope jackrabbit (*Lepus alleni*);

TABLE G.1 Identifiable skeletal elements, mostly incomplete

Species	Skull	Vertebra	Rib	Scapula	Front leg	Pelvis	Hind leg	Foot	Total
Lepus californicus[*]	8	5	8	7	21	15	19	10	93
Lepus alleni	9	1				2			12
Lepus sp.	10	11	15	7	8	10	14	12	87
Sylvilagus floridanus[*]				2	4		6		12
Sylvilagus sp.[*,†]	1	4	1	8	17	19	36	6	92
Odocoileus v. couesi[*]	7	4	3	4	9	1	12	14	54
Odocoileus hemionus[*]	1	2			1		1	2	7
Odocoileus sp.	8	14	5	5	5	3	20	31	91
Antilocapra	2				1		1	2	6
Ovis canadensis	4							4	8
Bison?		2							2
Felis (*concolor* or *onca*)								3	3
Felis pardalis	1								1
Lynx rufus					2		1		3
Vulpes				1	1				2
Procyon	1								1
Bassariscus	1								1
Canis (dog?)	10	6			5		7	25	53
Dipodomys sp.						1	2		3
Perognathus sp.	1								1
Citellus sp.	1					1			2
Cynomys sp.							1		1
Neotoma sp.							2		2
Castor	1								1
GRAND TOTAL									**538**

[*]Reported from Reeve Ruin.

[†]Some probably *auduboni*.

and the eastern cottontail (*Sylvilagus floridanus*) more common than the desert cottontail (*S. audu-boni*). Further, the implication is that the Indians did considerable hunting in the nearby mountains, as well as in the river valley.

In addition to the mammal remains, there were several bird elements and one frog. The birds, identified by Harrison B. Tordoff, consisted of five kinds of hawks (*Buteo*, *Parabuteo*, *Circus*, *Accipiter*, and *Falco*), the great horned owl (*Bubo*), raven (*Corvus*), dove (*Zenaidura*), two quail (*Lophortyx* and *Callipepla*), two ducks (*Mareca* and *Mergus*), a goose (*Anser*), and the thrush (*Turdus*). This is a considerably larger assemblage than found in the Reeve Ruin (five species). However, the absence of turkey (*Meleagris*) remains in the Davis Site (present in the Reeve Ruin) is difficult to explain.

The archaeologist is interested in the kinds of wild animals utilized by the particular Indian culture represented, and in the ecological conditions at the time of deposition as indicated by the animal remains. To the biologist, there are also zoogeographic implications and evidence of conditions that prevailed in prehistoric times.

Few zoologists are willing to take the time to identify archaeological material. It is time consuming, and the immediate rewards are not great. However, one never knows when something important will show up. But whether or not one finds something spectacular from a fauna, it is a definite link with the past, a link that we can get in no other way. With the present system of dating organic materials, these remains take on an added significance. They help close the gap between the latest fossil and the earliest historic records.—William H. Burt, Museum of Zoology, Univ. of Michigan, Ann Arbor. Received 21 March 1960.

APPENDIX H

Contextual Data for Fauna Identified by William H. Burt and Harrison B. Tordoff in 1958 and by Arthur H. Harris in 1970

[*Editor: In his dissertation, Rex Gerald (1975:Table 6) presents a summary table of mammalian faunal data that compares the assemblages from the Davis Ranch Site and Reeve Ruin. He indicates, through citations, that the sources of the data relating to the Davis Ranch Site are William Burt's (1961) published report on the mammalian fauna, which also summarizes information on birds provided by Harrison Tordoff, and "unpublished notes" by Arthur Harris dated 1970. Burt's (1961) publication, however, only reports site-level totals. There is no presentation of data by intrasite provenience. The data in table H.1, which are sorted by recovery context and bone bag number, are identifications made by Burt and Tordoff compiled from a series of four typewritten lists (Burt and Tordoff 1958) found at the Amerind Museum among materials transferred there from the University of Texas at El Paso, where Gerald was employed at the time of his death. These lists, which bear handwritten comments identified as "corrections by Art Harris," appear to represent the raw material from which Gerald constructed the summary table discussed above. Table H.2 presents identifications by Harris. The scientific names used by Burt, Tordoff, and Harris have been updated to conform to current conventions.*]

TABLE H.1 Mammalian and amphibian fauna identified by William H. Burt and avian fauna identified by Harrison B. Tordoff, in 1958, sorted by provenience and bone bag

Provenience	Bag no.	*n*	Element	Scientific name	Common name
House 1 fill	4	1	Humerus	*Lepus californicus*	Black-tailed jackrabbit
House 2 fill	8	1	Mandible	cf. *Canis lupus familiaris*	Probable dog
House 2 fill	8	1	Tibia	*Sylvilagus* sp.	Cottontail rabbit
House 2 fill	8	1	Humerus	*Sylvilagus* sp.	Cottontail rabbit
House 2 fill	8	1	Humerus frag	cf. Aves	Probable bird
House 2 fill	23	1	Femur shaft frag?	cf. *Odocoileus* sp.	Probable deer
House 2 fill	23	1	Tip of antler	*Odocoileus* sp.	Deer
House 2 fill	23	1	Frag		
House 2 fill	82	1	Rib	*Lepus* sp.	Jackrabbit
House 2 fill	82		Limb bone frags	Artiodactyla	Artiodactyl
House 2 fill	82		Frags	Aves	Bird
House 2 fill	124	1	Phalanx	*Odocoileus* cf. *hemionus*	Probable mule deer
House 3 fill	62	1	Tibia frag	Artiodactyla	Artiodactyl
House 3 fill	62	1	Vertebra frag	Mammalia	Mammal
House 3 fill	62		Frag	Mammalia	Mammal
House 3 fill	62	1	Fibula[a]	cf. Mammalia	Probable mammal
House 3 fill	88	1	Tip of right mandible	*Lepus* sp.	Jackrabbit
House 3 fill	88		Frags	Mammalia	Mammal
House 3 fill	88	1	Left mandible	*Odocoileus virginianus couesi*	White-tailed deer
House 3 fill	88	1	Left mandible	*Odocoileus virginianus couesi*	White-tailed deer
House 3 fill	88	1	Limb bone frag	cf. *Odocoileus* sp.	Probable deer
House 3 fill	88	1	Frag	Mammalia	Mammal

House 3 fill	88		Frags	Mammalia	Mammal
House 3 fill	88		Frag	Mammalia	Mammal
House 3 fill	88	2	Limb bone frags	cf. *Odocoileus* sp.	Probable deer
House 3 fill	88	1	Scapula frag	Mammalia	Mammal
House 3 fill	88	4	Pelvis frags	cf. *Odocoileus* sp.	Probable deer
House 3 fill	88	1	Tibia frag	cf. *Odocoileus* sp.	Probable deer
House 3 fill	88	1	Distal end of tibia	cf. *Antilocapra americana*	Probable pronghorn
House 3 fill	88	1	Right innominate	*Spermophilus* sp.	Ground squirrel
House 3 fill	88	2	Frags	Mammalia	Mammal
House 3 fill	88		Frags	Mammalia	Mammal
House 3 fill	88		Limb bone frags	*Artiodactyla*	Artiodactyl
House 3 fill	88	1	Right innominate	*Lepus* sp.	Jackrabbit
House 4 fill	102	1	Head of rib	*Odocoileus* cf. *virginianus couesi*	Probable white-tailed deer
House 4 fill	102		Limb bone frags	cf. *Odocoileus* sp.	Probable deer
House 4 floor	95	1	Femur shaft frag	cf. *Canis lupus familiaris*	Probable dog
House 4 floor	95	1	Ischium	*Lepus* sp.	Jackrabbit
House 4 floor	95	1	Rib	*Lepus* sp.	Jackrabbit
House 4 floor	95	1	Right mandible	*Lepus alleni*	Antelope jackrabbit
House 4 floor	95	1	Distal phalanx	cf. *Odocoileus* sp.	Probable deer
House 5 fill	10	1	Distal end of metacarpal	*Odocoileus* cf. *virginianus couesi*	Probable white-tailed deer
House 5 fill	10	3	Tibia? frags	cf. *Odocoileus* sp.	Probable deer
House 5 fill	10	1	Long bone frag	cf. *Odocoileus* sp.	Probable deer
House 5 fill	89	1	Phalanx	*Homo sapiens*	Human
House 5 fill	89	1	Scapula	*Lepus* sp.	Jackrabbit
House 5 fill	89	1	Humerus	*Lepus californicus*	Black-tailed jackrabbit

(*continued*)

TABLE H.1 *(continued)*

Provenience	Bag no.	*n*	Element	Scientific name	Common name
House 6 floor	103	1	Tip of ilium	*Sylvilagus* sp.	Cottontail rabbit
House 6 floor	103	1	Limb bone frag	Artiodactyla	Artiodactyl
House 6 floor	103	2	Frags[b]	cf. Mammalia	Probable mammal
House 7 pits 1 and 2	112	1	End of phalanx[c]		
House 7 pits 1 and 2	112	1	Frag		
House 7 fill	111	1	Phalanx	cf. *Odocoileus* sp.	Probable deer
House 7 fill	111	1	Tibia frag	*Sylvilagus* sp.	Cottontail rabbit
House 7 fill	125	1	Right innominate	*Lepus californicus*	Black-tailed jackrabbit
House 7 floor 1	119	1	Left innominate	*Sylvilagus* sp.	Cottontail rabbit
House 7 floor 1	119	1	Frag	Mammalia	Mammal
House 7 floor 1	120		Limb bone frags	cf. Artiodactyla	Probable artiodactyl
House 7 subfloor 1 fill	123	1	Cervical vertebra	*Lepus* sp.	Jackrabbit
House 7 subfloor 1 fill	123	1	Head of humerus	*Lepus* sp.	Jackrabbit
House 7 subfloor 1 fill	123		Frags[d]		
House 9 floor	127		Rib frags	*Lepus* sp.	Jackrabbit
House 9 floor	127	1	Tooth	*Lepus* sp.	Jackrabbit
House 9 floor	127	1	Head of femur	*Lepus* sp.	Jackrabbit
House 9 floor	127	1	Distal end of humerus	*Sylvilagus* sp.	Cottontail rabbit
House 9 floor	127	1	Distal end of tibia	*Sylvilagus* sp.	Cottontail rabbit
House 9 floor	127	1	Metapodial	*Lepus* sp.	Jackrabbit
House 9 floor	127	1	Rib head	*Lepus* sp.	Jackrabbit
House 9 floor	127	1	Distal end of femur	cf. *Canis lupus familiaris*	Probable dog
House 9 floor	127	1	Head of femur	cf. *Canis lupus familiaris*	Probable dog

House 9 floor	127	1	Mandible	*Bassariscus astutus*	Ringtail
House 9 floor	127	1	Auditory bulla	*Chaetodipus* cf. *baileyi*	Probable Bailey's pocket mouse
House 9 floor	127	1	Pectoral girdle	Anura	Frog
Kiva fill	48	1	Distal end of metacarpal	*Odocoileus* cf. *virginianus couesi*	Probable white-tailed deer
Kiva fill	48	1	Phalanx	*Odocoileus* sp.	Deer
Kiva fill	48	2	Distal ends of humeri	*Sylvilagus* cf. *floridanus*	Probable eastern cottontail rabbit
Kiva fill	48	1	Humerus	*Sylvilagus* cf. *floridanus*	Probable eastern cottontail rabbit
Kiva fill	48	3	Innominates	*Sylvilagus* sp.	Cottontail rabbit
Kiva fill	48	2	Scapulae	*Sylvilagus* cf. *floridanus*	Probable eastern cottontail rabbit
Kiva fill	48	2	Proximal ends of tibiae	*Sylvilagus* cf. *floridanus*	Probable eastern cottontail rabbit
Kiva fill	48	1	Head of rib	*Sylvilagus* sp.	Cottontail rabbit
Kiva fill	48	1	Metatarsal	*Sylvilagus* sp.	Cottontail rabbit
Kiva fill	48	2	Metatarsals	*Lepus* sp.	Jackrabbit
Kiva fill	48	1	Metacarpal	*Lepus* sp.	Jackrabbit
Kiva fill	48	2	Ulnae	*Lepus* cf. *californicus*	Probable black-tailed jackrabbit
Kiva fill	48	2	Scapulae	*Lepus* cf. *californicus*	Probable black-tailed jackrabbit
Kiva fill	48	1	Proximal end of femur	*Lepus* sp.	Jackrabbit
Kiva fill	48	1	Distal end of femur	*Lepus* sp.	Jackrabbit
Kiva fill	48	1	Maxillary	*Lepus alleni*	Antelope jackrabbit
Kiva fill	48	1	Right mandible	*Lepus alleni*	Antelope jackrabbit
Kiva fill	48	1	Pelvis frag	*Lepus* sp.	Jackrabbit
Kiva fill	48	1	Tibia	*Lepus californicus*	Black-tailed jackrabbit
Kiva fill	48	1	Radius frag	*Lepus californicus*	Black-tailed jackrabbit
Kiva fill	48	1	Radius	*Lepus californicus*	Black-tailed jackrabbit
Kiva fill	48	1	Lumbar vertebra	*Lepus* sp.	Jackrabbit

(*continued*)

TABLE H.1 *(continued)*

Provenience	Bag no.	*n*	Element	Scientific name	Common name
Kiva fill	48	4	Rib frags	*Lepus* sp.	Jackrabbit
Kiva fill	48	1	Sacrum	*Lepus* sp.	Jackrabbit
Kiva fill	48	1	Lumbar vertebra	*Sylvilagus* sp.	Cottontail rabbit
Kiva fill	48	2	Tibiae	*Sylvilagus* cf. *floridanus*	Probable eastern cottontail rabbit
Kiva fill	48	1	Distal end of femur	*Sylvilagus* cf. *floridanus*	Probable eastern cottontail rabbit
Kiva fill	48		Frags	Mammalia	Mammal
Kiva fill	48	1	Tibia	*Neotoma albigula*	White-throated woodrat
Kiva fill	48	1	Tibia	*Cynomys* sp.	Prairie dog
Kiva fill	50	1	Proximal end of ulna	cf. *Odocoileus* sp.	Probable deer
Kiva fill	50	1	Proximal end of ulna	cf. *Odocoileus* sp.	Probable deer
Kiva fill	50	1	Calcaneum	Artiodactyla	Artiodactyl
Kiva fill	50	1	Distal end of metacarpal	*Odocoileus virginianus couesi*	White-tailed deer
Kiva fill	50	1	Rib frag	Artiodactyla	Artiodactyl
Kiva fill	50	1	Proximal end of radius	Artiodactyla	Artiodactyl
Kiva fill	50	Several	Limb bone frags	Mammalia, mostly Artiodactyla	Mammal, mostly artiodactyl
Kiva fill	50	1	Phalanx	Artiodactyla	Artiodactyl
Kiva fill	50	1	Phalanx	*Ovis canadensis*	Bighorn sheep
Kiva fill	50	1	Pelvis frag	Artiodactyla	Artiodactyl
Kiva fill	50	1	Head of rib	Artiodactyla	Artiodactyl
Kiva fill	50	1	Mandible frag	cf. *Canis lupus familiaris*	Probable dog
Kiva fill	50	1	Pelvis frag	Artiodactyla	Artiodactyl
Kiva fill	50	1	Metacarpal frag	Artiodactyla	Artiodactyl
Kiva fill	50	1	Calcaneum frag	Artiodactyla	Artiodactyl

Kiva fill	50	1	Phalanx frag	Artiodactyla	Artiodactyl
Kiva fill	50	1	Rib frag	Artiodactyla	Artiodactyl
Kiva fill	50	1	Lumbar vertebra	Artiodactyla	Artiodactyl
Kiva fill	50	1	Phalanx	Artiodactyla	Artiodactyl
Kiva fill	50	1	Cervical vertebra	Artiodactyla	Artiodactyl
Kiva fill	50	1	Phalanx	cf. *Odocoileus* sp.	Probable deer
Kiva fill	50	1	Mandible frag	*Lepus californicus*	Black-tailed jackrabbit
Kiva fill	50	1	Calcaneum	*Lepus californicus*	Black-tailed jackrabbit
Kiva fill	50	1	Right femur	*Lepus californicus*	Black-tailed jackrabbit
Kiva fill	50	1	Limb bone	Anura	Frog
Kiva fill	50	1	Distal end of tibia	*Lepus californicus*	Black-tailed jackrabbit
Kiva fill	50	1	Proximal end of tibia	*Lepus californicus*	Black-tailed jackrabbit
Kiva fill	50	1	Distal end of scapula	*Lepus californicus*	Black-tailed jackrabbit
Kiva fill	50	1	Right innominate	*Lepus californicus*	Black-tailed jackrabbit
Kiva fill	50	2	Thoracic vertebrae	*Lepus californicus*	Black-tailed jackrabbit
Kiva fill	50	1	Lumbar vertebra	*Lepus californicus*	Black-tailed jackrabbit
Kiva fill	50	Several	Rib frags	*Lepus* sp.	Jackrabbit
Kiva fill	50	1	Proximal end of humerus	*Sylvilagus* sp.	Cottontail rabbit
Kiva fill	50	1	Distal end of humerus	*Sylvilagus* sp.	Cottontail rabbit
Kiva fill	50	1	Proximal end of femur	*Sylvilagus* sp.	Cottontail rabbit
Kiva fill	50	1	Distal end of femur	*Sylvilagus* sp.	Cottontail rabbit
Kiva fill	50	1	Proximal end of tibia	*Sylvilagus* sp.	Cottontail rabbit
Kiva fill	50	1	Scapula frag	*Sylvilagus* sp.	Cottontail rabbit
Kiva fill	50	1	Limb bone frag	cf. Leporidae	Probable hare or rabbit
Kiva fill	50	Several	Frags	Mammalia	Mammal

(*continued*)

TABLE H.1 *(continued)*

Provenience	Bag no.	*n*	Element	Scientific name	Common name
Kiva fill	50	3	Phalanges	*Homo sapiens*	Human
Kiva fill	50	1	Tooth	*Homo sapiens*	Human
Kiva fill	50	2	Frags	*Homo sapiens*	Human
Kiva fill	50	1	Femur	*Neotoma albigula*	White-throated woodrat
Kiva fill	50	2	Bird bones	cf. Accipitridae	Probable hawk
Kiva fill	55	1	Distal end of tibia	*Odocoileus* cf. *virginianus couesi*	Probable white-tailed deer
Kiva fill	55	1	Proximal end of tibia	*Odocoileus* cf. *virginianus couesi*	Probable white-tailed deer
Kiva fill	55	4	Metatarsals	cf. *Canis latrans*	Probable coyote[e]
Kiva fill	55	1	Calcaneum	cf. *Canis latrans*	Probable coyote[e]
Kiva fill	55	1	Astragalus	cf. *Canis latrans*	Probable coyote[e]
Kiva fill	55	1	Distal end of tibia	cf. *Canis latrans*	Probable coyote[e]
Kiva fill	55	1	Claw	cf. *Canis latrans*	Probable coyote[e]
Kiva fill	55	2	Phalanges	*Canis* sp.	Coyote or dog
Kiva fill	55	Several	Frags		
Kiva fill	55	2	Humeri	*Accipiter cooperii*	Cooper's hawk
Kiva fill	55	1	Frag	Aves	Bird
Kiva fill	58		Limb bone frags	Artiodactyla	Artiodactyl
Kiva fill	58	1	Neural spine of thoracic vertebra	Artiodactyla	Artiodactyl
Kiva fill	58	1	Phalanx	Artiodactyla	Artiodactyl
Kiva fill	58	1	Lumbar vertebra	Artiodactyla	Artiodactyl
Kiva fill	58	1	Centrum of vertebra	Artiodactyla	Artiodactyl
Kiva fill	58	1	Ilium frag	Artiodactyla	Artiodactyl
Kiva fill	58	1	Pelvis frag	Artiodactyla	Artiodactyl

Kiva fill	58	1	Distal end of metacarpal	Artiodactyla	Artiodactyl
Kiva fill	58	1	Axis	*Canis lupus familiaris*	Dog
Kiva fill	58	1	Cervical vertebra	*Canis lupus familiaris*	Dog
Kiva fill	58	1	Tibiotarsus	cf. Accipitridae	Probable hawk
Kiva fill	58	1	Tibiotarsus	Aves	Bird
Kiva fill	58	1	Tarsometatarsus	*Buteo jamaicensis*	Red-tailed hawk
Kiva fill	58	1	Left innominate	*Lepus* cf. *californicus*	Probable black-tailed jackrabbit
Kiva fill	58	1	Right innominate	*Lepus* cf. *californicus*	Probable black-tailed jackrabbit
Kiva fill	58	1	Proximal end of left tibia	*Lepus* cf. *californicus*	Probable black-tailed jackrabbit
Kiva fill	58	1	Proximal end of right tibia	*Lepus* cf. *californicus*	Probable black-tailed jackrabbit
Kiva fill	58	1	Head of humerus	*Lepus* cf. *californicus*	Black-tailed jackrabbit
Kiva fill	58	2	Right femora	*Sylvilagus* sp.	Cottontail rabbit
Kiva fill	58	1	Left femur	*Sylvilagus* sp.	Cottontail rabbit
Kiva fill	58	2	Metatarsals	*Homo sapiens*	Human
Kiva fill	58	2	Frags	cf. *Homo sapiens*	Probable human
Kiva fill	58	Several	Frags	Mammalia	Mammal
Kiva fill	61	1	Limb bone frag	cf. *Odocoileus* sp.	Probable deer
Kiva fill	61	1	Distal end of humerus	*Odocoileus hemionus*	Mule deer
Kiva fill	61	1	Pelvis frag	cf. *Odocoileus* sp.	Probable deer
Kiva fill	61	1	Centrum of vertebra	cf. *Odocoileus* sp.	Probable deer
Kiva fill	61	1	Pelvis frag	*Sylvilagus* sp.	Cottontail rabbit
Kiva fill	61	1	Distal end of femur	*Sylvilagus* sp.	Cottontail rabbit
Kiva fill	61	1	Scapula	*Lepus californicus*	Black-tailed jackrabbit
Kiva fill	61	1	Distal end of tibia	*Odocoileus* sp.	Deer
Kiva fill	61	1	Humerus frag	*Sylvilagus* sp.	Cottontail rabbit

(*continued*)

TABLE H.1 *(continued)*

Provenience	Bag no.	*n*	Element	Scientific name	Common name
Kiva fill	61	1	Distal end of metacarpal	cf. *Odocoileus* sp.	Probable deer
Kiva fill	61	1	Proximal end of humerus	*Sylvilagus* sp.	Cottontail rabbit
Kiva fill	61	1	Proximal end of femur	*Sylvilagus* sp.	Cottontail rabbit
Kiva fill	61	1	Radius	*Sylvilagus* sp.	Cottontail rabbit
Kiva fill	61	1	Left innominate	*Sylvilagus* sp.	Cottontail rabbit
Kiva fill	61	1	Ilium	*Lepus californicus*	Black-tailed jackrabbit
Kiva fill	61	1	Rib	*Lepus* sp.	Jackrabbit
Kiva fill	61	1	Rib	*Odocoileus* sp.	Deer
Kiva fill	61	1	Ulna	*Sylvilagus* sp.	Cottontail rabbit
Kiva fill	61	1	Proximal end of metacarpal	cf. *Odocoileus* sp.	Probable deer
Kiva fill	61	1	Lumbar vertebra	*Lepus* sp.	Jackrabbit
Kiva fill	61	2	Thoracic vertebrae	Artiodactyla	Artiodactyl
Kiva fill	61	1	Ilium	*Lepus* sp.	Jackrabbit
Kiva fill	61	1	Limb bone	Mammalia	Mammal
Kiva fill	61	1	Ilium	*Sylvilagus* sp.	Cottontail rabbit
Kiva fill	61	1	Pelvis frag	*Lepus californicus*	Black-tailed jackrabbit
Kiva fill	61	1	Distal end of radius	*Odocoileus* sp.	Deer
Kiva fill	61	1	Distal end of humerus	*Sylvilagus* sp.	Cottontail rabbit
Kiva fill	61	1	Rib frag	*Lepus* sp.	Jackrabbit
Kiva fill	61	1	Femur frag	Artiodactyla	Artiodactyl
Kiva fill	61	1	Humerus	*Zenaidura macroura*	Mourning dove
Kiva fill	61	1	Sternum	*Callipepla gambelii*	Gambel's quail
Kiva fill	61	1	Claw	cf. *Buteo jamaicensis*	Probable red-tailed hawk

Kiva fill	61	2	Frags	Aves	Bird
Kiva fill	61	1	Phalanx	*Lepus* sp.	Jackrabbit
Kiva fill	64	1	Scapula	*Odocoileus* cf. *virginianus couesi*	Probable white-tailed deer
Kiva fill	64	1	Scapula frag	cf. *Odocoileus* sp.	Probable deer
Kiva fill	64	1	Base of skull	*Lepus alleni*	Antelope jackrabbit
Kiva fill	64	1	Right mandible	*Lepus californicus*	Black-tailed jackrabbit
Kiva fill	64	11	Limb bone frags	Artiodactyla	Artiodactyl
Kiva fill	64	1	Rib frag	Artiodactyla	Artiodactyl
Kiva fill	64	1	Proximal end of ulna	*Antilocapra americana*	Pronghorn
Kiva fill	64	1	Auditory bulla	*Lepus* sp.	Jackrabbit
Kiva fill	64	1	Centrum of vertebra	Mammalia	Mammal
Kiva fill	64	1	Right innominate	*Sylvilagus* sp.	Cottontail rabbit
Kiva fill	64	14	Frags	Mammalia	Mammal
Kiva fill	64	1	Proximal end of metacarpal	Artiodactyla	Artiodactyl
Kiva fill	64	1	Metacarpal shaft frag	Artiodactyla	Artiodactyl
Kiva fill	64	1	Metacarpal	*Sylvilagus* sp.	Cottontail rabbit
Kiva fill	64	1	Distal end of tibia	*Odocoileus* cf. *virginianus couesi*	Probable white-tailed deer
Kiva fill	64	3	Frags		
Kiva fill	64	1	Metatarsal	*Lepus* sp.	Jackrabbit
Kiva fill	64	1	Palatine bone	*Lepus* sp.	Jackrabbit
Kiva fill	64	1	Ulna frag	*Lepus* sp.	Jackrabbit
Kiva fill	64	1	Distal end of femur	*Sylvilagus* sp.	Cottontail rabbit
Kiva fill	64	1	Ulna	*Sylvilagus* sp.	Cottontail rabbit
Kiva fill	64	1	Innominate frag	*Lepus californicus*	Black-tailed jackrabbit
Kiva fill	64	1	Phalanx	Artiodactyla	Artiodactyl

(continued)

TABLE H.1 *(continued)*

Provenience	Bag no.	*n*	Element	Scientific name	Common name
Kiva fill	64	1	Head of femur	*Lepus* sp.	Jackrabbit
Kiva fill	64	1	Ilium frag	*Lepus* sp.	Jackrabbit
Kiva fill	64	1	Proximal end of metacarpal	*Odocoileus* cf. *virginianus couesi*	Probable white-tailed deer
Kiva fill	64	1	Humerus	*Lynx rufus*	Bobcat
Kiva fill	64	1	Proximal end of ulna	Artiodactyla	Artiodactyl
Kiva fill	64	1	Frag	cf. *Homo sapiens*	Probable human
Kiva fill	64	1		cf. Aves	Probable bird
Kiva fill	64	1	Tibiotarsus	Aves	Bird
Kiva fill	64	1	Tibiotarsus	Aves	Bird
Kiva fill	64	1	Distal end of humerus	Aves	Bird
Kiva fill	65	1	Phalanx	*Homo sapiens*	Human
Kiva fill	65	Several	Frags	Mammalia	Mammal
Kiva fill	65	1	Phalanx	*Lepus* sp.	Jackrabbit
Kiva fill	65	1	Scapula frag	Artiodactyla	Artiodactyl
Kiva fill	65	1	Lumbar vertebra	cf. *Odocoileus* sp.	Probable deer
Kiva fill	65	1	Humeral condyle	*Odocoileus* sp.	Deer
Kiva fill	65	2	Neural spines of vertebrae	cf. *Odocoileus* sp.	Probable deer
Kiva fill	65	1	Head of tibia	*Odocoileus* sp.	Deer
Kiva fill	65	1	Distal end of metatarsal	*Odocoileus* cf. *virginianus couesi*	Probable white-tailed deer
Kiva fill	65	1	Thoracic vertebra	cf. *Odocoileus* sp.	Probable deer
Kiva fill	65	2	Distal ends of humeri	*Odocoileus* cf. *virginianus couesi*	Probable white-tailed deer
Kiva fill	65	1	Femur shaft frag	*Odocoileus* cf. *virginianus couesi*	Probable white-tailed deer
Kiva fill	65	1	Metatarsal shaft frag	cf. *Odocoileus* sp.	Probable deer

Kiva fill	65	1	Rib	*Lepus* sp.	Jackrabbit
Kiva fill	65	1	Antler burr	*Odocoileus* sp.	Deer
Kiva fill	65	1	Metatarsal frag	cf. *Odocoileus* sp.	Probable deer
Kiva fill	65	1	Scapula frag	cf. *Odocoileus* sp.	Probable deer
Kiva fill	65	1	Scapula frag	*Odocoileus* cf. *virginianus couesi*	Probable white-tailed deer
Kiva fill	65	1	Lumbar vertebra	*Odocoileus* cf. *virginianus couesi*	Probable white-tailed deer
Kiva fill	65	1	Cervical vertebra	*Lepus* sp.	Jackrabbit
Kiva fill	65	1	Scapula	*Sylvilagus* sp.	Cottontail rabbit
Kiva fill	65	1	Metatarsal	*Lepus* sp.	Jackrabbit
Kiva fill	65	1	Tooth	*Odocoileus* sp.	Deer
Kiva fill	65		Limb bone frags	cf. *Odocoileus* sp.	Probable deer
Kiva fill	65	1	Antler burr	*Odocoileus* sp.	Deer
Kiva fill	65	1	Left innominate	*Sylvilagus* sp.	Cottontail rabbit
Kiva fill	65	1	Distal end of right tibia	*Lepus californicus*	Black-tailed jackrabbit
Kiva fill	65	1	Metacarpal frag	cf. *Odocoileus* sp.	Probable deer
Kiva fill	65	1	Ulna	*Lynx rufus*	Bobcat
Kiva fill	65	1	Right mandible	*Procyon lotor*	Raccoon
Kiva fill	65	1	Vertebra frag	*Odocoileus* sp.	Deer
Kiva fill	65	1	Phalanx	*Odocoileus* sp.	Deer
Kiva fill	65	1	Antler frag	*Odocoileus* sp.	Deer
Kiva fill	65	1	Calcaneum	*Odocoileus* sp.	Deer
Kiva fill	65	1	Limb bone frag	cf. *Odocoileus* sp.	Probable deer
Kiva fill	65	Several	Cranial frags	*Odocoileus* sp.	Deer
Kiva fill	65	1	Proximal end of metatarsal	*Odocoileus* cf. *virginianus couesi*	Probable white-tailed deer
Kiva fill	65	1	Distal end of femur	*Lepus californicus*	Black-tailed jackrabbit

(continued)

TABLE H.1 *(continued)*

Provenience	Bag no.	*n*	Element	Scientific name	Common name
Kiva fill	70	1	Astragalus	*Odocoileus* cf. *virginianus couesi*	Probable white-tailed deer
Kiva fill	70	1	Tibia	*Canis lupus familiaris*	Dog
Kiva fill	70	1	Femur	*Canis lupus familiaris*	Dog
Kiva fill	70	1	Radius	*Canis lupus familiaris*	Dog
Kiva fill	70	1	Radius	*Canis lupus familiaris*	Dog
Kiva fill	70	1	Humerus	*Canis lupus familiaris*	Dog
Kiva fill	70	2	Thoracic vertebrae	*Canis lupus familiaris*	Dog
Kiva fill	70	1	Atlas	*Canis lupus familiaris*	Dog
Kiva fill	70	1	Sternum frag	*Canis lupus familiaris*	Dog
Kiva fill	70	1	Rib	*Lepus* sp.	Jackrabbit
Kiva fill	70	2	Metatarsals	*Lepus* sp.	Jackrabbit
Kiva fill	70	1	Metacarpal	cf. *Canis lupus familiaris*	Probable dog
Kiva fill	70	1	Metacarpal frag	cf. *Canis lupus familiaris*	Probable dog
Kiva fill	70	1	Distal end of humerus	*Mareca americana*	American wigeon
Kiva fill	70	1	Proximal end of coracoid	cf. *Anser albifrons*	Probable white-fronted goose
Kiva fill	70	1		cf. Aves	Probable bird
Kiva fill	70	Several	Frags	Mammalia	Mammal
Kiva fill	72	1	Right mandible	*Canis lupus familiaris*	Dog
Kiva fill (T8.5–9S 22–23E)	32	1	Innominate	*Lepus* sp.	Jackrabbit
Kiva fill (T8.5–9S 22–23E)	32	1	Head of femur	cf. *Homo sapiens*	Probable human
Kiva fill (T8.5–9S 22–23E)	32		Frag	cf. *Homo sapiens*	Probable human
Kiva fill (T8.5–9S 22–23E)	32	1	Axis frag	Artiodactyla	Artiodactyl
Kiva fill (T8.5–9S 22–23E)	32	1	Femur frag	Artiodactyla	Artiodactyl

Kiva fill (T8.5–9S 22–23E)	32		Limb bone frags	Artiodactyla	Artiodactyl
Kiva fill (T8.5–9S 22–23E)	32	1	Base of antler	cf. *Odocoileus* sp.	Probable deer
Kiva fill (T8.5–9S 24–25E L1)	17	1	Distal end of left tibia	*Odocoileus* sp.	Deer
Kiva fill (T8.5–9S 24–25E L1)	17	1	Limb bone frag	*Odocoileus* sp.	Deer
Kiva fill (T8.5–9S 24–25E L2)	18	1	Lumbar vertebra	*Sylvilagus* sp.	Cottontail rabbit
Kiva fill (T8.5–9S 24–25E L2)	18	1	Head of right femur	*Sylvilagus* sp.	Cottontail rabbit
Kiva fill (T8.5–9S 24–25E L2)	18	1	Left mandible frag	*Lepus californicus*	Black-tailed jackrabbit
Kiva fill (T8.5–9S 24–25E L2)	18	1	Proximal frag of metatarsal	*Odocoileus* cf. *virginianus couesi*	Probable white-tailed deer
Kiva fill (T8.5–9S 24–25E L2)	18	1	Pelvis frag	*Odocoileus* cf. *virginianus couesi*	Probable white-tailed deer
Kiva fill (T8.5–9S 24–25E L2)	18	1	Frag		
Kiva fill (T8.5–9S 24–25E L3)	20		Frags	Mammalia	Mammal
Kiva fill (T8.5–9S 24–25E L4)	22	1	Pelvis frag	Mammalia	Small mammal
Kiva fill (T8.5–9S 24–25E L4)	22	1	Mandible	cf. *Canis lupus familiaris*	Probable dog
Kiva fill (T8.5–9S 24–25E L4)	22	1	Distal end of metatarsal	*Odocoileus* cf. *virginianus couesi*	Probable white-tailed deer
Kiva fill (T8.5–9S 24–25E L4)	22	Several	Frags		
Kiva fill (T8.5–9S 24–25E L4)	22		Canine and incisors	cf. *Canis lupus familiaris*	Probable dog
Kiva fill (T10S 23–24E L1)	27	1	Proximal phalanx, first digit of foot	*Homo sapiens*	Human
Kiva fill (T10S 23–24E L1)	27	1	Proximal phalanx	cf. *Odocoileus* sp.	Probable deer
Kiva fill (T10S 23–24E L1)	27	1	Right innominate	*Sylvilagus* sp.	Cottontail rabbit
Kiva fill (T10S 23–24E L1)	27	1	Tibia frag	cf. *Lepus* sp.	Probable jackrabbit
Kiva fill (T10S 23–24E L1)	27	1	Metatarsal frag	cf. *Odocoileus* sp.	Probable deer
Kiva fill (T10S 23–24E L2)	28	1	Radius	*Lepus californicus*	Black-tailed jackrabbit
Kiva fill (T10S 23–24E L2)	28	1	Rib	*Lepus californicus*	Black-tailed jackrabbit
Kiva fill (T10S 23–24E L2)	28	1	Metacarpal	*Lepus californicus*	Black-tailed jackrabbit
Kiva fill (T10S 23–24E L2)	28	1	Mandible tip	*Lepus californicus*	Black-tailed jackrabbit

(continued)

TABLE H.1 *(continued)*

Provenience	Bag no.	*n*	Element	Scientific name	Common name
Kiva fill (T10S 23–24E L2)	28	1	Head of scapula	*Sylvilagus* sp.	Cottontail rabbit
Kiva fill (T10S 23–24E L2)	28	1	Phalanx	*Homo sapiens*	Human
Kiva fill (T10S 23–24E L2)	28	1	Metacarpal	*Puma concolor* or *Panthera onca*	Mountain lion or jaguar
Kiva fill (T10S 23–24E L2)	28	1	Phalanx	*Puma concolor* or *Panthera onca*	Mountain lion or jaguar
Kiva fill (T10S 23–24E L2)	28	1	Phalanx	cf. *Ovis canadensis*	Probable bighorn sheep
Kiva fill (T10S 23–24E L2)	28	1	Metatarsal frag	Artiodactyla	Artiodactyl
Kiva fill (T10S 23–24E L2)	28	1	Head of rib	Artiodactyla	Artiodactyl
Kiva fill (T10S 23–24E L2)	28		Frags		
Kiva fill (T10S 23–24E L2)	28	1	Tarsometatarsus	*Falco mexicanus*	Prairie falcon
Kiva fill (T10S 23–25E L2)	31	1	Proximal end of metacarpal	Artiodactyla	Artiodactyl
Kiva fill (T10S 23–25E L2)	31	1	Distal end of tibia	*Odocoileus* sp.	Deer
Kiva fill (T10S 23–25E L2)	31	1	Distal end of humerus	cf. *Odocoileus* sp.	Probable deer
Kiva fill (T10S 23–25E L2)	31	1	Phalanx	Artiodactyla	Artiodactyl
Kiva fill (T10S 23–25E L2)	31	1	Proximal end of scapula	Artiodactyla	Artiodactyl
Kiva fill (T10S 23–25E L2)	31	1	Rib frag	Artiodactyla	Artiodactyl
Kiva fill (T10S 23–25E L2)	31	1	Phalanx	*Homo sapiens*	Human
Kiva fill (T10S 23–25E L2)	31	1	Head of femur	*Sylvilagus* sp.	Cottontail rabbit
Kiva fill (T10S 23–25E L2)	31		Metapodials	*Sylvilagus* sp.	Cottontail rabbit
Kiva fill (T10S 23–25E L2)	31	1	Scapula frag	*Lepus* sp.	Jackrabbit
Kiva fill (T10S 23–25E L2)	31	1	Centrum of vertebra	*Lepus* sp.	Jackrabbit
Kiva fill (T10S 23–25E L2)	31		Unidentifiable	Aves	Bird
Kiva fill (T10S 23–25E L2)	31	1	Proximal end of metatarsal	Artiodactyla	Artiodactyl
Kiva fill (T10S 23–25E L2)	31	1	Radius	*Lepus* sp.	Jackrabbit

Kiva fill (T10S 23–25E L2)	31	1	Phalanx	*Puma concolor* or *Panthera onca*	Mountain lion or jaguar
Kiva fill (T10S 23–25E L3)	38	1	Head of right femur	*Odocoileus* cf. *virginianus couesi*	Probable white-tailed deer
Kiva fill (T10S 23–25E L3)	38	1	Right calcaneum	*Odocoileus* cf. *virginianus couesi*	Probable white-tailed deer
Kiva fill (T10S 23–25E L3)	38	1	Phalanx frag	*Odocoileus* sp.	Deer
Kiva fill (T10S 23–25E L3)	38	1	Proximal end of humerus	cf. *Lepus* sp.	Probable jackrabbit
Kiva fill (T10S 23–25E L3)	38	1	Left innominate frag	cf. *Lepus* sp.	Probable jackrabbit
Kiva fill (T10S 23–25E L3)	38	1	Proximal end of metatarsal	cf. *Lepus* sp.	Probable jackrabbit
Kiva fill (T10S 23–25E L3)	38	1	Proximal end of rib	cf. *Lepus* sp.	Probable jackrabbit
Kiva fill (T10S 23–25E L3)	38	1	Scapula frag	cf. *Lepus* sp.	Probable jackrabbit
Kiva fill (T10S 23–25E L3)	38	1	Ulna shaft frag	cf. *Lepus* sp.	Probable jackrabbit
Kiva fill (T10S 23–25E L3)	38	1	Coracoid	*Anas* sp.	Small duck, size of teal
Kiva fill (T10S 23–25E L3)	38	1	Frag		
Kiva fill (T10S 23E L4)	41	1	Sub-terminal phalanx	*Homo sapiens*	Human
Kiva fill (T12S 18–20E)	113	1	Vertebra frag	cf. *Odocoileus* sp.	Probable deer
Kiva fill (T12S 18–20E)	113	1	Phalanx	cf. *Odocoileus* sp.	Probable deer
Kiva fill (T12S 18–20E)	113	1	Metapodial frag	cf. *Odocoileus* sp.	Probable deer
Kiva fill (T12S 18–20E)	113	1	Head of right femur	*Sylvilagus* sp.	Cottontail rabbit
Kiva fill (T15S 22–24E)	36	1	Innominate	*Sylvilagus* sp.	Cottontail rabbit
Kiva fill (T15S 22–24E)	36	1	Metatarsal frag	cf. *Odocoileus* sp.	Probable deer
Kiva fill (T15S 22–24E)	36	2	Limb bone frags	cf. *Odocoileus* sp.	Probable deer
Kiva fill (T15S 22–24E)	36	1	Podial[a]	*Homo sapiens*	Human
Kiva fill (T15S 25E)	25a	2	Cervical vertebrae	Artiodactyla	Artiodactyl
Kiva fill (T15S 25E)	25a	Several	Vertebrae frags	Artiodactyla	Artiodactyl
Kiva fill (T15S 25E)	25a		Limb bone frags	Artiodactyla	Artiodactyl
Kiva fill (T15S 25E)	25a	2	Cervical vertebrae	*Lepus* sp.	Jackrabbit

(*continued*)

TABLE H.1 *(continued)*

Provenience	Bag no.	*n*	Element	Scientific name	Common name
Kiva fill (T15S 25E)	25a	1	Calcaneum	*Lepus* sp.	Jackrabbit
Kiva fill (T15S 25E)	25a	1	Distal end of femur	*Lepus* sp.	Jackrabbit
Kiva fill (T15S 25E)	25a	1	Radius	*Lepus* sp.	Jackrabbit
Kiva fill (T15S 25E)	25a	1	Innominate	*Sylvilagus* sp.	Cottontail rabbit
Kiva fill (T15S 25E)	25a	1	Head of femur	*Sylvilagus* sp.	Cottontail rabbit
Kiva fill (T15S 25E)	25a		Frags	Mammalia	Mammal
Kiva fill (T15S 25E)	25a	1	Carpometacarpus	cf. *Callipepla squamata*	Probable scaled quail
Kiva fill (T15S 25E)	25b		Maxillaries	*Lepus alleni*	Antelope jackrabbit
Kiva fill (T15S 25E)	25b	1	Mandible	*Lepus californicus*	Black-tailed jackrabbit
Kiva fill (T15S 25E)	25b		Skull frags	*Lepus* sp.	Jackrabbit
Kiva fill (T22E 8–11S)	46	1	Pelvis frag	Artiodactyla	Artiodactyl
Kiva fill (T22E 8–11S)	46	1	Distal end of femur	Artiodactyla	Artiodactyl
Kiva fill (T22E 8–11S)	46	1	Femur frag	Artiodactyla	Artiodactyl
Kiva fill (T22E 8–11S)	46	1	Distal end of metapodial	Artiodactyla	Artiodactyl
Kiva fill (T22E 8–11S)	46	Several	Frags	cf. Mammalia	Probable mammal
Kiva fill (T22E 8–11S)	46	1	Ulna	cf. Aves	Probable bird
Kiva fill (T22E 10–14S)	29	1	Occipital condyle	Artiodactyla	Artiodactyl
Kiva fill (T22E 10–14S)	29	1	Phalanx	cf. *Odocoileus* sp.	Probable deer
Kiva fill (T22E 10–14S)	29	1	Scapula frag	Artiodactyla	Artiodactyl
Kiva fill (T22E 10–14S)	29	1	Innominate	*Lepus* cf. *alleni*	Probable antelope jackrabbit
Kiva fill (T22E 10–14S)	29	1	Lumbar[f] vertebra	*Lepus* sp.	Jackrabbit
Kiva fill (T22E 10–14S)	29	5	Occipital condyles	*Lepus* sp.	Jackrabbit
Kiva fill (T22E 10–14S)	29	1	Auditory bulla	*Lepus* sp.	Jackrabbit

Kiva fill (T22E 10–14S)	29	1	Lumbar vertebra	*Sylvilagus* sp.	Cottontail rabbit
Kiva fill (T22E 10–14S)	29		Frags	Mammalia	Mammal
Kiva fill (T22E 10–14S)	29			*Parabuteo unicinctus*	Harris's hawk
Kiva fill (T22E 11–15S)	40	1	Axis	*Odocoileus* cf. *virginianus couesi*	Probable white-tailed deer
Kiva fill (T22E 11–15S)	40	1	Scapula	*Odocoileus* cf. *virginianus couesi*	Probable white-tailed deer
Kiva fill (T22E 11–15S)	40	1	Proximal end of radius	*Odocoileus* cf. *virginianus couesi*	Probable white-tailed deer
Kiva fill (T22E 11–15S)	40	1	Humerus	*Odocoileus* cf. *virginianus couesi*	Probable white-tailed deer
Kiva fill (T22E 11–15S)	40	1	Femur frag	cf. *Odocoileus* sp.	Probable deer
Kiva fill (T22E 11–15S)	40	1	Femur	cf. *Odocoileus* sp.	Probable deer
Kiva fill (T22E 11–15S)	40	1	Vertebra frag	cf. *Odocoileus* sp.	Probable deer
Kiva fill (T22E 11–15S)	40	1	Navicular-cuboid	cf. *Odocoileus* sp.	Probable deer
Kiva fill (T22E 11–15S)	40	1	Phalanx	cf. *Odocoileus* sp.	Probable deer
Kiva fill (T22E 11–15S)	40	1	Calcaneum	*Sylvilagus* sp.	Cottontail rabbit
Kiva fill (T22E 11–15S)	40	1	Astragalus	*Sylvilagus* sp.	Cottontail rabbit
Kiva fill (T22E 11–15S)	40		Occipital condyles	*Lepus alleni*	Antelope jackrabbit
Kiva fill (T22E 11–15S)	40	1	Left mandible	*Lepus alleni*	Antelope jackrabbit
Kiva fill (T22E 11–15S)	40	1	Proximal end of tibia	*Lepus californicus*	Black-tailed jackrabbit
Kiva fill (T22E 11–15S)	40	1	Distal end of tibia	*Lepus californicus*	Black-tailed jackrabbit
Kiva fill (T22E 11–15S)	40	1	Humerus	*Lepus californicus*	Black-tailed jackrabbit
Kiva fill (T22E 11–15S)	40	1	Sacrum	*Lepus californicus*	Black-tailed jackrabbit
Kiva fill (T22E 11–15S)	40	1	Innominate	*Lepus californicus*	Black-tailed jackrabbit
Kiva fill (T22E 11–15S)	40	1	Innominate	*Sylvilagus* cf. *floridanus*	Probable eastern cottontail rabbit
Kiva fill (T22E 11–15S)	40	2	Scapulae	*Sylvilagus* cf. *floridanus*	Probable eastern cottontail rabbit
Kiva fill (T22E 11–15S)	40	1	Rib	*Lepus* sp.	Jackrabbit
Kiva fill (T22E 11–15S)	40	1	Tibiotarsus	*Buteo jamaicensis*	Red-tailed hawk

(*continued*)

TABLE H.1 *(continued)*

Provenience	Bag no.	*n*	Element	Scientific name	Common name
Kiva fill (T22E 11–15S)	40	Several	Frags	Mammalia	Mammal
Kiva fill (T22E 11–15S)	40	1	Femur shaft	cf. *Sylvilagus* sp.	Probable cottontail rabbit
Kiva fill (T22E 11–15S)	40	1	Tooth	*Lepus* sp.	Jackrabbit
Kiva fill (T22E 11–15S)	47		Limb bone frags	Artiodactyla	Artiodactyl
Kiva fill (T22E 11–15S)	47	1	Scapula frag	Artiodactyla	Artiodactyl
Kiva fill (T22E 11–15S)	47	1	Distal end of humerus	Artiodactyla	Artiodactyl
Kiva fill (T22E 11–15S)	47	1	Ulna	*Lepus californicus*	Black-tailed jackrabbit
Kiva fill (T22E 11–15S)	47	2	Radii	*Lepus californicus*	Black-tailed jackrabbit
Kiva fill (T22E 11–15S)	47	1	Metatarsal	*Lepus californicus*	Black-tailed jackrabbit
Kiva fill (T22E 11–15S)	47	1	Tibia	*Lepus californicus*	Black-tailed jackrabbit
Kiva fill (T22E 11–15S)	47	1	Mandible	*Lepus californicus*	Black-tailed jackrabbit
Kiva fill (T22E 11–15S)	47	1	Bone	Mammalia	Mammal
Kiva fill (T23E 11–13S)	42	1	Antler base	*Odocoileus* cf. *virginianus couesi*	Probable white-tailed deer
Kiva fill (T23E 11–13S)	42	1	Atlas	*Odocoileus* cf. *hemionus*	Probable mule deer
Kiva fill (T23E 11–13S)	42	1	Distal end of radius	*Odocoileus* cf. *virginianus couesi*	Probable white-tailed deer
Kiva fill (T23E 11–13S)	42	1	Proximal end of metatarsal	*Odocoileus* cf. *virginianus couesi*	Probable white-tailed deer
Kiva fill (T23E 11–13S)	42	1	Right calcaneum	*Odocoileus* cf. *virginianus couesi*	Probable white-tailed deer
Kiva fill (T23E 11–13S)	42	1	Lumbar vertebra	*Odocoileus* cf. *virginianus couesi*	Probable white-tailed deer
Kiva fill (T23E 11–13S)	42	1	Proximal end of scapula	*Odocoileus* cf. *virginianus couesi*	Probable white-tailed deer
Kiva fill (T23E 11–13S)	42	1	Proximal end of phalanx	*Odocoileus* cf. *virginianus couesi*	Probable white-tailed deer
Kiva fill (T23E 11–13S)	42	1	Distal end of metapodial	*Odocoileus* cf. *virginianus couesi*	Probable white-tailed deer
Kiva fill (T23E 11–13S)	42	1	Femur frag	*Odocoileus* cf. *virginianus couesi*	Probable white-tailed deer
Kiva fill (T23E 11–13S)	42	5	Pelvis frags	Artiodactyla	Artiodactyl

Kiva fill (T23E 11–13S)	42	3	Femur frags	*Odocoileus* cf. *virginianus couesi*	Probable white-tailed deer
Kiva fill (T23E 11–13S)	42	2	Scapula frags	cf. *Odocoileus* sp.	Probable deer
Kiva fill (T23E 11–13S)	42	1	Rib frag	cf. *Odocoileus* sp.	Probable deer
Kiva fill (T23E 11–13S)	42	1	Proximal end of tibia	*Lepus californicus*	Black-tailed jackrabbit
Kiva fill (T23E 11–13S)	42	1	Right femur	*Sylvilagus* sp.	Cottontail rabbit
Kiva fill (T23E 11–13S)	42	2	Right femur frags	*Sylvilagus* sp.	Cottontail rabbit
Kiva fill (T23E 11–13S)	42	1	Humerus	*Sylvilagus* sp.	Cottontail rabbit
Kiva fill (T23E 11–13S)	42	1	Distal end of left femur	*Lepus californicus*	Black-tailed jackrabbit
Kiva fill (T23E 11–13S)	42	1	Lumbar vertebra	*Lepus californicus*	Black-tailed jackrabbit
Kiva fill (T23E 11–13S)	42	1	Metatarsal	*Lepus californicus*	Black-tailed jackrabbit
Kiva fill (T23E 11–13S)	42	3	Rib frags	*Lepus* sp.	Jackrabbit
Kiva fill (T23E 11–13S)	42	1	Cranium frag	*Sylvilagus* sp.	Cottontail rabbit
Kiva fill (T23E 11–13S)	42	1	Left upper molar	*Canis* sp.	Dog or coyote
Kiva fill (T23E 11–13S)	42	1	Proximal end of scapula	*Sylvilagus* sp.	Cottontail rabbit
Kiva fill (T23E 11–13S)	42	1	Frag of enamel from tooth?		
Kiva fill (T23E 11–13S)	42	1	Femur	*Buteo* sp.	Large hawk, size of red-tailed hawk
Kiva fill (T23E 11–13S)	42	1	Coracoid	*Corvus corax*	Common raven
Kiva fill (T23E 11–13S)	42	1	Tibiotarsus	Aves	Bird
Kiva fill (T22–23E 8–9S)	44	1	Fibula shaft	*Homo sapiens*	Human
Kiva fill (T22–23E 8–9S)	44	1	Lumbar vertebra	Artiodactyla	Artiodactyl
Kiva fill (T22–23E 8–9S)	44	1	Femur shaft frag	cf. *Odocoileus* sp.	Probable deer
Kiva fill (T22–23E 8–9S)	44	1	Proximal end of tibia	*Sylvilagus* sp.	Cottontail rabbit
Kiva fill (T22–23E 8–9S)	44	1	Frag	Mammalia	Mammal
Kiva fill (T26E 7–16S)	12	1	Frag	Mammalia	Mammal
Kiva stratitest level 5	67	2	Phalanges	cf. *Odocoileus* sp.	Probable deer

(*continued*)

TABLE H.1 *(continued)*

Provenience	Bag no.	*n*	Element	Scientific name	Common name
Kiva stratitest level 5	67	1	Distal end of metacarpal	cf. *Odocoileus* sp.	Probable deer
Kiva stratitest level 5	67	1	Distal end of tibia	cf. *Odocoileus* sp.	Probable deer
Kiva stratitest level 5	67	1	Phalanx	*Homo sapiens*	Human
Kiva stratitest level 5	67	1	Proximal end of humerus	*Sylvilagus* cf. *floridanus*	Probable eastern cottontail rabbit
Kiva stratitest level 5	67	1	Tibia shaft	*Lepus* sp.	Jackrabbit
Kiva stratitest level 5	67	1	Canine tooth	cf. *Canis lupus familiaris*	Probable dog
Kiva stratitest level 5	67	Several	Frags	Mammalia	Mammal
Kiva stratitest level 6	69	1	Proximal end of metapodial	Artiodactyla	Artiodactyl
Kiva stratitest level 7	71	1	Limb bone frag	Artiodactyla	Artiodactyl
Kiva SE corner (bird burial)	75	1	Premaxillary	*Spermophilus* sp.	Ground squirrel
Kiva SE corner (bird burial)	75		Bones	*Buteo* sp.	Probable red-tailed and/or Swainson's hawk
Kiva floor	51	5	Skull frags	*Canis lupus familiaris*	Dog (1 individual)
Kiva floor	51	1	Molar	*Odocoileus virginianus couesi*	White-tailed deer
Kiva floor	68	1	Thoracic vertebra	*Canis lupus familiaris*	Dog
Kiva floor	68	3	Phalanges	*Canis lupus familiaris*	Dog
Kiva floor	68	7	Metacarpals and metatarsals	*Canis lupus familiaris*	Dog
Kiva floor	68	1	Calcaneum	*Canis lupus familiaris*	Dog
Kiva floor	68	1	Mandible frag	*Canis lupus familiaris*	Dog
Kiva floor	68	1	Scapula frag	*Antilocapra americana* or *Odocoileus* sp.	Pronghorn or deer
Kiva floor	68	2	Femur frags	Artiodactyla	Artiodactyl
Kiva floor	68	1	Lumbar vertebra	*Sylvilagus* sp.	Cottontail rabbit

Kiva floor	68	1	Humerus frag	*Lepus californicus*	Black-tailed jackrabbit
Kiva floor	68	1	Frag		
Kiva foot drum	72	1	Distal end of metapodial	Artiodactyla	Artiodactyl
Kiva foot drum	74	1	Canine tooth	cf. *Canis lupus familiaris*	Probable dog
Kiva ventilator	73	1	Left innominate	*Lepus alleni*	Antelope jackrabbit
Kiva ventilator	73	1	Right innominate	*Lepus alleni*	Antelope jackrabbit
Kiva ventilator	73	2	Radii	*Lepus californicus*	Black-tailed jackrabbit
Kiva ventilator	73	1	Sacrum	*Lepus californicus*	Black-tailed jackrabbit
Kiva ventilator	73	1	Limb bone frag	cf. *Odocoileus* sp.	Probable deer
Room 2 floor	108		Frags	Mammalia	Mammal
Room 2 floor	108	2	Skull frags	*Castor canadensis*	Beaver
Room 2 floor	108	1	Coracoid	*Mergus merganser*	Common merganser
Room 2 fill	106	1	Astragalus	*Odocoileus* sp.	Deer
Room 2 fill	106	3	Frags	Artiodactyla	Artiodactyl
Room 3	11	1	Distal end of radius	*Lepus californicus*	Black-tailed jackrabbit
Room 3	11	1	Metatarsal	*Lepus californicus*	Black-tailed jackrabbit
Room 3	11	1	Limb bone frag	cf. *Odocoileus* sp.	Probable deer
Room 3	11	1	Ulna frag?	cf. *Lepus* sp.	Probable jackrabbit
Room 3 level 1	16		Metatarsal frags	cf. *Odocoileus* sp.	Probable deer
Room 3 level 1	16	1	Phalanx	cf. *Odocoileus* sp.	Probable deer
Room 3 floor	19	1	Head of femur	*Bubo virginianus*	Great horned owl
Room 3 floor	19	2	Heads of ribs	*Lepus californicus*	Black-tailed jackrabbit
Room 3 floor	19	1	Head of radius	*Lepus californicus*	Black-tailed jackrabbit
Room 3 floor	19	1	Head of scapula	*Lepus californicus*	Black-tailed jackrabbit
Room 3 floor	19	1	Metacarpal	*Lepus californicus*	Black-tailed jackrabbit

(*continued*)

TABLE H.1 *(continued)*

Provenience	Bag no.	*n*	Element	Scientific name	Common name
Room 3 floor	19	1	Head of scapula	*Sylvilagus* sp.	Cottontail rabbit
Room 3 floor	19	1	Proximal end of ulna	*Sylvilagus* sp.	Cottontail rabbit
Room 3 floor	19	1	Calcaneum	*Sylvilagus* sp.	Cottontail rabbit
Room 3 floor	19	1	Carpal	*Antilocapra americana*	Pronghorn
Room 3 floor	19	1	Phalanx	cf. *Odocoileus* sp.	Probable deer
Room 3 floor	19	1	Frag		
Room 3 floor	19	1	Tibia	*Dipodomys* cf. *merriami*	Probable Merriam's kangaroo rat
Room 3 floor	19	2	Humerus frags	*Sylvilagus* sp.	Cottontail rabbit
Room 3 floor	19	2	Tibia frags	*Sylvilagus* sp.	Cottontail rabbit
Room 3 floor	19	1	Pelvis frag	*Sylvilagus* sp.	Cottontail rabbit
Room 3 floor	19	1	Metatarsal	*Lepus californicus*	Black-tailed jackrabbit
Room 3 floor	19	Several	Limb bone frags	*Odocoileus* sp. or *Antilocapra americana*	Deer or pronghorn
Trench in front of Room 3	26	1	Head of rib	Artiodactyla	Artiodactyl
Trench in front of Room 3	26	1	Metapodial frag	Artiodactyla	Artiodactyl
Trench in front of Room 3	26	1	Lumbar vertebra	Artiodactyla	Artiodactyl
Trench in front of Room 3	26	3	Vertebrae frags	Artiodactyla	Artiodactyl
Trench in front of Room 3	26	1	Phalanx	Artiodactyla	Artiodactyl
Trench in front of Room 3	26	1	Humerus	*Lepus californicus*	Black-tailed jackrabbit
Trench in front of Room 3	26	1	Metatarsal	*Lepus californicus*	Black-tailed jackrabbit
Trench in front of Room 3	26	1	Innominate	*Lepus californicus*	Black-tailed jackrabbit
Trench in front of Room 3	26	1	Mandible	*Lepus californicus*	Black-tailed jackrabbit
Trench in front of Room 3	26	1	Femur frag	Artiodactyla	Artiodactyl

Trench in front of Room 3	26	3	Skull frags	cf. Artiodactyla	Probable artiodactyl
Room 4 stratitest level 1	76	2	Incisors	cf. *Ovis canadensis*	Probable bighorn sheep
Room 4 stratitest level 1	76	2	Molar frags	cf. *Ovis canadensis*	Probable bighorn sheep
Room 4 stratitest level 1	76	1	Phalanx	Artiodactyla	Artiodactyl
Room 4 stratitest level 1	76	1	Scapula	*Lepus* sp.	Jackrabbit
Room 4 stratitest level 1	76	1	Frag	Mammalia	Mammal
Room 4 stratitest level 3	78	1	Scapula	*Lepus* sp.	Jackrabbit
Room 4 stratitest level 3	78		Atlas frags	Mammalia	Mammal
Room 4 stratitest level 3	78	1	Mandible	*Lepus* sp.	Jackrabbit
Room 4 stratitest level 3	78	2	Frags	Mammalia	Mammal
Room 4 stratitest level 4	79	1	Distal end of femur	*Lepus* sp.	Jackrabbit
Room 4 stratitest level 4	79	1	Left mandible	*Antilocapra americana*	Pronghorn
Room 4 stratitest level 4	79	1	Condyle	cf. *Antilocapra americana*	Probable pronghorn
Room 4 stratitest level 4	79	1	Leg bone frag	cf. *Odocoileus* sp.	Probable deer
Room 4 stratitest level 4	79	1	Mandible frag	cf. *Odocoileus* sp.	Probable deer
Room 4 stratitest level 4	79	Several	Tooth frags	*Antilocapra americana*	Pronghorn
Room 4 stratitest level 4	79	1	Phalanx	cf. *Odocoileus* sp.	Probable deer
Room 5 fill	30	1	Phalanx	cf. *Odocoileus* sp.	Probable deer
Room 5 fill	30	1	Rib frag	cf. *Odocoileus* sp.	Probable deer
Room 5 fill	30	1	Radius frag	Carnivora	Carnivore
Room 5 fill	30	1	Head of right femur	*Lepus* sp.	Jackrabbit
Room 5 fill	30	1	Right innominate	*Lepus* sp.	Jackrabbit
Room 5 fill	30	1	Left innominate	*Lepus* sp.	Jackrabbit
Room 5 fill	101	1	Distal end of femur	*Sylvilagus* sp.	Cottontail rabbit
Room 5 fill	101	1	Proximal end of femur	*Sylvilagus* sp.	Cottontail rabbit

(continued)

TABLE H.1 *(continued)*

Provenience	Bag no.	*n*	Element	Scientific name	Common name
Room 5 fill	101	1	Tibia	*Lepus* sp.	Jackrabbit
Room 5 fill	101	1	Tibia shaft	cf. *Canis lupus familiaris*	Probable dog
Room 5 fill	101	1	Mandible	cf. *Leopardus pardalis*	Probable ocelot
Room 5 fill	116	1	Phalanx	cf. *Odocoileus* sp.	Probable deer
Room 5 fill	116	1	Tibia	*Sylvilagus* sp.	Cottontail rabbit
Room 5 fill	116	1	Scapula	*Lepus californicus*	Black-tailed jackrabbit
Room 5 fill	116	1	Distal end of tibia	*Odocoileus* sp.	Deer
Room 5 fill	116	1	Frag	Mammalia	Mammal
Room 6 fill	56	1	Auditory tube with meatus	cf. *Odocoileus* sp.	Probable deer
Room 6 fill	56	1	Mastoid	cf. *Odocoileus* sp.	Probable deer
Room 6 fill	56	2	Femur frags	cf. *Odocoileus* sp.	Probable deer
Room 6 fill	56	1	Right femur	*Sylvilagus* sp.	Cottontail rabbit
Room 6 fill	56	1	Distal end of femur	*Sylvilagus* sp.	Cottontail rabbit
Room 6 fill	93	1	Left tibia	*Lepus californicus*	Black-tailed jackrabbit
Room 6 fill	93	1	Scapula	*Lepus californicus*	Black-tailed jackrabbit
Room 6 fill	93	1	Limb bone frag	cf. *Lepus* sp.	Probable jackrabbit
Room 6 fill	93	2	Left femora	*Sylvilagus* sp.	Cottontail rabbit
Room 6 fill	93	1	Metatarsal frag	cf. *Odocoileus* sp.	Probable deer
Room 6 fill	93	1	Frag	Aves	Bird
Room 7 fill	33	1	Head of rib	*Odocoileus* cf. *virginianus couesi*	Probable white-tailed deer
Room 7 fill	39	1	Head of left femur	*Lepus californicus*	Black-tailed jackrabbit
Room 7 fill	39	1	Metatarsal frag	*Odocoileus* sp.	Deer
Room 7 fill	39	1	Scapula frag	*Odocoileus* sp.	Deer

Room 7 floor	43	1	Molar	*Odocoileus* cf. *virginianus couesi*	Probable white-tailed deer
Room 7 floor	43	1	Phalanx	cf. *Odocoileus* sp.	Probable deer
Room 7 floor	43	4	Frags	cf. *Odocoileus* sp.	Probable deer
Room 8 fill	60	1	Head of right femur	*Lepus californicus*	Black-tailed jackrabbit
Room 8 fill	60		Frags	Mammalia	Mammal
Room 8 subfloor	122	1	Proximal end of femur	*Lepus* sp.	Jackrabbit
Room 8 subfloor	122	1	Frag	cf. Aves	Probable bird
Trench in front of Room 8	34	1	Distal end of humerus	*Sylvilagus* sp.	Cottontail rabbit
Trench in front of Room 9	35	1	Right mandible	*Lepus* sp.	Jackrabbit
Room 10 fill	52	1	Ulna	*Circus cyaneus*	Northern harrier
Room 10 fill	52	1	Tip of antler	*Odocoileus* sp.	Deer
Room 10 stratitest level 3	57	2	Frags	Mammalia	Mammal
Room 10 stratitest level 3	57	1	Head of rib	Artiodactyla	Artiodactyl
Room 10 stratitest level 3	57	1	Scapula	*Vulpes velox*	Swift fox
Room 10 floor	63	1	Antler frag	*Odocoileus* sp.	Deer
Room 11 fill	45	1	Head of left tibia	*Lepus californicus*	Black-tailed jackrabbit
Room 11 fill	49	1	Mandible	*Lepus alleni*	Antelope jackrabbit
Room 11 fill	49	1	Distal end of femur	*Sylvilagus* sp.	Cottontail rabbit
Room 11 level 3	53	1	Thoracic vertebra	cf. *Odocoileus* sp.	Probable deer
Room 11 level 3	53	1	Rib frag	cf. *Odocoileus* sp.	Probable deer
Room 11 level 3	53	1	Frag		
Room 11 level 4	54	1	Calcaneum	*Odocoileus hemionus*	Mule deer
Room 11 level 4	54	4	Carpals	*Odocoileus* cf. *virginianus couesi*	Probable white-tailed deer
Room 11 level 4	54	1	Maxillary frag	*Odocoileus* sp.	Deer
Room 11 level 4	54	1	Femur shaft	*Odocoileus* sp.	Deer

(*continued*)

TABLE H.1 *(continued)*

Provenience	Bag no.	*n*	Element	Scientific name	Common name
Room 11 level 4	54	Several	Frags	Mammalia	Mammal
Room 11 level 4	54	1	Head of rib	cf. *Odocoileus* sp.	Probable deer
Room 11 floor	59	1	Distal end of radius	*Odocoileus* cf. *virginianus couesi*	Probable white-tailed deer
Room 11 floor	59	1	Tooth	*Odocoileus* cf. *virginianus couesi*	Probable white-tailed deer
Room 11 floor	59		Frags of femur, humerus, etc.	*Odocoileus* cf. *virginianus couesi*	Probable white-tailed deer
Room 14 fill	85	1	Head of scapula	Artiodactyla	Artiodactyl
Room 14 fill	85	1	Calcaneum	cf. *Odocoileus* sp.	Probable deer
Room 14 fill	85		Limb bone frags	Artiodactyla	Artiodactyl
Room 14 fill	85	1	Radius	*Sylvilagus* sp.	Cottontail rabbit
Room 14 fill	85	1	Proximal end of femur	*Sylvilagus* sp.	Cottontail rabbit
Room 14 fill	85	1	Proximal end of metacarpal	Artiodactyla	Artiodactyl
Room 14 fill	85	1	Left innominate	*Sylvilagus* sp.	Cottontail rabbit
Room 14 fill	85	1	Head of tibia frag	cf. *Odocoileus* sp.	Probable deer
Room 14 fill	85	1	Coracoid	*Buteo jamaicensis*	Red-tailed hawk
Room 14 fill	85	1	Ulna	Accipitridae	Hawk
Room 14 fill	85	2	Left mandibles	*Odocoileus virginianus couesi*	White-tailed deer
Room 14 fill	85	1	Limb bone frag	cf. *Odocoileus* sp.	Probable deer
Room 14 fill	85	1	Scapula frag	Mammalia	Mammal
Room 14 fill	85	1	Pelvis frag	cf. *Odocoileus* sp.	Probable deer
Room 14 fill	85	1	Tibia frag	cf. *Odocoileus* sp.	Probable deer
Room 14 fill	85	1	Right innominate	*Lepus* sp.	Jackrabbit
Room 14 fill	85	1	Pelvis frag	cf. *Odocoileus* sp.	Probable deer
Room 14 fill	85	1	Tip of right mandible	*Lepus* sp.	Jackrabbit

Room 14 fill	85	1	Distal end of tibia	cf. *Antilocapra americana*	Probable pronghorn
Room 14 fill	85	1	Right innominate	*Spermophilus* sp.	Ground squirrel
Room 16 fill	87	1	Humerus	*Lepus californicus*	Black-tailed jackrabbit
Room 16 stratitest level 3	128	1	Right innominate	*Sylvilagus* sp.	Cottontail rabbit
Room 16 stratitest level 3	128	1	Patella	cf. Artiodactyla	Probable artiodactyl
Room 18 fill	91		Frags		
Room 19 fill	92	1	Distal end of left femur	*Lepus californicus*	Black-tailed jackrabbit
Room 19 fill	100	1	Distal[g] end of radius	*Odocoileus* cf. *virginianus couesi*	Probable white-tailed deer
Room 19 fill	100	1	Sacrum	*Sylvilagus* sp.	Cottontail rabbit
Room 19 fill	100	1	Frag[h]		
Room 21 fill	97	1	Proximal end of metatarsal	cf. *Antilocapra americana*	Probable pronghorn
Room 34 fill	104	1	Right mandible	*Lepus californicus*	Black-tailed jackrabbit
Room 34 fill	104	1	Distal end of radius	*Odocoileus* cf. *virginianus couesi*	Probable white-tailed deer
Room 34 fill	104	1		cf. Aves	Probable bird
Room 34 fill	104	1	Femur frag	Artiodactyla	Artiodactyl
Room 34 fill	104	1	Scapula frag	*Lepus* sp.	Jackrabbit
Room 34 fill	104	1	Scapula frag	Artiodactyla	Artiodactyl
Room 34 fill	104	1	Left tibia	*Sylvilagus* sp.	Cottontail rabbit
Room 34 fill	104	1	Femur	Aves	Bird
Room 34 fill	104	1	Humerus	*Zenaidura macroura*	Mourning dove
Room 34 fill	104	1	Ilium	*Lepus* sp.	Jackrabbit
Room 34 fill	107	1	Metatarsal frag	*Odocoileus* sp. or *Antilocapra americana*	Deer or pronghorn
Room 34 fill (T13S 10–11E)	114	1	Distal end of tibia	*Odocoileus virginianus couesi*	White-tailed deer[e]
Room 34 fill (T13S 10–11E)	114	1	Astragalus	*Odocoileus virginianus couesi*	White-tailed deer[e]

(*continued*)

TABLE H.1 *(continued)*

Provenience	Bag no.	*n*	Element	Scientific name	Common name
Room 34 fill (T13S 10–11E)	114	2	Frags	cf. Mammalia	Probable mammal
Room 34 fill (T13S 10–11E)	114	1	Frag	cf. Aves	Probable bird
Room 35 fill	109	1	Phalanx	cf. *Ovis canadensis*	Probable bighorn sheep
Room 36 fill	110	1	Ulna	*Lynx rufus*	Bobcat
Room 44 subfloor	126	1	Radius	*Canis lupus familiaris*	Dog
Room 44 subfloor	126	1	Ulna	*Canis lupus familiaris*	Dog
Room 44 subfloor	126	1	Metacarpal	*Canis lupus familiaris*	Dog
Room 44 subfloor	126	1	Metacarpal	*Canis lupus familiaris*	Dog
Room 44 subfloor	126	1	Phalanx	*Canis lupus familiaris*	Dog
Room 44 subfloor	126	1	Head of humerus	*Sylvilagus* sp.	Cottontail rabbit
Room 44 subfloor	126		Frags		
Burial 10	90	1	Rib frag	Artiodactyla	Artiodactyl
Burial 10	90	1	Proximal end of femur	*Sylvilagus* sp.	Cottontail rabbit
Burial 10	90	1	Right innominate	*Dipodomys* sp.	Kangaroo rat
Burial 10	90	1	Tibia frag	cf. Rodentia	Probable rodent
Burial 10	90	1	Humerus	*Turdus migratorius*	American robin
Burial 11	115	1	Radius	*Lepus californicus*	Black-tailed jackrabbit
Burial 11	115	2	Centra of vertebrae	*Lepus* sp.	Jackrabbit
Burial 11	115	1	Navicular-cuboid	*Odocoileus* sp.	Deer
Burial 12	94	2	Caudal vertebrae	cf. *Bos* or *Bison*	Probable cow or bison
NE Trash	96	1	Proximal end of metacarpal	*Odocoileus* sp.	Deer
NE Trash	96	1	Antler? tip	*Odocoileus* sp.	Deer
NE Trash	96	1	Head of rib	Artiodactyla	Artiodactyl

NE Trash	96	1	Tibia	*Lepus* sp.	Jackrabbit
NE Trash	96	1	Head of femur	*Sylvilagus* sp.	Cottontail rabbit
NE Trash	96		Frags	Mammalia	Mammal
NE Trash	96	1	Metacarpal	*Homo sapiens*	Human
NE Trash	96	1	Phalanx	*Homo sapiens*	Human
NE Trash	96	1	Ulna frag	cf. Aves	Probable large bird
NE Trash	99	1	Tibia	*Dipodomys* sp.	Kangaroo rat
NE Trash	99	1	Fibula	*Dipodomys* sp.	Kangaroo rat
NE Trash	99	1	Distal end of tibia	*Odocoileus* cf. *hemionus*	Probable mule deer
NE Trash	99	1	Limb bone frag	Mammalia	Mammal
NE Trash	105	1	Innominate	*Lepus californicus*	Black-tailed jackrabbit
NE Trash	105	1	Limb bone frag	cf. Artiodactyla	Probable artiodactyl
NE Trash (T20E 39–40N)	83	1	Tarsometatarsus	*Accipiter cooperii*	Cooper's hawk
NE Trash (T20E 39–40N)	83	1	Calcaneum	*Odocoileus* sp. or *Ovis* sp.	Deer or sheep
Pit Oven 1	2	1	Radius	*Vulpes* cf. *velox*	Probable swift fox
Pit Oven 1	2	1	Tarsometatarsus	*Parabuteo unicinctus*	Harris's hawk
Pit Oven 1	2	3	Wing bones	cf. Accipitridae	Probable hawk
Pit Oven 1	7	1	Left innominate	*Lepus californicus*	Black-tailed jackrabbit
Pit Oven 1	7	1	Proximal end of left tibia	*Sylvilagus* sp.	Cottontail rabbit
Pit Oven 2	9	1	Lumbar vertebra	*Lepus* cf. *alleni*	Probable antelope jackrabbit
Stratitest 1 level 1	118	1	Left innominate	*Sylvilagus* sp.	Cottontail rabbit
Stratitest 1 level 1	118	1	Scapula	*Sylvilagus* sp.	Cottontail rabbit
Stratitest 1 level 1	118	1	Scapula	*Lepus* sp.	Jackrabbit
Stratitest 1 level 1	118	1	Innominate	*Lepus californicus*	Black-tailed jackrabbit
Stratitest 1 level 1	118	1	Ulna	*Lepus* sp.	Jackrabbit

(*continued*)

TABLE H.1 *(continued)*

Provenience	Bag no.	*n*	Element	Scientific name	Common name
Stratitest 1 level 1	118	2	Frags	Mammalia	Mammal
Stratitest 1 level 5	121	1	Atlas	*Odocoileus hemionus*	Mule deer
Stratitest 1 level 5	121	2	Neural spines of vertebrae	cf. *Odocoileus* sp.	Probable deer
Stratitest 1 level 5	121	Several	Frags	Mammalia	Mammal
T1S 20–14E	5		Teeth	*Odocoileus* cf. *virginianus couesi*	Probable white-tailed deer
T1S 20–14E	5	1	Tibia frag	*Odocoileus* cf. *virginianus couesi*	Probable white-tailed deer
T1S 20–14E	5	1	Lumbar vertebra	*Odocoileus* cf. *virginianus couesi*	Probable white-tailed deer
T1S 20–14E	5	1	Rib frag	*Odocoileus* cf. *virginianus couesi*	Probable white-tailed deer
T1S 20–14E	5	1	Distal end of right tibia	*Lepus californicus*	Black-tailed jackrabbit
T1S 20–14E	5	1	Proximal end of left tibia	*Sylvilagus* sp.	Cottontail rabbit
T1S 23–26E	13	2	Frags (larger long bone)		
T1S 23–26E	13	1	Hyoid frag	*Odocoileus* sp.	Deer
T1S 23–26E	13	1	Head of tibia	*Lepus californicus*	Black-tailed jackrabbit
T1S 23–26E	13	1	Phalanx	*Lepus californicus*	Black-tailed jackrabbit
T1S 30–46E	3	1	Limb bone frag?		
T1S 30–46E	3	1	Antler base	*Odocoileus* cf. *hemionus*	Probable mule deer
T19S 23–25E	80		Frags	Mammalia	Mammal
T20S 20E	81			cf. Aves	Probable bird
T20S 20E	81	Several	Frags[i]		
T17E 12S	117	1	Proximal end of radius	*Odocoileus* sp.	Deer
T17E 12S	117	1	Distal end of metacarpal	*Odocoileus* sp.	Deer
T17E 12S	117	1	Metatarsal	*Lepus* sp.	Jackrabbit
T17E 12S	117		Frags	Mammalia	Mammal

T24E 18–19S	77	1	Distal end of femur	*Lepus* sp.	Jackrabbit
T24E 18–19S	77	2	Ribs	*Lepus* sp.	Jackrabbit
T24E 18–19S	77	1	Cervical vertebra	*Lepus* sp.	Jackrabbit
T24E 18–19S	77	1	Frag	Mammalia	Mammal
T24E 18–19S	77	4	Cranial frags	*Homo sapiens*	Human
T26E 16S	21	1	Femur shaft	cf. *Odocoileus* sp.	Probable deer
T26E 16S	21		Limb bone frags	Artiodactyla	Artiodactyl
T26E 16S	24	1	Axis	*Odocoileus* cf. *virginianus couesi*	Probable white-tailed deer
T26E 16S	24	1	Rib head	*Odocoileus* cf. *virginianus couesi*	Probable white-tailed deer
T26E 16S	24	1	Phalanx	*Odocoileus* cf. *virginianus couesi*	Probable white-tailed deer
T26E 16S	24	1	Frag	*Odocoileus* cf. *virginianus couesi*	Probable white-tailed deer
T10N 0–7E	6	1	Femur	*Lepus* sp.	Jackrabbit
T10N 0–7E	6	1	Lumbar vertebra	*Lepus* sp.	Jackrabbit
T10N 0–7E	6	Several		*Parabuteo unicinctus* and *Buteo jamaicensis*	Harris's hawk and red-tailed hawk
T10N 0–7E	14	1	Tarsometatarsus	*Parabuteo unicinctus*	Harris's hawk
T10N 0–7E	14	3	Frags	cf. Mammalia	Probable mammal
T10N 14–20E	1	1	Metatarsal frag?	cf. *Odocoileus* sp.	Probable deer
T10N 15–17E	86	1	Humerus	*Lepus californicus*	Black-tailed jackrabbit
T10N 15–17E	86	1	Phalanx	*Homo sapiens*	Human
T10N 15–17E	86	1	Tibia	cf. *Lynx rufus*	Probable bobcat
T10N 15–17E	86		Limb bone frags	Artiodactyla	Artiodactyl
T10N 21–26E	15		Frags, probably femur	cf. *Odocoileus* sp.	Probable deer
T11N 16–17E	84	1	Phalanx	*Homo sapiens*	Human
T11N 16–17E	84	1	Limb bone frag	Mammalia	Mammal

(*continued*)

TABLE H.1 *(continued)*

Provenience	Bag no.	*n*	Element	Scientific name	Common name
T15N 25–26E	98	1	Proximal end of metacarpal	cf. *Ovis canadensis*	Probable bighorn sheep
T15N 25–26E	98		Frags		
No provenience	37	1	Cervical vertebra	cf. *Odocoileus* sp.	Probable deer
No provenience	37	1	Thoracic vertebra	cf. *Odocoileus* sp.	Probable deer
No provenience	37	1	Limb bone frag	cf. *Odocoileus* sp.	Probable deer

[a]Per Harris

[b]Probable antler frags, per Harris

[c]Posterior end of calcaneum, per Harris

[d]Includes skull frags of *Lepus* sp., per Harris

[e]Single individual

[f]Thoracic, per Harris

[g]Proximal, per Harris

[h]Ulna frag, per Harris

[i]Femur shaft and proximal end of femur of *Lepus* sp., per Harris

TABLE H.2 Mammalian fauna identified by Arthur H. Harris in 1970, sorted by provenience and bone bag

Provenience	Bag no.	*n*	Element	Scientific name	Common name
House 1 fill	4	1	Humerus	*Lepus* sp.	Jackrabbit
House 2 fill	8	1	Mandible	cf. *Canis lupus familiaris*	Probable dog
House 2 fill	8	1	Tibia	*Sylvilagus* sp.	Cottontail rabbit
House 2 fill	8	1	Humerus	*Sylvilagus* sp.	Cottontail rabbit
House 2 fill	23	1	Femur shaft frag?	cf. *Odocoileus* sp.	Probable deer
House 2 fill	23	1	Tip of antler	cf. *Odocoileus* sp.	Probable deer
House 2 fill	82	1	Rib	Mammalia	Medium-sized mammal
House 2 fill	82		Limb bone frags	Artiodactyla	Artiodactyl
House 2 fill	124	1	Phalanx	*Odocoileus* cf. *hemionus*	Probable mule deer
House 3 fill	62	1	Tibia frag	Artiodactyla	Artiodactyl
House 3 fill	62	1	Vertebra frag	Mammalia	Mammal
House 3 fill	62		Frag	Mammalia	Mammal
House 3 fill	88	1	Tip of right mandible	*Lepus* sp.	Jackrabbit
House 3 fill	88		Frags	Mammalia, including skull frags of *Lepus* sp.	Mammal, including skull frags of jackrabbit
House 3 fill	88	1	Left mandible	*Odocoileus virginianus couesi*	White-tailed deer
House 3 fill	88	1	Left mandible	*Odocoileus virginianus couesi*	White-tailed deer
House 3 fill	88	1	Limb bone frag	cf. *Odocoileus* sp.	Probable deer
House 3 fill	88	1	Frag	Mammalia	Mammal
House 3 fill	88		Frags	Mammalia	Mammal
House 3 fill	88		Frag	Mammalia	Mammal
House 3 fill	88	2	Limb bone frags	cf. *Odocoileus* sp.	Probable deer
House 3 fill	88	1	Scapula frag	cf. Artiodactyla	Probable artiodactyl

(*continued*)

TABLE H.2 *(continued)*

Provenience	Bag no.	*n*	Element	Scientific name	Common name
House 3 fill	88	4	Pelvis frags	*Odocoileus* sp.	Deer
House 3 fill	88	1	Tibia frag	Artiodactyla	Artiodactyl
House 3 fill	88	1	Distal end of tibia	cf. *Antilocapra americana*	Probable pronghorn
House 3 fill	88	1	Right innominate	*Spermophilus* sp.	Ground squirrel
House 3 fill	88	2	Frags	Mammalia	Mammal
House 3 fill	88		Frags	Mammalia	Mammal
House 3 fill	88		Limb bone frags	Artiodactyla	Artiodactyl
House 3 fill	88	1	Right innominate	*Lepus* sp.	Jackrabbit
House 4 fill	102	1	Head of rib	Artiodactyla	Artiodactyl
House 4 fill	102		Limb bone frags	cf. *Odocoileus* sp.	Probable deer
House 4 floor	95	1	Femur shaft frag	cf. *Canis lupus familiaris*	Probable dog
House 4 floor	95	1	Ischium	*Lepus* sp.	Jackrabbit
House 4 floor	95	1	Rib	*Lepus* sp.	Jackrabbit
House 4 floor	95	1	Right mandible	*Lepus alleni*	Antelope jackrabbit
House 4 floor	95	1	Distal phalanx	cf. *Odocoileus* sp.	Probable deer
House 5 fill	10	1	Distal end of metacarpal	*Odocoileus* cf. *virginianus couesi*	Probable white-tailed deer
House 5 fill	10	3	Tibia? frags	cf. *Odocoileus* sp.	Probable deer
House 5 fill	10	1	Long bone frag	cf. *Odocoileus* sp.	Probable deer
House 5 fill	89	1	Phalanx	*Homo sapiens*	Human
House 5 fill	89	1	Scapula	*Lepus* sp.	Jackrabbit
House 5 fill	89	1	Humerus	*Lepus* sp.	Jackrabbit
House 6 floor	103	1	Tip of ilium	*Sylvilagus* sp.	Cottontail rabbit
House 6 floor	103	1	Limb bone frag	Artiodactyla	Artiodactyl

House 6 floor	103	2	Probable antler frags	cf. *Odocoileus* sp.	Probable deer
House 7 pits 1 and 2	112	1	Posterior end of calcaneum	*Sylvilagus* sp.	Cottontail rabbit
House 7 fill	111	1	Phalanx	*Odocoileus* sp.	Deer
House 7 fill	111	1	Tibia frag	*Sylvilagus* sp.	Cottontail rabbit
House 7 fill	125	1	Right innominate	*Lepus californicus*	Black-tailed jackrabbit
House 7 floor 1	119	1	Left innominate	*Sylvilagus* sp.	Cottontail rabbit
House 7 floor 1	119	1	Frag	Mammalia	Mammal
House 7 floor 1	120		Limb bone frags	cf. Artiodactyla	Probable artiodactyl
House 7 subfloor 1 fill	123	1	Cervical vertebra	*Lepus* sp.	Jackrabbit
House 7 subfloor 1 fill	123	1	Head of humerus	*Lepus* sp.	Jackrabbit
House 7 subfloor 1 fill	123		Skull frags	*Lepus* sp.	Jackrabbit
House 9 floor	127		Rib frags	*Lepus* sp.	Jackrabbit
House 9 floor	127	1	Tooth	*Lepus* sp.	Jackrabbit
House 9 floor	127	1	Head of femur	*Lepus* sp.	Jackrabbit
House 9 floor	127	1	Distal end of humerus	*Sylvilagus* sp.	Cottontail rabbit
House 9 floor	127	1	Distal end of tibia	*Sylvilagus* sp.	Cottontail rabbit
House 9 floor	127	1	Metapodial	*Lepus* sp.	Jackrabbit
House 9 floor	127	1	Rib head	*Lepus* sp.	Jackrabbit
House 9 floor	127	1	Distal end of femur	cf. *Canis lupus familiaris*	Probable dog
House 9 floor	127	1	Head of femur	cf. *Canis lupus familiaris*	Probable dog
House 9 floor	127	1	Mandible	*Bassariscus astutus*	Ringtail
House 9 floor	127	1	Auditory bulla	*Chaetodipus* cf. *baileyi*	Probable Bailey's pocket mouse
Kiva fill	48	1	Distal end of metacarpal	*Odocoileus* cf. *virginianus couesi*	Probable white-tailed deer
Kiva fill	48	1	Phalanx	*Odocoileus* sp.	Deer
Kiva fill	48	2	Distal ends of humeri	*Sylvilagus* cf. *floridanus*	Probable eastern cottontail rabbit

(*continued*)

TABLE H.2 *(continued)*

Provenience	Bag no.	*n*	Element	Scientific name	Common name
Kiva fill	48	1	Humerus	*Sylvilagus* cf. *floridanus*	Probable eastern cottontail rabbit
Kiva fill	48	3	Innominates	*Sylvilagus* sp.	Cottontail rabbit
Kiva fill	48	2	Scapulae	*Sylvilagus* cf. *floridanus*	Probable eastern cottontail rabbit
Kiva fill	48	2	Proximal ends of tibiae	*Sylvilagus* cf. *floridanus*	Probable eastern cottontail rabbit
Kiva fill	48	1	Head of rib	*Sylvilagus* sp.	Cottontail rabbit
Kiva fill	48	1	Metatarsal	*Sylvilagus* sp.	Cottontail rabbit
Kiva fill	48	2	Metatarsals	*Lepus* sp.	Jackrabbit
Kiva fill	48	1	Metacarpal	*Lepus* sp.	Jackrabbit
Kiva fill	48	2	Ulnae	*Lepus* cf. *californicus*	Probable black-tailed jackrabbit
Kiva fill	48	2	Scapulae	*Lepus* cf. *californicus*	Probable black-tailed jackrabbit
Kiva fill	48	1	Proximal end of femur	*Lepus* sp.	Jackrabbit
Kiva fill	48	1	Distal end of femur	*Lepus* sp.	Jackrabbit
Kiva fill	48	1	Maxillary	*Lepus alleni*	Antelope jackrabbit
Kiva fill	48	1	Right mandible	*Lepus alleni*	Antelope jackrabbit
Kiva fill	48	1	Pelvis frag	*Lepus* sp.	Jackrabbit
Kiva fill	48	1	Tibia	*Lepus californicus*	Black-tailed jackrabbit
Kiva fill	48	1	Radius frag	*Lepus californicus*	Black-tailed jackrabbit
Kiva fill	48	1	Radius	*Lepus californicus*	Black-tailed jackrabbit
Kiva fill	48	1	Lumbar vertebra	*Lepus* sp.	Jackrabbit
Kiva fill	48	4	Rib frags	*Lepus* sp.	Jackrabbit
Kiva fill	48	1	Sacrum	*Lepus* sp.	Jackrabbit
Kiva fill	48	1	Lumbar vertebra	*Sylvilagus* sp.	Cottontail rabbit
Kiva fill	48	2	Tibiae	*Sylvilagus* cf. *floridanus*	Probable eastern cottontail rabbit
Kiva fill	48	1	Distal end of femur	*Sylvilagus* cf. *floridanus*	Probable eastern cottontail rabbit

Kiva fill	48		Frags	Mammalia	Mammal
Kiva fill	48	1	Tibia	*Neotoma albigula*	White-throated woodrat
Kiva fill	48	1	Tibia	*Cynomys* sp.	Prairie dog
Kiva fill	50	1	Proximal end of ulna	cf. *Odocoileus* sp.	Probable deer
Kiva fill	50	1	Proximal end of ulna	cf. *Odocoileus* sp.	Probable deer
Kiva fill	50	1	Calcaneum	Artiodactyla	Artiodactyl
Kiva fill	50	1	Distal end of metacarpal	*Odocoileus virginianus couesi*	White-tailed deer
Kiva fill	50	1	Rib frag	Artiodactyla	Artiodactyl
Kiva fill	50	1	Proximal end of radius	Artiodactyla	Artiodactyl
Kiva fill	50	Several	Limb bone frags	Mammalia, mostly Artiodactyla	Mammal, mostly artiodactyl
Kiva fill	50	1	Phalanx	Artiodactyla	Artiodactyl
Kiva fill	50	1	Phalanx	*Ovis canadensis*	Bighorn sheep
Kiva fill	50	1	Pelvis frag	Artiodactyla	Artiodactyl
Kiva fill	50	1	Head of rib	Artiodactyla	Artiodactyl
Kiva fill	50	1	Mandible frag	cf. *Canis lupus familiaris*	Probable dog
Kiva fill	50	1	Pelvis frag	Artiodactyla	Artiodactyl
Kiva fill	50	1	Metacarpal frag	Artiodactyla	Artiodactyl
Kiva fill	50	1	Calcaneum frag	Artiodactyla	Artiodactyl
Kiva fill	50	1	Phalanx frag	Artiodactyla	Artiodactyl
Kiva fill	50	1	Rib frag	Artiodactyla	Artiodactyl
Kiva fill	50	1	Lumbar vertebra	Artiodactyla	Artiodactyl
Kiva fill	50	1	Phalanx	Artiodactyla	Artiodactyl
Kiva fill	50	1	Cervical vertebra	Artiodactyla	Artiodactyl
Kiva fill	50	1	Phalanx	cf. *Odocoileus* sp.	Probable deer
Kiva fill	50	1	Mandible frag	*Lepus californicus*	Black-tailed jackrabbit

(*continued*)

TABLE H.2 *(continued)*

Provenience	Bag no.	*n*	Element	Scientific name	Common name
Kiva fill	50	1	Calcaneum	*Lepus californicus*	Black-tailed jackrabbit
Kiva fill	50	1	Right femur	*Lepus californicus*	Black-tailed jackrabbit
Kiva fill	50	1	Distal end of tibia	*Lepus californicus*	Black-tailed jackrabbit
Kiva fill	50	1	Proximal end of tibia	*Lepus californicus*	Black-tailed jackrabbit
Kiva fill	50	1	Distal end of scapula	*Lepus californicus*	Black-tailed jackrabbit
Kiva fill	50	1	Right innominate	*Lepus californicus*	Black-tailed jackrabbit
Kiva fill	50	2	Thoracic vertebrae	*Lepus californicus*	Black-tailed jackrabbit
Kiva fill	50	1	Lumbar vertebra	*Lepus californicus*	Black-tailed jackrabbit
Kiva fill	50	Several	Rib frags	*Lepus* sp.	Jackrabbit
Kiva fill	50	1	Proximal end of humerus	*Sylvilagus* sp.	Cottontail rabbit
Kiva fill	50	1	Distal end of humerus	*Sylvilagus* sp.	Cottontail rabbit
Kiva fill	50	1	Proximal end of femur	*Sylvilagus* sp.	Cottontail rabbit
Kiva fill	50	1	Distal end of femur	*Sylvilagus* sp.	Cottontail rabbit
Kiva fill	50	1	Proximal end of tibia	*Sylvilagus* sp.	Cottontail rabbit
Kiva fill	50	1	Scapula frag	*Sylvilagus* sp.	Cottontail rabbit
Kiva fill	50	1	Limb bone frag	cf. Leporidae	Probable hare or rabbit
Kiva fill	50	Several	Frags	Mammalia	Mammal
Kiva fill	50	3	Phalanges	*Homo sapiens*	Human
Kiva fill	50	1	Tooth	*Homo sapiens*	Human
Kiva fill	50	2	Frags	*Homo sapiens*	Human
Kiva fill	50	1	Femur	*Neotoma albigula*	White-throated woodrat
Kiva fill	55	1	Distal end of tibia	*Odocoileus* cf. *virginianus couesi*	Probable white-tailed deer
Kiva fill	55	1	Proximal end of tibia	Artiodactyla	Artiodactyl
Kiva fill	55	4	Metatarsals	cf. *Canis latrans*	Probable coyote[a]

Kiva fill	55	1	Calcaneum	cf. *Canis latrans*	Probable coyote[a]
Kiva fill	55	1	Astragalus	cf. *Canis latrans*	Probable coyote[a]
Kiva fill	55	1	Distal end of tibia	cf. *Canis latrans*	Probable coyote[a]
Kiva fill	55	1	Claw	cf. *Canis latrans*	Probable coyote[a]
Kiva fill	55	2	Phalanges	*Canis* sp.	Coyote or dog
Kiva fill	55	1	Frag	cf. Mammalia	Probable mammal
Kiva fill	58		Limb bone frags	Artiodactyla	Artiodactyl
Kiva fill	58	1	Neural spine of thoracic vertebra	Artiodactyla	Artiodactyl
Kiva fill	58	1	Phalanx	Artiodactyla	Artiodactyl
Kiva fill	58	1	Lumbar vertebra	Artiodactyla	Artiodactyl
Kiva fill	58	1	Centrum of vertebra	Artiodactyla	Artiodactyl
Kiva fill	58	1	Ilium frag	Artiodactyla	Artiodactyl
Kiva fill	58	1	Pelvis frag	Artiodactyla	Artiodactyl
Kiva fill	58	1	Distal end of metacarpal	Artiodactyla	Artiodactyl
Kiva fill	58	1	Axis	*Canis lupus familiaris*	Dog
Kiva fill	58	1	Cervical vertebra	*Canis lupus familiaris*	Dog
Kiva fill	58	1	Left innominate	*Lepus* cf. *californicus*	Probable black-tailed jackrabbit
Kiva fill	58	1	Right innominate	*Lepus* cf. *californicus*	Probable black-tailed jackrabbit
Kiva fill	58	1	Proximal end of left tibia	*Lepus* cf. *californicus*	Probable black-tailed jackrabbit
Kiva fill	58	1	Proximal end of right tibia	*Lepus* cf. *californicus*	Probable black-tailed jackrabbit
Kiva fill	58	1	Head of humerus	*Lepus californicus*	Black-tailed jackrabbit
Kiva fill	58	2	Right femora	*Sylvilagus* sp.	Cottontail rabbit
Kiva fill	58	1	Left femur	*Sylvilagus* sp.	Cottontail rabbit
Kiva fill	58	2	Metatarsals	*Homo sapiens*	Human

(continued)

TABLE H.2 *(continued)*

Provenience	Bag no.	*n*	Element	Scientific name	Common name
Kiva fill	58	2	Frags	cf. *Homo sapiens*	Probable human
Kiva fill	58	Several	Frags	Mammalia	Mammal
Kiva fill	61	1	Limb bone frag	cf. *Odocoileus* sp.	Probable deer
Kiva fill	61	1	Distal end of humerus	*Odocoileus hemionus*	Mule deer
Kiva fill	61	1	Pelvis frag	cf. *Odocoileus* sp.	Probable deer
Kiva fill	61	1	Centrum of vertebra	cf. *Odocoileus* sp.	Probable deer
Kiva fill	61	1	Pelvis frag	*Sylvilagus* sp.	Cottontail rabbit
Kiva fill	61	1	Distal end of femur	*Sylvilagus* sp.	Cottontail rabbit
Kiva fill	61	1	Scapula	*Lepus californicus*	Black-tailed jackrabbit
Kiva fill	61	1	Distal end of tibia	*Odocoileus* sp.	Deer
Kiva fill	61	1	Humerus frag	*Sylvilagus* sp.	Cottontail rabbit
Kiva fill	61	1	Distal end of metacarpal	cf. *Odocoileus* sp.	Probable deer
Kiva fill	61	1	Proximal end of humerus	*Sylvilagus* sp.	Cottontail rabbit
Kiva fill	61	1	Proximal end of femur	*Sylvilagus* sp.	Cottontail rabbit
Kiva fill	61	1	Radius	*Sylvilagus* sp.	Cottontail rabbit
Kiva fill	61	1	Left innominate	*Sylvilagus* sp.	Cottontail rabbit
Kiva fill	61	1	Ilium	*Lepus californicus*	Black-tailed jackrabbit
Kiva fill	61	1	Rib	*Lepus* sp.	Jackrabbit
Kiva fill	61	1	Rib	*Odocoileus* sp.	Deer
Kiva fill	61	1	Ulna	*Sylvilagus* sp.	Cottontail rabbit
Kiva fill	61	1	Proximal end of metacarpal	cf. *Odocoileus* sp.	Probable deer
Kiva fill	61	1	Lumbar vertebra	*Lepus* sp.	Jackrabbit
Kiva fill	61	2	Thoracic vertebrae	Artiodactyla	Artiodactyl
Kiva fill	61	1	Ilium	*Lepus* sp.	Jackrabbit

Kiva fill	61	1	Limb bone	Mammalia	Mammal
Kiva fill	61	1	Ilium	*Sylvilagus* sp.	Cottontail rabbit
Kiva fill	61	1	Pelvis frag	*Lepus californicus*	Black-tailed jackrabbit
Kiva fill	61	1	Distal end of radius	*Odocoileus* sp.	Deer
Kiva fill	61	1	Distal end of humerus	*Sylvilagus* sp.	Cottontail rabbit
Kiva fill	61	1	Rib frag	*Lepus* sp.	Jackrabbit
Kiva fill	61	1	Femur frag	Artiodactyla	Artiodactyl
Kiva fill	61	1	Phalanx	*Lepus* sp.	Jackrabbit
Kiva fill	64	1	Scapula	*Odocoileus* cf. *virginianus couesi*	Probable white-tailed deer
Kiva fill	64	1	Scapula frag	cf. *Odocoileus* sp.	Probable deer
Kiva fill	64	1	Base of skull	*Lepus alleni*	Antelope jackrabbit
Kiva fill	64	1	Right mandible	*Lepus californicus*	Black-tailed jackrabbit
Kiva fill	64	11	Limb bone frags	Artiodactyla	Artiodactyl
Kiva fill	64	1	Rib frag	Artiodactyla	Artiodactyl
Kiva fill	64	1	Proximal end of ulna	*Antilocapra americana*	Pronghorn
Kiva fill	64	1	Auditory bulla	*Lepus* sp.	Jackrabbit
Kiva fill	64	1	Centrum of vertebra	Mammalia	Mammal
Kiva fill	64	1	Right innominate	*Sylvilagus* sp.	Cottontail rabbit
Kiva fill	64	14	Frags	Mammalia	Mammal
Kiva fill	64	1	Proximal end of metacarpal	Artiodactyla	Artiodactyl
Kiva fill	64	1	Metacarpal shaft frag	Artiodactyla	Artiodactyl
Kiva fill	64	1	Metacarpal	*Sylvilagus* sp.	Cottontail rabbit
Kiva fill	64	1	Distal end of tibia	*Odocoileus* cf. *virginianus couesi*	Probable white-tailed deer
Kiva fill	64	1	Metatarsal	*Lepus* sp.	Jackrabbit
Kiva fill	64	1	Palatine bone	*Lepus* sp.	Jackrabbit

(*continued*)

TABLE H.2 *(continued)*

Provenience	Bag no.	*n*	Element	Scientific name	Common name
Kiva fill	64	1	Ulna frag	*Lepus* sp.	Jackrabbit
Kiva fill	64	1	Distal end of femur	*Sylvilagus* sp.	Cottontail rabbit
Kiva fill	64	1	Ulna	*Sylvilagus* sp.	Cottontail rabbit
Kiva fill	64	1	Innominate frag	*Lepus californicus*	Black-tailed jackrabbit
Kiva fill	64	1	Phalanx	Artiodactyla	Artiodactyl
Kiva fill	64	1	Head of femur	*Lepus* sp.	Jackrabbit
Kiva fill	64	1	Ilium frag	*Lepus* sp.	Jackrabbit
Kiva fill	64	1	Proximal end of metacarpal	*Odocoileus* cf. *virginianus couesi*	Probable white-tailed deer
Kiva fill	64	1	Humerus	*Lynx rufus*	Bobcat
Kiva fill	64	1	Proximal end of ulna	Artiodactyla	Artiodactyl
Kiva fill	64	1	Frag	cf. *Homo sapiens*	Probable human
Kiva fill	65	1	Phalanx	*Homo sapiens*	Human
Kiva fill	65	Several	Frags	Mammalia	Mammal
Kiva fill	65	1	Phalanx	*Lepus* sp.	Jackrabbit
Kiva fill	65	1	Scapula frag	Artiodactyla	Artiodactyl
Kiva fill	65	1	Lumbar vertebra	cf. *Odocoileus* sp.	Probable deer
Kiva fill	65	1	Humeral condyle	*Odocoileus* sp.	Deer
Kiva fill	65	2	Neural spines of vertebrae	cf. *Odocoileus* sp.	Probable deer
Kiva fill	65	1	Head of tibia	*Odocoileus* sp.	Deer
Kiva fill	65	1	Distal end of metatarsal	*Odocoileus* cf. *virginianus couesi*	Probable white-tailed deer
Kiva fill	65	1	Thoracic vertebra	cf. *Odocoileus* sp.	Probable deer
Kiva fill	65	2	Distal ends of humeri	*Odocoileus* cf. *virginianus couesi*	Probable white-tailed deer
Kiva fill	65	1	Femur shaft frag	*Odocoileus* cf. *virginianus couesi*	Probable white-tailed deer
Kiva fill	65	1	Metatarsal shaft frag	cf. *Odocoileus* sp.	Probable deer

Kiva fill	65	1	Rib	*Lepus* sp.	Jackrabbit
Kiva fill	65	1	Antler burr	*Odocoileus* sp.	Deer
Kiva fill	65	1	Metatarsal frag	cf. *Odocoileus* sp.	Probable deer
Kiva fill	65	1	Scapula frag	cf. *Odocoileus* sp.	Probable deer
Kiva fill	65	1	Scapula frag	*Odocoileus* cf. *virginianus couesi*	Probable white-tailed deer
Kiva fill	65	1	Lumbar vertebra	*Odocoileus* cf. *virginianus couesi*	Probable white-tailed deer
Kiva fill	65	1	Cervical vertebra	*Lepus* sp.	Jackrabbit
Kiva fill	65	1	Scapula	*Sylvilagus* sp.	Cottontail rabbit
Kiva fill	65	1	Metatarsal	*Lepus* sp.	Jackrabbit
Kiva fill	65	1	Tooth	*Odocoileus* sp.	Deer
Kiva fill	65		Limb bone frags	cf. *Odocoileus* sp.	Probable deer
Kiva fill	65	1	Antler burr	*Odocoileus* sp.	Deer
Kiva fill	65	1	Left innominate	*Sylvilagus* sp.	Cottontail rabbit
Kiva fill	65	1	Distal end of right tibia	*Lepus californicus*	Black-tailed jackrabbit
Kiva fill	65	1	Metacarpal frag	cf. *Odocoileus* sp.	Probable deer
Kiva fill	65	1	Ulna	*Lynx rufus*	Bobcat
Kiva fill	65	1	Right mandible	*Procyon lotor*	Raccoon
Kiva fill	65	1	Vertebra frag	*Odocoileus* sp.	Deer
Kiva fill	65	1	Phalanx	*Odocoileus* sp.	Deer
Kiva fill	65	1	Antler frag	*Odocoileus* sp.	Deer
Kiva fill	65	1	Calcaneum	*Odocoileus* sp.	Deer
Kiva fill	65	1	Limb bone frag	cf. *Odocoileus* sp.	Probable deer
Kiva fill	65	Several	Cranial frags	*Odocoileus* sp.	Deer
Kiva fill	65	1	Proximal end of metatarsal	*Odocoileus* cf. *virginianus couesi*	Probable white-tailed deer
Kiva fill	65	1	Distal end of femur	*Lepus californicus*	Black-tailed jackrabbit

(*continued*)

TABLE H.2 *(continued)*

Provenience	Bag no.	*n*	Element	Scientific name	Common name
Kiva fill	70	1	Astragalus	*Odocoileus* cf. *virginianus couesi*	Probable white-tailed deer
Kiva fill	70	1	Tibia	*Canis lupus familiaris*	Dog
Kiva fill	70	1	Femur	*Canis lupus familiaris*	Dog
Kiva fill	70	1	Radius	*Canis lupus familiaris*	Dog
Kiva fill	70	1	Radius	*Canis lupus familiaris*	Dog
Kiva fill	70	1	Humerus	*Canis lupus familiaris*	Dog
Kiva fill	70	2	Thoracic vertebrae	*Canis lupus familiaris*	Dog
Kiva fill	70	1	Atlas	*Canis lupus familiaris*	Dog
Kiva fill	70	1	Sternum frag	*Canis lupus familiaris*	Dog
Kiva fill	70	1	Rib	*Lepus* sp.	Jackrabbit
Kiva fill	70	2	Metatarsals	*Lepus* sp.	Jackrabbit
Kiva fill	70	1	Metacarpal	cf. *Canis lupus familiaris*	Probable dog
Kiva fill	70	1	Metacarpal frag	cf. *Canis lupus familiaris*	Probable dog
Kiva fill	70	Several	Frags	Mammalia	Mammal
Kiva fill	72	1	Right mandible	*Canis lupus familiaris*	Dog
Kiva fill (T8.5–9S 22–23E)	32	1	Innominate	*Lepus* sp.	Jackrabbit
Kiva fill (T8.5–9S 22–23E)	32	1	Head of femur	cf. *Homo sapiens*	Probable human
Kiva fill (T8.5–9S 22–23E)	32		Frag	cf. *Homo sapiens*	Probable human
Kiva fill (T8.5–9S 22–23E)	32	1	Axis frag	Artiodactyla	Artiodactyl
Kiva fill (T8.5–9S 22–23E)	32	1	Femur frag	Artiodactyla	Artiodactyl
Kiva fill (T8.5–9S 22–23E)	32		Limb bone frags	Artiodactyla	Artiodactyl
Kiva fill (T8.5–9S 22–23E)	32	1	Base of antler	cf. *Odocoileus* sp.	Probable deer
Kiva fill (T8.5–9S 24–25E L1)	17	1	Distal end of left tibia	*Odocoileus* sp.	Deer
Kiva fill (T8.5–9S 24–25E L1)	17	1	Limb bone frag	cf. *Odocoileus* sp.	Probable deer

Kiva fill (T8.5–9S 24–25E L2)	18	1	Lumbar vertebra	*Sylvilagus* sp.	Cottontail rabbit
Kiva fill (T8.5–9S 24–25E L2)	18	1	Head of right femur	*Sylvilagus* sp.	Cottontail rabbit
Kiva fill (T8.5–9S 24–25E L2)	18	1	Left mandible frag	*Sylvilagus* sp.	Cottontail rabbit
Kiva fill (T8.5–9S 24–25E L2)	18	1	Proximal frag of metatarsal	*Odocoileus* cf. *virginianus couesi*	Probable white-tailed deer
Kiva fill (T8.5–9S 24–25E L2)	18	1	Pelvis frag	*Odocoileus* cf. *virginianus couesi*	Probable white-tailed deer
Kiva fill (T8.5–9S 24–25E L2)	18	1	Frag	cf. *Odocoileus* sp.	Probable deer
Kiva fill (T8.5–9S 24–25E L3)	20		Frags	Mammalia	Mammal
Kiva fill (T8.5–9S 24–25E L4)	22	1	Pelvis frag	cf. *Sylvilagus* sp.	Probable cottontail rabbit
Kiva fill (T8.5–9S 24–25E L4)	22	1	Mandible	cf. *Canis lupus familiaris*	Probable dog
Kiva fill (T8.5–9S 24–25E L4)	22	1	Distal end of metatarsal	*Odocoileus* cf. *virginianus couesi*	Probable white-tailed deer
Kiva fill (T8.5–9S 24–25E L4)	22		Canine and incisors	cf. *Canis lupus familiaris*	Probable dog
Kiva fill (T10S 23–24E L1)	27	1	Proximal phalanx, first digit of foot	*Homo sapiens*	Human
Kiva fill (T10S 23–24E L1)	27	1	Proximal phalanx	*Odocoileus* cf. *virginianus couesi*	Probable white-tailed deer
Kiva fill (T10S 23–24E L1)	27	1	Right innominate	*Sylvilagus* sp.	Cottontail rabbit
Kiva fill (T10S 23–24E L1)	27	1	Tibia frag	cf. *Lepus* sp.	Probable jackrabbit
Kiva fill (T10S 23–24E L1)	27	1	Metatarsal frag	cf. *Odocoileus* sp.	Probable deer
Kiva fill (T10S 23–24E L2)	28	1	Radius	*Lepus californicus*	Black-tailed jackrabbit
Kiva fill (T10S 23–24E L2)	28	1	Rib	*Lepus californicus*	Black-tailed jackrabbit
Kiva fill (T10S 23–24E L2)	28	1	Metacarpal	*Lepus californicus*	Black-tailed jackrabbit
Kiva fill (T10S 23–24E L2)	28	1	Mandible tip	*Lepus californicus*	Black-tailed jackrabbit
Kiva fill (T10S 23–24E L2)	28	1	Head of scapula	*Sylvilagus* sp.	Cottontail rabbit
Kiva fill (T10S 23–24E L2)	28	1	Phalanx	*Homo sapiens*	Human
Kiva fill (T10S 23–24E L2)	28	1	Metacarpal	*Puma concolor* or *Panthera onca*	Mountain lion or jaguar
Kiva fill (T10S 23–24E L2)	28	1	Phalanx	*Puma concolor* or *Panthera onca*	Mountain lion or jaguar

(continued)

TABLE H.2 *(continued)*

Provenience	Bag no.	*n*	Element	Scientific name	Common name
Kiva fill (T10S 23–24E L2)	28	1	Phalanx	cf. *Ovis canadensis*	Probable bighorn sheep
Kiva fill (T10S 23–24E L2)	28	1	Metatarsal frag	Artiodactyla	Artiodactyl
Kiva fill (T10S 23–24E L2)	28	1	Head of rib	Artiodactyla	Artiodactyl
Kiva fill (T10S 23–25E L2)	31	1	Proximal end of metacarpal	Artiodactyla	Artiodactyl
Kiva fill (T10S 23–25E L2)	31	1	Distal end of tibia	*Odocoileus* sp.	Deer
Kiva fill (T10S 23–25E L2)	31	1	Distal end of humerus	cf. *Odocoileus* sp.	Probable deer
Kiva fill (T10S 23–25E L2)	31	1	Phalanx	Artiodactyla	Artiodactyl
Kiva fill (T10S 23–25E L2)	31	1	Proximal end of scapula	Artiodactyla	Artiodactyl
Kiva fill (T10S 23–25E L2)	31	1	Rib frag	Artiodactyla	Artiodactyl
Kiva fill (T10S 23–25E L2)	31	1	Phalanx	*Homo sapiens*	Human
Kiva fill (T10S 23–25E L2)	31	1	Head of femur	*Sylvilagus* sp.	Cottontail rabbit
Kiva fill (T10S 23–25E L2)	31		Metapodials	*Sylvilagus* sp.	Cottontail rabbit
Kiva fill (T10S 23–25E L2)	31	1	Scapula frag	*Lepus* sp.	Jackrabbit
Kiva fill (T10S 23–25E L2)	31	1	Centrum of vertebra	*Lepus* sp.	Jackrabbit
Kiva fill (T10S 23–25E L2)	31	1	Proximal end of metatarsal	Artiodactyla	Artiodactyl
Kiva fill (T10S 23–25E L2)	31	1	Radius	*Lepus* sp.	Jackrabbit
Kiva fill (T10S 23–25E L2)	31	1	Phalanx	*Puma concolor* or *Panthera onca*	Mountain lion or jaguar
Kiva fill (T10S 23–25E L3)	38	1	Head of right femur	cf. *Odocoileus* sp.	Probable deer
Kiva fill (T10S 23–25E L3)	38	1	Right calcaneum	cf. *Odocoileus* sp.	Probable deer
Kiva fill (T10S 23–25E L3)	38	1	Phalanx frag	*Odocoileus* sp.	Deer
Kiva fill (T10S 23–25E L3)	38	1	Proximal end of humerus	*Sylvilagus* sp.	Cottontail rabbit
Kiva fill (T10S 23–25E L3)	38	1	Left innominate frag	*Sylvilagus* sp.	Cottontail rabbit
Kiva fill (T10S 23–25E L3)	38	1	Proximal end of metatarsal	cf. *Lepus* sp.	Probable jackrabbit
Kiva fill (T10S 23–25E L3)	38	1	Proximal end of rib	cf. *Lepus* sp.	Probable jackrabbit

Kiva fill (T10S 23–25E L3)	38	1	Scapula frag	cf. *Lepus* sp.	Probable jackrabbit
Kiva fill (T10S 23–25E L3)	38	1	Ulna shaft frag	cf. *Lepus* sp.	Probable jackrabbit
Kiva fill (T10S 23E L4)	41	1	Sub-terminal phalanx	*Homo sapiens*	Human
Kiva fill (T12S 18–20E)	113	1	Vertebra frag	cf. Artiodactyla	Probable artiodactyl
Kiva fill (T12S 18–20E)	113	1	Phalanx	cf. *Odocoileus* sp.	Probable deer
Kiva fill (T12S 18–20E)	113	1	Metapodial frag	*Odocoileus* sp.	Deer
Kiva fill (T12S 18–20E)	113	1	Head of right femur	*Sylvilagus* sp.	Cottontail rabbit
Kiva fill (T15S 22–24E)	36	1	Innominate	*Sylvilagus* sp.	Cottontail rabbit
Kiva fill (T15S 22–24E)	36	1	Metatarsal frag	cf. *Odocoileus* sp.	Probable deer
Kiva fill (T15S 22–24E)	36	2	Limb bone frags	cf. *Odocoileus* sp.	Probable deer
Kiva fill (T15S 22–24E)	36	1	Podial	*Homo sapiens*	Human
Kiva fill (T15S 25E)	25a	2	Cervical vertebrae	Artiodactyla	Artiodactyl
Kiva fill (T15S 25E)	25a	Several	Vertebrae frags	Artiodactyla	Artiodactyl
Kiva fill (T15S 25E)	25a		Limb bone frags	Artiodactyla	Artiodactyl
Kiva fill (T15S 25E)	25a	2	Cervical vertebrae	*Lepus* sp.	Jackrabbit
Kiva fill (T15S 25E)	25a	1	Calcaneum	*Lepus* sp.	Jackrabbit
Kiva fill (T15S 25E)	25a	1	Distal end of femur	*Lepus* sp.	Jackrabbit
Kiva fill (T15S 25E)	25a	1	Radius	*Lepus* sp.	Jackrabbit
Kiva fill (T15S 25E)	25a	1	Innominate	*Sylvilagus* sp.	Cottontail rabbit
Kiva fill (T15S 25E)	25a	1	Head of femur	*Sylvilagus* sp.	Cottontail rabbit
Kiva fill (T15S 25E)	25a		Frags	Mammalia	Mammal
Kiva fill (T15S 25E)	25b		Maxillaries	*Lepus alleni*	Antelope jackrabbit
Kiva fill (T15S 25E)	25b	1	Mandible	*Lepus californicus*	Black-tailed jackrabbit
Kiva fill (T15S 25E)	25b		Skull frags	*Lepus* sp.	Jackrabbit
Kiva fill (T22E 8–11S)	46	1	Pelvis frag	Artiodactyla	Artiodactyl

(continued)

TABLE H.2 *(continued)*

Provenience	Bag no.	*n*	Element	Scientific name	Common name
Kiva fill (T22E 8–11S)	46	1	Distal end of femur	Artiodactyla	Artiodactyl
Kiva fill (T22E 8–11S)	46	1	Femur frag	Artiodactyla	Artiodactyl
Kiva fill (T22E 8–11S)	46	1	Distal end of metapodial	Artiodactyla	Artiodactyl
Kiva fill (T22E 8–11S)	46	Several	Frags	cf. Mammalia	Probable mammal
Kiva fill (T22E 10–14S)	29	1	Occipital condyle	Artiodactyla	Artiodactyl
Kiva fill (T22E 10–14S)	29	1	Phalanx	cf. *Odocoileus* sp.	Probable deer
Kiva fill (T22E 10–14S)	29	1	Scapula frag	Artiodactyla	Artiodactyl
Kiva fill (T22E 10–14S)	29	1	Innominate	*Lepus* cf. *alleni*	Probable antelope jackrabbit
Kiva fill (T22E 10–14S)	29	1	Thoracic vertebra	*Lepus* sp.	Jackrabbit
Kiva fill (T22E 10–14S)	29	5	Occipital condyles	*Lepus* sp.	Jackrabbit
Kiva fill (T22E 10–14S)	29	1	Auditory bulla	*Lepus* sp.	Jackrabbit
Kiva fill (T22E 10–14S)	29	1	Lumbar vertebra	*Sylvilagus* sp.	Cottontail rabbit
Kiva fill (T22E 10–14S)	29		Frags	Mammalia	Mammal
Kiva fill (T22E 11–15S)	40	1	Axis	*Odocoileus* cf. *virginianus couesi*	Probable white-tailed deer
Kiva fill (T22E 11–15S)	40	1	Scapula	*Odocoileus* cf. *virginianus couesi*	Probable white-tailed deer
Kiva fill (T22E 11–15S)	40	1	Proximal end of radius	*Odocoileus* cf. *virginianus couesi*	Probable white-tailed deer
Kiva fill (T22E 11–15S)	40	1	Humerus	*Odocoileus* cf. *virginianus couesi*	Probable white-tailed deer
Kiva fill (T22E 11–15S)	40	1	Femur frag	cf. *Odocoileus* sp.	Probable deer
Kiva fill (T22E 11–15S)	40	1	Femur	cf. *Odocoileus* sp.	Probable deer
Kiva fill (T22E 11–15S)	40	1	Vertebra frag	cf. *Odocoileus* sp.	Probable deer
Kiva fill (T22E 11–15S)	40	1	Navicular-cuboid	cf. *Odocoileus* sp.	Probable deer
Kiva fill (T22E 11–15S)	40	1	Phalanx	cf. *Odocoileus* sp.	Probable deer
Kiva fill (T22E 11–15S)	40	1	Calcaneum	*Sylvilagus* sp.	Cottontail rabbit
Kiva fill (T22E 11–15S)	40	1	Astragalus	*Sylvilagus* sp.	Cottontail rabbit

Kiva fill (T22E 11–15S)	40		Occipital condyles	*Lepus alleni*	Antelope jackrabbit
Kiva fill (T22E 11–15S)	40	1	Left mandible	*Lepus alleni*	Antelope jackrabbit
Kiva fill (T22E 11–15S)	40	1	Proximal end of tibia	*Lepus californicus*	Black-tailed jackrabbit
Kiva fill (T22E 11–15S)	40	1	Distal end of tibia	*Lepus californicus*	Black-tailed jackrabbit
Kiva fill (T22E 11–15S)	40	1	Humerus	*Lepus californicus*	Black-tailed jackrabbit
Kiva fill (T22E 11–15S)	40	1	Sacrum	*Lepus californicus*	Black-tailed jackrabbit
Kiva fill (T22E 11–15S)	40	1	Innominate	*Lepus californicus*	Black-tailed jackrabbit
Kiva fill (T22E 11–15S)	40	1	Innominate	*Sylvilagus* cf. *floridanus*	Probable eastern cottontail rabbit
Kiva fill (T22E 11–15S)	40	2	Scapulae	*Sylvilagus* cf. *floridanus*	Probable eastern cottontail rabbit
Kiva fill (T22E 11–15S)	40	1	Rib	*Lepus* sp.	Jackrabbit
Kiva fill (T22E 11–15S)	40	Several	Frags	Mammalia	Mammal
Kiva fill (T22E 11–15S)	40	1	Femur shaft	cf. *Sylvilagus* sp.	Probable cottontail rabbit
Kiva fill (T22E 11–15S)	40	1	Tooth	*Lepus* sp.	Jackrabbit
Kiva fill (T22E 11–15S)	47		Limb bone frags	Artiodactyla	Artiodactyl
Kiva fill (T22E 11–15S)	47	1	Scapula frag	Artiodactyla	Artiodactyl
Kiva fill (T22E 11–15S)	47	1	Distal end of humerus	Artiodactyla	Artiodactyl
Kiva fill (T22E 11–15S)	47	1	Ulna	*Lepus californicus*	Black-tailed jackrabbit
Kiva fill (T22E 11–15S)	47	2	Radii	*Lepus californicus*	Black-tailed jackrabbit
Kiva fill (T22E 11–15S)	47	1	Metatarsal	*Lepus californicus*	Black-tailed jackrabbit
Kiva fill (T22E 11–15S)	47	1	Tibia	*Lepus californicus*	Black-tailed jackrabbit
Kiva fill (T22E 11–15S)	47	1	Mandible	*Lepus californicus*	Black-tailed jackrabbit
Kiva fill (T22E 11–15S)	47	1	Bone	Mammalia	Mammal
Kiva fill (T23E 11–13S)	42	1	Antler base	*Odocoileus* cf. *virginianus couesi*	Probable white-tailed deer
Kiva fill (T23E 11–13S)	42	1	Atlas	*Antilocapra americana*	Pronghorn
Kiva fill (T23E 11–13S)	42	1	Distal end of radius	*Odocoileus* cf. *virginianus couesi*	Probable white-tailed deer

(*continued*)

TABLE H.2 *(continued)*

Provenience	Bag no.	*n*	Element	Scientific name	Common name
Kiva fill (T23E 11–13S)	42	1	Proximal end of metatarsal	*Odocoileus* cf. *virginianus couesi*	Probable white-tailed deer
Kiva fill (T23E 11–13S)	42	1	Right calcaneum	*Odocoileus* cf. *virginianus couesi*	Probable white-tailed deer
Kiva fill (T23E 11–13S)	42	1	Lumbar vertebra	*Odocoileus* cf. *virginianus couesi*	Probable white-tailed deer
Kiva fill (T23E 11–13S)	42	1	Proximal end of scapula	*Odocoileus* cf. *virginianus couesi*	Probable white-tailed deer
Kiva fill (T23E 11–13S)	42	1	Proximal end of phalanx	*Odocoileus* cf. *virginianus couesi*	Probable white-tailed deer
Kiva fill (T23E 11–13S)	42	1	Distal end of metapodial	*Odocoileus* cf. *virginianus couesi*	Probable white-tailed deer
Kiva fill (T23E 11–13S)	42	1	Femur frag	*Odocoileus* cf. *virginianus couesi*	Probable white-tailed deer
Kiva fill (T23E 11–13S)	42	5	Pelvis frags	Artiodactyla	Artiodactyl
Kiva fill (T23E 11–13S)	42	3	Femur frags	*Odocoileus* cf. *virginianus couesi*	Probable white-tailed deer
Kiva fill (T23E 11–13S)	42	2	Scapula frags	cf. *Odocoileus* sp.	Probable deer
Kiva fill (T23E 11–13S)	42	1	Rib frag	cf. *Odocoileus* sp.	Probable deer
Kiva fill (T23E 11–13S)	42	1	Proximal end of tibia	*Lepus* sp.	Jackrabbit
Kiva fill (T23E 11–13S)	42	1	Right femur	*Sylvilagus* sp.	Cottontail rabbit
Kiva fill (T23E 11–13S)	42	2	Right femur frags	*Sylvilagus* sp.	Cottontail rabbit
Kiva fill (T23E 11–13S)	42	1	Humerus	*Sylvilagus* sp.	Cottontail rabbit
Kiva fill (T23E 11–13S)	42	1	Distal end of left femur	*Lepus californicus*	Black-tailed jackrabbit
Kiva fill (T23E 11–13S)	42	1	Lumbar vertebra	*Lepus californicus*	Black-tailed jackrabbit
Kiva fill (T23E 11–13S)	42	1	Metatarsal	*Lepus californicus*	Black-tailed jackrabbit
Kiva fill (T23E 11–13S)	42	3	Rib frags	*Lepus* sp.	Jackrabbit
Kiva fill (T23E 11–13S)	42	1	Cranium frag	*Sylvilagus* sp.	Cottontail rabbit
Kiva fill (T23E 11–13S)	42	1	Left upper molar	*Canis* sp.	Dog or coyote
Kiva fill (T23E 11–13S)	42	1	Proximal end of scapula	*Sylvilagus* sp.	Cottontail rabbit
Kiva fill (T22–23E 8–9S)	44	1	Fibula shaft	*Homo sapiens*	Human
Kiva fill (T22–23E 8–9S)	44	1	Lumbar vertebra	Artiodactyla	Artiodactyl

Kiva fill (T22–23E 8–9S)	44	1	Femur shaft frag	cf. *Odocoileus* sp.	Probable deer
Kiva fill (T22–23E 8–9S)	44	1	Proximal end of tibia	*Sylvilagus* sp.	Cottontail rabbit
Kiva fill (T22–23E 8–9S)	44	1	Frag	Mammalia	Mammal
Kiva fill (T26E 7–16S)	12	1	Frag	Mammalia	Mammal
Kiva stratitest level 5	67	2	Phalanges	cf. *Odocoileus* sp.	Probable deer
Kiva stratitest level 5	67	1	Distal end of metacarpal	cf. *Odocoileus* sp.	Probable deer
Kiva stratitest level 5	67	1	Distal end of tibia	cf. *Odocoileus* sp.	Probable deer
Kiva stratitest level 5	67	1	Phalanx	*Homo sapiens*	Human
Kiva stratitest level 5	67	1	Proximal end of humerus	*Sylvilagus* cf. *floridanus*	Probable eastern cottontail rabbit
Kiva stratitest level 5	67	1	Tibia shaft	*Lepus* sp.	Jackrabbit
Kiva stratitest level 5	67	1	Canine tooth	cf. *Canis lupus familiaris*	Probable dog
Kiva stratitest level 5	67	Several	Frags	Mammalia	Mammal
Kiva stratitest level 6	69	1	Proximal end of metapodial	Artiodactyla	Artiodactyl
Kiva stratitest level 7	71	1	Limb bone frag	cf. Artiodactyla	Probable artiodactyl
Kiva SE corner (bird burial)	75	1	Premaxillary	*Spermophilus* sp.	Ground squirrel
Kiva floor	51	5	Skull frags	*Canis lupus familiaris*	Dog
Kiva floor	51	1	Molar	*Odocoileus virginianus couesi*	White-tailed deer
Kiva floor	68	1	Thoracic vertebra	*Canis lupus familiaris*	Dog
Kiva floor	68	3	Phalanges	*Canis lupus familiaris*	Dog
Kiva floor	68	7	Metacarpals and metatarsals	*Canis lupus familiaris*	Dog
Kiva floor	68	1	Calcaneum	*Canis lupus familiaris*	Dog
Kiva floor	68	1	Mandible frag	*Canis lupus familiaris*	Dog
Kiva floor	68	1	Scapula frag	*Antilocapra americana* or *Odocoileus* sp.	Pronghorn or deer
Kiva floor	68	2	Femur frags	Artiodactyla	Artiodactyl

(*continued*)

TABLE H.2 *(continued)*

Provenience	Bag no.	*n*	Element	Scientific name	Common name
Kiva floor	68	1	Lumbar vertebra	*Sylvilagus* sp.	Cottontail rabbit
Kiva floor	68	1	Humerus frag	*Lepus californicus*	Black-tailed jackrabbit
Kiva foot drum	72	1	Distal end of metapodial	Artiodactyla	Artiodactyl
Kiva foot drum	74	1	Canine tooth	cf. *Canis lupus familiaris*	Probable dog
Kiva ventilator	73	1	Left innominate	*Lepus alleni*	Antelope jackrabbit
Kiva ventilator	73	1	Right innominate	*Lepus alleni*	Antelope jackrabbit
Kiva ventilator	73	2	Radii	*Lepus californicus*	Black-tailed jackrabbit
Kiva ventilator	73	1	Sacrum	*Lepus californicus*	Black-tailed jackrabbit
Kiva ventilator	73	1	Limb bone frag	cf. *Odocoileus* sp.	Probable deer
Room 2 floor	108		Frags	Mammalia	Mammal
Room 2 floor	108	2	Skull frags	*Castor canadensis*	Beaver
Room 2 fill	106	1	Astragalus	*Odocoileus* sp.	Deer
Room 2 fill	106	3	Frags	Artiodactyla	Artiodactyl
Room 3	11	1	Distal end of radius	*Lepus* sp.	Jackrabbit
Room 3	11	1	Metatarsal	*Lepus* sp.	Jackrabbit
Room 3	11	1	Limb bone frag	?	
Room 3	11	1	Ulna frag?	cf. *Lepus* sp.	Probable jackrabbit
Room 3 level 1	16		Metatarsal frags	cf. *Odocoileus* sp.	Probable deer
Room 3 level 1	16	1	Phalanx	cf. *Odocoileus* sp.	Probable deer
Room 3 floor	19	2	Heads of ribs	*Lepus californicus*	Black-tailed jackrabbit
Room 3 floor	19	1	Head of radius	*Lepus* sp.	Jackrabbit
Room 3 floor	19	1	Head of scapula	*Lepus* sp.	Jackrabbit
Room 3 floor	19	1	Metacarpal	*Sylvilagus* sp.	Cottontail rabbit
Room 3 floor	19	1	Head of scapula	*Sylvilagus* sp.	Cottontail rabbit

Room 3 floor	19	1	Proximal end of ulna	*Sylvilagus* sp.	Cottontail rabbit
Room 3 floor	19	1	Calcaneum	*Sylvilagus* sp.	Cottontail rabbit
Room 3 floor	19	1	Carpal	*Antilocapra americana*	Pronghorn
Room 3 floor	19	1	Phalanx	cf. *Odocoileus* sp.	Probable deer
Room 3 floor	19	1	Tibia	*Dipodomys* cf. *merriami*	Probable Merriam's kangaroo rat
Room 3 floor	19	2	Humerus frags	*Sylvilagus* sp.	Cottontail rabbit
Room 3 floor	19	2	Tibia frags	*Sylvilagus* sp.	Cottontail rabbit
Room 3 floor	19	1	Pelvis frag	*Sylvilagus* sp.	Cottontail rabbit
Room 3 floor	19	1	Metatarsal	*Lepus californicus*	Black-tailed jackrabbit
Room 3 floor	19	Several	Limb bone frags	*Odocoileus* sp. or *Antilocapra americana*	Deer or pronghorn
Trench in front of Room 3	26	1	Head of rib	Artiodactyla	Artiodactyl
Trench in front of Room 3	26	1	Metapodial frag	Artiodactyla	Artiodactyl
Trench in front of Room 3	26	1	Lumbar vertebra	Artiodactyla	Artiodactyl
Trench in front of Room 3	26	3	Vertebrae frags	Artiodactyla	Artiodactyl
Trench in front of Room 3	26	1	Phalanx	Artiodactyla	Artiodactyl
Trench in front of Room 3	26	1	Humerus	*Lepus californicus*	Black-tailed jackrabbit
Trench in front of Room 3	26	1	Metatarsal	*Lepus californicus*	Black-tailed jackrabbit
Trench in front of Room 3	26	1	Innominate	*Lepus californicus*	Black-tailed jackrabbit
Trench in front of Room 3	26	1	Mandible	*Lepus californicus*	Black-tailed jackrabbit
Trench in front of Room 3	26	1	Femur frag	Artiodactyla	Artiodactyl
Trench in front of Room 3	26	3	Skull frags	cf. Artiodactyla	Probable artiodactyl
Room 4 stratitest level 1	76	2	Incisors	cf. *Ovis canadensis*	Probable bighorn sheep
Room 4 stratitest level 1	76	2	Molar frags	cf. *Ovis canadensis*	Probable bighorn sheep
Room 4 stratitest level 1	76	1	Phalanx	Artiodactyla	Artiodactyl

(*continued*)

TABLE H.2 *(continued)*

Provenience	Bag no.	*n*	Element	Scientific name	Common name
Room 4 stratitest level 1	76	1	Scapula	*Lepus* sp.	Jackrabbit
Room 4 stratitest level 1	76	1	Frag	Mammalia	Mammal
Room 4 stratitest level 3	78	1	Scapula	*Lepus* sp.	Jackrabbit
Room 4 stratitest level 3	78		Atlas frags	cf. *Sylvilagus* sp.	Probable cottontail rabbit
Room 4 stratitest level 3	78	1	Mandible	*Sylvilagus* sp.	Cottontail rabbit
Room 4 stratitest level 3	78	2	Frags	Mammalia	Mammal
Room 4 stratitest level 4	79	1	Distal end of femur	*Lepus* sp.	Jackrabbit
Room 4 stratitest level 4	79	1	Left mandible	*Antilocapra americana*	Pronghorn
Room 4 stratitest level 4	79	1	Condyle	cf. *Antilocapra americana*	Probable pronghorn
Room 4 stratitest level 4	79	1	Leg bone frag	cf. *Odocoileus* sp.	Probable deer
Room 4 stratitest level 4	79	1	Mandible frag	cf. *Odocoileus* sp.	Probable deer
Room 4 stratitest level 4	79	Several	Tooth frags	*Antilocapra americana*	Pronghorn
Room 4 stratitest level 4	79	1	Phalanx	cf. *Odocoileus* sp.	Probable deer
Room 5 fill	30	1	Phalanx	*Antilocapra americana*	Pronghorn
Room 5 fill	30	1	Rib frag	*Antilocapra americana*	Pronghorn
Room 5 fill	30	1	Radius frag	Carnivora	Carnivore
Room 5 fill	30	1	Head of right femur	*Lepus* sp.	Jackrabbit
Room 5 fill	30	1	Right innominate	*Lepus* sp.	Jackrabbit
Room 5 fill	30	1	Left innominate	*Lepus* sp.	Jackrabbit
Room 5 fill	101	1	Distal end of femur	*Sylvilagus* sp.	Cottontail rabbit
Room 5 fill	101	1	Proximal end of femur	*Sylvilagus* sp.	Cottontail rabbit
Room 5 fill	101	1	Tibia	*Lepus sp.*	Jackrabbit
Room 5 fill	101	1	Tibia shaft	*cf. Canis lupus familiaris*	Probable dog
Room 5 fill	101	1	Mandible	cf. *Leopardus pardalis*	Probable ocelot

Room 5 fill	116	1	Phalanx	*Odocoileus* sp.	Deer
Room 5 fill	116	1	Tibia	*Sylvilagus* sp.	Cottontail rabbit
Room 5 fill	116	1	Scapula	*Lepus* sp.	Jackrabbit
Room 5 fill	116	1	Distal end of tibia	*Odocoileus* sp.	Deer
Room 5 fill	116	1	Frag	Mammalia	Mammal
Room 6 fill	56	1	Auditory tube with meatus	cf. *Odocoileus* sp.	Probable deer
Room 6 fill	56	1	Mastoid	cf. *Odocoileus* sp.	Probable deer
Room 6 fill	56	2	Femur frags	cf. *Odocoileus* sp.	Probable deer
Room 6 fill	56	1	Right femur	*Sylvilagus* sp.	Cottontail rabbit
Room 6 fill	56	1	Distal end of femur	*Sylvilagus* sp.	Cottontail rabbit
Room 6 fill	93	1	Left tibia	*Lepus californicus*	Black-tailed jackrabbit
Room 6 fill	93	1	Scapula	*Lepus californicus*	Black-tailed jackrabbit
Room 6 fill	93	1	Limb bone frag	cf. *Lepus* sp.	Probable jackrabbit
Room 6 fill	93	2	Left femora	*Sylvilagus* sp.	Cottontail rabbit
Room 6 fill	93	1	Metatarsal frag	cf. *Odocoileus* sp.	Probable deer
Room 7 fill	33	1	Head of rib	cf. Artiodactyla	Probable artiodactyl
Room 7 fill	39	1	Head of left femur	*Lepus* sp.	Jackrabbit
Room 7 fill	39	1	Metatarsal frag	*Odocoileus* sp.	Deer
Room 7 fill	39	1	Scapula frag	*Odocoileus* sp.	Deer
Room 7 floor	43	1	Molar	*Odocoileus* sp.	Deer
Room 7 floor	43	1	Phalanx	cf. *Odocoileus* sp.	Probable deer
Room 7 floor	43	4	Frags	cf. *Odocoileus* sp.	Probable deer
Room 8 fill	60	1	Head of right femur	*Lepus* sp.	Jackrabbit
Room 8 fill	60		Frags	Mammalia	Mammal
Room 8 subfloor	122	1	Proximal end of femur	*Lepus* sp.	Jackrabbit

(*continued*)

TABLE H.2 *(continued)*

Provenience	Bag no.	*n*	Element	Scientific name	Common name
Trench in front of Room 8	34	1	Distal end of humerus	*Sylvilagus* sp.	Cottontail rabbit
Trench in front of Room 9	35	1	Right mandible	*Lepus* sp.	Jackrabbit
Room 10 fill	52	1	Tip of antler	*Odocoileus* sp.	Deer
Room 10 stratitest level 3	57	2	Frags	Mammalia	Mammal
Room 10 stratitest level 3	57	1	Head of rib	Artiodactyla	Artiodactyl
Room 10 stratitest level 3	57	1	Scapula	*Vulpes velox*	Swift fox
Room 10 floor	63	1	Antler frag	*Odocoileus* sp.	Deer
Room 11 fill	45	1	Head of left tibia	*Lepus* sp.	Jackrabbit
Room 11 fill	49	1	Mandible	*Lepus alleni*	Antelope jackrabbit
Room 11 fill	49	1	Distal end of femur	*Sylvilagus* sp.	Cottontail rabbit
Room 11 level 3	53	1	Thoracic vertebra	Artiodactyla	Artiodactyl
Room 11 level 3	53	1	Rib frag	Artiodactyla	Artiodactyl
Room 11 level 4	54	1	Calcaneum	*Odocoileus hemionus*	Mule deer
Room 11 level 4	54	4	Carpals	*Odocoileus* cf. *virginianus couesi*	Probable white-tailed deer
Room 11 level 4	54	1	Maxillary frag	*Odocoileus* sp.	Deer
Room 11 level 4	54	1	Femur shaft	*Odocoileus* sp.	Deer
Room 11 level 4	54	Several	Frags	Mammalia	Mammal
Room 11 level 4	54	1	Head of rib	cf. *Odocoileus* sp.	Probable deer
Room 11 floor	59	1	Distal end of radius	*Odocoileus* cf. *virginianus couesi*	Probable white-tailed deer
Room 11 floor	59	1	Tooth	*Odocoileus* cf. *virginianus couesi*	Probable white-tailed deer
Room 11 floor	59		Frags of femur, humerus, etc.	*Odocoileus* cf. *virginianus couesi*	Probable white-tailed deer
Room 14 fill	85	1	Head of scapula	Artiodactyla	Artiodactyl
Room 14 fill	85	1	Calcaneum	cf. *Odocoileus* sp.	Probable deer
Room 14 fill	85		Limb bone frags	Artiodactyla	Artiodactyl

Room 14 fill	85	1	Radius	*Sylvilagus* sp.	Cottontail rabbit
Room 14 fill	85	1	Proximal end of femur	*Sylvilagus* sp.	Cottontail rabbit
Room 14 fill	85	1	Proximal end of metacarpal	Artiodactyla	Artiodactyl
Room 14 fill	85	1	Left innominate	*Sylvilagus* sp.	Cottontail rabbit
Room 14 fill	85	1	Head of tibia frag	cf. *Odocoileus* sp.	Probable deer
Room 14 fill	85	2	Left mandibles	*Odocoileus virginianus couesi*	White-tailed deer
Room 14 fill	85	1	Limb bone frag	cf. *Odocoileus* sp.	Probable deer
Room 14 fill	85	1	Scapula frag	Mammalia	Mammal
Room 14 fill	85	1	Pelvis frag	cf. *Odocoileus* sp.	Probable deer
Room 14 fill	85	1	Tibia frag	cf. *Odocoileus* sp.	Probable deer
Room 14 fill	85	1	Right innominate	*Lepus* sp.	Jackrabbit
Room 14 fill	85	1	Pelvis frag	cf. *Odocoileus* sp.	Probable deer
Room 14 fill	85	1	Tip of right mandible	*Lepus* sp.	Jackrabbit
Room 14 fill	85	1	Distal end of tibia	cf. *Antilocapra americana*	Probable pronghorn
Room 14 fill	85	1	Right innominate	*Spermophilus* sp.	Ground squirrel
Room 16 fill	87	1	Humerus	*Lepus* sp.	Jackrabbit
Room 16 stratitest level 3	128	1	Right innominate	*Sylvilagus* sp.	Cottontail rabbit
Room 16 stratitest level 3	128	1	Patella	cf. Artiodactyla	Probable artiodactyl
Room 19 fill	92	1	Distal end of left femur	*Lepus* sp.	Jackrabbit
Room 19 fill	100	1	Proximal end of radius	*Odocoileus* cf. *virginianus couesi*	Probable white-tailed deer
Room 19 fill	100	1	Sacrum	*Sylvilagus* sp.	Cottontail rabbit
Room 19 fill	100	1	Ulna frag	*Odocoileus* cf. *virginianus couesi*	Probable white-tailed deer
Room 21 fill	97	1	Proximal end of metatarsal	cf. *Antilocapra americana*	Probable pronghorn
Room 34 fill	104	1	Right mandible	*Lepus californicus*	Black-tailed jackrabbit
Room 34 fill	104	1	Distal end of radius	*Odocoileus* cf. *virginianus couesi*	Probable white-tailed deer

(*continued*)

TABLE H.2 *(continued)*

Provenience	Bag no.	*n*	Element	Scientific name	Common name
Room 34 fill	104	1	Femur frag	Artiodactyla	Artiodactyl
Room 34 fill	104	1	Scapula frag	*Lepus* sp.	Jackrabbit
Room 34 fill	104	1	Scapula frag	Artiodactyla	Artiodactyl
Room 34 fill	104	1	Left tibia	*Sylvilagus* sp.	Cottontail rabbit
Room 34 fill	104	1	Ilium	*Lepus* sp.	Jackrabbit
Room 34 fill	107	1	Metatarsal frag	*Odocoileus* sp. or *Antilocapra americana*	Deer or pronghorn
Room 34 fill (T13S 10–11E)	114	1	Distal end of tibia	*Odocoileus virginianus couesi*	White-tailed deer[a]
Room 34 fill (T13S 10–11E)	114	1	Astragalus	*Odocoileus virginianus couesi*	White-tailed deer[a]
Room 34 fill (T13S 10–11E)	114	2	Frags	cf. Mammalia	Probable mammal
Room 35 fill	109	1	Phalanx	*Ovis canadensis*	Bighorn sheep
Room 36 fill	110	1	Ulna	*Lynx rufus*	Bobcat
Room 44 subfloor	126	1	Radius	*Canis lupus familiaris*	Dog
Room 44 subfloor	126	1	Ulna	*Canis lupus familiaris*	Dog
Room 44 subfloor	126	1	Metacarpal	*Canis lupus familiaris*	Dog
Room 44 subfloor	126	1	Metacarpal	*Canis lupus familiaris*	Dog
Room 44 subfloor	126	1	Phalanx	*Canis lupus familiaris*	Dog
Room 44 subfloor	126	1	Head of humerus	*Sylvilagus* sp.	Cottontail rabbit
Burial 10	90	1	Rib frag	Artiodactyla	Artiodactyl
Burial 10	90	1	Proximal end of femur	*Sylvilagus* sp.	Cottontail rabbit
Burial 10	90	1	Right innominate	*Dipodomys* sp.	Kangaroo rat
Burial 10	90	1	Tibia frag	cf. Rodentia	Probable rodent
Burial 11	115	1	Radius	*Lepus californicus*	Black-tailed jackrabbit
Burial 11	115	2	Centra of vertebrae	*Lepus* sp.	Jackrabbit

Burial 11	115	1	Navicular-cuboid	*Odocoileus* sp.	Deer
Burial 12	94	2	Caudal vertebrae	cf. *Bos* or *Bison*	Probable cow or bison
NE Trash	96	1	Proximal end of metacarpal	*Odocoileus* sp.	Deer
NE Trash	96	1	Antler? tip	*Odocoileus* sp.	Deer
NE Trash	96	1	Head of rib	Artiodactyla	Artiodactyl
NE Trash	96	1	Tibia	*Lepus* sp.	Jackrabbit
NE Trash	96	1	Head of femur	*Sylvilagus* sp.	Cottontail rabbit
NE Trash	96		Frags	Mammalia	Mammal
NE Trash	96	1	Metacarpal	*Homo sapiens*	Human
NE Trash	96	1	Phalanx	*Homo sapiens*	Human
NE Trash	99	1	Tibia	*Neotoma* sp.	Woodrat
NE Trash	99	1	Fibula	*Neotoma* sp.	Woodrat
NE Trash	99	1	Distal end of tibia	*Odocoileus* cf. *hemionus*	Probable mule deer
NE Trash	99	1	Limb bone frag	*Artiodactyla*	Artiodactyl
NE Trash	105	1	Innominate	*Lepus* sp.	Jackrabbit
NE Trash	105	1	Limb bone frag	cf. Artiodactyla	Probable artiodactyl
NE Trash (T20E 39–40N)	83	1	Calcaneum	*Odocoileus* sp. or *Ovis* sp.	Deer or sheep
Pit Oven 1	2	1	Radius	*Urocyon cinereoargenteus* or *Vulpes macrotis*	Gray fox or kit fox
Pit Oven 1	7	1	Left innominate	*Lepus* sp.	Jackrabbit
Pit Oven 1	7	1	Proximal end of left tibia	*Sylvilagus* sp.	Cottontail rabbit
Pit Oven 2	9	1	Lumbar vertebra	*Lepus* sp.	Jackrabbit
Stratitest 1 level 1	118	1	Left innominate	*Sylvilagus* sp.	Cottontail rabbit
Stratitest 1 level 1	118	1	Scapula	*Sylvilagus* sp.	Cottontail rabbit
Stratitest 1 level 1	118	1	Scapula	*Lepus* sp.	Jackrabbit

(continued)

TABLE H.2 *(continued)*

Provenience	Bag no.	*n*	Element	Scientific name	Common name
Stratitest 1 level 1	118	1	Innominate	*Lepus californicus*	Black-tailed jackrabbit
Stratitest 1 level 1	118	1	Ulna	*Lepus* sp.	Jackrabbit
Stratitest 1 level 1	118	2	Frags	Mammalia	Mammal
Stratitest 1 level 5	121	1	Atlas	*Odocoileus hemionus*	Mule deer
Stratitest 1 level 5	121	2	Neural spines of vertebrae	cf. *Odocoileus* sp.	Probable deer
Stratitest 1 level 5	121	Several	Frags	Mammalia	Mammal
T1S 20–14E	5		Teeth	*Odocoileus* cf. *virginianus couesi*	Probable white-tailed deer
T1S 20–14E	5	1	Tibia frag	?	
T1S 20–14E	5	1	Lumbar vertebra	?	
T1S 20–14E	5	1	Rib frag	?	
T1S 20–14E	5	1	Distal end of right tibia	*Lepus* sp.	Jackrabbit
T1S 20–14E	5	1	Proximal end of left tibia	*Sylvilagus* sp.	Cottontail rabbit
T1S 23–26E	13	1	Hyoid frag	cf. *Odocoileus* sp.	Probable deer
T1S 23–26E	13	1	Head of tibia	*Lepus* sp.	Jackrabbit
T1S 23–26E	13	1	Phalanx	*Lepus* sp.	Jackrabbit
T1S 30–46E	3	1	Antler base	*Odocoileus* sp.	Deer
T19S 23–25E	80		Frags	Mammalia	Mammal
T20S 20E	81	1	Femur shaft	*Lepus* sp.	Jackrabbit
T20S 20E	81	1	Proximal end of femur	*Lepus* sp.	Jackrabbit
T17E 12S	117	1	Proximal end of radius	*Odocoileus* sp.	Deer
T17E 12S	117	1	Distal end of metacarpal	*Odocoileus* sp.	Deer
T17E 12S	117	1	Metatarsal	*Lepus* sp.	Jackrabbit
T17E 12S	117		Frags	Mammalia	Mammal
T24E 18–19S	77	1	Distal end of femur	*Lepus* sp.	Jackrabbit

T24E 18–19S	77	2	Ribs	*Lepus* sp.	Jackrabbit
T24E 18–19S	77	1	Cervical vertebra	*Lepus* sp.	Jackrabbit
T24E 18–19S	77	1	Frag	Mammalia	Mammal
T24E 18–19S	77	4	Cranial frags	*Homo sapiens*	Human
T26E 16S	21	1	Femur shaft	cf. *Odocoileus* sp.	Probable deer
T26E 16S	21		Limb bone frags	Artiodactyla	Artiodactyl
T26E 16S	24	1	Axis	*Odocoileus* cf. *virginianus couesi*	Probable white-tailed deer
T26E 16S	24	1	Rib head	*Odocoileus* cf. *virginianus couesi*	Probable white-tailed deer
T26E 16S	24	1	Phalanx	*Odocoileus* cf. *virginianus couesi*	Probable white-tailed deer
T26E 16S	24	1	Frag	*Odocoileus* cf. *virginianus couesi*	Probable white-tailed deer
T10N 0–7E	6	1	Femur	*Lepus* sp.	Jackrabbit
T10N 0–7E	6	1	Lumbar vertebra	*Lepus* sp.	Jackrabbit
T10N 0–7E	14	3	Frags	cf. Mammalia	Probable mammal
T10N 14–20E	1	1	Metatarsal frag?	cf. *Odocoileus* sp.	Probable deer
T10N 15–17E	86	1	Humerus	*Lepus* sp.	Jackrabbit
T10N 15–17E	86	1	Phalanx	*Homo sapiens*	Human
T10N 15–17E	86	1	Tibia	cf. *Lynx rufus*	Probable bobcat
T10N 15–17E	86		Limb bone frags	Artiodactyla	Artiodactyl
T10N 21–26E	15		Frags, probably femur	?	
T11N 16–17E	84	1	Phalanx	*Homo sapiens*	Human
T11N 16–17E	84	1	Limb bone frag	Mammalia	Mammal
T15N 25–26E	98	1	Proximal end of metacarpal	cf. *Ovis canadensis*	Probable bighorn sheep
No provenience	37	1	Cervical vertebra	cf. *Odocoileus* sp.	Probable deer
No provenience	37	1	Thoracic vertebra	cf. *Odocoileus* sp.	Probable deer
No provenience	37	1	Limb bone frag	cf. *Odocoileus* sp.	Probable deer

[a]Single individual

APPENDIX I

Avifauna Identified by R. Roy Johnson in 1969

[*Editor: In his dissertation, Rex Gerald (1975:Table 3) presents a summary table of avian faunal data that compares the assemblages from the Davis Ranch Site and Reeve Ruin. He indicates, through citations, that the sources of the data relating to the Davis Ranch Site are an "unpublished manuscript" by Harrison Tordoff, dated 1958, and an "unpublished manuscript" by R. Roy Johnson, dated 1969. The data in table I.1, which are sorted by recovery context and bone bag number, are identifications made by Johnson compiled from a typewritten list found at the Amerind Museum among materials transferred there from the University of Texas at El Paso, where Gerald was employed at the time of his death. This list (Johnson 1969) and the documents used to compile table H.1 (Burt and Tordoff 1958) appear to represent the raw material from which Gerald constructed the summary table discussed above. The scientific names used by Johnson have been updated to conform to current conventions.*]

TABLE I.1 Avian fauna identified by R. Roy Johnson in 1969, sorted by provenience and bone bag

Provenience	Bag no.	Scientific name	Common name	Elements	*n*	MNI[a]
House2 fill	8	cf. *Nycticorax*	Probable black-crowned night heron	Humerus, distal 1/4, L	1	1
Kiva fill (T15S 25E)	25	*Callipepla squamata*	Scaled quail	Carpometacarpus, R	1	1
Kiva fill (T10S 23–24E L2)	28	*Falco peregrinus*	Peregrine falcon	Tarsometatarsus, L	1	1
Kiva fill (T22E 10–14S)	29	*Buteo* sp.	Large hawk[b]	Tibiotarsus, distal 1/3, L[c]	1	
Kiva fill (T10S 22–25E L2)	31	*Circus cyaneus*	Northern harrier	Humerus head, R	1	1
Kiva fill (T10S 22–25E L2)	31	Cerylinae	Kingfisher	Ulna, L	1	1
Kiva fill (T10S 23–25E L3)	38	*Anas* sp.	Teal-size duck	Coracoid, R	1	1
Kiva fill (T22E 11–15S)	40	*Buteo* sp.	Large hawk[b]	Tibiotarsus, R[c]	1	
Kiva fill (T23E 11–13S)	42	*Buteo* sp.	Large hawk[b]	Femur, R[c]	1	
Kiva fill (T23E 11–13S)	42	*Corvus corax*	Common raven	Coracoid, R	1	1
Kiva fill (T23E 11–13S)	42	Odontophoridae	Quail	Tibiotarsus, proximal 1/2, L	1	
Kiva fill (22E 8–11S)	46	*Buteo* sp.	Small hawk	Ulna, L	1	1
Kiva fill	50	*Corvus corax*	Common raven	Ulna, L[d]	1	
Kiva fill	55	*Buteo* sp.	Large hawk[b]	Tarsometatarsus, distal 2/3, R[c]	1	
Kiva fill	55	*Circus cyaneus*	Northern harrier	Humerus, L[e]	1	
Kiva fill	58	*Buteo* sp.	Large hawk[b]	Tarsometatarsus, distal 1/2, L[c]	1	
Kiva fill	58	*Buteo* sp.	Large hawk[b]	Tibiotarsus, proximal 2/3, R[c]	1	
Kiva fill	58	*Geococcyx californianus*	Greater roadrunner	Tibiotarsus, proximal 1/2, L	1	2
Kiva fill	61	*Falco mexicanus*	Prairie falcon	Tibiotarsus, proximal 1/2, L	1	1
Kiva fill	61	*Buteo*	Large hawk[b]	Claw[c]	1	

(continued)

TABLE I.1 *(continued)*

Provenience	Bag no.	Scientific name	Common name	Elements	*n*	MNI[a]
Kiva fill	61	*Zenaidura macroura*	Mourning dove	Humerus, R	1	1
Kiva fill	61	*Corvus cryptoleucus*	Chihuahuan raven	Ulna, proximal 1/3, R	1	1
Kiva fill	64	*Corvus corax*	Common raven	Tibiotarsus, proximal 1/2, R[d]	1	
Kiva fill	64	*Geococcyx californianus*	Greater roadrunner	Tibiotarsus, proximal 1/2, L[f]	1	
Kiva fill	64	Aves	Bird	Humerus, distal 1/2	1	
Kiva fill	70	*Branta* sp. or *Chen* sp.	Small goose	Coracoid, proximal 1/4	1	1
Kiva fill	70	Anatinae	Duck	Humerus, distal 1/2	1	1
Kiva SE corner (bird burial)	75	*Buteogallus anthracinus*	Common black hawk	Tarsometatarsus, R	1	1
Kiva SE corner (bird burial)	75	*Buteo* sp.	Large hawk[b]	Tarsometatarsi, L	2	6–12
Kiva SE corner (bird burial)	75	*Buteo* sp.	Large hawk[b]	Tarsometatarsus, distal 1/2, L	1	
Kiva SE corner (bird burial)	75	*Buteo* sp.	Large hawk[b]	Tarsometatarsus, proximal 1/2, L	1	
Kiva SE corner (bird burial)	75	*Buteo* sp.	Large hawk[b]	Ulna, L	1	
Kiva SE corner (bird burial)	75	*Buteo* sp.	Large hawk[b]	Carpometacarpus, L	1	
Kiva SE corner (bird burial)	75	*Buteo* sp.	Large hawk[b]	Tibiotarsus, distal 1/4, R	1	
Kiva SE corner (bird burial)	75	*Buteo* sp.	Large hawk[b]	Tarsometatarsus, distal 1/2, R	1	
Kiva SE corner (bird burial)	75	*Buteo* sp.	Large hawk[b]	Radius, R	1	
Kiva SE corner (bird burial)	75	*Buteo* sp.	Large hawk[b]	Carpometacarpus, R	1	
Kiva SE corner (bird burial)	75	*Buteo* sp.	Large hawk[b]	Digits	3	
Kiva SE corner (bird burial)	75	*Buteo* sp.	Large hawk[b]	Foot bones, at least 2 MNI	44	
Kiva SE corner (bird burial)	75	*Buteo* sp.	Large hawk[b]	Cranium	1	
Kiva SE corner (bird burial)	75	*Buteo* sp.	Large hawk[b]	Skull fragments	22	
Kiva SE corner (bird burial)	75	*Buteo* sp.	Large hawk[b]	Tarsometatarsus shaft fragment	1	
Room2 floor	108	*Mergus merganser*	Common merganser	Coracoid, L	1	1
Room3 floor	19	*Bubo virginianus*	Great horned owl	Femur head, L	1	1

Room6 fill	93	Aves	Bird	Fragment	1	
Room10 fill	52	*Circus* sp. or *Buteo* sp.	Hawk	Ulna	1	1
Room14 fill	85	*Buteo* sp.	Large hawk[b]	Coracoid, L	1	1–2
Room14 fill	85	*Buteo* sp.	Large hawk[b]	Ulna, R	1	
Room34 fill	104	*Zenaidura macroura*	Mourning dove	Humerus, proximal 1/2, R	1	1
Room34 fill	104	Aves	Bird	Femur fragment	1	
Room34 fill (T13S 10–11E)	114	Aves	Bird	Long bone fragment		
Burial10	90	*Turdus migratorius*	American robin	Humerus, shattered head, L	1	1
NE Trash (T20E 39–40N)	83	*Accipiter cooperii*	Cooper's hawk	Tarsometatarsus, R	1	1
NE Trash	96	*Aquila chrysaetos*	Golden eagle	Ulna shaft, L	1	1
Pit Oven1	2	*Buteo* sp.	Large hawk	Ulna, L	1	5
Pit Oven1	2	*Buteo* sp.	Large hawk	Ulnae, proximal 1/2, L	2	
Pit Oven1	2	*Buteo* sp.	Large hawk	Ulnae, distal 1/2, L	2	
Pit Oven1	2	*Buteo* sp.	Large hawk	Tarsometatarsus, L	1	
Pit Oven1	2	*Buteo* sp.	Large hawk	Ulna, distal 3/4, R	1	
Pit Oven1	2	*Buteo* sp.	Large hawk	Radius, R	1	
T20S 20E	81	Aves	Bird	Fragments		
T10N 0–7E	6	*Buteo* sp.	Large hawk[b]	Humerus, shaft, L	1	4+
T10N 0–7E	6	*Buteo* sp.	Large hawk[b]	Radii, L	2	
T10N 0–7E	6	*Buteo* sp.	Large hawk[b]	Ulnae, L	2	
T10N 0–7E	6	*Buteo* sp.	Large hawk[b]	Ulna, proximal 3/4, L	1	
T10N 0–7E	6	*Buteo* sp.	Large hawk[b]	Radius, proximal 1/2, L	1	
T10N 0–7E	6	*Buteo* sp.	Large hawk[b]	Humerus, distal 2/3, R	1	
T10N 0–7E	6	*Buteo* sp.	Large hawk[b]	Radii, R	2	

(*continued*)

TABLE I.1 *(continued)*

Provenience	Bag no.	Scientific name	Common name	Elements	*n*	MNI[a]
T10N 0–7E	6	*Buteo* sp.	Large hawk[b]	Ulnae, R	3	
T10N 0–7E	6	*Buteo* sp.	Large hawk[b]	Crescent, R	1	
T10N 0–7E	6	*Buteo* sp.	Large hawk[b]	Carpometacarpus, R	1	
T10N 0–7E	6	*Buteo* sp.	Large hawk[b]	Radius shaft, R	1	
T10N 0–7E	6	*Buteo* sp.	Large hawk[b]	Tibiotarsus, shaft fragment, L	1	
T10N 0–7E	6	*Buteo* sp.	Large hawk[b]	Femur shaft, L	1	
T10N 0–7E	6	*Buteo* sp.	Large hawk[b]	Tarsometatarsus, R	1	
T10N 0–7E	6	*Buteo* sp.	Large hawk[b]	Femur, proximal 2/3, R	1	
T10N 0–7E	6	*Buteo* sp.	Large hawk[b]	Tarsometatarsus, distal 1/2, R	1	
T10N 0–7E	6	*Buteo* sp.	Large hawk[b]	Skull roof fragment	1	
T10N 0–7E	6	*Buteo* sp.	Large hawk[b]	Vertebrae	3	
T10N 0–7E	6	*Buteo* sp.	Large hawk[b]	Miscellaneous fragments	7	
T10N 0–7E	6	*Parabuteo unicinctus*	Harris's hawk	Tarsometatarsus, L	1	1
T10N 0–7E	14	*Buteogallus anthracinus*	Common black hawk	Tarsometatarsus, R	1	1

[a]Mimimum number of individuals

[b]Size of red-tailed hawk

[c]Included in MNI of *Buteo* sp. reported for Bag No. 75

[d]Included in MNI of *Corvus corax* reported for Bag No. 42

[e]Included in MNI of *Circus cyaneus* reported for Bag No. 31

[f]Included in MNI of *Geococcyx californianus* reported for Bag No. 58

APPENDIX J

Archaeological Pollen Analysis at the Davis Ranch Site

James S. Schoenwetter

In January 2008, I received a letter from William Robinson suggesting that a manuscript I had prepared 43 years earlier might finally be published. In 1965, while directing the palynology laboratory of the Laboratory of Anthropology at the Museum of New Mexico, I had worked on the extraction and analysis of pollen from 58 sediment samples collected from archaeological contexts at the Davis Ranch Site and Reeve Ruin by Rex Gerald. Correspondence over the year following submission of my report focused on the question of Gerald's intentions regarding the report's use and publication. I believed the manuscript required editing, and perhaps revision, prior to dissemination as an appendix to Gerald's dissertation, and I preferred that he allow me to see any direct quotes he might make in context in his writings. He assured me he would only paraphrase my language or quote raw data, so the matter was dropped.

That report has now been made public (Schoenwetter 1965a), but the intervening years have generated bodies of palynological and archaeological information that significantly affect the archaeological value of the pollen study. Although the present analysis is focused on interpretation of the pollen record from the Davis Ranch Site, while the other gave priority to the pollen of samples from Reeve Ruin, comparison with the earlier study will prove relevant.

RESEARCH CONCERNS

In 1965, archaeological research was normally centered on three issues: identification of the cultural affiliations of sites and artifact assemblages, determination of chronological placement of artifact styles and fashions, and reconstruction of cultural patterns through ethnographic analogy and application of the direct historical approach. Perception of archaeological cultures as the product of systemically organized human populations was only dimly envisioned. General comprehension of what are now understood as cultural-ecological relationships was essentially limited to recognition that, given its technology, a prehistoric culture's economic options would be conditioned (if not controlled by) the climate of its environment.

In this intellectual context, the research questions the 1965 pollen study was expected to consider were: "Does the record identify or suggest climatic change during the occupations of these sites that may have had economic consequences?" and "Does the record provide independent information that suggests the antiquity of artifact assemblages associated with the pollen samples?" Today, a different intellectual context prompts identification of somewhat different principle research questions. The degree to which the pollen record can provide an independent estimate of the antiquity of the associated archaeological record remains relevant, but for different reasons. In 1965, dates were essential for proper classification of associated artifacts in appropriate time-space grid units and the construction of narratives of technological change and evolution. Determining the usage dates of artifact assemblages remains as significant today as it did then, but the then-prevalent concerns with analysis of artifact assemblages in terms of trait lists and mechanisms of diffusion seem quaint considerations of a nearly forgotten period in the intellectual history of archaeological research. Our interest today is to assess the antiquity of artifact assemblages in order to explore their cultural significance as expressions of behavior patterns with a wide range of sociological, economic, political, and ceremonial implications. Estimating the absolute antiquity of the pollen samples now seems less important than determining if differences in their relative ages may provide insight into interpretation of variations in their associated artifact assemblages.

The character and results of archaeological research in the San Pedro Valley over the past 40, and especially the past 20, years have also suggested new research concerns. When the earlier work was done, direct evidence of agricultural activity in the environs of these sites was lacking, although the inference that the sites' populations were supported by corn-beans-squash agriculture was unquestioned. Simple observation of maize and cucurbit pollen in the site's pollen record was adequate to support the inference established by the direct historical approach. Today, the research concern is oriented to recognition of palynological evidence for the role of irrigation and use of local plant resources.

During the intervening decades, there has been substantial development of evidence that the Davis Ranch Site and Reeve Ruin are members of a suite of "enclave" populations of migrants to the San Pedro Valley with cultural roots in the Kayenta/Tusayan district of northern Arizona. This finding encourages a research interest in palynological evidence of this pattern and/or ethnobotanical behavior that may be related to the migration event.

THE POLLEN RECORD

Tables J.1–J.4 present the palynological observations made in 1965, excluding those of two surface sediment samples collected from each site. The surface samples were collected with the intention of identifying the character of the modern pollen rain of the site areas. Their general similarity with the pollen spectra recovered from samples deposited during the occupation of the sites, however, and their regular inclusion of significant quantities of pollen of cultivated plants, plants adapted to human-disturbed habitats, plants adapted to irrigated fields, and plants exploited for their economic values, make the surface samples unsuitable as controls.

Most of the observed pollen was produced and disseminated by plants adapted to disturbed semi-arid habitats (e.g., Chenopodinneae, a pollen taxon produced by members of the goosefoot and amaranth families) and by prominent sunflower family plants of the Lower Sonoran Desert biome (Ambrosieae, Tubuliflorae). The geographic placement and sizes of the human populations that occupied the sites are sufficient evidence of the prehistoric existence of those ecosystem conditions. But because these pollen taxa make up such a large fraction of the record, the frequency values of each of the other pollen taxa are necessarily statistically constrained in the total pollen count. To compensate for this to some degree, and thus allow the other pollen taxa to be represented in frequencies amenable to statistical evaluation, I observed many more pollen grains per sample than was normally required. My goal was tabulation of at least 100 pollen grains per sample *exclusive* of the numbers of Chenopodinnae, Ambrosieae, and Tubuliflorae pollen also observed.

CHRONOLOGICAL CONCERNS

Thanks to the availability of an extensive dendrochronological record that has been carefully applied to determine the use-lives of ceramic styles, to the frequent archaeological occurrence of hearths and other materials responsive to archaeomagnetic dating, to the recovery of ceramic and obsidian artifacts responsive to thermoluminescence and hydration dating, and to a database of radiocarbon assay information, there has been little application of palynological research for dating southwestern artifact assemblages associated with pollen samples in sites younger than the second century AD. These research areas were all less advanced in 1965, however, and I was then very involved with the development of a pollen chronology that could be employed at southwestern archaeological sites where other dating information was absent or could benefit from an independent approach (Schoenwetter 1970; Schoenwetter and Dittert 1968). It is now clear that a number of the assumptions and inferences I used to assess the antiquity of the pollen records from the Davis Ranch Site and Reeve Ruin are untenable, and the estimates of absolute antiquity that I proposed at that time must be dismissed.

The raw data of the pollen study undertaken in 1965, however, retain their potential for assisting resolution of two chronological problems of archaeological relevance. One is the problem of the relative age of occupations of rooms at each site. The other is the relative antiquity of occupations of rooms at the two sites.

Palynologists approach such problems through establishment of a pollen sequence in which one set of pollen statistics can be recognized to vary through time. These variations identify a suite of pollen zones, or episodes. Ideally, the pollen zones reflect temporal variations in ecosystem conditions that occur at regional geographic scales, such as changes in forest types. When pollen samples have been recovered in stratigraphic order, as from lacustrine cores, assessment of the relative sequential order of the samples is not a concern. Here, the samples were collected from deposits within rooms at the sites. While the temporal order of samples collected from the same room is known as a result of their relative stratigraphy, the temporal order of samples from different rooms must be deduced from knowledge of the character of the artifactual assemblages directly associated with the samples and knowledge of the construction sequence of the architectural elements of the site.

In the present instance, the ceramic assemblages associated with the pollen samples provide no insight into their temporal order, since the pottery types recovered are all members of the same archaeological phase. There are temporal clues, however, provided by architectural evidence of which rooms and room blocks were constructed earlier and which were later.

Three of the four rooms from which pollen samples were collected at the Davis Ranch Site were part of the site's youngest houseblock. And of those three, Room 33 was constructed after Rooms 17 and 21. Room 46 was located in a separate houseblock, whose temporal relationship to the others at the site is not architecturally evidenced. Samples were collected in stratigraphic order in Room 17.

At Reeve Ruin, samples were collected from Rooms 8 and 9 in Houseblock 2 at Plaza 2. These rooms were constructed during the first building phase of this houseblock. Plaza 2 also contains Houseblock 1. Sampled Rooms 20, 22, and 23 were constructed during the first building phase of this houseblock, as well. Sampled Rooms 24 and 26, however, were added to the houseblock in the second building phase and are younger. The third plaza at Reeve Ruin contains a single houseblock. The sample from Room 29 comes from this context.

The temporal sequence of *room construction*, unfortunately, need not be equivalent to the temporal sequence of *pollen deposition* in sediments that accumulated in the rooms. The suggestion that the sediment of a floor, or floor contact, pollen sample accumulated during the room's occupation, coincident with the accumulation of associated artifacts, is probably true for most samples. It is possible, however, for the pollen of a sample to have been deposited on a use surface that existed before the space was roofed or enclosed within walls; in that

TABLE J.1 Arboreal pollen types at Reeve Ruin and the Davis Ranch Site

Site	Sample no.	Context	Upland *Pinus edulis*-type	Upland *Pinus ponderosa*-type
Reeve Ruin	10	Room 26 floor contact	8	
	35	Room 20 floor contact	9	2
	36	Room 20 6.0–7.0 cm below floor	11	
	37	Room 20 Floor 2	16	1
	8	Room 22 floor contact	10	4
	39	Room 29 floor contact	19	1
	29	Room 23 floor contact	20	4
	28	Room 24 floor contact	9	7
	19	Room 9 floor contact	18	7
	9	Room 8 floor plaster	14	3
Davis Ranch Site	48	Room 21 -40.0 cm to -45.0 cm	10	
	47	Room 21 -45.0 cm to -50.0 cm	8	
	46	Room 21 -50.0 cm to -55.0 cm	7	2
	34	Room 21 floor contact	6	1
	69	Room 46 floor contact	16	2
	57	Room 33 floor contact	15	6
	62	Room 17 6.0 cm above floor	18	
	64	Room 17 2.5 cm above floor	12	4
	65	Room 17 1.0 cm above floor	10	8
	66	Room 17 floor plaster	10	8

Upland		Lowland		Riparian		
Juniperus	*Quercus*	*Celtis*	*Prosopis*	*Betula*	*Alnus*	*Juglans*
2	1	1		1		
2	2	1				
7						
1	3		2			
	3		1			
2	2		1			
6	2		2			
	2					
2	4	1	2	1	1	
2	8					
2	2		2			
1						
1						
2						
4	2					1
		1				
4	1		2			
	3	2				
2	2		1			
2	1	1	2			

TABLE J.2 Shrub pollen types at Reeve Ruin and the Davis Ranch Site

Site	Sample no.	Context	*Artemisia*	Liliaceae
Reeve Ruin	10	Room 26 floor contact	3	6
	35	Room 20 floor contact	1	8
	36	Room 20 6.0–7.0 cm below floor	1	13
	37	Room 20 Floor 2	1	10
	8	Room 22 floor contact	4	
	39	Room 29 floor contact	1	6
	29	Room 23 floor contact	1	10
	28	Room 24 floor contact	1	1
	19	Room 9 floor contact	5	8
	9	Room 8 floor plaster	7	10
Davis Ranch Site	48	Room 21 -40.0 cm to -45.0 cm	2	8
	47	Room 21 -45.0 cm to -50.0 cm	3	10
	46	Room 21 -50.0 cm to -55.0 cm	1	4
	34	Room 21 floor contact	1	8
	69	Room 46 floor contact	1	3
	57	Room 33 floor contact	3	15
	62	Room 17 6.0 cm above floor	1	9
	64	Room 17 2.5 cm above floor	2	13
	65	Room 17 1.0 cm above floor	3	5
	66	Room 17 floor plaster		6

Ephedra nevadensis-type	*Ephedra torreyana*-type	*Cereus*-type	*Cylindropuntia*	*Platyopuntia*
		1		
	2			
			2	
1	3		24	
1	1		5	
1	1	1	5	5
1				
			5	2
1	2	2	21	
1	1		5	
2			1	
	3			
			1	
		1	1	
2	2	1	1	
1			4	
	1		1	
			4	
		1		

TABLE J.3 Herbaceous pollen types at Reeve Ruin and the Davis Ranch Site

Site	Sample no.	Context	Poaceae	Chenopodinneae	*Tidestromia*	Asteraceae		
						Ambrosieae	Tubuliflorae	Liguliflorae
Reeve Ruin	10	Room 26 floor contact	41	359	26	82	185	2
	35	Room 20 floor contact	46	1,482	7	80	125	
	36	Room 20 6.0–7.0 cm below floor	41	936	6	51	136	4
	37	Room 20 Floor 2	34	819	2	34	214	3
	8	Room 22 floor contact	38	402	5	54	126	3
	39	Room 29 floor contact	38	552	2	38	118	2
	29	Room 23 floor contact	28	299	5	37	155	1
	28	Room 24 floor contact	14	87		9	70	
	19	Room 9 floor contact	18	591	4	89	120	3
	9	Room 8 floor plaster	32	484	5	129	139	2
Davis Ranch Site	48	Room 21 -40.0 cm to -45.0 cm	38	1,102	3	86	137	1
	47	Room 21 -45.0 cm to -50.0 cm	37	978	3	75	148	
	46	Room 21 -50.0 cm to -55.0 cm	16	395	1	39	45	
	34	Room 21 floor contact	14	497		47	90	1
	69	Room 46 floor contact	23	1,052		33	283	
	57	Room 33 floor contact	23	549	5	36	146	4
	62	Room 17 6.0 cm above floor	33	689	2	48	67	1
	64	Room 17 2.5 cm above floor	17	318		31	91	2
	65	Room 17 1.0 cm above floor	17	380	1	33	67	1
	66	Room 17 floor plaster	19	345	2	37	57	2

(continued)

Site	Sample no.	Context	*Euphorbia*	Zygophyllaceae	Geraniaceae	Onagraceae	Malvaceae	*Acacia*	Unknown
Reeve Ruin	10	Room 26 floor contact	4			1			4
	35	Room 20 floor contact	6						4
	36	Room 20 6.0–7.0 cm below floor	6						5
	37	Room 20 Floor 2	5	1			1		3
	8	Room 22 floor contact	1		1	5		1	4
	39	Room 29 floor contact							6
	29	Room 23 floor contact	5				1		9
	28	Room 24 floor contact	3	1		5			3
	19	Room 9 floor contact	7			3	1		4
	9	Room 8 floor plaster	3			1			4
Davis Ranch Site	48	Room 21 –40.0 cm to –45.0 cm	3	1					4
	47	Room 21 –45.0 cm to –50.0 cm	1	1					3
	46	Room 21 –50.0 cm to –55.0 cm							2
	34	Room 21 floor contact	3						2
	69	Room 46 floor contact	4		2				1
	57	Room 33 floor contact	2	1		1			2
	62	Room 17 6.0 cm above floor	3		3				2
	64	Room 17 2.5 cm above floor	5	4	7				4
	65	Room 17 1.0 cm above floor	8	3	6				4
	66	Room 17 floor plaster	8	1	11				3

TABLE J.4 Economic pollen types at Reeve Ruin and the Davis Ranch Site

Site	Sample no.	Context	*Zea*	*Cucurbita*	*Cleome*	Cyperaceae	*Typha*	Cruciferae	Nyctaginaceae
Reeve Ruin	10	Room 26 floor contact	2			1		2	4
	35	Room 20 floor contact	1		8			7	5
	36	Room 20 6.0–7.0 cm below floor			3	1		6	3
	37	Room 20 Floor 2	2			3		4	10
	8	Room 22 floor contact	14			14	1	7	7
	39	Room 29 floor contact	1			4			16
	29	Room 23 floor contact	1			2		9	
	28	Room 24 floor contact	4			1			48
	19	Room 9 floor contact	10	1		4		5	9
	9	Room 8 floor plaster	1			2	1	4	7
Davis Ranch Site	48	Room 21 –40.0 cm to –45.0 cm						20	6
	47	Room 21 –45.0 cm to –50.0 cm	1			4		25	8
	46	Room 21 –50.0 cm to –55.0 cm	1					4	12
	34	Room 21 floor contact				1		3	9
	69	Room 46 floor contact	1			1		17	21
	57	Room 33 floor contact	2		1	2		10	15
	62	Room 17 6.0 cm above floor	5		2	4		11	12
	64	Room 17 2.5 cm above floor	2		1	1		9	23
	65	Room 17 1.0 cm above floor	8		1	1		14	16
	66	Room 17 floor plaster	4	2	4	2		9	19

case, its pollen would date to before the time of room construction.

Taking the construction sequence and the internal stratigraphy of samples into consideration, the pollen records of some samples from Reeve Ruin and some from the Davis Ranch Site can be placed in relative stratigraphic order (table J.5). Much of the pollen observed in this group of samples was produced by plants whose growth and development are adapted to human behavior patterns. Pollen of cultivars and other plants adapted to irrigated field habitats are the most obvious members of this flora, but pollen of plants that flourish on human-disturbed landscapes, such as the immediate environs of inhabited sites, are also prominent in the samples. The few pollen types in these samples that have any real potential to prove informative about regional ecosystem conditions are those disseminated by upland forest trees, desert and grassland shrubs, and grasses. If, over the course of time, significant variation occurred in the pollen statistics of these three categories, the differences can be interpreted to identify ecosystem changes. These changes, in turn, suggest distinct temporal episodes.

TABLE J.5 Stratigraphic ordering of selected samples from the Davis Ranch Site and Reeve Ruin

	Site and sample provenience	
Relative age	Davis Ranch Site	Reeve Ruin
Youngest	Room 33 floor contact	Rooms 26 and 24
	Room 17 +6.0 cm	Room 20 upper floor
	Room 17 +2.5 cm	Room 20 between floors
	Room 17 +1.0 cm	Room 20 lower floor
Oldest	Room 17 floor contact	Rooms 22, 23, 8, and 9

I explored the potential of the pollen record to identify such episodes by determining the ratio of observed pollen of upland trees (pines, oaks, junipers) and the observed pollen of grasses. The former category consists of plants that could not grow locally under current ecosystem conditions in the San Pedro Valley; the latter category consists of plants well adapted to local ecosystem conditions. A larger ratio (significantly more grass pollen) suggests ecosystem conditions more like those of the present; a smaller ratio (significantly more upland tree pollen) suggests ecosystem conditions that would allow more pollen to arrive at the sites from distant sources. This could occur because a greater production of upland plant pollen was precipitated by ecosystem changes taking place beyond the valley, or because the numbers and vigor of local grass populations were adversely affected by ecosystem changes occurring within the valley.

Plugging the ratio data into the sample sequence information recognized above produced the results in table J.6. Although the pattern is more pronounced at Reeve Ruin, the clear tendency is for the ratio to be greater in older samples and lesser in younger samples. Because the ratios are based on small actual numbers of observations (n ranges from 32 to 62 pollen grains), the distinctions between them are not always statistically significant. There seem to be, however, three sorts of ratios: the oldest ones that range from 1.72 to 0.84; those of middle age that range from 0.61 to 0.44; and the youngest sample with a ratio of 0.27.

The data are adequate to support the argument that each of these categories of ratios identifies distinct ecosystem conditions existing at different points in relative time. However, there are sufficient discrepancies in the general pattern to allow debate. Their architectural relationship suggests that Room 21 is older than Room 33 at the Davis Ranch Site, but the pollen ratios of their floor contact deposit samples indicate the opposite. Room 24 was built late in the construction sequence at Reeve Ruin, but the AP:Grass (upland arboreal to grass) pollen ratio of its floor contact sample suggests it

TABLE J.6 Stratigraphic patterning in the ratio of upland arboreal pollen to grass pollen in selected samples from the Davis Ranch Site and Reeve Ruin

	Davis Ranch Site		Reeve Ruin	
Relative age	UAP[a]: Grass	Provenience	UAP[a]: Grass	Provenience
Youngest	0.91	Room 33 floor contact	0.27, 1.29	Rooms 26 and 24
	1.35	Room 17 +6.0 cm	0.61	Room 20 upper floor
	1.12	Room 17 +2.5 cm	0.51	Room 20 between floors
	1.24	Room 17 +1.0 cm	0.61	Room 20 lower floor
			0.44, 1.14, 0.84, 1.72	Rooms 22, 23, 8, and 9
Oldest	1.16	Room 17 floor contact		

[a]Upland arboreal pollen (see table J.1)

was deposited significantly earlier than those from other sampled rooms in that houseblock. The architectural evidence suggests that Rooms 20, 22, and 23 were constructed at the same time, but the pollen record suggests that pollen was deposited on the floor of Room 23 before it was deposited on the floors of the other two rooms. And there is no architectural evidence suggesting any relative temporal order to Rooms 20, 22, 23, 8, and 9, but their pollen records argue that the two houseblocks involved were constructed during different horizons identified by distinctions in the AP:Grass pollen ratio.

At this juncture, the lack of modern surface pollen rain control data and the relatively small numbers of analyzed samples and observations significantly hamper development of firm conclusions. Because we do not have data that would allow us to assess whether or not variability in the AP:Grass ratio of pollen records from this district actually identifies distinct ecosystem conditions, because of the small numbers of pollen grains of upland trees and local grasses observed in the analysis, and because of the small number of sampled rooms that can be placed in relative temporal order on the basis of architectural evidence, we cannot *demonstrate* that those discrepancies are more significant to interpretation than the general pattern of ratio change over the course of time. Even so, I am willing to accept the latter as the conclusion appropriate to the palynological evidence. I also think it not unlikely that the surfaces sampled from Room 8 and Room 24 existed as use surfaces before they were enclosed by the walls of their respective rooms, and I suggest that although Rooms 20, 22, and 23 were built in the same construction phase, Room 23 was occupied earlier than the other two.

Acceptance of the validity of the general pattern requires a liberal interpretation of the palynological data but allows conclusions to be drawn about inter- and intrasite relative chronology. The samples would be dated in the relative order presented in table J.7. Two rather significant inferences may be drawn from this conclusion. First, since most of the sampled rooms at the Davis Ranch Site come from its youngest houseblock, construction at Reeve Ruin may not have been initiated until occupation of the Davis Ranch Site had mostly or totally ceased. Second, construction and occupation of Reeve Ruin took place under regional ecosystem conditions distinct from those that had occurred during most of the occupation of the Davis Ranch Site, conditions that increased the ratio of upland to local pollen.

The reason(s) for the ecosystem changes involved cannot be deduced from the data of this study. Nor can the available information support an argument that the change was a response to either climatic

TABLE J.7 Relative chronology of all samples from the Davis Ranch Site and Reeve Ruin based on the ratio of upland arboreal pollen to grass pollen

	Davis Ranch Site		Reeve Ruin	
Relative age	Provenience	UAP[a]: Grass	Provenience	UAP[a]: Grass
Youngest	Room 21 -40.0 cm to -45.0 cm	0.37	Room 26 floor contact	0.27
	Room 21 -45.0 cm to -50.0 cm	0.24		
Middle	Room 21 -50.0 cm to -55.0 cm	0.63	Room 20 upper floor	0.61
	Room 21 floor	0.64	Room 20 between floors	0.51
			Room 20 lower floor	0.61
			Room 22 floor contact	0.44
			Room 29 floor contact	0.47
Oldest	Room 33 floor contact	0.91	Room 8 floor contact	0.84
	Room 17 6.0 cm above floor	1.35	Room 24 floor contact	1.29
	Room 17 2.5 cm above floor	1.12	Room 9 floor	1.72
	Room 17 1.0 cm above floor	1.24		
	Room 17 floor	1.11		
	Room 46 floor	1.04		

[a]Upland arboreal pollen (see table J.1)

or human behavioral factors. It should be noted, however, that a parallel increase in the amount of nonlocal upland pollen has been documented for the San Pedro Valley during the historic era (Davis et al. 2002:406). Following the conclusion reached by Hastings and Turner (1965) and Davis and Turner (1986), this upland pollen increase is here attributed to reduced aboriginal burning of valley floor and grassland vegetation, with consequent development of more extensive stands of mesquite and juniper.

AGRICULTURAL AND ECONOMIC POLLEN TYPES

Agricultural activities are represented in the palynological record in two ways: by the occurrence of pollen of cultigens, and by the significant presence of the pollen of plants adapted to the habitats farmers create to encourage agricultural productivity. Both are recovered in the Davis Ranch Site pollen record.

The two crop plants that contributed pollen to the samples are *Zea* (maize) and *Cucurbita* (squash). Neither pollen type was observed as a statistically significant fraction of the pollen count of a given sample, but the maize pollen record is ubiquitous. Squash is represented by two pollen grains in one of the Davis Ranch Site samples and a single pollen grain in one of the Reeve Ruin samples.

Fish (1985, 1994) has argued that the statistically significant occurrence of *Boerhaavia* and Nyctaginaceae pollen in archaeological contexts constitutes the palynological "signature" of the sort of irrigation technology practiced by the Hohokam in the Salt and Gila Valleys of central Arizona. In this pollen record, *Boerhaavia* pollen is essentially absent. Nyctaginaceae and Cruciferae pollen, however, were recovered in significant quantities in the Davis

Ranch Site and Reeve Ruin samples. Both of these pollen taxa derive from insect-pollinated species that normally contribute much smaller amounts of pollen to local pollen rains. I strongly suspect that, in combination, they identify the occurrence of irrigation activity and that the replacement of *Boerhaavia* by Cruciferae in the signature is either a response to a difference in lowland ecosystem conditions or an indication that the irrigation technology used in the two regions was distinctive. The ubiquity and frequencies of *Prosopis* (mesquite), *Typha* (cattail), and Cyperaceae (sedge) pollen are also consistent with the occurrence of irrigation canals.

The Davis Ranch Site samples include a more ubiquitous record of Cylindropuntia pollen than can be explained by "natural" mechanisms of pollen dissemination and deposition. Cylindropuntia (cholla) pollen is frequently and consistently encountered in Hohokam and Salado habitation context samples, and its occurrence is traditionally interpreted as a product of collection and use of cholla fruits as a staple food. In the present case, more Cylindropuntia pollen occurs in the Reeve Ruin samples than in those from the Davis Ranch Site, particularly in the samples from the lower floor of Room 24 and the floor of Room 9. These samples are arguably from some of the earliest use surfaces of the site. I suggest the data indicate intensified food gathering at this stage in the history of Reeve, relative both to contemporary agricultural food production at the Davis Ranch Site and to subsequent years.

The unusual ubiquity and abundance of Liliaceae pollen in the Davis Ranch Site and Reeve Ruin samples is almost certainly the result of human manipulation of the insect-pollinated plant that produced this pollen. Unfortunately, in 1965, I did not have sufficient access to reference pollen types to be able to distinguish the pollen types of different genera of the lily family, and the primary reference for Arizona's flora I was using at the time (Kearney and Peebles 1951) classified *Agave* as a genus in the lily family. Today, Agave is classified to the family *Agavaceae*. Agave, sotol, or yucca are all ethnographically recognized sources of textile or cordage fiber, and *Agave* is known as a prehistorically cultivated food source, as well. Because the palynological identification is uncertain, I have not identified this pollen type as an indicator of economic activity in table J.4. The possibility that the pollen type is actually identifiable as *Agave* should be given very serious consideration, however.

CLEOME SERRULATA (BEEWEED) POLLEN

One of the more surprising features of the Davis Ranch Site and Reeve Ruin pollen records is the occurrence of beeweed pollen. While a common feature of the floras of northern Arizona, where it is frequently associated with the ruins of archaeological sites, the plant that produces this pollen type does not occur naturally in the state south of the Mogollon Rim—even in "sky island" high-elevation woodlands and forests. Commenting on the 1965 report, P. J. Mehringer (personal communication 1965) noted that it was difficult to credit this observation because of the range extension that would be involved. I am certain that misidentification of the pollen type has not occurred because I compared it with reference material available to me at the time and because I was very familiar with it as a product of prior research on site-context samples from northern New Mexico (e.g., Schoenwetter 1964, 1965b, 1965c).

When the earlier study was done, however, I was not aware that Roosevelt Red Ware (Salado polychrome pottery) designs incorporated carbon-based paint, nor had the Kayenta/Tusayan migrant link to the Davis Ranch Site and Reeve Ruin been generally accepted. *Cleome serrulata* is ethnographically used as a source of black pigment by Pueblo peoples (Whiting 1939). The plant is harvested when in flower, the black juice extracted from bruised plants, placed in boiling water, and the water boiled off to form a cake of pigment. A good deal of pollen must be released with the juice and retained in the pigment cake. Given the other archaeological evidence for contact with cultural populations in districts where *Cleome* is a native member of the vegetation, it seems likely that beeweed pigment cakes were traded to the San Pedro Valley. Spillage from the reconstituted paint would account for *Cleome* pollen on the floors of certain rooms.

Since evidence for irrigation exists in the local pollen record, it is possible that *Cleome* populations were maintained in the San Pedro Valley as cultivated exotics. This is a less parsimonious interpretation, however, and the localized distribution of the pollen type in the record argues against it at these sites.

SUMMARY

Many years ago, I analyzed a suite of pollen samples collected from archaeological deposits at the Davis Ranch Site and Reeve Ruin (Schoenwetter 1965a). This study presents a tabulation of my observations and reinterprets the results of that work in the light of more recent archaeological information and theory. I suggest that the Davis Ranch Site and Reeve Ruin pollen record provides adequate evidence for the following inferences of archaeological relevance:

1. Deposition of the samples and the pollen they contain occurred during three episodes of time within the span of the single archaeological phase recognized through ceramic analysis. The pollen of samples from Rooms 46, 33, and 17 at the Davis Ranch Site accumulated during the earliest of these episodes. The deposits sampled in Rooms 8 and 9 and the lower floor contact deposit in Room 24 at Reeve Ruin also date from this episode. I suspect the lower floor of Room 24 represents a use surface established prior to construction of the houseblock.

   The floor contact sample from Room 21 at the Davis Ranch Site and the deepest sample of fill from that room seem to have been deposited during the second of the three episodes. Pollen deposition in the rooms of Reeve Ruin mostly took place at this time, as represented by floor contact samples from Rooms 29, 22, 23, and the lower and upper floors of Room 20.

   Evidence that the occupation of the Davis Ranch Site had ceased before the third episode and the conclusion of the ceramic phase is reflected by the fact that the only samples deposited during this youngest episode derive from room fill in Room 21. Construction continued into this episode at Reeve Ruin, however, as evidenced by the pollen record of the floor contact sample from Room 26—which is one of the last rooms constructed in its houseblock at that site.
2. The character of the changes in regional ecosystem conditions that are identified by palynological distinctions between the temporal episodes is not adequately evidenced by the data considered in this study. The trend of increasing amounts in arboreal pollen over the course of the occupation, however, parallels a similar increase recognized for the historic era in pollen sequences collected throughout the San Pedro Valley (Davis et al. 2002). In that case, the trend is interpreted as an outcome of changes in human land use.
3. The pollen record provides evidence of food production through irrigation agriculture, though differences in the ways that irrigation is palynologically expressed in these sites and sites in central Arizona may be clues to distinctions in irrigation technology in the two districts.
4. The ubiquity and frequency of cholla pollen in the samples from these sites is similar to its occurrence in Hohokam and Salado sites, where it is interpreted as the product of wild food collection. The distribution of the pollen type in this record, however, suggests such collection may have been intensified at Reeve Ruin when its earliest rooms were occupied.
5. Unusual amounts of the pollen of some member of the lily or agave families occur in the pollen records from both the Davis Ranch Site and Reeve Ruin. Since all members of these families are insect pollinated, the ubiquity and frequency of this pollen type in the samples argues

for human manipulation of the plant. I was unable to identify the genus involved in 1965, and indeed, I cannot be sure that the pollen I observed is not *Agave* pollen. Given our present understanding of the significance of prehistoric *Agave* cultivation in central and southern Arizona, representation of this cultivar seems a more likely interpretation of the record than unusually intensive manipulation of yucca or sotol.

6. The abundance of pollen of beeweed (*Cleome serrulata*) in these samples is clear evidence of human manipulation of the plant, since it is both an insect-pollinated and an exotic taxon. It most probably owes its occurrence in the prehistoric pollen record of the San Pedro Valley to its use as a source of black pigment in the decoration of Roosevelt Red Ware. The pigment is more likely to have been obtained through trade than through local cultivation of the source plants. Although this suite of samples is too small to provide more than a hint of the true distribution of beeweed pollen in the two sites, it suggests that application of black paint during manufacture of this ceramic style was done inside rooms despite low light levels. Perhaps this activity was limited to specific places within the community as well.

REFERENCES CITED

Abbott, David R., and David A. Gregory. 1988. Hohokam Ceramic Wares and Types. In *The 1982–1984 Excavations at Las Colinas, Volume 4: Material Culture*, by David R. Abbott, Kim E. Beckwith, Patricia L. Crown, R. Thomas Euler, David A. Gregory, J. Ronald London, Marilyn B. Saul, Larry A. Schwalbe, Mary Bernard-Shaw, Christine R. Szuter, and Arthur W. Vokes, pp. 5–28. Archaeological Series No. 162. Arizona State Museum, University of Arizona, Tucson.

Abbott, R. Tucker. 1974. *American Seashells: The Marine Molluska of the Atlantic and Pacific Coasts of North America*. 2nd ed. Van Nostrand Reinhold, New York.

Adams, E. Charles. 1991. *The Origin and Development of the Pueblo Katsina Cult*. University of Arizona Press, Tucson.

Adams, E. Charles. 2002. *Homol'ovi: An Ancient Hopi Settlement Cluster*. University of Arizona Press, Tucson.

Adams, Jenny L. 1994. The Development of Prehistoric Grinding Technology in the Point of Pines Area, East-Central Arizona. PhD dissertation, Department of Anthropology, University of Arizona, Tucson. ProQuest, Ann Arbor, Michigan.

Adams, Jenny L. 2002. *Ground Stone Analysis: A Technological Approach*. University of Utah Press, Salt Lake City.

Adams, Jenny L. 2006. Ground Stone Artifacts. In *Rio Nuevo Archaeology, 2000–2003: Investigations at the San Agustín Mission and Mission Gardens, Tucson Presidio, Tucson Pressed Brick Company, and Clearwater Site*, edited by J. Homer Thiel and Jonathan B. Mabry, pp 9.1–9.32. Technical Report No. 2004-11. Desert Archaeology, Tucson, Arizona.

Adams, Jenny L. 2010. Engendering Households through Technological Identity. In *Engendering Households in the Prehistoric Southwest*, edited by Barbara J. Roth, pp. 208–228. University of Arizona Press, Tucson.

Adams, Jenny L. 2014. *Ground Stone Analysis: A Technological Approach*. 2nd ed. University of Utah Press, Salt Lake City.

Adams, Jenny L. 2015. San Pedro Phase Grinding Technology at Las Capas, AZ AA:12:111 (ASM). In *Implements of Change: Tools, Subsistence, and the Built Environment of Las Capas, an Early Agricultural Irrigation Community in Southern Arizona*, edited by James M. Vint, pp. 95–159. Anthropological Papers No. 51. Archaeology Southwest, Tucson, Arizona.

Ahlstrom, Richard V. N., Mark L. Chenault, Mark Zyniecki, and David H. Greenwald. 1995. Chronology, Compound Growth, and Demography. In *Early Desert Farming and Irrigation Settlements: Archaeological Investigations in the Phoenix Sky Harbor Center, Volume 3: Pueblo Salado*, edited by David H. Greenwald, Mark L. Chenault, and Dawn M. Greenwald, pp. 369–381. Anthropological Research Paper No. 4. SWCA Environmental Consultants, Flagstaff, Arizona.

Altschul, Jeffrey H., and Steven D. Shelley. 1996. Summary and Conclusions. In *On the Border: Analysis of Materials Recovered from the 1964 and 1991–1992 Excavations at the Garden Canyon Site (AZ EE:11:13 ASM)*, edited by Steven D. Shelley and Jeffrey H. Altschul, pp. 141–156. Technical Series No. 61. Statistical Research, Tucson, Arizona.

Altschul, Jeffrey H., Rein Vanderpot, César A. Quijada, and Robert Heckman. 2014. People of the Grassland: Archaic and Formative Cultures of the Upper and Middle San Pedro Valley. In *Between Mimbres and Hohokam: Exploring the Archaeology and History of Southeastern Arizona and Southwestern New Mexico*, edited by Henry D. Wallace, pp. 279–321. Anthropological Papers No. 52. Archaeology Southwest, Tucson, Arizona.

Ambler, J. Richard, Alexander J. Lindsay Jr., and Mary Anne Stein. 1964. *Survey and Excavations on Cummings Mesa, Arizona and Utah, 1960–1961*. Museum of Northern Arizona Bulletin No. 39. Glen Canyon Series No. 5. Northern Arizona Society of Science and Art, Flagstaff.

Anderson, Keith M. 1969. *Archaeology on the Shonto Plateau, Northeast Arizona*. Technical Series Vol. 7. Southwest Monuments Association, Gila Pueblo, Globe, Arizona.

Anyon, Roger, and Steven A. LeBlanc. 1984. *The Galaz Ruin: A Prehistoric Mimbres Village in Southwestern New Mexico*. Maxwell Museum of Anthropology, Albuquerque, New Mexico; University of New Mexico Press, Albuquerque.

Baldwin, Gordon C. 1934. The Prehistoric Pueblo of Kinishba. Master's thesis, College of Letters, Arts and Sciences, University of Arizona, Tucson.

Baldwin, Gordon C. 1938. A New Pottery Type from Eastern Arizona. *Southwestern Lore* 4(2):21–26.

Baldwin, Gordon C. 1939. The Material Culture of Kinishba. *American Antiquity* 4:314–327.

Baldwin, Gordon C. 1941. The Archaeology of the Upper Salt River Valley, Arizona: Its Sequence and Interrelationships. PhD dissertation, Department of Anthropology, University of Southern California, Los Angeles.

Baldwin, Gordon C. 1944. Mescal Knives from Southern Nevada. *American Antiquity* 9:330–332.

Bannister, Bryant, John W. Hannah, and William J. Robinson. 1970. *Tree-Ring Dates from New Mexico M-N, S, Z: Southwestern New Mexico Area*. Laboratory of Tree-Ring Research, University of Arizona, Tucson.

Barker, Claire S., and Patrick D. Lyons. 2011. Exploring the Meaning of the Late Prehispanic Yellow Ware Horizon. Paper presented at the 76th Annual Meeting of the Society for American Archaeology, Sacramento, California.

Bartlett, Katharine. 1933. *Pueblo Milling Stones of the Flagstaff Region and Their Relation to Others in the Southwest: A Study in Progressive Efficiency*. Museum of Northern Arizona Bulletin No. 3. Northern Arizona Society of Science and Art, Flagstaff.

Bayham, Frank E. 1976. Appendix III: Tools. In *Desert Resources and Hohokam Subsistence: The Conoco Florence Project*, by William H. Doelle, pp. 219–229. Archaeological Series No. 103. Arizona State Museum, University of Arizona, Tucson.

Beals, Ralph, George W. Brainard, and Watson Smith. 1945. *Archaeological Studies in Northeast Arizona*. University of California Publications in American Archaeology and Ethnology Vol. 44, No. 1. University of California Press, Berkeley.

Bequaert, Joseph C., and Walter B. Miller. 1973. *The Mollusks of the Arid Southwest: With an Arizona Check List*. University of Arizona Press, Tucson.

Bernard-Shaw, Mary. 1983. The Stone Tool Assemblage of the Salt-Gila Aqueduct Project Sites. In *Hohokam Archaeology Along the*

Salt-Gila Aqueduct Central Arizona Project, Volume 8: Material Culture, edited by Lynn S. Teague and Patricia L. Crown, pp. 373–443. Archaeological Series No. 150. Arizona State Museum, University of Arizona, Tucson.

Bernard-Shaw, Mary. 1988. Chipped Stone Artifacts. In *The 1982–1984 Excavations at Las Colinas, Volume 4: Material Culture*, by David R. Abbott, Kim E. Beckwith, Patricia L. Crown, R. Thomas Euler, David A. Gregory, J. Ronald London, Marilyn B. Saul, Larry A. Schwalbe, Mary Bernard-Shaw, Christine R. Szuter, and Arthur W. Vokes, pp. 273–297. Archaeological Series No. 162. Arizona State Museum, University of Arizona, Tucson.

Bernard-Shaw, Mary. 1990. Experimental Agave Fiber Extraction. In *Rincon Phase Seasonal Occupation in the Northern Tucson Basin*, by Mary Bernard-Shaw and Frederick W. Huntington, pp. 181–195. Technical Report No. 90-2. Center for Desert Archaeology, Tucson, Arizona.

Boggess, Douglas H. M., Mark E. Harlan, Deni J. Seymour, and Courtney Rose. 2003. *Prehistoric and Historic Homesteads and Ghost Towns: Data Recovery Along the Valley Telephone Fiber Optic Corridor in Southeastern Arizona*. Lone Mountain Report No. 683. Lone Mountain Archaeological Services, Albuquerque, New Mexico.

Bolton, Herbert E. 1936. *Rim of Christendom: A Biography of Eusebio Francisco Kino, Pacific Coast Pioneer*. Macmillan, New York.

Boone, Elizabeth H. 2003. A Web of Understanding: Pictorial Codices and the Shared Intellectual Culture of Late Postclassic Mesoamerica. In *The Postclassic Mesoamerican World*, edited by Michael E. Smith and Francis F. Berdan, pp. 207–226. University of Utah Press, Salt Lake City.

Bowen, Greg L. 1993. A Study of Tabular Tools. In *Classic Period Occupation on the Santa Cruz Flats: The Santa Cruz Flats Archaeological Project*, edited by T. Kathleen Henderson and Richard J. Martynec, pp. 385–393. Northland Research, Flagstaff, Arizona.

Bowen, Thomas. 1972. A Survey and Reevaluation of the Trincheras Culture, Sonora, Mexico. Manuscript on file, Library and Archives, Arizona State Museum, University of Arizona.

Bowen, Thomas. 1976. *Seri Prehistory: The Archaeology of the Central Coast of Sonora, Mexico*. Anthropological Papers of the University of Arizona No. 27. University of Arizona Press, Tucson.

Brainerd, George W. 1951. The Place of Chronological Ordering in Archaeological Analysis. *American Antiquity* 16:301–313.

Brand, Donald D. 1935. The Distribution of Pottery Types in Northwest Mexico. *American Anthropologist* 37:287–305.

Brandes, Raymond S. 1957. An Archaeological Survey Within Gila County, Arizona. Manuscript on file, Western Archeological and Conservation Center, National Park Service, Tucson, Arizona.

Breternitz, David A. 1966. *An Appraisal of Tree-Ring Dated Pottery in the Southwest*. Anthropological Papers of the University of Arizona No. 10. University of Arizona Press, Tucson.

Breternitz, David A., James C. Gifford, and Alan P. Olson. 1957. Point of Pines Phase Sequence and Utility Pottery Type Revisions. *American Antiquity* 22:412–416.

Brew, Susan A., and Bruce B. Huckell. 1987. A Protohistoric Piman Burial and a Consideration of Piman Burial Practices. *Kiva* 52:163–191.

Brody, J. J., and Rina Swentzell. 1996. *To Touch the Past: The Painted Pottery of the Mimbres People*. Hudson Hills Press, New York.

Bronitsky, Gordon, and James D. Merritt. 1986. *The Archaeology of Southeast Arizona: A Class I Cultural Resource Inventory*. Cultural Resource Series No. 2. Bureau of Land Management, Phoenix, Arizona.

Brown, Jeffrey L. 1973. The Origin and Nature of Salado: Evidence from the Safford Valley, Arizona. PhD dissertation, Department of

Anthropology, University of Arizona, Tucson. ProQuest, Ann Arbor, Michigan.

Brown, Jeffrey L. 1974. Pueblo Viejo Salado Sites and Their Relationship to Western Pueblo Culture. *Artifact* 12(2):1–53.

Brumfiel, Elizabeth. 1976. Specialization and Exchange at the Late Postclassic (Aztec) Community of Huexotla, Mexico. PhD dissertation, Department of Anthropology, University of Michigan, Ann Arbor. ProQuest, Ann Arbor, Michigan.

Brunson, Judy Lynn. 1989. The Social Organization of the Los Muertos Hohokam: A Reanalysis of Cushing's Hemenway Expedition Data. PhD dissertation, Department of Anthropology, Arizona State University, Tempe. ProQuest, Ann Arbor, Michigan.

Bunzel, Ruth L. 1932. Zuñi Katcinas: An Analytical Study. In *Forty-Seventh Annual Report of the Bureau of American Ethnology for the Years 1929–1930*, pp. 837–1086. Smithsonian Institution, Washington, D.C.

Burgett, Jessica Prue. 2006. El Paso Polychrome in the Casas Grandes Region, Chihuahua, Mexico: Ceramic Exchange between Paquimé and the Jornada Mogollon. PhD dissertation, Department of Anthropology, Pennsylvania State University, University Park. ProQuest, Ann Arbor. Michigan.

Burt, William H. 1961. A Fauna from an Indian Site near Redington, Arizona. *Journal of Mammalogy* 42:115–116.

Burt, William H., and Robert W. Storer. 1958. Animal Bones. In *The Reeve Ruin of Southeastern Arizona: A Study of a Prehistoric Western Pueblo Migration into the Middle San Pedro Valley*, by Charles C. Di Peso, p. 116. Amerind Foundation No. 8. Amerind Foundation, Dragoon, Arizona.

Burt, William H., and Harrison B. Tordoff. 1958. Identification of Mammal Bone from Davis Ruin (ARIZONA:BB:11:7) by William H. Burt, Birds Identified by Harrison B. Tordoff, Museum of Zoology, University of Michigan, 4/5/58. Manuscript on file, Archives, Amerind Museum, Dragoon, Arizona.

Bushnell, G. H. S. 1955. Some Pueblo IV Pottery Types From Kechipauan, New Mexico, U.S.A. In *Anais do 31 Congresso Internacional de Americanistas, São Paulo, 23 a 28 de Agôsto de 1954, Vol. 2*, compiled by Herbert Baldus, pp. 657–665. Editora Anhembi, São Paulo, Brazil.

Cable, John S. 1990. Who Were the Protohistoric Occupants of Ak-Chin? A Study Concerning the Relationship between Ethnicity and Ceramic Style. In *Archaeology of the Ak-Chin Indian Community West Side Farms Project, Volume 5: Subsistence Studies and Synthesis and Interpretation*, compiled by Robert E. Gasser, Christine K. Robinson, and Cory Dale Breternitz, pp. 23.1–23.65. Publications in Archaeology No. 9. Soil Systems, Phoenix, Arizona.

Carlson, Roy L. 1961. White Mountain Red Ware: A Stylistic Tradition in the Pottery of East Central Arizona. PhD dissertation, Department of Anthropology, University of Arizona, Tucson. ProQuest, Ann Arbor, Michigan.

Carlson, Roy L. 1970. *White Mountain Redware: A Pottery Tradition of East-Central Arizona and Western New Mexico*. Anthropological Papers of the University of Arizona No. 19. University of Arizona Press, Tucson.

Carlson, Roy L. 1982. The Polychrome Complexes. In *Southwestern Ceramics: A Comparative Review*, edited by Albert H. Schroeder, pp. 201–234. Arizona Archaeologist No. 15. Arizona Archaeological Society, Phoenix.

Carpenter, Alice H. 1996. The Feather Prince: A Personal Narrative of Southeastern Arizona Prehistory. Annotated by Linda M. Gregonis. *Journal of the Southwest* 38:299–342.

Carpenter, John P. 2002. The Animas Phase and Paquimé: Regional Differentiation and Integration at Joyce Well. In *The Joyce Well Site: On the Frontier of the Casas Grandes World*, by James M. Skibo, Eugene B. McCluney, and William H. Walker, pp. 148–166. University of Utah Press, Salt Lake City.

Carr, Christopher. 1995a. Building a Unified Middle-Range Theory of Artifact Design: Historical Perspectives and Tactics. In *Style, Society, and Person: Archaeological and Ethnological Perspectives*, edited by Christopher Carr and Jill E. Neitzel, pp. 151–170. Plenum Press, New York.

Carr, Christopher. 1995b. A Unified Middle-Range Theory of Artifact Design. In *Style, Society, and Person: Archaeological and Ethnological Perspectives*, edited by Christopher Carr and Jill E. Neitzel, pp. 171–258. Plenum Press, New York.

Castetter, Edward F., Willis H. Bell, and Alvin R. Grove. 1938. *Ethnobiological Studies in the American Southwest Volume VI: The Early Utilization and the Distribution of Agave in the American Southwest.* University of New Mexico Bulletin No. 335. Biological Series Vol. 5, No. 4. University of New Mexico Press, Albuquerque.

Christenson, Andrew L. 1991. Identifying Pukis or Potters' Turntables at Anasazi Sites. *Pottery Southwest* 18(1):1–6.

Christenson, Andrew L. 1994. Perforated and Unperforated Plates as Tools for Pottery Manufacture. In *Function and Technology of Anasazi Ceramics from Black Mesa, Arizona*, edited by Marion F. Smith Jr., pp. 55–65. Occasional Paper No. 15. Center for Archaeological Investigations, Southern Illinois University, Carbondale.

Ciolek-Torrello, Richard, Martha M. Callahan, and David H. Greenwald (editors). 1988. *Hohokam Settlement Along the Slopes of the Picacho Mountains, Volume 2: The Brady Wash Sites.* Museum of Northern Arizona Research Paper No. 35. Museum of Northern Arizona, Flagstaff.

Clark, Jeffery J. 2001. *Tracking Prehistoric Migrations: Pueblo Settlers Among the Tonto Basin Hohokam.* Anthropological Papers of the University of Arizona No. 65. University of Arizona Press, Tucson.

Clark, Jeffery J. (editor). 2004. *Ancient Farmers of the Safford Basin: Archaeology of the U.S. 70 Safford-to-Thatcher Project.* Anthropological Papers No. 39. Center for Desert Archaeology, Tucson, Arizona.

Clark, Jeffery J., Michael W. Diehl, Jennifer A. Waters, J. Brett Hill, and Jenny L. Adams. 2012. Plant and Animal Utilization. In *Migrants and Mounds: Classic Period Archaeology of the Lower San Pedro Valley*, edited by Jeffery J. Clark and Patrick D. Lyons, pp. 309–344. Anthropological Papers No. 45. Archaeology Southwest, Tucson, Arizona.

Clark, Jeffery J., and J. Brett Hill. 2012. Standardizing Artifact Counts for Intersite Comparisons, San Pedro Preservation Project. Electronic document, https://www.archaeologysouthwest.org/pdf/supplemental/ap45_clarkandhill.pdf, accessed August 22, 2018.

Clark, Jeffery J., J. Brett Hill, Patrick D. Lyons, and Stacey N. Lengyel. 2012. Of Migrants and Mounds. In *Migrants and Mounds: Classic Period Archaeology of the Lower San Pedro Valley*, edited by Jeffery J. Clark and Patrick D. Lyons, pp. 345–405. Anthropological Papers No. 45. Archaeology Southwest, Tucson, Arizona.

Clark, Jeffery J., Deborah J. Huntley, J. Brett Hill, and Patrick D. Lyons. 2013. The Kayenta Diaspora and Salado Meta-Identity in the Late Pre-Contact U.S. Southwest. In *The Archaeology of Hybrid Material Culture*, edited by Jeb J. Card, pp. 399–424. Occasional Paper No. 39. Center for Archaeological Investigations, Southern Illinois University, Carbondale.

Clark, Jeffery J., and Karl Laumbach. 2011. Ancestral Puebloan Migrations in the Southern Southwest: Perspectives from Arizona and New Mexico. In *Movement, Connectivity, and Landscape Change in the Ancient Southwest*, edited by Margaret C. Nelson and Colleen Strawhacker, pp. 297–320. University Press of Colorado, Boulder.

Clark, Jeffery J., and Patrick D. Lyons. 2012. How, Where, and What We Excavated. In *Migrants and Mounds: Classic Period Archaeology of the Lower San Pedro Valley*, edited by Jeffery J.

Clark and Patrick D. Lyons, pp. 67–210. Anthropological Papers No. 45. Archaeology Southwest, Tucson, Arizona.

Clark, Jeffery J., and Patrick D. Lyons (editors). 2012. *Migrants and Mounds: Classic Period Archaeology of the Lower San Pedro Valley*. Anthropological Papers No. 45. Archaeology Southwest, Tucson, Arizona.

Clark, Jeffery J., Patrick D. Lyons, J. Brett Hill, Stacey N. Lengyel, and Mark C. Slaughter. 2014. Migrants and Mounds in the Lower San Pedro Valley, A.D. 1200–1450. In *Between Mimbres and Hohokam: Exploring the Archaeology and History of Southeastern Arizona and Southwestern New Mexico*, edited by Henry D. Wallace, pp. 203–278. Anthropological Papers No. 52. Archaeology Southwest, Tucson, Arizona.

Clark, Jeffery J., Fred L. Nials, and James M. Vint. 2004. Introduction. In *Ancient Farmers of the Safford Basin: Archaeology of the U.S. 70 Safford-to-Thatcher Project*, edited by Jeffery J. Clark, pp. 1–22. Anthropological Papers No. 39. Center for Desert Archaeology, Tucson, Arizona.

Clarke, Eleanor P. 1933. Designs on the Prehistoric Pottery of Arizona. Master's thesis, College of Letters, Arts and Sciences, University of Arizona, Tucson.

Clarke, Eleanor P. 1935. *Designs on the Prehistoric Pottery of Arizona*. University of Arizona Bulletin Vol. 6, No. 4. Social Science Bulletin No. 9. University of Arizona, Tucson.

Colton, Harold S. 1939. *Prehistoric Culture Units and their Relationships in Northern Arizona*. Museum of Northern Arizona Bulletin No. 17. Northern Arizona Society of Science and Art, Flagstaff.

Colton, Harold S. 1941. *Winona and Ridge Ruin, Part II: Notes on the Technology and Taxonomy of the Pottery*. Museum of Northern Arizona Bulletin No. 19. Northern Arizona Society of Science and Art, Flagstaff.

Colton, Harold S. 1946. *The Sinagua: A Summary of the Archaeology of the Region of Flagstaff, Arizona*. Museum of Northern Arizona Bulletin No. 22. Northern Arizona Society of Science and Art, Flagstaff.

Colton, Harold S. 1953. *Potsherds: An Introduction to the Study of Prehistoric Southwestern Ceramics and Their Use in Historic Reconstruction*. Museum of Northern Arizona Bulletin No. 25. Northern Arizona Society of Science and Art, Flagstaff.

Colton, Harold S. 1955. *Check List of Southwestern Pottery Types*. Museum of Northern Arizona Ceramic Series No. 2. Northern Arizona Society of Science and Art, Flagstaff.

Colton, Harold S. 1965. *Check List of Southwestern Pottery Types*. Museum of Northern Arizona Ceramic Series No. 2, Revised. Northern Arizona Society of Science and Art, Flagstaff.

Colton, Harold S. (editor). 1956. *Pottery Types of the Southwest*. Museum of Northern Arizona Ceramic Series No. 3C. Northern Arizona Society of Science and Art, Flagstaff.

Colton, Harold S., and Lyndon L. Hargrave. 1935. Naming Pottery Types, and Rules of Priority. *Science* 82(2133):462–463.

Colton, Harold S., and Lyndon L. Hargrave. 1937. *Handbook of Northern Arizona Pottery Wares*. Museum of Northern Arizona Bulletin No. 11. Northern Arizona Society of Science and Art, Flagstaff.

Cosgrove, Harriet S., and Cornelius B. Cosgrove. 1932. *The Swarts Ruin: A Typical Mimbres Site in Southwestern New Mexico: Report of the Mimbres Valley Expedition, Seasons of 1924–1927*. Papers of the Peabody Museum of American Archaeology and Ethnology Vol. 15, Pt. 1. Harvard University, Cambridge. Massachusetts.

Cosner, Aaron J. 1951. Arrowshaft-Straightening with a Grooved Stone. *American Antiquity* 17:147–148.

Craig, Douglas B. 2001. Environmental and Cultural Setting. In *The Grewe Archaeological Research Project, Volume 1: Project Background and Feature Descriptions*, edited by Douglas B. Craig, pp. 7–16. Anthropological Research

Papers No. 99-1. Northland Research, Flagstaff, Arizona.

Craig, Douglas B. (editor). 2011. *Archaeological and Geoarchaeological Investigations Along the Santa Cruz River Floodplain: The Pima County Plant Interconnect Project*. Technical Report No. 09-47. Northland Research, Tempe, Arizona.

Crotty, Helen K. 1983. *Honoring the Dead: Anasazi Ceramics from the Rainbow Bridge-Monument Valley Expedition*. Monograph Series No. 22. Museum of Cultural History, University of California, Los Angeles.

Crown, Patricia L. 1981. Analysis of the Las Colinas Ceramics. In *The 1968 Excavations at Mound 8, Las Colinas Ruins Group, Phoenix, Arizona*, edited by Laurens C. Hammack and Alan P. Sullivan III, pp. 87–169. Archaeological Series No. 154. Arizona State Museum, University of Arizona, Tucson.

Crown, Patricia L. 1991. The Hohokam: Current Views of Prehistory and the Regional System. In *Chaco and Hohokam: Prehistoric Regional Systems in the American Southwest*, edited by Patricia L. Crown and W. James Judge, pp. 135–157. School of American Research Press, Santa Fe, New Mexico.

Crown, Patricia L. 1994. *Ceramics and Ideology: Salado Polychrome Pottery*. University of New Mexico Press, Albuquerque.

Culin, Stewart. 1907. Games of the North American Indians. In *Twenty-Fourth Annual Report of the Bureau of American Ethnology for the Years 1902–1903*, pp. 3–811. Government Printing Office, Washington, D.C.

Cummings, Byron. 1910. *The Ancient Inhabitants of the San Juan Valley*. Bulletin of the University of Utah, Vol. 3, No. 2, Pt. 2. Second Archaeological Number. University of Utah, Salt Lake City.

Cummings, Byron. 1940. *Kinishba: A Prehistoric Pueblo of the Great Pueblo Period*. Hohokam Museums Association, Tucson, Arizona; University of Arizona, Tucson.

Danson, Edward B. 1957. Appendix G: Pottery Type Descriptions. In *Excavations, 1940, at University Indian Ruin*, by Julian D. Hayden, pp. 219–231. Technical Series Vol. 5. Southwestern Monuments Association, Gila Pueblo, Globe, Arizona.

Danson, Edward B., and Roberts M. Wallace. 1956. A Petrographic Study of Gila Polychrome. *American Antiquity* 22:180–183.

Davis, Owen K., Tom Minckley, Tom Moutoux, Tim Jull, and Bob Kalin. 2002. The Transformation of Sonoran Desert Wetlands Following the Historic Decrease of Burning. *Journal of Arid Environments* 50:393–412.

Davis, Owen K., and Raymond M. Turner. 1986. Palynological Evidence for the Historic Expansion of Juniper and Desert Shrubs in Arizona, U.S.A. *Review of Palaeobotany and Palynology* 49:177–193.

Dean, Jeffrey S. 1969. *Chronological Analysis of Tsegi Phase Sites in Northeastern Arizona*. Papers of the Laboratory of Tree-Ring Research No. 3. University of Arizona Press, Tucson.

Dean, Jeffrey S. 2000. Introduction: The Salado Phenomenon. In *Salado*, edited by Jeffrey S. Dean, pp. 3–16. Amerind Foundation New World Studies Series No. 4. Amerind Foundation, Dragoon, Arizona; University of New Mexico Press, Albuquerque.

Dean, Jeffrey S. (editor). 2000. *Salado*. Amerind Foundation New World Studies Series No. 4. Amerind Foundation, Dragoon, Arizona; University of New Mexico Press, Albuquerque.

Dean, Jeffrey S., Mark C. Slaughter, and Dennie O. Bowden III. 1996. Desert Dendrochronology: Tree-Ring Dating Prehistoric Sites in the Tucson Basin. *Kiva* 62:7–26.

Deaver, William L. 1984. Pottery. In *Hohokam Habitation Sites in the Northern Santa Rita Mountains*, by Alan Ferg, Kenneth C. Rozen, William L. Deaver, Martyn D. Tagg, David A. Phillips Jr., and David A. Gregory, pp. 237–419. Archaeological Series No. 147, Vol. 2. Arizona State Museum, University of Arizona, Tucson.

Deaver, William L. 1989. Pottery and Other Ceramic Artifacts. In *The 1979–1983 Testing at*

Los Morteros (AZ AA:12:57): A Large Hohokam Village Site in the Tucson Basin, by Richard C. Lange and William L. Deaver, pp. 27–81. Archaeological Series No. 177. Arizona State Museum, University of Arizona, Tucson.

Deaver, William L. 1990. Native American Ceramics. In *Archaeology of the Ak-Chin Indian Community West Side Farms Project, Volume 4: Material Culture and Human Remains*, compiled by Robert E. Gasser, Christine K. Robinson, and Cory Dale Breternitz, pp. 15.1–15.21. Publications in Archaeology No. 9. Soil Systems, Phoenix, Arizona.

Deaver, William L., and Carla R. Van West (editors). 2001. *El Macayo: A Prehistoric Settlement in the Upper Santa Cruz River Valley.* Technical Series No. 74. Statistical Research, Tucson, Arizona.

Devitt, Mathew A. 2006. Potrests and the Potential of Worked Sherds in Migration Studies. *Glyphs* 56(7):6–7.

Devitt, Mathew A., and Patrick D. Lyons. 2012. Appendix D: Modified Sherds, San Pedro Preservation Project. In *Migrants and Mounds: Classic Period Archaeology of the Lower San Pedro Valley*, edited by Jeffery J. Clark and Patrick D. Lyons, pp. 443–456. Anthropological Papers No. 45. Archaeology Southwest, Tucson, Arizona.

Di Peso, Charles C. 1951a. *The Babocomari Village Site on the Babocomari River, Southeastern Arizona.* Amerind Foundation No. 5. Amerind Foundation, Dragoon, Arizona.

Di Peso, Charles C. 1951b. A Ball Court Located on the San Pedro River in Southeastern Arizona. *American Antiquity* 16:257–260.

Di Peso, Charles C. 1953. *The Sobaipuri Indians of the Upper San Pedro River Valley, Southeastern Arizona.* Amerind Foundation No. 6. Amerind Foundation, Dragoon, Arizona.

Di Peso, Charles C. 1956. *The Upper Pima of San Cayetano del Tumacacori: An Archaeohistorical Reconstruction of the Ootam of the Pimeria Alta.* Amerind Foundation No. 7. Amerind Foundation, Dragoon, Arizona.

Di Peso, Charles C. 1958a. *The Reeve Ruin of Southeastern Arizona: A Study of a Prehistoric Western Pueblo Migration into the Middle San Pedro Valley.* Amerind Foundation No. 8. Amerind Foundation, Dragoon, Arizona.

Di Peso, Charles C. 1958b. Western Pueblo Intrusion into the San Pedro Valley. *Kiva* 23(4):12–16.

Di Peso, Charles C. 1979. Prehistory: O'otam. In *Southwest*, edited by Alfonso Ortiz, pp. 91–99. Handbook of North American Indians, Volume 9, William C. Sturtevant, general editor. Smithsonian Institution, Washington, D.C.

Di Peso, Charles C. 1980. The Hohokam and the O'otam. In *Current Issues in Hohokam Prehistory: Proceedings of a Symposium*, edited by David E. Doyel and Fred Plog, pp. 224–230. Anthropological Research Papers No. 23. Department of Anthropology, Arizona State University, Tempe.

Di Peso, Charles C. 1981. Discussion of Masse, Doelle, Sheridan, and Reff Papers from Southwestern Protohistory Conference. In *The Protohistoric Period in the North American Southwest, A.D. 1450–1700*, edited by David R. Wilcox and W. Bruce Masse, pp. 113–122. Anthropological Research Papers No. 24. Department of Anthropology, Arizona State University, Tempe.

Di Peso, Charles C., John B. Rinaldo, and Gloria J. Fenner. 1974. *Casas Grandes: A Fallen Trading Center of the Gran Chichimeca*, Vol. 8. Amerind Foundation No. 9. Amerind Foundation, Dragoon, Arizona; Northland Press, Flagstaff, Arizona.

Dittert, Alfred E., Jr. 1959. Culture Change in the Cebolleta Mesa Region, Central Western New Mexico. PhD dissertation, Department of Anthropology, University of Arizona, Tucson. ProQuest, Ann Arbor, Michigan.

Dixon, Keith A. 1956. The Archaeological Significance of Certain Unusual Pottery Shapes of the Prehistoric Southwest. PhD dissertation, Department of Anthropology, University of California, Los Angeles.

Dixon, Keith A. 1963. The Interamerican Diffusion of a Cooking Technique: The Culinary Shoe-Pot. *American Anthropologist* 65:593–619.

Dixon, Keith A. 1976. Shoe-Pots, Patajos, and the Principle of Whimsy. *American Antiquity* 41:386–391.

Doelle, William H., Henry D. Wallace, and Jeffery J. Clark. 2012. Lower San Pedro Survey Results and Research Design for Test Excavations. In *Migrants and Mounds: Classic Period Archaeology of the Lower San Pedro Valley*, edited by Jeffery J. Clark and Patrick D. Lyons, pp. 29–65. Anthropological Papers No. 45. Archaeology Southwest, Tucson, Arizona.

Dongoske, Kurt E., Leigh Jenkins, and T. J. Ferguson. 1993. Understanding the Past through Hopi Oral History. *Native Peoples* 6(2):24–31.

Dorsey, George A., and Heinrich R. Voth. 1902. *The Mishongnovi Ceremonies of the Snake and Antelope Fraternities*. Field Columbian Museum Anthropological Series Vol. 3, No. 3. Field Columbian Museum, Chicago.

Douglas, John E. 1987. Late Prehistoric Archaeological Remains in the San Bernardino Valley, Southeastern Arizona. *Kiva* 53:35–51.

Douglas, John E. 1990. Regional Interaction in the Northern Sierra: An Analysis Based on the Late Prehistoric Occupation of the San Bernardino Valley, Southeastern Arizona. PhD Dissertation, Department of Anthropology, University of Arizona, Tucson. ProQuest, Ann Arbor, Michigan.

Douglas, John E. 1995. Autonomy and Regional Systems in the Late Prehistoric Southern Southwest. *American Antiquity* 60:240–257.

Douglas, John E. 1996. Distinguishing Change During the Animas Phase (A.D. 1150–1450) at the Boss Ranch Site, Southeastern Arizona. *North American Archaeologist* 17:183–202.

Douglas, John E. 2007. Making and Breaking Boundaries in the Hinterlands: The Social and Settlement Dynamics of Far Southeastern Arizona and Southwestern New Mexico. In *Hinterlands and Regional Dynamics in the Ancient Southwest*, edited by Alan P. Sullivan III and James M. Bayman, pp. 97–108. University of Arizona Press, Tucson.

Douglas, John E. 2014. Social Identity and Change at Ceramic Period Settlements in and near Far Southeastern Arizona. In *Between Mimbres and Hohokam: Exploring the Archaeology and History of Southeastern Arizona and Southwestern New Mexico*, edited by Henry D. Wallace, pp. 323–348. Anthropological Papers No. 52. Archaeology Southwest, Tucson, Arizona.

Douglass, A. E. 1935. *Dating Pueblo Bonito and Other Ruins of the Southwest*. Contributed Technical Papers, Pueblo Bonito Series No. 1. National Geographic Society, Washington, D.C.

Douglass, A. E. 1938. Southwestern Dated Ruins: V. *Tree-Ring Bulletin* 5(2):10–13.

Doyel, David E. 1974. *Excavations in the Escalante Ruin Group, Southern Arizona*. Archaeological Series No. 37. Arizona State Museum, University of Arizona, Tucson.

Doyel, David E. 1977. *Excavations in the Middle Santa Cruz River Valley, Southeastern Arizona*. Contribution to Highway Salvage Archaeology in Arizona No. 44. Arizona State Museum, University of Arizona, Tucson.

Doyel, David E. 1978. *The Miami Wash Project: Hohokam and Salado in the Globe-Miami Area, Central Arizona*. Contribution to Highway Salvage Archaeology in Arizona No. 52. Arizona State Museum, University of Arizona, Tucson.

Doyel, David E. 2000. In Pursuit of the Salado in the Sonoran Desert. In *Salado*, edited by Jeffrey S. Dean, pp. 295–314. Amerind Foundation New World Studies Series No. 4. Amerind Foundation, Dragoon, Arizona; University of New Mexico Press, Albuquerque.

Doyel, David E., and Emil W. Haury (editors). 1976. The 1976 Salado Conference. *Kiva* 42:1–134.

Duff, Andrew I. L. 2002. *Western Pueblo Identities*. University of Arizona Press, Tucson.

Duffen, William A. 1936a. 76 Ranch Site: Notes from the 1936 Excavations. Manuscript on file,

Library and Archives, Arizona State Museum, University of Arizona, Tucson.

Duffen, William A. 1936b. Development of Human Culture in the San Pedro River Valley, Arizona. Master's thesis, Department of Archaeology, University of Arizona, Tucson.

Duffen, William A. 1937. Some Notes on a Summer's Work near Bonita, Arizona. *Kiva* 2(4):13–16.

Duffen, William A., and William K. Hartmann. 1997. The 76 Ranch Ruin and the Location of Chichilticale. In *The Coronado Expedition to Tierra Nueva: The 1540–1542 Route Across the Southwest*, edited by Richard Flint and Shirley Cushing Flint, pp. 158–175. University Press of Colorado, Niwot.

Eighmy, Jeffrey L., and David E. Doyel. 1987. A Reanalysis of First Reported Archeomagnetic Dates from the Hohokam Area, Southern Arizona. *Journal of Field Archaeology* 14:331–342.

Eiseman, Fred B. 1959. The Hopi Salt Trail. *Plateau* 32(2):25–32.

Ellis, Florence Hawley. 1952. Jemez Kiva Magic and its Relation to Features of Prehistoric Kivas. *Southwestern Journal of Anthropology* 8:147–163.

Elson, Mark D., Miriam T. Stark, and David A. Gregory. 2000. Tonto Basin Local Systems: Implications for Cultural Affiliation and Migration. In *Salado*, edited by Jeffrey S. Dean, pp. 167–191. Amerind Foundation New World Studies Series No. 4. Amerind Foundation, Dragoon, Arizona; University of New Mexico Press, Albuquerque.

Fenner, Gloria J. 1977. History and Scope of the Amerind Foundation. *Kiva* 42:317–329.

Ferg, Alan. 1982. One page of typed notes documenting a personal communication from Emil W. Haury to Patricia L. Crown regarding the attributes of San Carlos Red-on-brown. Manuscript on file, Emil W. Haury Papers, MS 3, Library and Archives, Arizona State Museum, University of Arizona, Tucson.

Ferg, Alan. 1997. Cienega Phase Rare Artifacts: Finding Their Place in Prehistory. *Archaeology in Tucson* 11(3):8–9.

Ferg, Alan. 1998. Rare Stone, Fired Clay, Bone, and Shell Artifacts. In *Archaeological Investigations of Early Village Sites in the Middle Santa Cruz Valley: Analyses and Synthesis, Part II*, edited by Jonathan B. Mabry, pp. 545–654. Anthropological Papers No. 19. Center for Desert Archaeology, Tucson, Arizona.

Ferg, Alan. 2003. Traditional Western Apache Mescal Gathering as Recorded by Historical Photographs and Museum Collections. *Desert Plants* 19(2):1–56.

Ferguson, T. J., and Chip Colwell-Chanthaphonh. 2006. *History Is in the Land: Multivocal Tribal Traditions in Arizona's San Pedro Valley*. University of Arizona Press, Tucson.

Ferguson, T. J., and Micah Lomaomvaya. 1999. *Hoopoq'yaqam niqw Wukoskyavi (Those Who Went to the Northeast and Tonto Basin): Hopi-Salado Cultural Affiliation Study*. Hopi Cultural Preservation Office, Hopi Tribe, Kykotsmovi, Arizona.

Fewkes, J. Walter. 1892. A Few Summer Ceremonials at the Tusayan Pueblos. In *A Journal of American Ethnology and Archaeology*, Vol. 2, edited by J. Walter Fewkes, pp. 1–159. Houghton, Mifflin, Boston, Massachusetts.

Fewkes, J. Walter. 1898. Archeological Expedition to Arizona in 1895. In *Seventeenth Annual Report of the Bureau of American Ethnology for the Years 1895–1896, Part 2*, pp. 519–752. Government Printing Office, Washington, D.C.

Fewkes, J. Walter. 1899. The Alósaka Cult of the Hopi Indians. *American Anthropologist* (n.s.) 1:522–544.

Fewkes, J. Walter. 1904. Two Summers' Work in Pueblo Ruins. In *Twenty-Second Annual Report of the Bureau of American Ethnology for the Years 1900–1901, Part 1*, pp. 3–195. Smithsonian Institution, Washington, D.C.

Fewkes, J. Walter. 1908. Ventilators in Ceremonial Rooms of Prehistoric Cliff-Dwellings. *American Anthropologist* 10:387–398.

Fewkes, J. Walter. 1911. *Preliminary Report on a Visit to the Navaho National Monument, Arizona.* Bureau of American Ethnology Bulletin No. 50. Government Printing Office, Washington, D.C.

Fish, Paul R., and Suzanne K. Fish. 1999. Reflections on the Casas Grandes Regional System from the Northwestern Periphery. In *The Casas Grandes World*, edited by Curtis F. Schaafsma and Carroll L. Riley, pp. 27–42. University of Utah Press, Salt Lake City.

Fish, Paul R., and Suzanne K. Fish. 2006. Malpais Borderlands Prehistory. In *Prehistory and Early History of the Malpais Borderlands: Archaeological Synthesis and Recommendations*, by Paul R. Fish, Suzanne K. Fish, and John H. Madsen, pp. 23–43. Rocky Mountain Research Station General Technical Report RMRS-GTR-176. U.S. Department of Agriculture, U.S. Forest Service, Fort Collins, Colorado.

Fish, Suzanne K. 1985. Prehistoric Disturbance Floras of the Lower Sonoran Desert and Their Implications. In *Late Quaternary Vegetation and Climates of the American Southwest*, edited by Bonnie F. Jacobs, Patricia L. Fall, and Owen K. Davis, pp. 77–88. Contributions Series No. 16. American Association of Stratigraphic Palynologists Foundation, Dallas, Texas.

Fish, Suzanne K. 1994. Archaeological Palynology of Gardens and Fields. In *The Archaeology of Garden and Field*, edited by Naomi F. Miller and Kathryn L. Gleason, pp. 44–69. University of Pennsylvania Press, Philadelphia.

Fish, Suzanne K., Paul R. Fish, and John H. Madsen (editors). 1992. *The Marana Community in the Hohokam World.* Anthropological Papers of the University of Arizona No. 56. University of Arizona Press, Tucson.

Fontana, Bernard L., William J. Robinson, Charles W. Cormack, and Ernest E. Leavitt Jr. 1962. *Papago Indian Pottery.* Monographs of the American Ethnological Society No. 38. University of Washington Press, Seattle.

Fortenberry, Nanabell, and Gladys Bennett. 1968. Potsherd Study at Dutch Ruin. Manuscript on file, Library and Archives, Arizona State Museum, University of Arizona, Tucson.

Foster, Michael S. 1994. Intrusive Ceramics. In *The Pueblo Grande Project, Volume 4: Material Culture*, edited by Michael S. Foster, pp. 119–165. Publications in Archaeology No. 20. Soil Systems, Phoenix, Arizona.

Franklin, Hayward H. 1980. *Excavations at Second Canyon Ruin, San Pedro Valley, Arizona.* Contribution to Highway Salvage Archaeology in Arizona No. 60. Arizona State Museum, University of Arizona, Tucson.

Franklin, Hayward H., and W. Bruce Masse. 1976. The San Pedro Salado: A Case of Prehistoric Migration. *Kiva* 42:47–55.

Fulton, William S. 1934a. *Archeological Notes on Texas Canyon, Arizona.* Contributions from the Museum of the American Indian Heye Foundation Vol. 12, No. 1. Museum of the American Indian, New York.

Fulton, William S. 1934b. *Archeological Notes on Texas Canyon, Arizona.* Contributions from the Museum of the American Indian Heye Foundation Vol. 12, No. 2. Museum of the American Indian, New York.

Fulton, William S. 1938. *Archeological Notes on Texas Canyon, Arizona.* Contributions from the Museum of the American Indian Heye Foundation Vol. 12, No. 3. Museum of the American Indian, New York.

Fulton, William S., and Carr Tuthill. 1940. *An Archaeological Site Near Gleeson, Arizona.* Amerind Foundation No. 1. Amerind Foundation, Dragoon, Arizona.

Gabel, Norman. 1931. Martinez Hill Ruins: An Example of Prehistoric Culture of the Middle Gila. Master's thesis, College of Letters, Arts and Sciences, University of Arizona, Tucson.

Gann, Douglas W. 1995. The Adobe Pueblo Site: Investigations in Prehispanic Adobe Brick Architecture. Master's thesis, Department of Anthropology, University of Arizona, Tucson.

Geertz, Armin W., and Michael Lomatuway'ma. 1987. *Children of Cottonwood: Piety and*

Ceremonialism in Hopi Indian Puppetry. University of Nebraska Press, Lincoln.

Geib, Phil R. 1985. Site Descriptions. In *Archaeological Investigations near Rainbow City, Navajo Mountain, Utah*, edited by Phil R. Geib, J. Richard Ambler, and Martha M. Callahan, pp. 69–240. Northern Arizona University Archaeological Report No. 576. Northern Arizona University, Flagstaff.

Geib, Phil R. 1996. *Glen Canyon Revisited*. University of Utah Anthropological Papers No. 119. University of Utah Press, Salt Lake City.

Genovés, Santiago. 1967. Proportionality of the Long Bones and Their Relation to Stature Among Mesoamericans. *American Journal of Physical Anthropology* 26:67–77.

Gerald, Rex E. 1957a. Haby Dig Site-Field Notes (ARIZONA:BB:3:1[AF]). Manuscript on file, Archives, Amerind Museum, Dragoon, Arizona.

Gerald, Rex E. 1957b. A Historic House Excavation Near Janos, Northwest Chihuahua, Mexico. Master's thesis, Department of Anthropology, University of Pennsylvania, Philadelphia.

Gerald, Rex E. 1958. A Pueblo Kiva in Southeastern Arizona. Paper presented at the 23rd Annual Meeting of the Society for American Archaeology, Norman, Oklahoma.

Gerald, Rex E. 1968. *Spanish Presidios of the Late Eighteenth Century in Northern New Spain*. Museum of New Mexico Research Records No. 7. Museum of New Mexico Press, Santa Fe.

Gerald, Rex E. 1975. Drought Correlated Changes in Two Prehistoric Pueblo Communities in Southeastern Arizona. PhD dissertation, Department of Anthropology, University of Chicago, Chicago. ProQuest, Ann Arbor, Michigan

Germeshausen, Edward. 1972. Appendix II: Report of Test Excavations on Sites AA:5:6, AA:5:7, and AA:5:8. In *An Archaeological Survey of the Santa Rosa Wash Project*, assembled by Veletta Canouts, pp. 132–144. Archaeological Series No. 18. Arizona State Museum, University of Arizona, Tucson.

Gifford, Edward W. 1932. *The Southeastern Yavapai*. University of California Publications in American Archaeology and Ethnology Vol. 29, No. 3. University of California Press, Berkeley.

Gifford, Edward W. 1947. *Californian Shell Artifacts*. University of California Anthropological Records Vol. 9, No. 1. University of California Press, Berkley.

Gifford, James C. 1980. *Archaeological Explorations in Caves of the Point of Pines Region, Arizona*. Anthropological Papers of the University of Arizona No. 36. University of Arizona Press, Tucson.

Gifford, James C., and Watson Smith. 1978. *Gray Corrugated Pottery from Awatovi and Other Jeddito Sites in Northeastern Arizona*. Papers of the Peabody Museum of Archaeology and Ethnology Vol. 69. Harvard University, Cambridge, Massachusetts.

Gilman, Patricia A. 2011. Between Mimbres and Hohokam: The San Simon Basin During the Pit Structure Period. *Kiva* 76:277–295.

Gladwin, Harold S. 1936. Discussion. In *An Archaeological Survey of Chihuahua, Mexico*, by E. B. Sayles, pp. 89–107. Medallion Papers No. 22. Gila Pueblo, Globe, Arizona.

Gladwin, Harold S. 1957. *A History of the Ancient Southwest*. Bond Wheelwright Company, Portland, Maine.

Gladwin, Harold S., Emil W. Haury, E. B. Sayles, and Nora Gladwin. 1937. *Excavations at Snaketown: Material Culture*. Medallion Papers No. 25. Gila Pueblo, Globe, Arizona.

Gladwin, Winifred, and Harold S. Gladwin. 1929. *The Red-on-Buff Culture of the Gila Basin*. Medallion Papers No. 3. Gila Pueblo, Globe, Arizona.

Gladwin, Winifred, and Harold S. Gladwin. 1930. *Some Southwestern Pottery Types: Series I*. Medallion Papers No. 8. Gila Pueblo, Globe, Arizona.

Gladwin, Winifred, and Harold S. Gladwin. 1933. *Some Southwestern Pottery Types: Series III*. Medallion Papers No. 13. Gila Pueblo, Globe, Arizona.

Gladwin, Winifred, and Harold S. Gladwin. 1934. *A Method for Designation of Cultures and Their Variations*. Medallion Papers No. 15. Gila Pueblo, Globe, Arizona.

Gladwin, Winifred, and Harold S. Gladwin. 1935. *The Eastern Range of the Red-on-Buff Culture*. Medallion Papers No. 16. Gila Pueblo, Globe, Arizona.

Greenleaf, J. Cameron. 1975. *Excavations at Punta de Agua, in the Santa Cruz River Basin, Southeastern Arizona*. Anthropological Papers of the University of Arizona No. 26. University of Arizona Press, Tucson.

Greenwald, Dawn. 1988. Ground Stone. In *Hohokam Settlement Along the Slopes of the Picacho Mountains, Volume 4: Material Culture, Tucson Aqueduct Project*, edited by Martha M. Callahan, pp. 127–220. Museum of Northern Arizona Research Paper No. 35. Museum of Northern Arizona, Flagstaff.

Gregonis, Linda M. 1996. Cultural Interaction in the Northeastern Tucson Basin: The Gibbon Springs Ceramic Assemblage. In *Excavation of the Gibbon Springs Site: A Classic Period Village in the Northeastern Tucson Basin*, edited by Mark C. Slaughter and Heidi Roberts, pp. 183–258. Archaeological Report No. 94-87. SWCA Environmental Consultants, Tucson, Arizona.

Gregonis, Linda M. 2011. Shell. In *Whiptail Ruin (AZ BB:10:3[ASM]): A Classic Period Community in the Northeastern Tucson Basin*, edited by Linda M. Gregonis and Gayle Harrison Hartmann, pp. 203–218. Archaeological Series No. 203. Arizona State Museum, University of Arizona, Tucson.

Gregonis, Linda M., and W. Bruce Masse (editors). 1996. "Alice Hubbard Carpenter: The Legacy and Context of a Southwestern Avocational Archaeologist." Special issue, *Journal of the Southwest* 38.

Gregory, David A. 1995a. Research Orientation and Research Problems: Prehistoric Sites. In *The San Carlos Reservoir Cultural Resources Survey, Volume I*, edited by Andrew T. Black and Margerie Green, pp. 33–41. Cultural Resources Report No. 87. Archaeological Consulting Services, Tempe, Arizona.

Gregory, David A. 1995b. Prehistoric Ceramic Variability. In *The San Carlos Reservoir Cultural Resources Survey, Volume I*, edited by Andrew T. Black and Margerie Green, pp. 43–50. Cultural Resources Report No. 87. Archaeological Consulting Services, Tempe, Arizona.

Gregory, David A. (editor). 2001. *Excavations in the Santa Cruz River Floodplain: The Early Agricultural Period Component at Los Pozos*. Anthropological Papers No. 21. Center for Desert Archaeology, Tucson, Arizona.

Guernsey, Samuel J. 1931. *Explorations in Northeastern Arizona: Report on the Archaeological Fieldwork of 1920–1923*. Papers of the Peabody Museum of American Archaeology and Ethnology Vol. 12, Pt. 1. Harvard University, Cambridge, Massachusetts.

Guthe, Carl E. 1925. *Pueblo Pottery Making: A Study at the Village of San Ildefonso*. Yale University Press, New Haven, Connecticut.

Hammack, Laurens C. 1971. *The Peppersauce Wash Project: A Preliminary Report on the Salvage Excavation of Four Archaeological Sites in the San Pedro Valley, Southeastern Arizona*. Arizona State Museum, University of Arizona, Tucson.

Hargrave, Lyndon L. 1931. Excavations at Kin Tiel and Kokopnyama. In *Recently Dated Pueblo Ruins in Arizona*, by Emil W. Haury and Lyndon L. Hargrave, pp. 80–120. Smithsonian Miscellaneous Collections Vol. 82, No. 11. Smithsonian Institution, Washington, D.C.

Harlow, Francis H. 1968. Fourteenth Century Painted Pottery from near Cliff, New Mexico. Manuscript on file, Office of Archaeological Studies, Museum of New Mexico, Santa Fe.

Harrill, Bruce. 1986. Architecture. In *The Kayenta Anasazi: Archaeological Investigations Along the Black Mesa Railroad Corridor, Volume 1: Specialists' Reports*, by Sara Stebbins, Bruce Harrill, William D. Wade, Marsha V. Gallagher, Hugh

Cutler, and Leonard Blake, pp. 71–87. Research Paper No. 30. Museum of Northern Arizona, Flagstaff.

Harrington, Mark R. 1930. Paiute Cave. In *Archeological Explorations in Southern Nevada: Report of the First Sessions Expedition*, by Mark R. Harrington, Irwin Hayden, and Louis Schellbach III, pp. 106–126. Papers No. 4. Southwest Museum, Los Angeles.

Harris, Rachel M. 2009. Collecting, Protecting, and Sharing the Past: The History of the Terrence and Jean Reidhead Collection. Undergraduate honors thesis, Department of Anthropology, Brigham Young University, Provo, Utah.

Hastings, James R., and Raymond M. Turner. 1965. *The Changing Mile: An Ecological Study of Vegetation Change with Time in the Lower Mile of an Arid and Semiarid Region*. University of Arizona Press, Tucson.

Haury, Emil W. 1931. Showlow and Pinedale Ruins. In *Recently Dated Pueblo Ruins in Arizona*, by Emil W. Haury and Lyndon L. Hargrave, pp. 4–79. Smithsonian Miscellaneous Collections Vol. 82, No. 11. Smithsonian Institution, Washington, D.C.

Haury, Emil W. 1934. *The Canyon Creek Ruin and the Cliff Dwellings of the Sierra Ancha*. Medallion Papers No. 14. Gila Pueblo, Globe, Arizona.

Haury, Emil W. 1936. *The Mogollon Culture of Southwestern New Mexico*. Medallion Papers No. 20. Gila Pueblo, Globe, Arizona.

Haury, Emil W. 1937a. Pottery Types at Snaketown. In *Excavations at Snaketown: Material Culture*, by Harold S. Gladwin, Emil W. Haury, E. B. Sayles, and Nora Gladwin, pp. 169–229. Medallion Papers No. 25. Gila Pueblo, Globe, Arizona.

Haury, Emil W. 1937b. Stone: Palettes and Ornaments. In *Excavations at Snaketown: Material Culture*, by Harold S. Gladwin, Emil W. Haury, E. B. Sayles, and Nora Gladwin, pp. 121–134. Medallion Papers No. 25. Gila Pueblo, Globe, Arizona.

Haury, Emil W. 1937c. Shell. In *Excavations at Snaketown: Material Culture*, by Harold S. Gladwin, Emil W. Haury, E. B. Sayles, and Nora Gladwin, pp. 135–153. Medallion Papers No. 25. Gila Pueblo, Globe, Arizona.

Haury, Emil W. 1940. *Excavations in the Forestdale Valley, East-Central Arizona*. University of Arizona Bulletin Vol. 11, No. 4. Social Science Bulletin No. 12. University of Arizona, Tucson.

Haury, Emil W. 1945. *The Excavation of Los Muertos and Neighboring Ruins in the Salt River Valley, Southern Arizona, Based on the Work of the Hemenway Southwestern Archaeological Expedition of 1887–1888*. Papers of the Peabody Museum of American Archaeology and Ethnology Vol. 24, Pt. 1. Harvard University, Cambridge, Massachusetts.

Haury, Emil W. 1949. Sherds Identified by E. W. Haury. In *The Pendleton Ruin, Hidalgo County, New Mexico*, by Alfred V. Kidder, Harriet S. Cosgrove, and C. Burton Cosgrove, pp. 137–138. Contributions to American Anthropology and History 10, No. 50, Publication 585. Carnegie Institution of Washington, Washington, D.C.

Haury, Emil W. 1950. Material Culture. In *The Stratigraphy and Archaeology of Ventana Cave*, by Emil W. Haury, Kirk Bryan, Edwin H. Colbert, Norman E. Gabel, Clara Lee Tanner, and T. E. Buehrer, pp. 170–459. University of Arizona Press, Tucson.

Haury, Emil W. 1957. An Alluvial Site on the San Carlos Indian Reservation, Arizona. *American Antiquity* 23:2–27.

Haury, Emil W. 1958. Evidence at Point of Pines for a Prehistoric Migration from Northern Arizona. In *Migrations in New World Culture History*, edited by Raymond H. Thompson, pp. 1–6. University of Arizona Bulletin Vol. 29, No. 2. Social Science Bulletin No. 27. University of Arizona Press, Tucson.

Haury, Emil W. 1976. *The Hohokam, Desert Farmers and Craftsmen: Excavations at Snaketown, 1964–1965*. University of Arizona Press, Tucson.

Haury, Emil W. 1989. *Point of Pines, Arizona: A History of the University of Arizona Archaeological Field School.* Anthropological Papers of the University of Arizona No. 50. University of Arizona Press, Tucson.

Haury, Emil W., Kirk Bryan, Edwin H. Colbert, Norman E. Gabel, Clara Lee Tanner, and T. E. Buehrer. 1950. *The Stratigraphy and Archaeology of Ventana Cave.* University of Arizona Press, Tucson.

Hawley, Florence M. 1928. Pottery and Cultural Relations in the Middle Gila. Master's thesis, College of Letters, Arts, and Sciences, University of Arizona, Tucson.

Hawley, Florence M. 1932. The Bead Mountain Pueblos of Southern Arizona. *Art and Archaeology* 33(5):227–236.

Hawley, Florence M. 1936. *Field Manual of Prehistoric Southwestern Pottery Types.* University of New Mexico Bulletin No. 291. Anthropological Series Vol. 1, No. 4. University of New Mexico Press, Albuquerque.

Hawley, Florence M. 1950a. Big Kivas, Little Kivas, and Moiety Houses in Historical Reconstruction. *Southwestern Journal of Anthropology* 6:286–302.

Hawley, Florence M. 1950b. *Field Manual of Prehistoric Southwestern Pottery Types.* Rev. ed. University of New Mexico Bulletin No. 291. Anthropological Series Vol. 1, No. 4. University of New Mexico, Albuquerque.

Hawley, Fred G. 1937. Chemical Investigation of the Incrustation on Pottery Vessels and Palettes from Snaketown. In *Excavations at Snaketown: Material Culture*, by Harold S. Gladwin, Emil W. Haury, E. B. Sayles, and Nora Gladwin, pp. 282–289. Medallion Papers No. 25. Gila Pueblo, Globe, Arizona.

Hayden, Julian D. 1957. *Excavations, 1940, at University Indian Ruin.* Technical Series Vol. 5. Southwestern Monuments Association, Gila Pueblo, Globe, Arizona.

Heacock Erika, and Arthur Vokes. 2013. Analysis and Reanalysis of Ornament Assemblages in the Arizona State Museum Collections: Ash Terrace (AZ BB:2:19[ASM]), ASM Acc. AP-1995-123; Second Canyon Ruin (AZ BB:11:20[ASM]), ASM Acc. AP-2482; Rabid Ruin (AZ AA:12:46[ASM]), ASM Acc. AP-2165, AP-1990-120, AP-2008-136, AP-2010-396; University Indian Ruin (AZ BB:9:33[ASM]), ASM Acc. AP-CU, AP-70. Forms on file, Collections Division, Arizona State Museum, University of Arizona, Tucson.

Heckman, Robert A. 2000a. The Tucson Basin Tradition. In *Prehistoric Painted Pottery of Southeastern Arizona*, by Robert A. Heckman, Barbara K. Montgomery, and Stephanie M. Whittlesey, pp. 83–94. Technical Series No. 77. Statistical Research, Tucson, Arizona.

Heckman, Robert A. 2000b. The Babocomari Tradition. In *Prehistoric Painted Pottery of Southeastern Arizona*, by Robert A. Heckman, Barbara K. Montgomery, and Stephanie M. Whittlesey, pp. 23–41. Technical Series No. 77. Statistical Research, Tucson, Arizona.

Heckman, Robert A. 2000c. The San Simon Tradition. In *Prehistoric Painted Pottery of Southeastern Arizona*, by Robert A. Heckman, Barbara K. Montgomery, and Stephanie M. Whittlesey, pp. 63–74. Technical Series No. 77. Statistical Research, Tucson, Arizona.

Heckman, Robert A. 2000d. The Dragoon Tradition. In *Prehistoric Painted Pottery of Southeastern Arizona*, by Robert A. Heckman, Barbara K. Montgomery, and Stephanie M. Whittlesey, pp. 43–62. Technical Series No. 77. Statistical Research, Tucson, Arizona.

Heckman, Robert A. 2000e. The Trincheras Tradition. In *Prehistoric Painted Pottery of Southeastern Arizona*, by Robert A. Heckman, Barbara K. Montgomery, and Stephanie M. Whittlesey, pp. 75–81. Technical Series No. 77. Statistical Research, Tucson, Arizona.

Heckman, Robert A., and Stephanie M. Whittlesey. 1999. Ceramics. In *Investigations at Sunset Mesa Ruin*, edited by Richard Ciolek-Torrello, Edgar K. Huber, and Robert B. Neily, pp. 87–133. Technical Series No. 66. Statistical Research, Tucson, Arizona.

Heckman, Robert A., and Stephanie M. Whittlesey. 2000. Concluding Thoughts. In *Prehistoric Painted Pottery of Southeastern Arizona*, by Robert A. Heckman, Barbara K. Montgomery, and Stephanie M. Whittlesey, pp. 117–127. Technical Series No. 77. Statistical Research, Tucson, Arizona.

Hegmon, Michelle, Margaret C. Nelson, Roger Anyon, Darrell Creel, Steven A. LeBlanc, and Harry J. Shafer. 1999. Scale and Time-Space Systematics in the Post-A.D. 1100 Mimbres Region of the North American Southwest. *Kiva* 65:143–166.

Heidke, James M. 1995. Ceramic Analysis. In *Archaeological Investigations at Los Morteros, a Prehistoric Settlement in the Northern Tucson Basin*, edited by Henry D. Wallace, pp. 263–442. Anthropological Papers No. 17. Center for Desert Archaeology, Tucson, Arizona.

Heidke, James M. 2000. Middle Rincon Phase Ceramic Artifacts from Sunset Mesa. In *Excavations at Sunset Mesa Ruin*, edited by Michael W. Lindeman, pp. 75–117. Technical Report No. 2000-02. Desert Archaeology, Tucson, Arizona.

Henderson, T. Kathleen. 1993. Perspectives on the Classic Period Occupation of the Santa Cruz Flats. In *Classic Period Occupation on the Santa Cruz Flats: The Santa Cruz Flats Archaeological Project*, edited by T. Kathleen Henderson and Richard J. Martynec, pp. 579–596. Northland Research, Flagstaff, Arizona.

Henderson, T. Kathleen. 2002. Chronology. In *The Grewe Archaeological Research Project, Volume 1: Project Background and Feature Descriptions*, edited by Douglas B. Craig, pp. 163–207. Anthropological Research Papers No. 99-1. Northland Research, Flagstaff, Arizona.

Henderson, T. Kathleen, and Richard J. Martynec (editors). 1993. *Classic Period Occupation on the Santa Cruz Flats: The Santa Cruz Flats Archaeological Project*. Northland Research, Flagstaff, Arizona.

Herr, Sarah. 1993. Broken Pots as Tools. In *Across the Colorado Plateau: Anthropological Studies for the Transwestern Pipeline Expansion Project, Volume XVI: Interpretation of Ceramic Artifacts*, by Barbara J. Mills, Christine E. Goetze, and María Nieves Zedeño, pp. 347–376. Office of Contract Archaeology and Maxwell Museum of Anthropology, University of New Mexico, Albuquerque.

Hester, Thomas R., and Robert F. Heizer. 1972. Problems in the Functional Interpretation of Artifacts: Scraper Planes from Mitla and Yagul, Oaxaca. *Contributions of the University of California Archaeological Research Facility* 14:107–123.

Hewitt, Nancy J., and Joel M. Brisbin. 1989. Site AZ J-31-2. In *Kayenta Anasazi Archaeology and Navajo Ethnohistory on the Northwestern Shonto Plateau: The N-16 Project*, edited by Alan R. Schroedl, pp. 381–460. Cultural Resources Report 412-01-8909. P-III Associates, Salt Lake City, Utah.

Hill, J. Brett, Jeffery J. Clark, William H. Doelle, and Patrick D. Lyons. 2004. Prehistoric Demography in the Southwest: Migration, Coalescence, and Hohokam Population Decline. *American Antiquity* 69:689–716.

Hill, J. Brett, Patrick D. Lyons, Jeffery J. Clark, and William H. Doelle. 2015. The "Collapse" of Cooperative Hohokam Irrigation in the Lower Salt River Valley. *Journal of the Southwest* 57:609–673.

Hill, James N. 1970. *Broken K Pueblo: Prehistoric Social Organization in the American Southwest.* Anthropological Papers of the University of Arizona No. 18. University of Arizona Press, Tucson.

Hill, Kenneth C., Emory Sekaquaptewa, Mary E. Black, Ekkehart Malotki, and Michael Lomatuway'ma. 1998. *Hopi Dictionary (*Hopìikwa Lavàytutuveni*): A Hopi-English Dictionary of the Third Mesa Dialect.* University of Arizona Press, Tucson.

Hodge, F. W. 1921. *Turquois Work of Hawikuh, New Mexico.* Leaflets of the Museum of the

American Indian Heye Foundation No. 2. Museum of the American Indian, New York.

Hodge, F. W. 1939. A Square Kiva at Hawikuh. In *So Live the Works of Men: Seventieth Anniversary Volume Honoring Edgar Lee Hewett*, edited by Donald D. Brand and Fred E. Harvey, pp. 195–214. University of New Mexico Press, Albuquerque; School of American Research, Santa Fe, New Mexico.

Hodge, F. W. 1966. The Plaza Trench and Its Disclosures. In *The Excavation of Hawikuh by Frederick Webb Hodge: Report of the Hendricks-Hodge Expedition, 1917–1923*, edited by Watson Smith, Richard B. Woodbury, and Nathalie F. S. Woodbury, pp. 150–172. Contributions from the Museum of the American Indian Heye Foundation Vol. 20. Museum of the American Indian, New York.

Hoffman, Charles M. 1997. Alliance Formation and Social Interaction During the Sedentary Period: A Stylistic Analysis of Hohokam Arrowpoints. PhD dissertation, Department of Anthropology, Arizona State University, Tempe. ProQuest, Ann Arbor, Michigan.

Hohmann, John W., and David Eshbaugh. 1988. Investigations at Roger's Cliff Ruin. In *Erich F. Schmidt's Investigations of Salado Sites in Central Arizona*, by John W. Hohmann and Linda B. Kelley, pp. 91–108. Museum of Northern Arizona Bulletin No. 56. Museum of Northern Arizona Press, Flagstaff.

Hohmann, John W., Stephen Germick, and Christopher D. Adams. 1992. Discovery of a Salado Ceremonial Room. In *Proceedings of the Second Salado Conference, Globe, AZ, 1992*, edited by Richard C. Lange and Stephen Germick, pp. 92–102. Occasional Paper. Arizona Archaeological Society, Phoenix.

Holmer, Richard N., and Dennis G. Weder. 1980. Common Post-Archaic Projectile Points of the Fremont Area. In *Fremont Perspectives*, edited by David B. Madsen, pp. 55–68. Antiquities Section Selected Papers Vol. 7, No. 16. Division of State History, Utah State Historical Society, Salt Lake City.

Hough, Walter. 1903. Archeological Fieldwork in Northeastern Arizona: The Museum-Gates Expedition of 1901. In *Annual Report of the United States National Museum for 1901*, pp. 279–358. Government Printing Office, Washington, D.C.

Hough, Walter. 1918. The Hopi Indian Collection in the United States National Museum. *Proceedings of the United States National Museum* 54(2235):23–296.

Hough, Walter. 1930. Exploration of Ruins in the White Mountain Apache Indian Reservation, Arizona. *Proceedings of the United States National Museum* 78(13):1–21.

Howard, Ann Valdo. 1987. The La Ciudad Shell Assemblage. In *Specialized Studies in the Economy, Environment and Culture of La Ciudad*, edited by Jo Ann E. Kisselburg, Glen E. Rice, and Brenda L. Shears, pp. 75–174. Anthropological Field Studies No. 20. Office of Cultural Resource Management, Department of Anthropology, Arizona State University, Tempe.

Huckell, Bruce B. 1988. Late Archaic Archaeology of the Tucson Basin: A Status Report. In *Recent Research on Tucson Basin Prehistory*, edited by William H. Doelle and Paul R. Fish, pp. 57–80. Anthropological Papers No. 10. Institute for American Research, Tucson, Arizona.

Huckell, Bruce B. 1995. *Of Marshes and Maize: Preceramic Agricultural Settlements in the Cienega Valley, Southeastern Arizona*. Anthropological Papers of the University of Arizona No. 59. University of Arizona Press, Tucson.

Huckell, Bruce B., and Lisa W. Huckell. 1982. Archaeological Test Excavations at Tubac State Park, Arizona. In *Archaeological Test Excavations in Southern Arizona*, compiled by Susan A. Brew, pp. 63–102. Archaeological Series No. 152. Arizona State Museum, University of Arizona, Tucson.

Huckell, Lisa W. 1976. Analysis of the Shell Remains from the Rabid Ruin, Arizona. Manuscript on file, Library and Archives, Arizona State Museum, University of Arizona, Tucson.

Huntington, Frederick W. 1986. *Archaeological Investigations at the West Branch Site: Early and*

Middle Rincon Occupation in the Southern Tucson Basin. Anthropological Papers No. 5. Institute for American Research, Tucson, Arizona.

Huntley, Deborah L., Jeffery J. Clark, Robert Jones, and Katherine Dungan. 2010. Get Back: Kayenta and Salado Migrations into Southwest New Mexico. In *The Collected Papers from the 15th Biennial Mogollon Conference, Silver City, New Mexico*, edited by Lora Jackson Legare, pp. 51–72. Special Report No. 12. El Paso Archaeological Society, El Paso, Texas.

Huntley, Deborah L., Jeffery J. Clark, and Mary F. Ownby. 2016. Movement of People and Pots in the Upper Gila Region of the American Southwest. In *Exploring Cause and Explanation in Historical Ecology, Demography, and Movement in the American Southwest*, edited by Cynthia L. Herhahn and Ann F. Ramenofsky, pp. 275–295. University Press of Colorado, Boulder.

Jackson, Earl, and Sallie Pierce Van Valkenburgh. 1954. *Montezuma Castle Archaeology, Part I: Excavations*. Technical Series Vol. 3, No. 1. Southwestern Monuments Association, Gila Pueblo, Globe, Arizona.

James, Harry C. 1990. *Pages from Hopi History*. University of Arizona Press, Tucson.

Jeancon, Jean A. 1923. *Excavations in the Chama Valley, New Mexico*. Bureau of American Ethnology Bulletin No. 81. Government Printing Office, Washington, D.C.

Jennings, Calvin H. 1980. Further Investigations at the Puerco Site, Petrified Forest National Park, Arizona. Manuscript on file, Western Archeological and Conservation Center, National Park Service, U.S. Department of the Interior, Tucson, Arizona.

Jernigan, E. Wesley. 1978. *Jewelry of the Prehistoric Southwest*. School of American Research, Santa Fe, New Mexico; University of New Mexico Press, Albuquerque.

Jernigan, E. Wesley. 1993. Krider Kiva Site, AZ CC:1:43 (ASM) site card, site map, ceramic counts, and kiva plan and profile maps. Manuscript on file, Archaeological Records Office, Arizona State Museum, University of Arizona, Tucson.

Johnson, Alfred E., and Raymond H. Thompson. 1963. The Ringo Site, Southeastern Arizona. *American Antiquity* 28:465–481.

Johnson, Alfred E., and William W. Wasley. 1966. Archaeological Excavations near Bylas, Arizona. *Kiva* 31:205–253.

Johnson, Harvey L. 1957. The Archaeo-History of the Lower San Pedro River Valley, Showing the Transition from Salado to Sobaipuri at the Village of La Victoria. Manuscript on file, Archives, Amerind Museum, Dragoon, Arizona.

Johnson, R. Roy. 1969. Bird Bones Recovered from Davis Ranch Site (Ariz. BB:11:7), Identified by R. Roy Johnson. Manuscript on file, Archives, Amerind Museum, Dragoon, Arizona.

Jones, Robert. 1996. Ceramic Analysis. In *On the Border: Analysis of Materials Recovered from the 1964 and 1991–1992 Excavations at the Garden Canyon Site (AZ EE:11:13 ASM)*, edited by Steven D. Shelley and Jeffrey H. Altschul, pp. 15–63. Technical Series No. 61. Statistical Research, Tucson, Arizona.

Justice, Noel D. 2002. *Stone Age Spear and Arrow Points of the Southwestern United States*. Indiana University Press, Bloomington.

Kearney, Thomas H., and Robert H. Peebles. 1951. *Arizona Flora*. University of California Press, Berkeley.

Keen, A. Myra. 1971. *Sea Shells of Tropical West America: Marine Mollusks from Baja California to Peru*. 2nd ed. Stanford University Press, Stanford, California.

Kelly, Isabel T. 1938. The Hodges Site. Manuscript on file (folders A-105, 106, 107, 110, and 111), Library and Archives, Arizona State Museum, University of Arizona, Tucson.

Kelly, Isabel T., James E. Officer, and Emil W. Haury. 1978. *The Hodges Ruin: A Hohokam Community in the Tucson Basin*. Edited by Gayle Harrison Hartmann. Anthropological Papers of the University of Arizona No. 30. University of Arizona Press, Tucson.

Kidder, Alfred V. 1932. *The Artifacts of Pecos*. Papers of the Southwestern Expedition, Phillips Academy No. 6. Yale University Press, New Haven, Connecticut.

Kidder, Alfred V. 1936. I. The Glaze-Paint, Culinary, and Other Wares. In *The Pottery of Pecos Volume II: I. The Glaze-Paint, Culinary, and Other Wares, II. The Technology of Pecos Pottery*, by Alfred V. Kidder and Anna O. Shepard, pp. 1–388. Papers of the Southwestern Expedition, Phillips Academy No. 7. Yale University Press, New Haven, Connecticut.

Kidder, Alfred V. 1939. Notes on the Archaeology of the Babícora District, Chihuahua. In *So Live the Works of Men: Seventieth Anniversary Volume Honoring Edgar Lee Hewett*, edited by Donald D. Brand and Fred E. Harvey, pp. 221–230. University of New Mexico Press, Albuquerque; School of American Research, Santa Fe, New Mexico.

Kidder, Alfred V., Harriet S. Cosgrove, and C. Burton Cosgrove. 1949. *The Pendleton Ruin, Hidalgo County, New Mexico*. Contributions to American Anthropology and History 10, No. 50, Publication 585. Carnegie Institution of Washington, Washington, D.C.

Kidder, Alfred V., and Samuel J. Guernsey. 1919. *Archeological Explorations in Northeastern Arizona*. Bureau of American Ethnology Bulletin 65. Government Printing Office, Washington, D.C.

Kowta, Makoto. 1969. *The Sayles Complex: A Late Milling Stone Assemblage from Cajon Pass and the Ecological Implication of its Scraper Planes*. Publications in Anthropology 6. University of California Press, Berkeley.

Lange, Charles H. 1958. The Keresan Component of Southwestern Pueblo Culture. *Southwestern Journal of Anthropology* 14:34–50.

Lange, Richard C., and Stephen Germick (editors). 1992. *Proceedings of the Second Salado Conference, Globe, AZ 1992*. Occasional Paper. Arizona Archaeological Society, Phoenix.

Lekson, Stephen H. 1992. Salado of the East. In *Proceedings of the Second Salado Conference, Globe, AZ, 1992*, edited by Richard C. Lange and Stephen Germick, pp. 17–21. Occasional Paper. Arizona Archaeological Society, Phoenix.

Lekson, Stephen H. 2000. Salado in Chihuahua. In *Salado*, edited by Jeffrey S. Dean, pp. 275–294. Amerind Foundation New World Studies Series No. 4. Amerind Foundation, Dragoon, Arizona; University of New Mexico Press, Albuquerque.

Lekson, Stephen H. 2002. *Salado Archaeology of the Upper Gila, New Mexico*. Anthropological Papers of the University of Arizona No. 67. University of Arizona Press, Tucson.

Lekson, Stephen H. 2014. Southwest New Mexico and the Land Between. In *Between Mimbres and Hohokam: Exploring the Archaeology and History of Southeastern Arizona and Southwestern New Mexico*, edited by Henry D. Wallace, pp. 501–510. Anthropological Papers No. 52. Archaeology Southwest, Tucson, Arizona.

Light, Sara. 1990. A Preliminary Study of the Raptor Bones from the Point of Pines, Arizona Site. Master's report, Department of Anthropology, University of Arizona, Tucson.

Lindauer, Owen. 1996. *The Place of the Storehouses: Roosevelt Platform Mound Study Report on the Schoolhouse Point Mound, Pinto Creek Complex*. Anthropological Field Studies No. 35. Roosevelt Monograph Series No. 6. Office of Cultural Resource Management, Department of Anthropology, Arizona State University, Tempe.

Lindauer, Owen. 1997. *The Archaeology of Schoolhouse Point Mesa: Roosevelt Platform Mound Study Report on the Schoolhouse Point Mesa Sites, Schoolhouse Management Group, Pinto Creek Complex*. Anthropological Field Studies No. 37. Roosevelt Monograph Series No. 8. Office of Cultural Resource Management, Department of Anthropology, Arizona State University, Tempe.

Lindsay, Alexander J., Jr. 1969. The Tsegi Phase of the Kayenta Cultural Tradition in Northeastern

Arizona. PhD dissertation, Department of Anthropology, University of Arizona, Tucson. UMI, Ann Arbor, Michigan.

Lindsay, Alexander J., Jr. 1987. Anasazi Population Movements to Southeastern Arizona. *American Archeology* 6(3):190–198.

Lindsay, Alexander J., Jr. 1992. Tucson Polychrome: History, Dating, Distribution and Design. In *Proceedings of the Second Salado Conference, Globe, AZ, 1992*, edited by Richard C. Lange and Stephen Germick, pp. 230–237. Occasional Paper. Arizona Archaeological Society, Phoenix.

Lindsay, Alexander J., Jr., J. Richard Ambler, Mary Anne Stein, and Philip M. Hobler. 1968. *Survey and Excavations North and East of Navajo Mountain, Utah, 1959–1962*. Museum of Northern Arizona Bulletin No. 45. Glen Canyon Series No. 8. Northern Arizona Society of Science and Art, Flagstaff.

Lindsay, Alexander J., Jr., and Calvin H. Jennings (compilers). 1968. *Salado Red Ware Conference: Ninth Southwestern Ceramic Seminar, October 13–14, 1967*. Museum of Northern Arizona Ceramic Series No. 4. Northern Arizona Society of Science and Art, Flagstaff.

Lister, Florence C., and Robert H. Lister. 1989. *The Chinese of Early Tucson: Historic Archaeology from the Tucson Urban Renewal Project*. Anthropological Papers of the University of Arizona No. 52. University of Arizona Press, Tucson.

Lister, Robert H. 1955. *The Present Status of the Archaeology of Western Mexico: A Distributional Study*. University of Colorado Studies Series in Anthropology No. 5. University of Colorado Press, Boulder.

Lister, Robert H., and Florence C. Lister. 1978. *Anasazi Pottery: Ten Centuries of Prehistoric Ceramic Art in the Four Corners Country of the Southwestern United States as Illustrated by the Earl H. Morris Memorial Pottery Collection in the University of Colorado Museum*. Reprinted. Maxwell Museum of Anthropology, Albuquerque, New Mexico; University of New Mexico Press, Albuquerque.

Loendorf, Chris, and Glen E. Rice. 2004. *Projectile Point Typology, Gila River Indian Community, Arizona*. Anthropological Research Papers No. 2. Gila River Indian Community Cultural Resource Management Program, Sacaton, Arizona.

Longacre, William A. 1970. *Archaeology as Anthropology: A Case Study*. Anthropological Papers of the University of Arizona No. 17. University of Arizona Press, Tucson.

Luchetta, Sarah K. 2005. Soza Phase Sites in the Lower San Pedro Valley, Arizona. Master's thesis, Department of Anthropology, University of Arizona, Tucson.

Lumholtz, Carl. 1902. *Unknown Mexico: A Record of Five Years' Exploration Among the Tribes of the Western Sierra Madre; In the Tierra Caliente of Tepic and Jalisco; and Among the Tarascos of Michoacan*. 2 vols. Charles Scribner's Sons, New York.

Lyons, Patrick D. 1997. Excavation Report for the 1996 Field Season: Homol'ovi I (AZ J:14:3[ASM]), Structure 901. Manuscript on file, Homol'ovi Research Program, Arizona State Museum, University of Arizona, Tucson.

Lyons, Patrick D. 1999a. Davis Ruin Perforated Plate Data. Manuscript on file, Arizona State Museum, University of Arizona, Tucson.

Lyons, Patrick D. 1999b. New Perspectives on Hay Hollow Valley and the Upper Little Colorado: The View from Homol'ovi. Paper presented at the 64th Annual Meeting of the Society for American Archaeology, Chicago.

Lyons, Patrick D. 2001. Winslow Orange Ware and the Ancestral Hopi Migration Horizon. PhD dissertation, Department of Anthropology, University of Arizona, Tucson. ProQuest, Ann Arbor, Michigan.

Lyons, Patrick D. 2003. *Ancestral Hopi Migrations*. Anthropological Papers of the University of Arizona No. 68. University of Arizona Press, Tucson.

Lyons, Patrick D. 2004a. José Solas Ruin. *Kiva* 70:143–181.

Lyons, Patrick D. 2004b. Cliff Polychrome. *Kiva* 69:361–400.

Lyons, Patrick D. 2004c. Appendix B: Type Description of San Carlos Red-on-brown: Safford Variety. In *Ancient Farmers of the Safford Basin: Archaeology of the U.S. 70 Safford-to-Thatcher Project*, edited by Jeffery J. Clark, pp. 203–206. Anthropological Papers No. 39. Center for Desert Archaeology, Tucson, Arizona.

Lyons, Patrick D. 2004d. Ceramics. In *Ancient Farmers of the Safford Basin: Archaeology of the U.S. 70 Safford-to-Thatcher Project*, edited by Jeffery J. Clark, pp. 95–126. Anthropological Papers No. 39. Center for Desert Archaeology, Tucson, Arizona.

Lyons, Patrick D. 2004e. Review of "Centuries of Decline During the Hohokam Classic Period at Pueblo Grande," edited by David R. Abbott. *Journal of Field Archaeology* 29:486–494.

Lyons, Patrick D. 2007. The Kayenta Diaspora and Group Identities in the American Southwest. Paper presented at the 72nd Annual Meeting of the Society for American Archaeology, Austin, Texas.

Lyons, Patrick D. 2010. Norton Allen's Excavations in the San Pedro and Dripping Spring Valleys of Southeastern Arizona. *Journal of the Southwest* 52:323–361.

Lyons, Patrick D. 2012a. Appendix E: Type Description of San Carlos Red-on-brown: Aravaipa Variety. In *Migrants and Mounds: Classic Period Archaeology of the Lower San Pedro Valley*, edited by Jeffery J. Clark and Patrick D. Lyons, pp. 457–461. Anthropological Papers No. 45. Archaeology Southwest, Tucson, Arizona.

Lyons, Patrick D. 2012b. Ceramic Typology, Chronology, Production, and Circulation. In *Migrants and Mounds: Classic Period Archaeology of the Lower San Pedro Valley*, edited by Jeffery J. Clark and Patrick D. Lyons, pp. 211–308. Anthropological Papers No. 45. Archaeology Southwest, Tucson, Arizona.

Lyons, Patrick D. 2013a. "By their fruits ye shall know them": The Pottery of Kinishba Revisited. In *Kinishba Lost and Found: Mid-Century Excavations and Contemporary Perspectives*, edited by John R. Welch, pp. 145–208. Arizona State Museum Archaeological Series No. 206. Arizona State Museum, University of Arizona, Tucson.

Lyons, Patrick D. 2013b. Placing the Tonto Cliff Dwellings in the Larger Context of the Tonto Basin and the Southern US Southwest. Final Report of WNPA Research Project 06-09: Investigating Ancient Dynamics by Studying Salado Ceramics and Obsidian. Manuscript on file, Archaeology Southwest, Tucson, Arizona.

Lyons, Patrick D. 2014. Jeddito Yellow Ware, Migration, and the Kayenta Diaspora. *Kiva* 79:147–174.

Lyons, Patrick D. 2015. A Behavioral Archaeology of Ancient Migrations. In *Explorations in Behavioral Archaeology*, edited by William H. Walker and James M. Skibo, pp. 37–51. University of Utah Press, Salt Lake City.

Lyons, Patrick D., and Jeffery J. Clark. 2008. Interaction, Enculturation, Social Distance, and Ancient Ethnic Identities. In *Archaeology Without Borders: Contact, Commerce, and Change in the U.S. Southwest and Northwestern Mexico*, edited by Laurie D. Webster and Maxine McBrinn, pp. 185–207. University Press of Colorado, Boulder; INAH, Chihuahua, Mexico.

Lyons, Patrick D., and Jeffery J. Clark. 2012. A Community of Practice in Diaspora: The Rise and Demise of Roosevelt Red Ware. In *Potters and Communities of Practice: Glaze Paint and Polychrome Pottery in the American Southwest, A.D. 1250–1700*, edited by Linda S. Cordell and Judith A. Habicht-Mauche, pp. 19–33. Anthropological Papers of the University of Arizona No. 75. University of Arizona Press, Tucson.

Lyons, Patrick D., Jeffery J. Clark, and J. Brett Hill. 2011. Ancient Social Boundaries Inscribed on the Landscape of the Lower San Pedro Valley.

In *Contemporary Archaeologies of the Southwest*, edited by William H. Walker and Kathryn Venzor, pp. 175–196. University Press of Colorado, Boulder.

Lyons, Patrick D., J. Brett Hill, and Jeffery J. Clark. 2008. Demography, Agricultural Potential, and Identity Among Ancient Immigrants. In *The Social Construction of Communities: Agency, Structure, and Identity in the Prehispanic Southwest*, edited by Mark D. Varien and James Potter, pp. 191–213. AltaMira Press, Lanham, Maryland.

Lyons, Patrick D., J. Brett Hill, and Jeffery J. Clark. 2011. Irrigation Communities and Communities in Diaspora. In *Movement, Connectivity, and Landscape Change in the Ancient Southwest: The 20th Anniversary Southwest Symposium*, edited by Margaret C. Nelson and Colleen Strawhacker, pp. 375–401. University Press of Colorado, Boulder.

Lyons, Patrick D., J. Brett Hill, and Jeffery J. Clark. 2014. The Hohokam-Upper Piman Continuum Revisited. In *Building Transnational Archaeologies: The 11th Southwest Symposium, Hermosillo, Sonora, México*, edited by Elisa Villalpando and Randall H. McGuire, pp. 77–91. Archaeological Series No. 209. Arizona State Museum, University of Arizona, Tucson.

Lyons, Patrick D., and Alexander J. Lindsay Jr. 2006. Perforated Plates and the Salado Phenomenon. *Kiva* 72:5–54.

Lyons, Patrick D., and Anna A. Neuzil. 2006. Research on the Mills Collection. *Archaeology Southwest* 20(2):17.

Mabry, Jonathan B. 1998. Architectural Variability and Site Structures. In *Archaeological Investigations of Early Village Sites in the Middle Santa Cruz Valley: Analyses and Synthesis*, edited by Jonathan Mabry, pp. 209–243. Anthropological Papers No. 19. Center for Desert Archaeology, Tucson, Arizona.

Mabry, Jonathan B. 1999. A Rare Glimpse of the Sobaipuri from Colossal Cave. *Archaeology Southwest* 13(4):11.

Mabry, Jonathan, Deborah L. Swartz, Helga Wöcherl, Jeffery J. Clark, Gavin W. Archer, and Michael W. Lindeman. 1997. *Archaeological Investigations of Early Village Sites in the Middle Santa Cruz Valley: Descriptions of the Santa Cruz Bend, Square Hearth, Stone Pipe, and Canal Sites*. Anthropological Papers No. 18. Center for Desert Archaeology, Tucson, Arizona.

McCluney, Eugene B. 1962. *Clanton Draw and Box Canyon: An Interim Report on Two Prehistoric Sites in Hidalgo County, New Mexico, and Related Surveys*. Monograph No. 26. School of American Research, Santa Fe, New Mexico.

McGimsey, Charles R., III. 1980. *Mariana Mesa: Seven Prehistoric Settlements in West-Central New Mexico*. Papers of the Peabody Museum of Archaeology and Ethnology Vol. 72. Harvard University, Cambridge, Massachusetts.

McGregor, John C. 1965. *Southwestern Archaeology*. 2nd ed. University of Illinois Press, Urbana.

McGuire, Randall H. 1975. Central Heights: A Small Salado Site Near Globe. Manuscript on file, Arizona State Museum Archaeological Repository, University of Arizona, Tucson.

McGuire, Randall H., and María Elisa Villalpando C. 1993. *An Archaeological Survey of the Altar Valley, Sonora, Mexico*. Arizona State Museum Archaeological Series No. 184. Arizona State Museum, University of Arizona, Tucson.

McKusick, Charmion R. 1982. Avifauna from Grasshopper Pueblo. In *Multidisciplinary Research at Grasshopper Pueblo, Arizona*, edited by William A. Longacre, Sally J. Holbrook, and Michael W. Graves, pp. 87–96. Anthropological Papers of the University of Arizona No. 40. University of Arizona Press, Tucson.

McKusick, Charmion R. 2001. *Southwest Birds of Sacrifice*. Arizona Archaeologist No. 31. Arizona Archaeological Society, Phoenix.

Manje, Captain Juan Mateo. 1954. *Unknown Arizona and Sonora, 1693–1721: From the Francisco Fernández del Castillo Version of Luz de Tierra Incógnita, an English Translation of Part II.*

Translated by Harry J. Karns and associates. Arizona Silhouettes, Tucson.

Marmaduke, William S., and T. Kathleen Henderson. 1995. *Archaeology in the Distribution Division of the Central Arizona Project: Thoughts on the History of the Hohokam Culture in Southern Arizona, and on the Practice of Archaeology in the 1990s*. Northland Research, Flagstaff, Arizona.

Martin, Deborah. 1990. In Memoriam: Rex Ervin Gerald, 1928–1990. *Artifact* 28(3):iii–vii.

Martin, Deborah. 1997. Rex Gerald to Receive Award of Distinction. *El Paso Archaeology: The Official Newsletter of the El Paso Archaeological Society* 30(9):3–4.

Martin, Paul S. 1939. *Modified Basket Maker Sites, Ackmen-Lowry Area, Southwestern Colorado, 1938*. Anthropological Series Vol. 23, No. 3. Field Museum of Natural History, Chicago.

Martin, Paul S., William A. Longacre, and James N. Hill. 1967. *Chapters in the Prehistory of Eastern Arizona, III*. Fieldiana: Anthropology Vol. 57. Field Museum of Natural History, Chicago.

Martin, Paul S., and John B. Rinaldo. 1960. *Table Rock Pueblo, Arizona*. Fieldiana: Anthropology Vol. 51, No. 2. Chicago Natural History Museum, Chicago.

Martin, Paul S., John B. Rinaldo, Elaine A. Bluhm, Hugh C. Cutler, and Roger Grange Jr. 1952. *Mogollon Cultural Continuity and Change: The Stratigraphic Analysis of Tularosa and Cordova Caves*. Fieldiana: Anthropology Vol. 40. Chicago Natural History Museum, Chicago.

Martin, Paul S., John B. Rinaldo, William A. Longacre, Leslie G. Freeman Jr., James A. Brown, Richard H. Hevly, and M. E. Cooley. 1964. *Chapters in the Prehistory of Eastern Arizona, II*. Fieldiana: Anthropology Vol. 55. Chicago Natural History Museum, Chicago.

Martynec, Richard J. 1993. Decorated and Intrusive Ceramics from the SCFAP Sites. In *Classic Period Occupation on the Santa Cruz Flats: The Santa Cruz Flats Archaeological Project*, edited by T. Kathleen Henderson and Richard J. Martynec, pp. 277–311. Northland Research, Flagstaff, Arizona.

Masse, W. Bruce. 1980a. The Hohokam of the Lower San Pedro Valley and the Northern Papagueria: Continuity and Variability in Two Regional Populations. In *Current Issues in Hohokam Prehistory: Proceedings of a Symposium*, edited by David E. Doyel and Fred Plog, pp. 205–223. Anthropological Research Papers No. 23. Department of Anthropology, Arizona State University, Tempe.

Masse, W. Bruce. 1980b. *The Peppersauce Wash Project: Excavations at Three Multicomponent Sites in the Lower San Pedro Valley, Arizona*, by W. Bruce Masse, edited by Gayle H. Hartmann. Contribution to Highway Salvage Archaeology in Arizona No. 53. Manuscript on file, Library and Archives, Arizona State Museum, University of Arizona, Tucson.

Masse, W. Bruce. 1981. A Reappraisal of the Protohistoric Sobaipuri Indians of Southeastern Arizona. In *The Protohistoric Period in the North American Southwest, A.D. 1450–1700*, edited by David R. Wilcox and W. Bruce Masse, pp. 28–56. Anthropological Research Papers No. 24. Department of Anthropology, Arizona State University, Tempe.

Masse, W. Bruce. 1982. Hohokam Ceramic Art: Regionalism and the Imprint of Societal Change. In *Southwestern Ceramics: A Comparative Review*, edited by Albert H. Schroeder, pp. 70–105. Arizona Archaeologist No. 15. Arizona Archaeological Society, Phoenix.

Masse, W. Bruce. 1990. Whimsy Flat: AZ T:16:71 (ASM). In *Archaeology of the Ak-Chin Indian Community West Side Farms Project, Volume 3: The Archaeological Data Recovery Program*, compiled by Robert E. Gasser, Christine K. Robinson, and Cory Dale Breternitz, pp. 12.1–12.37. Publications in Archaeology No. 9. Soil Systems, Phoenix, Arizona.

Masse, W. Bruce, Linda M. Gregonis, and Mark C. Slaughter. 2014. Corridor, Frontier, Melting Pot, or Autonomous Systems: The Lower San

Pedro Valley, A.D. 600–1200. In *Between Mimbres and Hohokam: Exploring the Archaeology and History of Southeastern Arizona and Southwestern New Mexico*, edited by Henry D. Wallace, pp. 165–202. Anthropological Papers No. 52. Archaeology Southwest, Tucson, Arizona.

Mekeel, Scudder. 1935. Subsistence: Plant Foods and Preparation. In *Walapai Ethnography*, edited by Alfred L. Kroeber, pp. 48–57. Memoirs No. 42. American Anthropological Association, Menasha, Wisconsin.

Miksa, Elizabeth J. 2001. Temper Provenance Studies. In *The Grewe Archaeological Project Volume 2: Material Culture, Part I: Ceramic Studies*, edited by David R. Abbott, pp. 7–45. Anthropological Research Papers No. 99-1. Northland Research, Tempe, Arizona.

Miksa, Elizabeth J., Sergio F. Castro-Reino, and Carlos P. Lavayen. 2003. An Actualistic Sand Petrofacies Model for the San Pedro Valley, Arizona, with Application to Classic Period Ceramics. Manuscript on file, Archaeology Southwest, Tucson, Arizona.

Miksa, Elizabeth J., and James M. Heidke. 1995. Drawing a Line in the Sands: Models of Ceramic Temper Provenance. In *The Roosevelt Community Development Study, Volume 2: Ceramic Chronology, Technology, and Economics*, edited by James M. Heidke and Miriam T. Stark, pp. 133–205. Anthropological Papers No. 14. Center for Desert Archaeology, Tucson, Arizona.

Mills, Barbara J. 1998. Migration and Pueblo IV Community Reorganization in the Silver Creek Area, East-Central Arizona. In *Migration and Reorganization: The Pueblo IV Period in the American Southwest*, edited by Katherine A. Spielmann, pp. 65–80. Arizona State University Anthropological Research Papers No. 51. Department of Anthropology, Arizona State University, Tempe.

Mills, Barbara J. 2007. Performing the Feast: Visual Display and Suprahousehold Commensalism in the Puebloan Southwest. *American Antiquity* 72:210–239.

Mills, Barbara J., Jeffery J. Clark, Matthew A. Peeples, W. R. Haas Jr., John M. Roberts Jr., J. Brett Hill, Deborah L. Huntley, Lewis Borck, Ronald L. Breiger, Aaron Clauset, and M. Steven Shackley. 2013. Transformations of Social Networks in the Late Pre-Hispanic US Southwest. *Proceedings of the National Academy of Sciences of the United States of America* 1101(15):5785–5790.

Mills, Barbara J., and Sarah A. Herr. 1999. Chronology of the Mogollon Rim Region. In *Living on the Edge of the Rim: Excavations and Analysis of the Silver Creek Archaeological Research Project 1993–1998*, Vol. 1, edited by Barbara J. Mills, Sarah A. Herr, and Scott Van Keuren, pp. 269–293. Archaeological Series No. 192. Arizona State Museum, University of Arizona, Tucson.

Mills, Barbara J., Sarah A. Herr, Susan L. Stinson, and Daniela Triadan. 1999. Ceramic Production and Distribution. In *Living on the Edge of the Rim: Excavations and Analysis of the Silver Creek Archaeological Research Project 1993–1998*, Vol. 2, edited by Barbara J. Mills, Sarah A. Herr, and Scott Van Keuren, pp. 295–324. Archaeological Series No. 192. Arizona State Museum, University of Arizona, Tucson.

Mills, Barbara J., Scott Van Keuren, Susan L. Stinson, William M. Graves III, Eric J. Kaldahl, and Joanne M. Newcomb. 1999. Excavations at Bailey Ruin. In *Living on the Edge of the Rim: Excavations and Analysis of the Silver Creek Archaeological Research Project 1993–1998*, Vol. 1, edited by Barbara J. Mills, Sarah A. Herr, and Scott Van Keuren, pp. 149–242. Archaeological Series No. 192. Arizona State Museum, University of Arizona, Tucson.

Mills, Jack P., and Vera M. Mills. 1940–1949. Archaeological Notes on the Nine Mile Site. Manuscript on file, Archives, Amerind Museum, Dragoon, Arizona.

Mills, Jack P., and Vera M. Mills. 1955. The Webb Site: A Report on an Archaeological Salvage Operation. Manuscript on file, Library and Archives, Arizona State Museum, University of Arizona, Tucson.

Mills, Jack P., and Vera M. Mills. 1966. *The Glass Ranch Site*. Special Report No. 4. El Paso Archaeological Society, El Paso, Texas.

Mills, Jack P., and Vera M. Mills. 1969a. *The Kuykendall Site: A Prehistoric Salado Village in Southeastern Arizona*. Special Report No. 6. El Paso Archaeological Society, El Paso, Texas.

Mills, Jack P., and Vera M. Mills. 1969b. Burned House: An Additional Excavation at the Kuykendall Site. *Artifact* 7(3):21–32.

Mills, Jack P., and Vera M. Mills. 1971. The Slaughter Ranch Site: A Prehistoric Village Near the Mexican Border in Southeastern Arizona. *Artifact* 9(3):23–52.

Mills, Jack P., and Vera M. Mills. 1972. The Dinwiddie Site: A Prehistoric Salado Ruin on Duck Creek, Western New Mexico. *Artifact* 10(2):i–50.

Mills, Jack P., and Vera M. Mills. 1978. *The Curtis Site: A Pre-Historic Village in the Safford Valley*. Self-published, Elfrida, Arizona.

Mindeleff, Victor. 1891. A Study of Pueblo Architecture: Tusayan and Cibola. In *Eighth Annual Report of the Bureau of American Ethnology for the Years 1886–1887*, pp. 3–228. Smithsonian Institution, Washington, D.C.

Montell, Gösta. 1937. De Entografiska Undersökningarna. *Ethnos* 2:301–318.

Morris, Elizabeth Ann. 1957. Stratigraphic Evidence for a Cultural Continuum at the Point of Pines Ruin. Master's thesis, Department of Anthropology, University of Arizona, Tucson.

Morss, Noel. 1954. *Clay Figurines of the American Southwest with a Description of the New Pillings Find in Northeastern Utah and a Comparison with Certain Other North American Figurines*. Papers of the Peabody Museum of American Archaeology and Ethnology Vol. 49, Pt. 1. Harvard University, Cambridge, Massachusetts.

Munsell Color. 1994. *Munsell Soil Color Charts*. Rev. ed. Macbeth Division of Kollmorgen Instruments Corporation, New Windsor, New York.

Myers, Terry L. 2009. *Pre-historical, Historical, and Recent Distribution of Freshwater Mussels (Unionidae:* Anodonta*) in the Colorado River and Rio Yaqui Basins*. U.S. Fish and Wildlife Service, Arizona Ecological Services Field Office, Phoenix.

Neely, James A. 2005. Prehistoric Agricultural and Settlement Systems in Lefthand Canyon, Safford Valley, Southeastern Arizona. In *Inscriptions: Collected Papers in Honor of Richard B. and Nathalie F. S. Woodbury*, edited by Regge N. Wiseman, Thomas C. O'Laughlin, and Cordelia T. Snow, pp. 145–169. Papers No. 31. Archaeological Society of New Mexico, Albuquerque.

Neily, Robert B., Joseph S. Crary, Gay M. Kinkade, and Stephen Germick. 1993. The Owens-Colvin Site Revisited: A Preliminary Report of the Excavations of a Bylas Phase Settlement near Eden, Arizona. Paper presented at the 1993 Pecos Conference, Springerville, Arizona.

Nelson, Ben A., and Steven A. LeBlanc. 1986. *Short-Term Sedentism in the American Southwest: The Mimbres Valley Salado*. Maxwell Museum of Anthropology, Albuquerque, New Mexico; University of New Mexico Press, Albuquerque.

Nelson, Richard S. 1981. The Role of a Puchteca System in Hohokam Exchange. PhD Dissertation, Department of Anthropology, New York University, New York. ProQuest, Ann Arbor, Michigan.

Nelson, Richard S. 1991. *Hohokam Marine Shell Exchange and Artifacts*. Archaeological Series No. 179. Arizona State Museum, University of Arizona, Tucson.

Nequatewa, Edmund. 1936. *Truth of a Hopi and Other Clan Stories of Shungopovi*. Museum of Northern Arizona Bulletin No. 8. Northern Arizona Society of Science and Art, Flagstaff.

Neuzil, Anna A. 2005. In the Aftermath of Migration: Assessing the Social Consequences of Late 13th and 14th Century Population Movements into Southeastern Arizona. PhD dissertation, Department of Anthropology, University of Arizona, Tucson. ProQuest, Ann Arbor, Michigan.

Neuzil, Anna A. 2008. *In the Aftermath of Migration: Renegotiating Ancient Identity in Southeastern Arizona*. Anthropological Papers of the University of Arizona No. 73. University of Arizona Press, Tucson.

Neuzil, Anna A., and Patrick D. Lyons. 2006. *An Analysis of Whole Vessels from the Mills Collection Curated at Eastern Arizona College, Thatcher, Arizona*. Technical Report No. 2005-001. Center for Desert Archaeology, Tucson, Arizona.

Neuzil, Anna A., and M. Kyle Woodson. 2008. Migration and Identity in the Safford and Aravaipa Valleys of Southeastern Arizona. In *Crossroads of the Southwest: Culture, Identity, and Migration in Arizona's Safford Basin*, edited by David E. Purcell, pp. 13–38. Cambridge Scholars Publishing, Newcastle, England.

Neuzil, Anna A., and M. Kyle Woodson. 2014. The Safford Basin and Aravaipa Creek: A Cultural Melting Pot of the Ancient Past. In *Between Mimbres and Hohokam: Exploring the Archaeology and History of Southeastern Arizona and Southwestern New Mexico*, edited by Henry D. Wallace, pp. 349–400. Anthropological Papers No. 52. Archaeology Southwest, Tucson, Arizona.

Officer, James E. 1978. Shell. In *The Hodges Ruin: A Hohokam Community in the Tucson Basin*, by Isabel T. Kelly, James E. Officer, and Emil W. Haury, edited by Gayle H. Hartmann, pp. 110–122. Anthropological Papers of the University of Arizona No. 30. University of Arizona Press, Tucson, Arizona.

Olsen, Stanley J. 1978. The Faunal Analysis. In *Bones from Awatovi, Northeastern Arizona*, by Stanley J. Olsen and Richard Page Wheeler, pp. 1–34. Papers of the Peabody Museum of Archaeology and Ethnology Vol. 70, Pts. 1 and 2. Harvard University, Cambridge, Massachusetts.

Olson, Alan P. 1959. An Evaluation of the Phase Concept in Southwestern Archaeology. PhD dissertation, Department of Anthropology, University of Arizona, Tucson. ProQuest, Ann Arbor, Michigan.

Oppelt, Norman T. 1984. Worked Potsherds of the Prehistoric Southwest: Their Forms and Distribution. *Pottery Southwest* 11(1):1–6.

Parsons, Elsie Clews. 1939. *Pueblo Indian Religion*. 2 vols. University of Chicago Press, Chicago.

Parsons, Elsie Clews (editor). 1936. *Hopi Journal of Alexander M. Stephen*. 2 vols. Columbia University Contributions to Anthropology No. 23. Columbia University Press, New York.

Parsons, Jeffrey R., and Mary H. Parsons. 1985. Otomí Maguey Utilization: An Ethnoarchaeological Perspective. Preliminary Report to the National Geographic Society. Manuscript on file, Library and Archives, Arizona State Museum, University of Arizona, Tucson.

Parsons, Jeffrey R., and Mary H. Parsons 1990. *Maguey Utilization in Highland Central Mexico: An Archaeological Ethnography*. Anthropological Papers No. 82. Museum of Anthropology, University of Michigan, Ann Arbor.

Pierson, Lloyd M. 1962. Excavations at the Lower Ruin and Annex, Tonto National Monument, 1952. In *Archeological Studies at Tonto National Monument, Arizona*, edited by Louis R. Caywood, pp. 33–69. Technical Series Vol. 2. Southwestern Monuments Association, Gila Pueblo, Globe, Arizona.

Pilles, Peter J., Jr., and Edward B. Danson. 1974. The Prehistoric Pottery of Arizona. *Arizona Highways* 50(1):2–5, 10–15, 43–45.

Purcell, David E., and Jeffery J. Clark. 2008. Multi-Cultural Communities in the Safford Basin. In *Crossroads of the Southwest: Culture, Identity, and Migration in Arizona's Safford Basin*, edited by David E. Purcell, pp. 39–59. Cambridge Scholars Publishing, Newcastle, England.

Ravesloot, John C., and Stephanie M. Whittlesey. 1987. Inferring the Protohistoric Period in Southern Arizona. In *The Archaeology of the San Xavier Bridge Site (AZ BB:13:14), Tucson Basin, Southern Arizona*, edited by John C. Ravesloot, pp. 81–98. Archaeological Series No. 171. Arizona State Museum, University of Arizona, Tucson.

Reed, Erik K. 1948. The Western Pueblo Archaeological Complex. *El Palacio* 55:9–15.

Rice, Glen E. 1990. An Intellectual History of the Salado Concept. In *A Design for Salado Research*, edited by Glen E. Rice, pp. 21–29. Anthropological Field Studies No. 22. Roosevelt Monograph Series No. 1. Office of Cultural Resource Management, Department of Anthropology, Arizona State University, Tempe.

Rice, Glen E. 2016. *Sending the Spirits Home: The Archaeology of Hohokam Mortuary Practice*. University of Utah Press, Salt Lake City.

Riggs, Charles R., Jr. 2001. *The Architecture of Grasshopper Pueblo*. University of Utah Press, Salt Lake City.

Rinaldo, John B. 1952. Pottery. In *Mogollon Cultural Continuity and Change: The Stratigraphic Analysis of Tularosa and Cordova Caves*, by Paul S. Martin, John B. Rinaldo, Elaine Bluhm, Hugh C. Cutler, and Roger Grange Jr., pp. 51–101. Fieldiana: Anthropology Vol. 40. Chicago Natural History Museum, Chicago.

Rinaldo, John B. 1974a. Medio Period Stone Artifacts. In *Casas Grandes: A Fallen Trading Center of the Gran Chichimeca*, by Charles C. Di Peso, John B. Rinaldo, and Gloria J. Fenner, Vol. 7, pp. 38–481. Amerind Foundation No. 9. Amerind Foundation, Dragoon, Arizona; Northland Press, Flagstaff, Arizona.

Rinaldo, John B. 1974b. Trade Wares: Eastern Middle Gila Drainage. In *Casas Grandes: A Fallen Trading Center of the Gran Chichimeca*, by Charles C. Di Peso, John B. Rinaldo, and Gloria J. Fenner, Vol. 8, pp. 148–154. Amerind Foundation No. 9. Amerind Foundation, Dragoon, Arizona; Northland Press, Flagstaff, Arizona.

Rinaldo, John B., and Elaine A. Bluhm. 1956. *Late Mogollon Pottery Types of the Reserve Area*. Fieldiana: Anthropology Vol. 36, No. 7. Chicago Natural History Museum, Chicago.

Rinker, Jennifer. 1998. The Bryce-Smith Project: Irrigated Agriculture and Habitation from A.D. 1000 to 1450, Lefthand Canyon, Safford Valley, Arizona. Master's thesis, Department of Anthropology, University of Texas, Austin.

Robinson, William S. 1951. A Method for Chronologically Ordering Archaeological Deposits. *American Antiquity* 16:293–301.

Rogers, Malcolm. 1929. The Stone Art of the San Dieguito Plateau. *American Anthropologist* 31:454–467.

Rogers, Malcolm. 1939. *Early Lithic Industries of the Lower Basin of the Colorado River and Adjacent Desert Areas*. Papers No. 3. San Diego Museum, San Diego, California.

Salls, Roy A. 1985. The Scraper Plane: A Functional Interpretation. *Journal of Field Archaeology* 12:99–106.

Sauer, Carl O., and Donald D. Brand. 1931. *Prehistoric Settlements of Sonora with Special Reference to Cerros de Trincheras*. University of California Publications in Geography Vol. 5, No. 3. University of California Press, Berkeley.

Sayles, E. B. 1936. *An Archaeological Survey of Chihuahua, Mexico*. Medallion Papers No. 22. Gila Pueblo, Globe, Arizona.

Sayles, E. B. 1937. Stone Implements and Bowls. In *Excavations at Snaketown: Material Culture*, by Harold S. Gladwin, Emil W. Haury, E. B. Sayles, and Nora Gladwin, pp. 101–120. Medallion Papers No. 25. Gila Pueblo, Globe, Arizona.

Sayles, E. B. 1941. Archaeology of the Cochise Culture. In *The Cochise Culture*, by E. B. Sayles and Ernst Antevs, pp. 1–30. Medallion Papers No. 29. Gila Pueblo, Globe, Arizona.

Sayles, E. B. 1945. *The San Simon Branch: Excavations at Cave Creek and in the San Simon Valley, I: Material Culture*. Medallion Papers No. 34. Gila Pueblo, Globe, Arizona.

Sayles, E. B., and Ernst Antevs. 1941. *The Cochise Culture*. Medallion Papers No. 29. Gila Pueblo, Globe, Arizona.

Scantling, Frederick H. 1940. Excavations at the Jackrabbit Ruin, Papago Indian Reservation, Arizona. Master's thesis, Department of Anthropology, University of Arizona, Tucson.

Schachner, Gregson. 2006. The Decline of Zuni Glaze Ware Production in the Tumultuous Fifteenth Century. In *The Social Life of Pots: Glaze Wares and Cultural Dynamics in the Southwest, A.D. 1250–1680*, edited by Judith A. Habicht-Mauche, Suzanne L. Eckert, and Deborah L. Huntley, pp. 124–141. University of Arizona Press, Tucson.

Schaefer, Jerry. 1994. The Stuff of Creation: Recent Approaches to Ceramic Analysis in the Colorado Desert. In *Recent Research Along the Lower Colorado River: Proceedings from a Symposium Presented at the 59th Annual Meeting of the Society for American Archaeology, Anaheim, California, April 1994*, edited by Joseph A. Ezzo, pp. 81–100. Technical Series No. 51. Statistical Research, Tucson, Arizona.

Schmidt, Erich F. 1927. A Stratigraphic Study in the Gila-Salt Region, Arizona. *Proceedings of the National Academy of Sciences of the United States of America* 13(5):291–298.

Schmidt, Erich F. 1928. *Time-Relations of Prehistoric Pottery Types in Southern Arizona*. Anthropological Papers Vol. 30, No. 5. American Museum of Natural History, New York.

Schoenwetter, James. 1964. Pollen Analysis of Cochiti Project Materials: Preliminary Report. Electronic document, The Digital Archaeological Record (tDAR), https://core.tdar.org/document/5981/pollen-analysis-of-cochiti-project-materials-preliminary-report/, accessed June 18, 2018.

Schoenwetter, James. 1965a. Pollen Studies at Reeve Ruin and the Davis Ranch Site: Electronic document, The Digital Archaeological Record (tDAR), Preliminary Report. https://core.tdar.org/document/5986/pollen-studies-at-reeve-ruin-and-the-davis-ranch-site-preliminary-report, accessed June 18, 2018.

Schoenwetter, James. 1965b. Pollen Studies at Picuris Pueblo: Preliminary Report. Electronic document, The Digital Archaeological Record (tDAR), https://core.tdar.org/ document/5987/pollen-studies-at-picuris-pueblo-preliminary-report, accessed June 18, 2018.

Schoenwetter, James. 1965c. Pollen Studies at the Sapawe Site: Preliminary Report. Electronic document, The Digital Archaeological Record (tDAR), https://core.tdar.org/document/5985/pollen-studies-at-the-sapawe-site-preliminary-report, accessed June 18, 2018.

Schoenwetter, James. 1970. Archaeological Pollen Studies of the Colorado Plateau. *American Antiquity* 35:35–48.

Schoenwetter, James, and Alfred E. Dittert. 1968. An Ecological Interpretation of Anasazi Settlement Patterns. In *Anthropological Archaeology in the Americas*, edited by Betty J. Meggers, pp 41–66. Anthropological Society of Washington, Washington, D.C.

Schroeder, Albert H. 1940. A Stratigraphic Survey of Pre-Spanish Trash Mounds of the Salt River Valley, Arizona. Master's thesis, Department of Anthropology, University of Arizona, Tucson.

Schroeder, Albert H. 1952. The Bearing of Ceramics on Developments in the Hohokam Classic Period. *Southwestern Journal of Anthropology* 8:320–335.

Schroeder, Albert H. 1958. Lower Colorado Buff Ware: A Descriptive Revision. In *Pottery Types of the Southwest*, edited by Harold S. Colton, Ware 16. Museum of Northern Arizona Ceramic Series 3D. Northern Arizona Society of Science and Art, Flagstaff.

Schroedl, Alan R. (editor). 1989. *Kayenta Anasazi Archaeology and Navajo Ethnohistory on the Northwest Shonto Plateau: The N-16 Project*. 2 vols. Cultural Resources Report 412-01-8909. P-III Associates, Salt Lake City, Utah.

Second Southwestern Ceramic Seminar. 1959. *Second Southwestern Ceramic Seminar: White*

Mountain Red Ware and Shiwanna Red Ware. Museum of Northern Arizona, Flagstaff.

Seymour, Deni J. 1989. The Dynamics of Sobaipuri Settlement in the Eastern Pimería Alta. *Journal of the Southwest* 31:205–222.

Seymour, Deni J. 2009. The Canutillo Complex: Evidence of Protohistoric Mobile Occupants in the Southern Southwest. *Kiva* 74:421–446.

Seymour, Deni J. 2011. *Where the Earth and Sky Are Sewn Together: Sobaipuri-O'odham Contexts of Contact and Colonialism*. University of Utah Press, Salt Lake City.

Shafer, Harry J. 2003. *Mimbres Archaeology at the NAN Ranch Ruin*. University of New Mexico Press, Albuquerque.

Shafer, Harry J., and Robbie L. Brewington. 1995. Microstylistic Changes in Mimbres Black-on-white Pottery: Examples from the NAN Ruin, Grant County, New Mexico. *Kiva* 61: 5–29.

Sharer, Robert J., and Loa P. Traxler. 2006. *The Ancient Maya*. 6th ed. Stanford University Press, Stanford, California.

Shelley, Steven D., and Jeffrey H. Altschul. 1996. Introduction. In *On the Border: Analysis of Materials Recovered from the 1964 and 1991–1992 Excavations at the Garden Canyon Site (AZ EE:11:13 ASM)*, edited by Steven D. Shelley and Jeffrey H. Altschul, pp. 1–13. Technical Series No. 61. Statistical Research, Tucson, Arizona.

Shelley, Steven D., and Jeffrey H. Altschul (editors). 1996. *On the Border: Analysis of Materials Recovered from the 1964 and 1991–1992 Excavations at the Garden Canyon Site (AZ EE:11:13 ASM)*. Technical Series No. 61. Statistical Research, Tucson, Arizona.

Shenk, Lynette O., and George A. Teague. 1975. *Excavations at Tubac Presidio*. Archaeological Series No. 85. Arizona State Museum, University of Arizona, Tucson.

Shepard, Anna O. 1956. *Ceramics for the Archaeologist*. Publication No. 609. Carnegie Institution, Washington, D.C.

Simmons, Leo W. (editor). 1942. *Sun Chief: The Autobiography of a Hopi Indian*. Yale University Press, New Haven, Connecticut.

Skibo, James M., Eugene B. McCluney, and William H. Walker. 2002. *The Joyce Well Site: On the Frontier of the Casas Grandes World*. University of Utah Press, Salt Lake City.

Sliva, R. Jane. 1997. *An Introduction to the Study and Analysis of Flaked Stone Artifacts and Lithic Technology*. Center for Desert Archaeology, Tucson, Arizona.

Sliva, R. Jane. 2005. Developments in Flaked Stone Technology During the Transition to Agriculture. In *Material Cultures and Lifeways of Early Agricultural Communities in Southern Arizona*, edited by R. Jane Sliva, pp. 47–98. Anthropological Papers No. 35. Center for Desert Archaeology, Tucson, Arizona.

Smiley, Terah L. 1952a. *Four Late Prehistoric Kivas at Point of Pines, Arizona*. University of Arizona Bulletin Vol. 23, No. 3. Social Science Bulletin No. 21. University of Arizona Press, Tucson.

Smiley, Terah L. 1952b. *A Summary of Tree-Ring Dates from Southwestern Archaeological Sites*. University of Arizona Bulletin, Vol. 22, No. 4. Laboratory Bulletin of Tree-Ring Research No. 5. University of Arizona Press, Tucson.

Smith, Jimmy E., II, Louis "Pinky" Robertson, Art Tawater, Bryan Jameson, and Glynn Osburn. 2009. *Techado Spring Pueblo, West-Central New Mexico*. Tarrant County Archeological Society Special Publication No. 3. Tarrant County Archeological Society, Fort Worth, Texas.

Smith, Philip G. 1977. A Study of San Carlos Red-on-brown, a Prehistoric Ceramic Type. Student paper prepared for Anthropology 299 at the University of Arizona. Manuscript on file, Emil W. Haury Papers, MS 3, Library and Archives, Arizona State Museum, University of Arizona, Tucson.

Smith, Philip G. 1979. Salado Sites in the Dripping Springs Valley, Central Arizona. *Artifact* 17(2):38–69.

Smith, Watson. 1952a. *Excavations in Big Hawk Valley, Wupatki National Monument, Arizona.* Museum of Northern Arizona Bulletin No. 24. Northern Arizona Society of Science and Art, Flagstaff.

Smith, Watson. 1952b. *Kiva Mural Decorations at Awatovi and Kawaika-a with a Survey of Other Wall Paintings in the Pueblo Southwest.* Papers of the Peabody Museum of American Archaeology and Ethnology Vol. 37. Harvard University, Cambridge, Massachusetts.

Smith, Watson. 1959. Harvey L. Johnson, 1904–1959. *Kiva* 24(4):25.

Smith, Watson. 1971. *Painted Ceramics of the Western Mound at Awatovi.* Papers of the Peabody Museum of Archaeology and Ethnology Vol. 38. Harvard University, Cambridge, Massachusetts.

Smith, Watson. 1972 *Prehistoric Kivas of Antelope Mesa, Northeastern Arizona.* Papers of the Peabody Museum of Archaeology and Ethnology Vol. 39, Pt. 1. Harvard University, Cambridge, Massachusetts.

Smith, Watson, Richard B. Woodbury, and Nathalie F. S. Woodbury. 1966. *The Excavation of Hawikuh by Frederick Webb Hodge: Report of the Hendricks-Hodge Expedition, 1917–1923.* Contributions from the Museum of the American Indian Heye Foundation Vol. 20. Museum of the American Indian, New York.

Spier, Leslie. 1928. *Havasupai Ethnography.* Anthropological Papers Vol. 29, No. 3. American Museum of Natural History, New York.

Spurr, Kimberley. 2013. Mortuary Practices in the Homeland. *Archaeology Southwest* 27(3):15–16.

Stallings, W. S., Jr. 1931. *El Paso Polychrome.* Technical Series Bulletin No. 3. Laboratory of Anthropology, Santa Fe, New Mexico.

Stark, Miriam T., Mark D. Elson, and Jeffery J. Clark. 1998. Social Boundaries and Technical Choices in Tonto Basin Prehistory. In *The Archaeology of Social Boundaries*, edited by Miriam T. Stark, pp. 208–231. Smithsonian Institution, Washington, D.C.

Steen, Charlie R. 1962. Excavations at the Upper Ruin, Tonto National Monument, 1940. In *Archeological Studies at Tonto National Monument, Arizona*, edited by Louis R. Caywood, pp. vii–30. Technical Series Vol. 2. Southwestern Monuments Association, Gila Pueblo, Globe, Arizona.

Stewart, Joe D., and Karen R. Adams. 1999. Evaluating Visual Criteria for Identifying Carbon- and Iron-Based Pottery Paints from the Four Corners Region Using SEM-EDS. *American Antiquity* 64:675–696.

Stewart, Joe D., Karen R. Adams, Graham J. Borradaile, and Allan J. MacKenzie. 2002. Investigations of Paints on Ancestral Puebloan Black-on-white Pottery Using Magnetic and Microanalytic Methods. *Journal of Archaeological Science* 29:1309–1316.

Strand, Jennifer G. 1998. An Analysis of the Homol'ovi Fauna with Emphasis on Ritual Behavior. PhD dissertation, Department of Anthropology, University of Arizona, Tucson. UMI, Ann Arbor, Michigan.

Sullivan, Alan P., III. 1986. *Prehistory of the Upper Basin, Coconino County, Arizona.* Archaeological Series No. 167. Arizona State Museum, University of Arizona, Tucson.

Swartz, Deborah L. 2008. Introduction. In *Life in the Foothills: Archaeological Investigations in the Tortolita Mountains of Southern Arizona*, edited by Deborah L. Swartz, pp. 1–13. Anthropological Papers No. 46. Center for Desert Archaeology, Tucson, Arizona.

Taylor, Walter W. 1948. *A Study of Archeology.* Memoirs of the American Anthropological Association No. 69. American Anthropological Association, Menasha, Wisconsin.

Teague, George. 1980. Appendix B: Stone Artifacts from Alder Wash Ruin. In *The Peppersauce Wash Project: Excavations at Three Multicomponent Sites in the Lower San Pedro Valley, Arizona*, by W. Bruce Masse, pp. 297–322. Contribution to Highway Salvage Archaeology in Arizona No. 53. Manuscript on file, Library and

Archives, Arizona State Museum, University of Arizona, Tucson.

Teague, George. 1981. The Nonflaked Stone Artifacts from Las Colinas. In *The 1968 Excavations at Mound 8, Las Colinas Ruins Group, Phoenix, Arizona*, edited by Laurens C. Hammack and Alan P. Sullivan III, pp. 201–247. Archaeological Series No. 154. Arizona State Museum, University of Arizona, Tucson.

Thiel, J. Homer, and Michael W. Diehl. 2006. Cultural History of the Tucson Basin and the Project Area. In *Rio Nuevo Archaeology, 2000–2003: Investigations at the San Agustín Mission and Mission Gardens, Tucson Presidio, Tucson Pressed Brick Company, and Clearwater Site*, edited by J. Homer Thiel and Jonathan B. Mabry, pp 3.1–3.12. Technical Report No. 2004-11. Desert Archaeology, Tucson, Arizona.

Titiev, Mischa. 1944. *Old Oraibi: A Study of the Hopi Indians of Third Mesa*. Papers of the Peabody Museum of American Archaeology and Ethnology Vol. 22, Pt. 1. Harvard University, Cambridge, Massachusetts.

Toulouse, Joseph H., Jr. 1939. Arrow-Shaft Tools (With Notes on Their General Distribution). In *Preliminary Report on the 1937 Excavations, BC 50–51, Chaco Canyon, New Mexico, With Some Distributional Analyses*, edited by Clyde Kluckhohn and Paul Reiter, pp. 80–89. University of New Mexico Bulletin No. 345. Anthropological Series Vol. 3, No. 2. University of New Mexico Press, Albuquerque.

Triadan, Daniela. 1997. *Ceramic Commodities and Common Containers: Production and Distribution of White Mountain Red Ware in the Grasshopper Region, Arizona*. Anthropological Papers of the University of Arizona No. 61. University of Arizona Press, Tucson.

Triadan, Daniela. 2013. Compositional and Distributional Analyses of Some 14th Century Ceramics from Kinishba Pueblo: Implications for Pottery Production and Migration. In *Kinishba Lost and Found: Mid-Century Excavations and Contemporary Perspectives*, edited by John R. Welch, pp. 209–241. Archaeological Series No. 206. Arizona State Museum, University of Arizona, Tucson.

Triadan, Daniela, Barbara J. Mills, and Andrew I. Duff. 2002. From Compositional to Anthropological: Fourteenth-Century Red Ware Circulation and Its Implications for Pueblo Reorganization. In *Ceramic Production and Circulation in the Greater Southwest: Source Determination by INAA and Complementary Mineralogical Investigations*, edited by Donna M. Glowacki and Hector Neff, pp. 85–97. Monograph 44. Cotsen Institute of Archaeology, University of California, Los Angeles.

Trotter, Mildred, and Goldine C. Gleser. 1958. A Re-evaluation of Estimation of Stature Based on Measurements of Stature Taken During Life and of Long Bones After Death. *American Journal of Physical Anthropology* 16:79–123.

Tuthill, Carr. 1947. *The Tres Alamos Site on the San Pedro River, Southeastern Arizona*. Amerind Foundation No. 4. Amerind Foundation, Dragoon, Arizona.

Tuthill, Carr. 1950. Notes on the Dragoon Complex. In *For the Dean: Essays in Anthropology in Honor of Byron Cummings on His Eighty-Ninth Birthday, September 20, 1950*, edited by Erik K. Reed and Dale S. King, pp. 51–61. Hohokam Museums Association, Tucson, Arizona; Southwestern Monuments Association, Santa Fe, New Mexico.

Tyberg, Joel J. 2000. Influences, Occupation, and Salado Development at the Solomonsville Site. Master's thesis, Department of Anthropology, University of Colorado, Boulder.

Urban, Sharon F. 2003. *Glycymeris* Reigns: Shell at the Zanardelli Site (The shell analysis forms and notes for the Valley Telephone Project, Arizona State Museum Accession 2003-1513). Manuscript on file, Library and Archives, Arizona State Museum, University of Arizona, Tucson.

Valado, Martha Trenna. 1999. Ground Stone Technology in the Silver Creek Area, East-Central

Arizona. Master's thesis, Department of Anthropology, University of Arizona, Tucson. ProQuest, Ann Arbor, Michigan

Vanderpot, Rein, and Jeffrey H. Altschul. 2007. The Mescal Wash Site: A Persistent Place in Southeastern Arizona. In *Hinterlands and Regional Dynamics in the Ancient Southwest*, edited by Alan P. Sullivan III and James M. Bayman, pp. 50–69. University of Arizona Press, Tucson.

Vargas, Victoria D. 2000. Shell Artifacts. In *Archaeological Investigations at AZ V:13:201, Town of Kearny, Pinal County, Arizona*, compiled by Caven P. Clark, pp. 10.1–10.8. Cultural Resources Report No. 114. Archaeological Consulting Services, Tempe, Arizona.

Vickrey, Irene S. 1939. Draft description of San Carlos Redware. Manuscript on file, Emil W. Haury Papers, MS 3, Library and Archives, Arizona State Museum, University of Arizona, Tucson.

Vickrey, Irene S. 1962. Description of Types as Identified at Besh-Ba-Gowah. In *Archaeological Studies at Tonto National Monument, Arizona*, edited by Louis R. Caywood, p. 19. Technical Series Vol. 2. Southwestern Monuments Association, Gila Pueblo, Globe, Arizona.

Vint, James M. 2000. Fieldnotes and Forms Associated with Center For Desert Archaeology Excavations at José Solas Ruin (AZ BB:11:91[ASM]). Manuscript on file, Archaeology Southwest, Tucson, Arizona.

Vint, James M. 2017. Time and Place of the Early Agricultural Period in the Tucson Basin of Southern Arizona. PhD dissertation, School of Anthropology, University of Arizona, Tucson. ProQuest, Ann Arbor, Michigan.

Vokes, Arthur W. 1984. The Shell Assemblage of the Salt-Gila Aqueduct Project Sites. In *Hohokam Archaeology Along the Salt-Gila Aqueduct Central Arizona Project, Volume 8: Material Culture*, edited by Lynn S. Teague and Patricia L. Crown, pp. 465–574. Archaeological Series No. 150. Arizona State Museum, University of Arizona, Tucson.

Vokes, Arthur W. 1986. Shell. In *Archaeological Investigations at the West Branch Site: Early and Middle Rincon Occupation in the Southern Tucson Basin*, by Frederick W. Huntington, pp. 229–250. Anthropological Papers No. 5. Institute for American Research, Tucson, Arizona.

Vokes, Arthur W. 1988a. Shell Artifacts. In *The 1982–1984 Excavations at Las Colinas, Volume 4: Material Culture*, by David R. Abbott, Kim E. Beckwith, Patricia L. Crown, R. Thomas Euler, David A. Gregory, J. Ronald London, Marilyn B. Saul, Larry A. Schwalbe, Mary Bernard-Shaw, Christine R. Szuter, and Arthur W. Vokes, pp. 319–384. Archaeological Series No. 162. Arizona State Museum, University of Arizona, Tucson.

Vokes, Arthur W. 1988b. Shell Artifacts. In *Hohokam Archaeology Along Phase B of the Tucson Aqueduct, Central Arizona Project, Volume 2: Excavations at Fastimes (AZ AA:12:384), a Rillito Phase Site in the Avra Valley*, edited by Jon S. Czaplicki and John C. Ravesloot, pp. 223–233. Archaeological Series No. 178. Arizona State Museum, University of Arizona, Tucson.

Vokes, Arthur W. 1989a. Late Pioneer and Colonial Period Shell. In *Hohokam Archaeology Along Phase B of the Tucson Aqueduct, Central Arizona Project, Volume 1: Syntheses and Interpretations*, edited by Jon S. Czaplicki and John C. Ravesloot, pp. 477–487. Archaeological Series No. 178. Arizona State Museum, University of Arizona, Tucson.

Vokes, Arthur W. 1989b. Shell Artifacts. In *Archaeological Investigations at the Redtail Site, AA:12:149(ASM), in the Northern Tucson Basin*, by Mary Bernard-Shaw, pp. 191–198. Technical Report No. 89-8. Center for Desert Archaeology, Tucson, Arizona.

Vokes, Arthur W. 1989c. Shell Artifacts. In *Hohokam Archaeology Along Phase B of the Tucson Aqueduct, Central Arizona Project, Volume 3: Excavations at Water World (AZ AA:16:94), a Rillito Phase Ballcourt Village in the Avra*

Valley, edited by Jon S. Czaplicki and John C. Ravesloot, pp. 237–248. Archaeological Series No. 178. Arizona State Museum, University of Arizona, Tucson.

Vokes, Arthur W. 1993. Shell from AZ BB:9:50(ASM). In *Archaeological Test Excavations and Plan for Data Recovery at AZ BB:9:50(ASM), the Gibbon Springs Site, Pima County, Arizona*, by Mark C. Slaughter and David A. Phillips Jr., pp. 11.1–11.2. Archaeological Report No. 93-50. SWCA Environmental Consultants, Tucson, Arizona.

Vokes, Arthur W. 1995. Shell Artifacts. In *Archaeological Investigations at Los Morteros, a Prehistoric Settlement in the Northern Tucson Basin*, Vol. 2, by Henry D. Wallace, pp. 567–604. Anthropological Papers No. 17. Center for Desert Archaeology, Tucson, Arizona.

Vokes, Arthur W. 1996a. Marine Shell Artifacts at Early Villages in Southern Arizona and Implications for Long Distance Exchange. Paper presented at the 61st Annual Meeting of the Society for American Archaeology, New Orleans, Louisiana.

Vokes, Arthur W. 1996b. Shell Material from the Gibbon Springs Site. In *Excavation of the Gibbon Springs Site: A Classic Period Village in the Northeastern Tucson Basin*, edited by Mark C. Slaughter and Heidi Roberts, pp. 401–411. Archaeological Report No. 94-87. SWCA Environmental Consultants, Tucson, Arizona.

Vokes, Arthur W. 1997. Shell Material from AZ AA:12:311(ASM). In *Data Recovery at Site AZ AA:12:311(ASM) and Archaeological Monitoring for the Coventry Homes Pipeline Project*, by David B. Tucker, pp. 79–87. Archaeological Report No. 97-177. SWCA Environmental Consultants, Tucson, Arizona.

Vokes, Arthur W. 1998. Shell Artifacts. In *Archaeological Investigations of Early Village Sites in the Middle Santa Cruz Valley: Analyses and Synthesis*, edited by Jonathan B. Mabry, pp. 437–470. Anthropological Papers No. 19. Center for Desert Archaeology, Tucson, Arizona.

Vokes, Arthur W. 2001a. Shell Artifacts. In *Excavations in the Santa Cruz River Floodplain: The Early Agricultural Component at Los Pozos*, by David A. Gregory, pp. 135–152. Anthropological Papers No. 21. Center for Desert Archaeology, Tucson, Arizona.

Vokes, Arthur W. 2001b. Shell (The shell from the Yuma Wash Site: Silverbell Place Project). AP-2017-424: Data Recovery at a portion of AZ AA:12:311, southwest of Silverbell Road and west of Yuma Wash. Manuscript on file, Library and Archives, Arizona State Museum, University of Arizona, Tucson.

Vokes, Arthur W. 2001c. The Shell Ornament Assemblage. In *Tonto Creek Archaeological Project: Life and Death Along Tonto Creek*, edited by Jeffery J. Clark and Penny Dufoe Minturn, pp. 353–419. Anthropological Papers No. 24. Center for Desert Archaeology, Tucson, Arizona.

Vokes, Arthur W. 2005. Early Agricultural Period Shell Use. In *Material Cultures and Lifeways of Early Agricultural Communities in Southern Arizona*, edited by R. Jane Sliva, pp. 153–170. Anthropological Papers No. 35. Center for Desert Archaeology, Tucson, Arizona.

Vokes, Arthur W. 2008. Shell (The shell from the 2002–2003 Field Season of the Marana Heritage Program-Yuma Wash Site). AP-2010-296: Marana Heritage Program: Yuma Wash Field School and Bojórquez-Aguirre Ranch Data Recovery. Manuscript on file, Library and Archives, Arizona State Museum, University of Arizona, Tucson.

Vokes, Arthur W. 2009a. MSM Project Shell. In *Archaeological Investigations at Five Sites West of the Santa Cruz River in Marana, Arizona: Yuma Wash and Silverbell-Ina Hohokam Sites AZ AA:12:311(ASM), AZ AA:12:314(ASM), and AZ AA:12:315(ASM); & Bojórquez-Aguirre Ranch and Meador-Cañas Sites AZ AA:12:122(ASM) and AZ AA:12:313(ASM)*, edited by Arthur C. MacWilliams and Allen Dart, pp. 11.1–11.20. Old Pueblo Archaeology Center, Tucson, Arizona.

Vokes, Arthur W. 2009b. Shell Ornaments (The shell from Seasons 3 & 4 of the Marana Heritage Program-Yuma Wash Site). AP-2010-296: Marana Heritage Program: Yuma Wash Field School and Bojórquez-Aguirre Ranch Data Recovery. Manuscript on file, Library and Archives, Arizona State Museum, University of Arizona, Tucson.

Vokes, Arthur W. 2009c. A Synthesis of the Yuma Wash Site's Shell Material from the MHPY and Other Projects. In *Archaeological Investigations at Five Sites West of the Santa Cruz River in Marana, Arizona: Yuma Wash and Silverbell-Ina Hohokam Sites AZ AA:12:311(ASM), AZ AA:12:314(ASM), and AZ AA:12:315(ASM); & Bojórquez-Aguirre Ranch and Meador-Cañas Sites AZ AA:12:122(ASM) and AZ AA:12:313(ASM)*, edited by Arthur C. MacWilliams and Allen Dart, pp. 28.1–28.30. Old Pueblo Archaeology Center, Tucson, Arizona.

Vokes, Arthur W. 2009d. Shell Ornaments from the Zanardelli Site, AZ BB:13:1(ASM). In *Archaeological Excavations at the Zanardelli Site, AZ BB:13:1 (ASM)*, edited by Ellen C. Ruble, pp. 116–131. Technical Report No. 2004-01. Desert Archaeology, Tucson, Arizona.

Vokes, Arthur W. 2011. Shell Ornaments. In *Archaeological Data Recovery Excavations at a Portion of AZ BB:13:1(ASM), the Zanardelli Site, within the U.S. Highway 89 Right-of-way South of Tucson in Pima County, Arizona*, edited by Jeffrey T. Jones, pp. 187–207. Tierra Archaeological Report No. 2005-124. Tierra Right of Way Services, Tucson, Arizona.

Vokes, Arthur W. 2016. The Shell Assemblage. In *Archaeological Investigations at the Yuma Wash Site and Outlying Settlements, Part 2*, edited by Deborah L. Swartz, pp. 707–754. Anthropological Papers No. 49. Archaeology Southwest, Tucson, Arizona.

Vokes, Arthur W., and Jenny L. Adams. 2016. Ornaments Among Mortuary Contexts, Yuma Wash. In *Archaeological Investigations at the Yuma Wash Site and Outlying Settlements, Part 2*, edited by Deborah L. Swartz, pp. 755–785. Anthropological Papers No. 49. Archaeology Southwest, Tucson, Arizona.

Voth, Heinrich R. 1905. *The Traditions of the Hopi*. Publication 96. Anthropological Series Vol. 8. Field Colombian Museum, Chicago.

Walker, William H. 1995. Ceremonial Trash? In *Expanding Archaeology*, edited by James M. Skibo, William H. Walker, and Axel E. Nielsen, pp. 67–79. University of Utah Press, Salt Lake City.

Walker, William H. 1999. Ritual Prehistory: A Pueblo Case Study. PhD dissertation, Department of Anthropology, University of Arizona, Tucson. UMI, Ann Arbor, Michigan.

Wallace, Henry D. 1986. *Rincon Phase Decorated Ceramics in the Tucson Basin: A Focus on the West Branch Site*. Anthropological Papers No. 1. Institute for American Research, Tucson, Arizona.

Wallace, Henry D. 1995. Decorated Buffware and Brownware Ceramics. In *The Roosevelt Community Development Study Volume 2: Ceramic Chronology, Technology, and Economics*, edited by James M. Heidke and Miriam T. Stark, pp. 19–84. Anthropological Papers No. 14. Center for Desert Archaeology, Tucson, Arizona.

Wallace, Henry D. 1996. Notes on the Alice Hubbard Carpenter Collection. *Journal of the Southwest* 38:351–365.

Wallace, Henry D. 2001. Time Seriation and Typological Refinement of the Middle Gila Buffware Sequence: Snaketown Through Soho Phases. In *The Grewe Archaeological Research Project Volume 2: Material Culture, Part I: Ceramic Studies*, edited by David R. Abbott, pp. 177–261. Anthropological Research Papers 99-1. Northland Research, Tempe, Arizona.

Wallace, Henry D. 2003. Ballcourts and Buff Wares. *Archaeology Southwest* 17(3):5–6.

Wallace, Henry D. 2004. Update to the Middle Gila Buff Ware Ceramic Sequence. In *Hohokam Farming on the Salt River Floodplain: Refining*

Models and Analytical Methods, edited by T. Kathleen Henderson, pp. 45–124. Anthropological Papers No. 43. Center for Desert Archaeology, Tucson, Arizona.

Wallace, Henry D. 2014. Introduction to the Land Between. In *Between Mimbres and Hohokam: Exploring the Archaeology and History of Southeastern Arizona and Southwestern New Mexico*, edited by Henry D. Wallace, pp. 1–13. Anthropological Papers No. 52. Archaeology Southwest, Tucson, Arizona.

Wallace, Henry D., and William H. Doelle. 2001. Classic Period Warfare in Southern Arizona. In *Deadly Landscapes: Case Studies in Prehistoric Southwestern Warfare*, edited by Glen E. Rice and Steven A. LeBlanc, pp. 239–287. University of Utah Press, Salt Lake City.

Wallace, Henry D., James M. Heidke, and William H. Doelle. 1995. Hohokam Origins. *Kiva* 60:575–618.

Wallace, Laurel T. 1998. *The Ormand Village: Final Report on the 1965–1966 Excavation*. Archaeology Notes 229. Office of Archaeological Studies, Museum of New Mexico, Santa Fe.

Ward, Albert E. 1975. *Inscription House: Two Research Reports*. Museum of Northern Arizona Technical Series No. 16. Northern Arizona Society of Science and Art, Flagstaff.

Wasley, William W. 1957. *The Archaeological Survey of the Arizona State Museum*. Arizona State Museum, University of Arizona, Tucson.

Waters, Michael R. 1982a. The Lowland Patayan Ceramic Tradition. In *Hohokam and Patayan: Prehistory of Southwestern Arizona*, edited by Randall H. McGuire and Michael B. Schiffer, pp. 275–297. Academic Press, New York.

Waters, Michael R. 1982b. Appendix G: The Lowland Patayan Ceramic Typology. In *Hohokam and Patayan: Prehistory of Southwestern Arizona*, edited by Randall H. McGuire and Michael B. Schiffer, pp. 537–570. Academic Press, New York.

Wauchope, Robert (editor). 1956. *Seminars in Archaeology: 1955*. Memoirs No. 11. Society for American Archaeology, Salt Lake City, Utah.

Welch, John R. 1995. Preservation, Research, and Public Interpretation at Pueblo Devol, an Arizona Cliff Dwelling. *Kiva* 61:121–143.

Wendorf, Fred. 1950. *A Report on the Excavation of a Small Ruin Near Point of Pines, East Central Arizona*. University of Arizona Bulletin Vol. 21, No. 3. Social Science Bulletin No. 19. University of Arizona Press, Tucson.

Wheat, Joe Ben. 1955. *Mogollon Culture Prior to A.D. 1000*. American Anthropological Association Memoir No. 82. Memoirs of the Society for American Archaeology No. 10. American Anthropological Association, Menasha, Wisconsin; Society for American Archaeology, Salt Lake City, Utah.

Wheat, Joe Ben. 1956. Review of "The Sobaipuri Indians of the Upper San Pedro River Valley, Southeastern Arizona." *American Antiquity* 21:430–431.

White, Devin Alan. 2004. *Hohokam Palettes*. Archaeological Series No. 196. Arizona State Museum, University of Arizona, Tucson.

Whiting, Alfred F. 1939. *Ethnobotany of the Hopi*. Museum of Northern Arizona Bulletin No. 15. Northern Arizona Society of Science and Art, Flagstaff.

Whittlesey, Stephanie M., Richard S. Ciolek-Torrello, and Matthew A. Sterner. 1994. Prehistory of the San Pedro River Valley. In *Southern Arizona, the Last 12,000 Years: A Cultural Historic Overview for the Western Army National Guard Aviation Training Site*, by Stephanie M. Whittlesey, Richard S. Ciolek-Torrello, and Matthew A. Sterner, pp. 45–108. Technical Series No. 48. Statistical Research, Tucson, Arizona.

Whittlesey, Stephanie M., and Robert A. Heckman. 2000. Other Painted Ceramics of Southeastern Arizona. In *Prehistoric Painted Pottery of Southeastern Arizona*, by Robert A. Heckman, Barbara K. Montgomery, and Stephanie M. Whittlesey, pp. 95–115. Technical Series No. 77. Statistical Research, Tucson, Arizona.

Wilcox, David R. 1979. The Hohokam Regional System. In *An Archaeological Test of Sites in the Gila Butte-Santan Region, South-Central Arizona*, by Glen E. Rice, David R. Wilcox, Kevin Rafferty, and James Schoenwetter, pp. 77–116. Anthropological Research Papers No. 18. Technical Paper No. 3. Department of Anthropology, Arizona State University, Tempe.

Wilcox, David R. 1980. The Current Status of the Hohokam Concept. In *Current Issues in Hohokam Prehistory: Proceedings of a Symposium*, edited by David E. Doyel and Fred G. Plog, pp. 236–242. Arizona State University Anthropological Research Papers No. 23. Department of Anthropology, Arizona State University, Tempe.

Wilcox, David R., and James Holmlund. 2007. *The Archaeology of Perry Mesa and Its World*. Bilby Research Center Occasional Papers No. 3. Northern Arizona University, Flagstaff.

Wilcox, David R., and Lynette O. Shenk. 1977. *The Architecture of Casa Grande and Its Interpretations*. Archaeological Series No. 115. Arizona State Museum, University of Arizona, Tucson.

Wilcox, David R., and Charles Sternberg. 1983. *Hohokam Ballcourts and Their Interpretation*. Arizona State Museum Archaeological Series No. 160. Arizona State Museum, University of Arizona, Tucson.

Willey, Gordon R., Charles C. Di Peso, William A. Ritchie, Irving Rouse, John H. Rowe, and Donald W. Lathrap. 1956. An Archaeological Classification of Culture Contact Situations. In *Seminars in Archaeology: 1955*, edited by Robert Wauchope, pp. 1–30. Memoirs No. 11. Society for American Archaeology, Salt Lake City, Utah.

Williams, Jack. 1986. The Presidio of Santa Cruz de Terrenate: A Forgotten Fortress of Southern Arizona. *Smoke Signal* 47–48:129–148.

Wilson, C. Dean. 1998a. Ormand Ceramic Analysis Part I: Methodology and Categories. In *The Ormand Village: Final Report on the 1965–1966 Excavation*, by Laurel T. Wallace, pp. 195–251. Archaeology Notes 229. Office of Archaeological Studies, Museum of New Mexico, Santa Fe.

Wilson, C. Dean. 1998b. Ormand Ceramic Analyses Part II: Ceramic Trends from the Ormand Village. In *The Ormand Village: Final Report on the 1965–1966 Excavation*, by Laurel T. Wallace, pp. 253–290. Archaeology Notes 229. Office of Archaeological Studies, Museum of New Mexico, Santa Fe.

Windmiller, Ric. 1972. *Ta-e-wun: A Colonial Period Hohokam Campsite in East-Central Arizona*. Archaeological Series No. 11. Arizona State Museum, University of Arizona, Tucson.

Windmiller, Ric. 1974. *Contributions to Pinto Valley Archaeology*. Archaeological Series No. 51. Arizona State Museum, University of Arizona, Tucson.

Withers, Arnold M. 1941. Excavations at Valshni Village, Papago Indian Reservation, Arizona. Master's thesis, Department of Anthropology, University of Arizona, Tucson.

Withers, Arnold M. 1973. *Excavations at Valshni Village, Arizona*. Edited by Walter Thomas Duering. Arizona Archaeologist No. 7. Arizona Archaeological Society, Phoenix.

Wöcherl, Helga (editor). 2007. *Archaeological Investigations at the El Taller, AZ AA:12:92 (ASM), and Rillito Fan, AZ AA:12:788, Sites Along Eastbound I-10 Between Sunset and Ruthrauff Roads, Tucson, Pima County, Arizona*. Technical Report No. 2003-08. Desert Archaeology, Tucson, Arizona.

Wood, J. Scott. 1987. *Checklist of Pottery Types for the Tonto National Forest: An Introduction to the Archaeological Ceramics of Central Arizona*. Arizona Archaeologist No. 21. Arizona Archaeological Society, Phoenix.

Woodbury, Richard B. 1954. *Prehistoric Stone Implements of Northeastern Arizona*. Papers of the Peabody Museum of American Archaeology and Ethnology Vol. 34. Harvard University, Cambridge, Massachusetts.

Woodbury, Richard B., and Nathalie F. S. Woodbury. 1966. Decorated Pottery of the Zuni Area. In *The*

Excavation of Hawikuh by Frederick Webb Hodge: Report of the Hendricks-Hodge Expedition, 1917–1923, by Watson Smith, Richard B. Woodbury, and Nathalie F. S. Woodbury, pp. 302–336. Contributions from the Museum of the American Indian Heye Foundation Vol. 20. Museum of the American Indian, New York.

Woodson, M. Kyle. 1995. The Goat Hill Site: A Western Anasazi Pueblo in the Safford Valley of Southeastern Arizona. Master's thesis, Department of Anthropology, University of Texas, Austin.

Woodson, M. Kyle. 1999. Migrations in Late Anasazi Prehistory: The Evidence from the Goat Hill Site. *Kiva* 65:63–84.

Woodson, M. Kyle. 2002. Synthesis and Conclusions. In *Archaeological Investigations at the Sweetwater Site on the Gila River Indian Community*, edited by M. Kyle Woodson, pp. 233–260. CRMP Technical Report No. 2002-14. Cultural Resource Management Program, Gila River Indian Community, Sacaton, Arizona.

Woodward, Arthur. 1931. *The Grewe Site, Gila Valley, Arizona*. Van Bergen-Los Angeles Museum Expedition Occasional Papers No. 1. Los Angeles Museum of History, Science, and Art, Los Angeles.

Woosley, Anne I., and Bart Olinger. 1993. The Casas Grandes Ceramic Tradition: Production and Interregional Exchange of Ramos Polychrome. In *Culture and Contact: Charles C. Di Peso's Gran Chichimeca*, edited by Anne I. Woosley and John C. Ravesloot, pp. 105–131. New World Studies Series No. 2. Amerind Foundation, Dragoon, Arizona; University of New Mexico Press, Albuquerque.

WoRMS. 2018. World Register of Marine Species. http://www.marinespecies.org/, accessed June 18, 2018.

Wright, Barton A., and Rex E. Gerald. 1950. The Zanardelli Site, Arizona BB:13:12. *Kiva* 16(3):8–15.

Zedeño, María Nieves. 1994. *Sourcing Prehistoric Ceramics at Chodistaas Pueblo, Arizona: The Circulation of People and Pots in the Grasshopper Region*. Anthropological Papers of the University of Arizona No. 58. University of Arizona Press, Tucson.

Zedeño, María Nieves. 2002. Artifact Design, Composition, and Context: Updating the Analysis of Ceramic Circulation at Point of Pines, Arizona. In *Ceramic Production and Circulation in the Greater Southwest: Source Determination by INAA and Complementary Mineralogical Investigations*, edited by Donna M. Glowacki and Hector Neff, pp. 74–84. Monograph 44. Cotsen Institute of Archaeology, University of California, Los Angeles.

CONTRIBUTORS

Ethne Barnes is a private consultant and researcher in physical anthropology/paleopathology recognized for establishing the morphogenetic approach to analyzing developmental anomalies/defects of the human skeleton. She received her PhD in anthropology from Arizona State University in 1991 and is now based in Tucson, Arizona. Her research and consultations have included archaeological projects in Greece, Turkey, China, northern Mexico, South America, and the southwestern and midwestern United States. Her most significant publications include *Atlas of Developmental Field Anomalies of the Human Skeleton: A Paleopathology Perspective* (2012, Wiley-Blackwell), *Diseases and Human Evolution* (2005, University of New Mexico Press), *Developmental Defects of the Axial Skeleton in Paleopathology* (1994, University Press of Colorado), "Developmental Disorders in the Skeleton," in *A Companion to Paleopathology* (2012, edited by Anne Grauer, Wiley-Blackwell), and "Congenital Anomalies," in *Advances in Human Paleopathology* (2008, edited by Ron Pinhasi and Simon Mays, John Wiley and Sons).

William H. Burt (1903–1987) analyzed the mammalian fauna from the Davis Ranch Site at Rex Gerald's request in 1958. At that time, Burt was curator of mammals at the Museum of Zoology and professor in the Department of Zoology at the University of Michigan. He earned his bachelor's (1926) and master's (1927) degrees at the University of Kansas and received his PhD from the University of California, Berkeley (1930). After working as a research fellow at the California Institute of Technology (1931–1935), he came to the University of Michigan. An expert on the systematics, distribution, and ecology of mammals, Burt served as editor of the Museum of Zoology's publication series, as well as the *Journal of Mammalogy*, and twice was elected president of the American Society of Mammalogists. His publications include *The Mammals of Michigan* (1946, University of Michigan Press), *The Mammals of the Great Lakes Region* (1957, University of Michigan Press), and a volume in the Roger Tory Peterson Field Guide Series, *A Field Guide to the Mammals, Giving Field Marks of All Species Found North of the Mexican Boundary* (1952, Houghton Mifflin).

Jeffery J. Clark has been a preservation archaeologist at Archaeology Southwest for 20 years. He is also an adjunct associate professor in the School of Anthropology at the University of Arizona. Jeff received his PhD (1997) and MA (1990) from the University of Arizona and his BA (1983) from Cornell University. During the 1980s and early 1990s, he worked extensively in southwest Asia, including Israel, Syria, and Iraq. Over the past 25 years, Jeff has directed projects in southern Arizona and southwestern New

Mexico through Archaeology Southwest and Desert Archaeology Inc. His research has examined the scale and impact of human migration, focusing on the Salado phenomenon in the late precontact U.S. Southwest. Over the past 10 years, Clark has been a principal investigator, in collaboration with the University of Arizona and other institutions, on several projects that have resulted in large databases used to reconstruct ancient regional social networks.

Jeffrey S. Dean, professor emeritus of dendrochronology in the Laboratory of Tree-Ring Research at the University of Arizona (UA), has PhD (1967) and BA degrees (1961) in anthropology from UA. His interests include the U.S. Southwest, archaeological theory and method, chronometry, dendroarchaeology, paleoenvironmental reconstruction, and relationships between human behavior and environmental stability, variability, and change. His publications include *Chronological Analysis of Tsegi Phase Sites in Northeastern Arizona* (1969, UA Press), "Aspects of Tsegi Phase Social Organization: A Trial Reconstruction" in *Reconstructing Prehistoric Pueblo Societies* (1970, edited by William A. Longacre, University of New Mexico Press), "A Model of Anasazi Behavioral Adaption" in *The Anasazi in a Changing Environment* (1988, edited by George J. Gumerman, Cambridge University Press), and "Late Pueblo II–Pueblo III in Kayenta-Branch Prehistory" in *Prehistoric Culture Change on the Colorado Plateau: Ten Thousand Years on Black Mesa* (2002, edited by Shirley Powell and Francis E. Smiley, UA Press). Volumes he has edited or co-edited include *Tree Rings, Environment, and Humanity* (1996, *Radiocarbon*, Department of Geosciences, UA), *Salado* (2000, Amerind Foundation and University of New Mexico Press), and *Environmental Change and Human Adaptation in the Ancient American Southwest* (2006, University of Utah Press). His work has also appeared in *Science*, *Proceedings of the National Academy of Sciences of the United States of America*, *Nature Climate Change*, *American Antiquity*, *Journal of Anthropological Archaeology*, *Radiocarbon*, *Artificial Life*, *Journal of Archaeological Science*, and *Tree-Ring Research*.

Gloria J. Fenner earned her BA (1958) and MA (1962) degrees in anthropology at the University of Illinois. She joined the staff of the Amerind Foundation in 1963 as an assistant archaeologist. She would later hold the position of archaeologist (1969–1977) and archaeologist/lab chief (1977–1979) at the Amerind, before working as an associate curator at the Arizona State Museum (1979–1982) and curator of the National Park Service's Museum Collections Repository at the Western Archeological and Conservation Center (1982–2006). Fenner edited volumes 1–8 and co-authored volumes 4–8 of *Casas Grandes: A Fallen Trading Center of the Gran Chichimeca* (1974, Amerind Foundation and Northland Press). Her work has also appeared in the Illinois Archaeological Survey Bulletin series, the Western Archeological and Conservation Center's Publications in Anthropology series, *Kiva*, and *Curator*. Her areas of expertise include the archaeology of the U.S. Southwest and northern Mexico, the ethnography of the U.S. Southwest, and museum collections management.

Rex E. Gerald (1928–1990) excavated the Davis Ranch Site in 1957 as a predoctoral research fellow at the Amerind Foundation. He later served 22 years as director of the Centennial Museum at the University of Texas at El Paso (UTEP). At the time of his death, he was an associate professor of anthropology at UTEP. Gerald received his BA in anthropology from the University of Arizona (1951) and his AM in anthropology from the University of Pennsylvania (1957). He was awarded a PhD in anthropology by the University of Chicago in 1975. In his dissertation, he used palynological and faunal data, as well as the spatial distribution of ceramic design elements, to examine social responses to climate change at the Davis Ranch Site and Reeve Ruin. After completing his dissertation, Gerald very seldom turned his attention to archaeology in Arizona, focusing instead on the cultural resources of Texas and northern Chihuahua. He was a pioneer in the field of cultural resource management archaeology in Texas and a key contributor to Spanish presidio studies. He is also remembered as the researcher largely responsible for the government's 1987 decision to restore federal recognition of the Tigua Tribe of Ysleta del Sur Pueblo.

Arthur H. Harris is professor emeritus of biological sciences at the University of Texas at El Paso (UTEP) and curator of paleobiology of the UTEP Biodiversity Collections. Trained as a mammalogist at the University of New Mexico, with additional coursework at the University of Arizona, he added interests in zooarchaeology and late Quaternary vertebrate paleontology early on. Co-authorships of *Mammals of New Mexico* (1975, University of New Mexico Press) and *The Faunal Remains from Arroyo Hondo Pueblo, New Mexico* (1984, School of American Research Press) grew from the first two of these interests, as did a series of shorter papers. Harris's studies of paleontology focus largely on faunas retrieved from southern New Mexico and Trans-Pecos Texas and document late Pleistocene changes through time and space. In recent years, much of his effort has been concentrated on producing and maintaining a web publication, *Pleistocene Vertebrates of Southwestern USA and Northwestern Mexico*, an outgrowth of an earlier book, *Late Pleistocene Vertebrate Paleoecology of the West* (1985, University of Texas Press).

Erika Heacock received her BA (2010) and MA (2015) degrees from the School of Anthropology at the University of Arizona, where she focused on the U.S. Southwest and applied archaeology. Heacock worked as a curatorial assistant (2009–2013) and a curatorial specialist (2013–2017) in the Archaeological Repository at the Arizona State Museum (ASM), at the University of Arizona. Her primary role was documenting and facilitating the transfer of several large collections, pursuant to the Native American Graves Protection and Repatriation Act. While at ASM, she was mentored in archaeomalacology by Arthur W. Vokes. Together, she and Vokes analyzed and wrote reports on several shell assemblages, including material from the Harris Site, in southwestern New Mexico. Heacock incorporated data from Gila Pueblo's 1930s excavations at the Harris Site, as well as the results of recent work by the University of Nevada, Las Vegas, in her MA thesis on the use of shell in the Mimbres region. She currently lives in Arvada, Colorado, and works for Tetra Tech Inc. as a cultural resource management professional.

R. Roy Johnson, an ornithologist and botanist, reanalyzed the avifauna from the Davis Ranch Site, producing a report in 1969. Gerald knew Johnson when they were both faculty members at the University of Texas at El Paso (UTEP). Johnson earned his BS in biology at Arizona State University (1955), his MS in zoology at the University of Arizona (1960), and his PhD in botany at the University of Kansas (1964). He held positions as a professor of biology at Western New Mexico University (assistant professor, 1964–1965), UTEP (assistant, then associate professor, 1965–1968), and Prescott College (associate professor, then professor, 1968–1973). From 1973 to 1979, he was a research scientist at Grand Canyon National Park, and from 1979 to 1992, he served both as unit leader for the National Park Service Cooperative Studies Unit at the University of Arizona (UA) and as a UA professor of natural resources. Johnson is currently a research associate of the Museum of Northern Arizona and is especially interested in avian populations living along the rivers of the Southwest. He has authored or co-authored more than 200 scientific publications. His recent contributions include *Requiem for the Santa Cruz: An Environmental History of an Arizona River*, co-authored with Robert H. Webb, Julio L. Betancourt, and Raymond M. Turner (2014, UA Press).

Patrick D. Lyons is director of the Arizona State Museum, an associate professor in the School of Anthropology at the University of Arizona, and a research associate at Archaeology Southwest. Lyons earned his BA (1991) and MA (1992) in anthropology (specializing in archaeology) at the University of Illinois, Chicago. He received his

PhD in anthropology from the University of Arizona (2001). His research focuses on ancient population movements in the U.S. Southwest and the archaeology, history, ethnography, and ethnohistory of the Hopi people. Lyons has primarily conducted fieldwork in the Homol'ovi settlement cluster, near present-day Winslow, in northeastern Arizona, and in the San Pedro Valley of southeastern Arizona. He is the author of *Ancestral Hopi Migrations* (2003, University of Arizona Press) and co-editor of *Migrants and Mounds: Classic Period Archaeology of the Lower San Pedro Valley* (2012, Archaeology Southwest). His work has also appeared in a number of journals, including *American Antiquity*, *Proceedings of the National Academy of Sciences of the United States of America*, *Heritage Management*, *Journal of Anthropological Archaeology*, *Journal of the Southwest*, and *Kiva*, as well as numerous scholarly edited volumes.

William J. Robinson earned all three of his degrees in anthropology (BA, 1957; MA, 1959; PhD, 1967) at the University of Arizona (UA). He attended the UA archaeological field school at Point of Pines in 1956 and 1957, working with Rex Gerald at AZ W:9:39(ASM) in 1956. Robinson joined the Laboratory of Tree-Ring Research (LTRR) at UA in 1963 as a research associate, becoming a faculty member in 1969 (assistant professor of dendrochronology, 1969–1971; associate, 1971–1976; professor, 1976–1989). He also served as LTRR's assistant director (1972–1981) and director (1982–1986). Robinson was lead author or co-author of 13 of the 16 quadrangle reports (compilations of tree-ring dates) issued by LTRR between 1966 and 1975 and editor of the *Tree-Ring Bulletin* from 1969 to 1983. Between 1969 and 1978, he collaborated with Jeffrey S. Dean and Alexander J. Lindsay Jr. on the Long House Valley Project, a survey that resulted in the recording of more than 820 sites in the Kayenta region. He has also made significant contributions to Spanish mission archaeology in southern Arizona, with excavations at San Xavier del Bac and Guevavi, and he co-authored the classic treatment of Tohono O'odham traditional ceramics, *Papago Indian Pottery* (1962, University of Washington Press).

James S. Schoenwetter (1935–2015), then professor emeritus of anthropology at Arizona State University, contributed an update, written in 2008, of his 1965 report on the analysis of pollen samples from the Davis Ranch Site. Schoenwetter had processed samples from the site when he was director of the Palynology Laboratory of the Laboratory of Anthropology at the Museum of New Mexico. Schoenwetter earned two AB degrees at the University of Chicago (1955, 1956) before obtaining an MS in botany (1960) at the University of Arizona. He received his PhD in anthropology from Southern Illinois University in 1967. Schoenwetter joined the faculty of the Department of Anthropology at Arizona State University in 1967 and retired in 2000. A pioneer in the field of archaeological palynology, Schoenwetter's many publications include "Pollen Analysis of Eighteen Archaeological Sites in Arizona and New Mexico" in *Chapters in the Prehistory of Eastern Arizona, I* (1962, by Paul S. Martin et al., Chicago Natural History Museum), *Alluvial and Palynological Reconstruction of Environments, Navajo Reservoir District* (1964, with Frank W. Eddy, Museum of New Mexico Press), "Archaeological Pollen Studies of the Colorado Plateau" (1970, *American Antiquity*), and "A Palynological Approach to a Chronometry Problem on the Colorado Plateau" (1987, *Journal of Ethnobiology*).

Harrison B. Tordoff (1923–2008), then curator of birds at the Museum of Zoology and assistant professor in the Department of Zoology at the University of Michigan, was responsible for the 1958 identification of avifauna from the Davis Ranch Site reported by William Burt in 1961. Tordoff earned his BA in zoology at Cornell (1946) and his AM (1949) and PhD (1952) in zoology at the University of Michigan. From 1950 to 1957, he was a faculty member in the Department of Zoology at the University of Kansas and a curator at the University of Kansas Natural History Museum. He held positions at the University of Michigan from 1957 until 1970. In 1970, he came to the University of Minnesota as a professor of ecology and behavioral biology (1970–1991) and director of the Bell Museum of Natural History (1970–1983). He was an expert on the systematics of cardueline finches and the driving force behind the restoration of the peregrine falcon in the Upper Mississippi. He also helped to initiate and raised money to support the *Birds of North America* project, a comprehensive encyclopedia that is now an online database curated by the Cornell Lab of Ornithology.

Arthur W. Vokes earned his BA (1971) and MA (1995) degrees in anthropology at the University of Arizona (UA). Since 1990, he has been manager of the Archaeological Repository at the Arizona State Museum at UA. He has been involved in archaeological research in the U.S. Southwest for more than 45 years, focusing mainly on the analysis of shell and stone artifacts. He has authored more than 120 reports on shell assemblages from across the region, but the majority of his contributions address material recovered from sites in southern Arizona. He is also a recognized expert in museum collections management. His recent major publications include "Exchange Networks for Exotic Goods in the Southwest and Zuni's Place in Them" in *Zuni Origins: Toward a New Synthesis of Southwestern Archaeology* (2007, with David A. Gregory, UA Press), "The Role of Fee Structures in Repository Sustainability" (2010, with Patrick D. Lyons, *Heritage Management*), and "Dusting Off the Data: Curating and Rehabilitating Archaeological Legacy and Orphaned Collections" (2016, with Kathryn MacFarland, *Advances in Archaeological Practice*).

INDEX

Page numbers followed by *f* indicate figures. Page numbers followed by *t* indicate tables.

AMERIND STUDIES IN ANTHROPOLOGY

Series Editor **Christine R. Szuter**

Trincheras Sites in Time, Space, and Society
Edited by Suzanne K. Fish, Paul R. Fish, and M. Elisa Villalpando

Collaborating at the Trowel's Edge: Teaching and Learning in Indigenous Archaeology
Edited by Stephen W. Silliman

Warfare in Cultural Context: Practice, Agency, and the Archaeology of Violence
Edited by Axel E. Nielsen and William H. Walker

Across a Great Divide: Continuity and Change in Native North American Societies, 1400–1900
Edited by Laura L. Scheiber and Mark D. Mitchell

Leaving Mesa Verde: Peril and Change in the Thirteenth-Century Southwest
Edited by Timothy A. Kohler, Mark D. Varien, and Aaron M. Wright

Becoming Villagers: Comparing Early Village Society
Edited by Matthew S. Bandy and Jake R. Fox

Hunter-Gatherer Archaeology as Historical Process
Edited by Kenneth E. Sassaman and Donald H. Holly Jr.

Religious Transformation in the Late Pre-Hispanic Pueblo World
Edited by Donna M. Glowacki and Scott Van Keuren

Crow-Omaha: New Light on a Classic Problem of Kinship Analysis
Edited by Thomas R. Trautmann and Peter M. Whiteley

Native and Spanish New Worlds: Sixteenth-Century Entradas in the American Southwest and Southeast
Edited by Clay Mathers, Jeffrey M. Mitchem, and Charles M. Haecker

Transformation by Fire: The Archaeology of Cremation in Cultural Context
Edited by Ian Kuijt, Colin P. Quinn, and Gabriel Cooney

Chaco Revisited: New Research on the Prehistory of Chaco Canyon
Edited by Carrie C. Heitman and Stephen Plog

Ancient Paquimé and the Casas Grandes World
Edited by Paul E. Minnis and Michael E. Whalen

Beyond Germs: Native Depopulation in North America
Edited by Catherine M. Cameron, Paul Kelton, and Alan C. Swedlund

Knowledge in Motion: Constellations of Learning Across Time and Place
Edited by Andrew P. Roddick and Ann B. Stahl

Rethinking the Aztec Economy
Edited by Deborah L. Nichols, Frances F. Berdan, and Michael E. Smith

Ten Thousand Years of Inequality: The Archaeology of Wealth Differences
Edited by Timothy A. Kohler and Michael E. Smith

The Continuous Path: Pueblo Movement and the Archaeology of Becoming
Edited by Samuel Duwe and Robert W. Preucel

The Davis Ranch Site: A Kayenta Immigrant Enclave in Southeastern Arizona
Rex E. Gerald; Edited by Patrick D. Lyons